Lecture Notes in Computer Science   16054

Founding Editors

Gerhard Goos
Juris Hartmanis

Editorial Board Members

Elisa Bertino, *Purdue University, West Lafayette, IN, USA*
Wen Gao, *Peking University, Beijing, China*
Bernhard Steffen , *TU Dortmund University, Dortmund, Germany*
Moti Yung , *Columbia University, New York, NY, USA*

The series Lecture Notes in Computer Science (LNCS), including its subseries Lecture Notes in Artificial Intelligence (LNAI) and Lecture Notes in Bioinformatics (LNBI), has established itself as a medium for the publication of new developments in computer science and information technology research, teaching, and education.

LNCS enjoys close cooperation with the computer science R & D community, the series counts many renowned academics among its volume editors and paper authors, and collaborates with prestigious societies. Its mission is to serve this international community by providing an invaluable service, mainly focused on the publication of conference and workshop proceedings and postproceedings. LNCS commenced publication in 1973.

Vincent Nicomette · Abdelmalek Benzekri ·
Nora Boulahia-Cuppens · Jaideep Vaidya
Editors

Computer Security – ESORICS 2025

30th European Symposium
on Research in Computer Security
Toulouse, France, September 22–24, 2025
Proceedings, Part II

Editors
Vincent Nicomette
INSA Toulouse
Toulouse, France

Abdelmalek Benzekri
Université Toulouse - Paul Sabatier
Toulouse, France

Nora Boulahia-Cuppens
Polytechnique Montreal
Montreal, QC, Canada

Jaideep Vaidya
Rutgers University
Newark, NJ, USA

ISSN 0302-9743　　　　　　　ISSN 1611-3349　(electronic)
Lecture Notes in Computer Science
ISBN 978-3-032-07890-2　　　ISBN 978-3-032-07891-9　(eBook)
https://doi.org/10.1007/978-3-032-07891-9

© The Editor(s) (if applicable) and The Author(s), under exclusive license to Springer Nature Switzerland AG 2026

This work is subject to copyright. All rights are solely and exclusively licensed by the Publisher, whether the whole or part of the material is concerned, specifically the rights of translation, reprinting, reuse of illustrations, recitation, broadcasting, reproduction on microfilms or in any other physical way, and transmission or information storage and retrieval, electronic adaptation, computer software, or by similar or dissimilar methodology now known or hereafter developed.
The use of general descriptive names, registered names, trademarks, service marks, etc. in this publication does not imply, even in the absence of a specific statement, that such names are exempt from the relevant protective laws and regulations and therefore free for general use.
The publisher, the authors and the editors are safe to assume that the advice and information in this book are believed to be true and accurate at the date of publication. Neither the publisher nor the authors or the editors give a warranty, expressed or implied, with respect to the material contained herein or for any errors or omissions that may have been made. The publisher remains neutral with regard to jurisdictional claims in published maps and institutional affiliations.

This Springer imprint is published by the registered company Springer Nature Switzerland AG
The registered company address is: Gewerbestrasse 11, 6330 Cham, Switzerland

If disposing of this product, please recycle the paper.

Preface

It is our great pleasure to welcome you to the thirtieth edition of the European Symposium on Research in Computer Security (ESORICS 2025). This symposium was founded to further the progress of research in computer, information and cyber security and in privacy, by establishing a European forum for bringing together researchers in this area, by promoting the exchange of ideas with system developers and by encouraging links with researchers in related areas.

Since its inception in 1990, ESORICS has been hosted in a series of European countries and has established itself as the premiere European research event in computer security. Starting biannually in 1990 in Toulouse, the symposium has been held annually since 2002. We are delighted to welcome you to the 30th edition of the symposium in Toulouse, where it was first held.

As one of the longest-running reputable conferences focused on security research, ESORICS 2025 attracted numerous high-quality submissions from all over the world, with authors affiliated with diverse academic, non-profit, governmental, and industrial entities. After two rounds of submissions, each followed by an extensive reviewing period, we wound up with an excellent program, covering a broad range of timely and interesting topics. A total of 605 unique submissions were received: 150 in the first round and 475 in the second (of which 20 were invited resubmissions). Three to four reviewers per submission in a single-blind review driven by selfless and dedicated PC members (and external reviewers) collectively did an amazing job providing thorough and insightful reviews. Some PC members even "went the extra mile" by reviewing more than their share. The end result was 100 accepted submissions: 10 and 90, in the first and second rounds, respectively – giving an overall acceptance rate of 16.52%.

The ESORICS 2025 technical program was organized into 27 tracks held in 3 parallel sessions as well as 3 impressive keynote talks by internationally prominent and active researchers across academia and industry: Carlos Aguilar, Pierangela Samarati, and V. S. Subrahmanian. The program testifies to the level of excellence and stature of ESORICS.

Putting together ESORICS 2025 was a team effort. We would like to express our sincere gratitude to:

- Authors and contributors: without high-quality submissions from the authors, the success of the conference would not have been possible.
- PC members and additional reviewers: for the effort they put into the evaluation and high-quality in-depth reviews.
- Organization Chairs: Denise Gross from ICO, Justine Praneuf from LAAS-CNRS, Charlotte Sébastien from Université de Toulouse, and Tifanny Vest from Université de Toulouse for all of their efforts in organizing the conference and managing all of the logistics.
- Publicity Chairs: Paria Shirani from the University of Ottawa, Canada, Wenjuan Li from Hong Kong Polytechnic University, China, and Sebastien Bardin from Software

Safety and Security Lab, CEA, France, for their efforts in spreading the word about ESORICS 2025.
- Web Chairs: Charlotte Sébastien from Université de Toulouse and Tifanny Vest from Université de Toulouse for their efforts and continuous and quick updates of the website.
- Workshops Chair Romain Laborde from IRIT, Université de Toulouse for handling the workshops organization and being involved in other organizational aspects.
- Sponsor Chair Giorgia Macilotti from Airbus Protect for helping to arrange sponsorship for the symposium.
- The ESORICS Steering Committee and in particular, the Steering Committee Chair Joaquin Garcia-Alfaro for providing advice with numerous organizational issues.
- Easychair for providing an excellent conference management system.

In closing, we believe that ESORICS 2025 was an overall success and we hope that all attendees enjoyed the symposium and their stay in Toulouse, France.

July 2025

Jaideep Vaidya
Abdelmalek Benzekri
Nora Boulahia-Cuppens
Vincent Nicomette

Organization

General Chairs

Vincent Nicomette   LAAS-CNRS, INSA de Toulouse, France
Abdelmalek Benzekri   IRIT, Université de Toulouse, France

Program Chairs

Nora Boulahia-Cuppens   Polytechnique Montréal, Canada
Jaideep Vaidya   Rutgers University, USA

Publicity Chairs

Paria Shirani   University of Ottawa, Canada
Wenjuan Li   Education University of Hong Kong, China
Sebastien Bardin   CEA, France

Organization Chairs

Denise Gross   ICO, France
Justine Praneuf   LAAS-CNRS, France
Charlotte Sébastien   Université de Toulouse, France
Tifanny Vest   Université de Toulouse, France

Workshops Chair

Romain Laborde   IRIT, Université de Toulouse, France

Sponsor Chair

Giorgia Macilotti   Airbus Protect, France

Web Chairs

Charlotte Sébastien — Université de Toulouse, France
Tifanny Vest — Université de Toulouse, France

Steering Committee

Joachim Biskup — University of Dortmund, Germany
Frédéric Cuppens — Polytechnique Montréal, Canada
Sabrina De Capitani di Vimercati — Università degli Studi di Milano, Italy
Joaquin Garcia-Alfaro (Chair) — Institut Polytechnique de Paris, France
Dieter Gollmann — Hamburg University of Technology, Germany
Sushil Jajodia — George Mason University, USA
Sokratis Katsikas — Norwegian University of Science and Technology, Norway
Mirek Kutyłowski — Wrocław University of Technology, Poland
Javier Lopez — Universidad de Málaga, Spain
Jean-Jacques Quisquater — Université catholique de Louvain, Belgium
Peter Y. A. Ryan — University of Luxembourg, Luxembourg
Pierangela Samarati — Università degli Studi di Milano, Italy
Einar Snekkenes — Norwegian University of Science and Technology, Norway
Michael Waidner — Technische Universität Darmstadt, Germany
Edgar Weippl — University of Vienna & SBA Research, Austria

Program Committee

Andrea Agiollo (Round 2) — TU Delft, The Netherlands
Massimiliano Albanese — George Mason University, USA
Cristina Alcaraz — University of Málaga, Spain
Abdelrahaman Aly — Technology Innovation Institute, United Arab Emirates
Shengwei An (Round 2) — Virginia Tech, USA
Hafiz Asif (Round 2) — Hofstra University, Rutgers University, USA
Mikael Asplund — Linköping University, Sweden
Vijay Atluri — Rutgers University, USA
Daniel Augot (Round 1) — Inria Saclay, France
Samiha Ayed (Round 2) — Université de technologie de Troyes, France
Sebastien Bardin — CEA LIST, France
Alessandro Barenghi — Politecnico di Milano, Italy

Ken Barker (Round 1)	University of Calgary, Canada
Giampaolo Bella (Round 2)	University of Catania, Italy
Abdelmalek Benzekri	Université de Toulouse, France
Elisa Bertino	Purdue University, USA
Clara Bertolissi (Round 2)	Aix-Marseille University, France
Bruhadeshwar Bezawada (Round 2)	Southern Arkansas University, USA
Smriti Bhatt (Round 2)	Purdue University, USA
Giuseppe Bianchi (Round 2)	University of Rome "Tor Vergata", Italy
Alex Biryukov	University of Luxembourg, Luxembourg
Jorge Blasco (Round 1)	Universidad Politécnica de Madrid, Spain
Carlo Blundo	Università degli Studi di Salerno, Italy
Tamara Bonaci (Round 2)	Northeastern University, USA
Rainer Böhme (Round 2)	University of Innsbruck, Austria
Pino Caballero-Gil	University of La Laguna, Spain
Maurantonio Caprolu (Round 2)	King Abdullah University of Science and Technology, Saudi Arabia
Xavier Carpent	University of Nottingham, UK
Aldar C.-F. Chan (Round 2)	University of Hong Kong, China
Bo Chen (Round 2)	Michigan Technological University, USA
Rongmao Chen (Round 2)	National University of Defense Technology, China
Xiaofeng Chen (Round 2)	Xidian University, China
Yuan Cheng (Round 2)	University of Nottingham Ningbo China, China
Sherman S. M. Chow (Round 2)	Chinese University of Hong Kong, China
Pietro Colombo (Round 2)	Università dell'Insubria, Italy
Michal Choras (Round 1)	Bydgoszcz University of Science and Technology, Poland
Mauro Conti	University of Padua, Italy
Bruno Crispo (Round 2)	University of Trento, Italy
Michel Cukier (Round 2)	University of Maryland, USA
Frédéric Cuppens	Polytechnique Montréal, Canada
Tooska Dargahi	Manchester Metropolitan University, UK
Saptarshi Das (Round 2)	Pennsylvania State University, USA
Sabrina De Capitani di Vimercati	Universita' degli Studi di Milano, Italy
Hervé Debar	Télécom SudParis, France
Jose Maria De Fuentes (Round 1)	Universidad Carlos III de Madrid, Spain
Soumyadeep Dey (Round 2)	IIT Kharagpur, India
Roberto Di Pietro (Round 2)	King Abdullah University of Science and Technology, Saudi Arabia
Tassos Dimitriou (Round 2)	Kuwait University, Kuwait
Xuhua Ding (Round 1)	Singapore Management University, Singapore

Josep Domingo-Ferrer	Universitat Rovira i Virgili, Spain
Andreas Ekelhart (Round 1)	Secure Business Austria, Austria
Santiago Escobar (Round 2)	Universitat Politècnica de València, Spain
David Espes (Round 2)	Université de Bretagne Ouest, France
Shuya Feng (Round 2)	University of Connecticut, USA
Anna Lisa Ferrara	Università degli studi del Molise, Italy
Josep Lluís Ferrer Gomila (Round 2)	Universitat de les Illes Balears, Spain
Philip W. L. Fong (Round 2)	University of Calgary, Canada
Olga Gadyatskaya	University of Leiden, The Netherlands
Debin Gao	Singapore Management University, Singapore
Joaquin Garcia-Alfaro	Institut Polytechnique de Paris, France
Essam Ghadafi	Newcastle University, UK
Giorgio Giacinto	University of Cagliari, Italy
Alberto Giaretta (Round 1)	Örebro Universitet, Sweden
Dieter Gollmann	Hamburg University of Technology, Germany
Lorena González Manzano	Universidad Carlos III de Madrid, Spain
Dimitris Gritzalis (Round 1)	Athens University of Economics & Business, Greece
Stefanos Gritzalis (Round 2)	University of Piraeus, Greece
Maanak Gupta (Round 2)	Tennessee Tech University, USA
M. Emre Gursoy (Round 2)	Koç University, Turkey
Gregory Gutin (Round 2)	Royal Holloway, University of London, UK
Hannes Hartenstein (Round 2)	Karlsruhe Institute of Technology, Germany
Hongxin Hu (Round 2)	University at Buffalo, SUNY, USA
Xinyi Huang (Round 2)	Fujian Normal University, China
Hugo Jonker	Open University of the Netherlands, The Netherlands
Sokratis Katsikas	Norwegian University of Science and Technology, Norway
Stefan Katzenbeisser	University of Passau, Germany
Jörg Keller	FernUniversität in Hagen, Germany
Latifur Khan (Round 2)	University of Texas at Dallas, USA
Hiroaki Kikuchi	Meiji University, Japan
Hyoungshick Kim (Round 2)	Sungkyunkwan University, South Korea
Ram Krishnan (Round 2)	University of Texas at San Antonio, USA
Marina Krotofil	Maersk, Switzerland
Christopher Kruegel (Round 2)	University of California Santa Barbara, USA
Alptekin Küpçü	Koç University, Turkey
Romain Laborde	Université de Toulouse, France
Peeter Laud	Cybernetica AS, Estonia
Maryline Laurent	Télécom SudParis, France

Zeyu Lei (Round 2)	Purdue University, USA
Shujun Li (Round 2)	University of Kent, UK
Wenting Li (Round 2)	Peking University, China
Jun Li (Round 2)	University of Oregon, USA
Kaitai Liang	Delft University of Technology, The Netherlands
Hoon Wei Lim (Round 2)	NCS Group, Singapore
Dan Lin (Round 2)	Vanderbilt University, USA
Peng Liu (Round 2)	Pennsylvania State University, USA
Giovanni Livraga	University of Milan, Italy
Valeria Loscri	Inria, France
Wenjing Lou (Round 2)	Virginia Tech, USA
Rongxing Lu (Round 2)	Queen's University, Canada
Haibing Lu (Round 2)	Santa Clara University, USA
Xiapu Luo (Round 2)	Hong Kong Polytechnic University, China
Eduard Marin	Telefónica Research, Spain
Jean-Yves Marion	Université de Lorraine, France
Fabio Martinelli (Round 2)	IIT-CNR, Italy
Amir Masoumzadeh (Round 2)	University at Albany - SUNY, USA
Barbara Masucci	University of Salerno, Italy
Wojciech Mazurczyk	Warsaw University of Technology, Poland
David Megías	Universitat Oberta de Catalunya, Spain
Weizhi Meng	Lancaster University, UK
Donika Mirdita (Round 2)	Fraunhofer Secure Information Technology, Germany
Chris Mitchell (Round 2)	Royal Holloway, University of London, UK
Barsha Mitra (Round 2)	BITS Pilani Hyderabad Campus, India
Sudip Mittal (Round 2)	Mississippi State University, USA
Meisam Mohammady (Round 2)	Iowa State University, USA
Haralambos Mouratidis (Round 2)	University of Essex, UK
Guillermo Navarro-Arribas	Autonomous University of Barcelona, Spain
Jianting Ning (Round 2)	Singapore Management University, Singapore
Antonino Nocera	University of Pavia, Italy
Gabriele Oligeri	Hamad Bin Khalifa University, Qatar
Melek Önen (Round 2)	EURECOM, France
Philippe Owezarski	LAAS-CNRS, France
Balaji Palanisamy (Round 2)	University of Pittsburgh, USA
Stefano Paraboschi (Round 2)	Università di Bergamo, Italy
Sikhar Patranabis (Round 2)	IBM Research India, India
Günther Pernul (Round 2)	Universität Regensburg, Germany
Josef Pieprzyk	CSIRO/Data61, Australia
Joachim Posegga	University of Passau, Germany
Mir Mehedi Pritom (Round 2)	Tennessee Tech University, USA

Megha Quamara (Round 2)	King's College London, UK
Silvio Ranise (Round 2)	University of Trento, Italy
Kai Rannenberg (Round 2)	Goethe University Frankfurt, Germany
Siddharth Prakash Rao (Round 2)	Nokia Bell Labs, Finland
Danda B. Rawat (Round 2)	Howard University, USA
Indrakshi Ray (Round 1)	Colorado State University, USA
Indrajit Ray (Round 2)	Colorado State University, USA
Peter Rønne	University of Luxembourg, Luxembourg
Carlos Rubio Medrano (Round 2)	Texas A&M University, USA
Peter Y. A. Ryan	University of Luxembourg, Luxembourg
Reihaneh Safavi-Naini	University of Calgary, Canada
Pierangela Samarati	Università degli Studi di Milano, Italy
Neetesh Saxena	Cardiff University, UK
Neta Rozen-Schiff (Round 2)	Hebrew University of Jerusalem, Israel
Dominique Schröder	Universität Erlangen-Nürnberg, Germany
Jörg Schwenk	Ruhr-Universität Bochum, Germany
Savio Sciancalepore	Eindhoven University of Technology, The Netherlands
R. Sekar (Round 2)	Stony Brook University, USA
Basit Shafiq (Round 2)	Lahore University of Management Sciences, Pakistan
Ankit Shah (Round 2)	Indiana University, USA
Siamak Shahandashti	University of York, UK
Alessandro Sorniotti (Round 1)	IBM Research Europe, Switzerland
Shantanu Sharma (Round 2)	New Jersey Institute of Technology, USA
Wenbo Shen (Round 2)	Zhejiang University, China
Weidong Shi (Round 2)	University of Houston, USA
Arunesh Sinha (Round 2)	Rutgers University, USA
Jayesh Soni (Round 2)	Florida International University, USA
Angelo Spognardi	Sapienza Università di Roma, Italy
Riccardo Spolaor	Shandong University, China
Natalia Stakhanova (Round 2)	University of Saskatchewan, Canada
Thorsten Strufe (Round 2)	Karlsruhe Institute of Technology, Germany
Wenhai Sun (Round 2)	Purdue University, USA
Shamik Sural (Round 2)	Indian Institute of Technology Kharagpur, India
Luis Suárez (Round 2)	Ericsson, Canada
Qiang Tang (Round 2)	University of Sydney, Australia
Nadia Tawbi	Laval University, Canada
Vicenc Torra	Umeå University, Sweden
Jacob Torrey (Round 2)	Thinkst Applied Research, USA
Ari Trachtenberg (Round 2)	Boston University, USA
Stacey Truex (Round 2)	Denison University, USA

Jalaj Upadhyay (Round 2)   Johns Hopkins University, USA
Tobias Urban (Round 2)   Westphalian University of Applied Sciences, Germany
Daniele Venturi   Sapienza University of Rome, Italy
Rakesh Verma (Round 2)   University of Houston, USA
Tran Viet Xuan Phuong (Round 2)   University of Arkansas at Little Rock, USA
Joao P. Vilela (Round 2)   University of Porto, Portugal
Di Wang (Round 2)   State University of New York at Buffalo, USA
Haining Wang (Round 2)   Virginia Tech, USA
Cong Wang (Round 2)   City University of Hong Kong, China
Xinyue Wang (Round 2)   Renmin University of China, China
Lingyu Wang (Round 2)   Concordia University, Canada
Han Wang (Round 2)   University of Kansas, USA
Wenqi Wei (Round 2)   Fordham University, USA
Edgar Weippl   University of Vienna, Austria
Avishai Wool (Round 1)   Tel Aviv University, Israel
Christos Xenakis (Round 2)   University of Piraeus, Greece
Yang Xiang (Round 2)   Swinburne University of Technology, Australia
Yue Xiao (Round 2)   IBM Research, USA
Shouhuai Xu (Round 2)   University of Colorado Colorado Springs, USA
Runhua Xu (Round 2)   Beihang University, China
Peng Xu (Round 2)   Huazhong University of Science and Technology, China

Guomin Yang (Round 2)   Singapore Management University, Singapore
Zhihao Yao (Round 2)   New Jersey Institute of Technology, USA
Roland Yap (Round 2)   National University of Singapore, Singapore
Miuyin Yong Wong (Round 2)   Georgia Institute of Technology, USA
Chuan Yue (Round 2)   Colorado School of Mines, USA
Stefano Zanero (Round 1)   Politecnico di Milano, Italy
Yuan Zhang (Round 2)   Fudan University, China
Zhikun Zhang (Round 2)   Zhejiang University, China
Kehuan Zhang (Round 2)   Chinese University of Hong Kong, China
Liang Zhao (Round 2)   Emory University, USA
Ziming Zhao (Round 2)   Northeastern University, USA
Yunlei Zhao (Round 2)   Fudan University, China
Jianying Zhou (Round 2)   Singapore University of Technology and Design, Singapore
Sencun Zhu (Round 2)   Pennsylvania State University, USA
Rui Zhu (Round 2)   Indiana University, USA

Organization

Additional Reviewers

Abbadini, Marco
Abdelgawad, Mahmoud
Abdullahi, Ahmed
Abu Jabal, Amani
Afzal, Zeeshan
Aghayarzadeh, Hamed
Agrawal, Anand
Ahmed, Basharat
Ahmed, Faisal
Akbar, Khandakar Ashrafi
Akbarzadeh, Aida
Al Kadri, Mhd Omar
Al Mahmud, Tamim
Alborch Escobar, Ferran
Alhaidari, Abdulrahman
Allami, Ali
Almani, Dimah
Almasan, Paul
Almutaitri, Abeer
Amaral Simões, Sancho
Arazzi, Marco
Armanuzzaman, Md
Arriaga, Afonso
Arrus, Aurora
Aryal, Kshitiz
Aung, Yan Lin
Avizheh, Sepideh
Azizli, Elmaddin
Bacho, Renas
Baecker, Ruben
Bashir, Shadaab Kawnain
Belguith, Sana
Benaloh, Josh
Beneš, Martin
Beretta, Michele
Berlato, Stefano
Bertrand, Léo
Bertrand, Simon
Bezawada, Bruhadeshwar
Bianchi, Federica
Binosi, Lorenzo
Binte Haq, Hina
Birashk, Amin

Biswas, Chinmoy
Bisways, Chinmoy
Boyapally, Harishma
Carlson, Trevor E.
Carminati, Michele
Carvalho, Tânia
Casagrande, Marco
Castiglione, Arcangelo
Castiglione, Gianpietro
Catuogno, Luigi
Cecconello, Stefano
Charlès, Alex
Chaturvedi, Bhuvnesh
Chawla, Abhimanyu
Chekole, Eyasu Getahun
Chen, Depeng
Chen, Juntao
Chen, Yumin
Chen, Zeyu
Chong, Chun Jie
Chouchoulis, Ioannis
Chu, Hien Thi Thu
Cihangiroglu, Mert
Cimato, Stelvio
Collu, Matteo Gioele
Cui, Hui
Cunha, Mariana
Dai, Jiongyu
Dai, Xushu
Daneshmand, Arash
Dang, Hai-Van
Das, Debayan
Das, Prajit Kumar
Das Chowdhury, Partha
Daudén-Esmel, Cristòfol
Deidda, Nicola
Demetrio, Luca
Demir, Nurullah
Demirkiran, Ferhat
Dey, Kunal
Di Gennaro, Marco
Di Paolo, Edoardo
Ding, Weikang

Dipta, Debopriya Roy
Dolati, Mahdi
Donadel, Denis
Droll, Jan
Du, Linkang
Du, Minxin
Duck, Gregory
Dunbar, Arthur
Eichhammer, Philipp
Erinola, Nurullah
Esposito, Sergio
Facchinetti, Dario
Fadavi, Mojtaba
Falanji, Reyhane
Falebita, Oluwatosin
Faraj, Omair
Farasat, Talaya
Feng, Hanwen
Ferrari, Stefano
Ferré-Queralt, Joan
Flamini, Andrea
Fotiadis, Georgios
Fouotsa, Tako Boris
Galeazzi, Alessandro
Gao, Yang
Garbelini, Matheus
García Díaz, Jorge Francisco
García Fernández, Pablo
George, Aleena Elsa
Ghorbel, Bassem
Ghosh, Soumyadyuti
Giannakopoulos, Thrasyvoulos
Giapantzis, Konstantinos
Gimenez, Pierre-François
Glas, Magdalena
Golinelli, Matteo
Gomes, Catarina
Gowdanakatte, Shwetha
Grill, Johannes
Grisafi, Michele
Groszschaedl, Johann
Grundmann, Matthias
Guiot, Miquel
Guo, Jinduo
Gupta, Deepti

Haefner, Kyle
Haffar, Rami
Haffey, Preston
Hamm, Peter
Hamm And Lieberknecht, Two Subreviewers Peter And Ann-Kristin
Han, Qiang
Han, Yanni
Haque, Md Shahedul
Hassanpour, Seyedeh Bahereh
Herranz, Javier
Hopkins, Jacob
Hore, Soumyadeep
Hosseini, Henry
Hou, Chenxi
Howard, Samuel
Hu, Chengcong
Huang, Mengdie
Huang, Qiqing
Huang, Zhicheng
Huso, Ingrid
Ibarrondo, Alberto
In, Junbeom
Ioannidis, Thodoris
Irfan, Muhammad
Jacob, Florian
Jacqmin, Quentin
Jiang, Shan
Jiang, Yuning
Jin, Heng
Jorba, Josep
Kaaniche, Nesrine
Kammueller, Florian
Kanpak, Halil Ibrahim
Karim Imtiaz
Katsis Charalampos
Kei, Andes Y. L.
Kembu, Vignesh Kumar
Kermabon-Bobinnec, Hugo
Kern, Sascha
Khan, Younas
Kimm, Hanke
Koffas, Stefanos
Koohpayeh Araghi, Tanya
Korichi, Youcef

Kouko, Gildas
Kumar, Gulshan
Kumari, Komal
Kunwar, Pradip
Lalande, Jean-Francois
Lara, Carlos
Laura Madison, Axel Durbet
Le Mouel, Florian
Leinweber, Marc
Lerch-Hostalot, Daniel
Li, Adrian Shuai
Li, Fagen
Li, Xiang
Li, Xiaoguo
Li, Yamin
Li Calsi, Davide
Liang, Yu
Ligier, Damien
Lin, Chao
Litzinger, Sebastian
Liu, Gaoxiang
Liu, Jiahao
Liu, Jianghua
Loh, Jia-Chng
Lombard-Platet, Marius
Longo, Riccardo
Lopez Morales, Efren
Lotto, Alessandro
Luchini, Chiara
Luo, Nanqing
Lybarger, Kevin
Löbner, Sascha
Ma, Jack P. K.
Ma, Jinhua
Ma, Wanlun
Ma, Zheyuan
Maehren, Marcel
Maffei, Ivo
Maitra, Sudip
Makropodis, Ioannis
Maldonado, Mark
Manzanares-Salor, Benet
Martins, Óscar
Marty, Pierre
Massidda, Emmanuele

McCarthy, Andrew
Meadows, Catherine
Meng, Qiaoran
Mercer, Rebekah
Merzdovnik, Georg
Michaud, Quentin
Mishra, Nimish
Mishra, Sagar
Mitra, Shaswata
Mohammadi, Sareh
Mondragon, Jennifer
Mostafiz, Mir Imtiaz
Mura, Raffaele
Müller, Mathis
Nagasubramaniam, Piyush
Nath, Souradip
Nelson, Jonathan
Neudert, Raphael
Nguyen, Hieu
Nicolazzo, Serena
Niknia, Ahad
Niow, Choon Hock
Noble, Daniel
P., Vinod
Palihawadana, Chamath
Pan, Ying-Yu
Panebianco, Francesco
Panja, Somnath
Patel, Raj
Paudel, Diwas
Persiano, Giuseppe
Pimpinella, Giovanni
Podder, Rakesh
Praharaj, Lopamudra
Preatoni, Riccardo
Psychogyiou, Aikaterini
Pucher, Michael
Puchta, Alexander
Pérez-Ramos, Edgar
Qiu, Tian Qu, Jiashu
Quadrio, Giacomo
Quinci, Arianna
Qureshi, Amna
Raciti, Mario
Rasul, Md Fazle

Regano, Leonardo
Reijsbergen, Daniel
Rizzi, Matteo
Rosenblattl, Jakob
Rossi, Matthew
Roy, Shovan
Russo, Luigi
Saadi Dadmarzi, Hamidreza
Sacchetta, Juri
Saha, Rahul
Samdaliri, Mahya
Sanna, Alessandro
Saqlain, Sabbir Ahmed
Sato, Shingo
Sauger, Gabriel
Senn, Judith
Serra-Ruiz, Jordi
Sha, Kailun
Shafir, Lior
Shahriar, Md Hasan
Sharif, Amir
Shen, Zilin
Shepherd, Carlton
Shi, Shanghao
Siemer, Jan Niklas
Singh, Animesh
Singh, Gurjot
Sinha, Sayani
Skandylas, Charilaos
Skrobot, Marjan
Song, Yongcheng
Song, Zirui
Soria-Comas, Jordi
Spadafora, Chiara
Spiesberger, Patrick
Srivastava, Gautam
Stifter, Nicholas
Streicher, Klaus
Stylianou, Ioannis
Sun, Shihua
Sözen Esen, Derya
Thomas, Julian
Thomas, Tony
Tian, Guohua
Tian, Jianwen

Tippe, Pascal
Todd, James
Torabi, Sadegh
Tripathi, Himanshu
Trombetta, Alberto
Tsado, Yakubu
Tuck, Bryan
Tureček, Philip
Udovenko, Aleksei
Valeriani, Lorenzo
Vasilopoulos, Dimitrios
Wan, Guoan
Wang, Cheng-Long
Wang, Hongxiao
Wang, Jingzhe
Wang, Lulu
Wang, Shuo
Wang, Wenli
Wang, Xinhai
Wang, Yuyu
Wazan, Ahmad Samer
Wen, Tian
Wong, Harry W. H.
Wu, Jiaojiao
Wu, Pengfei
Xie, Xinhong
Xu, Chenming
Xu, Difei
Xu, Peng
Xu, Shengmin
Xue, Haiyang
Yan, Yingfei
Yang, Fan
Yang, Yang
Yang, Zeyu
Yin, Zihao
Younas, Affan
Yu, Chia-Mu
Yu, Hexuan
Yu, Tianchi
Yuan, Quan
Yuan, Wei
Yuan, Yijun
Zari, Oualid
Zhang, Bokang

Zhang, Chaoyu
Zhang, Ke
Zhang, Zicheng
Zhao, Rui

Zhou, Ming
Zhu, Rui
Zhu, Xiaogang
Özfatura, Kerem

Contents – Part II

A Certified-Input Mixnet from Two-Party Mercurial Signatures
on Randomizable Ciphertexts 1
  Masayuki Abe, Masaya Nanri, Miyako Ohkubo,
  Octavio Perez-Kempner, Daniel Slamanig, and Mehdi Tibouchi

Tetris! Traceable Extendable Threshold Ring Signatures and More 22
  Gennaro Avitabile, Vincenzo Botta, and Dario Fiore

Efficient One-Pass Private Set Intersection from Pairings with Offline
Preprocessing 42
  Joonsang Baek, Seongbong Choi, Willy Susilo, Partha Sarathi Roy,
  and Hyung Tae Lee

Practical Robust Dynamic Searchable Symmetric Encryption Supporting
Conjunctive Queries 63
  Bingxue Bian, Qiaoer Xu, Jiatao Liu, and Jianfeng Wang

Security Analysis of Covercrypt: A Quantum-Safe Hybrid Key
Encapsulation Mechanism for Hidden Access Policies 84
  Théophile Brézot, Chloé Hébant, Paola de Perthuis,
  and David Pointcheval

Anamorphic Monero Transactions: The Threat of Bypassing Anti-money
Laundering Laws 103
  Adrian Cinal, Przemysław Kubiak, Mirosław Kutyłowski,
  and Gabriel Wechta

Hyperion: Transparent End-to-End Verifiable Voting with Coercion
Mitigation 124
  Aditya Damodaran, Simon Rastikian, Peter B. Rønne,
  and Peter Y. A. Ryan

Two-Factor Authenticated Key Exchange with Enhanced Security
from Post-quantum Assumptions 144
  Qijia Fan, Chenhao Bao, Xuanyu Shi, Shuai Han, and Shengli Liu

Concretely Efficient Parallel-Accessible DORAM for 100K-Sized Array 164
  Koki Hamada

A Symbolic Analysis of Hash Functions Vulnerabilities in Maude-NPA 186
    Arturo Hernández-Sánchez and Santiago Escobar

A Post-quantum Distributed OPRF from the Legendre PRF 205
    Novak Kaluđerović, Nan Cheng, and Aikaterini Mitrokotsa

TERRA: Trojan-Resilient Reverse-Firewall for Cryptographic
Applications 226
    Chandan Kumar, Nimish Mishra, Suvradip Chakraborty,
    Satrajit Ghosh, and Debdeep Mukhopadhyay

Reaction Attack on TFHE: Minimum Number of Oracle Queries
and Nearly Optimum Attacking Scheme 247
    Remma Kumazaki and Yuichi Kaji

Predicate-Private Asymmetric Searchable Encryption for Conjunctions
from Lattices 262
    Qinyi Li and Xavier Boyen

DEBridge: Towards Secure and Practical Plausibly Deniable Encryption
Based on USB Bridge Controller 282
    Chongyu Long, Yuewu Wang, Lingguang Lei, Haoyang Xing,
    and Jiwu Jing

Formalisation of the KZG Polynomial Commitment Schemes in EasyCrypt 303
    Palak and Thomas Haines

UTRA: Universal Token Reusability Attack and Token Unforgeable
Delegatable Order-Revealing Encryption 321
    Jaehwan Park, Hyeonbum Lee, Junbeom Hur, Jae Hong Seo,
    and Doowon Kim

Enhanced Key Mismatch Attacks on Lattice-Based KEMs: Multi-bit
Inference and Ciphertext Generalization 341
    Yan Shao, Yuejun Liu, Yongbin Zhou, and Mingyao Shao

Code Encryption with Intel TME-MK for Control-Flow Enforcement 359
    Martin Unterguggenberger, Lukas Lamster, Mathias Oberhuber,
    Simon Scherer, and Stefan Mangard

Optimized Privacy-Preserving Multi-signatures from Discrete Logarithm
Assumption 379
    Xiaoyang Wei, Shuai Han, and Shengli Liu

Polylogarithmic Polynomial Commitment Scheme over Galois Rings 400
  *Zhuo Wu, Xinxuan Zhang, Yi Deng, Yuanju Wei, Zhongliang Zhang,
  and Liuyu Yang*

Efficient Homomorphic Evaluation for Non-polynomial Functions 421
  Changhong Xu and Honggang Hu

Athena: Accelerating KeySwitch and Bootstrapping for Fully
Homomorphic Encryption on CUDA GPU 442
  *Yifan Yang, Kexin Zhang, Peng Xu, Zhaojun Lu, Wei Wang, Weiqi Wang,
  and Kaitai Liang*

Formally-Verified Security Against Forgery of Remote Attestation Using
SSProve 463
  Sara Zain, Jannik Mähn, Stefan Köpsell, and Sebastian Ertel

SAFEPATH: Encryption-Less On-Demand Input Path Protection for Mobile
Devices 485
  Xin Zhang and Yifan Zhang

Extending Groth16 for Disjunctive Statements 506
  *Xudong Zhu, Xinxuan Zhang, Xuyang Song, Yi Deng, Yuanju Wei,
  and Liuyu Yang*

Author Index 529

A Certified-Input Mixnet from Two-Party Mercurial Signatures on Randomizable Ciphertexts

Masayuki Abe[1,2], Masaya Nanri[2], Miyako Ohkubo[3],
Octavio Perez-Kempner[1(✉)], Daniel Slamanig[4], and Mehdi Tibouchi[1,2]

[1] NTT Social Informatics Laboratories, Tokyo, Japan
octavio.perezkempner@ntt.com
[2] Kyoto University, Kyoto, Japan
[3] Security Fundamentals Laboratory, CSRI, NICT, Tokyo, Japan
[4] Research Institute CODE, Universität der Bundeswehr München, Munich, Germany

Abstract. A certified-input mixnet introduced by Hébant et al. (PKC '20) employs homomorphically signed ciphertexts to reduce the complexity of shuffling arguments. However, the state-of-the-art construction relies on heavy Groth-Sahai proofs for key homomorphism, and only achieves honest-user security, limiting broader applicability.

This work proposes a novel certified-input mixnet achieving stronger security guarantees, alongside better efficiency. This is achieved by introducing a tailored signature scheme, *two-party mercurial signatures on randomizable ciphertexts*, that allows users and an authority to jointly sign ciphertexts supporting key, ciphertext, and signature randomization without compromising integrity and privacy.

We compare our approach to previous works that employ structured ciphertexts, implement our protocols, and provide performance benchmarks. Our results show that verifying the mixing process for 50,000 ciphertexts takes just 135 s on a commodity laptop using ten mixers, underscoring the practicality and efficiency of our approach.

Keywords: Mixnet · Certified Inputs · Mercurial Signatures · Voting

1 Introduction

Mixnets [19] use multiple servers to shuffle a set of encrypted messages in cascade to hide the relation between the initial input and resulting output. A central challenge has been how to efficiently guarantee the integrity of the messages. Hébant, Phan, and Pointcheval [34] introduced a new paradigm, *certified-input mixnets*, that takes homomorphically signed ciphertexts as input and outputs randomized yet signed ciphertexts with a lightweight proof of correctness of the randomization of the keys, which is aggregated over all users' keys, together preserving the integrity of the embedded messages after shuffling. In contrast to prior approaches, which incur linear overhead in the number of mix servers on top of the ciphertexts (already linear in the number of users), their work achieves constant overhead in the number of mix servers. Specifically, the verifier only needs to examine the input, the final output from the mixnet, and the proofs on the aggregated keys. These proofs can optionally be compressed into a single proof, eliminating the need for a linear number of proofs. Their approach requires a certification authority (CA) to certify inputs (as motivated by voting scenarios) and offers a highly scalable solution. This extended model also fits other practical applications such as oracle networks (*e.g.,* [17,38]) including those deployed in platforms such as Chainlink [18] that involve semi-trusted authorities and untrusted parties who run software as a service.

While promising, their state-of-the-art instantiation, referred to hereafter as HPP20, suffers from serious drawbacks, hindering real-world deployments. To clarify, we recap their construction at a high level. Each user holds a user-key uvk and a signature σ_a on it issued by the CA with its key avk. The user encrypts a message into a ciphertext ct and signs it with uvk into signature σ_u. The certified-input is thus structured as $(ct, \sigma_u, \sigma_a, \mathsf{uvk})$. Each mix-server randomize it into $(ct', \sigma'_u, \sigma'_a, \mathsf{uvk}')$ with shuffling, and provides a proof π of correct randomization of uvk in an aggregated form over all users' keys. The signatures and keys are to be homomorphic to allow randomization and aggregation. Unforgeability of σ_u guarantees that every signed output-ciphertext corresponds to a signed input-ciphertext. The proof π of correct randomization on aggregated keys ensures that every input user-key corresponds to an output user-key.

Firstly, we observe that their soundness and privacy are only guaranteed for *honest users*, and they actually break down in the presence of corrupt users. Suppose that there are corrupted users associated with keys $\mathsf{uvk}_1, \mathsf{uvk}_2$ and uvk_3 colluding with the first mix-server. They set up their keys to satisfy $\mathsf{uvk}_1 + \mathsf{uvk}_2 + \mathsf{uvk}_3 = 3 \cdot \mathsf{uvk}_1$ so that the first mix-server can replace their inputs with three randomized copies of the input from the first user without affecting to their aggregation. In the voting application, this is a serious threat for fairness as an adversary can replace some votes after other votes are cast.

Secondly, HPP20 involves several primitives: two linearly homomorphic signature schemes [37]–one for σ_u and the other for σ_a, a multi-signature scheme [14] and Groth-Sahai proofs [32] included in π issued by each mix server. This results in a complex setup and use of an ad-hoc unlinkability assumption.

1.1 Our Contribution

We present a certified-input mixnet addressing previous drawbacks. Figure 1 illustrates the diagram of our *base* scheme whose details appear in Sect. 3. Following HPP20, to remove linearity in the number of mix servers, we discuss alternatives for mix-servers to jointly prove the correctness of their processing. Our key contributions include a new signature scheme, *Mercurial Signature on Randomizable Ciphertexts* (MSoRC), and its two-party signature generation protocol. We detail the advantages of our construction and contributions as follows.

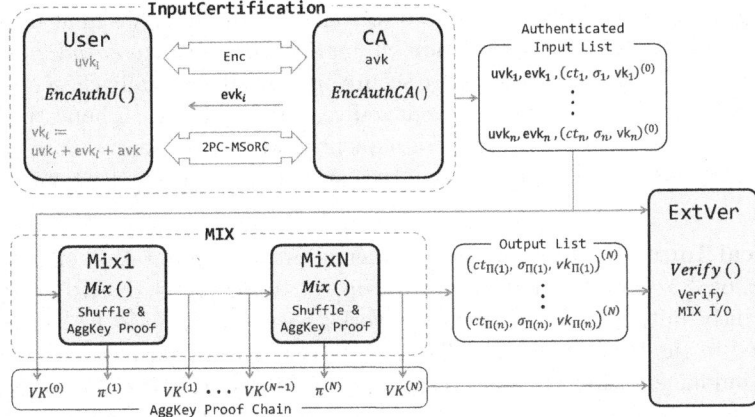

Fig. 1. Diagram of our *base* certified-input mixnet.

Malicious-User Security. Our mixnet ensures soundness even in the presence of corrupt users. As shown in Fig. 1, every ciphertext is signed using a joint key composed of the user's key (uvk_i), an ephemeral key (evk_i), and the authority's key (avk). The inclusion of evk prevents corrupt users from manipulating the distribution of the joint signature keys and ensures a one-to-one correspondence between input and output joint keys through a proof of correct key randomization on their aggregated form. We additionally allow the CA to randomize the ciphertexts, preventing the original user from opening them. While this does not directly enhance the standard security of mixnets, it is beneficial for achieving receipt-freeness in voting contexts, as discussed in the long version [4].

Simpler and More Efficient. Our approach replaces the two-layer structure of HPP20, where users sign ciphertexts and authorities sign user keys, with a two-party MSoRC signing protocol that produces a single signature verified by a joint key. This simplification eliminates the need for Groth-Sahai proofs executed by each mix-server. Instead, we simply require discrete logarithm proofs, further enhancing efficiency. Overall, our construction reduces setup complexity, computation, and verification costs compared to HPP20.

These desirable properties are attained with a moderate increase in complexity for the CA. Our two-party signing process necessitates two rounds of interaction, as opposed to the single round required in HPP20. Additionally, in HPP20, the CA's task can be completed independently of the ciphertext. While the CA's involvement is slightly more intensive in our approach, it's important to note that, in HPP20, users' keys are intended for one-time use and the CA must participate in each execution of the mixnet regardless.

New Mercurial Signature Scheme. Our new primitive, MSoRC, is an independent contribution that we anticipate will have applications beyond mixnets. We first present a base MSoRC construction, which extends *signatures on randomizable ciphertexts* (SoRC) in [11] to allow key randomization, similar to *mer-*

curial signatures (MS) [24]. Then, we introduce its two-party signature generation, incorporating techniques from *interactive threshold mercurial signatures* (TMS) in [3]. These constructions are secure against adversarially chosen encryption keys. However, for mixnets, a relaxed security notion with honestly generated encryption keys is sufficient. Consequently, we also present a more efficient variant that achieves an optimal signature size of three group elements [2].

Practical Implementation. Our mixnet improves computation efficiency by a factor of 3.5x and communication by up to 3x compared to HPP20. It also significantly outperforms all previous works based on Rand-RCCA encryption discussed in the long version [4]. To evaluate practical performance, we provide a Rust implementation. To the best of our knowledge, this is the first practical implementation of mixnets under the certified input paradigm. In the worst-case scenario, for $n = 50k$ ciphertexts and $N = 10$ mixers, the mixing process takes approximately 40 seconds, and verifying the final mixing result takes around 135 seconds on a commodity laptop, without parallelization. All of our cryptographic building blocks can be easily implemented using existing libraries. Additionally, our modular design makes implementation tasks less error-prone.

1.2 Related Work

Signatures on Equivalence Classes and Randomizable Ciphertexts. Signatures on Equivalence Classes (EQS) [28,33] are *malleable* structure-preserving signatures [1,2] (*i.e.*, pairing-based signatures with messages and public keys that are elements of a source group and whose verification is done using paring-product equations) defined over a message vector space. They allow a controlled form of malleability on message-signature pairs. EQS have further been studied to consider equivalence classes for the public key only [10] or both (latter introduced under the name of mercurial signatures in [24]). In addition, [11] considered a different equivalence relation for the message space and gave the first construction of SoRC [13] from EQS. In brief, it signs ElGamal ciphertexts and all randomizations of a ciphertext define an equivalence class. The motivation of SoRC is to build signatures on ciphertexts that could be adapted to randomizations of them. The SoRC construction from [11] (which is based on [28]) provides a strong notion of *class-hiding* where an adapted message-signature pair looks like a completely random message-signature pair even when knowing the original message-signature pair. However, it only provides the same weak public-key class hiding guarantees of early constructions [21,24,25] (*i.e.*, original signers can identify adapted signatures for an adapted public key using their secret key). A stronger class-hiding notion for the public key was recently addressed in [3] where TMS are introduced. As it allows parties to produce a signature on their combined public keys, key-randomizability of the resulting signature provides a stronger class-hiding notion as long as parties keep their signing key private. We follow their two-party construction that is simpler and suffices for our purpose.

Verifiable Mixnets. Efficient proofs of shuffling have been continuously improved in the literature. The proof size and the verification work could be sub-linear relative to the number of inputs, *e.g.,* [12]. In general, applying zk-SNARKs, *e.g.,* [6,29–31] to the shuffling relation the communication complexity can be reduced to poly-logarithmic. However, these approaches include several trade-offs, such as cumbersome setups, extensive common reference strings, heavy preprocessing requirements, or significant computational resource on the prover's side. Also, as noted in [34], the proof grows linearly in the number of mix servers at the end. Such conditions are not necessarily acceptable for a scenario where casual users act as mix servers to protect their privacy autonomously.

While we focus on the certified input paradigm, other approaches ease the workload of verifiable shuffling by enforcing a specific structure on input ciphertexts to prevent malicious behaviour by mix-servers. Faonio *et al.* [26,27] use Re-randomizable Replayable CCA (Rand-RCCA) encryption [16] to eliminate the need for a proof of shuffle, replacing it with NIZK proofs of plaintext knowledge for each ciphertext and NIZK proofs of membership at each mixing stage. Unfortunately, their approach requires a complex setup and incurs high computational costs. This is primarily because their Rand-RCCA scheme is based on Cramer-Shoup encryption [23], and the associated NIZK proofs involve elements in the target group of a pairing, significantly increasing proof size.

Another approach that diminishes a proof of shuffle appears in [20]. It uses an escrowed linkable ring signature scheme and a regular signature to sign ciphertexts, publishing the former while hiding the latter among mix servers. However, as the ring includes all potential users, it does not easily scale.

Finally, there are works that explore post-quantum secure mixnets, such as [5, 7–9,15,35]. Although these approaches require a careful selection of parameters and are far less efficient, exploring post-quantum security in the certified input paradigm remains a promising direction for future research.

1.3 Technical Overview

We provide a step-by-step overview of the two-party MSoRC construction and explain its role in our certified-input mixnet design.

1) SoRC. We begin by recalling SoRC from [11]. With verification key $(G, \hat{G}, \hat{X}_0, \hat{X}_1)$, its signature on ElGamal ciphertext (C_0, C_1) for encryption key (G, X) consists of group elements $(Z, S, \hat{S}, T)$. It is verified by three equations:

$$e(Z, \hat{S}) = e(C_0, \hat{X}_0)e(C_1, \hat{X}_1)e(G, \hat{G}),$$
$$e(S, \hat{G}) = e(G, \hat{S}), \text{ and } e(T, \hat{S}) = e(G, \hat{X}_0)e(X, \hat{X}_1)$$

where e is a bilinear map. The ciphertext and signature are malleable in the sense that anyone can re-randomize them; $(C_0', C_1') = (C_0 + rG, C_1 + rX)$ and $(Z', S', \hat{S}', T') = ((Z+rT)/s, sS, s\hat{S}, T/s)$ for any r and $s \in \mathbb{Z}_p^*$. However, the key space is not malleable, as the verification equation involves $e(G, \hat{G})$, which rules out any key randomizations of the form $(\hat{X}_0^\rho, \hat{X}_1^\rho)$ for any $\rho \leftarrow_\$ \mathbb{Z}_p^*$ that would pass the first verification equation: $e(Z^\rho, \hat{S}) \neq e(C_0, \hat{X}_0^\rho)e(C_1, \hat{X}_1^\rho)e(G, \hat{G})$.

2) From SoRC to MSoRC. To obtain malleability on the key space, we turn the SoRC from [11] into a full-fledged MSoRC. Our MSoRC extends the signing key with one more element, $\hat{X}_2$, using it to sign a fixed generator G. The first verification equation changes to $e(Z, \hat{S}) = e(C_0, \hat{X}_0)e(C_1, \hat{X}_1)e(G, \hat{X}_2)$, and the key can be randomized within the equivalence class with factor ρ as $e(Z^\rho, \hat{S}) = e(C_0, \hat{X}_0^\rho)e(C_1, \hat{X}_1^\rho)e(G, \hat{X}_2^\rho)$. This prevents the ciphertext from being altered with $(C_0^{\rho'}, C_1^{\rho'})$ since G in $e(G, \hat{X}_2)$ must remain fixed. We prove security of our base MSoRC giving a reduction to the original SoRC.

3) Optimizing MSoRC. For honestly generated encryption key X, our MSoRC can be optimized to yield a signature, $(Z, \hat{S}, T)$, consisting of only three group elements without compromising the security. To see why, consider the case where x of $X = G^x$ is known to the adversary. Since the third verification equation is

$$e(T, \hat{S}) = e(G, \hat{X}_0)e(G^x, \hat{X}_1) = e(G, \hat{X}_0\hat{X}_1^x),$$

the adversary can compute T and $\hat{S}$ as $T = G$ and $\hat{S} = \hat{X}_0\hat{X}_1^x$ without knowing signing key x_0 and x_1. Thus, the second verification equation $e(S, \hat{G}) = e(G, \hat{S})$ has been involved to ensure that $\hat{S}$ has been computed with x_0 and x_1, even if decryption key x is known to the adversary. On the other hand, if x is not known to the adversary, the second equation is unnecessary and so does S. We prove this intuition rigorously in the Generic Group Model (GGM).

4) Two-party MSoRC. MSoRC provides the public key class-hiding only in a weak sense as the signer can trace randomized keys by using the signing key. Observe that the equivalence class of key $(\hat{X}_0, \hat{X}_1, \hat{X}_2)$ is defined by keys of the form $(\hat{X}_0^\rho, \hat{X}_1^\rho, \hat{X}_2^\rho)$. A key $(\hat{X}_0', \hat{X}_1', \hat{X}_2')$ is in the class if and only if $(\hat{X}_0')^{1/x_0} = (\hat{X}_1')^{1/x_1} = (\hat{X}_2')^{1/x_2} (= \hat{G}^\rho)$ holds for secret key (x_0, x_1, x_2). In [3], it is suggested to distribute the secret key among multiple parties, ensuring that no single party can perform tracing. However, achieving efficient distributed signing in the presence of malicious signers is a non-trivial challenge. Following the approach in [3], we additively distribute the secret key among two parties, a user and the CA, to fit to our certified-input mixnet scenario. The signing protocol for the two-party MSoRC follows a blind-compute-unblind structure, which allows us to simulate an honest party in the unforgeability proof when the other party is corrupted. We show that the unforgeability of the two-party MSoRC can be reduced to the unforgeability of the base MSoRC.

5) Mixnet from two-party MSoRC. We use the two-party MSoRC so that users and the CA jointly create a certified ciphertext as input to the mixnet. User i having ciphertext $(C_0, C_1)_i$ joins with the preliminary registered key, uvk_i, and the authority works with an ephemeral key evk_i and its long-term key avk. User key uvk_i as well as ephemeral key evk_i are published *in an authentic manner* so that joint verification key $\mathsf{vk}_i := \mathsf{uvk}_i + \mathsf{evk}_i + \mathsf{avk}$ can be computed in public. The ephemeral key is included to ensure that every vk_i is independent. The randomized ciphertext $(C'_0, C'_1)_i$, MSoRC signature σ'_i, and verification key vk'_i (all publicly randomizable through adaptation functions of MSoRC), are the user's input to the mixnet. For simplicity, our communication model assumes the presence of a publicly verifiable authenticated channel – *i.e.*, all messages are recorded in a way that their authenticity can be publicly verified. This is equivalent to a bulletin board with authenticated writing, which is a standard assumption in e-voting applications, and the setting we adopt as well.

Considering $s_1, \ldots, s_N$ mix servers, s_j delivers $\mathcal{SS}\mathsf{et}^{(j)} := \{(C'_0, C'_1)_{\Pi(i)}, \sigma'_{\Pi(i)}, \mathsf{vk}'_{\Pi(i)}\}_{i \in [n]}$ for permutation $\Pi : [n] \to [n]$ and an authenticated NIZK proof of correct mixing to s_{j+1} using the statement from the previous round as the base point. The proof is: $\mathsf{NIZK}\{(\sum_{i=1}^{i=n} \mathsf{vk}'^{(j-1)}_{\Pi(i)}, \rho) : \sum_{i=1}^{i=n} \mathsf{vk}'^{(j)}_{\Pi(i)} = \rho \cdot \sum_{i=1}^{i=n} \mathsf{vk}'^{(j-1)}_{\Pi(i)}\}$.

This is where we replace Groth-Sahai with more lightweight Schnorr proofs thanks to our MSoRC structure. All servers authenticate their NIZK proof, which can be batch verified. Everyone can publicly verify the authenticated proofs to confirm the participation of each mix server while batch verification validates the output tuple. Only the initial tuples, the final ones, all the N short NIZK proofs, and server's public keys are needed for verification. This is because if the authenticated proofs verify, the output tuple implicitly validates the intermediate randomizations performed by each mix server. Alternatively, as in HPP20, the mix servers could perform a second round to produce a multi-signature on a single proof, making the final verification independent of N (cf. Section 3).

Security of MSoRC ensures that no collusion between mix servers and the CA can break public key unlinkability of honest users as long as one mix server is honest (*i.e.*, it correctly randomizes the tuples and permutes them). This holds even if the CA colludes with a subset of mix servers *and users*. Correctness of this process is ensured proving the correct randomization of verification keys, which is a discrete log proof on the sum of all of them.

2 Mercurial Signatures on Randomizable Ciphertexts

Notation. The set of integers from 1 to n is denoted as $[n]$. $\mathbb{Z}_p$ represents the ring of integers modulo p. For a set $\mathcal{S}$, $r \leftarrow_\$ \mathcal{S}$ denotes that r is sampled uniformly at random from $\mathcal{S}$. The security parameter κ is usually passed in unary form. Let BGGen be a PPT algorithm that on input 1^κ, returns $\mathsf{pp} = (p, \mathbb{G}_1, \mathbb{G}_2, \mathbb{G}_T, G, \hat{G}, e)$, an asymmetric bilinear group where $\mathbb{G}_1, \mathbb{G}_2, \mathbb{G}_T$ are cyclic groups of prime order p with $\lceil \log_2 p \rceil = \kappa$, G and $\hat{G}$ are generators of $\mathbb{G}_1$ and $\mathbb{G}_2$, and $e : \mathbb{G}_1 \times \mathbb{G}_2 \to \mathbb{G}_T$ is an efficiently computable (non-degenerate) bilinear map. e is said to be of Type-3 if no efficiently computable isomorphisms between $\mathbb{G}_1$ and $\mathbb{G}_2$ are known. Let $\mathcal{PP}$ be the set of public parameters. For each $\mathsf{pp} \in \mathcal{PP}$, let $\mathcal{M}_\mathsf{pp}, \mathcal{DK}_\mathsf{pp}, \mathcal{EK}_\mathsf{pp}, \mathcal{C}_\mathsf{pp}, \mathcal{R}_\mathsf{pp}, \mathcal{SK}_\mathsf{pp}, \mathcal{VK}_\mathsf{pp}$, and $\mathcal{S}_\mathsf{pp}$ denote the sets of messages, decryption keys, encryption keys, ciphertexts, ciphertext randomness, signature keys, verification keys, and signatures, respectively.

Preliminaries. We refer the reader to the long version [4] for preliminaries on ElGamal encryption and zero-knowledge proofs as used in our constructions.

2.1 Definitions

Our definitions for MSoRC adapt the presentation from [11] to signatures on randomizable ciphertexts (similar to what [24] does for mercurial signatures when generalizing the ideas from [28]). Thus, they can be seen as a merge between the original syntax and security properties of SoRC and MS schemes. For completeness, we include an algorithm ConvertSK in the syntax (it is not required by our mixnet but it could be useful in other applications of MSoRC). As in [24], let $\mathcal{R}$ be an equivalence relation where $[x]_\mathcal{R} = \{y \mid \mathcal{R}(x,y)\}$ denotes the equivalence class of which x is a representative. We loosely consider parametrized relations and say they are well-defined as long as the corresponding parameters are well-defined. We recall that signatures on randomizable ciphertexts are EQS where Adapt is analogous to ChgRep. More precisely, the equivalence class $[c]_{\mathsf{ek}}$ of a ciphertext c under encryption key ek is defined as all randomizations of c, that is, $[c]_{\mathsf{ek}} := \{c' \mid \exists\, r \in \mathcal{R}_{\mathsf{pp}} : c' = \mathsf{Rndmz}(\mathsf{ek}, c; r)\}$. Similarly, equivalence classes of verification and secret keys are defined as $[\mathsf{vk}]_{\mathsf{vk}} := \{\mathsf{vk}' \mid \exists\, r \in \mathcal{R}_{\mathsf{pp}} : \mathsf{vk}' = r\mathsf{vk}\}$ and $[\mathsf{sk}]_{\mathsf{sk}} := \{\mathsf{sk}' \mid \exists\, r \in \mathcal{R}_{\mathsf{pp}} : \mathsf{sk}' = r\mathsf{sk}\}$, respectively.

Definition 1 (Mercurial Signature on Randomizable Ciphertexts). *A MSoRC scheme for parametrized equivalence relations $\mathcal{R}_c$, $\mathcal{R}_{\mathsf{pk}}$, $\mathcal{R}_{\mathsf{sk}}$ is a tuple of the following polynomial-time algorithms of which all except* Setup, KeyGen, *and* SKG *are implicitly parametrized by* pp *generated by* Setup:

Setup(1^κ) $\to$ pp: *Outputs public parameters.*
KeyGen(pp) $\to$ (ek, dk): *Outputs encryption and decryption keys.*
Enc(ek, $m; r$) $\to c$: *Outputs a ciphertext c for a message m using randomness r.*
Dec(dk, c) $\to m$: *Outputs a message m.*
Rndmz(ek, $c; \mu$) $\to c'$: *Randomizes a ciphertext c into c' using random μ.*
SKG(pp) $\to$ (sk, vk): *Outputs a signing key and a verification key.*
Sign(sk, ek, $c; s$) $\to \sigma$: *Outputs a signature σ for c under sk using random s.*
Verify(vk, ek, c, σ) $\to 0/1$: *Verifies (c, σ) w.r.t. vk and ek.*
Adapt($\sigma; \mu, \rho$) $\to \sigma'$: *Randomizes σ into σ' using random μ and ρ.*
ConvertSK(sk, ρ) $\to$ sk': *Randomizes sk into sk' using random ρ.*
ConvertVK(vk, ρ) $\to$ vk': *Randomizes vk into vk' using random ρ.*

Definition 2 (Correctness). *A MSoRC scheme is correct if for all sufficiently large κ,* pp $\in$ Setup(1^κ), (ek, dk) $\in$ KeyGen(pp), (sk, vk) $\in$ SKG(pp), $m \in \mathcal{M}_{\mathsf{pp}}$, $r, \mu, \rho \in \mathcal{R}_{\mathsf{pp}}$, $\sigma \in$ Sign(sk, ek, c) *and* $c \in \mathcal{C}_{\mathsf{pp}}$: Dec(dk, Enc(ek, $m; r$)) = m, Pr[Verify(vk, ek, c, σ) = 1] = 1, ConvertSK(sk, ρ) $\in [\mathsf{sk}]_{\mathsf{sk}} \wedge$ ConvertVK(vk, ρ) $\in [\mathsf{vk}]_{\mathsf{vk}} \wedge$ Pr[Verify(ConvertVK(vk, ρ), ek, Rndmz(ek, $c; \mu$), Adapt($\sigma; \mu, \rho$)) = 1] = 1.

Similar to mercurial signatures, MSoRC unforgeability should allow the adversary to output signatures under equivalent public keys (which are not considered a forgery). However, since MSoRC also deal with encryption keys, it is crucial to consider what happens to them and how they are managed in the unforgeability game. The unforgeability notion from BF20 [11] considers a forgery to be the case in which the adversary can produce a signature on an encryption of a message for an encryption key that has not been queried for that message. This strong unforgeability notion lets the adversary produce signatures under any encryption key pair of its choice. While such notion enables applications such as blind signatures [13], we observe that the encryption keys used in mixnets are either managed by the CA or by some other set of authorities (if a distributed key generation protocol is used to distribute trust) but not the users. Therefore, we can relax the unforgeability requirement so that it's the challenger who picks the encryption key pair instead of the adversary.[1] We formalize both variants as UNF-I and UNF-II in the long version of this work [4].

An MSoRC should also provide an encryption scheme with IND-CPA security and full class-hiding, as previously defined in [11].

Definition 3 (IND-CPA security &Full Class-Hiding [11]). *A MSoRC scheme is IND-CPA and full class-hiding if:*

- **IND-CPA:** *the advantage of any* PPT *adversary* $\mathcal{A}$ *defined by* $\mathbf{Adv}^{\mathsf{IND\text{-}CPA}}_{\mathsf{MSoRC},\mathcal{A}}(\kappa) := 2 \cdot Pr\left[\mathbf{Exp}^{\mathsf{IND\text{-}CPA}}_{\mathsf{MSoRC},\mathcal{A}}(\kappa) \Rightarrow \mathsf{true}\right] - 1 = \epsilon(\kappa).$
- **Full class-hiding:** *the advantage of any* PPT *adversary* $\mathcal{A}$ *defined by* $\mathbf{Adv}^{\mathsf{Full\text{-}CH}}_{\mathsf{MSoRC},\mathcal{A}}(\kappa) := 2 \cdot Pr\left[\mathbf{Exp}^{\mathsf{Full\text{-}CH}}_{\mathsf{MSoRC},\mathcal{A}}(\kappa) \Rightarrow \mathsf{true}\right] - 1 = \epsilon(\kappa).$

where $\mathbf{Exp}^{\mathsf{IND\text{-}CPA}}_{\mathsf{MSoRC},\mathcal{A}}(\kappa)$ *and* $\mathbf{Exp}^{\mathsf{Full\text{-}CH}}_{\mathsf{MSoRC},\mathcal{A}}(\kappa)$ *are defined as:*

Experiment $\mathbf{Exp}^{\mathsf{IND\text{-}CPA}}_{\mathsf{MSoRC},\mathcal{A}}(\kappa)$
―――――――――――――――――
$\mathsf{pp} \leftarrow_\$ \mathsf{Setup}(1^\kappa); b \leftarrow_\$ \{0,1\}; r \leftarrow_\$ \mathcal{R}_{\mathsf{pp}}$
$(\mathsf{dk}, \mathsf{ek}) \leftarrow_\$ \mathsf{KeyGen}(\mathsf{pp})$
$(\mathsf{st}, m_0, m_1) \leftarrow \mathcal{A}(\mathsf{ek}); c \leftarrow \mathsf{Enc}(\mathsf{ek}, m_b, r)$
$b' \leftarrow_\$ \mathcal{A}(\mathsf{st}, c); \mathbf{b}return = b'$

Experiment $\mathbf{Exp}^{\mathsf{Full\text{-}CH}}_{\mathsf{MSoRC},\mathcal{A}}(\kappa)$
―――――――――――――――――
$\mathsf{pp} \leftarrow_\$ \mathsf{Setup}(1^\kappa); b \leftarrow_\$ \{0,1\}; r \leftarrow_\$ \mathcal{R}_{\mathsf{pp}}$
$(\mathsf{dk}, \mathsf{ek}) \leftarrow_\$ \mathsf{KeyGen}(\mathsf{pp})$
$(\mathsf{st}, c) \leftarrow \mathcal{A}(\mathsf{ek}); c_0 \leftarrow_\$ \mathcal{C}_{\mathsf{pp}}; c_1 \leftarrow \mathsf{Rndmz}(\mathsf{ek}, c; r)$
$b' \leftarrow \mathcal{A}(\mathsf{st}, c_b); \mathbf{b}return = b'$

We consider signature adaptations for a new representative of the public key, extending the definition from [11].

Definition 4 (Adaption). *A MSoRC is adaptable (under malicious keys) if for all sufficiently large* κ, *all* $\mathsf{pp} \in \mathsf{Setup}(1^\kappa)$, $(\mathsf{vk}, \mathsf{ek}, c, \sigma) \in \mathcal{VK}_{\mathsf{pp}} \times \mathcal{EK}_{\mathsf{pp}} \times \mathcal{C}_{\mathsf{pp}} \times \mathcal{S}_{\mathsf{pp}}$ *that satisfy* $\mathsf{Verify}(\mathsf{vk}, \mathsf{ek}, c, \sigma) = 1$ *and all* $(\mu, \rho) \in \mathcal{R}^2_{\mathsf{pp}}$, *the output of* $\mathsf{Adapt}(\sigma; \mu, \rho)$ *is uniformly distributed over the set* $\{\sigma' \in \mathcal{S}_{\mathsf{pp}} | \mathsf{Verify}(\mathsf{ConvertVK}(\mathsf{vk}, \rho), \mathsf{ek}, \mathsf{Rndmz}(\mathsf{ek}, c, \mu), \sigma') = 1\}$.

We will also consider an interactive signing protocol as defined below.

$\mathsf{ISign}_{\mathsf{P}_0}(\mathsf{sk}_0, \mathsf{ek}, c) \leftrightarrow \mathsf{ISign}_{\mathsf{P}_1}(\mathsf{sk}_1, \mathsf{ek}, c) \to \sigma$: This algorithm is run interactively. It produces a signature σ for c under sk, implicitly defined as $\mathsf{sk}_0 + \mathsf{sk}_1$.

―――――――――――――
[1] This key observation allows us to obtain an even more efficient MSoRC construction.

Experiment $\mathbf{Exp}_{\mathsf{MSoRC}}^{\mathsf{UNF-III}}(1^\kappa, \mathcal{A})$
$Q \leftarrow \emptyset; \mathsf{pp} \leftarrow\!\!\$ \mathsf{Setup}(1^\kappa); (b, \mathsf{st}) \leftarrow \mathcal{A}(\mathsf{pp}); (\mathsf{dk}, \mathsf{ek}) \leftarrow\!\!\$ \mathsf{KeyGen}(\mathsf{pp})$
$(\mathsf{sk}_i, \mathsf{vk}_i)_{i \in \{0,1\}} \leftarrow\!\!\$ \mathsf{TKGen}(\mathsf{pp}); \mathsf{vk} \leftarrow \mathsf{vk}_0 + \mathsf{vk}_1$
$(\mathsf{vk}^*, c^*, \sigma^*) \leftarrow \mathcal{A}^{\mathsf{ISign}_{1-b}(\mathsf{sk}_{1-b}, \cdot, \cdot)}(\mathsf{st}, \mathsf{vk}_0, \mathsf{vk}_1, \mathsf{sk}_b, \mathsf{ek})$
return $c^* \notin Q \wedge [\mathsf{vk}^*]_{\mathsf{vk}} = [\mathsf{vk}]_{\mathsf{vk}} \wedge \mathsf{Verify}(\mathsf{vk}^*, \mathsf{ek}, c^*, \sigma^*) = 1$
Oracle $\mathsf{ISign}_{1-b}(\mathsf{sk}_{1-b}, \mathsf{ek}, c) : Q \leftarrow Q \cup [c]_{\mathsf{ek}};$ **return** $\mathsf{ISign}_{1-b}(\mathsf{sk}_{1-b}, \mathsf{ek}, c)$

Fig. 2. Unforgeability w.r.t an interactive signing protocol.

Consequently, we define unforgeability and public-key class-hiding assuming at least one honest signer. To prove security, we introduce a key generation algorithm that is run by a trusted third party that produces (vk, sk) as in SKG but such that $\mathsf{vk} = \mathsf{vk}_0 + \mathsf{vk}_1$ and $\mathsf{sk} = \mathsf{sk}_0 + \mathsf{sk}_1$ (in practice, each party will run SKG independently). We require the following property adapted from [3].

Definition 5 (Security of key generation). TKGen *is secure if it outputs* vk *with the same distribution as* SKG, *and there exists a simulator,* SimTKGen, *s.t. for any sufficiently large* κ, *any* $\mathsf{pp} \in \mathsf{Setup}(1^\kappa)$, $(\mathsf{vk}, \mathsf{sk}) \in \mathsf{SKG}(\mathsf{pp})$, *and* $b \in \{0,1\}$, $\mathsf{SimTKGen}(\mathsf{vk}, b)$ *outputs* sk_b *and* $\{\mathsf{vk}_0, \mathsf{vk}_1\}$. *The joint distribution of* $(\mathsf{vk}, \mathsf{vk}_0, \mathsf{vk}_1, \mathsf{sk}_b)$ *is indistinguishable from that of* $\mathsf{TKGen}(\mathsf{pp})$.

For unforgeability, we let the adversary choose one of the parties and leak its corresponding keys. The encryption key pair is generated by the challenger, which suffices for our application. However, we emphasize that the definition below can easily be generalized to adversarially chosen keys, as earlier discussed.

Definition 6 (UNF-III). *A* MSoRC *scheme is unforgeable if the advantage of any* PPT *adversary* $\mathcal{A}$ *having access to an interactive signing oracle defined by* $\mathbf{Adv}_{\mathsf{MSoRC}}^{\mathsf{UNF-III}}(1^\kappa, \mathcal{A}) := Pr[\mathbf{Exp}_{\mathsf{MSoRC}}^{\mathsf{UNF-III}}(1^\kappa, \mathcal{A}) \Rightarrow \mathsf{true}] \leq \epsilon(\kappa)$, *where* $\mathbf{Exp}_{\mathsf{MSoRC}}^{\mathsf{UNF-III}}(1^\kappa, \mathcal{A})$ *is shown in Fig. 2.*

For public key class-hiding, we adapt definitions from [24] and [3] (*i.e.*, considering an interactive signing protocol). This allows us to obtain a stronger notion of public key class-hiding when one of the parties is honest. In other words, full public key class hiding holds if the parties don't collude. Following the naming convention from [3], we formalize this notion as *public key unlinkability*. As we shall see, this notion suffices for the considered applications.

Definition 7 (PK-UNL). *A* MSoRC *scheme is public key unlinkable if the advantage of any* PPT *adversary* $\mathcal{A}$ *defined by* $\mathbf{Adv}_{\mathsf{MSoRC}}^{\mathsf{PK-UNL}}(1^\kappa, \mathcal{A}) := 2 \cdot Pr[\mathbf{Exp}_{\mathsf{MSoRC}}^{\mathsf{PK-UNL}}(1^\kappa, \mathcal{A}) \Rightarrow \mathsf{true}] - 1 \leq \epsilon(\kappa)$, *where* $\mathbf{Exp}_{\mathsf{MSoRC}}^{\mathsf{PK-UNL}}(1^\kappa, \mathcal{A})$ *is shown below.*

Experiment $\boldsymbol{Exp}^{\text{PK-UNL}}_{\text{MSoRC}}(1^\kappa, \mathcal{A})$

$\text{pp} \leftarrow_\$ \text{Setup}(1^\kappa); \rho \leftarrow_\$ \mathcal{R}_{\text{pp}}; b \leftarrow_\$ \{0,1\}; (\widetilde{\text{sk}}, \widetilde{\text{vk}}) \leftarrow_\$ \text{TKGen}(\text{pp})$
$(\text{sk}_i, \text{vk}_i)_{i \in \{0,1\}} \leftarrow_\$ \text{TKGen}(\text{pp}); \text{vk}' \leftarrow \text{ConvertVK}(\widetilde{\text{vk}} + \text{vk}_b, \rho)$
$b' \leftarrow_\$ \mathcal{A}^{\text{ISign}(\text{sk}_b, \cdot, \cdot)}(\widetilde{\text{sk}}, \widetilde{\text{vk}}, \text{vk}', \text{vk}_0, \text{vk}_1); \boldsymbol{b} return = b'$

Oracle $\text{ISign}(\text{sk}_b, \text{ek}, c, \text{vk})$
$\text{vk} if = \text{vk}' 1 =, 2 = \sigma[] then \leftarrow_\$ \text{ISign}_b(\text{sk}_b, \text{ek}, c)$
$\text{Adapt} return(\sigma; \rho)\, \text{vk} elseif = \text{vk}_i\ return ISign(\text{sk}_i, \text{ek}, c)$

2.2 Single-Signer Construction

In Fig. 3, we present the base MSoRC with a single signer. Our departure point is the SoRC from [11], which is an EQS based on [28] that signs ElGamal ciphertexts. In [11], a signature consists of four group elements $Z = \frac{1}{s}(x_0 C_0 + x_1 C_1 + G), S = sG, \hat{S} = s\hat{G}$ and $T = \frac{1}{s}(x_0 G + x_1 X)$, where (C_0, C_1) is the ciphertext, X it's encryption key, and (x_0, x_1) the scheme's signing key. Without G, $(Z, S, \hat{S})$ is the EQS from [28]. The idea from [11] was to embed G into Z so that Z can only be adapted to ciphertext randomizations using the additional element T. To turn the SoRC from [11] into a full-fledged MSoRC we extend the secret key to include one more element x_2 and use it to sign G in Z. This way, Z can be adapted to a new key representative, as well as to a ciphertext randomization if T is used.

$\mathsf{MSoRC.Setup}(1^\kappa): \text{pp} := (p, \mathbb{G}_1, \mathbb{G}_2, \mathbb{G}_T, G, \hat{G}, e) \leftarrow_\$ \mathsf{BGGen}(1^\kappa); \textbf{return}\ (\text{pp})$
$\mathsf{MSoRC.KeyGen}(\text{pp}): \text{dk} := x \leftarrow_\$ \mathbb{Z}_p^*; \text{ek} := X \leftarrow xG; \textbf{return}\ (\text{dk}, \text{ek})$
$\mathsf{MSoRC.SKG}(\text{pp}): \text{sk} := (x_0, x_1, x_2) \leftarrow \mathbb{Z}_p^*; \text{vk} := (x_0 \hat{G}, x_1 \hat{G}, x_2 \hat{G}); \textbf{return}\ (\text{sk}, \text{vk})$
$\mathsf{MSoRC.Enc}(X, M; r): \textbf{return}\ (rG, M + rX)$
$\mathsf{MSoRC.Dec}(x, (C_0, C_1)): \textbf{return}\ M := C_1 - xC_0$
$\mathsf{MSoRC.Rndmz}(X, (C_0, C_1); \mu): \textbf{return}\ (C_0 + \mu G, C_1 + \mu X)$
$\mathsf{MSoRC.Sign}((x_0, x_1, x_2), X, (C_0, C_1)):$
$s \leftarrow_\$ \mathbb{Z}_p^*; Z := \frac{1}{s}(x_0 C_0 + x_1 C_1 + x_2 G); S := sG; \hat{S} := s\hat{G}; T := \frac{1}{s}(x_0 G + x_1 X)$
$\textbf{return}\ (Z, S, \hat{S}, T)$
$\mathsf{MSoRC.ConvertSK}((x_0, x_1, x_2), \rho): \textbf{return}\ (\rho x_0, \rho x_1, \rho x_2)$
$\mathsf{MSoRC.ConvertVK}((\hat{X}_0, \hat{X}_1, \hat{X}_2), \rho): \textbf{return}\ (\rho \hat{X}_0, \rho \hat{X}_1, \rho \hat{X}_2)$
$\mathsf{MSoRC.Adapt}((Z, S, \hat{S}, T); \mu, \rho):$
$s' \leftarrow_\$ \mathbb{Z}_p^*; Z' := \frac{\rho}{s'}(Z + \mu T); S' := s'S; \hat{S}' := s'\hat{S}; T' := \frac{\rho}{s'}T; \textbf{return}\ (Z', S', \hat{S}', T')$
$\mathsf{MSoRC.Verify}((\hat{X}_0, \hat{X}_1, \hat{X}_2), X, (C_0, C_1), (Z, S, \hat{S}, T)):$
$\textbf{return}\ e(Z, \hat{S}) = e(C_0, \hat{X}_0)e(C_1, \hat{X}_1)e(G, \hat{X}_2)$
$\land\ e(T, \hat{S}) = e(G, \hat{X}_0)e(X, \hat{X}_1)\ \land\ e(S, \hat{G}) = e(G, \hat{S})$

Fig. 3. Our base MSoRC scheme.

Correctness of our base scheme follows by inspection. ElGamal is IND − CPA if the DDH assumption holds, which we assume. Full class-hiding was already proven in [11] giving a reduction to DDH. Likewise, signature adaption follows directly from that of the original SoRC ([11], Proposition 2). We prove unforgeability and public key unlinkability as stated below in the long version [4].

Theorem 1. *Our base* MSoRC *is unforgeable in the GGM, and public key unlinkable under corruption of at most one party.*

2.3 Two-Party Construction

We can extend our construction to support a two-party *interactive* signing protocol as shown in Fig. 4. We do so using the techniques from [3] to build TMS, and all elements are computed analogously (*e.g.*, we compute a blinded version of Z and T, with each party proving the correctness of each step via short ZKPoK's). ZKPoK's are defined as follows:

- ZKPoK$[s_0 : S_0 = s_0 G \wedge \hat{S}_0 = s_0 \hat{G}]$,
- ZKPoK$[(s_0, x_0^0, x_1^0, x_2^0) : T_0 = \frac{1}{s_0}(T_1 + x_0^0 G + x_1^0 X) \wedge S_0 = s_0 G \wedge Z_0 = \frac{1}{s_0}(Z_1 + x_0^0 C_0 + x_1^0 C_1 + x_2^0 G) \wedge \hat{X}_0^0 = x_0^0 \hat{G} \wedge \hat{X}_1^0 = x_1^0 \hat{G} \wedge \hat{X}_2^0 = x_2^0 \hat{G}]$,
- ZKPoK$[(r, x_0^1, x_1^1, x_2^1) : T_1 = rS_0 + x_0^1 G + x_1^1 X \wedge Z_1 = rS_0 + x_0^1 C_0 + x_1^1 C_1 + x_2^1 G \wedge \hat{X}_0^1 = x_0^1 \hat{G} \wedge \hat{X}_1^1 = x_1^1 \hat{G} \wedge \hat{X}_1^2 = x_2^1 \hat{G}]$,
- ZKPoK$[(r, s_1) : T = \frac{1}{s_1}(T_0 - rG) \wedge S = s_1 S_0 \wedge \hat{S} = s_1 \hat{S}_0 \wedge Z = \frac{1}{s_1}(Z_0 - rG)]$.

We stress that all ZKPoK involved are as simple to implement as a Schnorr proof. In the long version [4] we explain why the interactive variant produces signatures under the same distribution. It remains to be seen that our two-party

- ZKPoK$[s_0 : S_0 = s_0 G \wedge \hat{S}_0 = s_0 \hat{G}]$,
- ZKPoK$[(s_0, x_0^0, x_1^0, x_2^0) : T_0 = \frac{1}{s_0}(T_1 + x_0^0 G + x_1^0 X) \wedge S_0 = s_0 G \wedge Z_0 = \frac{1}{s_0}(Z_1 + x_0^0 C_0 + x_1^0 C_1 + x_2^0 G) \wedge \hat{X}_0^0 = x_0^0 \hat{G} \wedge \hat{X}_1^0 = x_1^0 \hat{G} \wedge \hat{X}_2^0 = x_2^0 \hat{G}]$,

P_0: $C_0, C_1, X, \{\hat{X}_i^0 = x_i^0 \hat{G}, x_i^0, \hat{X}_i^1\}_{i \in \{0,1,2\}}$	P_1: $C_0, C_1, X, \{\hat{X}_i^1 = x_i^1 \hat{G}, x_i^1, \hat{X}_i^1\}_{i \in \{0,1,2\}}$
$s_0 \leftarrow\!\!\$\ \mathbb{Z}_p^*$; $S_0 \leftarrow s_0 G$; $\hat{S}_0 \leftarrow s_0 \hat{G}$	$r \leftarrow\!\!\$\ \mathbb{Z}_p$; $s_1 \leftarrow\!\!\$\ \mathbb{Z}_p^*$
$\pi_0 \leftarrow \mathsf{ZKPoK}[s_0]$ $\xrightarrow{S_0, \hat{S}_0, \pi_0}$	$\hat{S} \leftarrow s_1 \hat{S}_0$; $Z_1 \leftarrow rS_0 + x_0^1 C_0 + x_1^1 C_1 + x_2^1 G$
	$T_1 \leftarrow rS_0 + x_0^1 G + x_1^1 X$
$T_0 \leftarrow \frac{1}{s_0}(T_1 + x_0^0 G + x_1^0 X)$ $\xleftarrow{T_1, Z_1, \pi_1}$	$\pi_1 \leftarrow \mathsf{ZKPoK}[r, x_0^1, x_1^1, x_2^1]$
$Z_0 \leftarrow \frac{1}{s_0}(Z_1 + x_0^0 C_0 + x_1^0 C_1 + x_2^0 G)$	
$\widetilde{\pi}_0 \leftarrow \mathsf{ZKPoK}[s_0, x_0^0, x_1^0, x_2^0]$ $\xrightarrow{Z_0, T_0, \widetilde{\pi}_0}$	$T \leftarrow \frac{1}{s_1}(T_0 - rG)$; $Z \leftarrow \frac{1}{s_1}(Z_0 - rG)$
	$\widetilde{\pi}_1 \leftarrow \mathsf{ZKPoK}[r, s_1]$
return $(\sigma, \widetilde{\pi}_1)$ $\xleftarrow{\sigma, \widetilde{\pi}_1}$	$\sigma \leftarrow (Z, \boxed{S}, \hat{S}, T)$; **return** $(\sigma, \widetilde{\pi}_1)$

Fig. 4. Our two-party interactive signing algorithm.

variant is also unforgeable (other properties are obviously taken over from the single-party construction). We reduce unforgeability of the two-party MSoRC to that of single-party MSoRC in a similar way as done in [3]. Consequently, we obtain the following theorem, which we prove in the long version [4].

Theorem 2. *Our two-party* MSoRC *from Fig. 4 is unforgeable if the single-party base* MSoRC *is unforgeable, and all* ZKPoK*'s are secure.*

We claim that signature element S (boxed value S in Fig. 4) can be removed if encryption keys are honestly generated, and use this optimization to instantiate MSoRC in our mixnet construction. Further details and corresponding security proofs for this optimization can be found in the long version [4].

3 Mixnet from Two-Party MSoRC

Entities and Communication Model. As outlined before, our mixnet considers three main entities: users, CA, and mixers. As for the trust model, any users may be corrupted and behave maliciously. The CA is trusted to adhere to the protocol and thus follows the protocol as specified, but it is not trusted in terms of privacy. Mixers are not trusted to follow the protocol but at least one of them is trusted in terms of privacy. Our mixnet involves two more entities; an external verifier and a polling authority (PA). The external verifier assures the correctness of the input and output lists for the sake of soundness, and the involvement of all mix servers for the sake of privacy. PA is an entity that is responsible to decrypt the output ciphertexts. It is trusted in terms of privacy but not for soundness. To ease the trust, PA could be distributed among a set of entities that hold the decryption key and decrypt the output tuples in a distributed manner. Since this is a common approach, we do not discuss it in detail. These entities communicate through a publicly verifiable authenticated channel.

Construction. Our mixnet operates in four main phases: Setup, Input Certification, Mixing, and Verification, as illustrated in Fig. 1. These are followed by a final decryption phase performed by PA, which we omit here as it is straightforward. Below, we describe each phase in detail.

Setup Phase. All parameters and keys are sampled in this phase. For ease of exposition, we present this phase as a single algorithm, $\mathsf{Setup}(1^\kappa)$, run by a trusted party. The public parameters pp are published, and the secret keys are delivered to the respective parties privately.

$\mathsf{Setup}(1^\kappa)$:
$\mathsf{pp}_1 \leftarrow_\$ \mathsf{MSoRC.Setup}(1^\kappa)$ // $\mathsf{pp}_1 = (p, \mathbb{G}_1, \mathbb{G}_2, \mathbb{G}_T, G, \hat{G}, e)$
$\mathsf{pp}_2 \leftarrow_\$ \mathsf{NIZK.Setup}(1^\kappa)$
$(\mathsf{dk}, \mathsf{ek}) \leftarrow \mathsf{MSoRC.KeyGen}(\mathsf{pp}_1)$ // to PA
$(\mathsf{ask}, \mathsf{avk}) \leftarrow \mathsf{MSoRC.SKG}(\mathsf{pp}_1)$ // to CA
foreach $i \in [n]$ $(\mathsf{usk}_i, \mathsf{uvk}_i) \leftarrow \mathsf{MSoRC.SKG}(\mathsf{pp}_1)$ // to user i
$\mathsf{pp} := (\mathsf{pp}_1, \mathsf{pp}_2, \mathsf{ek}, \mathsf{avk}, \mathsf{uvk}_{i \in [n]})$ // publish

In practice, each key generation algorithm is performed independently by the respective party, *i.e.*, PA, CA, and each user. This assumes the standard certified-key setting, where all entities must prove knowledge of their secret keys.

Input Certification Phase. In this phase, ciphertexts from users are certified to form the initial input for the subsequent mixing phase. Each user and the CA collaboratively execute the protocols $\mathsf{EncAuth}_{u_i}$ and $\mathsf{EncAuth}_{\mathsf{CA}}$, respectively. At a high level, this process consists of the user encrypting their message, followed by a two-party MSoRC signing protocol (as depicted in Fig. 4) on the resulting ciphertext. The protocol is detailed below.

$$\frac{\mathsf{EncAuth}_{u_i}(\mathsf{usk}_i, \mathsf{uvk}_i, \mathsf{avk}, M_i, \mathsf{ek}):}{\mathsf{ct}_i \leftarrow \mathsf{MSoRC.Enc}(\mathsf{ek}, M_i; \gamma)}$$

$\pi \leftarrow \mathsf{ZKPoK}[(\gamma, \mathsf{usk}_i) : \mathsf{st1}]$

$$\xrightarrow{\mathsf{ct}_i, \pi}$$

$$\frac{\mathsf{EncAuth}_{\mathsf{CA}}(\mathsf{ask}, \mathsf{avk}, \mathsf{uvk}_i, \mathsf{ek}):}{}$$

$\mathsf{ct}'_i \leftarrow \mathsf{MSoRC.Rndmz}(\mathsf{ek}, \mathsf{ct}_i; \mu)$
$\pi' \leftarrow \mathsf{ZKPoK}[\mu : \mathsf{st2}]$

$$\xleftarrow{\mathsf{ct}'_i, \pi', \mathsf{evk}_i}$$ $(\mathsf{esk}_i, \mathsf{evk}_i) \leftarrow_\$ \mathsf{MSoRC.SKG}()$

$\sigma_i \leftarrow \mathsf{MSoRC.ISign}_{\mathsf{P}_0}(\mathsf{usk}_i, \mathsf{ct}'_i)$ $\xleftrightarrow{\mathsf{MSoRC.ISign}}$ $\sigma_i \leftarrow \mathsf{MSoRC.ISign}_{\mathsf{P}_1}(\boxed{\mathsf{esk}_i + \mathsf{ask}}, \mathsf{ct}'_i)$
$(return \sigma_i, \mathsf{ct}'_i, \mathsf{evk}_i)$ $\qquad\qquad\qquad\qquad (return \sigma_i, \mathsf{ct}'_i, \mathsf{esk}_i, \mathsf{evk}_i)$

The protocol involves two zero-knowledge proofs, which are implicitly verified, and the protocol aborts if any verification fails. The first proof, provided by the user, establishes knowledge of (γ, usk_i) such that $\mathsf{st1} := (C_0 = \gamma G \wedge \mathsf{uvk}_i = \mathsf{usk}_i \hat{G})$, where C_0 is the first component of the ciphertext $\mathsf{ct}_i = (\gamma G, M_i + \gamma \mathsf{ek})$. The second proof, st2, demonstrates that ct'_i is a correct re-randomization of ct_i, i.e., $\mathsf{st2} := (\mathsf{ct}'_i = \mathsf{MSoRC.Rndmz}(\mathsf{ek}, \mathsf{ct}_i; \mu))$. In the following, we clarify the rationale behind our design choices:

Ciphertext Randomization by the CA is Optional. While not essential for our mixnet's soundness or privacy, randomizing the ciphertext by the CA is beneficial in applications such as receipt-free voting, as it prevents users from demonstrating that a ciphertext decrypts to a specific message.

User's ZKPoKEnsures Plaintext Knowledge and Authentication. This proof prevents replay attacks in which an adversarial user could wait for another to submit a ciphertext, randomize it, and then obtain a signature on the same message.

Ephemeral Key Pairs $(\mathsf{esk}_i, \mathsf{evk}_i)$ on theCA Side. Introduction of an ephemeral key pair by the CA protects against maliciously crafted user keys. Without this, a malicious user could generate keys in a correlated manner and collude with the first mix server to replace ciphertexts. The inclusion of the ephemeral public key ensures that each verification key is independent of the user's key generation. In the algorithm, we highlight this modification by indicating that the CA signs with $\mathsf{esk}_i + \mathsf{ask}$ instead of ask alone (boxed value in the protocol). Consequently, MSoRC.ISign produces a signature that verifies under $\mathsf{uvk}_i + \mathsf{evk}_i + \mathsf{avk}$.

Upon completion of the protocol between the CA and user i, the resulting tuple $(\sigma_i, \mathsf{ct}'_i, \mathsf{uvk}_i, \mathsf{evk}_i)$ is published in an authenticated manner. It is crucial to ensure that evk_i is the ephemeral key generated by the CA. For clarity and consistency, we assume that the CA is responsible for publishing these tuples.

Mix($\mathcal{SSet}^{(j-1)}$)
$(\text{ct}_i^{(j-1)}, \sigma_i^{(j-1)}, \text{vk}_i^{(j-1)})_{i \in [n]} \leftarrow \mathcal{SSet}^{(j-1)}$ //parse input list
$\mu, \rho \leftarrow_\$ \mathbb{Z}_p^*; \Pi_j \leftarrow_\$ \Pi[n]$ //sample random factors
foreach $i \in [n]$ **do**   //randomize & permute
   if MSoRC.Verify($\text{vk}_i^{(j-1)}, \text{ct}_i^{(j-1)}, \sigma_i^{(j-1)}) \neq 1$ **abort**
   $\text{vk}_{\Pi_j(i)}^{(j)} \leftarrow$ MSoRC.ConvertVK($\text{vk}_i^{(j-i)}, \rho$)
   $\sigma_{\Pi_j(i)}^{(j)} \leftarrow$ MSoRC.Adapt($\sigma_i^{(j-1)}; \mu, \rho$)
   $\text{ct}_{\Pi_j(i)}^{(j)} \leftarrow$ MSoRC.Rndmz(ek, $\text{ct}_i^{(j-1)}; \mu$)
$\mathcal{SSet}^{(j)} := (\text{ct}_i^{(j)}, \sigma_i^{(j)}, \text{vk}_i^{(j)})_{i \in [n]}$ //compose output list
$\text{VK}^{(j-1)} := \sum \text{vk}_i^{(j-1)}; \text{VK}^{(j)} := \sum \text{vk}_i^{(j)}$ //aggregate I/O keys
$\pi^{(j)} \leftarrow$ NIZK.Prove[ρ : st3]   //proof on aggregated keys
return ($\mathcal{SSet}^{(j)}, \text{VK}^{(j)}, \pi^{(j)}$)

Fig. 5. Mix algorithm.

This phase concludes once all users have completed the protocol with the CA. Let $\mathcal{CIL} := (\sigma_i, \text{ct}'_i, \text{uvk}_i, \text{evk}_i)_{i \in [n]}$ denote the certified input list. For each entry, define $\text{vk}_i := \text{uvk}_i + \text{evk}_i + \text{avk}$; we treat vk_i as a virtual value, computed in this way whenever referenced. From this point onward, each tuple $(\text{ct}'_i, \sigma_i, \text{vk}_i)$ produced in this phase is relabeled with the superscript (0) as $(\text{ct}_i^{(0)}, \sigma_i^{(0)}, \text{vk}_i^{(0)})$. We then define the initial shuffle set as $\mathcal{SSet}^{(0)} := (\text{ct}_i^{(0)}, \sigma_i^{(0)}, \text{vk}_i^{(0)})_{i \in [n]}$.

Mixing Phase. In this phase, the mix servers $1, \ldots, N$ operate sequentially in a cascade. Each mix server receives an input list, processes it, and passes the resulting output list to the next server. Let $\Pi[n]$ denote the set of all permutations over $[n]$, and let NIZK denote a non-interactive zero-knowledge proof system. Each mix server j executes the Mix algorithm as shown in Fig. 5. Statement st3 := ($\text{VK}^{(j)}$ = MSoRC.ConvertVK($\text{VK}^{(j-1)}, \rho$)), ensures correct transformation of the aggregated key. The algorithm proceeds as follows:

1. It first parses $\mathcal{SSet}^{(j-1)}$ (the previous mix server's output) and samples fresh randomness μ, ρ, and a permutation Π_j from their respective domains.
2. For each verified input tuple ($\text{ct}_i^{(j-1)}, \sigma_i^{(j-1)}, \text{vk}_i^{(j-1)}$), it randomizes the verification key, signature, and ciphertext using the random factors ρ and μ via the corresponding MSoRC functions, and stores the result in a position determined by Π_j in the output list.
3. Finally, it aggregates the verification keys in both the input and output, and proves that they are correctly related via the common randomness ρ. With our MSoRC, this proof reduces to a lightweight equality of discrete logarithms among three pairs of elements.

Each mix server j publishes its output ($\mathcal{SSet}^{(j)}, \text{VK}^{(j)}, \pi^{(j)}$). The output list $\mathcal{SSet}^{(j)}$ is then provided as input to the next mix server. The pair ($\text{VK}^{(j)}, \pi^{(j)}$)

$\mathsf{Verify}(\mathcal{CIL}, \pi^{(1)}, \ldots, \pi^{(N)}, \mathsf{VK}^{(1)}, \ldots, \mathsf{VK}^{(N-1)}, \mathcal{SS}\mathsf{et}^{(N)})$:
$(\sigma_i, \mathsf{ct}'_i, \mathsf{uvk}_i, \mathsf{evk}_i)_{i \in [n]} \leftarrow \mathcal{CIL}$ //parse I/O lists
$(\mathsf{ct}_i^{(N)}, \sigma_i^{(N)}, \mathsf{vk}_i^{(N)})_{i \in [n]} \leftarrow \mathcal{SS}\mathsf{et}^{(N)}$
foreach $i \in [n]$ **do**   //check I/O entries
    if $\mathsf{MSoRC.Verify}(\mathsf{uvk}_i + \mathsf{evk}_i + \mathsf{avk}, \mathsf{ct}'_i, \sigma_i) \neq 1$ **return** 0
    if $\mathsf{MSoRC.Verify}(\mathsf{vk}_i^{(N)}, \mathsf{ct}_i^{(N)}, \sigma_i^{(N)}) \neq 1$ **return** 0
$\mathsf{VK}^{(0)} := \sum_{i=1}^{n} \mathsf{uvk}_i + \mathsf{evk}_i + \mathsf{avk};\ \mathsf{VK}^{(N)} := \sum_{i=1}^{n} \mathsf{vk}_i^{(N)}$ //aggregate I/O keys
foreach $j \in [N]$ **do**   //check proof chain
    if $\mathsf{NIZK.Verify}(\pi^{(j)}, \mathsf{VK}^{(j-1)}, \mathsf{VK}^{(j)}) \neq 1$ **return** 0
return 1

Fig. 6. Verify algorithm.

forms a link in the proof chain that will be checked during the verification phase. The mixing phase concludes when the final mix server N publishes its output. Mix servers do not verify the proof from previous servers. While they could perform this check and abort early upon failure, we defer all proof verification to the final verification phase for simplicity. However, each server does verify every entry in its input list using MSoRC.Verify. Notably, this verification is essential for privacy rather than soundness, as detailed in the security proof.

Verification Phase. Any external party can verify the mixing process. Although all outputs are publicly available, the verifier only requires the certified input list $\mathcal{CIL}$, the sequence of proofs $(\pi^{(1)}, \ldots, \pi^{(N)})$, the aggregated keys $(\mathsf{VK}^{(1)}, \ldots, \mathsf{VK}^{(N-1)})$, and the final output list $\mathcal{SS}\mathsf{et}^{(N)}$ as input. Notably, the verifier does not need access to any intermediate output lists $\mathcal{SS}\mathsf{et}^{(j)}$ for $j = 1, \ldots, N-1$. The verification algorithm is shown in Fig. 6. The phase concludes when the verifier outputs 1 (success) or 0 (failure). In the event of failure, the application layer can determine the appropriate response. Since all data are authenticated and publicly available, identifying the source of any inconsistency is straightforward.

Constant-Size Proof. Following HPP20, we can eliminate the linear dependency on N by introducing a second round of interaction using the multi-signature from [14]. Each mixer computes its own proof and a partial proof π', which is updated by multiplying in its witness. Unlike HPP20, which relies on GS proofs, we use the more efficient updatable proof system from [22] (CH20) as detailed in [4]. The first mixer creates a proof, and each subsequent mixer updates it; at the end, π' attests to the relation between the initial and final tuples, allowing the entire process to be verified with a single proof. Mixers batch verify all proofs and jointly sign π' if they agree. Both the last individual proof and π' show knowledge of a witness for the final tuple, but π' relates it directly to the initial input. Batch verification ensures all servers participated honestly. Updating π' is efficient, requiring only a multiplication in $\mathbb{Z}_p$ and two exponentiations in $\mathbb{G}_2$ for the optimized two-key version of our MSoRC.

By allowing a second round of interaction, we can further simplify the above approach, originally envisioned in HPP20 and adapted to our setting. Since the NIZK proofs used in this work are simple discrete logarithm proofs, we can dispense with the CH20 proof system and instead rely on standard Schnorr proofs. Concretely, the process proceeds as follows:

1. Each mixer computes its individual proof $\pi^{(j)} \leftarrow$ NIZK.Prove($\mathsf{VK}^{(j-1)}, \mathsf{VK}^{(j)}, \rho^{(j)}$) as a Schnorr proof, and records the randomizer $\rho^{(j)}$ used.
2. After the mixing phase, the mixers engage in a second round of interaction. First, they batch-verify all individual proofs as before. Then, they jointly produce a distributed Schnorr proof $\pi' \leftarrow$ NIZK.Prove($\mathsf{VK}^{(0)}, \mathsf{VK}^{(N)}, \rho'$), where $\rho' = \prod_j \rho^{(j)}$. Finally, they sign π' using a multi-signature scheme.

Security Model and Extensions. We defer the presentation of the security model and proofs to the long version [4], where we also discuss how to extend our mixnet to support multiple ciphertexts with minimal overhead and discuss its application for e-voting.

3.1 Performance Evaluation

Comparison. We compare our mixnet with the works by Hébant et al. [34] and Faonio and Russo [27] (Rand-RCCA), presenting asymptotic computational and communication costs in the long version [4].

Experimental Results. We implemented a prototype of our protocols in Rust using the blasters library [36], which implements the pairing-friendly BLS12-381 curve. BLAKE3 [40] was used to instantiate hash functions. Source code and documentation to reproduce our results are available on GitHub [39]. We used Rust's Criterion library and the nightly compiler with no extra optimizations to run the benchmarks on a MacBook Pro M3 with 32GB of RAM. The (interactive) signing protocol of our MSoRC scheme (Fig. 4) takes 6.4ms while EncAuth (which includes the ZKPoK's) takes 8.1ms.

Running times of other protocols are summarized in Table 1, confirming the linear complexity of our mixnet scheme. In all cases, the standard deviation was below 1s. We note that a pairing takes around 380 microseconds while a multi-exponentiation for $N = 10$ takes 737 microseconds. Thus, for a small N, the difference between our standard Verify (where we verify N proofs in batch) and the constant-size variant of it (where a single proof is verified) is negligible.

Our prototype does not make use of parallelization libraries such as Rayon. However, our scheme is highly compatible with such techniques due to the individual processing of tuples during mixing and verification. Moreover, practical deployments would use proper servers, allowing our solution to scale further.

Table 1. Running times of each protocol in seconds.

n	InputVerification	Mix	Verify ($N=5$)	($N=10$)
1k	2.7	0.8	2.7	2.7
10k	27.1	8.3	27	27
25k	67.6	20.7	67.4	67.4
50k	135	41.3	134.6	134.5

4 Conclusion

In this work, we introduced a new certified-input mixnet construction based on the novel concept of mercurial signatures on randomizable ciphertexts (MSoRC). Our approach advances the state of the art by achieving both improved efficiency and stronger security guarantees compared to previous frameworks such as HPP20. In particular, our two-party MSoRC provides public-key unlinkability, which is crucial for protecting voter privacy in e-voting systems against collusion between users, mix servers, and the certificate authority.

The modularity of our construction facilitates integration and future improvements, making it adaptable to evolving cryptographic primitives. Through careful design and optimization, we demonstrated that our protocol is both scalable and practical. Our implementation and benchmarks show that, for 50k voters and 10 mix servers, the worst-case mixing time is around 40 s, and the entire process completes in under 5 min on a commodity laptop, without any parallelization. We believe our contributions will enable the development of more efficient and practical mixnet protocols for privacy-sensitive applications.

References

1. Abe, M., Fuchsbauer, G., Groth, J., Haralambiev, K., Ohkubo, M.: Structure-preserving signatures and commitments to group elements. In: Rabin, T. (ed.) CRYPTO 2010. LNCS, vol. 6223, pp. 209–236. Springer, Heidelberg (2010). https://doi.org/10.1007/978-3-642-14623-7_12
2. Abe, M., Groth, J., Haralambiev, K., Ohkubo, M.: Optimal structure-preserving signatures in asymmetric bilinear groups. In: Rogaway, P. (ed.) CRYPTO 2011. LNCS, vol. 6841, pp. 649–666. Springer, Heidelberg (2011). https://doi.org/10.1007/978-3-642-22792-9_37
3. Abe, M., Nanri, M., Kempner, O.P., Tibouchi, M.: Interactive threshold mercurial signatures and applications. In: Chung, K.M., Sasaki, Y. (eds.) Advances in Cryptology - ASIACRYPT 2024, pp. 69–103. Springer, Singapore (2025). https://doi.org/10.1007/978-981-96-0891-1_3
4. Abe, M., Nanri, M., Ohkubo, M., Perez Kempner, O., Slamanig, D., Tibouchi, M.: A certified-input mixnet from two-party mercurial signatures on randomizable ciphertexts. Cryptology ePrint Archive (2024). https://ia.cr/2024/1503

5. Ahmad, K., Kamal, A., Ahmad, K.A.B., Khari, M., Crespo, R.G.: Fast hybrid-mixnet for security and privacy using NTRU algorithm. J. Inf. Secur. Appl. **60**, 102872 (2021)
6. Ames, S., Hazay, C., Ishai, Y., Venkitasubramaniam, M.: Ligero: lightweight sublinear arguments without a trusted setup. In: Thuraisingham, B.M., Evans, D., Malkin, T., Xu, D. (eds.) ACM CCS 2017, pp. 2087–2104. ACM Press (2017). https://doi.org/10.1145/3133956.3134104
7. Aranha, D.F., Baum, C., Gjøsteen, K., Silde, T.: Verifiable mix-nets and distributed decryption for voting from lattice-based assumptions. In: Proceedings of the 2023 ACM SIGSAC Conference on Computer and Communications Security, CCS 2023, Copenhagen, Denmark, 26–30 November 2023, pp. 1467–1481. ACM (2023). https://doi.org/10.1145/3576915.3616683
8. Aranha, D.F., Baum, C., Gjøsteen, K., Silde, T.: Verifiable mix-nets and distributed decryption for voting from lattice-based assumptions. In: Proceedings of the 2023 ACM SIGSAC Conference on Computer and Communications Security, CCS '23, pp. 1467–1481. Association for Computing Machinery, New York (2023). https://doi.org/10.1145/3576915.3616683
9. Aranha, D.F., Baum, C., Gjøsteen, K., Silde, T., Tunge, T.: Lattice-based proof of shuffle and applications to electronic voting. In: Paterson, K.G. (ed.) CT-RSA 2021. LNCS, vol. 12704, pp. 227–251. Springer, Cham (2021). https://doi.org/10.1007/978-3-030-75539-3_10
10. Backes, M., Hanzlik, L., Kluczniak, K., Schneider, J.: Signatures with flexible public key: introducing equivalence classes for public keys. In: Peyrin, T., Galbraith, S. (eds.) ASIACRYPT 2018. LNCS, vol. 11273, pp. 405–434. Springer, Cham (2018). https://doi.org/10.1007/978-3-030-03329-3_14
11. Bauer, B., Fuchsbauer, G.: Efficient signatures on randomizable ciphertexts. In: Galdi, C., Kolesnikov, V. (eds.) SCN 2020. LNCS, vol. 12238, pp. 359–381. Springer, Cham (2020). https://doi.org/10.1007/978-3-030-57990-6_18
12. Bayer, S., Groth, J.: Efficient zero-knowledge argument for correctness of a shuffle. In: Pointcheval, D., Johansson, T. (eds.) EUROCRYPT 2012. LNCS, vol. 7237, pp. 263–280. Springer, Heidelberg (2012). https://doi.org/10.1007/978-3-642-29011-4_17
13. Blazy, O., Fuchsbauer, G., Pointcheval, D., Vergnaud, D.: Signatures on randomizable ciphertexts. In: Catalano, D., Fazio, N., Gennaro, R., Nicolosi, A. (eds.) PKC 2011. LNCS, vol. 6571, pp. 403–422. Springer, Heidelberg (2011). https://doi.org/10.1007/978-3-642-19379-8_25
14. Boneh, D., Drijvers, M., Neven, G.: Compact multi-signatures for smaller blockchains. In: Peyrin, T., Galbraith, S. (eds.) ASIACRYPT 2018. LNCS, vol. 11273, pp. 435–464. Springer, Cham (2018). https://doi.org/10.1007/978-3-030-03329-3_15
15. Boyen, X., Haines, T., Müller, J.: A verifiable and practical lattice-based decryption mix net with external auditing. In: Chen, L., Li, N., Liang, K., Schneider, S. (eds.) ESORICS 2020. LNCS, vol. 12309, pp. 336–356. Springer, Cham (2020). https://doi.org/10.1007/978-3-030-59013-0_17
16. Canetti, R., Krawczyk, H., Nielsen, J.B.: Relaxing chosen-ciphertext security. In: Boneh, D. (ed.) CRYPTO 2003. LNCS, vol. 2729, pp. 565–582. Springer, Heidelberg (2003). https://doi.org/10.1007/978-3-540-45146-4_33
17. Castejon-Molina, D., Vasilopoulos, D., Moreno-Sanchez, P.: Mixbuy: contingent payment in the presence of coin mixers. Proc. Priv. Enhancing Technol. **2025**(1), 671–706 (2025). https://doi.org/10.56553/POPETS-2025-0036

18. Chainlink: Chainlink network. Online (2025). https://chain.link/
19. Chaum, D.L.: Untraceable electronic mail, return addresses, and digital pseudonyms. Commun. ACM **24**(2), 84–90 (1981). https://doi.org/10.1145/358549.358563
20. Chow, S.S.M., Liu, J.K., Wong, D.S.: Robust receipt-free election system with ballot secrecy and verifiability. In: NDSS 2008. The Internet Society (2008)
21. Connolly, A., Lafourcade, P., Perez-Kempner, O.: Improved constructions of anonymous credentials from structure-preserving signatures on equivalence classes. In: Hanaoka, G., Shikata, J., Watanabe, Y. (eds.) PKC 2022, Part I. LNCS, vol. 13177, pp. 409–438. Springer, Heidelberg (2022). https://doi.org/10.1007/978-3-030-97121-2_15
22. Couteau, G., Hartmann, D.: Shorter non-interactive zero-knowledge arguments and ZAPs for algebraic languages. In: Micciancio, D., Ristenpart, T. (eds.) CRYPTO 2020. LNCS, vol. 12172, pp. 768–798. Springer, Cham (2020). https://doi.org/10.1007/978-3-030-56877-1_27
23. Cramer, R., Shoup, V.: Universal hash proofs and a paradigm for adaptive chosen ciphertext secure public-key encryption. In: Knudsen, L.R. (ed.) EUROCRYPT 2002. LNCS, vol. 2332, pp. 45–64. Springer, Heidelberg (2002). https://doi.org/10.1007/3-540-46035-7_4
24. Crites, E.C., Lysyanskaya, A.: Delegatable anonymous credentials from mercurial signatures. In: Matsui, M. (ed.) CT-RSA 2019. LNCS, vol. 11405, pp. 535–555. Springer, Cham (2019). https://doi.org/10.1007/978-3-030-12612-4_27
25. Crites, E.C., Lysyanskaya, A.: Mercurial signatures for variable-length messages. PoPETs **2021**(4), 441–463 (2021). https://doi.org/10.2478/popets-2021-0079
26. Faonio, A., Fiore, D., Herranz, J., Ràfols, C.: Structure-preserving and re-randomizable RCCA-secure public key encryption and its applications. In: Galbraith, S.D., Moriai, S. (eds.) ASIACRYPT 2019. LNCS, vol. 11923, pp. 159–190. Springer, Cham (2019). https://doi.org/10.1007/978-3-030-34618-8_6
27. Faonio, A., Russo, L.: Mix-nets from re-randomizable and replayable cca-secure public-key encryption. In: Galdi, C., Jarecki, S. (eds.) Security and Cryptography for Networks, pp. 172–196. Springer, Cham (2022). https://doi.org/10.1007/978-3-031-14791-3_8
28. Fuchsbauer, G., Hanser, C., Slamanig, D.: Structure-preserving signatures on equivalence classes and constant-size anonymous credentials. J. Cryptol. **32**(2), 498–546 (2019). https://doi.org/10.1007/s00145-018-9281-4
29. Gabizon, A., Williamson, Z.J., Ciobotaru, O.: PLONK: permutations over lagrange-bases for oecumenical noninteractive arguments of knowledge. Cryptology ePrint Archive, Report 2019/953 (2019). https://eprint.iacr.org/2019/953
30. Gennaro, R., Gentry, C., Parno, B., Raykova, M.: Quadratic span programs and succinct NIZKs without PCPs. In: Johansson, T., Nguyen, P.Q. (eds.) EUROCRYPT 2013. LNCS, vol. 7881, pp. 626–645. Springer, Heidelberg (2013). https://doi.org/10.1007/978-3-642-38348-9_37
31. Groth, J.: On the Size of pairing-based non-interactive arguments. In: Fischlin, M., Coron, J.-S. (eds.) EUROCRYPT 2016. LNCS, vol. 9666, pp. 305–326. Springer, Heidelberg (2016). https://doi.org/10.1007/978-3-662-49896-5_11
32. Groth, J., Sahai, A.: Efficient non-interactive proof systems for bilinear groups. In: Smart, N. (ed.) EUROCRYPT 2008. LNCS, vol. 4965, pp. 415–432. Springer, Heidelberg (2008). https://doi.org/10.1007/978-3-540-78967-3_24
33. Hanser, C., Slamanig, D.: Structure-preserving signatures on equivalence classes and their application to anonymous credentials. In: Sarkar, P., Iwata, T. (eds.)

ASIACRYPT 2014. LNCS, vol. 8873, pp. 491–511. Springer, Heidelberg (2014). https://doi.org/10.1007/978-3-662-45611-8_26
34. Hébant, C., Phan, D.H., Pointcheval, D.: Linearly-homomorphic signatures and scalable mix-nets. In: Kiayias, A., Kohlweiss, M., Wallden, P., Zikas, V. (eds.) PKC 2020. LNCS, vol. 12111, pp. 597–627. Springer, Cham (2020). https://doi.org/10.1007/978-3-030-45388-6_21
35. Herranz, J., Martínez, R., Sánchez, M.: Shorter lattice-based zero-knowledge proofs for the correctness of a shuffle. In: Bernhard, M., et al. (eds.) FC 2021. LNCS, vol. 12676, pp. 315–329. Springer, Heidelberg (2021). https://doi.org/10.1007/978-3-662-63958-0_27
36. Labs, P.: High performance implementation of bls12 381. Online (2021). https://github.com/filecoin-project/blstrs
37. Libert, B., Peters, T., Joye, M., Yung, M.: Linearly homomorphic structure-preserving signatures and their applications. In: Canetti, R., Garay, J.A. (eds.) CRYPTO 2013. LNCS, vol. 8043, pp. 289–307. Springer, Heidelberg (2013). https://doi.org/10.1007/978-3-642-40084-1_17
38. Madathil, V., et al.: Cryptographic oracle-based conditional payments. In: 30th Annual Network and Distributed System Security Symposium, NDSS 2023, San Diego, California, USA, 27 February–3 March 2023. The Internet Society (2023). https://www.ndss-symposium.org/ndss-paper/cryptographic-oracle-based-conditional-payments/
39. Nanri, M.: Implementation of mixnets from msorc (2025). https://github.com/octaviopk9/esorics_msorc
40. O'Connor, J., Aumasson, J.P., Neves, S., Wilcox-O'Hearn, Z.: Blake3. Online (2020). https://github.com/BLAKE3-team/BLAKE3

𝕿𝖊𝖙𝖗𝖎𝖘! Traceable Extendable Threshold Ring Signatures and More

Gennaro Avitabile[1](✉), Vincenzo Botta[2], and Dario Fiore[1]

[1] IMDEA Software Institute, Madrid, Spain
{gennaro.avitabile,dario.fiore}@imdea.org
[2] Sapienza University of Rome, Rome, Italy
vincenzo.botta@uniroma1.it

Abstract. Traceable ring signatures enhance ring signatures by adding an accountability layer. Specifically, if a party signs two different messages within the protocol, their identity is revealed. Another desirable feature is *extendability*. In particular, *extendable threshold* ring signatures (ETRS) allow to *non-interactively* update already finalized signatures by enlarging the ring or the set of signers.

Combining traceability and extendability in a single scheme is unexplored and would offer a new tool for privacy-preserving voting schemes in scenarios where the voters are not known in advance. In this paper, we show how to reconcile both properties by introducing and constructing a new cryptographic primitive called Tetris. Notably, our Tetris construction simultaneously achieves a strong flavor of anonymity and linear-size signatures, which is the main technical challenge in existing techniques. To solve this challenge, we develop a new approach to traceability that leads to several conceptual and technical contributions. Among those, we introduce and construct, based on Groth-Sahai proofs, *extendable* shuffle arguments that can be *non-interactively* updated by several provers.

1 Introduction

A ring signature scheme allows a signer to generate a signature on behalf of a publicly known group of potential signers called ring [42], the identity of the signer is hidden among all the possible signers in the ring. Ring signatures are crucial in many applications including anonymous authentication [40], privacy-protecting cryptocurrencies [45], whistleblowing [42], and e-voting [43,46]. Unfortunately, ring signatures offer an unlimited level of anonymity which is not always desirable: consider a simple voting protocol where voters have to pick between two choices. To cast a vote, a user produces a signature of her choice using her own secret key. A dishonest voter might exploit the anonymity of ring signatures to cast a double vote without being detected. To tackle these issues, variants of ring signatures known as *linkable* ring signatures [37] and *traceable* ring signatures have been proposed [27,28]. The former allows one to establish whether two signatures have been produced by the same user or not. The latter has additional features. In traceable ring signatures, a signature on a message m is also issued w.r.t. a topic τ (e.g., a unique identifier of an election). Given two valid signatures w.r.t. the same topic τ and different messages, one can trace the public key of the signer who generated both signatures. If τ and m are equal in both signatures, the tracing procedure just reveals that they were both generated by the same signer, without revealing their identity. Signatures issued w.r.t. different topics are unlinkable. A traceable ring signature must also be *exculpable*, meaning that it is unfeasible to produce two signatures to *falsely* accuse a user of having signed two different messages on the same topic.

Threshold ring signatures generalize ring signatures allowing $t \geq 1$ signers to hide their identity within a ring of size $n \geq t$. Generally, threshold ring signatures require fixing the ring and the threshold at signature generation time with no possibility of further modifying them without a new intervention of the signers themselves. This is a significant limitation as all the potential signers must be known in advance. More recently, the concept of Extendable Threshold Ring Signatures (ETRS) was introduced in [4]. ETRS allow to non-interactively update a threshold ring signature on a certain message so that the updated signature has a greater threshold and/or an augmented ring. A key property of ETRS is the *strong anonymity* notion defined in [7]. The adversary can see all the signature's updates resulting from threshold increments and ring extensions that a signature undergoes from when it is generated up until the protocol ends[1]. This property is crucial for voting since all the updates are publicly available. Despite the main application of ETRS being voting (when participants are not known in advance[2]), the known ETRS providing the even weaker notion of linkability [4] has "quadratic" $O(tn)$ size.

1.1 Our Contributions

Our first contribution is a general definition of traceability that takes into account the threshold setting as well as extendability. Indeed, to the best of our knowledge, previous definitions are only for (plain non-threshold i.e., with $t = 1$) ring signatures and allow tracing only between signatures having the same ring [27]. Simple adaptations of [27] fail at capturing the idea that *all* the misbehaving signers should be discovered (and not just a subset of them). Therefore, we adopt a fundamentally different approach in defining traceability.

The main challenge we solve is to construct a linear-size Tetris. Indeed, there are straightforward solutions to build a Tetris with signatures of "quadratic", $O(tn)$, size. On the other hand, linear-size traceability techniques for non-extendable ring signatures are not applicable as they break strong anonymity. Towards our Tetris, we introduce and construct the following building blocks:

1. Extendable shuffles, namely arguments proving that a t-size list of clear-text elements is a permuted subset of the values encrypted in a list of $n \geq t$

---

[1] In the anonymity notion proposed in [4], the adversary can only see the signature obtained after all the ring extensions and threshold increments are performed.

[2] An application is using a blockchain to vote on conflicting petitions. Here, not known in advance participants may endorse one proposal using their wallet key-pair.

ciphertexts. The proof can be updated by several (independent) provers that can re-randomize the ciphertexts, add a ciphertext to the list, or reveal a new clear-text element. The size of the proof is $O(n)$. Our extendable shuffle is constructed combining techniques from [7,34].
2. Doubly-authentication-preventing tags (DAPT) are *deterministic* tags that are tied to a public key, a topic, and a message. These tags are anonymous when issued on different topics, but two tags generated with the same key, on the same topic, and different messages reveal the public key.

1.2 Technical Overview

A Simple Quadratic Solution. An approach to get a Tetris consists of a folklore compiler transforming traceable ring signatures into traceable *threshold* ring signatures supporting the join operation (i.e., incrementation of the threshold). That is, whenever two traceable ring signatures over the same message and ring do not trace to a signer, they can be concatenated together to produce a 2-out-of-n signature. As a result, a signature with threshold t is composed of t ring signatures. If the base traceable ring signature also supports the extend operation (i.e., incrementation of the ring), then we immediately get a Tetris. However, existing methods for extendability [4,7] have a linear complexity in n, resulting in a Tetris of size $O(tn)$.

Towards a Linear-Size. Tetris. A natural starting point is to combine strongly anonymous $O(n)$-size ETRS [7] with known traceability techniques [16,26,27]. The key idea in [16,26,27] is to publish a pseudo-random tag for each public key in the ring. Whenever pk_i is one of the signers, its tag is uniquely determined by pk_i and the topic τ, while the tags of non-signers are just placeholders indistinguishable from legitimate tags. To trace a pair of signatures, it suffices to look for identical tags in both signatures. However, this approach is at odds with strong anonymity. Indeed, an adversary who has access to the full evolution of a signature can easily guess which signers have performed a join operation along the way. This is because once a *new* signer joins a signature, it is necessary to replace its placeholder tag with a new one as there exists only one valid tag for a key that is in the set of signers. Moreover, for the same reason, it is not possible to change the tags related to the previous signers. Given a pair of signatures (σ_{j-1}, σ_j) before and after the j-th join operation, the signers of σ_{j-1} are the public keys corresponding to the tags that have remained unchanged in σ_j.

An alternative approach is to break the link between tags and public keys and only publish t tags (i.e., one tag per signer). The signature also contains a non-interactive zero-knowledge (NIZK) proof[3] that the t tags come from t public keys in the ring, while hiding the actual correspondence between tags and public keys. Notice that the above attack is not applicable anymore, as no information is published about non-signers. We remark that the NIZK proof should be *extendable*, allowing future signers to extend the ring or to increase the threshold

---

[3] In this work, we interchangeably use proof and argument. Generally, unless specified, soundness is assumed to hold against a PPT adversary.

by providing a new tag. Known extendable proofs [7] support disjunctive threshold relations, that are proofs stating that t out of n base statements $(x_1, ..., x_n)$ are in a base language $\mathcal{L}$. These proofs have size $O(n\mathsf{S})^4$, where S is the size of a proof for $x_i \in \mathcal{L}$. For example, such relations can be used to express the above predicate via t disjunctive proofs stating that each of the t tags is generated w.r.t the topic τ and the message m using one of the public keys $\mathsf{pk}_1, ..., \mathsf{pk}_n$. This approach gives again a signature of size $O(tn)$ (i.e., t proofs of size $n\mathsf{S}$, with S independent from t and n). In this work, we start from the idea of publishing only t tags and we use our extendable shuffle to prove, *with a $O(n)$-size proof*, that such a correspondence between public keys and correctly generated tags exists.

1.3 Related Work

Ring signatures were introduced by Rivest et al. [42]. Several works have focused on improving the signature size [3,5,9,23,32,36,39,41,48,49], the minimal assumptions required [2,10,13,38], the security against quantum adversaries [3,11,12,16,25,36]. For some applications (e.g., e-voting) plain ring signatures are not enough and additional properties are required. Accountability properties based on trusted authorities were explored for both group and ring signatures [1,14,15,29,47]. Liu et al. [37] introduced likability allowing *anyone* to determine if multiple signature were made by the same user without revealing their identity. Fujisaki et al. [27] introduced traceable ring signatures allowing deanonymization of a signer that produces multiple signatures on different messages. Subsequent works focused on improving the size or the assumptions of traceable ring signatures [6,16,25,26,44]. Threshold ring signatures [3,5,17,39,50] were introduced by Bresson et al. [17], in which t members of a group of n parties can sign a message keeping their identity hidden. Aranha et al. [4] have enhanced the functionality of threshold ring signatures by proposing ETRS. Avitabile et al. [7] proposed a stricter anonymity definition for ETRS along with a new partially structure-preserving [30] ETRS based on Groth-Sahai (GS) proofs [24,31,35].

2 Traceable Extendable Threshold Ring Signatures

A 𝔗etris scheme $\mathfrak{T}$ consists of the following PPT algorithms and a poly-time relation $R_{\mathsf{key}}^{\mathfrak{T}}$. We model signatures as a pair $\sigma = (\mu, \mathsf{tinfo})$, where we call tinfo tracing information as it is used by the Trace algorithm.

- $(\mathsf{pp}, \mathsf{td}) \leftarrow \mathsf{Setup}(1^\lambda)$: outputs public parameters pp and trapdoor td.[5]
- $(\mathsf{pk}, \mathsf{sk}) \leftarrow \mathsf{KGen}()$: generates a new public and secret key pair.

---

[4] Although recursibe SNARKs might give succinct extendable proofs [19,21], those proof systems are costly in terms of proving time and memory and rely on strong assumptions. We are instead interested in efficient provers and standard assumptions.

[5] The pp parameters produced by Setup are implicitly available to all algorithms.

- $\sigma \leftarrow \mathsf{Sign}(\tau, m, \{\mathsf{pk}_i\}_{i \in \mathcal{R}}, \mathsf{sk})$: on input a topic τ, a message m, a secret key sk corresponding to a public key pk_i with $i \in \mathcal{R}$, returns a signature σ.
- $0/1 \leftarrow \mathsf{Verify}(t, \tau, m, \{\mathsf{pk}_i\}_{i \in \mathcal{R}}, \sigma)$: verifies a signature with threshold t, it outputs 1 to accept, and 0 to reject.
- $\sigma' \leftarrow \mathsf{Join}(\tau, m, \{\mathsf{pk}_i\}_{i \in \mathcal{R}}, \mathsf{sk}, \sigma)$: outputs a new signature with threshold $t+1$.
- $\sigma' \leftarrow \mathsf{Extend}(\tau, m, \sigma, \{\mathsf{pk}_i\}_{i \in \mathcal{R}}, \{\mathsf{pk}_i\}_{i \in \mathcal{R}'})$: outputs a new signature with threshold t for ring $\mathcal{R} \cup \mathcal{R}'$.
- $T \leftarrow \mathsf{Trace}(\tau, m_1, m_2, \mathsf{tinfo}_1, \mathsf{tinfo}_2, \{\mathsf{pk}_i\}_{i \in \mathcal{R}_1}, \{\mathsf{pk}_i\}_{i \in \mathcal{R}_2})$: it is a *deterministic* algorithm. It outputs T that takes one of the following values: (i) indep; (ii) (linked, n); (iii) a set $\mathsf{PK} = \{\mathsf{pk}_i\}_{i \in \mathcal{R} \subseteq \mathcal{R}_1 \cap \mathcal{R}_2}$. Where indep means that there are no common signers, (linked, n) means that $m_1 = m_2$ and there are n common signers, and when $m_1 \neq m_2$, PK is the set of traced keys.

We use the notion of ladder from [4]. A ladder lad is a sequence of tuples (action, input), where action $\in \{\mathsf{Sign}, \mathsf{Join}, \mathsf{Extend}\}$ and input depends on action. If action = Sign, then input is a pair $(\mathcal{R}, i)$, with $\mathcal{R}$ the ring for the signature and i the signer's identity. If action = Join, then input is an identifier i of the joining signer. If action = Extend, then input is a ring $\mathcal{R}$ used to extend the previous one. We denote by lad.$\mathcal{S}$ the set of signers of a ladder lad. A ladder uniquely determines a sequence of signatures, each with a specific ring and threshold. We define the Proc algorithm (see [8, Fig. 3]), which takes as input a topic, message, ladder, and list of keys, and outputs the corresponding sequence of signatures, returning $\bot$ if the ladder is malformed. A 𝔗etris must satisfy the following properties (Fig. 1 lists the oracles used by our definitions). We require correctness: any honestly generated and updated signature (via join or extend) must be accepted by Verify. We now introduce a property on keys that aids the definition of further notions.

Definition 1 (Verifiability of Keys). $\forall \lambda \in \mathbb{N}$, $(\mathsf{pp}, \mathsf{td}) \leftarrow \mathsf{Setup}(1^\lambda)$: $(\mathsf{pk}, \mathsf{sk}) \in \mathsf{KGen}()$ *iff* $(\mathsf{pk}, \mathsf{sk}) \in R^{\mathfrak{T}}_{\mathsf{key}}$, *and* $\forall$ pk *there is a unique sk:* $(\mathsf{pk}, \mathsf{sk}) \in R^{\mathfrak{T}}_{\mathsf{key}}$.

We define tracing correctness (Fig. 2) to model that, on honestly generated signatures from adversarially chosen keys, messages, and ladders, Trace should return the expected output (e.g., the set of common signers if $m_1 \neq m_2$).

Definition 2 (Tracing Correctness). $\forall$ PPT $\mathcal{A}$ $\Pr\left[\mathsf{Exp}^{\mathsf{Tcorr}}_{\mathcal{A}, \mathfrak{T}}(\lambda) = 1\right] \leq \mathsf{negl}(\lambda)$.

On Defining Traceability. Previous definitions for $t = 1$ [27] require the adversary to output a topic τ, a ring $\mathcal{R}$ of size n, and $n+1$ accepting message/signature pairs w.r.t. τ and $\mathcal{R}$. $\mathcal{A}$ generates all the keys by itself and wins the game if the signatures it produces look signed by different signers according to Trace. If the scheme is traceable, the adversary should not be able to win as there must exist at least a pair of signatures sharing the same signer. However, modeling traceability for general $t \geq 1$ is far more complicated. One may adapt the definition of [27]

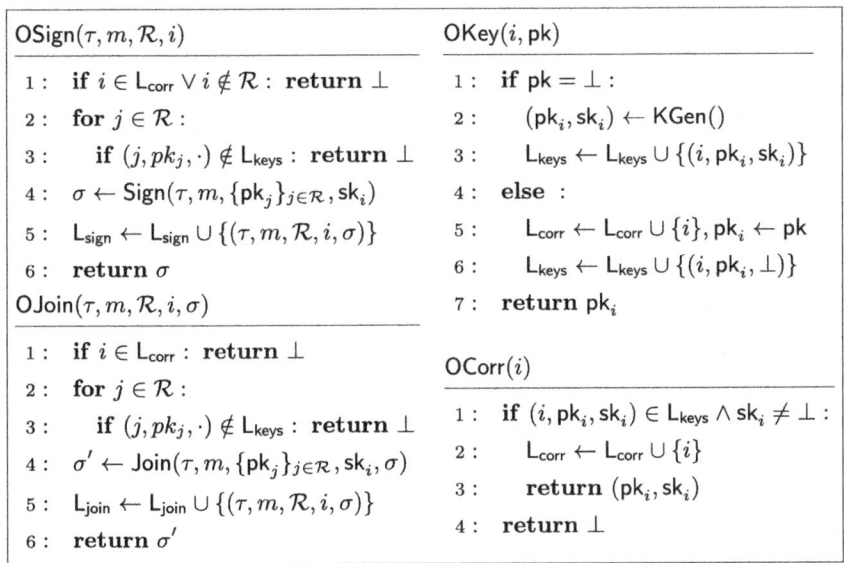

Fig. 1. Oracles for the security definitions of 𝔗etris.

requiring $\mathcal{A}$ to provide enough signatures so that at least two of them must have c overlapping signers at least. However, unlike the $t = 1$ case where the size of the overlap is fixed, $\mathcal{A}$ may produce signatures with $c' > c$ overlapping signers. Therefore, such a definition would allow schemes tracing c keys while we want to identify *all* the $c' > c$ malicious signers. We solve this issue proposing a definition featuring an extractor Ext which is able to perfectly identify the guilty signers and whose output should match the one of Trace. In the following definition, we require the existence of such extractor.

Definition 3 (Signers Extraction). $\exists$ PPT Ext *that* $\forall$ $(pp, td) \leftarrow \mathsf{Setup}(1^\lambda)$, $\Lambda = (t, \tau, m, \{pk_i\}_{i \in \mathcal{R}}, \sigma = (\mu, \mathsf{tinfo}))$ *s.t.* $\mathsf{Verify}(pp, \Lambda) = 1$: $\mathsf{Ext}(td, \Lambda) = \begin{cases} \bot \\ (\mathsf{PK}, \mathsf{Ind}) \end{cases}$. Ext *satisfies the following two properties (see [8, Definition 4] for a formal definition):*

1. *Whenever* Ext *does not return* $\bot$, *it outputs the signers' public keys in* PK *and the list of indexes* Ind *specifying the order in which they joined. Moreover, using the (unique) secret keys corresponding to* PK *and* Ind, *it is possible to generate a signature with the* same tinfo *as the one in input contained in* Λ.
2. *For all PPT* $\mathcal{A}$ *it is unfeasible to find an accepting* Λ *s.t.* $\mathsf{Ext}(td, \Lambda) = \bot$.

We define traceability requiring $\mathcal{A}$ to output a pair of signatures for keys of its choice. $\mathcal{A}$ wins if the output of Trace does not agree with Ext (Fig. 3).[6]

---

[6] The Ext in this definition works as the extractor of signers extraction Definition 3).

$\mathsf{Exp}_{\mathcal{A},\mathfrak{T}}^{\mathsf{Tcorr}}(\lambda)$

1: $(\mathsf{pp},\mathsf{td}) \leftarrow \mathsf{Setup}(\lambda), (\tau, m_0, m_1, \mathsf{lad}_0, \mathsf{lad}_1, \mathsf{L}_{\mathsf{keys}}) \leftarrow \mathcal{A}(\mathsf{pp})$
2: $\forall (i, \mathsf{pk}_i, \mathsf{sk}_i) \in \mathsf{L}_{\mathsf{keys}} \land \mathsf{sk}_i \neq \bot : \mathbf{if}\ (\mathsf{sk}_i, \mathsf{pk}_i) \notin R_{\mathsf{key}}^{\mathfrak{T}}\ :\ \mathbf{return}\ 0$
3: $\forall (i, \mathsf{pk}_i, \mathsf{sk}_i), (j, \mathsf{pk}_j, \mathsf{sk}_j) \in \mathsf{L}_{\mathsf{keys}} \land \mathsf{sk}_i, \mathsf{sk}_j \neq \bot \land i \neq j : \mathbf{if}\ \mathsf{pk}_i = \mathsf{pk}_j\ :\ \mathbf{return}\ 0$
4: $\forall b \in \{0,1\}\ \mathsf{val}_b \leftarrow \mathsf{Proc}(\tau, m_b, \mathsf{L}_{\mathsf{keys}}, \mathsf{lad}_b)$
5: $\mathbf{if}\ \exists b \in \{0,1\} : \mathsf{val}_b = \bot\ \mathbf{return}\ 0$
6: $\forall b \in \{0,1\} : \mathbf{parse}\ \mathsf{val}_b = (\Sigma_b, \mathsf{Th}_b, \mathcal{R}_b), \Sigma_b = \{\sigma_1^b, ..., \sigma_{\ell_b}^b = (\mu_b, \mathsf{tinfo}_b)\}$
7: $T \leftarrow \mathsf{Trace}(\tau, m_0, m_1, \mathsf{tinfo}_0, \mathsf{tinfo}_1, \{\mathsf{pk}_j\}_{j \in \mathcal{R}_0}, \{\mathsf{pk}_k\}_{k \in \mathcal{R}_1})$
8: $\mathbf{if}\ \mathsf{lad}_0.\mathcal{S} \cap \mathsf{lad}_1.\mathcal{S} = \emptyset \land T \neq \mathsf{indep} : \mathbf{return}\ 1$
9: $\mathbf{if}\ m_0 \neq m_1 \land T \neq \mathsf{lad}_0.\mathcal{S} \cap \mathsf{lad}_1.\mathcal{S} : \mathbf{return}\ 1$
10: $\mathbf{if}\ m_0 = m_1 \land T \neq (\mathsf{linked}, (|\mathsf{lad}_0.\mathcal{S} \cap \mathsf{lad}_1.\mathcal{S}|) : \mathbf{return}\ 1$
11: $\mathbf{return}\ 0$

Fig. 2. Tracing correctness game of 𝔗etris. In line 3, if public keys are tuples, we say that two public keys are equal if they are equal in at least one position. This is justified as sampling the same value in two public key tuples basically requires sampling the same value in two secret key tuples (e.g., discrete log of a group element).

Definition 4 (Traceability). $\exists$ PPT Ext: $\forall$ PPT $\mathcal{A}$ $\Pr\left[\mathsf{Exp}_{\mathsf{Ext},\mathcal{A},\mathfrak{T}}^{\mathsf{Trace}}(\lambda) = 1\right] \leq \mathsf{negl}(\lambda)$.

Finally, we define strong anonymity and exculpability. Strong anonymity models that $\mathcal{A}$ should not learn the signers of a signature. $\mathcal{A}$ chooses two ladders and gets the full evolution of the signature coming from one of the two ladders. $\mathcal{A}$ has to guess the correct ladder with probability non-negligibly better than $1/2$. We omit the formal definition as it is similar to the one of [7], but its description is given in [8, Fig. 6]. Exculpability (Fig. 4) models that $\mathcal{A}$ cannot falsely accuse a honest user of producing two signatures on the same τ.

Definition 5 (Exculpability). $\forall$ PPT $\mathcal{A}$ $\Pr\left[\mathsf{Exp}_{\mathcal{A},\mathfrak{T}}^{\mathsf{Exculp}}(\lambda) = 1\right] \leq \mathsf{negl}(\lambda)$.

We omit the definition of unforgeability since traceability and exculpability imply unforgeability. Additionally, tracing correctness and signers extraction imply traceability. We defer to [8, Lem. 1] for the proofs. As [4,7], we do not model malicious signers trying to prevent others from joining.

On the Admissible Adversaries of Exculpability. Line 8 of $\mathsf{Exp}_{\mathcal{A},\mathfrak{T}}^{\mathsf{Exculp}}(\lambda)$ ensures that any key for which $\mathcal{A}$ asked two queries over the same topic τ and different messages $m_0 \neq m_1$ is considered corrupted. Indeed, since the aim of traceable signatures is to prevent such behavior, we allow constructions with the additional feature that any signer who signs different messages loses any security guarantee.

$\mathsf{Exp}_{\mathsf{Ext},\mathcal{A},\mathfrak{T}}^{\mathsf{Trace}}(\lambda)$

1: $(\mathsf{pp},\mathsf{td}) \leftarrow \mathsf{Setup}(1^\lambda)$
2: $(\tau, t_0, t_1, \{\mathsf{pk}_i\}_{i \in \mathcal{R}_0}, \{\mathsf{pk}_j\}_{j \in \mathcal{R}_1}, m_0, m_1, \sigma_0, \sigma_1) \leftarrow \mathcal{A}(\mathsf{pp}, \mathsf{td})$
3: **if** $\exists b \in \{0,1\}$ s.t. $\mathsf{Verify}(t_b, \tau, m_b, \{\mathsf{pk}_i\}_{i \in \mathcal{R}_b}, \sigma_b) = 0$: **return** 0
4: $\forall b \in \{0,1\} : \mathsf{out}_b \leftarrow \mathsf{Ext}(\mathsf{td}, \tau, m_b, t_b, \{\mathsf{pk}_i\}_{i \in \mathcal{R}_b}, \sigma_b)$
5: **if** $\exists b \in \{0,1\}$ s.t. $\mathsf{out}_b = \bot$: **return** 1
6: $\forall b \in \{0,1\} : \mathbf{parse}\ \mathsf{out}_b = (\mathsf{PK}_b, \mathsf{Ind}_b), \sigma_b = (\mu_b, \mathsf{tinfo}_b)$
7: $T \leftarrow \mathsf{Trace}(\tau, m_0, m_1, \mathsf{tinfo}_0, \mathsf{tinfo}_1, \{\mathsf{pk}_i\}_{i \in \mathcal{R}_0}, \{\mathsf{pk}_j\}_{j \in \mathcal{R}_1})$
8: **if** $\mathsf{PK} = \mathsf{PK}_0 \cap \mathsf{PK}_1 = \emptyset \land T \neq \mathsf{indep}$: **return** 1 **else** : **return** 0
9: **if** $m_0 \neq m_1$:
10:     **if** $\mathsf{PK} \neq T$: **return** 1 **else** : **return** 0
11:     **else** : **parse** $T = (\mathsf{linked}, n)$, **if** $n \neq |\mathsf{PK}|$: **return** 1 **else** : **return** 0

Fig. 3. Traceability game of 𝔗etris.

3 Doubly-Authentication-Preventing Tags (DAPT)

Doubly-authentication-preventing tags (DAPT) are inspired by DAPS [18,22]. A DAPT consists of a triple of PPT algorithms (KGen, Tag, TagTrace). KGen is randomized and produces (pk, sk). Tag is deterministic and produces the tag e on input sk, a topic τ, and a message m. TagTrace is the deterministic tracing algorithm that on input two tags e_0, e_1 on the same topic τ and different messages $m_0 \neq m_1$, outputs 1 iff both tags were generated w.r.t. public key pk. The required properties are: (i) *verifiability of the keys* saying that there exists a relation R_{key} such that each (pk, sk) is valid iff it belongs to R_{key} and that for each pk there exists a single sk; (ii) *tag traceability* saying that if e_0, e_1 are honestly produced with the same sk, on the same τ, and $m_0 \neq m_1$, TagTrace returns 1 with probability negligibly close to 1; furthermore, the probability that the adversary $\mathcal{A}$ produces $(\tau, m_0, m_1, \mathsf{pk}_0, \mathsf{pk}_1, \mathsf{sk}_0, \mathsf{sk}_1)$ s.t. $\mathsf{TagTrace}(e_0, e_1, m_0, m_1, \mathsf{pk}_0) = 1$ where $e_b \leftarrow \mathsf{Tag}(\mathsf{sk}_b, \tau, m_b)$ with $b \in \{0,1\}$ is negligible; (iii) *pseudo-randomness* saying that $\mathcal{A}$ has negligible advantage in distinguishing a randomly sampled tag from a tag generated by Tag; (iv) *non-frameability* saying that $\mathcal{A}$ has negligible probability to produce a pair of tags tracing w.r.t pk without knowing sk. Unlike DAPS, DAPT hide the public key used to generate the tag. However, the tracing algorithm only exposes the public key but not the secret key.

Our DAPT. We use bilinear groups $(p, \hat{\mathbb{G}}, \breve{\mathbb{H}}, \mathbb{T}, e, \hat{g}, \breve{h}) \leftarrow \mathcal{G}(1^\lambda)$. $\mathcal{G}(1^\lambda)$ outputs the description of a bilinear group. $\hat{\mathbb{G}}, \breve{\mathbb{H}}, \mathbb{T}$ are prime p order groups, $\hat{g}, \breve{h}$ are generators of $\hat{\mathbb{G}}, \breve{\mathbb{H}}$ respectively, and $e : \hat{\mathbb{G}} \times \breve{\mathbb{H}} \to \mathbb{T}$ is a non-degenerate bilinear map. We use the additive notation for the group operations and multiplicative notation for the bilinear map e. The topic space is $\{0,1\}^*$, the message space is $\mathbb{Z}_p$, and the tag space is $\hat{\mathbb{G}}$. The algorithms work as follows:

$\mathsf{Exp}_{\mathcal{A},\mathfrak{T}}^{\mathsf{Exculp}}(\lambda)$
1 : $\quad\mathsf{L_{keys}, L_{corr}, L_{sign}, L_{join}} \leftarrow \emptyset, \mathsf{O} \leftarrow \{\mathsf{OSign}, \mathsf{OKey}, \mathsf{OCorr}, \mathsf{OJoin}\}$
2 : $\quad(\mathsf{pp}, \mathsf{td}) \leftarrow \mathsf{Setup}(1^\lambda), (\tau^*, t_0^*, t_1^*, \mathcal{R}_0^*, \mathcal{R}_1^*, m_0^*, m_1^*, \sigma_0^*, \sigma_1^*) \leftarrow \mathcal{A}^{\mathsf{O}}(\mathsf{pp})$
3 : $\quad\mathbf{if}\ \exists b \in \{0,1\}\ \mathsf{Verify}(t_b^*, \tau^*, m_b^*, \{\mathsf{pk}_i\}_{i \in \mathcal{R}_b^*}, \sigma_b^*) = 0 :\ \mathbf{return}\ 0$
4 : $\quad\mathsf{PK} \leftarrow \mathsf{Trace}(\tau^*, m_0^*, m_1^*, \sigma_0^*, \sigma_1^*, \{\mathsf{pk}_i\}_{i\in\mathcal{R}_0^*}, \{\mathsf{pk}_j\}_{j\in\mathcal{R}_1^*})$
5 : $\quad\mathbf{if}\ \mathsf{PK} = \mathsf{indep} \vee \mathsf{PK} = (\mathsf{linked}, \cdot) :\ \mathbf{return}\ 0$
6 : $\quad\forall\ \mathsf{pk}_i \in \mathsf{PK} :$
7 : $\quad\quad\mathbf{if}\ \mathsf{pk}_i \in \mathsf{L_{corr}} : \mathsf{PK} = \mathsf{PK} \setminus \mathsf{pk}_i$
8 : $\quad\quad\mathbf{elseif}\ \exists (\tau, m_0, \mathcal{R}', \sigma', j), (\tau, m_1, \mathcal{R}'', \sigma'', j) \in \mathsf{L_{sign}} \cup \mathsf{L_{join}}\ \text{s.t.}$
$\quad\quad\quad m_0 \neq m_1 \wedge j \in \mathcal{R}_0^* \wedge j \in \mathcal{R}_1^* \wedge \mathsf{pk}_i = \mathsf{pk}_j :$
9 : $\quad\quad\quad \mathsf{PK} = \mathsf{PK} \setminus \mathsf{pk}_i$
10 : $\quad\mathbf{if}\ \mathsf{PK} = \emptyset :\ \mathbf{return}\ 0\ \mathbf{else}\ :\ \mathbf{return}\ 1$

Fig. 4. Exculpability game of $\mathfrak{T}$etris.

- $(\mathsf{pk}, \mathsf{sk}) \leftarrow \mathsf{KGen}(\mathsf{gk}): \mathsf{sk} = (x, y) \leftarrow_{\$} \mathbb{Z}_p^2$, $\mathsf{pk} = (\hat{\mathsf{pk}}_1 = x\hat{g}, \hat{\mathsf{pk}}_2 = y\hat{g}, \check{\mathsf{pk}}_2 = y\check{h})$
- $\hat{e} \leftarrow \mathsf{Tag}(\mathsf{sk}, \tau, m): \hat{\tau} \leftarrow H(\tau)$, return $\hat{e} = x\hat{\tau} + mx\hat{\mathsf{pk}}_2$
- $0/1 \leftarrow \mathsf{TagTrace}(\hat{e}_0, \hat{e}_1, m_0, m_1, \mathsf{pk})$: If $(\hat{e}_0 - \hat{e}_1) \cdot \check{h} = \hat{\mathsf{pk}}_1 \cdot (m_0 - m_1)\check{\mathsf{pk}}_2$ return 1, else return 0
- $R_{\mathsf{key}} = \{((\hat{\mathsf{pk}}_1, \hat{\mathsf{pk}}_2, \check{\mathsf{pk}}_2), (x, y)) | \hat{\mathsf{pk}}_1 = x\hat{g}, \hat{\mathsf{pk}}_2 = y\hat{g}, \check{\mathsf{pk}}_2 = y\check{h}\}$

Theorem 1. *If DDH and Co-CDH hold relative to $\mathcal{G}$, then the scheme above, where H is a random oracle, is a* DAPT. *(See [8, Theorem 3] for the proof).*

4 Extendable Shuffle and ENIWI

The goal of an extendable shuffle is to prove that each element e_i of a public list $\{e_1, ..., e_t\}$ of $t \leq n$ elements is the value committed in a *different* commitment in a list $\{c_1, ..., c_n\}$ of n commitments. Formally, we define:

$$R_{\mathsf{SH}} = \{(c_1, ..., c_n, e_1, ..., e_t), (\phi, r_1, ..., r_n) | \forall\ i \in [t] : \phi\ \text{injective}\ [t] \to [n] \wedge c_{\phi(i)} \leftarrow \mathsf{Com}(e_i, r_i)\}. \tag{1}$$

An extendable shuffle allows one to update previously generated proofs via:

- **Extend**: On input a proof for $(c_1, ..., c_n, e_1, ..., e_t) \in \mathcal{L}_{\mathsf{SH}}$, and a new commitment c_{n+1}, output a proof for $(c'_1, ..., c'_n, c'_{n+1}, e_1, ..., e_t) \in \mathcal{L}_{\mathsf{SH}}$.
- **Add**: On input a proof for $(c_1, ..., c_n, e_1, ..., e_t) \in \mathcal{L}_{\mathsf{SH}}$, a new element e_{t+1}, a new commitment c'_i to e_{t+1} (along with its opening randomness) where position i has not been previously used, and an auxiliary value aux_i, output a proof for $(c'_1, ..., c'_n, e_1, ..., e_t, e_{t+1}) \in \mathcal{L}_{\mathsf{SH}}$.

Notice that when performing an add/extend operation all the commitments are re-randomized (i.e., we write c'_i to indicate that c'_i is the re-randomization of c_i). The extend operation can be executed without any private input from the previous provers. However, the same does not apply to the add operation. When a prover computes a proof Π for a statement $(c_1, ..., c_n, e_1, ..., e_t) \in \mathcal{L}_{\mathsf{SH}}$, it generates auxiliary values $\mathsf{AUX} = (\mathsf{aux}_1, ..., \mathsf{aux}_n)$ alongside the proof. The auxiliary value aux_i is used later to perform the add operation through an additional algorithm named ShAdd. Given an accepting proof Π for $(c_1, ..., c_n, e_1, ..., e_t) \in \mathcal{L}_{\mathsf{SH}}$, a new element e_{t+1} and an opening r_i of a fresh commitment c'_i to e_{t+1} for an unused index i, and the auxiliary value aux_i, ShAdd outputs a proof Π' for $(c'_1, ..., c'_n, e_1, ..., e_{t+1}) \in \mathcal{L}_{\mathsf{SH}}$. Similarly, the algorithm ShExtend is employed for the extend operation, which does not need any auxiliary value. When provided with an accepting proof for $(c_1, ..., c_n, e_1, ..., e_t) \in \mathcal{L}_{\mathsf{SH}}$ and a commitment c_{n+1}, ShExtend produces a proof Π' for $x = (c'_1, ..., c'_{n+1}, e_1, ..., e_t) \in \mathcal{L}_{\mathsf{SH}}$ and the auxiliary value aux_{n+1} associated with the index $n+1$. On input the randomness given to ShAdd (ShExtend) and all the previous auxiliary values, SHAuxUpd updates all the auxiliary values to enable further additions.

We build our extendable shuffle modifying the shuffle in [34] which is based on GS proofs. We adapt [34] to asymmetric groups and use techniques from [7] to turn the regular shuffle of [34] into an extendable one. As [7], we require that proofs after the extend/add operations are indistinguishable from proofs done from scratch with the whole witness. We introduce the property of extended zero knowledge (EZK) meaning that simulated and real proofs are indistinguishable, even when given the auxiliary values of the *unused* indeces. See [8, Sec. 4] for formal definitions. We now give an overview of the ENIWI of [7].

ENIWI. ENIWI [7] are defined w.r.t. a threshold relation $R_{\mathcal{L}_{tr}}$, which is in turn defined w.r.t. a poly-time relation $R_{\mathcal{L}}$. In words, the prover wants to prove that k *different* statements out of n are in the language $\mathcal{L}$. Let $\mathcal{L}_{tr}$ be the corresponding NP-language. In an ENIWI we can update a proof via:

Extend: turn a proof for $(t, x_1, ..., x_n) \in \mathcal{L}_{tr}$ into one for $(t, x_1, ..., x_{n+1}) \in \mathcal{L}_{tr}$.
Add: turn a proof for $(t, x_1, ..., x_n) \in \mathcal{L}_{tr}$ into one for $(t+1, x_1, ..., x_n) \in \mathcal{L}_{tr}$.

The ENIWI of [7] is based on the remarkable malleability of GS proofs [20,35]. GS proofs are a commit-and-prove framework to prove the satisfiability of several types of equations over bilinear groups. In GS, secret variables are committed, and the prover generates proof elements from the committed values and commitment randomnesses. The proof is verified based on the statement, commitments, and proof elements. Partial knowledge of satisfying assignments for t out of n equations is proved by introducing additional *binary* "switch" variables bit_i s.t. when $\mathsf{bit}_i = 1$ the i-th equation is left unaltered, while when $\mathsf{bit}_i = 0$ the i-th equation admits the trivial solution, thus allowing for simulation. Then, an additional equation proving that $\sum_{i=1}^{n} \mathsf{bit}_i = t$ guarantees that only $n - t$ equations can be simulated, while the prover must hold a satisfying assignment for t of them. The core idea of [7] is the observation that the proof elements of a GS proof are computed by linearly combining, along with some randomizers, the committed variables and the commitment randomnesses. This means that given (a function of) the values and the randomnesses of some committed variables, it is always possible to erase their contribution from a proof element in order to replace the old variables with freshly committed ones, assuming that the new assignment of the variables satisfies the new equation being proven[7]. Roughly speaking, auxiliary values correspond to commitment openings for these switch variables bit_i allowing to update a proof for $\sum_{i=1}^{n} \text{bit}_i = t$ into a proof for $\sum_{i=1}^{n} \text{bit}_i = t + 1$ without knowledge of the other bit_j with $j \neq i$. A key observation we use is that several extendable proofs can be connected to each other by sharing the same switch variables; this guarantees that the active indices (i.e., $i \in [n]$ s.t. $\text{bit}_i = 1$) are the same in all proofs.

In [7] the notion of EWI, i.e. extended (E) witness indistinguishability (WI), is introduced. It is a WI notion allowing the adversary to further get the auxiliary values corresponding to unused positions in both witnesses. We introduce two flavors of WI that are useful in proving the security of our Tetris, such flavors have some similarities with EWI but do not seem to imply each other. They are all satisfied by the ENIWI of [7]. Witness addition indistinguishability (WAI) ensures that two addition operations over the same index α, but with different witnesses for x_α are indistinguishable. Fixed position WI (FPWI) guarantees that two pairs of proofs and auxiliary values generated for the same statement with two different witnesses sharing the same used indices are indistinguishable. Finally, we introduce Perfect Δ-Extraction (similar to F-extraction [24, Definition 3])) that is a perfect but mild extraction property. Indeed, instead of extracting the full witness, the extractor perfectly extracts the used indices and a function Δ of the rest of the witness. A formal description is given in [8, Definition 16].

ENIWI and Extendable Shuffle. One could wonder why we do not directly use the ENIWI of [7] to construct the extendable shuffle. The reason is that to hide the concrete mapping between tags and public keys with a threshold relation one must *explicitly* relate *every* tag to *every* possible public key, leading to a final statement of size $O(tn)$; and thus proof size $O(tn)$. On the other hand, creating a proof system tailored for the shuffle gives us an $O(n)$ proof. We obtain this complexity by relying on the Groth and Lu's shuffle [34][8].

Our Extendable Shuffle. Our extendable shuffle argument is defined for R_{SH}:

$$R_{\mathsf{SH}} = \{(\mathsf{ck}, x = (t, \hat{z}_1, ..., \hat{z}_n, \tilde{m}_1, ..., \tilde{m}_n, \hat{e}_1, ..., \hat{e}_t), w = (\phi, r_1, ..., r_t,$$
$$r_{\tilde{m}_1}, ..., r_{\tilde{m}_n}))| \forall i \in [n] \ \tilde{m}_i \leftarrow \mathsf{Com}_{\mathsf{ck}}(\mathsf{bit}_i; r_{\tilde{m}_i}) \wedge \mathsf{bit}_i \in \{0,1\} \wedge \sum_{i=1}^{n} \mathsf{bit}_i = t \wedge$$
$$\forall_{i=1}^{t} (\mathsf{bit}_{\phi(i)} = 1 \wedge (\hat{z}_{\phi(i)} \leftarrow \mathsf{Com}_{\mathsf{ck}}(\hat{e}_i; r_i))) \wedge \phi \text{ is an injective map } [t] \to [n]\}.$$

As commitment scheme, we use ElGamal with commitment keys $\hat{\mathsf{ck}}$ and $\check{\mathsf{ck}}$:

---

[7] The techniques in [7] are applied only to Pairing-Product Equations, but the same techniques apply with minimal adjustments to all the other equation types in GS.

[8] Our work compares to [7] like Groth and Lu's shuffle [34] compares to GS proofs. In [34] they created a custom solution for shuffles while GS proofs could already handle them, but with a quadratic size proof.

- Commit to a group element $\hat{E}$: $\hat{\boldsymbol{z}} = (\hat{\boldsymbol{z}}^1, \hat{\boldsymbol{z}}^2) = (r_{\hat{z}}\hat{g}, \hat{E} + r_{\hat{z}}\hat{\mathsf{ck}})$.
- Commit to a bit bit: $\tilde{\boldsymbol{m}} = (\tilde{\boldsymbol{m}}^1, \tilde{\boldsymbol{m}}^2) = (r_{\tilde{m}}\check{h}, \mathsf{bit}\check{h} + r_{\tilde{m}}\check{\mathsf{ck}})$.

Let ψ be a committed variable that is 1 on a regular $\mathsf{crs_{SH}}$ and can be equivocated to 0 with the simulation trapdoor; such a variable is implicitly available in the crs of GS [34]. The variable ψ is only needed to achieve EZK, so it can be ignored in the following overview in which we describe all the equations we prove and why they give a shuffle argument.

To prove the correctness of the switch variables $\{\mathsf{bit}_i : i \in [n]\}$, i.e., that $\forall i \in [n] : \mathsf{bit}_i \in \{0,1\} \wedge \sum_{i=1}^{n} \mathsf{bit}_i = t$, we define the equations $\mathcal{B}_i : \mathsf{bit}_i(1 - \mathsf{bit}_i) = 0$ and $\mathcal{K} : \sum_{i=1}^{n} \mathsf{bit}_i = t\psi$. The main challenge is to devise a set of equations whose satisfiability, proven with GS, implies the statement in the third line of R_{SH}. Towards this goal, we first introduce new variables $\hat{E}_i, f_i, r_{\hat{z}_i}$ and define the following equations (with public constants $\check{\mathsf{ck}}, \hat{\mathsf{ck}}, \hat{g}, \check{h}, \hat{\boldsymbol{z}}_i, \tilde{\boldsymbol{m}}_i$):

$$(\forall i) \; \mathcal{D}_{i,1}^1 : f_i\hat{\boldsymbol{z}}_i^1 = r_{\hat{z}_i}\hat{g}, \quad \mathcal{D}_{i,2}^1 : f_i\hat{\boldsymbol{z}}_i^2 = f_i\hat{E}_i + r_{\hat{z}_i}\hat{\mathsf{ck}}, \quad \mathcal{F}_i : f_i = \mathsf{bit}_i\psi$$

$$(\forall i) \; \mathcal{D}_{i,1}^2 : \psi\tilde{\boldsymbol{m}}_i^1 = r_{\tilde{m}_i}\check{h}, \quad \mathcal{D}_{i,2}^2 : \psi\tilde{\boldsymbol{m}}_1^2 = \mathsf{bit}_i\check{h} + r_{\tilde{m}_i}\check{\mathsf{ck}}.$$

The equations in the first line guarantee that the prover can open t commitments to tags, while the equations in the second line guarantee that the i-th switch variable bit_i is correctly committed in $\tilde{\boldsymbol{m}}_i$.

To prove the shuffle w.r.t. the t public values $(\hat{e}_1, ..., \hat{e}_t)$, we extend the techniques of [34] as follows. First, let us state two assumptions which we rely on, namely the *subset* permutation pairing assumption (SPPA) and the *subset* simultaneous pairing assumption (SSPA). They are inspired (and clearly implied) by their non-subset (i.e., when $t = n$) analogues introduced in [34] for symmetric groups. The permutation pairing assumption was already adapted to the asymmetric setting by González [33].

Assumption 1 (SPPA). $\forall (p, \hat{\mathbb{G}}, \check{\mathbb{H}}, \mathbb{T}, e, \hat{g}, \check{h}) \leftarrow \mathcal{G}(1^\lambda), n \in \mathbb{N}, t \leq n$, and PPT $\mathcal{A}$:

$$\Pr\left[\begin{array}{l} (\{\breve{a}_i\}, \{\breve{b}_i\}, \{\hat{c}_i\}) \leftarrow \mathcal{A}(\mathsf{gk}, t, \{\hat{g}_i\}, \{\hat{\gamma}_i\}, \{\check{h}_i\}, \{\check{\delta}_i\}) \\ \sum_{i=1}^{t} \breve{a}_i = \sum_{i=1}^{t} \check{h}_i, \; \sum_{i=1}^{t} \breve{b}_i = \sum_{i=1}^{t} \check{\delta}_i \\ \forall i \in [t] \; \hat{g} \cdot \breve{a}_i = \hat{c}_i \cdot \check{h}, \hat{g} \cdot \breve{b}_i = \hat{c}_i \cdot \breve{a}_i \\ \{\breve{a}_i\}, \{\breve{b}_i\} \text{ not a permutation of } \{\check{h}_i\}, \{\check{\delta}_i\} \end{array} \middle| \begin{array}{l} x_1, ..., x_n \leftarrow \mathbb{Z}_p, \\ \{\hat{g}_i\} = \{x_i\hat{g}\}, \{\hat{\gamma}_i\} = \{x_i^2\hat{g}\} \\ \{\check{h}_i\} = \{x_i\check{h}\}, \{\check{\delta}_i\} = \{x_i^2\check{\delta}\} \end{array}\right] \leq \mathsf{negl}(\lambda).$$

Assumption 2 (SSPA). $\forall \mathsf{gk} = (p, \hat{\mathbb{G}}, \check{\mathbb{H}}, \mathbb{T}, e, \hat{g}, \check{h}) \leftarrow \mathcal{G}(1^\lambda), n \in \mathbb{N}, t \leq n$, and PPT $\mathcal{A}$:

$$\Pr\left[\begin{array}{l} \{\hat{\mu}_i\} \leftarrow \mathcal{A}(\mathsf{gk}, t, \{\hat{g}_i\}, \{\hat{\gamma}_i\}, \{\check{h}_i\}, \{\check{\delta}_i\}) \\ \sum_{i=1}^{t} \hat{\mu}_i \cdot \check{h} = 0_\mathbb{T}, \sum_{i=1}^{t} \hat{\mu}_i \cdot \check{\delta}_i = 0_\mathbb{T} \\ \exists i : \hat{\mu}_i \neq \hat{0} \end{array} \middle| \begin{array}{l} x_1, ..., x_n \leftarrow \mathbb{Z}_p, \\ \{\hat{g}_i\} = \{x_i\hat{g}\}, \{\hat{\gamma}_i\} = \{x_i^2\hat{g}\} \\ \{\check{h}_i\} = \{x_i\check{h}\}, \{\check{\delta}_i\} = \{x_i^2\check{\delta}\} \end{array}\right] \leq \mathsf{negl}(\lambda).$$

Second, we introduce new variables $\{\check{a}_i, \check{a}'_i, \check{b}_i, \check{b}'_i, \hat{c}_i : i \in [n]\}$ and define the following equations (with public constants $\hat{g}, \check{h}, \check{h}_i, \check{\delta}_i$), where all the $\check{h}_i, \check{\delta}_i$ with $i \in [n]$ are part of $\mathsf{crs}_{\mathsf{SH}}$ and are generated as stated in Assumption 1.

$$\mathcal{Q}^1_i : \check{a}_i = \mathsf{bit}_i \check{a}'_i \quad (\forall i) \; \mathcal{Q}^2_i : \check{b}_i = \mathsf{bit}_i \check{b}'_i$$

$$\mathcal{S}^1 : \sum_{i=1}^n \check{a}_i = \sum_{i=1}^t \psi \check{h}_i \quad \mathcal{S}^2 : \sum_{i=1}^n \check{b}_i = \sum_{i=1}^t \psi \check{\delta}_i$$

$$(\forall i) \; \mathcal{V}^1_i : \hat{g} \cdot \check{a}_i = \hat{c}_i \cdot \check{h} \quad (\forall i) \; \mathcal{V}^2_i : \hat{g} \cdot \check{b}_i = \hat{c}_i \cdot \check{a}_i$$

The above equations formulate a subset permutation pairing problem over the variables $\{\check{a}_i, \check{b}_i\}$ as stated in Assumption 1. In particular, for all $i \in [n]$ the equations $\mathcal{Q}^1_i, \mathcal{Q}^2_i$, together with equations $\mathcal{B}_i$ and $\mathcal{K}$ guarantee that at least t of the variables $\check{a}_i$ and $\check{b}_i$ are set to $\check{0}$. Additionally, if the equations $\mathcal{S}^1, \mathcal{S}^2, \mathcal{V}^1, \mathcal{V}^2$ are satisfied then, thanks to the subset permutation assumption, there exists except with negligible probability a set of indices $\mathcal{J} = \{\alpha_1, ..., \alpha_t\}$ with $1 \leq \alpha_i \leq n$ s.t. $\{(\check{a}_{\alpha_i}, \check{b}_{\alpha_i})\}_{i \in [t]}$ is a permutation of $\{(\check{h}_i, \check{\delta}_i)\}_{i \in [t]}$.

Namely, the switch variables bit_i modify the equations in such a way that setting $\mathsf{bit}_i = 1$ implies that $i \in \mathcal{J}$. Finally, we define the following equations with variables $\hat{o}, \hat{o}', \psi, \hat{E}_i, \check{a}_i, \check{b}_i$ and public constants $\hat{e}_i, \check{h}, \check{\delta}_i, \check{h}_i$.

$$\mathcal{E}^1 : \hat{o} \cdot \check{h} + \sum_{i=1}^n \hat{E}_i \cdot \check{a}_i = \sum_{i=1}^t \hat{e}_i \cdot \check{h}_i, \quad \mathcal{E}^2 : \hat{o}' \cdot \check{h} + \sum_{i=1}^n \hat{E}_i \cdot \check{b}_i = \sum_{i=1}^t \hat{e}_i \cdot \check{\delta}_i$$

$$\mathcal{P}^2 : \psi \hat{o} = \hat{0} \quad \mathcal{P}^3 : \psi \hat{o}' = \hat{0}$$

As for ψ, the introduction of the variables $\hat{o}$ and $\hat{o}'$ is only useful to the simulator. Let us look at the equations in the first line, we have that $\sum_{i=1}^n \hat{E}_i \cdot \check{a}_i = \sum_{i=1}^t \hat{e}_i \cdot \check{h}_i$ and $\sum_{i=1}^n \hat{E}_i \cdot \check{b}_i = \sum_{i=1}^t \hat{e}_i \cdot \check{\delta}_i$. Given that $\{(\check{a}_{\alpha_i}, \check{b}_{\alpha_i})\}_{i \in [t]}$ is a permutation of $\{(\check{h}_i, \check{\delta}_i)\}_{i \in [t]}$, there must exist a permutation π such that $\sum_{i=1}^t (\hat{E}_{\alpha_{\pi(i)}} - \hat{e}_i) \cdot \check{h}_i = \hat{0}$ and $\sum_{i=1}^t (\hat{E}_{\alpha_{\pi(i)}} - \hat{e}_i) \cdot \check{\delta}_i = \hat{0}$. This constitutes a subset simultaneous pairing problem (see Assumption 2), and assuming its computational hardness, we can infer that $\hat{E}_{\alpha_{\pi(i)}} = \hat{e}_i$ for all $i \in [t]$. To prove all the above equations the prover assigns the value to the variables in the following way:

- For all $i \in [n]$ set $r_{\tilde{m}_i}$ as the value given in the witness.
- Set $\mathcal{I} \leftarrow \emptyset$. For all $j \in [t]$ let $\phi(j) = i$, set $\check{a}_i = \check{a}'_i = \check{h}_j, \check{b}_i = \check{b}'_i = \check{\delta}_j, \hat{c}_i = \hat{g}_j, \hat{E}_i = \hat{e}_j, \mathsf{bit}_i = 1, f_1 = 1, r_{\hat{z}_i} = r_j, \mathcal{I} \leftarrow \mathcal{I} \cup \{i\}$.
- $\forall i \in [n] \setminus \mathcal{I}: \check{a}_i = \check{a}'_i = \check{0}, \check{b}_i = \check{b}'_i = \check{0}, \hat{c}_i = \hat{0}, \hat{E}_i = \hat{0}, \mathsf{bit}_i = 0, f_i = 0, r_{\hat{z}_i} = 0$.

The simulation trapdoor consists of the trapdoor of the GS proof system, that allows equivocating ψ to 0, and the discrete logs $\{p_i\}_{i \in [n]}$ of the elements $\{\hat{g}_i\}_{i \in [n]}$. To simulate a proof without knowledge of the witness it suffices to set variables $\hat{o} = \sum_{i=1}^t p_i \hat{e}_i, \hat{o}' = \sum_{i=1}^t p_i^2 \hat{e}_i, (\forall i) \; \check{a}_i = \check{a}'_i = \check{0}, \check{b}_i = \check{b}'_i = \check{0}, \hat{c}_i = \hat{0}, \hat{E}_i = \hat{0}, \mathsf{bit}_i = 0, f_i = 0, r_{\hat{z}_i} = 0, r_{\tilde{m}_i} = 0$. EZK follows from WI of GS proofs and from the fact that the variables corresponding to the inactive positions are assigned in the same way both for real and simulated proofs.

Extend and add operations can be implemented as in [7] since, as for their ENIWI, they only involve adding/removing the contribution of certain variables within a set of equations (i.e., $\mathcal{K}, \mathcal{S}^1, \mathcal{S}^2, \mathcal{E}^1, \mathcal{E}^2$). Whenever an extend/add operation is performed, the lists of commitments $\{\hat{z}_i\}_{i \in [n]}$ to group elements and commitments $\{\tilde{m}_i\}_{i \in [n]}$ to switch variables are also re-randomized (ElGamal is re-randomizable). Applying this re-randomization and updating the GS proofs consequently is straightforward given the malleability of all the components. We defer to [8, App. B] for a detailed description and the security proofs.

5 Our 𝔗etris

We define the relation R_D. The statement contains a commitment c, a DAPT public key pk_T, a topic τ, a message m, and a trapdoor theorem x_{trap}. A witness for R_D is a tuple (e, r, sk_T) such that (e, r) is an opening of c and e is a tag over the pair (τ, m) and the secret key sk_T. Alternatively, the witness can be w_{trap} such that $(x_{\mathsf{trap}}, w_{\mathsf{trap}}) \in R_{\mathcal{L}_{\mathsf{trap}}}$, where $\mathcal{L}_{\mathsf{trap}}$ is a language in NP∩ co-NP (e.g., Diffie-Hellman tuples). Introducing x_{trap} is useful to prove security.

$$R_D = \{(\mathsf{ck}, x = (c, \mathsf{pk}_T, \tau, m, x_{\mathsf{trap}}), w) | (w = (e, r, \mathsf{sk}_T) \land e \leftarrow \mathsf{Tag}(\mathsf{sk}_T, \tau, m) \land$$
$$c \leftarrow \mathsf{Com}_{\mathsf{ck}}(e; r) \land (\mathsf{pk}_T, \mathsf{sk}_T) \in R_{\mathsf{key}}) \lor (w = w_{\mathsf{trap}} \land (x_{\mathsf{trap}}, w_{\mathsf{trap}}) \in R_{\mathcal{L}_{\mathsf{trap}}})\}.$$

Then, we define the threshold relation over R_D as follows.

$$R_{D_{\mathsf{tr}}} = \{(\mathsf{ck}, x = (t, x_1, ..., x_n, \tilde{c}_1, ..., \tilde{c}_n), w = (\phi, w_1, ..., w_t, \tilde{r}_1, ..., \tilde{r}_n)) |$$
$$\forall i \in [n] \; \exists \; \mathsf{bit}_i : \; \tilde{c}_i \leftarrow \mathsf{Com}_{\mathsf{ck}}(\mathsf{bit}_i; \tilde{r}_i) \land \mathsf{bit}_i \in \{0, 1\} \land \sum_{i=1}^{n} \mathsf{bit}_i = t$$
$$\land \forall_{i=1}^{t}(\mathsf{bit}_{\phi(i)} = 1 \land (\mathsf{ck}, x_{\phi(i)}, w_i) \in R_D) \land \phi \text{ is an injective map } [t] \to [n]\}$$

Additionally, we define the extendable shuffle relation as

$$R_{\mathsf{SH}} = \{(\mathsf{ck}, x = (t, c_1, ..., c_n, \tilde{c}_1, ..., \tilde{c}_n, e_1, ..., e_t), w = (\phi, r_1, ..., r_t, \tilde{r}_1, ..., \tilde{r}_n)) |$$
$$\forall i \in [n] \; \exists \; \mathsf{bit}_i : \; \tilde{c}_i \leftarrow \mathsf{Com}_{\mathsf{ck}}(\mathsf{bit}_i; \tilde{r}_i) \land \mathsf{bit}_i \in \{0, 1\} \land \sum_{i=1}^{n} \mathsf{bit}_i = t \land$$
$$\forall_{i=1}^{t}(\mathsf{bit}_{\phi(i)} = 1 \land (c_{\phi(i)} \leftarrow \mathsf{Com}_{\mathsf{ck}}(e_i, r_i))) \land \phi \text{ is an injective map } [t] \to [n]\}.$$

The building blocks are: (i) a DAPT; (ii) an ENIWI for $R_{D_{\mathsf{tr}}}$ that we call EP; (iii) an extendable shuffle SH for R_{SH}; (iv) an IND-CPA public key encryption scheme PKE in which every public key has a unique secret key. PKE must be homomorphic w.r.t. EP.AuxUpd and SH.AuxUpd. Since in both EP and SH, updating the auxiliary values (AuxUpd) simply consists of applying the group operation between two elements of $\hat{\mathbb{G}}$ or $\check{\mathbb{H}}$, we can use ElGamal (in $\hat{\mathbb{G}}$ and $\check{\mathbb{H}}$) as PKE. We require EP and SH to work over the same perfectly binding $\mathsf{Com}_{\mathsf{ck}}$ (i.e., ElGamal). Our 𝔗etris works as follows (see [8, Fig. 11 and 12] for details):

- Setup: It just runs the setup of Com, EP and SH.[9] Additionally, it samples a random x_trap s.t. $x_\text{trap} \notin \mathcal{L}_\text{trap}$[10].
- KGen: The key-pair is composed by the key-pair of DAPT and the key-pair of PKE i.e., pk = ($\text{pk}_\text{T}, \text{pk}_\text{e}$) and sk = ($\text{sk}_\text{T}, \text{sk}_\text{e}$).
- Sign: To compute a signature on m with tag τ, the signer i computes $e \leftarrow \text{Tag}(\text{sk}_\text{T}^i, \tau, m)$, $c_i \leftarrow \text{Com}(e; r_i)$, and $\widetilde{c}_i \leftarrow \text{Com}_\text{ck}(1, \widetilde{r}_i)$. Then, it generates c_j and $\widetilde{c}_j$ $\forall j \in [n], j \neq i$ by committing to zero. It thus obtains $C = \{c_i\}_{i \in [n]}$, $\widetilde{C} = \{\widetilde{c}_i\}_{i \in [n]}$, and the tag e. The signer then proves that $(\text{ck}, (1, x_1, ..., x_n, \widetilde{C})) \in \mathcal{L}_\text{Dtr}$ with $x_i = (c_i, \text{pk}_\text{T}^i, \tau, m, x_\text{trap})$, and that $(\text{ck}, (1, C, \widetilde{C}, e)) \in \mathcal{L}_\text{SH}$, using EP and SH respectively, obtaining proofs Π_EP and Π_SH, along with their auxiliary values. The resulting auxiliary values are individually encrypted under the public keys of the corresponding ring members (i.e. aux_i, for both EP and SH, is encrypted under pk_i for each of the public keys in the ring), leading to lists of ciphertexts $\text{A}_\text{EP}, \text{A}_\text{SH}$. The signature in output is $\sigma = (\Pi_\text{EP}, \Pi_\text{SH}, \text{A}_\text{EP}, \text{A}_\text{SH}, C, \widetilde{C}, \text{E})$, where E is the list of the t tags; i.e., it contains only one tag when the signature is fist generated. Intuitively, Π_EP guarantees that 1 out of the n commitments in C commits to a tag that was honestly generated starting from τ, m, and one of the DAPT keys in the ring, and Π_SH proves that the tag e actually comes from C. Crucially both proofs are about the *same* C and switch variables $\widetilde{C}$. Thus, if both proof are accepting we know that they are both talking about the same active indeces, meaning that all the t (where $t = 1$ when the signature is first generated) clear-text tags of a valid signature actually correspond to honestly generated tags w.r.t. τ, m and t *different* keys in the ring.
- Verify: It just verifies the proofs Π_EP and Π_SH.
- Join: To join, the i-th signer computes $e_i \leftarrow \text{Tag}(\text{sk}_\text{T}^i, \tau, m)$, $c_i \leftarrow \text{Com}(e; r_i)$, and $\widetilde{c}_i \leftarrow \text{Com}_\text{ck}(1, \widetilde{r}_i)$, it decrypts its auxiliary value from A_EP and A_SH and runs the addition operation on both Π_EP and Π_SH getting Π'_EP and Π'_SH. It consequently homomorphically updates all the auxiliary values in A_EP and A_SH getting A'_EP and A'_SH. The addition operation on Π_EP and Π_SH is performed using some common randomness so that they both produce the *same* list of re-randomized commitments C' and $\widetilde{C}'$. E is updated to E' by adding the freshly generated tag e_i. It outputs $\sigma = (\Pi'_\text{EP}, \Pi'_\text{SH}, \text{A}'_\text{EP}, \text{A}'_\text{SH}, C', \widetilde{C}', \text{E}')$.
- Extend: It commits to zero in c_{n+1} and $\widetilde{c_{n+1}}$, runs the extend operation with shared randomness on both proofs, and updates the auxiliary values analogous to what done in Join.
- Trace: If the message is the same for both signatures, it counts the t identical tags and returns (linked, t), otherwise it runs the TagTrace algorithm of the DAPT on all possible triplets of tags and public keys and returns PK where PK is the set of all the traced public keys. If $|\text{PK}| = 0$, it returns indep.

---

[9] The setup of SH bounds the length of the commitments list. Thus our 𝔗etris supports rings of bounded size. Removing this limitation is an open problem.

[10] This can be done efficiently by sampling an instance in the complement of $\mathcal{L}_\text{trap}$.

Theorem 2. *Let* DAPT *be defined as in Sect. 3. Let* EP *be an* ENIWI *for* $R_{\mathsf{D}_{\mathsf{tr}}}$ *with WAI, FPWI, EWI, perfect Δ-Extraction. Let* SH *be an extendable shuffle for relation* R_{SH} *with EZK. Let* PKE *be* IND-CPA, *homomorphic w.r.t.* EP.AuxUpd *and* SH.AuxUpd, *and with verifiability of keys (defined analogously as the one of* DAPT*). Then, the above scheme is a* Tetris *(Sect. 2).* Δ *is defined as follows.*

$$\Delta(w_1...,w_k) = \begin{cases} \bot & \text{if } \exists i \in [k] : (x_{\mathsf{trap}}, w_i) \in R_{\mathcal{L}_{\mathsf{trap}}} \\ (e_1,...,e_k) & \text{otherwise} \end{cases} \quad (2)$$

We give a sketch and defer to [8, Thm. 2] for the formal proof. Furthermore, in [8, App. C] we instantiate EP using [7] and prove it enjoys all the required properties. The standard cryptographic tools we use are defined in [8, App. A].

Verifiability of Keys: It follows from the one of DAPT and PKE.
Tracing Correctness: It follows from the tag traceability of DAPT and the fact all the key pairs output by $\mathcal{A}$ are in $R_{\mathsf{key}}^{\mathfrak{T}}$.
Signers Extraction: The extractor Ext algorithm extracts the committed tags using the extractor of EP (the extractor cannot return $\bot$ since $x_{\mathsf{trap}} \notin \mathcal{L}_{\mathsf{trap}}$). Thanks to the soundness of SH they will be a permutation of the cleartext ones with overwhelming probability (otherwise it outputs $\bot$). From the permutation it is easy to compute (PK, Ind).
Traceability: It follows from the fact that every Tetris which has verifiability of keys, tracing correctness, and signers extraction is traceable.
Strong Anonymity: The proof is carried out through a series of hybrids starting from the game processing lad_0 and ending up to the game processing lad_1. First x_{trap} is sampled with a witness w_{trap} so that $(x_{\mathsf{trap}}, w_{\mathsf{trap}}) \in R_{\mathcal{L}_{\mathsf{trap}}}$, and w_{trap} is used to reply to sign and join queries. This replies are indistinguishable from regular replies thanks to FPWI and WAI of EP and the hardness of $\mathcal{L}_{\mathsf{trap}}$. Then, sign and join operations in lad_0 are processed using w_{trap} as well (indistinguishability follows again from FPWI and WAI of EP). Then, all the cleartext tags resulting from processing the ladders are switched with uniformly random tags (tag pseudo-randomness of DAPT). Then, all the extension and addition actions on EP and SH coming from lad_0 are done recomputing the proofs from scratch (while preserving their connection w.r.t C and $\widetilde{C}$) so that the auxiliary values are not necessary anymore to process the ladder. Then, the ciphertexts of all the signers' in lad_0 and lad_1 are set to encrypt $\bot$. Recall that an admissible $\mathcal{A}$ cannot corrupt any of the signers. Indistinguishability follows from the IND-CPA property of PKE. Now the shuffle proof is simulated instead and indistinguishability follows from EZK of SH. Then, the commitments in C are set according to the correct tags induced by lad_1 (hiding of the commitment), and the clear-text tags are switched to the tags induced by lad_1 as well (tag pseudo-randomness). Then, we remove the use of w_{trap} while processing the ladder and use the DAPT secret keys as witness instead (EWI of EP). Finally, we start a sequence of hybrids that progressively removes the use of SH.Sim, of w_{trap}, and that switches back to using the extension and addition algorithms for Extend and Join queries/actions ending up with the real game using lad_1.

Exculpability: We construct an adversary $\mathcal{B}$ for the non-frameability of DAPT. $\mathcal{B}$ guesses an index i^* s.t. $\mathsf{pk}_{i^*} \in \mathsf{PK}$ at the end of the exculpability experiment (Fig. 4; i^* must exist otherwise $\mathcal{A}$ is not admissible). $\mathcal{B}$ uses $(x_{\mathsf{trap}}, w_{\mathsf{trap}})$ to reply to $\mathcal{A}$'s queries without knowing $\mathsf{sk}_\mathsf{T}^{i^*}$. Finally, $\mathcal{B}$ incorporates $\mathsf{pk}_\mathsf{T}^{i^*}$ from the non-frameability game of DAPT and uses the output of $\mathcal{A}$ to extract two tags (i.e., the ones tracing to $\mathsf{pk}_\mathsf{T}^{i^*}$) and message pairs to play in the non-frameability game..

Acknowledgements. This work is supported by the PICOCRYPT project that has received funding from the European Research Council (ERC) under the European Unions Horizon 2020 research and innovation programme (Grant agreement No. 101001283), partially supported by projects PRODIGY (TED2021-132464B- I00) and ESPADA (PID2022-142290OB-I00) funded by MCIN/AEI/10.13039/501100011033/. This work is also part of the grants CEX2024-001471-M funded by MICIU/AEI/10.13039/501100011033, and JDC2023-050791-I funded by MCIN/AEI/10.13039/501100 011033 and the ESF+. This work was also supported by PE11-Made in Italy–Circular and Sustainable (MICS)–European Union Next-Generation-EU (Piano Nazionale di Ripresa e Resilienza–PNRR).

References

1. Abe, M., Chow, S.S.M., Haralambiev, K., Ohkubo, M.: Double-trapdoor anonymous tags for traceable signatures. In: Lopez, J., Tsudik, G. (eds.) ACNS 2011. LNCS, vol. 6715, pp. 183–200. Springer, Heidelberg (2011). https://doi.org/10.1007/978-3-642-21554-4_11
2. Abe, M., Ohkubo, M., Suzuki, K.: 1-out-of-n signatures from a variety of keys. In: Zheng, Y. (ed.) ASIACRYPT 2002. LNCS, vol. 2501, pp. 415–432. Springer, Heidelberg (2002). https://doi.org/10.1007/3-540-36178-2_26
3. Aguilar Melchor, C., Cayrel, P.-L., Gaborit, P.: A new efficient threshold ring signature scheme based on coding theory. In: Buchmann, J., Ding, J. (eds.) PQCrypto 2008. LNCS, vol. 5299, pp. 1–16. Springer, Heidelberg (2008). https://doi.org/10.1007/978-3-540-88403-3_1
4. Aranha, D.F., Hall-Andersen, M., Nitulescu, A., Pagnin, E., Yakoubov, S.: Count me in! extendability for threshold ring signatures. In: Hanaoka, G., Shikata, J., Watanabe, Y. (eds.) PKC 2022, Part II. LNCS, vol. 13178, pp. 379–406. Springer, Heidelberg (2022). https://doi.org/10.1007/978-3-030-97131-1_13
5. Attema, T., Cramer, R., Rambaud, M.: Compressed Σ-Protocols for Bilinear Group Arithmetic Circuits and Application to Logarithmic Transparent Threshold Signatures. In: Tibouchi, M., Wang, H. (eds.) ASIACRYPT 2021. LNCS, vol. 13093, pp. 526–556. Springer, Cham (2021). https://doi.org/10.1007/978-3-030-92068-5_18
6. Au, M.H., Liu, J.K., Susilo, W., Yuen, T.H.: Secure id-based linkable and revocable-iff-linked ring signature with constant-size construction. Theor. Comput. Sci. **469**, 1–14 (2013)
7. Avitabile, G., Botta, V., Fiore, D.: Extendable threshold ring signatures with enhanced anonymity. In: Boldyreva, A., Kolesnikov, V. (eds.) PKC 2023, Part I. LNCS, vol. 13940, pp. 281–311. Springer, Heidelberg (2023). https://doi.org/10.1007/978-3-031-31368-4_11

8. Avitabile, G., Botta, V., Fiore, D.: Tetris! traceable extendable threshold ring signatures and more. Cryptology ePrint Archive, Paper 2025/730 (2025). https://eprint.iacr.org/2025/730
9. Avitabile, G., Botta, V., Friolo, D., Visconti, I.: Efficient proofs of knowledge for threshold relations. In: Atluri, V., Di Pietro, R., Jensen, C.D., Meng, W. (eds.) ESORICS 2022, Part III. LNCS, vol. 13556, pp. 42–62. Springer, Heidelberg (2022). https://doi.org/10.1007/978-3-031-17143-7_3
10. Backes, M., Döttling, N., Hanzlik, L., Kluczniak, K., Schneider, J.: Ring signatures: logarithmic-size, no setup—from standard assumptions. In: Ishai, Y., Rijmen, V. (eds.) EUROCRYPT 2019. LNCS, vol. 11478, pp. 281–311. Springer, Cham (2019). https://doi.org/10.1007/978-3-030-17659-4_10
11. Bettaieb, S., Schrek, J.: Improved lattice-based threshold ring signature scheme. In: Gaborit, P. (ed.) PQCrypto 2013. LNCS, vol. 7932, pp. 34–51. Springer, Heidelberg (2013). https://doi.org/10.1007/978-3-642-38616-9_3
12. Beullens, W., Katsumata, S., Pintore, F.: Calamari and Falafl: logarithmic (linkable) ring signatures from isogenies and lattices. In: Moriai, S., Wang, H. (eds.) ASIACRYPT 2020. LNCS, vol. 12492, pp. 464–492. Springer, Cham (2020). https://doi.org/10.1007/978-3-030-64834-3_16
13. Boneh, D., Gentry, C., Lynn, B., Shacham, H.: Aggregate and verifiably encrypted signatures from bilinear maps. In: Biham, E. (ed.) EUROCRYPT 2003. LNCS, vol. 2656, pp. 416–432. Springer, Heidelberg (2003). https://doi.org/10.1007/3-540-39200-9_26
14. Bootle, J., Cerulli, A., Chaidos, P., Ghadafi, E., Groth, J.: Foundations of fully dynamic group signatures. In: Manulis, M., Sadeghi, A.-R., Schneider, S. (eds.) ACNS 2016. LNCS, vol. 9696, pp. 117–136. Springer, Cham (2016). https://doi.org/10.1007/978-3-319-39555-5_7
15. Bootle, J., Cerulli, A., Chaidos, P., Ghadafi, E., Groth, J., Petit, C.: Short accountable ring signatures based on DDH. In: Pernul, G., Ryan, P.Y.A., Weippl, E. (eds.) ESORICS 2015. LNCS, vol. 9326, pp. 243–265. Springer, Cham (2015). https://doi.org/10.1007/978-3-319-24174-6_13
16. Branco, P., Mateus, P.: A traceable ring signature scheme based on coding theory. In: Ding, J., Steinwandt, R. (eds.) PQCrypto 2019. LNCS, vol. 11505, pp. 387–403. Springer, Cham (2019). https://doi.org/10.1007/978-3-030-25510-7_21
17. Bresson, E., Stern, J., Szydlo, M.: Threshold ring signatures and applications to ad-hoc groups. In: Yung, M. (ed.) CRYPTO 2002. LNCS, vol. 2442, pp. 465–480. Springer, Heidelberg (2002). https://doi.org/10.1007/3-540-45708-9_30
18. Catalano, D., Fuchsbauer, G., Soleimanian, A.: Double-authentication-preventing signatures in the standard model. In: Galdi, C., Kolesnikov, V. (eds.) SCN 2020. LNCS, vol. 12238, pp. 338–358. Springer, Cham (2020). https://doi.org/10.1007/978-3-030-57990-6_17
19. Chakraborty, S., Hofheinz, D., Langrehr, R., Nielsen, J.B., Striecks, C., Venturi, D.: Malleable SNARKs and their applications. Cryptology ePrint Archive, Paper 2025/311 (2025). https://eprint.iacr.org/2025/311
20. Chase, M., Kohlweiss, M., Lysyanskaya, A., Meiklejohn, S.: Malleable proof systems and applications. In: Pointcheval, D., Johansson, T. (eds.) EUROCRYPT 2012. LNCS, vol. 7237, pp. 281–300. Springer, Heidelberg (2012). https://doi.org/10.1007/978-3-642-29011-4_18
21. Chase, M., Kohlweiss, M., Lysyanskaya, A., Meiklejohn, S.: Succinct malleable NIZKs and an application to compact shuffles. In: Sahai, A. (ed.) TCC 2013. LNCS, vol. 7785, pp. 100–119. Springer, Heidelberg (2013). https://doi.org/10.1007/978-3-642-36594-2_6

22. Derler, D., Ramacher, S., Slamanig, D.: Generic double-authentication preventing signatures and a post-quantum instantiation. In: Baek, J., Susilo, W., Kim, J. (eds.) ProvSec 2018. LNCS, vol. 11192, pp. 258–276. Springer, Cham (2018). https://doi.org/10.1007/978-3-030-01446-9_15
23. Dodis, Y., Kiayias, A., Nicolosi, A., Shoup, V.: Anonymous identification in Ad Hoc groups. In: Cachin, C., Camenisch, J.L. (eds.) EUROCRYPT 2004. LNCS, vol. 3027, pp. 609–626. Springer, Heidelberg (2004). https://doi.org/10.1007/978-3-540-24676-3_36
24. Escala, A., Groth, J.: Fine-tuning groth-sahai proofs. In: Krawczyk, H. (ed.) PKC 2014. LNCS, vol. 8383, pp. 630–649. Springer, Heidelberg (2014). https://doi.org/10.1007/978-3-642-54631-0_36
25. Feng, H., Liu, J., Li, D., Li, Y., Wu, Q.: Traceable ring signatures: general framework and post-quantum security. Des. Codes Cryptogr. **89**(6), 1111–1145 (2021). https://doi.org/10.1007/s10623-021-00863-x
26. Fujisaki, E.: Sub-linear size traceable ring signatures without random oracles. In: Kiayias, A. (ed.) CT-RSA 2011. LNCS, vol. 6558, pp. 393–415. Springer, Heidelberg (2011). https://doi.org/10.1007/978-3-642-19074-2_25
27. Fujisaki, E., Suzuki, K.: Traceable ring signature. In: Okamoto, T., Wang, X. (eds.) PKC 2007. LNCS, vol. 4450, pp. 181–200. Springer, Heidelberg (2007). https://doi.org/10.1007/978-3-540-71677-8_13
28. Fujisaki, E., Suzuki, K.: Traceable ring signature. IEICE Trans. Fundam. Electron. Commun. Comput. Sci. **91-A**(1), 83–93 (2008). https://doi.org/10.1093/IETFEC/E91-A.1.83, https://doi.org/10.1093/ietfec/e91-a.1.83
29. Ghadafi, E.: Efficient distributed tag-based encryption and its application to group signatures with efficient distributed traceability. In: Aranha, D.F., Menezes, A. (eds.) LATINCRYPT 2014. LNCS, vol. 8895, pp. 327–347. Springer, Cham (2015). https://doi.org/10.1007/978-3-319-16295-9_18
30. Ghadafi, E.: Partially structure-preserving signatures: lower bounds, constructions and more. In: Sako, K., Tippenhauer, N.O. (eds.) ACNS 2021. LNCS, vol. 12726, pp. 284–312. Springer, Cham (2021). https://doi.org/10.1007/978-3-030-78372-3_11
31. Ghadafi, E., Smart, N.P., Warinschi, B.: Groth–sahai proofs revisited. In: Nguyen, P.Q., Pointcheval, D. (eds.) PKC 2010. LNCS, vol. 6056, pp. 177–192. Springer, Heidelberg (2010). https://doi.org/10.1007/978-3-642-13013-7_11
32. Goel, A., Green, M., Hall-Andersen, M., Kaptchuk, G.: Stacking sigmas: A framework to compose Σ-protocols for disjunctions. In: Dunkelman, O., Dziembowski, S. (eds.) EUROCRYPT 2022, Part II. LNCS, vol. 13276, pp. 458–487. Springer, Heidelberg (2022). https://doi.org/10.1007/978-3-031-07085-3_16
33. González, A.: Shorter ring signatures from standard assumptions. In: Lin, D., Sako, K. (eds.) PKC 2019. LNCS, vol. 11442, pp. 99–126. Springer, Cham (2019). https://doi.org/10.1007/978-3-030-17253-4_4
34. Groth, J., Lu, S.: A non-interactive shuffle with pairing based verifiability. In: Kurosawa, K. (ed.) ASIACRYPT 2007. LNCS, vol. 4833, pp. 51–67. Springer, Heidelberg (2007). https://doi.org/10.1007/978-3-540-76900-2_4
35. Groth, J., Sahai, A.: Efficient non-interactive proof systems for bilinear groups. In: Smart, N. (ed.) EUROCRYPT 2008. LNCS, vol. 4965, pp. 415–432. Springer, Heidelberg (2008). https://doi.org/10.1007/978-3-540-78967-3_24
36. Haque, A., Scafuro, A.: Threshold ring signatures: new definitions and post-quantum security. In: Kiayias, A., Kohlweiss, M., Wallden, P., Zikas, V. (eds.) PKC 2020. LNCS, vol. 12111, pp. 423–452. Springer, Cham (2020). https://doi.org/10.1007/978-3-030-45388-6_15

37. Liu, J.K., Wei, V.K., Wong, D.S.: Linkable spontaneous anonymous group signature for Ad Hoc groups. In: Wang, H., Pieprzyk, J., Varadharajan, V. (eds.) ACISP 2004. LNCS, vol. 3108, pp. 325–335. Springer, Heidelberg (2004). https://doi.org/10.1007/978-3-540-27800-9_28
38. Malavolta, G., Schröder, D.: Efficient ring signatures in the standard model. In: Takagi, T., Peyrin, T. (eds.) ASIACRYPT 2017. LNCS, vol. 10625, pp. 128–157. Springer, Cham (2017). https://doi.org/10.1007/978-3-319-70697-9_5
39. Munch-Hansen, A., Orlandi, C., Yakoubov, S.: Stronger notions and a more efficient construction of threshold ring signatures. In: Longa, P., Ràfols, C. (eds.) LATIN-CRYPT 2021. LNCS, vol. 12912, pp. 363–381. Springer, Cham (2021). https://doi.org/10.1007/978-3-030-88238-9_18
40. Naor, M.: Deniable ring authentication. In: Yung, M. (ed.) CRYPTO 2002. LNCS, vol. 2442, pp. 481–498. Springer, Heidelberg (2002). https://doi.org/10.1007/3-540-45708-9_31
41. Petzoldt, A., Bulygin, S., Buchmann, J.: A multivariate based threshold ring signature scheme. Appl. Algebra Eng. Commun. Comput. 24(3–4), 255–275 (2013)
42. Rivest, R.L., Shamir, A., Tauman, Y.: How to leak a secret. In: Boyd, C. (ed.) ASIACRYPT 2001. LNCS, vol. 2248, pp. 552–565. Springer, Heidelberg (2001). https://doi.org/10.1007/3-540-45682-1_32
43. Russo, A., Anta, A.F., Vasco, M.I.G., Romano, S.P.: Chirotonia: a scalable and secure e-Voting framework based on blockchains and linkable ring signatures. In: 2021 IEEE International Conference on Blockchain (Blockchain), pp. 417–424 (2021)
44. Scafuro, A., Zhang, B.: One-time traceable ring signatures. In: Bertino, E., Shulman, H., Waidner, M. (eds.) ESORICS 2021. LNCS, vol. 12973, pp. 481–500. Springer, Cham (2021). https://doi.org/10.1007/978-3-030-88428-4_24
45. Thyagarajan, S.A.K., Malavolta, G., Schmid, F., Schröder, D.: Verifiable timed linkable ring signatures for scalable payments for monero. In: Atluri, V., Di Pietro, R., Jensen, C.D., Meng, W. (eds.) ESORICS 2022, Part II. LNCS, vol. 13555, pp. 467–486. Springer, Heidelberg (2022). https://doi.org/10.1007/978-3-031-17146-8_23
46. Tsang, P.P., Wei, V.K.: Short linkable ring signatures for E-Voting, E-Cash and attestation. In: Deng, R.H., Bao, F., Pang, H.H., Zhou, J. (eds.) ISPEC 2005. LNCS, vol. 3439, pp. 48–60. Springer, Heidelberg (2005). https://doi.org/10.1007/978-3-540-31979-5_5
47. Xu, S., Yung, M.: Accountable ring signatures: a smart card approach. In: Smart Card Research and Advanced Applications VI, pp. 271–286. Springer US, Boston, MA (2004)
48. Yuen, T.H., Esgin, M.F., Liu, J.K., Au, M.H., Ding, Z.: *DualRing*: generic construction of ring signatures with efficient instantiations. In: Malkin, T., Peikert, C. (eds.) CRYPTO 2021. LNCS, vol. 12825, pp. 251–281. Springer, Cham (2021). https://doi.org/10.1007/978-3-030-84242-0_10
49. Yuen, T.H., Liu, J.K., Au, M.H., Susilo, W., Zhou, J.: Efficient linkable and/or threshold ring signature without random oracles. Comput. J. 56(4), 407–421 (2013)
50. Zhang, C., Yuen, T.H., Xiong, H., Chow, S.S.M., Yiu, S.M., He, Y.J.: Multi-key leakage-resilient threshold cryptography. In: Chen, K., Xie, Q., Qiu, W., Li, N., Tzeng, W.G. (eds.) ASIACCS 2013, pp. 61–70. ACM Press (May 2013)

Efficient One-Pass Private Set Intersection from Pairings with Offline Preprocessing

Joonsang Baek[1], Seongbong Choi[2], Willy Susilo[1], Partha Sarathi Roy[1], and Hyung Tae Lee[2(✉)]

[1] Institute of Cybersecurity and Cryptology, University of Wollongong, Wollongong, Australia
{baek,wsusilo,partha}@uow.edu.au
[2] Chung-Ang University, Seoul, Republic of Korea
{welq2st,hyungtaelee}@cau.ac.kr

Abstract. We present an efficient pairing-based private set intersection (PSI) protocol with offline preprocessing. Our protocol is *one-pass* as a receiver does not have to transmit any message to a sender for the entire PSI operation, implying that a sender can initiate a protocol execution anytime at will by sending a PSI message to the receiver. Moreover, the sender's computation and communication costs are independent of the size of the receiver's input set. We prove that our protocol is secure against semi-honest adversaries under the (standard) bilinear Diffie-Hellman assumption in the random oracle model. We also extend our semi-honest secure PSI protocol to achieve malicious security without compromising efficiency. Our experiments show that the receiver's intersection retrieval runs 100–1000 times faster than that of Aranha et al.'s protocol (ACM CCS '22), which is the state-of-the-art pairing-based PSI protocol, depending on the size of sets, and maintains a similar amount of computation and communication costs for the sender. Thanks to the much less computational burden for the receiver, our PSI protocols are expected to handle data sets of moderately large size well.

Keywords: Private set intersection · pairings · one-pass protocol · bilinear Diffie-Hellman assumption · random oracle · offline preprocessing

1 Introduction

Private set intersection (PSI) is a technique for enabling two parties to compute the intersection of their data sets without revealing anything to the counterparty other than the intersection. PSI is in the realm of secure multi-party computation and is regarded as highly relevant to the current cybersecurity applications, such as private contact discovery, password checkup, and voter registration [17].

There have been numerous PSI constructions based on various cryptographic primitives [15], but the PSI protocols based on Oblivious Transfer (OT) and the

Diffie-Hellman (DH) key exchange are the ones widely researched and used in practice. Usually, the DH-based protocols require less communication than the OT-based protocols, while the latter offer much faster computation. Despite the DH-based PSI having emerged decades ago [11,14], they have not been brought into focus until recently when Rosulek and Trieu [18] proposed an efficient DH-based PSI protocol, which we denote by "RT21". Soon after Rosulek and Trieu's work, Aranha et al. [2] constructed another DH-based PSI protocol using pairings, which we denote by "ALOS22".

The central theme of this work is DH-based PSI. According to Rosulek and Trieu [18], the reasons why we still need DH-based PSI protocols are the followings: First, reducing communication costs is more critical than computational costs in many applications since the CPUs can easily be attached to the shared network, as exemplified by Google's choice for their PSI solution [12]. Second, although saving computations is vital for environments where the PSI operation is performed over large sets, many situations only require PSI operations for small sets, such as the PSI application based on Apple's AirDrop [10] and calendar schedule sharing (up to 360 h per month).

1.1 Problem Statements

Reducing Communication Complexity. The first question of our PSI research is whether it is possible to reduce the communication complexity of the DH-based PSI protocols even further. In particular, we aim at constructing a *one-pass* PSI protocol between the sender and the receiver so that the protocol execution ends after one of them transmits a message in a single pass. One-pass PSI protocols can be advantageous in many applications that require low latency for real-time communications, where a sender, for example, does not have to wait for any message from a receiver. However, the aforementioned DH-based PSI protocols, RT21 and ALOS22 are three and two passes, respectively, as one party always needs to receive some messages from the other before proceeding to the next phase of the protocol.

Improving Laconic PSI. Another question is whether it is possible to design a laconic or laconic-like PSI protocol that significantly improves the efficiency and practical viability of the existing pairing-based PSI protocol, ALOS22 [2]. The heart of a laconic property of PSI protocols is that the computation and communication costs of a sender do not depend on the size of a receiver's input. Specifically, Aranha et al. describe a laconic (PSI) protocol run between a sender and a receiver as follows [2, Section 1]: 1) The protocol should only have two messages; 2) The total communication and the work of the sender do not depend on the size of the receiver's input; and 3) The receiver's first message can be reused by multiple senders. Note that laconic PSI protocols are useful for applications where the senders are client-side machines with constrained resources while the receiver is a powerful server with a large database. The ALOS22 protocol achieves the laconic properties using the pairing-based "accumulator" [16].

We realized that despite its elegant structure, ALOS22 has a notable deficiency in the receiver side computation: For example, according to [2], to process the receiver's input set of only 4,096 elements, the receiver's computation takes about 20 min[1]. Even if the receiver is a powerful server, the slow running time to this degree would make the protocol less viable in practice. We address this issue by taking a fresh approach to the design of laconic(-like) PSI.

1.2 Our Solutions

In this paper, we propose a *one-pass* PSI protocol based on pairings by leveraging an offline preprocessing phase. Our approach builds on observations from ALOS22, where the third party plays a crucial role in executing the PSI operation. Specifically, in their protocol, the third party generates a common reference string consisting of group elements whose size matches the receiver's set. Furthermore, these group elements are derived from a secret value selected by the third party. Consequently, if the third party is dishonest, it can potentially retrieve the sender's set. To ensure security, their protocol implicitly assumes that the third party is honest.

Our PSI protocol draws inspiration from a three-party (non-interactive) key agreement protocol involving the sender, the receiver and the third party, with assigning more roles to the third party. Concretely, in our protocol the third party begins by generating its public key $\Gamma = g_2^s$, where s is a corresponding secret key and g_2 is a generator of the underlying pairing group $\mathbb{G}_2$ for a pairing $e : \mathbb{G}_1 \times \mathbb{G}_2 \to \mathbb{G}_T$. It publishes Γ as a part of the common reference string. The third party then jointly runs the "receiver-set registration" process with the receiver. After this process, the receiver obtains $K_j = \mathsf{F}(y_j)^s$ for each element y_j in the receiver's set, where F is a hash function from $\{0,1\}^*$ to $\mathbb{G}_1$. It is worth noting that this process is independent of the sender and can be executed offline.

Once the sender wishes to compute the intersection, he selects a random secret value r, and computes $\psi = g_2^r$ and $\chi = \Gamma^r$. The sender calculates $\mu_i = e(\mathsf{F}(x_i), \chi)$ and $R_i = \mathsf{H}(\mu_i)$ for each element x_i in the sender's set where H is a pre-determined hash function. Then, the sender passes ψ and R_i's to the receiver. Upon receiving ψ and R_i's, the receiver extracts the intersection by identifying pairs (K_j, y_j) such that $\mathsf{H}(e(K_j, \psi)) = R_i$ for some R_i. If the sender and the receiver have the same element $x_i = y_j$, then the receiver can obtain such $x_i = y_j$ since $e(K_j, \psi) = e(\mathsf{F}(y_j), g_2)^{rs} = e(\mathsf{F}(x_i), \chi)$ from the bilinear property of the pairing.

The proposed PSI protocol is secure against semi-honest adversaries under the bilinear Diffie-Hellman (BDH) assumption in the random oracle model. Informally, for an adversary to retrieve any information about an element x that is not in the intersection, the adversary must know $e(\mathsf{F}(x), g_2)^{rs} = e(g_1, g_2)^{rst}$ where $\Gamma = g_2^s$, $\psi = g_2^r$ and $\mathsf{F}(x)$ are given, with $\mathsf{F}(x) = g_1^t$ for some t. However, it is infeasible under the BDH assumption. We formally demonstrate the security of our PSI protocol under the BDH assumption and random oracle heuristics in the semi-honest model.

---

[1] This measurement is taken from [2]. When we ran their protocol, the running time was much slower. (Readers are referred to Sect. 5 of this paper for the details).

We also extend our semi-honest PSI protocol to a malicious model by incorporating the technique proposed by Rosulek and Trieu in [18]. This involves modifying the input of the hash function H to include the associated element. In the modified protocol, $R_i = \mathsf{H}(\mu_i)$ is replaced with $R_i = \mathsf{H}(x_i, \mu_i)$ and the receiver retrieves the intersection by checking $\mathsf{H}(y_j, e(K_j, \psi)) = R_i$, instead of $\mathsf{H}(e(K_j, \psi)) = R_i$. Informally, if H is assumed to be a random oracle, from its query-answer list, a simulator can "extract" an ideal-world input that explains the input's effect in the real world. We confirm that this modification causes a slight incremental performance overhead compared to the semi-honest version. Additionally, we show that the protocol is secure against malicious adversaries under the BDH assumption in the random oracle model.

As mentioned earlier, introducing a third party to PSI protocols has security implications, as the third party could be a potential adversary that tries to compromise the sender and/or receiver's private sets. Our PSI protocol requires the third party to be trusted by the sender, like ALOS22. However, to protect the privacy of the receiver's input against the third party, which is implied in ALOS22, the receiver "masks" its elements of the input set using a randomization parameter in the receiver set registration. We prove that this masking technique provides privacy of the receiver's input against the third party.

Overall, as is the case with the laconic PSI protocols, our PSI protocol is beneficial for the "unbalanced PSI" [15] setting where numerous clients (the senders) with moderate-sized data cannot afford costly communications with servers (the receivers). Our PSI solution is unprecedented in that it is the first one-pass PSI protocol that renders communication overhead for the sender minimal while significantly reducing the receiver's computations for producing the intersection.

1.3 Summary of Our Contributions

In this work, we provide affirmative answers to the research questions we posed and make the following contributions:

- We present a one-pass PSI protocol based on pairings in Sect. 3, where the receiver does not transmit any message to the sender. Our protocol satisfies the efficiency requirements of the laconic PSI in the literature by keeping the sender's computation and communication overheads independent of the size of the receiver's input set. We prove that this protocol is secure against semi-honest adversaries under the BDH assumption in the random oracle model.
- We extend our base PSI protocol to achieve malicious security in Sect. 4. The transformation to the malicious-secure version, inspired by the RT21 protocol [18], is highly efficient and preserves all the requirements of the laconic PSI achieved by our based PSI protocol. The proposed malicious version is also secure under the (same) BDH assumption in the random oracle model.
- In Sect. 5, we provide implementations of our protocols in various sizes of input sets and compare the performance of the semi-honest secure version of our protocol with the most closely related protocols, ALOS22 [2] and

RT21 [18]. According to our experimental results, the receiver's running time of our protocol is 100–1000 times faster than that of ALOS22. Even costs for all other computation and communication are slightly less than those of ALOS22. Moreover, when the receiver's input set is sufficiently larger than the sender's, our protocol reduces the running time of the sender side at the cost of increased computation for the receiver. For example, with sender and receiver input set sizes of 2^{10} and 2^{16}, respectively, and a bandwidth limit of 10 Gbps, the sender's running time in our protocol is approximately 10.50 times faster than in RT21, while the receiver's total execution time is approximately 6.16 times slower.
- Regarding the security of our protocols in the presence of third-party involvement, we show in Sect. 6 that the receiver-set registration process provides the privacy of the receiver's input set against the third party.

1.4 Related Work

Numerous PSI protocols based on diverse cryptographic primitives have been proposed [3,5,11,13,18]. We only review DH-based and laconic PSI protocols exclusively, which are closely relevant to our work. For a more comprehensive summary of existing PSI protocols, readers are referred to [15].

DH-Based PSI Protocols. The DH-based PSI protocol can be traced back to the work of Meadows [14]. Later, Huberman et al. [11] proposed the DH-based PSI construction. Both are secure in the semi-honest model only. A DH-based PSI construction secure against malicious adversaries was first considered by De Cristofaro et al. [5]. They proposed the PSI protocol based on RSA groups, which is the first DH-based PSI protocol secure against malicious adversaries. Concurrently, Jarecki and Li [13] proposed an efficient PSI protocol under the One-More Gap DH assumption in the malicious model. Recently, Rosulek and Trieu [18] also proposed the DH-based PSI protocol. Their construction is secure against malicious adversaries and efficient, especially for small sets. They noted that despite the computational inefficiency compared with OT-based PSI protocols, the DH-based PSI protocols are still worth attention due to their very low communication cost and performance benefits for small sets.

Laconic PSI Protocols. In the realm of PSI, several laconic protocols have been proposed. Alamanti et al. [1] demonstrated that PSI protocols can be designed as laconic protocols and provided instantiations based on an RSA accumulator. Following their work, Aranha et al. [2] presented a laconic PSI protocol using a pairing-based accumulator. Later, Döttling et al. [6] proposed a laconic PSI protocol from lattices. Very recently, Wu et al. [20] proposed a laconic protocol for PSI cardinality employing two cloud servers.

2 Preliminaries

This section presents some preliminaries that help readers to understand our proposed PSI protocols in this paper.

2.1 Notations

Throughout this paper, we denote the security parameter by λ. We write $a \leftarrow_\$ A$ to denote an operation that a is assigned to a value from the set A uniformly at random. $[a]$ represents the set of integers x such that $1 \leq x \leq a$. More generally, $[a,b]$ represents the set of integers x such that $a \leq x \leq b$. $\mathcal{D}_1 \stackrel{c}{\approx} \mathcal{D}_2$ denotes that two distributions of $\mathcal{D}_1$ and $\mathcal{D}_2$ are computationally indistinguishable.

2.2 Definitions

We review the PSI ideal functionality and various definitions related to secure two-party computation. The detailed exposition of the definitions given in this paper can be found in [8].

Definition 1 (PSI Ideal Functionality f_{PSI}). *Let $X = \{x_1, \ldots, x_n\}$, where $x_i \in \{0,1\}^*$, be a party $\mathcal{P}_1$'s input set. Let $Y = \{y_1, \ldots, y_m\}$, where $y_i \in \{0,1\}^*$, be a party $\mathcal{P}_2$'s input set. Party $\mathcal{P}_2$ receives the intersection $Z = X \cap Y$.*

Semi-honest security assumes that an adversary corrupting the parties follows the protocol specification exactly but tries to get any information about the counterparty's input by observing the transcript of the message it has received and its internal state. The formal definition of semi-honest security is provided below.

Definition 2 (Semi-Honest Security). *Let $f = (f_1, f_2)$ be a functionality, which is assumed to be deterministic, and let Π be a protocol. Let $\mathsf{view}_1(X,Y)$ and $\mathsf{view}_2(X,Y)$ be the views of $\mathcal{P}_1$ and $\mathcal{P}_2$, respectively. Π securely computes f against semi-honest adversaries if there exist probabilistic polynomial-time algorithms Sim_1 and Sim_2 such that $\{\mathsf{Sim}_1(1^\lambda, X, f_1(X,Y))\} \stackrel{c}{\approx} \{\mathsf{view}_1^\Pi(X,Y)\}$ and $\{\mathsf{Sim}_2(1^\lambda, Y, f_2(X,Y))\} \stackrel{c}{\approx} \{\mathsf{view}_2^\Pi(X,Y)\}$.*

We now review the definition of malicious security [8]. The definition of malicious security assumes that the adversary may use any efficient attack strategy and arbitrarily deviate from the protocol specification. Unlike semi-honest security, the adversary may not use the input that is provided.

Definition 3 (Malicious Security). *Let $f = (f_1, f_2)$ be a functionality, which is assumed to be deterministic, and let Π be a protocol in which parties $\mathcal{P}_1$ and $\mathcal{P}_2$ are involved. Suppose that taking auxiliary input z as input, a malicious adversary $\mathcal{A}$ corrupts $\mathcal{P}_i$ where $i \in \{1,2\}$, which may either abort, send its received input or send some other input of the same length to the trusted party. Let (X', Y') be such input, where $X' = X$ if $i = 2$ and $Y' = Y$ if $i = 1$. Upon receiving (X', Y'), the trusted party computes $f_1(X',Y')$ and $f_2(X',Y')$, and sends $f_i(X',Y')$ to the corrupted party $\mathcal{P}_i$ and $f_j(X',Y')$ to the honest party $\mathcal{P}_j$ unless aborted.*

By $\mathsf{Ideal}_{f,\mathcal{A}(z),i}(X,Y)$, denote the output value the honest party received from the trusted party and $\mathcal{A}$'s any arbitrary (probabilistic polynomial-time computable) function of the initial input of the corrupted party. By $\mathsf{Real}_{\Pi,\mathcal{A},i}(X,Y)$, denote the output pair of the honest party and the adversary in the real execution of Π.

Π securely computes f against a malicious adversary $\mathcal{A}$ if there exists a probabilistic polynomial-time adversary Sim such that $\{\mathsf{Ideal}_{f,\mathsf{Sim}(z),i}(X,Y)\} \stackrel{c}{\approx} \{\mathsf{Real}_{\Pi,\mathcal{A},i}(X,Y)\}$ for every $i \in \{1, 2\}$.

Next, we review the definition of the bilinear Diffie-Hellman (BDH) assumption. Suppose that $\mathbb{G}_1$, $\mathbb{G}_2$, and $\mathbb{G}_T$ are cyclic groups of prime order p. A pairing is a bilinear map $e : \mathbb{G}_1 \times \mathbb{G}_2 \to \mathbb{G}_T$ that is non-degenerate and efficiently computable. In this paper, we consider the following version of the BDH assumption based on the Type-3 pairing as described in [4].

Definition 4 (Bilinear Diffie-Hellman (BDH) Assumption). Let $e : \mathbb{G}_1 \times \mathbb{G}_2 \to \mathbb{G}_T$ be an asymmetric pairing where $\mathbb{G}_1$, $\mathbb{G}_2$, and $\mathbb{G}_T$ are groups of order p. Let g_1, g_2 be generators of $\mathbb{G}_1$, $\mathbb{G}_2$, respectively. Given $(g_1^a, g_1^b, g_1^c, g_2^b, g_2^c)$ for $a, b, c \xleftarrow{\$} \mathbb{Z}_p^*$, the bilinear Diffie-Hellman (BDH) problem is to compute $e(g_1, g_2)^{abc}$. The BDH assumption states that the BDH problem is intractable.

3 Our PSI Protocol Secure in the Semi-honest Model

In this section, we present our pairing-based PSI protocol in the semi-honest model, followed by its correctness, efficiency, and security analysis.

3.1 Description and Correctness

Description. In our basic PSI protocol, there are three parties involved: a sender, a receiver, and a third party[2]. The common reference string $\mathsf{crs} = (e, \mathbb{G}_1, \mathbb{G}_2, \mathbb{G}_T, g_1, g_2, p, \mathsf{F}, \mathsf{H}, \Gamma)$ is generated by the third party, where $e : \mathbb{G}_1 \times \mathbb{G}_2 \to \mathbb{G}_T$ denotes an asymmetric pairing; $\mathbb{G}_1, \mathbb{G}_2, \mathbb{G}_T$ are cyclic groups of order p; g_1, g_2 are generators of $\mathbb{G}_1, \mathbb{G}_2$, respectively; $\mathsf{F} : \{0,1\}^* \to \mathbb{G}_1$ and $\mathsf{H} : \mathbb{G}_T \to \{0,1\}^\lambda$ are hash functions; and $\Gamma = g_2^s$ for $s \xleftarrow{\$} \mathbb{Z}_p^*$.

Let $Y = \{y_1, \ldots, y_m\}$ be an input set of the receiver. First, the receiver picks $\rho \xleftarrow{\$} \mathbb{Z}_p^*$, computes $\Lambda_j = \mathsf{F}(y_j)^\rho$ for all $j \in [m]$, and passes $\{\Lambda_j\}_{j=1}^m$ to the third party. Upon receiving $\{\Lambda_j\}_{j=1}^m$ from the receiver, the third party computes $\Psi_j = \Lambda_j^s$ for all $j \in [m]$ and returns $\{\Psi_j\}_{j=1}^m$ to the receiver. Once receiving $\{\Psi_j\}_{j=1}^m$ from the third party, the receiver computes $K_j = \Psi_j^{\rho^{-1}}$ for all $j \in [m]$. Note that this step can be performed independently from the following steps, so K_j's can be precomputed in the *offline phase* after the common reference string is set. We also note that computing $\mathsf{F}(y_j)^\rho$ is to protect information about y_j even from the third party.

The sender, taking $X = \{x_1, \ldots, x_n\}$ as an input set, engages with the receiver in the following steps: The sender picks $r \xleftarrow{\$} \mathbb{Z}_p^*$, computes $\psi = g_2^r$,

---

[2] Other PSI protocols in the literature, such as [1,2], do involve a third party. We indicate it more explicitly.

> **Input:** A sender's private set $X = \{x_1, \ldots, x_n\}$ and a receiver's private set $Y = \{y_1, \ldots, y_m\}$
>
> **CRS Generation:** The third party generates an asymmetric pairing $e : \mathbb{G}_1 \times \mathbb{G}_2 \to \mathbb{G}_T$ where $\mathbb{G}_1, \mathbb{G}_2, \mathbb{G}_T$ are cyclic groups of order p. It selects random generators $g_1 \in \mathbb{G}_1$, $g_2 \in \mathbb{G}_2$. It picks a random element $s \leftarrow\!\!\$\, \mathbb{Z}_p^*$ and computes $\Gamma = g_2^s$. It generates two hash functions $\mathsf{F} : \{0,1\}^* \to \mathbb{G}_1$, $\mathsf{H} : \mathbb{G}_T \to \{0,1\}^\lambda$. It outputs a common reference string $\mathsf{crs} = (e, \mathbb{G}_1, \mathbb{G}_2, \mathbb{G}_T, g_1, g_2, p, \mathsf{F}, \mathsf{H}, \Gamma)$.
>
> **[Offline Phase: Receiver-Set Registration]**
>
> 1. The receiver performs as follows:
>   (a) Select a random element $\rho \leftarrow\!\!\$\, \mathbb{Z}_p^*$.
>   (b) Compute $\Lambda_j = \mathsf{F}(y_j)^\rho$ for each $j \in [m]$.
>   (c) Send $(\Lambda_1, \ldots, \Lambda_m)$ to the third party.
> 2. The third party computes $\Psi_j = \Lambda_j^s$ for each $j \in [m]$ and sends $(\Psi_1, \ldots, \Psi_m)$ to the receiver.
> 3. The receiver computes $K_j = \Psi_j^{\rho^{-1}}$ for each $j \in [m]$.
>
> **[Online Phase]**
>
> 1. The sender performs as follows:
>   (a) Sample $r \leftarrow\!\!\$\, \mathbb{Z}_p^*$, and compute $\psi = g_2^r$ and $\chi = \Gamma^r$.
>   (b) Compute $\mu_i = e(\mathsf{F}(x_i), \chi)$ and $R_i = \mathsf{H}(\mu_i)$ for each $i \in [n]$.
>   (c) Send $(\psi, R_1, \ldots, R_n)$ to the receiver.
> 2. The receiver initiates Z as an empty set and performs as follows:
>   (a) Find (K_j, y_j) such that $\mathsf{H}(e(K_j, \psi)) = R_i$ for all $j \in [m]$ and $i \in [n]$. If such a y_j exists, update $Z = Z \cup \{y_j\}$.
>   (b) Output Z.

Fig. 1. Our PSI Protocol Secure against Semi-Honest Adversaries

$\chi = \Gamma^r$, $\mu_i = e(\mathsf{F}(x_i), \chi)$, and $R_i = \mathsf{H}(\mu_i)$ for each $i \in [n]$. Then, the sender passes $\psi, \{R_i\}_{i=1}^n$ to the receiver.

Finally, upon receiving $\psi, \{R_i\}_{i=1}^n$ from the sender, the receiver finds all (K_j, y_j) such that $\mathsf{H}(e(K_j, \psi)) = R_i$ for some $i \in [n]$, retrieving the intersection.

The formal description of our PSI protocol in the semi-honest model is given in Fig. 1.

Correctness. For correctness of the protocol described in Fig. 1, we prove the following theorem.

Theorem 1. *The receiver in our PSI protocol of Fig. 1 obtains $X \cap Y$ at the end of the protocol if F and H are collision-resistant.*

Proof. If the sender follows the descriptions of the protocol in Fig. 1 faithfully, then it holds that for each $i \in [n]$,

$$R_i = \mathsf{H}(\mu_i) = \mathsf{H}(e(\mathsf{F}(x_i), \Gamma^r)) = \mathsf{H}(e(\mathsf{F}(x_i), g_2^{sr})) = \mathsf{H}(e(\mathsf{F}(x_i), g_2)^{sr}). \quad (1)$$

On the other hand, at the last step of the receiver, for each $j \in [m]$, the receiver obtains

$$\mathsf{H}(e(K_j, \psi)) = \mathsf{H}(e(\Psi_j^{\rho^{-1}}, g_2^r)) = \mathsf{H}(e((\Lambda_j^s)^{\rho^{-1}}, g_2^r)) = \mathsf{H}(e(\mathsf{F}(y_j)^\rho, g_2^r)^{s\rho^{-1}})$$
$$= \mathsf{H}(e(\mathsf{F}(y_j), g_2^r)^s) = \mathsf{H}(e(\mathsf{F}(y_j), g_2)^{sr}). \quad (2)$$

Thus, if $x_i = y_j$, then R_i obtained from Eq. (1) and $\mathsf{H}(e(K_j, \psi))$ obtained from Eq. (2) are the same. Otherwise, R_i and $\mathsf{H}(e(K_j, \psi))$ are different with overwhelming probability since it is assumed that F and H are collision-resistant. Therefore, the receiver obtains $X \cap Y$ correctly at the end of the protocol. □

Comments on Efficiency. On the sender's side, the most intensive computations are n pairing operations needed to compute μ_i's. Additionally, it requires 2 group exponentiations in $\mathbb{G}_2$ to compute ψ and χ, n map-to-point operations to compute $\mathsf{F}(x_i)$'s, and n hash computations to compute R_i's. For the receiver-set registration at the offline phase, the receiver undertakes m map-to-point operations to compute F and $2m$ group exponentiations in $\mathbb{G}_1$ to compute Λ_j's and K_j's, and the third party performs m group exponentiations in $\mathbb{G}_1$. For the intersection extraction at the online phase, the receiver takes m pairing computations and m hash computations, and then searches m elements from n items. To help estimate actual computation time, we provide the runtime of each operation. According to our experiments with the BLS12-381 curve, a single group operation in $\mathbb{G}_1$ takes 0.13 ms, in $\mathbb{G}_2$ takes 0.22 ms, a map-to-point operation into $\mathbb{G}_1$ takes 0.16 ms, and a pairing operation takes 0.86 ms. See Sect. 5 for detailed and comprehensive results.

The communication costs from the sender are 1 group element in $\mathbb{G}_2$ and n hash outputs at the online phase. The receiver and the third party send and receive m elements in $\mathbb{G}_1$ each at the offline phase. Therefore, the total communication costs of our protocol in Fig. 1 are 1 group element in $\mathbb{G}_2$, $2m$ group elements in $\mathbb{G}_1$, and n hash outputs. Table 1 provides a comparison of ours with ALOS22, which is the state-of-the-art pairing-based PSI protocol, in terms of computation and communication costs. We confirm that the sender's computational and communication costs are independent of the receiver's set size m, meeting a key efficiency requirement for laconic PSI.

3.2 Security Analysis in the Semi-honest Model

We now analyze the security of our base PSI protocol against semi-honest adversaries, as defined in Definition 2, by proving Theorem 2.

Theorem 2. *Our PSI protocol in Fig. 1 is secure against semi-honest adversaries under the BDH assumption in the random oracle model.*

Table 1. Efficiency Comparison of Ours with ALOS22 in the Semi-Honest Setting

		Communication costs	
Protocol	$\mathcal{R} \to \mathcal{S}$	$\mathcal{S} \to \mathcal{R}$	$\mathcal{T} \leftrightarrow \mathcal{R}^{\ddagger}$
ALOS22	$1|\mathbb{G}_2|$	$n|\mathbb{G}_1| + n|\mathsf{H}|$	$m|\mathbb{G}_2|$
Ours Offline	–	–	$2m|\mathbb{G}_1|$
Online	–	$1|\mathbb{G}_2| + n|\mathsf{H}|$	–
		Computational costs	
Protocol	$\mathcal{T}$	$\mathcal{S}$	$\mathcal{R}$
ALOS22	$1\mathsf{E}_{\mathbb{G}_1} + m\mathsf{E}_{\mathbb{G}_2}$	$n\mathsf{BP} + 3n\mathsf{E}_{\mathbb{G}_1}$	$mn\mathsf{BP} + m^2\mathsf{E}_{\mathbb{G}_2}$
Ours Offline	$m\mathsf{E}_{\mathbb{G}_1}$	–	$2m\mathsf{E}_{\mathbb{G}_1} + m\mathsf{MtP}$
Online	–	$n\mathsf{BP} + 2\mathsf{E}_{\mathbb{G}_2} + n\mathsf{MtP}$	$m\mathsf{BP}$

* $\mathcal{S}$: the sender, $\mathcal{R}$: the receiver, $\mathcal{T}$: the third party
** n: the size of sender's input set, m: the size of receiver's input set, $|\mathbb{G}_1|, |\mathbb{G}_2|, |\mathbb{G}_T|$: the bit sizes to represent elements in $\mathbb{G}_1, \mathbb{G}_2, \mathbb{G}_T$, respectively, $|\mathsf{H}|$: the output size of hash function
† BP: the cost for one pairing operation, $\mathsf{E}_\mathbb{G}$: the cost for one group exponentiation in a group $\mathbb{G}$, MtP: the cost for encoding a value into $\mathbb{G}_1$
‡ The common reference string in ALOS22 which is the parameter generated by the third party is included in the communication between $\mathcal{T}$ and $\mathcal{R}$

Sketch of Proof. The basic idea of constructing a simulator is as follows. Given the BDH parameter $(g_1, g_2, g_1^a, g_1^b, g_1^c, g_2^b, g_2^c)$, the simulator sets $\Gamma(= g_2^s) = g_2^c$ and $\psi(= g_2^r) = g_2^b$ (a variable contained in the sender's message). It then simulates the random oracle F as follows: Upon receiving $y \in Y$, the simulator picks $l \leftarrow\$ \mathbb{Z}_p^*$ and computes $\mathsf{F}(y) = g_1^l$ for $y \in Y$, while $\mathsf{F}(x) = \Phi^l$ for $x \notin Y$, where $\Phi = g_1^a$. Intuitively, this distinctive way of responding to the query results in the corrupted receiver (controlled by an adversary) not being able to distinguish the simulated view from the real one *unless* it solves the BDH problem since $\mathsf{H}(e((\Phi^l, g_2^s)^r)) = \mathsf{H}(e(g_1^{al}, g_2^{cb})) = \mathsf{H}(e(g_1, g_2)^{abcl})$, where l is known to the simulator.

Proof. We construct a simulator Sim_1 with the semi-honest sender's set X as input. The simulator generates $(e, \mathbb{G}_1, \mathbb{G}_2, \mathbb{G}_T, g_1, g_2, p, \Gamma)$, where $\Gamma = g_2^s$ for $s \leftarrow\$ \mathbb{Z}_p^*$, and simulates the random oracles F and H. Since the sender does not receive anything from the receiver in the protocol, Sim_1 returns an empty set.

We now construct a simulator Sim_2 that is provided with the semi-honest receiver's input $Y = \{y_1, \ldots, y_m\}$ and the output returned by the PSI functionality $Z = \{z_1, \ldots, z_\sigma\}$:

1. Generate and send $(e, \mathbb{G}_1, \mathbb{G}_2, \mathbb{G}_T, g_1, g_2, p, \Gamma)$, where $\Gamma = g_2^s$ for $s \leftarrow\$ \mathbb{Z}_p^*$, to the semi-honest receiver.
2. Random oracles for the semi-honest receiver are simulated as follows. Pick $\tau \leftarrow\$ \mathbb{Z}_p^*$ and compute $\Phi = g_1^\tau$. For each query $y_k \in Y$ to the random oracle F,

pick $l_k \leftarrow\!\!\$\, \mathbb{Z}_p^*$ and return $g_1^{l_k}$ as $\mathsf{F}(y_k)$. The values $(y_k, g_1^{l_k}, l_k)$ are recorded in $\mathsf{List}_Y(\mathcal{O}_\mathsf{F})$. For each query $x_k \notin Y$ to the random oracle F, pick $l_k \leftarrow\!\!\$\, \mathbb{Z}_p^*$ and return Φ^{l_k} as $\mathsf{F}(x_k)$. The values (x_k, Φ^{l_k}, l_k) are recorded in $\mathsf{List}_{\overline{Y}}(\mathcal{O}_\mathsf{F})$. For each query $\mu_k \in \mathbb{G}_T$ to the random oracle H, pick $R_k \leftarrow\!\!\$\, \{0,1\}^\lambda$ and return it as $\mathsf{H}(\mu_k)$. The values (μ_k, R_k) are recorded in $\mathsf{List}(\mathcal{O}_\mathsf{H})$.
3. Fetch all $(y_j, g_1^{l_j}, l_j)$'s from $\mathsf{List}_Y(\mathcal{O}_\mathsf{F})$, compute $K_j = (g_1^{l_j})^s (= \mathsf{F}(y_j)^s)$ for all $y_j \in Y$, and send $(K_1, \ldots, K_m)$ to the semi-honest receiver.
4. Compute $\psi = g_2^r$ and $\chi = \Gamma^r$ for $r \leftarrow\!\!\$\, \mathbb{Z}_p^*$.
5. Compute $R_i = \mathsf{H}(e(\mathsf{F}(z_i), \chi))$ for all $i \in [1, \sigma]$. (Note that since $Z \subseteq Y$, all z_i's and the random oracle responses to them should have been recorded in $\mathsf{List}_Y(\mathcal{O}_\mathsf{F})$.) Pick $R_i \leftarrow\!\!\$\, \{0,1\}^\lambda$ for all $i \in [\sigma+1, n]$.
6. Send $(\psi, (R_1, \ldots, R_n))$ to the semi-honest receiver.

Below, we show that the simulation provided above is computationally indistinguishable from the real protocol, assuming the BDH problem is hard. To prove this claim, we define hybrids as follows:

Hybrid 0: This is the real protocol in which the sender and the receiver run the protocol honestly with input X and Y, respectively.

Hybrid 1: In this hybrid, we simulate the random oracles F and H as described in Step 2 of the simulator. The simulation of the two random oracles is perfect. Hence, the distribution of this hybrid is the same as the view of *Hybrid 0*.

Hybrid 2: In this hybrid, we compute K_j slightly differently from Step 3 of the simulator. In this hybrid, we compute $K_j = (g_1^s)^{l_j}$, where l_j is from $\mathsf{List}_Y(\mathcal{O}_\mathsf{F})$. However, this is merely a conceptual change since $(g_1^s)^{l_j} = (g_1^{l_j})^s$. Hence, the distribution of this hybrid is the same as the view of *Hybrid 1*.

Hybrid 3: In this hybrid, we generate R_i for $i = \sigma+1, \ldots, n$ in the view of the semi-honest receiver, following Step 5 of the simulator. Since the above R_i was chosen uniformly and independently from the output of the random oracle H, as long as the semi-honest receiver has not queried $\mu_i = e(\mathsf{F}(x_i), \Gamma^r)$ to the random oracle H, the distribution of R_i's in this hybrid and that of those in the previous hybrid are indistinguishable. However, the probability that such an event happens is bounded by the probability of solving the BDH problem, as the following claim shows.

Claim. The simulation of the random oracle H for the value R_i for all $i \in [\sigma+1, n]$ is inconsistent if the solution to the BDH problem is queried to H.

Proof. To prove this claim, we construct a BDH adversary $\mathcal{B}$ that can compute the solution to the BDH problem using the corrupted receiver. Given an instance of the BDH problem $(g_1, g_2, g_1^a, g_1^b, g_1^c, g_2^b, g_2^c)$, $\mathcal{B}$ simulates the execution of the protocol like the above simulator Sim_2 except the following setting up of the parameters:

$$\Gamma = g_2^c,\ \Phi = g_1^a,\ \psi(=g_2^r) = g_2^b,\ g_1^s = g_1^c.$$

Despite the above parameter changes, $\mathcal{B}$ can execute the simulator for the semi-honest receiver. $\mathcal{B}$'s strategy to extract the solution to the BDH problem for a given instance is as follows: First, compute $\mu'_j = e(K_j, \psi)$ for all $j = 1, \ldots, m$ and discard all μ'_j's, which appear as input of the entries in $\mathsf{List}(\mathcal{O}_\mathsf{H})$. (Since $e(K_j, \psi) = e((g_1^s)^{l_j}, g_2^b) = e((g_1^c)^{l_j}, g_2^b) = e(\mathsf{F}(y_j)^c, g_2^b)$ for $y_j \in Y$, they cannot be the solution to the BDH problem for a given instance.) From the remaining queries, each of which is denoted by μ_i, $\mathcal{B}$ can extract the solution to the BDH problem for a given instance by computing $\mu_i^{l_i^{-1}}$ for some $i \in [\sigma+1, n]$, since $\mu_i = e(\mathsf{F}(x_i), \Gamma^r) = e(\Phi^{l_i}, \Gamma^r) = e(g_1^{al_i}, g_2^{cb}) = e(g_1, g_2)^{abcl_i}$ by simulation. (Note that l_i is known to $\mathcal{B}$.) As $\mathcal{B}$ needs to find a correct l_i from $\mathsf{List}(\mathcal{O}_\mathsf{F})$ minus Y and $\mathsf{F}(x_i) = \Phi$ for $x_i \notin Y$ by simulation of F, such the solution can be found with probability $\sum_{\sigma+1}^n \frac{1}{q_\mathsf{F}-m}$, where q_F is the number of queries to the random oracle F. □

4 Our PSI Protocol Secure in the Malicious Model

We extend our base PSI protocol presented in Fig. 1 to the malicious security setting. The technique we used to achieve this was motivated by the RT21 protocol [18], in which x_i's, the elements of the input set, are hashed by a random oracle to ensure no information about them is leaked and input set extraction is possible due to lazy sampling in the security analysis.

4.1 Description and Correctness

Description. The variant closely resembles the original PSI protocol: At the final step of the sender in the protocol, when calculating $R_i = \mathsf{H}(\mu_i)$ for each $i \in [n]$, the corresponding data x_i is additionally inserted as an input of the hash function. That is, $R_i = \mathsf{H}(\mu_i)$ is replaced by $R_i = \hat{\mathsf{H}}(x_i, \mu_i)$ where $\hat{\mathsf{H}}$ is a hash function from $\{0,1\}^* \times \mathbb{G}_T$ to $\{0,1\}^\lambda$, defined in the common reference string. Subsequently, when the receiver receives $(\psi, R_1, \ldots, R_n)$, the receiver calculates $\hat{\mathsf{H}}(y_j, e(K_j, \psi))$ instead of $\mathsf{H}(e(K_j, \psi))$ and searches for it among $R_1, \ldots, R_n$. A full description of our PSI protocol for the malicious setting is given in Fig. 2.

Correctness. The correctness of this variant of the PSI protocol is straightforward from that of the original construction. Theorem 1 demonstrates that if $x_i = y_j$, then $\mu_i = e(\mathsf{F}(x_i), \chi) = e(K_j, \psi)$ and hence $\hat{\mathsf{H}}(x_i, \mu_i) = \hat{\mathsf{H}}(y_j, e(K_j, \psi))$. Otherwise, i.e., if $x_i \neq y_j$, then the above relation does not hold with overwhelming probability since F and H are collision-resistant.

Comments on Efficiency. We observe that the computation and communication costs of our extended PSI protocol are almost unchanged, except for the increased length of inputs of the hash function associated with R_i's.

4.2 Security Analysis in the Malicious Model

Now, we prove the following theorem regarding security in the malicious model.

> **Input:** A sender's private set $X = \{x_1, \ldots, x_n\}$ and a receiver's private set $Y = \{y_1, \ldots, y_m\}$
>
> **CRS Generation:** A common reference string $\mathsf{crs} = (e, \mathbb{G}_1, \mathbb{G}_2, \mathbb{G}_T, g_1, g_2, p, \mathsf{F}, \hat{\mathsf{H}}, \Gamma)$ is generated in almost the same manner as in Figure 1, except that H is replaced by $\hat{\mathsf{H}} : \{0,1\}^* \times \mathbb{G}_T \to \{0,1\}^\lambda$.
>
> **[Offline Phase: Receiver-Set Registration]** This phase is exactly the same as in Figure 1.
>
> **[Online Phase]**
>
> 1. The sender performs as follows:
>   (a) Sample $r \leftarrow_\$ \mathbb{Z}_p^*$, and compute $\psi = g_2^r$ and $\chi = \Gamma^r$.
>   (b) Compute $\mu_i = e(\mathsf{F}(x_i), \chi)$ and $R_i = \hat{\mathsf{H}}(x_i, \mu_i)$ for each $j \in [n]$.
>   (c) Send $(\psi, R_1, \ldots, R_n)$ to the receiver.
> 2. The receiver initiates Z as an empty set and performs as follows:
>   (a) Find (K_j, y_j) such that $\hat{\mathsf{H}}(y_j, e(K_j, \psi)) = R_i$ for all $j \in [m]$ and $i \in [n]$. If such a y_j exists, update $Z = Z \cup \{y_j\}$.
>   (b) Output Z.

Fig. 2. Our PSI Protocol Secure against Malicious Adversaries

Theorem 3. *Our protocol proposed in Fig. 2 is a secure PSI against malicious adversaries under the BDH assumption in the random oracle model.*

Sketch of Proof. We analyze the malicious security of our proposed protocol by considering two cases.

Case 1: When the sender is corrupted. Upon receiving $M = (\psi, R_1, \ldots, R_n)$ from the corrupted sender controlled by an adversary, Sim should extract an input set X' that explains the effect of M on the honest party (receiver). Note that for each $R \in \{R_1, \ldots, R_n\}$ should be of the form $\hat{\mathsf{H}}(x, \mu)$, where $\mu = e(\mathsf{F}(x)^s, \psi)$. The simulator can search the inputs and outputs of the random oracles F and $\hat{\mathsf{H}}$ to find the "consistent" x and μ satisfying $\mu = e(\mathsf{F}(x)^s, \psi)$. The extracted x's will form a set X', which will be sent to the ideal functionality to compute $X' \cap Y$, where Y is a private set of the honest receiver.

Case 2: When the receiver is corrupted. As is the case of the malicious sender, we need to construct a simulator that extracts the corrupted receiver's input. Using the BDH parameter $(g_1, g_2, g_1^a, g_1^b, g_1^c, g_2^b, g_2^c)$, the simulator Sim sets $\Gamma(= g_2^s) = g_2^c$ and $\psi(= g_2^r) = g_2^b$ (a variable contained in the sender's message). The simulator will observe all the inputs and corresponding outputs of the random oracles F and $\hat{\mathsf{H}}$. Then it will output a set of queries (made by the adversary) to F as an extracted set Y' for the receiver. The random oracles continue to work as before, however, the simulation of F differs before and after the simulator comes up with Y': The answer to the query y was g_1^l, but after the Y' is produced, the answer to the query becomes $\varPhi^l = (g_1^a)^l$ for $a \leftarrow_\$ \mathbb{Z}_p^*$. There are two implications for such change: By returning g_1^l as an answer to the query y to F, the simulator can freely simulate the corrupted receiver's receiver-set registration by computing $K = (g_1^c)^l$, which must be possible as $l \leftarrow_\$ \mathbb{Z}_p^*$ is known to the simulator. However, as the receiver can register a finite number (m) of its sets with the third party, it cannot register for any more inputs to obtain K's, and hence it is legitimate to return $\varPhi^l = (g_1^a)^l$ (for unknown a) as an answer to the query y (That is, the simulator loses the ability to simulate K in this case, but this is acceptable as the receiver will not be able to obtain K anymore.) Another implication is that querying (y, μ) to the random oracle $\hat{\mathsf{H}}$ without having K causes the adversary to solve the BDH problem, which makes the distribution of the honest sender's message in simulation different from that in the real protocol. Then the simulator sends Y' to the PSI functionality to receive $Z = X \cap Y'$, where $|X| = n$ and $|Z| = \sigma$. Then the simulator finds $x \in Y'$ such that $x \in Z$ and makes use of the query-answer list of the random oracle $\hat{\mathsf{H}}$ to find values $R = \hat{\mathsf{H}}(x, \mu)$. The simulator then picks uniform random $n - \sigma$ R's to create the sender's simulated message $(\psi, R_1, \ldots, R_n)$. Note that this simulated message is computationally indistinguishable from the one in the real protocol as long as $\hat{\mathsf{H}}$ is queried on (x, μ) such that $\mu = e(\mathsf{F}(x), \psi^c) = e(\varPhi^l, \psi^c) = e(g_1^{al}, g_2^{bc}) = e(g_1, g_2)^{abcl}$. Since the simulator knows l, it can compute the BDH key by computing $\mu^{l^{-1}}$. □

5 Performance Evaluation

In this section, we compare the performance of our semi-honest secure PSI protocol with Rosulek and Trieu's [18] and Aranha et al.'s [2], two closely-related PSI protocols that also provide semi-honest security. Additionally, we present experimental results of our PSI protocols in both the semi-honest and malicious settings for various input set sizes.

5.1 Test Environment

For a fair comparison, we implemented our PSI protocols (both semi-honest and malicious secure ones) along with RT21 [18] and ALOS22 [2]. The source codes for our PSI protocols were written in C++ language and are available from the GitHub repository[3]. For RT21 and ALOS22, we utilized the source codes obtained from the MINIPSI[4] and the RELIC[5] repositories, written by the authors of [2, 18], respectively. The original source code for ALOS22 was written in C language, but we slightly modified it to adapt to C++ language. Furthermore, we replaced SHA-256 in their source code with the SHA3-256 hash function and resolved a memory error, which occurs when the size of the receiver's input set m is larger than or equal to 2^{12}. For our protocols and ALOS22, the OpenSSL library [19] was employed for cryptographic hash operations, and so was the RELIC library [7] for pairing computations. In the implementations of our protocols and ALOS22,

---

[3] https://github.com/CryptoLabCAU/One-Pass-PSI-from-Pairings.
[4] https://github.com/osu-crypto/MiniPSI.
[5] https://github.com/relic-toolkit/relic/tree/main/demo/psi-client-server.

the parameters were set for the 128-bit security level, and the BLS12-381 curve was used for pairing and other elliptic curve operations.

For the 128-bit security level for RT21, Ristretto [9] built on top of Curve25519 was used for elliptic curve operations. Additionally, we found and fixed an error in the source code of RT21, which occurs when the size of the sender's data n is smaller than that of the receiver's data m with Ristretto. We used the Linux TC (traffic control) tool to handle the bandwidth limit for all protocols.

All experiments were conducted on a virtual machine with 4 cores and 8 threads running Ubuntu 20.04 LTS, hosted on a system consisting of an Intel(R) Xeon(R) Silver 4215 CPU at 3.2 GHz and 128 GB RAM, operating on Windows Server 2019. However, we used only a single core and a single thread for all the experiments. All the running times presented in the tables of this section are averages of 10 experiments.

5.2 Experimental Results

First, we fixed the size of the sender's input set to $n = 2^8$ and varied the size of the receiver's input set to $m = 2^8, 2^{10}, 2^{12}$ to measure the running times of the semi-honest secure version of our PSI protocol and to compare them with those of the RT21 and ALOS22 protocols. The results are presented in Table 2, where the bandwidth limit is set to 10 Gbps.

According to the table, when comparing ours with ALOS22, which satisfies the laconic property and also uses pairings, the sender's running time of our PSI protocol was approximately 1.04–1.08 times faster than those of ALOS22. The improvement in the receiver's running time is even more significant: Across all input sizes, our PSI protocol offers *100–1,000 times faster* receiver execution, *even when including the running time required for the receiver-set registration at the offline phase*, compared to ALOS22. This significant improvements can be attributed to the substantial recalculation of the accumulator in the intersection retrieval process required by ALOS22, which our protocol avoids.

When comparing ours with the RT21 protocol, which is also a DH-based PSI protocol and has the best complexity for small sets, we observed that when the sizes of the sender's and receiver's input sets are similar, the sender's running times of ours are slower than those of RT21. However, when the receiver's input set is 16 times larger than the sender's, e.g., $n = 2^8$ and $m = 2^{12}$, the performance gaps shifts: Ours is approximately 2.47 times faster than RT21 for the sender's execution. On the other hand, in terms of receiver's running times, ours are 3.42–4.27 times slower than RT21 during the online phase and 5.12–5.99 times slower for total receiver execution. (Thus, the receiver's running times of ALOS22 are roughly 500–5,000 times slower than RT21.)

The table also compares the communication costs (in KB) among three protocols. For fair comparison, we include the common reference string in ALOS22 as part of the communication costs between the third party and the receiver, since its size depends on the receiver's set size in their protocol. For RT21, the communication costs from the sender to the receiver include all messages from the sender

Table 2. Performance Comparison of RT21, ALOS22, and Ours in the Semi-Honest Model (Bandwidth: 10 Gbps)

n	m	Protocol		Comm. Cost (KB)			Running Time (ms)		
				$\mathcal{R} \to \mathcal{S}$	$\mathcal{S} \to \mathcal{R}$	$\mathcal{T} \leftrightarrow \mathcal{R}$ †	$\mathcal{S}$	$\mathcal{R}$	$\mathcal{T}$
2^8	2^8	RT21		8.19	1.82	–	73.97	82.80	–
		ALOS22		0.10	32.77	49.15	293.04	64683.58	–
		Ours	Offline	–	–	49.15	–	111.44	31.02
			Online	–	8.38	–	271.21	353.44	–
			Total	–	8.38	49.15	271.21	464.88	31.02
	2^{10}	RT21		32.77	1.82	–	198.78	249.06	–
		ALOS22		0.10	32.77	196.61	290.76	418349.91	–
		Ours	Offline	–	–	196.61	279.93	422.75	123.95
			Online	–	8.38	–	–	851.82	–
			Total	–	8.38	196.61	279.93	1274.57	123.95
	2^{12}	RT21		131.07	1.82	–	672.14	848.17	–
		ALOS22		0.10	32.77	786.43	290.25	9090316.95	–
		Ours	Offline	–	–	786.43	–	1683.08	508.20
			Online	–	8.38	–	272.05	3400.32	–
			Total	–	8.38	786.43	272.05	5083.39	508.20

* $\mathcal{S}$: the sender, $\mathcal{R}$: the receiver, $\mathcal{T}$: the third party
** n: the size of sender's input set, m: the size of receiver's input set
† The common reference string in ALOS22 which is the parameter generated by $\mathcal{T}$ is included in the communication between $\mathcal{T}$ and $\mathcal{R}$.

to the receiver during the protocol execution. From the table, we observe that RT21 achieves the best total communication cost. However, when focusing on online communication costs, our protocol demonstrates superior performance, with costs approximately 4 times lower than those of ALSO22. Compared to RT21, when the sender's and receiver's set sizes are similar, the online communication costs of our protocol are comparable as the receiver's set size becomes significantly larger than the sender's, however, our protocol offers shorter online communication costs than RT21. This improvement arises because the communication cost of RT21 scales proportionally with the size of the receiver's set, whereas that in our protocol is independent of the receiver's set size.

We also provide a more detailed comparison between ours and the RT21 protocol [18] under various parameter settings in Table 3 where the bandwidth limit was set to 10 Gbps. The ALOS22 protocol [2] is excluded due to its high computational costs. Based on our estimation from the data of Table 2, a single execution of the PSI computation for a receiver dataset of size 2^{14} would take more than 10 h with ALOS22.

We observe similar trends when we extend the input set sizes. In terms of computational costs, the receiver's running times of ours are approximately 3.42–5.59 times slower than RT21 during the online phase and 5.11–7.32 times slower for the total receiver execution with respect to the sender's and receiver's input set sizes. Moreover, when the sender's and receiver's input set sizes are similar, the sender's running times of ours are also slower than RT21. However, when the receiver's input set is at least 16 times larger than the sender's, the situation changes. With a 16-fold difference in input set sizes, the sender's running time becomes approximately 2.47–2.54 times faster, and the gap grows to 64 times, the improvement increases to 9.81–10.50 times.

In terms of communication costs, our protocol incurs 5.60–6.00 times higher costs compared to RT21. However, when focusing on online communication costs, our protocol demonstrates 1.19–1.24 times lower costs when the sender's and receiver's input set sizes are the same. Furthermore, as the receiver's input set size increases relative to the sender's, the gap in online communication costs between ours and RT21 scales proportionally with the ratio of the sender's and receiver's input set sizes. For example, when the sender's set size is 2^8 and the receiver's set size is 2^{14}, the total communication cost of ours is approximately 6.00 times higher than those of RT21. However, the online communication cost of ours is approximately 62.78 times lower.

In Table 4, we present experimental results of our PSI protocols in both semi-honest and malicious settings for larger input sets and various bandwidth limits. The table shows that the running times for both sender and receiver are increased by a factor of 3.76–4.74 when the data size is scaled up by a factor of 4. Furthermore, our malicious protocol incurs less than 2% overhead compared to the semi-honest protocol under the same setting. We also observe that the short bandwidth limitation begins to impact performance when the input size reaches 2^{18} or more.

Table 3. Detailed Comparison between RT21 and Ours in the Semi-Honest Model (Bandwidth: 10 Gbps)

			Comm. Costs (KB)			Running Time (ms)		
n	m	Protocol	$\mathcal{R} \to \mathcal{S}$	$\mathcal{S} \to \mathcal{R}$	$\mathcal{T} \leftrightarrow \mathcal{R}$	$\mathcal{S}$	$\mathcal{R}$	$\mathcal{T}$
2^8	2^8	RT21	8.19	1.82	–	73.97	82.80	–
		Ours Offline	–	–	49.15	–	111.44	31.02
		Online	–	8.38	–	271.21	353.44	–
		Total	–	8.38	49.15	271.21	464.88	31.02
	2^{10}	RT21	32.77	1.82	–	198.78	249.06	–
		Ours Offline	–	–	196.61	–	422.75	123.95
		Online	–	8.38	–	279.93	851.82	–
		Total	–	8.38	196.61	279.93	1274.57	123.95
	2^{12}	RT21	131.07	1.82	–	672.14	848.17	–
		Ours Offline	–	–	786.43	–	1683.08	508.20
		Online	–	8.38	786.43	272.05	3400.32	–
		Total	–	8.38	786.43	272.05	5083.39	508.20
	2^{14}	RT21	524.29	1.82	–	2646.87	3277.78	–
		Ours Offline	–	–	3145.73	–	6654.91	1975.55
		Online	–	8.38	–	269.68	13541.66	–
		Total	–	8.38	3145.73	269.68	20196.57	1975.55
2^{10}	2^{10}	RT21	32.77	8.22	–	210.44	243.65	–
		Ours Offline	–	–	196.61	–	420.64	124.96
		Online	–	32.96	–	1048.34	1363.08	–
		Total	–	32.96	196.61	1048.34	1783.72	124.96
	2^{12}	RT21	131.07	8.22	–	696.97	856.80	–
		Ours Offline	–	–	786.43	–	1701.72	495.78
		Online	–	32.96	–	1034.72	3414.62	–
		Total	–	32.96	786.43	1034.72	5116.34	495.78
	2^{14}	RT21	524.29	8.22	–	2648.88	3270.94	–
		Ours Offline	–	–	3145.73	–	6704.97	1991.82
		Online	–	32.96	–	1044.15	13544.14	–
		Total	–	32.96	3145.73	1044.15	20249.11	1991.82
	2^{16}	RT21	2097.15	8.22	–	11025.42	13121.24	–
		Ours Offline	–	–	12582.91	–	26604.69	7973.40
		Online	–	32.96	–	1050.35	54240.24	–
		Total	–	32.96	12582.91	1050.35	80844.93	7973.40

* $\mathcal{S}$: the sender, $\mathcal{R}$: the receiver, $\mathcal{T}$: the third party
** n: the size of sender's input set, m: the size of receiver's input set

Table 4. Total Running Times of Our Protocols with Various Sizes of Input Sets

		Running Time (sec)								
		10 Gbps			50 Mbps			1 Mbps		
$n = m$	Protocol	$\mathcal{S}$	$\mathcal{R}$	$\mathcal{T}$	$\mathcal{S}$	$\mathcal{R}$	$\mathcal{T}$	$\mathcal{S}$	$\mathcal{R}$	$\mathcal{T}$
2^{10}	Ours-SH	1.05	1.78	0.12	1.03	1.76	0.12	1.04	1.77	0.13
	Ours-Mal	1.04	1.78	0.12	1.05	1.79	0.13	1.05	1.80	0.13
2^{12}	Ours-SH	4.07	7.00	0.50	4.09	6.99	0.51	4.09	7.04	0.50
	Ours-Mal	4.13	7.05	0.50	4.11	7.03	0.49	4.11	7.09	0.50
2^{14}	Ours-SH	16.33	27.82	2.01	16.30	27.86	2.01	16.35	31.69	2.02
	Ours-Mal	16.44	28.09	2.00	16.45	28.12	2.00	16.47	31.74	2.01
2^{16}	Ours-SH	65.18	111.28	8.05	65.21	111.27	8.07	65.21	127.66	8.04
	Ours-Mal	65.69	112.27	8.03	65.73	112.21	8.03	65.73	128.46	8.02
2^{18}	Ours-SH	260.75	445.07	32.19	261.78	446.68	32.27	308.90	512.84	32.15
	Ours-Mal	263.12	449.24	32.18	263.69	450.16	32.31	309.62	516.80	32.25
2^{20}	Ours-SH	1059.62	1804.92	130.01	1064.63	1815.01	130.91	1324.92	2106.99	132.79
	Ours-Mal	1068.12	1821.43	130.49	1069.80	1822.87	130.37	1344.47	2139.67	133.94

* $\mathcal{S}$: the sender, $\mathcal{R}$: the receiver, $\mathcal{T}$: the third party
** n: the size of sender's input set, m: the size of receiver's input set

6 Security Concerning the Third Party

The following theorem shows that the receiver-set registration does not leak any information about the receiver's set to the third party.

Theorem 4. *The receiver-set registration process in our PSI protocols presented in Figs. 1 and 2 provide privacy of the receiver's input against the semi-honest third party in the random oracle model.*

Sketch of Proof. The main idea of the proof is to show that the uniform random $\rho \in \mathbb{Z}_p^*$ chosen by the receiver will hide any information about the elements y_j's in the receiver input Y. Also, if the hash function F is a random oracle, $\mathsf{F}(y_j)$ is uniform and random in $\mathbb{G}_1$, so is $\mathsf{F}(y_j)^\rho$, which will hide information about y_j.

Proof. Let $\mathcal{A}$ be an adversary controlling the third party, which observes the communication of the receive-set registration protocol. Assume that the random oracle F is simulated by computing $\mathsf{F}(y) = g^l$ for $l \leftarrow_\$ \mathbb{Z}_p^*$. Note that from the simulation of F, the message sent by the receiver to the third party (in the receiver-set registration) can be denoted by $\mathsf{F}(y)^\rho = (g_2^l)^\rho = g_2^{l\rho}$ for $\rho \leftarrow_\$ \mathbb{Z}_p^*$, which is a uniform element in $\mathbb{G}_2$.

Now, assume that $Y_0 = \{y_1^0, \ldots, y_m^0\}$ and $Y_1 = \{y_1^1, \ldots, y_m^1\}$ are two distinct sets of the receiver. (Since $|Y_0| = m$, we assume that $y_j^0 \neq y_k^0$ for all distinct $j, k \in [m]$, so are $y_j^1, y_k^1 \in Y_1$.) Suppose that $\mathcal{A}$ is given $W_b = \{\mathsf{F}(y_i^b)^\rho | j = 1, \ldots, m\}$ for $b \leftarrow_\$ \{0, 1\}$. Later, $\mathcal{A}$ is to output its guess $b' \in \{0, 1\}$ on b. Note that in W_b,

$\mathsf{F}(y_j^b)^\rho = g_2^{l\rho}$ is uniform in $\mathbb{G}_1$ for any $j \in [m]$. So, the probability that $\mathcal{A}$ comes up with the correct b without randomly guessing depends on the intersection of the following two events: E_1 denotes the event that $\mathcal{A}$ has queried y_i^b to the random oracle F and E_2 denotes the event that $\mathcal{A}$ correctly guesses $\rho \leftarrow^{\$} \mathbb{Z}_p^*$.

If we denote the event by $E = E_1 \wedge E_2$, $\Pr[E] \leq \Pr[E_2] \leq \frac{1}{|\mathbb{Z}_p^*|} \leq \frac{1}{p-1}$. So, by splitting the event $b' = b$, we have $\Pr[b' = b] = \Pr[b' = b|E]\Pr[E] + \Pr[b' = b|\neg E]\Pr[\neg E] \leq \Pr[E] + \Pr[b' = b|\neg E] \leq \frac{1}{p-1} + \frac{1}{2}$. Thus, $\left|\Pr[b' = b] - \frac{1}{2}\right|$ is negligible for large p. □

7 Conclusion

We proposed one-pass PSI protocols based on pairings with offline preprocessing in both the semi-honest and malicious models, where the receiver does not transmit any messages to the sender. Our protocols ensure the sender's computation and communication costs remain independent of the size of the receiver's input set, achieved through offline preprocessing, which requires the receiver to register its set with the third party. We also presented experimental results and compared the performance of our protocol with two closely related recent DH-based PSI protocols. The results show that our protocol significantly outperforms ALOS22 in terms of receiver execution. Furthermore, when the receiver's input set is substantially larger than the sender's, our protocol offers better performance for the sender compared to RT21. Future research directions include extending our work to support other private set operations and developing specific applications.

Acknowledgements. The authors thank the anonymous reviewers for their helpful comments. S. Choi and H. T. Lee were supported by the Institute of Information & Communications Technology Planning & Evaluation (IITP) grant funded by the Korea government (MSIT) (No. RS-2024-00399491, 75%) and the National Research Foundation of Korea (NRF) grant funded by the Korea government (MSIT) (No. NRF-2022R1A4A5034130, 25%). W. Susilo is supported by the Australian Research Council (ARC) Laureate Fellowship (FL230100033).

References

1. Alamati, N., Branco, P., Döttling, N., Garg, S., Hajiabadi, M., Pu, S.: Laconic private set intersection and applications. In: Nissim, K., Waters, B. (eds.) TCC 2021. LNCS, vol. 13044, pp. 94–125. Springer, Cham (2021). https://doi.org/10.1007/978-3-030-90456-2_4
2. Aranha, D.F., Lin, C., Orlandi, C., Simkin, M.: Laconic private set-intersection from pairings. In ACM CCS **2022**, 111–124 (2022)
3. Bienstock, A., Patel, S., Seo, J.Y., Yeo, K.: Near-optimal oblivious key-value stores for efficient psi, PSU and volume-hiding multi-maps. In: USENIX Security 2023, pp. 301–318. USENIX Association (2023)
4. Chatterjee, S., Menezes, A.: On cryptographic protocols employing asymmetric pairings - the role of ψ revisited. Discret. Appl. Math. **159**, 1311–1322 (2011)

5. Cristofaro, E., Kim, J., Tsudik, G.: Linear-complexity private set intersection protocols secure in malicious model. In: Abe, M. (ed.) ASIACRYPT 2010. LNCS, vol. 6477, pp. 213–231. Springer, Heidelberg (2010). https://doi.org/10.1007/978-3-642-17373-8_13
6. Döttling, N., Kolonelos, D., Lai, R.W.F., Lin, C., Malavolta, G., Rahimi, A.: Efficient Laconic Cryptography from Learning with Errors. In: Hazay, C., Stam, M. (eds.) Advances in Cryptology – EUROCRYPT 2023. LNCS, vol. 14006. Springer, Cham (2023). https://doi.org/10.1007/978-3-031-30620-4_14
7. Aranha, D.F., et al.: relic–toolkit, Version 0.6.0 (2020). https://github.com/relic-toolkit Accessed 1 Apr 2024
8. Goldreich, O.: Foundations of Cryptography: Volume II Basic Applications. Cambridge University Press (2004)
9. T.R. Group. Ristretto (2024). https://ristretto.group/ristretto.html Accessed 1 Sep 2024
10. Heinrich, A., Matthias Hollick, T.S., Stute, M., Weinert, C.: Privatedrop: practical privacy-preserving authentication for apple airdrop. In: USENIX Security 2021, pp. 3577–3594. USENIX Association (2021)
11. Huberman, B.A., Franklin, M., Hogg, T.: Enhancing privacy and trust in electronic communities. In: ACM EC 1999, pp. 78–86. ACM (1999)
12. Ion, M., et al.: On deploying secure computing: Private intersection-sum-with-cardinality. Cryptology ePrint Archive, Paper 2019/723 (2019). https://eprint.iacr.org/2019/723
13. Jarecki, S., Liu, X.: Fast secure computation of set intersection. In: Garay, J.A., De Prisco, R. (eds.) SCN 2010. LNCS, vol. 6280, pp. 418–435. Springer, Heidelberg (2010). https://doi.org/10.1007/978-3-642-15317-4_26
14. Meadows, C.: A more efficient cryptographic matchmaking protocol for use in the absence of available third party. In: IEEE SP 1986, pp. 134–187. IEEE (1985)
15. Morales, D., Agudo, I., Lopez, J.: Private set intersection: a systematic literature review. Comput. Sci. Rev. **49**, 10567 (2023)
16. Nguyen, L.: Accumulators from bilinear pairings and applications. In: Menezes, A. (ed.) CT-RSA 2005. LNCS, vol. 3376, pp. 275–292. Springer, Heidelberg (2005). https://doi.org/10.1007/978-3-540-30574-3_19
17. Rosulek, M.: A brief overview of private set intersection. Special Topics on Privacy and Public Auditability (STPPA) series, National Institute of Standards and Technology (2021)
18. Rosulek, M., Trieu, N.: Compact and malicious private set intersection for small sets. In: ACM CCS 2021, pp. 1166–1181 (2021)
19. O. Team. OpenSSL–Cryptography and SSL/TLS Toolkit, Version 1.1.1w (2023). https://www.openssl.org Accessed 7 Mar 2024
20. Wu, A., Xin, X., Zhu, J., Liu, W., Song, C., Li, G.: Cloud-assisted laconic private set intersection cardinality. IEEE TCC **12**(1), 295–305 (2024)

Practical Robust Dynamic Searchable Symmetric Encryption Supporting Conjunctive Queries

Bingxue Bian, Qiaoer Xu, Jiatao Liu, and Jianfeng Wang[✉]

School of Cyber Engineering, Xidian University, Xi'an, China
{eqxu,jiataoliu,bxbian}@stu.xidian.edu.cn, jfwang@xidian.edu.cn

Abstract. Dynamic Searchable Symmetric Encryption (DSSE) allows clients to securely update encrypted data, in addition to performing queries. Although researchers developed the first conjunctive SSE with forward and backward privacy in 2021, the proposed scheme cannot fully achieve the desired dynamicity for conjunctive queries. Very recently, an enhanced conjunctive DSSE was presented with new backward privacy for conjunctive queries (i.e., Type-O). However, it incurs substantial computational overhead in both update and search operations. Furthermore, how to extend conjunctive DSSE to handle abnormal update operations (e.g., re-insertion of deleted entries) remains a challenging problem.

To tackle the above limitations, we propose ROXT, a robust and efficient conjunctive DSSE scheme with forward and enhanced Type-O backward security. ROXT ensures robustness through a tag verification mechanism based on the Counting Bloom Filter, which accurately identifies valid ciphertexts using locally maintained compressed deletion lists. To enhance efficiency, ROXT integrates a shared cache mechanism with the OXT framework for search optimization. Performance evaluations show that ROXT significantly outperforms the state-of-the-art SDSSE-CQ in both update and search efficiency. Specifically, ROXT achieves a $3.98\times$ speedup in update latency and improves search efficiency by up to $106.27\times$ on the client side and $3.25\times$ on the server side.

Keywords: Robust DSSE · Conjunctive query · Forward and backward privacy

1 Introduction

Searchable Symmetric Encryption (SSE) enables clients to securely outsource encrypted data to an untrusted server while allowing the server to perform efficient search directly over the encrypted data. Since the inception of SSE [17], significant efforts have been devoted to developing efficient solutions characterized by strong security, high performance and expressive queries

[1,3,5,8,10,13,19,21,22,27]. However, most early work [7,8,17] focus on SSE over static dataset. Some progress has been made on dynamic SSE (DSSE) [3,4,14,19] to satisfy practical requirements. In particular, DSSE enables the client not only to perform private search, but also to update the outsourced data (i.e., inserting and/or deleting data) efficiently. Nevertheless, it has been demonstrated that the information leaked during updates can be successfully leveraged (e.g., by file-injection attack [25]) to break query privacy.

To suppress update leakage, Stefanov et al. [19] first introduced the concepts of forward and backward DSSE, which were later formalized by Bost et al. [3]. More concretely, forward privacy guarantees that previous queries cannot be linked to newly updated data, while backward privacy ensures that the deleted data cannot be matched with the previous queries. Subsequently, various DSSE schemes have been studied extensively [6,11,18,20,21]. Note that most existing DSSEs focus on a single-keyword setting, limiting their practicality.

Recently, Patranabis et al. [16] first explored conjunctive DSSE with forward and backward privacy named ODXT, which is built on a novel dynamic cross-tags data structure for efficient updates in conjunctive queries. Unfortunately, Zuo et al. [27] claimed that ODXT does not always work for the case of deletions, as it does not add deletion tags for files that contain the least frequent keyword, which could lead to incomplete deletion. To this end, they further formalize the notion of backward privacy for conjunctive DSSE schemes and propose two flavors of backward privacy (i.e., Type-O and Type-O$^-$) according to the amount of information revealed during search and updates. Nevertheless, their schemes incur substantial computational overhead due to the invocation of computation-intensive cryptographic primitives. Moreover, their scheme cannot support the re-insertion of previously deleted entries within the same search epoch.

In addition, Xu et al. [23] observed that most existing DSSE schemes cannot handle abnormal update queries, such as inserting the same keyword/document identifier pair repeatedly or deleting a non-existing entry, and introduced the notion of robust DSSE. Informally, robust DSSE ensures query correctness and desired security even when incorrect updates occur. Furthermore, they presented the first robust DSSE scheme called ROSE by designing key-updatable PRF, which enables the search tokens for the same keyword to be obfuscated. However, ROSE suffers from heavy computation and storage burden. To achieve practical robustness, Zheng et al. [26] proposed a lightweight robust DSSE with constant client storage by leveraging misoperations alarm mechanism. Nevertheless, we note that the mentioned schemes support only single-keyword queries, whereas conjunctive queries typically involve more complex query patterns, making them susceptible to erroneous updates. Thus, a natural question arises:

How to design a practical robust conjunctive DSSE with forward and backward privacy?

1.1 Our Contribution

In this paper, we offer a positive answer to the aforementioned question. Specifically, we propose Robust OXT (ROXT), an efficient robust conjunctive SSE

Table 1. Comparison with the previous works

Scheme	Client Storage	Communication		Computation		Conjunctive	XSet	FP	BP	Robust
		Search	Update	Search	Update					
ODXT [16]	$O(|\mathbf{W}|\log D)$	$O(a_{w_1}+d_{w_1})$	$O(1)$	$O((a_{w_1}+d_{w_1})n)$	$O(1)$	✓	✗		II	✗
SDSSE-CQ [27]	$O(|\mathbf{W}|(\log D+d))$	$O(r_q)$	$O(h)$	$O(a_{w_1}n+ha_q+n_q)$	$O(h)$	✓	✓		O	✗
SDSSE-CQ-S [27]	$O(|\mathbf{W}|(\log D+d))$	$O(r_q)$	$O(h)$	$O(a_{w_1}n+ha_q+n_q+2a_q)$	$O(h)$	✓	✓		O⁻	✗
ROSE [23]	$O(|\mathbf{W}|\log D)$	$O(a_w-d_w)$	$O(1)$	$O((a_w-d_w+1)d_w)$	$O(1)$	✗	—		III	✓
Themis [26]	$O(1)$	$O(a_w-d_w)$	$O(\log^3 N)$	$O(a_w-d_w)\log i_w+\log^2|\mathbf{W}|)$	$O(\log^3 N)$	✗	—		III	✓
Our ROXT	$O(|\mathbf{W}|\log D+|\mathbf{W}_d|d)$	$O(r_q)$	$O(1)$	$O((2a_{w_1}-d_{w_1})n+ha_q)$	$O(h)$	✓	✓		O	✓

We denote by $|\mathbf{W}|$, D, and N the total numbers of keywords, files, and keyword-identifier pairs in the database, respectively. a_w (resp., a_q) and d_w (resp., d_q) is the numbers of additions and deletions for keyword w (resp., a conjunctive query q). $d = \max_w d_w$ is the maximum number of deletions allowed for w, and $|\mathbf{W}_d| \leq |\mathbf{W}|$ is the number of keywords deleted before the next search. Let $n_q = a_q - d_q$ denote the number of entries associated with all keywords in q that have been added but not deleted, and $r_q \leq a_{w_1}$ the number of search results matching q.
w_1 is the least frequent keyword in q, and n is the number of queried keywords.
h is the number of hash functions used in the BF/CBF.
Since some schemes [16,27] are not robust, our analysis assumes that a distinct file is added in each update.

scheme with forward security and enhanced Type-O backward security. Table 1 gives a comprehensive comparison between ROXT and the existing constructions. In summary, our contributions are outlined below:

- We propose ROXT, the first robust DSSE scheme supporting conjunctive queries, which ensures correctness and security even under client misoperations. Correspondingly, we extend the original definition of Type-O backward security to account for duplicate updates with multiple timestamps, allowing ROXT to achieve forward and enhanced Type-O backward security.[1]
- To achieve robustness, ROXT integrates a tag verification mechanism based on the Counting Bloom Filter to accurately filter out invalid ciphertexts during search. Moreover, ROXT utilizes a shared cache mechanism that stores valid ciphertexts retrieved in previous queries to enhance search efficiency.
- We evaluate ROXT against the state-of-the-art conjunctive DSSE schemes SDSSE-CQ and SDSSE-CQ-S [27]. Experimental results show that ROXT reduces update latency by 3.98× and 4.17× compared to SDSSE-CQ and SDSSE-CQ-S, respectively. For client-side search, it improves efficiency by up to 106.27× and 201.83×, and for server-side search, by up to 3.25× and 142.5×, over SDSSE-CQ and SDSSE-CQ-S, respectively.

1.2 Related Work

Song et al. [17] initially introduced the notion of SSE that was formalized by Curtmola et al. [8] later. Since then, extensive research has been carried out

---
[1] ROXT can be extended to achieve Type-O⁻ backward privacy.

to construct the SSE scheme in terms of enhanced security [3,8,18,19,22], high performance [18,20,21], and expressive queries [5,10,16]. Note that almost all the early SSE schemes focused on single keyword search. To capture practical search capability, Cash et al. [5] presented an elegant conjunctive SSE scheme (named OXT) with sublinear search complexity. Note that OXT supports only static data.

Stefanov et al. [19] first introduced the notion of forward and backward privacy for SSE, which is a desirable feature in dynamic database settings. Bost et al. [2] presented the formal definition of forward-secure SSE, which ensures that an update leaks nothing about the previously queried keyword. Subsequently, Bost et al. [3] formalized the notion of backward privacy and proposed three flavors of backward secure SSE schemes from constrained cryptographic primitives. To reduce search latency, Sun et al. [21] proposed a practical non-interactive backward-private scheme by introducing a new primitive named symmetric puncturable encryption. Recently, Demertzis et al. [9] proposed a new forward- and backward-secure SSE scheme with small client storage. Note that all the aforementioned dynamic SSE schemes focus on single-keyword search.

In 2021, Patranabis et al. [16] initially studied the problem of forward and backward private conjunctive SSE and proposed the first conjunctive DSSE scheme, ODXT. However, Zuo et al. [27] pointed out that ODXT cannot work in the case of data deletion because the deletion tag is missing for files associated with the least frequent keyword. To fix this drawback, they introduced two enhanced backward privacy for conjunctive queries (i.e., Type-O and Type-O$^-$) and presented two concrete conjunctive DSSE schemes, SDSSE-CQ and SDSSE-CQ-S. However, these constructions suffer from tremendous computational cost.

Another line of research is to design robust DSSE that ensures query soundness and desired security in the case of misoperations. Xu et al. [23] introduced the notion of robust DSSE and presented the first robust DSSE instance dubbed ROSE by leveraging a key-updatable PRF. Yuan et al. [24] presented a fault-tolerant DSSE scheme that can tolerate incorrect update queries with a forward privacy guarantee. Recently, Zheng et al. [26] proposed a novel lightweight, robust DSSE by introducing a misoperation alert mechanism, which achieves a constant client storage cost.

In this work, we aim to design an efficient and robust conjunctive SSE with forward and backward privacy.

2 Preliminaries

In this section, we present the primitives used throughout the paper, including Counting Bloom Filter and dynamic SSE.

2.1 Cryptographic Assumption

Definition 1 *(Decisional Diffie-Hellman (DDH) Assumption.)* *Let* $\mathbb{G}$ *be a cyclic group of prime order p with generator g. Let $a, b, c \in \mathbb{Z}_p^*$. The DDH* assumption holds if for all probabilistic polynomial time (PPT) adversaries, the advantage in distinguishing (g, g^a, g^b, g^{ab}) and (g, g^a, g^b, g^c) is negligible:

$$|\Pr[\mathcal{A}(g, g^a, g^b, g^{ab}) = 1] - \Pr[\mathcal{A}(g, g^a, g^b, g^c) = 1]| \leq \mathsf{negl}(\lambda).$$

2.2 Pseudorandom Function

A function $F : \mathcal{K} \times \mathcal{X} \to \mathcal{Y}$ is a Pseudorandom Function (PRF) from the key space $\mathcal{K}$, domain $\mathcal{X}$ to range $\mathcal{Y}$ if for any PPT adversary $\mathcal{A}$, its advantage

$$Adv_{\mathcal{A},F}^{\mathrm{PRF}}(\lambda) = |\Pr[\mathcal{A}^{F(k,\cdot)}(\lambda) = 1] - \Pr[\mathcal{A}^{f(\cdot)}(\lambda) = 1]|$$

is negligible in λ, where $k \in \mathcal{K}$ and f is a random function from $\mathcal{X}$ to $\mathcal{Y}$.

2.3 Symmetric Encryption

An symmetric encryption (SE) scheme with key space $\mathcal{K}$, message space $\mathcal{M}$ and ciphertext space $\mathcal{C}$ is defined as **SE**=(**SE.Setup, SE.Enc, SE.Dec**):

- $K \leftarrow$ **SE.Setup**(1^λ): Given a security parameter λ, output a key $K \in \mathcal{K}$.
- $ct \leftarrow$ **SE.Enc**(K, m): Given a secret key K and a plaintext message $m \in \mathcal{M}$, output a ciphertext $ct \in \mathcal{C}$.
- $m/\bot \leftarrow$ **SE.Enc**(K, ct): Given a secret key K and a ciphertext ct, output the corresponding plaintext m, or a error symbol $\bot$ if decryption fails.

Security. An SE is IND-CPA secure if for every PPT adversary $\mathcal{A}$, its advantage

$$Adv_{\mathcal{A},SE}^{\mathrm{IND\text{-}CPA}}(\lambda) = |\Pr[\mathcal{A}^{\mathrm{Enc}(K,\cdot)}(m_0) = 1] - \Pr[\mathcal{A}^{\mathrm{Enc}(K,\cdot)}(m_1) = 1]|$$

is negligible, where $K \in \mathcal{K}$ is kept secret, $\mathcal{A}$ chooses $m_0, m_1 \in \mathcal{M}$ of equal length and makes adaptive encryption queries, excluding m_0 and m_1.

2.4 Dynamic Searchable Symmetric Encryption

Following [16,27], our DSSE scheme $\Sigma_{\mathbf{DSSE}} = $ (**Setup, Search, Update**) supports conjunctive queries consisting of three algorithms. This design can be easily extended from single-keyword DSSE schemes, as pointed out in ODXT [16].

- $(K, \sigma, \mathbf{EDB}) \leftarrow$ **Setup**(1^λ): Given a security parameter λ, this algorithm outputs a secret key K, a client state σ, and an encrypted database **EDB**. K and σ are stored by the client, while **EDB** is stored on the server.
- $(\sigma', \mathbf{Res}; \mathbf{EDB}') \leftarrow$ **Search**($K, q, \sigma; \mathbf{EDB}$): A two-party protocol between the client and the server. The client inputs the key K, a conjunctive query q, and the state σ, while the server inputs the encrypted database **EDB**. After the search, the server returns the query results **Res**, and the client state and encrypted database are updated to σ' and $\mathbf{EDB}'$, respectively.

- $(\sigma'; \mathbf{EDB'}) \leftarrow \mathbf{Update}(K, \mathrm{op}, (w, ind), \sigma; \mathbf{EDB})$: In this protocol, the client inputs $(K, \mathrm{op}, (w, ind), \sigma)$, and the server inputs $\mathbf{EDB}$. The operation $\mathrm{op} \in \{\mathsf{add}, \mathsf{del}\}$ specifies whether to add or delete the keyword-identifier pair (w, ind). The update yields new states σ' on the client and $\mathbf{EDB'}$ on the server.

Security. The security of a DSSE scheme is formally captured by the leakage function $\mathcal{L} = (\mathcal{L}^{Stp}, \mathcal{L}^{Srch}, \mathcal{L}^{Updt})$, which indicates the information exposed to the adversary during each execution phase. Specifically, $\mathcal{L}^{\mathsf{Stp}}$, $\mathcal{L}^{\mathsf{Srch}}$, and $\mathcal{L}^{\mathsf{Updt}}$ denote leakage during the **Setup**, **Search**, and **Update** phases, respectively.

Definition 2 (*Adaptive security*). *Let* $\Sigma_{\mathrm{DSSE}} = (\mathbf{Setup}, \mathbf{Search}, \mathbf{Update})$ *be a DSSE scheme. The scheme* Σ_{DSSE} *is said to be* $\mathcal{L}$*-adaptively secure if for any PPT adversary* $\mathcal{A}$*, there exists a simulator* $\mathcal{S}$ *with leakage function* $\mathcal{L} = (\mathcal{L}^{Stp}, \mathcal{L}^{Srch}, \mathcal{L}^{Updt})$ *satisfying*

$$|\Pr[\mathbf{Real}_{\mathcal{A}}^{\Sigma_{\mathrm{DSSE}}}(\lambda) = 1] - \Pr[\mathbf{Ideal}_{\mathcal{A},\mathcal{S}}^{\Sigma_{\mathrm{DSSE}}}(\lambda) = 1]| \leq \mathsf{negl}(\lambda),$$

where $\mathbf{Real}_{\mathcal{A}}^{\Sigma_{\mathrm{DSSE}}}(\lambda)$ *and* $\mathbf{Ideal}_{\mathcal{A},\mathcal{S}}^{\Sigma_{\mathrm{DSSE}}}(\lambda)$ *are defined as follows:*

- $\mathbf{Real}_{\mathcal{A}}^{\Sigma_{\mathrm{DSSE}}}(\lambda)$: $\mathcal{A}$ *chooses a security parameter* λ. *The experiment runs* $\mathbf{Setup}(1^\lambda)$ *and returns* $\mathbf{EDB}$ *to* $\mathcal{A}$. *Then* $\mathcal{A}$ *adaptively issues search (resp., update) on* q *(resp.,* $\mathrm{op}, (w, ind)$*) and returns the corresponding transcript of each operation. Finally,* $\mathcal{A}$ *outputs a bit* b.
- $\mathbf{Ideal}_{\mathcal{A},\mathcal{S}}^{\Sigma_{\mathrm{DSSE}}}(\lambda)$: $\mathcal{A}$ *chooses a security parameter* λ. *The experiment returns* $\mathbf{EDB}$ *simulated by* $\mathcal{L}^{Stp}(\lambda)$. *Then* $\mathcal{A}$ *adaptively issues search (resp., update) on* q *(resp.,* $\mathrm{op}, (w, ind)$*), and receives the transcript simulated by* $\mathcal{S}(\mathcal{L}^{Updt}(q))$ *(resp.,* $\mathcal{S}(\mathcal{L}^{Srch}(q))$*). Finally,* $\mathcal{A}$ *outputs a bit* b.

2.5 Robust DSSE

The definition of robustness in DSSE was formalized by Xu et al. [23]. A DSSE scheme is robust if it ensures both security and correctness even when the client issues duplicate updates or deletions of non-existent entries. Moreover, robustness ensures that previously deleted entries can be safely re-added.

Definition 3 (*Robustness*). *Let* Σ *be a DSSE scheme.* Σ *is robust if it maintains its security and correctness guarantees even when the client issues duplicate updates, deletes non-existent entries, or re-adds previously deleted entries.*

2.6 Counting Bloom Filter

Counting Bloom Filter (CBF) [12], a variant of Bloom Filter (BF), is a probabilistic data structure to support efficient element deletion, in addition to membership test. To insert or delete an element, the CBF hashes it and increments or decrements the corresponding counters by one. To query an element, the CBF checks whether all corresponding counters are non-zero; if so, the element is considered present, otherwise absent. Formally, the CBF comprises three algorithms $\mathbf{CBF} = (\mathbf{CBF.Gen}, \mathbf{CBF.Upd}, \mathbf{CBF.Check})$, defined as follows:

- $(C, H) \leftarrow \mathbf{CBF.Gen}(c, h)$: Given two integers $c, h \in \mathbb{N}$, it samples a set of h hash functions $H = \{H_j\}_{j \in [h]}$ where each $H_j : \mathcal{X} \rightarrow [c]$ maps elements from universe $\mathcal{X}$ to range $[c]$. It then initializes a counter array $C = 0^c$.
- $C \leftarrow \mathbf{CBF.Upd}(H, C, \mathrm{op}, x)$: It inputs the hash function set $H = \{H_j\}_{j \in [h]}$, a counter array C, an operation $\mathrm{op} \in \{\mathrm{add}, \mathrm{del}\}$, and an element $x \in \mathcal{X}$. If $\mathrm{op} = \mathrm{add}$, it increments each counter $C[H_j(x)]$ by 1 for all $j \in [h]$. If $\mathrm{op} = \mathrm{del}$, it decrements each $C[H_j(x)]$ by 1 unless the counter is already zero, in which case the decrement is skipped. We denote by $C_R \leftarrow \mathbf{CBF.Upd}(H, C, \mathrm{op}, R)$ the result of applying this update to each $x \in R$ individually.
- $1/0 \leftarrow \mathbf{CBF.Check}(H, C, x)$: Given $H = \{H_j\}_{j \in [h]}$, C, and an element $x \in \mathcal{X}$, it returns 1 if $C[H_j(x)] \neq 0$ for all $j \in [h]$; otherwise, it returns 0.

A CBF has perfect completeness if for any integers $c, h \in \mathbb{N}$ and any $R \subseteq \mathcal{X}$, when $(H, C) \leftarrow \mathbf{CBF.Gen}(c, h)$ and $C_R \leftarrow \mathbf{CBF.Upd}(H, C, \mathrm{op}, R)$, it holds that

$$\Pr[\mathbf{CBF.Check}(H, C_R, x) = 1] = 1, \text{ for all } x \in R.$$

Formally, following [15], when n elements are inserted into a CBF of size m using k hash functions, the probability that a given counter takes the value l is $P = b(l, kn, \frac{1}{m}) = \binom{kn}{l}(\frac{1}{m})^l(1 - \frac{1}{m})^{kn-l}$, where $b(\cdot)$ denotes the binomial distribution. The probability that a counter is less than a threshold θ is given by the cumulative sum $\sum_{l < \theta} b(l, kn, \frac{1}{m})$. Thus, the false-positive probability for a counting threshold θ is $P_{fp}(\theta, k, n, m) = (1 - \sum_{l < \theta} b(l, kn, \frac{1}{m}))^k$.

3 Our Constructions: ROXT

In this section, we first give a high-level description of ROXT and then present it in detail, along with its correctness and complexity analysis.

3.1 Technical Overview

We first outline the high-level ideas of our construction, with a focus on supporting conjunctive queries with robustness under dynamic updates.

Existing DSSE schemes for conjunctive queries, such as ODXT and SDSSE-CQ, face trade-offs between performance and correctness under update operations. ODXT follows the OXT framework, deploying a TSet structure to retrieve candidates for the least frequent keyword and an XSet to refine the result based on other keywords. However, it lacks forward privacy for XSet, incurs increased communication due to reliance on client-side deletion, and suffers from correctness issues under deletions. SDSSE-CQ addresses these limitations by applying a DSSE scheme [20] with forward and backward privacy, which supports single-keyword queries with non-interactive deletion, to both the TSet and XSet. Nevertheless, SDSSE-CQ prevents the client from re-adding previously deleted items within the same search epoch, limiting its practicality in real-world deployments.

To ensure both security and correctness even under client misoperations, such as duplicate additions or deletions, deletion of non-existent entries, and re-adding previously deleted items, we propose a specialized tag verification mechanism. Specifically, each keyword-identifier pair is mapped to a unique tag. To track deletions, the client maintains a compressed deletion list for each keyword using CBFs, denoted C_t and C_x for TSet and XSet, respectively. These lists are kept locally and are not visible to the server. When adding, if the tag already exists in the deletion list, the client removes it to restore the item, thus addressing the limitation of SDSSE-CQ. When deleting, if the tag is not present, it is inserted into the deletion list; otherwise, the operation is ignored. These rules ensure that prior to each query, the deletion lists reflect only currently deleted entries. During a search, the client uploads the deletion lists of all query keywords, enabling the server to filter out invalid tags via fast CBF checks. This guarantees correctness in any redundant or conflicting update history. Figure 1 illustrates a timeline example that shows how our mechanism dynamically adapts to mixed and redundant updates to ensure consistent and robust query results. At time t_{10}, the conjunctive query returns $\{ind_1, ind_2\}$ as the final result.

ind_1	$\{t_1, add, (w_1, ind_1)\}$	$\{t_2, add, (w_2, ind_1)\}$	$\{t_3, add, (w_1, ind_1)\}$	$\{t_4, del, (w_1, ind_1)\}$	$\{t_5, add, (w_1, ind_2)\}$
ind_2	$\{t_6, del, (w_1, ind_1)\}$	$\{t_7, del, (w_2, ind_2)\}$	$\{t_8, add, (w_1, ind_1)\}$	$\{t_9, add, (w_2, ind_2)\}$	$\{t_{10}, search, (w_1, w_2)\}$
Timeline	$t_1 - t_3$	$t_4 - t_6$	t_7	t_8	t_9

Fig. 1. Example of local deletion lists under the tag verification mechanism

Based on this verification mechanism, our ROXT ensures robustness for conjunctive queries under updates. Moreover, ROXT achieves forward privacy by applying a forward-private DSSE scheme to both the TSet and XSet. Backward security is ensured by filtering additions through local CBF-based deletion lists, preventing the server from correlating deletions with past additions. To improve efficiency, ROXT introduces a shared cache that stores valid entries retrieved in previous queries. During the next query, this cache is cross-verified with the new deletion list to discard invalid entries and reuse still-valid ones, thereby reducing redundant candidate computation and communication overhead. ROXT further performs physical deletion on the retrieved ciphertexts from the TSet and XSet after each query, reducing server-side storage. On the client side, deletion lists are maintained only for keywords with outstanding deletions. If a re-addition cancels all deletions for a keyword, its deletion list is removed. Similarly, once a deletion list has been sent to the server for search, it is cleared from the client's

Algorithm 1. Setup and Update Phase of ROXT

Setup(1^λ)
1: $K, K_t, K_i, K_x, K_s, K_z \xleftarrow{\$} \{0,1\}^\lambda$
2: $\mathbf{Dict}, \mathbf{C}_t, \mathbf{C}_x, \mathbf{EDB}_{cache} \leftarrow \emptyset$
3: $(\mathbf{EDB}_{tset}, K_{tset}, \sigma_{tset}) \leftarrow \Sigma_{fp}.\mathbf{Setup}(1^\lambda)$
4: $(\mathbf{EDB}_{xset}, K_{xset}, \sigma_{xset}) \leftarrow \Sigma_{fp}.\mathbf{Setup}(1^\lambda)$
5: $K = (K_{tset}, K_{xset}, K_s, K_t, K, K_x, K_i, K_z)$
6: $\sigma = (\sigma_{tset}, \sigma_{xset}, \mathbf{Dict}, \mathbf{C}_t, \mathbf{C}_x)$
7: $\mathbf{EDB} = (\mathbf{EDB}_{tset}, \mathbf{EDB}_{xset}, \mathbf{EDB}_{cache})$
8: return $(K, \sigma, \mathbf{EDB})$

Update(K, op, $(w, ind), \sigma; \mathbf{EDB}$)
1: $(acnt_w, scnt_w, scnx_w) \leftarrow \mathbf{Dict}[w]$
2: $C_t \leftarrow \mathbf{C}_t[w], C_x \leftarrow \mathbf{C}_x[w]$
3: if $\mathbf{Dict}[w] = \perp$ then
4: $\quad acnt_w, scnt_w, scnx_w \leftarrow 0$
5: end if
6: $t \leftarrow F(K_t, w||ind)$
7: if op = add then
8: $\quad acnt_w \leftarrow acnt_w + 1$
9: $\quad \mathbf{Dict}[w] \leftarrow (acnt_w, scnt_w, scnx_w)$
10: $\quad xind \leftarrow F_p(K_i, ind)$
11: $\quad z \leftarrow F_p(K_z, w||acnt_w)$
12: $\quad y \leftarrow xind \cdot z^{-1}, xtag \leftarrow g^{F_p(K_x, w) \cdot xind}$
13: $\quad K_w \leftarrow F(K, w), e \leftarrow \mathbf{SE.Enc}(K_w, ind)$
14: $\quad$ Run $\Sigma_{fp}.\mathbf{Update}(K_{tset}, \mathrm{add}, (w||scnt_w,$
$\quad\quad (e, y, acnt_w, t)), \sigma_{tset}; \mathbf{EDB}_{tset})$
15: $\quad$ Run $\Sigma_{fp}.\mathbf{Update}(K_{xset}, \mathrm{add}, (w||scnx_w,$

16: $\quad (xtag, t)), \sigma_{xset}; \mathbf{EDB}_{xset})$
17: if $C_t \neq \perp$ then
18: $\quad$ if $\mathbf{CBF.Check}(H, C_t, t) = 1$ then
19: $\quad\quad C_t \leftarrow \mathbf{CBF.Upd}(H, C_t, \mathrm{del}, t)$
20: $\quad\quad \mathbf{C}_t[w] \leftarrow C_t$
21: $\quad$ end if
22: end if
23: if $C_x \neq \perp$ then
24: $\quad$ if $\mathbf{CBF.Check}(H, C_x, t) = 1$ then
25: $\quad\quad C_x \leftarrow \mathbf{CBF.Upd}(H, C_x, \mathrm{del}, t)$
26: $\quad\quad \mathbf{C}_x[w] \leftarrow C_x$
27: $\quad$ end if
28: end if
29: else if op = del then
30: $\quad$ if $C_t = \perp$ then
31: $\quad\quad (C_t, H) \leftarrow \mathbf{CBF.Gen}(c, h)$
32: $\quad\quad C_t \leftarrow \mathbf{CBF.Upd}(H, C_t, \mathrm{add}, t)$
33: $\quad$ else if $\mathbf{CBF.Check}(H, C_t, t) = 0$ then
34: $\quad\quad C_t \leftarrow \mathbf{CBF.Upd}(H, C_t, \mathrm{add}, t)$
35: $\quad$ end if
36: $\quad$ if $C_x = \perp$ then
37: $\quad\quad (C_x, H) \leftarrow \mathbf{CBF.Gen}(c, h)$
38: $\quad\quad C_x \leftarrow \mathbf{CBF.Upd}(H, C_x, \mathrm{add}, t)$
39: $\quad$ else if $\mathbf{CBF.Check}(H, C_x, t) = 0$ then
40: $\quad\quad C_x \leftarrow \mathbf{CBF.Upd}(H, C_x, \mathrm{add}, t)$
41: $\quad$ end if
42: $\quad \mathbf{C}_t[w] \leftarrow C_t, \mathbf{C}_x[w] \leftarrow C_x$
43: end if

local storage. These optimizations reduce both client and server storage costs while preserving robustness guarantees.

3.2 Concrete Construction

Let $\Sigma_{fp} = (\Sigma_{fp}.\mathbf{Setup}, \Sigma_{fp}.\mathbf{Search}, \Sigma_{fp}.\mathbf{Update})$ be an arbitrary SSE scheme with forward security. With two PRFs $F : \{0,1\}^\lambda \times \{0,1\}^* \rightarrow \{0,1\}^\lambda$ and $F_p : \{0,1\}^\lambda \times \{0,1\}^* \rightarrow \mathbb{Z}_p^*$ (p is a prime), our ROXT comprises three algorithms $\Pi = (\mathbf{Setup, Update, Search})$, as shown in Algorithms 1 and 2.

Setup(1^λ): Given a security parameter λ, the client samples keys K, K_t for the PRF F, and K_i, K_x, K_s, K_z for the PRF F_p. It then sets three empty maps **Dict**, $\mathbf{C}_t$, $\mathbf{C}_x$ for each keyword. The map **Dict** stores three counters: $acnt_w$ for additions, $scnt_w$ for TSet searches, and $scnx_w$ for XSet searches. $\mathbf{C}_t$ and $\mathbf{C}_x$ store compressed deletion lists for TSet and XSet, respectively. The server sets an empty cache, $\mathbf{EDB}_{cache}$, to store recent search results from TSet and XSet, improving subsequent query efficiency. The client then runs the $\Sigma_{fp}.\mathbf{Setup}$ algorithm to generate the encrypted database, the master key, and the local state associated with TSet and XSet. Finally, the client outputs the key set K and local state table σ, while the server retains the encrypted database **EDB**.

Update(K, op, $(w, ind), \sigma; \mathbf{EDB}$): To update a keyword-identifier pair (w, ind), the client retrieves the current addition counter $acnt_w$, TSet search counter

Algorithm 2. Search Phase of ROXT

Search$(K, q = (w_1, \cdots, w_n), \sigma; \textbf{EDB})$
Client:
1: $(acnt_{w_1}, scnt_{w_1}, scnx_{w_1}) \leftarrow \textbf{Dict}[w_1]$
2: **if** $acnt_{w_1} = \perp$ **then**
3:    return $\emptyset$
4: **end if**
5: $K_w \leftarrow F(K, w_1)$
6: $\textbf{C}_{w_1} \leftarrow \textbf{C}_t[w_1], tkn_{w_1} \leftarrow F(K_s, w_1)$
7: delete $\textbf{C}_t[w_1]$ to release client storage
8: $scnt_{w_1} \leftarrow scnt_{w_1} + 1$
9: $\textbf{Dict}[w_1] \leftarrow (acnt_{w_1}, scnt_{w_1}, scnx_{w_1})$
10: **for** $i = 1$ to $acnt_{w_1}$ **do**
11:    **for** $j = 2$ to n **do**
12:       $xtoken_{i,j} \leftarrow g^{F_p(K_z, w_1 || i) \cdot F_p(K_x, w_j)}$
13:    **end for**
14:    $xtoken_i = \{xtoken_{i,2}, \cdots, xtoken_{i,n}\}$
15: **end for**
16: $xtoken = \{xtoken_1, \cdots, xtoken_{acnt_{w_1}}\}$
17: **for** $j = 2$ to n **do**
18:    $(acnt_{w_j}, scnt_{w_j}, scnx_{w_j}) \leftarrow \textbf{Dict}[w_j]$
19:    $\textbf{C}_{w_j} \leftarrow \textbf{C}_x[w_j], tkn_{w_j} \leftarrow F(K_s, w_j)$
20:    delete $\textbf{C}_x[w_j]$ to release client storage
21:    $scnx_{w_j} \leftarrow scnx_{w_j} + 1$
22:    $\textbf{Dict}[w_j] \leftarrow (acnt_{w_j}, scnt_{w_j}, scnx_{w_j})$
23: **end for**
24: Send $(xtoken, \{(tkn_{w_i}, \textbf{C}_{w_i})\}_{i=1}^n)$ to the server

Client ↔ Server:
25: Run $\Sigma_{fp}.\textbf{Search}(K_{tset}, w_1 || scnt_{w_1}, \sigma_{tset}; \textbf{EDB}_{tset})$, and the server gets a list $((e_1, y_1, 1, t_1), \cdots, (e_l, y_l, l, t_l))$.
26: **for** $j = 2$ to n **do**
27:    Run $\Sigma_{fp}.\textbf{Search}(K_{xset}, w_j || scnx_{w_j}, \sigma_{xset}; \textbf{EDB}_{xset})$, and the server gets a list $((xtag_{j,1}, t_{j,1}), \cdots, (xtag_{j,l_j}, t_{j,l_j}))$.
28: **end for**

Server:
29: TSet, XSet, $\textbf{Res} \leftarrow \emptyset$
30: **for** $j = 2$ to n **do**
31:    $(\text{TSetOld}_j, \text{XSetOld}_j) \leftarrow \textbf{EDB}_{cache}[tkn_{w_j}]$
32:    **for** $i = 1$ to l_j **do**
33:       **if** $\textbf{C}_{w_j} \neq \perp$ **then**
34:          **if** $\textbf{CBF}.\text{Check}(H, \textbf{C}_{w_j}, t_{j,i}) = 0$ **then**
35:             $\text{XSetNew}_j \leftarrow \text{XSetNew}_j \cup \{(xtag_{j,i}, t_{j,i})\}$
36:          **else**
37:             $\text{XSetOld}_j \leftarrow \text{XSetOld}_j \setminus \{(xtag_{j,i}, t_{j,i})\}$
38:          **end if**
39:       **else**
40:          $\text{XSetNew}_j \leftarrow \text{XSetNew}_j \cup \{(xtag_{j,i}, t_{j,i})\}$
41:       **end if**
42:       delete $(xtag_{j,i}, t_{j,i})$ from $\textbf{EDB}_{xset}$ to release server storage
43:    **end for**
44:    $\textbf{Res}_{X_j} \leftarrow \text{XSetNew}_j \cup \text{XSetOld}_j$
45:    $\textbf{EDB}_{cache}[tkn_{w_j}] \leftarrow (\text{TSetOld}_j, \textbf{Res}_{X_j})$
46:    **if** $\textbf{Res}_{X_j} = \perp$ **then**
47:       return $\emptyset$
48:    **end if**
49:    XSet $\leftarrow$ XSet $\cup$ $\textbf{Res}_{X_j}$
50: **end for**
51: $(\text{TSetOld}, \text{XSetOld}) \leftarrow \textbf{EDB}_{cache}[tkn_{w_1}]$
52: **for** $c = 1$ to l **do**
53:    **if** $\textbf{C}_{w_1} \neq \perp$ **then**
54:       **if** $\textbf{CBF}.\text{Check}(H, \textbf{C}_{w_1}, t_c) = 0$ **then**
55:          $\text{TSetNew} \leftarrow \text{TSetNew} \cup \{(e_c, y_c, c, t_c)\}$
56:       **else**
57:          $\text{TSetOld} \leftarrow \text{TSetOld} \setminus \{(e_c, y_c, c, t_c)\}$
58:       **end if**
59:    **else**
60:       $\text{TSetNew} \leftarrow \text{TSetNew} \cup \{(e_c, y_c, c, t_c)\}$
61:    **end if**
62:    delete (e_c, y_c, c, t_c) from $\textbf{EDB}_{test}$ to release server storage
63: **end for**
64: TSet $\leftarrow$ TSetNew $\cup$ TSetOld
65: $\textbf{EDB}_{cache}[tkn_{w_1}] \leftarrow (\text{TSet}, \text{XSetOld})$
66: **for each** $(e, y, c, t) \in$ TSet **do**
67:    $flag \leftarrow true$
68:    **for** $j = 2$ to n **do**
69:       **if** $(xtoken_{c,j})^y \notin$ XSet **then**
70:          $flag \leftarrow false$
71:       **end if**
72:    **end for**
73:    **if** $flag$ **then**
74:       $\textbf{Res} \leftarrow \textbf{Res} \cup \{e\}$
75:    **end if**
76: **end for**
77: Send $\textbf{Res}$ to the client

Client:
78: **for each** $e \in \textbf{Res}$ **do**
79:    $ind \leftarrow \textbf{SE}.\textbf{Dec}(K_w, e)$
80: **end for**

$scnt_w$, and XSet search count $scnx_w$ from **Dict**. It then retrieves the compressed deletion lists C_t of TSet and C_x of XSet for w, and computes a tag t for (w, ind).

For additions, the client increments $acnt_w$ and computes the blind factor y, the cross-tag $xtag$, and the encrypted identifier e. It then executes $\Sigma_{fp}.\textbf{Update}$ for $(e, y, acnt_w, t)$ and $(xtag, t)$, respectively, and sends the resulting entries to the server. To ensure robustness, the client checks whether tag t exists in the deletion lists, if they are non-empty (indicating a prior deletion). If tag t is found, (w, ind) is previously deleted, and the client removes t to re-add this pair (Algorithm 1, lines 16–27). For deletions, if C_t and C_x are empty, the client initializes them and inserts the tag t of the deleted (w, ind). If C_t and C_x are not empty, the client checks whether the tag t already exists in C_t and C_x. If the tag is not found, (w, ind) is not deleted, and the client inserts t. Otherwise, no action is taken, thus preventing repeated deletions (Algorithm 1, lines 32–34 and 38–40).

Search$(K, q = (w_1, \cdots, w_n), \sigma; \mathbf{EDB})$: To perform a conjunctive query $q = w_1 \wedge \cdots \wedge w_n$, the client first retrieves $(acnt_{w_1}, scnt_{w_1}, scnx_{w_1})$ of the least frequently added keyword w_1 from **Dict**, and increments the counters $scnt_{w_1}$ and $scnx_{w_j}$ ($2 \le j \le n$). It also retrieves the compressed deletion lists $\{C_{w_i}\}_{1 \le i \le n}$, each of which records the keyword-identifier pairs effectively deleted before this search. Next, the client computes search tokens $xtoken$ and tkn_{w_i}, and sends them to the server along with $\{C_{w_i}\}$ for $1 \le i \le n$. It then deletes these lists $\{C_{w_i}\}$ to release local storage. The client and server execute the Σ_{fp}.**Search** protocol to obtain tuples (e, y, c, t) for w_1 and $(xtag, t)$ for w_j ($2 \le j \le n$), while ensuring forward security for both TSet and XSet.

Upon receiving tokens, the server removes any $xtag$ whose associated tag t appears in the corresponding deletion list C_{w_j} ($2 \le j \le n$) to discard invalid entries. The valid $xtag$s of the current query, along with valid ones from $\mathbf{EDB}_{cache}$, form XSet to speed up query execution. Similarly, valid tuples (e, y, c, t) are inserted into the TSet, including those cached in $\mathbf{EDB}_{cache}$. Thus, the TSet holds identifiers matching w_1, while the XSet contains valid $xtag$s of the remaining query keywords, ensuring search robustness. Finally, the server computes $xtoken^y$ to retrieve identifiers containing all queried keywords and returns the results.

3.3 Correctness and Robustness Analysis

In ROXT, the keyword-identifier pairs added are stored on the server, while the tags of pre-search deletions are recorded in the client's local deletion lists. If no client misoperation occurs, the client uploads the corresponding deletion lists, allowing the server to apply deletions and construct the TSet and XSet for accurate query results. For various client misoperations, the robustness of ROXT can be achieved via our CBF-based tag verification mechanism:

- Duplicate additions: If the same keyword-identifier pairs are added multiple times, the corresponding ciphertexts–though stored at different addresses–are deduplicated at query time (Algorithm 2, lines 33–44 and 53–64), ensuring that only unique identifiers are returned.
- Duplicate or non-existent deletions: For each deletion, ROXT checks whether its tag already exists in the local deletion list (Algorithm 1, lines 28–41) to ensure that each tag is recorded only once. This prevents redundant or erroneous deletions from affecting query correctness.
- Re-additions after deletions (including non-existent deletions): If a deleted previously keyword-identifier pair is re-added, the tag verification mechanism

revokes the corresponding deletion tag from its CBF (Algorithm 1, lines 17–19 and 23–25), restoring the entry and preventing false suppression.

Therefore, ROXT maintains correctness even under client misoperations.

3.4 Complexity Analysis

Table 1 compares the complexity of ROXT with prior schemes and explains all notations used in this analysis. For each *add* operation of a keyword-identifier pair in the update phase, the client generates and uploads index entries (Algorithm 1, lines 10–15), which incurs constant computational and communication overhead, i.e., $O(1)$. The client also checks deletion status via a CBF and updates the local deletion list accordingly (Algorithms 1, lines 16–27), incurring a computational cost of $O(h)$. Each *deletion* similarly incurs an $O(h)$ computation cost, as the client checks and updates the local CBF (Algorithm 1, lines 29–41). Thus, each update operation incurs $O(h)$ computational and $O(1)$ communication overhead. For each keyword, the client maintains search and update counters, along with a list of pending deletions prior to the next search. This list is bounded by d, the maximum allowed deletions per keyword. Hence, the client-side storage overhead is $O(|\mathbf{W}|\log D+|\mathbf{W}_d|d)$, where $|\mathbf{W}_d|$ is the number of keywords marked for deletion before the next search. During search, the client generates $O(a_{w_1}\cdot n)$ search tokens (Algorithms 2, lines 6–19), where w_1 is the keyword with the fewest additions in conjunctive query q. Using these tokens, the server retrieves candidate entries for each keyword in q and verifies them via CBFs, incurring $O(ha_q)$ cost (Algorithms 2, lines 30–64). It then filters out deleted entries and performs $O((a_{w_1}-d_{w_1})\cdot n)$ exponentiations to compute the final results. The forward-secure DSSE incurs an additional $O(a_q)$ computational cost. Therefore, the total computational complexity of **Search** is $O((2a_{w_1}-d_{w_1})n+ha_q)$. The server returns the final conjunctive query result with a result communication complexity of $O(r_q)$.

4 Security Analysis

To precisely characterize the leakage profile of conjunctive DSSE schemes, Zuo et al. [27] introduce the notions of Type-O and Type-O$^-$ backward security. Informally, for a conjunctive query $q = (w_1, w_2, \ldots, w_n)$, Type-O$^-$ leaks the search pattern and result pattern of q; the list of undeleted identifiers matching q with their insertion timestamps; the total number of update operation and their timestamps for each keyword w in q; and the number of files matching each $\{w_1, w_s\}_{w_s\in\mathcal{W}}$ pair, where $\mathcal{W}$ denotes any subset of $(w_2, \ldots, w_n)$. Type-O additionally leaks the number of files matching each $\{w^*, w_s\}_{w_s\in\mathcal{W}}$ pair beyond the Type-O$^-$ leakage, where w^* represents any historically least frequent keywords, including w_1 in the current query. Let Q be a sequence of search queries of the form (u, w) and update queries of the form $(u, \text{op}, (w, ind))$. The corresponding leakage functions and formal definitions are specified as follows.

- $\mathbf{sp}(q)$ denotes the search pattern of query q, revealing whether each keyword $w \in q$ has been previously queried, defined as $\mathbf{sp}(q) = \{u : \{\mathrm{sp}(w)\} \in Q\}$.
- $\mathbf{rp}(q)$ denotes the result pattern of query q, revealing the set of files matching all keywords in the conjunctive query, defined as $\mathbf{rp}(q) = \{\mathrm{DB}(q)\}$.
- $\mathbf{TimeDB}(q)$ denotes the set of file identifiers matching q that have not been deleted, along with their respective insertion timestamps, defined as:

$$\mathbf{TimeDB}(q) = \{(\{u_i\}_{i\in[n]}, ind) \mid (u_i, \mathrm{add}, (w_i, ind)) \in Q \text{ and } \\ \forall u'_i : (u'_i, \mathrm{del}, (w_i, ind)) \notin Q\}.$$

- $\mathbf{Time}(q)$ denotes the set of timestamps corresponding to additions of each keyword w in the query q, defined as: $\mathbf{Time}(q) = \{u : \{u, \mathrm{op}, (w, ind)\}_{w\in q}\}$.
- $\mathrm{size}(w^*, W)$ represents the number of files matching any conjunctive query of the form $\{w^*, w_s\}_{w_s \in W}$, defined as $\mathrm{size}(w^*, W) = \{|\mathrm{DB}(w^*, w_s)|\}_{w_s \in W}$.

Definition 4 (Forward Security). *A $\mathcal{L}$-adaptively-secure DSSE scheme Σ is said to be forward secure if its update leakage function $\mathcal{L}^{Updt}$ is defined as:*

$$\mathcal{L}^{Updt}(\mathrm{op}, (w, ind)) = \mathcal{L}'((\mathrm{op}, ind)_T, (\mathrm{op}, ind)_X),$$

where $\mathcal{L}'$ is a stateless function, $(\mathrm{op}, ind)_T$ and $(\mathrm{op}, ind)_X$ are the (op, ind) leakage for TSet and XSet, respectively.

Definition 5 (Backward Security). *A $\mathcal{L}$-adaptively-secure DSSE scheme Σ is said to achieve Type-O or O^- backward security if its update leakage function $\mathcal{L}^{Updt}$ and search leakage function $\mathcal{L}^{Srch}$ are defined as follows, respectively:*

Type-O : $\quad \mathcal{L}^{Updt}(\mathrm{op}, (w, ind)) = \mathcal{L}'(\mathrm{op})$ and
$$\mathcal{L}^{Srch}(q) = \mathcal{L}''(\mathbf{sp}(q), \mathbf{rp}(q), \mathbf{TimeDB}(q), \mathbf{Time}(q), \mathrm{size}(w^*, W)),$$

Type-O^- : $\quad \mathcal{L}^{Updt}(\mathrm{op}, (w, ind)) = \mathcal{L}'(\mathrm{op})$ and
$$\mathcal{L}^{Srch}(q) = \mathcal{L}''(\mathbf{sp}(q), \mathbf{rp}(q), \mathbf{TimeDB}(q), \mathbf{Time}(q), \mathrm{size}(w_1, W)).$$

where $\mathcal{L}'$ and $\mathcal{L}''$ are stateless functions.

Following [23], we refine the leakage function and extend original Type-O backward security to *general Type-O backward security*. The corresponding formal definitions are given below, where $\mathcal{U}$ denotes the set of relevant timestamps:

$$\mathbf{exTimeDB}(q) = \{(\{\mathcal{U}_i\}_{i\in[n]}, ind) \mid \forall u_i \in \mathcal{U}, (u_i, \mathrm{add}, (w_i, ind)) \in Q \text{ and } \\ \forall u'_i > u_i : (u'_i, \mathrm{del}, (w_i, ind)) \notin Q\}.$$

$$\mathbf{exTime}(q) = \{(\mathcal{U}) : \forall u \in \mathcal{U}, \{u, \mathrm{op}, (w, ind)\}_{w\in q}\}.$$

Definition 6 (General Type-O Backward Security). *A $\mathcal{L}$-adaptive-secure DSSE scheme Σ is considered to achieve general Type-O backward security if its update and search leakage functions $\mathcal{L}^{Updt}$ and $\mathcal{L}^{Srch}$ are formulated this way:*

$$\mathcal{L}^{Updt}(\mathrm{op}, (w, ind)) = \mathcal{L}'(\mathrm{op}) \text{ and}$$
$$\mathcal{L}^{Srch}(q) = \mathcal{L}''(\mathbf{sp}(q), \mathbf{rp}(q), \mathbf{exTimeDB}(q), \mathbf{exTime}(q), \mathrm{size}(w^*, W)).$$

Theorem 1. *ROXT satisfies $\mathcal{L}$-adaptively forward and general Type-O backward security, iff Σ_{fp} is an $\mathcal{L}$-adaptively forward security DSSE scheme, F, F_p are secure PRFs, DDH assumption holds in group $\mathbb{G}$ and **SE** is an IND-CPA secure symmetric encryption. The leakage profile of ROXT is defined as $\mathcal{L}_{ROXT} = (\mathcal{L}_{ROXT}^{Updt}, \mathcal{L}_{ROXT}^{Srch})$, where $\mathcal{L}_{ROXT}^{Updt}(op, w, ind) = op$ and $\mathcal{L}_{ROXT}^{Srch}(q) = (\mathbf{sp}(q), \mathbf{rp}(q), \mathbf{exTimeDB}(q), \mathbf{exTime}(q), \mathrm{size}(w^*, W))$.*

Due to space limitations, the complete proof is provided in the Appendix A.

5 Performance Evaluation

In this section, we present a detailed experimental comparison between ROXT and the state-of-the-art schemes, including SDSSE-CQ [27], SDSSE-CQ-S [27], and ODXT [16] in terms of update and search performance.

5.1 Implementation Settings

Our experiments are conducted in Java using a single thread on a machine with an Intel Core i5-11500 CPU @ 2.7 GHz and 16 GB of RAM. All reported execution times are averages over 20 runs. We adopt FB-DSSE [28] as the underlying forward-secure SSE scheme and AES-128 as the SE algorithm. For cyclic group operations, we use the $\mathbb{G}_T$ group from the JPBC library. Our experimental dataset is 379,881 keyword-identifier pairs covering 201 distinct keywords extracted from the Enron Email dataset[2]. Moreover, we use 13 hash functions to achieve a false positive rate of 10^{-4} for both BF and CBF.

5.2 Evaluation and Comparison

Storage Performance. We evaluate the client-side storage overhead of ROXT, SDSSE-CQ, SDSSE-CQ-S, and ODXT. The experiment involves 201 keyword addition operations, followed by deletion targeting 10% of the file identifiers associated with three queried keywords, which correspond to 10, 10^5, and 10^5 files, respectively. Although each local CBF in ROXT theoretically consumes 4 times more space than a BF used in SDSSE-CQ and SDSSE-CQ-S, Table 2 shows that ROXT still achieves lower actual client-side storage overhead. This is attributed to our optimization strategy, where CBFs are maintained only for keywords with pending deletions and are cleared after each search. As expected, ODXT incurs minimal local storage due to its lazy deletion strategy. Overall, ROXT achieves robustness with acceptable client-side storage overhead.

Update Performance. We evaluate the update time for a keyword-identifier pair across ROXT, SDSSE-CQ, SDSSE-CQ-S, and ODXT. As depicted in Table 1, ROXT incurs slightly higher update computation complexity than ODXT due to the 13 additional hash computations in CBF. Thus, ROXT

---

[2] Enron Email Dataset: online at https://www.cs.cmu.edu/ ./enron/.

Table 2. Client-Side Storage Performance Comparison

Scheme	ROXT	SDSSE-CQ	SDSSE-CQ-S	ODXT
Storage (KB)	644.54	9629.63	9629.7	21.23

achieves slightly higher average addition time, as Table 3 shows. Although ROXT's update computation complexity is comparable to SDSSE-CQ and SDSSE-CQ-S, as shown in Table 1, ROXT's actual addition time is 3.98× and 4.17× higher, respectively. This is because SDSSE-CQ and SDSSE-CQ-S apply heavy cryptographic primitives over both the TSet and XSet entries, thus incurring higher computational costs. For deletion, ROXT, SDSSE-CQ, and SDSSE-CQ-S require only 0.01 ms, as the operation involves only hash computations on the CBF or BF. In contrast, ODXT's lazy deletion introduces ciphertext generation and client-server interaction, leading to a deletion latency comparable to that of addition. Overall, ROXT achieves superior efficiency in both addition and deletion, demonstrating its practicality for dynamic update scenarios.

Table 3. Update Time Comparison

Scheme	ROXT	SDSSE-CQ	SDSSE-CQ-S	ODXT
Per Add (ms)	0.53	2.11	2.21	0.48
Per Del (ms)	0.01	0.01	0.01	0.48

Update Communication Cost. We evaluate the update communication cost for a keyword-identifier pair in ROXT, SDSSE-CQ, SDSSE-CQ-S, and ODXT. As depicted in Table 1, ROXT has the update communication complexity comparable to ODXT and lower than SDSSE-CQ and SDSSE-CQ-S. Table 4 shows that, for additions, the communication cost of ROXT is slightly higher than that of ODXT and significantly lower than that of SDSSE-CQ and SDSSE-CQ-S. The marginal increase over ODXT is due to ROXT uploading one additional SE ciphertext. In contrast, SDSSE-CQ and SDSSE-CQ-S upload as many ciphertexts from the heavy primitive as the number of hash functions used in the BF. For deletions, ROXT, SDSSE-CQ, and SDSSE-CQ-S do not incur communication cost, as these operations are performed entirely on the client side. In contrast, ODXT incurs the same cost as for additions due to server interaction.

Table 4. Update Communication Cost

Scheme	ROXT	SDSSE-CQ	SDSSE-CQ-S	ODXT
Add (Byte)	688	5664	7952	180
Del (Byte)	0	0	0	180

Search Performance. We evaluate the search performance of ROXT, SDSSE-CQ, SDSSE-CQ-S, and ODXT. Let n_{w_i} denote the number of files matching keyword w_i; we conduct three types of conjunctive queries. The first type sets $n_{w_1} = 10$ and varies n_{w_2} from 10 to 10^5. The second type sets $n_{w_2} = 10^5$ and varies n_{w_1} from 10 to 10^5. The third type sets $n_{w_1} = 10$ and varies both n_{w_2} and n_{w_3} from 10 to 10^5. We measure client-side and server-side search time under two settings: (1) insertion-only, and (2) 10% deletions followed by insertions.

Figure 2 shows the search time for the first type. With insertion-only, ROXT's client-side search latency is comparable to ODXT, and up to 8.79× and 86.64× faster than SDSSE-CQ and SDSSE-CQ-S, respectively. For server-side search latency, ODXT remains constant, while ROXT, SDSSE-CQ, and SDSSE-CQ-S scale with n_{w_2} due to the forward-secure mechanism in their XSet design. SDSSE-CQ and SDSSE-CQ-S incur 1.49–2.97× and 2.64–142.5× the server-side latency of ROXT, respectively. With 10% deletions, ROXT maintains near-constant client-side latency, and is 47.44× and 126.7× faster than SDSSE-CQ and SDSSE-CQ-S, respectively. The higher latency in SDSSE-CQ-S is due to its added randomness in $xtag$. ROXT's server-side latency grows with n_{w_2}, while SDSSE-CQ and SDSSE-CQ-S are 1.2–1.9× and 1.9–130.84× slower, respectively. ODXT remains constant due to its lack of forward security in XSet.

Figure 3 shows the search time for the second type. With insertion-only, client-side search time increases with n_{w_1} in all schemes. On small datasets, ROXT yields the lowest search latency, and the performance gap narrows as dataset size increases. For server-side search time, ODXT exhibits linear growth with n_{w_1}.

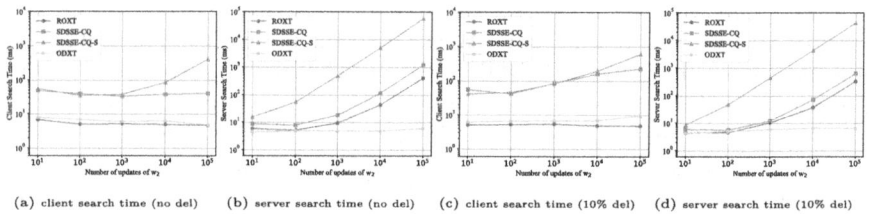

(a) client search time (no del) (b) server search time (no del) (c) client search time (10% del) (d) server search time (10% del)

Fig. 2. Two-conjunctive search query with constant w_1

Benefiting from lightweight hashes, ROXT is 1.12–3.25× and 2.7–121.26× faster than SDSSE-CQ and SDSSE-CQ-S, respectively. With 10% deletions, ROXT maintains client-side search time comparable to ODXT, while SDSSE-CQ and SDSSE-CQ-S are 106.27× and 201.83× slower, respectively, due to the use of computation-intensive primitives. On the server side, SDSSE-CQ and SDSSE-CQ-S are 1.05–2.35× and 2.6–132.47× slower than ROXT, respectively.

Figure 4 shows the search time for the third type. With addition-only, ROXT matches ODXT in client-side search time and outperforms SDSSE-CQ and SDSSE-CQ-S by up to 7.6× and 83.84×, respectively. For server-side search, ODXT remains stable, while ROXT, SDSSE-CQ, and SDSSE-CQ-S exhibit

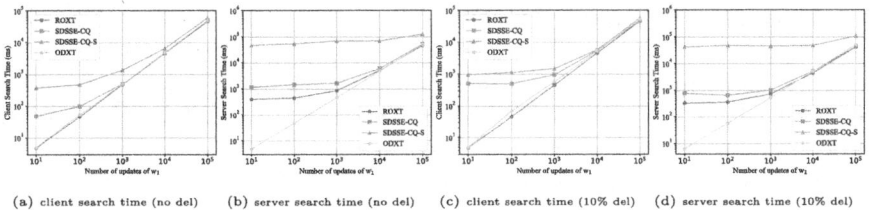

(a) client search time (no del) (b) server search time (no del) (c) client search time (10% del) (d) server search time (10% del)

Fig. 3. Two-conjunctive search query with constant w_2

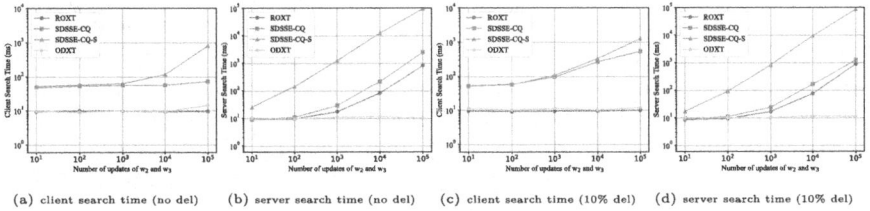

(a) client search time (no del) (b) server search time (no del) (c) client search time (10% del) (d) server search time (10% del)

Fig. 4. Three-conjunctive search query with constant w_1

increasing latency as n_{w_2} and n_{w_3} grow, due to their forward security guarantees for XSets. SDSSE-CQ and SDSSE-CQ-S incur 1–3× and 2.75–113.64× higher latency than ROXT. With 10% deletions, ROXT achieves slightly lower client-side latency than ODXT, while SDSSE-CQ and SDSSE-CQ-S suffer 54.24× and 126.71× slowdowns, respectively. On the server side, SDSSE-CQ and SDSSE-CQ-S are 1.1–2.18× and 2.0–126.4× slower than ROXT, respectively.

The evaluations demonstrate that ROXT offers robust support for conjunctive queries under dynamic updates while ensuring efficient search performance.

Conclusion

In this paper, we propose ROXT, a robust and efficient dynamic searchable encryption scheme that supports conjunctive queries with forward and enhanced Type-O backward security. With a tag verification mechanism based on CBFs, ROXT ensures robustness despite client misoperations. It further improves efficiency without compromising security guarantees through a shared cache mechanism. We formally prove that ROXT achieves enhanced Type-O backward security under robustness assumptions. Experimental results show that ROXT outperforms state-of-the-art conjunctive DSSE schemes in both search and update performance. Future work includes exploring new techniques to further improve search efficiency and advance the guarantees of backward security.

Acknowledgments. This work was supported by the National Cryptologic Science Fund of China (No. 2025NCSF02023).

A Proof of Security for ROXT

To prove Theorem 1, we define with a sequence of games, starting from the real experiment $\mathbf{Real}_{\mathcal{A}}^{\Pi}(\lambda)$, and ending with the ideal experiment $\mathbf{Ideal}_{\mathcal{A},\mathcal{L},\mathcal{S}}^{\Pi}(\lambda)$. We prove that each adjacent game pair is computationally indistinguishable.

Game G_0: the game is the same as real game $\mathbf{Real}_{\mathcal{A}}^{\Pi}(\lambda)$. Then

$$\Pr[\mathbf{Real}_{\mathcal{A}}^{\Pi}(\lambda) = 1] = \Pr[G_0 = 1].$$

Game G_1: In this game, we replace all keyed PRFs $F(K, \cdot), F(K_t, \cdot), F_p(K_i, \cdot), F_p(K_z, \cdot), F_p(K_x, \cdot), F(K_s, \cdot)$ with truly random functions defined over their respective domains. Specifically, for an updated entry $w\|ind$ (or $ind, w\|acnt_w, w$), a uniformly random value is sampled and stored in a table. For repeated updates, the table is consulted to return the same value. Thus, whether the adversary $\mathcal{A}$ can distinguish between Game G_1 and G_0 is equivalent to whether the adversary $\mathcal{B}_1$ can distinguish the keyed PRFs from truly random functions. Therefore, Game G_1 and Game G_0 are computationally indistinguishable.

$$|\Pr[G_1 = 1] - \Pr[G_0 = 1]| \leq 6 Adv_{\mathcal{B}_1, F}^{\mathrm{PRF}}(\lambda).$$

Game G_2: In this game, following the approach from [5], we modify the generation process of values y and $xtag$ in each update operation. Specifically, for every update, we sample $y, r \xleftarrow{\$} \mathbb{Z}_p$ and compute $xtag \leftarrow g^r$ for XSet verification. These generated values are subsequently stored in their corresponding tables. Therefore, whether the adversary $\mathcal{A}$ can distinguish between Game G_2 and G_1 is equivalent to whether the adversary $\mathcal{B}_2$ can break the DDH assumption. Consequently, Game G_2 and Game G_1 are computationally indistinguishable.

$$|\Pr[G_2 = 1] - \Pr[G_1 = 1]| \leq Adv_{\mathcal{B}_2}^{\mathrm{DDH}}(\lambda).$$

Game G_3: This game is identical to Game G_2 in all aspects except that it employs a symmetric encryption scheme to encrypt a constant string rather than file indices. Consequently, whether the adversary $\mathcal{A}$ can distinguish between Game G_3 and G_2 is equivalent to whether the adversary $\mathcal{B}_3$ can compromise the IND-CPA security of the symmetric encryption scheme. Therefore, Game G_3 and Game G_2 are computationally indistinguishable.

$$|\Pr[G_3 = 1] - \Pr[G_2 = 1]| \leq Adv_{\mathcal{B}_3, SE}^{\mathrm{IND\text{-}CPA}}(\lambda).$$

Game G_4: In this game, we replace Σ_{fp} with calls to its corresponding simulator $\mathcal{S}_{fp}$. Specifically, a bookkeeping mechanism is employed to actively record all Update queries, thereby eliminating reliance on server-side storage. All additions and deletions are deferred to subsequent Search queries. The game also maintains two lists, $\mathsf{L_{tset}}$ and $\mathsf{L_{xset}}$, to record the encrypted values of indices, associated tags, and insertion timestamps for each keyword w in TSet and XSet, respectively. They reconstruct the update history of each keyword and are provided as input to the simulator $\mathcal{S}_{fp}$. Therefore, whether the adversary $\mathcal{A}$ can distinguish between Game G_4 and G_3 equals whether the adversary $\mathcal{B}_4$ can break the forward security of Σ_{fp}. We conclude that Game G_4 and Game G_3 are computationally indistinguishable.

$$|Pr[G_4 = 1] - Pr[G_3 = 1]| \leq 2Adv_{\mathcal{B}_4, \Sigma_{fp}, S_{fp}}^{\mathcal{L}_{FS}}(\lambda).$$

Game G_5: In this game, we modify $xtoken$ generation during search. Specifically, for a query q containing n keywords, we first examine the adversary $\mathcal{A}$'s update query history to identify the set of update operations for the least frequently updated keyword w_1. Then, for each keyword w_i in the query, we compute the corresponding blinding factor $y_{i,j}$ and the oblivious cross-tag $xtag_{i,j}$, and generate the respective $xtoken_{i,j} = xtag_{i,j}^{1/y_{i,j}}$. From the adversary $\mathcal{A}$'s perspective, the distribution of each $xtoken$ value remains identical to that in Game G_4. We conclude that Game G_5 and Game G_4 are computationally indistinguishable.

$$\Pr[G_5 = 1] = \Pr[G_4 = 1].$$

Simulator: To simulate Game G_5, it suffices to avoid the explicit use of each keyword $w \in q$ when generating the corresponding search token $tokens[w]$. This can be achieved by simulating the search query using $\mathbf{sp}(q) = \{\mathrm{sp}(w)\}_{w \in q}$. Moreover, by utilizing the leakage functions $\mathbf{rp}(q), \mathbf{exTimeDB}(q), \mathbf{exTime}(q)$ and $\mathrm{size}(w^*, W)$ as inputs to the search algorithm, we can effectively simulate the construction process of the encrypted database EDB. Notably, the simulator no longer needs to track update operations during this process. We therefore conclude that the simulator can efficiently employ these well-defined leakage functions to successfully simulate Game G_5. Consequently, Game G_5 and the ideal game $\mathbf{Ideal}_{\mathcal{A}, \mathcal{L}, \mathcal{S}}^{\Pi}(\lambda)$ are computationally indistinguishable.

$$\Pr[\mathbf{Ideal}_{\mathcal{A}, \mathcal{L}, \mathcal{S}}^{\Pi}(\lambda) = 1] = \Pr[G_5 = 1].$$

At last, we could reach the conclusion that any PPT adversary $\mathcal{A}$ against our ROXT scheme is

$$|\Pr[\mathbf{Real}_{\mathcal{A}}^{\Pi}(\lambda) = 1] - \Pr[\mathbf{Ideal}_{\mathcal{A}, \mathcal{L}, \mathcal{S}}^{\Pi}(\lambda) = 1]| \leq 6Adv_{\mathcal{B}_1, F}^{PRF}(\lambda)$$
$$+ Adv_{\mathcal{B}_2}^{DDH}(\lambda) + Adv_{\mathcal{B}_3, SE}^{IND\text{-}CPA}(\lambda) + 2Adv_{\mathcal{B}_4, \Sigma_{fp}, S_{fp}}^{\mathcal{L}_{FS}}(\lambda).$$

Therefore, we complete the proof.

References

1. Bonomi, F., Mitzenmacher, M., Panigrahy, R., Singh, S., Varghese, G.: An improved construction for counting bloom filters. In: Azar, Y., Erlebach, T. (eds.) ESA 2006. LNCS, vol. 4168, pp. 684–695. Springer, Heidelberg (2006). https://doi.org/10.1007/11841036_61
2. Bost, R.: Σoφoς: forward secure searchable encryption. In: CCS 2016, pp. 1143–1154. ACM (2016). https://doi.org/10.1145/2976749.2978303

3. Bost, R., Minaud, B., Ohrimenko, O.: Forward and backward private searchable encryption from constrained cryptographic primitives. In: CCS 2017, pp. 1465–1482. ACM (2017). https://doi.org/10.1145/3133956.3133980
4. Cash, D., Jaeger, J., Jarecki, S., Jutla, C.S., Krawczyk, H., Rosu, M., Steiner, M.: Dynamic searchable encryption in very-large databases: Data structures and implementation. In: NDSS 2014. The Internet Society (2014)
5. Cash, D., Jarecki, S., Jutla, C., Krawczyk, H., Roşu, M.-C., Steiner, M.: Highly-scalable searchable symmetric encryption with support for boolean queries. In: Canetti, R., Garay, J.A. (eds.) CRYPTO 2013. LNCS, vol. 8042, pp. 353–373. Springer, Heidelberg (2013). https://doi.org/10.1007/978-3-642-40041-4_20
6. Chamani, J.G., Papadopoulos, D., Papamanthou, C., Jalili, R.: New constructions for forward and backward private symmetric searchable encryption. In: CCS 2018, pp. 1038–1055. ACM (2018). https://doi.org/10.1145/3243734.3243833
7. Chase, M., Kamara, S.: Structured encryption and controlled disclosure. In: Abe, M. (ed.) ASIACRYPT 2010. LNCS, vol. 6477, pp. 577–594. Springer, Heidelberg (2010). https://doi.org/10.1007/978-3-642-17373-8_33
8. Curtmola, R., Garay, J.A., Kamara, S., Ostrovsky, R.: Searchable symmetric encryption: improved definitions and efficient constructions. In: CCS 2006, pp. 79–88. ACM (2006). https://doi.org/10.1145/1180405.1180417
9. Demertzis, I., Chamani, J.G., Papadopoulos, D., Papamanthou, C.: Dynamic searchable encryption with small client storage. In: NDSS 2020. The Internet Society (2020)
10. Du, K., Wang, J., Wu, J., Wang, Y.: Scalable equi-join queries over encrypted database. In: CCS 2024, pp. 4002–4016. ACM (2024). https://doi.org/10.1145/3658644.3690377
11. Etemad, M., Küpçü, A., Papamanthou, C., Evans, D.: Efficient dynamic searchable encryption with forward privacy. Proc. Priv. Enhancing Technol. **2018**(1), 5–20 (2018). https://doi.org/10.1515/popets-2018-0002
12. Fan, L., Cao, P., Almeida, J.M., Broder, A.Z.: Summary cache: a scalable wide-area web cache sharing protocol. IEEE/ACM Trans. Netw. **8**(3), 281–293 (2000). https://doi.org/10.1109/90.851975
13. Kamara, S., Moataz, T.: Boolean searchable symmetric encryption with worst-case sub-linear complexity. In: Coron, J.-S., Nielsen, J.B. (eds.) EUROCRYPT 2017. LNCS, vol. 10212, pp. 94–124. Springer, Cham (2017). https://doi.org/10.1007/978-3-319-56617-7_4
14. Kamara, S., Papamanthou, C., Roeder, T.: Dynamic searchable symmetric encryption. In: CCS 2012, pp. 965–976. ACM (2012). https://doi.org/10.1145/2382196.2382298
15. Kim, K., Jeong, Y., Lee, Y., Lee, S.: Analysis of counting bloom filters used for count thresholding. Electronics **8**(7), 779 (2019)
16. Patranabis, S., Mukhopadhyay, D.: Forward and backward private conjunctive searchable symmetric encryption. In: NDSS 2021. The Internet Society (2021)
17. Song, D.X., Wagner, D.A., Perrig, A.: Practical techniques for searches on encrypted data. In: 2000 IEEE Symposium on Security and Privacy, Berkeley, California, USA, 14-17 May 2000. pp. 44–55. IEEE Computer Society (2000). https://doi.org/10.1109/SECPRI.2000.848445
18. Song, X., Dong, C., Yuan, D., Xu, Q., Zhao, M.: Forward private searchable symmetric encryption with optimized I/O efficiency. IEEE Trans. Dependable Secur. Comput. **17**(5), 912–927 (2020). https://doi.org/10.1109/TDSC.2018.2822294
19. Stefanov, E., Papamanthou, C., Shi, E.: Practical dynamic searchable encryption with small leakage. In: NDSS 2014. The Internet Society (2014)

20. Sun, S., et al.: Practical non-interactive searchable encryption with forward and backward privacy. In: 28th Annual Network and Distributed System Security Symposium, NDSS 2021. The Internet Society (2021)
21. Sun, S., et al.: Practical backward-secure searchable encryption from symmetric puncturable encryption. In: CCS 2018, pp. 763–780. ACM (2018), https://doi.org/10.1145/3243734.3243782
22. Wang, J., Sun, S., Li, T., Qi, S., Chen, X.: Practical volume-hiding encrypted multi-maps with optimal overhead and beyond. In: CCS 2022, pp. 2825–2839. ACM (2022). https://doi.org/10.1145/3548606.3559345
23. Xu, P., Susilo, W., Wang, W., Chen, T., Wu, Q., Liang, K., Jin, H.: ROSE: robust searchable encryption with forward and backward security. IEEE Trans. Inf. Forensics Secur. **17**, 1115–1130 (2022), https://doi.org/10.1109/TIFS.2022.3155977
24. Yuan, D., Cui, S., Russello, G.: We can make mistakes: fault-tolerant forward private verifiable dynamic searchable symmetric encryption. In: EuroS&P 2022, pp. 587–605. IEEE (2022). https://doi.org/10.1109/EuroSP53844.2022.00043
25. Zhang, Y., Katz, J., Papamanthou, C.: All your queries are belong to us: the power of file-injection attacks on searchable encryption. In: Holz, T., Savage, S. (eds.) USENIX Security 2016, pp. 707–720. USENIX Association (2016)
26. Zheng, Y., Xu, P., Wang, M., Xu, W., Wang, W., Chen, T., Jin, H.: Themis: robust and light-client dynamic searchable symmetric encryption. IEEE Trans. Inf. Forensics Secur. **19**, 8802–8816 (2024). https://doi.org/10.1109/TIFS.2024.3463971
27. Zuo, C., et al.: Searchable encryption for conjunctive queries with extended forward and backward privacy. Proc. Priv. Enhancing Technol. **2025**(1), 440–455 (2025). https://doi.org/10.56553/popets-2025-0024
28. Zuo, C., Sun, S.-F., Liu, J.K., Shao, J., Pieprzyk, J.: Dynamic searchable symmetric encryption with forward and stronger backward privacy. In: Sako, K., Schneider, S., Ryan, P.Y.A. (eds.) ESORICS 2019. LNCS, vol. 11736, pp. 283–303. Springer, Cham (2019). https://doi.org/10.1007/978-3-030-29962-0_14

Security Analysis of Covercrypt: A Quantum-Safe Hybrid Key Encapsulation Mechanism for Hidden Access Policies

Théophile Brézot[1], Chloé Hébant[1], Paola de Perthuis[2], and David Pointcheval[1,3]

[1] Cosmian, Paris, France
[2] Centrum Wiskunde and Informatica (CWI), Amsterdam, The Netherlands
[3] DIENS, École normale supérieure, université PSL, CNRS, Inria, Paris, France
david.pointcheval@ens.fr

Abstract. The ETSI Technical Specification 104 015 proposes a framework to build Key Encapsulation Mechanisms (KEMs) with access policies and attributes, in the Ciphertext-Policy Attribute-Based Encryption (CP-ABE) vein. Several security guarantees and functionalities are claimed, such as pre-quantum and post-quantum hybridization to achieve security against Chosen-Ciphertext Attacks (CCA), anonymity, and traceability. In this paper, we present a formal security analysis of a more generic construction, with application to the specific Covercrypt scheme, based on the pre-quantum ECDH and the post-quantum ML-KEM Key Encapsulation Mechanisms. We additionally provide an open-source library that implements the ETSI standard, in Rust, with high efficiency.

1 Introduction

Key Encapsulation Mechanisms (KEMs) are highly efficient when used in conjunction with Data Encryption Mechanisms (DEMs) to encrypt large volumes of data. The KEM-DEM paradigm, introduced by Shoup in [17], indeed combines a public-key scheme with a symmetric encryption scheme, resulting in ciphertexts that are similar in size to plaintexts. In essence, KEMs facilitate the secure transmission of session keys by allowing a user to perform the encapsulation procedure for a recipient or group of recipients, generating a session key and its encapsulation (the ciphertext). The recipients, if intended, can derive the session key from the ciphertext. The payload is then encrypted and decrypted using this session key with a DEM, which can be any authenticated encryption mechanism. This is determining for non-interactive communications between a sender and a recipient. KEMs may also be used as Interactive Key Exchange protocols, between two online parties.

To enhance security during the post-quantum transition, two KEMs may be hybridized, ensuring that the scheme's security depends on the best of both their securities. This approach maintains the privacy of encapsulated keys even if one

KEM algorithm is compromised. PQ/T hybridization as defined in [11] involves one pre-quantum and one post-quantum secure scheme, with the latter being presumably resistant to quantum adversaries while the former relies on more classical security assumptions, even if insecure against potential future quantum adversaries.

Attribute-Based Encryption (ABE), allows decryption based on attributes and policies in ciphertexts and user's keys [13]. Advanced ABE schemes support complex access policies but come with high computational costs and large ciphertexts, especially for post-quantum security. For fine-grained access control, one would be interested into strengthening the KEM to limit the access to the payload, in a similar vein.

ABE was initially introduced in [16], where decryption was possible if the number of common attributes in the key and ciphertext met a threshold. The more general work [13] introduced key-policy ABE (KP-ABE) and ciphertext-policy ABE (CP-ABE), associating a Boolean formula (policy) with either the user's key or the ciphertext. Decryption is possible if the Boolean formula accepts the attributes.

A desirable property for KP-ABE schemes (resp. CP-ABE) is for them to be *attribute-hiding* [15] (resp. *predicate-hiding*), meaning that ciphertexts should not allow users to learn anything of the attributes or the policies they were generated with, outside of their ability, or not, to successfully decrypt. State-of-the-art constructions for this property only do so for the limited class of inner-product predicates on attributes, with pre-quantum [15], or more recent post-quantum versions [9].

State-of-the-Art. For general purpose ABE, current post-quantum versions with implementable parameters [10, Table II], for the construction proposed in [4], led to encryption times in hundreds of milliseconds and decryption times (consisting in the application of the EvalCT, EvalPK, and Dec algorithms) of around a second on a CPU laptop, without attribute-hiding properties. A more recent post-quantum ABE-scheme was proposed last year [9] with a higher security, but incurring significantly higher costs than [4].

A first construction of ABE for polynomially-many logical attribute combinations, that can be built from any KEM, without pairings, and supporting efficient traditional/post-quantum hybridization, has been proposed two years ago [6], but with CPA security only. About functionalities, it was similar to [16], allowing decryption if some attributes are common in the key and ciphertext. It also attained a policy-hiding property ensuring that access policies in the ciphertexts were not revealed to users that did not fulfil them. More recently, a CCA construction has been standardized by ETSI [12]. However, its CCA security had never been proven nor analyzed.

Contributions. This paper first presents a formal security analysis of a generalization of the ETSI standard [12], and in particular, the CCA-secure Covercrypt scheme, based on the pre-quantum ECDH and the post-quantum ML-KEM. It targets specific access structures with multiple orthogonal dimensions, using a hybrid KEM for fine-grained access control, key rotation for dynamic user rights, and a traceability mechanism to detect user abuse. It is described in a black-box manner, allowing usage of various cryptographic algorithms. We have updated our library in Rust, from the CPA-version [6], that implements the standard, with additional features. The code is still open-source, and provides similar efficiency: half a millisecond for encrypting, and a millisecond for decrypting, for classical use, which is far better than [10].

2 Definitions

This paper targets Key Encapsulation Mechanism with Access Control (KEMAC), as introduced in [6]. We hereafter recall some formal definitions.

2.1 Computational Assumptions

Due to the lack of space, we will let the reader refer to the literature (and to full version of the paper [7]). But, we will rely on the *Decisional Diffie-Hellman Problem* in a group $\mathbb{G}$ (DDH$_\mathbb{G}$) of prime order p, with a generator P, or even the *Computational Diffie-Hellman Problem* (CDH$_\mathbb{G}$), for the ECDH construction, as well as the *Decisional Module Learning-with-Error Problem* (DMLWE) for the post-quantum Kyber encryption scheme [5], also known as ML-KEM [14].

2.2 Cryptographic Primitives

Key Encapsulation Mechanism. A Key Encapsulation Mechanism KEM is defined by three algorithms:

- KEM.KeyGen(1^κ): the *key generation algorithm* outputs a pair of public and secret keys (pk, sk);
- KEM.Enc(pk): the *encapsulation algorithm* generates a session key K and a ciphertext C of it, and outputs the pair (C, K);
- KEM.Dec(sk, C): the *decapsulation algorithm* outputs the key K encapsulated in C.

Again, for the sake of conciseness, we will let the reader refer to the literature (and to the full version of the paper [7]) for the correctness and the security notions of a KEM. We will consider classical indistinguishability of the encapsulated key (hereafter called *Session-Key Indistinguishability* (SK-IND)) [2], under either Chosen-Plaintext Attacks (CPA) or Chosen-Ciphertext Attacks (CCA). For anonymity, we will consider the *Public-Key Indistinguishability* (PK-IND) [1] in either the CPA or CCA settings.

Key Encapsulation Mechanism with Access Control. A KEM with Access Control allows multiple users to access the encapsulated key K from C, according to a rule $\mathcal{R}$ applied on Y in the user's key usk and X in the ciphertext C. It is defined by four algorithms:

- KEMAC.Setup($\mathcal{R}, 1^\kappa$) outputs the global public parameters MPK and the master secret key MSK;
- KEMAC.KeyGen(MSK, Y) outputs the user's secret key usk according to Y;
- KEMAC.Enc(MPK, X) generates a session key K and a ciphertext C of it according to X;
- KEMAC.Dec(usk, C) outputs the key K encapsulated in C.

Correctness. One expects KEMAC.Dec(usk, C) = K with overwhelming probability, for any X and Y such that $\mathcal{R}(X, Y) = 1$, where usk has been honestly generated for Y and K has been encapsulated in C for X, after an honest setup to generate (MPK, MSK).

1. $b \xleftarrow{\$} \{0, 1\}$
2. (MPK, MSK) ← KEMAC.Setup(1^κ)
3. $b' \leftarrow \mathcal{A}^{\mathcal{O}\text{KeyGen}(\cdot), \mathcal{O}\text{Dec}(\cdot), \mathcal{O}\text{EncChal}(\cdot)}$(MPK)
4. if there is a Y such that $\mathcal{R}(X^*, Y) = 1$, for X^* asked to $\mathcal{O}$EncChal, asked either to $\mathcal{O}$KeyGen or to $\mathcal{O}$Dec on the challenge C^*, then output a random bit $\beta \xleftarrow{\$} \{0, 1\}$, else output $\beta \leftarrow (b' = b)$

1. $b \xleftarrow{\$} \{0, 1\}$
2. (MPK, MSK) ← KEMAC.Setup(1^κ)
3. $b' \leftarrow \mathcal{A}^{\mathcal{O}\text{KeyGen}(\cdot), , \mathcal{O}\text{Dec}(\cdot), \mathcal{O}\text{EncChal}(\cdot, \cdot)}$(MPK)
4. if there is a Y such that $\mathcal{R}(X_0, Y) = 1$ or $\mathcal{R}(X_1, Y) = 1$, for (X^0, X^1) asked to $\mathcal{O}$EncChal, asked either to $\mathcal{O}$KeyGen or to $\mathcal{O}$Dec on the challenge C^*, then output a random bit $\beta \xleftarrow{\$} \{0, 1\}$, else output $\beta \leftarrow (b' = b)$

Fig. 1. Security Games for SK-IND-CCA and AC-IND-CCA for a KEMAC

Session-Key Privacy. As for the basic KEM, one may expect some privacy properties. Session-key privacy is modeled by indistinguishability of the actual session key from the ciphertext, even if the adversary has received some decryption keys and some decapsulations, as soon as some associated Y are incompatible with the challenge input X^* ($\mathcal{R}(X^*, Y) = 0$). More precisely, such a KEMAC is said to be SK-IND-CCA-secure in the key space $\mathcal{K}$ if for any adversary $\mathcal{A}$, that can ask *any* key usk using oracle $\mathcal{O}$KeyGen(Y), that outputs KEMAC.KeyGen(MSK, Y), *any* decapsulated key K using oracle $\mathcal{O}$Dec(Y, C), that outputs KEMAC.Dec(usk, C), for an ephemeral key usk obtained from $\mathcal{O}$KeyGen(Y), and one challenge on any X^*, using $\mathcal{O}$EncChal(X^*), that runs KEMAC.Enc(MPK, X^*) to get (C^*, K_0), chooses $K_1 \xleftarrow{\$} \mathcal{K}$, and outputs (C^*, K_b), for an initial random bit b, the advantage $\text{Adv}_{\text{KEMAC}}^{\text{sk-ind-cca}}(\mathcal{A})$ is negligible in the game presented on the left of Fig. 1. We stress that the bad situation where there is a Y such that $\mathcal{R}(X^*, Y) = 1$, for X^* asked to $\mathcal{O}$EncChal, asked either to $\mathcal{O}$KeyGen or to $\mathcal{O}$Dec on the challenge ciphertext C^* should be avoided by the adversary: as this leads to a trivial guess, this is considered as a non-legitimate attack.

As usual, we can restrict to chosen-plaintext attacks, where the adversary cannot ask for the decapsulation oracle.

Access-Control Privacy. One can also extend the anonymity notion, by hiding the parameter X used in the ciphertext C even if the adversary $\mathcal{A}$ can ask some decryption keys and some decapsulations, as soon as some associated Y are incompatible with the challenge input X^* ($\mathcal{R}(X,Y) = 0$). A KEMAC is said to be AC-IND-CCA-secure if for any adversary $\mathcal{A}$, that can ask *any* key usk using oracle $\mathcal{O}$KeyGen(Y), that outputs KEMAC.KeyGen(MSK, Y), *any* decapsulated key K using oracle $\mathcal{O}$Dec(Y,C), that outputs KEMAC.Dec(usk, C), for an ephemeral key usk obtained from $\mathcal{O}$KeyGen(Y), and one ciphertext on any pair (X_0, X_1), using $\mathcal{O}$EncChal(X_0, X_1), that runs KEMAC.Enc(MPK, X_b) to get (C^*, K), for an initial random bit b, $\text{Adv}_{\text{KEMAC}}^{\text{ac-ind-cca}}(\mathcal{A})$ is negligible in the game presented on the right of Fig. 1. As above, we can restrict to chosen-plaintext attacks, where the adversary cannot ask for the decapsulation oracle.

Traceability. In any multi-user setting, to avoid abuse of the decryption keys, one may want to be able to trace users (or their personal keys) from the decryption mechanism, and more generally from any *useful* pirate decoder, either given access to the key material in the device (white-box tracing) or just interacting with the device (black-box tracing) [8]. Without any keys, one expects session-key privacy, but as soon as one knows a key, one can distinguish the session-key. Then, we will call a *useful* pirate decoder $\mathcal{P}$ a good distinguisher against session-key privacy, that behaves differently with the real and a random key. But of course, this pirate decoder can be built from multiple user' keys, called traitors, and one would like to be able to trace at least one traitor from the collusion.

NIKE-Based KEM. A Non-Interactive Key Exchange (NIKE) is defined by two algorithms:

- NIKE.KeyGen(1^κ): on input of a security parameter κ, outputs a pair of public and secret keys (pk, sk);
- NIKE.SessionKey(sk, pk'): on input of a secret key sk and a public key pk', generates a session key K.

Again, due to the lack of space, we will let the reader refer to the literature (and to the full version of the paper [7]) for the correctness and the security notions of a NIKE. In short, we expect NIKE.SessionKey(sk_1, pk_0) = NIKE.SessionKey(sk_0, pk_1) for any two pairs of keys, and we will consider the basic one-wayness, as the SK-OW-security (for *Session-Key One-Wayness*), that is the computational problem of finding the session key from the two public keys.

Key-Homomorphic NIKE (KH-NIKE). A NIKE is said to be key-homomorphic, if the secret keys are in a ring $(\mathcal{R}, +, \times)$ and there is an internal group-law $\otimes$ and an external law $\odot$ on the public keys that make them correspond to each other: from $(\mathsf{pk}_0, \mathsf{sk}_0), (\mathsf{pk}_1, \mathsf{sk}_1) \leftarrow \mathsf{NIKE.KeyGen}(1^\kappa)$, the secret key $\mathsf{sk} \leftarrow \mathsf{sk}_0 + \mathsf{sk}_1$ corresponds to the public key $\mathsf{pk} \leftarrow \mathsf{pk}_0 \otimes \mathsf{pk}_1$, and the secret key $\mathsf{sk}' \leftarrow \mathsf{sk}_0 \times \mathsf{sk}_1$ corresponds to the public key $\mathsf{pk}' \leftarrow \mathsf{sk}_0 \odot \mathsf{pk}_1$. Furthermore, for any $(\mathsf{pk}'', \mathsf{sk}'') \leftarrow \mathsf{NIKE.KeyGen}(1^\kappa)$, we have

$$\mathsf{NIKE.SessionKey}(\mathsf{sk}'', \mathsf{sk}_0 \odot \mathsf{pk}_1) = \mathsf{NIKE.SessionKey}(\mathsf{sk}_0 \times \mathsf{sk}'', \mathsf{pk}_1).$$

3 Security Analysis of Covercrypt

In this section, we first present a generalization of Covercrypt, the ETSI TS 104 015 [12], that proposes to use a hybrid construction, combining a pre-quantum key-homomorphic NIKE and a post-quantum KEM, where the KEM is instantiated by the ML-KEM [14] and the NIKE is instantiated by the Hashed-ECDH. This provides hybridization of the security, with the best of both worlds: the post-quantum security of the KEM and the pre-quantum security of the KH-NIKE, at least for the session-key privacy.

3.1 Hybrid Traceable KEMAC with CCA Security

The generalization of Covercrypt combines any KH-NIKE with any KEM, the former being SK-OW-secure, and the latter being SK-IND-CCA and PK-IND-CCA-secure.

Detailled Description. Let Ω be $\{S_1, \ldots, S_N\}$, the set of rights; NIKE, a KH-NIKE scheme achieving SK-OW security, with secret keys in a ring $\mathcal{R}$ and public keys in a group $\mathbf{G}$; KEM, a KEM scheme achieving SK-IND-CCA and PK-IND-CCA security; $\mathcal{G}, \mathcal{H}$, and $\mathcal{J}$, hash functions, mapping elements to $\mathcal{R}$ elements, 2κ-bit strings, and 3κ-bit strings respectively. The scheme HTKEMAC is defined as follows:

- HTKEMAC.Setup$(\Omega, t, 1^\kappa)$: for a set Ω of rights and a threshold t for traceability:
  1. the algorithm samples $(P_1, s_1), \ldots, (P_t, s_t) \leftarrow \mathsf{NIKE.KeyGen}(1^\kappa)$;
  2. the algorithm samples $\alpha_1, \ldots, \alpha_t \xleftarrow{\$} \mathcal{R}$, and sets $s = \sum_k \alpha_k \cdot s_k$ and $H = \otimes_k(\alpha_k \odot P_k)$, with the constraint that s is invertible in $\mathcal{R}$;
  3. the set of user identities $\mathcal{ID}$ is initialized as an empty set, the tracing secret key is then set to $\mathsf{tsk} = (s, (s_k)_k, \mathcal{ID})$ and the tracing public key to $\mathsf{tpk} = (H, (P_k)_k)$;
  4. the set of users' secret keys showing their permissions is initialized as an empty set with $\mathcal{UP} \leftarrow \emptyset$;

5. for each right S_i of index i in Ω, the algorithm samples $(\mathsf{pk}_i, \mathsf{sk}_i) \leftarrow \mathsf{KEM.KeyGen}(1^\kappa)$, $(X_i, x_i) \leftarrow \mathsf{NIKE.KeyGen}(1^\kappa)$, computes $H_i \leftarrow s \odot X_i$, and sets $\mathsf{pk}'_i \leftarrow (H_i, \mathsf{pk}_i)$ and $\mathsf{sk}'_i \leftarrow (x_i, \mathsf{sk}_i)$;
6. finally, the global public key is set to $\mathsf{MPK} \leftarrow (\mathsf{tpk}, \{\mathsf{pk}'_i\}_i)$, and the master secret key to $\mathsf{MSK} \leftarrow (\mathsf{tsk}, \{\mathsf{sk}'_i\}_i, \mathcal{UP})$.

The algorithm returns $(\mathsf{MSK}, \mathsf{MPK})$.

- $\mathsf{HTKEMAC.KeyGen}(\mathsf{MSK}, U, Y)$: on input a username U, along with Y a set of indices corresponding to U's rights Ω, parsing the master secret key $\mathsf{MSK} = (\mathsf{tsk}, \{\mathsf{sk}'_i\}_i, \mathcal{UP})$ as an output of the Setup algorithm:
  1. it draws a random tuple $(\beta_k)_k$ such that $s = \sum_k \beta_k \cdot s_k$, and sets U's secret identifier to $\mathsf{uid} \leftarrow (\beta_k)_k$;
  2. it updates the tracing secret key by setting tsk' to be equal to tsk in which (U, uid) is added to $\mathcal{ID}$;
  3. U's secret key is defined as $\mathsf{usk} \leftarrow (\mathsf{uid}, \{\mathsf{sk}'_j\}_{j \in Y})$, and the master secret key is updated to MSK' equal to MSK in which usk was added to $\mathcal{UP}$.

  Finally, the algorithm outputs $(\mathsf{usk}, \mathsf{MSK}', \mathsf{tsk}')$.

- $\mathsf{HTKEMAC.Enc}(\mathsf{MPK}, X)$: parsing the public key $\mathsf{MPK} = (\mathsf{tpk}, \{\mathsf{pk}'_i\}_i)$ as an output of the Setup algorithm, and X as a set of indices of rights in Ω:
  1. denoting $\mathcal{K}$ the key space of KEM, the encryption algorithm draws $S \xleftarrow{\$} \mathcal{K}$, sets $r \leftarrow \mathcal{G}(S)$ and $(c_k \leftarrow r \odot P_k)_k$, and $c \leftarrow (c_k)_k$
  2. for each index $i \in X$, the algorithm sets $K_i \leftarrow \mathsf{NIKE.SessionKey}(r, H_i)$, $(E_i, K'_i) \leftarrow \mathsf{KEM.Enc}(\mathsf{pk}_i)$, and $E \leftarrow (E_\ell)_{\ell \in X}$;
  3. for each index $i \in X$, the algorithm sets $F_i \leftarrow S \oplus \mathcal{H}(K_i, K'_i, c, E)$, and $F \leftarrow (F_\ell)_{\ell \in X}$;
  4. the algorithm then computes $(K, V) \leftarrow \mathcal{J}(S, c, E, F)$, and sets the ciphertext as $C \leftarrow (c, E, F, V)$, and the encapsulated key to be K.

  The algorithm outputs (K, C).

- $\mathsf{HTKEMAC.Dec}(\mathsf{usk}, C)$: parsing usk as an output of the KeyGen algorithm, and $C = (c = (c_k)_k, E = (E_\ell)_\ell, F = (F_\ell)_\ell, V)$ as an output of the Enc algorithm, for a list of pairs (E_i, F_i), without knowing the corresponding keys. For each index i with such a pair (E_i, F_i) in C, and for each index $j \in Y$ with an element sk_j in usk, the decryption algorithm:
  1. runs $K'_{i,j} \leftarrow \mathsf{KEM.Dec}(\mathsf{sk}_j, E_i)$;
  2. computes $K_j \leftarrow \mathsf{NIKE.SessionKey}(x_j, \otimes_k (\beta_k \odot c_k))$;
  3. computes $S_{i,j} \leftarrow F_i \oplus \mathcal{H}(K_j, K'_{i,j}, c, E)$;
  4. computes both $r' \leftarrow \mathcal{G}(S_{i,j})$ and $(U'_{i,j}, V'_{i,j}) \leftarrow \mathcal{J}(S_{i,j}, c, E, F)$;
  5. checks whether $c = (r' \odot P_k)_k$ and $V'_{i,j} = V$: in the positive case, it returns $K \leftarrow U'_{i,j}$ and stops. Otherwise, it continues with the next pair (i, j).

  If for all indices i and j, no key was returned, the algorithm returns $\perp$.

The reader can check the correctness, when $X \cap Y \neq \emptyset$, using a common element.

3.2 Security Analysis

Let us prove the CCA security for the HTKEMAC scheme, for both session-key privacy and access-control privacy.

Session-Key Privacy. For the session-key privacy, we consider the SK-IND-CCA-game, where the adversary has access to the decryption oracle, excepted on the challenge ciphertext: HTKEMAC is said to be SK-IND-CCA-secure in the key space $\mathcal{K}$ if for any adversary $\mathcal{A}$, that can ask:

- any key usk, for access rights Y under user U, using the oracle $\mathcal{O}\mathsf{KeyGen}(U,Y)$ that outputs HTKEMAC.KeyGen(MSK, U,Y),
- any decryption on ciphertext C under access rights Y, using the oracle $\mathcal{O}\mathsf{Dec}(Y,C)$ that first gets usk from HTKEMAC.KeyGen(MSK, U,Y), and then outputs HTKEMAC.Dec(usk, C),
- and one ciphertext on any access rights X^*, using the oracle $\mathcal{O}\mathsf{EncChal}(X^*)$ that runs HTKEMAC.Enc(MPK, X^*) to get (C^*, K_0^*), chooses $K_1^* \xleftarrow{\$} \mathcal{K}$, and outputs (C^*, K_b^*), for the initial random bit b,

$\mathsf{Adv}^{\mathsf{sk-ind-cca}}_{\mathsf{HTKEMAC}}(\mathcal{A})$ is negligible in the security game presented on the left of Fig. 1, where the 4-th line is more precisely:

4. if there is a Y, either asked to $\mathcal{O}\mathsf{KeyGen}$ or with (Y, C^*) asked to $\mathcal{O}\mathsf{Dec}$, such that $X^* \cap Y \neq \emptyset$, for X^* asked to $\mathcal{O}\mathsf{EncChal}$, then output a random bit $\beta \xleftarrow{\$} \{0,1\}$, else output $\beta \leftarrow (b' = b)$.

Theorem 1 (Session-Key Privacy against Chosen-Ciphertext Attacks). *HTKEMAC achieves SK-IND-CCA security under either the SK-IND-CCA security of the underlying KEM or the SK-OW of the underlying KH-NIKE, in the random oracle model for $\mathcal{G}$, $\mathcal{H}$, and $\mathcal{J}$.*

Proof. To make the proof of HTKEMAC, we start from the initial security game:

Game G_0: At setup time, it chooses all the secret keys associated to all the rights in Ω (including s and $(s_k)_k$ that will be known all along this proof, as their privacy will only be used for tracing).
- For the $\mathcal{O}\mathsf{EncChal}$ query on $X^* \subseteq \Omega$, we denote $C^* = (c^* = (c_k^*)_k, E^* = (E_\ell^*)_\ell, F^* = (F_\ell^*)_\ell, V^*)$ the challenge ciphertext, honestly generated on X^*, with $S^* \xleftarrow{\$} \mathcal{K}$, $r^* \leftarrow \mathcal{G}(S^*)$, $(K_i^* \leftarrow \mathsf{NIKE.SessionKey}(r^*, H_i))_i$, $((E_i^*, K_i'^*) \leftarrow \mathsf{KEM.Enc}(\mathsf{pk}_i))_i$, and $(F_i^* \leftarrow S^* \oplus \mathcal{H}(K_i^*, K_i'^*, c^*, E^*))_i$. Eventually, K^* will denote the claimed encapsulated key, that is either real or random.
- For the $\mathcal{O}\mathsf{KeyGen}$ queries, one first generates a random tuple $(\beta_k)_k$ such that $\sum_k \beta_k \cdot s_k = s$, and then concatenates the secret keys generated in the setup;
- For a decryption query $\mathcal{O}\mathsf{Dec}(Y, C)$: one first generates a random tuple $(\beta_k)_k$ such that $\sum_k \beta_k \cdot s_k = s$; for each $j \in Y$ and every E_i in the ciphertext, it runs $\mathsf{KEM.Dec}(\mathsf{sk}_j, E_i)$ to get $K'_{i,j}$ or $\perp$, as well as $K_j = \mathsf{NIKE.SessionKey}(x_j, \otimes(\beta_k \odot c_k))$ and computes the candidate $S_{i,j} = F_i \oplus \mathcal{H}(K_j, K'_{i,j}, c, E)$. It then computes both $r' \leftarrow \mathcal{G}(S_{i,j})$ and $U'_{i,j}\|V'_{i,j} \leftarrow \mathcal{J}(S_{i,j}, c, E, F)$, and checks whether $c = (r' \odot P_k)_k$ and $V'_{i,j} = V$. In the positive case, it returns $U'_{i,j}$, otherwise it continues on the i, j indices.

In the end, the adversary must guess whether K^* is real or random. Note that from the constraints on the $\mathcal{O}$KeyGen-queries and $\mathcal{O}$Dec-queries, for the former, the Y's are disjoint from X^*, and for the latter, if the ciphertext is exactly the challenge ciphertext C^*, then $Y \cap X^* = \emptyset$ too. We stress that if for a given ciphertext C, $c = c^*$, then under the assumption public keys of NIKE have a huge entropy (negligible probability of collisions), and the absence of collisions for $\mathcal{G}$, $S = S^*$, to ensure the validity of the test $c^* = c = (r' \odot P_k)_k$ for $r' \leftarrow \mathcal{G}(S)$. Without having asked any of the challenge $\mathcal{H}$ queries, and thus on correct $(K_i^*, K_i'^*)$, S^* is hidden and the final check with $\mathcal{J}(S^*, c^*, E, F)$ would fail. This will be the intuition all along this proof.

Game G_1: In this game, for decryption queries, we stop and continue looping on the i, j indices if $\mathcal{J}(S_{i,j}, c, E, F)$ has not already been asked by the adversary. Indeed, without such query $V'_{i,j} = V$ would likely fail, as it cannot come from the challenge ciphertext. This makes no difference from the previous game. We stress that such $\mathcal{J}$ queries are specific to each ciphertext query.

Game G_2: As a consequence, for a decryption query C, we can enumerate on all the candidates S asked to $\mathcal{J}$, with answers U', V', and $S \leftarrow \mathcal{G}(S)$ such that $c = (r' \odot P_k)_k$ and $V' = V$. For each of these promising candidates S, and for each $j \in Y$, one computes $K_j \leftarrow$ NIKE.SessionKey(r', H_j), and for $K'_{i,j} \leftarrow$ KEM.Dec(sk_j, E_i). Then one eventually checks whether $S = F_i \oplus \mathcal{H}(K_j, K'_{i,j}, c, E)$. When it works for one candidate S and one index $j \in Y$, one returns U' as the decapsulated key. This makes no difference with the previous game as we were already expecting the $\mathcal{J}$-queries to be asked.

Game G_3: During the challenge ciphertext, we replace $\mathcal{H}(K_i^*, K'^*_i, c^*, E^*)$ by a random value, for all the indices i. This can only be detected by the adversary if it asks for one of theses $\mathcal{H}$-queries. We thus denotes AskH the event that some of these $\mathcal{H}$-queries is asked. Hence, unless event AskH happens, this game is perfectly indistinguishable from the previous one. We will now show this event is negligible.

Lemma 1. *Denoting the two events following events, during the above game,*

- Ev *the event that some* NIKE *key* K_i^* *generated during the challenge generation has been queried to the hash function* $\mathcal{H}(K_i^*, *, *, *)$ *by the adversary;*
- Ev' *the event that some* KEM *key* K'^*_i *generated during the challenge generation has been queried to the hash function* $\mathcal{H}(*, K'^*_i, *, *)$.

we can state that

- *if* Ev *is non-negligible, one can break the* SK-OW *security of* NIKE;
- *if* Ev' *is non-negligible, one can break the* SK-IND-CCA *security of* KEM.

We postpone the proof of this lemma to the end of the proof of Theorem 1. But as we clearly have AskH $\Rightarrow$ Ev and AskH $\Rightarrow$ Ev', if AskH would be non-negligible, then one could break both SK-OW security of NIKE and SK-IND-CCA security of KEM. Hence, AskH is negligible.

Game G_4: Eventually, we can replace all the F_i^*'s by random strings in $\{0,1\}^{2\kappa}$, for each index $i \in X^*$, in the challenge ciphertext. As in the previous game, they were all computed from S^* masked by truly independent random values, this makes no difference.

In this game, S^* is not used anymore, and thus, the probability to ask the $\mathcal{J}$-query is negligible: K^* is unpredictable. Hence, the advantage of the adversary in this last game is negligible, which concludes the proof.

□

Let us now prove the Lemma 1.

Proof (Proof of Lemma 1). Intuitively, for Ev to happen, the adversary must be able to break the SK-OW security of NIKE, and for Ev' to happen, the adversary must be able to break the SK-IND-CCA security of KEM. We thus split the proof according to these two cases.

Case 1: if Ev *is non-negligible, one can break the* SK-OW *security of* NIKE. We thus describe the simulation $\mathcal{B}$ of the challenger of the SK-IND-CCA of HTKEMAC in front of the adversary $\mathcal{A}$, using a challenger $\mathcal{C}$ of the SK-OW of NIKE. Eventually, the combination of $\mathcal{B}$ and $\mathcal{A}$ will be an adversary against the SK-OW security of NIKE. It will not exploit the output guess of the adversary $\mathcal{A}$, but the occurrence of event Ev.

From the SK-OW challenger $\mathcal{C}$, the simulator $\mathcal{B}$ receives two public keys (A, R) coming from $(A, a), (R, r) \leftarrow$ NIKE.KeyGen(1^κ). Its goal is to find $K =$ NIKE.SessionKey(a, R) = NIKE.SessionKey(r, A).

First, before the setup, the simulator $\mathcal{B}$ guesses for which index $I \in X^* \subseteq \Omega$, the event Ev happens (*i.e.*, K_I^* is queried to $\mathcal{H}$). As the real challenger would do, $\mathcal{B}$ generates all the secret keys s, $(s_k)_k$, and $(\mathsf{pk}_i, \mathsf{sk}_i)_i$, for all the rights in Ω. It also generates all the NIKE keys honestly, as $(X_i, x_i) \leftarrow$ NIKE.KeyGen(1^κ), excepted $X_I \leftarrow A$ that comes from the SK-OW challenger $\mathcal{C}$. During the generation of the challenge ciphertext, $\mathcal{B}$ first runs by itself $(E_i^*, K'^*_i) \leftarrow$ KEM.Enc(pk_i). After the choice of S^*, we implicitly set $r^* \leftarrow r/s$, as the output of the hash function $\mathcal{G}(S^*)$. Note that this is the reason why s must be invertible in $\mathcal{R}$. Then, we set $c_k^* \leftarrow (s_k/s) \odot R$, which is the correct value, as $(s_k/s) \odot R = (s_k \cdot r/s) \odot P = r^* \odot (s_k \cdot P) = r^* \odot P_k$. For the K_i^*'s, we do not need to explicitly compute $\mathcal{H}(K_i^*, K'^*_i, c^*, E^*)$, to mask S^* in the F_i's, as is has been replaced by a random value.

We stress that in this case, no information leaks about S^*, and whereas we do not know the answer, we should never be asked for $\mathcal{G}(S^*)$. Similarly, we should never be asked for $\mathcal{J}(S^*, c, E, F)$. Thus the above simulation of decapsulation queries can be used by $\mathcal{B}$, exploiting the knowledge of the sk_i's. This makes $\mathcal{A}$ behaving exactly as in an SK-IND-CCA game, until event Ev happens. And we actually do not care whether the simulation is not perfect after event Ev is raised.

As we assumed Ev to be non-negligible, in the initial game, it is still in this game: when $\mathcal{A}$ stops (or after a pre-determined polynomial-time limit) we can output a random element queried to $\mathcal{H}$. If Ev happened and the guess I

was correct, we output the correct value $K = K_I^*$ with non-negligible probability: the success probability is $\Pr[\mathsf{Ev}]/qn$ where n is the size of Ω (for the guess of I) and q the number of $\mathcal{H}$ queries (for the guess of the query). If Ev is non-negligible, we have built an efficient adversary (the combination of our simulator $\mathcal{B}$ and the adversary $\mathcal{A}$) against the SK-OW of NIKE. Indeed, $K_I^* = \mathsf{NIKE.SessionKey}(r^*, H_I) = \mathsf{NIKE.SessionKey}(r/s, s \odot X_I)$, which is equal to $\mathsf{NIKE.SessionKey}(r, X_I) = \mathsf{NIKE.SessionKey}(r, A)$.

Case 2: if Ev' is non-negligible, one can break the SK-IND-CCA security of KEM. We thus describe the simulation $\mathcal{B}$ of the challenger of the SK-IND-CCA of HTKEMAC in front of the adversary $\mathcal{A}$, using a challenger $\mathcal{C}$ of the SK-IND-CCA of KEM. Eventually, the combination of $\mathcal{B}$ and $\mathcal{A}$ will be an adversary against the SK-IND-CCA security of KEM. Again, it will not exploit the output guess of the adversary $\mathcal{A}$, but the occurrence of event Ev'.

First, the simulator $\mathcal{B}$ guesses for which index $I \in X^* \subseteq \Omega$, the event Ev' happens (K'^*_I is queried to $\mathcal{H}$). As the real challenger would do, $\mathcal{B}$ generates all the secret keys s, $(s_k)_k$, and $(X_i, x_i)_i$, for all the rights in Ω.

It also generates all the KEM keys honestly, as $(\mathsf{pk}_i, \mathsf{sk}_i) \leftarrow \mathsf{KEM.KeyGen}(1^\kappa)$, excepted pk_I that comes from the SK-IND-CCA challenger $\mathcal{C}$. During the generation of the challenge ciphertext, $\mathcal{B}$ first runs by itself $(E_i^*, K'^*_i) \leftarrow \mathsf{KEM.Enc}(\mathsf{pk}_i)$, excepted for $(E_I^* = E, K)$ that comes from the SK-IND-CCA challenger $\mathcal{C}$, if $I \in X^*$, with K that is either real or random. After the choice of S^*, $\mathcal{B}$ can generate r^* and $(c_k^*)_k$. But eventually, we can choose random values instead of $\mathcal{H}(K_i^*, K'^*_i, c^*, E^*)$, to mask S^* in the F_i's, as in the previous case.

This simulation of the challenge ciphertext by $\mathcal{B}$ makes no difference to the adversary unless it asks for some $\mathcal{H}(K_i^*, K'^*_i, c^*, E^*)$, for the real value K'^*_i. Then, the above simulation of decapsulation queries can be used by $\mathcal{B}$, exploiting the knowledge of the sk_i's, and K as the decapsulation of E_I^* under unknown sk_I. Indeed,

- if E_I^* is not involved, the simulation is easy, as in the previous game, possibly asking the decapsulation oracle under sk_I^* from the SK-IND-CCA security game against KEM.
- If E_I^* is involved, one uses K as the decapsulation of E_I^*.

In the real case, the simulation is perfect, as we decrypt E_I^* into the correct session key, until event Ev' happens. And we actually do not care whether the simulation is not perfect after event Ev' is raised. In the random case, the probability to ask K is negligible, as K is random and with no leakage. One may only reject a valid ciphertext if $\mathcal{H}(K_I, K'^*_I, c, E)$ has been queried, with correct K'^*_I. When the game ends (or after a pre-determined polynomial-time limit), the simulator $\mathcal{B}$ stops and outputs its answer (its guess whether K is real or random) against the SK-IND-CCA challenge of KEM as follows: if K has been queried to $\mathcal{H}$, then the simulator outputs 1 (meaning this is the real key); otherwise, it outputs a random bit.

If we are in an execution with event Ev' for $I \in X^*$, the simulator outputs 1 in the real case, but a random bit in the random case. In any situation, in the random case, the probability for K to have been queried is negligible, as it is random with no leakage, and so a random bit will be returned. So the advantage of our distinguisher (the combination of $\mathcal{B}$ and $\mathcal{A}$) is at least $\Pr[\mathsf{Ev}']/n$, where n is the size of Ω. If Ev' is non-negligible, we have built a successful distinguisher against the SK-IND-CCA security of KEM. □

Access-Control Privacy. In addition, we want to hide the set X^* used in the ciphertext C^*. More precisely, HTKEMAC is said to be AC-IND-CCA-secure if for any adversary $\mathcal{A}$, that can ask any key usk, for access rights Y, under user U, using oracle $\mathcal{O}\mathsf{KeyGen}(U,Y)$, and any decryption on ciphertext C under access rights Y, using oracle $\mathcal{O}\mathsf{Dec}(Y,C)$, as above, and one ciphertext on (X_0^*, X_1^*), using $\mathcal{O}\mathsf{EncChal}(X_0^*, X_1^*)$, that runs HTKEMAC.Enc(MPK, X_b^*) to get (C^*, K^*), for the initial random bit b, $\mathsf{Adv}_{\mathsf{HTKEMAC}}^{\mathsf{ac\text{-}ind\text{-}cca}}(\mathcal{A})$ is negligible in the security game presented on the right of Fig. 1, where the 4-th line is more precisely:

4. if $|X_0^*| \neq |X_1^*|$ or there is an Y, either asked to $\mathcal{O}\mathsf{KeyGen}$ or with (Y, C^*) asked to $\mathcal{O}\mathsf{Dec}$, such that $X_0^* \cap Y \neq \emptyset$ or $X_1^* \cap Y \neq \emptyset$, for the pair (X_0^*, X_1^*) asked to $\mathcal{O}\mathsf{EncChal}$ then output a random bit $\beta \xleftarrow{\$} \{0,1\}$, else output $\beta \leftarrow (b' = b)$.

We stress that the last step excludes trivial attacks, where the adversary would be able to check the challenge session key that helps to break privacy. As our ciphertexts are linear in X, the sets X_0^* and X_1^* must be of same sizes to expect privacy.

Theorem 2 (Access-Control Privacy against Chosen-Ciphertext Attacks). HTKEMAC *achieves* AC-IND-CCA-*security under the* PK-IND-CCA *security of* KEM, *the* SK-IND-CCA *security of* KEM, *and the* SK-OW *security of* NIKE, *in the random oracle model for* $\mathcal{G}$, $\mathcal{H}$, *and* $\mathcal{J}$.

Proof. To make the proof of HTKEMAC, we start from the initial security game:

Game G_0: At setup time, the simulator of the challenger will generate all the secret keys, including s and $(s_k)_k$ that will be known all along this proof, as their privacy will only be used for tracing. Then, we denote $C^* = (c^* = (c_k^*)_k, E^* = (E_\ell^*)_\ell, F^* = (F_\ell^*)_\ell, V^*)$ the challenge ciphertext, and K^* the encapsulated key, for the random bit b. For the $\mathcal{O}\mathsf{KeyGen}$ and $\mathcal{O}\mathsf{Dec}$ queries, one uses the secret keys. In the end, the adversary must guess whether X_0^* or X_1^* has been used to generate C^* (the bit b).

Game G_1: As in the previous proof, under the SK-IND-CCA of KEM and/or SK-OW of NIKE, Ev or Ev' is negligible, and so we can replace F_i^*'s by random values. This makes no difference to the adversary: S^* is perfectly hidden.

Game G_2: As S^* is hidden, any E_i^* involved during a decapsulation query can be safely skipped: without previous call to $\mathcal{H}(K_i, K_i'^*, c, E)$, the computed S will be random and then rejected by the $\mathcal{J}$-query. So during the simulation of the decapsulation queries, we skip the cases that involve an E_i^*. So only new ciphertexts can be queried under the keys from X_0^* or X_1^*.

Game G_3: As $|X_0^*| = |X_1^*|$, we can define a bijection B from X_0^* to X_1^*, where the common elements match with themselves, and different elements match with new elements. Now, we can make an hybrid sequence, where we change the public keys from X_b^* by the keys from X_0^*: in the k-th step of the sequence, we change E_k^* (involving pk_k from X_0^* or pk_k' from X_1^*, where we have previously guessed, during the setup, the two rights that will correspond to pk_k and pk_k', so that they are provided by the PK-IND-CCA-challenger), which is indistinguishable under the PK-IND-CCA security of KEM. Note that the difference between X_k from X_0^* and X_k' from X_1^* only impacts K_k^* which is never queried (as Ev is negligible, under SK-OW of NIKE). Again, we can always use the decryption oracle under pk_k from X_0^* or pk_k' from X_1^*, as E_k^* will never be queried during the simulation. At the end of the sequence, all the public keys are from X_0^*.

In this last game, the challenge ciphertext does not depend on b anymore: the adversary has zero-advantage. This concludes the proof. □

We can stress that the security analysis still holds even if we compute $F_i \leftarrow S \oplus \mathcal{H}(K_i, K'_i)$, as this still raises event AskH, in the above simulations. In the next section, we detail both implementations, with and without the ciphertext in the hash function $\mathcal{H}$.

Traceability. [6] already provided a traceable analysis in a black-box way, with only confirmation of traitors, following [3], when $\mathcal{R}$ is a field $\mathbb{F}$, and then $\mathbb{F}^t$ is a vector space of dimension t over $\mathbb{F}$.

Actually, as explained in [3], from n keys $\boldsymbol{\beta}_i = (\beta_{i,k})_k \in \mathbb{F}^t$, that satisfy $s = \boldsymbol{\beta}_i \cdot \boldsymbol{s}$, any new key that must satisfy the same relation can only be a convex combination, unless one can break the hardness of finding secret keys from public keys. And in the particular case of NIKE, this would break the SK-OW security.

Following [3] (and [6]), any collusion of less than t traitors can be confirmed in a black-box way: if we have a set of possible traitors in mind, we can confirm, whether this guess is correct or not, just by interacting with the pirate decoder.

Using multiples of codewords, from a specific linear space tracing code [3] for the secret keys $(\beta_{i,k})_k \in \mathbb{F}^t$, and the Berlekamp algorithm for decoding, any collusion of less than $t/2$ traitors can be efficiently traced in a white-box way: from the key $(\gamma_k)_k \in \mathbb{F}^t$ used by the pirate decoder, we can find the convex combination used to build it, and then know the keys used.

3.3 Covercrypt: an Efficient HTKEMAC with Hybrid CCA Security

In the ETSI standard [12], Covercrypt is proposed as a special case of HTKEMAC, with ECDH on any curve $\mathbb{G}$ of prime order p, spanned by a generator P, for the KH-NIKE, whose SK-OW security relies on the CDH, and ML-KEM [14] that is both SK-IND-CCA and PK-IND-CCA-secure under the DMLWE.

4 Access Structure

The previous sections focused on a specific case of ABE, where both keys and ciphertexts are associated to sets of rights, and decapsulation is possible if and only if the intersection of the two sets is not empty. However, a Ciphertext-Policy Attribute-Based Encryption (CP-ABE) should handle more general policies. For that, the ETSI standard describes a way to derive sets of rights from more advances policies, but more details are required for the implementation. We thus recall the general approach, and the rules to derive the sets of rights from the access structure. Some additional information is given to achieve backward compatibility after the evolution of some rights or with more users. Our implementation follows this approach.

4.1 High-Level Description

Let us first start with an example to illustrate the global approach, with an access structure described by three families, later called **dimensions**: CTR={EN, FR}, to deal with the countries England and France; DPT={DEV,MKG}, for the Development and Marketing departments, and SEC=(LOW,MED,HIG), for a hierarchy of security levels.

This defines the following **qualified attributes** along the 3 dimensions: along CTR, we have CTR::EN and CTR::FR; along DPT, we have DPT::DEV and DPT::MKG, and along SEC, we have SEC::LOW, SEC::MED, and SEC::HIG.

The two first dimensions CTR and DPT are defined by unordered sets (using {...}), whereas the last security level SEC is defined by an ordered set (using (...)), meaning that a user with the SEC::HIG attribute also possesses the SEC::LOW and SEC::MED qualified attributes, as SEC::HIG $\Rightarrow$ SEC::MED $\Rightarrow$ SEC::LOW, or equivalently SEC::LOW $\leq$ SEC::MED $\leq$ SEC::HIG, whereas attributes within the dimensions CTR and DPT are incomparable.

For backward compatibility reason, in each dimension, we introduce the *empty* attribute, leading to the qualified attributes CTR::, DPT:: and SEC::. This will indeed allow to dynamically add dimensions in the future, without having to re-encrypt all the data: new users' keys will remain compatible with the existing ciphertexts, as they will implicitly associate the empty attribute to the new dimensions. In addition, the empty attribute is smaller than any attribute in the same dimension: SEC:: $\Leftarrow$ SEC::LOW, and CTR:: $\Leftarrow$ CTR::EN as well as DPT:: $\Leftarrow$ DPT::MKG.

A **right** is a combination of attributes. Such a right is **valid** when represented as a conjunction of attributes if it involves (some or none) attributes of different dimensions only. One can then define Ω as the set of valid rights, that will be enough and necessary to define expected monotonous access policies in the specific context. In the general case, Ω contains all the possible combinations: this includes fully defined rights, such as CTR::FR && DPT::MKG && SEC::MED in the 3-dimension space, but also partially defined rights, such as CTR::FR which is equivalent to CTR::FR && DPT:: && SEC:: or SEC::HIG, equivalent to CTR:: && DPT:: && SEC::HIG.

These expansions will be used to optimize the ciphertext size: we expect a ciphertext for the right CTR::FR to be decapsulated by users with various rights, such as CTR::FR && DPT::DEV, CTR::FR && DPT::MKG && SEC::MED, and more. The sets X and Y will have to be carefully derived to allow decapsulation of a ciphertext under X by a user key under Y if and only if $X \cap Y \neq \emptyset$.

On the one hand, when one expresses the access policy for a given ciphertext, by any monotonous Boolean formula F, it can be converted into its Disjunctive Normal Form (DNF), that is a disjunction of (conjunctive) clauses. Such conjunctive clauses are exactly the above valid rights. The ciphertext will be associated to all the rights/clauses in the DNF, whereas the user's key will be associated to all the rights/clauses owned by the user, and the initial universe Ω will contain all the meaningful rights. We will define Ω to optimize the size of the ciphertext. In particular, all the possible combinations is a good choice in the most natural cases, where the number of clauses should be not so large.

The ordering along each dimension can be extended to a partial ordering between the rights, when the order is the same along each dimension.

Rule 1, from F to X: Once the Boolean formula F associated to a ciphertext has been converted into a list of clauses (DNF), one first removes the smaller clauses, and only keeps the remaining greater clauses for X.

If some clause CTR::FR && SEC::MED (completed into CTR::FR && DPT:: && SEC::MED, because of the empty dimension DPT::) is among those remaining clauses in X, for encrypting the ciphertext, Alice should be able to decapsulate it if she owns any right that is equal or greater than this right, which means:

CTR::FR && DPT::MKG && SEC::MED, CTR::FR && DPT::DEV && SEC::MED, CTR::FR && DPT::MKG && SEC::HIG, CTR::FR && DPT::DEV && SEC::HIG.

Hence, on the other hand, when generating keys for Alice, if she is explicitly given any of these 4 above rights, she should also implicitly own the right CTR::FR && DPT:: && SEC::MED to be able to decapsulate the above ciphertext without having to include more rights than the minimal ones in the ciphertext.

Rule 2, rights in Y (first hint): A user with explicit right R should also receive all the rights R' that are smaller than R in the partial order.

Furthermore, a missing dimension in such an explicit user's right R means "no restriction along this dimension". Then theses missing dimensions can be completed by any value: if Alice is given explicit right CTR::FR && SEC::MED, with no DPT restriction, she should be able to decapsulate any ciphertext with lower security level, or no security level (as SEC:: $\Leftarrow$ SEC::LOW $\Leftarrow$ SEC::MED) and CTR::FR, whatever DPT is.

Rule 2, rights in Y: A user with explicit right R should also receive all the rights R' that are smaller than R, and these rights $R' \Leftarrow R$ should also be completed by any value in the empty dimensions of R.

This is the main idea behind the optimization of the ciphertext size and the definition of the user-key rights, that are formalized in the full version of the paper [7].

Dynamic Access Structure and Users. Covercrypt [12] has been designed to allow a dynamic evolution of the access structure, by adding new dimensions, or new attributes in existing dimensions, as well as new users, without having to re-encrypt all the data. The specification precises when users' keys have to be renewed or refreshed, after some modification of the access structure. But in order not to loose old rights on old ciphertexts, our implementation considers users' secret keys as sets of keys for each right, keeping the old keys for the old rights, and adding new keys for the new rights. For decryption, the user tries each encapsulation against each secret for the current time period. If there is no matching, he tries again with the secrets for the previous time period, etc. For efficiency reasons, one could truncate each set of keys for each right.

4.2 Efficiency Considerations

It is easy to see that the running-time of a Covercrypt encapsulation is linear in the size of the target access policy: $T_{enc} = O(|X|)$.

However, in order to guarantee the policy-privacy and the attribute-hiding properties, in addition to the indistinguishability of the public keys, we need to avoid leakage during decryption: in our implementation, the rights in X and Y are first randomly permuted, so that timing attacks cannot help guessing which right has led to the decryption. However, as we stop as soon as decryption succeeds, the decryption time is not constant, but depends on the number of rights in X and Y, and the size of the $X \cap Y$:

$$E(T_{dec}^{cc}) = \left(\frac{|Y| - |X \cap Y|}{|X \cap Y| + 1} + \frac{1}{2} \right) \cdot |X| \cdot T_u.$$

More details can be found in the the full version of the paper [7].

5 Experimental Results

We have implemented the standard [12] in Rust, with additional features[1]. It uses the ml-kem library[2] and Diffie-Hellman, as well as SHA3 for the hash function. Thanks to the black-box design, we propose ML-KEM 512 or 768, and Diffie-Hellman on Ristretto255 (built on top of Curve25519) or P-256. More schemes can be easily added. Timings reported in Table 1 were measured on an Intel(R) Xeon(R) CPU @ 2.30GHz and correspond to a Covercrypt encapsulation and decapsulation, with ML-KEM 512 and Ristretto255, for a 32-byte symmetric key in function of $|X|$ and $|Y|$, with $|X \cap Y|$ growing one-by-one with the increase in $|Y|$ from 1 to $|X|$: the darker is the cell, the larger is the intersection, from 1 to 5. A comparison with timings measured using the GPSW pairing-based KEM [13] is also provided[3].

---

[1] https://github.com/Cosmian/cover_crypt/releases/tag/v15.0.0.
[2] https://docs.rs/ml-kem/latest/ml_kem/.
[3] https://github.com/Cosmian/abe_gpsw.

Table 1. Comparisons of Covercrypt and GPSW encapsulation/decapsulation times. For decapsulation, GPSW has a constant runtime of approximately 3880 µs.

Size of X	1	2	3	4	5
Covercrypt	271	378	515	652	794
[6] (CPA only)	191	272	329	401	487
GPSW KEM	4793	5431	6170	6607	7245

Covercrypt encapsulation time (in µs)

$\|Y\| \downarrow \ \backslash \ \|X\| \rightarrow$	1	2	3	4	5
12 [6] (CPA only)	508	896	1276	1688	2062
12	1100	1922	2640	3420	4360
18	1515	1520	2429	3214	4304
24	1908	2022	1955	2780	3547
30	2380	2324	2370	2394	3484
36	2828	2891	2776	2829	2817

$\|X \cap Y\|$	1	2	3	4	5

Covercrypt decapsulation time (in µs)

The CCA version is about twice as slow as the CPA version due to reliance on the Fujisaki-Okamoto transform both on the pre- and post-quantum encapsulations. Part of the slowdown can also be explained by the change of the underlying Kyber library. The change of the curve, from Ristretto255 to P-256, introduces a multiplicative factor between 3 and 4 in the encapsulation and decapsulation times. All the benches can be run from the GitHub repository[4].

Conclusion

This paper presented a formal security analysis of the Covercrypt scheme, as standardized by ETSI [12], a quantum-safe hybrid Key Encapsulation Mechanism designed for hidden access policies. Because of the anonymity property, the ciphertext cannot be constant-size, and we demonstrated the effectiveness of our approach in achieving strong security guarantees while maintaining efficiency: quite short ciphertexts, fast encapsulation and decapsulation, and a small number of public parameters.

Acknowledgments. This work was supported in part by the France 2030 ANR Project ANR-22-PECY-003 SecureCompute. Paola de Perthuis was supported by the NWO Gravitation Project QSC and the ERC Starting Grant 947821 (ARTICULATE).

---

[4] https://github.com/Cosmian/cover_crypt/releases/tag/v15.0.0.

References

1. Bellare, M., Boldyreva, A., Desai, A., Pointcheval, D.: Key-privacy in public-key encryption. In: Boyd, C. (ed.) ASIACRYPT 2001. LNCS, vol. 2248, pp. 566–582. Springer, Heidelberg (2001). https://doi.org/10.1007/3-540-45682-1_33
2. Bellare, M., Desai, A., Pointcheval, D., Rogaway, P.: Relations among notions of security for public-key encryption schemes. In: Krawczyk, H. (ed.) CRYPTO 1998. LNCS, vol. 1462, pp. 26–45. Springer, Heidelberg (1998). https://doi.org/10.1007/BFb0055718
3. Boneh, D., Franklin, M.: An efficient public key traitor tracing scheme. In: Wiener, M. (ed.) CRYPTO 1999. LNCS, vol. 1666, pp. 338–353. Springer, Heidelberg (1999). https://doi.org/10.1007/3-540-48405-1_22
4. Boneh, D., et al.: Fully key-homomorphic encryption, arithmetic circuit abe and compact garbled circuits. In: Nguyen, P.Q., Oswald, E. (eds.) EUROCRYPT 2014. LNCS, vol. 8441, pp. 533–556. Springer, Heidelberg (2014). https://doi.org/10.1007/978-3-642-55220-5_30
5. Bos, J.W., et al.: CRYSTALS - kyber: A CCA-secure module-lattice-based KEM. In: 2018 IEEE European Symposium on Security and Privacy. pp. 353–367. IEEE Computer Society Press (Apr 2018). https://doi.org/10.1109/EuroSP.2018.00032
6. Brézot, T., de Perthuis, P., Pointcheval, D.: Covercrypt: an efficient early-abort KEM for hidden access policies with traceability from the DDH and LWE. In: Tsudik, G., Conti, M., Liang, K., Smaragdakis, G. (eds.) ESORICS 2023, Part I. LNCS, vol. 14344, pp. 372–392. Springer, Cham (2023). https://doi.org/10.1007/978-3-031-50594-2_19
7. Brézot, T., Hébant, C., de Perthuis, P., Pointcheval, D.: Security analysis of covercrypt: A quantum-safe hybrid key encapsulation mechanism for hidden access policies. Cryptology ePrint Archive, Paper 2025/544 (2025). https://eprint.iacr.org/2025/544
8. Chor, B., Fiat, A., Naor, M.: Tracing traitors. In: Desmedt, Y.G. (ed.) CRYPTO 1994. LNCS, vol. 839, pp. 257–270. Springer, Heidelberg (1994). https://doi.org/10.1007/3-540-48658-5_25
9. Cini, V., Wee, H.: Unbounded ABE for circuits from LWE, revisited. In: Chung, K.M., Sasaki, Y. (eds.) ASIACRYPT 2024, Part IV. LNCS, vol. 15487, pp. 238–267. Springer, Singapore (2024). https://doi.org/10.1007/978-981-96-0894-2_8
10. Dai, W., et al.: Implementation and evaluation of a lattice-based key-policy ABE scheme. IEEE Trans. Inf. Forensics Secur. **13**(5), 1169–1184 (2018)
11. Driscoll, F., Parsons, M., Hale, B.: Terminology for Post-Quantum Traditional Hybrid Schemes (Jan 2025). https://datatracker.ietf.org/doc/draft-ietf-pquip-pqt-hybrid-terminology/
12. ETSI: TS 104 015: Efficient Quantum-Safe Hybrid Key Exchanges with Hidden Access Policies (Feb 2025), cyber Security (CYBER); Quantum-Safe Cryptography (QSC). https://www.etsi.org/deliver/etsi_ts/104000_104099/104015/01.01.01_60/ts_104015v010101p.pdf
13. Goyal, V., Pandey, O., Sahai, A., Waters, B.: Attribute-based encryption for fine-grained access control of encrypted data. In: Juels, A., Wright, R.N., De Capitani di Vimercati, S. (eds.) ACM CCS 2006, pp. 89–98. ACM Press (Oct / Nov 2006).https://doi.org/10.1145/1180405.1180418, available as Cryptology ePrint Archive Report 2006/309
14. NIST: Module-Lattice-Based Key-Encapsulation Mechanism Standard (2022). https://nvlpubs.nist.gov/nistpubs/fips/nist.fips.203.pdf

15. Okamoto, T., Takashima, K.: Fully secure unbounded inner-product and attribute-based encryption. In: Wang, X., Sako, K. (eds.) ASIACRYPT 2012. LNCS, vol. 7658, pp. 349–366. Springer, Heidelberg (2012). https://doi.org/10.1007/978-3-642-34961-4_22
16. Sahai, A., Waters, B.: Fuzzy identity-based encryption. In: Cramer, R. (ed.) EUROCRYPT 2005. LNCS, vol. 3494, pp. 457–473. Springer, Heidelberg (2005). https://doi.org/10.1007/11426639_27
17. Shoup, V.: A Proposal for an ISO Standard for Public Key Encryption (Dec 2001). https://shoup.net/papers/iso-2_1.pdf

Anamorphic Monero Transactions: The Threat of Bypassing Anti-money Laundering Laws

Adrian Cinal[✉], Przemysław Kubiak, Mirosław Kutyłowski, and Gabriel Wechta

NASK National Research Institute, Warsaw, Poland
{adrian.cinal,przemyslaw.kubiak,miroslaw.kutylowski,
gabriel.wechta}@nask.pl

Abstract. In this paper, we analyze the clash between privacy-oriented cryptocurrencies and emerging legal frameworks for combating financial crime, focusing in particular on the recent European Union regulations. We analyze Monero, a leading "privacy coin" and a major point of concern for crime-fighters, and study the scope of due diligence that must be exercised under the new law with regard to Monero trading platforms and how it translates to the technical capabilities of the Monero protocol. We both recognize flaws in the legislation and identify technical pitfalls threatening either the effective compliance of, say, Monero exchanges or the anonymity endeavour of Monero itself. Of independent interest is that we turn to anamorphic cryptography (marking one of the first practical applications of the concept) and leverage it to build a hidden transaction layer embedded in the Monero blockchain that obfuscates illegal money flow and circumvents transaction-level attempts at enforcing the EU law.

Keywords: Privacy coins · Anamorphic cryptography · Money laundering

1 Introduction

In the last decade, we have witnessed an emergence of cryptocurrency markets, and, although some level of maturity of the technology has been achieved, the upcoming years may still bring substantial changes to the crypto ecosystem. These will be driven by the growing concern about applications of cryptocurrencies to money laundering, illegal financial transfers, evading sanctions, etc. In particular, reports such as [8] suggest that anonymous cryptocurrencies, so-called "privacy coins," are increasingly being used by criminals. A possible response of state authorities to this threat might be a general ban on cryptocurrency trade; see, e.g., the decision of the People's Bank of China in 2021 outlawing virtual currency-related business activities. Before rushing to prohibition, however, opportunities for the economy, related to the use of cryptocurrencies, should be taken into account. For this reason, the European Union aims to find a compromise between strict rules eliminating pathology in cryptocurrency trading and keeping the market open for innovations. Unfortunately, building a simple legal framework for the extremely complex cryptocurrencies ecosystem (and the advanced cryptography involved in it) is a challenging task. Regardless of good intentions, regulating the market may fall short of the set goals, or worse: may have adverse effects.

1.1 Paper Contributions and Outline

We study the clash between privacy-preserving technologies as employed in cryptocurrencies and the law combating illegal financial trade. We specifically focus on the efforts of the regulators in Europe reflected in the recent crypto-assets regulation, MiCA [3], and the anti-money laundering directive, AML [2], but our core conclusions transfer to similar legislation elsewhere. We study the case of Monero (XMR), hailed as "the leading cryptocurrency focused on private and censorship-resistant transactions,"[1] and attempt to answer the following research questions:

> **RQ1**: Does the law discount privacy coins like Monero altogether, acknowledge and outlaw them, or open avenues for compliance without completely sacrificing the anonymity promises of the technology?
>
> **RQ2**: What are the technical solutions available in Monero today to comply with AML and MiCA and not sacrifice all anonymity?
>
> **RQ3**: Letter of the law notwithstanding, can provably air-tight controls be implemented for Monero today that could block illegal transactions and, if so, at what cost to user privacy?

As for **RQ1**, we argue in Sect. 2.1 that the law is overall vague and developed with cryptocurrencies like Bitcoin in mind and not a more technologically sophisticated Monero. Indeed, privacy-oriented cryptocurrencies are addressed in a single point (pertaining to trading platform operations) in MiCA [3] that only stipulates deanonymization of trading parties be possible. This, however, leaves the door open for compliance, if only mechanisms for such deanonymization and effective policies for their use can be identified in Monero today or developed in the future. We try to predict what case law will evolve out of the regulations and conclude that some form of *transaction-level auditing* [9] is likely to be settled upon. In Sects. 2.2 and 2.3, we then identify technical measures in the Monero protocol that can be expected to be used in implementing such auditing and map specific due diligence requirements onto them, thereby answering **RQ2**.[2] We do not explicate the exact framework for transaction-level auditing; instead,

---

[1] https://www.getmonero.org/get-started/what-is-monero/.
[2] Notably, we focus on Monero in its current form. Major updates, such as Seraphis and Jamtis, which have been work in progress for some years now but seem nowhere near completion, are out of scope.

we show that no matter how it is implemented, it will fail to keep track of transactions published by third parties on behalf of the criminals, cautioning against relying on it for financial oversight. Indeed, we consider an ideal-functionality adversary that can inspect *all* traffic sent from the criminal's machine and has access to auditing instruments afforded by Monero. We then give a construction, in Sects. 3 and 4, that enables the criminal's spending of moneroj[3] even in this extreme setting, thereby pointing to the futility of transaction-level auditing and partially answering **RQ3**. We finish by discussing a potential solution present in the Monero ecosystem, but conclude that, if applied at the required scale, it would substantially degrade Monero's privacy guarantees for *all* users, including non-EU residents. We conjecture that this cannot be avoided without substantial reworking of the Monero protocol, thus setting the direction of further Monero development. We devote most of the work to **RQ3** and, in answering it, develop what we call *anamorphic spending* that leverages *anamorphic signatures* [15] extended to the setting of ring signatures in order to thwart attempts at transaction-level auditing.

1.2 Notation

For the rest of the paper, let $\mathbb{G}$ denote the odd-order subgroup of the Edwards curve Ed25519. Let ℓ denote its (prime) order and G its distinguished generator. We write $u \cdot P$ to denote scalar multiplication of an elliptic curve point P by an integer u. We adopt the notation from [14] and use $\mathcal{H}_p$ and $\mathcal{H}_n$ to denote cryptographic hash functions mapping arbitrary strings to elliptic curve points in $\mathbb{G}$ and scalars in $\mathbb{Z}_\ell^*$, respectively.

2 European Legal System and Monero

This section gives an overview of the legal framework regulating the trade of cryptocurrencies in the European Union (EU), which is our main focus in this work, and introduces the relevant Monero features along the way. For details regarding the Monero protocol, see [1,14].

Before proceeding, note that the authors neither approve nor disapprove of the regulations in their current or future form. Instead, we aim to provide an account of the forseeable developments in the legislation and how it is being exercised, as well as provide a technical analysis of the capabilities and incapabilities of the underlying Monero system to comply with the law.

2.1 Markets in Crypto-Assets Regulation

The main legal act aiming to create a uniform and secure framework for the trade of *crypto-assets*[4] in the EU is Regulation 2023/1114 [3] on "markets in crypto-assets," or MiCA for short. We shall be concerned with *operating a trading*

---

[3] Units of the Monero currency.
[4] A crypto-asset is defined as "a digital representation of a value or a right that is able to be transferred and stored electronically using distributed ledger technology or similar technology" by [3]. In particular, this includes cryptocurrencies.

platform in the European Union (or wherever similar legislation may emerge) as defined in Article 3(1)(18) therein:

> *'operation of a trading platform for crypto-assets' means the management of ... systems, which bring together or facilitate the bringing together of multiple third-party purchasing and selling interests in crypto-assets ... in a way that results in a contract, either by exchanging crypto-assets for funds or by the exchange of crypto-assets for other crypto-assets.*

In particular, crypto *exchanges* fall into the category of trading platforms, even in the non-custodial setting, where they merely match asks and bids from an order book, and the actual trades get executed by the parties themselves without an intermediary.

Running a trading platform is regulated in Article 76 of MiCA [3], which requires that service providers

> *lay down, maintain and implement clear and transparent operating rules for the trading platform ... [that at least] set the approval processes, including customer due diligence requirements commensurate to the money laundering or terrorist financing risk presented by the applicant in accordance with Directive (EU) 2015/849, that are applied before admitting crypto-assets to the trading platform.*

Here, MICA [3] makes explicit reference to the "anti-money laundering" Directive 2015/849 [2], henceforth referred to simply as AML, giving legal grounds to obligating crypto trading platforms to exercise *due diligence* as defined by AML [2, Article 13(1)]:

> *Customer due diligence measures shall comprise:*
> *(a) identifying the customer and verifying the customer's identity ... obtained from a reliable and independent source;*
> *(b) identifying the beneficial owner and taking reasonable measures to verify that person's identity ...*
> *(c) assessing and, as appropriate, obtaining information on the purpose and intended nature of the business relationship;*
> *(d) conducting ongoing monitoring of the business relationship including scrutiny of transactions undertaken throughout the course of that relationship ...*

Möser [20] notes that, for Bitcoin, such customer due diligence could be exercised at the crypto-fiat boundary of the system, i.e., at an exchange platform, were it not for mixing services that obscure the transaction graph, preventing the identification of coin provenance (e.g., whether it is crime proceeds or not). In a privacy coin like Monero, however, the transaction graph is inherently secret (in a sense not much different from Bitcoin enhanced with mixing services), thereby making the utility of this kind of auditing questionable. At the same time, MiCA [3, Article 76(3)] reads:

The operating rules of the trading platform for crypto-assets shall prevent the admission to trading of crypto-assets that have an inbuilt anonymisation function unless the holders of those crypto-assets and their transaction history can be identified by the crypto-asset service providers operating a trading platform for crypto-assets.

This suggests that the only hope for Monero's survival on European trading platforms is effective technical measures for *transaction-level auditing* [9], where each trade involving Monero and at least one EU resident or legal person is inspected by the trading platform service provider (TPSP) according to AML's [2] due diligence rules. Indeed, many of the tools proposed in the literature for fighting cryptocurrency crime, such as tracing and blacklisting [19], cannot be applied to Monero unless transaction-level auditing is enforced. This answers **RQ1**.

In the following section, we identify existing mechanisms in Monero that could facilitate such oversight, assuming it to be a natural consequence of the existing legislation (and expecting it to soon be reflected either in case law or follow-up regulations). We do not give a concrete instantiation of an auditing framework, however; instead, we show that it cannot be effective no matter how it is implemented. For this, we show that even an all-powerful TPSP that inspects every single Monero transaction originating in the EU cannot be effective. We also remark that, in light of MiCA [3] being ambiguous about the TPSP's obligations, financial oversight institutions at member-state level could very well try to pursue a policy as stringent as this.

2.2 Anonymization Features of Monero

Monero uses a UTXO model, not unlike Bitcoin's, where each transaction points to heretofore unspent transaction outputs (UTXOs) as well as mints new UTXOs. A principal difference between Monero and, say, Bitcoin is that UTXOs are not directly addressed to *payment addresses*, which, in Monero, take the form $(K^v, K^s) \in \mathbb{G}^2$. Instead, a *one-time (stealth) address* $K^o \in \mathbb{G}$ is derived independently for each transaction output as

$$K^o = \mathcal{H}_n(r \cdot K^v) \cdot G + K^s,$$

where r is chosen uniformly at random from $\mathbb{Z}_\ell^*$ and $R = r \cdot G$ is published in the transaction.[5] Therefore, $S = r \cdot K^v$ is a Diffie-Hellman key that the recipient can recompute given R and their private *view key* k^v such that $K^v = k^v \cdot G$. The secret S shared between the sender and the recipient is also used to encrypt the output amount a as well a Pedersen commitment trapdoor x, both of which are later required to spend the output (see Sect. A for details on how the commitments are used). Spend authority is proved by signing the (hash of the) entire transaction with the *output key* $k^o = \mathcal{H}_n(k^v \cdot R) + k^s$, where k^s is

---

[5] We neglect the issue of diversification when multiple transaction outputs have the same recipient.

a private *spend key* such that $K^s = k^s \cdot G$. (Note that $K^o = k^o \cdot G$.) To hide the identity of the transaction's sender, a *ring signature* is used (see Sect. A) with $n-1$ *decoy* one-time addresses drawn at random from the Monero blockchain.

For each transaction input, the sender is also required by the protocol to reveal a *key image* $\tilde{K} = k^o \cdot \mathcal{H}_p(K^o)$ and prove consistency thereof. Monero nodes keep track of the set of revealed key images to detect and prevent *double-spending*, i.e., sending the same asset twice.

2.3 Transaction-Level Auditing in Monero

We now proceed to map the customer due diligence requirements defined by AML [2] and made applicable to, e.g., Monero exchanges by MiCA [3] onto the technical capabilities of Monero as it stands today, i.e., of Monero v0.18, thereby answering **RQ2**. The "scrutiny of transactions" from [2, Article 13(1)] is to be understood, in the broader context of the directive, as accounting for all transactions coming in to and going out from a user's permanent address (K^v, K^s), including their exact amounts.[6] True beneficiaries of outgoing transactions must also be identified. In the following paragraphs, we shall study these obligations one by one.

As argued in Sect. 2.1, it is natural to consider an edge case where an all-powerful TPSP acts as a watchdog, sitting between its clients and the public ledger, and inspects every transaction broadcast by or addressed to an EU citizen.[7] This could be seen as an ideal-functionality model for transaction-level auditing. We note that data collected this way (in compliance with AML) would be withheld from the public, thereby preserving anonymity in the eyes of other Monero network participants and making the policy seem a viable compromise between accountability and privacy. We must caution against relying on transaction-level auditing for MiCA [3] compliance, however. Indeed, below, we briefly identify mechanisms existing in Monero today that are natural candidates for implementing transaction-level auditing in such centralized, i.e., strongest possible, form, but follow this with a novel application of anamorphic cryptography that makes *all* transaction-level auditing attempts fail to detect transactions going out from the EU.

We keep the setting non-custodial assuming that (at least) the private spend key k^s remains solely with the client (and not the trading platform). Indeed, the directive [3] speaks of "ownership rights," and there exists a legal precedent in Europe to equate the owner of tokens to the "person who has the right to dispose of" them [6]. Importantly, however, we may consider, instead of a client and their trading platform service provider, an exchange subjected to a continuous audit by an external authority. Hiding the very fact of transacting or even just the truth about transaction amounts could allow such an exchange to, e.g., embezzle the funds escrowed with it without immediately revealing its insolvency. All reasoning that follows in Sects. 3 and 4 applies just the same to this case.

---

[6] Note that the platform service provider may be obligated by the law to disclose, e.g., to a revenue service, all transactions whose amounts exceed a certain threshold.

[7] In practice, the TPSP could block the transaction if not convinced of its legitimacy.

Finally, whenever we talk about identification of transaction's participants in this work, we are only concerned with finding their Monero addresses (K^v, K^s), thereby reducing the problem to the simpler case of identifying participants in, e.g., Bitcoin, for which there is extensive literature available [5,17,23].

Incoming Transactions with Amounts. A TPSP is obligated to analyze the transaction history of a client, hence, in particular, identify incoming assets. This can be achieved by disclosing the private view key k^v to the TPSP granting them insight into transactions sent to the client's payment address. The private view key also allows for the reconstruction of Diffie-Hellman keys $S = k^v \cdot R$ and the decryption of transaction amounts. We expect that, in light of MiCA [3], trading platforms will have a valid legal reason to request private view keys of their clients.

Outgoing Transactions with Amounts and True Beneficiaries. According to AML [2], a TPSP is obligated to identify the party originating a transaction as well as monitor the business relationship of the transaction participants. This also involves identification of the exact transaction amount and its true beneficiary. Identification of the amount is naturally achieved by disclosing to the TPSP the Diffie-Hellman key S that the sender computes as $r \cdot K^v$ for the recipient's view key K^v. A straightforward proof of equality of discrete logarithms can then be used to convince the TPSP that S corresponds to $R = r \cdot G$ (also included in the transaction) and K^v. Let $\mathsf{EqLog}_{G_1,\ldots,G_d}(K_1,\ldots,K_d)$ denote a non-interactive proof of equality of discrete logarithms of $K_1,\ldots,K_d$ to bases $G_1,\ldots,G_d$, respectively.[8] The sender can convince the TPSP that an output is addressed to (K^v, K^s) by presenting them with (S, π), where $\pi = \mathsf{EqLog}_{G,K^v}(R, S)$. Given this and the one-time address K^o of the output, the TPSP checks that $K^s = K^o - \mathcal{H}_n(S) \cdot G$ and verifies π. If both checks pass, the TPSP is convinced. This construction is referred to as an OutProof in [14]. Knowledge of S also immediately enables the TPSP to decrypt the transaction (output) amount.

One problem that remains to be addressed is that a user may hand the TPSP transactions originated by someone else. Since Monero uses ring signatures to authorize transactions, the TPSP's seeing in the ring a one-time address K^o corresponding to the client's permanent address (K^v, K^s) *does not* convince them that it is the client who is actually making a transfer. Any input in the ring could actually be getting spent in this transaction. The client should prove that the key image $\tilde{K}$ published in the transaction corresponds to K^o, i.e., that $\tilde{K} = k^o \cdot \mathcal{H}_p(K^o)$. This can be done by sending $\mathsf{EqLog}_{G,\mathcal{H}_p(K^o)}(K^o, \tilde{K})$ to the TPSP.[9]

---

[8] A description of such a proof can be found in [14, Section 3.1].
[9] A more complex proof for this is referred to as an UnspentProof in [14].

2.4 Pitfalls and Shortcomings

Having established the due diligence requirements following from [2,3], we will proceed to study the pitfalls awaiting implementers who turn to transaction-level auditing. Clearly, out-of-band channels, bypassing the TPSP, e.g., by means of a VPN, enable the evasion of transaction-level scrutiny. This could, in principle, be outlawed, but enforcing such ban would be non-trivial. We, however, choose to focus on a more fundamental problem, namely, that, even if a robust framework for transaction-level auditing is established and implements the above measures, it is *still* not enough to prevent money laundering or otherwise illegal transfers of moneroj (XMR). This result relies on the notion of *anamorphic cryptography* [15,21] and points to the futility of many regulatory efforts. Specifically, however the transaction-level auditing framework is implemented, even if every transaction broadcast by an EU citizen goes through the hands of the auditor (TPSP), then, still, in-band channels are available for criminals to send XMR offshore in a provably undetectable way.

Before proceeding, we also remark on a number of discrepancies between the legislation and the available technology. For one, in a privacy coin like Monero, the full provenance of funds can never be established, even if all EU residents are subjected to transaction-level auditing. This is due to transacting with non-EU residents. European platforms would have no legal grounds (nor technical capabilities) to request view keys or OutProof from foreign actors and so identifying incoming assets as, e.g., crime proceeds would remain impossible, all the while EU residents could not be held accountable for unsolicited reception of funds (note that Monero does not support any notion of a "refund"). This clashes with the intent of the lawmakers expressed in recital 77 of MiCA's [3] preamble:

> *In order to ensure the continued protection of the financial system of the Union against the risks of money laundering and terrorist financing, it is necessary to ensure that crypto-asset service providers carry out increased checks on financial operations involving customers and financial institutions from third countries listed as high-risk third countries ...*

Indeed, "increased checks" on operations involving transfer of Monero from third-country counterparties to the EU are hardly viable.

3 Anamorphic Channel in CLSAG Signatures

In this section, we construct an *anamorphic channel* [15,21,22] within the Monero protocol that shall enable in-band transfer of spending rights from an EU citizen, Alice, to an offshore accomplice, Bob, all without the TPSP's realizing, even if every single transaction broadcast by Alice goes through the TPSP's hands, and the TPSP implements the auditing mechanisms described above. To start, we give a construction that enables Alice, in possession of a *sender double key* sdk, to embed covert messages in Monero transactions in such a way that the *anamorphic transactions* carrying the secret messages are indistinguishable from regular Monero traffic even to a TPSP in possession of Alice's view key k^v and requiring OutProofs [14] for all transactions she broadcasts. In fact, the TPSP may also have possession of the double key sdk (the existence and knowledge of which Alice can plausibly deny and should deny). Only Bob (who need not coincide with any of the anamorphic transaction's recipients) with a matching *receiver double key* rdk is able to recover the covert messages.

Hybrid Encryption on Chain. For each input to a Monero transaction, a CLSAG ring signature [11] is produced (see Sect. A), each using $n > 1$ public keys that form a *ring*, with the signer's key at position π and $n-1$ *decoys*. Let $r_1, \ldots, r_n \in \mathbb{Z}_\ell^*$ denote the n nonces published as part of a CLSAG signature σ. Importantly, each r_i for $i \neq \pi$ is supposed to be drawn uniformly at random from $\mathbb{Z}_\ell^*$, while r_π is derived deterministically and depends on the other nonces. Instead of randomly choosing the decoy r_i's, we are going to use them for covert communication. This idea has been explored already by Alsalami and Zhang in [4], but instead of adopting their construction (designed for a signature scheme from an older version of Monero), we propose our own, which works in an asymmetric setting, enabling multiple mutually untrusted senders to communicate with the receiver holding rdk. We also enhance [4] by using a stream cipher-like construction for encryption, as opposed to a block cipher, making the relevant security reductions more immediate. Our construction uses one of the nonces r_i to run a Diffie-Hellman key exchange and the remaining $n-2$ random r_i's to hide ciphertexts. Given that, in practice, $n = 16$,[10] this results in a covert channel of bandwidth around 440 bytes per CLSAG signature, i.e., per one input to a transaction.

Let V denote the plaintext to be hidden in a CLSAG signature σ and assume the existence of an oracle (checksum verification) Valid that, for a given trial decryption V', returns 1 if V' is a valid plaintext and 0 otherwise (with high probability). The covert receiver will not know π a priori and thus will have to make up to n trial decryptions for different guesses, using Valid to recognize the correct one. Write V as an integer in base ℓ with at most $n-2$ digits:

$$V = (v_{n-2} v_{n-3} \cdots v_1)_\ell = \sum_{i=1}^{n-2} \ell^{i-1} v_i.$$

Generate *masks* $u_1, \ldots, u_{n-2} \in \mathbb{Z}_\ell$ using a PRNG seeded with a value ξ (defined below) and let

$$e_i = v_i + u_i \pmod{\ell} \quad \text{for } 1 \leq i \leq n-2. \tag{1}$$

The values e_i are indistinguishable from uniformly random on $\mathbb{Z}_\ell^*$ ($0 = e_i \notin \mathbb{Z}_\ell^*$ happens with negligible probability). We shall use an extra value e_0 to run an ephemeral-static Diffie-Hellman protocol with the sender double key sdk. Set ξ

---

[10] See, e.g., https://xmrchain.net.

to be the output of this protocol. Set the CLSAG nonces to

$$r_i = \begin{cases} e_{i-1} & \text{if } i < \pi, \\ e_{i-2} & \text{if } i > \pi. \end{cases}$$

Recall that r_π is produced deterministically as per CLSAG specification [11]. If the covert receiver knew π, they could correctly recover $e_0, \ldots, e_{n-2}$ (by excluding r_π) and, given rdk, complete the Diffie-Hellman protocol started in e_0, compute ξ, and recover the masks $u_1, \ldots, u_{n-2}$. This would enable them to undo Equation (1) and recover the plaintext V. Without a priori knowledge of π, the covert receiver can instead recover trial plaintexts $V' = (v'_{n-2}v'_{n-3}\cdots v'_1)_\ell$, for different guesses of $\pi \in \{1, \ldots, n\}$, and, for each of them, check if $\mathtt{Valid}(V') = 1$. (Note that, this way, the covert receiver, in possession of rdk, finds π, thus breaking the anonymity of the transaction sender.) We now proceed to give a construction for running the Diffie-Hellman protocol anamorphically in e_0, so that e_0 looks (unconditionally) uniformly random.

Random-Looking ECDH in CLSAG. We shall generalize Möller's construction for hybrid encryption with pseudorandom ciphertexts [18] to non-binary elliptic curves. Let $E_{a,b} : y^2 = x^3 + ax + b$ be an elliptic curve in short Weierstrass form over the field $\mathbb{Z}_\ell$, and let $d \in \mathbb{Z}_\ell^*$ be a non-square. The (quadratic) *twist* of $E_{a,b}$ by d is the curve $E_{a,b}^d : dy^2 = x^3 + ax + b$. Assume both curves give rise to groups of odd prime order (such curves can easily be found by the covert receiver and published). This precludes the existence of points of the form $(x, 0)$ on either curve (since they would have order 2) and hence forces $b \neq 0$. Note that every $x \in \mathbb{Z}_\ell$ corresponds either to a pair of points on $E_{a,b}$ (if $x^3 + ax + b$ is a square in $\mathbb{Z}_\ell$) or a pair of points on $E_{a,b}^d$ (otherwise). We give a construction (following [18]) that produces points (with known discrete logarithms) on either $E_{a,b}$ or $E_{a,b}^d$ in such a way that their x-coordinates are indistinguishable from values drawn uniformly at random from $\mathbb{Z}_\ell^*$.[11] Difficulty comes from the value $x = 0$ being a legitimate output of the algorithm in [18]. In our case, we must reject it, since we intend to use the output for e_0, and CLSAG nonces must be chosen from the multiplicative group $\mathbb{Z}_\ell^*$ only.[12] Observe how, for any pair of prime-order curves $E_{a,b}$ and $E_{a,b}^d$, $x = 0$ corresponds to a pair of points on one of the curves, since either b or b/d is a square in $\mathbb{Z}_\ell$. This pair of points must be explicitly rejected in the algorithm sampling x.

Let $\eta = |E_{a,b}| - 1$ denote the number of finite (excluding the point at infinity $\mathcal{O}$) points on $E_{a,b}$, and, similarly, let $\eta_d = |E_{a,b}^d| - 1$ denote the number of finite points on $E_{a,b}^d$. It can be shown that $\eta + \eta_d = 2\ell$ (see, e.g., [10]). Let the covert

---

[11] Choosing points on just one curve, say $E_{a,b}$, would not work, since the values of x for which $x^3 + ax + b$ is not a square in $\mathbb{Z}_\ell$ would occur with probability 0.

[12] See `random32_unbiased` at https://github.com/monero-project/monero/blob/341771ac3e65f88a6e78ca805f8dde2ae6ba7924/src/crypto/crypto.cpp#L123. Some sources [11,14] prescribe the nonces be chosen from the full field $\mathbb{Z}_\ell$ instead. This only simplifies the construction.

receiver, call him Bob, choose $a, b, d \in \mathbb{Z}_\ell^*$, with d square-free so that the curve $E_{a,b}$ *and* its quadratic twist $E_{a,b}^d$ are both secure. In particular, both orders $|E_{a,b}|$ and $|E_{a,b}^d|$ should be prime. Furthermore, let Bob fix two basepoints (generators of the groups), B and B_d, on $E_{a,b}$ and $E_{a,b}^d$, respectively. Bob can then generate a double key pair by drawing uniformly at random scalars $s \in \{1, \ldots, \eta\}$ and $s_d \in \{1, \ldots, \eta_d\}$ and computing $Y = s \cdot B$ and $Y_d = s_d \cdot B_d$. Finally, Bob sets $\mathsf{rdk} = (s, s_d)$ and $\mathsf{sdk} = (Y, Y_d)$. The domain parameters $(a, b, d, \eta, \eta_d, B, B_d)$ are published off chain, together with sdk, for Alice to read.[13] Suppose Alice wishes to send a message anamorphically to Bob. She shall randomly (with an appropriately skewed probability) choose one of the curves, $E_{a,b}$ or $E_{a,b}^d$, and a corresponding component of sdk, Y or Y_d, and use that to run an x-coordinate-only ephemeral-static Diffie-Hellman protocol in e_0. Note that, as per the discussion above, either $(0, \pm\sqrt{b}) \in E_{a,b}$, or $(0, \pm\sqrt{b/d}) \in E_{a,b}^d$, depending on whether b is a square in $\mathbb{Z}_\ell$ or not. But we cannot have $e_0 = 0$, and so we must skew the probabilities in Alice's choice even further than Möller does in [18]. Specifically, we must correct for the two points with zero x-coordinates on one of the curves. Let

$$(\eta', \eta_d') = \begin{cases} (\eta - 2, \eta_d) & \text{if } \sqrt{b} \in \mathbb{Z}_\ell, \\ (\eta, \eta_d - 2) & \text{otherwise}. \end{cases}$$

If b is a square, then $(0, \pm\sqrt{b})$ are two points on $E_{a,b}$, and so we exclude them from the count η. Otherwise, $(0, \pm\sqrt{b/d})$ are two points on $E_{a,b}^d$, and we exclude them from the count η_d. In the end, η' is the number of finite points $(x, y) \in E_{a,b}$, and η_d' is the number of finite points $(x, y) \in E_{a,b}^d$, with $x \in \mathbb{Z}_\ell^*$ in both cases. Each $x \in \mathbb{Z}_\ell^*$ appears exactly twice among the x-coordinates of the η' finite points of $E_{a,b}$ or twice among the x-coordinates of the η_d' finite points of $E_{a,b}^d$ (with points having $x = 0$ excluded from the relevant curve). Note that $\eta' + \eta_d' = 2\ell - 2$.

For each new anamorphic transfer addressed to Bob, Alice tosses an asymmetric coin and chooses the curve $E_{a,b}$ with probability $\eta'/(2\ell - 2)$ and the curve $E_{a,b}^d$ with probability $\eta_d'/(2\ell - 2)$. Let $\tilde{E} \in \{E_{a,b}, E_{a,b}^d\}$ denote the curve chosen for the transfer, $\tilde{B} \in \{B, B_d\}$ the corresponding basepoint of order $\tilde{\eta} + 1$, with $\tilde{\eta} \in \{\eta, \eta_d\}$, and $\tilde{Y} \in \{Y, Y_d\}$ the corresponding component of sdk. Let $\tilde{\eta}' \in \{\eta', \eta_d'\}$ denote the number of finite points on $\tilde{E}$ after correcting for the points with x-coordinate 0. Alice then chooses uniformly at random a scalar $q \in \{1, \ldots, \tilde{\eta}\}$ and computes an ephemeral public key $Q = q \cdot \tilde{B}$ as well as the corresponding shared secret $S = q \cdot \tilde{Y}$. If the x-coordinate $\mathbf{x}(Q) = 0$, Alice repeats this step. Finally, Alice sets $e_0 = \mathbf{x}(Q)$ and uses $\xi = \mathbf{x}(S)$ for the encryption of the anamorphic message V. Observe that e_0 is uniform in $\mathbb{Z}_\ell^*$. Indeed, for

---

[13] Bob can also publish them on chain, say, in an appropriately tagged transaction, since the knowledge of sdk does not help the TPSP convict Alice.

each $x \in \mathbb{Z}_\ell^*$, the "right" curve is chosen with probability $\tilde{\eta}'/(2\ell - 2)$, and, out of the $\tilde{\eta}'$ finite points $Q \in \tilde{E}$ with non-zero $\mathbf{x}(Q)$, two have $\mathbf{x}(Q) = x$.[14]

For each transaction published in the ledger, Bob checks the accompanying CLSAG signatures for hidden ciphertexts. Specifically, for each signature σ, Bob recovers $e_0, \ldots, e_{n-2}$ (there are n possibilities for r_π which must be excluded from σ to obtain this set). Given e_0, Bob checks if $e_0^3 + ae_0 + b$ is a square modulo ℓ. If so, Bob assumes $e_0 = \mathbf{x}(Q')$ for $Q' \in E_{a,b}$ and computes $\xi' = \mathbf{x}(s \cdot Q')$. Otherwise, Bob assumes Q' belongs to $E_{a,b}^d$ and computes $\xi' = \mathbf{x}(s_d \cdot Q')$. Bob seeds a PRNG with ξ', generates the masks $u_1, \ldots, u_{n-2}$ and solves Equation (1) for a trial decryption V'. If $\texttt{Valid}(V') = 0$ for all guesses of π, then σ did not contain a hidden ciphertext. Otherwise, Bob has recovered V.

In the theorem below, we extend the notion of signature anamorphism [15], formalized in terms of a distinguishing game with a *dictator* in possession of the signing key, to ring signatures in a natural way, i.e., we may, without loss of generality, assume the dictator chooses the decoy public keys.

Theorem 1. *CLSAG is an anamorphic (ring) signature scheme with anamorphic encryption/decryption algorithms given by the construction above.*

Proof. Without loss of generality assume that $\pi = n$, and it is E_d that contains the two points P with $\mathbf{x}(P) = 0$ (which immediately implies that there are no such points on E). Write G_0 for the *anamorphic game* [15,21], where an efficient dictator $\mathcal{D}$, in possession of the CLSAG signing key, interacts with an oracle implementing the above construction. Write p_i for the probability of $\mathcal{D}$ returning 1 in game G_i. Let G_1 be exactly like G_0 except the oracle seeds the PRNG with $\mathbf{x}(R)$ for R sampled uniformly from $\tilde{E} \setminus \{\mathcal{O}\}$ as opposed to with $\mathbf{x}(q \cdot \tilde{Y})$. Then,

$$|p_0 - p_1| \leq \epsilon_{\text{ddh}},$$

where ϵ_{ddh} is the maximum advantage an efficient adversary may have in deciding the Diffie-Hellman problem on $\tilde{E}$. Let G_2 be exactly like G_1 except the oracle seeds the PRNG with a uniformly random $\xi \in \mathbb{Z}_\ell$ as opposed to $\mathbf{x}(R)$. The adversary's advantage is bounded by the statistical distance between the two distributions on the seeds ξ in the two games, itself bounded by $1/(\ell - 1)$ (which, for brevity, we prove in Sect. B):

$$|p_1 - p_2| \leq \frac{1}{\ell - 1}.$$

Let G_3 be exactly like G_2 except that e_0 is chosen uniformly at random from $\mathbb{Z}_\ell^*$. As argued above, we have $p_2 = p_3$. Let G_4 differ from G_3 in that the oracle chooses the masks $u_1, \ldots, u_{n-2}$ uniformly at random from $\mathbb{Z}_\ell$. Then,

$$|p_3 - p_4| \leq \epsilon_{\text{prng}},$$

---

[14] Furthermore, each Q is chosen uniformly at random, since multiplication by the random q is a permutation of the prime-order cyclic group of points on $\tilde{E}$. Rejecting points Q with $\mathbf{x}(Q) = 0$ preserves the uniform distribution on the remaining elements.

where ϵ_prng is the maximum advantage an efficient adversary may have in distinguishing the PRNG output from a uniformly random string. Then, in G_5, let the oracle choose the *nonces* $e_1, \ldots, e_{n-2}$ uniformly at random from $\mathbb{Z}_\ell$ instead of the masks. Clearly, this is only a conceptual change, and $p_4 = p_5$. Finally, let G_6 be exactly like G_5 except the nonces are chosen from $\mathbb{Z}_\ell^*$ instead of $\mathbb{Z}_\ell$. The advantage in distinguishing a uniform distribution on $\mathbb{Z}_\ell$ from a uniform distribution on $\mathbb{Z}_\ell^*$ is bounded by their statistical distance $1/\ell$, giving

$$|p_5 - p_6| \leq \frac{n-2}{\ell} < \frac{n-2}{\ell - 1}.$$

Observe that G_6 corresponds exactly to the *real game* [15,21], in which $\mathcal{D}$ interacts with an honest CLSAG signer, and

$$|p_0 - p_6| \leq \epsilon_\text{ddh} + \epsilon_\text{prng} + \frac{n-1}{\ell - 1},$$

which is negligible in the security parameter $\lambda = |\ell|$. $\square$

4 Anamorphic Spending of XMR

We now show how the channel established above can be leveraged to transfer spending rights from Alice, subject to the TPSP's transaction-level auditing, to her offshore accomplices, who operate outside the EU's jurisdiction, i.e., have unencumbered access to the Monero network and ledger. Suppose direct transfer would be denied as violating AML control rules for transactions leaving the EU. We will have Alice broadcast *anamorphic transactions* that cannot be distinguished from regular transactions by the TPSP but contain tokens, most importantly the output key k^o, required to spend some other UTXO of Alice.

Consider a TPSP provisioned with the private view key k^v of every user that registers with the platform, including Alice. Furthermore, assume the extreme (centralized) case, where every transaction broadcast by Alice passes through the hands of this TPSP who has the right to request OutProofs [14] as described in Sect. 2.3 to identify the recipients of outgoing transactions.[15] We introduce the notion of *anamorphic spending* where Alice transfers the spending rights for a UTXO to her accomplice, Bob, via an anamorphic channel established in Sect. 3. The corresponding funds will, from the point of view of the TPSP engaging in transaction-level auditing, seem to have never been spent in the EU, but will nonetheless surface on a foreign market. Let a, x, and k^o be the amount, the output commitment trapdoor (see Sect. A), and the output key, respectively, of Alice's UTXO τ. Alice can create *any* transaction T, unrelated to τ, that sends some other UTXO to *anyone*, and embed a, x, and k^o in an anamorphic channel to Bob hidden within said transaction. Specifically, when signing (some input of) T, Alice, using Bob's double key sdk, follows the procedure laid out in

---

[15] The TPSP may also request $\mathsf{EqLog}_{G, \mathcal{H}_p(K^o)}(K^o, \tilde{K})$ (recall Sect. 2.3) to ensure the transactions Alice publishes actually spend Alice's funds.

Sect. 3 to produce an anamorphic signature (thus making T into an anamorphic transaction) that cannot be distinguished from a signature generated honestly according to the CLSAG specification (indeed, the TPSP here is subsumed by the even more capable dictator of Theorem 1) and therefore does not raise the suspicion of the TPSP (Alice is granted perfectly plausible denial).

Bob can now scan the Monero ledger, looking for transactions that carry anamorphic messages to him. Once Bob recognizes T, he can recover a, x, and k^o, and then be able to spend τ.[16] Since his access to the ledger is unencumbered by any trading platform's due diligence obligations, he can broadcast his transaction T' that takes τ as input. Anonymity mechanisms of Monero then work against the TPSP in Europe that cannot tell if τ was used as a decoy (recall Sect. 2.2) or actually spent in T'. Importantly, Bob does not learn Alice's long-term keys (k^v, k^s) and instead receives a token, namely, k^o, that only authorizes him to spend τ and no other UTXO. Note how this enables Alice to funnel XMR outside the EU without compromising her account. The money funneled offshore can later return to the EU using regular Monero channels (recall from Sect. 2.4 that such channels are hard to regulate and any reception of funds could be plausibly argued unsolicited), thus affording a money-laundering scheme. The Monero ledger serves here as a perfect anonymous communication channel—at no point does Alice communicate directly with Bob, except via the *bulletin board* afforded by the ledger, thwarting any wiretapping attempts by the authorities.

We note that it may be custodial crypto exchange services that engage in anamorphic spending and thus, e.g., successfully hide their insolvency from both the clients and the auditors equipped with view keys k^v to the exchange's accounts on the ledger. Also, given the trend to increase the ring size n, the anamorphic channel of Sect. 3 gets wider over time, enabling making many subliminal transfers, each possibly to a different recipient, all using a single anamorphic transaction, intuitively reducing the effectiveness of heuristics in detecting anamorphic spending.

In light of the above, we arrive at the following conclusion:

Conclusion 1 *Neither auditing at the crypto-fiat boundary nor transaction-level auditing is effective in the case of Monero. The former offers little insight into transaction history due to in-built anonymity features of the currency, and the latter remains susceptible to anamorphic spending with non-EU counterparties (which are given extra emphasis in the preamble of [3]; see, e.g., recital 77 therein), even if all out-of-band channels are shut.*

Note that we have assumed a model of the TPSP that is easily argued compliant with AML's [2] due diligence requirements and yet fails to account for the full scope of technical capabilities at the financial criminals' disposal, anamorphic cryptography included. This highlights a danger in implementing the regulations [2,3] carelessly (or maliciously).

---

[16] Bob can easily recognize τ by its one-time address $K^o = k^o \cdot G$.

4.1 Defecting Bob

In the above construction, we, importantly, assume that Bob remains "loyal" to Alice and does not collaborate with any of the trading platforms that know Alice's private view key k^v. Indeed, if Bob were to disclose k^o obtained from the anamorphic transaction to the platform's provider, they would compromise Alice's account. This is because a party in possession of both an output key k^o (for a transaction with public key R) and its corresponding private view key k^v immediately learns the spend key $k^s = k^o - \mathcal{H}_n(k^v \cdot R)$, granting them spend authority over *all* Alice's UTXOs.[17] If the law enforcement authorities in pursuit of Alice obtained k^s, they could effectively "freeze" her assets. To not run the risk of Bob turning rogue and "ratting" on her, Alice could use a straw man (a "mule"), Charlie. For a "cut," Charlie would forward to Bob, via the anamorphic channel, the output keys (together with a and x) for transactions coming, via the public ledger, from Alice to Charlie. Now, only Charlie's account in Monero would be at risk. A criminal organization could control multiple money mules like Charlie to further conceal its activities. Furthermore, if Charlie sells both his private keys to Alice, they need not ever again engage with the Monero network and can serve only as a front registered with the trading platform. Alice can make anamorphic transactions T addressed to Charlie, but secretly (through the anamorphic channel) authorize Bob to spend their outputs τ as well. Assuming some "honor among thieves," Charlie will not spend them before Bob does.

Interestingly, note that it is not clear who the legal owner of the coins is (and who is responsible for further activities involving them) after the execution of the anamorphic spending protocol as above. Equating the owner to the person technically capable of spending the funds (see [6] for a precedent) would suggest that Alice, Bob, and Charlie have joint ownership of the asset at this point. MiCA [3] takes the notion of crypto-asset ownership and custody for granted and gives the technical nuances no treatment.

4.2 Air-Tight Auditing and Consequences

We now revisit **RQ3** and briefly discuss the capacity of Monero (in its current form) to accommodate a more robust auditing framework. One way to satisfy the directive's [2] requirements would be for TPSPs to compel their clients to disclose key images $\tilde{K}$ of all their assets, on top of employing the tools of Sect. 2.3.[18] For honest users, this does not violate privacy any more than transaction-level auditing where the TPSP already knows when each UTXO gets spent. It does, however, thwart anamorphic spending as described above. Indeed, the auditor with knowledge of the key images of a user's assets can tell whenever any one of them gets spent, no matter who broadcasts the transaction or in what

---

[17] This is not prevented even by the use of *subaddresses*, which we chose not to introduce in this paper for brevity.

[18] This is a realistic concern considered by Monero developers, see Justin Berman's talk at MoneroKon 2022: https://www.youtube.com/watch?v=xGEBRQU1lzw.

jurisdiction. This is because the corresponding key image *must* be revealed on chain when spending a UTXO. We highlight here the alignment between the law and the technical requirements of the Monero protocol: key images' correspondence to spends is integral to double-spending prevention, therefore it is enforced by the protocol itself.

There are, however, two problems with this approach. First, it encroaches on the privacy of non-EU residents in that their anonymity guarantees are reduced, since collaborating EU-based TPSPs could rule out decoy keys of EU residents of which they know the key images. Second, there is no way to enforce the policy in a non-custodial setting, because a separate proof protocol (showing the consistency of the disclosed key image) must be played out between the user's wallet and the platform for each incoming asset. As long as the wallet remains offline, the account may accrue assets without revealing the key images, and the user cannot be held accountable for *not* using their wallet (e.g., keeping it "cold"). If Alice downloads her private keys, she may derive the output keys and transfer them anamorphically to Bob using an accomplice's, Charlie's, account.

Future of Monero. There have been numerous proposals for future directions of Monero, including empowering view-only wallets by changing the way key images are computed. This could, incidentally, grant auditors or TPSPs offline insight into outgoing transactions of their subjects or clients. There is, however, no official schedule as to when, if ever,[19] such changes may be made to Monero. Likewise, *full chain membership proofs*, that would extend the anonymity set to *all* UTXOs in the Monero ledger, are also on the development roadmap.[20]

5 Related Work

The study of establishing covert channels goes back to Simmons [24], with public blockchains only recently identified as perfect platforms for realizing them [4,7,12,16,25,26]. The notion of anamorphic cryptography is introduced in [21], with [15] further introducing anamorphic signatures and [22] introducing public-key anamorphic cryptography. Tiemann et al. [25] study using the Bitcoin blockchain as a secure chat (bulletin board). Their construction, however, requires the transaction creator to reveal to the receiver the private keys used to sign the transactions. Guo et al. [12] present a covert channel in Monero transactions with capacity of $n-1$ *bits* per transaction input, i.e., approximately $\lg(\ell) = 253$ *times* smaller than ours. In [16], the authors propose a covert channel in Monero transactions using the transaction amount as carrier. Alsalami and Zhang [4] study Monero in the context of covert broadcast and propose embedding ciphertexts in Monero's (old version of) ring signatures. Our construction in Sect. 3 can be viewed as an extension of their work that does away

---

[19] See https://gist.github.com/tevador/50160d160d24cfc6c52ae02eb3d17024?permalink_comment_id=5330787#gistcomment-5330787.

[20] See https://www.getmonero.org/resources/roadmap/.

with reliance on pre-shared symmetric keys. Keller et al. [13] show a scheme for proving a UTXO was only used as a decoy. It amounts to revealing the key image and proving its consistency.

6 Conclusions

We have highlighted the discordance between the emerging European law and the technological reality of Monero trading. In particular, we have considered the MiCA regulation [3] and argued that, in order to comply with Article 76(3) therein, some form of transaction-level auditing must be implemented to account for transaction histories of EU residents. We then considered the perfect functionality of an auditor that acts as a watchdog through the hands of which every transaction must pass and precluded the use of any out-of-band channels. In this extreme setting, we have shown that robust financial oversight remains elusive, despite on-paper compliance with the regulation [3] and the AML directive [2], due to a novel notion of anamorphic spending, which applies anamorphic signatures [15] to the blockchain setting. Anamorphic Monero transactions, indistinguishable from regular ones, can be leveraged to continue running money-laundering schemes with offshore accomplices largely unhindered, despite the Union's attempts at oversight.

A Ring Signatures in Monero

Monero transactions hide input and output amounts a_j using Pedersen commitments $C_j = x_j \cdot G + a_j \cdot H \in \mathbb{G}$ and rely on their being homomorphic to prove balance, i.e., that net input equals net output.[21] When spending some inputs, their commitments' trapdoors x_j are re-randomized, i.e., new commitments C'_j (referred to as *pseudo-output commitments* in [14]) with trapdoors x'_j are constructed, where each C'_j commits to the same amount as the corresponding input commitment C_j, and the output commitments' trapdoors y_t are selected so that the difference $\sum_j x'_j - \sum_t y_t$ vanishes modulo the group order ℓ. If the amounts balance (at least modulo ℓ), then the sum of the pseudo-output commitments must equal the sum of the output commitments, which can be verified by anyone.

What remains to be shown is the consistency of pseudo-output and input commitments. This is proved by showing the knowledge of $z_j = x_j - x'_j$ such that $C_j - C'_j = z_j \cdot G$. This, in turn, is done together with the proof of knowledge of the output key k_j^o (recall Sect. 2.2) by signing the transaction in question using a Concise Linkable Spontaneous Anonymous Group (CLSAG) signature scheme [11]. CLSAG signatures grant the signer anonymity by using a ring of n public keys with $n - 1$ *decoys*, but, importantly, also enable linking of any two signatures produced with the same key $K^o = k^o \cdot G$ by involving a *key image* $\tilde{K} = k^o \cdot \mathcal{H}_p(K^o)$ in the signature. This prevents double-spending, i.e., sending the same asset again in another transaction.

---
[21] For clarity of exposition, we neglect the miner's fee.

Each transaction input therefore comprises a set of n one-time addresses $\{K_1^o, \ldots, K_\pi^o, \ldots, K_n^o\}$ and n amount commitments $\{C_1, \ldots, C_\pi, \ldots, C_n\}$ with only the πth component in each corresponding to the actual input being spent. The user authorizes the transaction by revealing a pseudo-output commitment C' and signing with k_π^o and z_π where $C_\pi - C' = z_\pi \cdot G$. Write $Z_i = C_i - C'$. To produce a CLSAG signature, the signer chooses $n-1$ random nonces $r_i \in \mathbb{Z}_\ell^*$ for each $i \in \{1, \ldots, n\}$ excluding $i = \pi$, as well as a single random $\alpha \in \mathbb{Z}_\ell^*$, and computes *aggregate public keys*

$$W_i = \mathcal{H}_n(1\|\tilde{K}\|\tilde{Z}) \cdot K_i^o + \mathcal{H}_n(2\|\tilde{K}\|\tilde{Z}) \cdot Z_i$$

for each i. A single *aggregate key image* is computed as

$$\tilde{W} = \mathcal{H}_n(1\|\tilde{K}\|\tilde{Z}) \cdot \tilde{K} + \mathcal{H}_n(2\|\tilde{K}\|\tilde{Z}) \cdot \tilde{Z},$$

where $\tilde{K} = k_\pi^o \cdot \mathcal{H}_p(K_\pi^o)$ and $\tilde{Z} = z_\pi \cdot \mathcal{H}_p(K_\pi^o)$. Observe that the signer knows w_π such that $W_\pi = w_\pi \cdot G$ and $\tilde{W} = w_\pi \cdot \mathcal{H}_p(K_\pi^o)$. They proceed by computing

$$c_{(\pi \bmod n)+1} = \mathcal{H}_n\big(M\|(\alpha \cdot G)\|(\alpha \cdot \mathcal{H}_p(K_\pi^o))\big),$$

where M is a hash of the transaction data. The signer then traverses the ring of input transactions, starting with $i = (\pi \bmod n) + 1$, and computes

$$c_{(i \bmod n)+1} = \mathcal{H}_n\big(M\|(r_i \cdot G + c_i \cdot W_i)\|(r_i \cdot \mathcal{H}_p(K_i^o) + c_i \cdot \tilde{W})\big).$$

Finally, they set $r_\pi = \alpha - c_\pi w_\pi \pmod{\ell}$. The signature is

$$\sigma = (c_1, r_1, \ldots, r_n),$$

and the key images $\tilde{K}$ and $\tilde{Z}$ are published alongside it. Importantly for our purposes, out of the n nonces r_i, only one is derived deterministically, namely, r_π. The remaining ones are drawn uniformly at random from $\mathbb{Z}_\ell^*$. This is the basis for the anamorphic channel in Sect. 3.

B Bounding the Distance in Proof of Theorem 1

Claim. The statistical distance between ξ chosen uniformly at random from $\mathbb{Z}_\ell$ and $\xi = \mathbf{x}(R)$ for a uniform $R \in \tilde{E} \setminus \{\mathcal{O}\}$, where $\tilde{E}$ is chosen as specified in Sect. 3, is bounded above by $1/(\ell - 1)$.

Proof. Recall that the statistical distance is defined as

$$\Delta = \frac{1}{2} \sum_{x \in \mathbb{Z}_\ell} |\Pr[\xi = x] - \Pr[\mathbf{x}(R) = x]|.$$

Write $\mathbf{x}(E)$ for the set of x-coordinates of points on E, i.e., the set of $x \in \mathbb{Z}_\ell$ for which $x^3 + ax + b$ is a square. Similarly, let $\mathbf{x}(E_d)$ be the set of x-coordinates of points on E_d. Note that $\mathbb{Z}_\ell \setminus \mathbf{x}(E_d) = \mathbf{x}(E)$. The curve E is chosen with probability $\eta'/(2\ell - 2)$ and, for any $x \in \mathbf{x}(E)$, we have

$$\Pr[\mathbf{x}(R) = x] = \frac{\eta'}{2\ell - 2} \cdot \frac{2}{\eta} = \frac{1}{\ell - 1},$$

because $\eta' = \eta$. For $x \in \mathbf{x}(E_d)$, we have

$$\Pr[\mathbf{x}(R) = x] = \frac{\eta'_d}{2\ell - 2} \cdot \frac{2}{\eta_d} = \frac{\eta_d - 2}{\eta_d} \cdot \frac{1}{\ell - 1},$$

because $\eta'_d = \eta_d - 2$ accounts for the two points with x-coordinate 0 on E_d, and the curve E_d is chosen with probability $\eta'_d/(2\ell - 2)$. The statistical distance is therefore

$$\Delta = \frac{1}{2} \sum_{x \in \mathbf{x}(E)} \left| \frac{1}{\ell} - \frac{1}{\ell - 1} \right| + \frac{1}{2} \sum_{x \in \mathbf{x}(E_d)} \left| \frac{1}{\ell} - \left(1 - \frac{2}{\eta_d}\right) \cdot \frac{1}{\ell - 1} \right|.$$

Note that, because there are no points of order 2 on either curve, $|\mathbf{x}(E)| = \eta/2$, and, similarly, $|\mathbf{x}(E_d)| = \eta_d/2$, whence

$$\Delta = \frac{\eta}{4} \cdot \frac{1}{\ell(\ell - 1)} + \left| \frac{1}{2} \cdot \frac{1}{\ell - 1} - \frac{\eta_d}{4} \cdot \frac{1}{\ell(\ell - 1)} \right|.$$

Bounding the second term using the triangle inequality, we get

$$\Delta \leq \frac{\eta + \eta_d}{4} \cdot \frac{1}{\ell(\ell - 1)} + \frac{1}{2} \cdot \frac{1}{\ell - 1} = \frac{1}{2} \cdot \frac{1}{\ell - 1} + \frac{1}{2} \cdot \frac{1}{\ell - 1} = \frac{1}{\ell - 1},$$

where we used the fact that $\eta + \eta_d = 2\ell$. □

References

1. Monero Inflation Checker. https://www.moneroinflation.com/. Accessed 27 March 2025
2. Directive (EU) 2015/849 of the European Parliament and of the Council of 20 May 2015 on the prevention of the use of the financial system for the purposes of money laundering or terrorist financing, amending Regulation (EU) No 648/2012 of the European Parliament and of the Council, and repealing Directive 2005/60/EC of the European Parliament and of the Council and Commission Directive 2006/70/EC. Off. J. Euro. Union **L 141**, 73–117 (2015)
3. Regulation (EU) 2023/1114 of the European Parliament and of the Council of 31 May 2023 on markets in crypto-assets, and amending Regulations (EU) No 1093/2010 and (EU) no 1095/2010 and Directives 2013/36/EU and (EU) 2019/1937. Off. J. Euro. Union **L 150**, 40–205 (2023)
4. Alsalami, N., Zhang, B.: Uncontrolled randomness in blockchains: covert bulletin board for illicit activity. In: 28th IEEE/ACM International Symposium on Quality of Service, IWQoS 2020, Hangzhou, China, June 15-17, 2020, pp. 1–10. IEEE (2020). https://doi.org/10.1109/IWQOS49365.2020.9213064

5. Androulaki, E., Karame, G.O., Roeschlin, M., Scherer, T., Capkun, S.: Evaluating user privacy in Bitcoin. In: Sadeghi, A.R. (ed.) Financial Cryptography and Data Security, pp. 34–51. Springer, Berlin, Heidelberg (2013)
6. Benson, V., Adamyk, B., Chinnaswamy, A., Adamyk, O.: Harmonising cryptocurrency regulation in Europe: opportunities for preventing illicit transactions. Eur. J. Law Econ. **57**(1–2), 37–61 (2024). https://doi.org/10.1007/s10657-024-09797-w
7. Biryukov, A., Feher, D., Vitto, G.: Privacy aspects and subliminal channels in Zcash. In: Proceedings of the 2019 ACM SIGSAC Conference on Computer and Communications Security, pp. 1813–1830. CCS '19, Association for Computing Machinery, New York, NY, USA (2019). https://doi.org/10.1145/3319535.3345663
8. Chainanalysis: The 2024 crypto crime report (2024). https://go.chainalysis.com/crypto-crime-2024.html
9. Chatzigiannis, P., Baldimtsi, F., Chalkias, K.: SoK: auditability and accountability in distributed payment systems. In: International Conference on Applied Cryptography and Network Security (ACNS 2021), pp. 311–337. Springer (2021). https://doi.org/10.1007/978-3-030-78375-4_13
10. Fouque, P., Lercier, R., Réal, D., Valette, F.: Fault attack on elliptic curve Montgomery ladder implementation. In: Breveglieri, L., Gueron, S., Koren, I., Naccache, D., Seifert, J. (eds.) Fifth International Workshop on Fault Diagnosis and Tolerance in Cryptography, 2008, FDTC 2008, Washington, DC, USA, 10 August 2008, pp. 92–98. IEEE Computer Society (2008). https://doi.org/10.1109/FDTC.2008.15
11. Goodell, B., Noether, S., Blue, A.: Concise linkable ring signatures and forgery against adversarial keys (2020). https://api.semanticscholar.org/CorpusID:215542434
12. Guo, Z., Shi, L., Xu, M., Yin, H.: MRCC: a practical covert channel over Monero with provable security. IEEE Access **9**, 31816–31825 (2021). https://doi.org/10.1109/ACCESS.2021.3060285
13. Keller, P., Florian, M., Böhme, R.: Collaborative deanonymization. In: Financial Cryptography and Data Security. In: FC 2021 International Workshops: CoDecFin, DeFi, VOTING, and WTSC, Virtual Event, March 5, 2021, Revised Selected Papers, pp. 39–46. Springer, Berlin, Heidelberg (2021). https://doi.org/10.1007/978-3-662-63958-0_3
14. Koe, Alonso, K.M., Noether, S.: Zero to Monero: Second Edition (2020). https://www.getmonero.org/library/Zero-to-Monero-2-0-0.pdf
15. Kutyłowski, M., Persiano, G., Phan, D.H., Yung, M., Zawada, M.: Anamorphic signatures: secrecy from a dictator who only permits authentication! In: Handschuh, H., Lysyanskaya, A. (eds.) Advances in Cryptology - CRYPTO 2023, pp. 759–790. Springer, Cham (2023)
16. Liu, L., Liu, L., Li, B., Zhong, Y., Liao, S., Zhang, L.: MSCCS: a Monero-based security-enhanced covert communication system. Comput. Netw. **205**, 108759 (2022). https://doi.org/10.1016/j.comnet.2021.108759
17. Meiklejohn, S., et al.: A fistful of bitcoins: characterizing payments among men with no names. In: Proceedings of the 2013 Conference on Internet Measurement Conference, pp. 127–140. IMC '13, Association for Computing Machinery, New York, NY, USA (2013). https://doi.org/10.1145/2504730.2504747
18. Möller, B.: A public-key encryption scheme with pseudo-random Ciphertexts. In: Samarati, P., Ryan, P., Gollmann, D., Molva, R. (eds.) ESORICS 2004. LNCS, vol. 3193, pp. 335–351. Springer, Heidelberg (2004). https://doi.org/10.1007/978-3-540-30108-0_21

19. Möser, M., Böhme, R., Breuker, D.: Towards risk scoring of Bitcoin transactions. In: Financial Cryptography and Data Security, pp. 16–32. Springer (2014)
20. Möser, M., Böhme, R., Breuker, D.: An inquiry into money laundering tools in the Bitcoin ecosystem. In: 2013 APWG eCrime Researchers Summit, pp. 1–14 (2013). https://doi.org/10.1109/eCRS.2013.6805780
21. Persiano, G., Phan, D.H., Yung, M.: Anamorphic encryption: private communication against a dictator. In: Dunkelman, O., Dziembowski, S. (eds.) Advances in Cryptology - EUROCRYPT 2022, pp. 34–63. Springer, Cham (2022)
22. Persiano, G., Phan, D.H., Yung, M.: Public-key anamorphism in (CCA-secure) public-key encryption and beyond. In: Reyzin, L., Stebila, D. (eds.) Advances in Cryptology - CRYPTO 2024, pp. 422–455. Springer, Cham (2024)
23. Reid, F., Harrigan, M.: An analysis of anonymity in the Bitcoin system, pp. 197–223. Springer, New York, NY (2013). https://doi.org/10.1007/978-1-4614-4139-7_10
24. Simmons, G.J.: The prisoners' problem and the subliminal channel. In: Advances in Cryptology: Proceedings of CRYPTO '83, pp. 51–67. Plenum (1983)
25. Tiemann, T., Berndt, S., Eisenbarth, T., Liskiewicz, M.: Act natural! Exchanging private messages on public blockchains. In: 8th IEEE European Symposium on Security and Privacy, EuroS&P 2023, Delft, Netherlands, July 3–7, 2023, pp. 292–308. IEEE (2023). https://doi.org/10.1109/EUROSP57164.2023.00026
26. Zhang, T., Li, B., Zhu, Y., Han, T., Wu, Q.: Covert channels in blockchain and blockchain based covert communication: overview, state-of-the-art, and future directions. Comput. Commun. **205**, 136–146 (2023). https://doi.org/10.1016/j.comcom.2023.04.001

Hyperion: Transparent End-to-End Verifiable Voting with Coercion Mitigation

Aditya Damodaran[1], Simon Rastikian[2], Peter B. Rønne[1(✉)], and Peter Y. A. Ryan[1]

[1] SnT, University of Luxembourg, Esch-sur-Alzette, Luxembourg
peter.roenne@gmail.com, Peter.ryan@uni.lu
[2] Near One Limited, London, UK

Abstract. We present *Hyperion*, an end-to-end verifiable e-voting scheme that allows the voters to identify their votes in cleartext in the final tally. In contrast to schemes like *Selene* or *sElect*, identification is not via (private) tracker numbers but via cryptographic commitment terms. After publishing the tally, the *Election Authority* provides each voter with an individual dual key. Voters identify their votes by raising their dual key to their secret trapdoor key and finding the matching commitment term in the tally. The dual keys are self-certifying in that, without the voter's trapdoor key, it is intractable to forge a dual key that, when raised to the trapdoor key, will match an alternative commitment. On the other hand, a voter can use their own trapdoor key to forge a dual key to fool any would-be coercer.

We provide new improved definitions of privacy and verifiability for e-voting schemes and prove the scheme secure against these, as well as proving security with respect to earlier definitions in the literature.

We provide a prototype implementation and provide measurements which demonstrate that our scheme is practical for large scale elections.

1 Introduction

Many democracies are moving towards voting over the internet, and some, e.g. Estonia, has fully adopted it. While internet voting has many attractions it introduces new, poorly understood threats. The internet is inherently insecure and remote voting introduces coercion threats not present in in-person voting. To counter these threats, cryptographic mechanisms and protocols have been proposed. However, designing and analysing such protocols is very challenging, and we have not reached consensus on rigorous definitions of security properties such as *vote secrecy, verifiability, receipt-freeness, coercion-resistance* and *dispute resolution*.

A good voting system should not only deliver the correct result w.r.t. the legitimately cast votes, but also provide sufficient evidence to convince all observers of the announced result. Ensuring both vote secrecy and verifiability is complex, and indeed, many technologies sacrifice the latter, forcing the stakeholders to place total, blind trust in the correct behaviour of the code, for example direct-recording electronic (DRE) machines. Such observations motivated the development of end-to-end verifiable (E2E V) schemes [21] and the notion of software independence [28].

E2E V schemes usually involve the creation of an encryption or encoding of the vote at the time of casting, a copy of which is retained by the voter. Later the voter can check that her "receipt" appears correctly on an append-only public ledger called the *Bulletin Board* (BB). After this, a universally verifiable, anonymising tally is performed on the posted, encrypted ballots to reveal the result. Voters can also perform some form of ballot auditing before casting to gain assurance that their vote is correctly represented in their ballot. Putting these steps together ensures that the corruption of any vote during recording and tallying is detectable. Along with mechanisms to prevent ballot stuffing and clash attacks (ballot collisions) etc. we can detect any inaccuracy in the announced outcome.

Such schemes, while technically appealing, have at least two drawbacks. First, the fact that errors can be detected does not guarantee that they will be: it is essential that sufficient numbers of voters and observers actually perform the checks diligently and report anomalies. Second, a voting scheme must be easily understandable and usable by voters and voting officials. The assurance argument outlined above is rather subtle, and not easy for many voters or stakeholders to digest. Many find the idea of voters having to perform checks on encrypted ballots unreasonable.

These observations prompted the exploration of more direct and transparent forms of verification, in particular based on the idea of private tracker numbers to identify votes in cleartext in the tally. Examples of such schemes include the CNRS scheme [3], *Selene* [30] and sElect [25]. Of these, *Selene* is of particular interest as it provides mitigation of the coercion threats that tracker based schemes otherwise exhibit: the coercer demands the voter to reveal her tracker. Notably, the Selene construction has been trialled in elections in The Royal College of Nursing and The College of Podiatrists in the UK [32] and for elections in the ESORICS steering committee.

1.1 Contribution

We present a novel, E2E verifiable scheme, inspired by the *Selene* scheme [30], that not only provides a highly transparent verification, but also affords voters a greater sense of privacy than with *Selene*. *Hyperion* is significantly more efficient as it greatly simplifies the setup (Sect. 2.2) of *Selene*, eliminating all the encryption, mixing, decryption and ZK proofs computations implied by the use of tracker numbers.

Hyperion, in contrast to *Selene*, does not publicly reveal trackers, indeed, we do away entirely with trackers. Instead, the voter identifies her vote in the tally by identifying the row in the tally containing the commitment that opens, with her trapdoor secret key and dual key, to a constant, e.g. 1. This is rather like identifying your house by finding the door that opens to your key. This is still deniable, but the mechanism is now different: a coerced voter identifies a commitment paired with the coercer's required vote and, if necessary computes, using her trapdoor key, the fake dual key that opens the chosen commitment to 1. Doing away with the trackers also improves the situation for coerced voters, since they do not need to equivocate and lie about trackers that they have seen and which could have easy-to-remember or characteristic features. As an example, a voter might accidentally reveal having a tracker with consecutive numbers.

The *Hyperion* construction has further advantages over *Selene*. In particular, variants have been created that exploit the fact that the cryptographic commitments are perfectly randomly distributed to an observer only seeing the bulletin board. This can be used for quantum-safety against future attackers or even satisfying everlasting privacy (see the long version of this paper [14] where further variants are explored), and has even been used to construct the first scheme with everlasting receipt-freeness [26].

Importantly, we also contribute novel definitions, providing a ballot privacy definition allowing maliciously generated public keys by corrupted voters, and considering stronger adversaries with access to information about whether voters verify successfully or not. We also give a definition of verifiability against a malicious voting board and consider malware on the user side, and we prove verifiability when either the vote-casting or the vote-verification device is uncorrupted. We also provide proofs of security against established definitions in the literature, especially we prove privacy against a malicious board as in [12,16].

Finally we provide a prototype implementation along with performance data.

Structure of the Paper. We first discuss related work and introduce the notation used in the paper. We then describe the voter experience in Sect. 2: casting and verifying a vote and, where necessary, evading the coercer. The precise instantiation used for security proofs is presented in Sect. 3. The remainder of the paper presents the security definitions for ballot privacy (Sect. 4) and integrity (Sect. 5) followed by game-based proofs. These definitions are also novel and represent a contribution to the state of the art in the field. For the ballot privacy definition, we consider adversaries who get information on whether the verification of voters failed or not. Such information can lead to privacy attacks, as demonstrated in other protocols, and are important to counter in *Hyperion*. For verifiability, we craft a definition considering that each voter has two devices – one for vote casting and one for verification, and we demonstrate that both need to be corrupted for successful verifiability attacks against *Hyperion*.

Finally, we include some performance statistics for a prototype implementation that demonstrate that the scheme is practical for large scale elections, e.g. of the order of a million voters, see Appendix A.

Related Work. Most of the end-to-end verifiable schemes proposed to date involve a rather indirect verification by the voter: checking that an encryption of their vote appears on the BB in the input to a (universally verifiable) tally process. Some recent schemes seek a more direct and arguably more compelling voter verification process: identifying the vote in plaintext in the final tally. Here we focus on the latter class.

Schneier [33], proposes the idea of voters attaching a password to their vote which is then posted alongside the vote on the BB. Later, [3] elaborate on this in a boardroom context. sElect [25], is also tracker-based but with the additional feature of having an accountable tally process. All of these systems are vulnerable to the obvious threat of the coercer demanding the voter reveal her tracker. *Selene* [30] introduced the idea of delayed notification of the trackers to mitigate the coercion threat, along with constructions to guarantee uniqueness and deniability of the trackers.

Some adaptations of *Selene* have been presented in an in-person variant [29,38] and in a JCJ-like variant [22] which offers greater coercion-resistance. *Selene* has been analysed symbolically in [7] and implemented (using a distributed ledger) in [32].

Hyperion, like *Selene*, provides a direct and intuitive way for voters to verify their votes, however, it does away with the need for trackers. This modification greatly simplifies the setup and, more importantly, voters should feel much more comfortable about the privacy of their vote. Studies, [2,15,37] suggest that some voters are troubled by having their vote appear publicly beside their tracker. We hypothesise that voters will be more comfortable with the *Hyperion* verification, but this needs to be investigated by a complementary user study.

Selene has the problem that the coercer might claim ownership of a faked tracker offered by a coerced voter, or that it coincides with one offered by another victim. Several enhancements to *Selene* to counter this have been suggested including adding extra dummy trackers [30] and shrouding parts of the trackers or votes [23]. The *Hyperion* construction presented here, combined with a further innovation: individual bulletin boards, elaborated in the full version of this paper, provides a more elegant solution.

Regarding the definitions, our verifiability definition builds on [10], which following [11] is the best choice for our case. Our definition benefits from a detailed model that allows corruption of vote casting and usage of verification devices.

For the ballot privacy definition, the state of the art was summarised in the SoK paper [5] which also presented a game-based definition BPRIV that implies an ideal functionality under certain conditions and which covers all types of tally functions. This definition was further extended to considering more general attacks during vote casting and malicious boards in [12]. Unfortunately, that definition does not capture schemes where the verification happens after the tally as in *Hyperion*. Recently, a new definition was presented in [16] allowing late verification and which also included a machine-checked proof of ballot privacy for Selene. Whereas the last definition would be applicable to *Hyperion*, it does not capture attacks where the attacker has access to whether the voter's verification is successful or not. Since Hyperion allows a direct check of the tallied plaintext vote, this would immediately cause privacy problems if the adversary manages to cast a vote on behalf of the voter. However, the BPRIV type of definitions, especially [16], does not capture these types of attack, and are not well-suited to do this due to being based on a simulated view. Instead, we here go back to a very early definition by Benaloh [4], but update this with inspiration from [16], also taking into account that the adversary can register maliciously generated keys.

Notation. This paper includes writing program code. Besides standard notation for assigning ' $\leftarrow$ ' and random sampling ' $\twoheadleftarrow$ ', we will also use $X \overset{\cup}{\leftarrow} Y$ as shorthand for $X \leftarrow X \cup Y$. Similarly, we write $m \overset{\|}{\leftarrow} n$ shorthand for $m \leftarrow m \| n$. Security games invoke an efficient adversary $\mathcal{A}$ with access to some oracles. The games terminate when executing **Stop with** · command. Each game is associated to a certain winning probability. We write $\Pr[G(\mathcal{A})]$ for the probability that game G invoked with adversary $\mathcal{A}$ stops with $\top$. Game codes will be compacted by introducing the instructions **Require** · which stands for ' if not · then **Stop with** $\bot$ ' and **Promise** · which stands for ' if not · then **Stop with** $\top$ '.

2 Details of the Scheme

In this section, we describe the main variant of *Hyperion*. We note that the *Hyperion* verification mechanism is versatile and could be incorporated in an existing voting scheme. For concreteness, we present it as a self contained scheme. A protocol flow diagram can be found in the long version of this paper [14] (Fig. 7) along with additional details.

2.1 Parties Involved

Election Authority (EA). Performs the general election setup, i.e. defines the election parameters, the ballot styles etc. and sets up the initial Bulletin Board.

Bulletin Board (BB). We consider an append-only board with a consistent view for all participants.

Voters. Each voter i is identified uniquely with an id_i and holds two secret keys: a signing key used to authenticate the ballot and a verification trapdoor key used to verify the plaintext vote. These keys can be stored on two different devices/apps that assist the voters in casting and verifying their votes.

Registration Authority. Identifies the eligible voters and posts their public keys on BB.

Tally Tellers (TT). Are responsible for setting up a shared (threshold) public election key pk_{EA} which will be used for encryption. They also perform a verifiable decryption during the tally phase.

Mix-Tellers. Is a set of mix tellers that perform a verifiable parallel mix in order to anonymise the votes.

2.2 The Setup

The election authority publishes the relevant details of the election including a cryptographic setup of a secure prime order group on the BB. A set of tally tellers create a threshold public key pair for the election (sk_{EA}, pk_{EA}) and publishes pk_{EA}. We assume here that each eligible voter holds a valid private signing key with corresponding certification key pk_i published along with unique voter identifiers id_i on BB. The unique identifiers enable *universal eligibility verifiability*. We trust the registration authority to set this up correctly[1]. Note that the setup here is much simpler than that of *Selene* which requires additional verified generation, encryption and mixing of tracking numbers.

2.3 Voting

Each voter generates an ephemeral trapdoor key x_i using her device. The public component $h_i := g^{x_i}$ will be registered during vote casting, along with a Zero Knowledge Proof of Knowledge (ZKPoK) of x_i. For all proofs that follow, we assume that these proofs are non-malleable and include binding to a unique election identifier and the public election key pk_{EA}. The proofs here should also be bound to the identity id_i of the voters to prevent the public keys from being copied. In our case a simple Schnorr proof [34] is sufficient, made non-interactive via the (strong) Fiat-Shamir transformation [6,18] and including all the necessary information in the hash for non-malleability.

Voting proceeds as follows: voter i sends her trapdoor key h_i along with a ZKPoK of x_i, an encryption $\{v[i]\}_{pk_{EA}}$ of her vote v_i (e.g. ElGamal [17]) and the well-formedness ZK proofs of encryption, i.e. a proof of the vote be in the correct space and a proof of plaintext-knowledge[2]. Recall that these proofs are non-malleable and bound to the voter id_i to prevent vote copy attacks[3] [13]. The encryption scheme should support verifiable mixing and together with the ZKPs be IND-1-CCA (see Appendix A in [14]). We denote the concatenation of the ZK proofs by Π_i. Registering the (ephemeral) trapdoor keys at the same time as casting the vote avoids the need for an extra registration phase. All of this is signed, sent to the EA and appended next to the appropriate pk_i on the BB (for brevity sign(m) means the signature with the message m included):

$$id_i, pk_i, \text{sign}_i(\{v[i]\}_{pk_{EA}}, h_i, \Pi_i)$$

---

[1] In Estonia, each voter has her keys integrated in her identity card.
[2] A simple choice is Chaum-Pedersen proofs of discrete log equality using OR Sigma protocols for the different vote choices.
[3] Vote copy attacks would undermine coercion resistance with plaintext verification.

2.4 Tallying

Once the voting phase has closed, ballots posted to the BB with valid signatures and proofs are identified. For these, the Tally Tellers now take each public trapdoor key h_i and privately raise this to a fresh, random, secret r_i, encrypt it and post the output on BB together with Π_i^{TT}, a ZKPoK of honest construction with knowledge of r_i and the encryption random coins.[4] For ElGamal this proof can be efficiently implemented, see e.g. [8]. The Tellers keep the corresponding g^{r_i} (dual key) terms secret, for the verification phase. The BB now contains, for the rows with valid ballots, the following:

$$id_i,\ pk_i,\ \mathsf{sign}_i(\{v[i]\}_{pk_{\mathsf{EA}}},\ h_i,\ \Pi_i),\ \{h_i^{r_i}\}_{pk_{\mathsf{EA}}},\ \Pi_i^{\mathsf{TT}}$$

The pairs $(\{v[i]\}_{pk_{\mathsf{EA}}},\ \{h_i^{r_i}\}_{pk_{\mathsf{EA}}})$ are shuffled in parallel by a verifiable mix-net and verifiably decrypted to obtain the final Tally Board

$$v_i,\ h_i^{r_i}$$

together with the ZKP of correct parallel mixing and decryption, e.g. using Verificatum [36]. If an element $h_i^{r_i} = 1$ an error is output which only happens with negligible probability if at least one Tally Teller is honest.

2.5 Notification and Verification

After a suitable delay we move to the notification phase: g^{r_i} dual key is sent[5] to voter i over a private channel at a randomly chosen time during the notification period. The voter raises this to her secret trapdoor key x_i and finds the match among the $h_j^{r_j}$ terms, so identifying her vote in the tally column.

2.6 Coercion Mitigation

Suppose a coercer instructs voter i to submit the vote v^*.[6] Voter i identifies a row in the tally that contains the pair $(v_k,\ h_k^{r_k})$ s.t. $v_k = v^*$. Using her trapdoor key x_i, she computes the *fake* dual key that when raised to x_i will match this row $(h_k^{r_k})^{x_i^{-1}}$.

As with *Selene*, care has to be taken in designing the notification channel to avoid a coercer being able to observe the notification of the *real* dual key. In contexts in which we anticipate extreme coercion, where for example the coercer

---

[4] This can easily be distributed over the Tally Tellers for ElGamal. For instance, each TT_j posts $\{h_i^{r_{i,j}}\}_{pk_{\mathsf{EA}}}$ together with the appropriate ZKPoK, then these ciphertexts are multiplied together to obtain $\{h_i^{r_i}\}_{pk_{\mathsf{EA}}}$ where $\sum_j r_{i,j} = r_i$. Each Teller then keeps $g^{r_{i,j}}$.

[5] With multiple Tally Tellers, TT_j can send $g^{r_{i,j}}$ to the voter or they can be collected and sent to the voter under encryption of h_i.

[6] This presumes that some votes v^* are cast by other voters otherwise it will, in any case, be evident that voter i did not cast v^*. For techniques to deal with the situation of unpopular candidates, see [23,31].

demands access to the channel, coerced voters could be provided with means to request a fake dual key be sent over the channel instead of the real one.

We note that the vote casting method presented here is not fully coercion-resistant, but is software-dependent receipt-free, i.e. like Helios [1] would rely on the vote-casting device or app not leaking the randomness used in the vote encryption. However, *Hyperion* can be combined with different forms of vote-casting to achieve better receipt-freeness e.g. using the BeleniosRF construction, [9]. Also, better coercion-resistance can be achieved providing protection against a coercer even trying to vote on behalf of the coerced voter, e.g. by holding the signing key, for example using JCJ style credentials [24], see [22] but at the cost of an interactive vote verification.

2.7 Dispute Resolution

It is possible when verifying that a voter either fails to find the matching term or finds it but the associated vote does not match the vote they cast. The voter should notify this to the appropriate authority for the matter to be investigated.

Possible causes:

1. The voter's ballot was not correctly posted to the BB.
2. The voter's device did not encrypt the correct vote.
3. The voter's ballot was not correctly processed during the mixing and tallying.
4. The g^{r_i} term was corrupted.

Regarding the first, we should remark that voters should be encouraged to check the presence of their ballot on the BB before tallying starts, as with other E2E V schemes. Early detection of such problems makes them easier to resolve, but *Hyperion* (and indeed *Selene*) is less reliant than conventional E2E verifiable schemes on such checks being performed diligently.

It is of course possible that a voter claims falsely to have found a problem in which case we hit dispute resolution problems: it is not clear whether the problem is with the system, the voter's device or the voter, either lying or mis-remembering. We will discuss mechanisms to resolve disputes.

3 Hyperion Instantiation

We will here present the algorithms, EASetup, Setup, ValidCred, Vote, ValidBallot, Tally, GetSecret, Publish, Verify, VerifyVote and VerifyBallot, which we will use in security games, and how they are instantiated for Hyperion.

EASetup sets up the secure cyclic DH group (of prime order) (G, g) and creates the threshold public and secret keys (pk_{EA}, sk_{EA}). Setup uses the EA keys to generate for each id a "unique" signing key pair (sk, pk) along with the proof of well-formedness; the voter also picks a random exponent x_i and computes $h_i := g^{x_i}$ along with Π_{x_i} the proof of knowledge of x_i bound non-malleably to the voter id_i. The previous algorithms should be randomized when generating the keys. ValidCred outputs $\top$ if Π_{x_i} is valid, and $\bot$ otherwise. Vote extracts h_i

from pk and Π_{x_i}, encrypts the vote v with ElGamal encryption scheme using pk_{EA}, generates the proof of well-formedness and plaintext knowledge Π_v which is bound to the voter id_i, and signs these elements using sk. It finally outputs the signed elements along with the signature as a ballot blt and an empty state st. ValidBallot verifies the correctness of the signature using pk and the validity of Π_v and Π_x: if both verifications pass, then the function outputs $\top$, otherwise, it outputs $\bot$.

The Tally function has two main jobs, first computing the mix-net inputs while updating the BB, and second inserting some computed values to the decryption mix-nets and outputting the result along with the vote count. In its first functionality, Tally extracts h_i from BB, picks a random exponent r_i for each row i, computes $h_i^{r_i}$, g^{r_i}, internally stores g^{r_i}, then, it computes the encryption $\{h_i^{r_i}\}_{pk_{\mathsf{EA}}}$ with the proof of knowledge of r_i and correct encryption Π_i^{TT} and sends $(\{h_i^{r_i}\}_{pk_{\mathsf{EA}}}, \Pi_i^{\mathsf{TT}})$ to BB. In the second functionality, the pair $(\{h_i^{r_i}\}_{pk_{\mathsf{EA}}}, \{v_i\}_{pk_{\mathsf{EA}}})$ are put through the mix-net and decryption to output $(h_{\sigma_i}^{r_{\sigma_i}}, v_{\sigma_i}, \Pi_{\mathrm{mix}}, \Pi_{\mathrm{dec}})$ as the final tally.

Further, GetSecret outputs g^{r_i}. VerifyVote extracts $h_i^{r_i}$ from the bulletin board, raises the input g^{r_i} to the secret key input x_i and outputs the equality check. Publish outputs the verifiable mix and the decryption of $(v_i, h_i^{r_i})$ along with the BB.

Finally, Verify will verify all public evidence on BB, VerifyBallot will generally verify that a ballot appears correctly on BB for a given voter, however in Hyperion this can often be relaxed to check that some valid ballot has appeared for the given voter id which we denote VerifyVoted. In the privacy game we ignore this and it will always output $\top$. By ρ we denote the election result function.

In our privacy games we choose ρ to compute the array of votes created by extracting, from each element in the input array, the last submitted vote in the concatenated sequence.

4 Ballot Privacy

In this section, we introduce the game-based definition of ballot privacy Ballot-Priv. In this definition, we take into account voters having secret credentials sk_i and capture privacy leaks from verification, especially plaintext verification (as in *Hyperion, Selene* and the Estonian e-voting system).

Even though ballot privacy is a fundamental property in secure voting, it is hard to come up with a generic definition which supports standard proof techniques and encompasses large classes of voting systems and tally functions. A good overview of game-based definitions can be found in [5], which also concludes with a privacy definition (BPRIV) for general tally functions. BPRIV is however not directly applicable to the current context of post-tally verification. Instead we take advantage of *Hyperion* having a simple tally function, namely revealing all plaintext votes. This means we can use a much earlier definition as starting point, namely Benaloh's definition [4], which was rewritten in modern game-based notation in [5].

Figure 1 is a rework of Benaloh's definition, with inspiration from [12] and especially [16], allowing voters to hold secret key material and adding a verification phase. This verification phase has the potential to introduce privacy attacks, if the adversary has access to whether the verification was successful or not. This is a realistic real-world scenario even without compromised parties since voters might share a failed verification with others, perhaps even on social media.

For transparency and to detect wide-spread attacks such behaviour should even be endorsed, and hence better not invalidate privacy.

We also want to model robust voting systems in which the voting process proceeds even if individual verification fails (as would probably happen in larger elections). In the case where a covert attacker model against privacy is preferred, the definition can easily be updated to only let an adversary win the game if verification attempts are successful, which interestingly can still lead to an information leak of the vote. In the Ballot-Priv definition, Fig. 1, we assume a trusted BB and secure channels between the voters and BB, meaning that an honest ballot will arrive unchanged to BB. We also assume an initial setup giving each voter a unique identity id_i.

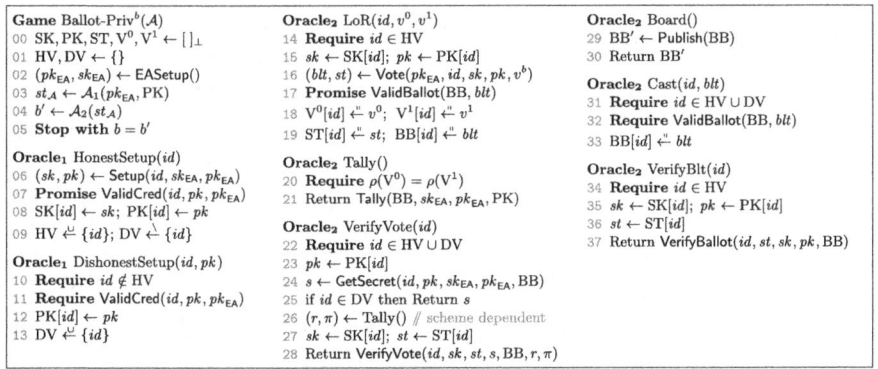

Fig. 1. The game-based security definition of Ballot Privacy. The adversary wins if it distinguishes the left world from the right one, by guessing bit b. In line 16, the Left-or-Right (LoR) oracle either inputs the left vote v^0 or the right one v^1 based on the bit b. We divide our adversary into $\mathcal{A}_1$ and $\mathcal{A}_2$ in 03, 04 and assume that they **respectively** have access to the oracles sub-indexed by 1 and 2.

First, in line 02, the EA prepares the master keys that are used to generate the voters credentials (lines 06–09), to verify a voter's credentials (lines 07, 11), to allow the voting process (line 16), to tally the BB (line 21) and to allow the generation of the voters' verification secrets (line 24).

Lines 10–13 give the adversary the possibility to dynamically register dishonest credentials for some voters: lines 09 and 10 prevent the adversary from registering a set of credentials as both honest and dishonest at the the same time e.g. by calling HonestSetup on a specific id and then DishonestSetup on the same id, causing the voter to be honest and dishonest at the same time. Notice that, for a voter $id \in \mathrm{ID}$, checks of honesty occur in lines 14, 25, 34.

Line 17 ensures that the ballots created in the left or right voting oracle are well-formed. Notice that in lines 18–19, the elements are concatenated to the history: this provides more generality then just overwriting the previous value using the $\leftarrow$ operator to accommodate elections that take into consideration the whole history of vote submissions.

In line 20, the ρ function guarantees that both V^0 and V^1 have the same count: this prevents $\mathcal{A}$ from trivially winning by querying $\mathrm{LoR}(v^0, v^1)$, $\mathrm{LoR}(v^0, v^0)$ and then querying Tally(). Additionally, $\mathcal{A}$ is capable of querying the ballot casting oracle (31–33), the board publishing oracle (29–30), the ballot verification oracle (34–37) and the vote verification oracle (22–28). The ballot verification oracle and the vote verification oracle, both, can provide the adversary with extra information about the honest and dishonest voters (secret s and/or verification output).

We define the advantage of the adversary $\mathrm{Adv}_{\mathcal{A}}^{\mathrm{Ballot\text{-}Priv}} := |\Pr[\mathrm{Ballot\text{-}Priv}^0(\mathcal{A})] - \Pr[\mathrm{Ballot\text{-}Priv}^1(\mathcal{A})]|$. The generality of this type of Benaloh definition is limited to certain types of result functions, see [11], which however is fulfilled for Hyperion where we output all votes after mixing. Especially, we notice that, a necessary condition on ρ is that it should fulfill the following relation $\rho(V_0) = \rho(V_1) \implies \rho(V_0 \| V') = \rho(V_1 \| V')$. Probably the definition could be extended to general cases, with an assumption of extraction properties of the ballots.

Theorem 1. *For all $\mathcal{A}$ playing* Ballot-Priv *(Fig. 1 instantiated with Hyperion, there exists adversaries $\mathcal{B}, \mathcal{C}, \mathcal{D}, \mathcal{E}, \mathcal{F}$ such that the following relation holds:*

$$\mathrm{Adv}_{\mathcal{A}}^{\mathrm{Ballot\text{-}Priv}} \leq \mathrm{Adv}_{\mathcal{B}}^{\mathrm{ZK}} + \mathrm{Adv}_{\mathcal{C}}^{\mathrm{EUF-CMA}} + \mathrm{Adv}_{\mathcal{D}}^{\mathrm{Mix}} + \mathrm{Adv}_{\mathcal{E}}^{\mathrm{ZK'}} + \mathrm{Adv}_{\mathcal{F}}^{\mathrm{poly\text{-}IND\text{-}1\text{-}CCA}}$$

Further, in the long version [14] we also prove that our scheme satisfies du-mb-BPRIV against a malicious board from [12,16]:

Theorem 2. *For all $\mathcal{A}$ playing* du-mb-BPRIV *[16] instantiated with Hyperion, there exists adversaries $\mathcal{B}, \mathcal{D}, \mathcal{D}', \mathcal{E}, \mathcal{F}$ such that the following relation holds:*

$$\mathrm{Adv}_{\mathcal{A}}^{\mathrm{du\text{-}mb\text{-}BPRIV}} \leq \mathrm{Adv}_{\mathcal{B}}^{\mathrm{ZK}} + \mathrm{Adv}_{\mathcal{D}}^{\mathrm{Mix}} + \mathrm{Adv}_{\mathcal{D}'}^{\mathrm{Mix}} + \mathrm{Adv}_{\mathcal{E}}^{\mathrm{ZK'}} + \mathrm{Adv}_{\mathcal{F}}^{\mathrm{poly\text{-}IND\text{-}1\text{-}CCA}}$$

The main difference for the bounding is that du-mb-BPRIV does not capture attacks for the verification success seen as a side-channel to the adversary, and hence the ballot signatures are not necessary.

4.1 Proof of Ballot Privacy

We now prove that our scheme meets Ballot-Priv property. In order to do so, we instantiate the algorithms as described in Sect. 3. We use game hopping technique to bound the adversary advantage. Since oracles can be called multiple times by the adversary, we will suppress pre-factors in the advantage bounds. We note by G_0 the instantiated Ballot-Priv game: $\mathsf{Adv}_{\mathcal{A}}^{\text{Ballot-Priv}} = \mathsf{Adv}_{\mathcal{A}}^{G_0}$.

In the first game hop, we remove line 07 in G_1. In fact under the assumption stated in Sect. 2.2 we have that line 07 will always pass, and thus $\mathsf{Adv}_{\mathcal{A}}^{G_0} = \mathsf{Adv}_{\mathcal{A}}^{G_1}$.

In G_2, by the zero knowledge property, the proofs Π_x and Π_{r_i} are simulated for honest voters. This is possible since these proofs are created by the challenger. Now, the adversary cannot extract any information from the simulated proofs and $\mathsf{Adv}_{\mathcal{A}}^{G_1} \leq \mathsf{Adv}_{\mathcal{A}}^{G_2} + \mathsf{Adv}_{\mathcal{B}}^{\text{ZK}}$ ($\mathsf{Adv}_{\mathcal{B}}^{\text{ZK}}$ is the advantage of $\mathcal{B}$ to distinguish simulation from real proofs).

In game G_3, we modify line 31 to require $id \in \mathsf{DV}$ only. In this case, because of the requirement in 32, when casting a ballot for an honest voter, the adversary has to be capable of forging a valid signature for the honest voter. If the signature scheme is existentially unforgeable, we have $\mathsf{Adv}_{\mathcal{A}}^{G_2} \leq \mathsf{Adv}_{\mathcal{A}}^{G_3} + \mathsf{Adv}_{\mathcal{C}}^{\text{EUF-CMA}}$.

In the fourth game G_4, we replace the verification step on line 28 to always output success. Because our scheme is correct, and since the adversary is not capable of submitting ballots on behalf of honest voters, then we have $\mathsf{Adv}_{\mathcal{A}}^{G_3} = \mathsf{Adv}_{\mathcal{A}}^{G_4}$.

In game G_5, we modify line 21 in the tally oracle: rather than picking r_i at random for each voter and computing $h_i^{r_i}$ then encrypting the computed value, we sample a uniformly random group element g_i and then encrypt it. Since we are working in a cyclic group of prime order, then the distributions of g_i and $h_i^{r_i}$ are exactly the same for all registered voters i, thus $\mathsf{Adv}_{\mathcal{A}}^{G_4} = \mathsf{Adv}_{\mathcal{A}}^{G_5}$.[7]

In the next game G_6, we modify again line 21, by replace the secure mix-net by its ideal functionality. We thus have $\mathsf{Adv}_{\mathcal{A}}^{G_5} \leq \mathsf{Adv}_{\mathcal{A}}^{G_6} + \mathsf{Adv}_{\mathcal{D}}^{\text{Mix}}$.[8]

In G_7, analogously to G_2, we simulate the decryption proofs Π_{dec} for all the ciphertexts output by the mix-net. Further, for the honest voters, the decryption values for the plaintext votes are taken from the calls to the LoR oracle. Due to the correctness of the encryption scheme, the adversary's advantage is $\mathsf{Adv}_{\mathcal{A}}^{G_6} \leq \mathsf{Adv}_{\mathcal{A}}^{G_7} + \mathsf{Adv}_{\mathcal{E}}^{\text{ZK}'}$.

In the final game hop, we require that the mix-nets in G_8 output the honest votes (taken from the LoR oracle) concatenated with the decryption of the dishonest votes. The views in the left world and the right world should be the same, thus we require the decryption mix to output $\rho(\mathbf{V}^b)$ concatenated with the dishonest votes. We have that $\mathsf{Adv}_{\mathcal{A}}^{G_8} = \mathsf{Adv}_{\mathcal{A}}^{G_7}$.

Finally, we argue that the advantage of the final game is exactly $\mathsf{Adv}_{\mathcal{F}}^{\text{poly-IND-1-CCA}}$ in poly-IND-1-CCA since we can remove all simulated proofs. The label is the id of the voters. We assume that the the encryption scheme with the non-malleable proofs of plaintext knowledge including the id satisfy poly-IND-1-CCA security.

---

[7] We can allow the adversary to have the dual key g^{r_i} for *all voters* in line 28 and still prove security of the scheme under the DDH assumptions: $h_i := g^{x_i}$ adversary cannot distinguish $(g^{x_i}, g^{r_i}, g^{x_i \cdot r_i})$ and (g^{x_i}, g^{r_i}, g_i).

[8] Alternatively, we could model the mix-net as a re-encryption mix with a NIZKP, and use IND-CPA of the encryptions of g_i to ignore these ciphertexts.

We conclude the following:

$$\mathsf{Adv}_{\mathcal{A}}^{\text{Ballot-Priv}} \leq \mathsf{Adv}_{\mathcal{B}}^{\text{ZK}} + \mathsf{Adv}_{\mathcal{C}}^{\text{EUF-CMA}} + \mathsf{Adv}_{\mathcal{D}}^{\text{Mix}} + \mathsf{Adv}_{\mathcal{E}}^{\text{ZK}'} + \mathsf{Adv}_{\mathcal{F}}^{\text{poly-IND-1-CCA}}$$

5 Integrity

5.1 Correctness

We first note that the scheme satisfies correctness in the sense that if the voting protocol is run honestly, the tally will give the correct result on the intended votes and all voters will verify correctly. This assumes correctness of the underlying zero-knowledge proofs, signatures, mix-net and correctness of the encryption scheme. This could be relaxed to non-perfect correctness if needed.

5.2 Verifiability

For an overview of verifiability definitions see [11], especially we will use the definition in [10]. This is because the specific voting-casting construction that we instantiate *Hyperion* with here is close to Helios-C (i.e. Helios with signatures) presented and proven verifiable in [10].

The election schemes in [10] are defined via algorithms Setup = EASetup, Credential = Setup, Vote, VerifyVote$_{\text{CGGI}}$, Validate = ValidBallot, Tally, Verify, where we have indicated by which algorithms they correspond to in our scheme, see Sect. 3. Verify will simply check all proofs on BB. The main difference is in VerifyVote: in Helios-like constructions this corresponds to checking that your actual ballot *blt* has appeared on BB. Here, it corresponds to performing the *Hyperion* verification and will involve getting the dual key from the EA. Since we will define security against a malicious BB, we further need that the voters check that a valid vote was registered under their *id*, but without having to check which specific cryptographic ballot is recorded (for improved usability). We denote this VerifyVoted. As in [10] we consider schemes without vote updates for simplicity.

In [10] combined individual and universal verifiability is defined against a malicious BB. This means the board is completely malicious up until the Tally, where it will be output by the adversary, and there will be a unified view of BB. This also models that vote casting channels might not be secure. The definition is via a game $\text{Exp}_{\mathcal{A}}^{verb}$ for which the adversary has negligible chance in creating a valid BB and tally where it is not true that 1) the vote count will contain the honest verifying voters' votes, 2) for the non-verifying honest voters their votes can maximally be deleted, and 3) there is maximally one vote per corrupted voter in the tally. To count this it is assumed that the result function ρ allows partial tally. The main assumption is that the Registration Authority is honest i.e. signing keys are setup honestly and not leaked and are existentially unforgeable, EUF-CMA. This will also hold for *Hyperion*.

Theorem 3. *Hyperion will satisfy Verifiability against a dishonest bulletin board [10] if the signing keys are not leaked, the signature scheme is EUF-CMA and the ballot verification is via* VerifyVoted, *i.e. the voter only checks if a valid vote was cast.*

The proof follows as for Helios-C, however, we use mix-nets instead of homomorphic tally, which still ensures one-vote per voter due to the soundness of the mixes. Also, we can replace VerifyVote$_{\text{CGGI}}$ with VerifyVoted since the adversary cannot forge a signature.[9]

However, this did not take into account the actual *Hyperion* verification check which also allows a voter to verify if the vote intent was captured directly in the tally. We now extend the verifiability definition to fully incorporate this. The main point will be that an honest checking voter can rely on her vote being counted correctly if either her signing key or *Hyperion* secret key is not compromised. In particular, we get a resistance against malware if we have separate devices for vote casting (containing the signing key) and vote verification (containing the *Hyperion* key), and not both devices are corrupted.

We now introduce a verifiability definition against a malicious voting bulletin board in the presence of malware with separate vote casting and vote verification devices. We stress that in the definition it is only the vote casting part of the bulletin board which is determined by the adversary, the registered public keys cannot be altered for honest devices.[10]

The security is defined via the experiment Verif-MBM in Fig. 2, where the advantage of the adversary is $\text{Adv}_{\mathcal{A}}^{\text{Verif-MBM}} = \Pr[\text{Verif-MBM}(\mathcal{A}) = 1]$ The malicious bulletin board and corrupted authorities are modeled by the adversary outputting the bulletin board as well as the tally result and proofs in line 05. $\mathcal{H}_c$ and $\mathcal{D}_c$ respectively denote the voter IDs with honest and corrupted vote casting devices which have registered public verification keys and hence constitute the eligible voters. Correspondingly, $\mathcal{H}_v$ and $\mathcal{D}_v$ are the voter IDs with honest and corrupted vote verification devices. We split the algorithm Setup into a part for the signing key and for the verification key denoted respectively Setup$_c$ and Setup$_v$, and we do the same split for the ValidCred algorithm.

$\mathcal{V}_i$ denotes the set of voters intending to vote and $\mathbf{V}_i$ captures their intended vote, with $\mathbb{V}$ the allowed vote space. $\mathcal{V}_{\text{Chkd}}$ denotes the voters who make successful verification checks. Failing checks would lead to complaints and the adversary loses the game. As in [10], the set of voters who are going to check can be input to the game to capture that not all voters verify. For simplicity we assume only voters with a vote intention will try to verify. Those who check will try to do both VerifyVote and VerifyBallot which we here simplify to VerifyVoted.[11]

We assume VerifyVoted is unaffected by malware since it just requires access to BB (and could be delegated). For VerifyVote, if the voter's verification device is corrupted, or the voter is not registered for verification, the check will be assumed successful.

---

[9] Since we are in a single pass setting this is particularly simple. With vote updates more care needs to be taken. Either we need to assume an append only board or that a vote update number is included in the signature and remembered by the voter.

[10] In practice this can be secured in a full malicious board setting by forwarding the public keys to proxies at registration time, who will check later that these appear correctly.

[11] The definition can use VerifyBallot by defining which part of the voter state the adversary can control.

```
Game Verif-MBM(𝒜)                         Oracle₁ HonestCastSetup(id)              Oracle₁ HonestVerSetup(id)
00  SK_c, PK_c ← [ ]_⊥                     23  Require id ∉ 𝒟_c                     32  Require id ∉ 𝒟_v
01  SK_v, PK_v, ST, V ← [ ]_⊥              24  (sk, pk) ← Setup_c(id, pk_EA)        33  (sk, pk) ← Setup_v(id, pk_EA)
02  ℋ_c, 𝒟_c, ℋ_v, 𝒟_v, 𝒱_i ← {}           25  Promise ValidCred_c(id, pk, pk_EA)   34  Promise ValidCred_v(id, pk, pk_EA)
03  (pk_EA, sk_EA) ← EASetup()             26  SK_c[id] ← sk; PK_c[id] ← pk         35  SK_v[id] ← sk; PK_v[id] ← pk
04  st_𝒜 ← 𝒜₁(pk_EA, PK)                   27  ℋ_c ←ᵘ {id}                          36  ℋ_v ←ᵘ {id}
05  (BB, r, π, st_𝒜) ← 𝒜₂(st_𝒜)
06  Require Verify(BB, r, π)               Oracle₁ DishonestCastSetup(id, pk)    Oracle₁ DishonestVerSetup(id, pk)
07  for id ∈ 𝒱_Chkd ∩ 𝒱_i                  28  Require id ∉ ℋ_c                     37  Require id ∉ ℋ_v
08    Require VerifyVoted(id, BB)          29  Require ValidCred_c(id, pk, pk_EA)   38  Require ValidCred_v(id, pk, pk_EA)
09    if id ∈ ℋ_v then:                    30  PK_c[id] ← pk                        39  PK_v[id] ← pk
10      sk ← SK_v[id], s ← 𝒜₃(st_𝒜)        31  𝒟_c ←ᵘ {id}                          40  𝒟_v ←ᵘ {id}
11      v ← V[id]
12      Require VerifyVote(id, sk, v, s, BB, r, π)                                 Oracle₂ Vote(id, v)
13  Require r = ⊤                                                                  41  Require id ∈ ℋ_c ∪ 𝒟_c
14  ℳ ← 𝒱_Chkd ∩ (ℋ_c ∪ ℋ_v)                                                        42  𝒱_i ←ᵘ {id}; V[id] ← v
15  a ← |𝒱_Chkd ∩ 𝒟_v|                                                              43  if id ∈ ℋ_c then
16  b ← |𝒟_c \ (𝒱_Chkd ∩ ℋ_v)|                                                      44    sk ← SK[id]; pk ← PK[id]
17  Require                                                                        45    (blt, st) ← Vote(pk_EA, id, sk, pk, v)
18    ∃n ∈ {a, ..., b}                                                             46    ST[id] ← st
19    ∃v₁, ..., v_n ∈ V // vote set                                                47    Return blt
20    ∃S ⊆ (𝒱_i \ 𝒱_Chkd) ∩ ℋ_c
21    s.t. r= ρ([V[j]]_{j∈S}) ⋆ ρ([v_j]_{j=1}^n) ⋆ ρ([V[j]]_{j∈ℳ})
22  Stop with ⊤
```

Fig. 2. The game-based definition of verifiability against a malicious voting board and malware. The indices on the oracles denote which adversary can use them. We use sub-index v to denote verify, c for cast and i for intended.

For uncorrupted devices, since EA is corrupted, the adversary can choose which dual key the voter receives. We do not need a corrupted category since if both devices are corrupted and the voter does not perform verifications then the voter is completely controlled by the adversary. A stronger version can let the adversary choose the election setup, but here it is honestly created.

Note that this definition does not capture the probability of detecting the presence of malware, but the guarantee given to a successfully verifying voter and what votes the adversary can choose for the rest. In particular, the adversary will win if he can output a valid BB and tally and manages to either 1) change the vote of a voter who has at least one honest device and who verified (line 14), or 2) for voters with honest vote casting devices, he manages to stuff votes or change a cast vote in another way than simply deleting it (line 20), or 3) for the remaining eligible voters can cast more than one vote per voter (line 18). The lower bound on votes in the last category comes from the voters with both devices being corrupted, and who are successfully verifying, will know that some vote arrived on their behalf, but not which plaintext vote it contains. Finally, in line 21 the $\star$ denotes the combination of partial tallies in the result function ρ.

The verifiability of *Hyperion* relies on the computational 1-Diffie-Hellman Inversion Problem (1-DHI) [27] for a cyclic prime order group of order q and generator (G, g).

Definition 1 (Computational 1-DHI). *Given $g^x \in G$ with $x \leftarrow \mathbb{Z}_q$ compute $g^{1/x}$. Under the 1-DHI assumption the advantage* $\mathsf{Adv}_{\mathcal{A}}^{1-DHI} = \Pr[x \leftarrow \mathbb{Z}_q : g^{1/x} = \mathcal{A}(g^x)]$ *is negligible for all PPT algorithms.*

If we use ballot verification VerifyBallot via VerifyVoted, i.e. the voter only checks if a valid vote was cast, then we have the following theorem

Theorem 4. *With EUF-CMA signatures, sound mix-nets, encryption correctness, simulation-sound extractability [6, 19] for the proofs of knowledge and under the 1-DHI assumption, the advantage in verifiability against a malicious BB and malware, $\mathsf{Adv}_\mathcal{A}^{\text{Verif-MBM}}$ is negligible.*

The proof can be found in Appendix B.

6 Conclusion

We present a new end-to-end verifiable scheme, inspired by the *Selene* tracker based scheme, that provides a similar, highly transparent, intuitive way for voters to verify their vote: by identifying their vote in cleartext in the tally. Our new construction however allows us to achieve this without the need for trackers and allows us to neatly avoid the tracker collision problem that undermined the *Selene* scheme. The collision threat however could re-emerge as collision of commitments rather than trackers. This prompts and enables a further innovation, described in the full version of this paper: the idea of individual voter views, that entirely avoids the collision threat of *Selene* and should afford voters a greater sense of privacy. Voters should feel more comfortable with *Hyperion* as it does not involve the public posting of all the tracker numbers paired with the votes.

While we do not advocate the use of *Hyperion* for high-stakes elections, we do believe that it is well suited to many less critical contexts. The transparency of the verification and the underlying simplicity of the constructions should be appealing to many stakeholders: the voters, the election officials, the candidates etc. The individual views version introduces some additional computation and complexity, but is efficient for small elections, and in any case could be done on demand when a voter seeks to verify their vote.

We have proven that the system satisfies ballot privacy and verifiability, the latter even under partial malware corruption of the voters' vote casting and verification devices. In the full version, [14], we sketch how the *Hyperion* scheme can be made everlasting private, see lso [26], or post-quantum secure. We also outline some possible variants of the core scheme, including the individual *BB* views, the re-introduction of trackers and the use of return or confirmation codes to address dispute resolution.

Future work will include full analysis of the current scheme and detailing the variants and formally proving them. We will also perform focus groups and user trials to gauge user response and preferences amongst the variants and w.r.t. to *Selene*.

Acknowledgments. This paper acknowledges the Luxembourg National Research Fund (FNR) CORE project EquiVox (C19/IS/13643617/EquiVox/Ryan) and the CORE project (C21/IS/16221219/ ImPAKT).

A Implementation

We implement and instantiate *Hyperion*[12] in Python, using the GNU Multiple Precision Arithmetic library, and evaluate its performance on a server equipped with a 32 core AMD EPYC 7302P CPU clocked at 3 GHz and 256 gigabytes of RAM. The implementation is parameterized by the P-256 curve. An implementation of a Terelius-Wikström mixnet [20,35] was employed for parallel shuffling in the tallying phase. Analogously, we also implement and instantiate *Selene*[13] in order to compare the performance of both schemes; these measurements are provided in Appendix E of [14]. Table 1 presents measurements collected during the course of 3 trial runs of the *Hyperion* scheme for 1000 voters, 10000 voters, and 100000 voters. We comment that though this is a prototype implementation, the mixnet code has been parallelised to run faster on multi-core systems. The explicit ZKPs employed in our implementation can be found in [14].

Table 1. Execution times of each phase of the Hyperion scheme in seconds.

Phase	$N = 1000$	$N = 10000$	$N = 100000$
Setup	0.0004 s	0.0005 s	0.0005 s
Voting	0.0085 s	0.0090 s	0.0160 s
Tallying (Mix)	42.205 s	1541.62 s	6886.90 s
Tallying (Decrypt)	5.4640 s	33.889 s	1092.32 s
Coercion-Mitigation	0.0008 s	0.0008 s	0.0007 s
Individual Views	14.091 s	256.72 s	3498.16 s

B Proof of Verifiability, Theorem 4

We here give a short proof, the finite advantage bound can easily be inferred. The proof is done without reference to whether a CRS or RO setup is used. By line 06 and 13 in Fig. 2 we can assume that the adversary outputs a valid BB with a result and valid proof. Since the mix-net proofs validate, by the soundness of the mix-net proofs, decryption proofs and correctness of the encryption scheme, we have that the resulting multiset of votes are equal to the plaintext inputs. For honestly cast ballots we have correctness and they will validate if added to BB. Also, honestly generated key will validate. All votes will be in the correct vote space, this can either be directly checked after decryption or derived from the soundness of the ballot proof of well-formedness.

For all voters in $\mathcal{H}_c$ we have valid signatures if they cast votes and by EUF-CMA the adversary cannot forge any signature. Hence for $\mathcal{H}_c$ no votes can be

---
[12] https://github.com/hyperion-voting/hyperion.
[13] https://github.com/hyperion-voting/selene.

stuffed and cast votes can never be altered, only deleted. Thus for successfully checking voters with honest vote casting device, $\mathcal{V}_{\mathrm{Chkd}} \cap \mathcal{H}_c$, all votes has to appear unaltered (remember $\mathcal{V}_{\mathrm{Chkd}} \subseteq \mathcal{V}_i$ i.e. the checking voters are part of the voters intending to vote), this proves the $\mathcal{V}_{\mathrm{Chkd}} \cap \mathcal{H}_c$ part of line 14. For the remaining cast votes from voters in $(\mathcal{V}_i \setminus \mathcal{V}_{\mathrm{Chkd}}) \cap \mathcal{H}_c$ the adversary can choose which to delete, ensuring line 20.

We can now consider the voters with a malicious vote-casting device $\mathcal{D}_c$. If these voters are not checking, we have no guarantees. If they check and have a corrupted verification device, then there has to be a ballot for their id due to VerifyVoted, however there is no guarantee which vote it contains. This explains the lower bound on the number of maliciously created ballots in line 18.

Finally, we need to consider voters successfully verifying with an uncorrupted verification device. We want to show that they will be able to verify their plaintext vote, hence proving the $\mathcal{V}_{\mathrm{Chkd}} \cap \mathcal{H}_v$ part of line 14 and the upper bound in line 18. We first simulate the ZKPoKs of x_i for the honestly registered Hyperion keys $h_i = g^{x_i}$.

We will give a proof by contradiction, i.e. we assume that a voter in $\mathcal{V}_{\mathrm{Chkd}} \cap \mathcal{H}_v$ will get pointed to another vote than her intended vote by the Hyperion verification with some non-negligible advantage $\mathsf{Adv}_{\mathcal{A}}$. We will use this to create an adversary against computations 1-DHI. To this end, we take a 1-DHI challenge g^x and use this as the key for a random voter in $\mathcal{V}_{\mathrm{Chkd}} \cap \mathcal{H}_v$ with a simulated proof. Since the key g^x is indistinguishable from random this voter will be targeted by the attack with probability at least $1/|\mathcal{V}_{\mathrm{Chkd}} \cap \mathcal{H}_v|$.

For all the voters with corrupted casting devices, we now extract their secret keys x_i from the ZKPoKs using the simulation sound extractability (for the honest verification devices, we know their secret keys). Let α denote the dual key term sent by the adversary to the voter. By the soundness of the ZKPoK for the encryption of the elements $h_i^{r_i}$, the soundness of the mix-net and the correctness of the encryption, the output commitments are all of the form $h_i^{r_i}$.

We further extract all r_is from the ZKPoKs. If the voter gets pointed to another vote we have that $\alpha^x = h_i^{r_i} = g^{x_i r_i}$ for some i with $x_i \neq x$. We don't know which i this is, but we guess at random between the k choices. Hence we can compute $\alpha^{1/(x_i r_i)}$ which will be equal $g^{1/x}$ with a non-negligible probability $\mathsf{Adv}_{\mathcal{A}}/(|\mathcal{V}_{\mathrm{Chkd}} \cap \mathcal{H}_v| \cdot k)$ breaking the computational 1-DHI assumption and concluding the proof.

References

1. Adida, B., De Marneffe, O., Pereira, O., Quisquater, J.J., et al.: Electing a university president using open-audit voting: analysis of real-world use of Helios. EVT/WOTE **9**(10) (2009)
2. Alsadi, M., Schneider, S.: Verify my vote: voter experience. E-Vote-ID 2020, 280 (2020)
3. Arnaud, M., Cortier, V., Wiedling, C.: Analysis of an electronic boardroom voting system. In: International Conference on E-Voting and Identity, pp. 109–126. Springer (2013)

4. Benaloh, J.D.C.: Verifiable secret-ballot elections, Ph.D. thesis, Yale University (1987)
5. Bernhard, D., Cortier, V., Galindo, D., Pereira, O., Warinschi, B.: Sok: a comprehensive analysis of game-based ballot privacy definitions. In: 2015 IEEE Symposium on Security and Privacy, pp. 499–516. IEEE (2015)
6. Bernhard, D., Pereira, O., Warinschi, B.: How not to prove yourself: pitfalls of the Fiat-Shamir heuristic and applications to Helios. In: International Conference on the Theory and Application of Cryptology and Information Security, pp. 626–643. Springer (2012)
7. Bruni, A., Drewsen, E., Schürmann, C.: Towards a mechanized proof of Selene receipt-freeness and vote-privacy. In: International Joint Conference on Electronic Voting, pp. 110–126. Springer (2017)
8. Camenisch, J.: Group signature schemes and payment systems based on the discrete logarithm problem, Ph.D. thesis, ETH Zurich (1998)
9. Chaidos, P., Cortier, V., Fuchsbauer, G., Galindo, D.: Beleniosrf: a non-interactive receipt-free electronic voting scheme. In: Proceedings of the 2016 ACM SIGSAC Conference on Computer and Communications Security, pp. 1614–1625 (2016)
10. Cortier, V., Galindo, D., Glondu, S., Izabachene, M.: Election verifiability for Helios under weaker trust assumptions. In: European Symposium on Research in Computer Security, pp. 327–344. Springer (2014)
11. Cortier, V., Galindo, D., Küsters, R., Müller, J., Truderung, T.: Sok: verifiability notions for e-voting protocols. In: 2016 IEEE Symposium on Security and Privacy (SP), pp. 779–798. IEEE (2016)
12. Cortier, V., Lallemand, J., Warinschi, B.: Fifty shades of ballot privacy: privacy against a malicious board. In: 2020 IEEE 33rd Computer Security Foundations Symposium (CSF), pp. 17–32. IEEE (2020)
13. Cortier, V., Smyth, B.: Attacking and fixing Helios: an analysis of ballot secrecy. J. Comput. Secur. **21**(1), 89–148 (2013)
14. Damodaran, A., Rastikian, S., Rønne, P.B., Ryan, P.Y.: Hyperion: transparent end-to-end verifiable voting with coercion mitigation. Cryptology ePrint Archive (2024)
15. Distler, V., Zollinger, M.L., Lallemand, C., Roenne, P.B., Ryan, P.Y., Koenig, V.: Security-visible, yet unseen? In: Proceedings of the 2019 CHI conference on human factors in computing systems, pp. 1–13 (2019)
16. Dragan, C.C., et al.: Machine-checked proofs of privacy against malicious boards for Selene & co. In: 35th IEEE Computer Security Foundations Symposium, CSF 2022, pp. 335–347. IEEE (2022)
17. ElGamal, T.: A public key cryptosystem and a signature scheme based on discrete logarithms. IEEE Trans. Inf. Theory **31**(4), 469–472 (1985)
18. Fiat, A., Shamir, A.: How to prove yourself: Practical solutions to identification and signature problems. In: Conference on the Theory and Application of Cryptographic Techniques, pp. 186–194. Springer (1986)
19. Groth, J.: Simulation-sound NIZK proofs for a practical language and constant size group signatures. In: International Conference on the Theory and Application of Cryptology and Information Security, pp. 444–459. Springer (2006)
20. Haenni, R., Locher, P., Koenig, R., Dubuis, E.: Pseudo-code algorithms for verifiable re-encryption mix-nets. In: Financial Cryptography and Data Security, pp. 370–384. Springer (2017)
21. Hao, F., Ryan, P.Y.: Real-World Electronic Voting: Design, Analysis and Deployment. CRC Press (2016)

22. Iovino, V., Rial, A., Rønne, P.B., Ryan, P.Y.: Using Selene to verify your vote in JCJ. In: International Conference on Financial Cryptography and Data Security, pp. 385–403. Springer (2017)
23. Jamroga, W., Roenne, P.B., Ryan, P.Y., Stark, P.B.: Risk-limiting tallies. In: International Joint Conference on Electronic Voting, pp. 183–199. Springer (2019)
24. Juels, A., Catalano, D., Jakobsson, M.: Coercion-resistant electronic elections. In: Towards Trustworthy Elections, pp. 37–63. Springer (2010)
25. Küsters, R., Müller, J., Scapin, E., Truderung, T.: sElect: a lightweight verifiable remote voting system. In: Computer Security Foundations Symposium (CSF), 2016 IEEE 29th, pp. 341–354. IEEE (2016)
26. Mosaheb, R., Rønne, P.B., Ryan, P.Y., Sarfaraz, S.: Direct and transparent voter verification with everlasting receipt-freeness. In: International Joint Conference on Electronic Voting, pp. 124–140. Springer, Cham (2024)
27. Pfitzmann, B.P., Sadeghi, A.R.: Anonymous fingerprinting with direct non-repudiation. In: International Conference on the Theory and Application of Cryptology and Information Security, pp. 401–414. Springer (2000)
28. Rivest, R.L.: On the notion of 'software independence' in voting systems. Philos. Trans. Roy. Soc. A Math. Phys. Eng. Sci. **366**(1881), 3759–3767 (2008)
29. Rønne, P.B., Ryan, P.Y., Zollinger, M.L.: Electryo, in-person voting with transparent voter verifiability and eligibility verifiability. arXiv preprint arXiv:2105.14783 (2021)
30. Ryan, P.Y.A., Rønne, P.B., Iovino, V.: Selene: voting with transparent verifiability and coercion-mitigation. In: International Conference on Financial Cryptography and Data Security, pp. 176–192. Springer (2016)
31. Ryan, P.Y., Roenne, P.B., Ostrev, D., Orche, F.E.E., Soroush, N., Stark, P.B.: Who was that masked voter? The tally won't tell! In: International Joint Conference on Electronic Voting, pp. 106–123. Springer (2021)
32. Sallal, M., et al.: Augmenting an internet voting system with Selene verifiability using permissioned distributed ledger. In: 2020 IEEE 40th International Conference on Distributed Computing Systems (ICDCS), pp. 1167–1168. IEEE (2020)
33. Schneier, B.: Applied Cryptography: Protocols, Algorithms, and Source Code in C. Wiley (2007)
34. Schnorr, C.P.: Efficient signature generation by smart cards. J. Cryptol. **4**(3), 161–174 (1991). https://doi.org/10.1007/BF00196725
35. Terelius, B., Wikström, D.: Proofs of restricted shuffles. In: Bernstein, D.J., Lange, T. (eds.) AFRICACRYPT 2010. LNCS, vol. 6055, pp. 100–113. Springer, Heidelberg (2010). https://doi.org/10.1007/978-3-642-12678-9_7
36. Wikström, D.: User Manual for the Verificatum Mix-Net Version 1.4.0. Verificatum AB, Stockholm, Sweden (2013)
37. Zollinger, M.L., Distler, V., Roenne, P.B., Ryan, P.Y., Lallemand, C., Koenig, V.: User experience design for e-voting: how mental models align with security mechanisms. arXiv preprint arXiv:2105.14901 (2021)
38. Zollinger, M.L., Rønne, P.B., Ryan, P.Y.: Short paper: mechanized proofs of verifiability and privacy in a paper-based e-voting scheme. In: International Conference on Financial Cryptography and Data Security, pp. 310–318. Springer (2020)

Two-Factor Authenticated Key Exchange with Enhanced Security from Post-quantum Assumptions

Qijia Fan, Chenhao Bao, Xuanyu Shi, Shuai Han[✉], and Shengli Liu[✉]

School of Computer Science, Shanghai Jiao Tong University, Shanghai 200240, China
{qweryy0566,bch123,shixuanyu,dalen17,slliu}@sjtu.edu.cn

Abstract. Two-factor authenticated key exchange (2fAKE) protocol requires a client to provide two authentication factors to authenticate itself and establish a shared session key with a server, thus providing double-insurance.

In this work, we focus on 2fAKE with *biometrics* and *passwords* serving as the two factors. Such 2fAKE might be the most convenient one for the client. However, the use of biometrics and passwords may increase the risk of their leakage. To protect the privacy of biometrics and passwords, we formalize an *enhanced* security model for 2fAKE. Specifically, we require *zero-knowledge* on the biometrics, namely the server database as well as the protocol transcripts do not reveal any information about the biometrics. As for passwords, we require that the compromise of the server database does not leak the passwords of clients.

We then propose a generic construction of 2fAKE, which enjoys both great convenience and enhanced security. It does not require the client to store any secrets, does not store the passwords in plain in the server database, and achieves zero-knowledge on the biometrics throughout the protocol. By instantiating the generic construction with post-quantum secure building blocks, we immediately get concrete 2fAKE protocol with enhanced security from *post-quantum assumptions*, which provides even stronger security guarantees. The experiments show that our 2fAKE instantiation achieves high efficiency, where the server stores just 3.1 KB in database for one client, the communication is only 3 rounds and costs 4.3 KB, the client runs in 25 ms and the server runs in only 0.2 ms.

1 Introduction

Authenticated Key Exchange (AKE) enables two parties to authenticate each other and establish a shared session key for secure communications. It is generally deployed in the client-server setting and enhances the security of various online services in our daily life, such as online shopping, online banking and online chatting. In these scenarios, a client authenticates herself/himself to the server by using some secret factor that only the client *knows*, like passwords or

---

© The Author(s), under exclusive license to Springer Nature Switzerland AG 2026
V. Nicomette et al. (Eds.): ESORICS 2025, LNCS 16054, pp. 144–163, 2026.
https://doi.org/10.1007/978-3-032-07891-9_8

secret keys, or that the client *has*, like biometrics, smart cards, or tokens. Accordingly, these give rise to variants of AKE, like password-based AKE (PAKE) [2,4,26], public-key-infrastructure (PKI)-based AKE [3,8,28], biometric-based AKE [22,35], etc. However, all these variants fall into the category of *single-factor* AKE, and once the client's secret factor is leaked or compromised by an adversary, the security of AKE can no longer be guaranteed.

A good way to decrease the risk is using *Two-Factor* AKE (2fAKE) [17–19,21, 32,38], where the client now makes use of two secret factors to do authentication and key establishment with the server. Only if the client possesses both factors, she/he can pass the authentication. Even if the adversary gets one factor of the client, it cannot impersonate the client to pass the authentication with the server. Thus 2fAKE provides stronger security guarantee and is preferable to single-factor AKE.

Different choices of the two factors lead to different types of 2fAKE, and among them, 2fAKE based on biometrics and passwords might be the most convenient one for the client. Biometrics (e.g., faces, fingerprints, palmprints, iris, voices) are features of client, and are naturally "carried" by client without effort. In contrast, smart cards or tokens usually impose management burden on the client, who has to carry them and access them whenever needed. Besides, passwords are usually easier-to-remember than cryptographic secret keys [26]. With the combination of biometrics and passwords as two factors, the client does not need to carry any additional device or store them in device, thus it provides a convenient and user-friendly manner to use 2fAKE.

However, the use of biometrics and passwords as two factors in 2fAKE might also increase the risk of their leakage. Biometrics are unique to the client and can hardly be changed, and once leaked, it would cause huge problems for the client. Moreover, in practice, the client tends to set the same password or related passwords for different services. Once one password is leaked, the security of other passwords would be compromised inevitably.

In summary, 2fAKE based on biometrics and passwords provides great convenience to the client, but on the other hand might increase the risk of leaking the factors. However, to the best of our knowledge, all existing biometric- and password-based 2fAKE schemes [17,21,32] do not take the protection of biometrics and passwords into account.

- The seminal work [32] by Pointcheval and Zimmer studies multi-factor AKE (a generalization of 2fAKE), where two of the multi-factors are biometrics and passwords and the others can be secret keys. However, their security model does not capture the protection of biometrics and passwords. Moreover, in their proposed scheme, the server stores the client's password in plain and encrypts the client's biometric using the client's key. If the server is compromised, the client's password is completely leaked, and moreover, if the adversary additionally gets the client's secret key, the client's biometric is also revealed by decryption. This is definitely unacceptable, since the leakage of secret key (one factor) should not lead to the leakage of biometric (another factor).

– The works [17,21] propose 2fAKE schemes, but they do not consider the protection of biometrics and passwords in their security model as well. Indeed, in the 2fAKE scheme in [21], the server stores g^b in the database, where g is a generator of a cyclic group G and b denotes the client's biometric. Even though the discrete logarithm in G might be hard to solve in general, it is still possible that one can recover the client's biometric b from g^b, since the client's biometric b is not uniformly distributed[1]. Besides, the 2fAKE scheme in [17] relies on trusted execution environment (TEE) for its security, which is vulnerable to side-channel attacks [13] and assumes completely trustworthy third-party (typically CPU manufacturer), thus limiting the application of their scheme.

Even worse, these existing schemes [17,21,32] all base their security on number-theoretic assumptions, such as the discrete logarithm or computational Diffie-Hellman (CDH) assumptions in cyclic groups, which are vulnerable to quantum adversaries. With the trend to migrate cryptographic algorithms to post-quantum ones (e.g., the NIST's post-quantum algorithm standardization [31]), it is desirable to build 2fAKE schemes from post-quantum assumptions. So it is natural to ask:

Can we construct biometric- and password-based 2fAKE which can additionally protect the privacy of biometrics and passwords, preferably based on post-quantum assumptions?

1.1 Our Contributions

In this paper, we answer the above question in the affirmative, by designing biometric- and password-based Two-Factor Authenticated Key Exchange (2fAKE) protocol with *enhanced* security and from *post-quantum* assumptions.
Enhanced Security Model for 2fAKE. Firstly, we establish an *enhanced* security model for 2fAKE, which provides three strong security guarantees: indistinguishability, authentication, and zero-knowledge. These three security notions are strong in the following sense:

- *Indistinguishability* requires that the session keys established by the client and the server are pseudorandom (i.e., computationally indistinguishable from uniformly random keys), even if the adversary later corrupts both the client and server, thus providing *perfect forward security* [16,27].
- *Authentication* guarantees that the client can authenticate herself/himself to the server only if she/he owns both of the two factors, and on the other hand, the server can authenticate itself to the client only if it possesses the enrollment data of the client, thus providing *mutually explicit authentication* [7,34]. Besides, it further ensures that, even if the adversary compromises the database of the server and obtains the enrollment data of the client, the adversary still cannot impersonate the client to pass the authentication with

---

[1] Recall that the well-accepted discrete logarithm problem is hard to solve only if the exponent b is uniformly distributed, e.g., see [25, Definition 8.62].

the server. In particular, the compromise of the server database should not leak the passwords of the client. This reduces the impact of server database leakage on client authentication and thus provides a strong guarantee.
- *Zero-knowledge* ensures that the 2fAKE protocol computationally hides the biometrics of the client in the whole process of the protocol. More precisely, no matter for the client's enrollment data stored by the server, or for the transcripts of the 2fAKE protocol, all of them do not reveal any information about the biometrics of the client, thus providing *zero-knowledge on the client's biometrics*. Even if the adversary compromises the database of the server, and sees all the communications between the client and server, the adversary cannot learn any information about the biometrics of the client.

Overall, the enhanced security for 2fAKE provides perfect forward security, mutually explicit authentication, and additionally takes the protection of biometrics and passwords into account, so that even if the server database is compromised, the client's biometrics and passwords are still hidden to the adversary.

Generic Construction of 2fAKE. Next, we propose a generic framework for constructing 2fAKE protocol with enhanced security in the random oracle model. Our generic construction uses three building blocks, i.e., a secure sketch (SS) [11], a digital signature (SIG) and an augmented/asymmetric PAKE (aPAKE) [5,14].

Roughly speaking, our generic 2fAKE works as follows (see also Fig. 3 in Sect. 4 for a graphical description):

- During the enrollment phase of 2fAKE (i.e., 2fAKE.Enroll in Fig. 3), the client generates a sampling w of her/his biometrics, and uses w to derive a signing key ssk of SIG and a hash value d via hash functions. Besides, the client uses her/his password pw to derive a password file rw according to the aPAKE protocol. Then the client sends the corresponding verification key vk, the password file rw and the hash value d to the server as the enrollment data.
- During the key exchange phase of 2fAKE (i.e., 2fAKE.Protocol in Fig. 3), the client and server first invoke the aPAKE protocol, using pw and rw as input respectively, and establish a shared aPAKE session key k^{aPAKE}. Then the server sends a hash value $t_S = \mathsf{H}_S(k^{\mathsf{aPAKE}} \| d)$ of k^{aPAKE} and d to the client to authenticate itself. Intuitively, the hash value $t_S = \mathsf{H}_S(k^{\mathsf{aPAKE}} \| d)$ functions as a proof of possession of rw and d, since without knowing rw, one cannot impersonate the server and get k^{aPAKE}, guaranteed by the security of aPAKE. Accordingly, the client sends another hash value $t_C = \mathsf{H}_C(k^{\mathsf{aPAKE}})$ of k^{aPAKE} to the server to authenticate herself/himself, and similarly, $t_C = \mathsf{H}_C(k^{\mathsf{aPAKE}})$ behaves as a proof of possession of pw.

Besides, the client generates a fresh biometric sampling w', which is different from the sampling w generated during the enrollment phase but close to w. To recover w, the client employs SS to correct the errors incurred by the different biometric samplings w, w'. After getting w, the client can re-derive the signing key ssk, and use it to sign the transcripts of the protocol, yielding a signature σ. Then the client sends the signature σ to the server, who can verify the validity of σ with vk stored in the enrollment data. Intuitively, the signature σ behaves as a proof of possession of the client's biometrics, since without knowing a biometric sampling w', one can hardly re-derive the signing key ssk, and without getting ssk, one can hardly output a valid signature σ, guaranteed by the security of SIG.

Finally, if the authentication checks pass, the client and server set a third hash value $k = \mathsf{H}_{\mathsf{key}}(k^{\mathsf{aPAKE}} \| d)$ of k^{aPAKE} and d as the session key of 2fAKE.

Intuitively, we rely on SS to make sure that the samplings w' of the biometric can be tuned to a unique sampling w, rely on SIG to authenticate the biometrics of the client, and rely on aPAKE to authenticate the password of the client as well as the enrollment data stored by the server. Overall, the client can pass the verification with the server (i.e., generating $t_\mathsf{C} = \mathsf{H}_\mathsf{C}(k^{\mathsf{aPAKE}})$ and valid σ) only if she/he owns both the biometrics and password pw, and the server can pass the verification with the client (i.e., generating $t_\mathsf{S} = \mathsf{H}_\mathsf{S}(k^{\mathsf{aPAKE}} \| d)$) only if it possesses rw and d contained in the enrollment data.

Moreover, we note that our proposed 2fAKE protocol achieves zero-knowledge on biometrics, since the server stores (vk, rw, d), which is just a verification key, a password file and a hash value, and the transcripts of 2fAKE include the transcripts of aPAKE together with two hash values $(t_\mathsf{S}, t_\mathsf{C})$ and a signature σ, all of which computationally hide the biometrics of the client in the random oracle model (cf. Section 5 for more details).

Instantiations from Post-quantum Assumptions. Finally, we obtain concrete 2fAKE protocol with enhanced security by instantiating our generic construction. Given that there are information-theoretical instantiations of SS [11,23,36,37] and instantiations of SIG and aPAKE from post-quantum assumptions like SIS (short-integer-solution)/LWE (learning-with-errors) [14,15], we immediately get 2fAKE protocol with enhanced security from post-quantum assumptions, which provides even stronger post-quantum security guarantees.

We implement our post-quantum secure 2fAKE protocol, and the experiments show that our concrete 2fAKE protocol achieves high efficiency, where the server stores just 3.1 KB in its database for one client, the communication is only 3

Table 1. Comparison of our 2fAKE protocol with the existing 2fAKE schemes [17,21,32]. The columns **Indistinguishability?**, **Authentication?** and **Zero-Knowledge?** ask whether the scheme achieves the corresponding security, where zero-knowledge means that the scheme computationally hides the biometrics of clients, and "–" indicates that it is unknown whether the scheme achieves the security. The column **Assumption** shows the computational assumption on which the security is based. The column **Rounds** shows the rounds of interactions between the client and the server.

Schemes	Indistinguishability?	Authentication?	Zero-Knowledge?	Assumption	Rounds
[32]	✓	✓	✗	CDH	4
[21]	✓	✓	✗	CDH	4
[17]	✓	✓	–	CDH + TEE	6
Our 2fAKE	✓	✓	✓	LWE/SIS	3

rounds and costs 4.3 KB, and the client runs in about 25 ms while the server runs in only 0.2 ms.

In Table 1, we compare our 2fAKE protocol with the existing biometric- and password-based 2fAKE schemes in terms of security and round efficiency.

2 Preliminaries

Notations. Let $\lambda \in \mathbb{N}$ denote the security parameter throughout the paper, and all algorithms, distributions, functions and adversaries take 1^λ as an implicit input. If x is defined by y or the value of y is assigned to x, we write $x := y$. For $n \in \mathbb{N}$, define $[n] := \{1, 2, ..., n\}$. For a set $\mathcal{X}$, denote by $x \leftarrow_\$ \mathcal{X}$ the procedure of sampling x from $\mathcal{X}$ uniformly at random. If $\mathcal{D}$ is distribution, $x \leftarrow_\$ \mathcal{D}$ means that x is sampled according to $\mathcal{D}$. For an algorithm $\mathcal{A}$, let $y \leftarrow \mathcal{A}(x; r)$ or simply $y \leftarrow \mathcal{A}(x)$ denote running $\mathcal{A}$ with input x and randomness r and assigning the output to y. "PPT" abbreviates probabilistic polynomial-time. Denote by poly some polynomial function and negl some negligible function in λ.

Due to space limitations, we refer to the full version of this paper for the definitions of secure sketch (SS), digital signature (SIG) and augmented/asymmetric password-based authenticated key exchange (aPAKE), which will serve as the core building blocks in our generic construction of 2fAKE.

3 Two-Factor Authenticated Key Exchange (2fAKE)

In this section, we present the formal definition of Two-Factor Authenticated Key Exchange (2fAKE) protocol, through which clients utilize their *biometrics* (e.g., faces, fingerprints, palmprints, iris, voices) and *passwords* to realize authentication and establish session keys with a server.

3.1 Definition of 2fAKE

Roughly speaking, Two-Factor Authenticated Key Exchange (2fAKE) is invoked between two parties, namely a client C and a server S, and consists of two phases, i.e., the enrollment phase and the key exchange phase.

During the *enrollment* phase, C can utilize its own biometric W and password pw to produce a pair of strings (edata, pub). Here edata is an enrollment data that will be sent to S and stored in S's database, and pub is a helper string stored by C locally and publicly.

Then during the *key exchange* phase, C can use its two factors (W, pw) and the public helper string pub to execute an interactive key exchange protocol with S who possesses edata, and they can compute a shared session key for later use.

Below we present the formal definition of 2fAKE (see also Fig. 1).

Definition 1 (Two-Factor Authenticated Key Exchange). *A Two-Factor Authenticated Key Exchange (2fAKE) protocol* 2fAKE = (2fAKE.Setup, 2fAKE.Enroll, 2fAKE.Protocol) *consists of two PPT algorithms and a PPT interactive protocol.*

- $pp_{2fAKE} \leftarrow$ 2fAKE.Setup: *The setup algorithm outputs a public parameter pp_{2fAKE}, which serves as an implicit input of other algorithms.*
- $(edata, pub) \leftarrow$ 2fAKE.Enroll(W, pw): *The enrollment algorithm takes as input a biometric W and a password pw of a client C, and outputs an enrollment data edata and a public helper string pub, where edata will be stored by a server S and pub will be stored by the client C itself.*
- $((\Psi_C, k_C), (\Psi_S, k_S)) \leftarrow$ 2fAKE.Protocol$(C(res_C) \leftrightarrow S(res_S))$: *The protocol is invoked by a client C and a server S, who have access to their own resources $res_C := (W, pw, pub)$ and $res_S := edata$, respectively. After the execution of the protocol, C outputs a flag $\Psi_C \in \{\emptyset, \textbf{accept}, \textbf{reject}\}$ and a session key $k_C \in \mathcal{K} \cup \{\emptyset\}$ (where $\mathcal{K}$ denotes the session key space), and similarly, S outputs Ψ_S and k_S.*

Correctness. If the client C and the server S execute the protocol 2fAKE.Protocol honestly, they will both accept the session and output a same session key, i.e., $\Psi_C = \Psi_S = \textbf{accept}$ and $k_C = k_S \neq \emptyset$.

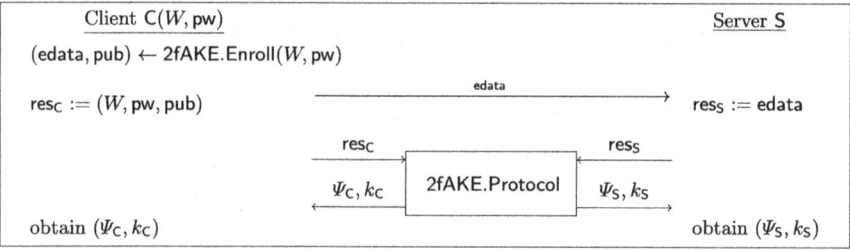

Fig. 1. A high-level illustration of 2fAKE.

3.2 Enhanced Security Model of 2fAKE

In this subsection, we formalize the enhanced security model for 2fAKE and define three important security notions, namely *indistinguishability, authentication, and zero-knowledge*. Roughly speaking,

- *Indistinguishability* requires that the session keys $k_C = k_S$ established by C and S are computationally indistinguishable from uniformly random keys.
- *Authentication* guarantees that S accepts a session only if C owns both of (W, pw), and on the other hand, C accepts a session only if S possesses edata.
- *Zero-knowledge* ensures that the strings edata and pub stored by S and C, as well as the transcripts of the protocol, do not reveal any information about the biometric W of C, and in fact, computationally hide it.

Our formalization follows a similar style to the existing security models for 2fAKE [17,21,32], and in particular, also uses the game-based definition in the Indistinguishability model (i.e., IND security), except that we additionally define zero-knowledge to protect the privacy of biometric of clients.

More precisely, indistinguishability and authentication will be defined in a common security experiment (i.e., $\mathsf{Exp}_{\mathsf{2fAKE},\ell,\mathcal{A}}$ shown in Fig. 2), while zero-knowledge will be defined in another slightly different security experiment (i.e., $\mathsf{Exp}^{\mathsf{ZK}}_{\mathsf{2fAKE},\ell,\mathcal{A},\mathsf{Sim}}$ shown in Fig. 2). These two security experiments are mostly the same except for slight differences, so we will describe them together and then explain the differences. Firstly, these two security experiments are both played between a challenger $\mathcal{C}$ and an adversary $\mathcal{A}$ (except that the latter also involves a simulator Sim, which we will explain later). During the experiments, $\mathcal{C}$ will execute multiple 2fAKE protocol instances between the client C and the server S, while $\mathcal{A}$ can implement passive attacks as well as the following active attacks:

- *Corruption attacks*: $\mathcal{A}$ can implement three kinds of corruption attacks, including the corruption of the client C to obtain a sampling of its biometric W (i.e., corruption of biometric) or to obtain its password pw (i.e., corruption of password), or the compromise of the server S to obtain the enrollment data edata (i.e., corruption of enrollment data).
- *Key reveal attacks*: $\mathcal{A}$ can obtain the session keys of some protocol instances.
- *Other active attacks*: $\mathcal{A}$ can interfere with all protocol instances by modifying, replacing, replaying, dropping, or injecting arbitrary messages.

Now we define oracles and their static variables in the security experiments.

Oracles and Security Experiments. Let $\mathsf{pp}_{\mathsf{2fAKE}} \leftarrow \mathsf{2fAKE.Setup}$ and $(\mathsf{edata}, \mathsf{pub}) \leftarrow \mathsf{2fAKE.Enroll}(W, \mathsf{pw})$. Suppose that C and S involve at most ℓ instances of the 2fAKE protocols. For party $U \in \{\mathsf{C},\mathsf{S}\}$, U's involvement in these protocol instances can be formalized by a series of oracles $\pi_U^1, \cdots, \pi_U^\ell$, where

- Oracle π_U^i ($i \in [\ell]$) formalizes U's execution of the i-th protocol instance.

Each oracle π_C^i for C has access to the client's resources $\mathsf{res}_\mathsf{C} := (W, \mathsf{pw}, \mathsf{pub})$, and each oracle π_S^i for S has access to the server's resources $\mathsf{res}_\mathsf{S} := \mathsf{edata}$. Besides, each π_U^i defines its own variables $\mathsf{var}_U^i := (k_U^i, \Psi_U^i)$ with initial values $(\emptyset, \emptyset)$.

- $k_U^i \in \mathcal{K} \cup \{\emptyset\}$: This variable records the session key computed by π_U^i.
- $\Psi_U^i \in \{\emptyset, \mathbf{accept}, \mathbf{reject}\}$: This variable indicates whether π_U^i has completed the protocol and accepted k_U^i. Note that $\Psi_U^i = \mathbf{accept}$ if and only if $k_U^i \neq \emptyset$.

Denote $\overline{U} := \{\mathsf{C},\mathsf{S}\} \setminus \{U\}$ as the other party, i.e., $\overline{U} = \mathsf{C}$ if $U = \mathsf{S}$ and $\overline{U} = \mathsf{S}$ if $U = \mathsf{C}$.

Formally, $\mathcal{A}$ has access to the following oracles via queries.

- $\mathsf{Send}(U, i, m)$. It formalizes active/passive attacks implemented by $\mathcal{A}$. If $m = \top$, it means that $\mathcal{A}$ asks oracle π_U^i to send the first protocol message to $\overline{U}$. Otherwise, $\mathcal{A}$ impersonates $\overline{U}$ to send message m to π_U^i. Then π_U^i executes the

2fAKE protocol with m just like U does, computes a message m', and updates its own variables $\mathsf{var}_U^i = (k_U^i, \Psi_U^i)$. The output message m' is returned to $\mathcal{A}$.

If $\mathsf{Send}(U, i, m)$ is the τ-th query asked by $\mathcal{A}$ and π_U^i changes Ψ_U^i to **accept** after that, then we say that π_U^i is τ-accept.

- CorruptBM. It formalizes the corruptions of C's biometric W. Upon this query, a sampling w of W is returned to $\mathcal{A}$.
- CorruptPW. It formalizes the corruption of C's password pw. Upon this query, pw is returned to $\mathcal{A}$.

If $\mathcal{A}$ queries both CorruptBM (in the τ-th query) and CorruptPW (in the τ'-th query), we say that C is $\max\{\tau, \tau'\}$-corrupted. Otherwise, if $\mathcal{A}$ never queries CorruptBM or CorruptPW, we say that C is ∞-corrupted.

- CorruptED. It formalizes the corruption of the enrollment data edata. Upon this query, edata is returned to $\mathcal{A}$.

If CorruptED is the τ-th query made by $\mathcal{A}$, we say that S is τ-corrupted. Otherwise, if $\mathcal{A}$ never queries CorruptED, we say that S is ∞-corrupted.

- KReveal(U, i). It formalizes session key reveal attacks implemented by $\mathcal{A}$, where $\mathcal{A}$ asks oracle π_U^i to reveal its session key k_U^i. If $\Psi_U^i \neq$ **accept** (i.e., $k_U^i = \emptyset$), $\bot$ is returned to $\mathcal{A}$. Otherwise, the session key k_U^i is returned to $\mathcal{A}$.
- Test(U, i). This oracle is used to define indistinguishability (and also authentication) for 2fAKE, so it appears only in the first experiment (i.e., $\mathsf{Exp}_{\mathsf{2fAKE},\ell,\mathcal{A}}$ in Fig. 2). If $\Psi_U^i \neq$ **accept** (i.e., $k_U^i = \emptyset$), the oracle returns $\bot$ to $\mathcal{A}$. Otherwise, the oracle sets $k_0 := k_U^i$, samples $k_1 \leftarrow_\$ \mathcal{K}$, and return $k_{b_{\mathsf{Ind}}}$ to $\mathcal{A}$. Here $b_{\mathsf{Ind}} \leftarrow_\$ \{0, 1\}$ is uniformly sampled challenge bit, chosen at the beginning of the experiment. The indistinguishability stipulates the hardness for $\mathcal{A}$ to guess the challenge bit b_{Ind} with probability non-negligibly better than $\frac{1}{2}$ (i.e., a random guess).

To characterize zero-knowledge on biometric for 2fAKE, we require that there exists a PPT simulator $\mathsf{Sim} = (\mathsf{Sim.Enroll}, \{\mathsf{Sim.}\pi_C^i\}_{i \in [\ell]})$, where $\mathsf{Sim.Enroll}$ can generate simulated $(\mathsf{edata}', \mathsf{pub}')$ and $\{\mathsf{Sim.}\pi_C^i\}_{i \in [\ell]}$ can generate simulated transcripts of the protocol instances for C, without using C's biometric W. The simulated $(\mathsf{edata}', \mathsf{pub}')$ and transcripts are required to be indistinguishable from honestly generated ones. More precisely,

- Sim.Enroll(pw): It takes as input the client's password pw (but without the biometric W), and outputs a pair of simulated edata' and public string pub'.
- $\mathsf{Sim.}\pi_C^i$ ($i \in [\ell]$): These are simulated oracles that have access to $\mathsf{Sim.res_C} := (\mathsf{pw}, \mathsf{pub}')$ with pub' produced by Sim.Enroll, but not to the biometric W, and generate simulated transcripts for C.

The experiment for zero-knowledge is slightly different (see $\mathsf{Exp}_{\mathsf{2fAKE},\ell,\mathcal{A},\mathsf{Sim}}^{\mathsf{ZK}}$ in Fig. 2), where the challenger $\mathcal{C}$ will choose another challenge bit $b_{\mathsf{ZK}} \leftarrow_\$ \{0, 1\}$, and if $b_{\mathsf{ZK}} = 1$, $\mathcal{C}$ gives the simulated $(\mathsf{edata}', \mathsf{pub}')$ instead of the honestly generated $(\mathsf{edata}, \mathsf{pub})$ to $\mathcal{A}$, and uses the simulated oracles $\mathsf{Sim.}\pi_C^i$ ($i \in [\ell]$) instead of the real oracles π_C^i ($i \in [\ell]$) to answer $\mathsf{Send}(U = C, i, m)$ queries made by $\mathcal{A}$. The zero-knowledge requires the hardness for $\mathcal{A}$ to guess the challenge bit b_{ZK} with probability non-negligibly better than $\frac{1}{2}$.

To define the security notions of 2fAKE formally, trivial attacks must be identified and excluded. For instances, the tested session keys must not be revealed. We will describe trivial attacks later and first introduce the concepts of original key and partner according to [29].

Definition 2. (Original Key [29]). *For two oracles π_C^i and π_S^j, the original key, denoted as $K(\pi_C^i, \pi_S^j)$ is the session key computed by the client and the server of the protocol under a passive adversary only.*

Definition 3. (Partner [29]). *Let $K(\cdot, \cdot)$ denote the original key function. For two oracles π_C^i and π_S^j, we say that π_C^i is partnered to π_S^j, denoted as $\mathsf{Partner}(\pi_C^i \leftarrow \pi_S^j)$, if $k_C^i = K(\pi_C^i, \pi_S^j) \neq \emptyset$. Similarly, we say that π_S^j is partnered to π_C^i, denoted as $\mathsf{Partner}(\pi_S^j \leftarrow \pi_C^i)$, if $k_S^j = K(\pi_C^i, \pi_S^j) \neq \emptyset$. We write $\mathsf{Partner}(\pi_C^i \leftrightarrow \pi_S^j)$ if $\mathsf{Partner}(\pi_C^i \leftarrow \pi_S^j)$ and $\mathsf{Partner}(\pi_S^j \leftarrow \pi_C^i)$.*

Trivial Attacks. To describe trivial attacks clearly, we define the following flags.

- pwCorr: whether C's password pw is corrupted;
- bmCorr: whether C's biometric W is corrupted;
- edCorr: whether the edata stored by S is corrupted;
- Aflag_C^i: whether the edata stored by S is corrupted when π_C^i accepts;
- Aflag_S^i: whether both pw and W are corrupted when π_S^i accepts;
- Bflag^i: whether both pw and W are corrupted when π_C^i accepts;
- T_U^i: whether π_U^i is tested;
- kRev_U^i: whether the session key k_U^i is revealed.

Based on that we give a list of trivial attacks **TA1-TA7** in Table 2.

Table 2. Trivial Attacks **TA1-TA7** for the security experiments of 2fAKE. Here $\overline{U} := \{C, S\} \setminus \{U\}$ denotes the party other than U, i.e., $\overline{U} = C$ if $U = S$ and $\overline{U} = S$ if $U = C$.

Types	Trivial attacks	Explanation
TA1	$T_C^i = \mathbf{true} \wedge \mathsf{Aflag}_C^i = \mathbf{true}$	π_C^i is tested but S has the enrollment data edata revealed before π_C^i accepts session key k_C^i
TA2	$T_S^i = \mathbf{true} \wedge \mathsf{Aflag}_S^i = \mathbf{true}$	π_S^i is tested but C has both its biometric and password revealed before π_S^i accepts session key k_S^i
TA3	$T_C^i = \mathbf{true} \wedge \mathsf{Bflag}^i = \mathbf{true}$	π_C^i is tested but C has both its biometric and password revealed before π_C^i accepts session key k_C^i
TA4	$T_U^i = \mathbf{true} \wedge \mathsf{kRev}_U^i = \mathbf{true}$	π_U^i is tested and its session key is revealed
TA5	$T_U^i = \mathbf{true}$ when $\mathsf{Test}(U, i)$ is queried	$\mathsf{Test}(U, i)$ is queried at least twice
TA6	$T_U^i = \mathbf{true} \wedge \mathsf{Partner}(\pi_U^i \leftrightarrow \pi_{\overline{U}}^j)$ $\wedge \mathsf{kRev}_{\overline{U}}^j = \mathbf{true}$	π_U^i is tested, π_U^i and $\pi_{\overline{U}}^j$ are partnered to each other, and $\pi_{\overline{U}}^j$'s session key is revealed
TA7	$T_U^i = \mathbf{true} \wedge \mathsf{Partner}(\pi_U^i \leftrightarrow \pi_{\overline{U}}^j)$ $\wedge T_{\overline{U}}^j = \mathbf{true}$	π_U^i is tested, π_U^i and $\pi_{\overline{U}}^j$ are partnered to each other, and $\pi_{\overline{U}}^j$ is tested

$\mathsf{Exp}_{\mathsf{2fAKE},\ell,\mathcal{A}}$ / $\mathsf{Exp}^{\mathsf{ZK}}_{\mathsf{2fAKE},\ell,\mathcal{A},\mathsf{Sim}}$:
$\mathsf{pp}_{\mathsf{2fAKE}} \leftarrow \mathsf{2fAKE.Setup}$; $W \leftarrow \mathbf{W}$; $\mathsf{pw} \leftarrow_\$ \mathcal{D}_{\mathsf{pw}}$
$b_{\mathsf{Ind}} \leftarrow_\$ \{0,1\}$ // challenge bit for pseudorandomness of session keys
$b_{\mathsf{ZK}} \leftarrow_\$ \{0,1\}$ // challenge bit for zero-knowledge of biometric
If $b_{\mathsf{ZK}} = 1$:
  (edata, pub) $\leftarrow$ Sim.Enroll(pw)
Else:
  (edata, pub) $\leftarrow$ 2fAKE.Enroll(W, pw)
pwCorr := false // whether C's password is corrupted
bmCorr := false // whether C's biometric is corrupted
edCorr := false // whether the enrollment data edata is corrupted
For $(U, i) \in \{\mathsf{C}, \mathsf{S}\} \times [\ell]$:
  $\mathsf{var}_U^i := (k_U^i, \Psi_U^i) := (\emptyset, \emptyset)$;
  $T_U^i := \mathsf{false}$; $\mathsf{kRev}_U^i := \mathsf{false}$; // Test, Key Reveal variables
  $\mathsf{Aflag}_U^i := \mathsf{false}$; // whether $\overline{U}$ is corrupted when π_U^i accepts
  $\mathsf{Bflag}^i := \mathsf{false}$ // whether C's password and biometric
  // are both corrupted when π_C^i accepts
$b^* \leftarrow \mathcal{A}^{\mathcal{O}_{\mathsf{2fAKE}}(\cdot)}(\mathsf{pp}_{\mathsf{2fAKE}}, \mathsf{pub})$

// Defining Authentication
$\mathsf{Win}_{\mathsf{Auth}} := \mathsf{false}$
$\mathsf{Win}_{\mathsf{Auth}} := \mathsf{true}$, If $\exists (U, i) \in \{\mathsf{C}, \mathsf{S}\} \times [\ell]$ s.t.
(1) $\Psi_U^i = \mathsf{accept}$
(2) (2.1) $\vee$ (2.2)
  (2.1) $U = \mathsf{S} \wedge \mathsf{Aflag}_\mathsf{S}^i = \mathsf{false}$
  (2.2) $U = \mathsf{C} \wedge \mathsf{Aflag}_\mathsf{C}^i = \mathsf{false} \wedge \mathsf{Bflag}^i = \mathsf{false}$
(3) (3.1) $\vee$ (3.2). Let $\overline{U} = \{\mathsf{C}, \mathsf{S}\} \setminus \{U\}$
  (3.1) $\not\exists j \in [\ell]$ s.t. Partner$(\pi_U^i \leftrightarrow \pi_{\overline{U}}^j)$
  (3.2) $\exists j \in [\ell], j' \in [\ell]$ with $j \neq j'$ s.t.
    Partner$(\pi_U^i \leftrightarrow \pi_{\overline{U}}^j) \wedge$ Partner$(\pi_U^i \leftrightarrow \pi_{\overline{U}}^{j'})$

// Defining Indistinguishability
$\mathsf{Win}_{\mathsf{Ind}} := \mathsf{false}$
If $b^* = b_{\mathsf{Ind}}$: $\mathsf{Win}_{\mathsf{Ind}} := \mathsf{true}$

// Defining Zero-Knowledge
$\mathsf{Win}_{\mathsf{ZK}} := \mathsf{false}$
If $b^* = b_{\mathsf{ZK}}$: $\mathsf{Win}_{\mathsf{ZK}} := \mathsf{true}$
Return 1

Partner$(\pi_\mathsf{C}^i \leftarrow \pi_\mathsf{S}^j)$: // checking whether Partner$(\pi_\mathsf{C}^i \leftarrow \pi_\mathsf{S}^j)$
If $k_\mathsf{C}^i = \mathsf{K}(\pi_\mathsf{C}^i, \pi_\mathsf{S}^j) \neq \emptyset$: Return 1

Partner$(\pi_\mathsf{S}^j \leftarrow \pi_\mathsf{C}^i)$: // checking whether Partner$(\pi_\mathsf{S}^j \leftarrow \pi_\mathsf{C}^i)$
If $k_\mathsf{S}^j = \mathsf{K}(\pi_\mathsf{C}^i, \pi_\mathsf{S}^j) \neq \emptyset$: Return 1

$\pi_U^i(m)$: // executing 2fAKE according to the protocol specification
π_U^i receives m and uses res_U, var_U^i to generate the next message m' of
2fAKE, and updates $\mathsf{var}_U^i := (k_U^i, \Psi_U^i)$;
If $m = \top$: π_U^i generates the first message m' as initiator;
If m is the last message of 2fAKE: $m' = \emptyset$;
Return m'

Sim.$\pi_\mathsf{C}^k(m)$: // executing 2fAKE according to the simulator without W
Sim.π_C^k receives m and uses Sim.res$_\mathsf{C} := (\mathsf{pw}, \mathsf{pub})$, $\mathsf{var}_\mathsf{C}^k$ to generate the
next simulated message m' of 2fAKE, and updates $\mathsf{var}_\mathsf{C}^k := (k_\mathsf{C}^k, \Psi_\mathsf{C}^k)$;
If $m = \top$: Sim.π_C^k generates the first message m' as initiator;
If m is the last message of 2fAKE: $m' = \emptyset$;
Return m'

$\mathcal{O}_{\mathsf{2fAKE}}(\mathsf{query})$:
If query = Send(U, i, m):
  If $(U, i) \notin \{\mathsf{C}, \mathsf{S}\} \times [\ell]$, Return $\perp$
  If $\Psi_U^i = \mathsf{accept}$: Return $\perp$
  If $b_{\mathsf{ZK}} = 1 \wedge U = \mathsf{C}$:
    $m' \leftarrow$ Sim.$\pi_\mathsf{C}^i(m)$
  Else:
    $m' \leftarrow \pi_U^i(m)$
  If $\Psi_U^i = \mathsf{accept}$:
    If $U = \mathsf{S}$:
      // determine whether C's password and biometric
      // are both corrupted when π_S^i accepts
      If pwCorr = true $\wedge$ bmCorr = true:
        $\mathsf{Aflag}_\mathsf{S}^i := \mathsf{true}$
    If $U = \mathsf{C}$:
      // determine whether the enrollment data edata
      // stored by S is corrupted when π_C^i accepts
      If edCorr = true:
        $\mathsf{Aflag}_\mathsf{C}^i := \mathsf{true}$
      // determine whether C's password and biometric
      // are both corrupted when π_C^i accepts
      If pwCorr = true $\wedge$ bmCorr = true:
        $\mathsf{Bflag}^i := \mathsf{true}$
  Return m'

If query = CorruptBM:
  bmCorr := true; $w \leftarrow W$; Return w

If query = CorruptPW:
  pwCorr := true; Return pw

If query = CorruptED:
  edCorr := true; Return edata

If query = KReveal(U, i):
  If $(U, i) \notin \{\mathsf{C}, \mathsf{S}\} \times [\ell]$, Return $\perp$
  If $\Psi_U^i \neq \mathsf{accept}$: Return $\perp$
  If $T_U^i = \mathsf{true}$: Return $\perp$ // Avoid TA4
  If $\exists j \in [\ell]$ s.t. Partner$(\pi_U^i \leftrightarrow \pi_{\overline{U}}^j)$:
    If $T_{\overline{U}}^j = \mathsf{true}$: Return $\perp$ // Avoid TA6
  $\mathsf{kRev}_U^i := \mathsf{true}$
  Return k_U^i

If query = Test(U, i):
  If $(U, i) \notin \{\mathsf{C}, \mathsf{S}\} \times [\ell]$, Return $\perp$
  If $\Psi_U^i \neq \mathsf{accept} \vee \mathsf{kRev}_U^i = \mathsf{true} \vee T_U^i = \mathsf{true}$:
    Return $\perp$ // Avoid TA4, TA5
  If $(U = \mathsf{C} \wedge (\mathsf{Aflag}_\mathsf{C}^i = \mathsf{true} \vee \mathsf{Bflag}^i = \mathsf{true}))$:
    Return $\perp$ // Avoid TA1, TA3
  If $(U = \mathsf{S} \wedge \mathsf{Aflag}_\mathsf{S}^i = \mathsf{true})$:
    Return $\perp$ // Avoid TA2
  If $\exists j \in [\ell]$ s.t. Partner$(\pi_U^i \leftrightarrow \pi_{\overline{U}}^j)$:
    If $(\mathsf{kRev}_{\overline{U}}^j = \mathsf{true}) \vee (T_{\overline{U}}^j = \mathsf{true})$:
      Return $\perp$ // Avoid TA6, TA7
  $T_U^i := \mathsf{true}$; $k_0 := k_U^i$; $k_1 \leftarrow_\$ \mathcal{K}$
  Return $k_{b_{\mathsf{Ind}}}$

Fig. 2. The security experiment $\mathsf{Exp}_{\mathsf{2fAKE},\ell,\mathcal{A}}$ (with dotted boxes) for defining authentication and indistinguishability of 2fAKE, and the security experiment $\mathsf{Exp}^{\mathsf{ZK}}_{\mathsf{2fAKE},\ell,\mathcal{A},\mathsf{Sim}}$ (with gray boxes) for defining zero-knowledge of 2fAKE.

Security Definition of 2fAKE. Based on the definitions of oracles and trivial attacks, we now give the formal definition for the security notions of 2fAKE.

Definition 4 (Enhanced Security of 2fAKE). *Let ℓ be the maximum number of protocol executions, $\mathbf{W}$ the distribution of biometrics, and $\mathcal{D}_{\mathsf{pw}}$ the password space.*

The security experiment $\mathsf{Exp}_{\mathsf{2fAKE},\ell,\mathcal{A}}$ for defining authentication and indistinguishability is described as follows (see also Fig. 2 with dotted boxes), which is played between a challenger $\mathcal{C}$ and an adversary $\mathcal{A}$.

1. $\mathcal{C}$ *invokes* 2fAKE.Setup *to get* $\mathsf{pp}_{\mathsf{2fAKE}}$, *and chooses a biometric* $W \leftarrow \mathbf{W}$ *and a password* $\mathsf{pw} \leftarrow_\$ \mathcal{D}_{\mathsf{pw}}$ *on behalf of the client. $\mathcal{C}$ also picks a challenge bit* $b_{\mathsf{Ind}} \leftarrow_\$ \{0,1\}$.
2. *Then $\mathcal{C}$ invokes* 2fAKE.Enroll(W, pw) *to get the enrollment data* edata *and public helper string* pub, *and provides $\mathcal{A}$ with* $\mathsf{pp}_{\mathsf{2fAKE}}$ *and public data* pub.
3. *Next $\mathcal{A}$ issues queries to oracles* Send, CorruptBM, CorruptPW, CorruptED, KReveal *and* Test *adaptively. In particular,*
   - *If $b_{\mathsf{Ind}} = 0$,* Test *responds with real session keys; if $b_{\mathsf{Ind}} = 1$,* Test *responds with uniformly sampled session keys.*
4. *Finally, $\mathcal{A}$ terminates with an output b^*.*

- **Authentication.** *Let* $\mathsf{Win}_{\mathsf{Auth}}$ *denote the event that $\mathcal{A}$ breaks authentication in the experiment $\mathsf{Exp}_{\mathsf{2fAKE},\ell,\mathcal{A}}$.* $\mathsf{Win}_{\mathsf{Auth}}$ *happens iff $\exists (U,i) \in \{\mathsf{C},\mathsf{S}\} \times [\ell]$ s.t.*
  (1) π_U^i is τ-accepted;
  (2) Either (2.1) or (2.2) happens.
    (2.1) $U = \mathsf{S}$, and $\overline{U} = \mathsf{C}$ is $\hat{\tau}$-corrupted with $\hat{\tau} > \tau$.
    (2.2) $U = \mathsf{C}$, $\overline{U} = \mathsf{S}$ is $\hat{\tau}$-corrupted with $\hat{\tau} > \tau$, and C is $\hat{\tau}'$-corrupted with $\hat{\tau}' > \tau$.
  (3) Either (3.1) or (3.2) happens.
    (3.1) There is no oracle $\pi_{\overline{U}}^j$ that π_U^i is partnered to.
    (3.2) There exist two $\pi_{\overline{U}}^j$ and $\pi_{\overline{U}}^{j'}$ with $j \neq j'$, to which π_U^i is partnered.
  2fAKE *achieves authentication if for any $\ell = $ poly, any PPT adversary $\mathcal{A}$ launching Q queries to oracle* Send *(i.e., online dictionary attacks), we have*

  $$\mathsf{Adv}^{\mathsf{Auth}}_{\mathsf{2fAKE},\ell,\mathcal{A}} := \Pr[\mathsf{Win}_{\mathsf{Auth}}] \leq \mathsf{negl} + \tfrac{Q}{|\mathcal{D}_{\mathsf{pw}}|}.$$

- **Indistinguishability.** *Let* $\mathsf{Win}_{\mathsf{Ind}}$ *denote the event that $b^* = b_{\mathsf{Ind}}$.* 2fAKE *achieves indistinguishability if for any $\ell = $ poly, any PPT adversary $\mathcal{A}$ launching Q queries to oracle* Send *(i.e., online dictionary attacks), we have*

  $$\mathsf{Adv}^{\mathsf{Ind}}_{\mathsf{2fAKE},\ell,\mathcal{A}} := \left|\Pr[\mathsf{Win}_{\mathsf{Ind}}] - \tfrac{1}{2}\right| \leq \mathsf{negl} + \tfrac{Q}{|\mathcal{D}_{\mathsf{pw}}|}.$$

The security experiment $\mathsf{Exp}^{\mathsf{ZK}}_{\mathsf{2fAKE},\ell,\mathcal{A},\mathsf{Sim}}$ for defining zero-knowledge is described as follows (see also Fig. 2 with gray boxes), played between $\mathcal{C}$ and $\mathcal{A}$.

1. $\mathcal{C}$ *invokes* 2fAKE.Setup *to get* $\mathsf{pp}_{\mathsf{2fAKE}}$, *and chooses a biometric* $W \leftarrow \mathbf{W}$ *and a password* $\mathsf{pw} \leftarrow_\$ \mathcal{D}_{\mathsf{pw}}$ *on behalf of the client. $\mathcal{C}$ also picks a challenge bit* $b_{\mathsf{ZK}} \leftarrow_\$ \{0,1\}$.

2. If $b_{\mathsf{ZK}} = 0$, $\mathcal{C}$ invokes 2fAKE.Enroll(W, pw) to get the enrollment data edata and public helper string pub; if $b_{\mathsf{ZK}} = 1$, $\mathcal{C}$ invokes Sim.Enroll(pw) to get the simulated edata and pub (here we omit the ′ symbols), without using the biometric W of C. Then $\mathcal{C}$ provides $\mathcal{A}$ with $\mathsf{pp}_{\mathsf{2fAKE}}$ and public data pub.
3. Next $\mathcal{A}$ issues queries to oracles Send, CorruptBM, CorruptPW, CorruptED and KReveal adaptively. In particular,
   - If $b_{\mathsf{ZK}} = 0$ or $U = \mathsf{S}$, Send responds by executing the real 2fAKE protocol; if $b_{\mathsf{ZK}} = 1$ and $U = \mathsf{C}$, Send responds by executing the simulator Sim without using the biometric W of C.
4. Finally, $\mathcal{A}$ terminates with an output b^*.

- **Zero-Knowledge.** Let $\mathsf{Win}_{\mathsf{ZK}}$ denote the event that $b^* = b_{\mathsf{ZK}}$. 2fAKE achieves zero-knowledge if for any $\ell = \mathrm{poly}$ and any PPT $\mathcal{A}$ that does not see the biometric W,[2] there exists a PPT simulator Sim = (Sim.Enroll, $\{\mathsf{Sim}.\pi_\mathsf{C}^i\}_{i \in [\ell]}$), such that

$$\mathsf{Adv}^{\mathsf{ZK}}_{\mathsf{2fAKE},\ell,\mathcal{A},\mathsf{Sim}} := \left|\Pr[\mathsf{Win}_{\mathsf{ZK}}] - \tfrac{1}{2}\right| \leq \mathsf{negl}.$$

Remark. In the above definition, the term "$\frac{Q}{|\mathcal{D}_{\mathsf{pw}}|}$" captures the advantage of online dictionary attacks against the password. Online dictionary attacks are always possible since $\mathcal{A}$ can simply guess C's password pw uniformly at random, and the guess will be correct with probability $\frac{1}{|\mathcal{D}_{\mathsf{pw}}|}$ each time. Our definition essentially ensures that these online attacks are the only efficient attacks. Such term also appears in the security for existing 2fAKE schemes [17,21].

4 Our 2fAKE Protocol

In this section, we present a generic construction of 2fAKE from a secure sketch SS, a digital signature scheme SIG, an augmented/asymmetric password-based authenticated key exchange protocol aPAKE and five hash functions $\mathsf{H}_{\mathsf{sig}}, \mathsf{H}_{\mathsf{d}}, \mathsf{H}_{\mathsf{S}}$, $\mathsf{H}_\mathsf{C}, \mathsf{H}_{\mathsf{key}}$.

More precisely, the underlying building blocks are as follows.

- Let SS = (SS.Gen, SS.Rec) be an $(\mathcal{W}, m, \tilde{m}, t)$-secure sketch with simulatable sketches.
- Let SIG = (SIG.Gen, Sign, Vrfy) be a signature scheme with message space $\{0,1\}^*$, signing key space $\mathcal{SK}$, and canonical verification key generation algorithm VK.Gen.
- Let aPAKE = (aPAKE.Setup, aPAKE.Enroll, aPAKE.Protocol) be an aPAKE protocol.
- Let $\mathsf{H}_{\mathsf{sig}} : \{0,1\}^* \to \mathcal{SK}$ and $\mathsf{H}_{\mathsf{d}}, \mathsf{H}_{\mathsf{S}}, \mathsf{H}_{\mathsf{C}}, \mathsf{H}_{\mathsf{key}} : \{0,1\}^* \to \{0,1\}^\lambda$ be five hash functions.

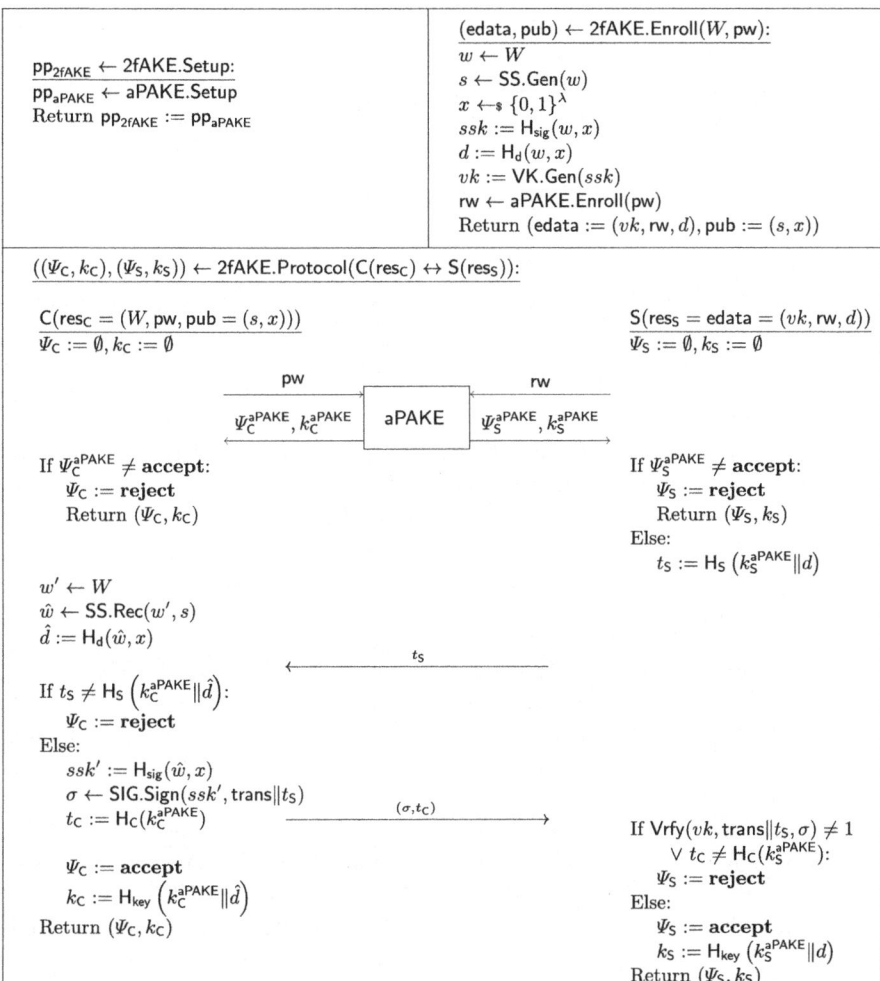

Fig. 3. Our generic construction of 2fAKE from secure sketch SS, signature scheme SIG, aPAKE protocol aPAKE and hash functions $H_{sig}, H_d, H_S, H_C, H_{key}$. Here trans denotes the transcripts of the underlying aPAKE protocol.

We show our 2fAKE scheme in Fig. 3 and refer to the full version for a textual description of our 2fAKE.

It is easy to check that the correctness of our 2fAKE protocol follows from the correctness of SS, SIG and aPAKE. Intuitively, we rely on SS to make sure that the samplings w' of a biometric W can be tuned to a unique sampling w. Then the hash function H_{sig} converts w into a signing key ssk of SIG, and the hash function H_d converts w into a hash value d, which is used in the generation

---

[2] This is reasonable, since if $\mathcal{A}$ already obtains a sampling w of W (e.g., by corrupting the client), it is meaningless to consider the zero-knowledge of biometric W.

of t_S and session key $k_C = k_S$. We stress that the signing key ssk and the hash value d are never stored locally by the client. Instead, the client will regenerate them from its own biometric W whenever needed. Consequently, the client stores only a public string $\mathsf{pub} = (s, x)$ which helps in the regeneration of ssk and d.

5 Security Proof of Our 2fAKE Protocol

In this section, we establish the security of our 2fAKE protocol on the security of the underlying building blocks SS, SIG, aPAKE via the following theorem.

Theorem 1. (Security of Our 2fAKE). *Suppose that (i) SS is an $(\mathcal{W}, m, \tilde{m}, t)$-secure sketch with $\tilde{m} = \omega(\log \lambda)$, has simulatable sketches, and the samplings of biometric W have min-entropy at least m;[3] (ii) SIG is a secure digital signature scheme; (iii) aPAKE is a secure aPAKE protocol; (iv) $\mathsf{H}_{sig}, \mathsf{H}_d, \mathsf{H}_S, \mathsf{H}_C, \mathsf{H}_{key}$ are modeled as random oracles. Then the 2fAKE proposed in Fig. 3 achieves indistinguishability, authentication, and zero-knowledge.*

Proof sketch. Due to space limitations, here we present a proof sketch and refer to the full version for the formal proof.

- *Authentication of our* 2fAKE: We prove the authentication for the client C and the authentication for the server S separately.

  Authentication for C means that an adversary $\mathcal{A}$ can not impersonate C to make S accept a session, unless $\mathcal{A}$ corrupts both C's password pw (via CorruptPW query) and biometric W (via CorruptBM query). Roughly speaking, we show the authentication for C by considering two cases. In the case that $\mathcal{A}$ does not get pw, $\mathcal{A}$ can hardly impersonate C to execute aPAKE.Protocol with S according to the security of aPAKE, and thus the resulting k_S^{aPAKE} is pseudorandom to $\mathcal{A}$. Consequently, $\mathcal{A}$ can hardly forge t_C satisfying $t_C = \mathsf{H}_C(k_S^{\mathsf{aPAKE}})$. In the other case that $\mathcal{A}$ does not get a sampling of C's biometric W, the sampling w of W has enough average conditional entropy conditioned on the sketch s, so that the value of $ssk = \mathsf{H}_{sig}(w, x)$ is uniformly random from $\mathcal{A}$'s view. Without knowing ssk, $\mathcal{A}$ can hardly produce a valid signature σ such that $\mathsf{Vrfy}(vk, \mathsf{trans}\|t_S, \sigma) = 1$ holds, guaranteed by the security of SIG.

  Authentication for S means that an adversary $\mathcal{A}$ can not impersonate S to make C accept a session, unless $\mathcal{A}$ corrupts the enrollment data $\mathsf{edata} = (vk, \mathsf{rw}, d)$ stored by S (via CorruptED query), or corrupts both C's password pw (via CorruptPW query) and biometric W (via CorruptBM query). Similarly, we show the authentication for S by considering two cases. In the case that $\mathcal{A}$ does not get edata and pw, $\mathcal{A}$ can hardly impersonate S to execute aPAKE.Protocol with C according to the security of aPAKE, and thus the

---

[3] According to the discussion in the full version, it is easy to have simulatable sketches for secure sketch. By [9,39], the biometrics like faces, fingerprints and iris have entropy of about 225 to 265 bits.

resulting $k_\mathsf{C}^\mathsf{aPAKE}$ is pseudorandom to $\mathcal{A}$. Consequently, $\mathcal{A}$ can hardly forge t_S satisfying $t_\mathsf{S} = \mathsf{H}_\mathsf{S}(k_\mathsf{C}^\mathsf{aPAKE} \| d)$. In the other case that $\mathcal{A}$ does not get edata and a sampling of C's biometric W, the sampling w of W has enough average entropy conditioned on the sketch s, and thus the value of $d = \mathsf{H}_\mathsf{d}(w, x)$ is uniformly random to $\mathcal{A}$. As a result, $\mathcal{A}$ can hardly forge t_S satisfying $t_\mathsf{S} = \mathsf{H}_\mathsf{S}(k_\mathsf{C}^\mathsf{aPAKE} \| d)$ either.

- *Indistinguishability of our* 2fAKE: If $\mathcal{A}$ corrupts C or S before a session key is accepted, the involved session key can not be tested, in order to avoid trivial attacks. On the other hand, if $\mathcal{A}$ does not corrupt C or S before a session key is accepted, by the authentication of our 2fAKE (as discussed above), $\mathcal{A}$ cannot impersonate C/S to make the other party accept. Consequently, for those tested session keys, $\mathcal{A}$ cannot interfere with the interactions between C and S, and in particular, cannot interfere with the executions of aPAKE.Protocol. There are two cases when C is not corrupted. If $\mathcal{A}$ does not have pw (and rw), then according to the security of aPAKE, the aPAKE session keys $k_\mathsf{C}^\mathsf{aPAKE} = k_\mathsf{S}^\mathsf{aPAKE}$ are pseudorandom to $\mathcal{A}$; if $\mathcal{A}$ has no samples of W, then according to the security of SS, the sampling w of W has enough average entropy conditioned on the sketch s, and thus the value of $d = \mathsf{H}_\mathsf{d}(w, x)$ is random to $\mathcal{A}$. In either case, the 2fAKE session keys $k_\mathsf{C} = \mathsf{H}_\mathsf{key}(k_\mathsf{C}^\mathsf{aPAKE} \| d) = \mathsf{H}_\mathsf{key}(k_\mathsf{S}^\mathsf{aPAKE} \| d) = k_\mathsf{S}$ are pseudorandom to $\mathcal{A}$. Consequently, the real session keys $k_0 = k_\mathsf{C} = k_\mathsf{S}$ are computationally indistinguishable from uniformly random keys $k_1 \leftarrow_\$ \mathcal{K}$.

- *Zero-knowledge of our* 2fAKE: We will show that the enrollment data $\mathsf{edata} = (vk, \mathsf{rw}, d)$, the public helper string $\mathsf{pub} = (s, x)$, and the transcripts of our 2fAKE protocol computationally hide the biometric W of C.

  Let us first analyze $\mathsf{edata} = (vk, \mathsf{rw}, d)$ and $\mathsf{pub} = (s, x)$. Recall that they are generated by the 2fAKE.Enroll algorithm in the following way: $w \leftarrow W$, $s \leftarrow \mathsf{SS.Gen}(w)$, $x \leftarrow_\$ \{0,1\}^\lambda$, $ssk := \mathsf{H}_\mathsf{sig}(w, x)$, $d := \mathsf{H}_\mathsf{d}(w, x)$, $vk := \mathsf{VK.Gen}(ssk)$ and $\mathsf{rw} \leftarrow \mathsf{aPAKE.Enroll}(\mathsf{pw})$. Note that if $\mathcal{A}$ never queries H_sig on (w, x), then $ssk = \mathsf{H}_\mathsf{sig}(w, x)$ is just a uniformly random signing key and contains no information about w since H_sig is modeled as random oracle, and so does vk. Indeed, $\mathcal{A}$ can hardly query H_sig on (w, x), since conditioned on s, the sampling w has enough average entropy according to the security of SS. Consequently, both ssk and vk contain no information about w. Similarly, d also contains no information about w. Moreover, rw and x do not involve w, and s can be efficiently simulated without knowing w. This shows the zero-knowledge of w in edata and pub.

  Next we analyze the transcripts of our 2fAKE protocol. Clearly, the transcripts of aPAKE involve only pw but not the biometric W. The only place where the biometric W is involved is that C uses W to regenerate ssk and d, and compute a signature $\sigma \leftarrow \mathsf{SIG.Sign}(ssk, \mathsf{trans} \| t_\mathsf{S})$. As we discussed above, ssk and d in fact contain no information about the biometric W, unless $\mathcal{A}$ can query H_sig or H_d on (w, x), which can hardly occur. Thus, the signature σ also contains no information about w. This shows the zero-knowledge of w in the transcripts of our 2fAKE.

In the formal proof in the full version, we will build a simulator to simulate edata, pub and the transcripts of our 2fAKE without using the biometric W.

6 Instantiation from Post-quantum Assumptions

We show how to instantiate our generic construction to obtain 2fAKE protocol from post-quantum assumptions.

- *Instantiations of* SS. Secure sketch is an information-theoretical primitive. The popular candidates are error-correction code-based SS [11,23,36,37].
- *Instantiations of* SIG. There are many secure digital signature schemes, and any instantiation with canonical key generation works. To obtain instantiations from post-quantum assumptions, we can use lattice-based signatures in [15,30] or CRYSTALS-Dilithium, Falcon in NIST Post-Quantum Cryptography (PQC) finalists [10,12], or isogeny-based ones [6].
- *Instantiations of* aPAKE. In [14], Gentry et al. propose a generic construction of aPAKE from digital signature and PAKE in the random oracle. By instantiating the underlying digital signature and PAKE with post-quantum secure ones like [1,6,10,12,15,30,33], respectively, we immediately obtain concrete aPAKE protocol from post-quantum assumptions.

Next we analyze the concrete efficiency of our 2fAKE protocol. For concreteness, we instantiate our 2fAKE with the secure sketch in [11], the digital signature Falcon [12,24], and the aPAKE protocol in [14] which is in turn instantiated with Falcon [12,24] and the PAKE protocol CAKE in [1]. (For completeness, we illustrate the resulting 2fAKE instantiation in the full version.) We implement our instantiation on Ubuntu 20.04 with two Intel(R) Core(TM) i7-11800H CPUs and 4 GB memory.

(1) **Storage size:** Our experiments show that the enrollment data edata = (vk, rw, d) stored by the server is just 3.1 KB for one client.

(2) **Rounds:** According to Fig. 3, our 2fAKE adds two extra rounds, t_S and (t_C, σ), to the underlying aPAKE. Fortunately, there are two cases in which our 2fAKE adds only one extra round to aPAKE, or even adds no round to aPAKE at all.

- If the last round of aPAKE is sent from server to client, we can merge t_S of our 2fAKE with it, and hence only one additional round is needed for our 2fAKE.
- If the last round of aPAKE is sent from client to server, and moreover, the server can compute aPAKE session key before the second last round, then we can merge t_S with the second last round of aPAKE and merge (t_C, σ) with the last round of aPAKE. In this case, no additional round is needed for 2fAKE.

Indeed, the aPAKE protocol in [14] falls into the second case, and then our 2fAKE protocol has the same number of rounds as the aPAKE in [14], i.e., 3 rounds. See the full version for a graphic description of our 2fAKE instantiation.

(3) Communication Complexity: By Fig. 3, our 2fAKE adds two hash values t_S, t_C and one signature σ to the communication of the underlying aPAKE. Note that t_C is designed for explicit authentication of the client's password, and thus we can eliminate it if the underlying aPAKE has already provided explicit authentication for the client's password, i.e., the server will abort if the client does not have the correct pw. This is achieved by many aPAKE protocols including the one in [14]. Consequently, the communication of our 2fAKE costs just 4.3 KB.

(4) Computation Complexity: Our experiments show that the running time of the client is about 25 ms and the running time of the server is about 0.2 ms. Here the client spends more time than the server, since the recovery algorithm of the secure sketch takes up about half of the running time of the client. We leave a more efficient instantiation as an interesting future work.

7 Conclusion

In this work, we presented a novel biometric- and password-based Two-Factor Authenticated Key Exchange (2fAKE) protocol that achieves enhanced security while maintaining practical efficiency. To address the privacy risks associated with biometric and password leakage, we formalized a new security model that simultaneously ensures indistinguishability, authentication, and zero-knowledge on biometrics. We then proposed a generic construction of 2fAKE using secure sketch, digital signature and aPAKE, and showed how to instantiate it from post-quantum assumptions. Our concrete implementation demonstrates that the protocol is lightweight in terms of storage, communication and computation, making it suitable for real-world deployment.

Acknowledgments. We would like to thank the reviewers for their valuable comments and suggestions. The authors were partially supported by National Cryptologic Science Fund of China (2025NCSF01009), National Natural Science Foundation of China (Grant No. 62372292), Guangdong Major Project of Basic and Applied Basic Research (2019B030302008), and the National Key R&D Program of China under Grant 2022YFB2701500.

References

1. Beguinet, H., Chevalier, C., Pointcheval, D., Ricosset, T., Rossi, M.: GeT a CAKE: generic transformations from key encaspulation mechanisms to password authenticated key exchanges. In: ACNS 2023, pp. 516–538 (2023)
2. Bellare, M., Pointcheval, D., Rogaway, P.: Authenticated key exchange secure against dictionary attacks. In: EUROCRYPT 2000, pp. 139–155 (2000)
3. Bellare, M., Rogaway, P.: Entity authentication and key distribution. In: CRYPTO 1993, pp. 232–249 (1993)
4. Bellovin, S.M., Merritt, M.: Encrypted key exchange: password-based protocols secure against dictionary attacks. In: IEEE SP 1992, pp. 72–84 (1992)

5. Bellovin, S.M., Merritt, M.: Augmented encrypted key exchange: a password-based protocol secure against dictionary attacks and password file compromise. In: ACM CCS 1993, pp. 244–250 (1993)
6. Beullens, W., Kleinjung, T., Vercauteren, F.: CSI-FiSh: efficient isogeny based signatures through class group computations. In: ASIACRYPT 2019, pp. 227–247 (2019)
7. Canetti, R., Krawczyk, H.: Security analysis of IKE's signature-based key-exchange protocol. In: CRYPTO 2002, pp. 143–161 (2002)
8. Canetti, R., Krawczyk, H.: Universally composable notions of key exchange and secure channels. In: EUROCRYPT 2002, pp. 337–351 (2002)
9. Daugman, J.: Understanding biometric entropy and iris capacity: avoiding identity collisions on national scales. Adv. Artif. Intell. Mach. Learn. **4**(2), 2152–2163 (2024)
10. Dilithium: NIST post-quantum cryptography standardization. https://pq-crystals.org/dilithium/
11. Dodis, Y., Ostrovsky, R., Reyzin, L., Smith, A.D.: Fuzzy extractors: how to generate strong keys from biometrics and other noisy data. SIAM J. Comput. **38**(1), 97–139 (2008)
12. Falcon: NIST post-quantum cryptography standardization. https://falcon-sign.info/
13. Fei, S., Yan, Z., Ding, W., Xie, H.: Security vulnerabilities of SGX and countermeasures: a survey. ACM Comput. Surv. **54**(6), 126:1-126:36 (2022)
14. Gentry, C., MacKenzie, P., Ramzan, Z.: A method for making password-based key exchange resilient to server compromise. In: CRYPTO 2006, pp. 142–159 (2006)
15. Gentry, C., Peikert, C., Vaikuntanathan, V.: Trapdoors for hard lattices and new cryptographic constructions. In: ACM STOC 2008, pp. 197–206 (2008)
16. Günther, C.G.: An identity-based key-exchange protocol. In: EUROCRYPT 1989, pp. 29–37 (1989)
17. Han, Y., Xu, C., Jiang, C., Chen, K.: A secure two-factor authentication key exchange scheme. IEEE Trans. Dependable Secur. Comput., 1–13 (2024)
18. Jarecki, S., Jubur, M., Krawczyk, H., Saxena, N., Shirvanian, M.: Two-factor password-authenticated key exchange with end-to-end security. ACM Trans. Priv. Secur. **24**(3) (2021)
19. Jarecki, S., Krawczyk, H., Shirvanian, M., Saxena, N.: Two-factor authentication with end-to-end password security. In: PKC 2018, pp. 431–461 (2018)
20. Jarecki, S., Krawczyk, H., Xu, J.: OPAQUE: an asymmetric PAKE protocol secure against pre-computation attacks. In: EUROCRYPT 2018, pp. 456–486 (2018)
21. Jiang, C., Xu, C., Han, Y., Zhang, Z., Chen, K.: Two-factor authenticated key exchange from biometrics with low entropy rates. IEEE Trans. Inf. Forensics Secur., 1–13 (2024)
22. Jiang, M., Liu, S., Han, S., Gu, D.: Fuzzy authenticated key exchange with tight security. In: ESORICS 2022, pp. 337–360 (2022)
23. Juels, A., Sudan, M.: A fuzzy vault scheme. Des. Codes Cryptogr. **38**(2), 237–257 (2006)
24. Kannwischer, M.J., Schwabe, P., Stebila, D., Wiggers, T.: Improving software quality in cryptography standardization projects. In: IEEE EuroS&P 2022, pp. 19–30 (2022)
25. Katz, J., Lindell, Y.: Introduction to Modern Cryptography, Second Edition. 2nd edn. (2014)
26. Katz, J., Ostrovsky, R., Yung, M.: Efficient password-authenticated key exchange using human-memorable passwords. In: EUROCRYPT 2001, pp. 475–494 (2001)

27. Krawczyk, H.: HMQV: a high-performance secure Diffie-Hellman protocol. In: CRYPTO 2005, pp. 546–566 (2005)
28. LaMacchia, B.A., Lauter, K., Mityagin, A.: Stronger security of authenticated key exchange. In: ProvSec 2007, pp. 1–16 (2007)
29. Li, Y., Schäge, S.: No-match attacks and robust partnering definitions: defining trivial attacks for security protocols is not trivial. In: ACM CCS 2017, pp. 1343–1360 (2017)
30. Lyubashevsky, V.: Lattice signatures without trapdoors. In: EUROCRYPT 2012, pp. 738–755 (2012)
31. NIST: NIST post-quantum cryptography standardization. https://csrc.nist.gov/projects/post-quantum-cryptography/
32. Pointcheval, D., Zimmer, S.: Multi-factor authenticated key exchange. In: ACNS 2008, pp. 277–295 (2008)
33. Santos, B.F.D., Gu, Y., Jarecki, S.: Randomized half-ideal cipher on groups with applications to UC (a)PAKE. In: EUROCRYPT 2023, pp. 128–156 (2023)
34. Shoup, V.: Security analysis of itSPAKE2+. In: TCC 2020, pp. 31–60 (2020)
35. Wang, M., He, K., Chen, J., Li, Z., Zhao, W., Du, R.: Biometrics-authenticated key exchange for secure messaging. In: ACM CCS 2021, pp. 2618–2631 (2021)
36. Wen, Y., Liu, S.: Robustly reusable fuzzy extractor from standard assumptions. In: ASIACRYPT 2018, pp. 459–489 (2018)
37. Woodage, J., Chatterjee, R., Dodis, Y., Juels, A., Ristenpart, T.: A new distribution-sensitive secure sketch and popularity-proportional hashing. In: CRYPTO 2017, pp. 682–710 (2017)
38. Xie, Q., Wong, D.S., Wang, G., Tan, X., Chen, K., Fang, L.: Provably secure dynamic ID-based anonymous two-factor authenticated key exchange protocol with extended security model. IEEE Trans. Inf. Forensics Secur. **12**(6), 1382–1392 (2017)
39. Yankov, M.P., Olsen, M.A., Stegmann, M.B., Christensen, S.S., Forchhammer, S.: Fingerprint entropy and identification capacity estimation based on pixel-level generative modelling. IEEE Trans. Inf. Forensics Secur. **15**, 56–65 (2020)

Concretely Efficient Parallel-Accessible DORAM for 100K-Sized Array

Koki Hamada[✉][iD]

NTT Social Informatics Laboratories, Tokyo 180-8585, Japan
koki.hamada@ntt.com

Abstract. We propose a concretely efficient parallel-accessible distributed oblivious RAM (DORAM). DORAM is a secure multi-party computation (MPC) protocol that enables private access to secret-shared arrays. Due to its wide application to more complex MPC protocols, many studies have been conducted on concretely efficient DORAMs. The best known concrete performance is about 900 accesses/second for arrays of sizes in the range 2^{13} to 2^{30}, achieved by a DORAM proposed by Falk et al.

In this paper, we propose a DORAM that provides concretely efficient parallel access for relatively small-sized arrays. Our DORAM is a three-party MPC protocol that is perfectly secure against a passive and static adversary who can corrupt up to one party. For an N-element array of D-bit elements, our DORAM accesses elements at k distinct addresses with $O(k\sqrt{N}(\log N + D))$ bits communication in 7 rounds and $O(kN(\log N + D))$ bits computation. When $D = 61$ and $N = 2^{17} \approx 100K$, the concrete performance of our DORAM is 452 accesses/second for sequential accesses. Thanks to the round complexity that is independent of the number of parallel access elements, the concrete performance of our protocol improves as k increases, achieving 1,076 accesses/second and 1,521 accesses/second in the cases of $k = 4$ and $k = 16$, respectively. As a byproduct, our DORAM simultaneously achieves information-theoretic security, constant round complexity, and sublinear communication complexity for the first time.

Keywords: Distributed oblivious RAM · Secure multi-party computation · Concrete efficiency

1 Introduction

Secure multi-party computation (MPC) is a cryptographic technique that allows multiple parties to compute while keeping their inputs private from each other. Since the inputs are not revealed to anyone during the computation, we can use MPC to ensure both privacy protection and data analysis. After the first study by Yao [25], improving the huge execution time has been a long-standing research topic for MPC. Up to now, efficient MPC protocols for various operations have been proposed. In addition to basic operations such as comparison [7] and floating-point arithmetic [19], in recent years, protocols that efficiently

Table 1. Comparison of constant round DORAMs.

	#Parties	Communication	Computation	Security
Trivial (linear scan)	3	$O(N)$	$O(N)$	Perfect
Floram [8]	2	$O(\sqrt{N})$	$O(N)$	Computational
Gordon et al. [12]	2	$O(\log N)$	$O(N)$	Computational
Bunn et al. [5]	3	$O(\sqrt{N})$	$O(N)$	Computational
Hamlin and Varia [13]	2	$O(\sqrt{N} \log N)$	$O(\sqrt{N} \log N)$	Computational
Ramen [4]	3	$O(\sqrt{N} \log N)$	$O(\sqrt{N} \log N)$	Computational
Ours	3	$O(\sqrt{N})$	$O(N)$	Perfect

perform applied operations such as machine learning [22] have also been proposed.

Distributed oblivious RAM (DORAM) is one of the MPC protocols that is still actively being studied for improving efficiency. It is an MPC protocol that enables private array access in MPC, and has a very wide range of applications: for example, it can be used as a component of secure data structures such as dictionaries and priority queues [16], as well as basic protocols such as binary search and breadth-first search [26], and it can also be used as memory to simulate RAM machines and convert arbitrary programs to MPC [15]. Due to such practical importance, there has been a lot of research on not only asymptotic improvements of DORAM's complexity, but also concretely efficient DORAM that directly improves execution time in real environments.

The concrete performance of DORAM has significantly improved over the years. For example, access speeds for arrays with around 2^{15} elements have improved from a few accesses per second [23,24] to tens of accesses per second [8,9,14,26], and even more recently to around 200 accesses per second [4,15,21]. Furthermore, the recently proposed GigaDORAM [10] showed a considerable improvement of about 900 accesses per second. GigaDORAM is also asymptotically efficient, maintaining its performance across array sizes from 2^{13} to 2^{30}.

It is beneficial in practice if access throughput could be increased by allowing parallel access to multiple addresses; since some applications require repeated read/write operations to multiple addresses. For example, in RAM machine simulations, multiple registers or memory addresses are accessed for each instruction execution, and in linked list operations, multiple pointers are updated in a single operation. Among existing concretely efficient DORAMs, only a few explicitly provides batch access [15,21], and none of them report access throughput better than that of GigaDORAM.

1.1 Contribution

In this paper, we propose a 3-party DORAM that can efficiently perform parallel access to medium-sized arrays. We also implement our protocol and show their concrete performance through benchmarking.

Our DORAM is a 3-party MPC protocol that is perfectly secure against a passive and static adversary who can corrupt up to one party. For an N-element array of D-bit elements, our DORAM accesses elements at k distinct addresses with $O(k\sqrt{N}(\log N + D))$ bits communication in 7 rounds and $O(kN(\log N + D))$ bits computation. Although our main interest is in concrete performance, from a theoretical perspective to the best of our knowledge, our DORAM is the first DORAM to simultaneously achieve information-theoretic security, constant round complexity, and sublinear communication complexity. A comparison of constant round DORAMs is shown in Table 1.

Focusing on concrete performance, our DORAM achieves a better concrete performance than GigaDORAM in some settings. For arrays of size $N \leq 2^{17} \approx 100K$ with each element of size $D = 61$ bits, our DORAM achieves 450 accesses/second for sequential access, 1076 accesses/second for $k = 4$ parallel access, and 1521 accesses/second for $k = 16$ parallel access. On the other hand, our DORAM requires linear local computation, so its performance degrades significantly for large N. In fact, at $N = 2^{24}$, the performances drop to 10 accesses/second, 32 accesses/second, and 69 accesses/second, respectively.

We also note that if k is sufficiently large, our protocol is not a good choice. For example, when $k = \Theta(N)$, our DORAM requires $O(N^2(\log N + D))$ bits of computation, which is quadratic with respect to N. An asymptotically efficient protocol [18] for large k has been proposed, which requires $O(N \log N(\log N+D))$ bits of communication/computation in $O(\log N)$ rounds even when $k = \Theta(N)$.

2 Preliminaries

We start with introducing some notation. Throughout this paper, the index of a vector or a matrix starts at 0. We refer to the i-th entry of a vector $\vec{v}$ by $\vec{v}[i]$ and the (i,j)-th entry of a matrix A by $A[i,j]$. That is, if $\vec{v}$ is a vector of length n, then $\vec{v} = (\vec{v}[0], \vec{v}[1], \ldots, \vec{v}[n-1])$. Also, if A is an $M \times N$ matrix, then the top most row is $(A[0,0], A[0,1], \ldots, A[0,N-1])$. Unless otherwise specified, we treat vectors as column vectors. For example, we interpret $\vec{v}$ as an $n \times 1$ matrix.

We also introduce operations related to vectors. We write the concatenation of vectors $\vec{a}$ and $\vec{b}$ as $\vec{a} \parallel \vec{b}$. $\mathrm{OneHot}(x,n)$ computes a one-hot vector $\vec{v}$ of length n such that $\vec{v}[i] = 1$ if $i = x$ and $\vec{v}[i] = 0$ otherwise. For example, $\mathrm{OneHot}(1,5) = (0,1,0,0,0)$. We write $\vec{v} >> d$ to represent a circular shift to $\vec{v}$ with amount d. That is, $\vec{u} := \vec{v} >> d$ satisfies $\vec{v}[i] = \vec{u}[i + d \bmod n]$ for $i \in [0,n)$, where $n := |\vec{v}| = |\vec{u}|$. For example, $(1,2,3,4,5) >> 3 = (3,4,5,1,2)$. Similarly, $\vec{v} << d$ represents a circular shift with reverse order. That is, $\vec{v} << d = \vec{v} >> -d$. For better readability, we summarize our notation in Table 3.

2.1 Secure Multi-party Computation Settings

We consider secret-sharing based three-party computation that is secure against a single static corruption. Let P_0, P_1, and P_2 be the three parties. We use the

Table 2. Costs of our $\mathcal{F}_{\text{MPC}}$ instantiation.

Command	Communication	Computation	Rounds	Source
Enc	$O(1)$	$O(1)$	1	Sect. 2.2
Mul	$O(1)$	$O(1)$	1	[2]
InnerProd (n elements)	$O(1)$	$O(n)$	1	[2]
Rotation (n elements)	$O(n)$	$O(n)$	$1+2$	Appendix B
TwoPCMul	$O(1)$	$O(1)$	$1+1$	Appendix B

perfect security version of the standard security definition in the presence of semi-honest adversaries [11]. The definition is shown in Appendix A.

We will prove the security of the protocols in a hybrid model. We assume that parties have access to a trusted party that compute a subfunctionality. When the subfunctionality is f, we say that the protocol works in the f-hybrid model.

Let p be an odd prime. We mainly use values on the prime field $\mathbb{Z}_p$, but for some protocols, we use values on a ring $\mathbb{Z}_M$ for some positive integers M. We write the multiplicative inverse of x in a prime field $\mathbb{Z}_p$ as $\text{ModInv}(x)$.

2.2 Secret Sharing Schemes

We use three types of secret sharing scheme: Shamir's scheme [20], replicated secret sharing scheme [6], and additive secret sharing scheme. We basically use Shamir's scheme, but often go through other schemes for efficiency.

For Shamir's scheme [20], we use the 2-out-of-3 version over $\mathbb{Z}_p$. With this parameter setting, no information about the secret can be leaked from any single share, but the secret can be recovered from any two shares. For a secret $s \in \mathbb{Z}_p$, we denote the share for P_i ($i \in \{0,1,2\}$) by $[\![s]\!]_i$. We write a triple of shares $([\![s]\!]_0, [\![s]\!]_1, [\![s]\!]_2)$ as $[\![s]\!]$. Each share $[\![s]\!]_i$ is an element in $\mathbb{Z}_p$.

For a replicated secret sharing scheme [6], letting M be a positive integer, we use the 2-out-of-3 version over a ring $\mathbb{Z}_M$. In this scheme, for a secret $s \in \mathbb{Z}_M$, the shares for parties P_0, P_1, and P_2 are defined as $\{\!\{s\}\!\}_0^{(M)} := (\{\!\{s\}\!\}_{20}^{(M)}, \{\!\{s\}\!\}_{01}^{(M)})$, $\{\!\{s\}\!\}_1^{(M)} := (\{\!\{s\}\!\}_{01}^{(M)}, \{\!\{s\}\!\}_{12}^{(M)})$, and $\{\!\{s\}\!\}_2^{(M)} := (\{\!\{s\}\!\}_{12}^{(M)}, \{\!\{s\}\!\}_{20}^{(M)})$, where $\{\!\{s\}\!\}_j^{(M)} \in \mathbb{Z}_M$ ($j \in \{01, 12, 20\}$) and $s = \{\!\{s\}\!\}_{01}^{(M)} + \{\!\{s\}\!\}_{12}^{(M)} + \{\!\{s\}\!\}_{20}^{(M)} \bmod M$. We write a triple of shares $(\{\!\{s\}\!\}_0^{(M)}, \{\!\{s\}\!\}_1^{(M)}, \{\!\{s\}\!\}_2^{(M)})$ as $\{\!\{s\}\!\}^{(M)}$.

For an additive secret-sharing scheme, we use a two-party version over $\mathbb{Z}_p$. We assume only P_0 and P_1 have a share. For a secret $s \in \mathbb{Z}_p$, we denote the share for P_i ($i \in \{0,1\}$) by $\langle s \rangle_i$. Each share is an element in $\mathbb{Z}_p$ and shares satisfy $s = \langle s \rangle_0 + \langle s \rangle_1 \bmod p$. We write a pair of shares $(\langle s \rangle_0, \langle s \rangle_1)$ as $\langle s \rangle$. Note that a secret shared value $[\![x]\!]$ of Shamir's scheme can be converted to a secret shared value $\langle x \rangle$ of this additive secret sharing scheme without any communication by each P_i ($i \in \{0,1\}$) performing local computation $\langle x \rangle_i := \lambda_i [\![x]\!]_i$. Here, λ_i is a public constant called the Lagrange coefficient used for reconstruction in Shamir's scheme.

All of these three schemes have linearity. That is, assuming that two values x and y are secret-shared, letting c be a public constant, we can construct secret shared values of $z_1 := x + y$, $z_2 := x - y$, and $z_3 := cx$ by performing $O(1)$ local computations at each party without communication. We describe the execution of these computations in Shamir's scheme as $[\![z_1]\!] \leftarrow [\![x]\!] + [\![y]\!]$, $[\![z_2]\!] \leftarrow [\![x]\!] - [\![y]\!]$, and $[\![z_3]\!] \leftarrow [\![x]\!] \times c$, respectively. The same notation is used for secret-shared values in replicated and additive schemes.

Functionality $\mathcal{F}_{\mathrm{MPC}}$

- $[\![z]\!] \leftarrow \mathsf{Enc}(x, P_i)$: On receiving x from a party P_i, output a fresh secret shared value $[\![z]\!]$ to all parties.
- $\{\!\{z\}\!\}^{(M)} \leftarrow \mathsf{Enc}(x, M, P_i)$: On receiving x and M from a party P_i, output a fresh secret shared value $\{\!\{z\}\!\}^{(M)}$ to all parties.
- $[\![z]\!] \leftarrow \mathsf{Mul}([\![x]\!], [\![y]\!])$: On receiving $[\![x]\!]$ and $[\![y]\!]$ from all parties, reconstruct x and y, compute $z := xy$, and output a fresh secret shared value $[\![z]\!]$ to all parties.
- $[\![z]\!] \leftarrow \mathsf{InnerProd}([\![\vec{x}]\!], [\![\vec{y}]\!])$: On receiving $[\![\vec{x}]\!]$ and $[\![\vec{y}]\!]$ s.t. $|\vec{x}| = |\vec{y}|$ from all parties, reconstruct $\vec{x}$ and $\vec{y}$, compute $z := \vec{x} \cdot \vec{y}$, and output a fresh secret shared value $[\![z]\!]$ to all parties.
- $[\![\vec{z}]\!] \leftarrow \mathsf{Rotation}(\langle \vec{x} \rangle, \{\!\{d\}\!\}^{(M)})$: On receiving $\{\!\{d\}\!\}^{(M)}$ from all parties and $\langle \vec{x} \rangle$ s.t. $|\vec{x}| = M$ from P_0 and P_1, reconstruct $\vec{x}$ and d, compute $\vec{z} := \vec{x} >> d$, and output a fresh secret shared vector $[\![\vec{z}]\!]$ to all parties.
- $\langle z \rangle \leftarrow \mathsf{TwoPCMul}(\langle x \rangle)$: On receiving $\langle x \rangle$ from P_0 and P_1, compute $z := \langle x \rangle_0 \langle x \rangle_1$, and output a fresh secret shared value $\langle z \rangle$ to P_0 and P_1.

Fig. 1. Functionality for the underlying MPC.

2.3 Secure Multi-party Computation Protocols

Our protocols rely on many existing protocols. We model a set of existing protocols as an ideal functionality called the underlying MPC and refer to it as $\mathcal{F}_{\mathrm{MPC}}$. We will construct our protocols in the $\mathcal{F}_{\mathrm{MPC}}$-hybrid model.

Underlying MPC. The underlying MPC functionality $\mathcal{F}_{\mathrm{MPC}}$ is shown in Fig. 1. For notational simplicity, $[\![z]\!] \leftarrow \mathsf{Mul}([\![x]\!], [\![y]\!])$ is also written as $[\![z]\!] \leftarrow [\![x]\!] \times [\![y]\!]$. Since $\mathcal{F}_{\mathrm{MPC}}$ does not define the efficiency of each command, we show examples of instantiating each command and their efficiency in Table 2. Here, round complexity in the form of $a + b$ represents that the first a rounds of the overall $a + b$ rounds are offline, meaning that they can be executed before receiving input. A detail of the instantiation appears in Appendix B. The cost analysis of our protocol uses the complexities shown in Table 2.

Subprotocols. We will also use some subprotocols that can be built on the underlying MPC as components. Here, we define them as follows.

- $\{\!\{z\}\!\}^{(M)} \leftarrow$ Additive2Replicated($\langle x \rangle, M$): It converts a secret shared value $\langle x \rangle$ to a fresh secret shared value $\{\!\{z\}\!\}^{(M)}$ s.t. $z = \langle x \rangle_0 + \langle x \rangle_1 \bmod M$. This can be implemented as follows:
    1. $\{\!\{y_0\}\!\}^{(M)} \leftarrow$ Enc($\langle x \rangle_0, M, P_0$) and $\{\!\{y_1\}\!\}^{(M)} \leftarrow$ Enc($\langle x \rangle_1, M, P_1$).
    2. $\{\!\{z\}\!\}^{(M)} := \{\!\{y_0\}\!\}^{(M)} + \{\!\{y_1\}\!\}^{(M)}$.
- $[\![z]\!] \leftarrow$ Additive2Shamir($\langle x \rangle$): It converts a secret shared value $\langle x \rangle$ to a fresh secret shared value $[\![z]\!]$ s.t. $z = x$. This can be implemented as follows:
    1. $[\![y_0]\!] \leftarrow$ Enc($\langle x \rangle_0, P_0$) and $[\![y_1]\!] \leftarrow$ Enc($\langle x \rangle_1, P_1$).
    2. $[\![z]\!] := [\![y_0]\!] + [\![y_1]\!]$.
- $[\![z]\!] \leftarrow$ IfElse($[\![c]\!], [\![t]\!], [\![f]\!]$): It receives three secret shared values $[\![c]\!]$, $[\![t]\!]$, and $[\![f]\!]$ s.t. $c \in \{0, 1\}$, and outputs a fresh secret shared value $[\![z]\!]$ s.t. $z = t$ if $c = 1$ and $z = f$ if $c = 0$. This can be implemented as:
    1. $[\![z]\!] \leftarrow [\![f]\!] + ([\![t]\!] - [\![f]\!]) \times [\![c]\!]$.
- $[\![C]\!] \leftarrow$ MatMul($[\![A]\!], [\![B]\!]$): It receives two secret shared matrices $[\![A]\!]$ and $[\![B]\!]$ and outputs a fresh secret shared matrix $[\![C]\!]$ s.t. $C = A \times B$. If the sizes of A and B are $m \times n$ and $n \times \ell$, respectively, this can be implemented as:
    1. $[\![C[i,j]]\!] \leftarrow$ InnerProd($[\![\vec{a}_i]\!], [\![\vec{b}_j]\!]$) for $i \in [0, m)$ and $j \in [0, \ell)$, where $[\![\vec{a}_i]\!]$ is the i-th row vector of $[\![A]\!]$ and $[\![\vec{b}_j]\!]$ is the j-th column vector of $[\![B]\!]$.

3 Our Constant Round DORAM

In this section, we describe the details of our DORAM. Our DORAM consists of three servers and is secure against passive and static single corruption. The functionality that our DORAM realizes is shown in Fig. 2. Extension to other MPC settings is discussed in Appendix D.

Functionality $\mathcal{F}_{\text{DORAM}}^{(N)}$

Parameters: Number of elements N.

Init($[\![\vec{a}]\!]$): On receiving a vector $[\![\vec{a}]\!]$ of length N from all parties, reconstruct $\vec{a}$ and store it.

$[\![\vec{z}]\!] \leftarrow$ Read($[\![\vec{x}]\!]$): On receiving $[\![\vec{x}]\!]$ such that $\vec{x}[i] \in [0, N)$ for all $i \in [0, |\vec{x}|)$ from all parties, do:
  1. Reconstruct addresses $\vec{x}$.
  2. For $i \in [0, |\vec{v}|)$, compute $\vec{z}[i] := \vec{a}[\vec{x}[i]]$.
  3. Output fresh secret shared vector $[\![\vec{z}]\!]$ to all parties.

Add($[\![\vec{x}]\!], [\![\vec{d}]\!]$): On receiving $[\![\vec{x}]\!]$ and $[\![\vec{d}]\!]$ such that $|\vec{x}| = |\vec{d}|$ and $\vec{x}[i] \in [0, N)$ for all $i \in [0, |\vec{x}|)$ from all parties, do:
  1. Reconstruct addresses $\vec{x}$ and values $\vec{d}$.
  2. For $i \in [0, |\vec{v}|)$, set $\vec{a}[\vec{x}[i]] := \vec{a}[\vec{x}[i]] + \vec{d}[i]$.

Write($[\![x]\!], [\![y]\!]$): On receiving $[\![\vec{x}]\!]$ and $[\![\vec{y}]\!]$ such that $|\vec{x}| = |\vec{y}|$, $\vec{x}[i] \in [0, N)$ for all $i \in [0, |\vec{x}|)$, and $\vec{x}[i] \neq \vec{x}[j]$ for $i \neq j$ from all parties, do:
  1. Reconstruct addresses $\vec{x}$ and values $\vec{y}$.
  2. For $i \in [0, |\vec{v}|)$, set $\vec{a}[\vec{x}[i]] := \vec{y}[i]$.

Fig. 2. Functionality for DORAM between three parties P_0, P_1, and P_2.

In addition to the read and write operations provided by many DORAMs, our DORAM provides an operation called addition. Unlike the *overwriting* of a value in a write operation, the add operation *adds* the given value to the specified element. Furthermore, our DORAM has a feature that it supports batch access to multiple addresses. The read and add operations can be called on multiple addresses (which may include the same address), and the write function can be called on multiple addresses (which should be distinct) at once.

3.1 Overview

Our DORAM provides the basic operations of reading and adding values at specified addresses in an array. This set of operations is an extension of standard DORAM, which provides reading and writing, since writing can be realized by combining reading and adding. Furthermore, our DORAM can perform reading, writing, or adding to multiple addresses in a batch. (More precisely, writing is limited to cases where addresses are distinct.) Thus, our DORAM is advantageous when performing a constant number of parallel reads and writes in series.

Our DORAM stores array of elements in three different locations: the main array $\vec{a}$, the stash, which records the addition queries, and the list U, which holds the addition queries that have not yet been stored in the stash. When initialized, the stash and U are empty, and the given array is set to $\vec{a}$. When adding, the address and the value to be added are simply added to U. When reading, if U is not empty, each element of U is converted and added to the stash. Then, the values from the main array $\vec{a}$ are read, and the differences from the stash are read, and finally these are added together and output. Reading values from the main array $\vec{a}$ is performed by calling the independent functionality $\mathcal{F}_{\text{RomRead}}$, which is shown in section Sect. 3.3. The stash grows larger as the addition is repeated, and the computational cost of each read and write also increases. To reduce this, a process called *flushing* is performed periodically to reflect the contents in the stash to the main array $\vec{a}$, in a similar way to the square-root oram.

One of the technical features of our DORAM is that it heavily uses *inner products*. The inner product functionality can be implemented in many honest-majority MPCs in one round with $O(1)$ communication and $O(n)$ computation, where n is the length of the vector. This property, where the communication complexity does not depend on the vector length, is very useful in designing low-communication protocols, and we also use inner products to construct a low-round and low-communication DORAM (at the cost of some computational cost). In order to smoothly perform the inner product, we introduce a functionality called $\mathcal{F}_{\text{Index2Bits}}$, which we use in many parts of our protocol. This functionality computes one-hot vectors for the corresponding row and column addresses when accessing array elements. By using this functionality, we can apply the technique of [3] to read from an array in two rounds of inner products. The protocol that realizes this functionality is shown in Sect. 3.2.

3.2 Instantiating $\mathcal{F}_{\text{Index2Bits}}$

Functionality $\mathcal{F}_{\text{Index2Bits}}^{(N,R,C)}$

Parameters: Upper bound N, number of rows R, and number of columns C.

$[\![\vec{r}]\!], [\![\vec{c}]\!] \leftarrow \text{Index2Bits}([\![x]\!])$: On receiving $[\![x]\!]$ s.t. $x \in [0, N)$ from all parties, do:
1. Reconstruct address x.
2. Compute $c := x \bmod C$, $r := \lfloor x/C \rfloor \bmod R$, $\vec{c} := \text{OneHot}(c, C)$, and $\vec{r} := \text{OneHot}(r, R)$.
3. Output fresh secret shared vectors $[\![\vec{r}]\!]$ and $[\![\vec{c}]\!]$ to all parties.

Fig. 3. Functionality for computing one-hot vectors of row and column addresses.

In this section, we present protocols that realize the functionality denoted by $\mathcal{F}_{\text{Index2Bits}}$ (Fig. 3). This functionality receives a secret shared address $[\![x]\!]$ and outputs two secret shared one-hot vectors $[\![\vec{r}]\!]$ and $[\![\vec{c}]\!]$ such that $\vec{c} = \text{OneHot}(c, C)$ and $\vec{r} = \text{OneHot}(r, R)$, where C and R are public constants, $c := x \bmod C$, and $r := \lfloor x/C \rfloor \bmod R$. As we will see in Sect. 3.3, we can read a specified element from an array by combining this ideal functionality with just two rounds of inner products.

We first show the protocol that realizes $\mathcal{F}_{\text{Index2Bits}}$ in a general case in Sect. 3.2. Then, we will show more efficient protocol for the case where the prime number p and the matrix size are limited in Sect. 3.2.

Protocol for the General Case. Here, we will show a protocol denoted by $\Pi_{\text{Index2BitsG}}$ that realizes $\mathcal{F}_{\text{Index2Bits}}$ in the general case. The parties are assumed to know that the address is less than $p/2$. In addition, we assume that the parameters R and C are natural numbers that satisfy $2C < p$, $2R < p$, and $CR < p$.

The outline of our protocol is as follows. We first convert $[\![x]\!]$ into the two-party additive secret sharing between P_0 and P_1. Then, by performing local computations on their own shares, P_0 and P_1 obtain additive secret sharing of the approximate row and column addresses. Next, we apply the private rotation functionality to convert these additively secret shared approximate addresses into secret shared one-hot vectors. Here, we use the property that we can convert an additively secret shared value into its one-hot vector by shifting a one-hot vector of zero. Finally, we shift these one-hot vectors by the errors between the approximate values we computed and the true values, and obtain the desired secret shared one-hot vectors.

To reduce the communication round, we introduce a new construction that compute the errors along with the approximate values of $x \bmod C$ and $\lfloor x/C \rfloor \bmod R$. In our construction, we use the fact that the desired computation on secret shared values can often be approximated well by the local computation for each party's share. Specifically, when calculating an approximation of the column addresses whose true value is $x \bmod C$, each party computes the remainder

172   K. Hamada

Algorithm 1: Protocol for $\Pi_{\text{Index2BitsG}}^{(N,R,C)}$, realizing $\mathcal{F}_{\text{Index2Bits}}^{(N,R,C)}$.

Parameters: Upper bound of index N, number of rows R, and number of columns C.
Require: p is an odd prime number, $2C < p$, $2R < p$, $CR < p$, and $2N \leq p$.
Notation: $[\![\vec{r}]\!], [\![\vec{c}]\!] \leftarrow \text{Index2Bits}([\![x]\!])$
Input: Address $[\![x]\!]$ such that $x \in [0, N)$.
Output: One-hot vectors $[\![\vec{r}]\!]$ and $[\![\vec{c}]\!]$ s.t. $r = \lfloor x/C \rfloor \bmod R$, $\vec{r} = \text{OneHot}(r, R)$,
$c = x \bmod C$, and $\vec{c} = \text{OneHot}(c, C)$.

1. Parties compute $[\![d]\!] \leftarrow 2 \times [\![x]\!]$ by local computation. Then, parties P_0 and P_1 locally compute an additive secret sharing $\langle d \rangle$ of $d = 2x$.
2. Parties securely compute approximations r'' and c'' of the row and column addresses of x. They are then converted to one-hot vectors $[\![\vec{r}'']\!]$ and $[\![\vec{c}'']\!]$.
   (a) Each party P_i ($i \in \{0,1\}$) locally computes $\langle c' \rangle_i := \lfloor \langle d \rangle_i/2 \rfloor \bmod C$ and $\langle r' \rangle_i := \lfloor \langle d \rangle_i/2C \rfloor \bmod R$.
   (b) Parties convert the approximate values of row and column addresses to replicated secret sharing as: $\{\!\{c''\}\!\}^{(C)} \leftarrow \text{Additive2Replicated}(\langle c' \rangle, C)$ and $\{\!\{r''\}\!\}^{(R)} \leftarrow \text{Additive2Replicated}(\langle r' \rangle, R)$.
   (c) Parties call Rotation() to compute the one-hot vectors of the approximate addresses as: $[\![\vec{c}'']\!] \leftarrow \text{Rotation}(\text{OneHot}(0, C), \{\!\{c''\}\!\}^{(C)})$ and
   $[\![\vec{r}'']\!] \leftarrow \text{Rotation}(\text{OneHot}(0, R), \{\!\{r''\}\!\}^{(R)})$.
3. Let l_i be the least significant bit of $\langle d \rangle_i$ ($i \in \{0,1\}$). There are three cases: Case 1 ($l_0 = l_1 = 0$), Case 2 ($l_0 = l_1 = 1$), and Case 3 ($l_0 \oplus l_1 = 1$). For $i \in \{1,2,3\}$, parties securely compute the flag $g_i \in \{0,1\}$ that indicates whether Case i applies.
   (a) Each party P_i ($i \in \{0,1\}$) sets $\langle l \rangle_i := l_i$.
   (b) Parties compute $\langle g_2 \rangle \leftarrow \text{TwoPCMul}(\langle l \rangle)$, $\langle g_3 \rangle \leftarrow \langle l \rangle - 2\langle g_2 \rangle$, and $\langle g_1 \rangle \leftarrow 1 - \langle l \rangle + \langle g_2 \rangle$.
   (c) For $i \in \{1,2,3\}$, parties converts the flags as $[\![g_i]\!] \leftarrow \text{Additive2Shamir}(\langle g_i \rangle)$.
4. Parties compute output for each case by correcting the one-hot vectors of approximate addresses.
   (a) Parties convert approximate addresses as $[\![c']\!] \leftarrow \text{Additive2Shamir}(\langle c' \rangle)$ and $[\![r']\!] \leftarrow \text{Additive2Shamir}(\langle r' \rangle)$.
   (b) Parties compute the output candidates $[\![\vec{c}_1]\!]$ and $[\![\vec{r}_1]\!]$ for Case 1 as: $[\![\vec{c}_1]\!] := [\![\vec{c}'']\!]$,
   $[\![c_1]\!] \leftarrow [\![\vec{c}_1]\!] \cdot (0,1,\ldots, C-1)$, $[\![e_1]\!] \leftarrow ([\![c']\!] - [\![c_1]\!]) \times \text{ModInv}(C)$, and
   $[\![\vec{r}_1]\!] \leftarrow \text{IfElse}([\![e_1]\!], [\![\vec{r}'']\!] \gg 1, [\![\vec{r}'']\!])$.
   (c) Parties compute the output candidates $[\![\vec{c}_2]\!]$ and $[\![\vec{r}_2]\!]$ for Case 2 as: $[\![\vec{c}_2]\!] := [\![\vec{c}'']\!] \gg 1$,
   $[\![c_2]\!] \leftarrow [\![\vec{c}_2]\!] \cdot (0,1,\ldots, C-1)$, $[\![e_2]\!] := ([\![c']\!] + 1 - [\![c_2]\!]) \times \text{ModInv}(C)$, and
   $[\![\vec{r}_2]\!] := \text{IfElse}([\![e_2]\!], [\![\vec{r}'']\!] \gg 1, [\![\vec{r}'']\!])$.
   (d) Parties compute the output candidates $[\![\vec{c}_3]\!]$ and $[\![\vec{r}_3]\!]$ for Case 3. First, parties compute $[\![\vec{c}_3]\!] := [\![\vec{c}'']\!] \ll c_p$, $[\![c_3]\!] \leftarrow [\![\vec{c}_3]\!] \cdot (0,1,\ldots, C-1)$, and
   $[\![e_3]\!] := ([\![c']\!] - c_p - [\![c_3]\!]) \times \text{ModInv}(C)$. Since $e_3 \in \{-1, 0, 1\}$, for each $k \in \{-1, 0, 1\}$, parties compute a flag $[\![f_k]\!]$ such that $f_k = 1$ iff $e_3 = k$ as:
   $[\![f_{-1}]\!] \leftarrow [\![e_3]\!] \times ([\![e_3]\!] - 1) \times \text{ModInv}(2)$, $[\![f_0]\!] \leftarrow (1 + [\![e_3]\!]) \times (1 - [\![e_3]\!])$, and
   $[\![f_1]\!] \leftarrow [\![e_3]\!] \times ([\![e_3]\!] + 1) \times \text{ModInv}(2)$. Parties compute $[\![\vec{r}_3]\!]$ for each possible value of e_3 and select the correct vector using the flags as
   $[\![\vec{r}_3]\!] \leftarrow ([\![\vec{r}'']\!] \ll (r_p + 1)) \times [\![f_{-1}]\!] + ([\![\vec{r}'']\!] \ll r_p) \times [\![f_0]\!] + ([\![\vec{r}'']\!] \ll (r_p - 1)) \times [\![f_1]\!]$.
5. Parties select the output according to the flags $[\![g_1]\!], [\![g_2]\!]$, and $[\![g_3]\!]$ as: $[\![\vec{c}]\!] \leftarrow \sum_{i=1}^{3} [\![\vec{c}_i]\!] \times [\![g_i]\!]$ and $[\![\vec{r}]\!] \leftarrow \sum_{i=1}^{3} [\![\vec{r}_i]\!] \times [\![g_i]\!]$.

---

of its own share, and regards this as the share of approximate remainder. Of course, the value reconstructed from these shares is not necessarily close to the desired $x \bmod C$, but we can show that there are only three possible candidates

Protocol and its correctness. Next, we will describe the details of our protocol. The protocol is shown in Algorithm 1. First, in Step 1, we compute $[\![d]\!]$ and convert it to additive secret sharing by local computation. Since $2x < p$, it follows that $d = 2x$. If we define $d_i := \langle d \rangle_i$ ($i \in \{0,1\}$), then either $d = d_0 + d_1$ or $d = d_0 + d_1 - p$, but since d is even and p is odd, we can see that the former is true if $l_0 = l_1$, and the latter is true otherwise [17]. In order to use this property, we compute the approximate values of c and r from the shares of $\langle d \rangle$, rather than from the shares of $\langle x \rangle$.

In Step 2, we first compute $\langle c' \rangle$ and $\langle r' \rangle$ by local computation in Step (a). We can uniquely decompose d_i into $d_i = 2CRa'_i + 2Cr'_i + 2c'_i + l_i$ ($l_i \in \{0,1\}$, $c'_i \in [0,C)$, $r'_i \in [0,R)$, $0 \le a'_i$). Then, the plaintexts of $\langle r' \rangle$ and $\langle c' \rangle$ satisfy $r' = r'_0 + r'_1$ and $c' = c'_0 + c'_1$, respectively. In Step (b), we convert $\langle c' \rangle$ into the replicated secret sharing of $c'' = c' \bmod C$. Then, by calling Rotation we obtain the secret sharing of $\vec{c}''' = \text{OneHot}(0, C) >> c'' = \text{OneHot}(c'', C)$. Similarly, we have $r'' = r' \bmod R$ and $\vec{r}''' = \text{OneHot}(r'', R)$.

In the following, we consider three cases: Case 1 ($l_0 = l_1 = 0$), Case 2 ($l_0 = l_1 = 1$), and Case 3 ($l_0 \oplus l_1 = 1$). Since $l = l_0 + l_1$ holds, flags g_1, g_2, and g_3 can be represented as $g_2 = l_0 \wedge l_1 = l_0 l_1$, $g_3 = l_0 \oplus l_1 = (l_0 + l_1) - l_0 l_1 = l - g_2$, and $g_1 = \neg l_0 \wedge \neg l_1 = 1 - (l_0 + l_1) + l_0 l_1 = 1 - l + g_2$. Thus, $[\![g_1]\!]$, $[\![g_2]\!]$, and $[\![g_3]\!]$ are obtained by the computation in Step 3.

Let's start by considering Case 1 ($l_0 = l_1 = 0$). Since $l_0 = l_1$, we have $d = d_0 + d_1$. Therefore, $x = d/2 = (d_0 + d_1)/2 = (2CRa' + 2Cr' + 2c')/2 = CRa' + Cr' + c'$ holds. Thus, since $c = $ x mod $C = c' \bmod C = c''$, we have that $\vec{c} = \vec{c}'''$. Also, since $(x - c)/C = Ra' + r' + (c' - c)/C$, if we define $e := (c' - c)/C$, then $r = (x - c)/C \bmod R = r' + (c' - c)/C \bmod R = r' + e \bmod R$ holds. Therefore, we have that $\vec{r} = \text{OneHot}(r, R) = \text{OneHot}(r' + e \bmod R, R) = \text{OneHot}(r' \bmod R, R) >> e = \text{OneHot}(r'', R) >> e = \vec{r}''' >> e$. Recall that $c = c' \bmod C$, $0 \le c \le C - 1$, $0 \le c' \le 2C - 2$, and $e = (c' - c)/C$. Then, we have $e \in \{0, 1\}$. Therefore, we can compute $\vec{r}$ by $\vec{r} = \text{IfElse}(e, \vec{r}''' >> 1, \vec{r}''')$. Thus, we can compute the candidate vectors $[\![\vec{r}_1]\!]$ and $[\![\vec{c}_1]\!]$ for Case 1 as Step 4(b).

In Case 2 ($l_0 = l_1 = 1$), we can use the fact that $d = d_0 + d_1$ to obtain $c = c' + 1 \bmod C$ and $r = r' + (c' + 1 - c)/C \bmod R$ by similar computations as in Case 1. If we set $e := (c' + 1 - c)/C$, we can derive $\vec{c} = \vec{c}''' >> 1$, $\vec{r} = \vec{r}''' >> e$, and $e \in \{0, 1\}$. Thus, we can compute the candidate vectors $[\![\vec{r}_2]\!]$ and $[\![\vec{c}_2]\!]$ for Case 2 as Step 4(c).

Case 3 ($l_0 \oplus l_1 = 1$) is a little more complicated. In this case, we use the fact that $d = d_0 + d_1 - p$. We uniquely decompose p as $p = 2CRa_p + 2Cr_p + 2c_p + 1$ ($0 \le a_p$, $c_p \in [0, C)$, $r_p \in [0, R)$). Then, we can obtain $c = c' - c_p \bmod C$ and $r = r' - r_p + (c' - c_p - c)/C \bmod R$. Let $e := (c' - c_p - c)/C$. Then, we can derive $\vec{c} = \vec{c}'' << c_p$, $\vec{r} = \vec{r}'' << (r_p - e)$, and $e \in \{-1, 0, 1\}$. Let $f_{-1} := e(e-1)/2$, $f_0 := (1+e)(1-e)$, and $f_1 := e(e+1)/2$. Then, we have that $f_k = 1$ iff $e = k$ for $e \in \{-1, 0, 1\}$. Therefore, we can compute $\vec{r}$ as $\vec{r} = (\vec{r}'' << (r_p+1)) \times f_{-1} + (\vec{r}'' << r_p) \times f_0 + (\vec{r}'' << (r_p-1)) \times f_2$. Thus, we can compute the candidate vectors $[\![\vec{r}_3]\!]$ and $[\![\vec{c}_3]\!]$ for Case 3 as Step 4(d).

Finally, in Step 5, the output corresponding to the current input is selected from the candidates computed in Step 4 using the flag computed in Step 3.

Security. The protocol consists only of calls to functionalities and local computations. Since the outputs of the functionalities are all fresh shares of secret-shared values, each party's view can be simulated by uniformly random values that are consistent with that party's output. Thus, we have the following theorem.

Theorem 1. *If p is an odd prime number, $2C < p$, $2R < p$, $CR < p$, and $2N \leq p$, then protocol $\Pi_{\text{Index2BitsG}}^{(N,R,C)}$ (Algorithm 1) computes $\mathcal{F}_{\text{Index2Bits}}^{(N,R,C)}$ (Fig. 3) with perfect security in the $\mathcal{F}_{\text{MPC}}$-hybrid model.*

Cost. The communication and computation costs are $O(C+R)$ and $O(C+R)$, respectively. $[\![\vec{c}]\!]$ and $[\![\vec{r}]\!]$ are computed in 4 and 6 rounds, respectively. The analysis is omitted due to page limitations.

Protocol for Power-of-Two Sized Matrix. Next, we propose a protocol denoted by $\Pi_{\text{Index2BitsS}}$ that realizes $\mathcal{F}_{\text{Index2Bits}}$ with lower communication rounds by limiting the size of the matrix to powers of 2. The parties are assumed to know that the address is less than $p/2$. In addition, the parameters R and C are powers of 2 that satisfy $2C < p$, $2R < p$, and $CR < p$. Furthermore, p is a prime number with the lower $\log_2 C + \log_2 R + 1$ bits are all 1, i.e., $p \equiv -1 \pmod{2RC}$. Examples of prime numbers that satisfy this condition include Mersenne primes.

The main idea of the protocol is the same as the protocol $\Pi_{\text{Index2BitsG}}$ for general case. In this protocol, the formulas for the addresses c and r can be simplified, so we will use this to make the protocol more efficient. Specifically, considering the same three cases as $\Pi_{\text{Index2BitsG}}$, using $c_p = C-1$ and $r_p = R-1$, we can compute $c = x \bmod C = c' \bmod C$ and $r = r' + (c'-c)/C \bmod R$ in Case 1, $c = c'+1 \bmod C$ and $r = r' + (c'+1-c)/C \bmod R$ in Case 2, and $c = c' - c_p \bmod C = c'+1 \bmod C$ and $r = r' - r_p + (c'-c_p-c)/C \bmod R = r' + (c'+1-c)/C \bmod R$ in Case 3. If we set $q := l_0 \vee l_1$, these equations can be expressed as

$$c = (c' + q \bmod C) \text{ and } r = (r' + (c'+q-c)/C \bmod R), \quad (1)$$

so there is no need to make a distinction between cases.

The protocol is shown in Algorithm 2. Like Algorithm 1, this protocol uses approximate row and column addresses to compute the one-hot vectors based on the derived equation in Equation (1). The main difference is in the computation of $[\![\vec{c}]\!]$. In Algorithm 1, when computing $[\![\vec{c}]\!]$, the one-hot vector of 0 was shifted by c'' and then corrected. In contrast, in this protocol, we first directly compute a one-hot vector of q from $\langle q \rangle$, and then shift this vector by c''. This change allows us to execute the preprocessing for both Rotation and TwoPCMul protocols in parallel, reducing the number of rounds.

Algorithm 2: Protocol for $\Pi_{\text{Index2BitsS}}^{(N,R,C)}$, realizing $\mathcal{F}_{\text{Index2Bits}}^{(N,R,C)}$.

Parameters: Upper bound of index N, number of rows R and number of columns C.

Require: p is an odd prime number, R and C are power of two, $2R < p$, $2C < p$, $p \equiv -1 \pmod{2CR}$, and $2N \leq p$.

Notation: $[\![\vec{r}]\!], [\![\vec{c}]\!] \leftarrow \text{Index2Bits}([\![x]\!])$

Input: Address $[\![x]\!]$ such that $x \in [0, N)$.

Output: One-hot vectors $[\![\vec{r}]\!]$ and $[\![\vec{c}]\!]$ s.t. $r = \lfloor x/C \rfloor \bmod R$, $\vec{r} = \text{OneHot}(r, R)$, $c = x \bmod C$, and $\vec{c} = \text{OneHot}(c, C)$.

1. Parties compute $[\![d]\!] \leftarrow 2 \times [\![x]\!]$ by local computation. Then, parties P_0 and P_1 locally compute an additive secret sharing $\langle d \rangle$ of $d := 2x$.
2. Let l_i be the least significant bit of $\langle d \rangle_i$ ($i \in \{0,1\}$). Parties securely computes a flag $q := (l_0 = 1 \vee l_1 = 1)$.
   (a) Each party P_i ($i \in \{0,1\}$) sets $\langle l \rangle_i := l_i$.
   (b) Parties compute $\langle q \rangle \leftarrow \langle l \rangle - \text{TwoPCMul}(\langle l \rangle)$.
3. Parties compute the one-hot vector $[\![\vec{c}]\!]$ of column address.
   (a) Each party P_i ($i \in \{0,1\}$) locally computes $\langle c' \rangle_i := \lfloor \langle d \rangle_i / 2 \rfloor \bmod C$.
   (b) Parties convert the approximate column address to replicated secret sharing as: $\{\!\{c''\}\!\}^{(C)} \leftarrow \text{Additive2Replicated}(\langle c' \rangle, C)$.
   (c) P_0 nad P_1 locally compute additive secret sharing of $\vec{q} := \text{OneHot}(q, C)$ as: $\langle \vec{q} \rangle \leftarrow (1 - \langle q \rangle, \langle q \rangle) \| 0^{C-2}$.
   (d) Parties call Rotation() to compute the one-hot vectors of the column address as: $[\![\vec{c}]\!] \leftarrow \text{Rotation}(\langle \vec{q} \rangle, \{\!\{c''\}\!\}^{(C)})$.
4. Parties compute the one-hot vector $[\![\vec{r}'']\!]$ of approximate row address.
   (a) Each party P_i ($i \in \{0,1\}$) locally computes $\langle r' \rangle_i := \lfloor \langle d \rangle_i / 2C \rfloor \bmod R$.
   (b) Parties convert the approximate row address to replicated secret sharing as: $\{\!\{r''\}\!\}^{(R)} \leftarrow \text{Additive2Replicated}(\langle r' \rangle, R)$.
   (c) Parties call Rotation() to compute the one-hot vector of the approximate row address as: $[\![\vec{r}'']\!] \leftarrow \text{Rotation}(\text{OneHot}(0, R), \{\!\{r''\}\!\}^{(R)})$.
5. Parties securely compute correction $e \in \{0,1\}$ for $\vec{r}''$.
   (a) Parties prepare required values as: $[q] \leftarrow \text{Additive2Shamir}(\langle q \rangle)$, $[c] \leftarrow [\![\vec{c}]\!] \cdot (0, 1, 2, \ldots, C-1)$, and $[c'] \leftarrow \text{Additive2Shamir}(\langle c' \rangle)$.
   (b) Parties compute correction as: $[e] \leftarrow ([c'] + [q] - [c]) \times \text{ModInv}(C)$.
6. Parties compute $[\![\vec{r}]\!]$ by correcting $[\![\vec{r}'']\!]$ as: $[\![\vec{r}]\!] \leftarrow \text{IfElse}([e], [\![\vec{r}'']\!] \gg 1, [\![\vec{r}'']\!])$.

Security. By the same argument as in Theorem 1, we have the following theorem.

Theorem 2. *If p is an odd prime number, R and C are power of two, $2R < p$, $2C < p$, $p \equiv -1 \pmod{2CR}$, and $2N \leq p$, then protocol $\Pi_{\text{Index2BitsS}}^{(N,R,C)}$ (Algorithm 2) computes $\mathcal{F}_{\text{Index2Bits}}^{(N,R,C)}$ (Fig. 3) with perfect security in the $\mathcal{F}_{\text{MPC}}$-hybrid model.*

Cost. The communication and computation costs are $O(C+R)$ and $O(C+R)$, respectively. $[\![e]\!]$ and $[\![\vec{r}]\!]$ are is computed in 1+3 and 1+4 rounds, respectively. The analysis is omitted due to page limitations.

3.3 Instantiating $\mathcal{F}_{\text{RomRead}}$

Functionality $\mathcal{F}_{\text{RomRead}}^{(N)}$

Parameters: Number of elements N.

$[\![\vec{z}]\!] \leftarrow \text{RomRead}([\![\vec{a}]\!], [\![\vec{x}]\!])$: Given a vector $[\![\vec{a}]\!]$ containing N elements and a vector $[\![\vec{x}]\!]$ containing k elements s.t. $\vec{x}[i] \in [0, N)$ for $i \in [0, k)$ from all parties. Do:

1. Reconstruct $\vec{a}$ and $\vec{x}$.
2. Let $\vec{z}$ be a vector of length k. Compute $\vec{z}[i] := \vec{a}[\vec{x}[i]]$ for $i \in [0, k)$.
3. Return a fresh secret-sharing $[\![\vec{z}]\!]$ of $\vec{z}$.

Fig. 4. Functionality for reading from an array between parties P_0, P_1, and P_2.

Algorithm 3: Protocol for $\Pi_{\text{RomRead}}^{(N,R,C)}$, realizing $\mathcal{F}_{\text{RomRead}}^{(N)}$.

Parameters: Number of elements N, number of rows R, and number of columns C.
Require: $N \leq CR$.
Notation: $[\![\vec{z}]\!] \leftarrow \text{RomRead}([\![\vec{a}]\!], [\![\vec{x}]\!])$
Input: A private vector $[\![\vec{a}]\!]$ of length N and a private indices $[\![\vec{x}]\!]$ of length k.
Output: A private vector $[\![z]\!]$ of length k s.t. $z[i] = a[x[i]]$ for $i \in [0, k)$.

1. Rearrange the elements of $[\![\vec{a}]\!]$ into an $R \times C$ matrix $[\![A]\!]$ in row-major order. If $N < CR$, compute $[\![0]\!]$'s locally and pad with them.
2. For each $i \in [0, k)$, do:
   (a) Compute one-hot vectors as: $[\![\vec{r}_i]\!], [\![\vec{c}_i]\!] \leftarrow \mathcal{F}_{\text{Index2Bits}}^{(N,R,C)} \cdot \text{Index2Bits}([\![\vec{x}[i]]\!])$.
   (b) Extract the corresponding column as: $[\![\vec{t}_i]\!] \leftarrow \text{MatMul}([\![A]\!], [\![\vec{c}_i]\!])$.
   (c) Extract the corresponding element as: $[\![\vec{z}[i]]\!] \leftarrow \text{InnerProd}([\![\vec{t}_i]\!], [\![\vec{r}_i]\!])$.

The ideal functionality $\mathcal{F}_{\text{RomRead}}$ receives a secret-shared array and secret-shared addresses, and returns a secret-shared vector of the values read from each address in the array. Our protocol, denoted by Π_{RomRead}, is an application of the binary search protocol in [3], and when instantiated with appropriate parameters, it realizes $\mathcal{F}_{\text{RomRead}}$ with linear communication in 1+5 rounds and $O(\sqrt{N})$ computation.

The protocol is shown in Algorithm 3. We first rearrange the array locally into a matrix according to R and C. Next, we call $\mathcal{F}_{\text{Index2Bits}}$ to obtain the one-hot vectors of the row and column addresses, $[\![\vec{r}_i]\!]$ and $[\![\vec{c}_i]\!]$. After that, we apply the technique of narrowing down the search target in [3] using inner product. If the $\vec{x}[i]$-th element of $\vec{a}$ corresponds to the (r,c) element of A, then $\vec{c}_i$ is a one-hot vector such that only the c-th element is 1. Therefore, by multiplying the matrix

A by $\vec{c}_i$ in step 2(b), the c-th column of A is extracted. Furthermore, since $\vec{r}_i$ is a one-hot vector in which only the r-th element is 1, by performing inner product with $\vec{r}_i$ in step 2(c), the (r,c) element of A, that is, the $\vec{x}[i]$-th element of $\vec{a}$ is extracted.

Security. By the same argument as in Theorem 1, we have the following theorem.

Theorem 3. *If $N \leq CR$, then protocol $\Pi_{\text{RomRead}}^{(N,R,C)}$ (Algorithm 3) computes $\mathcal{F}_{\text{RomRead}}^{(N)}$ (Fig. 4) with perfect security in the $(\mathcal{F}_{\text{MPC}}, \mathcal{F}_{\text{Index2Bits}}^{(N,R,C)})$-hybrid model.*

Cost. The protocol runs with $O(C+R)$ communication in $1+5$ rounds and $O(CR)$ local computation. The analysis is omitted due to page limitations.

3.4 Instantiating $\mathcal{F}_{\text{DORAM}}$

We propose a protocol, Π_{DORAM}, that realizes the functionality $\mathcal{F}_{\text{DORAM}}$. The protocol is shown in Algorithm 4. In the following, we describe each command.

The Init command is the first command to be called, and it realizes $\mathcal{F}_{\text{DORAM}}$.Init. It receives and stores the initial array, and initializes each variable.

The Add command realizes $\mathcal{F}_{\text{DORAM}}$.Add. This command adds the difference $\vec{d}[i]$ to the $\vec{x}[i]$-th element of $[\![\vec{a}]\!]$. This command does not actually update the values in the internal array, but the inputs are added to the list U as addition queries. They are later converted into a computation-friendly form in the Read command and added to the stash. When the Read command is called, the correct value at that time is computed by adding all the corresponding differences taken from the stash to the value taken from the array $[\![\vec{a}]\!]$.

The Read command realizes $\mathcal{F}_{\text{DORAM}}$.Read, and outputs the value of the specified address in DORAM. In Step 1, the addition queries stored in U, which are given by the Add command, are converted into a form that is easy to scan, and added to the stash. Specifically, for the query of adding $[\![d_*^{(j)}]\!]$ to the $[\![x_*^{(j)}]\!]$-th entry, which is stored in the j-th element of U, $[\![x_*^{(j)}]\!]$ is decomposed into one-hot vectors $[\![\vec{r}_*^{(j)}]\!]$ and $[\![\vec{c}_*^{(j)}]\!]$ by $\mathcal{F}_{\text{Index2Bits}}$, and $[\![\vec{r}_*^{(j)}]\!]$ and $[\![\vec{c}_*^{(j)}]\!]$ are stored as rows in $[\![S_{\text{row}}]\!]$ and $[\![S_{\text{col}}]\!]$, respectively. To make the later computations more efficient, we multiply $[\![d_*^{(j)}]\!]$ by $[\![\vec{c}_*^{(j)}]\!]$ before storing $[\![\vec{c}_*^{(j)}]\!]$ to $[\![S_{\text{col}}]\!]$.

In Step 2, given an address $[\![\vec{x}[i]]\!]$, we search for queries with the same address in the stash using linear scan, and compute the sum of the associated differences. First, $[\![\vec{x}[i]]\!]$ is decomposed into one-hot vectors $[\![\vec{r}^{(i)}]\!]$ and $[\![\vec{c}^{(i)}]\!]$. Let $\vec{r}_*^{(i)}$ and $\vec{c}_*^{(i)}$ be the j-th rows of $[\![S_{\text{row}}]\!]$ and $[\![S_{\text{col}}]\!]$, respectively. Since $(\vec{r}_*^{(i)} \cdot \vec{r}^{(i)}) \times (\vec{c}_*^{(i)} \cdot \vec{c}^{(i)})$ is equal to $d_*^{(i)}$ when $x_*^{(i)} = \vec{x}[j]$ and 0 otherwise, by performing this computation for each pair of rows in $[\![S_{\text{row}}]\!]$ and $[\![S_{\text{col}}]\!]$, the sum of the differences for $\vec{x}[i]$-th entry $[\![\vec{v}[j]]\!]$ is computed. In Step 2, this computation is performed all at once using matrix multiplication.

Algorithm 4: Protocol for $\Pi_{\text{DORAM}}^{(N,R,C,T)}$, realizing $\mathcal{F}_{\text{DORAM}}^{(N)}$

Parameters: Number of elements N, rows R, and columns C. Flush period T.
Command: Init($[\![\vec{a}_0]\!]$)
1. Store the initial array $[\![\vec{a}]\!] := [\![\vec{a}_0]\!]$.
2. Let U be a list of unprocessed addition queries and u be the size of U. Initialize $U := ()$ and $u := 0$.
3. Let $[\![S_{\text{row}}]\!]$ and $[\![S_{\text{col}}]\!]$ be matrices for the stash. Let s be the size of stash. Initialize $[\![S_{\text{row}}]\!]$ and $[\![S_{\text{col}}]\!]$ to $0 \times R$ and $0 \times C$ matrices. Initialize $s := 0$.

Command: $[\![\vec{z}]\!] \leftarrow$ Read($[\![\vec{x}]\!]$)

1. Add the unprocessed addition queries stored in U to the stash, and clear U. We refer to the j-th element of U as $([\![x_*^{(j)}]\!], [\![d_*^{(j)}]\!])$.
   (a) For $j \in [0, u)$, compute the one-hot vectors for the row and column addresses of the addition query as: $[\![\vec{r}_*^{(j)}]\!], [\![\vec{c}_*^{(j)}]\!] \leftarrow \mathcal{F}_{\text{Index2Bits}}^{(N,R,C)}$.Index2Bits($[\![x_*^{(j)}]\!]$).
   (b) For $j \in [0, u)$, multiply the column one-hot vector by the addition as $[\![\vec{c}_*^{(j)}]\!] \leftarrow [\![\vec{c}_*^{(j)}]\!] \times [\![d_*^{(j)}]\!]$.
   (c) For $j \in [0, u)$, set $[\![\vec{c}_*^{(j)}]\!]^T$ and $[\![\vec{r}_*^{(j)}]\!]^T$ to the $(s+j)$-th row of $[\![S_{\text{row}}]\!]$ and $[\![S_{\text{col}}]\!]$, respectively.
   (d) Set $s := s + u$, $U := ()$, and $u := 0$.
2. Read the sum of additions to each address in $\vec{x}$ from the stash. For $i \in [0, k)$, do:
   (a) Compute the one-hot vectors $[\![\vec{r}^{(i)}]\!], [\![\vec{c}^{(i)}]\!] \leftarrow \mathcal{F}_{\text{Index2Bits}}^{(N,R,C)}$.Index2Bits($[\![\vec{x}[i]]\!]$).
   (b) Detect matching of row address as: $[\![\vec{e}_{\text{col}}^{(i)}]\!] \leftarrow$ MatMul($[\![S_{\text{row}}]\!], [\![\vec{r}^{(i)}]\!]$).
   (c) Detect matching of column address as: $[\![\vec{e}_{\text{row}}^{(i)}]\!] \leftarrow$ MatMul($[\![S_{\text{col}}]\!], [\![\vec{c}^{(i)}]\!]$).
   (d) Compute the sum of additions $[\![\vec{v}[i]]\!] \leftarrow$ InnerProd($[\![\vec{e}_{\text{col}}^{(i)}]\!], [\![\vec{e}_{\text{row}}^{(i)}]\!]$).
3. Read from the array $[\![\vec{a}]\!]$ as $[\![\vec{t}]\!] \leftarrow \mathcal{F}_{\text{RomRead}}^{(N)}$.RomRead($[\![\vec{a}]\!], [\![\vec{x}]\!]$).
4. Compute the output $[\![\vec{z}]\!] \leftarrow [\![\vec{v}]\!] + [\![\vec{t}]\!]$.
5. If $s \geq T$, flush the stash.
   (a) Compute the addition of all elements as $[\![D]\!] \leftarrow$ MatMul($[\![S_{\text{col}}]\!]^T, [\![S_{\text{row}}]\!]$).
   (b) Store the first n elements of $[\![D]\!]$ to vector $[\![\vec{f}]\!]$ in row-major order and add it to $[\![\vec{a}]\!]$ as: $[\![\vec{a}]\!] \leftarrow [\![\vec{a}]\!] + [\![\vec{f}]\!]$.
   (c) Set $s := 0$. Delete all rows from $[\![S_{\text{row}}]\!]$ and $[\![S_{\text{col}}]\!]$.

Command: Add($[\![\vec{x}]\!], [\![\vec{d}]\!]$)

1. Append the queries to U as: $U := U \parallel (([\![\vec{x}[i]]\!], [\![\vec{d}[i]]\!]))_{i \in [0,k)}$. Update $u := u + k$.

Command: Write($[\![\vec{x}]\!], [\![\vec{y}]\!]$)

1. Read the current values and add as: $[\![\vec{z}]\!] \leftarrow$ Read($[\![\vec{x}]\!]$); Add($[\![\vec{x}]\!], [\![\vec{y}]\!] - [\![\vec{z}]\!]$).

In Step 3, a vector $[\![\vec{t}]\!]$ of elements in $[\![\vec{a}]\!]$ specified by $[\![\vec{x}]\!]$ is computed by calling $\mathcal{F}_{\mathsf{RomRead}}$. By adding this to the differences $[\![\vec{v}]\!]$ computed in Step 2, we can compute the current values $[\![\vec{z}]\!]$ at each address (Step 4).

If the size of the stash s exceeds the specified value $T-1$, the addition queries stored in the stash are reflected in array $[\![\vec{a}]\!]$ (Step 6). Let us explain the idea behind this process. Suppose that the ℓ-th unreflected addition query is (x,d). Then, this query is stored as the ℓ-th row vector of $[\![S_{\mathrm{row}}]\!]$ and the ℓ-the row vector of $[\![S_{\mathrm{col}}]\!]$, which we denote as $\vec{r}$ and $\vec{c}$, respectively. If the x-th element in the array corresponds to the (i,j)-entry of the matrix, then by computing $\vec{r}^T \times \vec{c}$, we can compute a $R \times C$ matrix such that only the (i,j)-entry is d and the rest are 0. By rearranging this matrix in row-major order and adding it to $[\![\vec{a}]\!]$, we can reflect the addition query. In Step 5, this process is performed for s rows at once using matrix multiplication. Thanks to the batch computation, the communication cost is $1/s$ compared to when computed one row by one row.

The Write command realizes $\mathcal{F}_{\mathsf{DORAM}}$.Write. As mentioned above, this command simply writes the values obtained by subtracting the values read from the values to be written.

Security. By the same argument as in Theorem 1, we have the following theorem.

Theorem 4. *Protocol $\Pi_{\mathsf{DORAM}}^{(N,R,C,T)}$ (Algorithm 4) computes $\mathcal{F}_{\mathsf{DORAM}}^{(N)}$ (Fig. 2) with perfect security in the ($\mathcal{F}_{\mathsf{MPC}}$, $\mathcal{F}_{\mathsf{Index2Bits}}^{(N,R,C)}$, $\mathcal{F}_{\mathsf{RomRead}}^{(N)}$)-hybrid model.*

Cost. We consider the case when R and C are power of two, and p is a prime number such that $p \equiv -1 \pmod{2RC}$ and $2N \leq p$. By selecting appropriate parameters, we can obtain the following costs. Init and Add commands require only $O(N)$ and $O(k)$ local computation, respectively. The costs for Read and Write are the same. The amortized cost for single read/write is $O(\sqrt{N})$ communication in 1+6 rounds and $O(N)$. The analysis is deferred to Appendix C.

4 Evaluation to Demonstrate Concrete Performance

We evaluate the concrete performance of our DORAM. We implemented our protocols on top of a three-party MPC that instantiates $\mathcal{F}_{\mathsf{MPC}}$ as described in Sect. 2.3. In order to use $\Pi_{\mathsf{Index2BitsS}}$, we chose the Mersenne prime field $\mathbb{Z}_p$ with $p = 2^{61} - 1$ as an underlying field, which is close to the 64-bit integer space. Our code was written in the C++ language and compiled on the Rocky Linux 9.2 OS using the g++ compiler with optimization options including -O3.

We ran benchmarks on a cluster of three servers connected by a ring topology network. Each server has two Intel Xeon Gold 6334 (3.60GHz 8cores/16threads) CPUs, 1 TB memory, and 2.5 TB SSD. Each server pair is connected via Intel Ethernet Controller X550 NICs with a bandwidth of 10 Gbps. The communication delay between servers was measured using the ping command, and min/avg/max/mdev was 0.159/0.243/0.301/0.049 ms.

We implemented the protocol proposed in Sect. 3 and ran benchmarks. For $\mathcal{F}_{\mathsf{Index2Bits}}$, we implemented $\Pi_{\mathsf{Index2BitsS}}$. Since our DORAM requires linear local

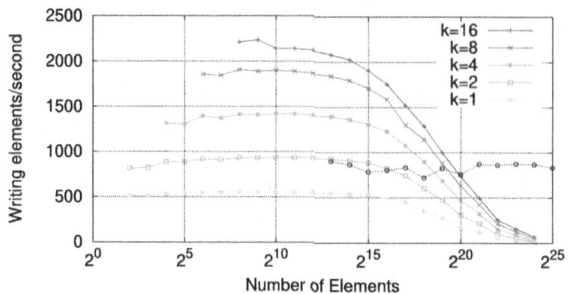

Fig. 5. Number of writing elements/second vs. number of elements. The plot with a dotted line is the numbers of GigaDORAM quoted from Fig. 5 in [10].

computation for N elements, it is expected that performance will decrease significantly for large N. In order to see the range of N where our DORAM can keep practical performance, we performed measurements with varying N. In addition, in order to see the performance improvement by parallel access, we also performed measurements with varying k, the number of parallel accesses.

We measured the performance of our DORAM write operation, rather than the read and add operations, since the write operation includes both of the other two operations. We measured the time until all write operations were reflected in the internal array by executing a flush, and calculated the average execution time. We set the data stored in a single address to be a single field element. In other words, the payload of the write operation is 61 bits.

First, let us observe the effect of each parameter on performance. Figure 5 shows the number of elements written per second when k and N are varied. We can see from the figure that performance improves as k increases, demonstrating the benefits of parallel execution. On the other hand, performance drops significantly as N increases. We will see how efficiency drops in Appendix E.

Next, we focus on the absolute performance. When $k = 1$, our write operation is about 450 writes/second even in the range $N \leq 2^{17}$, which is much slower than GigaDORAM's about 900 writes/second [10], plotted with dotted line in Fig. 5. On the other hand, when $k = 4$ and $N \leq 2^{17}$, our write operation achieves a performance of over 1000 writes/second, which even exceeds the reported performance of GigaDORAM [10]. To the best of our knowledge, the performance of 1000 writes/second is the fastest reported performance for $N \leq 2^{17}$ to date.

5 Conclusion

We proposed a three-party DORAM that can access multiple addresses in a batch. The protocols are perfectly secure against a semi-honest adversary that can corrupt at most one party. For an N-element array of D-bit elements, our DORAM accesses elements at k distinct addresses with $O(k\sqrt{N}(\log N + D))$ bits communication in 7 rounds and $O(kN(\log N + D))$ bits computation. Regarding

Algorithm 5: A realization of TwoPCMul() command.

Notation: $\langle z \rangle \leftarrow \mathsf{TwoPCMul}(\langle x \rangle)$

1. P_2 compute three random values $a, b, r \in \mathbb{Z}_p$.
2. P_2 sends a and $ab - r$ to P_0; P_2 sends b and r to P_1.
3. P_0 sends $\langle x \rangle_0 + a$ to P_1; P_1 sends $\langle x \rangle_1 + b$ to P_0.
4. P_0 computes $\langle z \rangle_0 := (ab - r) - a(\langle x \rangle_1 + b)$; P_1 computes $\langle z \rangle_1 := r + \langle x \rangle_1 (\langle x \rangle_0 + a)$.

concrete performance, our protocol outperformed the state of the art GigaDO-RAM [10], whose throughput is about 900 writes/second, in some settings. When $D = 61$, $N = 2^{17}$, and $k = 16$, our protocol achieved 1,521 writes/second.

A Formal Definition for Perfect Security

We give a formal security definition for three-party protocols. We assume a static single corruption by a semi-honest adversary. Let $f : (\{0,1\}^*)^3 \to (\{0,1\}^*)^3$ be a probabilistic 3-ary functionality, x_i be the input for party P_i ($i \in \{0,1,2\}$), $\vec{x} := (x_0, x_1, x_2)$, and $f_i(\vec{x})$ be the output for party P_i. Let Π be a three-party protocol for computing f, and let $\mathsf{view}_i^\Pi(\vec{x})$ and $\mathsf{output}^\Pi(\vec{x})$ denote the view of P_i and the output for all parties, respectively, during the execution of Π on $\vec{x}$. $\mathsf{view}_i^\Pi(\vec{x})$ consists of x_i, a random tape for P_i, and messages received by P_i.

Definition 1. *We say that Π computes f with perfect security if there exists an algorithm S such that for every $i \in \{0, 1, 2\}$ and every $\vec{x} \in (\{0,1\}^*)^3$, it holds that $\{(S(x_i, f_i(\vec{x})), f(\vec{x}))\} \equiv \{(\mathsf{view}_i^\Pi(\vec{x}), \mathsf{output}^\Pi(\vec{x}))\}$.*

B Detail of $\mathcal{F}_{\mathrm{MPC}}$ Instantiation

For Enc commands, we use the share operations provided by the underlying secret sharing schemes shown in Sect. 2.2. For Mul and InnerProd commands, we use the multiplication and inner product protocols in [2].

For Rotation command, we use the optimized shuffling protocol proposed as Protocol A.6 in [1]. Since the protocol in [1] has a different input/output format from our Rotation command, we have rewritten it in Algorithm 6, which is essentially the same as the original one. In the protocol, two shares of an additively secret-shared vector are respectively sent to other parties, masked with random numbers. Since the shift (permutation) is secret-shared by the replicated scheme, by applying the shifts of the shares before and after sending, a shifted additively secret-shared vector (between P_1 and P_2) is computed. When the length of the input vector is known in advance, Step 1 can be run in offline, so it runs with $O(n)$ communication and $O(n)$ local computation in $1+2$ rounds.

For TwoPCMul command, we use a simple protocol shown in Algorithm 5. The security of this protocol can be easily verified since the three values P_i ($i \in \{0, 1\}$) received are masked with three independent randoms and P_2 receives no value. This runs with $O(1)$ communication/computation in $1 + 1$ rounds.

Algorithm 6: A realization of Rotation() command. (Protocol A.6 in [1])

Notation: $[\![\vec{z}]\!] \leftarrow \mathsf{Rotation}(\langle \vec{x} \rangle, \{\!\{d\}\!\}^{(M)})$
Input: A private vector $\langle \vec{x} \rangle$ of length M and a private shift amount $\{\!\{d\}\!\}^{(M)}$.
Output: A private vector $[\![\vec{z}]\!]$ of length M s.t. $\vec{z} = \vec{x} \gg d$.

1. P_0 computes a vector of random values $\vec{r}_{20} \in \mathbb{Z}_p^M$ and sends it to P_2; P_1 computes a vector of random values $\vec{r}_{01} \in \mathbb{Z}_p^M$ and sends it to P_0.
2. For $j \in \{01, 12, 20\}$, let $\pi_j \in S_M$ be a permutation that shifts a vector of length M with amount $\{\!\{d\}\!\}_j^{(M)}$. We denote the operation of applying a permutation π to a vector $\vec{v}$ by $\pi \vec{v}$.
3. P_0 computes $\vec{y}_{01} := \pi_{20}\pi_{01}\langle \vec{x} \rangle_0 - \pi_{20}\vec{r}_{01} - \vec{r}_{20}$ and sends it to P_1; P_1 computes $\vec{y}_{12} := \pi_{01}\langle \vec{x} \rangle_1 + \vec{r}_{01}$ and sends it to P_2.
4. P_1 computes $\vec{z}_1 := \pi_{12}\vec{y}_{01}$; P_2 computes $\vec{z}_2 := \pi_{12}\pi_{20}\vec{y}_{12} + \pi_{12}\vec{r}_{20}$.
5. $[\![\vec{z}]\!] \leftarrow \mathsf{Enc}(\vec{z}_1, P_1) + \mathsf{Enc}(\vec{z}_2, P_2)$

C Deferred Cost Analysis of Algorithm 4

We set the parameters as follows. Let $w := \lceil \log_2 n \rceil$, $w_{\text{row}} := \lfloor w/2 \rfloor$, and $w_{\text{col}} := \lceil w/2 \rceil$. We set $R := 2^{w_{\text{row}}}$, $C := 2^{w_{\text{col}}}$, and $T := R$. Then, we instantiate $\mathcal{F}_{\text{Index2Bits}}$ and $\mathcal{F}_{\text{RomRead}}$ with $\Pi_{\text{Index2BitsS}}^{(N,R,C)}$ and $\Pi_{\text{RomRead}}^{(N,R,C)}$, respectively.

Neither the Init command nor the Add command requires communication. The local computations of Init and Add are $O(N)$ and $O(k)$, respectively.

Next, we will analyze the cost of the Read command. Taking into account that Steps 1(a) and 2(a) can be executed in parallel, $[\![\vec{v}]\!]$ and $[\![t]\!]$ can be computed in 1+6 rounds and 1+5 rounds, respectively. The flush in Step 5 can be completed in 1+5 rounds. Therefore, the communication round for Read is 1+6. By summing up the costs of each sub-protocol, we can see that, except for Step 5, Read requires $O(ks + (u+k)\sqrt{N})$ communication and $O((u+ks)\sqrt{N} + kN)$ local computation. The flush in Step 5 of the Read requires $O(N)$ communication and $O(TN)$ local computation. Finally, we will analyze the amortized cost of the Read command. Suppose that we perform tT writes, each time writing k items. Since the flush is performed kt times, the total cost is $O(kt(T^2 + T\sqrt{N} + N))$ communication and $O(ktT(T\sqrt{N} + N))$ local computation. Since we write ktT items, and $T = \Theta(\sqrt{N})$, the cost per single write is $O(\sqrt{N})$ communication and $O(N)$ local computation. In summary, the Read command runs in $1+6$ rounds. Its amortized costs are $O(k\sqrt{N})$ communication and $O(kN)$ local computation.

The cost of the Write command is the same as that of the Read command. That is, it runs in $1 + 6$ rounds and its amortized costs are $O(k\sqrt{N})$ communication and $O(kN)$ local computation.

D Extension to Other MPC Settings

Our protocols are constructed on Shamir's scheme under the condition of secure against a single corruption in three-party computation. Our protocol requires only properties such as the efficient realization of $\mathcal{F}_{\mathrm{MPC}}$, linear computation with local computation, and reconstruction via linear combination of shares. Therefore, it can also be constructed on other secret sharing schemes with similar properties, such as the 2-out-of-3 replicated scheme. In this paper, we decided to select one specific scheme for simplicity of description and implementation, and selected Shamir's scheme because of its small share size.

Our protocols will be extensible to cases where the number of parties and corruption tolerance vary, but efficiency will be significantly reduced. In particular, the protocols for $\mathcal{F}_{\mathrm{Index2Bits}}$ use the two-party additive scheme to minimize the number of cases, so increasing the corruption threshold increases the number of cases, making it difficult to maintain efficiency with a simple extension.

E Experimental Result to See How Efficiency Drops

To identify the N at which performance drops, we plot the running time for writing k elements on a log-log graph in Fig. 6. The slope of the curve represents the

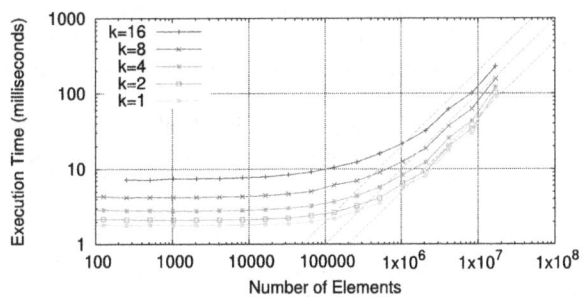

Fig. 6. Execution time vs. number of elements. The three diagonal dashed lines are $y = 0.000005x$, $y = 0.00001x$, and $y = 0.00002x$, which are auxiliary lines to help observe the slope.

Table 3. Summary of our notation.

Notation	Description
$\vec{v}[i]$	i-th entry of a vector $\vec{v}$
$A[i,j]$	(i,j)-th entry of a matrix A
$\mathrm{OneHot}(x,n)$	One-hot vector of length n s.t. only the x-th entry is 1
$\vec{v} >> d$	Circular right shift to a vector $\vec{v}$ with amount d
$\vec{v} << d$	Circular left shift to a vector $\vec{v}$ with amount d
$\mathrm{ModInv}(x)$	Multiplicative inverse of x in a prime field $\mathbb{Z}_p$
$[\![s]\!]$	Shares $([\![s]\!]_0, [\![s]\!]_1, [\![s]\!]_2)$ of $s \in \mathbb{Z}_p$ in the Shamir's scheme
$\{\!\{s\}\!\}^{(M)}$	Shares $(\{\!\{s\}\!\}_0^{(M)}, \{\!\{s\}\!\}_1^{(M)}, \{\!\{s\}\!\}_2^{(M)})$ of $s \in \mathbb{Z}_M$ in the replicated scheme
$\langle s \rangle$	Shares $(\langle s \rangle_0, \langle s \rangle_1)$ of $s \in \mathbb{Z}_p$ in the additive scheme

degree of the polynomial fit to the curve. As shown in the graph, the execution time remains nearly constant up to $N = 2^{17}$. The slope increases with increasing N and becomes nearly 1 for $N \geq 2^{20}$. Thus, the running time is nearly linear with respect to N when $N \geq 2^{20}$.

References

1. Asharov, G., et al.: Efficient secure three-party sorting with applications to data analysis and heavy hitters. In: CCS 2022, pp. 125–138. ACM (2022)
2. Ben-Or, M., Goldwasser, S., Wigderson, A.: Completeness theorems for non-cryptographic fault-tolerant distributed computation (extended abstract). In: STOC 1988, pp. 1–10. ACM (1988)
3. Blanton, M., Yuan, C.: Binary search in secure computation. In: NDSS 2022. The Internet Society (2022)
4. Braun, L., Pancholi, M., Rachuri, R., Simkin, M.: Ramen: souper fast three-party computation for RAM programs. In: CCS 2023, pp. 3284–3297. ACM (2023)
5. Bunn, P., Katz, J., Kushilevitz, E., Ostrovsky, R.: Efficient 3-party distributed ORAM. In: Galdi, C., Kolesnikov, V. (eds.) SCN 2020. LNCS, vol. 12238, pp. 215–232. Springer, Cham (2020). https://doi.org/10.1007/978-3-030-57990-6_11
6. Cramer, R., Damgård, I., Ishai, Y.: Share conversion, pseudorandom secret-sharing and applications to secure computation. In: Kilian, J. (ed.) TCC 2005. LNCS, vol. 3378, pp. 342–362. Springer, Heidelberg (2005). https://doi.org/10.1007/978-3-540-30576-7_19
7. Damgård, I., Escudero, D., Frederiksen, T.K., Keller, M., Scholl, P., Volgushev, N.: New primitives for actively-secure MPC over rings with applications to private machine learning. In: SP 2019, pp. 1102–1120. IEEE (2019)
8. Doerner, J., shelat, A.: Scaling ORAM for secure computation. In: CCS 2017, pp. 523–535. ACM (2017)
9. Faber, S., Jarecki, S., Kentros, S., Wei, B.: Three-party ORAM for secure computation. In: Iwata, T., Cheon, J.H. (eds.) ASIACRYPT 2015. LNCS, vol. 9452, pp. 360–385. Springer, Heidelberg (2015). https://doi.org/10.1007/978-3-662-48797-6_16
10. Falk, B.H., Ostrovsky, R., Shtepel, M., Zhang, J.: Gigadoram: breaking the billion address barrier. In: USENIX Security 2023, pp. 3871–3888 (2023)
11. Goldreich, O.: Foundations of Cryptography: Volume 2, Basic Applications, vol. 2. Cambridge University Press (2004)
12. Gordon, S.D., Katz, J., Wang, X.: Simple and efficient two-server ORAM. In: Peyrin, T., Galbraith, S. (eds.) ASIACRYPT 2018. LNCS, vol. 11274, pp. 141–157. Springer, Cham (2018). https://doi.org/10.1007/978-3-030-03332-3_6
13. Hamlin, A., Varia, M.: Two-server distributed ORAM with sublinear computation and constant rounds. In: Garay, J.A. (ed.) PKC 2021. LNCS, vol. 12711, pp. 499–527. Springer, Cham (2021). https://doi.org/10.1007/978-3-030-75248-4_18
14. Jarecki, S., Wei, B.: 3PC ORAM with low latency, low bandwidth, and fast batch retrieval. In: Preneel, B., Vercauteren, F. (eds.) ACNS 2018. LNCS, vol. 10892, pp. 360–378. Springer, Cham (2018). https://doi.org/10.1007/978-3-319-93387-0_19
15. Ji, K., Zhang, B., Lu, T., Ren, K.: Multi-party private function evaluation for RAM. IEEE Trans. Inf. Forensics Secur. **18**, 1252–1267 (2023)
16. Keller, M., Scholl, P.: Efficient, oblivious data structures for MPC. In: Sarkar, P., Iwata, T. (eds.) ASIACRYPT 2014. LNCS, vol. 8874, pp. 506–525. Springer, Heidelberg (2014). https://doi.org/10.1007/978-3-662-45608-8_27

17. Kikuchi, R., Ikarashi, D., Matsuda, T., Hamada, K., Chida, K.: Efficient bit-decomposition and modulus-conversion protocols with an honest majority. In: Susilo, W., Yang, G. (eds.) ACISP 2018. LNCS, vol. 10946, pp. 64–82. Springer, Cham (2018). https://doi.org/10.1007/978-3-319-93638-3_5
18. Laud, P.: Parallel oblivious array access for secure multiparty computation and privacy-preserving minimum spanning trees. Proc. Priv. Enhancing Technol. **2015**(2), 188–205 (2015)
19. Rathee, D., Bhattacharya, A., Sharma, R., Gupta, D., Chandran, N., Rastogi, A.: Secfloat: accurate floating-point meets secure 2-party computation. In: SP 2022, pp. 576–595. IEEE (2022)
20. Shamir, A.: How to share a secret. Commun. ACM **22**(11), 612–613 (1979)
21. Vadapalli, A., Henry, R., Goldberg, I.: Duoram: a bandwidth-efficient distributed ORAM for 2- and 3-party computation. In: USENIX Security 2023, pp. 3907–3924 (2023)
22. Wagh, S., Gupta, D., Chandran, N.: Securenn: 3-party secure computation for neural network training. Proc. Priv. Enhancing Technol. **2019**(3), 26–49 (2019)
23. Wang, X., Chan, T.H., Shi, E.: Circuit ORAM: on tightness of the goldreich-ostrovsky lower bound. In: CCS 2015, pp. 850–861. ACM (2015)
24. Wang, X.S., Huang, Y., Chan, T.H., Shelat, A., Shi, E.: SCORAM: oblivious RAM for secure computation. In: CCS 2014, pp. 191–202. ACM (2014)
25. Yao, A.C.: How to generate and exchange secrets (extended abstract). In: FOCS 1986, pp. 162–167. IEEE Computer Society (1986)
26. Zahur, S., et al.: Revisiting square-root ORAM: efficient random access in multi-party computation. In: SP 2016, pp. 218–234. IEEE Computer Society (2016)

A Symbolic Analysis of Hash Functions Vulnerabilities in Maude-NPA

Arturo Hernández-Sánchez[✉] and Santiago Escobar

VRAIN, Universitat Politècnica de València, València, Spain
{arthersan,sescobar}@upv.es

Abstract. Maude-NPA is an analysis tool for cryptographic security protocols that takes into account the algebraic properties of the cryptosystem. Some cryptographic properties and protocols using them have been beyond Maude-NPA capabilities. Hash functions have been extensively used as a key component in cryptographic protocols, but have never been analysed in Maude-NPA. In this paper, we study some hash vulnerabilities and analyze several protocols using Maude-NPA.

Keywords: Hash Functions · Cryptographic Protocols · Symbolic Analysis

1 Introduction

Maude-NPA [19] is an analysis tool for cryptographic security protocols that takes into account the algebraic properties of the cryptosystem. Sometimes algebraic properties can uncover weaknesses of cryptosystems and, in other cases, they are part of the protocol security assumptions. Maude-NPA is based on equational unification and performs backwards search from an attack state pattern to determine whether or not it is reachable. Maude-NPA can be used to reason about a wide range of cryptographic properties [20,23], including cancellation of encryption and decryption, Diffie-Hellman exponentiation [18], bilinear pairing [1], exclusive-or [36], and some approximations of homomorphic encryption [22,43]. Unfortunately, some cryptographic properties, and protocols using them, have been beyond Maude-NPA capabilities, either because the cryptographic properties cannot be expressed using its equational unification features or because the state space is unmanageable.

Hash functions have been extensively used as a key component in cryptographic protocols. They are expected to satisfy several security aspects such as

---

This work has been partially supported by the grant CIPROM/2022/6 funded by Generalitat Valenciana, by INCIBE's Chair funded by the EU-NextGenerationEU through the Spanish government's Plan de Recuperación, Transformación y Resiliencia, by the grant PID2021-122830OB-C42 funded by MCIN/AEI/10.13039/501100011033 and ERDF A way of making Europe and, by the NATO Science for Peace and Security Programme project SymSafe (grant number G6133).

collision resistant, i.e., the possibility of having two different inputs that produce the same output is extremely low, and *pre-image resistant*, i.e., the possibility of finding the right original input associated with a given hash output is extremely low. Moreover, they have commonly been assumed to be also *second pre-image resistant*, i.e., for a given input, the possibility of finding another input that produces the same hash is extremely low, and *length-extension resistant*, i.e., given an input, the possibility of finding another input such that, when concatenated to the former input, produces the same result is extremely low. Essentially, the hash functions are assumed to be *perfect*, i.e., every input/output combination is completely independent of all others, which corresponds to the *Random Oracle Model (ROM)*.

In [8], different vulnerabilities of hash functions are analyzed using Tamarin [40] and Proverif [7]. In this paper, we study some of those vulnerabilities and analyze several protocols using Maude-NPA. On the one hand, it is observed in [8] that, since Tamarin relies on the programming language Maude [9,15] as a backend to perform equational unification, it inherits two specific problems: infinitary unification for associative symbols (under some rare circumstances which are identified by issuing a warning) and, even if the number of unifiers may be finite in theory, a huge number of them, which makes protocol analysis impractical. On the other hand, an event-based approach is provided in [8] for Tamarin and Proverif as a solution to the use of associativity. Essentially, they define a dedicated process for computing the hash function with the peculiarities of the hash vulnerabilities they are interested in. In this paper, we follow a different approach. First, we consider the event-based approach by providing a Dolev-Yao capability that computes the hash function with the peculiarities of hash vulnerabilities. Second, despite of [8], we encode all the hash vulnerabilities as equational properties and analyze several protocols, finding some known and new attacks. We rely on order-sorted restrictions in order to obtain finitary equational unification, when associativity or variant equations are included, that work well in practice. We believe this order-sorted approach can easily be adopted by Tamarin and Proverif. Our specific contributions are:

1. We reproduce the attack $S1$ of the Sigma protocol [29] in [8] using an event-based approach.
2. We reproduce the attacks $S1$ and $S3$ of the Sigma protocol [29] in [8] using equational unification.
3. We identify a vulnerability of the Meadows protocol [30] not found in [8] using either pre-image or second pre-image with an inverse using equational unification.
4. We seamlessly combine different algebraic properties, including associativity, without incompleteness warnings and in reasonable analysis time.

After some preliminaries on rewriting logic in Sect. 2, we explain Maude-NPA in Sect. 3. Hash vulnerabilities are described in Sect. 4 but the modeling approaches adopted in this paper are described in Sect. 5. The Sigma and Meadows protocols are analyzed in Sect. 6. We conclude in Sect. 7.

2 Rewriting Logic

We follow the classical notation and terminology for term rewriting [39], and for rewriting logic and order-sorted notions [32]. We assume an order-sorted signature Σ with a poset of sorts $(\mathsf{S}, \leq)$. We also assume an S-sorted family $\mathcal{X} = \{\mathcal{X}_\mathsf{s}\}_{\mathsf{s} \in \mathsf{S}}$ of disjoint variable sets with each $\mathcal{X}_\mathsf{s}$ countably infinite. $\mathcal{T}_\Sigma(\mathcal{X})_\mathsf{s}$ is the set of terms of sort s, and $\mathcal{T}_{\Sigma,\mathsf{s}}$ is the set of ground terms of sort s. We write $\mathcal{T}_\Sigma(\mathcal{X})$ and $\mathcal{T}_\Sigma$ for the corresponding order-sorted term algebras. For a term t, $Var(t)$ denotes the set of variables in t. Throughout this paper, Σ is assumed to be *preregular*, so each term t has a least sort, denoted $ls(t)$.

A *substitution* $\sigma \in \mathcal{S}ubst(\Sigma, \mathcal{X})$ is a sorted mapping from a finite subset of $\mathcal{X}$ to $\mathcal{T}_\Sigma(\mathcal{X})$. Substitutions are written as $\sigma = \{X_1 \mapsto t_1, \ldots, X_n \mapsto t_n\}$, where the domain of σ is $Dom(\sigma) = \{X_1, \ldots, X_n\}$ and the set of variables introduced by terms $t_1, \ldots, t_n$ is written $Ran(\sigma)$. The identity substitution is denoted id. Substitutions are homomorphically extended to $\mathcal{T}_\Sigma(\mathcal{X})$. The application of a substitution σ to a term t is denoted by $t\sigma$ or $\sigma(t)$. The restriction of σ to a set of variables V is $\sigma|_V$. Composition of two substitutions σ and σ' is written $\sigma\sigma'$.

A Σ-*equation* is an unoriented pair $t = t'$, where $t, t' \in \mathcal{T}_\Sigma(\mathcal{X})_\mathsf{s}$ for some sort $\mathsf{s} \in \mathsf{S}$. Given Σ and a set E of Σ-equations, order-sorted equational logic induces a congruence relation $=_E$ on terms $t, t' \in \mathcal{T}_\Sigma(\mathcal{X})$. The E-equivalence class of a term t is denoted by $[t]_E$ and $\mathcal{T}_{\Sigma/E}(\mathcal{X})$ and $\mathcal{T}_{\Sigma/E}$ denote the corresponding order-sorted term algebras modulo E. Throughout this paper we assume that $\mathcal{T}_{\Sigma,\mathsf{s}} \neq \emptyset$ for every sort s, because this affords a simpler deduction system. An *equational theory* (Σ, E) is a pair with Σ an order-sorted signature and E a set of Σ-equations.

An E-*unifier* for a Σ-equation $t = t'$ is a substitution σ such that $t\sigma =_E t'\sigma$. A set of substitutions $CSU_E(t = t')$ is said to be a *complete* set of unifiers for the equality $t = t'$ modulo E iff: (i) each $\sigma \in CSU_E(t = t')$ is an E-unifier of $t = t'$; (ii) for any E-unifier ρ of $t = t'$ there is $\sigma \in CSU_E(t = t')$ and τ s.t. $\sigma\tau =_E \rho$; (iii) for all $\sigma \in CSU_E(t = t')$, $Dom(\sigma) \subseteq (Var(t) \cup Var(t'))$. An E-unification algorithm is *complete* if for any equation $t = t'$ it generates a complete set of E-unifiers. A unification algorithm is said to be *finitary* and complete if it always terminates after generating a finite and complete set of solutions. Unification modulo associativity is known to be infinitary, but the Maude programming language is able to provide a finitary and complete set of solutions under some circumstances and a finite approximation otherwise; see [9,16] for how it is used in Maude, see [17] for implementation details and see [15] when variant equations and associativity are combined.

A *rewrite rule* is an oriented pair $l \to r$, where $l \notin \mathcal{X}$ and $l, r \in \mathcal{T}_\Sigma(\mathcal{X})_\mathsf{s}$ for some sort $\mathsf{s} \in \mathsf{S}$. An *(unconditional) order-sorted rewrite theory* is a triple (Σ, E, R) with Σ an order-sorted signature, E a set of Σ-equations, and R a set of rewrite rules. The relation $\to_{R,E}$ on $\mathcal{T}_\Sigma(\mathcal{X})$ is defined as: $t \to_{p,R,E} t'$ (or just $t \to_{R,E} t'$) iff there exist $p \in Pos_\Sigma(t)$, a rule $l \to r$ in R, and a substitution σ such that $t|_p =_E l\sigma$ and $t' = t[r\sigma]_p$. The transitive (resp. transitive and reflexive) closure of $\to_{R,E}$ is denoted by $\to_{R,E}^+$ (resp. $\to_{R,E}^*$). A term t is (R, E)-irreducible if there is no t' s.t. $t \to_{R,E} t'$. The R, E-*narrowing* relation on $\mathcal{T}_\Sigma(\mathcal{X})$ is defined as

$t \leadsto_{p,\sigma,R,E} t'$ ($\leadsto_\sigma$ if R, E are understood, and $\leadsto$ if σ is also understood) if there is a non-variable position $p \in Pos_\Sigma(t)$, a rule $l \to r \in R$ standardized apart (i.e., contains no variable previously met during any previous computation) and a unifier $\sigma \in CSU_E(t|_p = l)$, such that $t' = (t[r]_p)\sigma$. The transitive (resp. transitive and reflexive) closure of $\leadsto$ is denoted by $\leadsto^+$ (resp. $\leadsto^*$).

3 The Maude-NPA

A protocol $\mathcal{P}$ is specified as an order-sorted equational theory $(\Sigma_\mathcal{P}, \mathcal{E}_\mathcal{P})$, where $\Sigma_\mathcal{P}$ is the set of symbols defining the protocol $\mathcal{P}$, which incorporates some pre-defined symbols for protocol infrastructure, and $\mathcal{E}_\mathcal{P}$ specifies the *algebraic properties* of the cryptographic functions $\Sigma_\mathcal{P}$, which may vary depending on different protocols. The set of equations $\mathcal{E}_\mathcal{P}$ can be decomposed into the disjoint union $\mathcal{E} = \overrightarrow{E} \uplus Ax$, where Ax is a set of axioms, which are implicitly expressed in Maude as operator attributes `assoc`, `comm`, and `id:` keywords, and $\overrightarrow{E}$ is a set of oriented equations which satisfy the following:

1. Ax is *regular*, i.e., for each $t = t'$ in Ax, we have $Var(t) = Var(t')$, and *linear*, i.e., for each $t = t'$ in Ax, each variable occurs only once in t and in t'.
2. Ax is *sort-preserving*, i.e., for each $t = t'$ in Ax and substitution σ, we have $t\sigma \in \mathcal{T}_{\Sigma_\mathcal{P}}(\mathcal{X})_s$ iff $t'\sigma \in \mathcal{T}_{\Sigma_\mathcal{P}}(\mathcal{X})_s$. for each equation $t = t'$ in Ax, all variables in $Var(t)$ and $Var(t')$ have a common top sort.
3. Ax has a finitary and complete unification algorithm.
4. The rewrite rules in $\overrightarrow{E}$ are *convergent*, i.e., confluent, terminating, and coherent modulo Ax, *sort-decreasing* and satisfy the finite variant property (see Definition 2).

In a decomposition, for each term $t \in \mathcal{T}_{\Sigma_\mathcal{P}}(\mathcal{X})$, there is a unique (up to Ax-equivalence) $(\overrightarrow{E}, Ax)$-irreducible term that can be obtained by rewriting t to its *normal* form, which is denoted by $t\downarrow_{\overrightarrow{E},Ax}$. The set of oriented equations $\overrightarrow{E}$ can be understood as a set of implicit rewrite rules, hence, we will denote the previous decomposition for the order-sorted equational theory $(\Sigma_\mathcal{P}, \mathcal{E}_\mathcal{P})$ as the rewriting system $(\Sigma_\mathcal{P}, Ax, \overrightarrow{E})$ In order to provide a finitary and complete unification algorithm for a decomposition $(\Sigma_\mathcal{P}, B, \overrightarrow{E})$, the *folding variant narrowing* strategy is defined in [25]. Intuitively, an $(\overrightarrow{E}, Ax)$-*variant* of a term t is the $(\overrightarrow{E}, Ax)$-irreducible form of an *instance* $t\sigma$ of t. That is, the variants of t are all of the possible $(\overrightarrow{E}, Ax)$-irreducible terms to which instances of t evaluate.

Definition 1. (Term Variant [10,25]). *Given a term t and a decomposition $(\Sigma, Ax, \overrightarrow{E})$, we say that (t', θ) is a variant of t if $t' =_{Ax} (t\theta)\downarrow_{\overrightarrow{E},Ax}$, where $Dom(\theta) \subseteq Var(t)$ and $Ran(\theta) \cap Var(t) = \emptyset$.*

It is possible to compute a complete and finite set of variants for some equational theories.

Definition 2. (Complete set of Variants [25]). *Given a decomposition* $(\Sigma, Ax, \vec{E})$ *and a term* t, *we write* $[\![t]\!]_{\vec{E},Ax}$ *for a* complete set of variants *of* t, *i.e., for any variant* (t_2, θ_2) *of* t, *there is a variant* $(t_1, \theta_1) \in [\![t]\!]_{\vec{E},Ax}$ *such that* $(t_1, \theta_1) \leq_{\vec{E},Ax} (t_2, \theta_2)$, *where* $(t_1, \theta_1) \leq_{\vec{E},Ax} (t_2, \theta_2)$ *iff there is a substitution* ρ *such that* $(\theta_1 \rho)|_{Var(t)} =_{Ax} (\theta_2 \downarrow_{\vec{E},Ax})|_{Var(t)}$ *and* $t_1 \rho =_{Ax} t_2$. *An equational theory has the* finite variant property *(FVP) (also called* finite variant theory*) iff for all* $t \in \mathcal{T}_\Sigma(\mathcal{X})$, $[\![t]\!]_{\vec{E},Ax}$ *is a finite set.*

The states of the protocol $\mathcal{P}$ are modeled as terms of an initial algebra $\mathcal{T}_{\Sigma_\mathcal{P}/\mathcal{E}_\mathcal{P}}$, i.e., each state is an equivalence class $[t]_{\mathcal{E}_\mathcal{P}} \in \mathcal{T}_{\Sigma_\mathcal{P}/\mathcal{E}_\mathcal{P}}$ of the form $\{S_1 \& \cdots \& S_n \& \{IK\}\}$ where & is an associative-commutative union operator with identity symbol $\emptyset$.

The *intruder knowledge IK* of a state $\{S_1 \& \cdots \& S_n \& \{IK\}\}$ is defined as a set of facts using the comma as an associative-commutative union operator with identity element $\emptyset$. There are two kinds of intruder facts: *positive* knowledge facts (the intruder knows m, i.e., $m \in \mathcal{I}$), and *negative* knowledge facts (the intruder *does not yet know* m but *will know it in a future state*, i.e., $m \notin \mathcal{I}$), where m is a message expression.

Each S_i of a state $\{S_1 \& \cdots \& S_n \& \{IK\}\}$ is called a strand and specifies the sequence of messages sent and received by a principal executing the protocol. *Strands* [26] are represented as a sequence of messages $[msg_1^\pm, msg_2^\pm, msg_3^\pm, \ldots, msg_{k-1}^\pm, msg_k^\pm]$ with $msg_i^\pm$ either msg_i^- (also written $-msg_i$) representing an input message, or msg_i^+ (also written $+msg_i$) representing an output message. Note that each msg_i is a term of a special sort **Msg**; this sort is extended by the user to allow any user-definable protocol syntax. Variables of a special sort **Fresh** are used to represent pseudo-random values (nonces) and Maude-NPA ensures that two distinct fresh variables will never be merged. Strands are extended with all the fresh variables $x_1, \ldots, x_k$ created by that strand, i.e., $::x_1, \ldots, x_k::[msg_1^\pm, msg_2^\pm, \ldots, msg_k^\pm]$. Strands are also extended [21] with constraints of the form "t_1 **eq** t_2" that can be inserted at any place and will be either solved during execution by equational unification or checked for satisfiability along the execution paths. Constraints of the form "t_1 **neq** t_2" indicate term disequality and are introduced during analysis [21].

Strands are used to represent both the actions of honest principals (with a strand specified for each protocol role) and the actions of an intruder (with a strand for each action an intruder is able to perform on messages). In Maude-NPA strands evolve over time; the symbol | is used to divide past and future. That is, given a strand [$msg_1^\pm$, ..., $msg_i^\pm$ | $msg_{i+1}^\pm$, ..., $msg_k^\pm$], messages $msg_1^\pm, \ldots, msg_i^\pm$ are the *past messages*, and messages $msg_{i+1}^\pm, \ldots, msg_k^\pm$ are the *future messages* ($msg_{i+1}^\pm$ is the immediate future message). A strand $[msg_1^\pm, \ldots, msg_k^\pm]$ is shorthand for $[nil \mid msg_1^\pm, \ldots, msg_k^\pm, nil]$. An *initial state* is a state where the bar is at the beginning for all strands in the state, and the intruder knowledge has no fact of the form $m \in \mathcal{I}$. A *final state* is a state where the bar is at the end for all strands in the state and there is no intruder fact of the form $m \notin \mathcal{I}$.

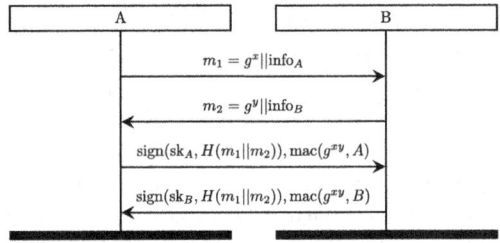

Fig. 1. The Sigma Protocol [6]

Example 1. Consider the variant of the Sign and MAC (Sigma) protocol [29] proposed in [6], depicted in Fig. 1. This authentication protocol allows two participants, A and B, to authenticate each other based on the hash values of their exchanged messages. The message suffixes inf_A and inf_B appearing in Fig. 1 depend on the protocol's instantiation and may include a nonce, a version, or the proposed ciphersuite. To bound the search space, we define these suffixes as the names of the honest participants in the strand specification within Maude-NPA. The strand syntax specification in Maude-NPA is as follows:

```
eq STRANDS-PROTOCOL =
:: rA :: [nil |
    +(exp(g, n(A, rA)) ; A:Name),
    -(EXPB ; MSJ2),
    +(sign(sk(A), H(exp(g, n(A, rA)) ; (A ; (EXPB ; MSJ2))))),
    -(sign(sk(B), H2)),
    (H(exp(g, n(A, rA)) ; (A ; (EXPB ; MSJ2))))
      eq
      (H2),
    +(ok),
    nil] &
:: rB :: [nil |
    -(EXPA ; MSJ1),
    +(exp(g, n(B, rB)) ; B),
    -(sign(sk(A), H1)),
    (H1)
      eq
      (H(EXPA ; (MSJ1 ; (exp(g, n(B, rB)) ; B)))),
    +(sign(sk(B), H(EXPA ; (MSJ1 ; (exp(g, n(B, rB)) ; B))))),
    -(ok),
    nil]
[nonexec] .
```

Notice that in our strand specification of the protocol, we did not include an explicit MAC operator, as two strand conditions already capture the verification process: they specify that the received digest must match the one obtained by hashing the previously sent and received messages.

Since the number of states $T_{\Sigma_\mathcal{P}/\mathcal{E}_\mathcal{P}}$ is in general infinite, rather than exploring concrete protocol states $[t]_{\mathcal{E}_\mathcal{P}} \in T_{\Sigma_\mathcal{P}/\mathcal{E}_\mathcal{P}}$ Maude-NPA explores *state patterns* $[t(x_1,\ldots,x_n)]_{\mathcal{E}_\mathcal{P}} \in T_{\Sigma_\mathcal{P}/\mathcal{E}_\mathcal{P}}(\mathcal{X})$ on the free $(\Sigma_\mathcal{P},\mathcal{E}_\mathcal{P})$-algebra over a set of variables $\mathcal{X}$. In this way, a state pattern $[t(x_1,\ldots,x_n)]_{\mathcal{E}_\mathcal{P}}$ represents not a single concrete state but a possibly infinite set of such states, namely all the *instances* of the pattern $[t(x_1,\ldots,x_n)]_{\mathcal{E}_\mathcal{P}}$ where the variables $x_1,\ldots,x_n$ have been instantiated by concrete ground terms.

The semantics of Maude-NPA is expressed in terms of a Maude rewrite theory, including *rewrite rules* that describe how a protocol moves from one state to another via the intruder's interaction with it [20]. One uses Maude-NPA to find an attack by specifying an insecure state pattern called an *attack pattern*. Maude-NPA attempts to find a path from an initial state to the attack pattern via *backwards narrowing* (using the narrowing capabilities of Maude [9] but with the reversed orientation of the rewrite rules). That is, a sequence from an initial state to an attack state is searched *in reverse* as a *backwards path* from an attack state pattern to an initial state. Maude-NPA attempts to find paths until it can no longer form any backwards narrowing steps, at which point it terminates. If at that point it has not found an initial state, the attack pattern is judged *unreachable*; providing a proof of security rather than finding attacks. However, note that Maude-NPA places *no bound on the number of sessions*, so reachability is undecidable in general. Maude-NPA does not achieve termination by any data abstraction, e.g. a bounded number of nonces. Instead, the tool makes use of a number of sound and complete state space reduction techniques that help to identify unreachable and redundant states [24], and thus make termination more likely.

4 Hash Functions

Hash functions are deterministic algorithms that allow us to compress an input string into a shorter one called a digest. In cryptography, they have various applications, such as creating message identifiers, constructing message authentication codes (MACs) [4,41] and acting as one-way functions to securely store sensitive data (e.g., passwords) without the need for decryption. Formally, a hash function is defined as follows [28]:

Definition 3. *A hash function with output length $\ell(n)$ is a pair of probabilistic polynomial time algorithms* (KGen, H) *satisfying the following:*

- KGen(1^n) $\to s$ *is a probabilistic algorithm that takes as input a security parameter 1^n and outputs a key s. We assume that n is implicit in s.*
- H *is a deterministic algorithm that takes as input a key s and a string $x \in \{0,1\}^*$ and outputs a string $H(s,x) \in \{0,1\}^{\ell(n)}$.*

If the function H is defined only for inputs $x \in \{0,1\}^{\ell'(n)}$ with $\ell'(n) > \ell(n)$, then H is called a compression function.

Notice that the key s used here differs from those in encryption or decryption functions since its secrecy is not required. In fact, the security properties we demand from H must hold even if an adversary is aware of s. Moreover, in many cryptographic protocol implementations, hash functions are instantiated without a key and have a fixed output length. Therefore, without loss of generality, we will consider unkeyed hash functions for the rest of the paper.

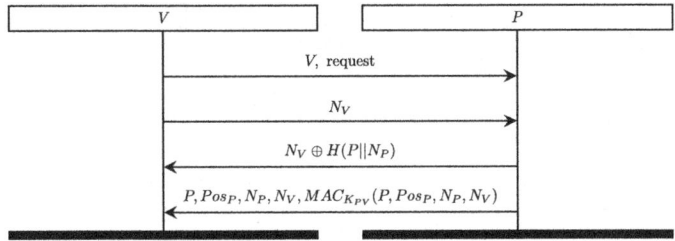

Fig. 2. Meadows et al. distance bounding protocol [30] instantiated with the function $F(N_V, P, N_P) = N_V \oplus H(P||N_P)$.

The first desirable security property of cryptographic hash functions is *collision-resistance*. Given two distinct inputs $x, y \in \{0,1\}^*$, we say that x and y collide if $H(x) = H(y)$. In general, collisions always exist for every hash functions, since the length of the input is arbitrary and the length of the output is fixed. However, a hash function is said to be *collision-resistant* if no probabilistic polynomial-time (PPT) adversary can find a collision with non-negligible probability. For some applications of cryptographic hash functions, it is enough to satisfy the following weaker collision-resistance security requirements:

- **Second preimage resistance (2ndPreImg):** Given an uniform $x \in \{0,1\}^*$, the probability for a PPT adversary to find $y \in \{0,1\}^*$ with $x \neq y$ such that $H(x) = H(y)$ is negligible.
- **First preimage resistance (1stPreImg):** Given $t = H(x)$, for an uniform $x \in \{0,1\}^*$, the probability for a PPT adversary to find a $y \in \{0,1\}^*$ (equal to x or not) such the $H(y) = t$ is negligible.

Clearly, any hash function that is second preimage resistant is also first preimage resistant.

Example 2. Consider the Distance Bounding Protocol proposed by Meadows et al. [30], depicted in Fig. 2, instantiated with the function $F(N_V, P, N_P) = N_V \oplus H(P||N_P)$, which is one example of a valid instantiation, as indicated by the authors. In this protocol, the verifier V initiates the exchange and, upon receiving the final message containing the MAC, computes F using the received values. Then it compares the computed result with the value received in the third step of the protocol. If both values match, V accepts the prover's response as valid. The security of this protocol relies on H being a collision-free hash function. If an adversary were able to find a first preimage—i.e., a value $y \in \text{Dom}(H)$ such that $H(y) = H(P||N_P)$, then the adversary could forge a valid hash, deceiving the verifier.

A specific type of collision known as a *Chosen-Prefix Collision (CPC)* [37] has been exploited in some deployed hash functions [38]. In this attack, given two prefixes $P, P' \in \{0,1\}^*$ of equal length, an adversary finds two suffixes

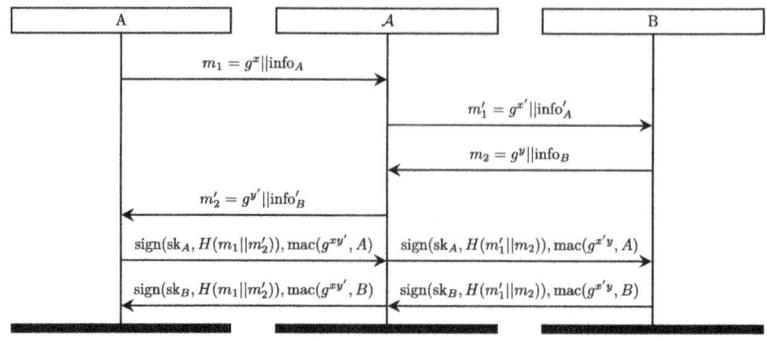

Fig. 3. Man-in-the-middle attack on the Sigma Protocol [6].

$C, C' \in \{0, 1\}^*$ (with $C \neq C'$) such that $H(P||C) = H(P'||C')$. If $P = P'$, this attack is called *Identical-Prefix Collision (IPC)* attack.

Another class of attacks are the *length extensions*. In these attacks, given $H(x)$ and the length of $x \in \{0, 1\}^*$, an adversary is able to compute $H(x||y)$ for $y \in \{0, 1\}^*$ without knowing x. Most hash functions based on the Merkle-Damgård (MD) construction [11,31]—such as MD4 [35], MD5 [34], SHA-1, or SHA-2 [33]—are susceptible to this attack [14]. Moreover, this construction allows adversaries to generate additional types of collisions due to the length extension property. Specifically, if two inputs $x, y \in \{0, 1\}^*$ of the same length produce the digest $H(x) = H(y)$ then $H(x||s) = H(y||s)$ for any suffix $s \in \{0, 1\}^*$, we will refer to this vulnerability as the *Collision Extension (ColExt)*.

Example 3. Consider the Sigma protocol described in Example 1. As noted in [6], if the used hash function were susceptible to CPC and based on the MD construction, the protocol will be susceptible to the Man-in-the-middle attack shown in Fig. 3. After intercepting message m_1, the adversary is able to compute the prefixes $P = m_1 || g^{y'}$ and $P' = g^{x'}$ and perform a CPC attack obtaining the suffixes $C = \text{infpart'}_B$ and $C' = \text{inf}'_A$ for which:

$$H = (m_1 || g^{y'} || \text{infpart'}_B) = H(g^{x'} || \text{inf}'_A)$$

Then, by the length extension properties, the adversary is able to append the message $S = m_2$ to both hashes, obtaining a collision due to the MD construction:

$$H = (m_1 || g^{y'} || \text{infpart'}_B || m_2) = H(g^{x'} || \text{inf}'_A || m_2)$$

Hence, if inf'_B is defined as $\text{inf}'_B = \text{infpart}'_B \parallel m_2$, then the adversary's forged messages for participants A and B are $m'_1 = g^{x'} \parallel \text{inf}'_A$ and $m'_2 = g^{y'} \parallel \text{inf}'_B$.

Despite these vulnerabilities, most security proofs for protocols using hash functions assume the **Random Oracle Model (ROM)** [5]. In this idealized model, a cryptographic hash function is treated as a truly random function, where an input $x \in \{0, 1\}^*$ is evaluated by querying an oracle, which returns the hash $H(x)$ as a black-box response. This abstraction simplifies security proofs for cryptographic protocols and ensures that any practical attacks stem from weaknesses in real-world hash function implementations rather than the model itself. Nevertheless, this idealization of hash functions may not accurately represent reality, as it assumes all hash functions to be good enough at emulating a random oracle. In practice, we need models that better reflect the real-world behavior of hash functions and the potential attacks they may be vulnerable to. These models could help identify which messages, keys, or other aspects of protocols could be compromised if an instantiated hash function is vulnerable to any of the previously mentioned attacks. As noted in [8], some hash functions once considered secure were later found to have vulnerabilities [3,42]. To address this, it is crucial to develop new models that extend beyond the idealized ROM by explicitly considering these vulnerabilities.

5 Modelling Hash Functions Vulnerabilities

To go beyond the ROM using the Maude-NPA tool, we need to think about how to model the hash function vulnerabilities mentioned above. One way could be translating them into equational properties for an operator H representing a hash function. Previous work [8] that proposed a symbolic analysis for hash function vulnerabilities considered an equational theory that models these weaknesses using Tamarin. For instance, to model 1stPreImg and 2ndPreImg collision vulnerabilities and the ability to guess the input value that produces a given digest of the hash function (InLeak), they considered the following equations:

$$\begin{aligned} \text{1stPreImg} \quad & H(\pi_1(H(z))) = H(z) \\ \text{2ndPreImg} \quad & H(\pi_2(H(z), z)) = H(z) \\ \text{InLeak} \quad & i(H(z)) = z \end{aligned} \quad (1)$$

where $\pi_1(.), \pi_2(.)$, and $i(.)$ are symbolic operators that allow to perform these attacks. The 1stPreImg and InLeak equations pose no problem for Maude-NPA. If we look at the 2ndPreImg equation, the operator π_2 has two arguments: a digest $H(z)$ and the input z that produced it. While this may seem redundant—since having access to z is sufficient to perform the attack—the authors in [8] used this form because they were unable to handle the more straightforward equation $H(\pi_2(z)) = H(z)$, which might seem like a naive way to model the vulnerability. The problem is that the equation $H(\pi_2(z)) = H(z)$ does not satisfy the FVP, since the set of variants $[\![H(x)]\!]_{\overrightarrow{E}, Ax}$ for a variable x, where $\{H(\pi_2(z)) \to H(z)\} \subset \overrightarrow{E}$, becomes infinite, as it includes all terms of the form $H(\pi_2(\ldots \pi_2(y) \ldots))$. To preserve this naive formulation while satisfying FVP in Maude-NPA, we can use subsorts as follows:

```
fmod 2ndPreImg is
    protecting DEFINITION-PROTOCOL-RULES .
    sorts Hash NNSet T1 T2 T3 T4 .
    subsort Hash T3 T4 < Msg .
    subsort T2 < T1 < Hash .

    op H : T3 -> T1 [frozen] .
    op H : T4 -> T2 [frozen] .
    op pi2 : T4 -> T3 [frozen] .
    var Y : T4 .

    eq H(pi2(Y)) = H(Y) [variant] .
endfm
```

Here, the equation H(pi2(Y)) = H(Y) satisfies FVP because the operator pi2 returns a term of sort T3, while it requires an input of sort T4. This prevents recursive applications of pi2, thus avoiding an infinite set of terms like H(pi2(... pi2(z)...)) within the equivalence class of H(Y). Additionally, this equational theory preserves the *sort-decreasing* property, as T2 < T1.

The main challenge that the authors faced in [8] was modeling hash function vulnerabilities that involve the concatenation operator ||, such as IPC, CPC, or length extension attacks. As they mentioned, to perform these attacks, the operator || needs to be an associative operator. This presents difficulties for tools that rely on unification because, given two messages, one must compute a finite and complete set of most general unifiers, which contains unifiers σ such that for any other unifier ρ, there exists a substitution μ satisfying $\rho = \sigma\mu$. However, for associative operators, this set is not guaranteed to be finite. To address this issue, the authors used the Maude language as a backend to perform equational unification when analyzing hash vulnerabilities involving the || operator. Maude returns a complete set of unifiers when finite, or a subset of them with a warning when the set is infinite [9,16,17]. They stopped the analysis when Maude raised this warning, assuming that the results would be incomplete in such cases. However, it is relatively simple to use order-sorted restrictions on variables in order to obtain a complete and manageable set of unifiers even if associativity is used.

Additionally, they faced challenges when analyzing protocols using equational theories due to non-termination and excessive verification times. To mitigate these issues, they proposed two alternative methods: an event based model using Tamarin and the use of recursive computation functions in Proverif to model hash function properties involving the || operator. One such property is inspired by the MD construction: $H(x||y) = h(H(x)||y)$, where h is the underlying compression function.

Maude-NPA can mitigate these issues by employing techniques to bound the search space, allowing us to obtain a complete set of most general unifiers for every unification problem appearing in the search space, reducing verification times and avoiding the potential state explosions due to the presence of the associative operation || in the equations of the equational theory. The key strategy, as we did with the 2ndPreImg vulnerability, is the use of subsorts. For instance, if we model the CPC attack using an equational theory with a single sort Msg denoting any payload:

```
eq H(X:Msg ; cp1(X:Msg,Y:Msg)) = H(Y:Msg ; cp2(X:Msg,Y:Msg)) [variant]
```

we may observe a substantial increase in the search space, as even extensive concatenation sequences may be used as prefixes for CPC attacks. Consequently, we could find unification problems where the set of most general unifiers is not finite when terms satisfying the CPC equation are generated. Additionally, this increases the cost of grammar generation. When a protocol specification is loaded into Maude-NPA, it automatically generates a set of grammars G, which represent unreachable states by the intruder. That is, for a given message m, if $m \in G$, there is no initial state S_{init} and substitution θ such that $\theta(m) \in \mathcal{I}$ in S_{init}. When the prefix length is unbounded, the time required to explore all possible patterns the intruder can generate using the cp1 and cp2 operator may grow significantly.

The order-sorted solution to manage this is by limiting the prefix length used in CPC attacks using dedicated sorts to restrict the length. This approach aligns with the CPC attack in Example 3, where the protocol instantiation determines the length of the message parts inf_A and inf_B and can be known by the intruder. To achieve this, we define the subsort MsgElem from the supersort Msg, which represents an isolated term that is not formed by the concatenation of any other term. For instance, as we will see in Sect. 6, the following equational theory modelling the CPC and ColExt attacks for a bounded length is enough for finding the attack mentioned in Example 3:

```
fmod CPC_ColExt is
    protecting DEFINITION-PROTOCOL-RULES .
    sorts Hash Name Nonce NeNonceSet Gen Exp Key GenvExp MsgElem .
    subsort Gen Exp < GenvExp .
    subsort Hash NeNonceSet GenvExp MsgElem < Msg .
    subsort Name Exp < MsgElem .
    op _;_ : Msg Msg -> Msg [frozen gather (e E) assoc] .
    op H : Msg -> Hash [frozen] .
    op cp1 : Msg Msg -> MsgElem [frozen] .
    op cp2 : Msg Msg -> MsgElem [frozen] .
    vars X1 X2 X3 Y1 S1 S2 : MsgElem .

    eq H((X1 ; X2 ; X3 ; cp1(X1 ; X2 ; X3,Y1)) ; S1 ; S2) =
       H((Y1 ; cp2(X1 ; X2 ; X3,Y1)) ; S1 ; S2) [variant] .
endfm
```

6 Sigma and Meadows Protocols

In this section, we exploit the vulnerabilities define in Sect. 4 to symbolically verify different attacks in two protocols: The Sigma and Meadow's Distance Bounding protocols. A summary of our analysis is provided in Table 1, including total execution times, the total number of generated states and the depth needed to find the attacks. The code for these experiments is available at [27].

6.1 Sigma Protocol

The Sigma protocol is an authentication protocol in which a participant A initiates the communication by sending an exponentiation g^x, following the principles

Table 1. Technical summary of protocol analysis.

Protocol	Hash Vul.	Approach	Algebraic Theory	Depth	States	Time
Sigma	CPC & ColExt	Eq. Theory	conc (assoc) exp (assoc, comm) cp1, cp2	11	6180	16.32 days
		Event-Based	conc (assoc) exp (assoc, comm)	13	618	1.14 h.
	CPC	Eq. Theory	conc (assoc) exp (assoc, comm) cp1, cp2	11	258	18 min.
Meadows	1stPreImg	Eq. Theory	conc (assoc[a]) XOR (assoc[a], conm) pi1	8	313	20.88 min.
	2ndPreImg & InLeak	Eq. Theory	conc (assoc[a]) XOR (assoc[a], comm) pi2, inLeak	8	698	2.37 h.

[a] Associativity was not needed to find the attacks shown in Figs. 6 and 7

of the Diffie-Hellman key exchange protocol [13], along with some auxiliary data $info_A$, which depends on the protocol's instantiation—such as the version of selected ciphersuite. Participant B responds with their own exponentiation g^y and associated information $info_B$. To ensure identity protection, both parties then exchange signed hashes of the previously exchanged messages, which are used to authenticate the subsequent MACs.

This reliance on hash functions makes the protocol vulnerable if those functions are susceptible to some of the attacks mentioned in Sect. 4 such as CPC or ColExt attacks. In our analysis, we focus on the variant of the Sigma protocol described in Example 1. As noted in [6,8], although this particular variant is not used in practice, its core structure closely resembles that of more complex, widely deployed protocols such as Transport Layer Security (TLS) [12] and Secure Shell (SSH) [44]. This makes it a useful and relevant protocol to analyze symbolically by considering potential hash function vulnerabilities.

First, we aimed to reproduce the attack S1, which is described in Example 3. As noted in [8], this attack becomes feasible if the used hash function is susceptible to CPC and ColExt vulnerabilities. We encoded these vulnerabilities using a bounded concatenation length within the equational theory, as detailed in the module `fmod CPC_ColExt` Sect. 3: the prefixes involved in the CPC attack are specified to a length of three concatenated terms for the first prefix and for the length of a single term for the second prefix. The suffix for the ColExt vulnerability is restricted to two terms. Additionally, we bounded the lengths of the message parts `info_A` and `info_B` in the attack state to one and three concatenated terms, respectively. We also included a never pattern to explicitly

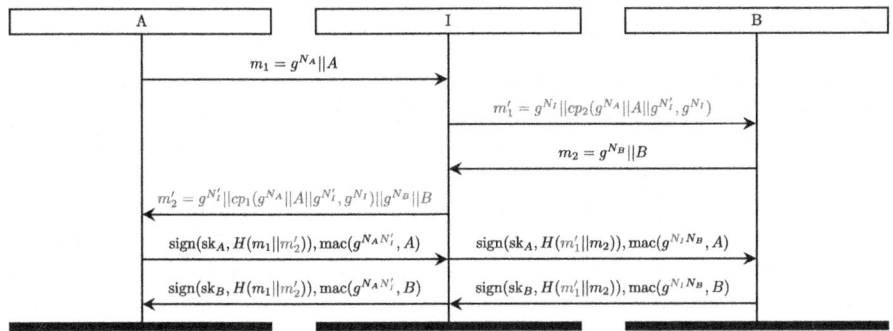

Fig. 4. Attack trace of the Man-in-the-middle attack on the Sigma Protocol found in Maude-NPA by considering the CPC and ColExt vulnerabilities.

exclude certain state patterns from the search space during symbolic analysis. In this case, we excluded patterns that correspond to regular protocol executions and trivial attacks that do not rely on vulnerabilities in the hash function, as discussed in [6]. Under these constraints, Maude-NPA was able to find the attack trace shown in Fig. 4. Notably, during this search, no unification warnings were reported, indicating that for all the unification problems found during the search, the set of most general unifiers was finite.

Another way by which we were able to find this attack—aligned with the event-based model proposed in [8] using Tamarin—is to avoid defining an equational theory that models the CPC in ColExt, and instead include the following intruder strand:

```
:: nil :: [ nil | -(sign(sk(A),H(X1 ; X2 ; X3 ; cp1(X1 ; X2 ; X3,Y1) ;
    S1 ; S2))), +(sign(sk(A),H(Y1 ; cp2(X1 ; X2 ; X3,Y1) ; S1 ; S2))),
    nil ]
```

We also reproduced the man-in-the-middle attack $S3$ presented in [8], in which the intruder positions itself between two initiators of the Sigma protocol. To model this attack, it was enough to consider only the CPC vulnerability without any bounded length of the prefixes, represented by the following equational theory:

```
fmod CPC is
    protecting DEFINITION-PROTOCOL-RULES .
    sorts Hash Name Nonce NeNonceSet Gen Exp Key GenvExp .
    subsort Gen Exp < GenvExp .
    subsort Hash NeNonceSet GenvExp Name Exp< Msg .
    op _;_ : Msg Msg -> Msg [frozen gather (e E) assoc] .
    op H : Msg -> Hash [frozen] .
    op cp1 : Msg Msg -> Msg [frozen] .
    op cp2 : Msg Msg -> Msg [frozen] .
    vars X Y : Msg .

    eq H((X ; cp1(X,Y))) = H((Y ; cp2(X,Y)) [variant] .
endfm
```

The resulting attack trace is shown in Fig. 5.

6.2 Meadows Distance Bounding Protocol

Distance Bounding Protocols are used to estimate a bound on the physical distance between two participants—typically a prover and a verifier. A fundamental security requirement for such protocols is that it must be computationally infeasible for an intruder to deceive the verifier about the prover's actual distance. In some protocol designs, this security relies on the security of specific cryptographic primitives, such as hash functions. Previous analyses on these protocols using Maude-NPA introduced a time and space process algebra that allows for the discovery of attacks which explicitly manipulate the protocol's real-time execution and distance bounds [2]. However, that work did not consider vulnerabilities in the hash functions, which we now explore as a new way for performing such attacks. For example, as showed in Example 2, the protocol proposed by Meadows et al. [30] becomes insecure if it is instantiated with a hash function that lacks first preimage resistance.

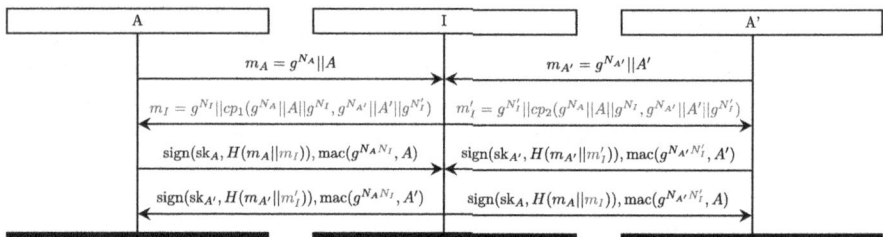

Fig. 5. Attack trace of the Man-in-the-middle attack on the Sigma Protocol with two initiators by considering the CPC vulnerability.

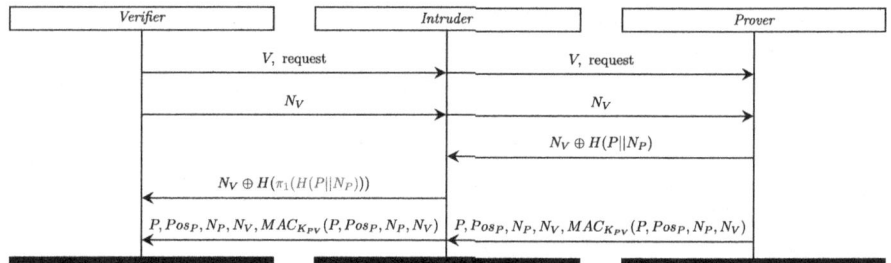

Fig. 6. An attack on the protocol by Meadows et al. [30], instantiated with the function $F(N_V, P, N_P) = N_V \oplus H(P|N_P)$, under the 1stPreImg vulnerability of the hash function H.

In this protocol instantiation, the verifier estimates an upper bound on the distance between the prover by measuring the time elapsed between sending his

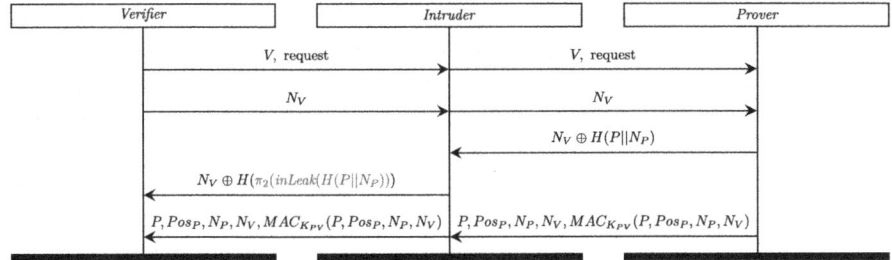

Fig. 7. An attack on the protocol by Meadows et al. [30], instantiated with the function $F(N_V, P, N_P) = N_V \oplus H(P|N_P)$, under the 2ndPreImg and InLeak vulnerabilities of the hash function H.

nonce N_V to the prover and receiving the rapid response, $N_v \oplus H(P||N_P)$. If the subsequently received MAC is valid—i.e., if the verifier computes the hash of the authenticated response and verifies that it matches the rapid response—the distance bound is accepted as valid.

However, if an intruder intercepts the rapid response and is able to find a collision for the digest $H(P|N_P)$—thus breaking the collision resistance assumption of [30]—they could forge a valid response that passes the MAC verification, as illustrated in Fig. 6. This manipulation could alter the actual communication time perceived by the verifier between the reception of the rapid response and the nonce, thereby compromising the correctness of the estimated distance bound in the protocol. In Maude-NPA, we were able to uncover this attack by modelling the first preimage vulnerability using the following equational theory:

```
fmod fstPreImg is
    sorts    Hash .
    subsort Hash < Msg .
    op pi1 : Hash -> Msg [frozen] .
    var H : Hash .
    eq H(pi1(H)) = H [variant] .
endfm
```

Following the approach of [8], we modelled this vulnerability by introducing the operator `pi1`, which represents a preimage of a given digest.

Another way for an intruder to construct a collision on the intercepted digest is under the 2ndPreImg and InLeak vulnerabilities, as illustrated in Fig. 7. We followed the approach described in Sect. 5 to model the 2ndPreImg and InLeak vulnerabilities, which enabled us to identify the attack illustrated in Fig. 7.

7 Conclusions and Future Work

In this paper, we reproduced the attack $S1$ of the Sigma protocol [29] in [8] using an event-based approach. Also, we reproduced the attacks $S1$ and $S3$ of the Sigma protocol [29] in [8] using equational unification. We identified a vulnerability of the Meadows protocol [30] not found in [8] using equational unification. Finally, we seamlessly combined different algebraic properties, including associativity, without incompleteness warnings and in reasonable analysis time. As future work, we plan to investigate other protocols and vulnerability dimensions from [8].

References

1. Aparicio-Sánchez, D., Escobar, S., Gutiérrez, R., Sapiña, J.: An optimizing protocol transformation for constructor finite variant theories in Maude-NPA. In: Chen, L., Li, N., Liang, K., Schneider, S. (eds.) ESORICS 2020. LNCS, vol. 12309, pp. 230–250. Springer, Cham (2020). https://doi.org/10.1007/978-3-030-59013-0_12
2. Aparicio-Sánchez, D., Escobar, S., Meadows, C., Meseguer, J., Sapiña, J.: Protocol analysis with time and space. In: Protocols, Strands, and Logic: Essays Dedicated to Joshua Guttman on the Occasion of his 66.66 th Birthday, pp. 22–49. Springer (2021)
3. Aurora, V.: Lifetimes of cryptographic hash functions (2017). https://valerieaurora.org/hash.html
4. Bellare, M., Canetti, R., Krawczyk, H.: Keying hash functions for message authentication. In: Koblitz, N. (ed.) CRYPTO 1996. LNCS, vol. 1109, pp. 1–15. Springer, Heidelberg (1996). https://doi.org/10.1007/3-540-68697-5_1
5. Bellare, M., Rogaway, P.: Random oracles are practical: a paradigm for designing efficient protocols. In: Proceedings of the 1st ACM Conference on Computer and Communications Security, pp. 62–73 (1993)
6. Bhargavan, K., Leurent, G.: Transcript collision attacks: breaking authentication in TLS, IKE, and SSH. In: Network and Distributed System Security Symposium–NDSS 2016 (2016)
7. Blanchet, B., Cheval, V., Cortier, V.: Proverif with lemmas, induction, fast subsumption, and much more. In: 43rd IEEE Symposium on Security and Privacy, SP 2022, San Francisco, CA, USA, May 22-26, 2022, pp. 69–86. IEEE (2022). https://doi.org/10.1109/SP46214.2022.9833653
8. Cheval, V., Cremers, C., Dax, A., Hirschi, L., Jacomme, C., Kremer, S.: Hash gone bad: automated discovery of protocol attacks that exploit hash function weaknesses. In: 32nd USENIX Security Symposium (USENIX Security 23), pp. 5899–5916 (2023)
9. Clavel, M., et al.: Maude manual (version 3.5) (2024). http://maude.cs.uiuc.edu
10. Comon-Lundh, H., Delaune, S.: The finite variant property: how to get rid of some algebraic properties. In: Proceedings of the 16th International Conference on Rewriting Techniques and Applications (RTA 2005). LNCS, vol. 3467, pp. 294–307. Springer (2005). https://doi.org/10.1007/978-3-540-32033-3_22
11. Damgård, I.B.: A design principle for hash functions. In: Conference on the Theory and Application of Cryptology, pp. 416–427. Springer (1989)
12. Dierks, T., Rescorla, E.: The transport layer security (TLS) protocol version 1.2, Technical report (2008)
13. Diffie, W., Hellman, M.: Exhaustive cryptanalysis of the NBS data encryption standard. Computer **10**(6), 74–84 (1997)
14. Duong, T., Rizzo, J.: Flickr's API signature forgery vulnerability, Technical report (2009)
15. Durán, F., et al.: Programming and symbolic computation in Maude. J. Log. Algebraic Methods Program. **110** (2020). https://doi.org/10.1016/J.JLAMP.2019.100497

16. Durán, F., Eker, S., Escobar, S., Martí-Oliet, N., Meseguer, J., Talcott, C.L.: Associative unification and symbolic reasoning modulo associativity in Maude. In: Rusu, V. (ed.) Rewriting Logic and Its Applications - 12th International Workshop, WRLA 2018, Held as a Satellite Event of ETAPS, Thessaloniki, Greece, June 14–15, 2018, Proceedings. LNCS, vol. 11152, pp. 98–114. Springer (2018). https://doi.org/10.1007/978-3-319-99840-4_6
17. Eker, S.: Associative unification in Maude. J. Log. Algebraic Methods Program. **126**, 100747 (2022). https://doi.org/10.1016/J.JLAMP.2021.100747
18. Escobar, S., Hendrix, J., Meadows, C., Meseguer, J.: Diffie-Hellman cryptographic reasoning in the Maude-NRL protocol analyzer. In: Proceedings of the 2nd International Workshop on Security and Rewriting Techniques (SecReT 2007) (2007)
19. Escobar, S., Meadows, C., Meseguer, J.: Maude-NPA: cryptographic protocol analysis modulo equational properties. In: Foundations of Security Analysis and Design V (FOSAD 2007/2008/2009 Tutorial Lectures). LNCS, vol. 5705, pp. 1–50. Springer (2009). https://doi.org/10.1007/978-3-642-03829-7_1
20. Escobar, S., Meadows, C., Meseguer, J.: Maude-NPA: cryptographic protocol analysis modulo equational properties. In: Aldini, A., Barthe, G., Gorrieri, R. (eds.) FOSAD 2008/2009 Tutorial Lectures. LNCS, vol. 5705, pp. 1–50. Springer (2009)
21. Escobar, S., Meadows, C., Meseguer, J., Santiago, S.: Symbolic protocol analysis with disequality constraints modulo equational theories. In: Bodei, C., Ferrari, G.-L., Priami, C. (eds.) Programming Languages with Applications to Biology and Security: Essays Dedicated to Pierpaolo Degano on the Occasion of his 65th Birthday. LNCS, vol. 9465, pp. 238–261. Springer, Cham (2015). https://doi.org/10.1007/978-3-319-25527-9_16
22. Escobar, S., et al.: Protocol analysis in Maude-NPA using unification modulo homomorphic encryption. In: Schneider-Kamp, P., Hanus, M. (eds.) Proceedings of the 13th International ACM SIGPLAN Conference on Principles and Practice of Declarative Programming, July 20–22, 2011, Odense, Denmark, pp. 65–76. ACM (2011). https://doi.org/10.1145/2003476.2003488
23. Escobar, S., Meadows, C., Meseguer, J.: Maude-NPA manual v3.1. http://maude.cs.illinois.edu/w/index.php/Maude_Tools:_Maude-NPA
24. Escobar, S., Meadows, C.A., Meseguer, J., Santiago, S.: State space reduction in the Maude-NRL protocol analyzer. Inf. Comput. **238**, 157–186 (2014). https://doi.org/10.1016/j.ic.2014.07.007
25. Escobar, S., Sasse, R., Meseguer, J.: Folding variant narrowing and optimal variant termination. J. Log. Algebr. Program. **81**(7–8), 898–928 (2012). https://doi.org/10.1016/j.jlap.2012.01.002
26. Fabrega, F.J.T., Herzog, J.C., Guttman, J.D.: Strand spaces: why is a security protocol correct? In: Proceedings. In: 1998 IEEE Symposium on Security and Privacy (Cat. No.98CB36186), pp. 160–171 (1998). https://doi.org/10.1109/SECPRI.1998.674832
27. Hernández-Sánchez, A., Escobar, S.: Hash vulnerabilities analysis in Maude-NPA (2025). https://personales.upv.es/sanesro/Maude-NPA_Protocols/Hash
28. Katz, J., Lindell, Y.: Introduction to Modern Cryptography: Principles and Protocols. Chapman and Hall/CRC (2007)
29. Krawczyk, H.: Sigma: the 'sign-and-mac' approach to authenticated Diffie-Hellman and its use in the IKE protocols. In: Annual International Cryptology Conference, pp. 400–425. Springer (2003)
30. Meadows, C., Poovendran, R., Pavlovic, D., Chang, L., Syverson, P.: Distance bounding protocols: authentication logic analysis and collusion attacks. In: Secure

Localization and Time Synchronization for Wireless Sensor and Ad Hoc Networks, pp. 279–298. Springer (2007)
31. Merkle, R.C.: One way hash functions and des. In: Conference on the Theory and Application of Cryptology, pp. 428–446. Springer (1989)
32. Meseguer, J.: Conditional rewriting logic as a unified model of concurrency. Theoret. Comput. Sci. **96**(1), 73–155 (1992)
33. National Institute of Standards and Technology (NIST): Secure Hash Standard (SHS) - FIPS PUB 180-4, Technical Report FIPS PUB 180-4, NIST (2015). https://nvlpubs.nist.gov/nistpubs/FIPS/NIST.FIPS.180-4.pdf
34. Rivest, R.L.: The MD5 message-digest algorithm. RFC 1321 (1992). https://doi.org/10.17487/RFC1321
35. Rivest, R.L.: The MD4 message digest algorithm. LNCS, Advances in Cryptography CRYPTO '90 (1998)
36. Sasse, R., Escobar, S., Meadows, C., Meseguer, J.: Protocol analysis modulo combination of theories: a case study in Maude-NPA. In: Cuellar, J., Lopez, J., Barthe, G., Pretschner, A. (eds.) Security and Trust Management, pp. 163–178. Springer, Berlin, Heidelberg (2011)
37. Stevens, M.: A survey of chosen-prefix collision attacks. In: London Mathematical Society Lecture Note Series, Cambridge University Press, pp. 182–220 (2021)
38. Stevens, M., Lenstra, A., De Weger, B.: Chosen-prefix collisions for MD5 and colliding x. 509 certificates for different identities. In: Advances in Cryptology-EUROCRYPT 2007: 26th Annual International Conference on the Theory and Applications of Cryptographic Techniques, Barcelona, Spain, May 20-24, 2007. Proceedings 26, pp. 1–22. Springer (2007)
39. TeReSe: Term Rewriting Systems. Cambridge University Press (2003). https://doi.org/10.1017/S095679680400526X
40. The Tamarin Team: The Tamarin-Prover Manual June 4 (2019). https://tamarin-prover.com/manual/master/tex/tamarin-manual.pdf
41. Turner, J.: The keyed-hash message authentication code (HMAC). FIPS PUB 198-1, National Institute of Standards and Technology (NIST) (2008)
42. Wilcox, Z.: Lessons from the history of attacks on secure hash functions (2017). https://electriccoin.co/blog/lessons-from-the-history-of-attacks-on-secure-hash-functions/
43. Yang, F., Escobar, S., Meadows, C.A., Meseguer, J., Narendran, P.: Theories of homomorphic encryption, unification, and the finite variant property. In: Chitil, O., King, A., Danvy, O. (eds.) Proceedings of the 16th International Symposium on Principles and Practice of Declarative Programming, Kent, Canterbury, United Kingdom, September 8–10, 2014, pp. 123–133. ACM (2014). https://doi.org/10.1145/2643135.2643154
44. Ylonen, T., Lonvick, C.: The secure shell (SSH) transport layer protocol, Technical report (2006)

A Post-quantum Distributed OPRF from the Legendre PRF

Novak Kaluđerović[1]([✉])[iD], Nan Cheng[2]([✉])[iD], and Aikaterini Mitrokotsa[2]([✉])[iD]

[1] Zircuit, Zürich, Switzerland
kolja@zircuit.com
[2] University of St. Gallen, St. Gallen, Switzerland
{nan.cheng,katerina.mitrokotsa}@unisg.ch

Abstract. A distributed OPRF enables a client to evaluate a pseudorandom function on a client-chosen input using a distributed key shared among multiple servers, ensuring that the servers learn nothing about the input or output, while the client learns nothing about the key. We present a post-quantum OPRF suitable for a distributed server setting, requiring only two rounds of communication between the client and servers, with server-to-server communication limited to a pre-computation phase. Our approach leverages the Legendre PRF, computed through a single MPC multiplication and opening during the online phase. We introduce a novel MPC technique that achieves multiplication and opening in one round using replicated secret sharing (RSS) in a malicious adversarial model. This allows for the quantum-secure, verifiable evaluation of the Legendre OPRF against malicious adversaries under a threshold assumption, without requiring inter-server communication. Beyond the Legendre PRF, this method is also of interest for general MPC operations. To our knowledge, our distributed OPRF (dOPRF) is the first post-quantum construction with these properties. We compare our approach to state-of-the-art MPC solutions and provide an implementation of our proposed dOPRF, benchmarking it against existing OPRF constructions. In practical settings, our results demonstrate superior efficiency.

Keywords: Distributed OPRF · Legendre PRF · MPC

1 Introduction

An oblivious PRF (OPRF) is a 2PC protocol that involves two parties, a client (receiver) and a server (sender) in which the server has a PRF key k and the client learns $F_k(x)$, where F is a PRF and x is the input chosen by the client. The design of the OPRF ensures that the server cannot gain any knowledge about the client's input or output, while it also prevents the client from learning anything about the server's key.

OPRFs were originally introduced by Freedman et al. [23], and have since found a wide range of applications. They serve as a fundamental building block for creating password-authenticated key exchange [2,3], password secret sharing [10,18], single sign-on protocols [4,10], and private set intersection [31,32], among many other use cases. Many existing practical OPRF constructions base their security on the difficulty of solving the discrete logarithm problem. This reliance makes such constructions vulnerable to attacks by quantum computers. Post-quantum OPRFs are an active area of research, and current constructions are either broken [9,12], inefficient [6,8], only presented in the semi-honest server model [5,19,21], or require many rounds of communication [11,12], and neither of them are distributed. While existing generic MPC protocols [14,15] offer strong security guarantees, they come with multiple rounds of communication between the client and servers, which can lead to delays as the client waits for the servers to exchange data before receiving the final output.

A variation of Oblivious Pseudorandom Functions (OPRFs) is the distributed OPRF (dOPRF), originally introduced by Jarecki et al. [30]. This model involves multiple servers that collaboratively evaluate the function. The secret key k is distributed among these servers, allowing them and the client to jointly compute the function $F_k(x)$ on the client's input x without revealing any information about x to the servers. Furthermore, the distributed nature of the key enhances protection against server breaches. This leads us to the question: *Is it possible to construct a distributed OPRF with optimized communication rounds?* In this work, we provide a positive answer by introducing a dOPRF protocol in merely two rounds with post-quantum security guarantees in a fully malicious model.

Our Contributions. *(i) We proposed a verifiable, non-interactive maliciously secure MPC multiply-and-open protocol.* This 2-round protocol is based on a Replicated Secret Sharing (RSS) scheme and serves as the foundation for our dOPRF protocol. This protocol can also be applied directly to compute other applications such as the inner product of two vectors, used in biometric authentication. *(ii) We proposed a 2-round dOPRF in the fully malicious adversarial model.* Leveraging above *multiply-and-open* protocol, we construct a dOPRF where a client and multiple servers collaboratively compute $\mathcal{C}_{\mathsf{PRF}} : (x, k, s^2) \mapsto (x+k)s^2$. The client shares their input with the servers and receives the output in just two communication rounds. Our proposed dOPRF ensures *output verification*, allowing the client to confirm the correctness of the output. Moreover, it also guarantees *input verification*, which protect honest servers from a malicious client, ensuring they do not leak sensitive data, resulting in a random output when the client misbehaves. *(iii) We performed detailed and comprehensive evaluation over our dOPRF primitive.* We did comprehensive comparision between our protocol and existing state-of-the-arts, and thus verified it's practical efficiency with small amount of servers.

1.1 Adversarial Model

We design our protocols to withstand malicious adversarial behavior, where an adversary is considered *malicious* if they can adopt any strategy within their capabilities, while being probabilistic polynomial-time bounded. The participants are the client and n servers, with t representing the threshold of corrupted servers. The client may or may not be corrupted, independent of t corrupted servers. Our protocols are provably secure when $t < n/3$ in a malicious setting. Non-corrupted servers are *honest*, adhering to the protocol without collusion.

We assume secure communication channels between the client and servers, including inter-server communication during pre-computation. Servers hold secret shares as randomness seeds, which can be generated via a non-interactive key exchange (NIKE) method. These seeds are utilized for generating random values during the protocol's setup. Finally, we assume a static adversary, meaning the set of corrupted parties is fixed at the protocol's start.

1.2 Highlevel Overview

The Legendre PRF can be computed using simple field arithmetic. We present an algorithm for the Legendre OPRF in a malicious setting (Sect. 5.2), structured in two phases as illustrated in Fig. 1. Both phases ensure post-quantum security, with the only non-information-theoretic components being hash functions and PRFs used for verification. The computation of the Legendre PRF function $F_k(x)$ is information-theoretically equivalent to revealing the field value $(x+k)s^2$, where s is a random non-zero field element unknown to both the client and servers. Thus, computing the Legendre PRF involves one squaring, one addition, and one multiplication.

We utilize replicated secret sharing (RSS) for secure computation, storing each field element x, k, s^2 as RSS shares among the servers. The linearity of RSS facilitates straightforward secure addition. For the efficient computation of the Legendre PRF, we focus on two operations: *RSS to RSS multiplication* (Sect. A) and *RSS to RSS multiplication-with-opening* (Sect. 4.1), corresponding to the square computation in the offline and online phase, respectively.

1.3 Related Work

Oblivious PRFs have been systematically studied by Casacuberta et al. [13]. The authors divide them into four main categories based on the underlying assumptions – Naor-Reingold (NR), Hashed Diffie-Hellman (HashDH and 2HashDH), and Dodis-Yampolskiy (DY), all of which are based on classical security assumptions. In Table 1 we compare some popular OPRFs against ours. *Partially oblivious* property means that the input provided by the client is split into a private part x_{priv} which remains secret, and public part x_{pub} which is revealed to the server(s). *Verifiabilty* allows the client to be convinced of the correctness of the received output. A *distributed* OPRF works in a multi-server setting (i.e., the secret key is distributed to multiple servers). In our case, the verifiability stems from the threshold assumption of a (super)majority of honest servers.

In Table 1, we compare our protocol with state-of-the-art oblivious pseudorandom functions (OPRFs) across various characteristics, including security and efficiency. The comparison highlights the partially oblivious and verifiable properties, as well as the ability to operate in a distributed manner. Our proposed protocol, based on the Legendre PRF, demonstrates significant advantages

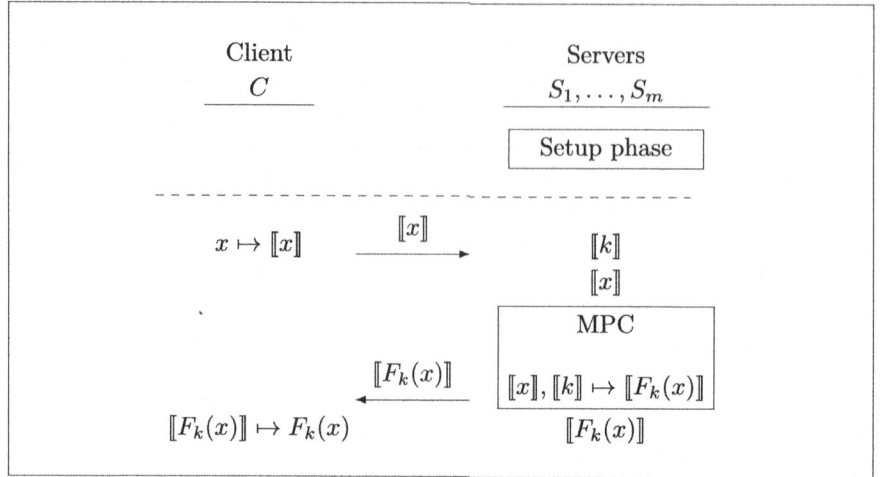

Fig. 1. MPC based distributed OPRF

with respect to both communication efficiency and computational performance, requiring only two rounds for its execution.

Recent research has explored various OPRF constructions. Notable works include lattice-based constructions by Albrecht et al. [6] and isogeny-based protocols by Boneh et al. [12]. Dodgson [20] established security for the Legendre OPRF in the UC model, while Beullens et al. [11] proposed a practical approach with significant communication rounds. Faller et al. [21] discussed efficient OPRFs using garbled circuits, and Albrecht et al. [5] provided a post-quantum OPRF that is efficient but incomplete without zero-knowledge proofs. In contrast, our dOPRF exhibits superior efficiency compared to existing protocols, requiring fewer communication rounds.

On Distributed Security. We note that our protocol offers different security properties in the distributed and threshold setting than previous classical constructions. Other dOPRFs preserve the secrecy of the input x when an adversary takes control of $> t$ servers. In our scenario a weaker security assumption holds – both the input x and the key k are revealed once a malicious party breaches a threshold of the servers. This may seem like a strong security relaxation, we argue that the benefits overweight the drawbacks. A malicious party that takes full ($> t$ threshold) control of the servers always learns the secret key k. This allows for a brute-force dictionary attack which can be used to reveal users' inputs. In general users' inputs are passwords (or hashes thereof) which are not assumed to be of high-entropy, and this attack would reveal any such inputs. A quantum computer would speed these attacks even further by employing a faster search algorithm such as Grover's search [26].

Table 1. Comparison to state-of-the-art OPRFs.

OPRF	PRF	Partially oblivious	Verifiable	Distributed	Quantum resistant
[27,29]	NR	✗	✓	✗	✗
[31]	DY	✗	✓	✗	✗
[10,28,30]	2HashDH	✓	✗	✓	✗
[6,12]	Isogenies	✗	✓	✗	✓
[21]	GC	✗	✗	✗	✓
[11,20]	Legendre PRF	✗	✓	✗	✓
Our work	Legendre PRF	✓	✓	✓	✓

2 Preliminaries

Notation. Let p be a prime. We assume that p is public and $p \approx 2^{2\lambda_c}$ or $p \approx 2^{3\lambda_q}$ where λ_c and λ_q are classical and quantum security parameters respectively. We denote with $\mathbb{F}_p$ the finite field of p elements. For any set S, we denote with $\#S$ the cardinality of S. We use subscripts to distinguish the terms of a sum ($a = \sum a_i$) or to index parties in a protocol (server S_i), while we use superscripts to denote values presumed to be equal and allocated to various parties (a^i given to party associated with index i).

Secret Sharing. Secret sharing is a method for distributing a secret value $x \in \mathbb{F}_p$ among multiple parties, so no single party, or a predefined group of parties, holds any information about the secret. We call t a threshold, and a corresponding secret sharing scheme a (t, n) scheme, if any group of at most t colluding parties cannot extract any information about the secret, while any group of $\geq t + 1$ parties can compute the secret x. We denote with $[\![x]\!]$ a generic secret sharing of a field element $x \in \mathbb{F}_p$, i.e., an n-tuple $(x_1, \ldots, x_n)$ such that each share x_i is owned by party i.

Distributed Oblivious PRFs. A *Pseudorandom Function* (PRF) family is a collection of functions $\{F_k\}_{k \in \mathcal{K}}$ with the same domain and co-domain, indexed by some key set $\mathcal{K}$, where a randomly sampled function from this family is difficult to be distinguished from a truly random function with the same domain and co-domain. An *Oblivious Pseudorandom Function* (OPRF) is a two-party privacy-preserving secure PRF protocol between a client and a server. An OPRF is called *distributed* (dOPRF) if there are multiple servers taking the role of the OPRF evaluator. A distributed (t,n) OPRF (dOPRF) is an OPRF variant which tolerates up to t malicious colluding servers among n servers.

2.1 The Legendre PRF

The Legendre PRF originated from Damgård [16]. Although initially impractical due to being significantly slower than generic PRF counterparts, interest in the Legendre PRF [22] increased after Grassi et al. [25] identified it as a suitable PRF for MPC, crediting to its homomorphic property of the Legendre symbol and its simple structure, making it MPC friendly.

Definition 1 (Legendre symbol). *We define the Legendre symbol:*

$$\left(\frac{a}{p}\right) = a^{\frac{p-1}{2}} = \begin{cases} 1 \text{ if } a \in \mathbb{F}_p \text{ is a square mod } p \\ -1 \text{ if } a \in \mathbb{F}_p \text{ is not a square mod } p. \end{cases}$$

In general, the Legendre symbol is defined by setting $\left(\frac{0}{p}\right) = 0$, which makes the symbol multiplicative, but comes at a cost of increasing the size of the co-domain. We will assume that $\left(\frac{0}{p}\right) = 1$ and that the symbol is multiplicative, which is a reasonable assumption, since for our use-case the inputs are random, and the probability that the input is $x = 0$ is negligible since the input is an element not known to the adversary. In particular, we assume

$$\left(\frac{a}{p}\right)\left(\frac{b}{p}\right) = \left(\frac{ab}{p}\right) \quad \text{for all } a, b \in \mathbb{F}_p. \tag{1}$$

Definition 2 (Legendre PRF). *We define the Legendre PRF to be the family of functions $\{F_k\}_{k \in \mathcal{K}}$ the key space being $\mathcal{K} = \mathbb{F}_p$, the functions parameterised as $F_k : \mathbb{F}_p \to \{-1, +1\}$ and defined as $F_k(x) := \left(\frac{x+k}{p}\right)$. Under this definition, the Legendre PRF outputs only a single bit. These functions can be expanded to a λ-bit output function by increasing the keyspace to $\mathcal{K}^\lambda$ and for each $k = (k_1, \ldots, k_\lambda) \in \mathcal{K}^\lambda$ defining*

$$F_k(x) := \left(\left(\frac{x+k_1}{p}\right), \left(\frac{x+k_2}{p}\right), \ldots, \left(\frac{x+k_\lambda}{p}\right)\right).$$

Multi-party Legendre Symbol Computation. The Legendre symbol $\left(\frac{a}{p}\right)$ of a secret shared input $[\![a]\!]$ can be computed via MPC. During the setup phase, the servers sample a random value $[\![s]\!]$ and compute $[\![s^2]\!]$. In the subsequent online evaluation, the servers compute $[\![a]\!], [\![s^2]\!] \mapsto [\![as^2]\!]$ and reveal the result to a designated receiver. This enables the receiver to locally compute the Legendre symbol as follows: $\left(\frac{as^2}{p}\right) = \left(\frac{a}{p}\right)\left(\frac{s^2}{p}\right) = \left(\frac{a}{p}\right)$.

Legendre PRF Hardness Assumptions. The security of the Legendre PRF relies on the Shifted Legendre Symbol Problem (SLSP) and the Decisional Shifted Legendre Symbol Problem (DSLSP) [35]. SLSP is at least as hard as DSLSP, indicating DSLSP $\leq$ SLSP under polynomial time reductions. For a more detailed security property of the Legendre PRF, please refere to the full version of this work [33].

3 Arithmetic MPC and Secret Sharing

We refer to the parties that hold secret shares and participate in multi-party computation as *servers*. The terms *server* and *server index* are used interchangeably to denote a server $S_1, \ldots, S_n$ or its corresponding index $i = 1, \ldots, n$. Similarly, we use *share* and *share index* to refer to a share of a secret held by some servers and the index of that share.

Additive Secret Sharing (ASS) [1] shares a field element $x \in \mathbb{F}_p$ among at least two servers indexed by some set $I \subseteq \{1, \ldots, n\}$, with the security threshold $t = \#I - 1$. Any $\leq t$ colluding parties have no information about x. We denote an ASS secret sharing of x as $[x]$, in this scheme, let $\mathcal{T} = I$ be the set of share indices, then each server S_i holds the term x_T where $T = i$ satisfying $x = \sum_{T \in \mathcal{T}} x_T$. **Replicated secret sharing (RSS)** is a generalisation of ASS, in which the same additive secret shares of an element are provided to multiple parties. Following the notation of [7], we have:

Definition 3 (Replicated secret sharing). *The (t, n)-Replicated secret sharing scheme among n servers is defined as follows: The set of share indices denoted as $\mathcal{T}$ is:*

$$\mathcal{T} := \{A \subseteq \{1, \ldots, n\} \mid \#A = t\},$$

and an element $x \in \mathbb{F}_p$ is secret shared by constructing an additive secret sharing of size $\#\mathcal{T} = \binom{n}{t}$, i.e.

$$x = \sum_{T \in \mathcal{T}} x_T$$

where all but one addends are sampled uniformly at random from $\mathbb{F}_p$, and the last one is selected so that the equation above is satisfied. The shares held by server S_i are exactly those x_T of index T where $i \notin T$. An RSS secret sharing of a field element x is denoted with $[\![x]\!]_R$.

Addtionally, we define $\mathcal{T}_i \subseteq \mathcal{T}$ to be the set of shares held by party S_i, i.e., $\mathcal{T}_i := \{T \in \mathcal{T} \mid i \notin T\}$; the shares held by any pair of servers S_i, S_j as $\mathcal{T}_{ij} := \mathcal{T}_i \cap \mathcal{T}_j$. Each server S_i holds exactly $\binom{n-1}{t}$ shares. $\mathcal{S}_T \subseteq \{1, \ldots, n\}$ is defined as the set of indices of servers holding the share T, $\mathcal{S}_T := \{i \in \{1, \ldots, n\} \mid T \in \mathcal{T}_i\} = \{1, \ldots, n\} \setminus T$; We further define the set of servers holding any pair of shares T_1, T_2 as $\mathcal{S}_{T_1 T_2} := \mathcal{S}_{T_1} \cap \mathcal{S}_{T_2}$. Each share T is held by exactly $n - t$ servers.

By abuse of notation, we denote with $[\![x]\!]_R := ((x_T^i)_{T \in \mathcal{T}_i})_{i=1,\ldots,n}$ the set of shares distributed to the servers by a (possibly corrupt) dealer. Each server S_i receives $(x_T^i)_{T \in \mathcal{T}_i}$ where x_T^i is the share associated to index T. We call $[\![x]\!]_R$ *valid* if $x_T^i = x_T^j$ for all $i, j \in \mathcal{S}_T$ and all $T \in \mathcal{T}$, then $[\![x]\!]_R$ is a replicated secret sharing $[\![x]\!]_R$ of $x = \sum_{T \in \mathcal{T}} x_T^i$; Otherwise the sharing is called *invalid*, and it does not correspond to an RSS sharing of a field element.

Theorem 1 (t-Privacy of Replicated Secret Sharing). *Let $[\![x]\!]_R$ be an RSS of x distributed to n parties. For any subset of parties $\mathcal{S}$, with $|\mathcal{S}| \leq t$, the following conditions hold:*

1. The view of the parties in $\mathcal{S}$ reveals no information about the secret x. Formally, for any secret x and any possible shares $s_1, s_2, \ldots, s_t$ held by the parties in $\mathcal{S}$,
$$\mathbb{P}[x | (x_T^1)_{T \in \mathcal{T}_1}, (x_T^2)_{T \in \mathcal{T}_2}, \ldots, (x_T^t)_{T \in \mathcal{T}_t}] = \mathbb{P}[x].$$

2. The shares of the parties in $\mathcal{S}$ can be perfectly simulated. That is, there exists a simulator Sim that generates shares $(\hat{x}_T^1)_{T \in \mathcal{T}_1}$, $(\hat{x}_T^2)_{T \in \mathcal{T}_2}$, …, $(\hat{x}_T^t)_{T \in \mathcal{T}_t}$ indistinguishable from the actual shares, without knowledge of the secret s.

3.1 Doubly Replicated Secret Sharing

We define *Doubly Replicated Secret Sharing* (DRSS) that is widely used in our dOPRF protocol. DRSS is a variation of RSS that maintains the same access structure but features a different distribution of shares. Consequently, it inherently preserves the same security and privacy properties as RSS; specifically, a (t,n)-DRSS scheme satisfies t-privacy and t-security, just like RSS.

Definition 4 (Doubly replicated secret sharing). *The (t,n)-Doubly replicated secret sharing scheme among n servers is defined similarly to RSS, with the exception that the set $\mathcal{T}^2$ is used instead of $\mathcal{T}$ as the set of share indices.*

An element $x \in \mathbb{F}_p$ is shared by constructing an additive secret sharing of size $\#\mathcal{T}^2 = \binom{n}{t}^2$,
$$x = \sum_{T_1, T_2 \in \mathcal{T}} x_{T_1 T_2},$$
where all but one addends are sampled uniformly at random from $\mathbb{F}_p$, and the last one is selected so that the equation above is satisfied. The shares held by server S_i are exactly those $x_{T_1 T_2}$ where $i \notin T_1 \cup T_2$.

Each server S_i holds shares $\{T_1 T_2 | T_1 \in \mathcal{T}_i, T_2 \in \mathcal{T}_i\}$, and that the share $x_{T_1 T_2}$ is held exactly by servers $\mathcal{S}_{T_1 T_2}$. In particular each $x_{T_1 T_2}$ is held by at least 1 server when $t < n/2$. Furthermore, as that $n - 2t \leq \#\mathcal{S}_{T_1 T_2}$ so when $t < n/3$, each share is held by at least $t+1$ servers, in particular by at least 1 *honest* server. By abuse of notation, we denote with $[\![x]\!]_D := ((x_{T_1 T_2}^i)_{T_1, T_2 \in \mathcal{T}_i})_{i=1,\ldots,n}$ the set of shares distributed to the servers by a (possibly corrupt) dealer. Each server S_i receives $(x_{T_1 T_2}^i)_{T_1 T_2 \in \mathcal{T}_i}$ where $x_{T_1 T_2}^i$ is the share associated to index $T_1 T_2$. We call $[\![x]\!]_D$ *valid* if $x_{T_1 T_2}^i = x_{T_1 T_2}^j$ for all $i, j \in \mathcal{S}_{T_1 T_2}$ and all $T_1, T_2 \in \mathcal{T}$. Then $[\![x]\!]_D$ is a doubly replicated secret sharing $[\![x]\!]_D$ of $x = \sum_{T_1, T_2 \in \mathcal{T}} x_{T_1 T_2}^i$. Otherwise the sharing is called *invalid*, and it does not correspond to a DRSS sharing of a field element.

4 Building Blocks

In this section, we present the building blocks (sub-protocols) for our full malicious dOPRF protocol in Sect. 5. We use the following notation for share indices, $\dot{\mathcal{T}} \subseteq \{1, \ldots, n\}$ (ASS), $\dot{\mathcal{T}} = \mathcal{T}$ (RSS) or $\dot{\mathcal{T}} = \mathcal{T}^2$ (DRSS), and the corresponding server set ($I \subseteq \dot{\mathcal{T}}$ for ASS or $\{1, \ldots, n\}$ for RSS/DRSS). We assume all protocols design in a RSS-(t,n) malicious setting, where there are up to t servers denoted as $\mathcal{S}_{\mathsf{Mal}}$ controlled by an adversary $\mathcal{A}$ that arbitrarily disrupts protocol execution, no less than $n - t$ servers denoted as $\mathcal{S}_{\mathsf{Hon}}$ honestly follow protocol.

Generating Random Secret Shares. Random secret shares are used both as common reference strings shared among different parties as well as to mask and hide data and secret shares. Due to page limit, we list those very basic primitives from which our protocols are built upon without showing their concrete construction. We assume all secret sharing are *Random secret sharing*; We define $\mathcal{F}_{\mathsf{GenRand}}$ as the ideal functionality that receives a command from a group of servers, and outputs corresponding random secret sharing of a random field element to all servers; we define $\mathcal{F}_{\mathsf{GenZero}}$ as the ideal functionality that receives a command from a group of servers and outputs corresponding random secret sharing of zero to all servers.

RSS to RSS Multiplication. The first multiplication for computing the Legendre PRF occurs during the setup phase, where servers compute $[\![s]\!]_R, [\![s]\!]_R \mapsto [\![s^2]\!]_R$, meaning that both the inputs and the output are RSS shares. We implement this using an optimization method based on [36]. We have included the detailed ideal functionality and its discussion in Appendix A.

4.1 RSS to RSS Multiplication with Opening

The second multiplication in Fig. 1 is computed in the online phase, where the servers compute $[\![x+k]\!]_R [\![s^2]\!]_R$ and the client is expecting a result $(x + k)s^2$ revealed to him. We define the ideal functionality of multiplication with opening in Fig. 2 as $\mathcal{F}_{\mathsf{MulOpen}}$, in which there are n servers $\{S_1, \cdots, S_n\}$ perform multiply-and-open to a receiver $S_j, j \in \{1, \cdots, n\}$. A naive way realizing $\mathcal{F}_{\mathsf{MulOpen}}$ is to first invoke $\mathcal{F}_{\mathsf{Mul}}$ which outputs $[\![(x+k)s^2]\!]_R$, and then reveal it to receiver S_j. However, we emphasize that this is communication inefficient (large communication volume in 2 rounds). Instead, we propose a new protocol 1 that computes $\mathcal{F}_{\mathsf{MulOpen}}$ in one round with fewer communication volumes.

In protocol 1, servers invoke $\mathcal{F}_{\mathsf{GenZero}}$ to obtain a DRSS share of zero $[\![z]\!]_D = (z_{T_1 T_2})_{T_1, T_2 \in \mathcal{T}}$ to mask later computed local products, additionally. Note this step can also be pre-computed in the setup phase for better online efficiency. With that, for $i \in \{1, \cdots, n\}$ each server i could locally compute the DRSS terms

$$o_{T_1 T_2} := a_{T_1} b_{T_2} + z_{T_1 T_2}, (T_1, T_2 \in \mathcal{T}_i)$$

for every $T_1, T_2 \in \mathcal{T}_i$. All these local terms from all servers in total constitute a random DRSS sharing of product ab, and they can be returned directly to receiver S_j. Upon receiving messages from all servers, the receiver S_j compares the consistency of $o^i_{T_1 T_2}$ for each $i \in \mathcal{S}_{T_1 T_2}, T_1 T_2 \in \mathcal{T}$. Only if all verification pass that S_j accepts the result $v = \sum_{T_1, T_2 \in \mathcal{T}} o_{T_1 T_2}$, otherwise it rejects.

Efficiency. Each server transmits $\binom{n-1}{t}^2$ elements to the receiver S_j. Let $D = \binom{n}{t}^2$ denote the number of Doubly Replicated Secret Sharing (DRSS) shares of zero in Π_{dOPRF}. Note that for one party holding $\binom{n-1}{t}^2$ DRSS shares, generating each DRSS share requires $D-1$ PRG calls. Therefore, generating DRSS shares of zero requires a total of $n\binom{n-1}{t}^2(D-1)$ PRG calls.

Security. Informally, we demonstrate how protocol 1 ensures both *verifiability* and *privacy*. $\mathcal{S}_{\mathsf{Hon}}$ has access to all RSS shares of a and b, enabling them to generate DRSS shares of ab for every share index pair $T_1, T_2 \in \mathcal{T}$. This redundancy allows for the detection of any additive attack from $\mathcal{S}_{\mathsf{Mal}}$ (verifiability).

We now address the privacy of (a,b) with respect to the receiver S_j, assuming $S_j \in \mathcal{S}_{\mathsf{Mal}}$. Assume in the worst case that $\mathcal{A}$ controls t servers, denote $\hat{s} := \{\alpha, \beta, \cdots\}$ as the set contains all indices of servers from $\mathcal{S}_{\mathsf{Mal}}$, note adversary $\mathcal{A}$ is able to learn all RSS shares of a or b except for the share index $\hat{T} := \hat{s}$. Thus, $\mathcal{A}$ learns nothing about DRSS shares of ab with those share indices in set

$$\hat{\mathcal{T}} = \{\hat{T}T_1, \ldots, \hat{T}T_{\max}\} \cup \{T_1\hat{T}, \ldots, T_{\max}\hat{T}\}.$$

Players: $S_1, \ldots, S_n$ and the ideal functionality $\mathcal{F}_{\mathsf{MulOpen}}$.
Input: $\mathcal{S}_{\mathsf{Hon}}$ inputs their shares $(a_T, b_T)_{T \in \mathcal{T}_i}$ to $\mathcal{F}_{\mathsf{MulOpen}}$, $\mathcal{S}_{\mathsf{Mal}}$ gives input $d \in \mathbb{F}_p$ to $\mathcal{F}_{\mathsf{MulOpen}}$.
Computation: $\mathcal{F}_{\mathsf{MulOpen}}$ reconstructs a, b from received RSS shares of $\mathcal{S}_{\mathsf{Hon}}$, computes $c = ab + d$.
Output: If $d = 0$, $\mathcal{F}_{\mathsf{MulOpen}}$ outputs (c, accept) to S_j. Otherwise, it outputs (c, reject) to S_j.

Fig. 2. Ideal functionality $\mathcal{F}_{\mathsf{MulOpen}}$ - RSS Multiplication with opening up to additive attack.

In another word, $\hat{\mathcal{T}}$ of size $2\binom{n}{t} - 1$ contains indices for which the corresponding DRSS terms that are known only to $\mathcal{S}_{\mathsf{Hon}}$. Each DRSS share with index in $\hat{\mathcal{T}}$ is masked by a random number that is known only to $\mathcal{S}_{\mathsf{Hon}}$, thus, $\mathcal{A}$ learns nothing about each individual product $a_{T_1} b_{T_2}$ for every $T_1, T_2 \in \hat{\mathcal{T}}$. Consequently, there is no leakage (*privacy*) in Protocol 1.

5 The Legendre dOPRF Protocol

In the framework of Fig. 1, if a malicious client colludes with $t' \leq t < n/3$ servers, protocol 1 is not applicable because we cannot guarantee that the input RSS of x is valid; that is, each server in $\mathcal{S}_{\mathsf{Hon}}$ must receive identical RSS shares corresponding to the same RSS index. For this reason, we first define the desired ideal functionality $\mathcal{F}_{\mathsf{dOPRF}}$ in Fig. 3 and then present our adapted protocol 2 that securely computes $\mathcal{F}_{\mathsf{dOPRF}}$ against an adversary $\mathcal{A}$ that controls both the client and $t' \leq t < n/3$ servers.

Protocol 1. Verifiable RSS multiplication with opening in the $\mathcal{F}_{\mathsf{GenZero}}$-hybrid model

Players: Server $S_1, \ldots, S_n$.
Input : $[\![a]\!]_R, [\![b]\!]_R$
Output: (v, accept) or (v, reject).

1 Servers invoke $\mathcal{F}_{\mathsf{GenZero}}$ to obtain $[\![z]\!]_D$.
2 **for** *each server from* $S_1, \ldots, S_n$ **do**
3   **for** $T_1, T_2 \in \mathcal{T}_i$ **do**
4   Compute $o^i_{T_1 T_2} = a^i_{T_1} b^i_{T_2} + z_{T_1 T_2}$.
5   **return** $\{o^i_{T_1 T_2}\}_{T_1, T_2 \in \mathcal{T}_i}$ to receiver S_R.
6 S_j proceeds once it receives all messages.
7 **for** $T_1, T_2 \in \mathcal{T}$ **do**
8   **for** $i \in \mathcal{S}_{T_1, T_2}$ **do**
9   **if** o_{T_1, T_2} *is not set* **then**
10   Set $o_{T_1, T_2} = o^i_{T_1, T_2}$.
11   **else**
12   **if** $o^i_{T_1, T_2} \neq o_{T_1, T_2}$ **then**
13   Outputs (v, reject) and aborts.
14 Outputs $(v = \sum_{T_1, T_2 \in \mathcal{T}} o_{T_1, T_2}, \mathsf{accept})$.

5.1 Ideal Functionality in the Malicious Setting

We assume that an adversary $\mathcal{A}$ corrupts $t' \leq t < n/3$ servers and the client in Fig. 1, and $\mathcal{A}$ might act arbitrarily the way he desires. Specifically, the adversary $\mathcal{A}$ may compromise the client to submit inconsistent replicated secret shares (RSS) of x to the honest servers in order to extract k. Additionally, $\mathcal{A}$ may corrupt t' servers to launch an additive attack during the multiply-and-open operations among the servers.

Thus, in Fig. 3 we are able to define the desired ideal functionality $\mathcal{F}_{\mathsf{dOPRF}}$ in the $(\mathcal{F}_{\mathsf{GenZero}}, \mathcal{F}_{\mathsf{GenRand}})$-hybrid model. $\mathcal{F}_{\mathsf{dOPRF}}$ interacts with the client and all n servers in the online phase. It serves as an ideal functionality that inputs $x \in \mathbb{F}_p$ or $\perp$ from the client, honest RSS shares of k, s^2 from $\mathcal{S}_{\mathsf{Hon}}$ and z from $\mathcal{A}$, and outputs to the client a computation result $(\alpha \in \{r \leftarrow_\$ \mathbb{F}_p, (x+k)s^2 + d\}, \mathsf{status} \in \{\mathsf{accept}, \mathsf{reject}\})$.

With the definition of the ideal functionality in Fig. 3, it is clear that when $\mathcal{A}$ inputs $\perp$ (modeling inconsistent RSS in real world) to $\mathcal{F}_{\mathsf{dOPRF}}$, the adversary learns only a random element $r \in \mathbb{F}_p$ after computation, thus gains no information of k or s^2. On the other hand, for $\mathcal{A}$ that controls t' servers, he cannot force an honest client to accept a computation result $c = (x+k)s^2 + d$ when $d \neq 0$.

Players: Server S_i; $i = 1, \ldots, n$, the client and $\mathcal{F}_{\mathsf{dOPRF}}$.
Input: Client inputs $x \in \mathbb{F}_p$ or $\perp$ to $\mathcal{F}_{\mathsf{dOPRF}}$. Denotes s^2 as b, $\mathcal{S}_{\mathsf{Hon}}$ inputs their shares $(k_T, b_T)_{T \in \mathcal{T}_i}$ to $\mathcal{F}_{\mathsf{dOPRF}}$, $\mathcal{A}$ gives input $d \in \mathbb{F}_p$ to $\mathcal{F}_{\mathsf{dOPRF}}$.
Computation: If the client inputs $x \in \mathbb{F}_p$, $\mathcal{F}_{\mathsf{dOPRF}}$ reconstructs k, b from received RSS shares of $\mathcal{S}_{\mathsf{Hon}}$, computes $c = (x + k)b + d$.
Output: If $x \in \mathbb{F}_p$, when $d = 0$, $\mathcal{F}_{\mathsf{dOPRF}}$ outputs (c, accept) to client and (c, reject) otherwise. When $x = \perp$, set $c = r$ where r is uniformly randomly selected from $\mathbb{F}_p$, $\mathcal{F}_{\mathsf{dOPRF}}$ outputs (r, reject) to the client.

Fig. 3. Ideal functionality $\mathcal{F}_{\mathsf{dOPRF}}$ up to additive attack.

5.2 Malicious Legendre dOPRF Protocol

A straightforward approach to implementing $\mathcal{F}_{\mathsf{dOPRF}}$ involves first verifying the consistency of the client's inputs among $\mathcal{S}_{\mathsf{Hon}}$. This verification process requires each participating server to confirm with every other server that holds the same RSS share. If any inconsistent RSS share of x is detected, the servers collectively output $[r]$, generated by $\mathcal{F}_{\mathsf{GenRand}}$, and then issue a reject signal. Otherwise, $\mathcal{F}_{\mathsf{MulOpen}}$ is invoked to compute $(x + k)s^2$. However, even realizing $\mathcal{F}_{\mathsf{MulOpen}}$ with our communication optimized protocol 1, this method of verifying client inputs leads to still three communication rounds.

In this subsection, we adapt protocol 1 to protocol 2 that realize $\mathcal{F}_{\mathsf{dOPRF}}$ in two rounds, which is also denoted as Π_{dOPRF} throughout. To check potential inconsistent RSS of x submitted to $\mathcal{S}_{\mathsf{Hon}}$, we introduce a small change in protocol 2: for every $T_1T_2 \in \mathcal{T}$, we have each server $i \in \mathcal{S}_{T_1T_2}$ send $v_{T_1T_2}^i = o_{T_1T_2}^i + (x_{T_1}^i + r_{T_1}^i)\hat{z}_{T_1T_2}^i$ to the client instead of $o_{T_1T_2}^i$ as in protocol 1, where $[r]$ is a random ASS among all servers and $\hat{z}_{T_1T_2}$ is an ASS shared among $\mathcal{S}_{T_1T_2}$. With this change, only if all honest parties receive consistent shares of x can the client reconstruct $o_{T_1T_2}$. Otherwise, the client receives random messages and learns nothing of k or s^2. In other words, if the client acts maliciously and sends an invalid RSS of x to $\mathcal{S}_{\mathsf{Hon}}$, the client will receive a random output, preventing the adversary from deducing any useful information. However, above change in protocol 2 breaks the verifiability by an honest client against additive attack. To remedy this loss, we have each server send additionally one single hash output h_i computed over $\{o_{T_1T_2}^i\}_{T_1,T_2 \in \mathcal{T}_i}$ to the client. After an honest client reconstructs $\{o_{T_1T_2}\}_{T_1,T_2 \in \mathcal{T}}$, for each $i \in [n]$ he recomputes his own hash output over $\{o_{T_1T_2}\}_{T_1,T_2 \in \mathcal{T}_i}$ and compares it to h_i, he accepts $\{o_{T_1T_2}\}_{T_1,T_2 \in \mathcal{T}}$ only if all checks pass. Here, altogether servers send $n\left(\binom{n-1}{t}^2 + 1\right)$ field elements to the client. For the detailed security proof of protocol 2, please refer it in Appendix B.

Client Verifiability. Consider a scenario where an honest client interacts with up to t servers that may be controlled by an adversary $\mathcal{A}$. In this setting, we assert

Protocol 2. Legendre dOPRF in the $(\mathcal{F}_{\mathsf{GenZero}}, \mathcal{F}_{\mathsf{GenRand}})$-hybrid model (Π_{dOPRF})

Players: Server S_i for $i = 1, \ldots, n$ and a client.
Input : $x \in \mathbb{F}_p$ by client, $[\![s^2]\!]_R$ and $[\![k]\!]_R$ by servers.
Output: (c, status).

1 Client computes a RSS of $x = \sum_{T \in \mathcal{T}} x_T$, then sends $(x_T)_{T \in \mathcal{T}_i}$ to server S_i for each $i \in \{1, \ldots, n\}$.
2 Servers invoke $\mathcal{F}_{\mathsf{GenZero}}$ to obtain $[\![z]\!]_D$, $[\![\hat{z}_{T_1 T_2}]\!]$ among $\mathcal{S}_{T_1 T_2}$ for each $T_1, T_2 \in \mathcal{T}$; additionally, they invoke $\mathcal{F}_{\mathsf{GenRand}}$ to obtain $[\![r]\!]_R$.
3 Let $[\![a]\!]_R = [\![x + k]\!]_R, [\![b]\!]_R = [\![s^2]\!]_R$.
4 **for** *each server i from $S_1, \ldots, S_n$* **do**
5   Set $H = \epsilon$.
6   **for** $T_1, T_2 \in \mathcal{T}_i$ **do**
7   Compute $o^i_{T_1 T_2} = a^i_{T_1} b^i_{T_2} + z_{T_1 T_2}$.
8   Update $H = H \| o^i_{T_1 T_2}$.
9   Compute $v^i_{T_1 T_2} = o^i_{T_1 T_2} + (x^i_{T_1} + r^i_{T_1}) \hat{z}^i_{T_1 T_2}$.
10   Compute $h_i = \mathsf{Hash}(H)$.
11   **return** $(\{v^i_{T_1 T_2}\}_{T_1, T_2 \in \mathcal{T}_i}, h_i)$ to client.
12 Once the client receives all messages, it proceeds as follows.
13 Set $v = 0$.
14 **for** $T_1, T_2 \in \mathcal{T}$ **do**
15   Computes $v_{T_1, T_2} = \frac{1}{\#\mathcal{S}_{T_1, T_2}} \sum_{i \in \mathcal{S}_{T_1, T_2}} v^i_{T_1, T_2}$.
16   Accumulates $v = v + v_{T_1, T_2}$.
17 **for** $i = 1, \ldots, n$ **do**
18   Set $H = \epsilon$.
19   **for** $T_1, T_2 \in \mathcal{T}_i$ **do**
20   Update $H = H \| v_{T_1 T_2}$.
21   If $h_i \neq \mathsf{Hash}(H)$, outputs (v, reject).
22 Outputs (v, accept).

the verification algorithm described in the reconstruction stage of protocol 2 is an efficient verification algorithm such that:

- If client inputs inconsistent RSS shares of x to $\mathcal{S}_{\mathsf{Hon}}$, client receives (r, reject);
- Otherwise, if $\mathcal{S}_{\mathsf{Mal}}$ inputs $d \in \mathbb{F}_p$ in the additive attack, client receives

$$c, \mathsf{status} = \begin{cases} (x+k)s^2 + d, \mathsf{reject} & \text{if } d \neq 0, \\ (x+k)s^2, \mathsf{accept} & \text{otherwise.} \end{cases}$$

This verifiability ensures that an honest client can reliably verify whether the protocol execution was free from disruptions, in the presence of up to t corrupted servers.

5.3 Full Security of the Legendre PRF

Theorem 2 establish that securely evaluating a single bit of the Legendre PRF in an oblivious manner is guaranteed, assuming up to $t < n/3$ malicious servers. This ensures that either the protocol runs honestly, or if there is a malicious party, no one gains any information about the secret values. As a result, the oblivious Legendre PRF effectively simulates an idealized Legendre PRF oracle $\mathcal{F}_{\mathsf{dOPRF}}$. The security of the PRF, where an attacker has access to the Legendre PRF oracle $\mathcal{F}_{\mathsf{dOPRF}}$, is based on the DSLSP Assumption. The most effective known attacks against the DSLSP Assumption are key-extraction attacks [24, 34, 35]. Given that an attacker can query the PRF M times, the classical attack requires $O(M^2 \log p)$ memory and has a runtime of $O(\frac{p \log p \log \log p}{M^2})$, while the quantum attack uses $\tilde{O}(M^2)$ classical memory with quantum random access and has a runtime of $\tilde{O}(\sqrt{\frac{p}{M^2}})$. Under these conditions, the protocol offers $\lambda_c = \lambda$ bits of classical security and $\lambda_q = 2\lambda/3$ bits of quantum security when the underlying prime p is of size 2λ.

On Partial Obliviousness. A partially oblivious PRF (pOPRF) is an OPRF whose input is divided into a private and a public part $x = (x_{\mathrm{pub}}, x_{\mathrm{priv}})$. There are generic transformations ([13], Sect. 3.1) to construct a pOPRF from an OPRF, which can also be employed in our construction. Let $\{F_k\}$ be an OPRF, let $\{G_k\}$ be a PRF. Then, the function $F'_k(x_{\mathrm{pub}}, x_{\mathrm{priv}}) := F_{G_k(x_{\mathrm{pub}})}(x_{\mathrm{priv}})$ is a pOPRF. Given a fixed RSS secret sharing of a key $k = \sum_{T \in \mathcal{T}} k_T$, we define $k' = \sum_{T \in \mathcal{T}} G_{k_T}(x_{\mathrm{pub}})$ to be an updated OPRF key, which we can also denote as $G'(k) = k'$. Here G' is a PRF function, which is not only a function on k, but on the randomness involved in splitting k into RSS shares. The new key k' can be computed from the public PRF G, the local shares k_T and the public part of the input x_{pub}. The partially oblivious Legendre PRF is defined to be the Legendre OPRF computed with the updated key k', both in the semi-honest and malicious setting.

On Adaptive Adversaries. An adaptive adversary is an adversarial model in which the set of corrupted servers can change over time. However, the adversary stays constrained to control at most t corrupted servers at a time. Our protocol can be made adaptively secure by updating all long term secret data at regular time intervals. These include the key $[\![k]\!]_R$, as well as random secret sharing generated from $\mathcal{F}_{\mathsf{GenZero}}$ and $\mathcal{F}_{\mathsf{GenRand}}$.

6 Evaluation

We first conduct an asymptotic comparison of our protocol Π_{dOPRF} with state-of-the-art MPC protocols for computing the Legendre symbol. Subsequently, we implemented Π_{dOPRF} in C++ and compared it to other OPRF solutions, in our implementation we use the BLAKE3 [37] as a hash function and also as a PRF for generating randomness. Our code is available at GitHub[1]. All our tests are on

---

[1] https://github.com/nann-cheng/d-OPRF.

a single server with 32GB RAM, 12th Gen Intel(R) Core(TM) i7-12700K CPU model that ran Ubuntu 22.04 LTS. Finally, in the same context, we performed local benchmarking on all sub-procedures of Π_{dOPRF}. Due to page limitations, the results are not included here; interested readers are referred to the full version [33].

6.1 Comparison to State-of-the-Art MPC

We compare our protocol Π_{dOPRF} to two state-of-the-art MPC solutions proposed by Dalskov et al. [15] and Chida et al. [14] and present our results in Table 2. Specifically, we consider the same but practical outsourced computation model with one client and a few servers, where one or two servers are corrupted. Note that we adapt the computation of $\mathcal{C}_{\mathsf{PRF}}$ to fit our desired outsourced computation model for [14,15].

Table 2. Concrete efficiency comparison to State-of-the-art MPC.

Reference	Scheme	Comm.	No Inter-Server Comm.	Rounds
Our Π_{dOPRF}	RSS-(1,4)	52	✓	2
Dalskov19[15]	RSS-(1,4)	36	✗	3
Chida23[14]	RSS-(1,3)	201	✗	9
Our Π_{dOPRF}	RSS-(2,7)	1687	✓	2
Chida23[14]	RSS-(2,5)	745	✗	9
Chida23[14]	SSS-(2,5)	445	✗	9

Table 3. Comparison between our work and state-of-the-art OPRF solutions. Superscript * indicates estimated numbers adapted to our WAN setting.

Protocol	λ	Primitive	Comm.[KB] Offline	Comm.[KB] Online	Rounds	Runtime [ms] Offline	Runtime [ms] Online
PESTO [10]	128	Pairing, ECDSA	–	–	2	–	260*
GC-OPRF [21]	128	GC, AES-128	–	4634	4	–	1842
Legendre-OPRF [11]	128	OT, ZK	–	911	9	–	1049*
Our Π_{dOPRF}	128	RSS-(1,4)	432	144	2	204	215
Our Π_{dOPRF}	128	RSS-(2,7)	93900	6303	2	1076	815
GC-OPRF [21]	256	GC, AES-256	–	6628	4	–	2320
Our Π_{dOPRF}	256	RSS-(1,4)	1728	579	2	208	637

In Chida et al. [14], the authors propose a general MPC framework designed for settings with an honest majority in the presence of $t < n/2$ malicious adversaries. This allows more room for adversarial behaviours than our work, which allows less corruptions with $t < n/3$. Their framework is modular and applicable to any arbitrary arithmetic circuit, and it consists four stages: *Input Sharing, Circuit Emulation, Verification,* and *Output Reconstruction.* However, their solution is not as efficient when applied to our proposed dOPRF. More precisely, for computing the circuit C_{PRF}, regardless of the underlying secret sharing scheme used, the framework requires 7 invocations of $\mathcal{F}_{rand}$, 6 invocations of $\mathcal{F}_{mul}$, and 8 invocations of $\mathcal{F}_{open}$ over 9 rounds. If using RSS-(t,n) where $(t, n) = (1, 3)$, assuming the underlying semi-honest sub-protocol $\mathcal{F}_{mul}$ is instantiated by a naive protocol consuming 24 elements in one round, $\mathcal{F}_{open}$ instantiated with 6 elements, this results in a total communication volume of 201 elements. When $(t, n) = (2, 5)$, assuming the underlying semi-honest sub-protocol $\mathcal{F}_{mul}$ is instantiated by the protocol in [17], which requires opening two masked elements among all parties, the communication volume would total 745 elements. Alternatively, if using Shamir Secret Sharing in the setting $(t, n) = (2, 5)$, communication-wise, the realization of $\mathcal{F}_{mul}$ requires 20 elements and $\mathcal{F}_{open}$ also requires 20 elements, resulting a total communication of 445 elements.

In the work of Dalskov et al. [15], they consider a setting of four parties where one party might be an active adversary, the authors propose a novel method performing multiplication as well as identifying cheating. This method incurs a total of 12 elements exchanged for each multiplication operation. Including the communication cost for the input and output stages, the total communication volume amounts to 36 elements over 3 rounds.

In Table 2, with one corrupt server, we compared our protocol to the solution built from Fantastic Four [15] that used both RSS-(1,4) and the solution from [14] built from RSS-(1,3); with two corrupt servers, we compared our protocol instantiated from RSS-(2,7) to the solution from [14] built from two secret sharing schemes, *i.e.* RSS-(2,5) and SSS-(2,5). As clearly shown in Table 2, only our work Π_{dOPRF} offers the advantage of no inter-server communication. In the setting of one corrupt server, since computation and communication are less dominant than communication delay, our protocol Π_{dOPRF} exhibits a clear advantage over the state-of-the-art. With two corrupt servers, our protocol Π_{dOPRF} requires roughly double or triple the communication volume than in [14], regardless of this higher volume cost, we argue with much fewer rounds required in our work: 2 rounds compared to 9 rounds, our protocol Π_{dOPRF} would be more efficient than [14] in this application scenario.

6.2 Comparison to State-of-the-Art OPRF

In Table 3, we compare our protocol against state-of-the-art works in terms of computation time and communication volume, covering both the offline and online phases for an output of 128 bits. All evaluations were performed in a simulated WAN environment (50 Mbits bandwidth and 100 ms delay) on a single machine. The compared works fall into two categories: two-party post-quantum OPRF protocols [11,21] and distributed classical OPRF protocols [10].

For each protocol, λ indicates the security level, *Comm* represents the total communication volume, *Rounds* denotes the number of sequential communication rounds in the online phase, and *Runtime* measures evaluation time at various stages. In the offline phase, *Runtime* reflects the total time taken by all parties to complete their tasks. In the online phase, we measure the time from the client's request initiation to obtaining the final OPRF/dOPRF result. The results for [10] are estimates based on figures from Table 1 of [10] (2 servers) adjusted for our WAN setting (200 ms RTT), while the numbers for [11] are sourced from their estimations in Sect. 5.2 under our WAN conditions. For GC-OPRF [21], we executed their code in the simulated WAN setting to obtain corresponding metrics. Notably, for our protocol Π_{dOPRF}, we revised the results to reflect a real distributed server setup, as it is expected to perform better with distributed computations.

Among all protocols that achieve $\lambda = 128$ bit security, our RSS-(1,4) Π_{dOPRF} instantiation protocol demonstrated the best computational and communication efficiency. Under $\lambda = 256$, our RSS-(1,4) Π_{dOPRF} protocol also outperforms the GC-OPRF protocol from [21].

Acknowledgments. This work was partially supported by the Stepping Stone Grant "Privacy-preserving & Distributed Authentication" funded by the University of St. Gallen.

A RSS to RSS Multiplication

Players: Server $S_1, \ldots, S_n$ and the functionality $\mathcal{F}_{\mathsf{Mul}}$.
Input: Every server $S_i \in \mathcal{S}_{\mathsf{Hon}}$ inputs their shares $(a_T, b_T)_{T \in \mathcal{T}_i}$ to $\mathcal{F}_{\mathsf{Mul}}$, while each malicious server inputs whatever input to $\mathcal{F}_{\mathsf{Mul}}$.
Computation: $\mathcal{F}_{\mathsf{Mul}}$ checks if every RSS share submitted by each $S_i \in \mathcal{S}_{\mathsf{Mal}}$ is equal to the one corresponds to the one hold by $\mathcal{S}_{\mathsf{Hon}}$, it outputs $\perp$ if there is any mismatch; otherwise $\mathcal{F}_{\mathsf{Mul}}$ reconstructs a, b from RSS shares sent by $\mathcal{S}_{\mathsf{Hon}}$ and computes $c = ab$, subsequentially a random RSS of c as $[\![c]\!]_R$.
Output: $\mathcal{F}_{\mathsf{Mul}}$ outputs corresponding RSS shares of $[\![c]\!]_R$ to all servers.

Fig. 4. Ideal functionality $\mathcal{F}_{\mathsf{Mul}}$ - RSS Multiplication with abort.

We define the ideal functionality of $\mathcal{F}_{\mathsf{Mul}}$ in Fig. 4. Maurer [36] in Protocol 6.2 provides maliciously secure multiplication in a similar fashion. They check for malicious behaviour by comparing the received shares and then opening the difference of all shares to confirm that parties indeed computed secret shares of the same product term $a_{T_1} b_{T_2}$. However, this approach takes three communication rounds and is communication costly.

We opt for a more efficient approach where the parties are assumed to hold a pre-shared DRSS random seed $[\![s]\!]_D$, and they use their seed share $s_{T_1 T_2}$ to compute the RSS sharing of each product term $[\![a_{T_1} b_{T_2}]\!]_R$. This way the parties can check for malicious behaviour without the need for additional communication. While this approach reduces the security to that of an underlying PRF function used for randomness generation, this trade-off is fine as the remainder of our protocol also relies on computational security (as opposed to information-theoretic in [36]). Specifically, assume that the servers hold a common seed distributed as a DRSS. In other words let $[\![s]\!]_D = (s_{T_1 T_2})_{T_1, T_2 \in \mathcal{T}}$ be held among the servers. Server i computes $c^{T_1 T_2} := a_{T_1} b_{T_2}$ for each $T_1, T_2 \in \mathcal{T}_i$, and then computes a secret sharing of c_i as $(c_T^{T_1 T_2})_{T \in \mathcal{T}} \leftarrow \mathrm{RSS}(c^{T_1 T_2}; s_{T_1 T_2})$. Each server distributes the RSS shares they computed to all other servers. Upon receiving all shares, the servers verify that the shares received from different parties corresponding to the same shares T_1, T_2, T are all equal, if not they abort, otherwise they compute the RSS of the product as $(ab)_T = \sum_{j=1}^{n} c_{j,T}$. Due to page limit, a detailed description of the protocol in the malicious adversarial setting with $t < n/3$, along with its associated proof, can be found in the full version of this work [33].

B The Security of Π_{dOPRF}

Theorem 2. *Protocol 2 securely computes $\mathcal{F}_{\mathsf{dOPRF}}$ in the $(\mathcal{F}_{\mathsf{GenZero}}, \mathcal{F}_{\mathsf{GenRand}})$-hybrid model with adversary $\mathcal{A}$ controls $t' \leq t < n/3$ servers and the client.*

Proof. We need to prove there exists a PPT simulator Sim, it inputs only the received output (c, status) by the client in the ideal functionality $\mathcal{F}_{\mathsf{dOPRF}}$, such that it's able to output a transcript whose distribution is indistinguishable to the one received by the client in protocol 2. Specifically, the goal is to simulate $v_{T_1 T_2}^i$ for every $i \in \mathcal{S}_{\mathsf{Hon}}, T_1, T_2 \in \hat{\mathcal{T}}$ and $\{h_i\}_{i \in \mathcal{S}_{\mathsf{Hon}}}$. w.l.o.g, assume $t' = t$, which indicates $|\mathcal{S}_{\mathsf{Hon}}| = n - t$, since each honest server holds RSS share index $\hat{T}$ and thus he holds $2\binom{t}{n-1}$ terms whose DRSS share indices are within $\hat{\mathcal{T}}$. Thus, there are in total $I = (n-t)(2\binom{t}{n-1})$ terms sent from $\mathcal{S}_{\mathsf{Hon}}$ corresponds to $\hat{\mathcal{T}}$.

In the case when the client submits consistent RSS of x to $\mathcal{S}_{\mathsf{Hon}}$, to simulate their distribution in this case, let Sim draws randomly field elements $\{r_i\}_{i \in [I-1]}$ from $\mathbb{F}_p$, where $\bar{r}$ is denoted as their sum. Denote $\bar{v} = c - d - \sum_{i \in [I-1]} r_i - \bar{r}$, the list $L = \{r_1, \cdots, r_{I-1}, \bar{v}\}$ of size I is exactly the generated simulation of $v_{T_1 T_2}^i$ for every $i \in \mathcal{S}_{\mathsf{Hon}}, T_1, T_2 \in \hat{\mathcal{T}}$, as the distribution of L is identical to what the client receives in the real world. Then, from L, the simulator is able to compute $o_{T_1 T_2}$ for every $T_1 T_2 \in \hat{\mathcal{T}}$ and hence perfectly computes $\hat{h}_i$ for every $i \in \mathcal{S}_{\mathsf{Hon}}$.

In contrast, when the client provides inconsistent RSS share of x to $\mathcal{S}_{\mathsf{Hon}}$, we analyze the message distribution in the real world. w.l.o.g, we assume that the client submits a valid $[\![x]\!]_R$ except at share index T_*. This means there are inconsistent values for the share x_{T_*} held by $\mathcal{S}_{T_*}$. Formally, we define $\bar{x}^i_{T_*} = e^i + x_{T_*}$, where there exist $i, j \in \mathcal{S}_{T_*}$ such that $e^i \neq e^j$. Here, e^i denotes the error in $\bar{x}^i_{T_*}$. Thus, $\bar{x}^i_{T_*}$ represents a potentially invalid share held by server S_i with share index T_*. Denote $\bar{\mathcal{T}} = \{T_*T_1, \ldots, T_*T_{\max}\}$, for every $T_1T_2 \in \bar{\mathcal{T}}$, observe that in protocol 2 the client reconstructs

$$v_{T_1T_2} = \frac{1}{\#\mathcal{S}_{T_1T_2}} \left(\sum_{i \in \mathcal{S}_{T_1T_2}} a^i_{T_1} b^i_{T_2} \right) + e_{T_1T_2}$$

where $e_{T_1T_2} = \frac{1}{\#\mathcal{S}_{T_1T_2}} \sum_{i \in \mathcal{S}_{T_1T_2}} e^i_{T_1} \hat{z}^i_{T_1T_2}$ is a linear combination result from random numbers that obeys a uniform distribution $\mathcal{U}$, thus the final reconstructed output $v_{T_1T_2}$ is independent of secret a or b. Finally, the client recovers $c = V + E$, where V is related to k and s^2 and $E = \sum_{T_1T_2 \in \bar{\mathcal{T}}} e_{T_1T_2}$ is a random number.

From above analysis, we present the simulator construction in the following, where the simulated view is indistinguishable to that in the execution of protocol 2. To simulate the transcript in the real world from $\mathcal{F}_{\mathsf{dOPRF}}$ output (r, reject):

- Let Sim draw randomly I field elements from $\mathbb{F}_p$ as simulated view transcript for $\hat{v}^i_{T_1T_2}, T_1T_2 \in \hat{\mathcal{T}}, i \in \mathcal{S}_{\mathsf{Hon}}$.
- For each $i \in \mathcal{S}_{\mathsf{Hon}}$, Let Sim draw a random element $\hat{h}_i$ from the output domain of Hash as simulated transcript of $\hat{h}_i$.

Finally, Sim is able to output $\{\{\hat{v}^{T_1T_2}_i\}_{T_1,T_2 \in \mathcal{T}_i}, \hat{h}_i\}_{i \in \mathcal{S}_{\mathsf{Hon}}}$. In the random oracle model, if we draw a random element $\hat{h}_i$ from the output domain of Hash, we argue that any PPT $\mathcal{A}$ cannot distinguish between $\hat{h}_i$ and the real execution output h_i. Thus, $\mathcal{A}$ simulates all transcripts sent from $\mathcal{S}_{\mathsf{Hon}}$ that is computationally indistinguishably to what he receives in the real world.

References

1. Secret sharing schemes realizing general access structures. In: Proceedings of the IEEE Global Telecommunication Conf., Globecom 87, LNCS (1987)
2. Unapproved IEEE draft standard for specifications for password based public key cryptographic techniques. In: IEEE Unapproved Std P1363.2 /D27 (2007)
3. ISO: Information technology — security techniques — key management — part 4: mechanisms based on weak secrets. ISO/IEC, International organization for standardization (2017). https://www.iso.org/standard/67933.html16
4. Agrawal, S., Miao, P., Mohassel, P., Mukherjee, P.: Pasta: password-based threshold authentication. Cryptology ePrint Archive, Paper 2018/885 (2018)
5. Albrecht, M.R., Davidson, A., Deo, A., Gardham, D." Crypto dark matter on the torus: oblivious prfs from shallow prfs and fhe. Cryptology ePrint Archive, Paper 2023/232 (2023)
6. Albrecht, M.R., Davidson, A., Deo, A., Smart, N.P.: Round-optimal verifiable oblivious pseudorandom functions from ideal lattices. Cryptology ePrint Archive, Paper 2019/1271 (2019)

7. Baccarini, A., Blanton, M., Yuan, C.: Multi-party replicated secret sharing over a ring with applications to privacy-preserving machine learning. Cryptology ePrint Archive, Paper 2020/1577 (2020)
8. Basso, A.: A post-quantum round-optimal oblivious prf from isogenies. Cryptology ePrint Archive, Paper 2023/225 (2023)
9. Basso, A., Kutas, P., Merz, S.P., Petit, C., Sanso, A.: Cryptanalysis of an oblivious prf from supersingular isogenies. In: Advances in Cryptology – ASIACRYPT (2021)
10. Baum, C., Frederiksen, T., Hesse, J., Lehmann, A., Yanai, A.: Pesto: proactively secure distributed single sign-on, or how to trust a hacked server. Cryptology ePrint Archive, Paper 2019/1470 (2019)
11. Beullens, W., Dodgson, L., Faller, S., Hesse, J.: The 2hash oprf framework and efficient post-quantum instantiations. Cryptology ePrint Archive, Paper 2024/450 (2024)
12. Boneh, D., Kogan, D., Woo, K.: Oblivious pseudorandom functions from isogenies. Cryptology ePrint Archive, Paper 2020/1532 (2020)
13. Casacuberta, S., Hesse, J., Lehmann, A.: Sok: oblivious pseudorandom functions. Cryptology ePrint Archive, Paper 2022/302 (2022)
14. Chida, K., et al.: Fast large-scale honest-majority mpc for malicious adversaries. J. Cryptol. **36**(3), 15 (2023)
15. Dalskov, A., Escudero, D., Keller, M.: Fantastic four:{Honest-Majority}{Four-Party} secure computation with malicious security. In: 30th USENIX Security Symposium (USENIX Security 21), pp. 2183–2200 (2021)
16. Damgård, I.: On the randomness of Legendre and Jacobi sequences. In: Proceedings of the 8th Annual International Cryptology Conference on Advances in Cryptology, CRYPTO 88, pp. 163–172, London, UK, UK, Springer-Verlag (1990)
17. Damgård, I., Nielsen, J.B.: Scalable and unconditionally secure multiparty computation. In: Annual International Cryptology Conference, pp. 572–590. Springer (2007)
18. Das, P., Hesse, J., Lehmann, A.: Dpase: distributed password-authenticated symmetric encryption. Cryptology ePrint Archive, Paper 2020/1443 (2020)
19. Dinur, I., et al.: Mpc-friendly symmetric cryptography from alternating moduli: candidates, protocols, and applications. In: Malkin, T., Peikert, C. (eds.) Advances in Cryptology – CRYPTO 2021 (2021)
20. Dodgson, L.: https://ethz.ch/content/dam/ethz/special-interest/infk/inst-infsec/appliedcrypto/education/theses/Master_Thesis_Post_Quantum_Building_blocks_for_secure_computation.pdf (2023)
21. Faller, S., Ottenhues, A., Ottenhues, J.: Composable oblivious pseudo-random functions via garbled circuits. Cryptology ePrint Archive, Paper 2023/1176 (2023)
22. Feist, D.: Legendre pseudo-random function (2019). https://legendreprf.org/bounties
23. Freedman, M.J., Ishai, Y., Pinkas, B., Reingold, O.: Keyword search and oblivious pseudorandom functions. In: Kilian, J. (ed.) Theory of Cryptography, pp. 303–324, Springer, Berlin, Heidelberg (2005)
24. Frixons, P., Schrottenloher, A.: Quantum security of the legendre prf. Cryptology ePrint Archive, Paper 2021/149 (2021)
25. Grassi, L., Rechberger, C., Rotaru, D., Scholl, P., Smart, N.P.: MPC-friendly symmetric key primitives. In: Proceedings of the 2016 ACM SIGSAC Conference on Computer and Communications Security, CCS 2016, pp. 430–443, New York, NY, USA, ACM (2016)
26. Grover, L.K.: A fast quantum mechanical algorithm for database search (1996)

27. Hazay, C., Lindell, Y.: Efficient protocols for set intersection and pattern matching with security against malicious and covert adversaries. Cryptology ePrint Archive, Paper 2009/045 (2009)
28. Bagherzandi, A., Jarecki, S., Saxena, N., Lu, Y.: Password-protected secret sharing. Cryptology ePrint Archive, Paper 2010/561 (2010)
29. Jarecki, S., Kiayias, A., Krawczyk, H.: Round-optimal password-protected secret sharing and t-pake in the password-only model. Cryptology ePrint Archive, Paper 2014/650 (2014)
30. Jarecki, S., Kiayias, A., Krawczyk, H., Xu, J.: Toppss: cost-minimal password-protected secret sharing based on threshold oprf. Cryptology ePrint Archive, Paper 2017/363 (2017)
31. Jarecki, S., Liu, X.: Efficient oblivious pseudorandom function with applications to adaptive ot and secure computation of set intersection (2009)
32. Jarecki, S., Liu, X.: Fast secure computation of set intersection (2010)
33. Kaluderovic, N., Cheng, N., Mitrokotsa, K.: A post-quantum distributed oprf from the legendre prf. *Cryptology ePrint Archive* (2024)
34. Kaluđerović, N., Kleinjung, T., Kostić, D.: Cryptanalysis of the generalised Legendre pseudorandom function. **4**, 267–282 (2020)
35. Kaluđerović, N., Kleinjung, T., Kostic, D.: Improved key recovery on the legendre prf. Cryptology ePrint Archive, Paper 2020/098 (2020)
36. Maurer, U.: Secure multi-party computation made simple. Discret. Appl. Math. **154**, 370–381 (2006)
37. O'Connor, J., Aumasson, J.-P., Neves, S., Zooko, W.-O.: Blake3, one function fast everywhere (2020)

TERRA: Trojan-Resilient Reverse-Firewall for Cryptographic Applications

Chandan Kumar[1(✉)], Nimish Mishra[1], Suvradip Chakraborty[2], Satrajit Ghosh[1], and Debdeep Mukhopadhyay[1]

[1] Indian Institute of Technology, Kharagpur, India
{cchaudhary278,nimish.mishra}@kgpian.iitkgp.ac.in,
{satrajit,debdeep}@cse.iitkgp.ac.in
[2] Visa Research, Palo Alto, California, USA
suvchakr@visa.com

Abstract. Reverse firewalls (RFs), introduced by Mironov and Stephens Davidowitz at Eurocrypt 2015, provide a defence mechanism for cryptographic protocols against subversion attacks. In a subversion setting, an adversary compromises the machines of honest parties, enabling the leakage of their secrets through the protocol transcript. Previous research in this area has established robust guarantees, including resistance against data exfiltration for an RF. In this work, we present a new perspective focused on the implementation specifics of RFs. The inherently untrusted nature of RFs exposes their real-world implementations to the risk of Trojan insertion—an especially pressing issue in today's outsourced supply chain ecosystem. We argue how Trojan-affected RF implementations can compromise their core exfiltration resistance property, leading to a complete breakdown of the RF's security guarantees.

Building on this perspective, we propose an enhanced definition for "Trojan-resilient Reverse Firewalls" (`Tr-RF`), incorporating an additional Trojan resilience property. We then present concrete instantiations of `Tr-RF`s for Coin Tossing (CT) and Oblivious Transfer (OT) protocols, utilizing techniques from Private Circuit III (CCS'16) to convert legacy RFs into `Tr-RF`s. We also give simulation-based proofs to claim the enhanced security guarantees of our `Tr-RF` instantiations. Additionally, we offer concrete implementations of our `Tr-RF` based CT and OT protocols utilizing the Open-Portable Trusted Execution Environment (OP-TEE). Through OP-TEE, we practically realize assumptions made in Private Circuit III that are critical to ensuring `Tr-RF` security, bridging the gap between theoretical models and real-world applications. To the best of our knowledge, this provides the *first* practical implementation of reverse firewalls for any cryptographic functionality. Our work emphasizes the importance of evaluating protocol specifications within *implementation-specific* contexts.

Keywords: Reverse Firewall · Split manufacturing · Trojan-Resilience

1 Introduction

The concept of **Reverse Firewall (RF)** was introduced by Ilya Mironov and Noah Stephens-Davidowitz in [15], addressing a pivotal question: *"Can we design cryptographic protocols that achieve meaningful security when the adversary may arbitrarily tamper with the victim's computer?"*

This concern became especially relevant in the post-Snowden era, which exposed that user hardware and software could be compromised to leak sensitive information, such as through backdoors, often without the user's knowledge [15]. Introduced in [15] and followed up in subsequent works [4-9,11], Reverse Firewalls (RF) serve as a solution to this problem. An RF acts as a firewall, between the user's machine and the external world, sanitizing messages sent and received during cryptographic protocols in a functionality-preserving way. Informally, it achieves the following key objectives:

- *Maintains functionality:* Assuming the user's machine is operating correctly, the RF should not alter the functionality of the protocol.
- *Preserves security:* If a cryptographic protocol ensures security based on the assumption that the user's protocol implementation is not tampered with, the RF maintains the same level of security, irrespective of the behavior of the user's computer.
- *Prevents exfiltration:* If the user's machine is compromised, the RF prevents it from leaking sensitive information to the external environment.

Trust Assumptions on RFs: Note that, in this setting, the RF is not considered a trusted third party and does not have access to the user's internal secrets or private states. Its access is strictly limited to the public parameters, as well as the incoming and outgoing messages of the protocol. The RF's primary role is to modify the protocol transcript in a manner that ensures no adversary, even one with control over the user's machine, can exfiltrate information or embed covert signals within the protocol transcripts via the RF. Consequently, in subversion settings, the security of a cryptographic protocol relies critically on the correct implementation of the RFs. More specifically, if an RF fails to modify the protocol transcript as prescribed, it can lead to information leakage, defeating the very purpose of using RFs. To further motivate this, let us consider the case of a simple two-party coin tossing protocol, where Alice and Bob engage in a protocol to agree on a random bit. Alice initially commits to a bit by sending a commitment com to Bob. Now if Alice's implementation is tampered, it may maliciously choose the commitment string com (say by choosing a bad randomness to commit or reverse sampling the commitment string until the commitment string starts with a fixed number of zeros) to covertly exfiltrate some signal or some information about Alice's internal secret state. In an RF setting, a correctly implemented RF randomises com and mitigates the possibility of such leakage. Thus, to provide security against such a malicious implementation, we implicitly assume that the RF will randomise the protocol transcript according to the specification. However, a subverted implementation of RF might not follow the protocol description and may not randomise com in the prescribed manner. That will break all the security guarantees of such a system. Furthermore, in today's outsourced supply chain ecosystem, malicious actors can embed Trojans [17] within RF implementations. Such Trojan-affected RF implementations can compromise their exfiltration resistance property, leading to a complete breakdown of the RF's security guarantees.

One might argue that composing multiple reverse firewalls $\{RF_1, \cdots, RF_m\}$, to form a single secure reverse firewall could address this issue, assuming that at least one RF_i maintains functional correctness and adheres to the protocol description—a property referred to as *stackability* in [15]. However, this approach still relies on the existence of at least one functionally correct and secure RF, which is challenging to ensure in practice. In this paper, we address this issue by considering the following question:

Is it possible to propose a generic and practical implementation framework that facilitates secure implementation of a reverse firewall?

We affirmatively answer this question and present the first practical implementation of reverse firewalls for two cryptographic functionalities: coin tossing and oblivious transfer. Our approach leverages a *split manufacturing* framework [12] for implementing reverse firewalls, where the RF circuit is divided into multiple sub-circuits connected through a simple master circuit. The master circuit, implemented in-house, serves as the root of trust. This framework ensures that even if the sub-circuits are tampered with, a correct implementation of the master circuit guarantees the functional correctness of the RF. We require the master circuit to be as *simple* as possible, comprising a minimal number of wires and basic gates. Importantly, the size of the master circuit remains independent of the complexity of the RF specification. Further, we define the concept of trojan-resilient RF (Tr-RF) and prove that one can take any RF specification and make it trojan-resilient using the proposed framework.

1.1 Our Contributions:

Trojan Resilient Reverse Firewall. We introduce the concept of a Trojan-Resilient Reverse Firewall (Tr-RF). In Sect. 3, we formally define the key properties required for a Tr-RF: *robust functionality maintenance, robust security preservation*, and *robust exfiltration resistance*. These properties generalize and strengthen the standard security requirements of a reverse firewall, namely functionality maintenance, security preservation, and exfiltration resistance. We show that any standard exfiltration-resistant RF [15] can be combined with a robust Trojan protection scheme (Definition 1) to obtain a Tr-RF that achieves robust exfiltration resistance.

An Implementation Framework for Tr-RF. We propose a framework for transforming any legacy RF into a Tr-RF using the robust trojan protection scheme, Private Circuit III [12]. This framework decomposes the RF specification into sub-circuit specifications, which are interconnected through a master circuit M. By designating M as the root of trust, the sub-circuits can be securely combined to construct a Tr-RF. The design of M is kept as simple as possible, as it is expected to be developed in-house, while the implementation of more complex

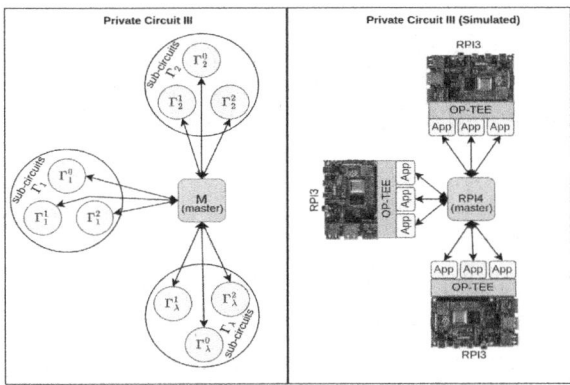

Fig. 1. Trojan-resilient circuit architecture and its simulation using the Raspberry Pi OP-TEE framework, where trusted components are shown in green and untrusted components in grey. (Color figure online)

sub-circuits can be outsourced to external agents. With a trusted implementation of M, the resulting Tr-RF remains secure even if the sub-circuits are compromised. Note that for our implementation, we extend the Trojan protection scheme for boolean addition and multiplication in Private Circuit III [12] to arithmetic circuits which support addition, multiplication, exponentiation and inversion.

Concrete Instantiation and Implementation. We have instantiated and implemented Tr-RF for two cryptographic protocols: coin tossing (CT) [3] and oblivious transfer (OT) [1,16]. To the best of our knowledge, this provides the *first* practical implementation of reverse firewalls for any cryptographic functionality. To instantiate coin-tossing, we start with Blum's protocol [3] and propose an RF construction based on it. We prove that this construction is a secure RF and, with a robust implementation, it results in a Tr-RF for the coin-tossing functionality. For OT, we consider the RF OT protocol from [15] and compile it to create a Tr-RF OT construction. Finally, we present a practical implementation of both Tr-RF CT and Tr-RF OT in the Open-Portable Trusted Execution Environment. We implement the framework for Tr-RFs by leveraging the Open Portable Trusted Execution Environment (OP-TEE) on ARM TrustZone (see Fig. 1). *We emphasize that we do not use TEEs to ensure functional correctness of RFs*. TEEs are used solely to realize certain specific assumptions of Private Circuit III by reducing them to collision-resistance of a cryptographic hash function. The functional correctness of Tr-RFs is guaranteed by Private Circuit III, along with some additional modifications that we introduce and discuss henceforth.

In this work, we implement Tr-RF in a distributed systems setting over a LAN network, leading to overheads in performance and communication. However, in the setting of split manufacturing, Tr-RF will be printed on a *single* Printed Circuit Board (PCB), thereby eliminating these overheads.

Organization. Section 2 provides notations. Section 3 introduces the background and formal definitions of Trojan-resilient Reverse Firewalls. Section 4 details their instantiations for Coin Tossing and Oblivious Transfer. Implementation aspects are covered in Sect. 5, and performance evaluation is presented in Sect. 6.

2 Preliminaries

Notations. $x \xleftarrow{\$} \mathcal{X}$ denotes that an element x is sampled randomly from a set $\mathcal{X}$. The output x of a randomized algorithm A is denoted by $x \leftarrow$ A. $k \in \mathbb{N}$ denotes the computational security parameter and $\mathsf{negl}(k)$ is a negligible function in k. All the necessary preliminaries for constructing Tr-RF CT and Tr-RF OT[1] are discussed in the full version of the paper [14]. For Tr-RF CT, we use a commitment scheme (com, reveal), where a sender commits to a message using com and later decommits using reveal to enable verification.

3 Trojan Resilient Reverse Firewall (Tr-RF)

In this section, we present our definitions of trojan resilience for reverse firewalls. Prior to that, we recall the definition of a trojan protection scheme from [12].

3.1 Trojan Protection Schemes [12].

A trojan protection scheme $\Pi = (\mathsf{TR}, \mathsf{T})$ consists of a circuit transformation algorithm TR and a testing algorithm T. The circuit transformation algorithm TR compiles an arbitrary functionality, described as an arithmetic circuit Γ, into a protected form that includes a trusted master circuit $\mathcal{M}$ and a set of circuit specifications $\Gamma_1, \ldots, \Gamma_\ell$. Importantly, the master circuit $\mathcal{M}$ contains only a few wires and simple gates, keeping its size independent of the complexity of Γ. This transformation is based on the "Split Manufacturing" principle proposed by Imeson et al. in [13]. The security of the trojan protection scheme Π against a malicious manufacturer is modeled through a robustness game, denoted as ROB_Π, as shown in Fig. 2. In the game, the transformation TR is first run to generate the specification of the protected circuit $(\mathcal{M}, \{\Gamma_i\}_i, \boldsymbol{m}')$. This specification is then provided to the malicious manufacturer $\mathcal{A}$, who produces a set of devices $\{D_i\}_i$. Following [12], we require that an implementation of D_i can be simulated.

Assumption 1. *Let D_i be the devices output by $\mathcal{A}$. We require that there exists (possibly probabilistic) circuit specifications $\widetilde{\Gamma}_i$ such that for all public inputs $\boldsymbol{x}$ and any initial state $\boldsymbol{m}$, the views of the circuit D_i and $\widetilde{\Gamma}_i$ are identically distributed.*

---

[1] In 1-out-of-2 OT the sender inputs $\{m_0, m_1\}$ and the receiver inputs $b \in \{0, 1\}$. Finally, the receiver learns m_b and the sender learns nothing.

The second component, the tester T is then run to verify that each device D_i correctly implements the functionality Γ_i, ensuring that its input/output behavior matches that of the honest specification. If the devices pass the tests, the adversary enters the second phase where they interact with a system consisting of the trusted master $\mathcal{M}$ and the device D_i. The evaluation of the sub-circuits $D_1, \ldots, D_\ell$ with master $\mathcal{M}$ on input $\boldsymbol{x}$ with initial state $\boldsymbol{m}$ to produce output $\boldsymbol{z}$ will be written as $\boldsymbol{z} \leftarrow (\mathcal{M} \Longleftrightarrow D_1, \cdots, D_\ell)[\boldsymbol{m}](\boldsymbol{x})$. This composition $(\mathcal{M} \Longleftrightarrow D_1, \cdots, D_\ell)$ can be viewed as a circuit $\mathcal{C_W}$ composed of the sub-circuits Γ_i and $\mathcal{M}$, where the composition is specified by the communication commands between Γ_i and $\mathcal{M}$. We say that an adversary $\mathcal{A}$ wins the game if and only if, after the testing succeeds, they produce an output $\boldsymbol{z}_i$ that deviates from the correct output $\boldsymbol{y}_i$ computed on input $\boldsymbol{x}_i$, i.e., $\boldsymbol{y}_i \leftarrow \Gamma[\boldsymbol{m}](\boldsymbol{x}_i)$. In other words, robustness guarantees that for identical inputs, the outputs in the second phase match those generated by the honest specification Γ. Robustness is parameterized by two values: t and n, where t represents the number of tests performed by T, and n is the number of executions in which the device's output align with the honest specification Γ. Following [12], constructing a robust trojan protection scheme requires that $t \gg n$.

Definition 1 (Trojan robustness). *Let ℓ, r, t, k be some natural parameters. A trojan protection scheme $\Pi = (\mathsf{TR}, \mathsf{T})$ is (t, r, ϵ)-trojan robust if the following two conditions hold:*

- *The tester T is t-bounded, i.e., each of the devices D_i is run by T at most t times, and at the end outputs a bit b indicating whether the test has passed or failed.*
- *For any (potentially malicious) manufacturer $\mathcal{A}$, any circuit Γ and any initial state $\boldsymbol{m}$ we have:*

$$\Pr[ROB_\Pi(\mathcal{A}, pub = (\ell, t, r, k), \Gamma, \boldsymbol{m}) = 1] \leq \epsilon,$$

where the probability is taken over the internal coin tosses of $\mathcal{A}$ and and the coin tosses of the game ROB_Π.

We will need the following theorem from [12].

Theorem 1. *Suppose $t, r, \ell, k \in \mathbb{N}$ with k is the computational security parameter, and let $\lambda = \ell/3$. Then $\Pi = (\mathsf{TR}, \mathsf{T})$ is (t, r, ϵ)-trojan robust for $\epsilon := F(\lceil \lambda/2 \rceil; \lambda, r/t) + \mathsf{negl}(k)$. In particular:*

- *For $r < 4t$ scheme Π is (t, r, ϵ)-trojan robust for $\epsilon := (4r/t)^{\lceil \lambda/2 \rceil} + \mathsf{negl}(k)$, and*
- *For $r < 2t$ scheme Π is (t, r, ϵ)-trojan robust with $\epsilon := e^{-2\lambda(1/2 - r/t)^2} + \mathsf{negl}(k)$.*

Here, $F(k; \lambda, p)$ is the tail of a binomial distribution with λ trails, p being the success probability and k being the minimal number of successes, i.e.:

$$F(k; \lambda, p) := \sum_{i=k}^{\lambda} \binom{\lambda}{i} p^i (1-p)^{\lambda - i} \tag{1}$$

In the next section we formally present our definition of trojan-resilient cryptographic reverse firewalls.

3.2 Trojan-Resilience for Cryptographic Reverse Firewalls

Before presenting our new definitions for trojan-resilient reverse firewalls, we establish notations and concepts related to cryptographic protocols and parties.

Game $\mathsf{ROB}_\Pi(\mathcal{A}, \mathsf{pub} = (\ell, t, r, k), \Gamma, \boldsymbol{m})$

1. $((\mathcal{M}, \{\Gamma_i\}_i), \boldsymbol{m}') \leftarrow (\mathsf{TR}_1(1^k, \ell, \Gamma), \mathsf{TR}_2(1^k, \ell, \boldsymbol{m}))$
2. $\{D_i\}_i \leftarrow \mathcal{A}(1^k, \mathcal{M}, \{\Gamma_i\}_i);$
3. Set the initial state of the devices $\mathsf{Init}(\{D_i\}_i, \boldsymbol{m}');$
4. If $\mathsf{T}^{D_1(\cdot),\ldots,D_\ell(\cdot)}(1^k, (\mathcal{M}, \{\Gamma_i\}_i)) = \mathit{false}$, return 0;
5. $x_1 \leftarrow \mathcal{A}(1^k);$
6. For $i = 1, \cdots, r$ repeat:
7. $\quad z_i \leftarrow (M \Longleftrightarrow D_1, \cdots, D_\ell)[\boldsymbol{m}'](x_i);$
8. $\quad y_i \leftarrow \Gamma[\boldsymbol{m}](x_i);$
9. $\quad$ If $y_i \neq z_i$ then return 1;
10. $\quad x_{i+1} \leftarrow \mathcal{A}(1^k, z_i);$
11. Return 0.

Fig. 2. The robustness game for a trojan protection scheme.

Definition 2 (Cryptographic Protocols [15]). *A cryptographic protocol $\mathcal{P} = (\mathsf{setup}, (P_i)_{i=1}^n)$ is an interaction between stateful parties $P_1, \ldots, P_n$ that begins with a setup procedure establishing initial states $(\sigma_{P_i})_{i=1}^n$, public parameter ρ, and a message schedule. Parties exchange messages using next-message and message-receipt algorithms $\mathsf{next}_{P_i}(\sigma_{P_i})$ and $\mathsf{receive}_{P_i}(\sigma_{P_i}, m)$ respectively, and produce results using output algorithms $\mathsf{output}_{P_i}(\sigma_{P_i})$ at the end. Each party is characterized by its defining algorithms: $P_i = (\mathsf{receive}_{P_i}, \mathsf{next}_{P_i}, \mathsf{output}_{P_i})$. Protocol runs must satisfy both functionality requirements $\mathcal{F}$ (constraining outputs for specific inputs) and security requirements $\mathcal{S}$ (constraining message distributions conditioned on particular inputs). A protocol is deemed secure for a party P if all security requirements relevant to P are satisfied.*

Definition 3 (Protocols and Parties). *Given a protocol $\mathcal{P} = (\mathsf{setup}, (P_i)_{i=1}^n)$, functionality $\mathcal{F}$, input I, party P, index j, and index set $J \subseteq \{1, \ldots, n\}$:*

– $\tau \leftarrow \mathcal{P}(I)$: *Transcript obtained by running $\mathcal{P}$ with input I.*

- $\mathcal{P}_{P_j} \Longrightarrow P$: *The protocol after replacing party P_j with P in $\mathcal{P}$.*
- $\mathcal{P}_J \Longrightarrow P$: *The protocol obtained by merging all parties $\{P_j\}_{j \in J}$ into a single implementation of P.*
- *If any party sends the special symbol $\perp$ as a message, the protocol terminates immediately, indicating a violation of functionality.*
- *P maintains $\mathcal{F}$ for P_j in $\mathcal{P}$ if $\mathcal{P}_{P_j} \Longrightarrow P$ satisfies $\mathcal{F}$ with negligible probability of failure over parties' and* setup *procedure's random coins for any fixed input.*

When $\mathcal{F}$, P_j', and $\mathcal{P}$ are understood from context, we simply state that P maintains functionality.

Next, we recall the definition of a cryptographic reverse firewall.

Definition 4 (Cryptographic reverse firewall [15]). *A cryptographic reverse firewall (RF) is a stateful algorithm $\mathcal{W}$ that takes its state and a message as input and outputs an updated state and message. For simplicity, we do not write the state of $\mathcal{W}$ explicitly. For a party $P = ($ receive, next, output$)$ and reverse firewall $\mathcal{W}$, the composed party with RF is defined as,*

$$\mathcal{W} \circ P := (\text{receive}_{\mathcal{W} \circ P}(\sigma, m) = \text{receive}_P(\sigma, \mathcal{W}(m)),$$
$$\text{next}_{\mathcal{W} \circ P}(\sigma) = \mathcal{W}(\text{next}_P(\sigma)),$$
$$\text{output}_{\mathcal{W} \circ P}(\sigma) = \text{output}_P(\sigma))$$

When the composed party engages in a protocol, the state of $\mathcal{W}$ is initialized to the public parameters σ. If $\mathcal{W}$ is meant to be composed with a party P, we call it reverse firewall for P.

With the relevant concepts established, we now define the properties that a trojan-resilient reverse firewall must fulfill:

Definition 5 (Robust Functionality-maintaining RFs) *Let $\mathcal{W}$ be a reverse firewall with circuit specification $\Gamma_{\mathcal{W}}$, and let $\mathcal{C}_{\mathcal{W}}$ be the circuit obtained from the circuit transformation algorithm of the trojan protection scheme, i.e., $\mathcal{C}_{\mathcal{W}} = (\mathcal{M} \iff D_1, \cdots, D_\ell)(\cdot)$. For any party P, let $\mathcal{C}_{\mathcal{W}}^1 \circ P = \mathcal{C}_{\mathcal{W}} \circ P$, and for $k \geq 2$, let $\mathcal{C}_{\mathcal{W}}^k \circ P = \mathcal{C}_{\mathcal{W}} \circ (\mathcal{C}_{\mathcal{W}}^{k-1} \circ P)$. For a protocol $\mathcal{P}$ that satisfies some functionality requirements $\mathcal{F}$, we say that a reverse firewall $\mathcal{W}$ maintains $\mathcal{F}$ for any party P in $\mathcal{P}$ if $\mathcal{C}_{\mathcal{W}}^k \circ P$ maintains $\mathcal{F}$ for P in $\mathcal{P}$ for any polynomially bounded $k \geq 1$. When $\mathcal{F}$, P, and $\mathcal{P}$ are clear from context, we simply say that the firewall $\mathcal{W}$ maintains functionality.*

Naturally, a firewall is only valuable if it offers a tangible benefit. The primary motivation for deploying a reverse firewall is to maintain a protocol's security, even in the event of a party's compromise (i.e., when the party's implementation is tampered with). In this work we define a stronger notion of *robust security preservation*, which extends this guarantee by requiring the protocol to remain secure not only when a party is compromised, but also when the reverse firewall's implementation is outsourced to a potentially malicious manufacturer.

Definition 6 (Robust Security-preserving RFs). *For a given protocol* $\mathcal{P} =$ *(setup, $(\mathsf{next}_{P_i}, \mathsf{receive}_{P_i}, \mathsf{output}_{P_i})_{i=1}^n$) that satisfies security requirements* $\mathcal{S}$ *and functionality* $\mathcal{F}$ *and a reverse firewall* $\mathcal{W}^{\mathrm{Tr-RF}}$ *with circuit specification* $\Gamma_{\mathcal{W}}$,

1. $\mathcal{W}^{\mathrm{Tr-RF}}$ *is robust strongly security preserving for* $\mathcal{S}$ *for party* P_j *in* $\mathcal{P}$ *if the protocol* $\mathcal{P}_{P_j} \Longrightarrow \mathcal{C}_\mathcal{W} \circ P_\mathcal{A}^*$ *satisfies* $\mathcal{S}$, *for any probabilistic polynomial-time* $P_\mathcal{A}^*$ *(potentially malicious implementation of* P_j). *Here*, $\mathcal{C}_\mathcal{W}(\cdot) = (\mathcal{M} \Longleftrightarrow D_1, \cdots, D_\ell)(\cdot)$ *as described above*.
2. $\mathcal{W}^{\mathrm{Tr-RF}}$ *is robust security preserving for party* P_j *in* $\mathcal{P}$ *against* $\mathcal{F}$-*maintaining adversaries if the protocol* $\mathcal{P}_{P_j} \Longrightarrow \mathcal{C}_\mathcal{W} \circ P_\mathcal{A}^*$ *satisfies* $\mathcal{S}$ *for any probabilistic polynomial-time* $P_\mathcal{A}^*$ *that maintains functionality* $\mathcal{F}$.

When the implementations of parties can be arbitrarily tampered with, the corresponding security notion is referred to as strong *(e.g., robust strong security-preserving or robust strong exfiltration-resistant). Conversely, if the tampering preserves the functionality of the parties, the term "strong" is omitted.*

When $\mathcal{S}, P_j, \mathcal{P}$ and $\mathcal{F}$ are clear from context, we simply say that $\mathcal{W}^{\mathrm{Tr-RF}}$ is robust strongly security-preserving and robust security-preserving, respectively.

Lastly, we require a trojan-resilient RF to meet the *robust exfiltration-resistance* property as defined below.

Definition 7 (Robust Exfiltration-resistant RFs). *For a protocol* $\mathcal{P}$ *satisfying functionality* $\mathcal{F}$ *and a reverse firewall* $\mathcal{W}^{\mathrm{Tr-RF}}$ *with circuit specification* $\Gamma_{\mathcal{W}}$,

- $\mathcal{W}^{\mathrm{Tr-RF}}$ *is robust strongly exfiltration-resistant for party* P_i *against party* P_j *in protocol* $\mathcal{P}$, *if no PPT adversary* $\mathcal{A}$ *achieves advantage that is non-negligible in the security parameter* k *in the game* ROBER($\mathcal{P}, P_i, P_j, \Gamma_\mathcal{W}, \boldsymbol{m}, k$), *as shown in Fig. 3. If* P_j *is empty, then we say that the firewall is robust strongly exfiltration resistant with respect to eavesdroppers.*
- $\mathcal{W}^{\mathrm{Tr-RF}}$ *is robust exfiltration-resistant for party* P_i *against party* P_j *in protocol* $\mathcal{P}$ *satisfying functionality* $\mathcal{F}$, *if no PPT adversary* $\mathcal{A}$ *achieves advantage that is non-negligible in the security parameter* k *in the game* ROBER($\mathcal{P}, P_i, P_j, \Gamma_\mathcal{W}, \boldsymbol{m}, k$), *as shown in Fig. 3. If* P_j *is empty, then we simply say that the firewall is robust exfiltration resistant with respect to eavesdroppers.*

In the first step of Game ROBER, the circuit transformation algorithm TR compiles the circuit specification $\Gamma_\mathcal{W}$ of the firewall $\mathcal{W}^{\mathrm{Tr-RF}}$ to produce $(\mathcal{M}, \{\Gamma_{\mathcal{W},i}\}_i, \boldsymbol{m}')$. This output is then provided to the malicious manufacturer $\mathcal{A}$, who generates a set of devices $\{D_i\}_i$ along with the tampered implementations $\bar{P}_i$ and $\bar{P}_j$ for parties P_i and P_j, respectively. The challenger then flips an unbiased coin b. If $b = 1$, the challenger replaces party P_i in the protocol $\mathcal{P}$ with the composed party $P_i^* = \mathcal{C}_\mathcal{W} \circ \bar{P}_i$, where $\bar{P}_i$ is the tampered implementation of P_i. If $b = 0$, the challenger replaces P_i with $P_i^* = \Gamma_\mathcal{W} \circ P_i$, the honest implementation

> **ROBER($\mathcal{P}, P_i, P_j, \Gamma_\mathcal{W}, m, k$)**
>
> 1. $((\mathcal{M}, \{\Gamma_{\mathcal{W},i}\}_i), m') \leftarrow (\mathsf{TR}_1(1^k, \ell, \Gamma_\mathcal{W}), \mathsf{TR}_2(1^k, \ell, m))$
> 2. $(D_1, \cdots, D_\ell, \bar{P}_i, \bar{P}_j, I) \leftarrow \mathcal{A}(1^k, \mathcal{M}, \{\Gamma_{\mathcal{W},i}\}_i)$
> 3. Set the initial state of the devices $\mathsf{Init}(\{D_i\}_i, m')$
> 4. $b \xleftarrow{\$} \{0, 1\}$;
> 5. If $b = 1$, set $P_i^* \leftarrow \mathcal{C}_\mathcal{W} \circ \bar{P}_i$
>   where $\mathcal{C}_\mathcal{W}(\cdot) = (\mathcal{M} \iff D_1, \cdots, D_\ell)[m'](\cdot)$
> 6. Else, $P_i^* \leftarrow \Gamma_\mathcal{W} \circ \bar{P}_i$.
> 7. $\tau^* \leftarrow \mathcal{P}_{P_i \implies P_i^*, P_j \implies \bar{P}_j}(I)$.
> 8. $b^* \leftarrow \mathcal{A}(\tau^*, \sigma_{\bar{P}_j})$.
> 9. If $b = b^*$ return 1; else return 0.

Fig. 3. The Robust Exfiltration Resistance security game for a reverse firewall $\mathcal{W}^{\mathrm{Tr-RF}}$ with specification $\Gamma_\mathcal{W}$ for party P_i in protocol $\mathcal{P}$ against party P_j with input I.

of P_i. The protocol $\mathcal{P}$ is then executed with P_i replaced by P_i^* and P_j replaced by $\bar{P}_j$. The adversary is given the transcript τ^* of the protocol execution along with the state $\sigma_{\bar{P}_j}$ of the tampered party $\bar{P}_j$. The adversary wins the game if it can guess the bit b with a probability significantly better than $\frac{1}{2}$.

Robust Exfiltration-resistance Implies Standard Exfiltration-Resistance. Our definition of robust exfiltration-resistance (ER) extends and generalizes the concept of standard exfiltration-resistance introduced in prior works. In standard ER, there are no circuit transformation steps; specifically, Step 1 in Fig. 3 is omitted, and in Step 2, the adversary outputs only the tampered implementations $\bar{P}_i$ and $\bar{P}_j$ and the input I. Furthermore, in Step 5, the circuit $\mathcal{C}_\mathcal{W}$ is defined as $\mathcal{C}_\mathcal{W}(\cdot) = \Gamma_\mathcal{W}(\cdot)$.

Having introduced our new definitions for trojan-resilient RF, we present two essential lemmas associated with them. First, we show that trojan *robustness* along with standard *exfiltration-resistance* for a RF implies robust exfiltration-resistance.

Lemma 1. *Let $\Pi = (\mathsf{TR}, \mathsf{T})$ be a trojan protection scheme that is (t, r, ϵ)-trojan robust, as defined in Definition 1. Also, let the firewall $\mathcal{W}^{\mathrm{Tr-RF}}$ with circuit specification $\Gamma_\mathcal{W}$ be (strongly) exfiltration-resistant for party P_i against party P_j in protocol $\mathcal{P}$ satisfying functionality $\mathcal{F}$. Then, circuit $\mathcal{C}_\mathcal{W}$ (see Fig. 3) derived by applying $\Pi = (\mathsf{TR}, \mathsf{T})$ to $\mathcal{W}^{\mathrm{Tr-RF}}$ is robust (strongly) exfiltration-resistant for party P_i against party P_j in the protocol $\mathcal{P}$ satisfying functionality $\mathcal{F}$.*

Due to space constraints, we provide the proof of this lemma in the full version of our paper [14].

Next, we show that robust exfiltration-resistance *implies* robust security-preservation for a reverse firewall when the underlying protocol has *simulation-based* (computational) security guarantees.

Lemma 2. *Let $\mathcal{F}$ be any functionality and let $\mathcal{P}$ be a protocol for realizing $\mathcal{F}$ with abort in presence of malicious adversaries. Let $\mathcal{W}^{\text{Tr-RF}}$ be a RF that is robust (strongly) exfiltration-resistant for party P_i against party P_j in protocol $\mathcal{P}$ satisfying functionality $\mathcal{F}$, then the firewall $\mathcal{W}^{\text{Tr-RF}}$ is robust security-preserving for protocol $\mathcal{P}$ according to Definition 6.*

Proof. The proof of this claim also follows from the trojan robustness property (see Def. 1) along with the result from [6]. In particular, [6] shows that standard (strong) exfiltration-resistance implies (strong) security preservation for a RF for simulation-based security notions. The trojan robustness guarantee implies that, with overwhelming probability in the robust exfiltration-resistance game, the circuit $C_\mathcal{W}$ can be replaced with the original specification $\Gamma_\mathcal{W}$ of the firewall $\mathcal{W}^{\text{Tr-RF}}$. The claim then follows from the result of [6]. □

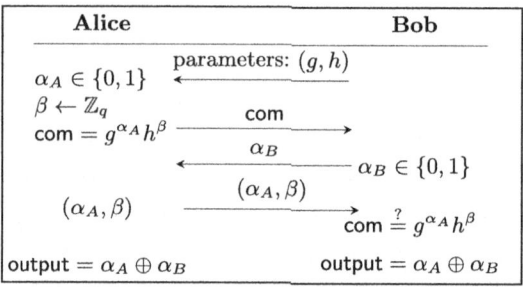

Fig. 4. Blum's coin tossing protocol using Pedersen commitment scheme.

4 Trojan-Resilient RFs for Coin Toss and Oblivious Transfer Protocol

In this section, we present trojan-resilient reverse firewalls for coin-tossing and oblivious transfer protocols sin the *semi-honest* setting. For the coin-tossing protocol, we require that the parties' implementations be tampered with in a *functionality-maintaining* manner [15], meaning that the tampered implementations do not disrupt the protocol's functionality. Most prior work on reverse firewalls adopts this tampering model, as it enables the attacker to exfiltrate information while remaining covert. In contrast, for the oblivious transfer protocol, we allow the adversary to tamper with the parties' implementations *arbitrarily*. We begin by presenting our two-party coin-tossing protocol, which is based on Blum's protocol [3] and instantiated using Pedersen commitments. Following this, we describe the reverse firewalls designed for each party in the protocol.

Finally, we propose a design model to upgrade these reverse firewalls into their trojan-resilient counterparts.

Two Party Coin Tossing Protocol [3]: We now present Blum's semi-honest secure two-party coin-tossing protocol, illustrated in Fig. 4. This protocol uses a bit commitment scheme and enables both parties to agree on a single bit that is uniformly distributed at random. The protocol follows the classic *commit-and-open* paradigm: Alice first commits to her bit, after which Bob sends his bit. Alice then reveals her committed bit, and the final coin toss outcome is computed as the XOR of their two bits.

Reverse Firewall for the Coin-Tossing Protocol. Figure 5 illustrates the coin-tossing protocol integrated with reverse firewalls, denoted as $\mathcal{W}_A$ for Alice and $\mathcal{W}_B$ for Bob. This protocol further requires the bit commitment scheme to be *additively homomorphic*, a property already satisfied by Pedersen commitments.

- *Setup:* Alice and Bob agree on a security parameter k and two generators $(g, h) \in \mathbb{G}^2$, where $(\mathbb{G}, \cdot)$ is a multiplicative cyclic group in which the discrete logarithm problem is assumed to be hard.
- *Protocol:* Alice samples a random bit $\alpha_A \in {0,1}$ and $\beta \in \mathbb{Z}_q$, and sends the Pedersen commitment $\mathsf{com} = g^{\alpha_A} h^\beta$. Her firewall $\mathcal{W}_A$ re-randomizes it using (α_1, r_1) to compute $\mathsf{com}' = \mathsf{com} \cdot g^{\alpha_1} h^{r_1}$, which is forwarded externally. Bob's firewall $\mathcal{W}_B$ similarly re-randomizes com' using (α_2, r_2) to obtain $\mathsf{com}'' = \mathsf{com}' \cdot g^{\alpha_2} h^{r_2}$ and sends it to Bob. Bob samples $\alpha_B \in \{0,1\}$, and $\mathcal{W}_B$ re-randomizes it as $\alpha'_B = \alpha_B + \alpha_2$ before forwarding it. $\mathcal{W}_A$ updates this to $\alpha''_B = \alpha'_B + \alpha_1$ and passes it to Alice. Alice then reveals (α_A, β) and computes $\mathsf{output_A} = (\alpha_A + \alpha''_B) \bmod 2$. Her firewall re-randomizes the opening as $(\alpha'_A, \beta') = (\alpha_A + \alpha_1, \beta + r_1)$ and sends it. $\mathcal{W}_B$ adjusts this to $(\alpha''_A, \beta'') = (\alpha'_A + \alpha_2, \beta' + r_2)$ and delivers it to Bob, who verifies $\mathsf{com}'' \stackrel{?}{=} g^{\alpha''_A} h^{\beta''}$. If valid, he outputs $\mathsf{output_B} = (\alpha''_A + \alpha_B) \bmod 2$; otherwise, he aborts.

Theorem 2. *Let $\prod$ be the reverse firewall enabled coin-tossing protocol depicted in Fig. 5. The firewalls $\mathcal{W}_A$ and $\mathcal{W}_B$ are functionality maintaining. If the commitment scheme* $\mathsf{COMMIT} = (\mathsf{Com}, \mathsf{Reveal})$ *is perfectly hiding, computationally binding and is homomorphic with respect to the operations as shown in Fig. 5, $\mathcal{W}_A$ and $\mathcal{W}_B$ preserve security and is exfiltration resistant.*

Proof. First, we show that the firewalls $\mathcal{W}_A$ and $\mathcal{W}_B$ are *functionality maintaining* and hence preserves correctness of the protocol. The output of Alice is: $\mathsf{output_A} = (\alpha_A + \alpha''_B) \bmod 2 = ((\alpha_A + \alpha_B) + (\alpha_1 + \alpha_2)) \bmod 2$. Similarly, the output of Bob is: $\mathsf{output_B} = (\alpha''_A + \alpha_B) \bmod 2 = ((\alpha_A + \alpha_B) + (\alpha_1 + \alpha_2)) \bmod 2$.

Hence, the output of both parties is the same. For proof of exfiltration resistance and security preservation, we would like to refer to the full version of our paper [14]. □

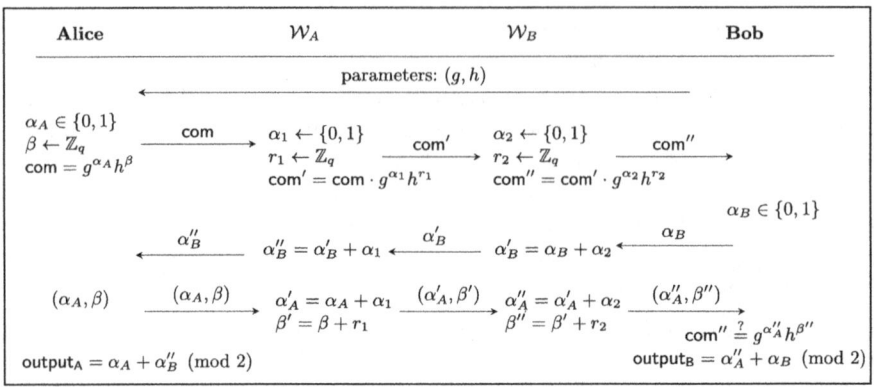

Fig. 5. Reverse firewall enabled coin tossing protocol

4.1 Trojan-Resilient Reverse Firewall for Coin Tossing Protocol

We present a transformation from a legacy Reverse Firewall (RF) to a Trojan-resilient RF (Tr-RF), inspired by the circuit-transformation approach of [12]. The construction comprises two components: a circuit transformation algorithm (TR) and a testing procedure (T). The original circuit Γ is decomposed into three mini-circuits $\Gamma_0, \Gamma_1, \Gamma_2$, which simulate Γ via a passively secure 3-party computation protocol. The transformation is executed by a trusted master node (M), which also secret-shares the inputs, while an untrusted manufacturer fabricates the mini-circuits. The transformation employs standard MPC primitives such as secure addition, multiplication, exponentiation, and modular inversion. These include operations like BEAVER.TRIPLE(q) for generating random multiplication triples, SECRET.SHARE(x) for additive sharing, MULT($\cdot$) for secure multiplication, and MOD.INVERSE(x, q) for computing modular inverses. Security is captured via a robustness game (Fig. 2), modelling a malicious manufacturer attempting to insert hardware trojans. The construction ensures high-probability detection or mitigation of such adversarial behavior.

Design Model. In our model, the master circuit M is capable of sampling a random value and securely distributing it to all mini-circuits ($\Gamma_0, \Gamma_1, \Gamma_2$). This setup assumes that M can transmit values of arbitrary length to the mini-circuits, enabling strong security guarantees with minimal computational overhead. Now, we build trojan-resilient $\mathcal{W}_A$ and $\mathcal{W}_B$ below:

Trojan-Resilient $\mathcal{W}_A$. In the coin-tossing protocol, the reverse firewall $\mathcal{W}_A$ ① computes commitment com′, ② computes α_B'' and ③ computes α_A' and β'. We discuss the functionality of master and mini-circuit computations below.

1. Distributed computation of com′:
   - **Master Circuit** (M): It randomly selects a 16-byte Advanced Encryption Standards (AES) key k_1. Then it chooses two 16-byte input strings, let's say str1 and str2. It then generates the pseudo-random value,

$r_1 = AES(k_1, \text{str1})$. After that, it generates another random bit, $\alpha_1 = AES(k_1, \text{str2}) \mod 2$ and Secret shares the commitment com as $[\text{com}]_p$ and shares the values r_1 and α_1 as $[r_1]_p$, $[\alpha_1]_p$ respectively among the mini-circuits.
- **Mini Circuit** (Γ^i): Each mini-circuit invokes the public exponentiation protocol and computes: $[g^\alpha]_p$ and $[h^{r_1}]_p$. It then invokes the secure multiplication protocol and computes: $[g^{\alpha_1} \cdot h^{r_1}]_p$ and uses the result from the previous step and the shared value $[\text{com}]_p$ to compute: $[\text{com} \cdot g^{\alpha_1} \cdot h^{r_1}]_p$.
- **Master Circuit** ($\mathcal{M}$): It now performs reconstruction over $[\text{com} \cdot g^{\alpha_1} \cdot h^{r_1}]_p$ to produce the final value $\text{com} \cdot g^{\alpha_1} \cdot h^{r_1}$.

2. Distributed computation of α''_B:
   - **Master Circuit** ($\mathcal{M}$): It generates shares of α'_B and α_1 as $[\alpha'_B]_p$ and $[\alpha_1]_p$ and sends it to the mini-circuits.
   - **Mini Circuits**(Γ^i): Each mini circuit invokes secure addition protocol and returns share $[\alpha'_B + \alpha_1]_p$ to master circuit.
   - **Master Circuit**($\mathcal{M}$): Finally, it runs a reconstruction over the values received from the mini-circuits to compute α''_B.

3. Distributed Computation of α'_A and β':
   - **Master Circuit** ($\mathcal{M}$): It generates shares of α_A and α_1 as $[\alpha'_B]_p$ and $[\alpha_1]_p$ and shares of β and r_1 as $[\beta]_p$ and $[r_1]_p$ sends them to the mini-circuits.
   - **Mini Circuits**(Γ^i): Each mini circuit invokes secure addition protocol over input pair $([\alpha'_B]_p, [\alpha_1]_p)$ and $([\beta]_p, [r_1]_p)$ and returns share $[\alpha_A + \alpha_1]_p$ and $[\beta + r_1]_p$ to master circuit.
   - **Master Circuit**($\mathcal{M}$): Finally, it runs the reconstruction over share $[\alpha_A + \alpha_1]_p$ and $[\beta + r_1]_p$ independently to compute α'_A and β'.

Trojan-resilient $\mathcal{W}_B$. The reverse firewall $\mathcal{W}_B$ implements the computation of com'', α'_B, α''_A and β''. However, these computation follows similar steps as the computations by $\mathcal{W}_A$, so we do not discuss $\mathcal{W}_B$ in detail here.

Theorem 3. *Let Σ be the coin tossing protocol which is exfiltration-resistant and $\Pi = (\text{TR}, \text{T})$ be a trojan protection scheme that is (t, r, ϵ)-trojan robust, as defined in Definition 1. For reverse firewalls $\mathcal{W}_A$ and $\mathcal{W}_B$ if transformed into $\mathcal{W}_A^{\text{Tr}-\text{RF}}$ and $\mathcal{W}_B^{\text{Tr}-\text{RF}}$ by applying Π on $\mathcal{W}_A$ and $\mathcal{W}_B$ as shown above, then $\mathcal{W}_A^{\text{Tr}-\text{RF}}$ and $\mathcal{W}_B^{\text{Tr}-\text{RF}}$ are robust-exfiltration resistant.*

Proof. The proof of the above theorem follows from Theorem 2 and Lemma 1. □

Theorem 4. *Let Σ be the coin tossing protocol and $\mathcal{W}_A$ and $\mathcal{W}_B$ be the robust exfiltration-resistant reverse firewalls for Alice and Bob, respectively, then $\mathcal{W}_A$ and $\mathcal{W}_B$ are also robust-security-preserving RFs.*

Proof. The proof of the above theorem follows from Theorem 3 and Lemma 2. □

4.2 Trojan-Resilient Reverse Firewall for Oblivious Transfer Protocol

We follow the reverse firewall for OT protocol from [15] and transform legacy RF for OT protocol into trojan-resilient RF following our design methodology. We provide the details OT protocol and its trojan-resileint RF in the Appendix A.

5 Implementation

We implement a Trojan-resilient reverse firewall for coin tossing and oblivious transfer protocols on Open-Portable Trusted Execution Environment (OP-TEE), writing approx 5000 lines of code in C language, ensuring the communication among mini circuits and master circuit through a LAN network.

Practical Realization. The Trojan protection scheme in Private Circuit III employs different types of circuits, each with distinct functionality. We outline the realizations of the *master circuit, sub-circuits*, and *mini-circuits*:

- *Master Circuit:* The master component, M, serves as the sole trusted hardware element, crucial for Trojan resilience. Its integrity must be ensured either through trusted fabrication or verifiability via reactive Trojan detection, requiring minimal gate complexity. M interfaces directly with the adversary, handles secret sharing and reconstruction, and performs majority voting across sub-circuits. We implement M using a Raspberry Pi 4 (RPI4) running Raspbian OS, utilizing the `mbedtls` library for cryptographic operations and `arpa` for socket-based communication.
- *Sub-Circuits:* Each sub-circuit Γ_i comprises λ independent instances executing a semi-honest three-party computation protocol on isolated shares, ensuring no cross-instance leakage. We adopt a semi-honest MPC protocol supporting secure addition, multiplication, and exponentiation. Correctness is reinforced via a testing phase. Sub-circuits are realized on Raspberry Pi 3 (RPI3) devices within the OP-TEE framework to guarantee isolation and security.
- *Mini-Circuits:* Each Γ_i consists of three mini-circuits ($\Gamma_i^1, \Gamma_i^2, \Gamma_i^3$), collectively implementing the target functionality under the semi-honest model. The master M ensures synchronized inputs and controls inter-mini-circuit communication. In practice, mini-circuits Γ_i^j are produced by a polynomially-bounded manufacturer $\mathcal{A}$, resulting in devices D_i^j treated as untrusted hardware. Mini-circuits are deployed as independent Trusted Applications within OP-TEE, enforcing strong isolation and master-mediated communication.

Realizing Private Circuit III Assumptions. Our use of a Trusted Execution Environment (TEE) aims to practically instantiate the compiler from [12], *without relying on OP-TEE's hardware trust* for Trojan-resilience guarantees. A fundamental assumption in [12] is the absence of direct communication between mini-circuits without master intervention. We enforce this by implementing mini-circuits as attested Trusted Applications in OP-TEE, leveraging remote attestation[2]. Thus, two mini-circuits can only interact if they can forge valid attestation reports—an event reduced to finding collisions in a collision-resistant hash function. Formally, our implementation reduces the communication assumption in [12] to the well-studied hardness of hash-collision resistance, a standard security assumption in cryptography. This reduction forms the core of our practical realization of a Trojan-resilient Reverse Firewall and its associated Coin Tossing and OT protocols.

Implementation Challenges. During the implementation of the Private Circuit III assumption, we encountered challenges with OP-TEE, developed by *Linaro*. Specifically, OP-TEE requires additional patches to operate on the Raspberry Pi 4 (RPI4) and suffers from network communication issues. Due to these limitations, we selected the Raspberry Pi 3 (RPI3) as our standard platform. However, even on RPI3, OP-TEE does not support cryptographic libraries such as *OpenSSL* or *mbedTLS* in the application, posing further constraints. To overcome this, we confined the large numbers in our framework as strings.

6 Performance Evaluation

We evaluate the performance of our proposed Trojan-resilient reverse firewall (Tr-RF) implementations for the coin tossing and oblivious transfer protocols. The evaluation benchmarks Tr-RF against two baselines: (1) the legacy reverse firewall, and (2) the plain protocol implementation without any reverse firewall. Our comparison focuses on both computational and communication overheads across all three variants for each protocol.

Experimental Setup. Our testbed comprises two Raspberry Pi models: (1) Raspberry Pi 4 Model B featuring a Broadcom BCM2711 Quad-core Cortex-A72 (ARM v8) 64-bit SoC @ 1.8 GHz and 8 GB RAM, and (2) Raspberry Pi 3 Model B v2 with a Broadcom BCM2837 Quad-core 64-bit CPU @ 1.2 GHz and 1 GB RAM. The setup utilizes 9 Raspberry Pi 3 boards as sub-circuits, with each sub-circuit executing 3 mini-circuits deployed as Trusted Applications within the OP-TEE framework. A Raspberry Pi 4 board acts as the trusted master node, responsible for minimal computations that remain independent of the circuit size. It also facilitates LAN-based socket communication among the mini-circuits.

System and Security Parameters. We employ the mbedtls library to support 2048-bit modular arithmetic and implement AES in counter mode as a pseudorandom generator. For the cryptographic operations, we use the same parameter settings as openssl, specifically selecting a group of prime order close to 2^{2048} that satisfies the Decisional Diffie-Hellman (DDH) assumption. This configuration supports our implementation of Pedersen commitments, which underpin the

---

[2] Remote Attestation combines hardware measurements and application state, signed by the OEM's private key.

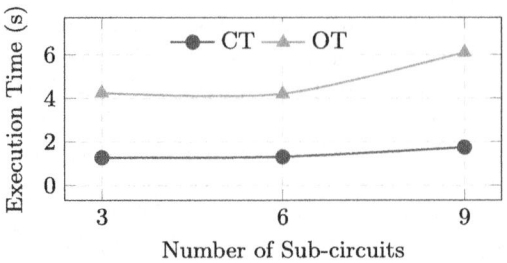

Fig. 6. Execution time (in seconds) for CT and OT protocols with varying sub-circuits.

coin tossing and oblivious transfer protocols. For robustness, we fix the number of sub-circuits at 9, which corresponds to a total of 27 mini-circuits (devices) as per the methodology in [12]. The security analysis therein ensures that, under a testing budget of $t = 10^9$ executions per sub-circuit and an operational workload of $n = 10^5$ actual executions, the overall computation remains correct with a soundness error bounded by 10^{-17}.

Baseline Implementations. We evaluate the performance of our Tr-RF constructions by comparing them against two baselines. The first is the Plain Protocol Baseline, where the protocol is executed without any reverse firewall, making it vulnerable to exfiltration if a party is compromised. For this, we use Blum's protocol [3] for coin tossing and the Naor-Pinkas/Aiello-Ishai-Raingold protocol [1,16] for oblivious transfer. The second is the Legacy Reverse Firewall Baseline, where the protocol is equipped with a conventional reverse firewall. In this case, we implement the RF-based coin tossing protocol described in Sect. 4.2, and for oblivious transfer, we adopt the RF construction from [15].

Building Blocks. We describe core building blocks for trojan-resilient protocol implementations, namely secure addition, secure multiplication, and secure exponentiation, along with their computation (see Table 1 (left)) and communication costs. Secure addition and multiplication are based on Araki's semi-honest three-party computation protocol [2], while public exponentiation uses techniques from [10]. For more details, refer to the full version of the paper [14].

Table 1. (**Left**) Execution time for (1) local operations and (2) building blocks of MPC on OP-TEE. (**Right**) Computation time for Coin Tossing (CT) and Oblivious Transfer (OT) across Plain, Legacy RF, and Tr-RF implementations.

Operations	(1)	(2)
Add	1.3 ms	27.95 ms
Mult	3.7 ms	63.45 ms
Exp	7.5 ms	69.89 ms

	CT	OT
Plain	0.028 s	0.078 s
Legacy RF	0.048 s	0.154 s
Tr-RF	0.746 s	2.561 s

Experimental Results. Figure 6 presents execution times of the coin tossing and oblivious transfer protocols as the number of sub-circuits increases from 3 to 9. We observe minimal execution overheads while significantly boosting Trojan-resilience. For instance, using 9 sub-circuits achieves a failure probability of 10^{-17} with practical computation costs. Table 1 (left) reports execution times for basic MPC building blocks under OP-TEE, while Table 1 (right) compares computation costs across three protocol variants: plain, legacy RF, and our Trojan-resilient RF (Tr-RF). Notably, our Tr-RF prototype on RPi3 incurs network overhead absent in practical deployments, where Tr-RF would ideally be implemented on a single PCB, eliminating communication latency. Exploring this PCB-based implementation remains an exciting direction for future work.

Acknowledgments. The authors would like to thank the anonymous reviewers whose comments helped in improving the final version of the manuscript. Chandan Kumar would like to thank Google Asia Pacific Pte Ltd. for partially supporting this project as part of the Google PhD fellowship program. Nimish Mishra and Debdeep Mukhopadhyay would like to acknowledge the Centre on Hardware-Security Entrepreneurship Research and Development (C-HERD), MeitY, Govt. of India, and Information Security Education and Awareness (ISEA) initiative, MeitY, Govt. of India, for partially funding this research. Satrajit Ghosh acknowledges the support of the Science and Engineering Research Board (SERB), India, for partially funding this work through the Start-up Research Grant IPT (Grant ID: SRG/2023/002154).

A   Trojan-Resilient Reverse Firewall for OT Protocol

This section briefly describes the reverse firewall for oblivious transfer protocol as given in [15], followed by its trojan-resilient instantiation.

OT Protocol [15]. Alice has inputs (m_0, m_1), and Bob has a choice bit b as input. Bob randomly samples generators $(g, c) \xleftarrow{\$} (\mathbb{G} \setminus \{1_\mathbb{G}\})^2$ and $y \xleftarrow{\$} \mathbb{Z}_q$. It computes and sends $(g, c, d = g^y, h = c^y g^b)$ to Alice. Then, Alice randomly samples $(r_0, s_0, r_1, s_1) \xleftarrow{\$} \mathbb{Z}_q^4$ and computes $(u_i, e_i)_{i=0}^1 \leftarrow (g^{r_i} c^{s_i}, d^{r_i}(h/g^i)^{s_i} m_i)_{i=0}^1$. It forwards $(u_i, e_i)_{i=0}^1$ to Bob. At the end, Bob computes $m_b = e_b/u_b^y$ to retrieve the message as per his choice bit.

Bob's Firewall: To re-randomize (g, c, d, h), the firewall samples $\alpha \xleftarrow{\$} \mathbb{Z}_q^*$ and $(x', y') \xleftarrow{\$} \mathbb{Z}_q^2$. It computes $g' \leftarrow g^\alpha$, $c' \leftarrow c^\alpha g'^{x'}$, $d' \leftarrow d^\alpha g'^{y'}$, and $h' \leftarrow h^\alpha c^{\alpha y'} d^{\alpha x'} g'^{x'y'}$. It forwards these values to Alice. Upon receiving (u_0, e_0, u_1, e_1), the firewall de-randomizes by computing $e'_0 \leftarrow e_0/u_0^{y'}$, and $e'_1 \leftarrow e_1/u_1^{y'}$. It then forwards (u_0, e'_0, u_1, e'_1) to Bob.

Alice's Firewall: Alice's firewall checks if $g = 1_\mathbb{G}$ and aborts if true. Otherwise, forwards (g, c, d, h) to Alice. When Alice revert back with its computation, it re-randomizes (u_0, e_0, u_1, e_1) by sampling $(r'_0, s'_0, r'_1, s'_1) \xleftarrow{\$} \mathbb{Z}_q^4$ and computing $(u'_i, e'_i)_{i=0}^1 \leftarrow (u_i g^{r'_i} c^{s'_i}, e_i d^{r'_i}(h/g^i)^{s'_i})_{i=0}^1$. The firewall forwards $(u'_i, e'_i)_{i=0}^1$ to Bob. The correctness and security guarantees are inferred directly from [15].

Trojan-resilient RF for OT Protocol: We implement Bob's reverse firewall with a master circuit ($\mathcal{M}$) and three mini-circuits ($\Gamma^0, \Gamma^1, \Gamma^2$), operating under the trojan-resilient model. We provide the step-wise computations of Alice's RF and Bob's RF below.

Trojan-Resilient $\mathcal{W}_B$ for OT. In the OT protocol, the reverse firewall $\mathcal{W}_B$ ① computes g', c', d', h' and ② computes e'_0, e'_1. Below, we describe the functionality of master and mini-circuits for these computations.

1. Distributed computation of g', c', d' and h':
   - **Master Circuit (M):** It randomly selects a $\alpha \in \mathbb{Z}_p^*$ and $(x', y') \xleftarrow{\$} \mathbb{Z}_p^2$. It secret shares g, c, d and h as $[g]_p, [c]_p, [d]_p$ and $[h]_p$ respectively among mini-circuits. It then shares α, x', y' to all mini-circuits.
   - **Mini Circuit (Γ^i):** Each mini-circuit invokes the public exponentiation protocol as $\text{Exp}([g]_p, \alpha)$, $\text{Exp}([c]_p, \alpha)$, $\text{Exp}([d]_p, \alpha)$, and $\text{Exp}([h]_p, \alpha)$ to compute $[g^\alpha]_p, [c^\alpha]_p, [d^\alpha]_p$ and $[h^\alpha]_p$ respectively. Now, they invoke public exponentiation protocol as $\text{Exp}([g^\alpha]_p, x')$, $\text{Exp}([g^\alpha]_p, y')$, $\text{Exp}([c^\alpha]_p, y')$, $\text{Exp}([d^\alpha]_p, x')$ and $\text{Exp}([g^\alpha]_p, x'y')$ to computes $[g^{\alpha x'}]_p, [g^{\alpha y'}]_p, [c^{\alpha y'}]_p, [d^{\alpha x'}]_p$ and $[g^{\alpha x' y'}]_p$. Afterwards, each mini-circuit invokes a secure multiplication protocol as $\text{Mult}([c^\alpha]_p, [g^{\alpha x'}]_p)$, $\text{Mult}([d^\alpha]_p, [g^{\alpha y'}]_p)$, $\text{Mult}([h^\alpha]_p, [c^{\alpha y'}]_p)$, and $\text{Mult}([d^{\alpha x'}]_p, [g^{\alpha x' y'}]_p)$ to compute shares of c', d', h'. Note that the shares of h' are computed by applying another $\text{Mult}(.)$ on the results of the last two multiplications.
   - **Master Circuit (M):** It now performs reconstruction over shares like, $g' = \text{Reconstruct}([g^\alpha]_p)$. to produce the final value g', c', d' and h'.

2. Distributed computation of e'_0 and e'_1:
   - **Master Circuit (M):** It generates shares of e_0, e_1 and u_0, u_1 as $[e_0]_p, [e_1]_p$ and $[u_0]_p, [u_1]_p$ respectively and sends it to the mini-circuits along with the value y'.
   - **Mini Circuits(Γ^i):** Each mini circuit invokes secure public exponentiation protocol as $\text{Exp}([u_0]_p, y')$ and $\text{Exp}([u_1]_p, y')$ to compute $[u_0^{y'}]_p$ and $[u_1^{y'}]_p$. After that, they perform private inverse protocol as $\text{Inv}([u_0^{y'}]_p)$ and $\text{Inv}([u_1^{y'}]_p)$ to compute $[u_0^{-y'}]_p$ and $[u_1^{-y'}]_p$. Finally, each mini-circuit perform secure multiplication as $\text{Mult}([e_0]_p, [u_0^{-y'}]_p)$ and $\text{Mult}([e_1]_p, [u_1^{-y'}]_p)$ to compute $[e'_0]_p$ and $[e'_1]_p$.
   - **Master Circuit($\mathcal{M}$):** Finally, it runs a reconstruction over the values received from the mini-circuits to compute e'_0 and e'_1.

Trojan-Resilient $\mathcal{W}_A$ for OT. The trojan-resilient Alice's firewall is implemented using a master circuit and three mini-circuits. While there are replicas of mini-circuits performing identical computations and participating in majority voting, we focus on a single replica to illustrate the computation steps.

The master circuit first checks if $g = 1_\mathbb{G}$ and aborts if true; otherwise, it forwards (g, c, d, h) to Alice. Upon receiving (u_0, e_0, u_1, e_1) from Alice, the master circuit randomly selects (r'_0, s'_0, r'_1, s'_1). To compute u'_i, it secret-shares g and

c, along with exponents r'_i and s'_i, respectively, with all mini-circuits. Using these shares, the mini-circuits perform secure multiplication to compute shares of $g^{r'_i}c^{s'_i}$. The secret shares of u_i are then combined with these results to compute shares of $u_i g^{r'_i}c^{s'_i}$. For the second part, the master circuit first computes shares of g raised to the power i using the public exponentiation algorithm. It then computes the inverse of g^i using the private inverse protocol and performs secure multiplication with the shares of h to compute shares of h/g^i. Subsequently, it uses public exponentiation on the shares of h/g^i with the exponent s'_i to compute shares of $(h/g^i)^{s'_i}$. Parallelly, it computes shares of $d^{r'_i}$ and performs secure multiplication to obtain shares of $d^{r'_i}(h/g^i)^{s'_i}$. Finally, the master circuit generates shares of e_i and combines them with the previously computed shares of $d^{r'_i}(h/g^i)^{s'_i}$ using secure multiplication to compute shares of $e_i d^{r'_i}(h/g^i)^{s'_i}$.

Theorem 5. *Let Σ be the oblivious transfer protocol, which is exfiltration-resistant, and the reverse firewall $\mathcal{W}$ for both Alice and Bob are transformed into $\mathcal{W}^{\text{Tr}-\text{RF}}$ applying Π on $\mathcal{W}$ as shown above, then $\mathcal{W}^{\text{Tr}-\text{RF}}$ is robust-exfiltration resistant.*

Proof. The proof of the above theorem follows from Lemma 1. □

Theorem 6. *Let Σ be the oblivious transfer protocol and $\mathcal{W}_A$ and $\mathcal{W}_B$ be the robust exfiltration-resistant reverse firewalls for Alice and Bob, respectively; then $\mathcal{W}_A$ and $\mathcal{W}_B$ are also robust-security-preserving RFs.*

Proof. The proof of the above theorem follows from Lemma 2. □

References

1. Aiello, B., Ishai, Y., Reingold, O.: Priced oblivious transfer: how to sell digital goods. In: Pfitzmann, B. (ed.) EUROCRYPT 2001. LNCS, vol. 2045, pp. 119–135. Springer, Heidelberg (2001). https://doi.org/10.1007/3-540-44987-6_8
2. Araki, T., Furukawa, J., Lindell, Y., Nof, A., Ohara, K.: High-throughput semi-honest secure three-party computation with an honest majority. In: Proceedings of the 2016 ACM SIGSAC Conference on Computer and Communications Security, CCS 2016, pp. 805–817. ACM, New York, NY, USA (2016). https://doi.org/10.1145/2976749.2978331
3. Blum, M.: Coin flipping by telephone. In: Advances in Cryptology: A Report on CRYPTO 81, pp. 11–15 (1981), /archive/crypto81/11_blum.pdf
4. Bossuat, A., Bultel, X., Fouque, P.-A., Onete, C., der Merwe, T.: Designing reverse firewalls for the real world. In: Chen, L., Li, N., Liang, K., Schneider, S. (eds.) ESORICS 2020. LNCS, vol. 12308, pp. 193–213. Springer, Cham (2020). https://doi.org/10.1007/978-3-030-58951-6_10
5. Chakraborty, S., Dziembowski, S., Nielsen, J.B.: Reverse firewalls for actively secure mpcs. In: Annual international cryptology conference, pp. 732–762. Springer (2020)
6. Chakraborty, S., Ganesh, C., Pancholi, M., Sarkar, P.: Reverse firewalls for adaptively secure mpc without setup. In: International Conference on the Theory and Application of Cryptology and Information Security, pp. 335–364. Springer (2021). https://doi.org/10.1007/978-3-030-92075-3_12

7. Chakraborty, S., Ganesh, C., Sarkar, P.: Reverse firewalls for oblivious transfer extension and applications to zero-knowledge. In: Annual International Conference on the Theory and Applications of Cryptographic Techniques, pp. 239–270. Springer (2023). https://doi.org/10.1007/978-3-031-30545-0_9
8. Chakraborty, S., Magliocco, L., Magri, B., Venturi, D.: Key exchange in the post-snowden era: Universally composable subversion-resilient pake. In: International Conference on the Theory and Application of Cryptology and Information Security, pp. 101–133. Springer (2025). https://doi.org/10.1007/978-981-96-0935-2_4
9. Chakraborty, S., Magri, B., Nielsen, J.B., Venturi, D.: Universally composable subversion-resilient cryptography. In: Annual International Conference on the Theory and Applications of Cryptographic Techniques, pp. 272–302. Springer (2022)
10. Damgård, I., Fitzi, M., Kiltz, E., Nielsen, J.B., Toft, T.: Unconditionally secure constant-rounds multi-party computation for equality, comparison, bits and exponentiation. In: Halevi, S., Rabin, T. (eds.) TCC 2006. LNCS, vol. 3876, pp. 285–304. Springer, Heidelberg (2006). https://doi.org/10.1007/11681878_15
11. Dodis, Y., Mironov, I., Stephens-Davidowitz, N.: Message transmission with reverse firewalls—secure communication on corrupted machines. In: Robshaw, M., Katz, J. (eds.) CRYPTO 2016. LNCS, vol. 9814, pp. 341–372. Springer, Heidelberg (2016). https://doi.org/10.1007/978-3-662-53018-4_13
12. Dziembowski, S., Faust, S., Standaert, F.X.: Private circuits iii: hardware trojan-resilience via testing amplification. In: Proceedings of the 2016 ACM SIGSAC Conference on Computer and Communications Security, CCS 2016, pp. 142–153. ACM, New York, NY, USA (2016). https://doi.org/10.1145/2976749.2978419
13. Imeson, F., Emtenan, A., Garg, S., Tripunitara, M.V.: Securing computer hardware using 3d integrated circuit (ic) technology and split manufacturing for obfuscation. In: Proceedings of the 22nd USENIX Conference on Security, SEC 2013, pp. 495–510. USENIX Association, USA (2013). https://doi.org/10.5555/2534766.2534809
14. Kumar, C., Mishra, N., Chakraborty, S., Ghosh, S., Mukhopadhyay, D.: TERRA : trojan-resilient reverse-firewall for cryptographic applications. Cryptology ePrint Archive, Paper 2025/761 (2025), https://eprint.iacr.org/2025/761
15. Mironov, I., Stephens-Davidowitz, N.: Cryptographic reverse firewalls. In: Oswald, E., Fischlin, M. (eds.) EUROCRYPT 2015. LNCS, vol. 9057, pp. 657–686. Springer, Heidelberg (2015). https://doi.org/10.1007/978-3-662-46803-6_22
16. Naor, M., Pinkas, B.: Efficient oblivious transfer protocols. In: Proceedings of the Twelfth Annual ACM-SIAM Symposium on Discrete Algorithms, SODA 2001, pp. 448–457. Society for Industrial and Applied Mathematics, USA (2001). https://doi.org/10.5555/365411.365502
17. Waksman, A., Sethumadhavan, S.: Tamper evident microprocessors. In: 2010 IEEE Symposium on Security and Privacy, pp. 173–188 (2010). https://doi.org/10.1109/SP.2010.19

Reaction Attack on TFHE: Minimum Number of Oracle Queries and Nearly Optimum Attacking Scheme

Remma Kumazaki and Yuichi Kaji[✉]

Nagoya University, Furo-cho, Chikusa-ku, Nagoya 4648601, Japan
kaji.yuichi.a0@f.mail.nagoya-u.ac.jp

Abstract. This study clarifies the minimum number of queries necessary for a reaction attack on the fully homomorphic encryption over the torus (TFHE). Homomorphic encryption is crucial to ensure both the confidentiality of data and the flexibility for computation. The unique usage of homomorphic encryption allows a reaction attack by a malicious homomorphic server, in which a legitimate client is abused as a ciphertext verification oracle. This study uses an information-theoretical approach to derive a lower bound on the number of queries, an essential measure of the threat of a reaction attack. The tightness of the lower bound is then shown by constructing a nearly optimum attacking scheme that almost achieves the bound. The lower bound is numerically calculated for a commonly used implementation of TFHE, where the computed value clearly and explicitly indicates the borderline which a TFHE client should not pass.

Keywords: homomorphic encryption · TFHE · reaction attack · entropy · information theoretical security

1 Introduction

1.1 Homomorphic Encryption

With the wide diffusion of cloud-based services, it is common for one's data to be possessed and processed by unidentifiable servers on the cloud. Ensuring both the confidentiality of the data and the flexibility for computation becomes crucial, and *homomorphic encryption* [5] is expected to play an essential role in various contexts [10, 14]. Homomorphic encryption enables us to perform calculations on encrypted data while keeping the data encrypted; For encrypted data $E(x)$ and $E(y)$ and an operation $\circ$ on plaintexts, one can perform, without a key, another operation $*$ on ciphertexts that satisfies $E(x) * E(y) = E(x \circ y)$. If we provide $E(x)$ and $E(y)$ to a cloud server and let the server calculate $E(x) * E(y)$, we can obtain the computation result $x \circ y$ without exposing x and y to the server.

The realization of secure and practical homomorphic encryption has been a longstanding problem since its first proposal in 1978 [13]. Homomorphic encryption must involve a mathematical structure to enable homomorphic operations, but such a structure often makes the encryption scheme vulnerable. A breakthrough was brought in

2006 by the study on the problem of learning-with-errors (LWE) [9]. People found that LWE provides both the robustness to secure encryption and the flexibility necessary to realize homomorphic operations [9], and several LWE-based homomorphic encryptions were discussed thereafter. However, those schemes suffer from the noise accumulated through homomorphic operations, which limits the applicable number of homomorphic operations. The control of noise becomes a focal point for realizing a *fully* homomorphic encryption, which should allow an unlimited number of applications of homomorphic operations. In 2009, Gentry overcame the problem by introducing *bootstrapping* [5], an operation to lower the magnitude of the noise accumulated through homomorphic operations. A fully homomorphic encryption scheme was developed using bootstrapping operations [5], but it was not sufficiently practical because the implementation of bootstrapping was costly and takes a long time. Later, Chillotti et al. demonstrated that using the LWE problem over a *torus* enables an efficient implementation of bootstrapping [3]. They proposed the *fully homomorphic encryption over the torus*, abbreviated as *TFHE* [3], which is now recognized as one of the most secure and practical fully homomorphic encryption schemes. It has been shown that breaking TFHE through a chosen-plaintext attack is equivalent to solving an LWE problem [3], which suggests that TFHE is secure against the usual attacking method in both classic and quantum frameworks. On the other hand, we need to remark that the unique usage of homomorphic encryption may allow a more powerful type of attack, which is named a reaction attack.

In a *reaction attack*, an adversary sends forged or altered ciphertexts to a computer system and tries to infer the information hidden in the system by observing the system's *reaction* [8]. Suppose the ciphertext sent to the system is malformed or decrypted to an abnormal value. In that case, the system may show an unusual reaction, such as issuing an error message, a longer response time, or a halt by exception. Such a reaction does not leak the hidden information directly, but the adversary might be able to learn something about the key or the encrypted data from that reaction. The reaction attack might be restrained if the system ignores all data coming from suspicious entities. However, such an approach is pointless in homomorphic encryption because it is a framework for attaining security in utilizing possibly suspicious computation servers (if the server is completely confident, we do not need to use homomorphic encryption). This means that reaction attacks are inevitable for homomorphic encryption, and the attack's threat should be investigated carefully.

It has been shown in [1] that TFHE is vulnerable if the server for homomorphic operations mounts a reaction attack. In the attack, the server tries to identify the error in the LWE problem in a binary search manner, where error values are compared with pivots by sending an altered ciphertext to a legitimate receiver and observing its reaction. Once errors are identified through these attempts, the key of TFHE is easily calculated. In this framework, the legitimate receiver is abused as a *ciphertext verification oracle* (*CVO*) [12], and the altered ciphertexts are used as *queries* to the oracle. The threat of the attack is measured by the number of queries used in the attack. If the attack succeeds with a few queries, clients hardly notice the attack, and the key can be revealed easily. The number of queries is discussed in [1] and its follow-up study [11], but the discussion ends with the superficial comparison of numbers and does not delve into insightful consideration.

1.2 Contribution of This Study

This paper shows that the number of queries necessary for the reaction attack on TFHE is lower bounded by the entropy of the plaintext messages and the noises used in ciphertexts of TFHE. The bound seems trivial at a glance, but a substantial point in our discussion is that the lower bound is tight: if we allow a reaction attacker to send queries more than the lower bound, then the key of TFHE is revealed to that attacker. The tightness is shown by constructing an attacking scheme by modifying the algorithm in [1]. We analyze the number of queries of the proposed scheme and show that the number almost coincides with the lower bound determined by the entropy. In other words, the proposed attacking scheme is nearly *optimum* for the number of queries. Because the gap between the theoretical bound and the number of queries our attacking scheme makes is so small, we conjecture that no attacking scheme uses a smaller number of queries than the proposed scheme. These results imply that the lower bound gives the minimum number of queries with which a reaction attacker obtains the key. The minimum number shows a clear and explicit threshold of how many queries TFHE can tolerate. The key remains safe if the number of queries is fewer than the threshold, but is seriously threatened once the number exceeds the threshold.

It is also emphasized that the lower bound we show is not conceptual but a concrete value that can be calculated numerically. Consider, for example, the reference implementation [2] of TFHE maintained by the authors of [3]. In this implementation, torus elements and noises are represented as 32-bit integers, and the noise is generated by rounding a continuous value that obeys the normal distribution with standard deviation 2^{17}. Calculation shows that the entropy of the message and the noise used in a ciphertext of this implementation of TFHE is 20.05 bits. Our result implies that this value, 20.05, is the lower bound on the number of queries required to identify the message and the noise used in a ciphertext of TFHE. The key length in the implementation of [2] is $n = 630$, and a 630-bit key is revealed when the messages and noises in 630 ciphertexts are identified. Therefore, the lower bound guarantees that the reaction attack does not reveal the key with queries less than $20.05n = 12,631.5$ for this implementation. For the same implementation, the nearly optimal attacking scheme that we propose uses 20.12 queries on average to identify the message and the noise in a ciphertext. The scheme therefore reveals a key with $20.12n = 12,675.6$ queries on average, which is only forty more than the lower bound and should be seriously considered when discussing a key's lifetime in TFHE. It is worth noting that the theoretical approach from information theory provides a practical and quantitative characterization of the security of TFHE.

2 TFHE and Reaction Attack

2.1 LWE over the Torus

In [3], a real *torus* is defined as $\mathbb{T} = \mathbb{R}/\mathbb{Z}$ mod 1, and thus as the set of real values in $[0, 1)$. An addition $+$ of two torus elements $a, b \in \mathbb{T}$ is defined as $a + b$ mod 1, with

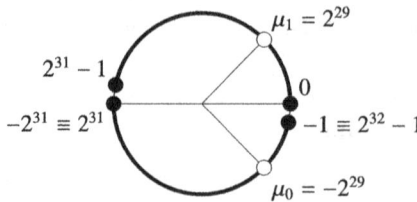

Fig. 1. illustration of the torus and encodings

which we can define a multiplication of an integer $k \in \mathbb{Z}$ and a torus element $a \in \mathbb{T}$ by $ka = ak = a + \cdots + a$. For an n-tuple (or a vector) $\boldsymbol{u} = (u_1, \ldots, u_n) \in \mathbb{Z}^n$ of integers and an n-tuple $\boldsymbol{v} = (v_1, \ldots, v_n) \in \mathbb{T}^n$ of torus elements, the dot product is defined as $\boldsymbol{u} \cdot \boldsymbol{v} = \boldsymbol{v} \cdot \boldsymbol{u} = \sum_{i=1}^{n} u_i v_i$. It is often useful to treat the torus as the set of reals in $[-1/2, 1/2)$ by regarding a torus element $1 - a$ with $0 < a \le 1/2$ as $-a$.

Let n be an integer, $S \subset \mathbb{Z}^n$ be a finite subset of n-tuples of integers, and μ and σ be parameters that are used as the mean and the standard deviation of a normal distribution. Choose a *key vector* $\boldsymbol{s} \in S$ uniformly, and also choose $\boldsymbol{a}_i \in \mathbb{T}^n$ uniformly and independently for $1 \le i \le n$. Sample n values $e_1, \ldots, e_n$ independently according to the normal distribution $\mathcal{N}(\mu, \sigma^2)$, and define $b_i = \boldsymbol{a}_i \cdot \boldsymbol{s} + e_i$ for $1 \le i \le n$. The values $e_1, \ldots, e_n$ are called *errors* or *noises*. The *learning-with-errors* over the torus is a problem of finding the key vector $\boldsymbol{s}$ from given $(\boldsymbol{a}_i, b_i)$ with $1 \le i \le n$[9] (if the rank of $\boldsymbol{a}_1, \ldots, \boldsymbol{a}_n$ is less than n, then additional tuples can be provided). It is believed that LWE is difficult to solve, though we can solve the problem easily once the values of noises $e_1, \ldots, e_n$ are identified.

2.2 TFHE and Its Parameters

This section briefly reviews the encryption mechanism of *TFHE*, the fully homomorphic encryption over the torus [3]. We omit many aspects such as homomorphic operations and the bootstrapping mechanism in TFHE because they have little relevance to the discussion in this paper.

Let μ_0 and μ_1 be two torus elements that are called the *encodings* of a 1-bit message 0 and 1, respectively. For a key vector $\boldsymbol{s} \in S$, TFHE encrypts a 1-bit plaintext message $m \in \{0, 1\}$ to a ciphertext $(\boldsymbol{a}, b)$ where $\boldsymbol{a} \in \mathbb{T}^n$ is chosen uniformly and $b = \boldsymbol{a} \cdot \boldsymbol{s} + \mu_m + e$ with the noise e sampled according to $\mathcal{N}(0, \sigma^2)$ (we may regard that $b = \boldsymbol{a} \cdot \boldsymbol{s} + e'$ with e' sampled according to $\mathcal{N}(\mu_m, \sigma^2)$). To decrypt $(\boldsymbol{a}, b)$, one computes $\mu = b - \boldsymbol{a} \cdot \boldsymbol{s}$ and sees if which of μ_0 or μ_1 is closer to μ; the decryption result is 0 if $|\mu_0 - \mu| \le |\mu_1 - \mu|$, and 1 otherwise. Notice that $\mu = b - \boldsymbol{a} \cdot \boldsymbol{s} = \mu_m + e$ with m the encoded plaintext bit and e the noise. To make this decryption work, the standard deviation σ of the noise is chosen so that e has a relatively small magnitude compared to μ_0 and μ_1.

In the reference implementation of TFHE [2], the torus elements and noises are scaled by 2^{32} and rounded to 32-bit integers in $\mathbb{Z}_{2^{32}} = [0, 2^{32} - 1]$. It is common to regard the integers as signed, and therefore, we consider a torus as the set of integers in $[-2^{31}, 2^{31} - 1]$. The encodings used in [2] are $\mu_0 = -2^{29}$ and $\mu_1 = 2^{29}$, which correspond to $\pm 1/8$ in the real torus $\mathbb{T}$. Figure 1 illustrates the torus and the encodings in [2]. Torus elements are points on the circumference of the circle, and $2^{32} - a$ with $1 \leq a \leq 2^{31}$ is regarded as a negative number $-a$. A ciphertext is decrypted to 0 if $\mu = b - \boldsymbol{a} \cdot \boldsymbol{s} \in [-2^{31}, -1] \equiv [2^{31}, 2^{32} - 1]$, and to 1 if $\mu \in [0, 2^{31} - 1]$. The standard deviation σ of the normal distribution for the noise is $\sigma = 2^{17}$. Notice that σ is so small that sampled noises are expected to have small magnitude compared to the encoding values $\pm 2^{29}$, making $\mu_m + e$ remain close to μ_m. The length of the key vector is $n = 630$, and the space of the keys is taken as $S = \mathbb{Z}_{2^{32}}^n$.

2.3 Reaction Attack on TFHE

In typical TFHE usage, a client has a secret key while a server does not have the key. The client sends encrypted data to the server and requests the server to perform homomorphic operations on the encrypted data. The server returns the operation's result in encrypted form, which the client decrypts and utilizes the result in the subsequent computation. Assume that the server is malicious and alters the ciphertext to be returned to the client. The client will continue the usual computation if the alteration does not change the decryption result. On the other hand, the client may show unusual reactions if the alteration of the ciphertext changes the decryption result. The unusual reaction can be observed in many different ways such as an emission of an error message, inconsistent behavior, abortion of computation, or a slight fluctuation of side information that the client does not concern. It seems complicated and unrealistic to eliminate the difference in reactions entirely. The reactions themselves do not expose secret information directly, but the differences in reactions may allow an adversary to learn about the key that is used in the client. The attack focusing on the target's reactions is generally called a *reaction attack* [8].

Chaturvedi et al. showed in [1] that TFHE is vulnerable to a reaction attack. In the framework of [1], the homomorphic server sends altered ciphertexts to the client. Upon receiving a ciphertext, the client shows either of two reactions depending on the decryption result of the received ciphertext. The server's attack in [1] consists of three phases: (1) selection of target ciphertexts, (2) identification of the noise in a target ciphertext, and (3) calculation of the key vector. In Phase 1, from ciphertexts computed by the homomorphic operations, the adversary (server) selects n *qualifying* ciphertexts that are encryptions of $m = 1$ and have non-negative noises. In Phase 2, the adversary determines the value of the noise used in the qualifying ciphertext in a binary search manner. In Phases 1 and 2, the computation is carried out by sending altered ciphertexts to the client and observing its reaction. Once the messages and noises are determined for n qualifying ciphertexts, the LWE problem turns into a system of equations from which the key vector is easily calculated (Phase 3).

In a formal discussion, the client in the above attack can be regarded as an *oracle* that answers whether a given ciphertext, which is called a *query*, is decrypted to an expected result. More specifically, the client plays the role of a *ciphertext verification oracle* [12], which we will define more formally later. The reaction attack is formalized as an interaction between the adversary (server) and the oracle (client), and the efficiency of an attack is measured by the number of queries necessary to complete the attack. Simple analysis shows that $6n$ queries are required in Phase 1 of [1]. The number of queries in Phase 2 is calculated as $31n$ if 32-bit integers are used to represent noises.

No query is necessary in Phase 3; therefore, $37n$ is the total number of queries made by the attack in [1] for the TFHE implementation of [2]. Walter proposes to reduce the number of queries to $27n$ by ignoring noises that rarely happen [11]. However, the number is not comparable to that of [1] because the attack in [11] fails with more probability than the attack in [1].

2.4 Formalization of the Oracle

To avoid possible confusion in the following discussion, we formalize the *ciphertext verification oracle*, abbreviated as *CVO*, as an abstract machine that receives a pair of ciphertexts (c, c') as a *query*, and answers "yes" if c and c' decrypt to the same result, and "no" otherwise.

We note that there is a small gap between the real client of TFHE and the above-defined CVO, but the gap does not change the essential points of the discussion while contributing to making it more transparent and more explicit. For example, a query to CVO is formalized as a pair of ciphertexts, while it is a single altered ciphertext that is sent from the adversary to the client. This difference is justified as follows: In the reaction attack, including the discussions in [1, 11], it is implicitly assumed that there is a correct ciphertext and the client unconsciously distinguishes whether the received ciphertext decrypts to the same result as the implicitly assumed correct ciphertext. By formalizing the query as a pair of correct and altered ciphertexts, we can clarify what the client verifies. We also remark that the real client may not always show unusual reactions when it receives wrong ciphertexts, while we assume that CVO always answers correctly whether c and c' decrypt to the same result. This difference is not substantial, as the assumption on CVO is regarded as the formalization of a cautious attacker who never misses minor differences in reactions.

3 Lower-Bound on the Number of Queries

3.1 Lower-Bound by Entropy

In this section, we investigate the lower bound on the number of queries necessary in the reaction attack on TFHE. The lower bound is essential because the reaction attack cannot be completed with fewer queries than the bound.

Let M and E be random variables of the one-bit message and the noise used in a ciphertext, respectively, and denote the entropy of a random variable of X by $H(X)$.

Theorem 1. *Let (a, b) be a ciphertext of TFHE with $b = a \cdot s + \mu_m + e$, where s is the key vector, $m \in \{0, 1\}$ is a plaintext message and e is the noise. We need $H(M) + H(E)$ or more queries to identify m and e through a reaction attack.*

Proof: Let t be the number of queries with which m and e are identified through a reaction attack. Write by X_i the answer of the CVO for the i-th query ($1 \leq i \leq t$) in the attack. As for the joint entropy $H(M, E, X_1, \ldots, X_t)$, we have

$$H(M, E, X_1, \ldots, X_t) = H(X_1) + H(X_2|X_1) + \cdots + H(X_t|X_1, \ldots, X_{t-1})$$
$$+ H(M, E|X_1, \ldots, X_t).$$

Note that, for $1 \leq i \leq t$, $H(X_i|X_1,\ldots,X_{i-1}) \leq 1$ because X_i, the answer from CVO, takes one of two values. Also notice that $H(M, E|X_1,\ldots,X_t) = 0$ because we have assumed that the values of M and E are identified from the t answers from CVO. Consequently we have $H(M, E, X_1, \ldots, X_t) \leq t$. As for the joint entropy, there is another transformation:

$$H(M, E, X_1, \ldots, X_t) = H(M, E) + H(X_1, \ldots, X_t|M, E)$$
$$= H(M) + H(E) + H(X_1, \ldots, X_t|M, E)$$
$$\geq H(M) + H(E),$$

where $H(M, E) = H(M) + H(E)$ holds because the message and the noise are chosen independently. With this inequality, $H(M) + H(E) \leq t$ is derived. □

The theorem guarantees that the key of TFHE is not revealed solely by a reaction attack if the number of queries is restricted to less than $H(M)+H(E)$. This means that the client can deter the reaction attack by replacing the key of TFHE before $H(M) + H(E)$ results of the homomorphic operations are received. This gives an essential insight into discussing the appropriate lifetime of a key.

Another point we notice is that the lower bound $H(M) + H(E)$ seems very small. In a sense, $H(M) + H(E)$ is trivial as a lower bound on the number of queries to identify M and E. In a discussion on cryptography, we often anticipate an encryption scheme to have *exponential* robustness in the size of secrets. If, for example, the secret key is n bits in length and has an n-bit entropy, then the encryption scheme should stay secure against all adversaries that do not have computational resources (number of steps, for example) smaller than 2^n. However, the lower bound on the number of queries for a reaction attack is $H(M) + H(E)$, which is in a proportional order in the size of secrets rather than exponential, and is irrelevant to the key size. This seems helpless, and a simple question arises naturally: is the lower bound of Theorem 1 tight or meaninglessly loose? Our answer is that the lower bound is tight. In the subsequent Sect. 4, we will focus on the tightness of the lower bound by showing an attacking method that uses almost the same number of queries as the lower bound.

3.2 Lower Bound in the Real System

Theorem 1 shows that a reaction attack needs $H(M) + H(E)$ or more queries to identify the message and the noise used in a ciphertext. It is reasonable to assume that the message M distributes uniformly over $\{0, 1\}$ and hence $H(M) = 1$. On the other hand, the calculation of the noise's entropy $H(E)$ is not apparent because it depends on how the noises are created. This section is devoted to calculating the precise value of $H(E)$ for the reference implementation [2] of TFHE.

In the formalization over a real torus $\mathbb{T}$, a noise is sampled according to a continuous normal distribution. In the implementation [2], torus elements and noises are scaled by 2^{32} and rounded to 32-bit integers. Specifically, a noise is obtained by sampling a continuous value according to a normal distribution with scaled standard deviation and by rounding the sampled continuous value. In this case, we need to convert the *differential entropy* [4] of a continuous random variable to the usual Shannon entropy of a discrete random variable. Let $h(X)$ denote the differential entropy of a continuous random variable X, and let Y^Δ be a discrete random variable which is defined by quantizing the value of X with the quantization step $\Delta(>0)$. The following relation holds between the entropy $H(Y^\Delta)$ of Y^Δ and the differential entropy $h(X)$ of X[4, Theorem 8.3.1].

$$\lim_{\Delta \to 0} H(Y^\Delta) \to h(X) - \log_2 \Delta. \tag{1}$$

If X obeys a normal distribution with standard deviation σ, then its differential entropy is given by

$$h(X) = \frac{1}{2} \log_2 2\pi e \sigma^2$$

as shown in [4, Example 8.1.2]. In the implementation in [2], the standard deviation and the quantization step are taken as $\sigma = 2^{17}$ and $\Delta = 1$, respectively. The relation (1) is valid only if $\Delta \to 0$, but $\Delta = 1$ is so large and $H(Y^\Delta)$ and $h(X)$ cannot be correlated with this setting. To get around this issue, introduce another continuous random variable $X' = 2^{-32}X$ and define Y^Δ by quantizing the value of X' with the quantization step 2^{-32}. Obviously $P_E(e) = P_{Y^\Delta}(e2^{-32})$ holds for any realized value e of E, and we have $H(E) = H(Y^\Delta)$. The quantization step of $\Delta = 2^{-32}$ is tiny, and the relation of (1) holds for this case, that is, we have

$$H(E) = H(Y^\Delta) = h(X') - \log_2 2^{-32} = h(X') + 32.$$

The new random variable X' obeys a normal distribution with standard deviation $2^{17} \times 2^{-32} = 2^{-15}$, and its differential entropy is

$$h(X') = \frac{1}{2} \log_2 2\pi e (2^{-15})^2 = -12.95.$$

The entropy of the discrete noise E is therefore calculated as $H(E) = H(Y^\Delta) = h(X') + 32 = 19.05$.

As we have stated, it is reasonable to assume that $H(M) = 1$. Consequently, the lower bound that is given in Theorem 1 is $H(M) + H(E) = 1 + 19.05 = 20.05$. A reaction attack needs 20.05 or more queries to identify the message and the noise used in a ciphertext of the implementation [2].

Compare this lower bound 20.05 with the number of queries used in existing reaction attacks. In the reaction attack considered in [1], 6 and 31 queries are necessary in the first and the second phases of the attack, and thus 37 queries are required to identify the message and the noise in a ciphertext. This is nearly double 20.05 and far from the lower bound. It is shown in [11] that the number of queries in the second phase can be reduced to 21 by ignoring rarely occurring noises. The modification degrades the probability of success of the attack, while the total number of queries, 6+21=27, is still far from the lower bound. These results suggest that more efficient reaction attacks can exist.

4 Nearly Optimum Attack and the Tightness of Lower Bound

There is a gap between the lower bound in Theorem 1 and the numbers of queries that are necessary for the attacks in [1,11]. We show in this section that the gap can be

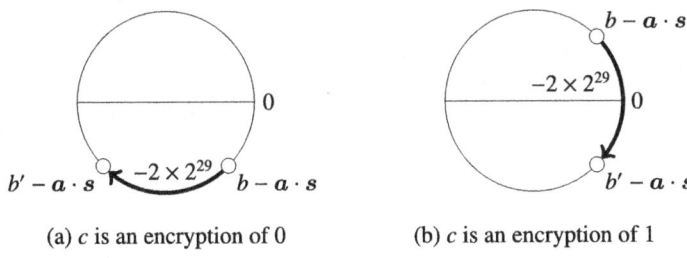

(a) c is an encryption of 0 (b) c is an encryption of 1

Fig. 2. phase 1 of the attack

eliminated by proposing a reaction attack that is nearly optimum with respect to the number of queries. It is shown that the number of queries used in the proposed attack almost coincides with the lower bound stated in Theorem 1, meaning that the bound is tight and represents the minimum number of queries that bring a reaction attack success. In this section, we assume the implementation [2] of TFHE where plaintext messages are encoded to $\mu_0 = -2^{29}$ and $\mu_1 = 2^{29}$, which correspond to $-1/8$ and $+1/8$ of the real torus, respectively.

4.1 The Attack

The attacking scheme we consider is a modification of the attack in [1]. Similar to [1], our attacking scheme consists of three phases: (1) identification of the messages in ciphertexts, (2) identification of the noises in ciphertexts, and (3) calculation of the key vector.

In TFHE usage, an adversary, typically the server that performs homomorphic operations, has access to many ciphertexts to be returned to a client. In Phase 1 of the attack, the adversary selects n of such ciphertexts and identifies the message bits that are encrypted in them. Let $c = (a, b)$ be one of the ciphertexts that the adversary selects. For this ciphertext, the adversary computes $b' = b - 2 \times 2^{29}$ and $c' = (a, b')$, and sends CVO (ciphertext verification oracle) with the query (c, c') asking whether c and c' are decrypted to the same result. If c was an encryption of a message bit 0, then $b = a \cdot s - 2^{29} + e$ and $b' = a \cdot s - 3 \times 2^{29} + e$. In this case, both c and c' are decrypted to 0 and CVO answers "yes" for the query (c, c') (Fig. 2(a)). On the other hand, if c was an encryption of a message bit 1, then $b = a \cdot s + 2^{29} + e$ and $b' = a \cdot s - 2^{29} + e$. In this case c is decrypted to 1 while c' is decrypted to 0, and CVO answers "no" for the query (c, c') (Fig. 2(b)). Therefore, the adversary can identify the message bit encrypted in a ciphertext c with only one query to CVO.

In Phase 2 of the attack, the adversary tries to identify the noise used in a ciphertext. Assume meanwhile that $c = (a, b)$ is an encryption of a message bit 1, and therefore $b = a \cdot s + 2^{29} + e$. In a practical setting, including [2], parameters are chosen so that c is correctly decrypted to 1. This is to say, $b - a \cdot s = 2^{29} + e$ belongs to the section $[0, 2^{31} - 1]$, and consequently the noise e belongs to the section $[-2^{29}, 2^{31} - 2^{29} - 1] = [-2^{29}, 3 \times 2^{29} - 1]$. Consider a slightly general situation where the adversary knows that the noise e belongs to a section $[l, r]$. In this case, the adversary can take a *pivot* integer

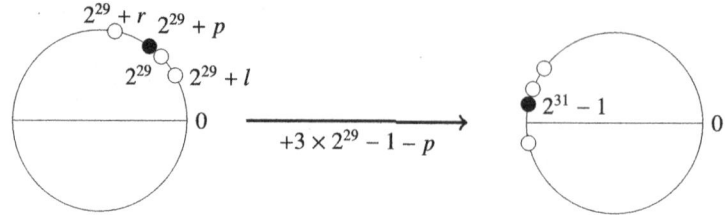

Fig. 3. phase 2 of the attack (points illustrate values of $b - a \cdot s$ and $b' - a \cdot s$).

p with $l < p < r$ and send CVO the query (c, c') where

$$c' = (a, b + 3 \times 2^{29} - 1 - p)$$
$$= (a, a \cdot s + 2^{29} + e + 3 \times 2^{29} - 1 - p)$$
$$= (a, a \cdot s + 2^{31} - 1 + e - p)$$
$$= (a, b').$$

The operation on the second component is intended to bring the value of b with noise p goes to $2^{31} - 1$, the maximum of the positive values in the torus. With this operation, a value of b with noise greater than p "overflows" to the negative region, while the value stays positive if its noise is p or less (Fig. 3). Indeed, if $e \leq p$ holds for the chosen pivot p, then

$$b' - a \cdot s = 2^{31} - 1 + e - p \leq 2^{31} - 1$$

and c' is decrypted to 1. If $p < e$, then

$$b' - a \cdot s = 2^{31} - 1 + e - p > 2^{31} - 1$$

and c' is decrypted to 0. As c is assumed to be an encryption of 1, CVO answers "yes" if $e \leq p$, and "no" if $p < e$. In the former case, the range of the noise is narrowed down to $[l, p]$. In the latter case, the range is narrowed to $[p + 1, r]$. In this way, we can identify the value of the noise e in a binary search manner by utilizing CVO.

The discussion so far is almost the same as in [1], but we add a twist here. In [1], the pivot p of the binary search is chosen so that $p = \lfloor (l + r)/2 \rfloor$. Our idea is to choose the pivot p so that the probability of $e \in [l, p]$ equals the probability of $e \in [p + 1, r]$ by referring to the probability density function of the noise. Let F be the cumulative distribution function of the normal distribution that the noise obeys. A noise in [2] is obtained by rounding a fractional part of a continuous noise, and therefore the probability of having a noise $e \in \mathbb{Z}$ is specified by $F(e + 1) - F(e)$. The probability of $e \in [l, p]$ is $F(p + 1) - F(l)$ and the probability of $e \in [p + 1, r]$ is $F(r + 1) - F(p + 1)$. To make the two probabilities as equal as possible, we choose the pivot integer p so that $p = \lfloor F^{-1}((F(l) + F(r + 1))/2) \rfloor$.

So far, we have discussed under the assumption that the ciphertext c is an encryption of 1, but a similar discussion holds for another case of c being an encryption of 0. If $c = (a, b)$ is an encryption of 0, then $b = a \cdot s - 2^{29} + e$ and the noise e belongs to the section $[-3 \times 2^{29}, 2^{29} - 1]$. Starting from this section, we can identify the value of e by the binary search as the case of c an encryption of 1.

The computation in Phase 2 is summarized as a pseudo-code in Fig. 4, where $o \leftarrow CVO(c, c')$ in the code represents that the answer of the oracle is o for the query (c, c') and we are assuming that the plaintext bit m of the ciphertext c has been computed in Phase 1 of the attack.

In Phase 3 of the attack, we can eliminate the fluctuations in the LWE problem because unknown μ_m and e have been identified in the preceding phases. Solve the system of equations, and we can calculate the key vector s.

Algorithm 1 Phase 2: search of the noise e

Require: a ciphertext $c = (a, b)$ and its plaintext bit m
Ensure: the noise e in the ciphertext c
1: **if** $m == 0$ **then**
2: $\quad [l, r] \leftarrow [-3 \times 2^{29}, 2^{29} - 1]$
3: **else**
4: $\quad [l, r] \leftarrow [-2^{29}, 3 \times 2^{29} - 1]$
5: **end if**
6: **while** $r - l > 0$ **do**
7: $\quad p = \lfloor F^{-1}((F(l) + F(r + 1))/2) \rfloor$
8: $\quad$ **if** $m == 0$ **then**
9: $\quad\quad c' \leftarrow (a, b - 3 \times 2^{29} + p)$
10: $\quad\quad o \leftarrow CVO(c, c')$
11: $\quad\quad$ **if** $o =$ "yes" **then**
12: $\quad\quad\quad [l, r] \leftarrow [p, r]$
13: $\quad\quad$ **else**
14: $\quad\quad\quad [l, r] \leftarrow [l, p - 1]$
15: $\quad\quad$ **end if**
16: $\quad$ **else**
17: $\quad\quad c' \leftarrow (a, b + 3 \times 2^{29} - 1 - p)$
18: $\quad\quad o \leftarrow CVO(c, c')$
19: $\quad\quad$ **if** $o =$ "yes" **then**
20: $\quad\quad\quad [l, r] \leftarrow [l, p]$
21: $\quad\quad$ **else**
22: $\quad\quad\quad [l, r] \leftarrow [p + 1, r]$
23: $\quad\quad$ **end if**
24: $\quad$ **end if**
25: **end while**
26: **return** l

Fig. 4. pseudo-code of the computation in Phase 2

4.2 The Number of Queries in the Attack

In this section, we investigate how many queries are made by the proposed attacking scheme for a single ciphertext.

Lemma 1. *Let (a, b) be a ciphertext of TFHE with $b = a \cdot s + \mu_m + e$, where s is the key vector, $m \in \{0, 1\}$ is a plaintext message and e is the noise. We need approximately $1 + H(E)$ queries on average to identify m and e through a proposed reaction attack.*

Proof: For the single ciphertext $c = (a, b)$, only one query is used in Phase 1 to identify the plaintext message bit m of c. Therefore, it suffices to show that the number of queries in Phase 2 is approximately $H(E)$ on average. For the recursive proof, we introduce an auxiliary random variable $Y_{l,r}$, where l and r are integers with $l \leq r$. The realized value of $Y_{l,r}$ is determined so that $Y_{l,r} = 1$ if the noise e is included in the section $[l, r]$ and $Y_{l,r} = 0$ otherwise. Under the condition that e is included in $[l, r]$ (i.e. $Y_{l,r} = 1$), the probability distribution of the noise is characterized by the conditional probability function $P_{E|Y_{l,r}}(x|1)$. The entropy of E under the condition $Y_{l,r} = 1$ is thus

$$H(E|Y_{l,r} = 1) = \sum_{x=l}^{r} -P_{E|Y_{l,r}}(x|1) \log_2 P_{E|Y_{l,r}}(x|1).$$

In the sequel, we show that if the binary search of Phase 2 is performed for the section $[l, r]$, then the search makes approximately $H(E|Y_{l,r} = 1)$ queries on average.

The proof is obtained by induction on the size of the section. For the basis of the proof, consider that the section $[l, r]$ contains only one integer, that is, $[l, r] = [l, l]$. In this case, the value of the noise e must be l, and no query is necessary. The conditional probability for this case is given by $P_{E|Y_{l,l}}(l|1) = 1$, and $H(E|Y_{l,l}) = 0$, which coincides with the number of queries in this case.

Assume that the inductive hypothesis holds for any section smaller than s. We consider that the section $[l, r]$ contains s integers. In Phase 2 of the proposed attacking scheme, the pivot p is selected so that the probabilities of $e \in [l, p]$ and $e \in [p + 1, r]$ are equally likely. For the selected pivot p, one CVO query is made to determine which of (case 1) $e \in [l, p]$ or (case 2) $e \in [p + 1, r]$ holds. Introduce another random variable $Y_{l,p}$ so that $Y_{l,p} = 1$ if $e \in [l, p]$, and $Y_{l,p} = 0$ otherwise. If $e \in [l, p]$ in the binary search (case 1), then the noise is characterized by the conditional probability function $P_{E|Y_{l,p}, Y_{l,r}}(x|1, 1)$. The binary search for the section $[l, p]$ will make $H(E|Y_{l,p} = 1, Y_{l,r} = 1)$ queries approximately on average because of the inductive hypothesis for the section $[l, p]$. Similarly, if $e \in [p + 1, r]$ (case 2), then the binary search for the section $[p + 1, r]$ will make $H(E|Y_{l,p} = 0, Y_{l,r} = 1)$ queries approximately on average. The expected number of queries is therefore approximated by

$$\begin{aligned} & 1 + P_{X_{l,p}|X_{l,r}}(1|1) H(E|X_{l,p} = 1, X_{l,r} = 1) \\ & + P_{X_{l,p}|X_{l,r}}(0|1) H(E|X_{l,p} = 0, X_{l,r} = 1) \\ & = 1 + H(E|X_{l,p}, X_{l,r} = 1) \end{aligned} \qquad (2)$$

where 1 counts the query to determine whether $e \in [l, p]$ or not. Remind that the pivot p is chosen so that $P_{Y_{l,p}|Y_{l,r}}(0|1) \approx P_{Y_{l,p}|Y_{l,r}}(1|1)$. In this case $H(Y_{l,p}|Y_{l,r} = 1) \approx 1$, and we can substitute the constant 1 in (2) by $H(Y_{l,p}|Y_{l,r} = 1)$. Therefore, the number of queries indicated by (2) is written as

$$\begin{aligned} H(X_{l,p}|X_{l,r} = 1) + H(E|X_{l,p}, X_{l,r} = 1) &= H(E, X_{l,p}|X_{l,r} = 1) \\ &= H(E|X_{l,r} = 1) + H(X_{l,p}|E, X_{l,r} = 1) \quad (3) \\ &= H(E|X_{l,r} = 1). \end{aligned}$$

The last transformation follows because the value of $X_{l,p}$ is uniquely determined if the value of E is known, and hence $H(X_{l,p}|E, X_{l,r} = 1) = 0$.

Now, we have shown that if the binary search of Phase 2 is performed for the section $[l, r]$, then the search makes approximately $H(E|Y_{l,r} = 1)$ queries on average. If l is very small and r is very large, then the noise e rarely goes out of $[l, r]$ and $P_{Y_{l,r}}(1) \approx 1$. In this case

$$H(E) = P_{Y_{l,r}}(1)H(E|Y_{l,r} = 1) + P_{Y_{l,r}}(0)H(E|Y_{l,r} = 0) \approx H(E|Y_{l,r} = 1).$$

This is the case of $[l, r] = [-3 \times 2^{29}, 2^{29} - 1]$ or $[l, r] = [-2^{29}, 3 \times 2^{29} - 1]$ and $\sigma = 2^{17}$, and therefore we can conclude that the number of queries in Phase 2 is approximated as $H(E)$ on average. □

Theorem 1 showed that a reaction attack needs $H(M) + H(E)$ or more queries to identify m and e in a ciphertext. Lemma 1 showed that the proposed reaction attack uses approximately $1 + H(E)$ queries on average. If a plaintext bit m is chosen uniformly from $\{0, 1\}$, then $H(M) = 1$ and the lower bound in Theorem 1 and the number of queries in Lemma 1 coincide. This implies that the lower bound in Theorem 1 is tight, and that the proposed reaction attack is nearly optimum in terms of the number of queries to the CVO, where we are saying "nearly" because we are using some approximations in the proof.

4.3 Effect of Approximations

In the proof of Lemma 1, we have used two approximations. The first approximation we used is $H(Y_{l,p}|Y_{l,r} = 1) \approx 1$. This approximation, not an equation, is introduced because noises take discrete values and the pivot p in the binary search cannot make the probability $P_{Y_{l,p}|Y_{l,r}}(1|1)$ of $e \in [l, p]$ and the probability $P_{Y_{l,p}|Y_{l,r}}(0|1)$ of $e \in [p+1, r]$ exactly the same. A small bias of the two probabilities makes the entropy $H(Y_{l,p}|Y_{l,r} = 1)$ slightly smaller than one, and therefore replacing the constant 1 in (2) by $H(Y_{l,p}|Y_{l,r} = 1)$ brings (3) slightly smaller than the number of queries actually used by the proposed attacking scheme. The second approximation used in the proof is $P_{Y_{l,r}}(1) \approx 1$. This approximation eliminates the contribution of $H(E|Y_{l,r} = 0)$ to $H(E)$, and makes the relation between $H(E)$ and (3) vague.

To evaluate the effect of these approximations, we implemented the binary search in Phase 2 and measured the number of queries necessary to identify the noise in a ciphertext. In the implementation, we used the same parameter setting as [2]: torus elements are represented by signed 32-bit integers, plaintext bits 0 and 1 are encoded to -2^{29} and 2^{29}, respectively, and noises are generated by rounding a continuous value that is sampled according to $\mathcal{N}(0, 2^{17})$. Under this setting, our investigation showed that the average number of queries necessary for Phase 2 of our attack is 19.12 for one ciphertext. One more query is needed for the preceding Phase 1 of the attack, and hence $1 + 19.12 = 20.12$ is the number of queries necessary to identify both the message and the noise in one ciphertext. To derive the key of length n, we need to identify messages and noises of n ciphertexts. Therefore, $20.12n$ is the number of queries that are required by the proposed attacking method.

Remind that the entropy $H(M) + H(E)$, which gives the lower bound on the number of queries, was 20.05 for the implementation [2]. The number 20.12 obtained in the above investigation is slightly greater than the lower bound, but not so much. It is therefore conjectured that the effect of the approximation is minor as far as the attack is used for practical implementations including [2].

5 Conclusion

This study investigated the number of queries necessary in the reaction attack on TFHE. It is shown that the number of queries needed to determine the message and the noise in a ciphertext is lower bounded by $H(M)+H(E)$, where $H(M)$ and $H(E)$ are the entropies of the messages and noises used in a ciphertext of TFHE, respectively. We also presented an attacking scheme and showed that the number of queries used by the scheme is almost the same as the lower bound, suggesting that the lower bound is tight and that the attacking scheme is nearly optimum.

For the practical implementation [2], the lower bound is calculated as 20.05, while the proposed attacking scheme uses 20.12 queries on average. To identify the key, which is an n-tuple of integers, we need to collect messages and noises of n different ciphertexts and turn an LWE problem into a system of equations. If $n = 630$ as in [2], then the lower bound suggests that less than $20.05n = 12,631.5$ queries are too few to complete the attack, while our attacking scheme demonstrates that $20.12n = 12,675.6$ queries suffice. A perspective of this kind helps in discussing the lifetime of a key in TFHE in a practical system.

We can apply the approach and technique used in this study to other homomorphic encryptions that have a similar structure to TFHE. Indeed, the preceding work [1] considers using the binary search technique on another homomorphic encryption known as the Fastest Homomorphic Encryption in the West (FHEW) [6]. Our investigation can naturally extend to FHEW, and numerical results should be obtained for the published implementation [7] of FHEW.

References

1. Chaturvedi, B., Chakraborty, A., Chatterjee, A., Mukhopadhyay, D.: A practical full key recovery attack on TFHE and FHEW by inducing decryption errors, Cryptology ePrint Archive, Report 2022/1563 (2022). https://eprint.iacr.org/2022/1563
2. Chillotti, I., Gama, N., Georgieva, M., Izabachène, M.: TFHE: fast fully homomorphic encryption library over the torus (2016). https://github.com/tfhe/tfhe
3. Chillotti, I., Gama, N., Georgieva, M., Izabachène, M.: TFHE: fast fully homomorphic encryption over the torus. J. Cryptol. **33**, 34–91 (2020)
4. Cover, T.M., Thomas, J.A.: Elements of Information Theory. Wiley (2006)
5. Gentry, C.: Fully homomorphic encryption using ideal lattices. In: Forty-First Annual ACM Symposium on Theory of Computer, pp. 169–178 (2009)
6. Ducas, L., Micciancio, D.: FHEW: bootstrapping homomorphic encryption in less than a second. In: Oswald, E., Fischlin, M. (eds.) EUROCRYPT 2015. LNCS, vol. 9056, pp. 617–640. Springer, Heidelberg (2015). https://doi.org/10.1007/978-3-662-46800-5_24

7. Ducas, L., Micciancio, D.: FHEW: a fully homomorphic encryption library (2017). https://github.com/lducas/FHEW
8. Hall, C., Goldberg, I., Schneier, B.: Reaction attacks against several public-key cryptosystem. In: Second International Conference on Information and Communication Security, pp. 2–12 (1999)
9. Regev, O.: On lattices, learning with errors, random linear codes, and cryptography. J. ACM **56**(6), 1–40 (2006)
10. Tebaa, M., Hajji, S.: Secure cloud computing through homomorphic encryption. Int. J. Adv. Comput. Technol. **5**(16), 29–38 (2013)
11. Walter, M.: On side-channel and CVO attacks against TFHE and FHEW, Cryptology ePrint Archive, Report 2022/1722 (2022). https://eprint.iacr.org/2022/1722
12. Hu, Z., Sun, F., Jiang, J.: Ciphertext verification security of symmetric encryption schemes. Sci. China Ser. F Inf. Sci. **52**(9), 1617–1631 (2009)
13. Rivest, R., Adleman, L., Dertouzos, M.L.: On data banks and privacy homomorphisms. Found. Secure Comput. **4**(11), 169–179 (1973)
14. Zhao, M.E., Geng, Y.: Homomorphic encryption technology for cloud computing. In: Eighth International Congress of Information and Communication Technology, pp. 73–83 (2019)

Predicate-Private Asymmetric Searchable Encryption for Conjunctions from Lattices

Qinyi Li[1]($\boxtimes$) and Xavier Boyen[2]($\boxtimes$)

[1] Griffith University, Brisbane, Australia
qinyi.li@griffith.edu.au
[2] Queensland University of Technology, Brisbane, Australia
xavier.boyen@qut.edu.au

Abstract. Searchable encryption (SE) enables searching encrypted data for useful information without full decryption. Asymmetric searchable encryption (ASE) allows anyone to encrypt data $\mathbf{y}$ with a public key, producing ciphertext $\mathsf{ct}_\mathbf{y}$. Given a predicate $P_\mathbf{x}(\cdot)$ over an attribute $\mathbf{x}$, a testing token $\mathsf{Tk}_\mathbf{x}$ can be generated to evaluate $P_\mathbf{x}(\mathbf{y})$ from $\mathsf{ct}_\mathbf{y}$. It is crucial to ensure that the token holder cannot infer information about $\mathbf{x}$ from $\mathsf{Tk}_\mathbf{x}$, even after evaluating the predicate on multiple ciphertexts. An ASE system meeting this requirement is called an enhanced predicate-private ASE. This paper proposes an enhanced predicate-private ASE system for conjunction predicates, based on standard lattice-based hard problems. This is the first post-quantum enhanced predicate-private ASE system supporting predicates beyond equality. At its core is a predicate-private Hidden Vector Encryption (HVE) scheme that handles large attribute universes. Our system enables privacy-preserving pattern matching on encrypted data, making it practical for various secure applications.

Keywords: searchable encryption · public key · token privacy

1 Introduction

Asymmetric searchable encryption (ASE) [7] is a cryptographic primitive that enables searching for specific patterns in encrypted data without requiring decryption. Formally, let $P : \mathcal{X} \times \mathcal{Y} \to \{0, 1\}$ be a predicate over two sets of vectors $\mathcal{X}$ and $\mathcal{Y}$, where we say $\mathbf{y}$ satisfies $\mathbf{x}$ if $P_\mathbf{x}(\mathbf{y}) = 1$. An ASE system for the predicate P consists of a public key and private key pair $(\mathsf{Pk}, \mathsf{Sk})$. The private key Sk generates a searching token $\mathsf{Tk}_\mathbf{x}$ for a given $\mathbf{x} \in \mathcal{X}$. A ciphertext $\mathsf{Ct}_\mathbf{y}$ is the encryption of data $\mathbf{y} \in \mathcal{Y}$ using the public key Pk. With $\mathsf{Tk}_\mathbf{x}$, one can evaluate $P_\mathbf{x}(\mathbf{y})$, determining whether the encrypted data $\mathbf{y}$ satisfies the pattern specified by $\mathbf{x}$. For simplicity, we refer to a search where $P_\mathbf{x}(\mathbf{y}) = 1$ as a matching search, and where $P_\mathbf{x}(\mathbf{y}) = 0$ as a mismatching search. Besides semantic security, i.e., $\mathsf{Ct}_\mathbf{y}$ reveals no information about $\mathbf{y}$ to eavesdroppers, ASE must guarantee that $\mathsf{Tk}_\mathbf{x}$ does not reveal any information about $\mathbf{y}$ in mismatching searches [7].

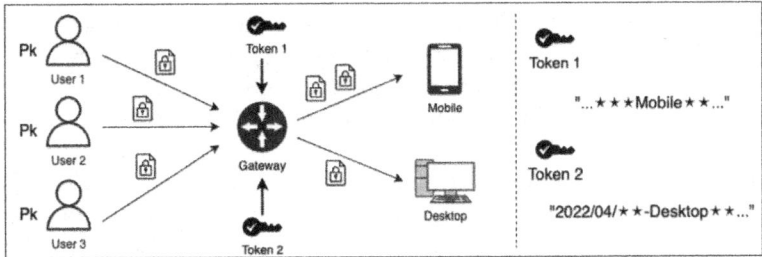

Fig. 1. Application of ASE

The prototype application of ASE, illustrated in Fig. 1, involves a routing gateway being granted searching tokens $\mathsf{Tk_x}$. This enables the gateway to determine whether the plaintexts of incoming ciphertexts contain specific patterns. The gateway then forwards the ciphertexts to the preferred destinations. With more expressive predicates P, ASE can support more complex pattern searches.

Constructing ASE. ASE schemes are constructed using the cryptographic primitive known as public-key predicate encryption (PE) [1,10,15]. A PE scheme consists of public parameters pub and a master key msk. Messages are encrypted using pub along with attributes, denoted $\mathbf{y}$. The decryption key is associated with a predicate $P_\mathbf{x}(\cdot)$, and decryption succeeds if and only if $P_\mathbf{x}(\mathbf{y}) = 1$. In addition to protecting the messages, PE ciphertexts also hide the attributes $\mathbf{y}$. An ASE scheme for a predicate P is derived from a PE scheme with the same predicate. Specifically, let pub and msk denote the public parameters and master private key of a PE scheme, respectively. In the ASE scheme, (Pk, Sk) is set to (pub, msk), and a token $\mathsf{Tk_x}$ corresponds to the decryption key $\mathsf{sk_x}$ of the PE scheme. An ASE ciphertext for an attribute $\mathbf{y}$ is simply a PE ciphertext under $\mathbf{y}$ with a constant message. To test a ciphertext, the ASE token decrypts the PE ciphertext. If the constant message is successfully recovered, it concludes $P_\mathbf{x}(\mathbf{y}) = 1$; otherwise, $P_\mathbf{x}(\mathbf{y}) = 0$. This indicates that ASE systems are PE systems with a constant message.

Predicate Privacy of ASE. In most ASE applications, gateways are required to be trusted. Otherwise, the system may encounter a privacy issue—specifically, the gateway could extract $\mathbf{x}$ from the token $\mathsf{Tk_x}$ and deduce the type of data $\mathbf{y}$ that the destination expects. Even more concerning, access to multiple tokens for different attributes could allow the gateway to reconstruct the data receiver's profile based on the incoming data. The security notion designed to address this problem is called predicate privacy (also referred to more generally as function privacy or function hiding [8,9,20]).[1] Defining predicate privacy for ASE is challenging [6,8]. A malicious gateway can generate ciphertexts for chosen attributes and test them against tokens $\mathsf{Tk_x}$, potentially inferring information about $\mathbf{x}$. Predicate privacy is achievable only when $\mathbf{x}$ has high min-entropy, ensuring that

---

[1] We use the term "predicate privacy" because we focus exclusively on predicate.

blindly chosen ciphertexts fail. Moreover, the standard semantic security definition for ASE (e.g., [7]) does not protect $\mathbf{y}$ from $\mathsf{ct_y}$ if the adversary possesses a token $\mathsf{Tk_x}$ such that $\mathbf{x}$ matches $\mathbf{y}$, thus breaking predicate privacy.

This issue is not unique to ASE but extends to other searchable encryption schemes, such as symmetric searchable encryption [16]. For example, the predicate-private ASE systems of Meng et al. [16] and Arruaga et al. [5] only guarantee predicate privacy for mismatching searches, leaving them vulnerable in matching cases. Similarly, the PE systems by Patranabis et al. [18] for inner-product and conjunction predicates fail to ensure predicate privacy in searchable encryption contexts. Boneh et al. [8] formalised enhanced predicate privacy for PE in equality predicates (anonymous identity-based encryption), and Bartusek et al. [6] extended this to hidden vector encryption for conjunctions. These definitions capture the essence of predicate privacy for ASE, ensuring that $\mathsf{Tk_x}$ reveals no meaningful information about $\mathbf{x}$, even when ciphertexts $\mathsf{ct_y}$ for matching tests (i.e., $P_\mathbf{x}(\mathbf{y}) = 1$) are available. We refer to ASE schemes satisfying such definitions as enhanced predicate-private ASE (EPP-ASE).

1.1 Our Contributions

The Research Gap. Enhanced predicate-private ASE (EPP-ASE) schemes are rare, with existing constructions supporting only limited predicate classes. Boneh et al. [8] proposed enhanced predicate-private anonymous identity-based encryption schemes based on standard assumptions from pairings and lattices, resulting in EPP-ASE schemes for equality predicates. Bartusek et al. [6] extended this to conjunctions (with wildcards) using a predicate-private hidden vector encryption (HVE) system, though their security relies on the generic group model (GGM). This raises an important question: "How can we construct a lattice-based predicate-private ASE scheme that supports predicates beyond equality?"

Our Results. We address the challenge by constructing the first enhanced predicate-private hidden-vector encryption (HVE) scheme from lattices, supporting large attribute universes. HVE, as a special case of PE, enables conjunctions of attributes with wildcards. Let $\mathcal{U}$ be the attribute universe, $\star$ be the wildcard symbol, and $\mathbf{x} = (x_1, ..., x_\ell) \in (\mathcal{U} \cup \star)^\ell$, $\mathbf{y} = (y_1, ..., y_\ell) \in \mathcal{U}^\ell$ be two vectors. The predicate for HVE $P_\mathbf{x}(\mathbf{y}) = 1$ if $x_i = y_i$ or $x_i = \star$ for all $i \in [\ell]$; in this case, we say $\mathbf{y}$ matches $\mathbf{x}$. Our HVE scheme gives an EPP-ASE system supporting pattern matching over encrypted attributes drawn from exponentially large sets. We prove its semantic security and enhanced predicate privacy in selective security models (Sect. 5), relying on the standard LWE assumption without random oracles. Table 1 compares existing predicate-private PE schemes, demonstrating that our HVE scheme advances the state-of-the-art by supporting conjunctions under post-quantum assumptions.

Limitations and Challenges. While our scheme significantly advances the state-of-the-art in enhanced predicate-private PE, it requires an a priori bound on the number of keys whose patterns can match the encrypted attributes (while allowing an unbounded number of keys for non-matching patterns). Such a PE

Table 1. Comparison of Predicate Private Public-Key PE Schemes

Scheme	Predicate	Assumptions	# of Matching Keys Allowed for Enhanced Predicate Privacy	Post-Quantum?
[8]	Equality	DLIN/LWE	Unbounded	✔
[6]	Conjunctions	GGM	Unbounded	✗
Ours	Conjunctions	LWE	Bounded	✔

system is known as bounded-key function-hiding functional encryption (for predicate functions). In practice, this means the derived ASE system can issue a bounded number of tokens whose patterns match the attributes of ciphertexts. This is sufficient for applications of ASE where the maximum number of matching tokens can be known. Enhancing the scheme's expressiveness and removing the bound are natural directions. However, the impossibility result of Ünal [20] indicates that constructing such a system using current lattice techniques faces insurmountable challenges, even for relatively simple functions like quadratic and inner-product functions. Thus, we anticipate that achieving further improvements will necessitate new techniques in lattice-based cryptography.

Applications. Our ASE system enables privacy-enhanced `grep` functionality over large encrypted domains, making it highly suitable for applications requiring privacy-preserving pattern matching on encrypted data, such as deep-packet inspection (DPI). Furthermore, leveraging the efficient conversion method by Bouscati'e et al. [11], our HVE scheme can also be used to Stream Encryption supporting Pattern Matching (SEPM) with enhanced predicate privacy.

1.2 Our Approaches

Our construction is inspired by the works of Boneh et al. [8] and Agrawal [2], and it is based on the classical dual-Regev encryption structure. Recall that the absolute minimum requirement for predicate privacy in the public-key setting is that the key attributes are sufficiently unpredictable. Let q be a prime which is polynomial in the security parameter, $\mathcal{U} = \mathbb{Z}_q$ be the (small) attribute universe, and $\mathbf{A}, \mathbf{U}, \{\mathbf{A}_i\}_{i \in [\ell]}$ be public matrices. To provide predicate privacy, we use a linear (inner product) randomness extractor $\mathsf{Ext}_\mathbf{h}(\cdot)$ with random seed $\mathbf{h}$. Using this setup, we design the following HVE scheme based on GPV encryption [13]. The ciphertext for the attribute $\mathbf{y} \in \mathcal{U}^\ell$ and message msg is set as

$$\mathbf{c}^\mathsf{T} = \mathbf{s}^\mathsf{T}\mathbf{A} + \mathbf{e}^\mathsf{T}; \quad \mathbf{c}_0^\mathsf{T} = \mathbf{s}^\mathsf{T}\mathbf{U} + \mathbf{e}^\mathsf{T} + \mathsf{msg}; \quad \{\mathbf{c}_i^\mathsf{T} = \mathbf{s}^\mathsf{T}(\mathbf{A}_i + y_i\mathbf{G}) + \mathbf{e}_i^\mathsf{T}\}_{i \in [\ell]}$$

The decryption key $\mathsf{sk}_\mathbf{x}$ for a pattern $\mathbf{x} \in (\mathcal{U} \cup \star)^\ell$ contains an index set $S \subseteq [\ell]$ (which includes the positions of $\mathbf{x}$ that are not wildcards), a low-norm matrix $\mathbf{D}$ and a random seed $\mathbf{h} \in \mathcal{U}^\ell$ such that:

$$\left[\mathbf{A} \mid \sum_{i \in S} \mathbf{B}_i h_i + (x_i \cdot h_i)\mathbf{G}\right]\mathbf{D} = [\mathbf{A} \mid \mathbf{B}_\mathbf{h} + \mathsf{Ext}_\mathbf{h}(\mathbf{x})\mathbf{G}]\mathbf{D} = \mathbf{U}$$

Decryption proceeds by applying the secret key $\mathbf{h}$ to linearly transform the ciphertext components $\mathbf{c}_{i\,i\in[\ell]}$ into $\mathbf{B_h} + \mathsf{Ext_h}(\mathbf{x})\mathbf{G}$. The scheme hides $\mathbf{y}_i$ and the message msg under the LWE assumption. Predicate privacy is achieved when $\mathbf{x}$ possesses high min-entropy, in which case the pair $(\mathbf{h}, \mathsf{Ext_h}(\mathbf{x}))$ is statistically close to uniform. However, the scheme exhibits two significant shortcomings. First, it does not necessarily guarantee correctness. Specifically, decrypting a ciphertext associated with an input $\mathbf{y}' \neq \mathbf{y}$ may still succeed, since the equality $\mathsf{Ext_h}(\mathbf{y}) = \mathsf{Ext_h}(\mathbf{y}')$ occurs with non-negligible probability $1/q$. Second, the attribute universe $\mathcal{U} = \mathbb{Z}_q$ is of polynomial size, which limits the ability to achieve high min-entropy, thus weakening the statistical privacy guarantees.

The idea of making a large universe is to use the full-rank difference FRD encoding [3,21] $\mathsf{FRD} : \mathbb{Z}_q^n \to \mathbb{Z}_q^{n \times n}$ to encode up to q^n values for each coordinate of $\mathbf{y}$ (and $\mathbf{x}$, $\mathbf{h}$), making $\mathcal{U} = \mathbb{Z}_q^n$. Our observation is that the homomorphisms of FRD maintain the randomness extraction property. More specifically, let $\mathcal{R}_q = \mathbb{Z}_q[X]/(f(X))$ be a polynomial ring where $f(X)$ is a degree-n polynomial irreducible over $\mathbb{Z}_q$, $\mathbb{Z}_q^n$ is isomorphic to $\mathcal{R}_q$, and every $\mathbb{Z}_q^n$-element has a unique correspondence in $\mathcal{R}_q$ via the coefficient embedding. The FRD function given in [3,21] is homomorphic both multiplicatively and additively, rendering $\mathsf{FRD}(h) + \mathsf{FRD}(x) = \mathsf{FRD}(h+x)$ and $\mathsf{FRD}(h)\mathsf{FRD}(x) = \mathsf{FRD}(h \cdot x)$ where $+$ and $\cdot$ are the polynomial addition and multiplication over $\mathcal{R}_q$, respectively. With this we have $\mathsf{Ext_h}(\mathbf{x}) = \sum_{i \in S} \mathsf{FRD}(h_i)\mathsf{FRD}(x_i) = \mathsf{FRD}(\sum_{i \in S} h_i \cdot x_i)$ and $\sum_{i \in S} h_i \cdot x_i$ is a well-known universal hashing, and so, a randomness extractor, as we needed.

A new challenge arises from the fact that the outputs of the extractor are now in $\mathbb{Z}_q^n$ for which $\mathbf{x}$ needs to have roughly $n \log q$ bits of min-entropy to meet predicate privacy, which is a strong requirement. To solve the problem, we resort to the extended FRD [12], which maps $\mathbb{Z}_q^k$ to $\mathbb{Z}_q^{n \times n}$ for any k divides n. We refer to Sect. 4.1 for more details. This approach offers a "two birds with one stone" solution. By setting $k = \lambda / \log q$ for security parameter λ, we achieve both $1/2^\lambda$ false positive decryption error and λ-bit min-entropy requirement from $\mathbf{x}$.

The construction so far supports simulating only a single private key $\mathsf{sk_x}$ for $\mathbf{x}$ matching the challenge ciphertext attributes, by programming the matrix $\mathbf{U}$ via a carefully chosen $\mathbf{D}$. To simulate up to (an a priori bound) Q such keys, we use a cover-free set to construct each $\mathbf{U}_i$ as a subset-sum of a set of public random matrices. With suitable parameters, the $\mathbf{U}_i$ are independently random, allowing us to program the corresponding decryption keys without collision.

2 Preliminaries

Notations. Let $\mathbf{R}$ be a matrix in $\mathbb{Z}^{m \times k}$. We use $\|\mathbf{R}\|$ to denote ℓ_2 norm of the longest column of $\mathbf{R}$, and $\|\mathbf{R}\|_\infty$ to denote the largest magnitude of the entries in $\mathbf{R}$. Let $s_1(\mathbf{R})$ denote the operator norm of $\mathbf{R}$, i.e., $s_1(\mathbf{R}) = \sup_{\|\mathbf{x}\|=1} \|\mathbf{R}\mathbf{x}\|$. We denote by $x \leftarrow X$ the process of sampling x according to the distribution X. We use $U(X)$ to denote the uniform distribution over the set X. We use standard asymptotic notations, e.g., O, Θ, ω. Let $\lambda \in \mathbb{N}$, the function $f : \mathbb{N} \to \mathbb{R}$ is said to be negligible if $f(\lambda) = \lambda^{-\omega(1)}$ and is written as $f(\lambda) = \mathsf{negl}(\lambda)$.

Let $\mathcal{U}$ be an attribute set and $\{1, 2, ..., \ell\}$ be the index set for strings with length ℓ. For a vector $\mathbf{v} = (v_1, ..., v_t) \in \mathcal{U}^t$ where $1 \le t \le \ell$, we define the function $\mathsf{ind} : \mathcal{U} \to \{1, 2, ..., \ell\}$ that maps an $\mathcal{U}$-element v_j into its index.

Let q be a prime, $\mathbf{A} \in \mathbb{Z}_q^{n \times m}$ and $\mathbf{u} \in \mathbb{Z}_q^n$. A random integer lattice for $\mathbf{A}$ is $\Lambda_q^\perp(\mathbf{A}) = \{\mathbf{e} \in \mathbb{Z}^m : \mathbf{Ae} = \mathbf{0} \pmod{q}\}$. $\Lambda_q^\mathbf{u}(\mathbf{A}) = \{\mathbf{e} \in \mathbb{Z}^m : \mathbf{Ae} = \mathbf{u} \pmod{q}\}$ is $\Lambda_q^\perp(\mathbf{A})$'s shift. We follow the cover-freeness approaches established in [2,14].

Lemma 1 (Cover-Freeness, [14]). *Let $\Delta_1, .., \Delta_q \subseteq [S]$ be randomly chosen subsets of size v. Let $v(\lambda) = \Theta(\lambda)$ and $S(\lambda) = \Theta(vq^2)$. Then, for all $i \in [q]$,*

$$\Pr[\Delta_i \setminus (\sup_{j \ne i} \Delta_j) \ne \emptyset] = 1 - \mathsf{negl}(\lambda)$$

where the probability is over the random choice of the subsets $\Delta_1, ..., \Delta_q$.

3 Lattice Trapdoors and the LWE Problem

We recall the following lemmas on lattice trapdoors developed through a series of works, e.g., [3,13,17]. Let n, m, q be positive integers, where $m \ge 2n \log q + \omega(\sqrt{\log n})$. Let $w = n\lceil \log q \rceil$, define $\mathbf{g}^\mathsf{T} = (1, 2, 4, \ldots, 2^{\lceil \log q \rceil - 1})$. Define the n-by-$n\lceil \log q \rceil$ gadget matrix [17] as

$$\mathbf{G} = [\mathbf{g}^\mathsf{T} \otimes \mathbf{I}_n] = \begin{bmatrix} \mathbf{g}^\mathsf{T} & & & \\ & \mathbf{g}^\mathsf{T} & & \\ & & \ddots & \\ & & & \mathbf{g}^\mathsf{T} \end{bmatrix} \in \mathbb{Z}_q^{n \times n \lceil \log q \rceil}.$$

We denote by $\mathbf{G}^{-1}() : \mathbb{Z}_q^{n \times \ell} \to \{0,1\}^{nw \times \ell}$, $\ell \ge 0$, the component-wise binary decomposition function.

The lemmas below state efficiently generating lattice trapdoors and sampling low-norm matrices from $\Lambda_q^\mathbf{U}(\mathbf{A})$.

Lemma 2 ([17]). *There is a p.p.t algorithm $\mathsf{TrapGen}(1^n, 1^m, q)$ returns matrices $\mathbf{A}, \mathbf{R}$ such that $(\mathbf{AR}$ distributes statistically close to $(U(\mathbb{Z}_q^{n \times m}), D_{\mathbb{Z},\omega(\sqrt{\log n})}^{(m-w) \times w})$, and $\mathbf{R}$ is called a $\mathbf{G}$-trapdoor of $\mathbf{A}$.*

Lemma 3 ([3]). *There is a p.p.t algorithm $\mathsf{SampleLeft}(\mathbf{A}, \mathbf{B}, \mathbf{R}, \mathbf{U}, s)$ takes as input $\mathbf{A} \in \mathbb{Z}_q^{n \times m}$ with its $\mathbf{G}$-trapdoor $\mathbf{R}$, $\mathbf{B} \in \mathbb{Z}_q^{n \times w}$, $\mathbf{U} \in \mathbb{Z}_q^{n \times \ell}$, and $s \ge \omega(\sqrt{\log n}) \cdot s_1(\mathbf{R})$, and returns $\mathbf{D} \in \mathbb{Z}^{(m+w) \times \ell}$ which has a distribution statistically close to $D_{\mathbb{Z},s}^{(m+w) \times \ell}$, conditioned on $\mathbf{AD} = \mathbf{U} \pmod{q}$, i.e., $D_{\Lambda_q^\mathbf{U}(\mathbf{A}), s}$.*

Lemma 4 ([3], Theorem 10, and [17], Theorem 5.1). *There exists a p.p.t algorithm $\mathsf{SampleRight}(\mathbf{A}, \mathbf{B}, \mathbf{R}', \mathbf{H}, \mathbf{U}, s)$ takes as input $\mathbf{A} \in \mathbb{Z}_q^{n \times m}$, $\mathbf{B} = \mathbf{AR}' + \mathbf{HG}$ where $\mathbf{R}' \in \mathbb{Z}^{m \times w}$, $\mathbf{H} \in \mathbb{Z}_q^{n \times n}$ is invertible over $\mathbb{Z}_q$, and $s > 5 \cdot s_1(\mathbf{R}') \cdot \omega(\sqrt{\log n}))$. It outputs $\mathbf{D} \in \mathbb{Z}^{(m+w) \times \ell}$ distributed statistically close to $D_{\mathbb{Z},s}^{(m+w) \times \ell}$, conditioned on $\mathbf{AD} = \mathbf{U} \pmod{q}$, i.e., $D_{\Lambda_q^\mathbf{U}(\mathbf{A}), s}$.*

The following regularity lemma by [13] is crucial to our security proofs.

Lemma 5. *For $\mathbf{A} \leftarrow U(\mathbb{Z}_q^{n\times m})$ and $\mathbf{e} \leftarrow D_{\mathbb{Z},s}^m$ with any $s \geq \omega(\sqrt{\log n})$, the distribution of $\mathbf{Ae} \bmod q$ is statistically close to $U(\mathbb{Z}_q^n)$. Furthermore, for a fixed $\mathbf{u} \in \mathbb{Z}_q^n$, the distribution of $\mathbf{e} \leftarrow D_{\mathbb{Z},s}^m$ given $\mathbf{Ae} = \mathbf{u} \bmod q$ is $D_{\Lambda_q^{\mathbf{u}}(\mathbf{A}),s}$.*

Definition 1 (The LWE Assumption). *Let λ be the security parameter and $n = n(\lambda)$. For integers $q = q(n) \geq 2$ and an error distribution $\chi = \chi(n)$ over $\mathbb{Z}_q$, the advantage of an adversary $\mathcal{A}$ against the learning with errors problem $\mathsf{LWE}_{n,m,q,\chi}$ is defined as*

$$\mathsf{Adv}_{\mathcal{A}}^{\mathsf{LWE}_{n,m,q,\chi}}(\lambda) := |\Pr[\mathcal{A}(\mathbf{A}, \mathbf{s}^\mathsf{T}\mathbf{A} + \mathbf{e}^\mathsf{T}) = 1] - \Pr[\mathcal{A}(\mathbf{A}, \mathbf{b}^\mathsf{T}) = 1]|$$

where $\mathbf{A} \leftarrow U(\mathbb{Z}_q^{n\times m})$, $\mathbf{s} \leftarrow U(\mathbb{Z}_q^n)$, $\mathbf{e} \leftarrow \chi^m$ and $\mathbf{b} \leftarrow U(\mathbb{Z}_q^n)$. We say $\mathsf{LWE}_{n,m,q,\chi}$ assumption holds if for all p.p.t adversary $\mathcal{A}$, $\mathsf{Adv}_{\mathcal{A}}^{\mathsf{LWE}_{n,m,q,\chi}}(\lambda) \leq \mathsf{negl}(\lambda)$.

4 Universal Hashing and Randomness Extraction

Let X and Y be two random variables over some finite set S. The statistical distance between X and Y is defined as $\Delta(X, Y) = \frac{1}{2}\sum_{s \in S}|\Pr[X = s] - \Pr[Y = s]|$. Let X_λ and Y_λ be ensembles of random variables indexed by the security parameter λ. We say that X and Y are $\mathsf{negl}(\lambda)$-statistically close (or simply statistically close) if $\Delta(X_\lambda, Y_\lambda) = \mathsf{negl}(\lambda)$. Let $\mathrm{H}_\infty(X) = -\log(\max_x \Pr[X = x])$ be the min-entropy the random variable X.

Definition 2 ((T,κ)-Block Sources). *We say a random variable $X = (X_1, ..., X_T)$ is a (T, κ)-block source if $\mathrm{H}_\infty(X_i|_{X_1=x_1,...,X_{i-1}=x_{i-1}}) \geq \kappa$ for every $i \in [T]$ and $x_1, ..., x_{i-1}$.*

We recall the following lemma due to Boneh et al. [8], which states that universal hash functions are randomness extractors for block sources.

Lemma 6 (lemma 2.3, [8]). *Let $\mathcal{H}$ be a universal collection of functions $H : U \to V$, and let $X = (X_1, ..., X_T)$ be (T, k)-block-source where $k \geq \log|V| + 2\log(1/\epsilon) + \Theta(1)$. Then, the distribution $(H_1, H_1(X_1), ..., H_T, H_T(X_T))$, where $(H_1, \cdots, H_T) \leftarrow \mathcal{H}^T$, is ϵT-close to the $U(H \times V)^T$.*

Let q be a prime, $d > 1$ be an integer, and $f(X)$ be a degree-d polynomial, irreducible over $\mathbb{Z}_q$. Define $\mathcal{R} = \mathbb{Z}[X]/(f(X))$ and $\mathcal{R}_q = \mathcal{R}/q\mathcal{R}$, i.e., $\mathcal{R}_q$ is a finite field. We define a hash family $\mathsf{Hash}_{\mathbf{s}}(\mathbf{v}) := \sum_{i=1}^\ell s_i \cdot v_i$ where $\mathbf{s} = (s_1, s_2, ..., s_\ell) \leftarrow U(\mathcal{R}_q^\ell)$, and $\mathbf{v} = (v_1, v_2, ..., v_\ell) \in \mathcal{R}_q^\ell$. We show Hash is universal.

Lemma 7. *The hash function family $\mathsf{Hash}_{\mathbf{s}}(\cdot)$ with $\mathbf{s} \leftarrow U(\mathcal{R}_q^\ell)$ is universal.*

Proof. Let $\mathbf{v} = \{v_1, ..., v_\ell\}, \mathbf{v}' = \{v_1', ..., v_\ell'\} \in \mathcal{R}_q^\ell$ satisfying $\mathbf{v} \neq \mathbf{v}'$ and $\mathsf{Hash}_{\mathbf{s}}(\mathbf{v}) = \mathsf{Hash}_{\mathbf{s}}(\mathbf{v})$. Without loss of generality, we assume that $v_i \neq v_i'$. So, we have $s_i \cdot (v_i - v_i') = \sum_{j \neq i} s_j \cdot (v_j - v_j') = h$, which gives $v_i - v_i' = s_i^{-1} \cdot h$ where s_i^{-1} is the inverse of s_i (recall $\mathcal{R}$ is a field, so s_i^{-1} exists). Hence, for randomly chosen $\mathbf{v}$ and $\mathbf{v}'$, $\Pr[\mathsf{Hash}_{\mathbf{s}}(\mathbf{v}) = \mathsf{Hash}_{\mathbf{s}}(\mathbf{v}')] \leq 1/|\mathcal{R}_q| = q^{-d}$. □

4.1 Full-Rank Difference Encoding

Let $1 < d \leq n$, and $f(X)$ be a degree-d irreducible polynomial over $\mathbb{Z}_q$. Define ring $\mathcal{R} = \mathbb{Z}[X]/(f(X))$ and $\mathcal{R}_q = \mathcal{R}/q\mathcal{R}$. We use the full-rank difference encoding $\varphi : \mathcal{R}_q \to \mathbb{Z}_q^{d \times d}$ [3,21]. Note that $\mathcal{R}_q$ is isomorphic to $\mathbb{Z}_q^d$, so any $\mathbb{Z}_q^d$-element can be uniquely identified as an $\mathcal{R}$-element via coefficient embeddings. We use $\mathcal{R}_q$ as the attribute universe for our HVE to accommodate exponentially many attributes (with $\omega(\log \lambda) \leq d \leq n$). φ is efficiently computable as has:

1. For any $u, v \in \mathcal{R}_q$ with $u \neq v$, $\varphi(u) - \varphi(v)$ is invertible in $\mathbb{Z}_q$.
2. For $u, v \in \mathcal{R}_q$, $\varphi(u) + \varphi(v) = \varphi(u+v)$, $\varphi(u) \cdot \varphi(v) = \varphi(uv)$.

Our HVE scheme uses the extended FRD by Boyen [12]. Let the integer $d|n$. For any $u \in \mathcal{R}_q$, we defined the extended FRD $H : \mathcal{R}_q \to \mathbb{Z}_q^{n \times n}$ as

$$H(u) := \begin{bmatrix} \boxed{\varphi(u)} & & & \\ & \boxed{\varphi(u)} & & \\ & & \ddots & \\ & & & \boxed{\varphi(u)} \end{bmatrix} \in \mathbb{Z}_q^{n \times n} \quad (1)$$

and here $\varphi(u)$ is a d-by-d matrix and other places of $H(u)$ are zeros.

We note that we use the extended FRD for a completely different purpose than that of Boyen [12], which is to refine the partitioning proofs for adaptively secure digital signatures for more efficient reductions.

5 Hidden Vector Encryption

Definition 3 (Hidden Vector Encryption). *Let λ be the security parameter, $\ell = \ell(\lambda)$, $\mathcal{U} = \mathcal{U}(\lambda)$ be the attribute universe and $\star$ denotes the wildcard. Let $\mathbf{x} = (x_1, ..., x_\ell) \in (\mathcal{U} \cup \{\star\})^\ell$ and $\mathbf{y} = \{y_1, ..., y_\ell\} \in \mathcal{U}^\ell$. Define predicate*

$$P_{\mathbf{x}}(\mathbf{y}) = \begin{cases} 1, & \text{if } x_i = y_i \text{ or } x_i = \star \text{ for all } i \in [\ell] \\ 0, & \text{otherwise} \end{cases}$$

An HVE system with attribute universe $\mathcal{U}$, message space $\mathcal{M}_\lambda$, and ciphertext space $\mathcal{C}_\lambda$ consists of four p.p.t algorithms. $\mathsf{Setup}(1^\lambda, 1^\ell, \mathcal{U})$ outputs public parameters pub and a master key msk. $\mathsf{KeyGen}(\mathsf{pub}, \mathsf{msk}, \mathbf{x})$ return a decryption key $\mathsf{sk}_\mathbf{x}$ for $\mathbf{x} = (x_1, ..., x_\ell) \in (\mathcal{U} \cup \{\star\})^\ell$. $\mathsf{Enc}(\mathsf{pub}, \mathbf{y}, \mathsf{msg})$ encrypts attributes $\mathbf{y} = (y_1, ..., y_\ell) \in \mathcal{U}^\ell$ and $\mathsf{msg} \in \mathcal{M}_\lambda$, and outputs a ciphertext $\mathsf{ct}_\mathbf{y}$. $\mathsf{Dec}(\mathsf{pub}, \mathsf{sk}_\mathbf{x}, \mathsf{ct}_\mathbf{y})$ returns a message or a special symbol $\perp$.

Definition 4 (Correctness of HVE). *We say that an HVE system is correct if for all $\lambda \in \mathbb{N}$, $\ell = \ell(\lambda)$, $(\mathsf{pub}, \mathsf{msk}) \leftarrow \mathsf{Setup}(1^\lambda, 1^\ell, \mathcal{U})$, $\mathsf{sk}_\mathbf{x} \leftarrow (\mathsf{pub}, \mathsf{msk}, \mathbf{x})$, and all $\mathsf{ct}_\mathbf{y} \leftarrow \mathsf{Enc}(\mathsf{pub}, \mathbf{y}, \mathsf{msg})$, $\Pr[\mathsf{Dec}(\mathsf{pub}, \mathsf{sk}_\mathbf{x}, \mathsf{ct}_\mathbf{y}) \to \mathsf{msg}] \geq 1 - \mathsf{negl}(\lambda)$ if $P_\mathbf{x}(\mathbf{y}) = 1$, where the probability is taken over the random coins of the algorithms.*

We require two security properties from HVE: attribute-data privacy and enhanced predicate privacy. Attribute-data privacy ensures that ciphertexts reveal no information about either the encrypted data or the associated attributes. Enhanced predicate privacy guarantees that, given a decryption key $\mathsf{sk}_\mathbf{x}$, no information about the vector $\mathbf{x}$ is leaked. We formalise both notions below.

Definition 5 (($Q, \mathbf{poly}$)-Selective-Simulation Attribute-Data Privacy). *We say an HVE scheme Π has (Q, poly)-SS attribute-data privacy if there exists a p.p.t simulator $\mathcal{S}$ such that for every p.p.t admissible adversary $\mathcal{A}$,*

$$\mathsf{Adv}^{\mathsf{DP}}_{\Pi,\mathcal{A}}(\lambda) := |\Pr[\mathsf{Exp}^{\mathsf{DP\text{-}real}}_{\Pi,\mathcal{A}}(\lambda) = 1] - \Pr[\mathsf{Exp}^{\mathsf{DP-rand}}_{\Pi,\mathcal{A},\mathcal{S}}(\lambda) = 1]$$

where the security experiments are defined in Fig. 2. We say an adversary $\mathcal{A}$ is admissible if for all it's queries $\mathbf{x}$ to KeyGen: 1) $P_\mathbf{x}(\mathbf{y}^*) = 1$ if $\mathbf{x} = \mathbf{x}_i$ for $i \in [Q]$, and 2) $P_\mathbf{x}(\mathbf{y}^*) = 0$ for all $\mathbf{x} \neq \mathbf{x}_i$, $i \in [Q]$.

Experiment $\mathsf{Exp}^{\mathsf{DP-real}}_{\Pi,\mathcal{A}}(\lambda)$:

1. $(\mathbf{y}^*, \mathbf{x}_1, .., \mathbf{x}_Q) \leftarrow \mathcal{A}(1^\lambda, 1^\ell)$
2. $(\mathsf{pub}, \mathsf{msk}) \leftarrow \mathsf{Setup}(1^\lambda)$
3. $\mathsf{msg} \leftarrow \mathcal{A}^{\mathsf{KeyGen}(\mathsf{pub},\mathsf{msk},\cdot)}(\mathsf{pub})$
4. $\mathsf{ct}^* \leftarrow \mathsf{Enc}(\mathsf{pub}, \mathbf{y}^*, \mathsf{msg})$
5. $b \leftarrow \mathcal{A}^{\mathsf{KeyGen}(\mathsf{pub},\mathsf{msk},\cdot)}(\mathsf{ct}^*)$
6. Output b

Experiment $\mathsf{Exp}^{\mathsf{DP-ideal}}_{\Pi,\mathcal{S}}(\lambda)$:

1. $(\mathbf{y}^*, \mathbf{x}_1, .., \mathbf{x}_Q) \leftarrow \mathcal{A}(1^\lambda, 1^\ell)$
2. $\mathsf{pub} \leftarrow \mathcal{S}(1^\lambda)$
3. $\mathsf{msg} \leftarrow \mathcal{A}^{\mathcal{S}(\mathsf{pub},\cdot)}(\mathsf{pub})$
4. $\mathsf{ct}^* \leftarrow \mathcal{S}(\mathsf{pub}, 1^{\ell|\mathcal{U}|}, 1^{|\mathsf{msg}|})$
5. $b \leftarrow \mathcal{A}^{\mathcal{S}(\mathsf{pub},\cdot)}(\mathsf{ct}^*)$
6. Output b

Fig. 2. Selective Attribute-Data Privacy Experiments

Definition 6 (Predicate-Privacy Oracles). *Let $\mathcal{U}$ be the attribute universe. Given $\mathbf{y}^* \in \mathcal{U}^\ell$, let $\bar{\mathcal{X}}_{|\mathbf{y}^*}$ be a circuit representing a joint distribution conditioned on $\mathbf{y}^*$ that $P_{\mathbf{x}_i}(\mathbf{y}) = 1$ for $(\mathbf{x}_1, ..., \mathbf{x}_Q) \leftarrow \bar{\mathcal{X}}_{|\mathbf{y}^*}$. The oracle $\mathsf{RoR}(\mathsf{real}, \cdot)$ takes as input an distribution $\tilde{\mathcal{X}}$ over $((\mathcal{U} \cup \{\star\})^\ell)^{T-Q}$, samples $(\mathbf{x}_{Q+1}, ..., \mathbf{x}_T) \leftarrow \tilde{\mathcal{X}}$, and returns $\mathsf{sk}_{\mathbf{x}_i} \leftarrow \mathsf{KeyGen}(\mathsf{pub}, \mathsf{msk}, \mathbf{x}_i)$ for $i \in [Q+1, T]$. The oracle $\mathsf{RoR}(\mathsf{rand}, \cdot)$ is identical to $\mathsf{RoR}(\mathsf{real}, \cdot)$ except that it draws random samples $(\mathbf{x}_{Q+1}, ..., \mathbf{x}_T) \leftarrow U(((\mathcal{U} \cup \{\star\})^\ell)^{T-Q})$ to generate $\mathsf{sk}_{\mathbf{x}_i}$. We require $\mathsf{sk}_{\mathbf{x}_i}$ contains the index set S_i of $\mathbf{x}_i$, i.e., $S_i = \{\mathsf{ind}(x_{i,j} \neq \star)\}_{j \in [\ell]}$.*

Definition 7 (Enhanced Predicate Privacy). *Let $\lambda \in \mathbb{N}$ be the security parameter. An HVE scheme $\Pi = (\mathsf{Setup}, \mathsf{KeyGen}, \mathsf{Enc}, \mathsf{Dec})$ has Q-enhanced predicate privacy if for any polynomial-time (T, κ)-admissible adversary $\mathcal{A}$,*

$$\mathsf{Adv}^{\mathsf{PP}}_{\Pi,\mathcal{A}}(\lambda) := |\Pr[\mathsf{Exp}^{\mathsf{PP-real}}_{\Pi,\mathcal{A}}(\lambda) = 1] - \Pr[\mathsf{Exp}^{\mathsf{PP-rand}}_{\Pi,\mathcal{A}}(\lambda) = 1]|$$

is negligible in λ where for $\mathsf{mode} \in \{\mathsf{real}, \mathsf{rand}\}$ the experiment $\mathsf{Exp}^{\mathsf{PP-mode}}_{\Pi,\mathcal{A}}(\lambda)$ is defined in Fig. 3 where $U((\mathcal{U} \cup \{\star\})^T)$ samples random $\mathbf{x}_i$ conditioned on

$P_{\mathbf{x}_i}(\mathbf{y}^*) = 1$, and the index sets $\{S_i\}$ for $\{\mathbf{x}_i\}_{i \in [T]}$ are identical in $\mathsf{Exp}_{\Pi,\mathcal{A}}^{\mathsf{PP-real}}(\lambda)$ and $\mathsf{Exp}_{\Pi,\mathcal{A}}^{\mathsf{PP-rand}}(\lambda)$. We say that an adversary is a (T,κ)-admissible predicate private adversary if the joint distribution $(\bar{\mathcal{X}}_{|\mathbf{y}^*}, \bar{\mathcal{X}})$ queried to the oracles $\mathsf{RoR}(\mathsf{real}, \cdot)$ is a (T, κ)-block source (Definition 2).

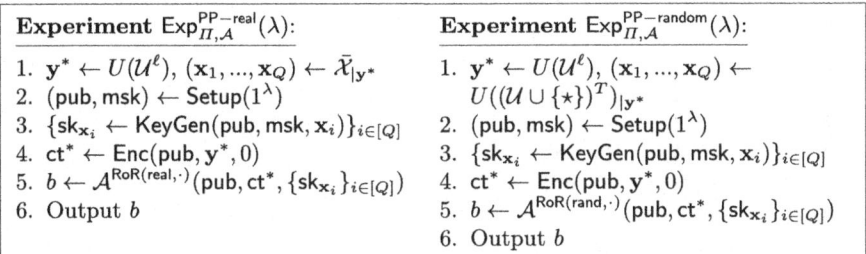

Fig. 3. Predicate Privacy Experiments

Remark 1 (Multi-Attribute Challenges). Definitions 5 and 7 consider a single challenge attribute $\mathbf{y}^*$. This can be naturally extended to the case where the adversary commits to multiple challenge attributes $\mathbf{y}_j^*$, each satisfying the condition $P_{\mathbf{x}_i}(\mathbf{y}_j^*) = 1$ for all issued keys $\mathsf{sk}_{\mathbf{x}_i}$. This generalised formulation is polynomially equivalent to the single-challenge case via a routine hybrid argument.

Remark 2 (Multi-Shot Adversaries). The above definition allows the adversary to query the oracle RoR once. We can modify the oracle so that the adversary gets $(\mathbf{x}_1, ..., \mathbf{x}_Q, \mathbf{x}_{Q+1}, ..., \mathbf{x}_T) \leftarrow \mathcal{X}_{|\mathbf{y}^*}$ for its first RoR-query, and more samples from the distribution $\mathcal{X}$ conditioned on these samples do not satisfy the predicate P with $\mathbf{y}^*$, as long as the samples $\{\mathbf{x}_i\}$ form a block source. As noted by Boneh et al. [8], this is equivalent to the one-shot definition via a routine hybrid argument.

6 Predicate-Private HVE from Lattices

Let λ be the security parameter. We used the extended FRD $H : \mathcal{R}_q \to \mathbb{Z}_q^{n \times n}$ defined in Sect. 4.1 where $1 < d = \omega(\log \lambda) \le n$ and $d|n$. The attribute universe $\mathcal{U} = \mathcal{R}_q$. Recall the function $\mathsf{ind} : \mathcal{U} \to \{1, 2, ..., \ell\}$ maps an $\mathcal{U}$-element v_j of a vector $\mathbf{v} \in \mathcal{U}^\ell$ into its index. Our HVE construction is given below.

- $\mathsf{Setup}(1^\lambda, 1^\ell)$:
    1. $(\mathbf{A}, \mathbf{R}) \leftarrow \mathsf{TrapGen}(n, m)$.
    2. $\mathbf{A}_i \leftarrow U(\mathbb{Z}_q^{n \times w})$ for $i \in [\ell]$, $\mathbf{U}_i \leftarrow U(\mathbb{Z}_q^{n \times \lambda})$ for $i \in [k]$.
    3. $\mathsf{pub} = (\mathbf{A}, \{\mathbf{U}_i\}_{i \in [k]}, \{\mathbf{A}_i\}_{i \in [\ell]})$, $\mathsf{msk} = \mathbf{R}$.

- $\mathsf{KeyGen}(\mathsf{pub}, \mathsf{msk}, \mathbf{x} = (x_1, ..., x_\ell) \in (\mathcal{R}_q \cup \{\star\})^\ell)$:

1. Let $S = \{\text{ind}(x_i \neq \star)\} \subseteq [\ell]$ be the receiver's attribute index set.
2. $h_{\text{ind}(x_i)} \leftarrow U(\mathcal{R}_q)$ for $\text{ind}(x_i) \in S$.
3. Set $\mathbf{B} = \sum_{\text{ind}(x_i) \in S} (\mathbf{A}_{\text{ind}(x_i)} + H(x_i)\mathbf{G}) \cdot \mathbf{G}^{-1}(H(h_{\text{ind}(x_i)})\mathbf{G})$.
4. Sample $\mathbf{r} = (r_1, ..., r_k) \leftarrow U(\{0,1\}^k)$ with hamming weight $v = \lambda$; Set $\mathbf{U}^* = \sum_{j=1}^{k} r_j \mathbf{U}_i$.
5. $\mathbf{D} \leftarrow \textsf{SampleLeft}(\mathbf{A}, \mathbf{B}, \mathbf{R}, \mathbf{U}^*, s)$.
6. Return $\textsf{sk}_\mathbf{x} := (\mathbf{D}, \{h_{\text{ind}(x_i)}\}_{\text{ind}(x_i) \in S}, S, \mathbf{r},)$.

- $\textsf{Enc}(\textsf{pub}, \mathbf{y} = (y_1, ... y_\ell) \in \mathcal{R}_q^\ell, \textsf{msg} \in \{0,1\}^\lambda)$:
  1. $\mathbf{e} \leftarrow D_{\mathbb{Z}, \alpha q}^m$, $\tilde{\mathbf{e}}_j \leftarrow D_{\mathbb{Z},\gamma}^\lambda$ for $j \in [k]$ with $\gamma = \alpha q \ell^{3/2} m^3 \cdot \omega(\log^{3/2} n)$, $\mathbf{e}_i \leftarrow D_{\mathbb{Z},\tau}^w$ for $i \in [\ell]$ with $\tau = 2\sqrt{m}(\alpha q) \cdot \omega(\log n)$, $\mathbf{s} \leftarrow U(\mathbb{Z}_q^n)$.
  2. $\mathbf{c}^\mathsf{T} \leftarrow \mathbf{s}^\mathsf{T} \mathbf{A} + \mathbf{e}^\mathsf{T}$, $\{\tilde{\mathbf{c}}_j^\mathsf{T} \leftarrow \mathbf{s}^\mathsf{T} \mathbf{U}_j + \tilde{\mathbf{e}}_j^\mathsf{T} + \textsf{msg}^\mathsf{T} \lfloor q/p \rfloor\}_{j \in [k]}$ where $p = k + 1$.
  3. $\{\mathbf{c}_i^\mathsf{T} \leftarrow \mathbf{s}^\mathsf{T}(\mathbf{A}_i + H(y_i)\mathbf{G}) + \mathbf{e}_i^\mathsf{T}\}_{i \in [\ell]}$.
  4. $\textsf{ct}_\mathbf{y} := (\mathbf{c}, \{\mathbf{c}_i\}_{i \in [\ell]}, \{\tilde{\mathbf{c}}_j\}_{j \in [k]})$.

- $\textsf{Dec}(\textsf{pub}, \textsf{sk}_\mathbf{x}, \textsf{ct}_\mathbf{y})$:
  1. Parse $\textsf{sk}_\mathbf{x} \rightarrow (\mathbf{D}, \{h_{\text{ind}(x_i)}\}_{\text{ind}(x_i) \in S}, S, \mathbf{r})$; Return $\perp$ if it does not parse.
  2. Parse $\textsf{ct}_\mathbf{y} \rightarrow (\mathbf{c}, \{\mathbf{c}_i\}_{i \in [\ell]}, \{\tilde{\mathbf{c}}_j\}_{j \in [k]})$; Return $\perp$ if it does not parse.
  3. With $S = \{\text{ind}(x_i \neq \star)\}$. Set

$$\mathbf{z} \leftarrow \sum_{j=1}^{k} r_j \tilde{\mathbf{c}}_j^\mathsf{T} - \left[\mathbf{c}^\mathsf{T} | \sum_{\text{ind}(x_i) \in S} \mathbf{c}_{\text{ind}(x_i)}^\mathsf{T} \cdot \mathbf{G}^{-1}(H(h_{\text{ind}(x_i)})\mathbf{G})\right] \mathbf{D}$$

  4. Round the coordinates of $\mathbf{z}$ to their closest integer in $\mathbb{Z}_p$ to get $\mathbf{z}' \in \mathbb{Z}_p^\lambda$; Return $\textsf{msg}' = \mathbf{z}'/(\sum_{i=j}^{k} r_i)$.

Correctness. We show the correctness of our construction as follows. Let $\mathbf{x} = \{x_1, ..., x_\ell\}$ be the set associated with the decryption key $\textsf{sk}_\mathbf{x}$ and $S = \{ind(x_i \neq \star)\}$ be the set of indexes of $\mathbf{x}$ over $[\ell]$ with $x_i \neq \star$. Let $\mathbf{y} = \{y_1, ..., y_\ell\}$ be the set associated with the ciphertext. Let $r^* = \sum_j^k r_j$ and $\mathbf{R}_{\text{ind}(x_i)} = \mathbf{G}^{-1}(H(h_{\text{ind}(x_i)})\mathbf{G})$

$$\begin{aligned}
\mathbf{z} &= \sum_j^k r_j \tilde{\mathbf{c}}_j^\mathsf{T} - \left[\mathbf{c}_0^\mathsf{T} | \sum_{\text{ind}(x_i) \in S} \mathbf{c}_{\text{ind}(x_i)}^\mathsf{T} \cdot \mathbf{G}^{-1}(H(h_{\text{ind}(x_i)})\mathbf{G})\right] \mathbf{D} \\
&= \sum_j^k r_j \tilde{\mathbf{c}}_j^\mathsf{T} - \left[\mathbf{c}_0^\mathsf{T} | \sum_{\text{ind}(x_i) \in S} \mathbf{s}^\mathsf{T}(\mathbf{A}_{\text{ind}(x_i)} + H(x_i)\mathbf{G}) \cdot \mathbf{R}_{\text{ind}(x_i)} + \mathbf{e}_{\text{ind}(x_i)}^\mathsf{T} \mathbf{R}_{\text{ind}(x_i)}\right] \mathbf{D} \\
&= \sum_j^k r_j \tilde{\mathbf{c}}_j^\mathsf{T} - \mathbf{s}^\mathsf{T} [\mathbf{A}|\mathbf{B}]\mathbf{D} + (\sum_{\text{ind}(x_i) \in S} \mathbf{e}_{\text{ind}(x_i)}^\mathsf{T} \cdot \mathbf{R}_{\text{ind}(x_i)}) \cdot \mathbf{D} \\
&= \mathbf{s}^\mathsf{T} \mathbf{U}^* + \sum_j^k r_j \tilde{\mathbf{e}}_j^\mathsf{T} - r^* \textsf{msg}^\mathsf{T} \lfloor q/p \rfloor - \mathbf{s}^\mathsf{T} \mathbf{U}^* - \bar{\mathbf{e}}^\mathsf{T} \\
&= r^* \textsf{msg}^\mathsf{T} \lfloor q/p \rfloor + r^* \tilde{\mathbf{e}}_j^\mathsf{T} + \bar{\mathbf{e}}^\mathsf{T}
\end{aligned}$$

Since $\|\mathbf{R}_{\text{ind}(v_i)}\|_\infty \leq \sqrt{m}$, $\|\mathbf{D}\|_\infty \leq s\sqrt{m+w}$, $\|\mathbf{e}_{\text{ind}(v_i)}\|_\infty \leq \tau\sqrt{w}$, and $\|\mathbf{e}_0\|_\infty \leq \alpha q \sqrt{\lambda}$, $\|\mathbf{e}_0\|_\infty \leq \alpha q \sqrt{m}$, we have

$$\begin{aligned}
\|r^* \mathbf{e} - \tilde{\mathbf{e}}\|_\infty &\leq v \|\mathbf{e}\|_\infty + \|\tilde{\mathbf{e}}\|_\infty \leq \lambda \cdot \alpha q \sqrt{\lambda} + t \cdot \tau \sqrt{w} \cdot \sqrt{m} \cdot s\sqrt{m+w} \\
&\leq O(\lambda \cdot \ell \cdot \tau \cdot s \cdot m^{3/2}) \leq q/(4p)
\end{aligned}$$

So, $r^* \cdot \mathsf{msg}$, and hence, msg can be recovered with all but negligible probability.

Parameters. We set the parameters as follows to satisfy the algorithms SampleLeft, SampleRight and the requirement for LWE hardness $q\alpha > 2\sqrt{n}$:

$$v = \lambda \quad ; \quad k = \Theta(v \cdot Q^2) \quad ; \quad s = \ell \cdot m^2 \cdot \omega(\log n) \quad ;$$
$$q = 2\lambda\ell n m^2 \cdot \omega(\log n) \quad ; \quad \alpha = \left(\lambda \ell m^2 \cdot \omega(\log n)\right)^{-1}$$

Table 2 gives the parameter sizes for our HVE scheme. As required by Lemma 1, the number of $\mathbf{U}_i$ matrices, e.g., $k = \Theta(vQ^2)$ for the hamming weight v and number of keys allowed for matching search Q. Concrete parameters can be derived by using the formulas for correctness and a hardness estimator, e.g., [4], for the LWE problem.

Table 2. Key and Ciphertext Sizes of the HVE Scheme

pub-size	msk-size	$\mathsf{sk_x}$-size	$\mathsf{ct_y}$-size
$(w\ell + \lambda k + m) \log_2 q$	$mw \log_2 q$	$(n + m + (d+1)\ell) \log_2 q + k$	$(m + \ell w + \lambda k) \log_2 q$

7 Security Proofs

7.1 Simulation Algorithms

We describe three simulation algorithms $\widetilde{\mathsf{Setup}}$, $\widetilde{\mathsf{KeyGen}}$, and $\widetilde{\mathsf{Enc}}$, which are used to facilitate our security proofs.

Simulating pub. The algorithm $\widetilde{\mathsf{Setup}}(1^\lambda, \mathbf{A}, \mathbf{y}, \mathbf{x}_1, ..., \mathbf{x}_Q)$ is used by a simulator $\mathcal{S}$ to simulate pub. Its input contains a $\mathbb{Z}_q^{n \times m}$-matrix $\mathbf{A}$, $\mathbf{y}^* = (y_1, ..., y_\ell) \in \mathcal{R}_q^\ell$, $\{\mathbf{x}_\iota = (x_{\iota 1}, ..., x_{\iota \ell})\}_{\iota \in [Q]}$ with $P_{\mathbf{x}_\iota}(\mathbf{y}^*) = 1$. For $\iota \in [Q]$, denote $S_\iota = \{\mathsf{ind}(x_{\iota i} \neq \star)\}$ and $\mathbf{R}_{\mathsf{ind}(x_{\iota i})} = \mathbf{G}^{-1}(H(h_{\mathsf{ind}(x_{\iota i})})\mathbf{G})$. The algorithm does:

1. $\bar{\mathbf{R}}_i \leftarrow D_{\mathbb{Z}, \omega(\sqrt{\log n})}$ and set $\mathbf{A}_i \leftarrow \mathbf{A}\bar{\mathbf{R}}_i - H(y_i)\mathbf{G}$ for $i \in [\ell]$.
2. It generates $\{\mathbf{U}_j\}_{j \in [k]}$ as follows.
   - For $\iota \in [Q]$, set
   $$\mathbf{B}_\iota = \sum\nolimits_{\mathsf{ind}(x_{\iota i}) \in S_\iota} \left(\mathbf{A}_{\mathsf{ind}(x_{\iota i})} + H(x_{\iota i})\mathbf{G}\right) \cdot \mathbf{G}^{-1}(H(h_{\mathsf{ind}(x_{\iota i})})\mathbf{G})$$
   $$= \mathbf{A} \sum\nolimits_{\mathsf{ind}(x_{\iota i}) \in S_\iota} \bar{\mathbf{R}}_{\mathsf{ind}(x_{\iota i})} \mathbf{R}_{\mathsf{ind}(x_{\iota i})} = \mathbf{A}\mathbf{T}_\iota$$

   - For $\iota \in [Q]$, set $\mathbf{D}_\iota^* = [\mathbf{D}_{\iota 1}^\mathsf{T} | \mathbf{D}_{\iota 2}^\mathsf{T}]^\mathsf{T}$ where $\mathbf{D}_{\iota 1} \leftarrow D_{\mathbb{Z}, s}^{m \times \lambda}$, $\mathbf{D}_{\iota 2} \leftarrow D_{\mathbb{Z}, s}^{w \times \lambda}$.
   - Compute $\mathbf{U}_\iota^* = [\mathbf{A} | \mathbf{B}_\iota] \mathbf{D}_\iota^* = \mathbf{A}\mathbf{D}_{\iota 1} + \mathbf{A}\mathbf{T}_\iota \mathbf{D}_{\iota 2}$.
   - For $\iota \in [Q]$, choose $\mathbf{r}_\iota \leftarrow U(\{0,1\})^k$ with hamming weight v.

- For $\iota \in [Q]$, write down the following equations in variables $\mathbf{X}_1, ..., \mathbf{X}_k$ over $\mathbb{Z}^{m \times \lambda}$:

$$\left\{ \mathbf{AD}_{\iota 1} + \mathbf{AT}_\iota \mathbf{D}_{\iota 2} = \mathbf{A}\left(\sum\nolimits_{j \in [k]} r_{\iota j} \mathbf{X}_j\right) \right\}_{\iota \in [Q]}$$

This is satisfied by $\mathbf{X}_1, ..., \mathbf{X}_k$ with

$$\left\{ \mathbf{D}_{\iota 1} + \mathbf{T}_\iota \mathbf{D}_{\iota 2} = \sum\nolimits_{j \in [k]} r_{\iota j} \mathbf{X}_j \right\}_{\iota \in [Q]} \quad (2)$$

The algorithm aborts if one of the matrices in $\{\mathbf{X}_1, ... \mathbf{X}_k\}$ appeared more than once in the RHS of the equations from (2); Otherwise, the algorithm proceeds to the next step.
- For each equation in (2), get the matrix, e.g., $\mathbf{X}_{\iota j'}$ that does not appear in the RHS of the other equations, and write

$$\mathbf{X}_{j'} = (\mathbf{D}_{\iota 1} + \mathbf{T}_\iota \mathbf{D}_{\iota 2}) - \sum\nolimits_{j \neq j'} r_{\iota j} \mathbf{X}_j$$

and then randomly sample $\mathbf{X}_j \leftarrow D^{m \times \lambda}_{\mathbb{Z}, \omega(\sqrt{\log n})}$ and set the Q values $\mathbf{X}_{j'}$ in the LHS to satisfy the above equation. Let $L = \{\mathbf{X}_j\}$ (resp. $R = \{\mathbf{X}_j\}$) be the set that contains all $\mathbf{X}_j$ from the LHS (resp. RHS) of the above equation. This lets us obtain $\{\mathbf{X}_j\}_{j \in [k]} = L \cup R$.
- With the values $\mathbf{X}_1, ..., \mathbf{X}_k$, set $\mathbf{U}_j = \mathbf{A}\mathbf{X}_j$ for $j \in [k]$.
3. It returns $\mathsf{pub} = (\mathbf{A}, \{\mathbf{U}\}_{i \in [k]}, \{\mathbf{A}_i\}_{i \in [\ell]})$ and state

$$st = \left(\{\bar{\mathbf{R}}_i\}_{i \in [\ell]}, , \{S_\iota, \{h_{\mathsf{ind}(x_{\iota i})}\}_{\mathsf{ind}(x_{\iota i}) \in S_\iota}, \mathbf{r}_\iota, \mathbf{D}^*_\iota\}_{\iota \in [Q]}, \{\mathbf{X}_j\}_{j \in [k]} := L \cup R \right).$$

We note that L contains $\mathbf{X}_j$ that have larger entries than those $\mathbf{X}_j$ in R.

Simulating Predicate Keys $\mathsf{sk}_\mathbf{x}$. This simulation algorithm takes two types of input, i.e., $\mathbf{x}_\iota$ for $\iota \in [Q]$ satisfying $\mathbf{x} \neq \mathbf{x}_\iota$, $P_{\mathbf{x}_\iota}(\mathbf{y}^*) = 1$, and $\mathbf{x} \in (\mathcal{U} \cup \{\star\})^\ell$ satisfying $P_\mathbf{x}(\mathbf{y}^*) = 0$. KeyGen($\mathsf{pub}, st, \mathbf{x}$)'s input st was generated in Setup. For $\mathbf{x}_\iota$ where $\iota \in [Q]$, the algorithm does:

1. Get $\mathbf{D}^*_\iota, \{h_{\mathsf{ind}(x_{\iota i})}\}_{\mathsf{ind}(x_{\iota i}) \in S_\iota}, S_\iota$, and $\mathbf{r}_\iota$ from st.
2. Return $\mathsf{sk}_{\mathbf{x}_\iota} := (\mathbf{D}^*_\iota, \{h_{\mathsf{ind}(x_{\iota i})}\}_{\mathsf{ind}(x_{\iota i}) \in S_\iota}, S_\iota, \mathbf{r}_\iota)$.

For $\mathbf{x}$, the algorithm does:

1. Let $S = \{\mathsf{ind}(x_i \neq \star)\} \subseteq [\ell]$ be the receiver's attribute index set.
2. $h_{\mathsf{ind}(x_i)} \leftarrow U(\mathcal{R}_q)$ for $\mathsf{ind}(x_i) \in S$.
3. Set

$$\mathbf{B} = \sum\nolimits_{\mathsf{ind}(x_i) \in S} \left(\mathbf{A}_{\mathsf{ind}(x_i)} + H(x_i)\mathbf{G}\right) \cdot \mathbf{G}^{-1}(H(h_{\mathsf{ind}(x_i)})\mathbf{G})$$
$$= \mathbf{A} \sum\nolimits_{\mathsf{ind}(x_i) \in S} \bar{\mathbf{R}}_{\mathsf{ind}(x_i)} \mathbf{R}_{\mathsf{ind}(x_i)} + H(\sum\nolimits_{\mathsf{ind}(x_i) \in S}(x_i - y_{\mathsf{ind}(x_i)}) \cdot h_{\mathsf{ind}(x_i)})\mathbf{G}$$
$$= \mathbf{AT}_\mathbf{x} + \mathbf{HG}$$

The algorithm aborts if $\sum_{\mathsf{ind}(x_i) \in S}(x_i - y_{\mathsf{ind}(x_i)}) \cdot h_{\mathsf{ind}(x_i)} = 0 \in \mathcal{R}_q$, i.e., $\mathbf{H} = \mathbf{0} \in \mathbb{Z}_q^{n \times n}$. Otherwise, it moves to the next step.

4. Sample random $\mathbf{r} = (r_1, ..., r_k) \in \{0,1\}^k$ with hamming weight v and set $\mathbf{U}^* = \sum_{j=1}^{k} r_j \mathbf{U}_i$.
5. $\mathbf{D} \leftarrow \mathsf{SampleRight}(\mathbf{A}, \mathbf{B}, \mathbf{T_x}, \mathbf{H}, \mathbf{U}^*, s)$.
6. Return $\mathsf{sk}_\mathbf{x} := (\mathbf{D}, \{h_{\mathsf{ind}(x_i)}\}_{\mathsf{ind}(x_i) \in S}, S, \mathbf{r})$.

Simulating the Challenge Ciphertext $\mathsf{ct}_{\mathbf{y}^*}$. We describe the algorithm $\widetilde{\mathsf{Enc}}(1^{\ell|\mathcal{U}|}, 1^{|\mathsf{msg}|})$ which is used to simulate the challenge ciphertext. $\widetilde{\mathsf{Enc}}$ does:

1. Select $\mathbf{c} \leftarrow U(\mathbb{Z}_q^m)$, $\mathbf{c}_i \leftarrow U(\mathbb{Z}_q^w)$ for $i \in [\ell]$, and $\tilde{\mathbf{c}}_j \leftarrow U(\mathbb{Z}_q^\lambda)$ for $j \in [k]$.
2. Return $\mathsf{ct}^* = (\mathbf{c}, \{\mathbf{c}_i\}_{i \in [\ell]}, \{\tilde{\mathbf{c}}_j\}_{j \in [k]})$.

7.2 Security Proof for Data-Attribute Privacy

Theorem 1. *The HVE scheme Π has (Q, poly)-selective simulation attribute-data privacy (Definition 5) if the $\mathsf{LWE}_{n,m,q,D_{\alpha q}}$ problem (Definition 1) is hard.*

Proof. We prove the Theorem by a sequence of security experiments G_0, G_1, G_2, and G_3. Each experiment outputs a well-defined binary value b. We denote the event that experiment G_i outputs 1 by S_0.

The first experiment G_0 is identical to $\mathsf{Exp}_{\Pi,\mathcal{A}}^{\mathsf{DP-real}}(\lambda)$. In particular, the adversary announces $(\mathbf{y}, \mathbf{x}_1, ... \mathbf{x}_Q)$ where $\mathbf{y}^* \in \mathcal{U}^\ell$ and $\mathbf{x}_i \in (\mathcal{U} \cup \{*\})^\ell$. With pub, $\mathcal{A}$ gets access to $\mathsf{KeyGen}(\mathsf{pub}, \mathsf{msk}, \cdot)$ with vectors $\mathbf{x} \in (\mathcal{U} \cup \{*\})^\ell$ subject to $P_\mathbf{x}(\mathbf{y}^*) = 0$. Then, $\mathcal{A}$ returns a chosen message msg and receives $\mathsf{ct}^* = \mathsf{Enc}(\mathsf{pub}, \mathbf{y}^*, \mathsf{msg})$. Continuing getting access to $\mathsf{KeyGen}(\mathsf{pub}, \mathsf{msk}, \cdot)$ with the same restriction, $\mathcal{A}$ eventually returns b. By definition,

$$\Pr[S_0] = \Pr[\mathsf{Exp}_{\Pi,\mathcal{A}}^{\mathsf{DP-real}}(\lambda) = 1] \qquad (3)$$

G_1 is identical G_0 except that the algorithms $\widetilde{\mathsf{Setup}}$ and $\widetilde{\mathsf{KeyGen}}$ are used to generate pub and reply to key generation queries. We argue that the changes only introduce negligible statistical differences from G_0. We first show that pub generated in both games is statistically indistinguishable, provided the algorithm $\widetilde{\mathsf{Setup}}$ does not abort. The matrix $\mathbf{A}$ was generated using TrapGen which bears a distribution statistically close to $U(\mathbb{Z}_q^{n \times m})$, according to Lemma 2. The matrices $\mathbf{A}_i$ is randomly chosen in G_0 and it is computed as $\mathbf{A}\bar{\mathbf{R}}_i - H(y_i)\mathbf{G}$. According to Lemma 5, the two distributions of $\mathbf{A}_i$ are statistically indistinguishable. Moreover, in G_0, $\mathbf{U}_j$ where $j \in [k]$ are chosen uniformly at random, i.e., from $U(\mathbb{Z}_q^{n \times \lambda})$. In G_1, we consider two cases with the equation

$$\mathbf{X}_{j'} = (\mathbf{D}_{\iota 1} + \mathbf{T}_\iota \mathbf{D}_{\iota 2}) - \sum_{j \neq j'} r_{\iota j} \mathbf{X}_j$$

from the algorithm $\widetilde{\mathsf{Setup}}$. The values $\mathbf{X}_j \in R$ (i.e., the $\mathbf{X}_j$ values appeared in the RHS of the equation) are independently chosen from $D_{\mathbb{Z},\omega(\sqrt{\log n})}^{m \times \lambda}$, according to Lemma 5, $\mathbf{U}_j = \mathbf{A}\mathbf{X}_j$ distributes statistically close to $U(\mathbb{Z}_q^{n \times \lambda})$. For values $X_{j'} \in L$, we have $\mathbf{U}_{j'} = \mathbf{A}\mathbf{X}_{j'} = (\mathbf{D}_{\iota 1} + \mathbf{T}_\iota \mathbf{D}_{\iota 2}) - \sum_{j \neq j'} r_{\iota j} \mathbf{X}_j$. Since $\mathbf{D}_{\iota 1} \leftarrow D_{\mathbb{Z},s}^{m \times \lambda}$, again, using Lemma 5, $\mathbf{U}_{j'}$ is statistically close to $U(\mathbb{Z}_q^{n \times \lambda})$. Finally, according to our parameter selection and Lemma 1 on cover-freeness, the algorithm $\widetilde{\mathsf{Setup}}$ aborts with only negligible probability. Hence, pub's distribution in G_1 is statistically close to its distribution in G_0.

We argue that the distributions $\mathsf{KeyGen}(\mathsf{pub},\mathsf{msk},\cdot)$ and $\widetilde{\mathsf{KeyGen}}(\mathsf{pub},st,\cdot)$ are statistically close. We consider $\mathbf{x}_\iota$, and $\mathsf{sk}_{\mathbf{x}_\iota} := (\mathbf{D}_\iota^*, \{h_{\mathsf{ind}(x_{\iota i})}\}_{\mathsf{ind}(x_{\iota i}) \in S_\iota}, S_\iota, \mathbf{r}_\iota)$. The last three components of $\mathsf{sk}_{\mathbf{x}_\iota}$ are distributed exactly as in G_0. Following the algorithm $\widetilde{\mathsf{Setup}}$, it is also easy to see that $\mathbf{D}_\iota$ has the distribution $D_{\mathbb{Z},s}^{(m+w) \times \lambda}$ conditioned on $[\mathbf{A}|\mathbf{B}_\iota]\mathbf{D}_\iota = \sum_{j \in [k]} r_{\iota,j}\mathbf{U}_j = \mathbf{U}_\iota^*$, i.e., $D_{\Lambda_q^{\mathbf{U}_\iota^*}([\mathbf{A}|\mathbf{B}_\iota]),s}$ which, according to Lemma 3, is statistically close to the distribution generated via SampleLeft as in G_0. Then, we consider the inputs $\mathbf{x}$ such that $P_\mathbf{x}(\mathbf{y}^*) = 0$. Following $\widetilde{\mathsf{KeyGen}}$, $\mathbf{B} = \mathbf{AT}_\mathbf{x} + \mathbf{HG}$ where $\mathbf{H} = H(\sum_{\mathsf{ind}(x_i) \in S}(x_i - y_{\mathsf{ind}(x_i)}) \cdot h_{\mathsf{ind}(x_i)})$. If $\mathbf{H} \neq \mathbf{0}$, the algorithm SampleRight enabled. To see the Gaussian parameter s is sufficiently large for SampleRight as required by Lemma 4, we have

$$s_1(\mathbf{T}) \leq w \|\mathbf{T}\| \leq w \cdot \left\|\left(\sum_{\mathsf{ind}(x_i) \in S} \bar{\mathbf{R}}_{\mathsf{ind}(x_i)}\right) \cdot \mathbf{R}_{\mathsf{ind}(x_i)}\right\|$$
$$\leq w \cdot \ell \cdot \sqrt{m} \cdot \omega(\sqrt{\log n}) \cdot \sqrt{w} \leq \ell \cdot m^2 \cdot \omega(\sqrt{\log n})$$

According to Lemma 4, the distributions of $\mathbf{D}_\iota$, i.e., $\mathsf{SampleLeft}(\mathbf{A},\mathbf{B},\mathbf{R},\mathbf{U}^*,s)$ in G_0 and $\mathsf{SampleRight}(\mathbf{A},\mathbf{B},\mathbf{T},\mathbf{H},\mathbf{U}^*,s)$ in G_1 are statistically close. For the probability that $\widetilde{\mathsf{KeyGen}}$ aborts, noticed that $P_\mathbf{x}(\mathbf{y}^*) = 0$, there must be one index, say $\mathsf{ind}(x_i)$ that $x_i \neq y_{\mathsf{ind}(x_i)}$. Since $h_{\mathsf{ind}(x_i)}$ is randomly chosen, $\sum_{\mathsf{ind}(x_i) \in S}(x_i - y_{\mathsf{ind}(x_i)}) \cdot h_{\mathsf{ind}(x_i)}$ is uniformly random over $\mathcal{R}_q$, the probability that $\mathbf{H} = \mathbf{0}$ is $1/q^d$. Assuming the adversary makes polynomial Q^* such queries, a union bound shows that the algorithm aborts during the simulation with no more than Q^*/q^k probability, which is negligible as $d = \omega(\log \lambda)$.

As a result, G_0 and G_1 are distributed statistically close and therefore

$$|\Pr[S_1] - \Pr[S_0]| \leq \mathsf{negl}(\lambda) \tag{4}$$

where $\mathsf{negl}(\lambda)$ accounts for the negligible statistical errors and the negligible probabilities that $\widetilde{\mathsf{Setup}}$ and $\widetilde{\mathsf{Enc}}$ abort.

G_2 is identical to G_1 except that the matrix $\mathbf{A}$ is uniformly random over $\mathbb{Z}_q^{n \times m}$. We note that the trapdoor $\mathbf{R}$ of $\mathbf{A}$ was not used anywhere in G_1. According to Lemma 2, $\mathbf{A}$'s distributions in G_1 and G_2 are statistically close. Hence,

$$|\Pr[S_2] - \Pr[S_1]| \leq \mathsf{negl}(\lambda) \tag{5}$$

for some negligible $\mathsf{negl}(\lambda)$.

G_3 is identical G_2 except the challenge ciphertext is produced by $\widetilde{\mathsf{Enc}}$. We constructed an algorithm $\mathcal{B}$ that uses the distinguisher of G_2 and G_3 to solve the $\mathsf{LWE}_{n,m,q D_{\alpha q}}$ problem. $\mathcal{B}$ receives an instance $(\mathbf{A} \in \mathbb{Z}_q^{n \times m}, \mathbf{b} \in \mathbb{Z}_q^m)$. It needs to decide, if $\mathbf{b}^\intercal = \mathbf{s}^\intercal \mathbf{A} + \mathbf{e}^\intercal$ or $(\mathbf{A}, \mathbf{b})$ are uniformly random. $\mathcal{B}$ dose so by simulating either G_2 or G_3 to the adversary $\mathcal{A}$ as follows. $\mathcal{B}$ generates the master public key pub and responds to the key generation queries as in G_2.

1. $\mathcal{B}$ uses $\mathbf{A}$ from the LWE challenge to run $\widetilde{\mathsf{Setup}}$ and $\widetilde{\mathsf{KeyGen}}$.
2. On receiving the challenge message msg, $\mathcal{B}$ samples
   - $\mathbf{v}_i \leftarrow D_{\mathbb{Z},\bar{\tau}}^w$ for $i \in [\ell]$ where $\bar{\tau} = \alpha q \sqrt{m} \cdot \omega(\sqrt{\log n})$
   - $\tilde{\mathbf{v}}_j \leftarrow D_{\mathbb{Z},\tilde{\tau}}^\lambda$ for the indexes j where $\tilde{\tau} = \alpha q \cdot \ell^{3/2} \cdot m^3 \cdot \omega(\log^{3/2} n)$
3. $\mathcal{B}$ then sets $\mathbf{c}^\intercal = \mathbf{b}^\intercal$, $\mathbf{c}_i^\intercal = \mathbf{b}^\intercal \bar{\mathbf{R}}_i + \mathbf{v}_i^\intercal$ for $i \in [\ell]$, and $\tilde{\mathbf{c}}_j^\intercal = \mathbf{b}^\intercal \mathbf{X}_j + \tilde{\mathbf{v}}_j^\intercal +$ msg$^\intercal \lfloor q/p \rfloor$ for $j \in [k]$, and returns $\mathsf{ct}^* = (\mathbf{c}, \{\mathbf{c}_i\}_{i\in[\ell]}, \{\tilde{\mathbf{c}}_j\}_{j\in[k]})$.4
4. $\mathcal{B}$ keeps interacting with $\mathcal{A}$ using $\widetilde{\mathsf{KeyGen}}$ and returns what $\mathcal{A}$ returns.

We analyse $\mathcal{B}$. First, the runtime of $\mathcal{B}$ is bounded by the runtime of $\mathcal{A}$ plus some polynomial, i.e., $\mathcal{B}$ is a p.p.t algorithm. Second, the public parameters pub and key generation queries are simulated as required by G_2 and G_3. For the ciphertext ct^*, if $\mathbf{b}^\intercal = \mathbf{s}^\intercal \mathbf{A} + \mathbf{e}^\intercal$, we can see that $\mathbf{c}$ is distributed properly; And for $i \in [\ell]$ and $j \in [k]$,

$$\mathbf{c}_i^\intercal = \mathbf{b}^\intercal \bar{\mathbf{R}}_i + \mathbf{v}_i^\intercal = \mathbf{s}^\intercal \mathbf{A} \bar{\mathbf{R}}_i + \mathbf{e}^\intercal \bar{\mathbf{R}}_i \mathbf{v}_i^\intercal$$
$$= \mathbf{s}^\intercal (\mathbf{A}_i + H(y_i)\mathbf{G}) + \mathbf{e}_i^\intercal$$

and

$$\tilde{\mathbf{c}}_j^\intercal = \mathbf{b}^\intercal \mathbf{X}_j + \tilde{\mathbf{v}}_j^\intercal = \mathbf{s}^\intercal \mathbf{A} \mathbf{X}_j + \mathbf{e}^\intercal \mathbf{X}_j + \tilde{\mathbf{v}}_j^\intercal$$
$$= \mathbf{s}^\intercal \mathbf{U}_j + \tilde{\mathbf{e}}_j^\intercal$$

Using Theorem 3.1, [19], conditioned on $\mathbf{A}\bar{\mathbf{R}}_i$ and $\mathbf{A}\mathbf{X}_j$, the noise terms $\mathbf{e}_i$ and $\tilde{\mathbf{e}}_j$ are distributed properly as in the G_2. This shows that $\mathcal{B}$ simulates G_2. So,

$$\Pr[S_2] = \Pr[\mathcal{B}(\mathbf{A}, \mathbf{s}^\intercal \mathbf{A} + \mathbf{e}^\intercal) = 1]$$

On the other hand, if $(\mathbf{A}, \mathbf{b})$ is uniformly random, all ciphertext components are uniformly random. So, $\mathcal{B}$ simulates G_3, and

$$\Pr[S_3] = \Pr[\mathcal{B}(\mathbf{A}, \mathbf{b}^\intercal) = 1]$$

Using the above two equations, we get

$$|\Pr[S_3] - \Pr[S_2]| \leq \mathsf{Adv}_\mathcal{B}^{\mathsf{LWE}_{n,m,q,D_{\mathbb{Z},\alpha q}}}(\lambda) \qquad (6)$$

We see that in G_3, ct^* contains no information about the challenge $\mathbf{y}^*$ and msg. Therefore, we have used the algorithm $\widetilde{\mathsf{Setup}}$, $\widetilde{\mathsf{KeyGen}}$ and $\widetilde{\mathsf{Enc}}$ to construct a simulator $\mathcal{S}$ such that

$$\Pr[S_3] = \Pr[\mathsf{Exp}_{\Pi,\mathcal{S}}^{\mathsf{DP-rand}}(\lambda) = 1] \qquad (7)$$

Combining inequalities (3), 4, 5, (6), and (7) leads to

$$\mathsf{Adv}_{\Pi,\mathcal{A}}^{\mathsf{DP}}(\lambda) \leq \mathsf{Adv}_\mathcal{B}^{\mathsf{LWE}_{n,m,q,D_{\mathbb{Z},\alpha q}}}(\lambda) + \mathsf{negl}(\lambda)$$

for some LWE solver $\mathcal{B}$. This proves the Theorem. □

7.3 Security Proof for Predicate Privacy

Theorem 2. *Let λ be the security parameter. The HVE scheme Π has predicate privacy (Definition 7) against any (T, κ)-admissible adversary with $\kappa \geq d \log q + 2 \log(1/\mathsf{negl}(\lambda)) + \Theta(1)$ for some negligible $\mathsf{negl}(\lambda)$.*

Proof. Let $\mathcal{A}$ be a (T, κ)-admissible adversary against the predicate privacy. We show that the distribution of $\mathcal{A}$'s view on $\mathsf{Exp}_{\Pi,\mathcal{A}}^{\mathsf{PP-real}}(\lambda)$, denoted by $\mathsf{View}_{\mathsf{real}}$, and the distribution of $\mathcal{A}$'s view on $\mathsf{Exp}_{\Pi,\mathcal{A}}^{\mathsf{PP-rand}}(\lambda)$, denoted by $\mathsf{View}_{\mathsf{rand}}$, are computationally indistinguishable. We proceed with a sequence of security games. Again, each of the games has a well-defined binary output.

The first game G_0 is identical to $\mathsf{Exp}_{\Pi,\mathcal{A}}^{\mathsf{PP-real}}(\lambda)$. At the beginning of the game, a random $\mathbf{y}^* \in \mathcal{U}^\ell$ is chosen and $(\mathbf{x}_1, ..., \mathbf{x}_Q)$ are drawn. After received pub, $\mathcal{A}$ makes query to the oracles $\mathsf{RoR}(\mathsf{real}, \cdot)$ to get $(\mathbf{x}_{Q+1}, ..., \mathbf{x}_T)$ sampled according $\mathcal{X}_{|\mathbf{y}^*}$ which are then used to obtained $\mathsf{sk}_{\mathbf{x}_i} \leftarrow \mathsf{KeyGen}(\mathsf{pub}, \mathsf{msk}, \mathbf{x}_i)$. So,

$$\Pr[S_0] = \Pr[\mathsf{Exp}_{\Pi,\mathcal{A}}^{\mathsf{PP-real}}(\lambda) = 1] \tag{8}$$

G_1 is identical to G_0 except that Setup, KeyGen and Enc are replaced by the simulation algorithms, $\widetilde{\mathsf{Setup}}$, $\widetilde{\mathsf{KeyGen}}$ and $\widetilde{\mathsf{Enc}}$, respectively. By the proof of Theorem 1, The distribution of G_1 is computationally indistinguishable from G_0, under the hardness of the $\mathsf{LWE}_{n,m,q,D_{\mathbb{Z},\alpha q}}$ problem, i.e.,

$$|\Pr[S_1] - \Pr[S_0]| \leq \mathsf{Adv}_{\mathcal{B}}^{\mathsf{LWE}_{n,m,q,D_{\mathbb{Z},\alpha q}}}(\lambda) + \mathsf{negl}(\lambda) \tag{9}$$

where $\mathsf{negl}(\lambda)$ accounts for the negligible statistical errors introduced by using the simulation algorithms and $\mathcal{B}$ is some LWE problem solver. We emphasise that the simulated ciphertext $\mathsf{ct}_{\mathbf{y}^*}$ does not carry over any information about $\mathbf{y}^*$ and but can be properly decrypted by the simulated keys $\mathsf{sk}_{\mathbf{x}_i}$ for $i \in [Q]$.

G_2 is identical to G_1 except that the algorithms $\widetilde{\mathsf{Setup}}$ and $\widetilde{\mathsf{KeyGen}}$ are respectively replaced by the normal algorithms Setup and KeyGen. Using the same proof for inequality (4) for Theorem 1, we have

$$|\Pr[S_2] - \Pr[G_1]| \leq \mathsf{negl}(\lambda) \tag{10}$$

where $\mathsf{negl}(\lambda)$ accounts for the negligible statistical errors.

G_3 is identical to G_2 except that $(\mathbf{x}_1, ..., \mathbf{x}_T)$ is now sampled from uniform distribution $U((\mathcal{U} \cup \{\star\})^T)$ instead of the (T, κ)-block source $(\bar{\mathcal{X}}_{|\mathbf{y}^*}, \tilde{\mathcal{X}})$, Recall that in G_2, the ciphertexts of the samples are independent of $\mathbf{y}^*$, and hence, independent of $\mathcal{A}$'s view. We examine the matrix $\mathbf{B}$ as it has all information about $\mathbf{x}_\iota = (x_{\iota 1}, ..., x_{\iota \ell})$ that could be available to $\mathcal{A}$. Following our construction and using the isomorphism from the extended FRD H,

$$\mathbf{B}_\iota = \sum\nolimits_{\mathsf{ind}(x_{\iota i}) \in S_\iota} \left(\mathbf{A}_{\mathsf{ind}(x_{\iota i})} + H(x_{\iota i})\mathbf{G}\right) \cdot \mathbf{G}^{-1}(H(h_{\mathsf{ind}(x_{\iota i})})\mathbf{G})$$

$$= \sum\nolimits_{\mathsf{ind}(x_{\iota i}) \in S_\iota} \mathbf{A}_i \mathbf{G}^{-1}(H(h_{\mathsf{ind}(x_{\iota i})})\mathbf{G} + H(\sum\nolimits_{\mathsf{ind}(x_{\iota i}) \in S} x_{\iota i} \cdot h_{\mathsf{ind}(x_{\iota i})})\mathbf{G}$$

Fixing the public parameters and noting $h_{\mathsf{ind}(x_{\iota i})}$ are random over $\mathcal{R}_q$, it suffices to assume that $\mathcal{A}$'s view to be

$$\mathsf{View}_{\mathsf{real}} = \left\{ \left(h_{\mathsf{ind}(x_{\iota i})}, \sum\nolimits_{\mathsf{ind}(x_{\iota i}) \in S_\iota} x_{\iota i} \cdot h_{\mathsf{ind}(x_{\iota i})} \right) \right\}_{\iota \in [T]}$$

By our hypothesis, $\{\mathbf{x}_\iota = (x_{\iota 1}, ..., x_{\iota \ell})\}_{\iota \in [T]}$ is ample from a (T, κ)-source. According to Lemma 7, the function $\mathsf{Hash}_{\mathbf{x}_\iota}(\cdot) : \mathcal{R}_q^\ell \to \mathcal{R}_q$ is universal. So, $\mathsf{View}_{\mathsf{real}}$ is statistically close to

$$\mathsf{View}_{\mathsf{rand}} = \left\{ \left(h_{\mathsf{ind}(x_{\iota i})}, \sum\nolimits_{\mathsf{ind}(x_{\iota i}) \in S_\iota} r_{\iota i} \cdot h_{\mathsf{ind}(x_{\iota i})} \right) \right\}_{\iota \in [T]}$$

where $\{(r_{\iota 1}, ..., r_{\iota \ell})\}_{\iota \in [T]}$ are sampled from $U((\mathcal{U} \cup \{\star\})^T)_{|\mathbf{y}^*}$. Hence, we derived

$$|\Pr[S_3] - \Pr[S_2]| \leq \mathsf{negl}(\lambda) \tag{11}$$

where $\mathsf{negl}(\lambda)$ accounts for the negligible statistical errors.

Finally, G_4 is identical to G_3 except that the simulation algorithms $\widetilde{\mathsf{Enc}}$ and is replaced the real algorithms Enc. Using the proofs of (4), (5) and (6), we have

$$|\Pr[S_4] - \Pr[S_3]| \leq \mathsf{Adv}_{\mathcal{B}}^{\mathsf{LWE}_{n,m,q,D_{\mathbb{Z},\alpha q}}}(\lambda) + \mathsf{negl}(\lambda) \tag{12}$$

where $\mathsf{negl}(\lambda)$ accounts for the negligible statistical errors.

Finally, by definition,

$$\Pr[S_4] = \Pr[\mathsf{Exp}_{\Pi,\mathcal{A}}^{\mathsf{PP-random}}(\lambda) = 1] \tag{13}$$

Combining relations (8)–(13), we have

$$\mathsf{Adv}_{\Pi,\mathcal{A}}^{\mathsf{PP}}(\lambda) \leq 2 \cdot \mathsf{Adv}_{\mathcal{B}}^{\mathsf{LWE}_{n,m,q,D_{\mathbb{Z},\alpha q}}}(\lambda) + \mathsf{negl}(\lambda)$$

And this proves the Theorem. □

8 Conclusion

We present an enhanced predicate-private hidden vector encryption (HVE) scheme based on lattices, capable of supporting a large attribute universe. This is the first predicate encryption scheme achieving enhanced predicate privacy for predicates beyond simple equality. The attribute-data privacy and enhanced predicate privacy of our construction enable the design of an asymmetric searchable encryption (ASE) scheme that offers robust privacy guarantees for both ciphertexts and search tokens. By supporting pattern matching with wildcards, our ASE scheme is particularly well-suited for conducting privacy-preserving pattern searches over encrypted data.

Due to the security of our HVE scheme, the ASE scheme supports the issuance of an a priori bounded number of matching search tokens. While this limitation is relatively mild in the context of searchable encryption—for example, the number of search tokens can be managed—it remains an interesting and valuable direction to explore for removing this restriction. We leave this as an open problem for future work.

References

1. Abdalla, M., et al.: Searchable encryption revisited: consistency properties, relation to anonymous IBE, and extensions. In: Shoup, V. (ed.) CRYPTO 2005. LNCS, vol. 3621, pp. 205–222. Springer, Heidelberg (2005). https://doi.org/10.1007/11535218_13
2. Agrawal, S.: Stronger security for reusable garbled circuits, general definitions and attacks. In: Katz, J., Shacham, H. (eds.) CRYPTO 2017. LNCS, vol. 10401, pp. 3–35. Springer, Cham (2017). https://doi.org/10.1007/978-3-319-63688-7_1
3. Agrawal, S., Boneh, D., Boyen, X.: Efficient lattice (H)IBE in the standard model. In: Gilbert, H. (ed.) EUROCRYPT 2010. LNCS, vol. 6110, pp. 553–572. Springer, Heidelberg (2010). https://doi.org/10.1007/978-3-642-13190-5_28
4. Albrecht, M.R., Player, R., Scott, S.: On the concrete hardness of learning with errors. J. Math. Cryptol. **9**(3), 169–203 (2015)
5. Arriaga, A., Tang, Q., Ryan, P.: Trapdoor privacy in asymmetric searchable encryption schemes. In: Pointcheval, D., Vergnaud, D. (eds.) AFRICACRYPT 2014. LNCS, vol. 8469, pp. 31–50. Springer, Cham (2014). https://doi.org/10.1007/978-3-319-06734-6_3
6. Bartusek, J., et al.: Public-key function-private hidden vector encryption (and more). In: Galbraith, S.D., Moriai, S. (eds.) ASIACRYPT 2019. LNCS, vol. 11923, pp. 489–519. Springer, Cham (2019). https://doi.org/10.1007/978-3-030-34618-8_17
7. Boneh, D., Crescenzo, G., Ostrovsky, R., Persiano, G.: Public key encryption with keyword search. In: Cachin, C., Camenisch, J.L. (eds.) EUROCRYPT 2004. LNCS, vol. 3027, pp. 506–522. Springer, Heidelberg (2004). https://doi.org/10.1007/978-3-540-24676-3_30
8. Boneh, D., Raghunathan, A., Segev, G.: Function-private identity-based encryption: hiding the function in functional encryption. In: Canetti, R., Garay, J.A. (eds.) CRYPTO 2013. LNCS, vol. 8043, pp. 461–478. Springer, Heidelberg (2013). https://doi.org/10.1007/978-3-642-40084-1_26
9. Boneh, D., Raghunathan, A., Segev, G.: Function-private subspace-membership encryption and its applications. In: Sako, K., Sarkar, P. (eds.) ASIACRYPT 2013. LNCS, vol. 8269, pp. 255–275. Springer, Heidelberg (2013). https://doi.org/10.1007/978-3-642-42033-7_14
10. Boneh, D., Waters, B.: Conjunctive, subset, and range queries on encrypted data. In: Vadhan, S.P. (ed.) TCC 2007. LNCS, vol. 4392, pp. 535–554. Springer, Heidelberg (2007). https://doi.org/10.1007/978-3-540-70936-7_29
11. Bouscatié, É., Castagnos, G., Sanders, O.: Pattern matching in encrypted stream from inner product encryption. In: Boldyreva, A., Kolesnikov, V. (eds.) PKC 2023. LNCS, vol. 13940, pp. 774–801. Springer, Cham (2023). https://doi.org/10.1007/978-3-031-31368-4_27
12. Boyen, X.: Lattice mixing and vanishing trapdoors: a framework for fully secure short signatures and more. In: Nguyen, P.Q., Pointcheval, D. (eds.) PKC 2010. LNCS, vol. 6056, pp. 499–517. Springer, Heidelberg (2010). https://doi.org/10.1007/978-3-642-13013-7_29
13. Gentry, C., Peikert, C., Vaikuntanathan, V.: Trapdoors for hard lattices and new cryptographic constructions. In: Proceedings of the 40th Annual ACM Symposium on Theory of Computing, STOC 2008, pp. 197–206. ACM, New York, NY, USA (2008)

14. Gorbunov, S., Vaikuntanathan, V., Wee, H.: Functional encryption with bounded collusions via multi-party computation. In: Safavi-Naini, R., Canetti, R. (eds.) CRYPTO 2012. LNCS, vol. 7417, pp. 162–179. Springer, Heidelberg (2012). https://doi.org/10.1007/978-3-642-32009-5_11
15. Gorbunov, S., Vaikuntanathan, V., Wee, H.: Predicate encryption for circuits from LWE. In: Gennaro, R., Robshaw, M. (eds.) CRYPTO 2015. LNCS, vol. 9216, pp. 503–523. Springer, Heidelberg (2015). https://doi.org/10.1007/978-3-662-48000-7_25
16. Meng, L., Chen, L., Tian, Y., Manulis, M., Liu, S.: FEASE: fast and expressive asymmetric searchable encryption. In: 33rd USENIX Security Symposium (USENIX Security 24), pp. 2545–2562 (2024)
17. Micciancio, D., Peikert, C.: Trapdoors for lattices: simpler, tighter, faster, smaller. In: Pointcheval, D., Johansson, T. (eds.) EUROCRYPT 2012. LNCS, vol. 7237, pp. 700–718. Springer, Heidelberg (2012). https://doi.org/10.1007/978-3-642-29011-4_41
18. Patranabis, S., Mukhopadhyay, D., Ramanna, S.C.: Function private predicate encryption for low min-entropy predicates. In: Lin, D., Sako, K. (eds.) PKC 2019. LNCS, vol. 11443, pp. 189–219. Springer, Cham (2019). https://doi.org/10.1007/978-3-030-17259-6_7
19. Peikert, C.: An efficient and parallel Gaussian sampler for lattices. In: Rabin, T. (ed.) CRYPTO 2010. LNCS, vol. 6223, pp. 80–97. Springer, Heidelberg (2010). https://doi.org/10.1007/978-3-642-14623-7_5
20. Ünal, A.: Impossibility results for lattice-based functional encryption schemes. In: Canteaut, A., Ishai, Y. (eds.) EUROCRYPT 2020. LNCS, vol. 12105, pp. 169–199. Springer, Cham (2020). https://doi.org/10.1007/978-3-030-45721-1_7
21. Xagawa, K.: Improved (Hierarchical) inner-product encryption from lattices. In: Kurosawa, K., Hanaoka, G. (eds.) PKC 2013. LNCS, vol. 7778, pp. 235–252. Springer, Heidelberg (2013). https://doi.org/10.1007/978-3-642-36362-7_15

DEBridge: Towards Secure and Practical Plausibly Deniable Encryption Based on USB Bridge Controller

Chongyu Long[1], Yuewu Wang[1]([✉]), Lingguang Lei[2,3], Haoyang Xing[1], and Jiwu Jing[1]

[1] School of Cryptology, University of Chinese Academy of Sciences, Beijing 100049, China
wangyuewu@ucas.ac.cn
[2] Key Laboratory of Cyberspace Security Defense, Institute of Information Engineering, CAS, Beijing 100089, China
[3] School of Cyber Security, University of Chinese Academy of Sciences, Beijing 100043, China

Abstract. Plausibly deniable encryption (PDE) systems have been developed to enable users to securely store sensitive data while plausibly denying its existence under coercion to disclose encryption keys. However, the majority of existing PDE systems are software-based, lacking hardware-level security protection for keys. Additionally, they often require the installation of additional supporting software and depend on specific operating systems (OS), file systems (FS), or storage media, significantly limiting their practicality.

To address these limitations, we present DEBridge, the first PDE system based on the USB bridge controller—a component that supports and controls data transfer between a host and a storage device. With the help of USB bridge controller, DEBridge introduces hardware security modules to provide hardware-level security protection for keys. We implement the "pseudo disk" as an interface for users to interact with the device, thereby avoiding the installation of additional software. Furthermore, DEBridge integrates hidden volume technology that supports multi-level deniability into the firmware of the USB bridge controller, thereby eliminating the dependence on OS, FS or storage media. We implement DEBridge on the TUSB9261 USB bridge controller and evaluate its feasibility and performance. Given the peculiarities and sensitivities of PDE systems themselves, we believe that the security and practicality brought by DEBridge are of significant value.

Keywords: Plausibly Deniable Encryption · Bridge Controller · Privacy · Coercive Attack

1 Introduction

Storage devices are increasingly used to store sensitive data, making the protection of this data crucial for every user. Conventional data protection methodologies, such as file-level or disk-level encryption, have been employed to address the challenges posed by unauthorized access due to theft or loss. However, these approaches merely serve to transfer the problem from data protection to key protection. They have been shown to be inadequate when confronted with more sophisticated adversaries who may capture both the devices and the users, using legal or coercive tactics (e.g., psychological or rubber hose cryptanalysis) to force the users into revealing their encryption keys [6]. In such cases, there is often a compromise of sensitive data, and the safety of the user is at risk [30,32,39].

To address this issue, the concept of PDE was introduced [8]. PDE enables encryption in a way that, when decrypted with the real key, the original sensitive data is revealed, but when decrypted with a decoy key, the harmless and decoy data is revealed. If captured, the users can expose the decoy key to avoid further harm while concealing the existence of their sensitive data. Although several PDE systems have been developed, they exhibit key limitations:

1) Lack of Hardware-Level Security. Most PDE systems depend on software-based disk encryption [2,9,10,16,36–38,41], a factor which renders them vulnerable to specific vulnerabilities. Firstly, the encryption is typically performed in the host's RAM, exposing it to threats such as cold boot and direct memory access (DMA) attacks, which can extract encryption keys from RAM [5,18]. Secondly, integrating secure hardware without compromising deniability is challenging for these systems. Consequently, key protection often relies solely on a single-factor password, leaving systems vulnerable to offline password-guessing attacks, including dictionary and rainbow table attacks, which can retrieve user passwords and keys. However, many existing schemes overlook these vulnerabilities and underestimate the capabilities of real-world adversaries in their adversarial models [13,19,20,30].

2) Requirements on Additional Software. It is evident that several PDE systems, including TrueCrypt [37], VeraCrypt [38] and Shufflecake [2] function as software tools in and of themselves. Moreover, MobiGyges [16], DEFTL [19] and MDEFTL [20] require the installation of client software to enable the hidden volume. However, the presence of such software can potentially raise suspicion if discovered by adversaries, thereby undermining the deniability [31]. Furthermore, transferring data between devices frequently requires the pre-installation of corresponding software, which can be both inconvenient and potentially risky, especially if the software has not been subjected to rigorous security scrutiny.

3) Dependencies on OS, FS or Storage Media. OS: Systems like MobiPluto [9], MobiGyges [16] and MobiCeal [10] depend on Linux's "thin provisioning" mechanism. Shufflecake [2], INVISILINE [31] and INFUSE [11] are implemented as Linux-specific kernel modules. StegFS [26] relies on certain older Linux kernel and APIs. This dependency limits their compatibility with certain other operating systems; **FS:** DEFY [30] relies on the YAFFS flash file system. Mobiflage [36] and MobiHydra [41] rely on the FAT file system's sequential write feature. These systems are incompatible with mainstream file systems such as NTFS and EXT4; **Storage Media:** PEARL [12], DEFTL [19] and MDEFTL [20] require customized flash translation layer (FTL) in flash storage devices, and

INFUSE [11] depends on specialized NAND chips, making them unsuitable for traditional hard disk drives (HDD).

Existing solutions fail to address these limitations simultaneously, which motivates us to design DEBridge. DEBridge is founded on several key insights:

1) Plausible Access to Security Hardware. The USB bridge controller is a widely utilised hardware component that can support and control data transmission between the host and storage device. In addition, in encrypted storage applications, it seamlessly integrates hardware security modules such as encryption components, true random number generators (TRNGs) and device-specific security keys [1,24,27]. With their help, all encryption is performed directly on the bridge controller, thereby significantly mitigating the threat of RAM as a potential attack vector. Furthermore, encryption keys can be plausibly protected by multiple factors, such as device-specific fingerprints and keys without compromising deniability, rendering offline attacks infeasible [22,24].

2) Eliminating Additional Software. A pseudo file system, named "pseudo disk", is introduced directly within the USB bridge controller firmware. The "pseudo disk" serves as a user interface for DEBridge, thereby eliminating the need for additional software. This offers a seamless plug-and-play solution for password and key management with high practicability.

3) Highly Compatible PDE Solution. Currently, almost all PDE solutions are implemented on the host side or disk side. In contrast, we integrate hidden volume technology into the firmware of the bridge controller to achieve plausible deniability. Due to the USB bridge controller sits between the host and the storage device on the physical pathway, it remains entirely independent of the OS, FS, and storage medium. This is unmatched by previous PDE solutions.

The **Main Contributions** of this paper are summarized as follows:

- We propose DEBridge, a secure and practical PDE storage solution based on USB bridge controller. DEBridge is the first design to incorporate deniability into the USB bridge controller, providing hardware-level security protection for keys. Furthermore, it does not rely on any additional software, OS, FS, or storage media, thereby offering enhanced compatibility and practicality.
- We implement a "pseudo disk" user interface, enabling DEBridge to handle password and key management independently. DEBridge supports multiple hidden volumes, and users can independently control the number of hidden volumes, thus achieving multi-level deniability.
- We theoretically analyze the security of DEBridge. We also implement a prototype system of DEBridge on TUSB9261 and evaluated its performance and usability through experiments. Given the particular and sensitive nature of PDE systems, we believe DEBridge is a significant and notable design.

2 Background

2.1 USB Bridge Controller

The USB bridge controller is designed to bridge storage devices (e.g., SSDs and HDDs) to the host USB bus. It typically comprises a USB control module and a storage device control module, which are responsible for managing data transfer between the host and the storage device. The USB bridge controller can intercept, modify and forward instructions and data during communication, and can independently send commands to both the host and the storage device. The firmware of a USB bridge controller is typically stored in its flash memory, which generally leaves free space for developers to do secondary development. Besides, many USB bridge controllers seamlessly integrate hardware security modules, such as encryption components, TRNG and device-specific security elements [1,24]. We can use them to provide hardware support for mainstream cryptographic algorithms to protect the security of stored data without raising suspicion.

2.2 Full Disk Encryption

Full Disk Encryption (FDE) is a foundational security technology that prevents sensitive data on storage devices from being compromised [23]. FDE encrypts all data stored on a device, requiring users to provide a valid key to decrypt the data each time they access the device. Based on its implementation, FDE can be categorized into two distinct types: software-based FDE and hardware-based FDE. Common software-based FDE includes BitLocker [3] (for Windows) and LUKS [40] (for Linux). Conversely, hardware-based FDE performs encryption directly within the drive itself. This can be achieved through the disk drive controller or the USB bridge controller [27], thereby ensuring that encryption and decryption processes are transparent to the user without detracting from the performance of the host system. Modern storage devices increasingly support hardware-accelerated encryption and demonstrate strong performance. For example, Fujitsu's MB86C30A USB bridge controller has a throughput of 270MB/s with the hardware-accelerated AES-XTS-256 [17]. Besides, both the SanDisk Extreme Portable SSD and Western Digital My Passport SSD have throughput of up to 1000MB/s when hardware-accelerated encryption [15,33].

2.3 Hidden Volume Technology

Hidden volume technology can provide plausible deniability for sensitive data, allowing users to protect data security when under threat [37,38]. The process begins by filling the entire storage device with random data. Two encrypted volumes are then created: a public volume and a hidden volume. The public volume spans the entire device and is encrypted using a public volume key. The hidden volume is embedded within the device at a secret offset and extends to the end of the disk, encrypted with a separate hidden volume key. Sensitive data is stored exclusively within the hidden volume. In the event of coercion, users can disclose only the public volume key without revealing the existence of the hidden volume. This is because the hidden volume is indistinguishable from the random data that was originally filled throughout the device.

3 Models and Assumptions

3.1 System Model

The primary focus of this study is on storage devices controlled by the USB bridge controllers. These include external disk drives based on USB bridge controllers (e.g., My Passport and Samsung T3/T5), as well as the combination of disk enclosures based on USB bridge controllers (e.g., RTL9210B and TUSB9261) and conventional disk drives (e.g., SSDs and HDDs). These storage devices are commonly used as external storage devices, which are very portable and ubiquitous.

3.2 Adversarial Model

We assume the presence of an adversary with limited computational resources but with coercive capabilities [8]. The adversary can capture both the victims and their storage device, using coercive means to extract the decryption key and reveal sensitive data. Additionally, the adversary may take a complete snapshot of the storage device and perform forensic analysis. However, we do not consider adversaries who can repeatedly capture the victims and their storage device or secretly take multiple snapshots over time. That is, we only consider single-snapshot adversary and do not consider multi-snapshot adversary.

Although multi-snapshot security is theoretically stronger, its exclusion remains justified for the following reasons: (1) No legal cases of conviction for a multi-snapshot attack has been found in the existing public literature. In contrast, even a relatively simple system with single-snapshot security like True-Crypt has been shown to help suspects secure acquittals [2]. (2) While a few schemes for implementing multi-snapshot security exist, their high throughput and space costs often make them impractical in most scenarios [13].

3.3 Assumptions

DEBridge relies on several key assumptions, as summarized in the following:

- The adversaries cannot capture a storage device in the PDE mode or after a crash of the PDE mode. Otherwise, the adversaries can easily obtain the sensitive data or detect the existence of PDE.
- The adversaries are aware of the design of DEBridge, but do not know the key and password for PDE mode.
- The adversaries are rational and will cease coercive actions if they are convinced that the decryption key has been revealed or if no conclusive evidence of sensitive data exists.
- The host operating system, bootloader, and USB bridge controller firmware are assumed to be free from malware. Specifically, in PDE mode, the users do not run any malicious applications controlled by the adversaries.

– The hardware device running DEBridge is assumed to be secure. While side-channel and fault injection attacks against cryptographic devices are known threats, efforts to enhance resistance to them have been actively addressed by orthogonal works [25,29,34,35], and are not the primary focus of this work. A brief discussion of mitigation strategies will be provided in Sect. 7.4.

4 DEBridge Design

4.1 Overview

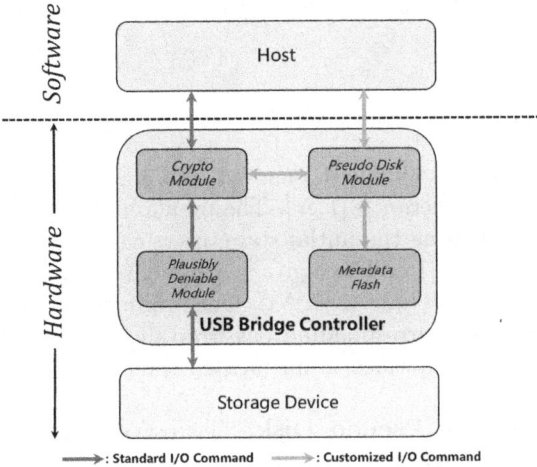

Fig. 1. Schematic Diagram of DEBridge's Workflow.

DEBridge enables the creation of two types of volumes on the storage device: **public volume** and **hidden volumes**. The hidden volumes reside within the free space of the public volume, beginning at a secret offset specified by the user. Both types volumes are encrypted with randomly generated keys, which are protected using the USB bridge controller's hardware security module. DEBridge operates in two modes: **standard mode**, which manages public volume, and **PDE mode**, which manages hidden volumes. The mode is selected by the user at startup by entering the corresponding password. A built-in "pseudo disk" in the bridge controller handles user interaction with DEBridge, eliminating the need for any additional software installation.

DEBridge achieves plausible deniability by encrypting sensitive data and storing it in the hidden volumes. To illustrate, consider a scenario with one public volume and one hidden volume. The public volume stores decoy data (regular data or relatively insensitive data), while the hidden volume stores sensitive data. Since the device is pre-filled with random data, the encrypted hidden volume data is indistinguishable from the random data when using the public volume. When coerced by an adversary, the user can pretend to comply by providing access to the public volume, thereby denying the existence of the hidden volume (sensitive data).

In practice, however, a single public volume may not fully convince an informed adversary aware of DEBridge's design, potentially leading to continued coercion. To address this, DEBridge supports the creation of multiple hidden volumes, offering **multi-level deniability**. The user can specify the number of hidden volumes (up to a maximum of N) during initialization. Each hidden volume represents a different level of deniability, with higher levels corresponding to more critical sensitive data. Under further coercion, the user can disclose L ($L < N$) passwords for lower-deniability hidden volumes to convince the adversary while protecting the most sensitive data. DEBridge's workflow is shown in Fig. 1.

4.2 "Pseudo Disk"

In DEBridge, the public volume is denoted as V_0, and the $i-th$ hidden volume is denoted as V_i, where $i \in [1, N]$. The pseudo disk operates in two states: initial and running. During the initial state, users can set the password of each volume (pwd_i, $i \in [0, N]$) and assign a percentage of the total storage space to each hidden volume (len_i, $i \in [1, N]$). Once initialized, users can activate a volume by entering the corresponding password. This interaction is facilitated through a pseudo disk interface, implemented directly within the bridge controller firmware.

Mechanism of the Pseudo Disk. The pseudo disk emulates the data structure of a real storage device, including capacity, partition tables, file systems, and specific files, all pre-stored in the bridge controller firmware. When a host queries the storage device for its data, the bridge controller intercepts and replaces the actual data with preconfigured pseudo disk data. In this way, a pseudo disk and a pseudo file were formed on the host. The pseudo file can use text or graphics to prompt the user to enter the corresponding information. And the "pseudo" just means that it is not a real physical storage device. The schematic diagram is shown in Fig. 2.

A global variable, $STATE_1$, tracks the states. In the initial state ($STATE_1 = 0$), the pseudo file prompts the user to set passwords (pwd_i, $i \in [0, N]$) and storage percentages (len_i, $i \in [1, N]$) for the corresponding volume. Once saved, the bridge controller captures this information and calculates the starting offset $offset_i$ for each hidden volume using (1):

$$offset_i = Dlen(1 - \sum_{j=i}^{N} len_j), i \in [1, N] \quad (1)$$

Here $Dlen$ represents the total number of 512-byte sectors on the device. The secondary hash of the password ($H_2(pwd_i)$) and the encrypted ciphertext of

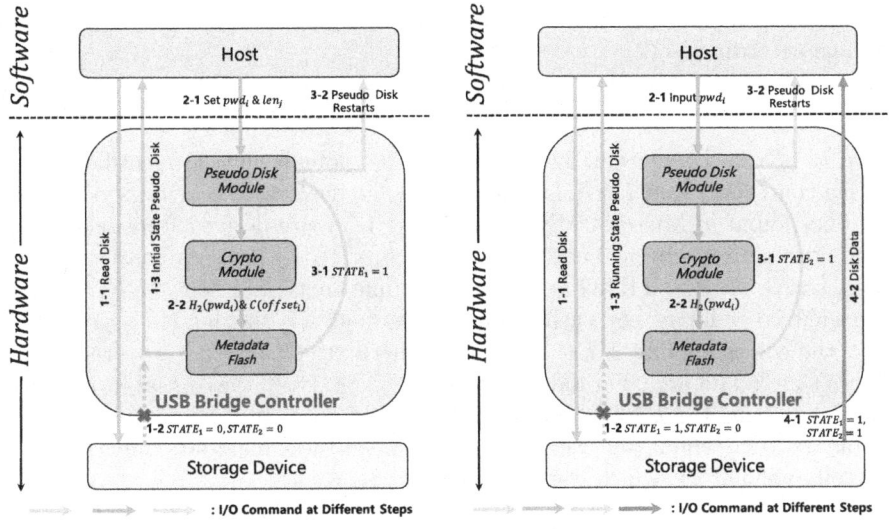

Fig. 2. Schematic Diagram of the Pseudo Disk

$offset_i$ are stored in the device's metadata area for password authentication and volume activation. The encryption of $offset_i$ ($C(offset_i)$) can be found in Sect. 4.3. Once the initial state is complete, $STATE_1$ is set to 1, indicating the running state, and the pseudo disk restarts.

In the running state, the pseudo file prompts the user to enter a password for the desired volume. A global variable, $STATE_2$, tracks the matching results (default $STATE_2 = 0$). The bridge controller retrieves the entered password, computes its secondary hash, and compares it with stored metadata. If a match is found, authentication succeeds, $STATE_2$ is set to 1. And the pseudo disk closes, the corresponding volume is activated.

Advantages of the Pseudo Disk. Unlike previous systems that require additional software for password management [2,37,38], pseudo disk eliminates the need for external tools, reducing security risks and minimizing adversarial suspicion. The pseudo disk also supports seamless operation across multiple hosts, offering plug-and-play functionality for diverse data transfer scenarios.

4.3 Key Management

DEBridge employs a hardware-level secure key management solution where each volume is encrypted with a unique key, and each key is protected by a distinct user-defined password. The processes for key and password management are tightly synchronized.

During the initial state, DEBridge captures the passwords $pwd_i, i \in [0, N]$ and offsets $offset_i, i \in [1, N]$ for corresponding volume via the pseudo disk.

Using these inputs, DEBridge generates a key-encryption-key KEK_i for each volume according to (2):

$$KEK_i = H(pwd_i || ID || HSK), i \in [0, N] \quad (2)$$

Here H is a hash function, ID represents the globally unique identifier of the bridge controller. And HSK is a device-specific hardware security keys such as the ones found in Micron's MX series SSDs. They are derived from secure elements like eFuses, physical unclonable functions (PUF) chips, or similar components [7,27]. Next, a TRNG generates a volume encryption key VEK_i for each user-enabled volume. For each volume $V_i, i \in [0, N]$, the VEK_i is encrypted with the corresponding KEK_i, and its ciphertext ($C(VEK_i)$) is stored in the device's metadata area. For hidden volumes $V_i, i \in [1, N]$, the $offset_i$ is similarly encrypted using the KEK_i, and its ciphertext ($C(offset_i)$) is also stored in the metadata area. The layout relationships between these metadata and $H_2(pwd_i)$ are self-explanatory, which were described in Sect. 4.4.

In the running state, DEBridge identifies the location of $C(VEK_i)$ (and $C(offset_i)$ for hidden volumes) based on the index of corresponding $H_2(pwd_i)$. Then using the pwd_i entered by the user, DEBridge can regenerate the KEK_i with (2) and decrypt the stored ciphertexts to retrieve the plaintext VEK_i. VEK_i is then used to decrypt and enable the selected volume.

The **Advantages of the Key Management** are summarized as follows:

1) The plaintext of KEK_i and VEK_i are stored exclusively in the volatile memory of the bridge controller and never reach the host's RAM. The on-chip RAM of the bridge controller is tightly integrated with the hardware, making physical extraction highly challenging.

2) The KEK_i of each volume is bound to the device-specific hardware security key HSK, making offline attacks like dictionary or rainbow table attacks exceedingly difficult. An adversary will be compelled to use devices as an oracle for online attacks, while the bridge controller can readily restrict the number of password attempts and time intervals for online brute-force attacks.

3) By decoupling the volume passwords from the keys, users can change a volume's password without requiring re-encryption of the volume's entire contents.

4.4 Storage Layout

Metadata Storage Layout. The metadata in DEBridge is stored within the flash of the bridge controller, encapsulating all password-related data. The layout of metadata is illustrated in Fig. 3 (assuming $N = 3$). The public volume V_0 and hidden volumes $V_i, i \in [1, N]$ are managed using distinct metadata entries: For the public volume V_0, the metadata includes: $H_2(pwd_0)$ and $C(VEK_0)$. For each hidden volume $V_i, i \in [1, N]$, the metadata includes: $H_2(pwd_i)$, $C(VEK_i)$ and $C(offset_i)$. The index i of each volume $V_i, i \in [0, N]$ determines a self-explanatory logical relationship for the storage address of its metadata.

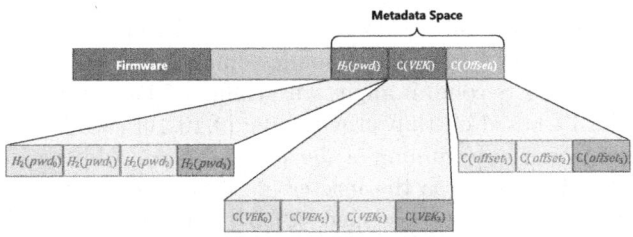

Fig. 3. DEBridge's Metadata Storage Layout.

Regardless of how many volumes the user creates during the initial state, the size of the metadata storage area is always equal to the metadata size when creating the maximum number of volumes that DEBridge can support. This slight waste of space is necessary to prevent an adversary from easily inferring the number of volumes through the size of the metadata storage area. Additionally, the metadata storage area is pre-filled with random data, effectively serving as a PDE system for metadata.

Data Storage Layout. In the data storage area, the public volume V_0 spans the entire storage space, while hidden volumes are embedded within its unused regions (as shown in Fig. 4a). The layout design incorporates three key principles, illustrated using hidden volume V_1:

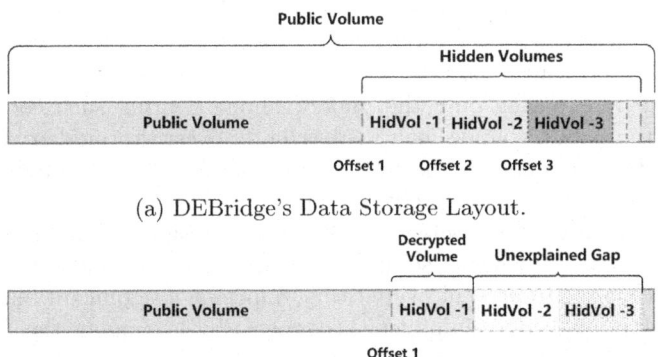

Fig. 4. Schematic Diagram of DEBridge's Data Storage Layout.

1) $offset_1$ is positioned beyond the halfway mark of the public volume, ensuring that hidden volumes occupy the latter half of the storage space. This arrangement is achieved by limiting the cumulative size of all hidden volumes

$\sum_{i=1}^{N} len_i$ to less than 50%. This design serves two purposes: First, it reserves sufficient space (over 50%) for the public volume, which is used frequently in regular operations. Second, it aligns with common file system behaviors (e.g., FAT and EXT4 based on thin provisioning [9,10,16]), where data is written sequentially from the beginning of the storage space. Additionally, the metadata of the NTFS, such as the master file table (MFT), is typically stored at the beginning of the storage space [21,37]. Our experimental observations also indicate that the NTFS generally writes data sequentially, too. Therefore, this approach can maximize storage efficiency and minimize data corruption.

2) Hidden volumes are embedded within the preceding hidden volume's unused space. For instance, V_1 extends from $offset_1$ toward the end of the public volume, while V_2 is nested within V_1. This containment prevents adversaries from identifying unexplained gap in storage (as shown in Fig. 4b), preserving the multi-level deniability feature. It is easy to find that the deniability level of V_i increases as i increases. We stipulate that the deniability level of the public volume V_0 is 0, and the deniability level of hidden volume V_i ($i \in [1, N]$) is i.

3) To avoid damaging critical metadata, such as the GPT header and partition table backup stored in the last sectors of the storage device, a small space is reserved between the end of the volumes. This point is critical to deniability, but has been overlooked in some previous literature [9,41].

4.5 Data Corruption

When employing the hidden volume mechanism to achieve deniability, the physical storage spaces of the public and hidden volumes inevitably overlap. Similarly, the storage spaces of different hidden volumes also overlap. This overlap is an inherent characteristic of the hidden volume mechanism [2,9,16,36–38,41].

In scenarios where a user is coerced by an adversary, the hidden volume is concealed by exposing only the public volume. During such coercion, data written to the public volume may inadvertently overwrite hidden volume data since the hidden volume remains entirely invisible. We do not address data overwriting issues under these coercive circumstances. However, in the absence of coercion, such overwriting between volumes can result in data loss and compromise deniability. Previous solutions require users to continuously monitor storage space usage to prevent overwriting, imposing a significant burden on the user [9,36,41]. DEBridge simplifies this process by leveraging the USB bridge controller's capability to read, intercept, and forward instructions, offering a user-friendly solution.

In particular, taking the public volume as an example, DEBridge introduces a "public volume (protecting hidden volume data)" mode. When not under coercion, users can activate this mode using a dedicated password. In this mode, the bridge controller examines the logical block address (LBA) of the host's write instruction. If the LBA falls within the storage space allocated to a hidden volume, the bridge controller returns a SCSI sense code with the value $LBA\_OUT\_OF\_RANGE$, halting the write operation and preventing data from overwriting the hidden volume. Similarly, users can enable protection modes for hidden volumes with higher levels of deniability. The password, key, and metadata management for these protection modes follow the same principles as outlined earlier and are not reiterated here.

5 Security Analysis

5.1 Single Snapshot Security

As previously discussed, DEBridge ensures that the storage device is pre-filled with random data. When users is coerced by an adversary, they can decrypt V_0 and directly access all plaintext data stored in it. The only part of the device that remains unexplained is the free space. This does not compromise deniability because this approach is consistent with basic FDE practices. In FDE, the initial step in formatting a storage device is to overwrite it entirely with random data. This prevents space analysis attacks by making it difficult to distinguish between genuinely unused space and encrypted data.

5.2 Robust Hardware-Level Security

The integration of hardware security modules is a common feature of USB bridge controllers. These modules enable encryption to be executed directly within the bridge controller, thereby significantly reducing vulnerabilities to host RAM attacks. Furthermore, encryption keys are protected through multi-factor authentication, including device-specific fingerprints and keys. In summary, DEBridge provides robust hardware-level security without compromising deniability. Additionally, DEBridge eliminates the need for additional software and employs a standard disk data layout, ensuring compatibility with widely used systems. Furthermore, DEBridge can be implemented to meet the Level 3 security requirements of FIPS 140-3 to prevent unauthorized physical access or tampering [28]. These features render DEBridge nearly invisible to adversaries [31], further enhancing its security by minimizing the risk of detection.

5.3 Other Security Issues

After using a storage device, users will leave traces on the host. These include disk event logs and USB logs of OS, Windows registry files and shortcuts, temporary files, previews of sensitive documents and records created by common applications like word processors and search agents [2,14]. When examined by the forensic techniques, these residual traces could compromise the deniability of the system. To strengthen DEBridge's real-world applicability, we recommend that users clean the traces of PDE mode immediately after exiting the hidden volumes.

6 Implementation and Evaluation

6.1 Implementation

The DEBridge prototype is implemented using the TUSB9261, a USB 3.0 to Serial ATA bridge based on the ARM Cortex-M3 microcontroller, developed by Texas Instruments (TI). This controller is one of the few open-source bridge controllers available, making it an ideal platform for customization. TI also provides a TUSB9261 demonstration kit for firmware development and testing.

Specifically, approximately 3,000 lines of C code were added to the TUSB9261 firmware (version 1.06). Additionally, we designed a custom disk enclosure. This enclosure incorporates an M.2 disk interface and a USB Type-C interface, resulting in a compact, portable design that emphasizes the practicability of DEBridge. For testing, we used this disk enclosure with a FANXIANG S201PRO SATA SSD (2TB capacity), pre-filled with random data.

Cryptography. The TUSB9261 lacks built-in hardware security modules such as encryption components, TRNGs, or secure elements. To address this, we implemented cryptographic algorithms directly in the firmware. The SM3 algorithm was used for hash operations, while SM4 with XTS block cipher mode was employed for data encryption. Device-specific hardware security keys and volume encryption keys were generated using a host-side random number generator. They are entered into DEBridge through the pseudo disk.

Pseudo Disk. To facilitate the pseudo disk functionality, we utilized the FAT12 file system and TXT file format due to their simplicity, minimal storage requirements, and universal compatibility across mainstream operating systems.

Volume Operation. For the public volume V_0, the default firmware settings are retained. For hidden volumes $V_i, i \in [1,3]$, which begin at $offset_i$ and extend to the end of the storage space allocated to the lower-deniability volume, firmware modifications are required. Taking V_1 as an example: When the V_1 is enabled, the TUSB9261 determines the command type sent by the host. For **capacity queries**, the TUSB9261 calculates the storage capacity $length_1$ using $offset_1$ and returns it to the host. This ensures LBA of read and write instructions are confined to the range $[0, length_1 - 1]$. For **read/write commands**, the TUSB9261 redirects instructions by adding $offset_1$ to the LBA, ensuring operations target $[offset_1, offset_1 + length_1 - 1]$.

In **protection mode**, if a write instruction's LBA exceeds $offset_2$, the TUSB9261 returns a SCSI sense code $LBA\_OUT\_OF\_RANGE$, terminating the operation and preventing data overwrites.

6.2 Evaluation

We evaluated the DEBridge implementation across two aspects: throughput and compatibility. The tests were performed on a Lenovo laptop with a 2.30 GHz Intel i7-11800H CPU and 32 GB of dual-channel RAM, running Windows 11 and Ubuntu 24.04 with Linux kernel 6.8.0.

Throughput. The primary difference between the DEBridge implementation and the default TUSB9261 lies in DEBridge's use of SM4-XTS algorithm for data encryption and decryption and its redirection of read/write instructions to support hidden volumes. SM3, used for password and key management, does not affect throughput. To evaluate throughput, we conducted four experiments: **1)** Default TUSB9261, **2)** TUSB9261 with instruction redirection, **3)** DEBridge's public volume (using SM4-XTS without redirection), **4)** DEBridge's hidden volume (using SM4-XTS with redirection).

Tests were conducted on both Linux and Windows. We used CrystalDiskMark for Windows and fio for Linux, maintaining consistent parameters across all tests: a 512 MB file size, 32-operation queue depth, and block sizes of 4KiB for random read/write (RR/RW) and 1MiB for sequential read/write (SR/SW). These parameters are generally recommended for evaluating the performance of a disk. All results represent averages of ten independent runs.

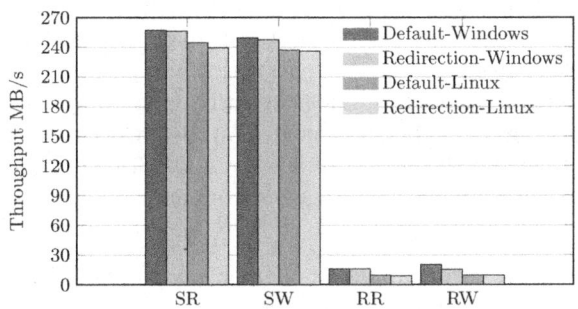

Fig. 5. Throughput comparison of default TUSB9261 vs. TUSB9261 with instruction redirection in Windows (blue series) and Linux (red series). (Color figure online)

Figure 5 shows the throughput of the default TUSB9261 and TUSB9261 with instruction redirection in Windows (blue series) and Linux (red series). Figure 6 shows the throughput of the public volume of the DEBridge implementation and the hidden volume of the DEBridge implementation in Windows (green series) and Linux (orange series). Comparing the two figures, we can see that the use of SM4-XTS significantly reduced throughput, with SR/SW throughput decreasing by two orders of magnitude and RR/RW by one order of magnitude compared to the default TUSB9261. Serial port analysis revealed that encrypting or decrypting 64KiB of data took approximately 47 ms (about 1394 KB/s), aligning closely with observed throughput of DEBridge implementation. This indicates that, without hardware acceleration, the SM4-XTS software implementation consumes nearly all CPU resources, severely limiting performance.

Comparative analysis within the same color series indicates that the redirection of read/write instructions in DEBridge results in a throughput loss of no more than 1%, regardless of whether SM4-XTS encryption is used (low throughput case in Fig. 6) or not (high throughput case in Fig. 5). In addition, the results

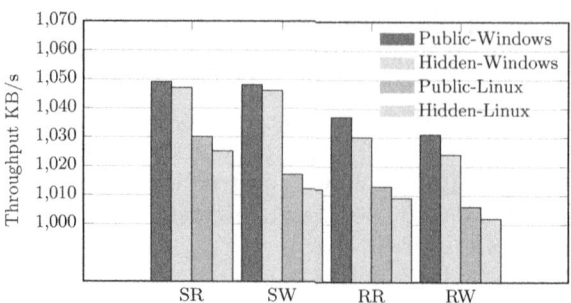

Fig. 6. Throughput comparison of DEBridge implementation's public volume vs. hidden volume in Windows (green series) and Linux (orange series). (Color figure online)

shown in Fig. 5 serve as a throughput reference for implementing high-speed versions of DEBridge on USB bridge controllers that support hardware-accelerated encryption. Because as discussed in Sect. 2.2, many modern USB bridge controllers support hardware-accelerated encryption and demonstrate high throughput. Although such controllers are not currently open source, it is reasonable to expect that DEBridge could be implemented on them with little overhead. Therefore, despite the current throughput limitations, DEBridge offers a practical and scalable solution for high-speed storage environments.

Compatibility. Our throughput tests demonstrated DEBridge's compatibility with both Windows and Linux operating systems. To further assess compatibility, we evaluated its usability with various file systems and storage devices. In addition to our custom-designed hard disk enclosure combined with FANXIANG's S201PRO SATA SSD, we tested a TUSB9261 demonstration kit combined with Western Digital's WD Green SATA SSD (2TB) and Toshiba's SATA HDD MQ04ABD200 (2TB).

We created a 2TB public volume and a 120 GB hidden volume using FAT32, NTFS and EXT4 file systems on these devices. Then We conducted a compatibility test on the volumes. The test results are summarized in Table 1, confirm that DEBridge is compatible with multiple operating systems, file systems and storage media, further validating its practicality.

Table 1. Compatibility Test Results.

	Operating System		File System			Storage Media	
Tests	Windows	Linux	FAT32	NTFS	EXT4	SSD	HDD
Results	✓	✓	✓	✓	✓	✓	✓

7 Discussion

7.1 EXT4 Support

The distributed metadata structure of the EXT4 file system prevents direct application of the DEBridge solution, as it could lead to data conflicts. To address this issue, we utilized thin provisioning in the Linux kernel to create thin volumes [2,9,36]. These volumes ensure that storage space is allocated linearly. This approach is transparent to DEBridge and does not compromise DEBridge's compatibility with other operating system or file systems.

7.2 Extension to Other Platforms

While DEBridge is currently tailored for external storage devices using USB bridge controllers, its design principles are also applicable to internal storage devices connected via PC slots, such as the Samsung 950 PRO, SanDisk X600, and Crucial MX300 [27]. These internal storage devices often incorporate protocol conversion functions similar to those in bridge controllers, making DEBridge readily portable to such platforms. Future work will focus on extending DEBridge to support internal storage solutions and implementing it with bridge controllers that support hardware-accelerated encryption to improve throughput.

7.3 Multi-snapshot Adversary Model

DEBridge can't protect against multi-snapshot adversaries, who can periodically access the victim's storage device. If the user updates the hidden volumes' data, the adversary can detect changes by comparing snapshots taken at different times. Specifically, modifications to the so-called "free" space will reveal the presence of the hidden volumes. Potential countermeasures like data re-randomization [2], dummy writes [10], and oblivious random access machines (ORAM) [4] can help, but they typically introduce significant overhead in throughput and space. Future work will focus on finding feasible solutions that balance enhanced security with system utility.

7.4 Side-Channel Attacks and Fault Injection Attacks

Side-channel attacks (e.g., timing attacks, energy analysis, cache attacks, and electromagnetic attacks) and fault injection attacks (e.g., clock glitch, voltage glitch, electromagnetic interference, and laser injection) are significant threats to cryptographic devices. These attacks can disrupt DEBridge's cryptographic calculations or extract sensitive information. Potential countermeasures include noise injection, masking schemes, design partitioning, and physical shielding for side-channel attacks [25,29,34], and standard cell hardening, time redundancy, and sensor-based fault detection for fault injection attacks [35]. However, system designers must make trade-offs between the added security from countermeasures and the costs in terms of delay, area, and power consumption.

8 Related Work

Starting from the selection of the layer where the PDE system works, different solutions have been proposed:

File System Layer: DEFY [30] and INFUSE [11] leverage the unique properties of YAFFS, a flash file system for Linux, to provide deniability. INFUSE, however, remains readable by off-the-shelf software. Similarly, StegFS [26] modifies the EXT2 file system to hide the sensitive data within cover files.

Block Device Layer: TrueCrypt [37] is a software-based PDE solution compatible with multiple operating systems and storage media, but it lacks support for EXT4. Mobile-device-focused schemes like Mobiflage [36] and MobiHydra [41] rely on the sequential write characteristics of FAT32 and require supporting software. Advanced solutions such as MobiPluto [9], MobiGyges [16], and MobiCeal [10] utilize thin provisioning in the Linux kernel to enable file-system-friendly sequential read and write operations but also necessitate client software. Shufflecake [2] and INVISILINE [31], implemented as Linux-specific kernel modules, are compatible with various file systems and storage media. INVISILINE is readable by off-the-shelf software and additionally supports invisibility. HIVE [4] introduced write-only ORAM for deniability and is deployed as a Linux kernel module with user management tools, maintaining compatibility across file systems and storage media.

Flash Translation Layer: Solutions like DEFTL [19] and PEARL [12] operate at the flash translation layer (FTL) and rely on customized FTL in flash-based storage media. Therefore, these approaches are incompatible with HDDs. Additionally, client support software needs to be installed.

Despite their contributions, none of these systems incorporate secure hardware at their respective layers, leaving them without hardware-level security. A detailed comparison of these solutions and DEBridge is provided in Table 2.

Table 2. Comparison of PDE Systems

Design	Layer	Hardware-level Security	Software-free	FS Compatible	OS Compatible	Media Compatible
DEFY [30]	FS	○	○	○	○	○
StegFS [26]	FS	○	●	○	○	●
INFUSE [11]	FS	○	●	○	○	○
TrueCrypt [37]	BD	○	○	○	●	●
Mobiflage [36]	BD	○	○	○	○	●
MobiHydra [41]	BD	○	○	○	○	●
MobiPluto [9]	BD	○	○	●	○	●
MobiGyges [16]	BD	○	○	●	○	●
MobiCeal [10]	BD	○	○	●	○	●
Shufflecake [2]	BD	○	○	●	○	●
INVISILINE [31]	BD	○	●	●	○	●
HIVE [4]	BD	○	○	●	○	●
PEARL [12]	FTL	○	○	●	●	○
DEFTL [19]	FTL	○	○	●	●	○
MDEFTL [20]	FTL	○	○	●	●	○
DEBridge	**Interface**	●	●	●	●	●

9 Conclusion

This paper introduces DEBridge, a pioneering plausibly deniable encryption storage system based on the USB bridge controller. DEBridge attains high security through its hardware security module, which provides robust, hardware-level protection for the keys. The system is also highly practical, leveraging the inherent advantages of USB bridge controllers: it requires no additional software, operates independently of specific operating systems, file systems, or storage media. The experimental results obtained from implementing a DEBridge prototype using TI's TUSB9261 and conducting extensive testing validate both the security and practicality of DEBridge.

Acknowledgments. This work was supported by the National Key Research and Development Program of China under Grant No. 2022YFB3103301.

References

1. Alendal, G., Kison, C., modg: got HW crypto? On the (in)security of a self-encrypting drive series. Cryptology ePrint Archive, Paper 2015/1002 (2015)
2. Anzuoni, E., Gagliardoni, T.: Shufflecake: plausible deniability for multiple hidden filesystems on Linux. In: Proceedings of the 2023 ACM SIGSAC Conference on Computer and Communications Security, pp. 3033–3047 (2023). https://doi.org/10.1145/3576915.3623126

3. BitLocker Team: Bitlocker overview (2024). https://learn.microsoft.com/en-us/windows/security/operating-system-security/data-protection/bitlocker/. Accessed 15 Aug 2024
4. Blass, E.O., Mayberry, T., Noubir, G., Onarlioglu, K.: Toward robust hidden volumes using write-only oblivious ram. In: Proceedings of the 2014 ACM SIGSAC Conference on Computer and Communications Security, pp. 203–214 (2014). https://doi.org/10.1145/2660267.2660313
5. Böck, B., Austria, S.B.: Firewire-based physical security attacks on Windows 7, EFS and BitLocker. Secure Business Austria Research Lab (2009)
6. Bojinov, H., Sanchez, D., Reber, P., Boneh, D., Lincoln, P.: Neuroscience meets cryptography: crypto primitives secure against rubber hose attacks. Commun. ACM **57**(5), 110–118 (2014). https://doi.org/10.1145/2594445
7. Braeken, A.: PUF based authentication protocol for IoT. Symmetry **10**(8), 352 (2018). https://doi.org/10.3390/sym10080352
8. Canetti, R., Dwork, C., Naor, M., Ostrovsky, R.: Deniable encryption. In: Kaliski, B.S. (ed.) CRYPTO 1997. LNCS, vol. 1294, pp. 90–104. Springer, Heidelberg (1997). https://doi.org/10.1007/BFb0052229
9. Chang, B., Wang, Z., Chen, B., Zhang, F.: MobiPluto: file system friendly deniable storage for mobile devices. In: Proceedings of the 31st Annual Computer Security Applications Conference, pp. 381–390 (2015). https://doi.org/10.1145/2818000.2818046
10. Chang, B., et al.: MobiCeal: towards secure and practical plausibly deniable encryption on mobile devices. In: 2018 48th Annual IEEE/IFIP International Conference on Dependable Systems and Networks (DSN), pp. 454–465. IEEE (2018). https://doi.org/10.1109/DSN.2018.00054
11. Chen, C., Chakraborti, A., Sion, R.: INFUSE: invisible plausibly-deniable file system for NAND flash. In: Proceedings on Privacy Enhancing Technologies (2020). https://doi.org/10.2478/popets-2020-0071
12. Chen, C., Chakraborti, A., Sion, R.: PEARL: plausibly deniable flash translation layer using WOM coding. In: 30th USENIX Security Symposium (USENIX Security 21), pp. 1109–1126 (2021)
13. Chen, C., Liang, X., Carbunar, B., Sion, R.: SoK: plausibly deniable storage. arXiv preprint arXiv:2111.12809 (2021). https://doi.org/10.48550/arXiv.2111.12809
14. Czeskis, A., Hilaire, D.J.S., Koscher, K., Gribble, S.D., Kohno, T., Schneier, B.: Defeating encrypted and deniable file systems: TrueCrypt V5. 1a and the case of the tattling OS and applications. In: HotSec (2008)
15. Digital, W.: My passport SSD data sheet (2023). https://documents.westerndigital.com/content/dam/doc-library/en_us/assets/public/wd/product/external-storage/my_passport/my_passport_ssd/data-sheet-my-passport-ssd.pdf
16. Feng, W., et al.: MobiGyges: a mobile hidden volume for preventing data loss, improving storage utilization, and avoiding device reboot. Futur. Gener. Comput. Syst. **109**, 158–171 (2020). https://doi.org/10.1016/j.future.2020.03.048
17. Fujitsu: Key specifications of the USB 3.0 - SATA bridge IC, MB86C30A. https://www.fujitsu.com/tw/Images/USB3_English_Attachement.pdf. Accessed 10 Apr 2025
18. Halderman, J.A., et al.: Lest we remember: cold-boot attacks on encryption keys. Commun. ACM **52**(5), 91–98 (2009). https://doi.org/10.1145/1506409.1506429
19. Jia, S., Xia, L., Chen, B., Liu, P.: DEFTL: implementing plausibly deniable encryption in flash translation layer. In: Proceedings of the 2017 ACM SIGSAC Confer-

ence on Computer and Communications Security, pp. 2217–2229 (2017). https://doi.org/10.1145/3133956.3134011
20. Jia, S., Zhang, Q., Xia, L., Jing, J., Liu, P.: MDEFTL: incorporating multi-snapshot plausible deniability into flash translation layer. IEEE Trans. Dependable Secure Comput. **19**(5), 3494–3507 (2021). https://doi.org/10.1109/TDSC.2021.3100897
21. Karresand, M., Axelsson, S., Dyrkolbotn, G.O.: Using NTFS cluster allocation behavior to find the location of user data. Digit. Investig. **29**, S51–S60 (2019). https://doi.org/10.1016/j.diin.2019.04.018
22. Khati, L.: Full disk encryption and beyond. Ph.D. thesis, Université Paris sciences et lettres (2019)
23. Khati, L., Mouha, N., Vergnaud, D.: Full disk encryption: bridging theory and practice. In: Handschuh, H. (ed.) CT-RSA 2017. LNCS, vol. 10159, pp. 241–257. Springer, Cham (2017). https://doi.org/10.1007/978-3-319-52153-4_14
24. Kim, J., et al.: Self-encrypting drive evolving toward multitenant cloud computing. Computer **57**(2), 79–90 (2024). https://doi.org/10.1109/MC.2023.3308955
25. Mai, K.: Side channel attacks and countermeasures. In: Tehranipoor, M., Wang, C. (eds.) Introduction to Hardware Security and Trust, pp. 175–194. Springer, New York (2011). https://doi.org/10.1007/978-1-4419-8080-9_8
26. McDonald, A.D., Kuhn, M.G.: StegFS: a steganographic file system for Linux. In: Pfitzmann, A. (ed.) IH 1999. LNCS, vol. 1768, pp. 463–477. Springer, Heidelberg (2000). https://doi.org/10.1007/10719724_32
27. Meijer, C., Van Gastel, B.: Self-encrypting deception: weaknesses in the encryption of solid state drives. In: 2019 IEEE Symposium on Security and Privacy (SP), pp. 72–87. IEEE (2019). https://doi.org/10.1109/SP.2019.00088
28. National Institute of Standards and Technology: FIPS 140-3: Security requirements for cryptographic modules. NIST Special Publication 800-140-3 (2022). https://doi.org/10.6028/NIST.SP.800-140. Accessed 5 Jan 2025
29. Ouladj, M., Guilley, S.: Side-Channel Analysis of Embedded Systems. Springer, Cham (2021). https://doi.org/10.1007/978-3-030-77222-2
30. Peters, T., Gondree, M.A., Peterson, Z.N.: DEFY: a deniable, encrypted file system for log-structured storage. In: NDSS (2015). https://doi.org/10.14722/ndss.2015.23078
31. Pinjala, S.K., Carbunar, B., Chakraborti, A., Sion, R.: INVISILINE: invisible plausibly-deniable storage. In: 2024 IEEE Symposium on Security and Privacy (SP), pp. 18. IEEE Computer Society (2023). https://doi.org/10.1109/SP54263.2024.00018
32. Westhead, R.: How a Syrian refugee risked his life to bear witness to atrocities (2012). http://www.thestar.com/news/world/2012/03/14/howasyrianrefugeeriskedhislifetobearwitnesstoatrocities.html
33. SanDisk: SanDisk extreme portable SSD data sheet (2024). https://documents.westerndigital.com/content/dam/doc-library/en_us/assets/public/sandisk/product/portable-drives/extreme-usb-3-2-ssd/data-sheet-sandisk-extreme-usb-3-2-ssd.pdf
34. Shepherd, C., et al.: Physical fault injection and side-channel attacks on mobile devices: a comprehensive analysis. Comput. Secur. **111**, 102471 (2021). https://doi.org/10.1016/j.cose.2021.102471
35. Shuvo, A.M., Zhang, T., Farahmandi, F., Tehranipoor, M.: A comprehensive survey on non-invasive fault injection attacks. Cryptology ePrint Archive (2023)

36. Skillen, A., Mannan, M.: Mobiflage: deniable storage encryption for mobile devices. IEEE Trans. Dependable Secure Comput. **11**(3), 224–237 (2013). https://doi.org/10.1109/TDSC.2013.56
37. TrueCrypt Team: Free open-source disk encryption software (2024). https://www.truecrypt71a.com/. Accessed 15 Aug 2024
38. VeraCrypt Team: Free open source disk encryption software (2024). https://www.veracrypt.fr/en/Home.html. Accessed 15 Aug 2024
39. Wikipedia contributors: Key disclosure law (2024). https://en.wikipedia.org/w/index.php?title=Key_disclosure_law. Accessed 15 Aug 2024
40. Wikipedia contributors: Linux unified key setup (2024). https://en.wikipedia.org/w/index.php?title=Linux_Unified_Key_Setup. Accessed 27 Aug 2024
41. Yu, X., Chen, B., Wang, Z., Chang, B., Zhu, W.T., Jing, J.: MobiHydra: pragmatic and multi-level plausibly deniable encryption storage for mobile devices. In: Chow, S.S.M., Camenisch, J., Hui, L.C.K., Yiu, S.M. (eds.) ISC 2014. LNCS, vol. 8783, pp. 555–567. Springer, Cham (2014). https://doi.org/10.1007/978-3-319-13257-0_36

Formalisation of the KZG Polynomial Commitment Schemes in EasyCrypt

Palak and Thomas Haines[✉]

The Australian National University, Canberra, Australia
{palak.palak,thomas.haines}@anu.edu.au

Abstract. In this paper, we present formally verified proofs of the popular KZG Polynomial Commitment Schemes (PCSs), including the security proofs for the properties of correctness, polynomial binding, evaluation binding and hiding. Polynomial commitment schemes have various applications in cryptography and computer science, including verifiable computation, blockchain and cryptocurrencies, secure multi-party computation as well as in the construction of ZK-SNARKs. To validate security, we utilise EasyCrypt, an interactive theorem prover that allows for formal verification of cryptographic primitives and protocols. This approach enforces correct proofs which cover all required cases and formalising assumptions reducing the risk of overlooked vulnerabilities. This formalisation validates the current understanding of KZG's PCSs as secure while clarifying various issues in the original claims.

1 Introduction

Formal verification plays a crucial role in cryptography by providing detailed methodologies to guarantee the correctness and security of cryptographic protocols. Formal verification, particularly theorem proving, uses formal logic for mathematically proving that a system adheres to its specifications and security properties, eliminates ambiguities and potential flaws. By providing us with an elaborate mathematical proof, formal verification helps in constructing secure cryptographic protocols, which can be deployed in real world applications.

Several tools have been developed to aid in the formal verification of cryptographic protocols using theorem proving. Some of the proof assistants specifically used for cryptography are CryptoVerif, EasyCrypt, CertiCrypt-Coq, and CryptHOL-Isabelle. Among all of these proof assistants EasyCrypt [1], is the closest to traditional pen-and-paper proofs, which makes it easy to write proofs that look like traditional cryptographic arguments and helps cryptographers who are used to working on paper. EasyCrypt has special features and libraries that make it easier to verify cryptographic schemes, whereas general-purpose tools can be more cumbersome and less efficient for this specific task. Additionally, EasyCrypt supports probabilistic reasoning and modelling adversarial behaviour, which are crucial for accurately capturing the security aspects of cryptographic protocols. These features are not as seamlessly integrated into more general tools. There are other prominent tools for cryptographic protocol verification such as ProVerif, and Tamarin but they are orthogonal to the verification of cryptography primitives.

Despite significant progress, formal verification is still not widely adopted across all areas of cryptography. This gap is primarily due to the complexity of cryptographic protocols and the intricate nature of formal methods. Several notable works (e.g., [2–7]) have applied formal verification to real-world cryptographic protocols. EasyCrypt has been used to give the security proofs of Cramer-Shoup and Hashed ElGamal cryptosystems [8]. The formalisation of game-based proofs was given by Nowak in 2007 by providing machine-checked proof of ElGamal semantic security and unpredictability of a pseudo-random generator in Coq [9]. Another significant work [10], uses CryptoVerif to prove unforgeability of the Full-Domain Hash signature scheme using game-based approach.

In this paper, we present formally verified proofs of the Kate-Zaverucha-Goldberg (KZG) [11] polynomial commitment schemes (PCSs), these two schemes we will refer to as **PolyCommit$_{DL}$** and **PolyCommit$_{Ped}$** in line with the original paper; the first of these already had proofs in the CryptHOL framework [12] but the second more complicated scheme did not. Our work includes security proofs for the properties of correctness, polynomial binding, evaluation binding, and hiding in EasyCrypt. Polynomial commitment schemes (PCSs) are fundamental cryptographic primitives that allow one to commit to a polynomial in constant size and later reveal and prove its evaluations at various points. They play a crucial role in a wide range of cryptographic protocols, including zero-knowledge proofs, verifiable secret sharing, and secure multiparty computation. Among the various PCS constructions, the Kate-Zaverucha-Goldberg (KZG) polynomial commitment schemes have gained popularity due to their efficiency and strong security properties; particularly prominent is their use in SNARKs, as we discuss in the next section. By presenting formally verified proofs of the KZG PCSs, this paper not only validates the current understanding of these schemes but also provides a foundation for future formal verification efforts in cryptography, as we explain in our conclusion. The use of EasyCrypt in our formalisation highlights the practical benefits of employing interactive theorem provers in ensuring the robustness and reliability of cryptographic protocols.

Polynomial commitment schemes (PCS) are critical components in various cryptographic protocols, particularly in zero-knowledge succinct non-interactive arguments of knowledge (ZK-SNARKs). ZK-SNARKs enable parties to prove the validity of statements without revealing any additional information beyond the fact that the statement is true, making them invaluable for applications where privacy is paramount and they do so with very short and easily verifiable proofs. Some notable SNARKS using PCS include Sonic [13], AuroraLight [14], Marlin [15] and Plonk [16].

Despite the importance of polynomial commitment schemes and ZK-SNARKs in modern cryptography, there is currently a lack of formalisation of these concepts and their security properties in tools like EasyCrypt. Regarding

SNARKs, formal verification is still an emerging field. While there have been some attempts to apply formal methods to components of SNARKs, comprehensive formal verification of SNARKs in their entirety is less common. For instance, some works like [17–19] have focused on formally verifying specific aspects of the underlying algebraic structures and cryptographic assumptions using proof assistants Coq, EasyCrypt and Certicrypt respectively, but a full formal verification pipeline for SNARKs is still a challenging and ongoing area of research. Some seminal works like [20,21] have formalised the correctness and soundness properties respectively of various SNARKs (variants of the fastest pairing based SNARK introduced by Groth in 2016 [22]) using the Lean theorem prover. However, there remains a growing need for the formalisation of the construction of more practically applicable and highly efficient SNARKs, such as Plonk, Sonic and Marlin, along with all of their associated security properties.

The most closely related work to ours is that of Rothmann and Kreuzer [12] which appeared at Foundations of Computer Security workshop 2024. In their work they verified the correctness, binding, and hiding of **PolyCommit$_{DL}$** using the CryptHOL [23] framework in the interactive theorem prover Isabele [24]. We expand on this work in several ways:

We verify PolyCommit$_{Ped}$: we verified the scheme **PolyCommit$_{DL}$** but also the more complicated scheme **PolyCommit$_{Ped}$**. Most of our contributions and insights relate to **PolyCommit$_{Ped}$**.

Stronger hiding definition: Rothmann and Kreuzer [12] improve upon the original hiding proof by allowing the evaluation points to be arbitrary rather than uniformly random. However, the proof still assumes the evaluation points are independent of the commitment. This means the game does not capture any advantage the adversary might have breaking hiding if it chooses the evaluation points based on the commitment. In contrast, our definition explicitly gives the adversary acesss to both the commitment key and commitment before it chooses the evaluation points.

1.1 Contributions

The primary contributions of this paper are threefold.

- First, we provide a detailed formalisation of polynomial commitment schemes including their security properties. We formalise the KZG constructions **PolyCommit$_{DL}$** and **PolyCommit$_{Ped}$** within the EasyCrypt framework. This includes the definitions and assumptions underlying the KZG schemes, ensuring an unambiguous representation of components and operations.
- Second, we deliver formally verified security proofs for the key properties of the KZG schemes: correctness, polynomial binding, evaluation binding, and hiding. These proofs are crucial for establishing the reliability and robustness of the scheme against various types of adversarial attacks.
- Third, we discuss the implications of our formalisation and verification efforts, particularly on the ambiguities in the original definitions and resulting security implications. For example, we discovered that the polynomial binding of

the **PolyCommit$_{\text{Ped}}$** does not reduce to the discrete log problem as claimed but to the stronger t-SDH assumption; this does not invalidate the security theorem for **PolyCommit$_{\text{Ped}}$** since it already assumed that t-SDH was hard.

We also highlight potential areas of improvement and future research directions. Specifically, we propose future work on verifying the highly efficient ZK-SNARKs which use polynomial commitment schemes.

To avoid any ambiguity, we do not think the imperfections we raise in the original analysis of KZG scheme in anyway undermines the contributions of Kate et al. [11]. To the contrary, our analysis shows the techniques introduced provide strong security.

1.2 Outline

This paper aims to provide as comprehensive an overview of the formal verification of the commitment schemes **PolyCommit$_{\text{DL}}$** and **PolyCommit$_{\text{Ped}}$** within the EasyCrypt framework as space allows; it is structured in five main sections.

In the following sections, first we provide a background section (Sect. 2) that covers the foundational concepts of polynomial commitment schemes including the mathematical foundations and operational mechanics. In the Details of Formalisation section (Sect. 3), we detail the formal verification process for both the **PolyCommit$_{\text{DL}}$** and **PolyCommit$_{\text{Ped}}$** commitment schemes, including their algorithms, modelling approaches, and security properties as implemented in EasyCrypt. The Insights from the Formalisation section (Sect. 4) examines key differences between our formalisation and the original definition, such as variations in hiding definitions, the impact of transitioning to the t-SDH assumption, and the significance of addressing missing subcases in evaluation binding. The paper concludes with a Conclusion (Sect. 5) that summarises the findings and suggests directions for future research in the field of formal verification of cryptographic protocols.

2 Background

This section provides an overview of bilinear maps and commitment schemes. We delve into polynomial commitment schemes (Sect. 2.3), detailing their structure and the basic algorithms that underpin their functionality. This is followed by a discussion on the modeling of PCS within the Easycrypt framework, which helps in formally verifying the security and correctness of these schemes. Lastly, we discuss the security properties of PCS.

2.1 Notation

We will use $\leftarrow$ to denote the assigning the output of a function to a variable, reserving $=$ for equality. We will use $\leftarrow_R$ to denote the sampling according to some distribution; when we write $\leftarrow_R S$ for some set S we mean the full, uniform and independent distribution over this set. When considering an algorithm we distinguish between normal inputs and random coins which are used by the algorithm; for example, $\mathcal{A}(i;r)$ denotes the algorithm $\mathcal{A}$ on input i using random coins r. We write $a \in \mathcal{A}(i)$ to denote that there exist random coins r such that the value a is produced by some algorithm $a \leftarrow \mathcal{A}(i;r)$. We will use $a \leftarrow_R \mathcal{A}(i)$ to denote sampling from the distribution defined by $\mathcal{A}(i)$ over the set of its random coins.

2.2 Bilinear Maps

For three cyclic groups $\mathbb{G}_1, \mathbb{G}_2$, and $\mathbb{G}_T$ of the same order prime p, a bilinear pairing is a map $e : \mathbb{G}_1 \to \mathbb{G}_2 \to \mathbb{G}_T$ with the following properties.

Bilinearity: For $g_1 \in \mathbb{G}_1$, $g_2 \in \mathbb{G}_2$ and $a, b \in \mathbb{Z}_p$, $e(g_1^a, g_2^b) = e(g_1, g_2)^{ab}$
Non-degeneracy: The map does not send all pairs in $\mathbb{G}_1 \times \mathbb{G}_2$ to unity $\in \mathbb{G}_T$

When $\mathbb{G}_1 = \mathbb{G}_2$ we say the pairing is symmetric.

We define symmetric bilinear maps in EasyCrypt based on an earlier encoding of asymmetric bilinear maps in the ZooCrypt project [25].

2.3 Polynomial Commitment Schemes

Polynomial Commitment Schemes, first introduced by Kate, Zaverucha, and Goldberg [11], can be defined as the functional commitment schemes where the function family is the family of polynomials of bounded degree. These schemes enable the committer to commit to a univariate polynomial in constant size. This is done by generating a commitment value, $C \leftarrow \texttt{Commit}(\phi(x))$ corresponding to the committed polynomial $\phi(x)$. At a later stage, the committer can open the polynomial at any specific point and the verifier can verify the correctness of the committed value.

Polynomial Commitment Schemes are comprised of the following six algorithms:

1. $Setup(1^\kappa, t)$
   Generates a commitment key PK for the commitment scheme with regards to a security parameters κ supporting polynomials up to degree t.
2. $Commit(PK, \phi(x))$
   Computes the commitment value C to a polynomial $\phi(x)$ along with an opening value d.
3. $Open(PK, C, \phi(x), d)$
   Returns the committed polynomial $\phi(x)$, if the commitment is correct for the committed polynomial, else it outputs $\bot$.
4. $VerifyPoly(PK, C, \phi(x), d)$
   Outputs 1 if the commitment is correct for the committed polynomial, else it outputs 0.

5. $CreateWitness(PK, \phi(x), i, d)$
   Generates and outputs a witness w_i corresponding to the evaluation of the polynomial $\phi(x)$ at a specific point i.
6. $VerifyEval(PK, C, i, \phi(i), w_i)$
   Outputs 1 if the evaluation $\phi(i)$ and witness w_i are correct for C, else 0.

Kate et al. introduced two instantiations of a polynomial commitment scheme in their paper, namely **PolyCommit$_{\mathbf{DL}}$** and **PolyCommit$_{\mathbf{Ped}}$**. **PolyCommit$_{\mathbf{DL}}$** is named so because its hiding property reduces to the discrete log problem whereas **PolyCommit$_{\mathbf{Ped}}$** takes its name for the resemblance to the famous Pedersen commitment scheme [26]. The current proof of hiding we have for **PolyCommit$_{\mathbf{DL}}$** under our stronger hiding definition reduces to a stronger assumption than discrete log, though we conjecture this is not necessary (see Sect. 3.2 for details).

2.4 Assumptions

Here we define the assumptions that we have used to prove the security properties of **PolyCommit$_{\mathbf{DL}}$** and **PolyCommit$_{\mathbf{Ped}}$** commitment schemes. Consider a cyclic group $\mathbb{G}$ of prime order p, where $p \geq 2^{2\kappa}$, for some security parameter κ, and $g \in \mathbb{G}$ such that $\mathbb{G} = \langle g \rangle$, that is, g is a generator of the prime order group $\mathbb{G}$. Here, $\epsilon(\kappa)$ represents a negligible function.[1]

Discrete logarithm assumption (DL)

The discrete logarithm assumption states that given a group element g^a, for $a \leftarrow_R \mathbb{Z}_p$, no PPT (Probabilistic Polynomial Time) adversary $\mathcal{A}$ can compute the exponent a with probability better than negligible in κ. That is,

$$Pr[\mathcal{A}(g, g^a) = a] \leq \epsilon(\kappa).$$

The definition of the discrete log experiment we use is identical to that in the standard library of EasyCrypt, with the group taken as the base group of the bilinear map.

t-Strong Diffie-Hellman assumption (t-SDH

Given a $(t+1)$-tuple of group elements $\langle g, g^a, g^{a^2}, \ldots g^{a^t} \rangle$, for some $a \leftarrow_R \mathbb{Z}_p$, the probability for any PPT adversary $\mathcal{A}$ to successfully output a pair (c, d), such that,

- $c \in \mathbb{Z}_p \setminus \{-a\}$, and,
- $d = g^{\frac{1}{a+c}}$

is negligible. That is,

$$Pr[\mathcal{A}(g, g^a, g^{a^2}, \ldots g^{a^t}) = \langle c, g^{\frac{1}{a+c}} \rangle] \leq \epsilon(\kappa).$$

---

[1] A function $\epsilon : \mathbb{N} \to [0,1]$ is said to be negligible if $\forall$ polynomials $p, \exists n_0 \in \mathbb{N}$, such that $\forall n \geq n_0, \epsilon(n) \leq \frac{1}{p(n)}$.

A variant of the t-SDH assumption

This new variant is defined specifically for the polynomial binding and evaluation binding of **PolyCommit$_{\text{Ped}}$**. These proofs would normally contain two cases: one of which reduces to discrete log, and the other to t-SDH; to simplify the proofs we introduce a hybrid assumption which encodes both a discrete log challenge and a t-SDH challenge. The adversary wins if it can solve either challenge given the answer to the other. The knowledge of the non-targeted secret is modeled by the adversary returning a function which given the non-targeted secret produces the targeted secret.

The adversary is challenged with two different exponents a and a'. The adversary's goal is either to compute the discrete logarithm value a' or to solve the t-SDH problem. For $a, a' \in_R \mathbb{Z}_p$ given a list of group elements $\langle g^{a^i}, (g^{a'})^{a^i} \rangle$ for i ranging from 0 to t, the adversary outputs a pair of polynomial time functions $(c(\cdot), d(\cdot))$, where $c : \mathbb{Z}_p \to \mathbb{Z}_p$ and $d : \mathbb{Z}_p \to \mathbb{G}$. This assumption states that for any PPT adversary $\mathcal{A}$, the probability that $\mathcal{A}$ can successfully satisfy either of the following conditions is negligible.

- Computes $c(a) = a'$, the discrete logarithm.
- Outputs $d(a') = g^{\frac{1}{a+c(a')}}$ for $c(a') \neq -a$.

We are able to prove in EasyCrypt the expected bound that the adversary's advantage against our new variant is bound by its advantage against t-SDH and DL. In summary, the variant simplifies analysis without any loss of rigiour or tightness. This would be of limited value in a paper proof but in a mechanised proof the new variant simplifies the proof and increased re-useability.

2.5 Security of PCSs

A PCS, defined by the six algorithms in Sect. 2.3, is said to be secure if it satisfies the following four properties.

1. **Correctness** - ensures reliability and trustworthiness.
   A polynomial commitment scheme is said to be correct if: for all κ and $t < 2^\kappa$, $PK \in \text{Setup}(1^\kappa, t)$, where κ is security parameter and $(C, d) \in \text{Commit}(PK, \phi(x))$, and all $\phi(x) \leftarrow_R \mathbb{Z}_p[x]$ of degree at most t,
   - VerifyPoly$(PK, C, \phi(x), d)$ successfully verifies the opening value produced by Open$(PK, C, \phi(x), d)$, and,
   - VerifyEval$(PK, C, i, \phi(i), w_i)$ successfully verifies the witness produced by CreateWitness$(PK, \phi(x), i, d)$ algorithm.
2. **Polynomial Binding:**
   For all κ, $t < 2^\kappa$, and polynomial-time adversaries $\mathcal{A}$:

$$Pr \begin{pmatrix} PK \leftarrow_R \text{Setup}(1^\kappa, t), \\ (C, \langle \phi(x), \phi'(x), d, d' \rangle) \leftarrow_R \mathcal{A}(PK) : \\ \text{VerifyPoly}(PK, C, \phi(x), d) = 1 \land \\ \text{VerifyPoly}(PK, C, \phi'(x), d') = 1 \land \\ \phi(x) \neq \phi'(x) \end{pmatrix} = \epsilon(\kappa)$$

No efficient adversary $\mathcal{A}$ can open a commitment to two different polynomials. That is, the probability that VerifyPoly$(PK, C, \phi(x), d)$ outputs 1 for polynomials $\phi(x)$ and $\phi'(x)$, given that $\phi(x) \neq \phi'(x)$, is negligible.

3. **Evaluation Binding**:
   For all κ, $t < 2^\kappa$, and polynomial-time adversaries $\mathcal{A}$:

$$Pr\begin{pmatrix} PK \leftarrow_R \text{Setup}(1^\kappa, t), \\ (C, i, \langle \phi(i), w_i \rangle, \langle \phi(i)', w_i' \rangle) \leftarrow_R \mathcal{A}(PK): \\ \text{VerifyEval}(PK, C, i, \phi(i), w_i) = 1 \wedge \\ \text{VerifyEval}(PK, C, i, \phi(i)', w_i') = 1 \wedge \\ \phi(i) \neq \phi(i)' \end{pmatrix} = \epsilon(\kappa)$$

No efficient adversary can produce two different evaluations and valid witnesses for a commitment at the same point. That is, the probability that VerifyEval$(PK, C, i, \phi(i), w_i)$ outputs 1 for two evaluations $\phi(i)$ and $\phi(i)'$ at a specific index i, such that, $\phi(i) \neq \phi(i)'$, is negligible.

4. **Hiding** - no efficient adversary can gain any useful information about the evaluation of the polynomial at any unqueried index, given the commitment value and $t - 1$ evaluations and witnesses, with high probability.
   That is, given $\langle PK, C \rangle$ and $\{\langle i_j, \phi(i_j), w_{\phi_{i_j}} \rangle : j \in [1, deg(\phi)]\}$ for a polynomial $\phi(x) \leftarrow_R \mathbb{Z}_p[x]$ such that VerifyEval$(PK, C, i_j, \phi(i_j), w_{\phi_{i_j}})$ outputs 1 for every queried index j, we have:
   - **Computational hiding**:
     probability that an adversary can determine $\phi(j')$ for any unqueried index j' is negligible.
   - **Unconditional hiding**:
     adversary gains any information about $\phi(j')$ for any unqueried index j'.

The paper definition of hiding is confused as we shall discuss in Section 4. Our definition in EasyCrypt is stronger than the paper definition particularly with regards to point d) below.

For the actual EasyCrypt definition (and proofs) please refer to our code https://github.com/gerlion/kzg_pcs. However, we will present the structure of the game below for clarity. We begin by defining the type of the adversary, unlike the previous adversaries we have seen this one is allowed two different actions in the game. First, given knowledge of PK and C it is allowed to choose the evaluation points. Second, given knowledge of the evaluations of the polynomial and corresponding witnesses the adversary is asked to return the evaluation of the polynomial at some other point. The security experiment procceds as follows:

(a) a polynomial is chosen at random,
(b) a commitment key is honestly generated,
(c) the commitment is honestly generated,
(d) $t - 1$ evaluation points are *chosen by the adversary with knowledge of the commitment key and commitment*,
(e) evaluations and witnesses to these points are created,
(f) and the adversary (with knowledge of the evaluations and witnesses) gives an evaluation and point.

(g) The adversary wins if the evaluation it gives is correct at the point it chose and that point was not one of those given to it.

Our EasyCrypt definition is stronger than the definition used in HOL by [5], since it captures the adversary's knowledge of PK and C. In the non-interactive variants of SNARKs is likely that the weaker definition suffices since in the Random Oracle Model the challenges (which become evaluation points) are chosen at random; however, in general it would be strange to assume that the adversary did not get to choose the evaluation points and could not use it's knowledge of commitment key and commitment when doing so.

To illustrate this point, consider a lottery where the aim is to correctly guess a number. One option would be to follow the normal convention and choose the winning number after the guesses are in; however, this requires a random beacon which can be tricky to implement. Consider an alternative where the host first commits to the correct response, and then the guesses come in. Using a PCS for this purpose has the nice property that the host can prove a particular guess is correct or not without leaking the correct answer. However, without the stronger definition of hiding the guesser could choose their guess to leak the correct answer.

3 Details of Formalisation

In the section, we will outline the core algorithms of both the **PolyCommit$_{DL}$** (Sect. 3.1) and **PolyCommit$_{Ped}$** commitment schemes (Sect. 3.3). Following the algorithmic modeling, we present the corresponding lemmas that were proven in EasyCrypt to capture each security property associated with these commitment schemes.

3.1 Formal Verification of PolyCommit$_{DL}$

For this particular commitment scheme, the commitment value is generated by raising $g \in \mathbb{G}$ to the power of an evaluation of the committed polynomial, where g is a generator of a prime order group $\mathbb{G}$. We detail how the various algorithms work below:

Setup($1^\kappa, t$) :
- Generates a bilinear pairing group $\mathcal{G} = \langle e, \mathbb{G}, \mathbb{G}_T \rangle$, where $e : \mathbb{G} \times \mathbb{G} \to \mathbb{G}_T$ is a symmetric bilinear mapping.
- Generates a $(t+1)$ - tuple $\langle g, g^\alpha, g^{\alpha^2}, \ldots, g^{\alpha^t} \rangle \in \mathbb{G}^{t+1}$, where g is a random generator of $\mathbb{G}$ and $\alpha \in \mathbb{Z}_p^*$ is the secret key SK.
- Returns the public key, $PK \leftarrow \langle \mathcal{G}, g, g^\alpha, g^{\alpha^2}, \ldots, g^{\alpha^t} \rangle$.

Commit($PK, \phi(X)$) : Computes the commitment value $C \leftarrow g^{\phi(\alpha)} = \prod_{j=0}^{deg(\phi)} (g^{\alpha^j})^{\phi_j} \in \mathbb{G}$ for the polynomial $\phi(X) \leftarrow \sum_{j=0}^{deg(\phi)} \phi_j x^j \in \mathbb{Z}_p[X]$ of degree less than or equal to t.

Open($PK, C, \phi(X)$) : Returns the committed polynomial $\phi(X)$.

VerifyPoly($PK, C, \phi(X)$) : Outputs 1 if $C = \prod_{j=0}^{deg(\phi)}(g^{\alpha^j})^{\phi_j}$ for $\phi(X) = \sum_{j=0}^{deg(\phi)} \phi_j x^j$, else it outputs 0.
CreateWitness($PK, \phi(X), i$):
- Computes $\psi_i(x) \leftarrow \frac{\phi(X) - \phi(i)}{(x-i)} \in \mathbb{Z}_p[X]$.
- Outputs $\langle i, \phi(i), w_i \rangle$, where $w_i = g^{\psi_i(\alpha)}$ is the witness.

VerifyEval($PK, C, i, \phi(i), w_i$): Outputs 1 if $e(C, g) = e(w_i, g^\alpha/g^i)e(g,g)^{\phi(i)}$, else it outputs 0.

Note, that **PolyCommit$_{\mathbf{DL}}$** does not use any witness to the opening so for simplicity we drop these from the text presentation and use the type unit in EasyCrypt. These witnesses are unnecessary because Commit is deterministic in **PolyCommit$_{\mathbf{DL}}$** (unlike **PolyCommit$_{\mathbf{Ped}}$**) and so the verifier once it has the polynomial can simply rerun the commitment function without any assistance.
Formalisation Note: The difference between the asymptotic notation in the paper and concrete notation in EasyCrypt is particularly noticeable in setup. Where in the asymptotic the various algebraic structures need to be generated based on the security parameters 1^κ in EasyCrypt these are instances of the corresponding theories. The value t rather than being given as input to every function is handled as a global constant.

3.2 Security Theorems Modelled in EasyCrypt (Sect. 2.5)

We have proved the **PolyCommit$_{\mathbf{DL}}$** satisfies the four properties we expect of a PCS. We adopt the convention of explaining the security result in prose while also including the EasyCrypt lemma. To understand these lemmas fully would require reviewing our scripts, particularly the definitions of the security experiments and reductions. We have decided to include them because there is a subset of the intended audience of this paper who will find the inclusion of the lemmas in the paper useful, while the remainder can ignore them at little cost.

1. Correctness: The correctness of **PolyCommit$_{\mathbf{DL}}$** is perfect. The proof in EasyCrypt is short and algebraic, similar to the paper proof. The main challenge was extending the EasyCrypt standard polynomial library with division and the associated lemmas.

   ```
   lemma DLScheme_Correctness :
   hoare [ Correctness (DLScheme).main : true ==> res ].
   ```

   The EasyCrypt lemma says that correctness experiment (Correctness) running on **PolyCommit$_{\mathbf{DL}}$** (captured by DLScheme) always returns true.

2. Polynomial Binding: Polynomial Binding is proved to bound by the adversary's success in the t-SDH problem. This means that if there exists an efficient adversary that breaks polynomial binding then that adversary is capable of solving the t-SDH problem. The proof is again very short in EasyCrypt and algebraic, very similar to the paper proof.

```
lemma DLScheme_PolyBinding (A <: AdvPB) &m :
    Pr[PolyBinding(DLScheme, A).main()
    @ &m : res] <=
    Pr[Bl.Tsdh(Adv(A)).main() @ &m : res].
```

The EasyCrypt lemma says that for any adversary A against the polynomial binding experiment, the probability of the adversary winning is less than or equal to that of the same adversary against t-SDH experiment (Bl.Tsdh) using the reduction Adv.

3. Evaluation Binding: Similarly for Evaluation binding we define the security lemma in terms of t-SDH adversary game. In comparison to the two prior proofs this is much longer but at around sixty lines, still fairly short; the added length comes from additional cases which we need to account for. The reduction is again straightforward though it branches based on if the point the adversary chooses i is the same point embed in the commitment key a, this first case was missing in the original proof as we discuss in 4.3 but otherwise the proofs are very similar.

```
lemma DLScheme_EvalBinding (A <: AdvEB) &m :
    Pr[EvalBinding(DLScheme, A).main()
    @ &m : res] <=
    Pr[Bl.Tsdh(Adv2(A)).main() @ &m : res].
```

4. Hiding: The adversary's advantage against hiding is proved to be bound by it's advantage in the discrete log experiment plus the adversary advantage against t-SDH. This proof, at nearly three hundred lines, is longest of the **PolyCommit$_{DL}$** proofs. Due to our stronger hiding definition this lemma and proofs are very far from the original paper. One of our sub-lemmas (called d_log) is very similar to the original paper proof but we can only use this once we have made several game hops. We start by switching from the security definition into a game in which much of the input the adversary sees is randomly sampled. We then branch that game into two based on if the point embed in the commitment key is among those the adversary asks for an evaluation of. If it is we show that this breaks the t-SDH assumption; if it isn't we show that adversary breaking hiding means it must be able to break the discrete log.

We believe the reduction to t-SDH should be unnecessary for **PolyCommit$_{DL}$** but have not been able to prove this despite spending several weeks; in contrast, in the case of **PolyCommit$_{Ped}$** we are quite certain the t-SDH is necessary for polynomial binding. We believe it should be unnecessary for **PolyCommit$_{DL}$** because conceptually, if the adversary asks for an evaluation of the polynomial at point embed in the commitment key this weakens the adversary since this value is already embedded in the commitment; the adversary then only gets information related to degree minus one points and the polynomial should be indeterminate. The sticking point trying to prove this was calculating the witness which the reduction should give the adversary for the point embedded in the commitment; much of our time was spent proving lemmas about polynomial division which allowed us to make the goal much cleaner but not actually discharge it.

```
lemma DLScheme_Hiding    &m :
    islossless A.guess =>
  Pr[ Hiding(DLScheme, A).real() @ &m : res ] <=
  Pr[ Bl.DLogExp(Adv3(A)).main() @ &m : res ] +
  Pr[ Bl.Tsdh(Adv3(A)).main() @ &m : res ]
```

3.3 Formal Verification of PolyCommit$_{Ped}$

For this particular commitment scheme, the commitment value is generated by using two generators of the group and two polynomials for enhanced security. Pedersen commitment scheme basically combines two commitment values from **PolyCommit$_{DL}$** using the homomorphic property of the scheme. Analogously to the famous Pedersen commitment scheme this provides prefect privacy.

1. Setup($1^\kappa, t$) :
    - Generates a bilinear pairing group $\mathcal{G} = \langle e, \mathbb{G}, \mathbb{G}_T \rangle$, where $e : \mathbb{G} \times \mathbb{G} \to \mathbb{G}_T$ is a symmetric bilinear mapping.
    - Generates a $(2t+2)$ - tuple $\langle g, g^\alpha, g^{\alpha^2}, \ldots, g^{\alpha^t}, h, h^\alpha, h^{\alpha^2}, \ldots, h^{\alpha^t} \rangle \in \mathbb{G}^{2t+2}$, where g and h are random generators of $\mathbb{G}$ and $\alpha \in \mathbb{Z}_p^*$ is the secret key.
    - Returns the public key, $PK \leftarrow \langle \mathcal{G}, g, g^\alpha, g^{\alpha^2}, \ldots, g^{\alpha^t}, h, h^\alpha, h^{\alpha^2}, \ldots, h^{\alpha^t} \rangle$.
2. Commit($PK, \phi(x)$) :
    Computes the commitment value $C \leftarrow g^{\phi(\alpha)} h^{\hat{\phi}(\alpha)} = \prod_{j=0}^{deg(\phi)}(g^{\alpha^j})^{\phi_j} \prod_{j=0}^{deg(\hat{\phi})}(h^{\alpha^j})^{\hat{\phi}_j} \in \mathbb{G}$ for the polynomials $\phi(x) \leftarrow \sum_{j=0}^{deg(\phi)} \phi_j x^j \in \mathbb{Z}_p[X]$ of degree less than or equal to t and $\hat{\phi}(x) \leftarrow \sum_{j=0}^{deg(\hat{\phi})} \hat{\phi}_j x^j \in \mathbb{Z}_p[X]$ of degree t.
3. Open($PK, C, \phi(x), \hat{\phi}(x)$) :
    Outputs the committed polynomials $\phi(x)$ and $\hat{\phi}(x)$.
4. VerifyPoly($PK, C, \phi(x), \hat{\phi}(x)$) :
    Outputs 1 if $C = \prod_{j=0}^{deg(\phi)}(g^{\alpha^j})^{\phi_j} \prod_{j=0}^{deg(\hat{\phi})}(h^{\alpha^j})^{\hat{\phi}_j}$, else it outputs 0.
5. CreateWitness($PK, \phi(x), \hat{\phi}(x), i$) :
    - Computes $\psi_i(x) \leftarrow \frac{\phi(x) - \phi(i)}{(x-i)}$ and $\hat{\psi}_i(x) \leftarrow \frac{\hat{\phi}(x) - \hat{\phi}(i)}{(x-i)}$.
    - Outputs $\langle i, \phi(i), \hat{\phi}(i), w_i \rangle$, where $w_i \leftarrow g^{\psi_i(\alpha)} h^{\hat{\psi}_i(\alpha)}$ is the witness.
6. VerifyEval($PK, C, i, \phi(i), \hat{\phi}(x), w_i$) :
    Outputs 1 if $e(C, g) = e(w_i, g^\alpha/g^i) e(g^{\phi(i)} h^{\hat{\phi}(i)}, g)$, else it outputs 0.

3.4 Security Properties Modelled in EasyCrypt (Sect. 2.5)

In this section, we describe how the security properties corresponding to the Pedersen commitment scheme have been modelled in EasyCrypt through a series of lemmas and provide a brief, intuitive explanation of what each lemma represents.

1. Correctness.
   The correctness of **PolyCommit$_{Ped}$** is perfect. The EasyCrypt proof is about fifty lines long and algebraic; it is very similar to the paper proof.
   ```
   lemma PedScheme_Corr :
   hoare[Correctness(PolyComPed).main : true ==> res].
   ```

2. Polynomial Binding.
   Polynomial Binding is proved to be bound by the adversary's success in our variant of the t-SDH problem. This means that if there exists an adversary that breaks polynomial binding then that adversary is capable of solving the t-SDH problem or the DL problem. The proof is about twenty lines long and algebraic, the second case of the proof is very similar to the original paper proof which omits the first case. The reduction Adv is essentially the same as used for **PolyCommit$_{DL}$** but with additional branching to handle case where DL challenge is solved.
   ```
   lemma PedScheme_PolyBinding (A <: AdvPB) &m :
   Pr[PolyBinding(PolyComPed, A).main() @ &m : res]
   <= Pr[B1.Tsdh2(Adv(A)).main(t) @ &m : res].
   ```

3. Evaluation Binding.
   Similarly for Evaluation binding we define the security lemma in terms of our variant t-SDH adversary game. The proof is about fifty lines long and algebraic, it is very similar to the original paper proof.
   ```
   lemma PedScheme_EvalBinding (Adv <: AdvEB) &m :
   Pr[EvalBinding(PolyComPed, Adv).main() @ &m : res]
   <= Pr[B1.Tsdh2(Adv2(Adv)).main(t) @ &m : res].
   ```

4. Unconditional Hiding. Hiding has been defined and proved by showing that the adversary's success probability in breaking the hiding property is essentially no better than guessing. Specifically, it is bounded above by two times the inverse of the order of the group, which is a very small number if the group order is large. The two times denotes two different cases where the adversary might win the game: firstly, it might win if it simply guesses the evaluation correctly, secondly it might win if the discrete log value between the 'generators' g and h is zero. One could sample the discrete log value b between g and h such that it is never equal to zero and so remove this second case; however, this significantly complicates other parts of the analysis.
   The proof is around four hundred lines long. We begin by switching through two games in which increasingly more of the values the adversary sees are randomly sampled or calculated without knowledge of the polynomial. We then

branch based on if the commitment key has zero as the discrete log between the two "generators" g and h. Both of these branches are then shown to occur with probability at most one over the order of the group. Our sub-lemma called Hiding_Bound is similar to the original paper proof we need our other game hopes to be able to apply it.

```
lemma PedScheme_Hiding &m :
  islossless A_H.guess =>
  Pr[Hiding(PolyCommitPed,A_H).real() @ &m : res]
    <= 2 / order.
```

4 Clarifications and Insights from the Formalisation

As is normal when engaging in formal verification we dealt with various cases in the proofs which were not covered in the original paper; most of these cases where comparatively trivial. However, several cases were either more complicated or had bearing on the definitions or assumptions; we highlight these more interesting cases below.

4.1 The Original Proof of Polynomial Binding for PolyCommit$_{\text{DL}}$ is Incorrect

In the original paper, the polynomial binding property of the Pedersen commitment scheme was "proved" under the Discrete Logarithm (DL) assumption. However, during the formalisation of this proof in EasyCrypt, we ended up with a proof which relied on the t-Strong Diffie-Hellman (t-SDH) assumption instead of the DL assumption. We conjecture that the original lemma is unsalvageable, that is unprovable.

The original proof, which can be found in the extended version of the KZG paper, proceeds in the standard manner for binding of Pedersen commitments. The discrete log challenge is embed in the commitment key and when the adversary returns valid openings for two different messages we extract the discrete log from these messages and openings. The extraction of the discrete log challenge λ from the messages $\phi(x)$ and $\phi'(x)$ and openings $\hat{\phi}(x)$ and $\hat{\phi}'(x)$ is computed as $\lambda = \frac{\phi'(\alpha) - \phi(\alpha)}{\hat{\phi}(\alpha) - \hat{\phi}'(\alpha)}$; where α is the point of evaluation embed in the commitment key. *There is no reasoning in the paper as to why this equation is well defined, that is why $\hat{\phi}(a) - \hat{\phi}'(a)$ is non-zero*. This is the point where the original proof fails to go through. This would normally follow directly from the messages being different but in this case just because $\phi(x)$ and $\phi'(x)$ are different doesn't mean that $\phi(\alpha)$ and $\phi'(\alpha)$ are. Particularly since the adversary sees the commitment key before choosing the messages there does not seem to be any reason under the discrete log assumption why this should be hard or unlikely.

By switching to the t-SDH assumption the adversary finding two different polynomials which agree at α allows us to make a reduction. Since the overall security theorem for **PolyCommit**$_{\text{Ped}}$ already relies on t-SDH there does not seem to be any effect on deployed systems of this incorrect lemma, for which we are thankful given how widely KZG commitment schemes are deployed.

4.2 Clarification: Hiding Definition

The definition of the hiding in the original paper by Kate et al. [11], which we included in Sect. 2.3, is somewhat underdefined in particular, it is unclear where the commitment key, commitment, evaluations, and openings come from. This issue is avoided in the example of Verifiable Secret Sharing since that protocol involves a trusted dealer.

Cleaning up the Original Definition. We clarify the original definition by saying that the commitment key, commitment, evaluations, and openings are honestly generated. In contrast, the evaluation points are chosen by the adversary with knowledge of the commitment key and commitment. As we have noted this differs from the interpretation by [12] which models the adversary choosing the evaluation points without knowledge of the commitment.

Going Beyond Trusted Dealers The comments in the original paper, particularly at the end of Sect. 3, suggest that it is necessary to either have a trusted dealer or to distribute setup: "In absence of a single trusted party, computing Setup can be distributed."

It seems likely that it should be possible to do better based on the perfect hiding of **PolyCommit**$_{\text{Ped}}$ and the ability to check the validity of the commitment key. We introduce a stronger definition of hiding, creatively called Strong Hiding to distinguish it from regular Hiding. Strong Hiding gives the adversary the ability to choose the commitment key but only allows them to win if the key is "valid". This stronger property allows the use of the **PolyCommit**$_{\text{Ped}}$ in two party protocols where the challenging party generates the commitment key on their own.

We are able to prove the hoped for result that **PolyCommit**$_{\text{Ped}}$ satisfies this strong definition of hiding. The prover is essentially identical to that for normal hiding with the additional logic that a key being valid means it has the structure required for the later algebraic reasoning.

```
lemma PolyComPed_Strong_Hiding &m :
  islossless A_SH.setup =>
  islossless A_SH.guess =>
  Pr[Strong_Hiding(PolyCommitPed,PolyCommitPed_A,A_SH)
    .real() @ &m : res] <= (1/ order).
```

4.3 Missing Subcase in Evaluation Binding of PolyCommit$_{\text{DL}}$ and PolyCommit$_{\text{Ped}}$

In the paper's proofs of evaluation binding, there is a case that isn't explicitly covered. The formal proof introduces a specific subcase analysis under the condition $w_i \neq w'_i$, that is that witnesses the adversary provides to the claimed polynomial evaluations are different. The issue occurs in the first of these subcases; the analysis assumes that $i \neq \alpha$, that is that the evaluation point i is not the point embedded in the commitment key α. Our EasyCrpyt proof includes additional steps to handle this subcase explicitly.

5 Conclusion

In this paper, we have provided a comprehensive formalisation of the Kate-Zaverucha-Goldberg (KZG) polynomial commitment schemes within the EasyCrypt framework. Our work meticulously details the formal definitions and assumptions underlying the KZG schemes, ensuring a clear and unambiguous representation of its components and operations. Through our formally verified security proofs of correctness, polynomial binding, evaluation binding, and hiding, we have established the robustness and reliability of the KZG scheme against various adversarial attacks.

An essential aspect of our work is the consideration of cases that were previously unclear in the original KZG paper. By addressing these ambiguous scenarios, we have further strengthened confidence in the security guarantees of the KZG schemes. This consideration reduces the risk of potential vulnerabilities and enhances the trustworthiness of the commitment schemes in practical applications. By leveraging the capabilities of EasyCrypt, we have demonstrated the practical benefits of employing interactive theorem provers in cryptographic formal verification, ensuring that all possible cases and assumptions are thoroughly considered and reducing the risk of overlooked vulnerabilities.

5.1 Future Work

While our formalisation and verification of the KZG polynomial commitment schemes mark a significant step forward, there are several avenues for future research and development. Building on our formalisation efforts, future work can focus on constructing highly efficient ZK-SNARKs using polynomial commitment schemes. By combining these schemes with interactive oracle proofs (IOPs), it is possible to achieve more succinct proofs and efficient verification while maintaining strong security guarantees. For example future work could aim to formalise the IOPs introduced by Antonio Faonio et al. [27], along with the formalisation of the combination of IOPs with PCSs. This can lead to practical and scalable solutions for privacy-preserving applications, particularly in e-voting, blockchain and secure multi-party computation.

References

1. Barthe, G., Dupressoir, F., Grégoire, B., Kunz, C., Schmidt, B., Strub, P.-Y.: EasyCrypt: a tutorial. In: Aldini, A., Lopez, J., Martinelli, F. (eds.) FOSAD 2012-2013. LNCS, vol. 8604, pp. 146–166. Springer, Cham (2014). https://doi.org/10.1007/978-3-319-10082-1_6

2. Haines, T., Goré, R., Sharma, B.: Did you mix me? Formally verifying verifiable mix nets in electronic voting. In: SP, pp. 1748–1765. IEEE (2021)
3. Basin, D.A., Cremers, C., Dreier, J., Sasse, R.: Tamarin: verification of large-scale, real-world, cryptographic protocols. IEEE Secur. Priv. **20**(3), 24–32 (2022)
4. Sprenger, C., Backes, M., Basin, D.A., Pfitzmann, B., Waidner, M.: Cryptographically sound theorem proving. In: CSFW, pp. 153–166. IEEE Computer Society (2006)
5. Baritel-Ruet, C.: Formal security proofs of cryptographic: a necessity achieved using easycrypt, Ph.D. dissertation, Université côte d'azur (2020)
6. Almeida, J.B., et al.: Machine-checked proofs for cryptographic standards: in differentiability of sponge and secure high-assurance implementations of SHA-3. In: CCS, pp. 1607–1622. ACM (2019)
7. Bosshard, A.G., Bootle, J., Sprenger, C.: Formal verification of the sum check protocol. CoRR, vol. abs/2402.06093 (2024)
8. Barthe, G., Grégoire, B., Heraud, S., Béguelin, S.Z.: Computer-aided security proofs for the working cryptographer. In: Rogaway, P. (ed.) CRYPTO 2011. LNCS, vol. 6841, pp. 71–90. Springer, Heidelberg (2011). https://doi.org/10.1007/978-3-642-22792-9_5
9. Nowak, D.: On formal verification of arithmetic-based cryptographic primitives. CoRR, vol. abs/0904.1110 (2009)
10. Blanchet, B., Pointcheval, D.: Automated security proofs with sequences of games. In: Dwork, C. (ed.) CRYPTO 2006. LNCS, vol. 4117, pp. 537–554. Springer, Heidelberg (2006). https://doi.org/10.1007/11818175_32
11. Kate, A., Zaverucha, G.M., Goldberg, I.: Constant-size commitments to polynomials and their applications. In: Abe, M. (ed.) ASIACRYPT 2010. LNCS, vol. 6477, pp. 177–194. Springer, Heidelberg (2010). https://doi.org/10.1007/978-3-642-17373-8_11
12. Rothmann, T., Kreuzer, K.: Formal verification of the kate-zaverucha-goldberg polynomial commitment scheme (2024)
13. Maller, M., Bowe, S., Kohlweiss, M., Meiklejohn, S.: Sonic: zero-knowledge snarks from linear-size universal and updatable structured reference strings. In: CCS, pp. 2111–2128. ACM (2019)
14. Gabizon, A.: Improved prover efficiency and SRS size in a sonic-like system. IACR Cryptol. ePrint Arch., 601 (2019)
15. Chiesa, A., Hu, Y., Maller, M., Mishra, P., Vesely, N., Ward, N.: Marlin: preprocessing zkSNARKs with universal and updatable SRS. In: Canteaut, A., Ishai, Y. (eds.) EUROCRYPT 2020. LNCS, vol. 12105, pp. 738–768. Springer, Cham (2020). https://doi.org/10.1007/978-3-030-45721-1_26
16. Gabizon, A., Williamson, Z.J., Ciobotaru, O.: PLONK: permutations over lagrange-bases for oecumenical noninteractive arguments of knowledge. IACR Cryptol. ePrint Arch., 953 (2019)
17. Metere, R., Dong, C.: Automated cryptographic analysis of the Pedersen commitment scheme. In: Rak, J., Bay, J., Kotenko, I., Popyack, L., Skormin, V., Szczypiorski, K. (eds.) MMM-ACNS 2017. LNCS, vol. 10446, pp. 275–287. Springer, Cham (2017). https://doi.org/10.1007/978-3-319-65127-9_22
18. Butler, D., Lochbihler, A., Aspinall, D., Gascón, A.: Formalising ς-protocols and commitment schemes using crypthol. J. Autom. Reason. **65**(4), 521–567 (2021)
19. Barthe, G., Hedin, D., Béguelin, S.Z., Grégoire, B., Heraud, S.: A machine-checked formalization of sigma-protocols. In: CSF, pp. 246–260. IEEE Computer Society (2010)

20. Avigad, J., Goldberg, L., Levit, D., Seginer, Y., Titelman, A.: A verified algebraic representation of Cairo program execution. In: CPP, pp. 153–165. ACM (2022)
21. Bailey, B., Miller, A.: Formalizing soundness proofs of linear PCP snarks. In: USENIX Security Symposium. USENIX Association (2024)
22. Groth, J.: On the size of pairing-based non-interactive arguments. In: Fischlin, M., Coron, J.-S. (eds.) EUROCRYPT 2016. LNCS, vol. 9666, pp. 305–326. Springer, Heidelberg (2016). https://doi.org/10.1007/978-3-662-49896-5_11
23. Basin, D.A., Lochbihler, A., Sefidgar, S.R.: CryptHOL: game-based proofs in higher-order logic. J. Cryptol. **33**(2), 494–566 (2020)
24. Nipkow, T., Paulson, L.C., Wenzel, M.: Isabelle/HOL - A Proof Assistant for Higher-Order Logic, ser. Lecture Notes in Computer Science, vol. 2283. Springer (2002)
25. Barthe, G., et al.: Fully automated analysis of padding-based encryption in the computational model. In: CCS, pp. 1247–1260. ACM (2013)
26. Pedersen, T.P.: Non-interactive and information-theoretic secure verifiable secret sharing. In: CRYPTO, series Lecture Notes in Computer Science, vol. 576, pp. 129–140. Springer (1991)
27. Faonio, A., Fiore, D., Kohlweiss, M., Russo, L., Zajac, M.: From polynomial IOP and commitments to non-malleable zksnarks. In: TCC (3), series Lecture Notes in Computer Science, vol. 14371, pp. 455–485. Springer (2023)

UTRA: Universal Token Reusability Attack and Token Unforgeable Delegatable Order-Revealing Encryption

Jaehwan Park[1], Hyeonbum Lee[2], Junbeom Hur[3], Jae Hong Seo[2(✉)], and Doowon Kim[1(✉)]

[1] University of Tennessee, Knoxville, USA
{jpark127,doowon}@utk.edu
[2] Hanyang University, Seoul, South Korea
{leehb3706,jaehongseo}@hanyang.ac.kr
[3] Korea University, Seoul, South Korea
jbhur@isslab.korea.ac.kr

Abstract. As datasets grow, users increasingly rely on cloud services for data storage and processing. Consequently, concerns regarding data protection and the practical use of encrypted data have emerged as significant challenges. One promising solution is order-revealing encryption (ORE), which enables efficient operations on encrypted numerical data. To support distributed environments with different users, delegatable ORE (DORE) extends this functionality to multi-client settings, enabling order comparisons between ciphertexts encrypted under different secret keys. However, Hahn et al. proposed a token forgery attack against DORE with a threat model and introduced the secure DORE (SEDORE) scheme as a countermeasure. Despite this enhancement, we claim that SEDORE remains vulnerable under the same threat model.

In this paper, we present a novel Universal Token Reusability Attack, which exposes a critical vulnerability in SEDORE with the identical threat model. To mitigate this, we introduce the concept of verifiable delegatable order-revealing encryption (VDORE), along with a formal definition of token unforgeability. Building on this, we design a new scheme, Token Unforgeable DORE (TUDORE), which ensures token unforgeability. Moreover, TUDORE achieves 1.5× faster token generation than SEDORE with enhanced security.

Keywords: Order-revealing encryption · Cross-database system · Token-based authentication

1 Introduction

With the increasing size of datasets, processing tasks on local machines are becoming impractical, thereby driving the demand for cloud-based services.

J. Park and H. Lee—Equal contribution.
H. Lee is now with Seoul National University (email: hyeonbumlee@snu.ac.kr). This work was completed while the author was at Hanyang University.

However, uploading data to cloud services without protections raises privacy concerns. Clients encrypt their data before outsourcing it to servers to address these issues. However, even after encryption, there remains a need to support efficient queries, particularly range queries, which are fundamental in applications such as health service [20,33], finance [30], and location-based service (LBS) [10,32]. For instance, doctors may need to determine whether a patient's HIV viral load exceeds a clinical threshold, financial systems may compare encrypted bids to identify those above the current maximum, and location-based services may retrieve nearby points of interest within a specified distance for route planning.

Since standard encryption schemes do not preserve the order of values, specialized cryptographic constructions are required to support range queries. Typical solutions include fully homomorphic encryption (FHE), order-preserving encryption (OPE), and order-revealing encryption (ORE). FHE provides strong privacy by allowing computations over encrypted data without leakage, but its high computational cost limits practical use [13]. OPE is a symmetric scheme that allows direct ciphertext comparison by preserving plaintext order with low overhead. However, OPE leaks more information than ideal ORE schemes [6].

To strike a better balance between efficiency and security, ORE has been proposed as a means to support such secure operations [5,8,11,14,16,17,22,25]. ORE is a method that reveals only the order by using a publicly disclosed comparison function, without leaking any information about the numerical datasets. For instance, ORE takes two ciphertexts as input and returns the order associated with the underlying plaintexts. With the advancement of ORE, Li et al. [16] proposed a delegatable ORE (DORE) scheme, which supports comparisons across different encryption keys. DORE enables data owners to issue one-time authorization tokens to users based on their secret keys.

However, Hahn et al. [14] identified vulnerabilities in DORE, demonstrating that authorization tokens could be forged by unauthorized users under a practical threat model, which was later adopted by [25]. In these attacks, an authorized user (traitor) who receives an access token from the data owner (victim) collaborates with an unauthorized user (attacker) to enable illegal query execution on the victim's database. These attacks result not only in unauthorized data access but also in financial losses for victims. Because many modern cloud service providers (CSPs) [9,19] adopt a pay-per-query model. Furthermore, such attacks are stealthy since the data owner cannot identify the traitor. In response to these risks, Hahn et al. proposed secure DORE (SEDORE), which strengthens token unforgeability. Building on this, Xu et al. [31] introduced efficient DORE (EDORE), which enhances performance compared to SEDORE.

1.1 Our Contribution

Despite the improvements in SEDORE and EDORE to mitigate practical forgery attacks, we discover that the same vulnerability exists in DORE [16], SEDORE [14], and EDORE [31] under the identical threat model proposed by [14]. We term this vulnerability as *universal token reusability*. This attack remains highly threatening, as it adheres to the practical and reasonable threat model defined by [14], even though the traitor provides the attacker with one additional piece of information in our scenario compared to that of [14].

Given the limitations of prior work, we propose a revised DORE scheme incorporating a verification algorithm, termed verifiable DORE (VDORE). We formally define the token unforgeability of the VDORE scheme for provable security and also explain the limitations of [14]'s security analysis. Moreover, we propose TUDORE, a novel token-unforgeable DORE scheme, built upon VDORE. Like SEDORE [14], our scheme retains the original algorithms of DORE [16] for setup, key generation, encryption, and test, while modifying the token generation algorithm to prevent attacks. This ensures minimal computational and storage overhead. Additionally, we incorporate digital signature schemes [7,27] into the token generation process to guarantee token unforgeability. We provide security analysis and experimental results showing that TUDORE achieves competitive efficiency compared to previous works [14,16,31]. In summary, we make the following main contributions:

1. **Universal Token Reusability Attack.** We first highlight that token-based DORE schemes [14,16,31] remain vulnerable to token forgery attacks. Specifically, under the same threat model described in [14], we introduce a new attack called *universal token reusability attack* in Sect. 4.
2. **Token Verification and Security Definition.** To counter the security threats revealed by the attack scenario, we revise the token-based DORE scheme by integrating a token verification algorithm. We explain the necessity of verification and shortcomings of [14]'s security analysis in Sect. 4. This revision introduces verifiable DORE (VDORE), which ensures provable security through three properties: *correctness, data privacy,* and *token unforgeability* in Sect. 5.
3. **Token Unforgeable VDORE Scheme.** We present a new secure VDORE scheme, named token unforgeable DORE (TUDORE), which leverages digital signature schemes [7,27]. Especially, we prove that TUDORE satisfies the properties of *correctness, data privacy,* and *token unforgeability* in Sect. 6.
4. **Implementation of TUDORE.** We provide implementation results to compare existing schemes [14,16,31] with our proposed method (TUDORE). Our experimental evaluation demonstrates that TUDORE is not only practical and feasible but also enhances security compared to prior schemes, as detailed in Sect. 7.

1.2 Related Works

Homomorphic Comparison from Fully Homomorphic Encryption. Cheon et al. [13] introduced homomorphic comparison for private queries based on fully homomorphic encryption (FHE), which has been further improved in subsequent works [12,28]. These approaches encode the comparison function as an arithmetic circuit and evaluate it homomorphically using FHE. Owing to the strong cryptographic guarantees of FHE, the protocols achieve post-quantum security. However, evaluating even a single 64-bit comparison typically takes several seconds [12,13,28], which is impractical in real-world scenarios. Moreover, to the best of our knowledge, no existing FHE-based construction has been proposed that supports delegatability. This limitation renders such methods impractical in multi-client scenarios where secret key sharing is undesirable or infeasible.

Order-Preserving Encryption. Order-preserving Encryption (OPE) was initially introduced by Agrawal et al. [4]. Subsequently, Boldyreva et al. [6] introduced the notion of "best possible" security, referred to as indistinguishability under ordered chosen-plaintext attack (IND-OCPA). This property ensures that two ciphertexts reveal no information about plaintexts other than their order. However, Boldyreva also pointed out that achieving this ideal security is not feasible for stateless and immutable OPE schemes. Therefore, as an effort to resolve these limitations, Popa et al. [24] proposed an interactive order-preserving encoding method via server state. However, their scheme is interactive, requiring $\mathcal{O}(\log N)$ communication rounds for both database updates and query execution. To address this, alternative solutions impose a trade-off by incurring client-side storage costs ranging from $\mathcal{O}(N)$ [15] to $\mathcal{O}(N^\delta)$ [26], where $0 < \delta < 1$. Nonetheless, despite improvements, OPE remains limited by interaction and trade-offs between performance and security.

Order-Revealing Encryption. Order-revealing encryption (ORE) is a technique that encrypts numerical data without preserving the order of the plaintext, allowing the comparison of two ciphertexts using a public function to determine their order. To improve efficiency, Chenette et al. [11] proposed a practical ORE scheme that supports bitwise encryption and comparison. Cash et al. [8] introduced a parameter-hiding ORE (pORE) that reveals only the equality pattern of the most significant differing bit (msdb). However, these schemes are limited to a single-user environment. Subsequently, various schemes have been proposed to support multi-client settings [5,16,17,22,25,31]. Especially, [16] proposed delegatable ORE (DORE), which supports comparisons over ciphertexts encrypted under different keys. Moreover, recent research [5] on ORE extends beyond traditional database applications and explores its use in machine learning algorithms.

Organization. This paper is organized as follows. In Sect. 2, we present the background of cross-database systems, delegatable ORE, and our system and threat model. Section 3 reviews existing token-based DORE schemes. In Sect. 4, we introduce a new attack called the universal token reusability attack targeting these schemes and the weaknesses in [14]'s security analysis. To address this, we propose the concept of verifiable DORE along with a formal security definition in Sect. 5. Finally, Sect. 6 and Sect. 7 describe the construction of a novel token-unforgeable DORE scheme and its experimental evaluation.

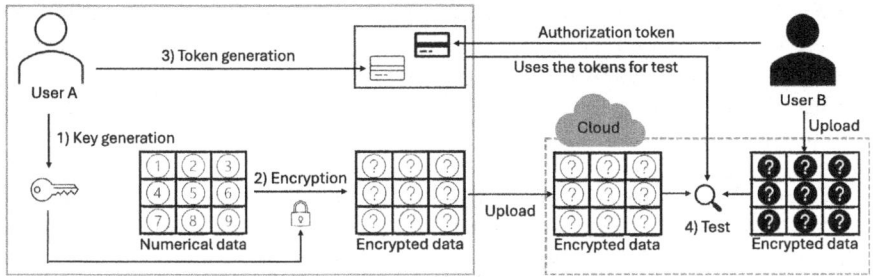

Fig. 1. The description of delegatable order-revealing encryption. The orange box with a solid line indicates the operations executed by User A, whereas the blue box with a dotted line represents the processes handled by the cloud. (Color figure online)

2 Background and Models

2.1 Background

Cross-Database Systems. In our system, similar to DORE [16], SEDORE [14], and EDORE [31], we consider a cross-database scenario. The cross-database system allows multiple users to upload their encrypted databases onto the server, based on their raw data. Users who want to collaborate and share datasets can perform relevant operations by sending queries to each other's databases. However, it is essential to note that not all users on the cloud server can access all databases; only those users authorized by the database owner can utilize specific databases. From this, the database owner distributes authorization tokens to grant authorized users access.

Delegatable Order-Revealing Encryption. DORE scheme has been introduced in a multi-client environment [16]. This scheme allows the data owner to grant authorization tokens to other users, enabling them to perform operations on each other's databases based on different secret keys.

In Fig. 1, we show the process of delegatable order-revealing encryption and explain it as follows: 1) User A generates their secret key using a key generation algorithm. 2) Afterward, they encrypt their numerical data with the key and upload it to the cloud. 3) If User A wishes to perform computations on User B's dataset, they obtain an authorization token from User B and then generate a token related to their dataset using the token generation algorithm. 4) When the server receives the tokens, it compares the encrypted data of User A and B with the tokens using a test algorithm. Finally, it determines the orders. Note that, the token is not issued per query but only once and remains valid thereafter.

2.2 System Model

We consider a scenario involving cross-database environments with encrypted databases. In this context, there are three entities with the following roles:

- **The Data Owner**: Encrypts data using the secret key and uploads it to the server. The data owner also provides authorization tokens to users who are authorized to access its databases.

- **The User**: Requests an authorization token from the data owner. Upon receiving the token, the user can use it to perform computations involving their own database and the data owner's database.
- **The Server**: Acts as a storage system for encrypted data uploaded by multiple data owners and processes incoming range queries from users.

Note that the entities uploading data to the server can all become data owners. Moreover, entities obtaining authorization tokens from different data owners can also access other databases.

2.3 Threat Model

Following the attack scenario described in [14], we consider two threat models related to data privacy violations and token forgeability, as follows:

- **Data Privacy Violation**: The server might attempt to disclose the content of the stored data, along with trying to acquire not only the ordering information and the index of the first differing bit between the two ciphertexts but also to recover the data.
- **Token Forgeability**: The server and unauthorized users may attempt to access the victim's database by creating forged tokens.

From this perspective, we focus on the notion of *token forgeability*. There are three entities involved in token forgery attacks: a victim ($\mathcal{V}$), who owns the database; an unauthorized user ($\mathcal{A}$) who tried to access victim's database without any permission; an authorized user ($\mathcal{M}$), who may illegally assist the unauthorized user ($\mathcal{A}$) in generating forged tokens.

Importantly, we assume that $\mathcal{M}$ never shares its secret key with $\mathcal{A}$, as such disclosure would allow $\mathcal{A}$ to exploit not only $\mathcal{V}$'s database, but also $\mathcal{M}$'s database by enabling the generation of tokens derived from $\mathcal{M}$'s secret key.

3 Overview of Token-Based DORE Schemes

3.1 Basic Notation

We first define some notations before revisiting the schemes. We denote $\mathbb{Z}_p$ as a prime field that is isomorphic to the integers mod p. Uniform sampling is denoted by $\xleftarrow{\$}$. For instance, $a \xleftarrow{\$} \mathbb{Z}_p$ indicates that a is uniformly chosen from $\mathbb{Z}_p$. H and F denote a cryptographic hash function whose range will be specified from the context. To describe bilinear groups, we denote $\langle p, \mathbb{G}_1, \mathbb{G}_2, g_1, g_2, \mathbb{G}_T, e \rangle$, that stands for prime p and cyclic groups $\mathbb{G}_1, \mathbb{G}_2, \mathbb{G}_T$ of order p, generators $g_1 \in \mathbb{G}_1$ and $g_2 \in \mathbb{G}_2$, and bilinear map $e : \mathbb{G}_1 \times \mathbb{G}_2 \to \mathbb{G}_T$, which is non-degenerate and a computable function satisfies $e(P^a, K^b) = e(P, K)^{ab}$ for all $a, b \in Z_p$. Hereafter, we assume that the prime p is sufficiently large because the security of DORE schemes relies on the discrete logarithm assumption.

3.2 Token-Based DORE Schemes

Li et al. [16] first proposed a token-based delegatable ORE scheme. The data owner delegates the management of data, but can manage authorization through the tokens. DORE scheme consists of 5 algorithms as follows:

- pp $\leftarrow$ DORE.Setup(1^λ): It takes the security parameter 1^λ as input and returns the public parameter pp.
- (pk, sk) $\leftarrow$ DORE.Keygen(pp) : It receives a public parameter pp as input and returns a pair of public key and secret key (pk, sk).
- ct $\leftarrow$ DORE.Enc(pp, m, sk): It takes a message $m \in \{0,1\}^*$ and sk as input and returns a ciphertext ct.
- $\text{tok}_{(v \to u)}$ $\leftarrow$ DORE.Token(pp, $\text{pk}_{(v)}$, $\text{sk}_{(u)}$): It takes the public key $\text{pk}_{(v)}$ of user v and the secret key $\text{sk}_{(u)}$ of user u as input and returns an authorization token $\text{tok}_{(v \to u)}$, indicating that user v is authorized by user u.
- res $\leftarrow$ DORE.Test(pp, $\text{ct}_{(u)}$, $\text{ct}_{(v)}$, $\text{tok}_{(v \to u)}$, $\text{tok}_{(u \to v)}$): It takes the two ciphertext $\text{ct}_{(u)}$ and $\text{ct}_{(v)}$, along with two tokens, $\text{tok}_{(v \to u)}$ and $\text{tok}_{(u \to v)}$, as input and returns the comparison result $res \in \{-1, 0, 1\}$. The output values represent the following: 1 indicates $m_u > m_v$, 0 indicates $m_u = m_v$, and -1 indicates $m_u < m_v$, where $m_\square$ denotes the plaintext of $\text{ct}_{(\square)}$ for $\square = u, v$.

Li et al. [16] introduced two security properties for DORE: correctness and IND-OCPA. Furthermore, Hahn et al. [14] emphasized that token forgeability is a critical security concern in the DORE scheme. Building on these works, token-based DORE schemes should satisfy three essential properties: correctness, data privacy, and soundness. We formalize and refine these properties in Sect. 5.

DERE-to-DORE Framework. In [16], Li et al. proposed a framework for constructing a DORE scheme from a token-based Delegatable Equality-Revealing Encoding (DERE). The primary difference lies in the test algorithm: the DERE test algorithm is restricted to checking only the equality between two ciphertexts. From a DERE scheme, DORE leverages the key generation, encryption, and testing algorithms of DERE and constructs its own encryption and test algorithms by iteratively running the encryption and test algorithms of DERE. Subsequent researches [14,31] follow this framework. For this reason, we now focus on the DERE scheme rather than the DORE scheme itself.

Li et al. constructed the DERE scheme based on the bilinear setting under the generic group model (GGM) [16]. To prevent a token forging attack, Hahn et al. revised the token generation of DERE and then proposed a new DERE scheme, SEDERE [14]. We describe the DERE and SEDERE schemes in Fig. 2.

One-Sided Token is Sufficient. In the Test algorithm, it currently requires two-sided tokens, $\text{tok}_{(v \to u)}$ and $\text{tok}_{(u \to v)}$. When a user u queries a ciphertext $\text{ct}_{(v)}$ stored in v's database, u first generates $\text{tok}_{(v \to u)}$ locally. Since the public key $\text{pk}_{(v)}$ is openly available, u can compute $\text{tok}_{(v \to u)}$ independently, without needing v's secret key. Subsequently, u uses the pair of tokens, $\text{tok}_{(v \to u)}$ (generated locally) and $\text{tok}_{(u \to v)}$ (received from user v), to perform the Test algorithm.

- pp ← DERE.Setup(1^λ): It takes the security parameter 1^λ as input and returns the public parameter pp $= (\langle p, \mathbb{G}_1, \mathbb{G}_2, g_1, g_2, \mathbb{G}_T, e \rangle, H, F)$.
- (pk, sk) ← DERE.Keygen(pp) : It takes a public parameter pp as input and uniformly chooses $a, b \xleftarrow{\$} \mathbb{Z}_p$. After that, it returns a pair of public key and secret key (pk, sk) $= (g_2^a, (a, b))$. Additionally, We denote a key pair of user u as $(\mathsf{pk}_{(u)}, \mathsf{sk}_{(u)}) = (g_2^{a_{(u)}}, (a_{(u)}, b_{(u)}))$.
- ct ← DERE.Enc(pp, m, sk): It takes a message $m \in \{0,1\}^*$ and sk as input. It randomly picks $r \xleftarrow{\$} \mathbb{Z}_p$ and return ct $:= (c^0, c^1) = ((g_1^{rb} H(m))^a, c^1 = g_1^r)$. For user u, we rewrite ct as $\mathsf{ct}_{(u)} = (c_{(u)}^0, c_{(u)}^1)$.
- $\mathsf{tok}_{(v \to u)}$ ← DERE.Token(pp, $\mathsf{pk}_{(v)}$, $\mathsf{sk}_{(u)}$): It takes the public key $\mathsf{pk}_{(v)} = g_2^{a_{(v)}}$ of user v and the secret key $\mathsf{sk}_{(u)} = (a_{(u)}, b_{(u)})$ of user u and returns an authorization token $\mathsf{tok}_{(v \to u)}$. ($v \to u$) from $\mathsf{tok}_{(v \to u)}$ means that the user u sends the authorization token to user v and $\mathsf{tok}_{(v \to u)}$ consists of $t^0_{(v \to u)}$ and $t^1_{(v \to u)}$.

    - (type-1, DERE [16]): $t^0_{(v \to u)} = \mathsf{pk}_{(v)}$, $t^1_{(v \to u)} = \mathsf{pk}_{(v)}^{a_{(u)} b_{(u)}}$
    - (type-2, SEDERE [14]): $t^0_{(v \to u)} = F\left(\mathsf{pk}_{(v)}^{a_{(u)}}\right)^{a_{(u)}^{-1}}$, $t^1_{(v \to u)} = F\left(\mathsf{pk}_{(v)}^{a_{(u)}}\right)^{b_{(v)}}$

    Finally, it returns $\mathsf{tok}_{(v \to u)} := (t^0_{(v \to u)}, t^1_{(v \to u)})$.
- $0 \backslash 1$ ← DERE.Test(pp, $\mathsf{ct}_{(u)}$, $\mathsf{ct}_{(v)}$, $\mathsf{tok}_{(v \to u)}$, $\mathsf{tok}_{(u \to v)}$): It takes the ciphertexts from user v and u, $\mathsf{ct}_{(v)}$ and $\mathsf{ct}_{(u)}$, and the tokens, $\mathsf{tok}_{(v \to u)}$ and $\mathsf{tok}_{(u \to v)}$ as input. After that, it computes $d_0 = \frac{e(c^0_{(u)}, t^0_{(v \to u)})}{e(c^1_{(u)}, t^1_{(v \to u)})}$, $d_1 = \frac{e(c^0_{(v)}, t^0_{(u \to v)})}{e(c^1_{(v)}, t^1_{(u \to v)})}$. It then compares them: if $d_0 = d_1$, it returns 1; otherwise, it returns 0.

Fig. 2. DERE and SEDERE Scheme.

4 Concrete Attack and Security Analysis of SEDORE

In this section, we present a concrete attack, named the Universal Token Reusability Attack, on the SEDORE scheme, demonstrating its vulnerability under the threat model described in Sect. 2.3. We then discuss how this attack relates to the soundness guarantees of SEDORE as proven in [14].

4.1 Universal Token Reusability Attack

Following the DERE-to-DORE framework, the vulnerability in SEDERE also leads to SEDORE. For this reason, we present an attack on the SEDERE scheme in Fig. 2, to validate the existence of the vulnerability in SEDORE. Before explaining the attack, we propose the notion of a universal forged token in the bilinear setting. A universal forged token $\mathsf{uft}_{(\mathcal{V}), h_2}$ is a forged token to access $\mathcal{V}$ based on group element h_2. Using $\mathsf{uft}_{(\mathcal{V}), h_2}$ and h_2, any adversary can query the database of $\mathcal{V}$ without authorized token from $\mathcal{V}$. We define a universal forged token as $\mathsf{uft}_{(\mathcal{V}), h_2} = (h_2^{a_{(\mathcal{V})}^{-1}}, h_2^{b_{(\mathcal{V})}})$ in our attack. We introduce it as follows:

Step 1: The user $\mathcal{V}$ creates authorization token $\text{tok}_{(\mathcal{M} \to \mathcal{V})}$ by using (type-2) DERE.Token algorithm[1] in Fig. 2 and sends it to user $\mathcal{M}$ as below:

$$\text{tok}_{(\mathcal{M} \to \mathcal{V})} = \left(F\left(\text{pk}_{(\mathcal{M})}^{a_{(\mathcal{V})}}\right)^{a_{(\mathcal{V})}^{-1}}, F\left(\text{pk}_{(\mathcal{M})}^{a_{(\mathcal{V})}}\right)^{b_{(\mathcal{V})}} \right)$$

Step 2: After $\mathcal{M}$ receives it, $\mathcal{M}$ randomly picks $r \xleftarrow{\$} \mathbb{Z}_p$ and sets a group element $h_2 = F(\text{pk}_{(\mathcal{V})}^{a_{(\mathcal{M})}})^r$. And then $\mathcal{M}$ computes a universal forged token $\text{uft}_{(\mathcal{V}), h_2}$ as following:

$$\text{uft}_{(\mathcal{V}), h_2} = \text{tok}_{(\mathcal{M} \to \mathcal{V})}^r = \left(\left(F(\text{pk}_{(\mathcal{M})}^{a_{(\mathcal{V})}})^r\right)^{a_{(\mathcal{V})}^{-1}}, \left(F(\text{pk}_{(\mathcal{M})}^{a_{(\mathcal{V})}})^r\right)^{b_{(\mathcal{V})}} \right)$$

After then, $\mathcal{M}$ sends h_2 and $\text{uft}_{(\mathcal{V}), h_2}$ to $\mathcal{A}$. Note that $\mathcal{M}$ can compute $\text{uft}_{(\mathcal{V}), h_2}$ by symmetric property $\text{pk}_{(\mathcal{M})}^{a_{(\mathcal{V})}} = g_2^{a_{\mathcal{V}} a_{\mathcal{M}}} = \text{pk}_{(\mathcal{V})}^{a_{(\mathcal{M})}}$. Since h_2 is randomized by $\mathcal{M}$'s randomness r, $(h_2, \text{uft}_{(\mathcal{V}), h_2}) \in \mathbb{G}_2^3$ look like uniformly random in the view of $\mathcal{A}$. By DL assumption, it is intractable for the $\mathcal{A}$ to find $\mathcal{M}$'s secret key $(a_{(\mathcal{M})}, b_{(\mathcal{M})})$ from h_2 and $\text{uft}_{(\mathcal{V}), h_2}$. For this reason, $\mathcal{M}$ may help adversary $\mathcal{A}$ without concern about leaking $\mathcal{M}$'s secret.

Step 3: After receiving $(h_2, \text{uft}_{(\mathcal{V}), h_2})$, $\mathcal{A}$ samples $\text{sk}_{(\mathcal{A})} = (a_{(\mathcal{A})}, b_{(\mathcal{A})}) \xleftarrow{\$} \mathbb{Z}_p^2$. And it computes the counterpart forged token $\text{uft}_{(\mathcal{A}), h_2}$ as follows:

$$\text{uft}_{(\mathcal{A}), h_2} = (h_2^{a_{(\mathcal{A})}^{-1}}, h_2^{b_{(\mathcal{A})}})$$

For the query, $\mathcal{A}$ generates $\text{ct}_{(\mathcal{A})} \leftarrow \text{DERE.Enc}(\text{pp}, m, \text{sk}_{(\mathcal{A})})$ using her secret key $(a_{(\mathcal{A})}, b_{(\mathcal{A})})$ and then use a pair of forged tokens $\text{uft}_{(\mathcal{A}), h_2}$ and $\text{uft}_{(\mathcal{V}), h_2}$.

For a given message m, let us denote the victim's ciphertext as $\text{ct}_{(\mathcal{V})} = ((g_1^{b_{(\mathcal{V})} r_{(\mathcal{V})}} H(m))^{a_{(\mathcal{V})}}, g_1^{r_{(\mathcal{V})}})$. Then we can get $\text{DERE.Test}(\text{ct}_{(\mathcal{V})}, \text{ct}_{(\mathcal{A})}, \text{uft}_{(\mathcal{V}), h_2}, \text{uft}_{(\mathcal{A}), h_2}) = 1$ by the following equations: For $i = 0, 1$, $\alpha_0 = \mathcal{V}$ and $\alpha_1 = \mathcal{A}$,

$$d_i = \frac{e(c_{(\alpha_i)}^0, \text{uft}_{(\alpha_i), h_2}^0)}{e(c_{(\alpha_i)}^1, \text{uft}_{(\alpha_i), h_2}^1)} = \frac{e((g_1^{b_{(\alpha_i)} r_{(\alpha_i)}} H(m))^{a_{(\alpha_i)}}, h_2^{a_{(\alpha_i)}^{-1}})}{e(g_1^{r_{(\alpha_i)}}, h_2^{b_{(\alpha_i)}})}$$

$$= \frac{e(g_1^{b_{(\alpha_i)} r_{(\alpha_i)}} H(m), h_2)}{e(g_1^{b_{(\alpha_i)} r_{(\alpha_i)}}, h_2)} = e(H(m), h_2).$$

In other words, $\mathcal{A}$ can be identified as equality between $\text{ct}_{(\mathcal{V})}$ and $\text{ct}_{(\mathcal{A})}$ plaintexts by the Test algorithm without the authorized token. The universal token reusability attack can also be applied to EDORE, but we defer the attack to the full version [23] due to space limitations.

---

[1] If the map F is the identity map on $\mathbb{G}_2$, type-2 DERE scheme becomes identical to the type-1 DERE scheme. Thus, the following attack against the type-2 DERE scheme can naturally be applied to the type-1 DERE scheme.

4.2 Limitation of Security Analysis in [14].

In [14], the authors proposed a soundness game to evaluate the resilience of SEDORE against token forgery attacks. In this game, the adversary aims to construct a *forged token* $\mathsf{tok}^*_{(\mathcal{C} \to \mathcal{A})}$ which, when used with a valid token $\mathsf{tok}_{(\mathcal{A} \to \mathcal{C})}$ generated by DERE.Token, yields a valid result under DERE.Test in Fig. 2. They incorporated cryptographic hash functions into the token generation to ensure soundness, making it computationally infeasible to construct $\mathsf{tok}^*_{(\mathcal{C} \to \mathcal{A})}$.

However, the structure of the soundness game limits the capabilities of the adversary. In practice, an adversary may generate a pair of forged tokens $(\mathsf{tok}^*_{(\mathcal{V} \to \mathcal{A})}, \mathsf{tok}^*_{(\mathcal{A} \to \mathcal{V})})$, that deviate from the expected structure in Fig. 2. Although the protocol assumes that only properly generated token pairs can be used to query the database, our findings from the attack described above demonstrate that even malformed tokens can still produce valid results under the DERE.Test algorithm. Therefore, the soundness definition in [14] should be revised to account for such adversarial behavior.

The main reason for this vulnerability is that the DERE.Test algorithm does not verify the validity of tokens by itself. Therefore, before executing the test, the server (i.e., the tester) must ensure that the tokens were genuinely issued by authorized users and have not been forged.

5 Verifiable DORE (VDORE) and Token Unforgeability

As we mentioned in Sect. 4, the tester should check the validity of the tokens to prevent universal token reusability attacks. To give a verifiability on DORE scheme (Section 3.2), we revise the Keygen algorithm to output verification key vk and we newly propose a verification algorithm Vfy. We define a verifiable DORE scheme VDORE := (Setup, Keygen, Enc, Token, Test, Vfy) as follows:

- pp ← VDORE.Setup(1^λ): It takes the security parameter 1^λ as input and returns the public parameter pp.
- (pk, sk) ← DORE.Keygen(pp): It takes a public parameter as input and returns a key tuple of public key, verification key, and secret key, (pk, vk, sk). The verification key is used to verify the validity of tokens. Both pk and vk may be managed publicly, but sk should be managed privately.
- ct ← VDORE.Enc(pp, m, sk): It takes a message $m \in \{0,1\}^*$ and sk as input and returns a ciphertext ct.
- $\mathsf{tok}_{(v \to u)}$ ← VDORE.Token(pp, $\mathsf{pk}_{(v)}$, $\mathsf{sk}_{(u)}$): It takes the public key $\mathsf{pk}_{(v)}$ of user v and the secret key $\mathsf{sk}_{(u)}$ of user u as input and returns an authorization token $\mathsf{tok}_{(v \to u)}$, indicating that user v is authorized by user u.
- res ← VDORE.Test(pp, $\mathsf{ct}_{(u)}$, $\mathsf{ct}_{(v)}$, $\mathsf{tok}_{(v \to u)}$, $\mathsf{tok}_{(u \to v)}$): It takes the two ciphertext $\mathsf{ct}_{(u)}$ and $\mathsf{ct}_{(v)}$, along with two tokens, $\mathsf{tok}_{(v \to u)}$ and $\mathsf{tok}_{(u \to v)}$, as input and returns the comparison result $res \in \{-1, 0, 1\}$. The output values represent the following: 1 indicates $m_u > m_v$, 0 indicates $m_u = m_v$, and -1 indicates $m_u < m_v$, where $m_\square$ denotes the plaintext of $\mathsf{ct}_{(\square)}$ for $\square = u, v$.

1. **Setting Phase**: $\mathcal{C}$ runs the setup algorithm $\mathsf{pp} \leftarrow \mathsf{Setup}(1^\lambda)$ and the key generation algorithm $(\mathsf{sk}_{(\mathcal{C})}, \mathsf{vk}_{(\mathcal{C})}, \mathsf{pk}_{(\mathcal{C})}) \leftarrow \mathsf{Keygen}(\mathsf{pp})$. It then sends $(\mathsf{pp}, \mathsf{vk}_{(\mathcal{C})}, \mathsf{pk}_{(\mathcal{C})})$ to $\mathcal{A}$ and keeps $\mathsf{sk}_{(\mathcal{C})}$ local storage.
2. **Query Phase**: $\mathcal{A}$ can query to $\mathcal{C}$:
   (a) **Key Query**: $\mathcal{A}$ sends a query with index i. Upon receiving the query, $\mathcal{C}$ checks whether $(i, \mathsf{pk}_{(i)}, \mathsf{vk}_{(i)}) \in S_{\mathsf{key}}$. If so, it returns $(i, \mathsf{pk}_{(i)}, \mathsf{vk}_{(i)})$ to $\mathcal{A}$. Otherwise, it generates a new key triple by running $(\mathsf{pk}_{(i)}, \mathsf{vk}_{(i)}, \mathsf{sk}_{(i)}) \leftarrow \mathsf{Keygen}(\mathsf{pp})$, returns $(\mathsf{pk}_{(i)}, \mathsf{vk}_{(i)})$ to $\mathcal{A}$, and adds the tuple $(i, \mathsf{pk}_{(i)}, \mathsf{vk}_{(i)})$ to the key query set S_{key}.
   (b) **Token Query**: If $\mathcal{A}$ sends a query with a received public key $\mathsf{pk}_{(i)} \in S_{\mathsf{key}}$, $\mathcal{C}$ generates an authorized token $\mathsf{tok}_{(i \to \mathcal{C})} \leftarrow \mathsf{Token}(\mathsf{pp}, \mathsf{pk}_{(i)}, \mathsf{sk}_{(\mathcal{C})})$ and then sends $\mathsf{tok}_{(i \to \mathcal{C})}$ to $\mathcal{A}$ and adds $\mathsf{tok}_{(i \to \mathcal{C})}$ to token query set S_{tok}.
   (c) **One-way function Query**: If $\mathcal{A}$ sends a query with index i and one-way function f, $\mathcal{C}$ output $f(\mathsf{sk}_{(i)})$.
3. **Challenge Phase**: $\mathcal{A}$ outputs a verification key $\mathsf{vk}^*_{(\mathcal{A})}$ and a pair of tokens $(\mathsf{tok}^*_{(\mathcal{C} \to \mathcal{A})}, \mathsf{tok}^*_{(\mathcal{A} \to \mathcal{C})})$. The $\mathcal{A}$ wins if $\mathsf{Vfy}(\mathsf{pp}, \mathsf{vk}_{(\mathcal{C})}, \mathsf{vk}^*_{(\mathcal{A})}, \mathsf{tok}^*_{(\mathcal{A} \to \mathcal{C})}, \mathsf{tok}^*_{(\mathcal{C} \to \mathcal{A})}) = 1$.

Fig. 3. Token forging Game.

- $0 \backslash 1 \leftarrow \boxed{\mathsf{VDORE.Vfy}(\mathsf{pp}, \mathsf{vk}_{(u)}, \mathsf{vk}_{(v)}, \mathsf{tok}_{(v \to u)}, \mathsf{tok}_{(u \to v)})}$: It takes the two verification keys $\mathsf{vk}_{(u)}$ and $\mathsf{vk}_{(v)}$, and two tokens $\mathsf{tok}_{(v \to u)}$ and $\mathsf{tok}_{(u \to v)}$ as input. If both tokens $\mathsf{tok}_{(v \to u)}$ and $\mathsf{tok}_{(u \to v)}$ go through (token validity) verification, it returns 1 (accept); otherwise, it returns 0 (reject).

To ensure a secure VDORE scheme, we consider three properties: *correctness*, *data privacy*, and *token unforgeability*.

Correctness. The correctness of VDORE ensures that the test algorithm accurately discerns the sequence of two ciphertexts provided by two mutually authenticated users. Let $(m_{(u)}, m_{(v)})$ be a pair of messages, $(\mathsf{pk}_{(u)}, \mathsf{vk}_{(u)}, \mathsf{sk}_{(u)})$, $(\mathsf{pk}_{(v)}, \mathsf{vk}_{(v)}, \mathsf{sk}_{(v)})$ be a pair of keys generated by Keygen algorithm, and $\mathsf{ct}_{(u)}$, $\mathsf{ct}_{(v)}$ be a ciphertext of $m_{(u)}$ and $m_{(v)}$ with key $\mathsf{sk}_{(u)}$ and $\mathsf{sk}_{(v)}$ respectively. We say VDORE scheme is correct if for any pair of messages $(m_{(u)}, m_{(v)})$ and keys $(\mathsf{pk}_{(u)}, \mathsf{vk}_{(u)}, \mathsf{sk}_{(u)})$, $(\mathsf{pk}_{(v)}, \mathsf{vk}_{(v)}, \mathsf{sk}_{(v)})$, the following holds:

- $\mathsf{VDORE.Vfy}(\mathsf{pp}, \mathsf{vk}_{(u)}, \mathsf{vk}_{(v)}, \mathsf{tok}_{(v \to u)}, \mathsf{tok}_{(u \to v)}) = 1$
- $\mathsf{VDORE.Test}(\mathsf{pp}, \mathsf{ct}_{(u)}, \mathsf{ct}_{(v)}, \mathsf{tok}_{(v \to u)}, \mathsf{tok}_{(u \to v)}) = res$
  - If $m_{(u)} > m_{(v)}$, then $res = 1$
  - If $m_{(u)} < m_{(v)}$, then $res = -1$
  - Otherwise, $res = 0$

Data Privacy. The data privacy of VDORE ensures that the ciphertexts ct generated by Enc algorithm do not leak information except order. VDORE provides data privacy if Enc algorithm satisfies indistinguishability under an ordered chosen plaintext attack (IND-OCPA) [16].

Token Unforgeability. Vfy algorithm of the VDORE scheme should detect forged tokens. To give provable security, we propose a new definition of token unforgeability. First, we construct a token forging game to give a game-based security. We describe the roles of adversary and challenger in Fig. 3.

We denote the $\mathcal{A}$'s advantage to the token forging game of VDORE scheme(or Vdere scheme) $\mathsf{Adv}^{\mathsf{TF}}[\mathcal{A}, \mathsf{VDORE}]$(or $\mathsf{Adv}^{\mathsf{TF}}[\mathcal{A}, \mathsf{VDERE}]$), which is a probability that $\mathcal{A}$ wins the token forging game under the VDORE(or VDERE) scheme.

Definition 1 (Token Unforgeability). *Let* (Setup, Keygen, Enc, Token, Test, Vfy) *be a* VDORE *(or* VDERE*) scheme. We say that* VDORE *(or* VDERE*) satisfies token unforgeability if for any PPT adversary $\mathcal{A}$ against token forging game in Fig. 3, the $\mathcal{A}$'s advantage to the game* $\mathsf{Adv}^{\mathsf{TF}}[\mathcal{A}, \mathsf{VDORE}]$ *(or* $\mathsf{Adv}^{\mathsf{TF}}[\mathcal{A}, \mathsf{VDERE}]$*) is less than* $\mathsf{negl}(\lambda)$.

Token Forging Game and Attack Scenario. In this paragraph, we explain the relationship between the token forging game and the attack scenario. The key pair $(\mathsf{pk}_{(\mathcal{C})}, \mathsf{vk}_{(\mathcal{C})})$ sent by $\mathcal{C}$ represents the public and verification keys of the victim $\mathcal{V}$. Note that other users, including the adversary, may know the public key $\mathsf{pk}_{(\mathcal{V})}$ and verification key $\mathsf{vk}_{(\mathcal{V})}$ of $\mathcal{V}$.

After that, we allow the adversary $\mathcal{A}$ to make three types of queries: key queries, token queries, and one-way function queries. Through key and token queries, $\mathcal{A}$ can obtain multiple public and verification keys along with their corresponding authorized tokens—representing resources obtained from colluding users. Additionally, we allow $\mathcal{A}$ to make one-way function queries to obtain specific values derived from the secret keys of colluding users. Due to the one-wayness of the function, it remains computationally hard for $\mathcal{A}$ to recover the secret key from the output, thereby modeling feasible collusion scenarios without revealing the users' secret keys.

The goal of $\mathcal{A}$ is to find a pair of forged tokens that successfully pass the verification algorithm Vfy. The difficulty of producing such a pair directly corresponds to the difficulty of forging tokens. Therefore, our definition of token unforgeability captures the security of the scheme against token forgery attacks.

Comparison with the Attack Game in [14]. As discussed in Sect. 4, the security game should account for a broader class of adversarial strategies. To this end, our token-forging game in Fig. 3 allows the adversary to output an arbitrary pair of tokens, $(\mathsf{tok}^*_{(\mathcal{A} \to \mathcal{C})}, \mathsf{tok}^*_{(\mathcal{C} \to \mathcal{A})})$. In contrast, the soundness game in [14] only allows the adversary to output a forged token $\mathsf{tok}^*_{(\mathcal{A} \to \mathcal{C})}$ corresponding to a given valid token $\mathsf{tok}_{(\mathcal{C} \to \mathcal{A})}$, which fails to capture the UTRA attack.

Furthermore, by incorporating a verification algorithm Vfy, we revise the adversary's winning condition—from obtaining a valid output from the test algorithm Test to receiving an acceptance from Vfy. To analyze previous schemes such as DORE and SEDORE within our framework, one can adapt the winning condition in the token-forging game accordingly: replacing acceptance from Vfy with the ability to obtain a valid output from Test. For further details, please refer to the full version [23].

6 TUDORE: Token Unforgeable DORE

In this section, we first construct our novel VDERE scheme TUDERE. And then, following the framework in [16], we complete the TUDORE scheme by using the TUDERE scheme. One of the main concerns is how to construct a verification algorithm. To guarantee token unforgeability, we apply digital signature schemes.

6.1 Signature Schemes Compatible with DERE Scheme.

A digital signature is a cryptographic scheme for the authenticity of digital messages. A valid digital signature on a message gives a recipient confidence that the message came from a sender known to the recipient. In our scenario, a signature scheme can give a token validity due to its unforgeability property. Signature schemes consists of four algorithms Sig = (Setup, Keygen, Sign, Verify) as follows:

- $pp_{sig} \leftarrow$ Sig.Setup(λ): This algorithm takes the security parameter λ as input and returns the public parameter pp_{sig}.
- $(vk_{sig}, sk_{sig}) \leftarrow$ Sig.Keygen(pp_{sig}): It takes a public parameter as input and outputs a key tuple of signing key sk_{sig} and verifying key vk_{sig}.
- $\sigma \leftarrow$ Sig.Sign(pp_{sig}, sk_{sig}, m): It takes public parameter pp_{sig}, signing key sk_{sig} and message as input and outputs signature σ.
- $0\backslash 1 \leftarrow$ Sig.Verify($pp_{sig}, vk_{sig}, m, \sigma$): It takes public parameter pp_{sig}, the verifying key vk_{sig} , message m, and signature σ as input. If the signature is valid, it returns 1; otherwise, it returns 0.

DERE scheme in Fig. 2 utilize discrete logarithmic (DL)-related keys: $pk = g_2^a$ and $sk = (a, b)$. To utilize the secret key as a signing key, we consider signature schemes with DL-related keys, e.g. Schnorr's signature [27] and BLS signature [7]. Concretely, both signature schemes utilize the signing key $sk_{sig} = b$ and verification key $vk_{sig} = g_1^b$. Furthermore, both schemes satisfy existential unforgeability under chosen message attack (EUF-CMA). For more details about both signature schemes, please refer to the full version [23].

6.2 Construct TUDORE Using Signature Scheme

By combining type-1 DERE scheme in Fig. 2 with signature schemes Sig, we construct a token unforgeable DORE scheme: TUDERE = (Setup, Keygen, Enc, Token, Test, Vfy). The main difference between DERE and TUDERE lie in Keygen, Token, and Vfy. In Keygen, an additional token verification key $vk = g_1^b$ is generated. The Token algorithm outputs a token that includes a signature. Finally, the Vfy algorithm checks the token using the verification algorithm of the signature scheme Sig. We describe TUDERE in Fig. 4.

In a similar way in the DERE-to-DORE framework [16], we construct TUDORE scheme using TUDERE scheme in Fig. 4; iteratively running Enc and Test algorithms but keeping other algorithms of TUDERE. We describe the scheme TUDORE in Fig. 6 in the Appendix.

- pp ← TUDERE.Setup(1^λ): This algorithm takes the security parameter 1^λ as input and returns the public parameter pp = $(\langle p, \mathbb{G}_1, \mathbb{G}_2, g_1, g_2, \mathbb{G}_T, e \rangle, H, T)$. Additionally, it sets pp$_{sig}$:= $(\langle p, \mathbb{G}_1, g_1 \rangle, T)$.
- (pk, vk , sk) ← TUDERE.Keygen(pp): This algorithm takes the public parameter pp as input and randomly chooses $a, b \stackrel{\$}{\leftarrow} \mathbb{Z}_p$. After that, it returns a tuple of keys as sk = (a, b), pk = g_2^a, and vk = g_1^b. Additionally, it sets signature keys as sk$_{sig}$:= b, and vk$_{sig}$:= vk.
- ct ← TUDERE.Enc(pp, m, sk): This algorithm takes a public parameter pp, a message $m \in \{0,1\}^*$, and sk = $(a, b) \in \mathbb{Z}_p^2$ as input and randomly picks $r \stackrel{\$}{\leftarrow} \mathbb{Z}_p$ and computes c^0 and c^1 as below:

$$c^0 = \left(g_1^{rb} H(m) \right)^a, \quad c^1 = g_1^r.$$

Finally, it returns $ct = (c^0, c^1)$.
- tok$_{(u \to v)}$ ← TUDERE.Token(pp, pk$_{(u)}$, sk$_{(v)}$): This algorithm takes the public key pk$_{(u)} \in \mathbb{G}_2$ of u and the secret key sk$_{(v)} = (a_{(v)}, b_{(v)}) \in \mathbb{Z}_p^2$ of v as input and returns the token tok$_{(u \to v)} = (t^0_{(u \to v)}, t^1_{(u \to v)}, \boxed{\sigma_v})$ as follows:

$$t^0_{(u \to v)} = \mathsf{pk}_{(u)}, \quad t^1_{(u \to v)} = \mathsf{pk}_{(u)}^{a_{(v)} b_{(v)}}$$
$$\sigma_v \leftarrow \mathsf{Sig.Sign}(\mathsf{pp}_{sig}, \mathsf{sk}_{sig,(v)}, (t^0_{(u \to v)}, t^1_{(u \to v)}))$$

- 0\1 ← TUDERE.Test(pp, ct$_{(u)}$, ct$_{(v)}$, tok$_{(v \to u)}$, tok$_{(u \to v)}$):
This algorithm takes the two ciphertexts and tokens for u and v and computes

$$d_0 = \frac{e\left(c^0_{(u)}, t^0_{(v \to u)}\right)}{e\left(c^1_{(u)}, t^1_{(v \to u)}\right)}, \quad d_1 = \frac{e\left(c^0_{(v)}, t^0_{(u \to v)}\right)}{e\left(c^1_{(v)}, t^1_{(u \to v)}\right)}$$

Finally, it compares d_0 and d_1, and if $d_0 = d_1$, it returns 1 and 0 otherwise.
- 0\1 ← TUDERE.Vfy(pp, vk$_{(u)}$, vk$_{(v)}$, tok$_{(v \to u)}$, tok$_{(u \to v)}$): This algorithm takes a public parameter pp, a pair of verification keys vk$_{(u)}$, vk$_{(v)}$ and tokens tok$_{(u \to v)}$, tok$_{(v \to u)}$. It parses tok$_{(u \to v)}$ and tok$_{(v \to u)}$ to $((t^0_{(u \to v)}, t^1_{(u \to v)}), \sigma_v)$ and $((t^0_{(v \to u)}, t^1_{(v \to u)}), \sigma_u)$ respectively. Then, run verification algorithms as follows:
  - $res_v \leftarrow \mathsf{Sig.Vfy}(\mathsf{pp}_{sig}, \mathsf{vk}_{(v)}, (t^0_{(u \to v)}, t^1_{(u \to v)}), \sigma_v)$
  - $res_u \leftarrow \mathsf{Sig.Vfy}(\mathsf{pp}_{sig}, \mathsf{vk}_{(u)}, (t^0_{(v \to u)}, t^1_{(v \to u)}), \sigma_u)$
  If $res_v = res_u = 1$, then it outputs 1. Otherwise, outputs 0.

Fig. 4. TUDERE Scheme.

6.3 Security Analysis

In [16], the authors provided a security proof for the correctness and IND-OCPA for the DORE scheme in the GGM. With the proof in [16] and the EUF-CMA signature scheme, we can conclude the following theorem.

Theorem 1. *Assume H and T are modeled as a random oracle and Sig is an EUF-CMA signature scheme. Then, the TUDORE scheme (Fig. 6) under*

Table 1. A comparative analysis for element and n-bit comparison

Schemes	Storage cost		Computational Cost			
	Enc	Token	Enc	Test	Token	Vfy
DORE [16]	$4n|\mathbb{G}_1|$	$2|\mathbb{G}_2|$	$6nE_{\mathbb{G}_1}$	$8nP_{\mathbb{G}_T}$	$E_{\mathbb{G}_2}$	×
SEDORE [14]	$4n|\mathbb{G}_1|$	$2|\mathbb{G}_2|$	$6nE_{\mathbb{G}_1}$	$8nP_{\mathbb{G}_T}$	$3E_{\mathbb{G}_2}$	×
EDORE [31]	$4n|\mathbb{Z}_p| + 2n|\mathbb{G}_2|$	$2|\mathbb{G}_1|$	$2nE_{\mathbb{G}_2}$	$8nE_{\mathbb{G}_1} + 4nP_{\mathbb{G}_T}$	$3E_{\mathbb{G}_1}$	×
TUDORE (Schnorr)	$4n|\mathbb{G}_1|$	$1|\mathbb{G}_1| + 2|\mathbb{G}_2| + 1|\mathbb{Z}_p|$	$6nE_{\mathbb{G}_1}$	$8nP_{\mathbb{G}_T}$	$E_{\mathbb{G}_1} + E_{\mathbb{G}_2}$	$4E_{\mathbb{G}_1}$
TUDORE (BLS)	$4n|\mathbb{G}_1|$	$1|\mathbb{G}_1| + 2|\mathbb{G}_2|$	$6nE_{\mathbb{G}_1}$	$8nP_{\mathbb{G}_T}$	$E_{\mathbb{G}_1} + E_{\mathbb{G}_2}$	$4P_{\mathbb{G}_T}$

$|\mathbb{G}_i|$: size of a group element in $\mathbb{G}_i$, $|\mathbb{Z}_p|$: size of a field element in $\mathbb{Z}_p$,
$E_{\mathbb{G}_i}$: group exponentiation on $\mathbb{G}_i$, $P_{\mathbb{G}_T}$: bilinear pairing operation,
× indicates the Verification algorithm is not available.

the TUDERE scheme (Fig. 4) satisfies the correctness, data privacy, and token unforgeability under the generic group model.

Proof Sketch. *(Correctness)* The correctness of TUDERE holds in the similar way of [16]. Concretely, for a valid token and ciphertext, the intermediate values d_0 and d_1 of Test should be equal by the bilinearity of the pairing operation. Additionally, from the correctness of the signature scheme, Vfy should output 1 so that TUDERE satisfies the correctness. Since TUDORE.Test consists of several correct TUDERE.Test algorithms, it follows that TUDORE satisfies correctness.
(Data privacy) Since our underlying encryption algorithm is the same as DERE [16], we can prove IND-OCPA in a similar way in [16]. Since DORE encryption underlying the DERE scheme satisfies IND-OCPA in the generic group model, our TUDORE encryption underlying the TUDERE scheme satisfies IND-OCPA. Therefore, our TUDORE scheme satisfies Data privacy.
(Token Unforgeability) Because the Vfy algorithm contains sign verification, TUDERE satisfies the token unforgeability of the EUF-CMA signature scheme.

Concretely, to complete the proof, we construct an EUF-CMA adversary $\mathcal{B}$ using the token forgeability adversary $\mathcal{A}$. To simulate the token query of $\mathcal{A}$, we should restrict $\mathcal{A}$ not get the public key locally. Since the public keys consist of group elements and the adversary does not get the group element itself in GGM, we ensure $\mathcal{A}$ does not get an arbitrary token $\mathsf{tok}_{(i \to \mathcal{C})}$ without the corresponding key query for $\mathsf{pk}_{(i)}$. Therefore, we claim that TUDERE satisfies token unforgeability if the underlying signature scheme satisfies EUF-CMA. For the complete proof, please refer to the full version [23]. □

7 Performance

7.1 Theoretical Performance

In Table 1, we present a comparative analysis of storage and computational costs, where the left side (group elements) shows storage costs and the right side (group/pairings) shows computational costs. Since the Enc and Test algorithms in SEDORE and TUDORE are identical to those in DORE, their performance remains the same. EDORE improves efficiency by reducing the number of group elements and pairing operations. TUDORE increases the token size due to the use of Schnorr or BLS signatures, reflecting a trade-off between security and efficiency. For the Token algorithm, DORE requires only a single group exponentiation, while SEDORE and EDORE require three, and TUDORE requires two. Consequently, TUDORE is approximately twice as slow as DORE, but 1.5× faster than both SEDORE and EDORE.

Notably, only TUDORE includes a verification algorithm that ensures token unforgeability. Verifying Schnorr and BLS signatures requires four exponentiations and four pairings, respectively. Based on their priorities, users can choose the scheme that best balances token size and computational efficiency.

7.2 Implementation and Performance.

In this section, we present the implementation results of token-based DORE schemes: DORE, SEDORE, EDORE, and our proposed TUDORE.

Environment. To ensure realistic evaluation, we conducted experiments in two environments: a server (Linux desktop with a 5.20 GHz Intel i9-12900K CPU and 64GB RAM for testing and verification) and a user device (Linux laptop with a 1.4 GHz AMD Ryzen 7 4700U CPU and 16GB RAM for token generation). We implemented TUDORE and the baseline schemes for comparison. Our implementation uses OpenSSL for hashing, the PBC library (in C) with the MNT224 curve for bilinear maps [18], and the GMP library for large integer arithmetic. For the verification algorithm, we adopt both Schnorr and BLS signatures [7,27], allowing users to select based on their computational environment.

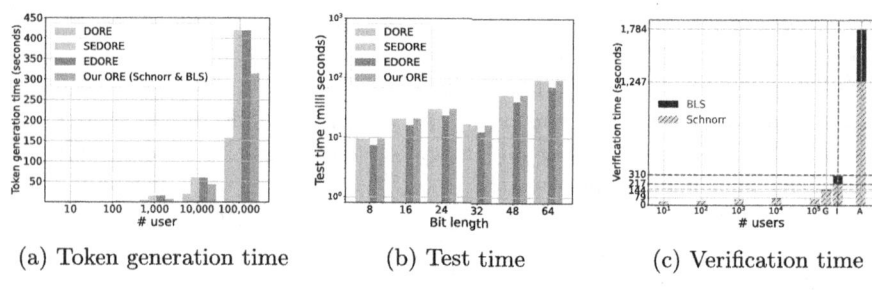

(a) Token generation time (b) Test time (c) Verification time

Fig. 5. The performance graphs for DORE, SEDORE, and our TUDORE.

Dataset. We utilize the dataset from the United Nations [29], which provides population estimates across five-year age groups. However, due to its limited range, we also incorporate real stock volume data from FAANG companies [21]. We use 10,000 samples for our experiments, comprising 5,000 from each dataset.

Token Generation Time. We compare the token generation time for issuing tokens to different numbers of users (10, 100, 1,000, 10,000, and 100,000). As shown in Fig. 5a , SEDORE and EDORE take approximately 3 times longer than DORE, while TUDORE is about 1.5 times faster than SEDORE and EDORE. Therefore, our method improves both security and token generation efficiency.

Test Time. As shown in Fig. 5b and consistent with Table 1, in each dataset, the computational time increases linearly with the bit size due to paddings. The test times for DORE, SEDORE, and TUDORE are identical, while EDORE is the fastest. Moreover, it can be observed that the computational time at 32 bits is faster than that at 16 and 24 bits. This is because the order in the 32-bit dataset is determined by the bits closer to the most significant bit (MSB).

Verification Time. We evaluate the verification algorithm using Schnorr and BLS signatures [7,27] across varying user counts (10, 100, 1,000, 10,000, and 100,000). To assess real-world applicability, we simulate cloud service provider (CSP) environments based on employee numbers at Google (182,502) [2], Amazon (1,608,000) [1], and IBM (282,200) [3]. Figure 5c shows that verification times with 100,000 users are 79 s / 84 s (Schnorr / BLS). In CSP-scale scenarios, the times are 144 s / 164 s for Google, 217 s / 310 s for IBM, and 1,247 s / 1,783 s (20.8min / 29.7min) for Amazon. Despite Amazon's high total time, the amortized cost remains low at 0.77ms / 1.1ms, demonstrating practical efficiency.

Range Query and Test Algorithm. From the token-based DORE query via the test algorithm, one can obtain the order information, whether a value is less than or greater than the encrypted data. Leveraging this property, a range query can be implemented by performing the DORE test twice for a single encrypted value, separately comparing the encrypted value against the lower and upper query. Although we do not directly evaluate range queries, their cost can be inferred from our experiments with the DORE scheme. Since each range query involves two comparisons per encrypted data point, the cost per encrypted value is approximately twice that of a single test execution.

8 Conclusion

We demonstrate the vulnerability of DORE, SEDORE, and EDORE within the identical threat model of token forgeability, as suggested by [14]. Although SEDORE and EDORE aim to achieve the token unforgeability property, we identify that both schemes are still vulnerable. To illustrate this vulnerability, we propose an attack strategy called the universal token reusability attack under the same threat model. From the attack, SEDORE and EDORE remain vulnerable to token forgery. To address these security concerns, we propose the VDORE with an enhanced security notion. We introduce TUDORE, which leverages the Schnorr and BLS signature schemes to prevent universal token reusability attacks. We provide a formalized definition and proof to clarify the unclear definitions and proofs of token unforgeability in previous work. Moreover, our scheme offers a faster token generation algorithm than SEDORE and EDORE.

Since the ORE scheme itself aims to compare numerical values, the input data is limited to numerical datasets. However, to apply it to various applications with other types, one can consider an appropriate encoding/decoding process to convert the data type to a numerical type. Additionally, considering the significance of range queries, exploring the integration of TUDORE-based range queries into real-world applications remains an important direction. We leave these as future work.

Acknowledgments. This research was supported in part by the Institute of Information and Communications Technology Planning and Evaluation (IITP), grant funded by the Korea Government (MSIT) (No.2022-0-00411, 50% & RS-2021-II210727, 40%), in part by Culture, Sports and Tourism R&D Program through the Korea Creative Content Agency grant funded by the Ministry of Culture, Sports and Tourism (RS-2024-00332210, 10%), the NSF (2335798), and the Tennessee Department of Economic and Community Development.

A Deffered Figures

A.1 TUDORE from the TUDERE

Following the DERE-to-DORE framework, we construct TUDORE from TUDERE as shown in Fig. 4. The conversion process is described in the following figure.

- $pp \leftarrow \mathsf{TUDORE.Setup}(1^\lambda)$: With the inputs, run TUDERE.Setup algorithm and output pp.
- $(\mathsf{pk}, \mathsf{vk}, \mathsf{sk}) \leftarrow \mathsf{TUDORE.Keygen}(\mathsf{pp})$: With the inputs, run TUDERE.Keygen(pp) algorithm and output $(\mathsf{pk}, \mathsf{vk}, \mathsf{vk})$.
- $\mathsf{tok}_{(u \to v)} \leftarrow \mathsf{TUDORE.Token}(\mathsf{pp}, \mathsf{pk}_{(u)}, \mathsf{sk}_{(v)})$: With the inputs, run TUDERE.Token algorithm and output $\mathsf{tok}_{(u \to v)}$.
- $0 \backslash 1 \leftarrow \mathsf{TUDERE.Vfy}(\mathsf{pp}, \mathsf{vk}_{(u)}, \mathsf{vk}_{(v)}, \mathsf{tok}_{(v \to u)}, \mathsf{tok}_{(u \to v)})$: With the inputs, run TUDERE.Vfy algorithm and output decision bit $0 \backslash 1$.
- $\mathsf{ct} \leftarrow \mathsf{TUDORE.Enc}(\mathsf{pp}, m, \mathsf{sk})$: It takes a message $m \in \{0, 1\}^*$ and sk as input. It encrypts message bit encodings $\epsilon(m_i, a)$, which is defined as $\epsilon(m_i, a) = (i, m_1 m_2 \ldots m_i || 0^{n-i}, a)$ for $a \in \{0, 1, 2\}$, as follows:
  If $m_i = 0$, it computes ciphertexts $\mathsf{ct}[i] = (\mathsf{ct}[i, 0], \mathsf{ct}[i, 1])$ as follows:

  $\mathsf{ct}[i, 0] = \mathsf{TUDERE.Enc}(\mathsf{pp}, \epsilon(m_i, 0), \mathsf{sk})$, $\mathsf{ct}[i, 1] = \mathsf{TUDERE.Enc}(\mathsf{pp}, \epsilon(m_i, 1), \mathsf{sk})$.

  Else if $m_i = 1$, it computes ciphertexts $\mathsf{ct}[i] = (\mathsf{ct}[i, 0], \mathsf{ct}[i, 1])$ as follows:

  $\mathsf{ct}[i, 0] = \mathsf{TUDERE.Enc}(\mathsf{pp}, \epsilon(m_i, 1), \mathsf{sk})$, $\mathsf{ct}[i, 1] = \mathsf{TUDERE.Enc}(\mathsf{pp}, \epsilon(m_i, 2), \mathsf{sk})$.

  Finally, this algorithm returns $\mathsf{ct} = (\mathsf{ct}[1], \ldots \mathsf{ct}[n])$.
- $res \leftarrow \mathsf{TUDORE.Test}(\mathsf{pp}, \mathsf{ct}_{(u)}, \mathsf{ct}_{(v)}, \mathsf{tok}_{(v \to u)}, \mathsf{tok}_{(u \to v)})$: It takes a pair of ciphertexts $\mathsf{ct}_{(u)}, \mathsf{ct}_{(v)}$ and tokens $\mathsf{tok}_{(v \to u)}, \mathsf{tok}_{(u \to v)}$ as input. Test algorithm runs TUDERE.Test iteratively. For $i = 1$ to n, the algorithm follows it:
  1. **If** $i = n+1$, then return 0
  2. **Else** Compute res_u^i and res_v^i as follows:
     - $res_u^i \leftarrow \mathsf{TUDERE.Test}(\mathsf{ct}_{(u)}[i, 0], \mathsf{ct}_{(v)}[i, 1])$
     - $res_v^i \leftarrow \mathsf{TUDERE.Test}(\mathsf{ct}_{(u)}[i, 1], \mathsf{ct}_{(v)}[i, 0])$
     (a) **If** $res_u^i = 1$, then returns 1
     (b) **Else if** $res_v^i = 1$, then return -1
     (c) **Else** $i \leftarrow i + 1$

Fig. 6. TUDORE scheme from TUDERE

References

1. Amazon employee. https://explodingtopics.com/blog/amazon-employees. Accessed 30 May 2024
2. Google employee. https://seo.ai/blog/how-many-people-work-at-google. Accessed 30 May 2024
3. IBM employee. https://stockanalysis.com/stocks/ibm/employees/. Accessed 30 May 2024
4. Agrawal, R., Kiernan, J., Srikant, R., Xu, Y.: Order preserving encryption for numeric data. In: Proceedings of the 2004 ACM SIGMOD International Conference on Management of data, pp. 563–574 (2004)
5. Berger, R., Dörre, F., Koch, A.: Two-party decision tree training from updatable order-revealing encryption. In: International Conference on Applied Cryptography and Network Security, pp. 288–317. Springer (2024)
6. Boldyreva, A., Chenette, N., Lee, Y., O'Neill, A.: Order-preserving symmetric encryption. In: Joux, A. (ed.) EUROCRYPT 2009. LNCS, vol. 5479, pp. 224–241. Springer, Heidelberg (2009). https://doi.org/10.1007/978-3-642-01001-9_13
7. Boneh, D., Lynn, B., Shacham, H.: Short signatures from the Weil pairing. J. Cryptol. **17**, 297–319 (2004)
8. Cash, D., Liu, F.-H., O'Neill, A., Zhandry, M., Zhang, C.: Parameter-hiding order revealing encryption. In: Peyrin, T., Galbraith, S. (eds.) ASIACRYPT 2018. LNCS, vol. 11272, pp. 181–210. Springer, Cham (2018). https://doi.org/10.1007/978-3-030-03326-2_7
9. Challita, S., Zalila, F., Gourdin, C., Merle, P.: A precise model for google cloud platform. In: 2018 IEEE International Conference on Cloud Engineering (IC2E), pp. 177–183. IEEE (2018)
10. Chen, Z., Nie, J., Li, Z., Susilo, W., Ge, C.: Geometric searchable encryption for privacy-preserving location-based services. IEEE Trans. Serv. Comput. **16**(4), 2672–2684 (2023)
11. Chenette, N., Lewi, K., Weis, S.A., Wu, D.J.: Practical order-revealing encryption with limited leakage. In: Peyrin, T. (ed.) FSE 2016. LNCS, vol. 9783, pp. 474–493. Springer, Heidelberg (2016). https://doi.org/10.1007/978-3-662-52993-5_24
12. Cheon, J.H., Kim, D., Kim, D.: Efficient homomorphic comparison methods with optimal complexity. In: Moriai, S., Wang, H. (eds.) ASIACRYPT 2020. LNCS, vol. 12492, pp. 221–256. Springer, Cham (2020). https://doi.org/10.1007/978-3-030-64834-3_8
13. Cheon, J.H., Kim, M., Kim, M.: Optimized search-and-compute circuits and their application to query evaluation on encrypted data. IEEE Trans. Inf. Forensics Secur. **11**(1), 188–199 (2015)
14. Hahn, C., Hur, J.: Delegatable order-revealing encryption for reliable cross-database query. IEEE Trans. Serv. Comput. (2022)
15. Kerschbaum, F., Schröpfer, A.: Optimal average-complexity ideal-security order-preserving encryption. In: Proceedings of the 2014 ACM SIGSAC Conference on Computer and Communications Security, pp. 275–286 (2014)
16. Li, Y., Wang, H., Zhao, Y.: Delegatable order-revealing encryption. In: Proceedings of the 2019 ACM Asia Conference on Computer and Communications Security, pp. 134–147 (2019)
17. Lv, C., Wang, J., Sun, S.-F., Wang, Y., Qi, S., Chen, X.: Efficient multi-client order-revealing encryption and its applications. In: Bertino, E., Shulman, H., Waidner, M. (eds.) ESORICS 2021. LNCS, vol. 12973, pp. 44–63. Springer, Cham (2021). https://doi.org/10.1007/978-3-030-88428-4_3

18. Lynn, B.: Pairing-based cryptography library. https://crypto.stanford.edu/pbc/ (2006)
19. Mathew, S., Varia, J.: Overview of amazon web services. Amazon Whitepapers **105**(1), 22 (2014)
20. Miao, Y., et al.: Time-controllable keyword search scheme with efficient revocation in mobile e-health cloud. IEEE Trans. Mob. Comput. **23**(5), 3650–3665 (2023)
21. MISHRA, A.: Faang- complete stock data. https://www.kaggle.com/datasets/aayushmishra1512/faang-complete-stock-data (2020). Accessed 30 May 2024
22. Park, J.H., Rezaeifar, Z., Hahn, C.: Securing multi-client range queries over encrypted data. Cluster Comput., 1–14 (2024)
23. Park, J., Lee, H., Hur, J., Seo, J.H., Kim, D.: UTRA: universe token reusability attack and verifiable delegatable order-revealing encryption. Cryptol. ePrint Arch. (2024)
24. Popa, R.A., Li, F.H., Zeldovich, N.: An ideal-security protocol for order-preserving encoding. In: 2013 IEEE Symposium on Security and Privacy, pp. 463–477. IEEE (2013)
25. Qiao, H., Peng, C., Feng, Q., Luo, M., He, D.: Ciphertext range query scheme against agent transfer and permission extension attacks for cloud computing. IEEE Internet Things J. (2024)
26. Roche, D.S., Apon, D., Choi, S.G., Yerukhimovich, A.: Pope: partial order preserving encoding. In: Proceedings of the 2016 ACM SIGSAC Conference on Computer and Communications Security, pp. 1131–1142 (2016)
27. Schnorr, C.P.: Efficient identification and signatures for smart cards. In: Advances in Cryptology—CRYPTO'89 Proceedings 9, pp. 239–252. Springer (1990)
28. Tan, B.H.M., Lee, H.T., Wang, H., Ren, S., Aung, K.M.M.: Efficient private comparison queries over encrypted databases using fully homomorphic encryption with finite fields. IEEE Trans. Dependable Secure Comput. **18**(6), 2861–2874 (2020)
29. United Nations: World population prospects - population division - united nations. https://population.un.org/wpp/ (2022). Accessed 30 May 2024
30. Xiao, J., et al.: Cloak: hiding retrieval information in blockchain systems via distributed query requests. IEEE Trans. Serv. Comput. (2024)
31. Xu, J., Peng, C., Li, R., Fu, J., Luo, M.: An efficient delegatable order-revealing encryption scheme for multi-user range queries. IEEE Trans. Cloud Comput. (2024)
32. Xu, Y., Cheng, H., Liu, X., Jiang, C., Zhang, X., Wang, M.: PCSE: privacy-preserving collaborative searchable encryption for group data sharing in cloud computing. IEEE Trans. Mobile Comput. (2025)
33. Yu, P., Ni, W., Liu, R.P., Zhang, Z., Zhang, H., Wen, Q.: Efficient encrypted range query on cloud platforms. ACM Trans. Cyber-Phys. Syst. (TCPS) **6**(3), 1–23 (2022)

Enhanced Key Mismatch Attacks on Lattice-Based KEMs: Multi-bit Inference and Ciphertext Generalization

Yan Shao[1], Yuejun Liu[1(✉)], Yongbin Zhou[1,2(✉)], and Mingyao Shao[2,3]

[1] School of Cyber Science and Engineering, Nanjing University of Science and Technology, Nanjing, China
{yan.shao,liuyuejun,zhouyongbin}@njust.edu.cn
[2] Institute of Information Engineering, Chinese Academy of Sciences, Beijing, China
shaomingyao@iie.ac.cn
[3] School of Cyber Security, University of Chinese Academy of Sciences, Beijing, China

Abstract. Key Mismatch Attacks (KMA) pose a significant threat to lattice-based key encapsulation mechanisms (KEMs), such as CRYSTALS-Kyber (Kyber), standardized as NIST FIPS 203. Despite advancements in KMA, including multi-positional strategies and enhanced oracles like the Multi-Value Key Mismatch Oracle (MV-KMO), existing methods suffer from high query counts and detectable ciphertexts, limiting their practicality. This paper proposes techniques to enhance KMA efficiency and stealth against Kyber and Saber. First, for CPA-secure KEMs, we propose a multi-bit inference strategy that uses crafted ciphertexts to extract information about multiple private key coefficients per Key Mismatch Oracle (KMO) query, reducing the required queries for Kyber1024 from 2368 to 2268 and for FireSaber from 2623 to 2571. Second, for CCA-secure KEMs, we present a minimal-query KMA method leveraging the Hamming Weight Incremental (HWI) leakage model to recover the full decapsulated message, thereby reducing queries from 2176 to 12 for Kyber1024 and from 2433 to 16 for FireSaber. Third, we develop a stealthy KMA variant for CCA-secure KEMs that reconstructs the noise vector to recover the private key, generating ciphertexts statistically indistinguishable from legitimate ones, as confirmed by entropy and Kullback-Leibler (KL) divergence analyses. These advancements improve KMA performance and covertness, revealing critical vulnerabilities in lattice-based KEMs and informing future cryptographic defenses.

Keywords: Lattice-based KEMs · Key mismatch attack · Multi-bit inference · Hamming weight incremental leakage · Undetectable attack

1 Introduction

The rapid advancements in quantum computing have made Shor's algorithm [13] a serious challenge to traditional public-key cryptosystems, jeopardizing the security foundations of widely used schemes like RSA and ECC. To address this challenge, NIST launched the Post-Quantum Cryptography Standardization Project [15] to develop quantum-resistant cryptographic algorithms, ensuring the long-term security of information in the quantum era.

Lattice-based KEMs, such as Kyber [2] and Saber [1], have emerged as promising solutions due to their strong security properties and computational efficiency. Notably, Kyber has been standardized by NIST as FIPS 203 [16], highlighting its importance for future secure communications. However, despite their theoretical robustness, lattice-based KEMs like Kyber and Saber remain susceptible to practical attacks, including KMA. KMA exploits key reuse [4,8] by analyzing multiple ciphertexts encapsulated under the same public key to determine whether the derived shared keys match, gradually revealing information about the private key and enabling efficient key recovery.

In a KMA, an adversary leverages the reuse of a private key across multiple encapsulation-decapsulation queries to recover the key, relying solely on key mismatch information. Attacks against Kyber can be classified into two categories. The first targets CPA-secure Kyber variants, utilizing a KMO to deduce key bits through mismatched ciphertexts. The second addresses CCA-secure Kyber implementations, employing Plaintext-Checking Oracle (PCO) with side-channel assistance to verify plaintexts and recover the private key. Although these approaches share some conceptual overlap, KMA distinguishes itself by not requiring side-channel techniques.

Research on KMA has progressed significantly. In 2021, Qin et al. [9] provided the first systematic analysis of KMA using KMO against CPA-secure KEMs. The KMO accepts a ciphertext c and a shared key K, computes $K' \leftarrow \text{KEM.Dec}(c)$, and outputs 1 if $K' = K$, or 0 otherwise. In 2023, Guo et al. [5] advanced this work by introducing a two-positional KMA based on KMO, improving efficiency by targeting multiple private key coefficients simultaneously. Both studies utilize the standard KMO, often instantiated via handshake behaviors in protocols like TLS [14]. In 2024, Shao et al. [12] proposed the MV-KMO, which exposes multiple bits of the decapsulated plaintext, enabling parallel KMA with enhanced efficiency. Further improvements by Li et al. [7] and Guo et al. [6] introduced adaptive parallel strategies to skip redundant queries caused by coefficient misalignment. In the CCA-secure KEMs, Li et al. [7] integrated a PCO with side-channel techniques, achieving the Huffman bound.

Despite these developments, existing KMA methods exhibit practical limitations, such as requiring numerous oracle queries (e.g., 2368 for Kyber1024) and producing detectable, non-standard ciphertexts, which limits their real-world applicability. This paper proposes a suite of techniques to improve the efficiency and stealth of KMA against Kyber, with potential applicability to other lattice-based KEMs. Our contributions are as follows:

– For CPA-secure KEMs, we introduce a multi-bit inference KMA strategy that utilizes carefully crafted ciphertexts to extract information about multiple key coefficients per query. This reduces the required KMO queries for Kyber1024 from 2368 to 2268 and for FireSaber from 2623 to 2571.

- For CCA-secure KEMs, we present a minimal-query KMA approach based on the HWI leakage model to recover the full decapsulated message m', lowering the query count for Kyber1024 from 2176 to 12 and for FireSaber from 2433 to 16.
- We develop a stealthy KMA variant for CCA-secure KEMs that reconstructs the noise vector e to derive the private key via $P_A = A \circ s_A + e$, generating ciphertexts statistically indistinguishable from legitimate ones, as confirmed by entropy and KL divergence analyses.

These contributions offer practical advancements in KMA research, exposing vulnerabilities in lattice-based KEMs while suggesting paths for enhanced defenses. Unlike prior works relying on enhanced oracles (e.g., MV-KMO [12]), our CPA-secure strategy maximizes the standard KMO's potential through algorithmic innovation. For CCA-secure settings, we leverage the HWI leakage model to achieve substantial query reductions.

The paper is structured as follows: Sect. 2 outlines notations and overviews Kyber and Saber. Section 3 details the multi-bit inference KMA for CPA-secure KEMs. Section 4 presents the minimal-query KMA for CCA-secure KEMs. Section 5 introduces the stealthy noise recovery method. Section 6 provides experimental results, and Sect. 7 concludes with implications and future directions.

2 Preliminaries

2.1 Notation

In this paper, we denote by R the ring $\mathbb{Z}[x]/(X^n + 1)$ and by R_q the ring $\mathbb{Z}_q[x]/(X^n + 1)$, where $n = 2^{n'-1}$ such that $X^n + 1$ is the $2^{n'}$-th cyclotomic polynomial. Through this paper, the values of n, n' and q are fixed to $n = 256$, $n' = 9$, and $q = 3329$. Regular font letters denote elements in R or R_q (which includes elements in $\mathbb{Z}$ and $\mathbb{Z}_q$) and bold lower-case letters represent vectors with coefficients in R or R_q. By default, all vectors will be column vectors. Bold upper-case letters are matrices. For a vector u (or matrix A), we denote by u^T (or A^T) its transpose. The polynomial $f(x) = f_0 + f_1 x + ... + f_{n-1}x^{n-1}$ in R_q can be expressed as the vector form $(f_0, f_1, ..., f_{n-1})$. For functions where the input and output are byte arrays, we denote them by B the set $\{0, ..., 255\}$, i.e., the set of 8-bit unsigned integers (bytes). We denote by B^k the set of byte arrays of length of k. For two byte arrays a and b we denote by $(a||b)$ the concatenation of a and b. The symbol $\lfloor a \rceil$ represents rounding the number a.

2.2 Kyber

Kyber [2] is a lattice-based KEM standardized by NIST as FIPS 203 [16] for its resilience against quantum attacks. Its security is rooted in the Module Learning With Errors (MLWE) problem, which introduces small noise into polynomials over a ring, rendering direct correlation between the private key and

Table 1. Parameter sets for Kyber.

Variant	Security Level	n	k	q	η_1	η_2	(d_u, d_v)
Kyber512	128-bit	256	2	3329	3	2	(10,4)
Kyber768	192-bit	256	3	3329	2	2	(10,4)
Kyber1024	256-bit	256	4	3329	2	2	(11,5)

ciphertext computationally infeasible. Kyber includes three variants–Kyber512, Kyber768, and Kyber1024, each with distinct security levels, as shown in Table 1.

Kyber combines a CPA-secure public-key encryption (PKE) scheme with the Fujisaki-Okamoto (FO) transformation [3] to achieve CCA security. The scheme comprises three phases–key generation, encapsulation, and decapsulation–illustrated in Fig. 1.

Bob

5. $m \xleftarrow{\$} \{0,1\}^{256}$
6. $m \leftarrow H(m)$
7. $(\overline{K}, r) := G(m \| H(P_A))$
8. ▷ $Kyber.CPAPKE.Enc(P_A, m, r)$
8.1 Generate matrix $A \in \mathcal{R}_q^{k \times k}$
8.2 Sample $r \in B_{\eta_1}^k, e_1 \in B_{\eta_2}^k, e_2 \in B_{\eta_2}$
8.3 $u_B \leftarrow A^T \circ r + e_1$
8.4 $v_B \leftarrow P_A^T \circ r + e_2 + Decompress_q(m,1)$
8.5 $c_1 \leftarrow Compress_q(u_B, d_u)$
8.6 $c_2 \leftarrow Compress_q(v_B, d_v)$
8.7 Output: (c_1, c_2)
9. $K_B \leftarrow KDF(\overline{K} \| H(c_1, c_2))$

$\xrightarrow{P_A}$ (reverse)
$\xrightarrow{(c_1, c_2)}$

Alice

1. $z \xleftarrow{\$} \{0,1\}^{256}$
2. ▷ $Kyber.CPAPKE.KeyGen()$
2.1 Generate matrix $A \in \mathcal{R}_q^{k \times k}$
2.2 Sample $s_A, e \in B_\eta^k$
2.3 $P_A \leftarrow A \circ s_A + e$
3. $S_A \leftarrow s_A \| P_A \| H(P_A) \| z$
4. Output: (S_A, P_A)

10. ▷ $Kyber.CPAPKE.Dec(S_A, (c_1, c_2))$
10.1 $u_A \leftarrow Decompress_q(c_1, d_u)$
10.2 $v_A \leftarrow Decompress_q(c_2, d_v)$
10.3 $m' \leftarrow Compress_q(v_A - s_A^T \circ u_A, 1)$
10.4 Output: m'
11. $(\overline{K'}, r') := G(m' \| H(P_A))$
CPA-secure:
12. $K_A \leftarrow KDF(\overline{K'} \| H(c_1, c_2))$
CCA-secure:
13. $(c'_1, c'_2) \leftarrow Kyber.CPAPKE.Enc(P_A, m', r')$
14. $K_A \leftarrow (c_1, c_2) == (c'_1, c'_2)$
    ? $KDF(\overline{K'} \| H(c_1, c_2))$
    : $KDF(z \| H(c_1, c_2))$

Fig. 1. Overview of Kyber KEM phases.

In key generation, Kyber produces a public-private key pair. The private key is a polynomial vector with coefficients sampled from a centered binomial distribution, while the public key is derived from the private key, a random noise vector, and a pre-generated public parameter matrix. This randomness ensures key unpredictability and quantum resistance.

During encapsulation, a random message is encoded as a polynomial and encrypted using the recipient's public key, yielding a fixed-length through compression encoding. In decapsulation, the recipient uses the private key to solve the MLWE problem, recovering the shared key. Compression encoding represents polynomial coefficients as compact bit sequences, enhancing transmission efficiency.

2.3 Saber

Saber [1] is a post-quantum KEM based on the Module Learning With Rounding (MLWR) problem, a variant of the Ring Learning With Errors (RLWE) problem. As a third round in NIST's post-quantum cryptography standardization process, Saber offers robust security against both classical and quantum attacks.

Saber includes three variants–LightSaber, Saber, and FireSaber, each with distinct security levels, as shown in Table 2. Similar to Kyber, Saber employs a CPA-secure PKE scheme combined with the FO transformation to achieve CCA-security, operating across key generation, encapsulation, and decapsulation phases.

Table 2. Parameter sets for Saber.

Variant	Security Level	Module Dimension	Noise Parameter
LightSaber	128-bit	2	Small
Saber	192-bit	3	Medium
FireSaber	256-bit	4	Large

3 Multi-bit Inference KMA for CPA-Secure KEMs

3.1 Key Mismatch Oracle

The KMO is a critical tool in key misuse attacks against lattice-based KEMs. It takes as input a private key s_A, a ciphertext $\bar{c}$, and a shared key K_B, computing $K_A \leftarrow \text{KEM.Dec}(s_A, \bar{c})$. The oracle returns 1 if $K_A = K_B$, indicating a key match, and 0 otherwise, signifying a mismatch. This binary output enables an adversary to infer information about the private key by observing decapsulation outcomes. The operation of the KMO is formalized in Algorithm 1.

In practice, the KMO can be instantiated through protocol behaviors, such as the TLS handshake with CPA-secure Kyber [17]. During the TLS handshake, the client and server derive a shared session key from the KEM output. A successful handshake indicates a key match ($K_A = K_B$), while a failure (e.g., due to a rejected session key) suggests a mismatch. This allows an adversary to infer the KMO's output indirectly, demonstrating its practical realizability without direct access to the decapsulation process.

Algorithm 1.. Key Mismatch Oracle

Input: $s_A, \bar{c}, K$
Output: 0 or 1

1 **Function** KeyMismatchOracle($s_A, \bar{c}, K_B$):
2 $\quad K_A \leftarrow$ KEM.Dec($s_A, \bar{c}$) **if** $K_A = K_B$ **then**
3 $\quad\quad$ | return *1*
4 $\quad$ **else**
5 $\quad\quad$ | return *0*
6 $\quad$ **end**

3.2 Review of Existing Key Mismatch Attacks

KMA exploit the KMO to recover the private key s_A by submitting crafted ciphertexts. We illustrate this with Kyber1024, where the private key $s_A = (s[0], s[1], s[2], s[3])$, with each $s[i] \in R_q^{256}$ and coefficients in $\{-2, -1, 0, 1, 2\}$, is recovered coefficient by coefficient.

Consider an adversary, Bob, aiming to recover Alice's private key s_A. To recover $s[0][0]$, Bob selects a message $m = (1, 0, \ldots, 0)$, constructs $u_B = ((\lfloor \frac{q}{32} \rceil, 0, \ldots, 0), 0, 0, 0)^T$ and $c_2 = (h, 0, \ldots, 0)$, then computes $c_1 = Compress_q(u_B, d_u)$ and sends the forged ciphertext (c_1, c_2) to Alice.

Upon receiving (c_1, c_2), Alice computes

$$u_A = Decompress_q(c_1, d_u) = ((\lfloor \frac{q}{32} \rceil, 0, \ldots, 0), 0, 0, 0)^T, \quad (1)$$

$$v_A = Decompress_q(c_2, d_v) = (\lfloor \frac{q}{32} h \rceil, 0, \ldots, 0), \quad (2)$$

and the decapsulated message

$$m' = Compress_q(v_A - s_A^T \cdot u_A, 1). \quad (3)$$

The first coefficient of m' is

$$m'[0] = \left\lfloor \frac{2}{q} \left(\lfloor \frac{q}{32} h \rceil - s[0][0] \lfloor \frac{q}{32} \rceil \right) \right\rceil \mod 2, \quad (4)$$

and the others are

$$m'[i] = \left\lfloor \frac{2}{q} \left(0 - s[0][i] \lfloor \frac{q}{32} \rceil \right) \right\rceil \mod 2 = 0, \quad 1 \le i \le 255. \quad (5)$$

For Kyber1024 ($q = 3329$), setting $h = 8$ yields $\lfloor \frac{q}{32}h \rceil = 832$ and $\lfloor \frac{q}{32} \rceil = 104$. The value of $m'[0]$ depends on whether $832 - 104 \cdot s[0][0]$ falls within $[0, q/2)$ or $[q/2, q)$, allowing the adversary to deduce $s[0][0]$ by testing different h values (e.g., 7, 8, 9, 10) and observing the KMO output, as shown in Fig. 2.

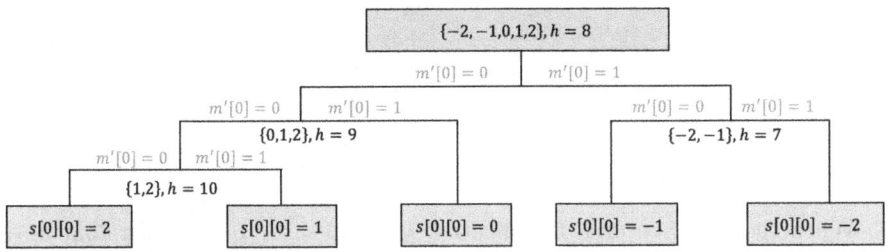

Fig. 2. Relationships of $m'[0]$ with $s[0][0]$ and h for Kyber1024.

To recover $s[0][i]$ ($i \geq 1$), Bob sets $\boldsymbol{u_B}[0][256 - i] = -\lfloor \frac{q}{32} \rceil$, yielding:

$$m'[0] = \left\lfloor \frac{2}{q}\left(\lfloor \frac{q}{32}h \rceil - s[0][i]\lfloor \frac{q}{32} \rceil\right) \right\rceil \mod 2. \tag{6}$$

This process is repeated for all coefficients across $s[0], s[1], s[2], s[3]$. The attack's complexity, based on the coefficient distribution $\{-2, -1, 0, 1, 2\}$, yields an average of 2.3125 queries per coefficient:

$$EX = \frac{3}{8} \cdot 2 + \frac{1}{4} \cdot 3 + \frac{1}{4} \cdot 2 + \frac{1}{16} \cdot 3 + \frac{1}{16} \cdot 2 = 2.3125. \tag{7}$$

3.3 Proposed Efficient KMA via Multi-bit Inference

Building on existing KMA described in Sect. 3.2, we propose a novel approach that enhances efficiency by inferring multiple bits from a single KMO query. Unlike parallel KMA, which relies on stronger oracles like the MV-KMO returning multiple bits [12], our method uses the standard KMO instantiated in protocols like TLS [14]. By crafting ciphertexts such that the KMO response provides information about multiple private key coefficients, we enable the KMO's response to constrain several coefficients simultaneously, improving information utilization per query.

For Kyber1024, the adversary selects a message $m = (0, 0, \ldots, 0)$ and constructs $\boldsymbol{u_B} = ((\lfloor \frac{q}{32} \rceil, 0, \ldots, 0), 0, 0, 0)^T$ and $c_2 = (h_0, h_1, 0, \ldots, 0)$. The forged ciphertext $(\boldsymbol{c_1}, c_2)$, where $\boldsymbol{c_1} = Compress_q(\boldsymbol{u_B}, d_u)$, is sent to the victim, who computes

$$\boldsymbol{u_A} = Decompress_q(\boldsymbol{c_1}, d_u) = ((\lfloor \frac{q}{32} \rceil, 0, \ldots, 0), 0, 0, 0)^T, \tag{8}$$

$$v_A = Decompress_q(c_2, d_v) = (\lfloor \frac{q}{32}h_0 \rceil, \lfloor \frac{q}{32}h_1 \rceil, 0, \ldots, 0), \tag{9}$$

and the decapsulated message

$$m' = Compress_q(v_A - s_A^T \cdot u_A, 1), \tag{10}$$

with

$$m'[0] = \left\lfloor \frac{2}{q}\left(\lfloor \frac{q}{32}h_0 \rceil - s[0][0]\lfloor \frac{q}{32}\rceil\right)\right\rceil \mod 2, \tag{11}$$

$$m'[1] = \left\lfloor \frac{2}{q}\left(\lfloor \frac{q}{32}h_1 \rceil - s[0][1]\lfloor \frac{q}{32}\rceil\right)\right\rceil \mod 2, \tag{12}$$

$$m'[i] = \left\lfloor \frac{2}{q}\left(0 - s[0][i]\lfloor \frac{q}{32}\rceil\right)\right\rceil \mod 2 = 0, \quad 2 \le i \le 255. \tag{13}$$

When the KMO returns 1, indicating $m' = [0, 0, \ldots, 0]$, we infer that both $s[0][0]$ and $s[0][1]$ are in $\{0, 1, 2\}$ for $h_0 = h_1 = 8$. For example, if $s[0][0] = 1$, $s[0][1] = 2$, and $h_0 = h_1 = 8$, the KMO returns 1, constraining both coefficients to $\{0, 1, 2\}$. If the KMO returns 0, m' has at least one non-zero bit $((m'[0], m'[1]) \in \{(1, 0), (0, 1), (1, 1)\})$. A second query with $h_0 = 8, h_1 = 0$ distinguishes these cases: a return of 1 implies $(m'[0], m'[1]) = (0, 1)$, constraining $s[0][0] \in \{0, 1, 2\}$ and $s[0][1] \in \{-1, -2\}$; otherwise, $s[0][0] \in \{-1, -2\}$ and $s[0][1] \in \{-2, -1, 0, 1, 2\}$.

Our recursive querying strategy, shown in Fig. 3, targets coefficient pairs (e.g., $s[k][i], s[k][i+1]$) and adapts based on the KMO response. If both coefficients are in $\{0, 1, 2\}$, the next query targets $s[k][i+2], s[k][i+3]$; otherwise, it shifts to $s[k][i+1], s[k][i+2]$. This approach reduces the average queries per coefficient to 2.2324 for Kyber1024, compared to 2.3125 for existing KMA:

$$EX = \frac{\frac{36}{256} \cdot 3 + \frac{24}{256} \cdot 17 + \frac{16}{256} \cdot 21 + \frac{6}{256} \cdot 17 + \frac{4}{256} \cdot 42 + \frac{1}{256} \cdot 21}{2} = 2.2324. \tag{14}$$

Our method extracts multi-bit information from a single-bit oracle, unlike parallel KMA, which requires a stronger oracle. This efficiency gain stems from leveraging dependencies in the decapsulated message, making our method both practical and distinct from existing techniques.

The multi-bit information inference method we propose can also be combined with the two-positional KMA introduced by Guo et al. [5]. By utilizing our method, we can not only recover $(s[k][i], s[k][128 + i])$ but also infer the information of $(s[k][i + 1], s[k][128 + i + 1])$ simultaneously.

This approach not only enhances efficiency but also broadens the applicability of KMA by relying solely on practical, standard oracles like those in TLS handshakes.

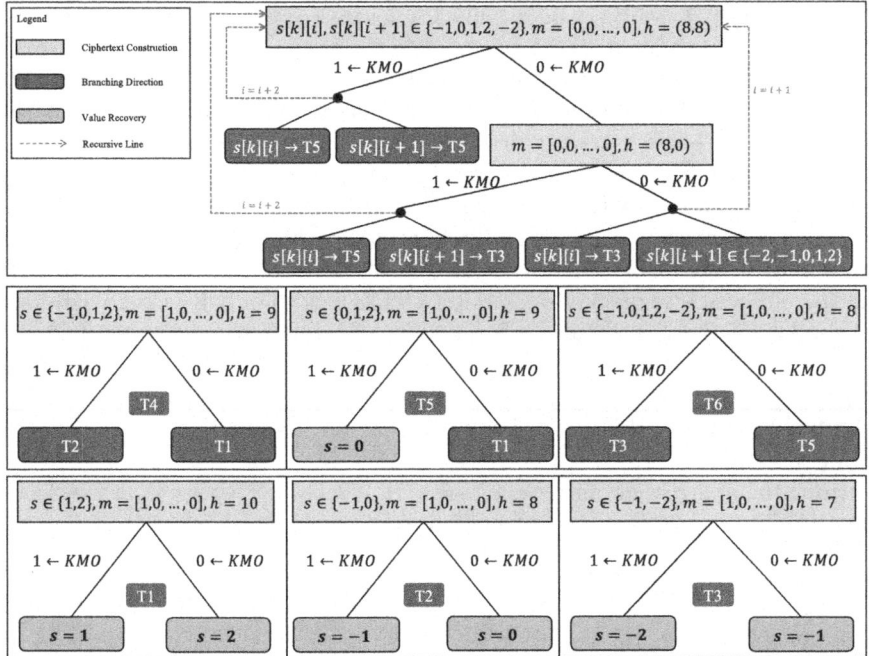

Fig. 3. Efficient KMA framework via two-bit inference for Kyber1024.

4 Minimal-Query KMA for CCA-Secure KEMs via HWI Leakage

In this section, we present a novel key recovery method for CCA-secure KEMs, leveraging side-channel information to achieve private key extraction with a minimal number of queries. Unlike prior approaches that either rely on computationally infeasible parallelism or underutilize leakage information, our method fully exploits the HWI leakage model to recover all coefficients of the decapsulated message m', enabling efficient deduction of the private key s_A.

4.1 Hamming Weight Incremental Leakage Model

The HWI leakage model, introduced by Ravi et al. [11], enables coefficient-by-coefficient recovery of the decapsulated message m' by exploiting side-channel information during decapsulation. This model monitors the Hamming weight of cumulative intermediate states during the decapsulation process. Specifically, for each coefficient i, the model observes whether the Hamming weight of the state t_i (representing the cumulative sum of message bits up to position i) increases compared to t_{i-1}. An increase indicates $m'[i] = 1$, as the addition of a new bit alters the power consumption profile, which can be detected via side-channel analysis.

Mathematically, $t_i = \sum_{j=0}^{i} m'[j]$, and the leakage reveals whether $m'[i] = 1$ if $HW(t_i) > HW(t_{i-1})$.

The HWI leakage model is implemented through fine-grained side-channel attacks, such as high-resolution power analysis or electromagnetic emanation measurements. These attacks detect bit transitions (e.g., $0 \to 1$ or $1 \to 0$) during decapsulation, which manifest as distinct power consumption patterns in hardware. By observing these transitions in a single (or very few) decapsulation traces, an adversary can sequentially reconstruct the entire m' vector, making it a powerful tool for message recovery. Specifically, Ravi et al. [11] have shown that the success rate quickly ramps up to 98.24% with only five averaged power traces, achieving full message recovery with a brute-force complexity of 2^6.

Algorithm 2.. The Hamming Weight Incremental Model

Input: $m'[256]$
Output: Hamming weight incremental array $HW[256]$
1 Function Hamming Weight Incremental Leakage Model(m'):
2     $HW[0] = m'[0]$ for $i \leftarrow 1$ to 255 do
3 | $HW[i] = m'[i] + HW[i-1]$
4   end
5   return HW

4.2 Private Key Recovery for CCA-Secure KEMs

While Ravi et al. [11] utilized the HWI leakage model for message recovery, we extend it to recover the private key s_A of CCA-secure KEMs, such as Kyber, with very few queries. Unlike [7], which also employs the HWI leakage model to attack CCA-secure Kyber and achieves the Huffman bound but relies solely on the first coefficient of the message m, our method leverages all coefficients of m'. This comprehensive utilization of m' enables efficient key recovery using only a minimal number of ciphertexts. Our method integrates the HWI leakage model's ability to recover m' with the KMA strategy, where each bit $m'[i]$ depends solely on a corresponding private key coefficient $s[0][i]$, achieving practicality without the computational overhead of traditional methods.

In contrast to parallel KMA [12], which achieves high parallelism (e.g., 256) at the cost of infeasible offline computation $O(2^{256})$, our method leverages the HWI leakage model to directly obtain m' via side-channel leakage, eliminating this bottleneck. For Kyber1024, the adversary constructs a ciphertext to expose the private key coefficients as follows:

The adversary selects $m = (0, 0, \ldots, 0)$, sets $\boldsymbol{u_B} = ((\lfloor \frac{q}{32} \rceil, 0, \ldots, 0), 0, 0, 0)^{\mathrm{T}}$, and defines $c_2 = (h_0, h_1, \ldots, h_{255})$, where h_i are integers. The forged ciphertext $(\boldsymbol{c_1}, c_2)$ is computed with $\boldsymbol{c_1} = Compress_q(\boldsymbol{u_B}, d_u)$ and sent to the target. During decapsulation, the recipient computes

$$\boldsymbol{u_A} = Decompress_q(\boldsymbol{c_1}, d_u) = ((\lfloor \frac{q}{32} \rceil, 0, ..., 0), 0, 0, 0)^{\mathrm{T}}, \tag{15}$$

$$v_A = Decompress_q(c_2, d_v) = (\lfloor \frac{q}{32} h_0 \rceil, \lfloor \frac{q}{32} h_1 \rceil, ..., \lfloor \frac{q}{32} h_{255} \rceil). \quad (16)$$

and derives the decapsulated message

$$m'[i] = \lfloor \frac{2}{q}(\lfloor \frac{q}{32} h_i \rceil - s[0][i]\lfloor \frac{q}{32} \rceil) \rceil \bmod 2, \text{ for } 0 \leq i \leq 255. \quad (17)$$

Using the HWI leakage model, the adversary recovers the full m' vector from a single decapsulation trace. By setting $h_i = 8$ initially and observing $m'[i]$, the range of $s[0][i]$ is determined. Subsequent queries adjust h_i (e.g., to 9 or 10), requiring at most three queries per coefficient vector to fully recover $s[0]$. For Kyber1024, with $k = 4$ coefficient vectors $(s[0], s[1], s[2], s[3])$, the total query count is $3 \times k = 12$.

This method mirrors parallel KMA with parallelism 256 but avoids its $O(2^{256})$ complexity by directly obtaining m' through the HWI leakage model. Thus, it achieves practical and efficient private key recovery for CCA-secure KEMs with very few queries.

5 Stealthy KMA for CCA-Secure KEMs via Ciphertext Generalization

This section introduces a stealthy variant of KMA for CCA-secure KEMs through ciphertext generalization, addressing the detectability issues inherent in traditional KMA. By recovering the noise vector e and leveraging the public key relation $\boldsymbol{P_A} = \boldsymbol{A} \circ \boldsymbol{s_A} + \boldsymbol{e}$, our method enables private key recovery while generating ciphertexts that are statistically indistinguishable from legitimate ones. We validate the stealthiness of this approach using entropy and Kullback-Leibler divergence analyses, demonstrating that our forged ciphertexts maintain randomness akin to genuine communications.

5.1 Overview of Ciphertext Generalization in KMA

Traditional KMA suffer from a critical limitation: their forged ciphertexts often exhibit low entropy and decapsulation into predictable plaintexts, such as all-zero vectors, rendering them easily detectable. To overcome this, we propose a stealthy KMA variant that introduces ciphertext generalization. This method removes the restrictive formatting of traditional KMA ciphertexts, generating ciphertexts statistically indistinguishable from legitimate ones. Our method leverages the encapsulation algorithm to produce a ciphertext for a message $m = (0, ..., 0)$, with the critical distinction that specially crafted random numbers ensure the decapsulated message m' depends solely on the noise vector e. By recovering e and solving $\boldsymbol{P_A} = \boldsymbol{A} \circ \boldsymbol{s_A} + \boldsymbol{e}$, we extract the private key $\boldsymbol{s_A}$, achieving a dual to conventional KMA focused on $\boldsymbol{s_A}$. This technique also ensures the decapsulated message m' appears random, enhancing attack stealthiness, and is tailored for CCA-secure KEMs like Kyber.

5.2 Noise Vector Recovery Technique

Taking Kyber1024 as an example, we demonstrate how the adversary recovers the noise vector e to deduce the private key s_A. The adversary forges a ciphertext that, upon decapsulation, yields a message m' tied exclusively to e. Using side-channel attacks, such as the HWI leakage model from Sect. 4, the adversary determines $m'[i]$ to infer $e[i]$.

Focusing on recovering $e[0][0]$, the adversary selects $m = (0, \ldots, 0)$ and sets $r = ((a, 0, \ldots, 0), 0, 0, 0)$, $e_1 = (0, 0, 0, 0)$, and $e_2 = (b, 0, \ldots, 0)$, where integers a and b are to achieve the Huffman bound [7] for each $e[i]$, minimizing the number of queries required. The forged ciphertext components are computed as

$$u_B = A^T r, \tag{18}$$

$$v_B = (As_A + e)^T r + e_2 + Decompress_q(m, 1) = s_A^T A^T r + e^T r + e_2, \tag{19}$$

yielding $c_1 = Compress_q(u_B, d_u)$ and $c_2 = Compress_q(v_B, d_v)$. The victim receives (c_1, c_2) and computes

$$u_A = Decompress_q(c_1, d_u) = A^T r, \tag{20}$$

$$v_A = Decompress_q(c_2, d_v) = s_A^T A^T r + e^T r + e_2. \tag{21}$$

with the decapsulated message

$$\begin{aligned} m' &= Compress_q(v_A - s_A^T \cdot u_A, 1) \\ &= Compress_q(s_A^T A^T r + e^T r - s_A^T A^T r + e_2, 1) \\ &= Compress_q(e^T r + e_2, 1). \end{aligned} \tag{22}$$

Specifically,

$$m'[0] = \lfloor \frac{2}{q}(e[0][0] \cdot a + b) \rceil \bmod 2, \tag{23}$$

$$m'[i] = \lfloor \frac{2}{q}(e[0][i] \cdot a) \rceil \bmod 2, \text{ for } 1 \leq i \leq 255. \tag{24}$$

Using the same oracle as Li et al. [7], the adversary gets $m'[0]$ and, by adjusting a and b, deduces $e[0][0]$, as illustrated in Fig. 4. This process extends to all coefficients of e. To recover the complete e, a total of 2176, 1632, and 1215 queries are required for Kyber1024, Kyber768, and Kyber512, respectively.

Similarly, as described in Sect. 4, by utilizing the HWI leakage model to obtain the full message m', the complete e can be recovered with just $3 \times k$ queries. Specifically, we modify e_2 to be $(b_0, b_1, \ldots, b_{255})$. In the first query, set $a = 1500$ and $b_0 = b_1 = \cdots = b_{255} = 312$, which partitions the range of each $e[i]$. In the second query, set $a = 1000$; if $e[i] \in \{0, -2, 2\}$, set $b[i] = 0$, otherwise set $b[i] = 416$. In the third query, set $a = 168$ and $b[i] = 900$.

Once e is fully recovered, the private key s_A is obtained by solving $P_A = A \circ s_A + e$.

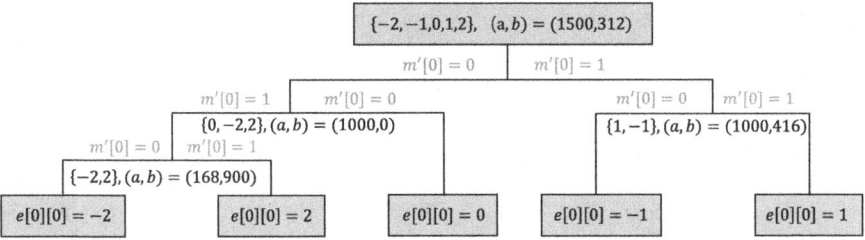

Fig. 4. Relationships of $m'[0]$ with $e[0][0]$ and (a,b) for Kyber1024.

5.3 Evaluation of Ciphertext Stealthiness

We assess the stealthiness of our generalized ciphertexts by comparing their statistical properties to legitimate ones using entropy and KL divergence [10].

Entropy Distribution. Shannon entropy, defined as $H(X) = -\sum_x P(x) \log_2 P(x)$, quantifies randomness. As illustrated in Fig. 5, we analyzed 1000 legitimate and 1000 forged ciphertexts bytes stream, computing entropies in bytes of approximately **7.9999 bits** for both, indicating near-perfect randomness. In contrast, traditional KMA ciphertexts, often decapsulating to all-zero messages, exhibit significantly lower entropy, making them detectable.

KL Divergence. KL divergence, $D_{KL}(P \parallel Q) = \sum_x P(x) \log_2 \frac{P(x)}{Q(x)}$, measures distribution similarity. For legitimate (P) and forged (Q) ciphertexts, we obtained $D_{KL} \approx \mathbf{0.00024}$ bits, a negligible difference confirming their indistinguishability. This starkly contrasts with traditional KMA ciphertexts, which deviate markedly from legitimate distributions.

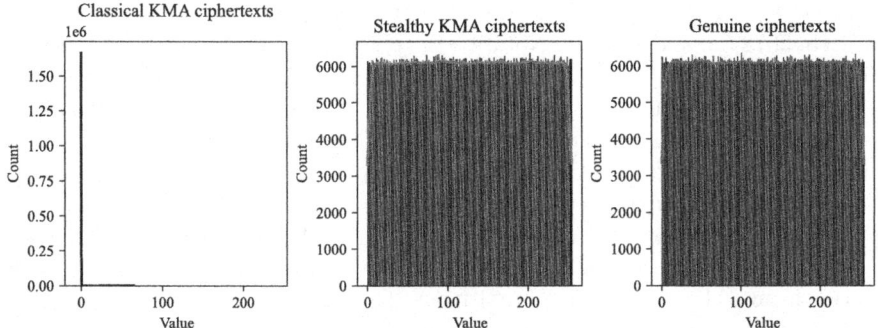

Fig. 5. Entropy distribution of legitimate and forged ciphertexts.

Our method thus achieves ciphertext generalization, producing random-looking ciphertexts that evade detection while enabling efficient private key recovery.

6 Experimental Evaluation

To validate the effectiveness of our proposed methods, we conducted a series of experiments on Kyber and Saber, two prominent lattice-based KEMs. The experiments were performed on a system with a 3.1 GHz 2-core Intel Core i5 CPU and 8 GB 2133 MHz RAM running macOS Ventura 13.7.1. Our evaluation focuses on the methods introduced in Sect. 3 and 4, providing detailed results and comparisons with state-of-the-art approaches.

The multi-bit inference KMA is suited for CPA-secure KEMs, where the attacker leverages the KMO to infer multiple bits of the decrypted message per query, thereby improving attack efficiency. In contrast, the minimal-query KMA targets CCA-secure KEMs and employs the HWI leakage model to recover the full decrypted message from a single (or very few) decapsulation traces, thus achieving minimal KMA queries. These two approaches are tailored to different security models, effectively extending the applicability of key mismatch attacks in real-world scenarios.

6.1 Evaluation of Multi-bit Inference KMA for CPA-Secure KEMs

We first evaluate the performance of our multi-bit inference KMA strategy for CPA-secure KEMs, as introduced in Sect. 3. The results are presented in Table 3, where we compare the average number of oracle queries required to recover private key coefficients against existing works.

In the one-positional KMA setting, our method consistently reduces query complexity across all tested configurations. For Kyber1024, Kyber768, and Kyber512, our method reduces the query counts from 2368.11, 1775.92, and 1309.25 to 2268.94, 1703.61, and 1283.34, respectively. Similarly, for Saber variants (e.g., FireSaber, Saber, LightSaber), the query counts are reduced to 2571.15, 2072.33, and 1416.14. Notably, the efficiency gain is more pronounced in higher-dimensional parameter sets, such as Kyber1024, demonstrating the scalability of our multi-bit inference strategy. This scalability advantage is attributed to our recursive multi-bit inference design, which leverages structured patterns in higher-dimensional key vectors more effectively.

Additionally, we extended our method to a two-positional KMA by incorporating pair-wise recovery techniques, as shown in Table 4. For Kyber1024 and Kyber768, our method slightly outperforms the state-of-the-art [5], reducing queries from 2118.10 to 2109.68 and from 1588.32 to 1582.14, respectively. For Kyber512, the query count increases marginally from 1205.36 to 1208.85 due to its smaller coefficient space and larger sampling range, where our method's advantages are less pronounced. This is because Kyber512 has only 512 coefficients, and each coefficient's sampling range is larger compared to the other two Kyber versions, limiting the effectiveness of our method in this specific case.

Table 3. One-positional KMA on CPA-secure KEMs.

	Kyber1024	Kyber768	Kyber512	FireSaber	Saber	LightSaber
Qin et al. [9]	2368.11	1775.92	1309.25	2623.14	2090.21	1557.89
Shao et al. (P = 1) [12]	2368.11	1775.92	1309.25	–	–	–
Li et al. (P = 1) [7]	2368.11	1775.92	1309.25	2623.14	2090.21	1557.89
Ours (multi-bit inference)	**2268.94**	**1703.61**	**1283.34**	**2571.15**	**2072.33**	**1416.14**

Table 4. Two-positional KMA on CPA-secure Kyber.

	Kyber1024	Kyber768	Kyber512
Guo et al. [5]	2118.10	1588.32	**1205.36**
Ours (multi-bit inference)	**2109.68**	**1582.14**	1208.85

6.2 Evaluation of Minimal-Query KMA for CCA-Secure KEMs

For the minimal-query KMA targeting CCA-secure KEMs, as introduced in Sect. 4, we evaluated our method on both Kyber and Saber, comparing it with the state-of-the-art approach [7]. As shown in Table 5, our method drastically reduces the number of queries required for key recovery. For Kyber1024, Kyber768, and Kyber512, the query counts are reduced to 12, 9, and 6, respectively, compared to 2176.24, 1632.10, and 1215.78 in [7]. Similarly, for Saber variants (FireSaber, Saber, LightSaber), our method requires only 16, 15, and 10 queries, significantly lower than the prior approach.

Table 5. KMA on CCA-secure KEMs.

	Kyber1024	Kyber768	Kyber512	FireSaber	Saber	LightSaber
Li et al. [7]	2176.24	1632.10	1215.78	2433.39	2016.42	1438.79
Ours	**12**	**9**	**6**	**16**	**15**	**10**

These results demonstrate that our method, which leverages the HWI leakage model to recover the full message m', achieves a substantial reduction in query complexity compared to existing techniques. This efficiency is particularly evident in higher-dimensional KEMs, underscoring the practical impact of our method.

7 Conclusion

This paper advances the KMA methods on lattice-based KEMs, such as Kyber and Saber, by addressing critical challenges in efficiency, query complexity, and detectability. Our work demonstrates that even with standard oracles, significant improvements in attack performance and stealth can be achieved through innovative strategies. The multi-bit inference approach reduces query complexity for CPA-secure KEMs, while the minimal-query method for CCA-secure KEMs leverages side-channel leakage to drastically lower the number of required queries. Additionally, the stealthy KMA variant ensures that forged ciphertexts are statistically indistinguishable from legitimate communications, enhancing the attack's covertness.

These findings not only highlight vulnerabilities in current post-quantum cryptographic schemes but also provide new perspectives for the field. Future research could explore further optimizations in attack strategies, develop enhanced defenses, or extend these methods to other post-quantum cryptographic primitives. Ultimately, this work underscores the need for continued scrutiny and improvement of post-quantum KEM security to withstand sophisticated oracle-based attacks.

Acknowledgements. This work is supported in part by National Key R&D Program of China (No. 2022YFB3103800), National Natural Science Foundation of China (No. U2336205, No. 62202230, No. 62202231, No. 62302224, No. 62302226) and Innovation Guidance and Technology Enterprise Cultivation Program (No. 202404BQ040148).

References

1. Basso, A., et al.: Saber: Mod-LWR based kem (round 3 submission) (2020). https://www.esat.kuleuven.be/cosic/pqcrypto/saber/
2. Bos, J.W., et al.: CRYSTALS - kyber: a cca-secure module-lattice-based KEM. In: 2018 IEEE European Symposium on Security and Privacy, EuroS&P 2018, London, United Kingdom, 24–26 April 2018, pp. 353–367. IEEE (2018). https://doi.org/10.1109/EUROSP.2018.00032
3. Fujisaki, E., Okamoto, T.: Secure integration of asymmetric and symmetric encryption schemes. In: Wiener, M. (ed.) CRYPTO 1999. LNCS, vol. 1666, pp. 537–554. Springer, Heidelberg (1999). https://doi.org/10.1007/3-540-48405-1_34
4. Greuet, A., Montoya, S., Renault, G.: Attack on LAC key exchange in misuse situation. In: Krenn, S., Shulman, H., Vaudenay, S. (eds.) CANS 2020. LNCS, vol. 12579, pp. 549–569. Springer, Cham (2020). https://doi.org/10.1007/978-3-030-65411-5_27
5. Guo, Q., Mårtensson, E.: Do not bound to a single position: near-optimal multi-positional mismatch attacks against kyber and saber. In: Johansson, T., Smith-Tone, D. (eds.) Post-Quantum Cryptography - 14th International Workshop, PQCrypto 2023, College Park, MD, USA, 16–18 August 2023, Proceedings. Lecture Notes in Computer Science, vol. 14154, pp. 291–320. Springer, Heidelberg (2023). https://doi.org/10.1007/978-3-031-40003-2_11

6. Guo, Q., Mårtensson, E., Åström, A.: The perils of limited key reuse: adaptive and parallel mismatch attacks with post-processing against kyber. IACR Commun. Cryptol. 1(3), 21 (2024). https://doi.org/10.62056/A3N5QJ888
7. Li, Z., Xu, J., Zou, Y., Hu, L.: Key recovery attack on crystals-kyber and saber kems in key reuse scenario. In: García-Alfaro, J., Kozik, R., Choras, M., Katsikas, S.K. (eds.) Computer Security - ESORICS 2024 - 29th European Symposium on Research in Computer Security, Bydgoszcz, Poland, 16–20 September 2024, Proceedings, Part III. Lecture Notes in Computer Science, vol. 14984, pp. 259–278. Springer, Heidelberg (2024). https://doi.org/10.1007/978-3-031-70896-1_13
8. Patton, C., Shrimpton, T.: Security in the presence of key reuse: context-separable interfaces and their applications. In: Boldyreva, A., Micciancio, D. (eds.) CRYPTO 2019. LNCS, vol. 11692, pp. 738–768. Springer, Cham (2019). https://doi.org/10.1007/978-3-030-26948-7_26
9. Qin, Y., Cheng, C., Zhang, X., Pan, Y., Hu, L., Ding, J.: A systematic approach and analysis of key mismatch attacks on lattice-based NIST candidate kems. In: Tibouchi, M., Wang, H. (eds.) Advances in Cryptology - ASIACRYPT 2021 - 27th International Conference on the Theory and Application of Cryptology and Information Security, Singapore, 6–10 December 2021, Proceedings, Part IV. Lecture Notes in Computer Science, vol. 13093, pp. 92–121. Springer, Heidelberg (2021). https://doi.org/10.1007/978-3-030-92068-5_4
10. Raiber, F., Kurland, O.: Kullback-leibler divergence revisited. In: Kamps, J., Kanoulas, E., de Rijke, M., Fang, H., Yilmaz, E. (eds.) Proceedings of the ACM SIGIR International Conference on Theory of Information Retrieval, ICTIR 2017, Amsterdam, The Netherlands, 1–4 October 2017, pp. 117–124. ACM (2017). https://doi.org/10.1145/3121050.3121062
11. Ravi, P., Bhasin, S., Roy, S.S., Chattopadhyay, A.: On exploiting message leakage in (few) NIST PQC candidates for practical message recovery attacks. IEEE Trans. Inf. Forensics Secur. 17, 684–699 (2022). https://doi.org/10.1109/TIFS.2021.3139268
12. Shao, M., Liu, Y., Zhou, Y.: Pairwise and parallel: enhancing the key mismatch attacks on kyber and beyond. In: Zhou, J., Quek, T.Q.S., Gao, D., Cárdenas, A.A. (eds.) Proceedings of the 19th ACM Asia Conference on Computer and Communications Security, ASIA CCS 2024, Singapore, 1–5 July 2024. ACM (2024). https://doi.org/10.1145/3634737.3637661
13. Shor, P.W.: Algorithms for quantum computation: discrete logarithms and factoring. In: 35th Annual Symposium on Foundations of Computer Science, Santa Fe, New Mexico, USA, 20–22 November 1994, pp. 124–134. IEEE Computer Society (1994). https://doi.org/10.1109/SFCS.1994.365700
14. Sosnowski, M., et al.: The performance of post-quantum TLS 1.3. In: Rossi, D., Secci, S., Bonaventure, O., Qiu, L. (eds.) Companion of the 19th International Conference on emerging Networking EXperiments and Technologies, CoNEXT 2023, Paris, France, 5–8 December 2023, pp. 19–27. ACM (2023). https://doi.org/10.1145/3624354.3630585
15. National Institute of Standards and Technology: Post-quantum cryptography standardization project (2016). https://csrc.nist.gov/projects/post-quantum-cryptography
16. National Institute of Standards and Technology: Fips 203: Module-lattice-based key-encapsulation mechanism standard (2024). https://doi.org/10.6028/NIST.FIPS.203

17. Zhou, B., Jiang, H., Zhao, Y.: CPA-secure KEMs are also sufficient for post-quantum TLS 1.3. In: Chung, K., Sasaki, Y. (eds.) Advances in Cryptology - ASIACRYPT 2024 - 30th International Conference on the Theory and Application of Cryptology and Information Security, Kolkata, India, 9–13 December 2024, Proceedings, Part III. Lecture Notes in Computer Science, vol. 15486, pp. 433–464. Springer, Heidelberg (2024). https://doi.org/10.1007/978-981-96-0891-1_14

Code Encryption with Intel TME-MK for Control-Flow Enforcement

Martin Unterguggenberger[✉], Lukas Lamster, Mathias Oberhuber, Simon Scherer, and Stefan Mangard

Graz University of Technology, Graz, Austria
martin.unterguggenberger@tugraz.at

Abstract. Memory safety errors enable an adversary to corrupt code pointers, diverting the program's control flow. Recent CPU features, such as Intel CET/IBT, harden software systems against exploitation attempts that maliciously redirect control flow operations. While IBT limits valid indirect branch targets, forward-edge transfers can still be redirected to any IBT-marked function. Thus, IBT cannot provide fine-grained protection against forward-edge control-flow attacks.

This paper presents code encryption with Intel TME-MK, a novel approach for control-flow enforcement against software exploitation on off-the-shelf x86 machines. We repurpose the Intel TME-MK runtime encryption to achieve function-level code encryption. Encrypted functions are only accessible through function pointers associated with the correct key, thereby enforcing fine-grained restrictions for control-flow transfers. We demonstrate two new encryption-based techniques for software hardening in practice: forward-edge control-flow integrity and library encryption. We implement a security-hardened toolchain that combines compiler instrumentation and a loader extension to ensure the validity of the program's execution flow through efficient hardware-backed encryption. Our prototype shows a geomean performance overhead of 7.8 % for forward-edge control-flow integrity and 2.2 % for library encryption evaluated with the SPEC CPU2017 benchmark suite.

Keywords: Code Encryption · Control-Flow Integrity · Intel TME-MK

1 Introduction

Coding errors that introduce memory safety bugs into software systems are a severe threat to platform security [45,49,63]. Such memory errors are a main root cause for enabling critical zero-day exploits [22,25,50]. A malicious actor can exploit how (non-memory safe) C/C++ software interacts with memory [53,61]. This way, an adversary can overwrite a code pointer, e.g., a function pointer or a return address, to divert the program's execution flow. Control-flow redirection allows for advanced exploitation techniques that are generally classified as code-reuse attacks. For instance, return-into-libc [59] overwrites a return address to redirect the control flow to a library function (e.g., system in libc). Furthermore, ROP [11,54] and COP/JOP [9,15] are powerful attacks that allow for arbitrary attack flows by chaining existing code gadgets located in executable memory.

Software-hardening defenses, such as security-enhancing compiler options, are essential for exploit mitigation throughout the entire low-level software stack. Security extensions need to harden legacy and future C/C++ codebases while being constrained to strict system requirements, e.g., minor performance impact and compatibility with legacy x86 software. To maintain efficiency and compatibility while preventing the exploitation of vulnerabilities, defense mechanisms must be integrated into the processor and enforced in hardware [38,51,60,66].

CPU features, such as Intel Control-flow Enforcement Technology (CET) [60], address specific sub-classes of control-flow hijacking attacks. Intel CET provides a shadow stack feature that ensures the integrity of return addresses. This strong protection against return address manipulation enables backward-edge control-flow integrity (CFI) [1,12,14]. Moreover, Intel CET introduces the Indirect Branch Tracking (IBT) feature, which explicitly marks valid destinations for the program's execution flow. Thus, forward-edge control-flow transfers, such as indirect jumps and calls, are exclusively limited to IBT-marked functions, which are identified via designated landing pad instructions. Any indirect branch to an unmarked address is interpreted as a control-flow hijacking attempt and causes an exception. However, IBT can only provide coarse-grained CFI. As all valid targets are marked using the same landing pad instruction, IBT cannot distinguish between multiple valid indirect branch targets. Thus, while IBT makes exploitation harder, this imprecision still allows an attacker to divert the control flow to any IBT-marked location anywhere in the program's code region [14,56].

In this paper, we present a novel approach for control-flow enforcement through fine-grained code encryption on off-the-shelf x86 machines. We repurpose Intel's encryption technology, Total Memory Encryption Multi-Key (TME-MK) [27,29], for function-granular code encryption. Intel TME-MK implements efficient runtime encryption, which is typically used for page-granular encryption of confidential virtual machines (VM) [28,30]. Our design builds on top of the TME-MK feature to encrypt code on a function granularity through the use of page aliasing, a technique that allows multiple virtual addresses to refer to the same physical memory. Function-granular code encryption enables two new toolchain hardening techniques: forward-edge CFI and library encryption.

Code encryption and linking function pointers with encryption keys restrict access to application or library functions. This approach limits available functions within the program, thereby mitigating control-flow attacks by enforcing fine-grained CFI policies or preventing the code reuse of security-critical library functions. The forced use of encryption keys for function pointers restricts control-flow transfers, as incorrect decryption leads to garbled code and, thus, results in the execution of arbitrary pseudo-random instructions, which likely causes a fault [33]. Compared to IBT, which limits indirect branches to any marked function entry, our design restricts the overall set of accessible functions by leveraging up to 32K encryption keys. Moreover, combining our code encryption with IBT offers synergies, *i.e.*, confining indirect branches to the function entry and reducing the set of accessible functions. Also, violations are detected, as the incorrect decryption of code is unlikely to lead to valid landing pads.

We implement a hardened toolchain consisting of an LLVM [37] extension, a modified loader, and a kernel patch, enabling control-flow enforcement through compiler instrumentation with hardware-backed encryption. Moreover, we provide an in-depth security analysis of our design and a performance evaluation using SPEC CPU2017 [10]. Our prototype shows practical results with a geomean overhead of 7.8 % for forward-edge CFI and 2.2 % for library encryption.

Contributions. In summary, we make the following contributions:

1. We present code encryption with Intel TME-MK, a novel approach that enforces fine-grained security policies on control-flow transfers by encrypting functions and linking function pointers to encryption keys.
2. We provide new insights on the application of code encryption: We detail two software hardening techniques, *i.e.*, forward-edge CFI and library encryption. In addition, we outline synergies of our encryption approach, resulting in garbled code, with detection through wrongly decrypted IBT landing pads.
3. We develop a prototype of our security-hardened toolchain and evaluate the performance, showcasing practical results for SPEC CPU2017.
4. We conduct an in-depth security analysis, highlighting the security properties and efficacy of our encryption-based design.

Outline. The paper is organized as follows. Section 2 provides the background of this work. Section 3 defines our threat model. Section 4 presents the design, and Sect. 5 describes the implementation of our prototype. Section 6 and Sect. 7 provide the security analysis and performance evaluation. Section 8 discusses related and future work. Section 9 concludes this work.

2 Background

This section provides the background on control-flow hijacking attacks, Intel Control-flow Enforcement Technology (CET), and Intel Total Memory Encryption Multi-Key (TME-MK).

2.1 Control-Flow Attacks

Software that is developed in non-memory safe programming languages (e.g., C and C++) is vulnerable to memory safety errors. These memory safety vulnerabilities, introduced by coding errors, enable a malicious actor to corrupt data located in memory. Consequently, this also allows an adversary to modify code pointers (e.g., function pointers or return addresses) through illegitimate memory interactions. These code pointers are then used by control flow instructions (e.g., ret, call, or jmp instructions). Hence, the corruption of the target address allows the redirection of the program's execution, hijacking the control flow.

In addition, more advanced exploitation techniques, such as return-oriented programming (ROP) [11,16], aim to reuse existing code from the executable memory to achieve arbitrary attack flows. Specifically, ROP attacks chain together multiple instruction sequences, called ROP gadgets, to achieve arbitrary attack flows through the exploitation of return instructions. Note that the return instruction retrieves the address of the next instruction from the stack and resumes the program execution from that address. By carefully chaining together these gadgets, also referred to as crafting an ROP chain, and manipulating return addresses located on the stack, the attacker can execute a sequence of gadgets to achieve arbitrary code execution flows.

Similarly, call/jmp-oriented programming (COP/JOP) [9,15] reuses existing code in memory through the redirection of indirect calls and jumps. For instance, these techniques achieve an arbitrary attack flow through the help of a dispatcher function [9]. Due to their use of gadgets in executable memory, ROP and COP/JOP attacks are generally classified as so-called code reuse attacks.

2.2 Intel Control-Flow Enforcement Technology

Intel Control-flow Enforcement Technology (CET) [60] is a set of architectural elements developed to help ensure the integrity of control-flow transfers within a program. Thereby, the processor is extended with capabilities to enforce control-flow integrity (CFI) [1,12,14] for both forward-edge and backward-edge transfers.

First, Intel CET provides a hardware-based shadow stack feature that offers strong protection against return address modification, thereby providing backward-edge CFI. Specifically, the shadow stack organizes and manages a separate stack that exclusively contains return addresses. On each function call, a copy of the return address is stored on the shadow stack, thus becoming inaccessible to the adversary. When exiting the called function, the return address is taken from the regular stack. In addition, this (potentially modified) address is then compared to the return address stored on the shadow stack. A mismatch during this comparison indicates a corrupted return address and results in an exception. Thus, return-based code-reuse attacks, e.g., return-into-libc [59] and ROP [11,54] attacks, are detected and mitigated.

Second, Intel CET provides forward-edge CFI through the integration of Indirect Branch Tracking (IBT). IBT extends the x86 ISA with landing pad instructions (e.g., endbr64). Typically, a compiler inserts landing pads in function entries to mark valid indirect call/jump targets in executable memory. Since IBT reduces the potential destinations of indirect branches to valid landing pad instructions, it greatly reduces the attack surface for control-flow hijacking attacks such as COP/JOP [9,15]. However, IBT can only provide coarse-grained CFI. As all valid function entries are identified using the same landing pad instructions, an attacker can still divert the control flow to all function entries marked with IBT within the application or (shared) libraries [56].

2.3 Intel Total Memory Encryption Multi-Key

Intel's memory encryption technology, Total Memory Encryption (TME) [27], allows transparent encryption of the system's entire physical memory with a single encryption key. The Total Memory Encryption Multi-Key (TME-MK) [27] extension provides DRAM encryption with multiple encryption keys, enabling the selection of page-granular encryption keys through the processor page tables [27,29]. Intel TME-MK is an architectural element mainly used for the encryption of virtual machines (VMs) and containers, thereby ensuring the confidentiality of DRAM data and helping to counteract physical attacks [26,28].

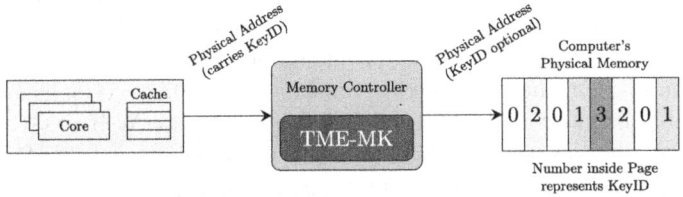

Fig. 1. Overview of the Intel TME-MK memory encryption.

Figure 1 shows an overview of Intel TME-MK's memory encryption. TME-MK operates transparently on memory transactions between the CPU core and the DRAM memory controller. Writing to memory encrypts the data, and subsequently, reading from memory decrypts the previously encrypted data. TME-MK organizes its cryptographic key material using a key table that maps the key identifiers (keyIDs) to their respective encryption keys. To offer more flexibility, TME-MK supports different encryption modes, such as 128-bit and 256-bit AES-XTS [20,21,43,55] encryption. Additionally, the Intel Trust Domain Extensions (TDX) [28,30] add support for authenticated encryption with cryptographic integrity through a message authentication code (MAC).

Memory pages are encrypted depending on the keyID encoded into the upper part of the physical address of the memory request. Thus, the physical address carries the keyID to the encryption engine in the memory controller, controlling the encryption key and mode used for the memory interactions. Note that TME-MK is specified for up to 2^{15} encryption keys [27]. As the encoding of keyIDs results in a reduction of addressable physical memory, the size of the keyID is platform-dependent and varies across processors with TME-MK support.

3 Threat Model

We consider an attacker that intends to exploit a memory safety vulnerability to corrupt a code pointer (e.g., a function pointer located in memory), hijacking

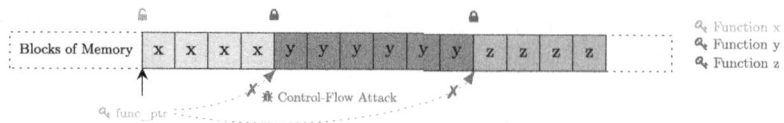

Fig. 2. High-level concept of the function-granular code encryption.

the control flow of an unprivileged user space program. Thereby, the adversary exploits a vulnerability in an attempt to modify the program state or behavior through the redirection of the program's execution flow. Moreover, we assume that the attacker knows the address space layout of the target program, *i.e.*, the attacker knows the addresses of potentially lucrative branch targets.

Intel CET [60] and comparable security features from other CPU vendors (e.g., AMD Shadow Stack [4] and ARM Guarded Control Stack [5]) are widely available. Thus, we assume that the Intel CET shadow stack feature is enabled and provides us with backward-edge control-flow integrity.

We assume that the privileged operating system/hypervisor is benign and that writable memory is marked as non-executable (see Write-XOR-Execute). We consider other attack vectors, such as side-channel attacks [35,41] and fault injection attacks [34,46,62], to be out of the scope of this work.

4 Design

In this section, we present our novel technique for control-flow enforcement through code encryption that effectively hardens software against control-flow hijacking attacks. We repurpose the Intel TME-MK encryption engine, available on off-the-shelf Intel x86 CPUs, to encrypt individual functions for the fine-grained restriction of forward-edge control-flow transfers.

4.1 High-Level Overview

At its core, our design encrypts individual functions with designated encryption keys. Encrypted functions are only available for call sites with a matching key that correctly decrypts the function. When performing an indirect call, the key associated with the functions pointer is used to decrypt the call target. Only functions encrypted with the associated key will be decrypted into meaningful code. Thus, our design enables fine-grained control-flow enforcement through code encryption. We repurpose the Intel TME-MK hardware feature to achieve function-granular code encryption on commodity x86 CPUs. Moreover, our hardened toolchain identifies function pointers and applies compiler-based code instrumentation *to enforce the use of designated encryption keys*, depending on the defined security policy. Note that our generic code encryption scheme enables a variety of security policies based on the underlying code encryption mechanism. While this work focuses on a function signature-based policy as a proof-of-concept, other CFI policies [42,64,67] can also be implemented.

Figure 2 illustrates a high-level overview of the function-granular code encryption employed by our design. In the example, individual 16B memory blocks of the code section are encrypted with the different encryption keys assigned to the functions x, y, and z. Moreover, control-flow transfers are instrumented to enforce the usage of a dedicated encryption key defined by the security policy. The example shows a function pointer associated with the encryption key of function x that is dereferenced by an indirect function call. Enforcing the usage of the encryption key for function x limits the valid call targets to destinations encrypted with the respective key. This way, any redirection of the control flow by tampering with the function pointer, e.g., to the functions y or z, leads to a decryption with a wrong key. Decrypting code with an incorrect key leads to garbled code due to a pseudo-random decryption result, which the attacker cannot control. Hence, executing instructions of a function encrypted with a different key is impossible as the attacker can only receive garbled code.

Furthermore, we assume that backward-edge control-flow transfers are protected by Intel CET's shadow stack feature. Note that code encryption also synergizes with the Intel IBT landing pads. Particularly, our encryption approach results in garbled code that is then detected through IBT, as the incorrect decryption of code is very unlikely to produce a valid landing pad instruction.

4.2 Code Encryption with Intel TME-MK

Our design repurposes the Intel TME-MK feature to efficiently encrypt executable code in memory. Intel TME-MK, originally intended for the encryption of entire virtual machines, enables page-granular encryption of memory. The encryption uses up to 15-bit keyIDs encoded in the physical address field of the page table entry to select up to 32K encryption keys [27]. All memory transactions between the CPU core and the main memory (*i.e.*, the DRAM) are transparently encrypted using the selected key. Our design advances this page-level encryption and allows the assignment of different encryption keys to individual functions.

Function-Granular Encryption. While TME-MK operates on page granularity, we can achieve function-granular encryption through page aliasing [57,58,65]. Figure 3 illustrates the function-granular code encryption with Intel TME-MK. Aliasing allows multiple virtual addresses to refer to the same physical memory and is typically used for shared memory. For every keyID, the program's code region is mapped into the virtual address space using a different virtual base address. However, all mapped regions reference the same physical memory. Thus, each keyID has a unique alias that maps to the physical memory using the associated keyID. Note that the alias mappings are chosen so that the code regions do not overlap with each other or with other regions in the virtual address space. At program startup, each function in the code is encrypted by writing it to memory using the corresponding alias for the intended keyID. As the setup of mappings and encryption of individual functions must precede the regular program execution, these steps are performed by the loader. After initialization, the loader sets

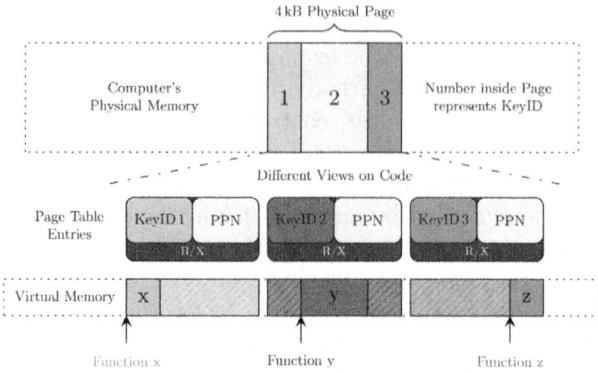

Fig. 3. Overview of the function-granular code encryption through Intel TME-MK. Aliasing creates different views on the computer's physical memory. Here, three functions, x, y, and z, are located on the same physical page while each function is encrypted with its respective encryption key (*i.e.*, keyID 1, 2, and 3). The compiler enforces the usage of keyIDs; thus, code can only be executed through function pointers associated with the correct keyID. This limits control-flow transfers as access with an incorrect keyID results in garbled code.

the permissions of code pages back to *read-only* and *executable*. While the loader ensures that each function is encrypted with the intended keyID, we must also ensure that the program uses the correct keyID for function calls at runtime. We achieve this through compiler instrumentation that forces indirect branches to use the virtual base address of the designated alias mappings and, thus, the corresponding encryption keys for forward-edge control-flow transfers.

The example given in Fig. 3 shows a 4 kB code page containing three distinct functions: x, y, and z. Memory aliasing creates different views on the program's code region, *i.e.*, it allows multiple virtual addresses to refer to the same physical memory location using different keyIDs. The functions x, y, and z can be accessed through the three mappings with the corresponding keyIDs 1, 2, and 3, respectively. Thus, function x can only be called when accessed through keyID 1 since other aliases result in garbled code and crash on execution.

The compiler enforces the usage of a specific keyID associated with the function pointer, depending on the security policy. Precisely, our design instruments the virtual addresses of the function pointers to refer to the alias mapping of the code section associated with their designated keyIDs. Depending on the security policy, the control-flow enforcement of our mechanism provides toolchain hardening for forward-edge CFI or library code encryption.

4.3 Control-Flow Enforcement

We leverage our code encryption approach to harden C/C++ software. First, our design allows the enforcement of fine-grained CFI policies to protect forward-edge control-flow transfers. Second, our design enables the encryption of library code that helps to protect against code reuse of security-critical library functions.

Forward-Edge Control-Flow Integrity. Control-flow attacks allow a malicious actor to redirect program execution to different destinations. When an adversary manages to corrupt the address of a function pointer used by a control-flow operation, they can divert the control flow to arbitrary code locations.

To counteract this threat, our design confines indirect branches to individual functions. We achieve this restriction of valid destinations for control-flow transfers by associating keyIDs (that correspond to a specific encryption key) with function pointers. This limits potential branch targets, as functions can only be executed through the use of a function pointer with the correct keyID. In general, our generic design can enforce a variety of CFI policies, e.g., type-based CFI [64]. For our proof-of-concept, we derive the CFI policy from the *function signature* of the target destination. Therefore, the compiler toolchain identifies function pointers and derives the keyIDs from their function signature. The mapping from function signatures to keyIDs is used to associate function pointers with encryption keys through compiler instrumentation. Subsequently, the function signatures and corresponding keyIDs are encoded as metadata into the ELF binary. The modified loader relies on this metadata and is responsible for creating the mappings for all available keyIDs of the code region, and encrypting the functions with the associated encryption keys upon program startup.

Even with Intel IBT, the state-of-the-art for CFI in commodity systems, an attacker can divert the control flow to any marked function entry. Our code encryption technique provides more fine-grained CFI, as forward-edge control-flow transfers only result in meaningful code if the target is decrypted with the intended key. Further, forward-edge CFI within libraries can be easily achieved by statically compiling and linking the application and libraries with our toolchain. In the case of our proof-of-concept CFI policy, attackers are confined to functions of the same function signature, *i.e.*, function signature-granular CFI. For other functions, CFI violations result in garbled code. In such a case, the attacker would force the program to execute arbitrary pseudo-random instructions that likely crash the program [33]. We can additionally improve the reliability by combining our encryption-based approach with IBT. As function entries must be marked by landing pads, most CFI violations are detected by IBT as the incorrectly decrypted code is highly unlikely to result in a valid landing pad. Alternatively, our code encryption approach can use Intel TME-MK with integrity support, detecting incorrect code accesses through a cryptographic MAC.

Library Code Encryption. The redirection of control-flow transfers can also be misused to call or jump into library functions. Library functions are a welcoming exploitation target as they often contain security-critical code, e.g., code reuse of functions in the C standard library [59].

To help protect against code reuse attacks of library functions, we restrict control-flow transfers from the application into shared libraries through security policies. Similar to our CFI scheme discussed above, we instrument the control-flow operations of the application to use a designated encryption key. Here, the application's code is assigned a default encryption key. We allow the selective hardening of software libraries to restrict access to a subset of functions that execute security-critical code. Security-critical library functions, such as system or exec, are encrypted with dedicated encryption keys that differ from the default key. Thus, invalid paths in the control-flow graph targeting critical library functions are restricted, as the matching key is required for correct decryption.

Library functions that are invoked via indirect branches are confined as the corresponding function pointer is associated with an encryption key due to our instrumentation. This encryption key defines which functions within the library can be accessed. Moreover, library calls are also instrumented, enforcing the usage of the associated encryption key for the library function. Note that shared libraries also need to be accessible for unprotected programs. Thus, our toolchain uses dedicated versions of the hardened shared libraries for our code encryption to maintain compatibility with unprotected programs.

5 Implementation

In the following, we describe the prototype implementation of our toolchain, which consists of an LLVM extension, a modified loader, and a kernel patch.

5.1 Compiler Extension

We implement our code encryption scheme as an extension to the LLVM [37] compiler (version 17.0.0). Our prototype integrates a set of compiler passes to the LLVM optimizer and the x86 backend. The backend passes insert a custom ELF section for metadata and perform the code instrumentation. Specifically, we implement a compiler pass that creates a custom ELF section and encodes metadata for all functions depending on the used security policy. For forward-edge CFI, our prototype derives the keyID from the function signature by generating a truncated hash value of the LLVM IR type information that maps to a dedicated keyID. For library encryption, the compiler pass allows the selection of keyIDs for individual library functions that are considered security critical.

Moreover, we implement a compiler pass that retrieves the keyIDs and instruments the corresponding control-flow instructions, linking them to the correct alias mappings. To achieve this, we analyze and identify all indirect function calls and instrument the target address by setting its alias bits associated with the above-identified keyID; e.g., the corresponding function signature. Concretely, we implement this by manipulating a specific bit range of the virtual address according to the keyID, depending on the security policy. For indirect branches, the function pointer is instrumented through logical operations, *i.e.*, by clearing the bit range and subsequently inserting the keyID into the alias bit range. This procedure forces the function pointers to use their intended virtual address alias corresponding to the policies' designated encryption key. Note that our compiler framework is fully parameterizable in regard to the bit range of the virtual address space to achieve compatibility with different memory layouts. Therefore, our extension offers two compiler options to define the number of available keyIDs and the bit range of the aliased code mappings. The compiler pass also needs to correct the target addresses for direct function calls within the program. As all functions are encrypted with their associated encryption keys to enforce our CFI policies, direct function calls also need to use the intended virtual address alias (e.g., keyID derived by the function signature) to decrypt functions correctly. Therefore, we patch the content of the `rip` register to use the intended virtual address to access the function with the correct keyID.

We also implement optimization passes operating on the LLVM IR. We need to handle statically allocated data that contain a function pointer in their initializer value, such as function pointers stored in global/static variables. Thus, we invoke a compiler-generated startup routine that correctly initializes global data containing function pointers with the correct keyID. In addition, we assign all static functions a unique function name (being able to differentiate functions with the same name but different signatures) and handle non-compatible operations like comparisons of function pointers. To optimize the performance of forward-edge CFI, our compiler toolchain additionally aligns and pads functions to the cache line size of 64B. This alignment is essential, as accessing an already cached memory region using a different memory alias forces the hardware to evict the currently cached version [2]. The LLVM compiler already provides an interface for this function alignment. In addition, we use the LLVM support for Intel IBT to insert landing pads for function entries.

For library code encryption, control-flow operations of the program are instrumented similarly to the CFI policy. Here, the compiler either enforces the use of the default encryption key (*i.e.*, keyID 0) or a designated encryption key associated with a security-critical function. Special care is required for shared libraries as these function calls are performed through the PLT. We also map the shared library with all available keyIDs and separately encrypt security-critical functions according to the security policy. The PLT stub uses the GOT entry to either call the dynamic linker to resolve the destination, or already contains the address of the library function. We instrument the PLT stub to enforce the use of the keyID associated with the defined security policy. This way, security-critical functions can only be called from their respective PLT entry or function pointers that are allowed to target this library function.

Note that we use an Intel Xeon Gold 6530 processor as our main development and evaluation platform. While Intel TME-MK supports up to 15-bit keyIDs, our processor supports 6-bit keyIDs, resulting in a total of 64 encryption keys. For our prototype, this means that keyID collisions for some function signatures can occur, which is a limitation of our evaluation platform. However, our compiler extension can also be configured in regards to the supported number of keyIDs of the processor, allowing the use of up to 15-bit keyIDs for future processors.

5.2 ELF Loader

We provide toolchain support for our code encryption scheme with a modified ELF loader. The loader is responsible for creating alias mappings to the code section for all available keyIDs (*i.e.*, 6-bit keyIDs on our evaluation platform). This allows access to the code section through all the associated encryption keys.

Moreover, the loader needs to encrypt individual functions depending on the used security policy. Therefore, the loader relies on the metadata encoded in our custom ELF section previously inserted by the compiler. The loader parses this metadata and encrypts the code of individual functions depending on the security policy, *i.e.*, by writing the function's code with the designated keyID to memory. During this initial setup, we flush cache lines when updating the associated keyID to ensure all writes are done with a single active keyID, as recommended by the TME-MK specification [27]. After code encryption, we change the page permissions of the code section back to *read-only* and *executable*.

In addition, the loader maps the PLT/GOT for every aliased code section. This is required since PLT calls are performed through instruction pointer relative-addressing. For our prototype, the loader also initializes shared libraries and maps them for all available keyIDs. However, dynamic linker support could be added to achieve an on-demand mapping and encryption of shared libraries.

5.3 Linux Kernel Patch

Operating system support is necessary to provide a software interface to control the Intel TME-MK memory encryption. Intel TME-MK repurposes up to 15-bit of the physical address (starting with the highest order bit available) located in the PTE to encode the keyID. We use an experimental Linux kernel patch provided by Intel Labs that allows to assign keyIDs through a syscall interface [31]. Specifically, the kernel patch enables additional arguments for the mprotect system call to associate a keyID with a specific range of memory pages.

6 Security Analysis

This section analyzes the derived security properties of our encryption-based design. We assume an adversary that manipulates a code pointer to redirect the program's control flow (see Sect. 3). We further distinguish between control-flow attacks that target forward-edge and backward-edge control-flow transfers. For backward-edge control-flow transfers, we assume that the Intel CET shadow stack efficiently protects the return address. Thus, corrupting the return addresses becomes infeasible, *i.e.*, the attacker cannot overwrite return addresses on the shadow stack. Furthermore, the adversary can attempt to gain control over a function pointer to divert the forward-edge control-flow transfer. Here, the attacker exploits a memory safety vulnerability to corrupt a function pointer and hijack the control flow, e.g., a buffer overflow that allows to overwrite and manipulate the function pointer and function arguments.

Function Pointer. Our generic code encryption design ensures fine-grained control-flow enforcement by linking function pointers with encryption keys. If an adversary gains control of a function pointer and manipulates its address to redirect control flow, the attack surface is confined. The compiler ensures that function pointers are instrumented to use their designated keyID, restricting forward-edge control-flow transfers solely to destinations that are permitted by the defined security policy. Furthermore, keyID forgery is prevented through our code instrumentation since the correct alias bits are explicitly set depending on the security policy directly before dereferencing the function pointer.

CFI Policy. Our generic design enables the implementation of different policies, such as CFI and library encryption. The prototype implements a CFI policy that derives valid indirect control-flow targets from *function signatures*. This signature-based CFI policy associates a designated keyID (mapping to an encryption key) for each function signature. This way, function pointers are limited to solely target destinations with their intended function signature, *i.e.*, signature-granular CFI confining the control flow to matching signatures. Note, however, that other CFI policies [42,64,67] can also be implemented on top of our code encryption scheme. In theory, our design can take advantage of up to 32K encryption keys, as Intel TME-MK is specified for up to 15-bit keyIDs, representing the total number of distinct encrypted functions leveraged by the CFI policy. Nevertheless, the number of available keyIDs is platform-specific, e.g., our evaluation platform supports 6-bit keyIDs. This can result in keyID collisions for some function signatures, which is a limitation of our evaluation platform.

Code Encryption. Our design enforces that program execution receives code decrypted with the encryption key that corresponds to the used keyID. For policy violations, this results in the (incorrect) decryption of garbled code and, subsequently, the execution of arbitrary pseudo-random instructions. Precisely, the use of the wrong keyID leads to a cache miss and results in the data being served from DRAM, where the TME-MK encryption engine decrypts the data. The use of an incorrect keyID causes the first instruction fetch to be decrypted with the wrong encryption key, executing garbled code and very likely causing a fault [33]. Moreover, our design uses IBT landing pads to detect control-flow attacks violating our security policies. It is highly unlikely that garbled code, due to the incorrect decryption, results in a valid landing pad instruction. Precisely, the probability that uniformly distributed data exactly matches a specific byte value is $\frac{1}{256}$. The endbr64 instruction uses a 4B instruction encoding. Thus, the probability of a decryption with a wrong key resulting in an endbr64 instruction can be given as $(\frac{1}{256})^4$, *i.e.*, 2^{-32}.

Authenticated Encryption. Moreover, our design can also take advantage of Intel TME-MK with integrity. Intel TDX [17,28,30] adds support for cryptographic integrity through authenticated encryption. Here, TME-MK provides an encryption mode that associates cache lines with a cryptographic MAC. This cryptographic integrity provides detection when functions are accessed with the incorrect key. Precisely, Intel TME-MK leverages a 28-bit MAC, resulting in a probability of $1 - 2^{-28}$ for detecting the violation and throwing an exception [65].

7 Performance Evaluation

In this section, we provide the performance evaluation of our design. We evaluate and discuss the overhead of our design with the SPEC CPU2017 [10] benchmark suite compiled with our LLVM extension and -O3 optimization level.

Evaluation Setup. We perform our evaluation on an Intel Xeon Gold 6530 processor with support for the Intel TME-MK memory encryption. The CPU features 32 cores, where each core has a 32 kB L1I/48kB L1D cache and a 2 MB L2 cache. All cores share a 160 kB L3 last-level cache (LLC). Moreover, our system configuration uses 512 GB DDR5-4800 DRAM with ECC memory. The given CPU provides 6-bit keyIDs that are usable for our code encryption scheme.

SPEC CPU2017 Results. For our evaluation, we benchmark our two security-hardened configurations and compare them to a baseline configuration, showcasing the performance overheads. Note that we use the *ref* input to evaluate all SPEC CPU2017 benchmarks. Our security-hardened configurations demonstrate the runtime overhead for forward-edge CFI and library code encryption, as detailed in Sect. 4. As our toolchain targets the hardening of C and C++ software, all Fortran benchmarks of SPEC CPU2017 are excluded. Furthermore, we exclude benchmarks with compatibility issues, e.g., the nab benchmark uses different function signatures for the forward declaration of external functions.

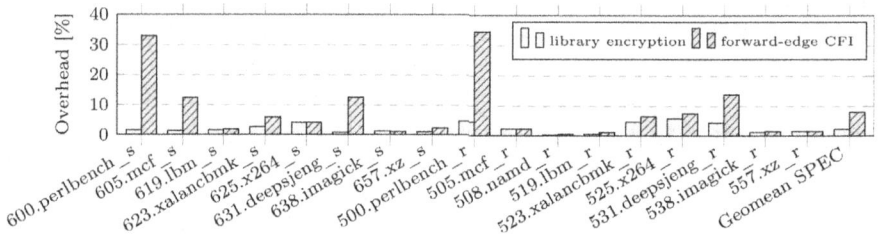

Fig. 4. The relative performance overhead of our design for SPEC CPU2017.

Figure 4 showcases the relative performance overhead of our design for the SPEC CPU2017 benchmark suite. We find that library code encryption imposes a low geomean overhead of 2.2 % for confining forward-edge control-flow transfers targeting security-critical library functions. Furthermore, signature-based

CFI imposes a geomean overhead of 7.8 % for fine-grained control-flow enforcement. The results vary across benchmarks. We find that the overhead mainly stems from two sources: the compiler instrumentation and the increased translation lookaside buffer (TLB) pressure caused by page aliasing. For example, our code encryption scheme imposes the largest performance overhead for the perlbench benchmark, which performs a higher relative number of function calls and returns than other benchmarks. In addition, we use the perf tool to further analyze the underlying causes of the incurred overhead. The results indicate that the overhead of the library encryption reflects the overhead of our compiler instrumentation. Moreover, page aliasing reduces TLB efficiency and increases the TLB miss rate, resulting in page table walks that increase memory latency. Note that the additional overhead of the signature-based CFI (compared to library encryption) strongly correlates with the increase in TLB pressure for all benchmarks. For instance, we find that the majority of the overhead for perlbench is due to the increase in the number of TLB misses by an order of magnitude.

8 Discussion

In this section, we compare our design with related work on control-flow enforcement, and discuss limitations and potential future work.

8.1 Related Work

FineIBT [23] provides fine-grained forward-edge CFI using Intel Indirect Branch Tracking (IBT) with compiler support for logical integrity checks to restrict valid indirect control-flow targets. Microsoft's Control Flow Guard (CFG) [8] enables forward-edge CFI through compiler instrumentation for runtime checks to validate the destinations of indirect control-flow transfers. In contrast, our design repurposes Intel TME-MK's hardware-backed encryption (*i.e.*, correctly decrypted code) instead of instrumenting logical integrity checks in software.

Code-pointer integrity (CPI) [36] ensures forward-edge CFI by enforcing integrity for code pointers. CPI identifies sensitive pointers (*i.e.*, code pointers and pointers that may access code pointers indirectly) through static analysis and instruments the program to store sensitive pointers and associated metadata at a protected memory region. The metadata of sensitive pointers is then checked on pointer dereferences. CPI also provides a safe stack [36] for provensafe objects.

In addition to CFI measures through logical integrity, CFI techniques based on cryptographic primitives have also been explored in prior work. For instance, ARM pointer authentication (PAuth) [51] and CCFI [44] provide CFI measures through the use of cryptographic message authentication codes (MACs). Also, PointGuard [19] enables pointer protection through the encryption of pointers.

The overall concept of ARM PAuth is to protect (code and data) pointers stored in memory from corruption [39,40]. Therefore, the cryptographic MAC, so-called pointer authentication code (PAC), of the pointer is generated and encoded into the upper bits of the pointer. This PAC ensures the pointer's integrity while stored in memory. Moreover, after loading the pointer from memory, the pointer is authenticated, detecting any potential manipulation (with probabilistic security depending on the size of the MAC [51]). ARM PAuth has been extensively studied, resulting in the outlining of potential weaknesses [13], e.g., PAC reuse [32,39] or PAC forgery [6]. Additionally, the PACMAN [52] vulnerability showcased how to brute-force PAC values through speculative execution.

Intel TME-MK has been used to help protect data in memory, e.g., by enforcing memory safety [57,58] and in-process isolation [65]. In addition, EC-CFI [48] presents control-flow integrity counteracting fault attacks by combining Intel TME-MK with the Intel virtualization technology. However, it is important to clarify that this approach is designed to protect against fault attacks [7]. This threat model includes a physical attacker that actively induces faults into the processor, e.g., through laser fault injection [7]. Contrarily, our approach targets a software attacker that exploits memory safety errors to hijack the control flow.

Other CFI schemes introduce custom hardware extensions for code encryption to primarily counteract fault attacks [18,24,47,68]. For example, SCFP [68] offers instruction granular control-flow protection by integrating an additional pipeline stage into the processor to decrypt the instructions during runtime. This protects the control flow against logical and physical attacks since the tampering of instructions leads to incorrect decryption and execution of pseudo-random instructions. In contrast, our design targets software attackers, while SCFP's instruction granular protection primarily focuses on counteracting fault attacks.

8.2 Limitations and Future Work

Our code encryption design requires an increased number of TLB entries, as each encryption key used within a page requires a separate TLB entry. This increases the TLB pressure, leading to a decrease in performance. Future optimizations can use 2MB-sized pages to lessen the overhead incurred by TLB pressure. Moreover, our design does not address fault injection attacks. An adversary with fault injection capabilities or physical access to the CPU poses a potential threat; thus, orthogonal countermeasures might be required.

This work implements signature-based CFI as a proof-of-concept; however, our generic design allows to enforce different security policies on top of the underlying code encryption mechanism. Future work could explore other CFI policies [42,64,67] to limit control-flow transfers. In addition, the AMD Secure Memory Encryption (SME) [33] feature enables memory encryption on AMD machines, leveraging a single encryption key. Recently, AMD also introduced Secure Memory Encryption Multi-Key (SME-MK) [3,4], an extension of AMD SME that supports multiple encryption keys. Future work could explore the implementation of a comparable code encryption scheme on AMD CPUs.

9 Conclusion

In this paper, we presented code encryption with Intel TME-MK, a novel approach for fine-grained control-flow enforcement on off-the-shelf x86 machines. We repurpose the Intel TME-MK hardware feature to encrypt individual functions and to associate control-flow operations with designated encryption keys. This restricts control-flow transfers solely to destinations that are permitted by our security policies, *i.e.*, encrypted with their respective encryption key.

This way, we enforce software hardening techniques for forward-edge CFI and library encryption by securing executable code via TME-MK's encryption. More concretely, our generic scheme allows us to efficiently encrypt individual functions through the use of up to 32K encryption keys. Control-flow hijacking leads to incorrect decryption and, thus, to garbled code, preventing software attacks that aim to illegitimately divert the program's execution flow through function pointer manipulation. This cryptographic restriction of control-flow transfers also achieves detection through wrongly decrypted IBT landing pads.

We implement a prototype of our security-hardened toolchain, consisting of an LLVM compiler extension, a modified ELF loader, and a kernel patch. Our performance evaluation showcases a geomean overhead of 7.8 % for forward-edge CFI and 2.2 % for library encryption using the SPEC CPU2017 benchmark suite.

Acknowledgments. We thank the anonymous reviewers for their valuable feedback that improved this work. This project has received funding from the Austrian Research Promotion Agency (FFG) via the AWARE project (FFG grant number 891092) and the RESIST project (FFG grant number 915106). Additional funding was provided by a generous gift from Intel.

References

1. Abadi, M., Budiu, M., Erlingsson, Ú., Ligatti, J.: Control-flow integrity. In: CCS (2005)
2. Aktas, E., Cohen, C., Eads, J., Forshaw, J., Wilhelm, F.: Intel Trust Domain Extensions (TDX) Security Review (2023). https://services.google.com/fh/files/misc/intel_tdx_-_full_report_041423.pdf. Accessed 10 June 2024
3. AMD: 4th Gen AMD EPYC Processor Architecture (2023). https://www.amd.com/en/products/processors/server/epyc/4th-generation-architecture.html. Accessed 27 May 2024
4. AMD: AMD64 Architecture Programmer's Manual Volume 2: System Programming (2025). https://www.amd.com/content/dam/amd/en/documents/processor-tech-docs/programmer-references/24593.pdf. Accessed 26 Feb 2025
5. Arm: Arm Architecture Reference Manual for A-profile architecture (2025). https://developer.arm.com/documentation/ddi0487. Accessed 26 Feb 2025
6. Azad, B.: Google Project Zero: Examining Pointer Authentication on the iPhone XS (2019). https://googleprojectzero.blogspot.com/2019/02/examining-pointer-authentication-on.html. Accessed 10 June 2024
7. Bar-El, H., Choukri, H., Naccache, D., Tunstall, M., Whelan, C.: The sorcerer's apprentice guide to fault attacks. Proc. IEEE **94**, 370–382 (2006)

8. Biondo, A., Conti, M., Lain, D.: Back to the epilogue: evading control flow guard via unaligned targets. In: NDSS (2018)
9. Bletsch, T.K., Jiang, X., Freeh, V.W., Liang, Z.: Jump-oriented programming: a new class of code-reuse attack. In: ASIACCS (2011)
10. Bucek, J., Lange, K., von Kistowski, J.: SPEC CPU2017: next-generation compute benchmark. In: ICPE (2018)
11. Buchanan, E., Roemer, R., Shacham, H., Savage, S.: When good instructions go bad: generalizing return-oriented programming to RISC. In: CCS (2008)
12. Burow, N., et al.: Control-flow integrity: precision, security, and performance. ACM Comput. Surv. **50**, 16:1–16:33 (2017)
13. Cai, Z., et al.: Demystifying pointer authentication on apple M1. In: USENIX Security (2023)
14. Carlini, N., Barresi, A., Payer, M., Wagner, D.A., Gross, T.R.: Control-flow bending: on the effectiveness of control-flow integrity. In: USENIX Security (2015)
15. Carlini, N., Wagner, D.A.: ROP is still dangerous: breaking modern defenses. In: USENIX Security (2014)
16. Checkoway, S., Davi, L., Dmitrienko, A., Sadeghi, A., Shacham, H., Winandy, M.: Return-oriented programming without returns. In: CCS (2010)
17. Cheng, P., et al.: Intel TDX demystified: a top-down approach. ACM Comput. Surv. **56**, 238:1–238:33 (2024)
18. de Clercq, R., et al.: SOFIA: software and control flow integrity architecture. In: DATE (2016)
19. Cowan, C., Beattie, S., Johansen, J., Wagle, P.: PointGuard^{TM}: protecting pointers from buffer overflow vulnerabilities. In: USENIX Security (2003)
20. Daemen, J., Rijmen, V.: The block cipher rijndael. In: CARDIS (1998)
21. Daemen, J., Rijmen, V.: The design of rijndael: AES - the advanced encryption standard. In: Information Security and Cryptography (2002)
22. Durumeric, Z., et al.: The matter of heartbleed. In: IMC (2014)
23. Gaidis, A.J., Moreira, J., Sun, K., Milburn, A., Atlidakis, V., Kemerlis, V.P.: FineIBT: fine-grain control-flow enforcement with indirect branch tracking. In: RAID (2023)
24. Gousselot, T., Dutertre, J., Potin, O., Rigaud, J.: Code encryption for confidentiality and execution integrity down to control signals. In: HOST (2025)
25. Graham-Cumming, J.: Incident report on memory leak caused by Cloudflare parser bug (2017). https://blog.cloudflare.com/incident-report-on-memory-leak-caused-by-cloudflare-parser-bug. Accessed 10 June 2024
26. Halderman, J.A., et al.: Lest we remember: cold boot attacks on encryption keys. In: USENIX Security (2008)
27. Intel: Intel Architecture Memory Encryption Technologies (2022). https://www.intel.com/content/www/us/en/content-details/679154/intel-architecture-memory-encryption-technologies-specification.html. Revision 1.4. Accessed 31 Jan 2023
28. Intel: Intel Trust Domain Extensions (2022). https://cdrdv2-public.intel.com/690419/TDX-Whitepaper-February2022.pdf. Accessed 27 May 2024
29. Intel: Runtime Encryption of Memory with Intel Total Memory Encryption-Multi-Key (Intel TME-MK) (2022). https://www.intel.com/content/www/us/en/developer/articles/news/runtime-encryption-of-memory-with-intel-tme-mk.html. Accessed 27 May 2024
30. Intel: Architecture Specification: Intel Trust Domain Extensions (Intel TDX) Module (2023). https://cdrdv2-public.intel.com/733568/tdx-module-1.0-public-spec-344425005.pdf. Accessed 27 May 2024

31. Intel Labs: TME-MK-i for Memory Safety (2024). https://github.com/intellabs/tme-mk-fine-grained-encryption-integrity. Accessed 20 May 2024
32. Ismail, M., Quach, A., Jelesnianski, C., Jang, Y., Min, C.: Tightly seal your sensitive pointers with PACTight. In: USENIX Security (2022)
33. Kaplan, D., Powell, J., Woller, T.: AMD Memory Encryption (2021). https://www.amd.com/content/dam/amd/en/documents/epyc-business-docs/white-papers/memory-encryption-white-paper.pdf. Accessed 27 May 2024
34. Kim, Yet al.: Flipping bits in memory without accessing them: an experimental study of DRAM disturbance errors. In: ISCA (2014)
35. Kocher, P., et al.: Spectre attacks: exploiting speculative execution. In: S&P (2019)
36. Kuznetsov, V., Szekeres, L., Payer, M., Candea, G., Sekar, R., Song, D.: Code-pointer integrity. In: OSDI (2014)
37. Lattner, C., Adve, V.S.: LLVM: a compilation framework for lifelong program analysis & transformation. In: CGO (2004)
38. LeMay, M., et al.: Cryptographic capability computing. In: MICRO (2021)
39. Liljestrand, H., Nyman, T., Gunn, L.J., Ekberg, J., Asokan, N.: PACStack: an authenticated call stack. In: USENIX Security (2021)
40. Liljestrand, H., Nyman, T., Wang, K., Perez, C.C., Ekberg, J., Asokan, N.: PAC it up: towards pointer integrity using ARM pointer authentication. In: USENIX Security (2019)
41. Lipp, M., et al.: Meltdown: reading kernel memory from user space. In: USENIX Security (2018)
42. Lu, K., Hu, H.: Where does it go?: refining indirect-call targets with multi-layer type analysis. In: CCS (2019)
43. Martin, L.: XTS: a mode of AES for encrypting hard disks. IEEE Secur. Priv. **8**, 68–69 (2010)
44. Mashtizadeh, A.J., Bittau, A., Boneh, D., Mazières, D.: CCFI: cryptographically enforced control flow integrity. In: CCS (2015)
45. Miller, M.: Trends, challenges, and strategic shifts in the software vulnerability mitigation landscape (2019). https://github.com/Microsoft/MSRC-Security-Research/blob/master/presentations/2019_02_BlueHatIL/2019_01%20-%20BlueHatIL%20-%20Tren. Accessed 26 Feb 2023
46. Murdock, K., Oswald, D.F., Garcia, F.D., Bulck, J.V., Gruss, D., Piessens, F.: Plundervolt: software-based fault injection attacks against intel SGX. In: S&P (2020)
47. Nasahl, P., Mangard, S.: SCRAMBLE-CFI: mitigating fault-induced control-flow attacks on OpenTitan. In: GLSVLSI (2023)
48. Nasahl, P., et al.: EC-CFI: control-flow integrity via code encryption counteracting fault attacks. In: HOST (2023)
49. National Security Agency: NSA Cybersecurity Information Sheet: Software Memory Safety (2022). https://media.defense.gov/2022/Nov/10/2003112742/-1/-1/0/CSI_SOFTWARE_MEMORY_SAFETY.PDF. Accessed 26 Feb 2023
50. Prince, M.: Quantifying the Impact of "Cloudbleed" (2017). https://blog.cloudflare.com/quantifying-the-impact-of-cloudbleed. Accessed 10 June 2024
51. Qualcomm: Pointer Authentication on ARMv8.3 (2017). https://www.qualcomm.com/content/dam/qcomm-martech/dm-assets/documents/pointer-auth-v7.pdf. Accessed 26 Feb 2023
52. Ravichandran, J., Na, W.T., Lang, J., Yan, M.: PACMAN: attacking ARM pointer authentication with speculative execution. In: ISCA (2022)
53. Rebert, A., Kern, C.: Secure by Design: Google's Perspective on Memory Safety. Technical report, Google Security Engineering (2024)

54. Roemer, R., Buchanan, E., Shacham, H., Savage, S.: Return-oriented programming: systems, languages, and applications. ACM Trans. Priv. Secur. **15**, 2:1–2:34 (2012)
55. Rogaway, P., Bellare, M., Black, J., Krovetz, T.: OCB: a block-cipher mode of operation for efficient authenticated encryption. In: CCS (2001)
56. Röttger, S.: Control-flow Integrity in V8 (2023). https://v8.dev/blog/control-flow-integrity. Accessed 10 June 2024
57. Schrammel, D., et al.: MEMES: memory encryption-based memory safety on commodity hardware. In: SECRYPT (2023)
58. Schrammel, D., et al.: Memory tagging using cryptographic integrity on commodity x86 CPUs. In: EuroS&P (2024)
59. Shacham, H.: The geometry of innocent flesh on the bone: return-into-libc without function calls (on the x86). In: CCS (2007)
60. Shanbhogue, V., Gupta, D., Sahita, R.: Security analysis of processor instruction set architecture for enforcing control-flow integrity. In: HASP (2019)
61. Szekeres, L., Payer, M., Wei, T., Song, D.: SoK: eternal war in memory. In: S&P (2013)
62. Tang, A., Sethumadhavan, S., Stolfo, S.J.: CLKSCREW: exposing the perils of security-oblivious energy management. In: USENIX Security (2017)
63. Taylor, A., Whalley, A., Jansens, D., Oskov, N.: An update on Memory Safety in Chrome (2021). https://security.googleblog.com/2021/09/an-update-on-memory-safety-in-chrome.html. Accessed 26 June 2023
64. Tice, C., et al.: Enforcing forward-edge control-flow integrity in GCC & LLVM. In: USENIX Security (2014)
65. Unterguggenberger, M., Lamster, L., Schrammel, D., Schwarzl, M., Mangard, S.: TME-Box: scalable in-process isolation through intel TME-MK memory encryption. In: NDSS (2025)
66. Unterguggenberger, M., Schrammel, D., Lamster, L., Nasahl, P., Mangard, S.: Cryptographically enforced memory safety. In: CCS (2023)
67. van der Veen, V., et al.: A tough call: mitigating advanced code-reuse attacks at the binary level. In: S&P (2016)
68. Werner, M., Unterluggauer, T., Schaffenrath, D., Mangard, S.: Sponge-based control-flow protection for IoT devices. In: EuroS&P (2018)

Optimized Privacy-Preserving Multi-signatures from Discrete Logarithm Assumption

Xiaoyang Wei[1,2], Shuai Han[1,2(✉)], and Shengli Liu[1(✉)]

[1] School of Computer Science, Shanghai Jiao Tong University, Shanghai 200240, China
{weixy02,dalen17,slliu}@sjtu.edu.cn
[2] State Key Laboratory of Integrated Services Networks, Xidian University, Xi'an 710071, China

Abstract. Multi-signatures allow a set of signers to generate a joint signature for the same message, which have been a popular realm in recent years. Tessaro and Zhu (EUROCRYPT'23) proposed an optimized version of a two-round multi-signature scheme MuSig2 (CRYPTO'21), called MuSig2-H, whose security relies on the plain discrete logarithm assumption. However, heavy computational overhead cannot be avoided during aggregated key generation, due to multiple exponentiations. Crites et al. (CRYPTO'22) proposed SpeedyMuSig, a more efficient version of MuSig2. Unfortunately, its proof relies on a non-standard assumption (the OMDL assumption) in an idealized model (the AGM). In a very recent work, Abou Haidar et al. (PKC'25) presented PP-MuSig2, a privacy-preserving version of MuSig2 which satisfies the strongest unforgeability and privacy, but failed to optimize efficiency and provide detailed proof of security reduction under the AOMDL assumption.

In this paper, we propose an optimized multi-signature scheme, called PP-SpeedyMuSig2-H, with high efficiency, strong security and privacy. Firstly, we use proofs of possession during key generation and verification, to improve the efficiency. Then, we revisit the framework of PP-MuSig2 and add privacy to the original MuSig2-H scheme. Moreover, we prove the strongest security and privacy of the new scheme in detail, where its security proof relies on the discrete logarithm assumption and the random oracle model, without using the AGM. Finally, we instantiate PP-SpeedyMuSig2-H based on the discrete logarithm assumption.

1 Introduction

Multi-signature schemes combine individual signatures from multiple signers into a single aggregated signature through interactive protocols, enabling applications like digital wallets [12] and Unmanned Aerial Vehicle Network [17] while relying on various cryptographic assumptions. Multi-signature schemes based on RSA problem [16], Schnorr signature [4], BLS signature [5] and other underlying cryptographic primitives and security assumptions are widely studied recently.

Among them, Schnorr signature (and its variants) is one of the most popular primitives in public key cryptography. In this work, we focus on constructing a new multi-signature scheme and proving its security [1,3,4,9,10,14,15,18].

The MuSig Scheme and its Variants. MuSig is the first Schnorr multi-signature scheme with provable security under the discrete logarithm assumption in the "Plain Public-key" model, where public keys can be aggregated without checking their validity, which was proposed by Maxwell et al. [14]. During key generation of the scheme, apk is the aggregated public key corresponding to the set of all public keys $PK = \{pk_1, ..., pk_n\}$. It is defined as $apk := \prod_{i=1}^{n} pk_i^{a_i}$, where $a_i := \mathsf{H}_{\mathsf{agg}}(pk_i, PK)$ is the key aggregation coefficient for the corresponding public key pk_i. Moreover, the signing protocol of MuSig requires three communication rounds. In order to reduce the number of signing rounds, Nick et al. [15] proposed an optimized version of MuSig called MuSig2, with public key aggregation and two signing rounds. However, its security is based on the non-standard algebraic one-more discrete logarithm (AOMDL) assumption, a weaker and falsifiable variant of the one-more discrete logarithm (OMDL) assumption. To prove the security under the plain discrete logarithm assumption, Tessaro and Zhu [18] proposed a variant of MuSig2 called MuSig2-H, which is a generic construction of multi-signature schemes from linear hash functions. Unfortunately, the above multi-signature schemes cause significant computational overhead during public key aggregation because of extra multi-exponentiations.

For the purpose of improving the efficiency of key aggregation, Crites et al. [3,9] proposed SimpleMuSig with three signing rounds. The "Proof of Possession" technique is used to check the validity of signers during key aggregation of the scheme, thus the aggregated public key is the product of all public keys without key aggregation coefficients. They also proposed SpeedyMuSig, an optimized version of SimpleMuSig with two signing rounds. However, its security proof is based on the OMDL assumption and the Schnorr knowledge of exponent assumption, which holds in the algebraic group model (AGM).

In conclusion, none of the above recent Schnorr multi-signature schemes meets all three specified criteria (a) based on a standard assumption, (b) high efficiency (fewer number of exponentiations during key aggregation) and (c) the security proof without relying on an idealized model, simultaneously. Thus, it is natural to ask:

Q1: *Can we construct a multi-signature scheme with high efficiency, and prove its security under the discrete logarithm assumption (preferably without relying on the AGM)?*

Privacy-Preserving Multi-signature Schemes. Recently, Lehmann et al. [13] proposed three privacy properties for multi-signature schemes. The strongest property is called "full privacy" (which will be formally recapped and introduced in Sect. 3), which ensures that the adversary cannot tell whether a public key and a signature are an aggregated key and a multi-signature, respectively, or stem from a standard signature algorithm. They [13] also proposed two adversarial models for defining the privacy properties. In the "Known Public-Key" (KPK) model, the adversary can freely interact with all signers and know all their public keys. In the "All-but-One-PK" (AbOPK) model, the adversary will no longer receive all public keys, but all but one.

Unfortunately, Lehmann et al. [13] provided formal proofs to indicate that MuSig and its variants cannot achieve the above privacy properties in the KPK model, because those schemes have deterministic key aggregation. In order to achieve privacy properties in the KPK model, a core method is transforming the key aggregation algorithm from deterministic to probabilistic (but verifiable). In a more recent work, Abou Haidar et al. [1] presented a generic enhancement for multi-signature schemes with deterministic key aggregation and proposed a privacy-preserving version of MuSig2, but without modification of key aggregation and formal analysis of unforgeability and security loss under the AOMDL assumption. Therefore, we propose a new question:

Q2: *Can we construct a privacy-preserving multi-signature scheme with the above advantages?*

Related Works. A variety of multi-signature schemes based on the discrete logarithm assumption (and its variants) have been widely studied in recent years. In [4], Bellare et al. designed a three-round Schnorr multi-signature scheme with a method of attack called "rogue-key attack". To resist the attack, the multi-signature scheme can be applied in the "Plain Public-key" model so that the legality of the signers need not be verified during key aggregation. Maxwell et al. [14] designed a Schnorr multi-signature scheme with provable security called MuSig (with its variant MuSigDN). Compared with the above schemes, MuSig expands the process of key aggregation, but without optimization in communication rounds. Unfortunately, MuSigDN relies on heavy zero-knowledge proofs which increase the complexity of the implementation significantly. Therefore, most subsequent works were improved on the basis of MuSig. Nick et al. [15] designed a two-round efficient multi-signature scheme MuSig2 based on the AOMDL assumption, a weaker and falsifiable version of the OMDL assumption. Later, Tessaro and Zhu [18] proposed MuSig2-H, a general construction of multi-signature schemes, whose security relies on the AOMPR assumption.

In addition to the basis of MuSig, researchers proposed other multi-signature schemes. Drijvers et al. [10] proposed a two-round multi-signature scheme called mBCJ, whose security only relies on the discrete logarithm assumption and the random oracle model, but is less efficient compared with MuSig2-H.

In order to remove the restriction of the "Plain Public-key" model, "Proof of Possession" (PoP) is widely applied into the construction of multi-signature schemes as a technical means to ensure the legitimacy of the signers. Boneh et al. [6] proposed a three-round multi-signature scheme MSDL-pop, which includes PoPs and is secure under the discrete logarithm assumption. MSDL-pop was claimed to have a security proof similar to that of DG-CoSi [11], which was proposed by Drijvers et al. However, in a follow-up work [10], the proof of DG-CoSi was determined to be flawed. In order to fill the gap, Crites et al. [3,9] proposed a multi-signature scheme SimpleMuSig, but without reducing the number of signing rounds. They also proposed a two-round multi-signature scheme SpeedyMuSig with PoPs, which improves efficiency compared with MuSig2-H. Unfortunately, SpeedyMuSig was secure under a weaker one-more discrete logarithm (OMDL) assumption and the Schnorr knowledge of exponent (schnorr-koe) assumption, which is true in the algebraic group model (AGM).

For privacy-preserving multi-signature schemes, Lehmann et al. [13] proposed two privacy-preserving variants of the BLS scheme, which satisfy the strongest unforgeability and privacy respectively. In a more recent work, Abou Haidar et al. [1] proposed two privacy-preserving multi-signature schemes PP-MuSig2 and PP-DualMS, which are based on the popular scheme MuSig2 and a lattice-based scheme DualMS [7], respectively.

Our Contributions. Our work answers the above questions by introducing an optimized multi-signature scheme which ensures the strongest privacy and unforgeability, while proving its security without relying on the AGM. In more detail, our work makes the following contributions.

- *Efficient Multi-signature Scheme with strong privacy and unforgeability.* We introduce a two-round multi-signature scheme called PP-SpeedyMuSig2-H, with proofs of possession in order to reduce the number of multi-exponentiations. PP-SpeedyMuSig2-H preserves privacy for signers, which provides the strongest privacy (full-privacy) and unforgeability (UNF-3) in the framework of [13], with almost no overhead compared to the original scheme.
- *Detailed Proof under the plain DL Assumption without Relying on the AGM.* We prove the unforgeability of PP-SpeedyMuSig2-H under the algebraic one-more preimage resistance (AOMPR) assumption (which will be finally reduced to the DL assumption), without relying on the AGM. The solution to avoid idealized models and significant security loss is using the combination of two types of forking lemmas to extract multiple PoPs of signers. Compared with MuSig2-H, the security loss of PP-SpeedyMuSig2-H has been reduced by half.

See Table 1 for a comparison with known (Schnorr) multi-signature schemes.

Technical Overview of Our Multi-signature Scheme. The goal of our work is to (1) construct a multi-signature scheme PP-SpeedyMuSig2-H with high efficiency, strong security and privacy; (2) prove the unforgeability and privacy of PP-SpeedyMuSig2-H under the AOMPR assumption without relying on the AGM. Below we explain the high-level ideas behind our scheme.

- **Reducing the number of multi-exponentiations.** From the analysis above, the key aggregation algorithms of MuSig scheme (and its variants) will cause significant computational overhead of multi-exponentiations. A straightforward idea to improve the efficiency is modifying the aggregated key to the product of all public keys without key aggregation coefficients. However, this will be subject to "rogue-key attacks", where a corrupted signer can maliciously set its public key and generate forged signatures by itself. To avoid the attacks, we have to ensure the legitimacy of the signers. Thus, we modify the key aggregation algorithm with proofs of possession, that is, the

Table 1. Comparison of different multi-signature schemes. The column **Round** shows the total number of communication rounds in the signing algorithm. The column **Verifiable Key Aggregation?** asks whether the key aggregation of multi-signature schemes is verifiable or not (deterministic). The column **Privacy** shows whether the scheme provides the privacy guarantees. The column **Assumption** indicates the assumptions that the security of the scheme is based on. The column **Without AGM?** asks whether the security proof of multi-signature schemes is relying on the algebraic group model (AGM) or not. The column **Multi-Exponentiations** shows the number of exponentiations in the group $\mathbb{G}$ for key generation (KGen), key aggregation (KAg) and signature signing (MulSign). n denotes the number of the signers.

Scheme	Round	Verifiable Key Aggregation?	Privacy	Assumption (ROM+...)	Without AGM?	Multi-Exponentiations KGen	KAg	MulSign
BN [4]	3	×	×	DL	✓	1	-	1
mBCJ [10]	3	×	×	DL	✓	2	2	4
MuSig [14]	3	×	×	DL	✓	1	n	$n+1$
MuSig2($\nu=2$) [15]	2	×	×	AOMDL	×	1	n	$n+3$
MuSig2($\nu=4$) [15]	2	×	×	AOMDL	✓	1	n	$n+4$
SimpleMuSig [3,9]	3	×	×	DL	×	1	2	0
SpeedyMuSig [3,9]	2	×	×	OMDL	×	2	0	4
PP-MuSig2 [1]	2	✓	✓	AOMDL	✓	1	$n+1$	1
MuSig2-H [18]	2	×	×	DL	✓	1	n	$n+3$
PP-SpeedyMuSig2-H	2	✓	✓	DL	✓	2	1	1

signers prove in zero knowledge that they know the corresponding secret keys. In short, each signer generates a public/secret key pair (pk, sk). In contrast to the original algorithm, pk consists of a standard public key component X and its proof of possession π, which is essentially the (Schnorr) signature of X. Along with the associated key verification algorithm, the legitimacy of a signer will be verified if the proof π is a legal signature of its key X, which can effectively resist "rogue-key attacks".

- **Adding privacy-preserving properties.** However, the modified scheme mentioned above has deterministic key aggregation, which fails to satisfy any privacy properties of the aggregated keys in a setting where the adversary knows all signers' individual public keys, from the framework of a recent work [13]. Therefore, to convert deterministic key aggregation into verifiable key aggregation, we introduce a dummy key pair (dsk, dpk) which is used as a "randomizer" in the aggregated keys and signatures. The specific algorithms will be introduced in Sect. 4.
- **Derivative problems caused by algorithm modification.** With proofs of possession and privacy properties, the security proof of the scheme should be adjusted. Similar to the proof of SpeedyMuSig [3,9], we have to solve the share of each signer's secret key x_i and the dummy secret key dsk to win the game. The security proof of SpeedyMuSig relies on the one-more discrete logarithm assumption and the Schnorr knowledge of exponent (schnorr-koe) assumption, which resorts to the AGM. It is a challenging task to provide a proof with fewer non-standard assumptions and idealized models.

– **How to avoid relying on the AGM ?** We would like to prove the unforgeability of the new scheme under the plain DL assumption without relying on the AGM. Making full use of forking lemmas is a natural approach to avoid the AGM and extract the keys. However, the known types of forking lemmas [2,4] cannot be used solely and directly. For instance, the forking lemma of Bellare and Neven (BN) [4] starts only two executions of the adversary. Applying this technique repeatedly to extract n times (from $n-1$ PoPs of $n-1$ corrupted signers plus one forgery) leads to 2^n simultaneous algorithm executions, which will incur an exponential loss. To overcome the difficulty, we are inspired by the security proof of a threshold signature scheme Olaf proposed in [8], and firstly embed the "mixed-forking" technique in the proof of a multi-signature scheme.

2 Preliminaries

Notations. Let κ denote the security parameter throughout the paper, and all algorithms, functions and adversaries take 1^κ as an implicit input. If x is defined by y or the value of y is assigned to x, we write $x := y$. For $i, j \in \mathbb{N}$ with $i < j$, define $[i, j] := \{i, i+1, ..., j\}$ and $[j] := \{1, 2, ..., j\}$. For a set $\mathcal{X}$, denote by $x \leftarrow_\$ \mathcal{X}$ the procedure of sampling x from $\mathcal{X}$ uniformly at random. If $\mathcal{D}$ is distribution, $x \leftarrow_\$ \mathcal{D}$ means that x is sampled according to $\mathcal{D}$. If $\mathcal{A}$ is a randomized algorithm, we let $y := \mathcal{A}(x; \rho)$ denote the operation of running $\mathcal{A}$ on inputs of x and random coins ρ and assigning its output to y, and $y \leftarrow \mathcal{A}(x)$ when coins ρ are chosen uniformly at random. "PPT" abbreviates probabilistic polynomial-time. Denote by negl some negligible function.

Linear Hash Functions and Algebraic One-More Preimage Resistance. We recall their definitions from [18].

Definition 1 (Linear Hash Functions). *A linear hash function family consists of two PPT algorithms* LHF $=$ (PGen, F) *such that*

– PGen *is a randomized algorithm that returns a public parameter par, which implicitly defines a field* $\mathcal{S} = \mathcal{S}(par)$, *and two* $\mathcal{S}$-*modules* $\mathcal{D} = \mathcal{D}(par)$ *and* $\mathcal{R} = \mathcal{R}(par)$. *We require* $|\mathcal{S}| \geq 2^\kappa$, $|\mathcal{D}| \geq 2^\kappa$, *and* $|\mathcal{R}| \geq 2^\kappa$.
– F *is a deterministic function from* $\mathcal{D}$ *to* $\mathcal{R}$ *such that* F $: \mathcal{D} \to \mathcal{R}$ *is a epimorphism of* $\mathcal{S}$-*modules. Moreover,* F *is not a monomorphism, i.e., there exists* $z^* \in \mathcal{D}$ *such that* $z^* \neq 0$ *and* F$(z^*) = 0$.

Definition 2 (AOMPR for Linear Hash Functions). *A linear hash function family* LHF $=$ (PGen, F) *has algebraic one-more preimage resistance (AOMPR), if for any PPT adversary* $\mathcal{A}$, *it holds that* $\mathsf{Adv}_{\mathsf{LHF},\mathcal{A}}^{\mathsf{AOMPR}}(\kappa) :=$ $\Pr[\mathsf{Exp}_{\mathsf{LHF},\mathcal{A}}^{\mathsf{AOMPR}} \Rightarrow 1] \leq \mathsf{negl}(\kappa)$, *where the experiment* $\mathsf{Exp}_{\mathsf{LHF},\mathcal{A}}^{\mathsf{AOMPR}}$ *is defined in Fig. 1.*

$\mathsf{Exp}^{\mathsf{AOMPR}}_{\mathsf{LHF},\mathcal{A}}$:	$\mathcal{O}_{\mathrm{CHAL}}()$:
$par \leftarrow \mathsf{PGen}$	$cid := cid + 1$
$cid := 0;\ l := 0$	$x_{cid} \leftarrow_{\$} \mathcal{D};\ X_{cid} := \mathsf{F}(x_{cid})$
$\{y_i\}_{i \in [cid]} \leftarrow \mathcal{A}^{\mathcal{O}_{\mathrm{CHAL}},\mathcal{O}_{\mathrm{PI}}}(par)$	Return X_{cid}
If $l \geq cid$: Return 0	$\mathcal{O}_{\mathrm{PI}}(Y \in \mathcal{R}, \alpha \in \mathcal{D}, \{\beta_i \in \mathcal{S}\}_{i \in [cid]})$:
If $\forall i \in [cid], \mathsf{F}(y_i) = X_i$:	Require: $Y = \mathsf{F}(\alpha) + \sum_{i \in [cid]} \beta_i X_i$
Return 1	$l := l + 1$
Else: Return 0	Return $\alpha + \sum_{i \in [cid]} \beta_i x_i$

Fig. 1. The AOMPR experiment for a linear hash function family $\mathsf{LHF} = (\mathsf{PGen}, \mathsf{F})$.

Remark. We note that our approach does not employ the algebraic group model (AGM). More concretely, similar to [8], our reduction to the AOMPR assumption is conceptually different from utilizing the AGM. The AGM offers the advantage of assuming the adversary against a cryptographic scheme is algebraic, which simplifies the reduction. However, for a security proof based on the AOMPR assumption, we are required to construct an algebraic reduction, which is a more challenging task. Furthermore, as will be shown in Sect. 5, for certain instantiations of linear hash functions, the associated AOMPR can be further reduced to the plain DL assumption. Consequently, the security of our scheme can be eventually reduced to the DL assumption, without using the AGM.

Forking Lemmas. We recall two types of forking lemmas, i.e., the general forking lemma by Bellare et al. [4] and the multi-forking lemma by Bagherzandi et al. [2], which represent different trade-offs between tightness and time complexity.

Lemma 1 (BN Forking Lemma [4]). *Let $q \geq 1$ be an integer. Let $\mathcal{A}$ be a probabilistic algorithm that takes as input a main input inp generated by some probabilistic algorithm $\mathsf{InpGen}()$, elements $h_1, ..., h_q$ from some sampleable set H, and random coins from some sampleable set $R_{\mathcal{A}}$, and returns either a distinguished failure symbol $\bot$, or a tuple (f, ϕ), where $f \in \{1, ..., q\}$ and ϕ is some side output. The accepting probability of $\mathcal{A}$, denoted as acc, is defined as the probability that $\mathcal{A}$ returns a non-$\bot$ output. Consider the algorithm $\mathsf{Fork}_H^{\mathcal{A}}$ defined in the left figure of Fig. 2, and let frk be the probability (over inp $\leftarrow \mathsf{InpGen}()$ and the random coins of $\mathsf{Fork}_H^{\mathcal{A}}$) that $\mathsf{Fork}_H^{\mathcal{A}}$ returns a non-$\bot$ output. Then $frk \geq acc \cdot (\frac{acc}{q} - \frac{1}{|H|})$.*

Lemma 2 (BCJ Multi-Forking Lemma [2]). *Let $q \geq 1$ be an integer. Let $\mathcal{A}$ be a probabilistic algorithm that takes as input a main input inp generated by some probabilistic algorithm $\mathsf{InpGen}()$, elements $h_1, ..., h_q$ from some sampleable set H, and random coins from some sampleable set $R_{\mathcal{A}}$, and returns either a distinguished failure symbol $\bot$, or a tuple $(F, \{\phi_f\}_{f \in F}, \theta)$, where $F \subseteq \{1, ..., q\}$, $F \neq \emptyset$, and $\{\phi_f\}_{f \in F}$ and θ are some side outputs. The accepting probability of $\mathcal{A}$, denoted as acc, is defined as the probability that $\mathcal{A}$ returns a non-$\bot$ output. Consider the algorithm $\mathsf{MFork}_H^{\mathcal{A}}$ defined in the right figure of Fig. 2, and let mfrk be the probability (over inp $\leftarrow \mathsf{InpGen}()$ and the random coins of $\mathsf{MFork}_H^{\mathcal{A}}$) that $\mathsf{MFork}_H^{\mathcal{A}}$ returns a non-$\bot$ output. Assume $|H| > |F| \cdot 8q/acc$. Then $mfrk \geq \frac{acc}{8}$.*

$\mathsf{Fork}_H^{\mathcal{A}}(inp)$:	$\mathsf{MFork}_H^{\mathcal{A}}(inp)$:
$\rho \twoheadleftarrow R_{\mathcal{A}}$	$\rho \twoheadleftarrow R_{\mathcal{A}}; h_1, ..., h_q \twoheadleftarrow H$
$h_1, ..., h_q \twoheadleftarrow H$	$\omega \leftarrow \mathcal{A}(inp, (h_1, ..., h_q); \rho)$
$\omega \leftarrow \mathcal{A}(inp, (h_1, ..., h_q); \rho)$	If $\omega = \perp$ then return $\perp$
If $\omega = \perp$ then return $\perp$	Parse $\omega = (F, \{\phi_f\}_{f \in F}, \theta)$
Parse $\omega = (f, \phi)$	$mout := \{(h_f, \phi_f)\}_{f \in F}$; $mout' := \emptyset$
$h'_1, ..., h'_q \twoheadleftarrow H$	For each $f \in F$ do
$\omega' \leftarrow \mathcal{A}(inp, (h_1, ..., h_{f-1}, h'_f, ..., h'_q); \rho)$	$\quad suc :=$ false; $j := 0$; $j_{max} := \lvert F \rvert \cdot 8q/acc \cdot \ln(\lvert F \rvert \cdot 8/acc)$
If $\omega' = \perp$ then return $\perp$	$\quad$ Repeat
Parse $\omega' = (f', \phi')$	$\quad\quad j := j+1$; $h'_f, ..., h'_q \twoheadleftarrow H$
If $f \neq f' \vee h_f = h'_f$ then return $\perp$	$\quad\quad \omega' \leftarrow \mathcal{A}(inp, (h_1, ..., h_{f-1}, h'_f, ..., h'_q); \rho)$
$out := (h_f, \phi)$	$\quad\quad$ If $\omega' = \perp$ then continue
$out' := (h'_f, \phi')$	$\quad\quad$ Parse $\omega' = (F', \{\phi'_f\}_{f \in F'}, \theta')$
Return (f, out, out')	$\quad\quad$ If $f \in F' \wedge h'_f \neq h_f$ then
	$\quad\quad\quad mout' := mout' \cup \{(h'_f, \phi'_f)\}$; $suc :=$ true
	$\quad$ until $suc =$ true $\vee j > j_{max}$
	$\quad$ If $suc =$ false then return $\perp$
	Return $(F, mout, mout', \theta)$

Fig. 2. The forking algorithms $\mathsf{Fork}_H^{\mathcal{A}}$ and $\mathsf{MFork}_H^{\mathcal{A}}$ in Lemma 1 and 2, respectively.

3 Multi-signatures with Verifiable Key Aggregation and Proofs of Possession

In this section, we introduce the syntax of a two-round multi-signature scheme MS with verifiable key aggregation and proofs of possession, and formalize the security properties accordingly. The syntax is defined below, which is a partial combination of different multi-signature definitions from [9], [18] and [13].

Definition 3 (MS with Verifiable Key Aggregation and Proofs of Possession). *A multi-signature scheme consists of a tuple of PPT algorithms* MS = (Setup, KGen, KVrfy, KAg, AgVrfy, PreSign, MulSign, Combine, Vrfy) *s.t.:*

- $pp \leftarrow$ Setup : *The setup algorithm outputs a public parameter pp, which serves as an implicit input of other algorithms.*
- $(pk = (X, \pi), sk) \leftarrow$ KGen : *The key generation algorithm generates a pair of public key and secret key (pk, sk), where pk contains a standard public key component X and its proof of possession π.*
- $0/1 \leftarrow$ KVrfy$(pk = (X, \pi))$: *The public key verification algorithm takes as input a public key $pk = (X, \pi)$ as input, and outputs a bit indicating whether pk is a valid public key. (If the verification succeeds, the public key component X will be added into a set PK for legal signers.)*
- $(apk, \Pi) \leftarrow$ KAg(PK) : *The public key aggregation algorithm takes a set of public key components $PK = \{X_i\}$ as input, and outputs an aggregated public key apk along with a proof of aggregation Π.*
- $0/1 \leftarrow$ AgVrfy(PK, apk, Π) : *The aggregated public key verification algorithm takes a set of public key components PK, an aggregated public key apk*

and a proof of aggregation Π as input, and outputs a bit indicating whether apk is valid aggregated public key w.r.t. PK.
- $(\rho_i, st_i) \leftarrow$ PreSign : The pre-signing algorithm generates a signer's first-round output ρ_i and state st_i.
- $\hat{z}_i \leftarrow$ MulSign$(st_i, sk_i, m, apk, \{\rho_j\})$: The multi-signing algorithm is a partially non-interactive algorithm, that on input the state st_i and the secret key sk_i of a signer, a message m, an aggregated public key apk and the outputs from all signers $\{\rho_j\}$, outputs a signature share $\hat{z}_i$.
- $\sigma \leftarrow$ Combine$(PK, \Pi, m, \{\hat{z}_i\})$: The signature combining algorithm takes as input a set of public key components PK, a proof of aggregation Π, a message m and a set of shares $\{\hat{z}_i\}$, and outputs a combined signature σ.
- $0/1 \leftarrow$ Vrfy(apk, m, σ) : The signature verification algorithms takes an aggregated public key apk, a message m and a signature σ as input, and outputs a bit indicating whether σ is valid signature on m w.r.t. apk.

Correctness. For any message m, any number of signers n, any $pp \leftarrow$ Setup, any $(pk_i = (X_i, \pi_i), sk_i) \leftarrow$ KGen for $i \in [n]$, let $PK = \{X_i\}_{i \in [n]}$, for any $(apk, \Pi) \leftarrow$ KAg(PK), any $(\rho_i, st_i) \leftarrow$ PreSign for $i \in [n]$, any $\hat{z}_i \leftarrow$ MulSign$(st_i, sk_i, m, apk, \{\rho_j\}_{j \in [n]})$ for $i \in [n]$, and any $\sigma \leftarrow$ Combine$(PK, \Pi, m, \{\hat{z}_i\}_{i \in [n]})$, it holds that (1) KVrfy$(X_i, \pi_i) = 1$ for all $i \in [n]$; (2) AgVrfy$(PK, apk, \Pi) = 1$; and (3) Vrfy$(apk, m, \sigma) = 1$.

We require unforgeability and privacy for a multi-signature scheme as follows.

Unforgeability. We revisit the notion of all unforgeability definitions with verifiable key aggregation from [13] and expand its syntax with proofs of possession. The main experiment structure is similar to the definitions from [13]: the adversary gets a public key pk^* for an honest signer, which contains a standard public key component X^* and its proof of possession π^*, and has access to a register oracle $\mathcal{O}_{\text{REG}}$ and two signing oracles $\mathcal{O}_{\text{PRESIGN}}$ and $\mathcal{O}_{\text{MULSIGN}}$. The register oracle $\mathcal{O}_{\text{REG}}$ expects a public key pk and parses pk into X and π. Then the oracle invokes the public key verification algorithm KVrfy to check the validity of pk. If the verification succeeds, the component X will be added into a set LPK. After generating the set LPK, the signing oracle $\mathcal{O}_{\text{MULSIGN}}$ expects a set PK, a message m, the aggregated public key apk and a proof Π which shows that apk and PK belong together and contain X^*. After checking the validity of Π, the oracle outputs the honest signer's signature share $\hat{z}_i$. The adversary must outputs a new message m^*, signature σ^*, claimed group PK^*- now along with the aggregated public key apk^* and its proof Π^*. For the new framework of unforgeability experiments, it is necessary to check that apk^* belongs to the group PK^* that includes the honest signer.

The unforgeability of MS schemes is defined in three levels with different freshness checks on the adversary's forgery. Group unforgeability is related to the strongest notion of the framework (UNF-3), which provides guarantees for the signer group and the aggregated key.

	UNF-1	UNF-2	UNF-3
$\mathsf{fresh}(m^*, PK^*, apk^*, Q) = 1$ if	$(m^*, \cdot, \cdot) \notin Q$	$(m^*, PK^*, \cdot) \notin Q$	$(m^*, PK^*, apk^*) \notin Q$

Fig. 3. Definitions of fresh for different levels of unforgeability.

$\mathsf{Exp}_{\mathsf{MS},\mathcal{A}}^{\mathsf{UNF-X}}$:
$pp \leftarrow \mathsf{Setup}; \ (pk^* = (X^*, \pi^*), sk^*) \leftarrow \mathsf{KGen}$
$S := \emptyset; \ Q := \emptyset$
$LPK := \{X^*\}$ //Record valid public key components
$\mathcal{O} := \{\mathcal{O}_{\mathsf{REG}}, \mathcal{O}_{\mathsf{PRESIGN}}, \mathcal{O}_{\mathsf{MULSIGN}}\}$
$(\sigma^*, m^*, apk^*, \Pi^*, PK^*) \leftarrow \mathcal{A}^{\mathcal{O}}(pp, pk^*)$
Return 1 if $PK^* \subseteq LPK \land \mathsf{Vrfy}(apk^*, m^*, \sigma^*) = 1$
$\quad \land \ \mathsf{AgVrfy}(PK^*, apk^*, \Pi^*) = 1 \land X^* \in PK^*$
$\quad \land \ \mathsf{fresh}(m^*, PK^*, apk^*, Q) = 1$

$\mathcal{O}_{\mathsf{REG}}(pk)$:
Parse $pk = (X, \pi)$
If $\mathsf{KVrfy}(X, \pi) = 1: \ LPK := LPK \cup \{X\};$ Return 1
Else: Return 0

$\mathcal{O}_{\mathsf{PRESIGN}}()$:
$j := j + 1$
$S := S \cup \{j\}$
$(\rho, st_j) \leftarrow \mathsf{PreSign}$
Return ρ

$\mathcal{O}_{\mathsf{MULSIGN}}(j, PK, apk, \Pi, m, \{\rho_i\}_{i \in [n]})$:
If $j \notin S \lor X^* \notin PK \lor PK \not\subseteq LPK$
$\quad \lor \ \mathsf{AgVrfy}(PK, apk, \Pi) \neq 1:$
$\quad$ Return $\bot$
$Q := Q \cup \{(m, PK, apk)\}$
$\hat{z} \leftarrow \mathsf{MulSign}(st_j, sk^*, m, apk, \{\rho_i\}_{i \in [n]})$
$S := S \setminus \{j\}$
Return $\hat{z}$

Fig. 4. The unforgeability experiment for a multi-signature scheme MS with verifiable key aggregation and proofs of possession, where fresh is defined in Fig. 3.

Definition 4 (Unforgeability for MS). *MS is* UNF-X *secure for* $X \in \{1, 2, 3\}$, *if for any PPT adversary* $\mathcal{A}$, *it holds that* $\mathsf{Adv}_{\mathsf{MS},\mathcal{A}}^{\mathsf{UNF-X}}(\kappa) := \Pr[\mathsf{Exp}_{\mathsf{MS},\mathcal{A}}^{\mathsf{UNF-X}} \Rightarrow 1] \leq \mathsf{negl}(\kappa)$, *where the experiment* $\mathsf{Exp}_{\mathsf{MS},\mathcal{A}}^{\mathsf{UNF-X}}$ *is defined in Fig. 4.*

Privacy. In this paper, we recap the strongest privacy definitions (full privacy) from [13] in the "Known-Public-Key" (KPK) model, which allows revealing all public keys. Full privacy ensures that the aggregated key does not reveal to the outsiders if it is an aggregated key or a single public key, which requires an indistinguishability game between an aggregated key and a single public key over an adversarially chosen signer group. Furthermore, in the $\mathsf{Exp}_{\mathsf{MS},\mathcal{A}}^{\mathsf{FullPriv}}$ experiment, a signing algorithm Sign is required, which outputs valid signatures corresponding to the individual public keys.

Definition 5 (Full Privacy for MS). *MS has full privacy in the* KPK *model, if there exists a PPT signing algorithm* Sign *(which takes as input a signer's secret key sk and a message m, and outputs a signature* σ*), such that for any PPT adversary* $\mathcal{A}$, *it holds that* $\mathsf{Adv}_{\mathsf{MS},\mathcal{A}}^{\mathsf{FullPriv}}(\kappa) := |\Pr[\mathsf{Exp}_{\mathsf{MS},\mathcal{A}}^{\mathsf{FullPriv}} \Rightarrow 1] - \frac{1}{2}| \leq \mathsf{negl}(\kappa)$, *where the experiment* $\mathsf{Exp}_{\mathsf{MS},\mathcal{A}}^{\mathsf{FullPriv}}$ *is defined in Fig. 5.*

$\mathsf{Exp}_{\mathsf{MS},\mathcal{A}}^{\mathsf{FullPriv}}$:	$\mathcal{O}_{\mathrm{CHL}}(m)$:
$b \leftarrow_\$ \{0,1\}$; $pp \leftarrow \mathsf{Setup}$; $n \leftarrow \mathcal{A}(pp)$	For $i \in S^*$:
For $i \in [n]$: $(pk_i = (X_i, \pi_i), sk_i) \leftarrow \mathsf{KGen}$	$(\rho_i, st_i) \leftarrow \mathsf{PreSign}$
$S^* \leftarrow \mathcal{A}(pp, \{pk_i, sk_i\}_{i \in [n]})$	For $i \in S^*$:
$PK_{S^*} = \{X_i\}_{i \in S^*}$	$\hat{z}_i \leftarrow \mathsf{MulSign}(st_i, sk_i, m, apk^*, \{\rho_j\}_{j \in [S^*]})$
If $b = 0$: $(apk^*, \Pi^*) \leftarrow \mathsf{KAg}(PK_{S^*})$, $pk^* := apk^*$	If $b = 0$:
If $b = 1$: $(pk, sk) \leftarrow \mathsf{KGen}$, $pk^* := pk$	Return $\sigma \leftarrow \mathsf{Combine}(PK_{S^*}, \Pi^*, m, \{\hat{z}_i\}_{i \in S^*})$
$b' \leftarrow \mathcal{A}^{\mathcal{O}_{\mathrm{CHL}}(\cdot)}(pk^*)$	If $b = 1$:
If $b' = b$: Return 1; Else: Return 0	Return $\sigma \leftarrow \mathsf{Sign}(sk, m)$

Fig. 5. Full privacy experiment for a multi-signature scheme MS in the KPK model.

4 PP-SpeedyMuSig2-H: More Efficient and Privacy-Preserving Multi-signature Scheme

MuSig2-H [18] is a two-round multi-signature scheme constructed from linear hash functions, whose security relies on the plain DL assumption. In this section, we propose a more efficient and privacy-preserving multi-signature scheme called PP-SpeedyMuSig2-H, which retains all advantages of MuSig2-H while improving its efficiency and enabling its use for privacy-preserving group signing. More precisely, we present our PP-SpeedyMuSig2-H in Subsect. 4.1. Then in Subsect. 4.2, we prove that PP-SpeedyMuSig2-H satisfies the strongest unforgeability UNF-3, under the AOMPR assumption without relying on the AGM. Finally, we prove the strongest privacy notions "full-privacy" for our PP-SpeedyMuSig2-H in Subsect. 4.3.

4.1 PP-SpeedyMuSig2-H Construction

We propose a two-round multi-signature scheme PP-SpeedyMuSig2-H from a linear hash function family $\mathsf{LHF} = (\mathsf{PGen}, \mathsf{F})$, with the help of four hash functions $\mathsf{H}_{\mathsf{sig}}, \mathsf{H}_{\mathsf{reg}}, \mathsf{H}_{\mathsf{non}} : \{0,1\}^* \to \mathcal{S}$ and $\mathsf{H}_{\mathsf{dm}} : \{0,1\}^* \to \mathcal{D}$, as shown in Fig. 6. It is straightforward to verify the correctness of our PP-SpeedyMuSig2-H.

4.2 Security Analysis of PP-SpeedyMuSig2-H

We prove the strongest unforgeability UNF-3 of PP-SpeedyMuSig2-H under the AOMPR assumption in the random oracle model, without relying on the AGM.

Theorem 1. *For any PPT UNF-3 adversary $\mathcal{A}$ making at most q_s queries to $\mathcal{O}_{\mathrm{REG}}, \mathcal{O}_{\mathrm{PRESIGN}}, \mathcal{O}_{\mathrm{MULSIGN}}$ and q_h queries to $\mathcal{O}_{\mathrm{RO}}$ with advantage $\epsilon = \mathsf{Adv}_{\mathsf{MS},\mathcal{A}}^{\mathsf{UNF-3}}(\kappa)$, there exists a PPT AOMPR adversary $\mathcal{D}^*$ making at most $2q_s + 1$ queries to $\mathcal{O}_{\mathrm{CHAL}}$, such that $\mathsf{Adv}_{\mathsf{LHF},\mathcal{D}^*}^{\mathsf{AOMPR}}(\kappa) \geq \frac{\epsilon^2}{8q} - \frac{q^2 + 4q + 6}{2^{\kappa - 2}}$, where $q = 4q_h + 2q_s + q_u + 1$. We require that $\mathsf{char}(\mathcal{S}) \geq 2^\kappa$ and q_u denotes the number of registered signers.*

Setup:	KAg(PK):	$\hat{R} := \bar{R} + b \cdot \bar{S}$
$pp \leftarrow$ PGen	$\Pi \leftarrow_\$ \{0,1\}^\kappa$	$c := \mathsf{H}_{\mathsf{sig}}(apk, m, \hat{R})$
Return pp	$dsk := \mathsf{H}_{\mathsf{dm}}(\Pi, PK)$	$z_i := r_i + b \cdot s_i + c \cdot x_i$
	$apk := \mathsf{F}(dsk) + \sum_{X_i \in PK} X_i$	$\hat{z}_i := ((R_i, S_i), z_i)$
KGen:	Return (apk, Π)	Return $\hat{z}_i$
$x \leftarrow_\$ \mathcal{D};\ X := \mathsf{F}(x)$	AgVrfy(PK, apk, Π):	Combine($PK, \Pi, m, \{\hat{z}_i\}_{i \in [n]}$):
$\tilde{r} \leftarrow_\$ \mathcal{D};\ \tilde{R} := \mathsf{F}(\tilde{r})$	$dsk := \mathsf{H}_{\mathsf{dm}}(\Pi, PK)$	Parse $\hat{z}_i = ((R_i, S_i), z_i)$ for $i \in [n]$
$\tilde{c} := \mathsf{H}_{\mathsf{reg}}(X, X, \tilde{R})$	If $apk \stackrel{?}{=} \mathsf{F}(dsk) + \sum_{X_i \in PK} X_i$:	$dsk := \mathsf{H}_{\mathsf{dm}}(\Pi, PK)$
$\tilde{z} := \tilde{r} + \tilde{c} \cdot x$	Return 1	$apk := \mathsf{F}(dsk) + \sum_{X_i \in PK} X_i$
$\pi := (\tilde{R}, \tilde{z})$	Else: Return 0	$\bar{R} := \sum_{i=1}^n R_i,\ \bar{S} := \sum_{i=1}^n S_i$
$pk := (X, \pi)$	PreSign:	$b := \mathsf{H}_{\mathsf{non}}(apk, m, \bar{R}, \bar{S})$
$sk := x$	$r_i \leftarrow_\$ \mathcal{D};\ R_i := \mathsf{F}(r_i)$	$\hat{R} := \bar{R} + b \cdot \bar{S}$
Return (pk, sk)	$s_i \leftarrow_\$ \mathcal{D};\ S_i := \mathsf{F}(s_i)$	$c := \mathsf{H}_{\mathsf{sig}}(apk, m, \hat{R})$
	$\rho_i := (R_i, S_i);\ st_i := (r_i, s_i)$	$z := c \cdot dsk + \sum_{i=1}^n z_i$
KVrfy(X, π):	Return (ρ_i, st_i)	$\sigma := (\hat{R}, z)$
Parse $\pi = (\tilde{R}, \tilde{z})$		Return σ
$\tilde{c} := \mathsf{H}_{\mathsf{reg}}(X, X, \tilde{R})$	MulSign($st_i, sk_i, m, apk, \{\rho_j\}_{j \in [n]}$):	Vrfy(apk, m, σ):
If $\mathsf{F}(\tilde{z}) \stackrel{?}{=} \tilde{R} + \tilde{c} \cdot X$:	Parse $st_i = (r_i, s_i)$ and $sk_i = x_i$	Parse $\sigma = (\hat{R}, z)$
Return 1	Parse $\rho_j = (R_j, S_j)$ for $j \in [n]$	$c := \mathsf{H}_{\mathsf{sig}}(apk, m, \hat{R})$
Else: Return 0	$\bar{R} := \sum_{j=1}^n R_j;\ \bar{S} := \sum_{j=1}^n S_j$	If $\mathsf{F}(z) \stackrel{?}{=} \hat{R} + c \cdot apk$: Return 1
	$b := \mathsf{H}_{\mathsf{non}}(apk, m, \bar{R}, \bar{S})$	Else: Return 0

Fig. 6. Description of our multi-signature scheme PP-SpeedyMuSig2-H from a linear hash function family LHF = (PGen, F) and four hash functions $\mathsf{H}_{\mathsf{sig}}, \mathsf{H}_{\mathsf{reg}}, \mathsf{H}_{\mathsf{non}}, \mathsf{H}_{\mathsf{dm}}$.

Proof overview. Our proof goes with several steps. First, we construct a wrapper $\mathcal{B}$ around $\mathcal{A}$, by simulating the $\mathsf{Exp}_{\mathsf{PP\text{-}SpeedyMuSig2\text{-}H}}^{\mathsf{UNF\text{-}3}}$ experiment towards $\mathcal{A}$. Algorithm $\mathcal{B}$ embeds a challenge X^* as the public key component of the honest signer, and returns all PoPs $\{\pi_i\}$ sent by $\mathcal{A}$ during key registration, the forgery $(\sigma^* = (\hat{R}^*, z^*), m^*, apk^*, \Pi^*, PK^*)$ output by $\mathcal{A}$ where $X^* \in PK^* = \{X_1, ..., X_{n-1}, X^*\}$ for n signers, and some extra information. If $\mathcal{A}$ wins, then AgVrfy(PK^*, apk^*, Π^*) = 1 holds, i.e.,

$$apk^* = \mathsf{F}(dsk^*) + \sum_{i=1}^{n-1} X_i + X^* \quad \text{with} \quad dsk^* := \mathsf{H}_{\mathsf{dm}}(\Pi^*, PK^*). \tag{1}$$

Then, during the first forking, we construct an algorithm $\mathcal{C}$ by invoking $\mathcal{B}$. Algorithm $\mathcal{C}$ runs the forking algorithm $\mathsf{Fork}_H^{\mathcal{B}}$ (cf. Lemma 1 and Fig. 2) and forks $\mathcal{B}$ on the $\mathsf{H}_{\mathsf{sig}}$ queries corresponding to the forgery. $\mathcal{C}$ will compute and output the preimage ask^* of the aggregated public key apk^* contained in the forgery so that $apk^* = \mathsf{F}(ask^*)$, and output $dsk^* := \mathsf{H}_{\mathsf{dm}}(\Pi^*, PK^*)$.

Next, during the second forking, we construct the AOMPR algorithm $\mathcal{D}$ by invoking $\mathcal{C}$. Algorithm $\mathcal{D}$ runs the multi-forking algorithm $\mathsf{MFork}_H^{\mathcal{C}}$ (cf. Lemma 2 and Fig. 2) and forks $\mathcal{C}$ on all $\mathsf{H}_{\mathsf{reg}}$ queries corresponding to PoPs sent by $\mathcal{A}$. $\mathcal{D}$ will compute the preimage $\{x_1, ..., x_{n-1}\}$ of the $\{X_1, ..., X_{n-1}\}$ in PK^* output by $\mathcal{C}$. By subtracting these $\{x_i\}$ and dsk^* from ask^*, $\mathcal{D}$ computes $x^* := ask^* - \sum_{i=1}^{n-1} x_i - dsk^*$, which will in fact be the preimage of the challenge X^*, since $\mathsf{F}(x^*) = \mathsf{F}(ask^*) - \sum_{i=1}^{n-1}\mathsf{F}(x_i) - \mathsf{F}(dsk^*) = apk^* - \sum_{i=1}^{n-1} X_i - \mathsf{F}(dsk^*) = X^*$ according to (1). Furthermore, $\mathcal{D}$ can solve the preimages of other $2q_s$ challenges during the simulation of signing queries. However, the above forking strategy will query the $\mathcal{O}_{\mathrm{PI}}$ oracle too many times.

To solve this problem, we construct the algorithm $\mathcal{D}^*$ by slightly modifying $\mathcal{D}$: $\mathcal{D}^*$ aborts all but one execution of $\mathcal{C}$ after (aggregated) key generation, i.e., after all PoPs from $\mathcal{A}$ have been received and dsk^* has been chosen. After the modification, $\mathcal{D}^*$ only makes two queries to $\mathcal{O}_{\mathrm{PI}}$ per signing query during the full execution of $\mathcal{C}$, which are as many as $\mathcal{O}_{\mathrm{CHAL}}$ queries made. Thus, $\mathcal{D}^*$ successfully wins the AOMPR game. We refer to Appendix A for the formal proof.

4.3 Privacy Analysis of PP-SpeedyMuSig2-H

We prove that PP-SpeedyMuSig2-H satisfies FullPriv to guarantee that the multi-signatures and aggregated keys of PP-SpeedyMuSig2-H are indistinguishable from stand-alone signatures and keys. In contrast to the analysis of [1], PP-SpeedyMuSig2-H is a generic construction of multi-signatures with proofs of possession from linear hash functions. Thus, we will first propose a stand-alone signature scheme "Linear Hash Function Signatures" LHFSign and then prove their indistinguishability. The description of LHFSign is as follows.

- **Key Generation.** The signer randomly chooses the secret key $sk \leftarrow_\$ \mathcal{D}$ and computes the public key $pk := \mathsf{F}(sk)$.
- **Signing.** To sign a message $m \in \{0,1\}^*$, the signer randomly chooses $r \leftarrow_\$ \mathcal{D}$, computes $\hat{R} := \mathsf{F}(r)$ and $c := \mathsf{H}_{\mathsf{sig}}(pk, m, \hat{R})$. The signature has format $\sigma = (\hat{R}, z)$ where $z := r + c \cdot sk$.
- **Signature Verification.** Verification is done by checking $\mathsf{F}(z) \stackrel{?}{=} \hat{R} + c \cdot pk$, where F and $\mathsf{H}_{\mathsf{sig}}$ are the same functions as used in PP-SpeedyMuSig2-H.

Theorem 2. *PP-SpeedyMuSig2-H is FullPriv if H_{dm} and $\mathsf{H}_{\mathsf{non}}$ are random oracles and for* $\mathsf{Sign} = \mathsf{LHFSign}$, *where we require* $\mathrm{char}(\mathcal{D}) \geq 2^\kappa$ *and* $\mathrm{char}(\mathcal{S}) \geq 2^\kappa$.

Proof of Theorem 2. We present a series of games to prove the FullPriv property of PP-SpeedyMuSig2-H where Game_0 is identical to $\mathsf{Exp}^{\mathsf{FullPriv}}_{\mathsf{PP\text{-}SpeedyMuSig2\text{-}H},\mathcal{A}}$. Let Ev_i be the event that $\mathcal{A}$ wins Game_i.

- Game_1: It is the same as the original FullPriv game except how we compute the challenge aggregated key apk^*. We compute an *aggregated secret key* $ask^* := dsk^* + \sum_{i \in S^*} sk_i$ where $dsk^* := \mathsf{H}_{\mathsf{dm}}(\Pi^*, PK_{S^*})$ and sk_i denotes the corresponding secret key of a legal signer. This change is internal and does not impact $\mathcal{A}$'s view, so $\Pr[Ev_1] = \Pr[Ev_0]$.
- Game_2: This game introduces an abort condition to $\mathcal{O}_{\mathrm{CHL}}$. Let $\bar{R}, \bar{S}$ be the aggregated random parameters when $\mathcal{O}_{\mathrm{CHL}}$ is running the Combine algorithm. If there exists a previous $\mathsf{H}_{\mathsf{non}}$ query with $\bar{R}$ and $\bar{S}$, then Game_2 aborts. Let $q_{\mathsf{H}_{\mathsf{non}}}$ and q_{CHL} be the number of $\mathsf{H}_{\mathsf{non}}$ and $\mathcal{O}_{\mathrm{CHL}}$ queries that $\mathcal{A}$ makes. Both $\bar{R}$ and $\bar{S}$ are uniformly random in $\mathcal{R}$, so $|\Pr[Ev_2] - \Pr[Ev_1]| \leq q_{\mathsf{CHL}} \cdot q_{\mathsf{H}_{\mathsf{non}}}/2^\kappa$.

- Game$_3$: This game is identical to Game$_2$, except that it changes the behavior of $\mathcal{O}_{\text{CHL}}$ to use LHFSign instead of multi-signature signing. Thus, $\mathcal{O}_{\text{CHL}}(m)$ runs $\sigma \leftarrow \text{LHFSign}(ask^*, m)$ when the challenge bit $b = 0$. A linear hash function signature σ can be parsed as $(\hat{R}, z)$. $\hat{R}$ is sampled uniformly random in both cases. PP-SpeedyMuSig2-H sets $r := \sum_{i \in [n]} (r_i + b' \cdot s_i)$ for $b' := \mathsf{H}_{\text{non}}(apk^*, m, \bar{R}, \bar{S})$ and random r_i, s_i values. By Game$_2$, there is no H_{non} query made by $\mathcal{A}$ for $\bar{R}$ and $\bar{S}$, so b' is uniformly random to $\mathcal{A}$. We have the following equations: $z = dsk^* \cdot c + \sum_{i \in S^*} z_i = dsk^* \cdot c + \sum_{i \in S^*} (r_i + b' \cdot s_i + c \cdot sk_i) = dsk^* \cdot c + \sum_{i \in S^*} (r_i + b' \cdot s_i) + c \cdot \sum_{i \in S^*} sk_i = r + c \cdot ask^*$, where $R_i := \mathsf{F}(r_i), S_i := \mathsf{F}(s_i), \hat{R} := \mathsf{F}(r)$ and $c := \mathsf{H}_{\text{sig}}(apk^*, m, \hat{R})$. We show that the z value is consistent with r value, so that $\Pr[Ev_3] = \Pr[Ev_2]$.
- Game$_4$: This game introduces an abort condition to H_{dm} queries. At the beginning of the game, we sample the challenge key aggregation proof Π^* and abort if $\mathcal{A}$ makes a H_{dm} query with Π^*. Π^* is sampled uniformly and the only related value of Π^* is $\mathsf{H}_{\text{dm}}(\Pi^*, PK_{S^*})$, which is sampled independently in $\mathcal{D}$ by the random oracle. Thus, the upper bound that $\mathcal{A}$ aborts is $q_{\mathsf{H}_{\text{dm}}}/2^\kappa$ and $|\Pr[Ev_4] - \Pr[Ev_3]| \leq q_{\mathsf{H}_{\text{dm}}}/2^\kappa$.
- Game$_5$: This game reflects the indistinguishability of ask^* and an honest secret key. In Game$_5$, we sample (apk^*, ask^*) as a fresh key pair, that $(apk^*, ask^*) \leftarrow \text{KGen}(pp)$. By Game$_4$, $\mathcal{A}$ does not make any H_{dm} query for Π^* so that $dsk^* := \mathsf{H}_{\text{dm}}(\Pi^*, PK_{S^*})$ is uniformly random. Thus, the change in Game$_5$ does not impact $\mathcal{A}$'s view and $\Pr[Ev_5] = \Pr[Ev_4]$.

In Game$_5$, the challenge public key pk^* is generated as an individual key and $\mathcal{O}_{\text{CHL}}$ queries are always answered with LHFSign, so Game$_5$ reveals no information about the challenge bit b and $\Pr[Ev_5] = 1/2$. Thus, we have the following conclusion: $|\Pr[\text{Exp}_{\text{PP-SpeedyMuSig2-H}, \mathcal{A}}^{\text{FullPriv}} \Rightarrow 1] - \frac{1}{2}| \leq \frac{q_{\text{CHL}} \cdot q_{\mathsf{H}_{\text{non}}} + q_{\mathsf{H}_{\text{dm}}}}{2^\kappa}$. $\square$

5 Instantiations from Discrete Logarithm Assumption

Now we show how to instantiate our multi-signature scheme PP-SpeedyMuSig2-H proposed in Sect. 4 from the discrete logarithm (DL) assumption. We can directly use the DL-based LHF_{DL} proposed in [18] as the underlying linear hash function needed in our PP-SpeedyMuSig2-H. For completeness, we present the details of LHF_{DL} as follows.

LHF from Discrete Logarithm Assumption. Let $(\mathbb{G}, p, g)$ be a group description where $\mathbb{G}$ is a cyclic group with prime order p and generator g.

The discrete logarithm (DL) assumption holds over $\mathbb{G}$, if for any PPT adversary $\mathcal{A}$, $\text{Adv}_{\mathbb{G}, \mathcal{A}}^{\text{DL}}(\kappa) := \Pr[Z \leftarrow_\$ \mathbb{G}, z \leftarrow \mathcal{A}(\mathbb{G}, p, g, Z) : g^z = Z] \leq \text{negl}(\kappa)$.

The linear hash function family LHF_{DL} proposed in [18] is as follows.

- **Parameter Generation** (PGen). The parameter generation algorithm uniformly samples $Z \in \mathbb{G}$ and returns $pp := (\mathbb{G}, p, g, Z)$.
- **Hash Function** (F). The function $\mathsf{F} : \mathcal{D} \to \mathcal{R}$ has $\mathcal{S} := \mathbb{Z}_p, \mathcal{D} := \mathbb{Z}_p^2, \mathcal{R} := \mathbb{G}$, and is defined by $\mathsf{F}(x_1, x_2) := g^{x_1} Z^{x_2}$ for any input $(x_1, x_2) \in \mathbb{Z}_p^2$.

As shown in [18, Theorem 1, Lemma 8], $\mathsf{LHF_{DL}}$ has algebraic one-more preimage resistance (AOMPR) based on the DL assumption, as recalled below.

Lemma 3 ([18]). *For any PPT adversary $\mathcal{A}$ against the AOMPR security of $\mathsf{LHF_{DL}}$, there exists a PPT adversary $\mathcal{B}$ against the DL assumption such that $\mathsf{Adv}^{\mathsf{AOMPR}}_{\mathsf{LHF},\mathcal{A}}(\kappa) \leq 2\mathsf{Adv}^{\mathsf{DL}}_{\mathbb{G},\mathcal{B}}(\kappa)$.*

To instantiate PP-SpeedyMuSig2-H, we set $x, \widetilde{r} \leftarrow_\$ \mathcal{D}_{key} := \{(y, 0) : y \in \mathbb{Z}_p\}$ during key generation. It is clear that $\mathsf{char}(\mathcal{S}) = p \geq 2^\kappa$, $|\mathcal{S}| \geq 2^\kappa$ and F is a bijection from $\mathcal{D}_{key}$ to $\mathcal{R}$. By combining Theorem 1 and Lemma 3, we can show the security of PP-SpeedyMuSig2-H instantiated from $\mathsf{LHF_{DL}}$ under the discrete logarithm assumption in the random oracle model.

Acknowledgments. We would like to thank the reviewers for their valuable comments and suggestions. The authors were partially supported by National Natural Science Foundation of China (Grant No. 62372292), National Cryptologic Science Fund of China (2025NCSF01009), Guangdong Major Project of Basic and Applied Basic Research (2019B030302008), and the National Key R&D Program of China under Grant 2022YFB2701500.

A Proof of Theorem 1

According to the proof overview, our proof will go with several steps. We will first construct an algorithm $\mathcal{B}$ by invoking $\mathcal{A}$, then construct an algorithm $\mathcal{C}$ by invoking $\mathcal{B}$, and then construct an algorithm $\mathcal{D}$ by invoking $\mathcal{C}$. Finally, we construct the AOMPR adversary $\mathcal{D}^*$, which is like $\mathcal{D}$ but aborts all but one execution of $\mathcal{C}$ after key generation and aggregation. Note that $\mathcal{D}^*$ has access to $\mathcal{O}_{\mathrm{CHAL}}$ and $\mathcal{O}_{\mathrm{PI}}$ oracles in the AOMPR game (cf. Fig. 1). During the proof, we call the probability that $\mathcal{A}$ returns a non-$\perp$ output the *accepting probability* $acc_{\mathcal{A}}$.

Construction of Algorithm $\mathcal{B}$. We first construct a "wrapping" algorithm $\mathcal{B}$ by simulating the $\mathsf{Exp}^{\mathsf{UNF\text{-}3}}_{\mathsf{PP\text{-}SpeedyMuSig2\text{-}H}}$ experiment (cf. Fig. 4 and Fig. 3) for $\mathcal{A}$, and returns $\mathcal{A}$'s forgery with some auxiliary information, unless some bad events happen.

$\mathcal{B}$ takes $inp_\mathcal{B} = (X^*, U_1, ..., U_{2q_s}, (h_{\mathrm{reg},1}, ..., h_{\mathrm{reg},q}))$ as input, where $X^*, U_1, ..., U_{2q_s} \leftarrow_\$ \mathcal{R}$ and $h_{\mathrm{reg},1}, ..., h_{\mathrm{reg},q} \leftarrow_\$ \mathcal{S}$. It also takes as input $h_1, ..., h_q \leftarrow_\$ \mathcal{S}$. Here $X^*, U_1, ..., U_{2q_s}$ are $2q_s + 1$ uniform elements in $\mathcal{R}$, which will be obtained via $2q_s + 1$ queries to the $\mathcal{O}_{\mathrm{CHAL}}$ oracle by the caller of $\mathcal{B}$ (i.e., $\mathcal{C}$ and $\mathcal{D}$ as described later). Thus, $\mathcal{B}$ has also access to the $\mathcal{O}_{\mathrm{PI}}$ oracle provided by the caller.

Firstly, $\mathcal{B}$ initializes related arrays $\mathsf{T}_{\mathrm{reg}}, \mathsf{T}_{\mathrm{non}}$ and $\mathsf{T}_{\mathrm{sig}}$ to store values from $\mathsf{H}_{\mathrm{reg}}, \mathsf{H}_{\mathrm{non}}$ and $\mathsf{H}_{\mathrm{sig}}$ respectively, and initializes $\mathsf{T}_{\mathrm{apk}}$ and T_{dm} to store values related to apk and dsk. Then, it initializes three counters $ctrh := 0$, $ctrs := 0$ and $ctr_{\mathrm{reg}} := 0$. Finally, it initializes a set LPK to store the public key components that have been verified, and dt to record the results of the $\mathcal{O}_{\mathrm{PI}}$ oracle queries related to each challenge. We use two flags $\mathsf{BadError}$ and $\mathsf{KeyColl}$ initially set to false, to keep track of bad events.

Then $\mathcal{B}$ generates a public key $pk^* = (X^*, \pi^*)$ for the honest signer as follows: it randomly sampled $\tilde{z}^*, \tilde{c}^* \leftarrow_\$ \mathcal{D}$, computes $\tilde{R}^* := \mathsf{F}(\tilde{z}^*) - \tilde{c}^* \cdot X^*$ and sets $\tilde{c}^* := \mathsf{H}_\mathsf{reg}(X^*, X^*, \tilde{R}^*), \pi^* := (\tilde{R}^*, \tilde{z}^*)$ and $pk^* := (X^*, \pi^*)$. If $\mathsf{T}_\mathsf{reg}(X^*, X^*, \tilde{R}^*) \neq \bot$, then BadError := true and $\mathcal{B}$ returns $\bot$.

Next $\mathcal{B}$ runs $\mathcal{A}(pp, pk^*)$, and simulates the oracles $\mathcal{O}_\mathrm{REG}, \mathcal{O}_\mathrm{RO}, \mathcal{O}_\mathrm{PRESIGN}$ and $\mathcal{O}_\mathrm{MULSIGN}$ in the $\mathsf{Exp}^{\mathsf{UNF\text{-}3}}_{\mathsf{PP\text{-}SpeedyMuSig2\text{-}H}}$ experiment for $\mathcal{A}$ as follows.

- **Register queries** $\mathcal{O}_\mathrm{REG}(pk)$. Parse $pk = (X, \pi = (\tilde{R}, \tilde{z}))$. If $\mathsf{T}_\mathsf{reg}(X, X, \tilde{R}) = \bot$, then $\mathcal{B}$ makes an internal query to $\mathsf{H}_\mathsf{reg}(X, X, \tilde{R})$ to make sure $\mathsf{T}_\mathsf{reg}(X, X, \tilde{R})$ is defined. Let $\tilde{c} := \mathsf{H}_\mathsf{reg}(X, X, \tilde{R})$, if $\mathsf{F}(\tilde{z}) \neq \tilde{R} + \tilde{c} \cdot X$, $\mathcal{B}$ returns 0. Otherwise, $\mathcal{B}$ adds X into LPK and returns 1.
- **Hash queries** $\mathsf{H}_\mathsf{dm}(\Pi, PK)$. $\mathcal{B}$ randomly chooses $dsk \leftarrow_\$ \mathcal{D}$ and computes the aggregated key $apk := \mathsf{F}(dsk) + \sum_{X_i \in PK} X_i$. If $\mathsf{T}_\mathsf{apk}(apk) \neq \bot$, then the event KeyColl := true and $\mathcal{B}$ returns $\bot$. Otherwise, $\mathcal{B}$ sets $\mathsf{T}_\mathsf{apk}(apk) := (\Pi, PK)$ and $\mathsf{T}_\mathsf{dm}(\Pi, PK) := dsk$ and returns $\mathsf{T}_\mathsf{dm}(\Pi, PK)$.
- **Hash queries** $\mathsf{H}_\mathsf{reg}(X, X, \tilde{R})$. If $\mathsf{T}_\mathsf{reg}(X, X, \tilde{R}) = \bot$, then $\mathcal{B}$ increments ctr_reg and assigns $\mathsf{T}_\mathsf{reg}(X, X, \tilde{R}) := h_{\mathsf{reg}, ctr_\mathsf{reg}}$. Finally, $\mathcal{B}$ returns $\mathsf{T}_\mathsf{reg}(X, X, \tilde{R})$.
- **Hash queries** $\mathsf{H}_\mathsf{non}(apk, m, \bar{R}, \bar{S})$. If $\mathsf{T}_\mathsf{non}(apk, m, \bar{R}, \bar{S}) = \bot$, then $\mathcal{B}$ increments $ctrh$ and assigns $\mathsf{T}_\mathsf{non}(apk, m, \bar{R}, \bar{S}) := h_{ctrh}$. Let $b := \mathsf{T}_\mathsf{non}(apk, m, \bar{R}, \bar{S})$, then $\mathcal{B}$ computes $\hat{R} := \bar{R} + b \cdot \bar{S}$. If $\mathsf{T}_\mathsf{sig}(apk, m, \hat{R}) = \bot$, then $\mathcal{B}$ makes an internal query to $\mathsf{H}_\mathsf{sig}(apk, m, \hat{R})$. Finally, $\mathcal{B}$ returns b.
- **Hash queries** $\mathsf{H}_\mathsf{sig}(apk, m, \hat{R})$. If $\mathsf{T}_\mathsf{sig}(apk, m, \hat{R}) = \bot$, then $\mathcal{B}$ increments $ctrh$ and assigns $\mathsf{T}_\mathsf{sig}(apk, m, \hat{R}) := h_{ctrh}$. Finally, $\mathcal{B}$ returns $\mathsf{T}_\mathsf{sig}(apk, m, \hat{R})$.
- **Pre-signing queries** $\mathcal{O}_\mathrm{PRESIGN}()$. $\mathcal{B}$ increments $ctrs$ and sets $R := U_{2ctrs-1}$, $S := U_{2ctrs}$ and $\rho := (R, S)$. Finally, $\mathcal{B}$ returns ρ.
- **Signing queries** $\mathcal{O}_\mathrm{MULSIGN}(j, PK, apk, \Pi, m, \{\rho_i\}_{i \in [n]})$. Same as in the experiment $\mathsf{Exp}^{\mathsf{UNF\text{-}3}}_{\mathsf{PP\text{-}SpeedyMuSig2\text{-}H}}$, except that in the simulation of MulSign, $\mathcal{B}$ first computes $\bar{R} := \sum_{i=1}^n R_i, \bar{S} := \sum_{i=1}^n S_i, b := \mathsf{H}_\mathsf{non}(apk, m, \bar{R}, \bar{S}), \hat{R} := \bar{R} + b \cdot \bar{S}$ and $c := \mathsf{H}_\mathsf{sig}(apk, m, \hat{R})$. Then, $\mathcal{B}$ sets $z := \mathcal{O}_\mathrm{PI}(U_{2j-1} + b \cdot U_{2j} + c \cdot X)$ by querying its own $\mathcal{O}_\mathrm{PI}$ oracle, and sets $\mathsf{dt}(j) := (b, c, z)$. Finally, $\mathcal{B}$ returns $\hat{z} := ((U_{2j-1}, U_{2j}), z)$.

Finally, $\mathcal{B}$ receives a forgery $(\sigma^* = (\hat{R}^*, z^*), m^*, apk^*, \Pi^*, PK^*)$ from $\mathcal{A}$, outputs $\bot$ directly if BadError = true or KeyColl = true or $\mathcal{A}$ does not succeed in the $\mathsf{Exp}^{\mathsf{UNF\text{-}3}}_{\mathsf{PP\text{-}SpeedyMuSig2\text{-}H}}$ experiment. Otherwise, we know that BadError = false, KeyColl = false and $\mathcal{A}$ succeeds, i.e., $PK^* \subseteq LPK \wedge \mathsf{Vrfy}(apk^*, m^*, \sigma^*) = 1 \wedge \mathsf{AgVrfy}(PK^*, apk^*, \Pi^*) = 1 \wedge X^* \in PK^* \wedge (m^*, PK^*, apk^*) \notin Q$. W.l.o.g., suppose $PK^* = \{X_1, ..., X_{n-1}, X^*\}$. We have the following observations.

Valid public keys. $PK^* \subseteq LPK$ means that each X_i ($i \in [n-1]$) in PK^* is registered by $\mathcal{A}$ through $\mathcal{O}_\mathrm{REG}(pk_i)$ query for some $pk_i = (X_i, \pi_i = (\tilde{R}_i, \tilde{z}_i))$, and satisfies $\mathsf{F}(\tilde{z}_i) = \tilde{R}_i + \tilde{c}_i \cdot X_i$ where $\tilde{c}_i := \mathsf{H}_\mathsf{reg}(X_i, X_i, \tilde{R}_i)$.

Valid signature. $\mathsf{Vrfy}(apk^*, m^*, \sigma^*) = 1$ means that $\mathsf{F}(z^*) = \hat{R}^* + c^* \cdot apk^*$ where $c^* := \mathsf{H}_\mathsf{sig}(apk^*, m^*, \hat{R}^*)$.

Valid aggregated key. $\mathsf{AgVrfy}(PK^*, apk^*, \Pi^*) = 1$ means that $apk^* = \mathsf{F}(dsk^*) + \sum_{i=1}^{n-1} X_i + X^*$ where $dsk^* := \mathsf{H}_\mathsf{dm}(\Pi^*, PK^*)$.

Then $\mathcal{B}$ prepares its own output as follows.

- Define $F := [n-1]$, and for each $i \in F = [n-1]$, define $\phi_i := (\tilde{z}_i, ctr_i)$ where ctr_i denotes the value of ctr_{reg} when $\mathsf{T}_{\mathsf{reg}}(X_i, X_i, \tilde{R}_i) := h_{\mathsf{reg}, ctr_{\mathsf{reg}}}$ is set so that $\tilde{c}_i = \mathsf{H}_{\mathsf{reg}}(X_i, X_i, \tilde{R}_i) = h_{\mathsf{reg}, ctr_{\mathsf{reg}}}$.
- Define f_{sig} as the value of $ctrh$ when $\mathsf{T}_{\mathsf{sig}}(apk^*, m^*, \hat{R}^*) := h_{ctrh}$ is set so that $c^* = \mathsf{H}_{\mathsf{sig}}(apk^*, m^*, \hat{R}^*) = h_{ctrh}$.

Finally, $\mathcal{B}$ outputs $(f_{sig}, (z^*, \mathsf{dt}, dsk^*, F, \{\phi_i = (\tilde{z}_i, ctr_i)\}_{i \in F}))$ to its caller.

We now show that $\mathcal{B}$ simulates the $\mathsf{Exp}^{\mathsf{UNF\text{-}3}}_{\mathsf{PP\text{-}SpeedyMuSig2\text{-}H}}$ experiment perfectly for $\mathcal{A}$. In the real game, x^* and $\tilde{r}^*$ are uniformly sampled from $\mathcal{D}$, then X^* and $\tilde{R}^*$ are uniformly distributed over $\mathcal{R}$ which are identical to the simulation. In the simulation of $\mathcal{B}$, if $\mathsf{BadError} = \mathsf{false}$, then $\pi^* := (\tilde{R}^*, \tilde{z}^*)$ is a valid proof of X^* with $\mathsf{F}(\tilde{z}^*) = \tilde{R}^* + \tilde{c}^* \cdot X^*$ holds, which is identical to the real game. Also, the output distributions of each hash query and each $\mathcal{O}_{\mathsf{PRESIGN}}$ query are identical to those of the real game. For the simulation of $\mathcal{O}_{\mathsf{MULSIGN}}$ queries, from the $\mathsf{Exp}^{\mathsf{UNF\text{-}3}}_{\mathsf{PP\text{-}SpeedyMuSig2\text{-}H}}$ experiment, $\mathcal{B}$ makes at most one query to $\mathcal{O}_{\mathsf{PI}}$ for each session j. Thus, z^* is uniformly distributed over the preimage of $U_{2j-1} + b \cdot U_{2j} + c \cdot X^*$ given the view of the adversary from the AOMPR game, which is also identical to the real game.

We also show that $\mathcal{B}$ receives enough values for programming random oracles by bounding ctr_{reg} and $ctrh$. $\mathsf{H}_{\mathsf{reg}}$ is called at most q_h times by $\mathcal{A}$ and at most q_u times when answering register queries $\mathcal{O}_{\mathsf{REG}}$, hence $ctr_{\mathsf{reg}} \leq q_h + q_u < q$ at the end of the execution. H_{dm} does not involve $ctrh$. $\mathsf{H}_{\mathsf{non}}$ is called at most q_h times by $\mathcal{A}$ and at most once per $\mathcal{O}_{\mathsf{MULSIGN}}$ query, hence at most $q_h + q_s$ times in total. Finally, $\mathsf{H}_{\mathsf{sig}}$ is called at most q_h times by $\mathcal{A}$, at most once per $\mathsf{H}_{\mathsf{non}}$ query, at most once per $\mathcal{O}_{\mathsf{MULSIGN}}$ query and at most once when verifying the forgery, hence at most $2q_h + q_s + 1$ times in total. In summary, $ctrh \leq 4q_h + 2q_s + q_u + 1 = q$ at the end of the execution.

To compute the accepting probability of $\mathcal{B}$, we analyze the probabilities of BadError and KeyColl.

- BadError. Recall that in the generation of pk^*, $\tilde{R}^* := \mathsf{F}(\tilde{z}^*) - \tilde{c}^* \cdot X^*$ with $\tilde{z}^* \leftarrow_\$ \mathcal{D}$, so it is uniformly distributed in $\mathcal{R}$. Moreover, $\mathcal{A}$ can query the $\mathsf{H}_{\mathsf{reg}}$ oracle at most q times, thus $\Pr[\mathsf{BadError}] \leq q/2^\kappa$.
- KeyColl. Recall that in $\mathsf{H}_{\mathsf{dm}}(\Pi, PK)$ query, dsk is sampled randomly in $\mathcal{D}$, then $apk := \mathsf{F}(dsk) + \sum_{X_i \in PK} X_i$ is uniformly distributed in $\mathcal{R}$. Thus, for each H_{dm} query, KeyColl can occur with probability at most $q/2^\kappa$. Then by a union bound, we have $\Pr[\mathsf{KeyColl}] \leq q^2/2^\kappa$.

Consequently, the accepting probability of $\mathcal{B}$ is $acc_\mathcal{B} \geq \mathsf{Adv}^{\mathsf{UNF\text{-}3}}_{\mathsf{MS}, \mathcal{A}}(\kappa) - \Pr[\mathsf{BadError}] - \Pr[\mathsf{KeyColl}] \geq \epsilon - (q + q^2)/2^\kappa$.

Construction of Algorithm $\mathcal{C}$. Next, using $\mathcal{B}$, we construct an algorithm $\mathcal{C}$ which computes the preimage of the aggregated public key apk^* from the forgery.

$\mathcal{C}$ takes $inp_\mathcal{C} = (X^*, U_1, ..., U_{2q_s})$ as input, where $X^*, U_1, ..., U_{2q_s} \leftarrow_\$ \mathcal{R}$. Analogously to $\mathcal{B}$, $(X^*, U_1, ..., U_{2q_s})$ will be obtained via $2q_s + 1$ queries to the $\mathcal{O}_{\mathsf{CHAL}}$

oracle by the caller of $\mathcal{C}$ (i.e., $\mathcal{D}$ as described later). Thus, $\mathcal{C}$ has also access to the $\mathcal{O}_{\mathrm{PI}}$ oracle provided by the caller.

Algorithm $\mathcal{C}$ is defined in the left side of Fig. 7, where $\mathcal{C}$ invokes the $\mathsf{Fork}_H^{\mathcal{B}}$ as defined in Lemma 1 and Fig. 2 with $H = \mathcal{S}$. All $\mathcal{O}_{\mathrm{PI}}$ oracle queries made by $\mathcal{B}$ in $\mathsf{Fork}_H^{\mathcal{B}}$ are relayed by $\mathcal{C}$ to its own $\mathcal{O}_{\mathrm{PI}}$ oracle. According to the definition of $\mathsf{Fork}_H^{\mathcal{B}}$ (cf. Fig. 2), $\mathsf{Fork}_H^{\mathcal{B}}$ will execute $\mathcal{B}$ two times, the first time resulting $\omega = (f_{sig}, (z^*, \mathsf{dt}, \mathsf{dsk}^*, F, \{\phi_i\}_{i \in F}))$ and the second time resulting $\omega' = (f'_{sig}, (z^{*\prime}, \mathsf{dt}', \mathsf{dsk}^{*\prime}, F', \{\phi'_i\}_{i \in F'}))$, and $\mathsf{Fork}_H^{\mathcal{B}}$ will output $(f_{sig}, out = (h_{f_{sig}}, (z^*, \mathsf{dt}, \mathsf{dsk}^*, F, \{\phi_i\}_{i \in F})), out' = (h'_{f_{sig}}, (z^{*\prime}, \mathsf{dt}', \mathsf{dsk}^{*\prime}, F', \{\phi'_i\}_{i \in F'})))$ only when $f_{sig} = f'_{sig}$ and $h_{f_{sig}} \neq h'_{f_{sig}}$ hold. The (out, out') returned by $\mathsf{Fork}_H^{\mathcal{B}}$ is derived from two successful forgeries according to $\mathcal{B}$'s strategy, and thus according to "**Valid signature**", it satisfies

$$\mathsf{F}(z^*) = \hat{R}^* + h_{f_{sig}} \cdot apk^* \text{ and } \mathsf{F}(z^{*\prime}) = \hat{R}^{*\prime} + h'_{f_{sig}} \cdot apk^{*\prime}. \quad (2)$$

Note that the two executions of $\mathcal{B}$ run by $\mathsf{Fork}_H^{\mathcal{B}}$ are identical before two assignments $\mathsf{T}_{\mathsf{sig}}(apk^*, m^*, \hat{R}^*) := h_{f_{sig}}$ and $\mathsf{T}_{\mathsf{sig}}(apk^{*\prime}, m^{*\prime}, \hat{R}^{*\prime}) := h'_{f_{sig}}$ in $\mathsf{H}_{\mathsf{sig}}$ queries, thus it must hold that $apk^* = apk^{*\prime}$, $m^* = m^{*\prime}$ and $\hat{R}^* = \hat{R}^{*\prime}$. Then by subtracting the two equations in (2), we get that $\mathsf{F}(z^* - z^{*\prime}) = (h_{f_{sig}} - h'_{f_{sig}}) \cdot apk^*$. Thus $ask^* := (z^* - z^{*\prime})/(h_{f_{sig}} - h'_{f_{sig}})$ is the preimage of the aggregated key apk^* so that $\mathsf{F}(ask^*) = apk^*$ holds, and $\mathcal{C}$ can compute ask^* as part of its output.

Algorithm $\mathcal{C}(inp_\mathcal{C}, (h_{\mathrm{reg},1}, ..., h_{\mathrm{reg},q}))$:	Algorithm $\mathcal{D}$:
Parse $inp_\mathcal{C} = (X^*, U_1, ..., U_{2q_s})$	$X^* \leftarrow \mathcal{O}_{\mathrm{CHAL}}$
$inp_\mathcal{B} := (X^*, U_1, ..., U_{2q_s}, (h_{\mathrm{reg},1}, ..., h_{\mathrm{reg},q}))$	For $i \in \{1, ..., 2q_s\}$: $U_i \leftarrow \mathcal{O}_{\mathrm{CHAL}}$
$\omega \leftarrow \mathsf{Fork}_H^{\mathcal{B}}(inp_\mathcal{B})$ with $H = \mathcal{S}$	$inp_\mathcal{C} := (X^*, U_1, ..., U_{2q_s})$
If $\omega = \bot$ then return $\bot$	$\omega \leftarrow \mathsf{MFork}_H^{\mathcal{C}}(inp_\mathcal{C})$ with $H = \mathcal{S}$
Parse $\omega = (f_{sig}, out, out')$	If $\omega = \bot$ then return $\bot$
Parse $out = (h_{f_{sig}}, (z^*, \mathsf{dt}, \mathsf{dsk}^*, F, \{\phi_i\}_{i \in F}))$	Parse $\omega = (F, mout, mout', \theta), \theta = (ask^*, dsk^*, \mathsf{dt}, \mathsf{dt}')$
Parse $out' = (h'_{f_{sig}}, (z^{*\prime}, \mathsf{dt}', \mathsf{dsk}^{*\prime}, F', \{\phi'_i\}_{i \in F'}))$	Parse $mout = \{(h_{\mathrm{reg},ctr_i}, \{\phi_i = (\tilde{z}_i, ctr_i)\})\}_{i \in F}$
$ask^* := (z^* - z^{*\prime})/(h_{f_{sig}} - h'_{f_{sig}})$	Parse $mout' = \{(h'_{\mathrm{reg},ctr_i}, \{\phi'_i = (\tilde{z}'_i, ctr'_i)\})\}_{i \in F'}$
$\theta := (ask^*, dsk^*, \mathsf{dt}, \mathsf{dt}')$	For $i \in F$:
Return $(F, \{\phi_i\}_{i \in F}, \theta)$	$x_i := (\tilde{z}_i - \tilde{z}'_i)/(h_{\mathrm{reg},ctr_i} - h'_{\mathrm{reg},ctr_i})$
	$x^* := ask^* - (\sum_{i \in F} x_i) - dsk^*$
	Compute $\{u_1, ..., u_{2q_s}\}$ from dt and dt'
	Return $(x^*, u_1, ..., u_{2q_s})$

Fig. 7. Algorithms $\mathcal{C}$ and $\mathcal{D}$ used in the proof of Theorem 1.

From Lemma 1, the accepting probability $acc_\mathcal{C}$ of $\mathcal{C}$ is the probability $frk_\mathcal{B}$ that $\mathsf{Fork}_H^{\mathcal{B}}$ does not output $\bot$, and thus $acc_\mathcal{C} = frk_\mathcal{B} \geq acc_\mathcal{B} \cdot (\frac{acc_\mathcal{B}}{q} - \frac{1}{|H|}) \geq (\epsilon - \frac{q+q^2}{2^\kappa}) \cdot (\frac{\epsilon}{q} - \frac{q+2}{2^\kappa}) \geq \frac{\epsilon^2}{q} - \frac{2q+3}{2^\kappa}$.

Construction of Algorithm $\mathcal{D}$. Then, we construct an algorithm $\mathcal{D}$ by invoking $\mathcal{C}$. More precisely, $\mathcal{D}$ is defined in the right side of Fig. 7, where $\mathcal{D}$ invokes the $\mathsf{MFork}_H^{\mathcal{C}}$ as defined in Lemma 2 and Fig. 2 with $H = \mathcal{S}$. Note that $\mathcal{D}$ has access to $\mathcal{O}_{\text{CHAL}}$ and $\mathcal{O}_{\text{PI}}$ oracles in the AOMPR game (cf. Fig. 1).

According to the definition of $\mathsf{MFork}_H^{\mathcal{C}}$ (cf. Fig. 2), $\mathsf{MFork}_H^{\mathcal{C}}$ will repeatedly execute $\mathcal{C}$, the first time resulting $\omega = (F, \{\phi_i = (\tilde{z}_i, ctr_i)\}_{i \in F}, \theta = (ask^*, dsk^*, \mathsf{dt}, \mathsf{dt}'))$ and other times resulting $\omega' = (F', \{\phi_i' = (\tilde{z}_i', ctr_i')\}_{i \in F'}, \theta')$. Thus, if for each $i \in F$, $i \in F'$ and $h_{\text{reg},ctr_i} \neq h'_{\text{reg},ctr_i}$ hold, $\mathsf{MFork}_H^{\mathcal{C}}$ outputs $(F, mout = \{(h_{\text{reg},ctr_i}, \phi_i)\}_{i \in F}, mout' = (h'_{\text{reg},ctr_i}, \phi_i')\}_{i \in F'}, \theta = (ask^*, dsk^*, \mathsf{dt}, \mathsf{dt}'))$, where $mout$ is from the first execution of $\mathcal{B}$ within the first execution of $\mathcal{C}$ and $mout'$ is from the first execution of $\mathcal{B}$ within other successful executions of $\mathcal{C}$. The $(F, mout, mout', \theta)$ returned by $\mathsf{MFork}_H^{\mathcal{C}}$ is derived from multiple successful forgeries according to $\mathcal{C}$'s strategy, and thus according to "**Valid public keys**", it satisfies

$$\mathsf{F}(\tilde{z}_i) = \tilde{R}_i + h_{\text{reg},ctr_i} \cdot X_i \text{ and } \mathsf{F}(\tilde{z}_i') = \tilde{R}_i' + h'_{\text{reg},ctr_i} \cdot X_i. \quad (3)$$

Note that the first and other successful executions of $\mathcal{C}$ within the first execution of $\mathcal{B}$ are identical before two assignments $\mathsf{T}_{\text{reg}}(X_i, X_i, \tilde{R}_i) := h_{\text{reg},ctr_i}$ and $\mathsf{T}_{\text{reg}}(X_i', X_i', \tilde{R}_i') := h'_{\text{reg},ctr_i}$ in H_{reg} queries, thus it must hold that $X_i = X_i'$ and $R_i = R_i'$ for $i \in [n-1]$. Then by subtracting the two equations in 3, we get that $\mathsf{F}(\tilde{z}_i - \tilde{z}_i') = (h_{\text{reg},ctr_i} - h'_{\text{reg},ctr_i}) \cdot X_i$. Thus $x_i := (\tilde{z}_i - \tilde{z}_i')/(h_{\text{reg},ctr_i} - h'_{\text{reg},ctr_i})$ is the preimage of the public key component X_i for $i \in [n-1]$ so that $\mathsf{F}(x_i) = X_i$.

According to "**Valid aggregated key**", apk^* is a valid aggregated public key so that $apk^* = \mathsf{F}(dsk^*) + \sum_{i=1}^{n-1} X_i + X^*$ holds, and ask^* is its preimage from the output of $\mathcal{C}$. Then, from the above analysis, $\sum_{i \in [n-1]} x_i$ is the preimage of $\sum_{i=1}^{n-1} X_i$. Thus, $\mathcal{D}$ can compute $x^* = ask^* - \sum_{i=1}^{n-1} x_i - dsk^*$ as the preimage of the challenge X^* so that $\mathsf{F}(x^*) = X^*$.

We then explain how $\mathcal{D}$ computes values $u_1, ..., u_{2q_s}$ to satisfy the equation $\mathsf{F}(u_i) = U_i$ respectively. Algorithm $\mathcal{D}$ initializes a flag $\mathsf{BadError}_2 := \mathsf{false}$ to keep track of another bad event. From the two executions of $\mathcal{B}$ run by $\mathsf{Fork}_H^{\mathcal{B}}$ (cf. Fig. 2) within the first execution of $\mathcal{C}$, $\mathcal{D}$ can obtain sets dt and dt' from θ, which keep track of $\mathcal{O}_{\text{PI}}$ queries. $\mathcal{D}$ iterates over $j \in [q_s]$ and looks for two tuples which satisfy $\mathsf{dt}(j) = (b, c, z)$ and $\mathsf{dt}'(j) = (b', c', z')$. They correspond to $\mathcal{O}_{\text{MULSIGN}}$ queries handles in the two executions, such that the pair of group elements (U_{2j-1}, U_{2j}) was assigned to (R, S) and (R', S') respectively by the $\mathcal{O}_{\text{PRESIGN}}$ query. During the first execution of $\mathcal{C}$, we can only find at most one tuple $(b, c, z) \in \mathsf{dt}$ and $(b', c', z') \in \mathsf{dt}'$ as two results of $\mathcal{O}_{\text{PI}}$ queries from the two executions of $\mathcal{B}$: $z \leftarrow \mathcal{O}_{\text{PI}}(U_{2j-1} + b \cdot U_{2j} + c \cdot X^*)$ and $z' \leftarrow \mathcal{O}_{\text{PI}}(U_{2j-1} + b' \cdot U_{2j} + c' \cdot X^*)$.

For each $j \in [q_s]$, $\mathsf{dt}(j) = (b, c, z) \neq \perp$ if and only if $\mathcal{B}$ makes a $\mathcal{O}_{\text{PI}}$ query with the input $U_{2j-1} + b \cdot U_{2j} + c \cdot X$. For any two tuples (b, c, z) and (b', c', z') of dt, if $b = b'$, then $c = c'$ and $z = z'$. In any case, $\mathcal{D}$ has now made two $\mathcal{O}_{\text{PI}}$ queries and can construct two linear equations with unknowns u_{2j-1} and u_{2j}, which are the preimages of U_{2j-1} and U_{2j}. Since $b \neq b'$, $\mathcal{D}$ can compute the unique solution of (u_{2j-1}, u_{2j}) from (4).

$$\mathsf{F}(z) = U_{2j-1} + b \cdot U_{2j} + c \cdot X^* \text{ and } \mathsf{F}(z') = U_{2j-1} + b' \cdot U_{2j} + c' \cdot X^*. \quad (4)$$

We analyze the upper bound of $\mathsf{BadError}_2$. $\mathsf{BadError}_2$ is set to true if there are two identical parameters $b = b'$ in the two executions of $\mathcal{B}$ during the first execution of $\mathcal{C}$. At most $2q_s$ scalars are used during $\mathcal{O}_{\mathrm{MULSIGN}}$ queries, which are uniformly distributed in $\mathcal{S}$ with $|\mathcal{S}| \geq 2^\kappa$ and $q_s \leq q$, we have $\Pr[\mathsf{BadError}_2] \leq \frac{4q^2}{|\mathcal{S}|} \leq \frac{4q^2}{2^\kappa}$. By Lemma 2, $\mathsf{MFork}_H^\mathcal{C}$ returns a non-$\bot$ output with probability $frk_\mathcal{C} \geq \frac{acc_\mathcal{C}}{8} \geq \frac{\epsilon^2}{8q} - \frac{2q+3}{2^{\kappa-3}}$. Thus, the accepting probability of $\mathcal{D}$ is $acc_\mathcal{D} \geq frk_\mathcal{C} - \Pr[\mathsf{BadError}_2] = \frac{\epsilon^2}{8q} - \frac{2q+3}{2^{\kappa-3}} - \frac{4q^2}{2^\kappa} = \frac{\epsilon^2}{8q} - \frac{q^2+4q+6}{2^{\kappa-2}}$.

Construction of Algorithm $\mathcal{D}^*$. Finally, we construct algorithm $\mathcal{D}^*$, which is a valid adversary against the AOMPR game, by slightly modifying $\mathcal{D}$ as follows: After the first execution of $\mathcal{C}$, $\mathcal{D}^*$ aborts any executions of $\mathcal{B}$ whenever it has collected all PoPs sent by $\mathcal{A}$ during $\mathcal{O}_{\mathrm{REG}}$ queries and the corresponding aggregated key apk^*. We show that the above modification does not change the accepting probability of $\mathcal{D}$ as compared to $\mathcal{D}^*$. Firstly, algorithm $\mathcal{D}$ uses values $F, mout = \{(h_{\mathrm{reg},ctr_i}, \phi_i)\}_{i \in F}$ and $mout' = (h'_{\mathrm{reg},ctr_i}, \phi'_i)\}_{i \in F'}$, but these values are already determined when $\mathcal{B}$ is aborted. Then, $\mathcal{D}$ uses the related dummy secret key dsk^*, which has already sampled randomly as well before $\mathcal{B}$ aborts, thus multiple forkings will not change the value of dsk. $\mathcal{D}$ also uses value θ, which is from the first execution of $\mathcal{C}$. Moreover, to compute values u_i for $i \in [2q_s]$, $\mathcal{D}$ uses sets dt and dt', which are part of θ. In summary, the modification does not affect any values used by $\mathcal{D}$, and thus $acc_{\mathcal{D}^*} = acc_\mathcal{D}$.

Let us count the number of $\mathcal{O}_{\mathrm{CHAL}}$ and $\mathcal{O}_{\mathrm{PI}}$ queries made by algorithm $\mathcal{D}^*$ after the modification: $\mathcal{D}^*$ makes $2q_s + 1$ $\mathcal{O}_{\mathrm{CHAL}}$ queries. $\mathcal{D}^*$ aborts executions of $\mathcal{B}$ early, $\mathcal{B}$ only makes $\mathcal{O}_{\mathrm{PI}}$ queries during the first execution of $\mathcal{C}$. Since one execution of $\mathcal{C}$ runs two executions of $\mathcal{B}$ (via $\mathsf{Fork}_H^\mathcal{B}$) and each $\mathcal{B}$ makes q_s queries $\mathcal{O}_{\mathrm{PI}}$ queries, $\mathcal{D}^*$ makes $2q_s$ $\mathcal{O}_{\mathrm{PI}}$ queries. If $\mathcal{D}^*$ returns a non-$\bot$ output, it successfully solves the AOMPR problem with the advantage $\mathsf{Adv}^{\mathrm{AOMPR}}_{\mathrm{LHF},\mathcal{D}^*}(\kappa) = acc_{\mathcal{D}^*} \geq \frac{\epsilon^2}{8q} - \frac{q^2+4q+6}{2^{\kappa-2}}$. □

References

1. Abou Haidar, C., Das, D., Lehmann, A., Özbay, C., Kempner, O.P.: Privacy-preserving multi-signatures: generic techniques and constructions without pairings. In: Jager, T., Pan, J. (eds.) PKC 2025. LNCS, vol. 15675, pp. 66–98. Springer, Cham (2025). https://doi.org/10.1007/978-3-031-91823-0_3
2. Bagherzandi, A., Cheon, J.H., Jarecki, S.: Multisignatures secure under the discrete logarithm assumption and a generalized forking lemma. In: ACM CCS 2008, pp. 449–458 (2008)
3. Bellare, M., Crites, E.C., Komlo, C., Maller, M., Tessaro, S., Zhu, C.: Better than advertised security for non-interactive threshold signatures. In: Dodis, Y., Shrimpton, T. (eds.) CRYPTO 2022. LNCS, pp. 517–550. Springer, Cham (2022). https://doi.org/10.1007/978-3-031-15985-5_18
4. Bellare, M., Neven, G.: Multi-signatures in the plain public-key model and a general forking lemma. In: ACM CCS 2006, pp. 390–399 (2006)
5. Boldyreva, A.: Threshold signatures, multisignatures and blind signatures based on the Gap-Diffie-Hellman-group signature scheme. In: PKC 2003, pp. 31–46 (2003)

6. Boneh, D., Drijvers, M., Neven, G.: Compact multi-signatures for smaller blockchains. In: Peyrin, T., Galbraith, S. (eds.) ASIACRYPT 2018. LNCS, vol. 11273, pp. 435–464. Springer, Cham (2018). https://doi.org/10.1007/978-3-030-03329-3_15
7. Chen, Y.: : Efficient lattice-based two-round multi-signature with trapdoor-free simulation. In: CRYPTO 2023, pp. 716–747 (2023)
8. Chu, H., Gerhart, P., Ruffing, T., Schröder, D.: Practical Schnorr threshold signatures without the algebraic group model. In: CRYPTO 2023, pp. 743–773 (2023)
9. Crites, E., Komlo, C., Maller, M.: How to prove Schnorr assuming Schnorr: security of multi-and threshold signatures. Cryptology ePrint Archive (2021)
10. Drijvers, M., et al.: On the security of two-round multi-signatures. In: IEEE SP 2019, pp. 1084–1101 (2019)
11. Drijvers, M., Edalatnejad, K., Ford, B., Neven, G.: Okamoto beats Schnorr: on the provable security of multi-signatures. IACR Cryptol. ePrint Arch., 417 (2018)
12. Gennaro, R., Goldfeder, S., Narayanan, A.: Threshold-optimal DSA/ECDSA signatures and an application to bitcoin wallet security. In: ACNS 2016, pp. 156–174 (2016)
13. Lehmann, A., Özbay, C.: Multi-signatures for ad-hoc and privacy-preserving group signing. In: PKC 2024, pp. 196–228 (2024)
14. Maxwell, G., Poelstra, A., Seurin, Y., Wuille, P.: Simple schnorr multi-signatures with applications to bitcoin. Des. Codes Cryptogr. **2019**, 2139–2164 (2019)
15. Nick, J., Ruffing, T., Seurin, Y.: MuSig2: simple two-round schnorr multi-signatures. In: Malkin, T., Peikert, C. (eds.) CRYPTO 2021. LNCS, vol. 12825, pp. 189–221. Springer, Cham (2021). https://doi.org/10.1007/978-3-030-84242-0_8
16. Ohta, K., Okamoto, T.: A digital multisignature scheme based on the Fiat-Shamir scheme. In: Imai, H., Rivest, R.L., Matsumoto, T. (eds.) ASIACRYPT 1991. LNCS, vol. 739, pp. 139–148. Springer, Heidelberg (1993). https://doi.org/10.1007/3-540-57332-1_11
17. Shin, Y.A., Jeong, I.R., Byun, J.W.: Identity-based multiproxy signature with proxy signing key for internet of drones. IEEE Internet Things J. **2024**, 4191–4205 (2024)
18. Tessaro, S., Zhu, C.: Threshold and multi-signature schemes from linear hash functions. In: EUROCRYPT 2023, pp. 628–658 (2023)

Polylogarithmic Polynomial Commitment Scheme over Galois Rings

Zhuo Wu[1,2], Xinxuan Zhang[1,2], Yi Deng[1,2(✉)], Yuanju Wei[1,2], Zhongliang Zhang[1,2], and Liuyu Yang[1,2]

[1] Key Laboratory of Cyberspace Security Defense, Institute of Information Engineering, Chinese Academy of Sciences, Beijing, China
[2] School of Cyber Security, University of Chinese Academy of Sciences, Beijing, China
{wuzhuo,zhangxinxuan,deng,weiyuanju,
zhangzhongliang,yangliuyu}@iie.ac.cn

Abstract. This paper introduces the first multilinear polynomial commitment scheme (PCS) over Galois rings achieving $\mathcal{O}(\log^2 n)$ verification cost. It achieves $\mathcal{O}(n \log n)$ committing time and $\mathcal{O}(n)$ evaluation opening prover time. This PCS can be used to construct zero-knowledge proofs for arithmetic circuits over Galois rings, facilitating verifiable computation in applications requiring proofs of polynomial ring operations (e.g., verifiable fully homomorphic encryption). First we construct random foldable linear codes over Galois rings with sufficient code distance and present a distance preservation theorem over Galois rings. Second we extend the Basefold commitment (Zeilberger et al., Crypto 2024) to multilinear polynomials over Galois rings. Our approach reduces proof size and verifier time from $\mathcal{O}(\sqrt{n})$ to $\mathcal{O}(\log^2 n)$ compared to Wei et al., PKC 2025. Furthermore, we give a batched multipoint opening protocol for evaluation phase that collapses the proof size and verifier time of N polynomials at M points from $\mathcal{O}(NM \log^2 n)$ to $\mathcal{O}(\log^2 n)$, prover time from $\mathcal{O}(NMn)$ to $\mathcal{O}(n)$, further enhancing efficiency.

Keywords: Polynomial Commitment · Galois Ring · zk-SNARK

1 Introduction

Polynomial commitment schemes serve as foundational building blocks for zero-knowledge succinct non-interactive argument of knowledge (zk-SNARKs) (e.g. [1,6,8,10,12,19]), with critical applications in privacy-preserving computation and blockchain systems. Existing PCS constructions primarily operate over finite fields. However, the emergence of lattice-based cryptographic protocols involving polynomial rings necessitates efficient PCS constructions over Galois rings. These non-field rings introduce unique challenges, including zero divisors and complex distance metrics, which render conventional finite-field-based techniques inapplicable. Despite recent progress in building proofs over polynomial rings [7,11,13,18], they extended Brakedown PCS [12] and Pinocchio [15] to rings, no prior works achieve logarithmic verification cost for ring arithmetic circuits without trusted setup. While Rinocchio [11] offers constant verification, it necessitates a circuit-specific trusted setup, and each proof for different circuit requires executing a precompile process. Our PCS is transparent, requiring only a single initial setup that is applicable to commitments over different polynomials.

Motivation. Existing PCS over Galois rings face two primary limitations: (1) verification complexity are limited to $\mathcal{O}(\sqrt{n})$, and (2) they lack support for batched evaluation of multiple polynomials and points. To achieve a more efficient PCS, we extend the Basefold commitment scheme for polynomials over finite fields [19] to polynomials over Galois rings. And we present a bached variant for Basefold to support multi-point opening.

Our Approach. Our goal is to construct a scheme for committing to a multilinear polynomial f over Galois rings and proving the correctness of its evaluation at a point x, i.e., $f(x) = y$. A multilinear polynomial is a multivariate polynomial that the degree of the polynomial in each variable is at most one. Any multilinear polynomial $f(X_1, X_2, \cdots, X_d)$ can be uniquely expressed as $\sum_{\mathbf{b}\in\{0,1\}^d} f(\mathbf{b})\tilde{e}q_{\mathbf{b}}(X_1, X_2, \cdots, X_d)$, where $\tilde{e}q_{\mathbf{b}}$ is the multilinear Lagrange basis polynomial with interpolating set $\{0,1\}^d$. Thus, proving $f(x) = y$ reduces to proving a sum. We leverage the sum-check protocol ([14], Chapter 4 from [17]) to prove this sum. However, the final step of the sum-check protocol requires evaluating f at a random point. Here, we introduce IOPP [2,16]. In this context, an IOPP is an interactive proof (in random oracle model) demonstrating that a vector is close to a codeword in a given code. A key observation in the Basefold commitment construction [19], is that IOPP execution can be viewed as opening a polynomial at a random point. This directly addresses the need to evaluate f at a random point in the final step of the sum-check protocol. We exploit this insight to construct a PCS for multilinear polynomials over Galois rings.

Our Contributions. The main contributions of this work are as follows:

- **Random Foldable Codes over Galois Rings:** By constructing (c, k_0, d)-foldable linear codes with provable minimum distance bounds via homomorphic reduction to finite fields (Lemma 1), we enable $\mathcal{O}(n \log n)$-time encoding and sufficient minimum code distance for following constructions.
- **Basefold Polynomial Commitment over Galois rings:** By introducing a linear proximity gap theorem (Theorem 1) for linear codes over Galois rings and combining IOPP with the sum-check protocol, we obtain a multilinear PCS (Fig. 3) over Galois rings with $\mathcal{O}(\log^2 n)$ proof size and verifier time, $\mathcal{O}(n \log n)$ committing time, and $\mathcal{O}(n)$ evaluation opening proof time.
- **Multipoint opening Protocol:** A batched evaluation protocol leveraging polynomial linearization (Fig. 4) to reduce N-polynomial M-point verification costs from $\mathcal{O}(NM \log^2 n)$ to $\mathcal{O}(\log^2 n + N + M)$, and prover cost from $\mathcal{O}(NMn)$ to $\mathcal{O}(n + N + M)$, thereby further enhancing efficiency.

2 Preliminaries

Definition 1 (Galois Ring). *Let p be a prime number and $s, r \in \mathbb{N}$. The Galois ring $GR = GR(p^s, r)$ is the finite commutative ring with p^{sr} elements,* constructed as: $GR(p^s, r) \cong \mathbb{Z}_{p^s}[X]/(f(X))$, where $f(X)$ is a monic polynomial of degree r which is irreducible modulo p. We denote $GR^\times(p^s, r)$ as the set of all invertible elements in $GR(p^s, r)$, and we have $|GR^\times(p^s, r)| = p^{r(s-1)}(p^r - 1)$.

Definition 2 (Multilinear Polynomial over Galois Rings). *A multilinear polynomial f in d variables $X_1, \ldots, X_d$ over Galois ring $GR(p^s, r)$ is represented as $f \in GR(p^s, r)[X_1, \ldots, X_d]$, where the coefficient vector $\mathbf{f} \in GR(p^s, r)^{2^d}$ encodes the 2^d coefficients, corresponding to all possible terms with each variable X_i appearing to degree 0 or 1.*

Definition 3 (Relative Minimum Distance of Linear Codes over Galois Rings). *Let C be an $[n, k, d]$-linear code over the Galois ring $GR(p^s, r)$, where n is the codeword length, k is the message length and d is the minimum Hamming distance. The Hamming distance between two codewords $\mathbf{c}, \mathbf{d} \in C$, denoted by $\Delta(\mathbf{c}, \mathbf{d})$, is the number of positions where they differ: $\Delta(\mathbf{c}, \mathbf{d}) = |\{i \mid c_i \neq d_i, 1 \leq i \leq N\}|$. The relative minimum distance Δ_C of code C is:*

$$\Delta_C = \frac{\min\{\Delta(\mathbf{c}, \mathbf{d}) \mid \mathbf{c}, \mathbf{d} \in C, \mathbf{c} \neq \mathbf{d}\}}{N}.$$

Definition 4 (Coset Relative Minimum Distance [19]). *Let n be an even integer and let C be an $[n, k, d]$-linear code over $GR(p^s, r)$. Let $\mathbf{v} \in GR(p^s, r)^n$ be a vector and let $\mathbf{c} \in C$ be a codeword. The coset relative distance $\Delta^*(\mathbf{v}, \mathbf{c})$ between $\mathbf{v}$ and $\mathbf{c}$ is defined as:*

$$\Delta^*(\mathbf{v}, \mathbf{c}) = \frac{2|\{j \in [1, n/2] : \mathbf{v}[j] \neq \mathbf{c}[j] \vee \mathbf{v}[j + n/2] \neq \mathbf{c}[j + n/2]\}|}{n}.$$

The relative minimum distance of $\mathbf{v} \in GR(p^s, r)^n$ to the code C is defined as: $\Delta^*(\mathbf{v}, C) = \min_{\mathbf{c} \in C} \Delta^*(\mathbf{v}, \mathbf{c})$, and $\Delta(\mathbf{v}, C) \leq \Delta^*(\mathbf{v}, C)$ (lemma 6 [19]).

Definition 5 (Maximum Distance Separable Code). *A linear code with length n, dimension k, and minimum distance d satisfies $d \leq n - k + 1$ (the Singleton Bound). It is called Maximum Distance Separable (MDS) if and only if $d = n - k + 1$.*

Definition 6 (Johnson Bound [19]). *For every $\gamma \in (0, 1)$, define $J_\gamma : [0, 1] \to [0, 1]$ as the function $J_\gamma(\lambda) := 1 - \sqrt{1 - \lambda(1 - \gamma)}$.*

Definition 7 (Free Module). *Let R be a ring. An R-module F is called free if there exists a subset $B \subseteq F$, called a basis, such that:*

1. *B is linearly independent: for any distinct $b_1, \ldots, b_n \in B$ and $r_1, \ldots, r_n \in R$,*

$$r_1 b_1 + \cdots + r_n b_n = 0_F \implies r_1 = \cdots = r_n = 0_R.$$

2. *B spans F: every $x \in F$ can be expressed as*

$$x = s_1 b_1 + \cdots + s_m b_m,$$

for some $b_1, \ldots, b_m \in B$ and $s_1, \ldots, s_m \in R$.

Free modules are defined to capture and generalize the essential property of vector spaces over fields. A free module over a ring extends the notions of "basis" and "linear combination" to the more general setting of modules.

Definition 8 (Polynomial commitment scheme [12]). *A polynomial commitment scheme for multilinear polynomials over a Galois ring $GR(p^s, r)$ is a tuple of four protocols PC = (Gen, Commit, Open, Eval):*

- *$Gen(1^\lambda, \mu)$: Generate public parameters pp, taking security parameter λ and number of variables μ as input.*
- *$Commit(pp, G, \gamma)$: Takes public parameters pp, randomness γ and a μ-variate multilinear polynomial $G \in GR(p^s, r)[\mu]$, outputs a commitment C.*
- *$Open(pp, C, G, \gamma)$: Verifies if commitment C corresponds to polynomial G and randomness γ, outputs a boolean $b \in \{0, 1\}$.*
- *$Eval(pp, C, z, v, \mu, G)$: A protocol between a prover $\mathcal{P}$ and verifier $\mathcal{V}$. $\mathcal{P}$ and $\mathcal{V}$ hold $pp, C, z \in GR(p^s, r)^\mu, v \in GR(p^s, r), \mu$, only $\mathcal{P}$ holds G. $\mathcal{P}$ attempts to convince $\mathcal{V}$ that $G(z) = v$. The verifier outputs a boolean $b \in \{0, 1\}$.*

A tuple of four protocols (Gen, Commit, Open, Eval) is an extractable polynomial commitment scheme for multilinear polynomials over a Galois ring $GR(p^s, r)$ if the following conditions hold:

- **Completeness.** *For any valid polynomial G and evaluation point r, if $v = G(r)$, an honest prover can convince the verifier to output 1 in the Eval protocol with probability at least 1.*
- **Binding.** *It is computationally hard for any PPT adversary to find a commitment C and two distinct polynomials $G_0 \neq G_1$ such that $Open(pp, C, G_0) = 1$ and $Open(pp, C, G_1) = 1$, except with negligible probability ($\leq negl(\lambda)$).*
- **Knowledge Soundness.** *Eval is a succinct argument of knowledge for the NP relation $R_{Eval} \subseteq (\{0,1\}^* \times GR(p^s, r)^\mu \times GR(p^s, r)) \times GR(p^s, r)[\mu]$ defined as: A pair $((C, r, v), G)$ is in R_{Eval} if and only if $G \in GR(p^s, r)[\mu]$, $G(r) = v$, and $Open(pp, C, G) = 1$. The statement is (C, r, v) and the witness is G.*

Definition 9 (Foldable linear codes over Galois rings adapted from Definition 5 in [19]). *For Galois ring $GR(p^s, r)$ and let $c, k_0, d \in \mathbb{N}$. A linear code $C_d : GR(p^s, r)^{k_0 \cdot 2^d} \to GR(p^s, r)^{ck_0 \cdot 2^d}$ with generator matrix $\mathbf{G}_d$ over Galois ring $GR(p^s, r)$ is called foldable if there exists a list of matrices $(\mathbf{G}_0, \ldots, \mathbf{G}_{d-1})$ and diagonal matrices $(T_0, \ldots, T_{d-1})$ and $(T'_0, \ldots, T'_{d-1})$ over $GR(p^s, r)$, such that for every $i \in [1, d]$ satisfy 1,2 and for every $i \in [0, d]$ satisfy 3:*

1. *The diagonal matrices $T_{i-1}, T'_{i-1} \in (GR(p^s, r))^{ck_0 \cdot 2^{i-1} \times ck_0 \cdot 2^{i-1}}$ satisfies that $diag(T_{i-1})[j] \neq diag(T'_{i-1})[j]$ for every $j \in [ck_0 \cdot 2^{i-1}]$;*
2. *The matrix $\mathbf{G}_i \in (GR(p^s, r))^{ck_0 \cdot 2^i \times ck_0 \cdot 2^i}$ equals:*

$$\mathbf{G}_i = \begin{bmatrix} \mathbf{G}_{i-1} & \mathbf{G}_{i-1} \\ \mathbf{G}_{i-1} \cdot T_{i-1} & \mathbf{G}_{i-1} \cdot T'_{i-1} \end{bmatrix}.$$

3. $\mathsf{Im}(\mathbf{G}_i) = \{m \cdot \mathbf{G}_i \mid m \in GR(p^s, r)^{k_0 \cdot 2^i}\}$ are free GR-modules.

Fact 1. *For Galois ring $GR(p^s, r)$ and let $a, b \in GR(p^s, r)$ with $a, b \neq 0$. Then the linear equation $ax = b$ has at most $p^{r(s-1)}$ solutions.*

Fact 2. *For Galois ring $GR(p^s, r)$ and let $f(x)$ be a non-zero polynomial of degree d over $GR(p^s, r)$. Then for a randomly chosen element $x \in GR(p^s, r)$, the probability that $f(x) = 0$ is at most $\frac{d}{p^r}$.*

3 Random Foldable Codes over Galois Rings

In this section, we present a foldable linear code over Galois rings. We present its encoding algorithm and analysis of its relative minimum distance.

Definition 10 (Random Foldable Linear Codes). *Fixed the Galois ring $GR(p^s, r)$, $c, k_0 \in \mathbb{N}$. For $i = 0$, define $\mathbf{G_0}$ as a one row, c columns matrix: $(v_1, v_2, \cdots, v_c)$, where $v_j \in GR^\times(p^s, r)$ for $1 \leq j \leq c$. For every $i > 0$, define foldable linear codes by sampling generator matrices $(\mathbf{G_1}, \mathbf{G_2}, \cdots, \mathbf{G_i})$ as follows:*

Sample $\mathsf{diag}(T_{i-1}) \xleftarrow{\$} GR^\times(p^s, r)$ and define $\mathbf{G_i}$ as

$$\mathbf{G_i} = \begin{bmatrix} \mathbf{G_{i-1}} & \mathbf{G_{i-1}} \\ \mathbf{G_{i-1}} \cdot T_{i-1} & \& \mathbf{G_{i-1}} \cdot (-T_{i-1}) \end{bmatrix}$$

where $\mathbf{G_i} \in (GR^\times(p^s, r))^{k_i \times n_{i-1}}$, $k_i = 2^i k_0$, $n_i = ck_i$ ($n_0 = c$, $k_0 = 1$). For a $d \in \mathbb{N}$, denote C_d as the $[c, k_0, d]$-foldable linear code with generator matrix $\mathbf{G_d}$.

For $0 \leq i \leq d$, since the entries of each G_i are invertible, we can perform Gaussian elimination on $\mathbf{G_i}$ to obtain its row-echelon form. The columns within the row-echelon submatrix of $\mathbf{G_i}$ then form a basis. The span of this basis in $GR(p^s, r)$ is the set $\mathsf{Im}(\mathbf{G_i}) = \{m \cdot \mathbf{G_i} \mid m \in GR(p^s, r)^{k_i}\}$, which constitutes a free GR-module (Definition 7).

Encoding Algorithms for Random Foldable Codes. The encoding logic of this algorithm is based on a divide-and-conquer recursion, achieving an encoding complexity of $\mathcal{O}(n \log n)$, where n denotes the codeword length. Specifically, to encode $m \in GR(p^s, r)^{k_d}$ with generator matrix $\mathbf{G_d}$, the computation cost is $(1 + \frac{d}{2}) \cdot n_d$ multiplications and n_d additions over Galois ring $GR(p^s, r)$.

Algorithm 1: Encoding of Random Foldable Codes over $GR(p^s, r)$

Input: $m \in GR(p^s, r)^{k_d}$.
output: $w \in GR(p^s, r)^{n_d}$ such that $w = \mathsf{Enc}_d(m) = m \cdot \mathbf{G}_d$.
Parameters: $\mathbf{G}_0$ and Diagonal matrices $(T_0, T_1, \ldots, T_{d-1})$ over $GR(p^s, r)$.

if $d = 0$ then
    return $\mathsf{Enc}_0(m)$
else
    1. parse $m = (\mathbf{m}_l, \mathbf{m}_r)$ where $\mathbf{m}_l, \mathbf{m}_r \in GR(p^s, r)^{k_d-1}$ are of equal length;
    2. set: $\mathbf{l} \leftarrow \mathsf{Enc}_{d-1}(\mathbf{m}_l)$; $\mathbf{r} \leftarrow \mathsf{Enc}_{d-1}(\mathbf{m}_r)$; $\mathbf{t} \leftarrow \mathsf{diag}(T_{d-1})$;
    3. return $(\mathbf{l} + \mathbf{t} \circ \mathbf{r}, \mathbf{l} - \mathbf{t} \circ \mathbf{r})$.

3.1 Relative Minimum Distance

Directly computing the minimum code distance for large linear codes is computationally intractable. Thus, we theoretically analyze a lower bound on the code distance. However, zero divisors significantly impact the probability of zero elements appearing in codewords. Precisely characterizing the distribution of zero divisors in codewords is laborious with limited gains, as different types of zero divisors belong to distinct ideals with varying proportions. Therefore, we take a different approach: demonstrating that the minimum distance of codes over $GR(p^s, r)$ is no less than the minimum distance of foldable random linear codes over $GR(p, r)$ which is a finite field of size $|p^r|$. In essence, this approach is equivalent to treating zero divisors within $GR(p^s, r)$ as zero elements, which slightly reduces the analyzed minimum distance. The actual minimum distance will be somewhat larger, but this difference is minor, because in practice zero divisors constitute only a very small fraction of the elements in the ring.

For a linear code, analyzing the minimum distance between any two codewords is equivalent to evaluating the maximum number of zero entries in any individual codeword. Therefore, we present an analysis of the number of zero entries in random foldable linear codes over Galois rings.

Lemma 1. *For $v \in GR(p^s, r)^k$, let $v' = v \pmod{p}$. Let $\mathsf{num0}(v)$ denote the number of zero entries in v, i.e., $\mathsf{num0}(v) = |\{i \mid v_i = 0\}|$. Then, we have $\mathsf{num0}(v) \leq \mathsf{num0}(v')$.*

Proof. Let $v' = v \pmod{p}$. If $v_i = 0$ in $GR(p^s, r)$, then $v'_i = v_i \pmod{p} = 0 \pmod{p} = 0$ in $GR(p, r)$. Thus, the set of indices $\{i \mid v_i = 0\}$ is a subset of $\{i \mid v'_i = 0\}$. Taking the cardinality of these sets gives $\mathsf{num0}(v) \leq \mathsf{num0}(v')$. $\square$

For (c, k_0, d)-foldable linear code C_d generated by $\mathbf{G_0}, T_0, T_1, \ldots, T_{d-1}$, given any $\mathbf{m} \in GR(p^s, r)^{k_d} \setminus \mathbf{0}$, let $e = \mathsf{Enc}_d(\mathbf{m})$, and by Definition 10 $e_p = e \bmod p$ is:

$$\mathbf{m} \cdot \mathbf{G_d} \bmod p = (\mathbf{m} \bmod p) \cdot \begin{pmatrix} \mathbf{G_{d-1}} \bmod p & \mathbf{G_{d-1}} \bmod p \\ \mathbf{G_{d-1}} \cdot T_{d-1} \bmod p & \mathbf{G_{d-1}} \cdot (-T_{d-1}) \bmod p \end{pmatrix}.$$

By Lemma 1, we have $\mathsf{num0}(e) \leq \mathsf{num0}(e_p)$, and the relative minimum distance of Δ_{C_d} has a lower bound:

$$\Delta C_d = \frac{ck_d - \mathsf{num0}(e)}{ck_d} \geq \frac{ck_d - \mathsf{num0}(e_p)}{ck_d},$$

Next, to lower bound Δ_{C_d}, we derive the following upper bound on $\mathsf{num0}(e_p)$:

$$\mathsf{num0}(e_p) \leq ck_d \left(\frac{\epsilon_{GR}^d}{c} + \frac{\epsilon_{GR}}{\log p^r} \sum_{i=1}^{d} (\epsilon_{GR})^{d-i} \left(0.6 + \frac{2\log(ck_i/2) + \lambda}{ck_i} \right) \right).$$

where $\epsilon_{GR} = \frac{\log p^r}{\log p^r - 1.001}$. This bound follows directly from Theorem 2 in [19].

Let $\pi : GR(p^s, r) \to GR(p, r) \cong \mathbb{F}_{p^r}$ be the natural ring homomorphism defined by reduction modulo p. We have $\pi(ab) = \pi(a) \cdot \pi(b)$ for $a, b \in GR(p^s, r)$.

Specifically, if $\mathrm{GR}(p^s, r) \cong \mathbb{Z}_{p^s}[x]/(f(X))$ where $f(X)$ is a monic basic irreducible polynomial of degree r over $\mathbb{Z}_{p^s}[X]$, then π can be viewed as reducing the coefficients of polynomials in $\mathbb{Z}_{p^s}[X]/(f(X))$ modulo p to obtain elements in $\mathbb{Z}_p[X]/(f(X)) \cong \mathrm{GR}(p, r) \cong \mathbb{F}_{p^r}$. $\mathrm{GR}(p, r)$ can also be treated as a finite field $\mathbb{F}_{p^r}$, which is the extension field of $\mathbb{F}_p$.

Let $\mathbf{m}' = \pi(\mathbf{m})$, we have $\mathbf{m}' \in \mathbb{F}_{p^r}^{k_d}$. Next, we consider linear codes C'_d over the finite field $\mathbb{F}_{p^r}$. The generator matrix of C'_d is $\mathbf{G}'_\mathbf{d}$ constructed as follows:

Let $\mathbf{G}'_\mathbf{0} = \pi(\mathbf{G_0})$ and codes generated by $\mathbf{G}'_\mathbf{0}$ are MDS (Definition 5)[1]. Recursively generate $\{\mathbf{G}'_\mathbf{i}\}_{1 \leq i \leq d}$ as:

$$\mathbf{G}'_\mathbf{i} = \begin{bmatrix} \mathbf{G}'_{\mathbf{i-1}} & \mathbf{G}'_{\mathbf{i-1}} \\ \mathbf{G}'_{\mathbf{i-1}} \cdot \pi(T_{i-1}) & \mathbf{G}'_{\mathbf{i-1}} \cdot (-\pi(T_{i-1})) \end{bmatrix} = \begin{bmatrix} \pi(\mathbf{G_{i-1}}) & \pi(\mathbf{G_{i-1}}) \\ \pi(\mathbf{G_{i-1}} \cdot T_{i-1}) & \pi(\mathbf{G_{i-1}} \cdot (-T_{i-1})) \end{bmatrix}$$

To show C'_d is (c, k_0, d)-foldable random linear code over $\mathbb{F}_{p^r}$ with random folding elements from $\mathbb{F}_{p^r}^\times$ (Definition 9 in [19]), we need to prove that if T_i is uniformly sampled from $\mathrm{GR}^\times(p^s, r)$, then $\pi(T_i)$ is uniformly distributed over $\mathbb{F}_{p^r}^\times$.

For any $\alpha \in \mathbb{F}_{p^r}^\times$, α can be written as a polynomial: $a_0 + a_1 X + \cdots + a_{r-1} X^{r-1}$, where $\{a_i\}_{0 \leq i \leq r-1}$ are the coefficients in $\mathbb{F}_p$. For elements β in $\mathrm{GR}(p^s, r)$ of the patter: $b_0 + b_1 X + \cdots + b_{r-1} X^{r-1}$, where $b_i \in \{p \cdot q + a_i \mid q \in [0, p^{s-1} - 1]\}$, $\pi(\beta) = y$ and $\beta \in \mathrm{GR}^\times(p^s, r)$. When T_i is uniformly sampled from $\mathrm{GR}^\times(p^s, r)$, for any $\alpha \in \mathbb{F}_{p^r}^\times$, the probability that $\pi(T_i) = \alpha$ is:

$$\Pr(\pi(T_i) = \alpha) = \frac{|\{x \in \mathrm{GR}^\times \mid \pi(x) = \alpha\}|}{|\mathrm{GR}^\times|} = \frac{|\beta|}{|\mathrm{GR}^\times|} = \frac{p^{r(s-1)}}{p^{r(s-1)}(p^r - 1)} = \frac{1}{|\mathbb{F}_{p^r}^\times|}.$$

This confirms that $\pi(T_i)$ is uniformly distributed over $\mathbb{F}_{p^r}^\times$. Since we assume the folding elements T'_i for random codes over $\mathbb{F}_{p^r}$ are also uniformly sampled from $\mathbb{F}_{p^r}^\times$, the distribution of $\pi(T_i)$ matches the distribution of T'_i. Thus, C'_d is indeed a (c, k_0, d)-foldable random linear code over $\mathbb{F}_{p^r}$ by Definition 9 in [19]. And $\mathbf{G}'_\mathbf{i} = \pi(\mathbf{G_i})$, so $\mathbf{m}'\mathbf{G}'_\mathbf{d} = \mathbf{m}\mathbf{G_d} \mod p$. We can now apply Theorem 2 from [19] to bound the zero entries in C'_d, which is exactly the upper bound of $\mathrm{num0}(e_p)$ and consequently we have the lower bound of Δ_{C_d}. We show concrete code distances in Table 1, and $t_0 = 1$ by Definition 10.

4 Polylogarithmic Polynomial Commitment

In this section, we generalize the Basefold IOPP for foldable codes over Galois rings $\mathrm{GR}(p^s, r)$ and combined with a sum-check protocol over Galois rings $\mathrm{GR}(p^s, r)$, construct a multilinear polynomial commitment scheme with logarithmic verification. Importantly, this construction applies to any foldable code over Galois rings, not just the random foldable codes introduced in the previous section. For the random foldable codes we achieve $\mathcal{O}(n \log n)$ encoding time.

---

[1] This can easily be verified by Definition 10, as $\mathbf{G}'_\mathbf{0}$ can be viewed as a generator matrix for a Reed-Solomon code over a finite field.

Table 1. Practical performance on the relative minimum distance of random foldable codes over Galois rings $GR(p^s, r)$. The security parameter λ is 128.

k_0	k_d	c	$\|p^r\|$	Δ_{C_d}
1	2^8	16	2^{32}	0.4176
1	2^{10}	16	2^{64}	0.6728
1	2^{10}	8	2^{128}	0.6760
1	2^{25}	16	2^{128}	0.7144
1	2^{25}	8	2^{256}	0.7288

4.1 BaseFold IOPPs for Foldable Codes over Galois Rings

For some integer $d \geq 0$, a foldable linear code C_d over $GR(p^s, r)$ is specified by a sequence of generator matrices $(\mathbf{G_0}, \mathbf{G_1}, \ldots, \mathbf{G_d})$, where for each $i \in [1, d]$, $\mathbf{G_i} \in GR(p^s, r)^{k_i \times n_i}$ has the following structure:

$$\mathbf{G_i} = \begin{bmatrix} \mathbf{G_{i-1}} & \mathbf{G_{i-1}} \\ \mathbf{G_{i-1}} \cdot T_{i-1} & \mathbf{G_{i-1}} \cdot T'_{i-1} \end{bmatrix}$$

where $T_{i-1}, T'_{i-1} \in GR(p^s, r)^{n_{i-1} \times n_{i-1}}$ are diagonal matrices. For each index $j \in [n_{i-1}]$, we require the diagonal difference $\mathsf{diag}(T_{i-1})[j] - \mathsf{diag}(T'_{i-1})[j]$ is invertible in $GR(p^s, r)^{n_{i-1}}$. This requirement stems from the fact that interpolation is not directly applicable over a ring. The Basefold folding process relies on linear interpolation, where deriving a third point on a line from two known points on the same line. By Definition 10, $T'_{i-1} = -T_{i-1}$ and T_{i-1} sampled from $GR^{\times}(p^s, r)$, we have $\mathsf{diag}(T_{i-1})[j] - \mathsf{diag}(T'_{i-1})[j] = 2\mathsf{diag}(T_{i-1})[j]$, which is invertible in $GR(p^s, r)$ if $p \neq 2$. This is analogous to the requirement in Basefold [19] that $2\mathsf{diag}(T_{i-1})[j]$ is invertible in a field of characteristic not 2. The goal of IOPP is to verify that a given vector $\pi_d \in GR(p^s, r)^{n_d}$ is close to a codeword in C_d. We present the protocol in two phases: commit and query in Fig. 1

Completeness guarantees that if π_d is a codeword in C_d, and the prover follows the commit protocol honestly, then the verifier always accepts in the query phase. This property stems from the foldability and linearity of the code.

Soundness guarantees that if π_d is significantly distant from any valid codeword in the code C_d, then with overwhelming probability after the IOPP.Commit phase, the initial oracle π_0 will also be demonstrably distant from any codeword in C_0. Consequently, during the IOPP.Query phase, the verifier will output accept with only negligible probability.

The central challenge in establishing soundness lies in ensuring a sufficient distance preservation gap throughout the IOPP.Commit phase. This requires a quantifiable proximity gap for the underlying random linear codes over Galois rings, a concept frequently utilized in the proximity error analysis of IOPP protocols [4,5]. Existing literature, however, lacks a proven distance preservation gap specifically for linear codes defined over Galois rings. To address this, we present the first proximity gap analysis (Theorem 1), extending Theorem 4.4

from [5]. This theorem serves as the foundation for guaranteeing the soundness of our proposed IOPP protocol. Free module over rings play a role like linear space over fields.

Theorem 1 (Linear proximity gap for linear codes over Galois Rings). *Let $V \subseteq GR(p^s, r)^n$ be a free module over the Galois ring $GR(p^s, r)$ with $\Delta_V = \zeta$. Let $u^* \in GR(p^s, r)^n$ and let $\gamma > 0$ satisfy $\delta < J_\gamma(J_\gamma(\zeta))$. For $u \in GR(p^s, r)^n$, define $A = A_{u,\gamma} = \{\alpha \in GR(p^s, r) \mid \Delta(u^* + \alpha u, V) < \delta - \gamma\}$. If $|A| > \frac{2p^{r(s-1)}}{\gamma^3}$, then there exist $v^*, v \in V$ such that $|\{i \in [n] \mid (u_i = v_i) \land (u^* = v^*)\}| \geq (1 - \delta)n$.*

Theorem 2 (Soundness adapted from Theorem 3 [19]). *Let C_d be a (c, k_0, d)-foldable linear code defined over Galois ring $GR(p^s, r)$. Let C_i denote the code generated by $\mathbf{G}_i$ for $0 \leq i \leq d$, with $\Delta_{C_{i+1}} < \Delta_{C_i}$. Define a constant $\gamma > 0$ and set $\delta := \min(\Delta^*(\pi_d, C_d), J_\gamma(J_\gamma(\Delta_{C_d})))$, where $\Delta^*(\pi_d, C_d)$ is the relative coset minimum distance (Definition 4). Then, with a probability of at least $1 - \frac{2d}{\gamma^3 p^r}$ over the randomly sampled challenges $(\alpha_0, \ldots, \alpha_{d-1})$ in the IOPP.commit phase, for any prover oracles $\{\pi_{d-1}, \ldots, \pi_0\}$, the probability that the verifier outputs "accept" in all l repetitions of the IOPP.query phase is upper-bounded by $(1 - \delta + \gamma d)^l$.*

We present proofs for Theorem 1 and Theorem 2 in Appendix A.1 and A.2.

Remark 1. We remove the interactions in our construction using the Fiat-Shamir Heuristic [3,9] in the random oracle model. The transformation only incurs a negligible soundness loss [3]. Specifically, vectors sent by the prover in the IOP can be substituted with Merkle commitments to those vectors. Correspondingly, each query from the verifier to a vector is answered by the prover by providing the requested value along with a Merkle tree authentication path.

4.2 Sumcheck Protocol over Galois Rings

Let us briefly review sum-check protocol ([14], Chapter 4 from [17]). To efficiently verify equation $\sum_{\mathbf{b} \in \{0,1\}^l} f(\mathbf{b}) = H$ over all binary inputs, where $f : \mathbb{F}^l \to \mathbb{F}$ is a d-degree multivariate polynomial, the prover and verifier engage in an l-round protocol with soundness error $\frac{dl}{|\mathbb{F}|}$. In each round i, the prover sends a univariate polynomial f_i, and the verifier responds with a random challenge r_i, checking that $f_i(0) + f_i(1)$ equals a given value. In the final round, the verifier queries the prover for the evaluation of $f(r_1, \ldots, r_l)$ and outputs accept or reject. The sum-check protocol over Galois rings presents in Fig. 2.

Soundness of Sumcheck Protocol. In the sumcheck protocol for multivariate polynomial $f : GR^l \to GR$ over $GR(p^s, r)$, the verifier can sample challenges from $GR(p^s, r)$. If the prover is dishonest, in at least one round the claimed polynomial is not correct, and by Fact 2 the probability that the verifier accepts in a given round is at most $\frac{\deg(f)}{p^r}$. Since the total degree is at most d and there are l rounds, a union bound shows that the overall soundness error is $\frac{dl}{p^r}$.

IOPP.Commit Phase

Input Oracles: $\pi_d \in \mathrm{GR}(p^s, r)^{n_d}$
Output Oracles: $(\pi_{d-1}, \ldots, \pi_0)$.

From $i = d - 1$ down to 0:

1. <u>Verifier:</u> sample $\alpha_i \leftarrow \mathrm{GR}(p^s, r)$, send α_i to prover.

2. For each $j \in [1, n_{i-1}]$:
   <u>Prover:</u>
   construct a polynomial $f(X)$ of degree ≤ 1 over $\mathrm{GR}(p^s, r)$ as:
   $$f(X) = \pi_{i+1}[j] + \frac{\pi_{i+1}[j] - \pi_{i+1}[j + n_i]}{\mathrm{diag}(T_i)[j] - \mathrm{diag}(T_i')[j]} (X - \mathrm{diag}(T_i)[j]).$$
   Set $\pi_i[j] = f(\alpha_i)$.

3. <u>Prover:</u> send oracle $\pi_i \in \mathrm{GR}(p^s, r)^{n_i}$ to verifier.

IOPP.Query Phase

Oracles: $(\pi_d, \ldots, \pi_1, \pi_0)$.

1. <u>Verifier:</u> sample query index $\mu \leftarrow [1, n_{d-1}]$.

2. From $i = d - 1$ down to 0,
   <u>Verifier:</u>

   Query oracles $\pi_{i+1}[\mu]$ and $\pi_{i+1}[\mu + n_i]$ and compute $p(X)$ as:
   $$p(X) = \pi_{i+1}[\mu] + \frac{\pi_{i+1}[\mu] - \pi_{i+1}[\mu + n_i]}{\mathrm{diag}(T_i)[\mu] - \mathrm{diag}(T_i')[\mu]} (X - \mathrm{diag}(T_i)[\mu]).$$
   Check if $p(\alpha_i) = \pi_i[\mu]$. If not, **Reject**;
   If $i > 0$ and $\mu \geq n_{i-1}$, update $\mu = \mu - n_{i-1}$.

3. <u>Verifier:</u> if π_0 is a valid codeword w.r.t. G_0 over $\mathrm{GR}(p^s, r)$, **Accept**; else **Reject**.

Fig. 1. IOPP for foldable codes over $\mathrm{GR}(p^s, r)$

4.3 Multilinear Polynomial Commitment

We present a multilinear polynomial commitment scheme over Galois rings with polylogarithmic proof size and verification time in Fig. 3. The construction combines the Basefold IOPP (Fig. 1) and sumcheck protocol (Fig. 2), and the coefficients of f are ordered consistently in both protocols.

Completeness. For an honest prover, denote f_i as the i-variate multilinear polynomial $f(X_1, \ldots, X_i, r_i, \ldots, r_{d-1})$ such that $\mathsf{Enc}_i(\mathbf{f}_i) = \pi_i$ in the evaluation protocol, where $\mathbf{f}_i \in \mathrm{GR}(p^s, r)^{2^i}$ as coefficients. For $i \in [0, d-1]$, by the Definition 2, we can order the coefficients $\mathbf{f}_{i+1} = (\mathbf{f}_{i+1,l}, \mathbf{f}_{i+1,r})$ such that $\mathbf{f}_i = \mathbf{f}_{i+1,l} + r_i \cdot \mathbf{f}_{i+1,r}$, then $\mathbf{f}_0 = f(\mathbf{r})$ implies $\pi_0 \cdot \tilde{eq}_{\mathbf{z}}(\mathbf{r}) = \mathsf{Enc}_0(\mathbf{f}_0) \cdot \tilde{eq}_{\mathbf{z}}(\mathbf{r}) =$

> **Sumcheck Protocol over Galois Ring GR(p^s, r)**
>
> **Input:** $\sum_{b_1, b_2, \ldots, b_l \in \{0,1\}} f(b_1, b_2, \ldots, b_l) = H$.
>
> For $i = 1$:
>
> > **Prover:** send univariate $f_1(x_1) = \sum_{b_2, \ldots, b_l \in \{0,1\}} f(x_1, b_2, \ldots, b_l)$ to verifier.
> > **Verifier:** check $H = f_1(0) + f_1(1)$, send random $r_1 \in \mathrm{GR}(p^s, r)$ to prover.
>
> From $i = 2$ to $l - 1$:
>
> > **Prover:** send univariate $f_i(x_i) = \sum_{b_{i+1}, \ldots, b_l \in \{0,1\}} f(r_1, \ldots, r_{i-1}, x_i, b_{i+1} \ldots, b_l)$ to verifier.
> > **Verifier:** check $f_{i-1}(r_{i-1}) = f_i(0) + f_i(1)$, send random $r_i \in \mathrm{GR}(p^s, r)$ to prover.
>
> For $i = l$:
>
> > **Prover:** send univariate $f_l(x_l) = f(r_1, r_2, \ldots, r_{l-1}, x_l)$ to verifier.
> > **Verifier:** check $f_{l-1}(r_{l-1}) = f_l(0) + f_l(1)$, send random $r_l \in \mathrm{GR}(p^s, r)$ to prover.
>
> Assume an oracle access to an evaluation $f(r_1, r_2, \ldots, r_l)$ of f. The verifier accepts if and only if the evaluation at the final round satisfies: $f_l(r_l) = f(r_1, r_2, \ldots, r_l)$. Note that the specific instantiation of this oracle is determined by the application of the sumcheck protocol.

Fig. 2. Sumcheck Protocol. Sumcheck Protocol. The verifier accepts if and only if the evaluation at the final round satisfies: $f_l(r_l) = f(r_1, r_2, \ldots, r_l)$. Note that the specific instantiation of this oracle is determined by the application of the sumcheck protocol.

$\mathsf{Enc}_0(\mathbf{f}_0 \cdot \tilde{eq}_\mathbf{z}(r_0, \ldots, r_{d-1})) = \pi'_0 = \mathsf{Enc}_0(h_1(r_0))$ holds.

Binding. Assume an adversary can open a commitment Ct to two distinct polynomials f_1 and f_2, with corresponding codewords π_1 and π_2. This implies the Merkle commit of π_1 and π_2 are the same. Consequently, either $\pi_1 = \pi_2$ or the adversary has found a hash collision. If $\pi_1 = \pi_2$, then given that $\Delta^*(\mathsf{Enc}_d(\mathbf{f}_1), \pi_1)$, $\Delta^*(\mathsf{Enc}_d(\mathbf{f}_2), \pi_1) < \frac{\Delta_{C_d}}{2}$, by triangle inequality and lemma 6 in [19], we have $\Delta(\mathsf{Enc}_d(\mathbf{f}_1), \mathsf{Enc}_d(\mathbf{f}_2)) \leq \Delta^*(\mathsf{Enc}_d(\mathbf{f}_1), \mathsf{Enc}_d(\mathbf{f}_2)) < \Delta_{C_d}$, therefore $f_1 = f_2$.

Theorem 3 (Soundness of Polynomial Commitment). Let $\gamma, \delta \in (0,1)$ such that $3\delta - \gamma d < \Delta_{C_d}$ and $\frac{2d}{\gamma^3 p^r} + (1 - \delta + \gamma d)^l < 2^{-\lambda}$, where λ is the security parameter. Let C_i denote the code generated by $\mathbf{G}_i$ with $\Delta_{C_{i+1}} < \Delta_{C_i}$ for $0 \leq i \leq d$. In the evaluation protocol (Fig. 3), for any malicious prover, the probability that verifier passes the checks in Step 3 is upper-bounded by $\frac{2d}{p^r}$.

We present the proof for Theorem 3 and Extractablity in Appendix B.1 and B.2.

Prover Time. In commitment phase, the cost of encoding of multilinear polynomial f is dominated by $\mathcal{O}(n_d \log n_d) = \mathcal{O}(ck_d \log ck_d)$ multiplications over $\mathrm{GR}(p^s, r)$ and then hashes the ck_d elements of corresponding codeword. c is fixed constant defined in code C_0. In evaluation phase, the prover runs IOPP.Commit and sumcheck protocol. In sumcheck protocol, the prover computes polynomial $h_i(X)$, let T_h denote the cost of an evaluation of $f(\mathbf{b}, X, \mathbf{r}) \cdot \tilde{eq}_{\mathbf{z}}(\mathbf{b}, X, \mathbf{r})$ at point $(\mathbf{b},X,\mathbf{r})$. Then the cost of computing $h_i(X)$ is $2^{i-1}T_h$, the totol cost of prover to compute $\{h_i\}_{1\leq i\leq d}$ is $(2^d-1)T_h$. T_h depends on the sparsity of specific f, since f is multilinear(the degree for each variable is 1 or 0), so if we precompute $\prod_{i=1}^d r_i$, then computing f and $\tilde{eq}_z$ only consists of constant additions over $GR(p^s, r)$ and compute $f \cdot \tilde{eq}_z$(two degree-1 polynomials) only envolves 4 multiplications and 1 addition over $GR(p^s,r)$. Thus $(2^d-1)T_h \approx 4(2^d-1) \approx 4k_d$ multiplications. In IOPP.Commit, the prover computes $\{g_j(r_i)\}_{1\leq j\leq n_i}$ and obtain π_i then computes each merkle roots of π_i. These evolves $\mathcal{O}(ck_i)$ ring operations and hashes. So over all d rounds, the prover complexity is $\mathcal{O}(ck_d) + \mathcal{O}(4k_d) \approx \mathcal{O}(k_d)$.

Proof Size. The proof size consists of {Merkle.Commit(π_i)}, $\{h_i(X)\}$ and $\{r_i\}$, the merkle roots are outputs of hash functions where one output is hundreds of bits, and $\{h_i(X)\}$ consists at most 3 ring elements since $h_i(X)$ is degree-2 polynomials. Additionally in the IOPP.Query phase, μ and a merkle tree authentication path of each oracle π_i, the path for the opening of π_i consists of $\log n_i$ hash outputs. And there are $\log n_d$ oracles to be opened, thus resulting in $\mathcal{O}(\log^2 n_d) = \mathcal{O}(\log^2 ck_d) \approx \mathcal{O}(\log^2 k_d)$ complexity in proof size.

Verifier Time. Verifier needs to perform $\mathcal{O}(d)$ ring operations for sumcheck protocol and IOPP.Query phase, verifier needs to check the merkle tree authentication paths which for one path verification needs at most $\mathcal{O}(d)$ hash computations, thus for l runs of query, the verifier complexity if $\mathcal{O}(l\log^2 n_d) \approx \mathcal{O}(\log^2 k_d)$.

4.4 Multipoint Opening Protocol

Additionally, we give a method to further accelerate the efficiency of our polynomial commitment scheme when there are many polynomials and they are queried to evaluate at multiple points. For polynomials $\{f_i\}_{1\leq i\leq N}$ and points $\{\mathbf{z}_j\}_{1\leq j\leq M}$, we show the multipoint protocol in Fig. 4, which is designed for opening multiple polynomials at the same set of points.

In the evaluation phase in Fig. 4, when prover runs IOPP.Commit for the polynomial ϕ, it uses $\pi_{\phi,d}$ to compute $\pi_{\phi,d-1}$, so in the IOPP.Query the verifier has to query $\pi_{\phi,d}$, but verifier only has oracle accesses to $\{\pi_{f_i,d}\}_{1\leq i\leq N}$. So we slightly change the query phase, on input oracles $\{\pi_{f_i,d}\}_{1\leq i\leq N}, \{\pi_{\phi,i}\}_{d-1\geq i\geq 0}$:

- Verifier sample query index $\mu \in [n_{d-1}]$.
- From $i = d-1$ down to 0: $i = d-1$, query oracles $\{\pi_{f_i,d}\}_{1\leq i\leq N}$, compute $\pi_{\phi,d}[\mu] = \sum_{i=1}^N \alpha^{i-1}\pi_{f_i,d}[\mu]$ and $\pi_{\phi,d}[\mu + n_{d-1}] = \sum_{i=1}^N \alpha^{i-1}\pi_{f_i,d}[\mu + n_{d-1}]$; Else if $0 \leq i \leq d-2$, query $\pi_{\phi,i+1}$. Then compute $p(X)$ and check if $p(r_i) = \pi_{\phi,i}[\mu]$, update $\mu = \mu - n_{i-1}$.
- if $\pi_{\phi,0}$ is a valid codeword output accept; else reject.

Multilinear Polynomial Commitment over Galois Ring $\mathrm{GR}(p^s, r)$

Prover inputs: $f \in \mathrm{GR}(p^s, r)[X_1, X_2, \ldots, X_d]$ with coefficients $\mathbf{f} \in \mathrm{GR}(p^s, r)^{2^d}$.
Code Parameters: $\mathbf{G_0}$ and diagnal matrices $T_0, T_1, \ldots, T_{d-1}$ and $T_0', T_1', \ldots, T_{d-1}'$.
$\tilde{eq}_{b_1,\ldots,b_d}(X_1,\ldots,X_d) = \prod_{i=1}^{d}(b_i x_i + (1-b_i)(1-x_i))$ and $\tilde{eq}_{b_1,\ldots,b_d}(X_1,\ldots,X_d) = \tilde{eq}_{X_1,\ldots,X_d}(b_1,\ldots,b_d)$.

Commit Phase:

<u>Prover:</u> compute the oracle $\pi_f = \mathrm{Enc}_d(\mathbf{f})$ and send the oracle π_f as the commitment Ct to verifier.
(The derived commitment in the random oracle model is the root of merkle tree.)

Opening Phase:
For opening polynomial f given commitment Ct:

<u>Prover:</u> send polynomial f and a word π_f to verifier.

<u>Verifier:</u> perform the following checks:

- Check if the Merkle commitment of π_f equals Ct;
- Check if $\Delta(\pi_f, \mathrm{Enc}_d(\mathbf{f}))$ is less than $\frac{\Delta_{C_d}}{2}$.

Evaluation Phase:
For opening polynomial f at point $\mathbf{z} \in \mathrm{GR}(p^s, r)^d$ with claimed value $y \in \mathrm{GR}(p^s, r)$ given commitment Ct:

1. <u>Prover:</u> send $h_d(X) = \sum_{\mathbf{b} \in \{0,1\}^{d-1}} f(\mathbf{b}, X) \cdot \tilde{eq}_{\mathbf{z}}(\mathbf{b}, X)$.

2. For $i = d-1$ down to 0:

   <u>Verifier:</u> send random $r_i \in \mathrm{GR}(p^s, r)$ to prover.

   <u>Prover:</u> perform as follows:

   - for each $j \in [1, n_i]$, set $g_j(X)$ as:

   $$g_j(X) = \pi_{i+1}[j] + \frac{\pi_{i+1}[j] - \pi_{i+1}[j + n_i]}{\mathrm{diag}(T_i)[j] - \mathrm{diag}(T_i')[j]}(X - \mathrm{diag}(T_i)[j])$$

   and set $\pi_i[j] = g_j(r_i)$, send oracle $\pi_i \in \mathrm{GR}(p^s, r)^{n_i}$.
   - if $i > 0$, send h_i as:

   $$h_i(X) = \sum_{\mathbf{b} \in \{0,1\}^{i-1}} f(\mathbf{b}, X, r_i, \ldots, r_{d-1}) \cdot \tilde{eq}_{\mathbf{z}}(\mathbf{b}, X, r_i, \ldots, r_{d-1})$$

3. <u>Verifier:</u> perform the following checks:

   - Check if $\mathrm{IOPP.Query}^{(\pi_d, \ldots, \pi_1, \pi_0)}$ outputs accept.
   - Check if $h_d(0) + h_d(1) = y$ and for every $i \in [1, d-1]$, $h_i(0) + h_i(1) = h_{i+1}(r_i)$.
   - Check if $\mathrm{Enc}_0(h_1(r_0))$ equals π_0', where $\pi_0' = \pi_0 \cdot \tilde{eq}_{\mathbf{z}}(r_0, \ldots, r_{d-1}) = (\pi_{0,1} \cdot \tilde{eq}_{\mathbf{z}}(\mathbf{r}), \pi_{0,2} \cdot \tilde{eq}_{\mathbf{z}}(\mathbf{r}), \ldots, \pi_{0,c} \cdot \tilde{eq}_{\mathbf{z}}(\mathbf{r}))$.

Fig. 3. Multilinear Polynomial Commitment Scheme

Efficiency Analysis. The commitment cost is simply N times the cost of committing to a polynomial of length k_d. In the evaluation phase of the sum-check protocol, the prover needs to additionally compute M instances of $\tilde{eq}_{\mathbf{z}_j}$ and their linear combination per round. The proof size in the IOPP.Query phase only increases by N openings for $\{\pi_{f_i,d}\}_{1 \leq i \leq N}$. The verifier's cost only increases by the hash computation during the openings of $\{\pi_{f_i,d}\}_{1 \leq i \leq N}$ and the computation of $\sum_{j=1}^{M} \beta^{j-1} \tilde{eq}_{\mathbf{z}_j}(r_0, \ldots, r_{d-1})$.

Soundness of Multipoint Opening Protocol. Conditioned on the soundness of the sumcheck protocol holding within the evaluation protocol, and then assuming there exists $1 \leq u \leq N$ and $1 \leq v \leq M$ such that $f_u(\mathbf{z}_v) \neq y_{uv}$, the probability that the verifier passes the check is at most a negligible probability plus the following probability:

$$\Pr[h_d(0) + h_d(1) = \sum_{j=1}^{M} \beta^{j-1} \sum_{i=1}^{N} \alpha^{i-1} y_{ij}]$$

$$\leq \Pr[\sum_{\mathbf{b} \in \{0,1\}^d} (\phi(\mathbf{b}) \cdot \sum_{j=1}^{M} \beta^{j-1} \cdot \tilde{eq}_{\mathbf{z}_j}(\mathbf{b})) = \sum_{j=1}^{M} \beta^{j-1} \sum_{i=1}^{N} \alpha^{i-1} y_{ij}]$$

$$= \Pr[\sum_{j=1}^{M} \beta^{j-1} \sum_{\mathbf{b} \in \{0,1\}^d} (\phi(\mathbf{b}) \cdot \tilde{eq}_{\mathbf{z}_j}(\mathbf{b})) = \sum_{j=1}^{M} \beta^{j-1} \sum_{i=1}^{N} \alpha^{i-1} y_{ij}]$$

$$= \Pr[\sum_{j=1}^{M} \beta^{j-1} \sum_{\mathbf{b} \in \{0,1\}^d} (\sum_{i=1}^{N} \alpha^{i-1} f_i(\mathbf{b}) \cdot \tilde{eq}_{\mathbf{z}_j}(\mathbf{b})) = \sum_{j=1}^{M} \beta^{j-1} \sum_{i=1}^{N} \alpha^{i-1} y_{ij}]$$

$$= \Pr[\sum_{j=1}^{M} \beta^{j-1} \sum_{i=1}^{N} \alpha^{i-1} (\sum_{\mathbf{b} \in \{0,1\}^d} f_i(\mathbf{b}) \cdot \tilde{eq}_{\mathbf{z}_j}(\mathbf{b}) - y_{ij}) = 0]$$

Let polynomial $A(x) = \sum_{i=1}^{N} x^{i-1} (\sum_{\mathbf{b} \in \{0,1\}^d} f_i(\mathbf{b}) \cdot \tilde{eq}_{\mathbf{z}_v}(\mathbf{b}) - y_{iv})$ over $GR(p^s, r)$, we have $\sum_{\mathbf{b} \in \{0,1\}^d} f_u(\mathbf{b}) \cdot \tilde{eq}_{\mathbf{z}_v}(\mathbf{b}) - y_{uv} \neq 0$, so $A(x)$ is not a zero polynomial, by Fact 2 we have $\Pr_{x \xleftarrow{\$} GR(p^s,r)}[A(x) = 0] \leq \frac{N-1}{p^r}$. Let polynomial $B(x) = \sum_{j=1}^{M} x^{j-1} (\sum_{i=1}^{N} \alpha^{i-1} (\sum_{\mathbf{b} \in \{0,1\}^d} f_i(\mathbf{b}) \cdot \tilde{eq}_{\mathbf{z}_j}(\mathbf{b}) - y_{ij}))$.
Thus we have:

$$\Pr[\sum_{j=1}^{M} \beta^{j-1} \sum_{i=1}^{N} \alpha^{i-1} (\sum_{\mathbf{b} \in \{0,1\}^d} f_i(\mathbf{b}) \cdot \tilde{eq}_{\mathbf{z}_j}(\mathbf{b}) - y_{ij}) = 0] = \Pr_{x \xleftarrow{\$} GR(p^s,r)}[B(x) = 0]$$

$$= \Pr_{x,y \xleftarrow{\$} GR(p^s,r)}[B(x) = 0 \mid A(y) = 0] + \Pr_{x,y \xleftarrow{\$} GR(p^s,r)}[B(x) = 0 \mid A(y) \neq 0]$$

$$\leq \frac{N-1}{p^r} + (1 - \frac{N-1}{p^r}) \cdot \frac{M-1}{p^r} \leq \frac{M+N-2}{p^r}$$

Thus if p^r is large enough such that $\frac{M+N-2}{p^r} < 2^{-\lambda}$, a malicious prover can only success with negligible probability.

Multipoint Opening of Polynomial Commitments

Prover inputs: For N multilinear polynomials $f_1, \ldots, f_N \in \mathrm{GR}(p^s, r)[X_1, X_2, \ldots, X_d]$ with coefficients $\mathbf{f}_1, \ldots, \mathbf{f}_N \in \mathrm{GR}(p^s, r)^{2^d}$.
Code Parameters: $\mathbf{G_0}$ and diagnal matrices $T_0, T_1, \ldots, T_{d-1}$ and $T'_0, T'_1, \ldots, T'_{d-1}$.

Commit Phase:

  Prover: For $1 \leq i \leq N$, compute the oracle $\pi_{f_i,d} = \mathrm{Enc}_d(\mathbf{f}_i)$ and send the oracles $\{\pi_{f_i,d}\}_{1 \leq i \leq N}$ as the commitment $\{\mathsf{Ct}_i\}_{1 \leq i \leq N}$ to verifier

  Verifier: send random $\alpha, \beta \in \mathrm{GR}(p^s, r)$ to prover.

  Define: $\phi = \sum_{i=1}^{N} \alpha^{i-1} f_i$, $\pi_{\phi,d} = \sum_{i=1}^{N} \alpha^{i-1} \pi_{f_i,d} = \mathrm{Enc}_d(\phi)$(Linear Code).

Evaluation Phase:
For opening polynomials $\{f_i\}_{1 \leq i \leq N}$ at points $\{\mathbf{z}_j\}_{1 \leq j \leq M}$ for each $\mathbf{z}_j \in \mathrm{GR}(p^s, r)^d$ with claimed values $f_i(\mathbf{z}_j) = y_{ij} \in \mathrm{GR}(p^s, r)$ given commitments $\{\mathsf{Ct}_i\}_{1 \leq i \leq N}$:

1.Prover: send $h_d(X) = \sum_{\mathbf{b} \in \{0,1\}^{d-1}} (\phi(\mathbf{b}, X) \cdot \sum_{j=1}^{M} \beta^{j-1} \cdot \tilde{eq}_{\mathbf{z}_j}(\mathbf{b}, X))$.

2. For $i = d - 1$ down to 0:

  Verifier: send random $r_i \in \mathrm{GR}(p^s, r)$ to prover.

  Prover: perform as follows:

  – for each $j \in [1, n_i]$, set $g_j(X)$ as:

  $$g_j(X) = \pi_{\phi, i+1}[j] + \frac{\pi_{\phi, i+1}[j] - \pi_{\phi, i+1}[j + n_i]}{\mathrm{diag}(T_i)[j] - \mathrm{diag}(T'_i)[j]}(X - \mathrm{diag}(T_i)[j])$$

  and set $\pi_{\phi,i}[j] = g_j(r_i)$, send oracle $\pi_{\phi,i} \in \mathrm{GR}(p^s, r)^{n_i}$.
  – if $i > 0$, send h_i as:

  $$h_i(X) = \sum_{\mathbf{b} \in \{0,1\}^{i-1}} (\phi(\mathbf{b}, X, r_i, \ldots, r_{d-1}) \sum_{j=1}^{M} \beta^{j-1} \cdot \tilde{eq}_{\mathbf{z}_j}(\mathbf{b}, X, r_i, \ldots, r_{d-1}))$$

3.Verifier: perform the following checks:

  – Check if $\mathsf{IOPP.Query}^{(\{\pi_{f_i,d}\}_{1 \leq i \leq N}, \{\pi_{\phi,i}\}_{d-1 \geq i \geq 0})}$ outputs **accept**.
  – Check if $h_d(0) + h_d(1) = \sum_{j=1}^{M} \beta^{j-1} \sum_{i=1}^{N} \alpha^{i-1} y_{ij}$ and for every $i \in [1, d-1]$, $h_i(0) + h_i(1) = h_{i+1}(r_i)$
  – Check if $\mathrm{Enc}_0(h_1(r_0))$ equals $\pi'_{\phi,0}$, where $\pi'_{\phi,0} = \pi_{\phi,0} \cdot \sum_{j=1}^{M} \beta^{j-1} \tilde{eq}_{\mathbf{z}_j}(\mathbf{r}) = (\pi_{\phi,0,1} \cdot \sum_{j=1}^{M} \beta^{j-1} \tilde{eq}_{\mathbf{z}_j}(\mathbf{r}), \ldots, \pi_{\phi,0,c} \cdot \sum_{j=1}^{M} \beta^{j-1} \tilde{eq}_{\mathbf{z}_j}(\mathbf{r}))$.

Fig. 4. Multipoint opening Protocol

Remark 2 (Sample Challenges in Extension Rings). The soundness error of the aforementioned PCS, IOPP depend on p^r. Therefore, if p^r is not sufficiently large, resulting in a soundness error no smaller than $2^{-\lambda}$, we can sample challenges from a sufficiently large extension ring $\mathrm{GR}(p^s, rk)$ obtained by extending $\mathrm{GR}(p^s, r)$. This is a common practice in many SNARKs based on small fields. In this case, for an encoding $\mathrm{Enc}(\mathbf{m})$, we can treat $\mathbf{m} \in \mathrm{GR}(p^s, r)$ as a constant term in the extension ring $\mathrm{GR}(p^s, rk)$. Consequently, for a message $\mathbf{m} \in (\mathrm{GR}(p^s, r))^{k_d}$, the encoding of $\mathbf{m}$ over the small ring $\mathrm{GR}(p^s, r)$ is exactly the encoding of $\mathbf{m}$ over the extension ring $\mathrm{GR}(p^s, rk)$. Thus, the prover's computational cost in the commitment phase remains based on the small ring; we treat the commitment as being over the large ring during the opening phase and then select random challenges in the extension ring to enhance soundness.

5 Conclusion

Combining our PCS with interactive oracle proofs (IOPs) yields efficient zkSNARKs for polynomial ring arithmetic (Theorem 1 from [8]), significantly impacting real-world applications. For example, it accelerates verifiable fully homomorphic encryption (VFHE), enabling verifiable computations over encrypted data. VFHE applications include privacy-preserving cloud computing with auditable FHE operations, secure multi-party neural network inference on ciphertexts, and regulatory-compliant financial derivatives calculations demanding cryptographically certified privacy and arithmetic correctness.

We compare our work with existing polynomial commitment schemes over Galois rings in Table 2. To highlight the efficiency gains in multi-opening scenarios, we contrast the straightforward approach of independent evaluations with our batched protocol.

Table 2. Comparisons of different polynomial commitment schemes over Galois rings. The first two rows compares a multilinear polynomial with n coefficients and evaluate on one point. The next two rows illustrate multipoint openings on N polynomials and M points. The last row show the complexity of our multipoint opening protocol.

Scheme	Commit Phase	Evaluation Phase		
	Commit time	Prover time	Proof size	Verifier time
Brakedown$_{\mathrm{GR}}$ [13,18]	$\mathcal{O}(n)$	$\mathcal{O}(n)$	$\mathcal{O}(\sqrt{n})$	$\mathcal{O}(\sqrt{n})$
Basefold$_{\mathrm{GR}}$ (**This Work**)	$\mathcal{O}(n \log n)$	$\mathcal{O}(n)$	$\mathcal{O}(\log^2 n)$	$\mathcal{O}(\log^2 n)$
This Work(Unbatched)	$\mathcal{O}(Nn \log n)$	$\mathcal{O}(NMn)$	$\mathcal{O}(NM \log^2 n)$	$\mathcal{O}(NM \log^2 n)$
This Work(Batched)	$\mathcal{O}(Nn \log n)$	$\mathcal{O}(n)$ $+\mathcal{O}(M \log n)$	$\mathcal{O}(\log^2 n)$ $+\mathcal{O}(N \log n)$	$\mathcal{O}(\log^2 n)$ $+\mathcal{O}(M) +$ $\mathcal{O}(N \log n)$

Acknowledgement. We are supported by the Strategic Priority Research Program of Chinese Academy of Sciences (Grant No. XDB0690200), andÂăthe National Key Research and Development Program of China (Grant No. 2023YFB4503203).

A Soundness of IOPP for Foldable Codes

A.1 Proof of Theorem 1

Proof. For each $\alpha \in A$, there exists $v^\alpha \in V$ such that $\Delta(u^* + \alpha u, v^\alpha) < \delta - \gamma$. This implies that $\Delta(u^*, v^\alpha - \alpha u) < \delta - \gamma$. We construct a graph with vertex set A; two vertices α and α' are adjacent if $\Delta(v^\alpha - \alpha u, v^{\alpha'} - \alpha' u) < J_\gamma^{-1}(\delta)$.

By the Johnson bound from Theorem 2.2 [5], this graph cannot have an independent set of size $\frac{1}{\gamma}$. Applying Turán's theorem, we find a vertex α_0 with degree at least $\gamma|A| - 1$. Hence, there exists a subset $B \subseteq A$ with $|B| \geq \gamma|A| - 1$ such that for all $\alpha \in B$, $\Delta(v^{\alpha_0} - \alpha_0 u, v^\alpha) \leq J_\gamma^{-1}(\delta)$.

Define $C = C_{\alpha_0, N} = \{\alpha \in B \mid \alpha - \alpha_0 \notin (p)\}$. (p) denotes the maximal ideal consisting of non-invertible elements. For all $\alpha \in C$, we have $\Delta(u, \frac{1}{\alpha - \alpha_0}(v^\alpha - v^{\alpha_0})) \leq J_\gamma^{-1}(\delta)$. Since V has distance ζ and $J_\gamma(\zeta) > J_\gamma^{-1}(\delta)$, we apply the Johnson bound again, there can be at most $\frac{1}{\gamma}$ distinct vectors $v \in V$ such that $\Delta(u, v) < J_\gamma^{-1}(\delta)$. By the pigeonhole principle, there exists a vector $v \in V$ and a subset $D \subseteq C$ with $|D| \geq \gamma|C|$ such that for all $\alpha \in D$, we have $v = \frac{1}{\alpha - \alpha_0}(v^\alpha - v^{\alpha_0})$. Thus, for all $\alpha \in D$, we have $v^\alpha = (v^{\alpha_0} - \alpha_0 v) + \alpha v$.

Denote $v^\alpha = v^* + \alpha v$, where $v^*, v \in V$. Substituting back into the definition of v^α, we obtain for all $\alpha \in D$: $\Delta(u^*, v^* + \alpha(v - u)) < \delta - \gamma$. Rewriting gives: $\Delta(u^* - v^*, \alpha(v-u)) < \delta - \gamma$. For any coordinate $i \in [n]$ where $u_i \neq v_i$ or $u_i^* \neq v_i^*$, there can be at most $p^{r(s-1)}$ values of $\alpha \in \mathrm{GR}(p^s, r)$ satisfying $u_i^* - v_i^* = \alpha(v_i - u_i)$ (Fact 1). Consequently, there must exist an $\alpha \in D$ such that:

$$\Delta(u^* - v^*, \alpha(v - u)) \geq 1 - \frac{|\{i \in [n] \mid (u_i = v_i) \wedge (u_i^* = v_i^*)\}|}{n} - \frac{p^{r(s-1)}}{|D|}.$$

Combining this with our upper bound on $\Delta(u^* - v^*, \alpha(v - u))$, we conclude:

$$\frac{|\{i \in [n] \mid (u_i = v_i) \wedge (u_i^* = v_i^*)\}|}{n} \geq 1 - \delta + \gamma - \frac{p^{r(s-1)}}{|D|}.$$

From the inequality $|D| \geq \gamma|C| = \gamma(|B| - p^{r(s-1)}) \geq \gamma^2|A| - \gamma(p^{r(s-1)} + 1)$, and given that:

$$|A| \geq \frac{2p^{r(s-1)}}{\gamma^3} \geq \frac{p^{r(s-1)}}{\gamma^3} + \frac{p^{r(s-1)} + 1}{\gamma},$$

with the easily satisfied condition $\gamma \leq \sqrt{\frac{p^{r(s-1)}}{p^{r(s-1)}+1}}$, we deduce: $\frac{|D|}{p^{r(s-1)}} \geq \frac{1}{\gamma}$. This completes the proof. □

A.2 Proof of Theorem 2

Proof. To bound the probability that a malicious prover significantly reduces the Hamming distance to the codeword space in the IOPP.commit phase, we analyze a single interaction round (where the verifier sends a random challenge $\alpha_i \in \mathrm{GR}(p^s, r)$ and the prover responds with π_i) and then apply a union bound over all d rounds. Specifically, we bound the probability that $\Delta^*(\pi_i, C_i)$ is significantly smaller than $\Delta^*(\pi_{i+1}, C_{i+1})$. Let $\mathsf{fold}_\alpha(\pi_{i+1}) = \mathbf{u} + \alpha \mathbf{u}^*$ be the result of the folding operation with challenge α, where $\mathbf{u}$ and $\mathbf{u}^*$ are the unique interpolated vectors such that $\pi_{i+1} = (\mathbf{u} + \mathsf{diag}(T_i) \circ \mathbf{u}^*, \mathbf{u} + \mathsf{diag}(T_i') \circ \mathbf{u}^*)$. Define the set $A = \{\alpha \in \mathrm{GR}(p^s, r) \mid \Delta^*(\mathbf{u} + \alpha \mathbf{u}^*, C_i) < \delta^{(i+1)} - \gamma\}$. Here, $\delta^{(i)} = \min(\Delta^*(\pi_i, C_i), J_\gamma(J_\gamma(\Delta_{C_d})))$.

We next argue the probability that for randomly chosen challenge α_i such that $\alpha_i \in A$ is bounded by $\frac{2p^{r(s-1)}}{\gamma^3}$.

If $|A| > \frac{2p^{r(s-1)}}{\gamma^3}$, we know $\delta^{(i+1)} \leq J_\gamma(J_\gamma(\Delta_{C_d}))$ and $\Delta_{C_i} \geq \Delta_{C_{i+1}}$ for all $i \in [0, d-1]$, thus $\delta^{(i+1)} \leq J_\gamma(J_\gamma(\Delta_{C_i})))$, by Theorem 1, there exists $\mathbf{v}$ and $\mathbf{v}^*$ in C_i and a subset $S \subseteq [1, n_i]$, $|S| \geq (1 - \delta^{i+1}) n_i$ such that $\mathbf{u}[s] = \mathbf{v}[s]$ and $\mathbf{u}^*[s] = \mathbf{v}^*[s]$ for all $s \in S$. By linearility of the code, $c_w = (\mathbf{v} + \mathsf{diag}(T_{i-1}) \circ \mathbf{v}^*, \mathbf{v} + \mathsf{diag}(T_{i-1}') \circ \mathbf{v}^*)$ is a codeword in C_{i+1}. Therefore, c_w agrees with π_{i+1} at positions s and $s + n_i$ for $s \in S$, thus $\Delta^*(\pi_{i+1}, C_{i+1}) < \frac{2\delta^{i+1} n_i}{n_{i+1}} = \delta^{(i+1)}$, which contracts $\Delta^*(\pi_{i+1}, C_{i+1}) \geq \delta^{(i+1)}$. Then, the probability a randomly chosen α_i belongs to A is upper bounded by:

$$P(\alpha_{d-1} \in A) = \frac{|A|}{|\mathrm{GR}(p^s, r)|} \leq \frac{\frac{2p^{r(s-1)}}{\gamma^3}}{p^{rs}} = \frac{2}{\gamma^3 p^r}$$

This implies that in round i, after the verifier sends challenge α_i, the probability that a cheating prover can successfully send an oracle π_i whose Hamming distance to C_i is notably smaller than $\Delta^*(\pi_{i+1}, \Delta_{C_{i+1}})$ is at most $\frac{2}{\gamma^3 p^r}$.

By applying the union bound over all d rounds, the probability that the verifier is cheated in any round $i \in [0, d-1]$ is bounded by $\sum_{i=0}^{d-1} \frac{2}{\gamma^3 p^r} = \frac{2d}{\gamma^3 p^r}$. Thus, with probability at most $\frac{2d}{\gamma^3 p^r}$, for all rounds of folding, there exists one round that $\Delta(\mathsf{fold}_{\alpha_i}(\pi_{i+1}), C_i) < \delta^{i+1} - \gamma$. We can demonstrate that the rejection probability in the IOPP.Query phase is upper-bounded by the expression $P = \sum_{i=0}^{d-1} \Delta(\pi_i, \mathsf{fold}_{\alpha_i}(\pi_{i+1}))$. Claim 2 of [19] then implies that $P \geq \delta - \gamma d$. Thus considering l repetitions of the query phase, the probability that the verifier outputs accept in all l repetitions upper-bounded by $(1 - \delta + \gamma d)^l$. □

B Soundness of Polynomial Commitment

B.1 Proof of Theorem 3

Proof. By IOPP soundness (Theorem 2), with overwhelming probability we have $\Delta^*(\pi_d, C_d) < \delta$, by lemma 6 in [19] we have $\Delta(\pi_d, C_d) \leq \Delta^*(\pi_d, C_d) \leq \delta < \frac{1}{2}\Delta_{C_d}$, thus there exists a unique vector $\mathbf{f} \in \mathrm{GR}(p^s, r)^{k_d}$ such that $\Delta(\mathsf{Enc}_d(\mathbf{f}), \pi_d) < \frac{1}{2}\Delta_{C_d}$. For the unique multilinear polynomial f with coefficients $\mathbf{f}$, assume that $f(\mathbf{z}) \neq y$, we prove that for any malicious prover, the probability that verifier passes the check in step **3** of evaluation protocol is negligible.

First we address the probability of $A = \{\pi_0 \neq \mathsf{Enc}_0(f(\mathbf{r})) \wedge \pi_0 \in C_0\}$ is negligible, for the random challenges $\mathbf{r} = (r_1,..,r_{d-1})$ in the evaluation protocol. Let f_i be the i-variate multilinear polynomial $f(X_1,\ldots,X_i,r_i,\ldots,r_{d-1}) \in \mathsf{GR}(p^s,r)[X_1,X_2,\ldots,X_i]$. Since $\Delta^*(\pi_d, C_d) \leq \delta$, if A holds, then there exists at least one round $k \in [0, d-1]$ such that $\Delta^*(\pi_k, \mathsf{Enc}_k(\mathbf{g}_k)) < \delta$ for $\mathbf{g}_k \neq \mathbf{f}_k$, $g_k \in \mathsf{GR}(p^s,r)[X_1,X_2,\ldots,X_k]$ and $\Delta^*(\pi_{k+1}, \mathsf{Enc}_{k+1}(\mathbf{f}_{k+1})) < \delta$. Then by definition of minimum relative distance, $\Delta(\mathsf{Enc}_k(\mathbf{g}_k), \mathsf{Enc}_k(\mathbf{f}_k)) \geq \Delta_{C_k}$, and the different positions between π_{k+1} and $\mathsf{Enc}_{k+1}(\mathbf{f}_{k+1})$ is at most $n_{k+1} \cdot \delta$, thus:

$$\Delta^*(\mathsf{fold}_{r_k}(\pi_{k+1}), \mathsf{Enc}_k(\mathbf{f}_k))$$
$$= \Delta^*(\mathsf{fold}_{r_k}(\pi_{k+1}), \mathsf{fold}_{r_k}(\mathsf{Enc}_{k+1}(\mathbf{f}_{k+1})))$$
$$< \frac{n_{k+1}\delta}{n_k} = 2\delta < \Delta_{C_d} < \Delta_{C_k}$$

Again by IOPP soundness, we have $\Delta^*(\mathsf{fold}_{r_k}(\pi_{k+1}), C_k) < \delta - \gamma$, and according to above inequality we have $\Delta^*(\mathsf{fold}_{r_k}(\pi_{k+1}), \mathsf{Enc}_k(\mathbf{f}_k)) < \Delta_{C_k}$, since Δ_{C_k} is the minimum relative distance between any codewords in C_k, thus $\mathsf{Enc}_k(\mathbf{f}_k)$ is the only codeword satisfy $\Delta^*(\mathsf{fold}_{r_k}(\pi_{k+1}), \mathsf{Enc}_k(\mathbf{f}_k)) < \delta - \gamma < \delta$. Then by triangle inequality and $3\delta - \gamma d < \Delta_{C_d}$, we have:

$$\Delta(\pi_k, \mathsf{fold}_{r_k}(\pi_{k+1}))$$
$$\geq \Delta(\pi_k, \mathsf{Enc}_k(\mathbf{f}_k)) - \Delta(\mathsf{Enc}_k(\mathbf{f}_k), \mathsf{fold}_{r_k}(\pi_{k+1}))$$
$$\geq \Delta(\mathsf{Enc}_k(\mathbf{g}_k), \mathsf{Enc}_k(\mathbf{f}_k)) - \Delta(\pi_k, \mathsf{Enc}_k(\mathbf{g}_k)) - \Delta(\mathsf{Enc}_k(\mathbf{f}_k), \mathsf{fold}_{r_k}(\pi_{k+1}))$$
$$\geq \Delta_{C_k} - \delta - \delta \geq \Delta_{C_d} - 2\delta > \delta - \gamma d$$

Thus in the IOPP.Query phase, if A holds, the accepting probability of verifier over l repetition runs is at most $(1 - (\Delta_{C_d} - 2\delta))^l < (1 - (\delta - \gamma d))^l < 2^{-\lambda}$ (by $3\delta - \gamma d < \Delta_{C_d}$), which is negligible. Finally, under the condition that $\pi_0 = \mathsf{Enc}_0(f(\mathbf{r}))$, the validity of the equation $\mathsf{Enc}_0(h_1(r_0)) = \pi_0 \cdot \tilde{eq}_{\mathbf{z}}(r_0,\ldots,r_{d-1})$ implies the validity of the equation $h_1(r_0)) = f(\mathbf{r}) \cdot \tilde{eq}_{\mathbf{z}}(r_0,\ldots,r_{d-1}$. If $f(\mathbf{z}) = \sum_{\mathbf{b} \in \{0,1\}^d} f(\mathbf{b}) \cdot \tilde{eq}_{\mathbf{z}}(\mathbf{b}) \neq y$, by soundness of sumcheck protocol, for any malicious prover, the probability that verifier passes the check in step **3** is at most $\frac{2d}{p^r}$, where the individual degree of each variable of $f(X)$ and $\tilde{eq}_{\mathbf{z}}(X)$ is 1 and the univariate polynomial $h_i(X)$ has degree 2 of variable X. □

B.2 Extractability

Knowledge soundness involves extraction to obtain an invertible matrix. Gaussian elimination can then be applied to recover coefficients of the multilinear polynomial used in the commitment scheme. For example, given $g(x,y) = a_1 + a_2 x + a_3 y + a_4 xy$, recovering $\mathbf{g} = (a_1, a_2, a_3, a_4)$ requires four evaluations of $g(x, y)$. However the presence of zero divisors among the monomials of a multilinear polynomial over Galois rings can lead to a non-invertible matrix. We next analyze the probability of invertible matrices. For a d-variate multilinear polynomial f, the probability that randomly chosen points $r_1, r_2, \ldots, r_d$

in the evaluation protocol are invertible elements is at most $\xi = (1 - \frac{d}{p^r})$, as $\Pr[r_i \in \mathrm{GR}(p^s,r) \setminus \mathrm{GR}^\times(p^s,r)] = \frac{1}{p^r}$. Therefore, in polynomial time $\mathcal{O}(2^d \cdot \frac{1}{\xi})$, one can extract a matrix consisting of invertible elements, ensuring the matrix is invertible, and enabling successful recovery via Gaussian elimination.

References

1. Ben-Sasson, E., Bentov, I., Horesh, Y., Riabzev, M.: Scalable, transparent, and post-quantum secure computational integrity. http://eprint.iacr.org/2018/046
2. Ben-Sasson, E., Chiesa, A., Gabizon, A., Riabzev, M., Spooner, N.: Short interactive oracle proofs with constant query complexity, via composition and sumcheck. https://eccc.weizmann.ac.il/report/2016/046
3. Ben-Sasson, E., Chiesa, A., Spooner, N.: Interactive oracle proofs. In: Hirt, M., Smith, A. (eds.) TCC 2016. LNCS, vol. 9986, pp. 31–60. Springer, Heidelberg (2016). https://doi.org/10.1007/978-3-662-53644-5_2
4. Ben-Sasson, E., Goldberg, L., Kopparty, S., Saraf, S.: DEEP-FRI: sampling outside the box improves soundness. In: Vidick, T. (ed.) 11th Innovations in Theoretical Computer Science Conference, ITCS 2020, January 12-14, 2020, Seattle, Washington, USA. https://doi.org/10.4230/LIPIcs.ITCS.2020.5
5. Ben-Sasson, E., Kopparty, S., Saraf, S.: Worst-case to average case reductions for the distance to a code. In: Servedio, R.A. (ed.) CCC 2018, June 22-24, 2018, San Diego, CA, USA. https://doi.org/10.4230/LIPIcs.CCC.2018.24
6. Bünz, B., Bootle, J., Boneh, D., Poelstra, A., Wuille, P., Maxwell, G.: Bulletproofs: short proofs for confidential transactions and more. In: SP 2018, 21-23 May 2018, San Francisco, California, USA. https://doi.org/10.1109/SP.2018.00020
7. Cascudo, I., Costache, A., Cozzo, D., Fiore, D., Guimarães, A., Soria-Vazquez, E.: Verifiable computation for approximate homomorphic encryption schemes. https://eprint.iacr.org/2025/286
8. Chiesa, A., Hu, Y., Maller, M., Mishra, P., Vesely, N., Ward, N.: Marlin: preprocessing zkSNARKs with universal and updatable SRS. In: Canteaut, A., Ishai, Y. (eds.) EUROCRYPT 2020. LNCS, vol. 12105, pp. 738–768. Springer, Cham (2020). https://doi.org/10.1007/978-3-030-45721-1_26
9. Fiat, A., Shamir, A.: How to prove yourself: practical solutions to identification and signature problems. In: Odlyzko, A.M. (ed.) CRYPTO '86, Santa Barbara, California, USA (1986). https://doi.org/10.1007/3-540-47721-7_12
10. Gabizon, A., Williamson, Z.J., Ciobotaru, O.: PLONK: permutations over lagrange-bases for oecumenical noninteractive arguments of knowledge. https://eprint.iacr.org/2019/953
11. Ganesh, C., Nitulescu, A., Soria-Vazquez, E.: Rinocchio: Snarks for ring arithmetic. https://doi.org/10.1007/s00145-023-09481-3
12. Golovnev, A., Lee, J., Setty, S.T.V., Thaler, J., Wahby, R.S.: Brakedown: linear-time and field-agnostic snarks for R1CS. In: Handschuh, H., Lysyanskaya, A. (eds.) CRYPTO 2023, Santa Barbara, CA, USA, August 20-24, 2023, Proceedings, Part II. https://doi.org/10.1007/978-3-031-38545-2_7
13. Huang, M.M., Mao, X., Zhang, J.: Sublinear proofs over polynomial rings. https://eprint.iacr.org/2025/199
14. Lund, C., Fortnow, L., Karloff, H.J., Nisan, N.: Algebraic methods for interactive proof systems. In: 31st Annual Symposium on Foundations of Computer Science, St. Louis, Missouri, USA, October 22-24, 1990, Volume I. https://doi.org/10.1109/FSCS.1990.89518

15. Parno, B., Howell, J., Gentry, C., Raykova, M.: Pinocchio: Nearly practical verifiable computation. In: SP 2013, Berkeley, CA, USA, May 19-22, 2013. https://doi.org/10.1109/SP.2013.47
16. Reingold, O., Rothblum, G.N., Rothblum, R.D.: Constant-round interactive proofs for delegating computation. In: Wichs, D., Mansour, Y. (eds.) STOC 2016, Cambridge, MA, USA, June 18-21, 2016. https://doi.org/10.1145/2897518.2897652
17. Thaler, J.: Proofs, arguments, and zero-knowledge, Foundations and Trends® in Privacy and Security, vol. 4. Now Publishers Inc. (2022)
18. Wei, Y., Zhang, X., Deng, Y.: Transparent snarks over galois rings. In: Jager, T., Pan, J. (eds.) PKC 2025, Røros, Norway, May 12-15, 2025, Proceedings, Part I. https://doi.org/10.1007/978-3-031-91820-9_14
19. Zeilberger, H., Chen, B., Fisch, B.: Basefold: Efficient field-agnostic polynomial commitment schemes from foldable codes. In: Reyzin, L., Stebila, D. (eds.) CRYPTO 2024, Santa Barbara, CA, USA, August 18-22, 2024, Proceedings, Part X. https://doi.org/10.1007/978-3-031-68403-6_5

Efficient Homomorphic Evaluation for Non-polynomial Functions

Changhong Xu[1] and Honggang Hu[1,2](✉)

[1] School of Cyber Science and Technology, University of Science and Technology of China, Hefei 230027, China
xuchangh@mail.ustc.edu.cn, hghu2005@ustc.edu.cn
[2] Hefei National Laboratory, University of Science and Technology of China, Hefei 230088, China

Abstract. Efficient computation of non-polynomial functions in homomorphic encryption schemes is important for secure operations across various fields. Recent studies have focused on developing efficient algorithms for these computations. In this paper, we extend the Remez algorithm to derive an approximate polynomial with minimal relative error, enabling the homomorphic evaluation of non-polynomial functions such as the reciprocal m-th root function $f(x) = x^{-1/m}$ where $m \in \mathbb{Z}^+$ and the exponential function $f(x) = e^x$. Additionally, we introduce a novel approximate polynomial $u(x) = \sum_{i=0}^{n} c_i r^i x^{mi+1}$ designed to further refine the approximation range for $f(x) = x^{-1/m}$. Utilizing these methods, we introduce new algorithms for the homomorphic evaluation of inverse, square root, and exponential functions, which are subsequently implemented with the SEAL library. The experimental results demonstrate the superiority of our algorithms, requiring only 20% of the execution time for the inverse function and 15% for the square root function compared to previous method. Furthermore, based on our approximate inverse and exponential algorithms, we propose a new algorithm for the softmax function that exhibits reduced computation time and significantly smaller maximum and average errors.

Keywords: Homomorphic encryption · CKKS scheme · Non-polynomial functions · Minimax approximation

1 Introduction

Fully homomorphic encryption (FHE) is an encryption scheme that enables algebraic computations on encrypted data without decrypting it. The concept of homomorphic encryption was first proposed by Rivest, Adleman, and Dertouzos in 1978 [32]. In 2009, Gentry's breakthrough work [14] solved the problem of constructing a fully homomorphic encryption system. This innovation has since gained significant attention in various privacy-preserving applications. Since then, several FHE schemes have been proposed [5,7,11–13,15].

FHE schemes are broadly categorized as bit-wise (e.g., FHEW [12], TFHE [11]) and word-wise (e.g., BGV [5], CKKS [7]). Bit-wise schemes operate on individual bits using logical gates, while word-wise schemes support batched SIMD polynomial operations. Recent hybrid approaches such as CHIMERA [4] and PEGASUS [29] seek to leverage the advantages of both.

This work focuses on the CKKS scheme, which supports approximate arithmetic over real and complex numbers. However, a limitation of the CKKS scheme is its restriction to polynomial operations. Non-polynomial operations such as comparison and inverse must be approximated.

Non-polynomial functions play an important role in domains like machine learning [1,34], secure genome analysis [3,21,35], and financial computation [17], where operations like inverse, square root, and exponential functions are frequently used. Hence, efficient polynomial approximation of these functions is crucial for practical FHE applications.

In these approximations, relative error is typically preferred over absolute error, especially when function values vary over large ranges. This approach is widely adopted in works like fast inverse square root [28] and exponential function approximation [33]. Therefore, in the rest of this paper, we primarily consider the relative error of the approximate polynomial.

1.1 Our Contributions

Approximate Polynomial with Minimal Relative Error. We extend the classical Remez algorithm to a relative-error variant that minimizes the relative error of approximation. The resulting polynomial $p(x)$ provides the closest approximation to a target function $f(x)$ in terms of relative error.

Improved Polynomial Approximation for $f(x) = x^{-1/m}$. We propose a novel type of approximate polynomial $u(x) = \sum_{i=0}^{n} c_i r^i x^{mi+1}$ designed to refine the approximation range for $f(r) = r^{-1/m}$, where r is the ciphertext input of the homomorphic evaluation. Across all possible values of r, the relative error between $u(x)$ and $r^{-1/m}$ remain consistent, enabling $u(x)$ to tightly minimize the output range. By computing the composite polynomial $u_k \circ \cdots \circ u_1$, any desired precision can be achieved.

Improved Performance of Homomorphic Non-polynomial Operations. We develop efficient homomorphic algorithms for inverse, square root, and exponential functions, supporting broader input ranges without additional comparisons. Implemented in Microsoft SEAL [30], our methods significantly outperform prior work. Compared to Algorithm 1 in [27], our NewInv and NewSqrt algorithms reduce runtime to less than 20% and 15%, respectively. We also evaluate softmax homomorphically using our approximations, achieving lower error and faster computation than [19,26].

1.2 Related Works

Polynomial approximation of non-polynomial functions is essential in the CKKS scheme. For example, CKKS bootstrapping necessitates the homomorphic evaluation of a modular reduction function. Numerous studies [18,20,24,25] have concentrated on reducing errors and improving computational efficiency of the approximation for the modular reduction function. Substantial research [8,22] has also been directed toward approximating the sign function within the CKKS framework, considering its potential transformation into comparison and maximum functions.

For the inverse functions, lots of paper [7,10] approximates the multiplicative inverse of $x \in [0, 2]$ using Goldschmidt's division algorithm [16]. For the square root function, [10] applied a two-variable iterative method from [36]. Recently, [27] proposed a method to find the approximate value of $f(x) = x^{-1/m}$.

The exponential function $f(x) = exp(x)$ has been approximated using Taylor series [7], scaled power functions [19], and L^2-approximation [23]. Combining Goldschmidt's method with the approaches in [19,23], several softmax approximations have been developed [26]. In particular, [26] improved accuracy and extended the input range using a domain extension technique from [9].

2 Preliminaries

2.1 Notations

Throughout this paper, we utilize several notations and conventions for clarity and consistency. All logarithms are taken to be base 2. The symbols $\mathbb{Z}$, $\mathbb{C}$, and $\mathbb{R}$ represent the integer ring, the complex number field, and the real number field, respectively. The composite polynomial $p_k (p_{k-1} (\cdots p_1(x)))$ is denoted as $p_k \circ p_{k-1} \circ \cdots \circ p_1(x)$. The interval notation $[a, b]$ is used for intervals where $b > a > 0$, and a real number r belongs to either $[a, b]$ or $[-b, -a] \cup [a, b]$. For the approximation of the function $f(x)$, the interval $I(e, r)$ is defined as $[c, d]$, where c and d are determined using: $c = min((1 - e) r, (1 + e) r)$ and $d = max((1 - e) r, (1 + e) r)$. The precision parameter is denoted as μ.

2.2 Homomorphic Encryption

In this paper, we focus primarily on the CKKS scheme. Unlike other FHE schemes, the CKKS(Cheon-Kim-Kim-Song) scheme [7] is a homomorphic encryption scheme that allows for approximate arithmetic operations. It enables homomorphic evaluations of both real and complex numbers. The CKKS scheme is defined as follows:

Definition 1 (CKKS scheme [7]). Let $R = \mathbb{Z}[X] / (X^N + 1)$ and $R_q = R/qR = \mathbb{Z}_q[X] / (X^N + 1)$. Let $DG(\sigma^2)$ denote the discrete Gaussian over $\mathbb{Z}^N$ with variance σ^2. Let $HWT(h)$ denote the set of signed binary vectors in $\{0, \pm 1\}^N$ with Hamming weight h. Let Δ be the scaling factor, and let φ denote the canonical embedding from R to $\mathbb{C}^{N/2}$. A CKKS scheme consists of the following algorithms:

- **KeyGen(λ):** Sample a secret value $s \leftarrow HWT(h)$, a random value $a \leftarrow R_{q_L}$, and a Gaussian noise $e \leftarrow DG(\sigma^2)$. Set the secret key as $sk = (1, s)$, and the public key as $pk = (b = -as+e, a)$. Similarly, generate the evaluation key $evk = (b', a') \in R_{P \cdot q_L}^2$ with $a' \leftarrow R_{P \cdot q_L}$, $e' \leftarrow DG(\sigma^2)$. Output pk, sk, and evk.

- **Ecd(z)**: Encode $z \in \mathbb{C}^{N/2}$ to $m(x) \in R$ via $m(x) = (\lfloor \Delta \cdot \varphi^{-1}(z) \rceil)$.
- **Dcd(m(X))**: Decode $m(x) \in R$ to $z \in \mathbb{C}^{N/2}$ via $\Delta^{-1} \cdot \varphi(m)$.
- **Enc(m, pk)**: Output ciphertext $c = v \cdot pk + (m + e_0, e_1) \pmod{q_L}$ with random vector v and $e_0, e_1 \leftarrow DG(\sigma^2)$.
- **Dec(c, sk)**: Outputs plaintext $m = c_0 + c_1 \cdot sk \pmod{q_l}$.
- **Add(c_1, c_2)**: Output $c_{add} = c_1 + c_2 \pmod{q_l}$.
- **Mult(c_1, c_2, evk)**: Perform multiplication with relinearization using evk.
- **RS(c)**: Rescale $c \in R_{q_l}^2$ to modulus q'_l, output $c' = \lfloor \frac{q_{l'}}{q_l} \cdot c \rceil \pmod{q_{l'}} \in R_{q_{l'}}^2$.

In the CKKS scheme, multiplications can be either scalar (with plaintexts) or non-scalar (between ciphertexts), where the latter incurs significantly higher computational costs due to the relinearization and rescaling steps. In practical libraries such as SEAL, the costs of key-switching and modulus-switching are closely tied to the number of non-scalar multiplications. To optimize performance, our approach focuses on minimizing both the multiplicative depth and the number of non-scalar multiplications.

2.3 Minimax Polynomial Approximation Method

In this paper, we use the minimax polynomial approximation method to approximate the inverse and square root functions. To provide a foundation for our approach, we introduce some basic concepts about approximation theory [6] and the Remez algorithm [31] for minimax approximation.

Definition 2 (Haar's condition [6]). A set of functions $\{g_1, \cdots, g_n\}$ is said to satisfy Haar's condition if each g_i is continuous on $[a, b]$, and any n distinct vectors in $\{\boldsymbol{v} = (g_1(x), \cdots, g_n(x)); x \in [a, b]\}$ are linearly independent. In other words, for any n different numbers $x_1, \cdots, x_n \in [a, b]$, the determinant of the matrix formed by evaluating the functions at those points

$$D[x_1, \cdots, x_n] = \begin{vmatrix} g_1(x_1) & \cdots & g_n(x_1) \\ \vdots & \ddots & \vdots \\ g_1(x_n) & \cdots & g_n(x_n) \end{vmatrix} \quad (1)$$

is not equal to zero.

Definition 3 (Minimax approximate polynomial [6]). Given a set of functions $\{g_1, \cdots, g_n\}$ satisfying Haar's condition on $[a, b]$, let X be a closed subset of $[a, b]$. The function f is a continuous function defined on X. Let polynomial $p_a(x) = \sum_{i=1}^{n} c_{a,i} g_i(x)$ and $e(x) = p_a(x) - f(x)$. Then the polynomial $p(x) = \sum_{i=1}^{n} c_i g_i(x)$ is the minimax approximate polynomial on X for f if it minimizes $max_{x \in X} |e(x)|$ among any polynomial $p_a(x)$.

Algorithm 1. Remez Algorithm [31]

Require: A domain $[a,b]$, a set of functions $\{g_1, \cdots, g_n\}$ which satisfies Haar's condition, a continuous function f defined on the interval $[a,b]$, and an approximate parameter γ.
Ensure: The minimax approximate polynomial p on $[a,b]$ for f.
1: Choose $n+1$ numbers $x_1, \cdots, x_{n+1} \in [a,b]$, where $x_1 < \cdots < x_{n+1}$;
2: Find a polynomial $p(x) = \sum_{i=1}^{n} c_i g_i(x)$, such that for $1 \le i \le n+1$, $p(x_i) - f(x_i) = (-1)^i E$, where E is an unknown real number;
3: Find n zeros $z_1, \cdots, z_n$ of $e(x) = p(x) - f(x)$ in $[a,b]$, where for $1 \le i \le n$, $x_i < z_i < x_{i+1}$. Let $z_0 = a$ and $z_{n+1} = b$;
4: Find the maximum point y_i of $|e(x)|$ in $[z_{i-1}, z_i]$, $i = 1, \cdots, n+1$ respectively;
5: $\epsilon_{max} = max(|e(y_1)|, \cdots, |e(y_{n+1})|)$;
6: $\epsilon_{min} = min(|e(y_1)|, \cdots, |e(y_{n+1})|)$;
7: **if** $(\epsilon_{max} - \epsilon_{min})/\epsilon_{min} < \gamma$ **then**
8:     return $p(x)$;
9: **else**
10:     $x_i = y_i, i = 1, \cdots, n+1$;
11:     Go to line 2;
12: **end if**

We can use the Remez algorithm, as described in Algorithm 1, to compute the minimax polynomial approximation of a continuous function f defined on the interval $[a,b]$. The Remez algorithm is supported by the following theorems.

Theorem 1 (Chebyshev alternation theorem [6]). *Given a set of functions $\{g_1, \cdots, g_n\}$ satisfying Haar's condition on $[a,b]$, let X be a closed subset of $[a,b]$. The function f is a continuous function defined on X. Let polynomial $p(x) = \sum_{i=1}^{n} c_i g_i(x)$ and $e(x) = p(x) - f(x)$. Then we say that $p(x)$ is the minimax approximate polynomial on X for function f if and only if there exist $n+1$ different points $x_0 < \cdots < x_n, x_i \in X$ such that $e(x_i) = -e(x_{i-1}) = \pm max_{x \in X} |e(x)|$, for $1 \le i \le n$.*

Theorem 2 (Uniqueness theorem [6]). *Given a set of functions $\{g_1, \cdots, g_n\}$ satisfying Haar's condition on $[a,b]$. Then for any continuous function f defined on the interval $[a,b]$, its minimax approximate polynomial $p(x) = \sum_{i=1}^{n} c_i g_i(x)$ is unique.*

3 Our Approximate Method

In this section, we extend the Remez algorithm to derive an approximate polynomial p with minimal relative error. Through homomorphic evaluation of p, we can find approximate values for non-polynomial functions such as the reciprocal m-th root function $f(x) = x^{-1/m}$ where $m \in \mathbb{Z}^+$ and the exponential function $f(x) = e^x$. In addition, for $f(x) = x^{-1/m}$, we introduce a novel polynomial designed to further enhance the accuracy of the approximation. Furthermore, we conduct an analysis of the depth consumption and the number of non-scalar multiplications required by these polynomials.

Algorithm 2. Relative Remez Algorithm

Require: A domain $[a,b]$, a set of functions $\{g_0(x), \cdots, g_n(x)\}$, a continuous function $f(x)$ defined on the interval $[a,b]$, and an approximate parameter γ.
Ensure: The approximate polynomial $p(x)$ on $[a,b]$ for $f(x)$.
1: For $x_0, x_1, \cdots, x_{n+1} \in [a,b]$, let $x_i = i \cdot \frac{b-a}{n+1} + a$;
2: Find a polynomial $p(x) = \sum_{i=0}^{n} c_i g_i(x)$, such that for $0 \le i \le n+1$, $(p(x_i) - f(x_i))/f(x_i) = -1^i \cdot E$, where E is an unknown real number;
3: Find $n+1$ zeros $z_1, \cdots, z_{n+1}$ of $re(x) = (p(x) - f(x))/f(x)$ in $[a,b]$, where for $1 \le i \le n+1$, $x_{i-1} < z_i < x_i$. Let $z_0 = a$ and $z_{n+2} = b$;
4: Find the maximum point y_i of $|re(x)|$ in $[z_i, z_{i+1}]$, $i = 0, 1, \cdots, n+1$ respectively;
5: $\epsilon_{max} = max(|re(y_0)|, \cdots, |re(y_{n+1})|)$;
6: $\epsilon_{min} = min(|re(y_0)|, \cdots, |re(y_{n+1})|)$;
7: **if** $\frac{\epsilon_{max} - \epsilon_{min}}{\epsilon_{min}} < \gamma$ **then**
8:    **return** $p(x)$;
9: **else**
10:    For $i = 0, \cdots, n+1$, $x_i = y_i$;
11:    Go to line 2;
12: **end if**

3.1 Initial Guess

In this paper, we extend the Remez algorithm to obtain an initial guess with minimal relative error. For the continuous function $f(x)$ defined on the interval $[a,b]$, our algorithm aims to find a polynomial $p(x)$ with the basis $g_0(x), \cdots, g_n(x)$ that approximates $f(x)$. Unlike the original Remez Algorithm, which minimizes the absolute error, our algorithm aims to minimize the relative error between $p(x)$ and $f(x)$. To formalize this, we introduce the concept of the minimax relative error approximate polynomial:

Definition 4 (Minimax relative error approximate polynomial). Given a set of functions $\{g_1, \cdots, g_n\}$, let X be a closed subset of $[a,b]$. The function f is a continuous function defined on X. Let polynomial $p_a(x) = \sum_{i=1}^{n} c_{a,i} g_i(x)$ and $re(x) = (p_a(x) - f(x))/f(x)$. Then $p(x) = \sum_{i=1}^{n} c_i g_i(x)$ is the minimax relative error approximate polynomial on X for f if it minimizes the relative error $max_{x \in X} |re(x)|$ among any polynomial $p_a(x)$.

The relative Remez algorithm, as described in Algorithm 2, is designed to determine such minimax relative error approximate polynomials. Algorithm 2 outputs a polynomial $p(x)$ such that $e_0 = max_{x \in [a,b]} |re(x)| = |re(y_i)|$ for $0 \le i \le n+1$, where $y_0 < y_1 < \cdots < y_{n+1}$ are the points in the interval $[a,b]$ at which the maximum relative error occurs. To ensure that $p(x)$ is the minimax relative error approximate polynomial for $f(x)$, certain conditions must be met for the function $f(x)$ and the basis $g_0(x), \ldots, g_n(x)$. The following theorem provides conditions under which the output of Algorithm 2 is the minimax relative error approximate polynomial for the function $f(x)$ with the basis $g_0(x), \ldots, g_n(x)$.

Theorem 3. *Given the domain $[a,b]$ for Algorithm 2, the function $f(x)$ is continuous on $[a,b]$. The output $p(x)$ of Algorithm 2 is the minimax relative* error approximate polynomial for $f(x)$ on $[a,b]$, as long as the set of functions $\{g_0/f, \cdots, g_n/f\}$ is a set of continuous functions defined on $[a,b]$ which satisfies Haar's condition.

Proof. Since the set $\{g_0/f, \cdots, g_n/f\}$ satisfies Haar's condition on $[a,b]$, we can apply the Remez algorithm with this basis to determine the minimax approximate polynomial $p_r(x) = \sum_{i=0}^{n} c_{r,i} g_i(x)/f(x)$ for $f_1(x) = 1$ on $[a,b]$.

When using the Remez algorithm, an initial step is choose interpolation points $x_i = i \cdot \frac{b-a}{n+1} + a$ for $0 \le i \le n+1$, and solve $p_r(x_i) - 1 = -1^i \cdot E$ where $c_{r,i}$ and E are the unknown variables. In Algorithm 2, solving

$$\frac{p(x_i) - f(x_1)}{f(x_i)} = \sum_{i=0}^{n} c_i \frac{g_i(x_i)}{f_i(x_i)} - 1 = -1^i \cdot E$$

yields the same coefficients as above, hence $c_i = c_{r,i}$ for $0 \le i \le n$. This implies that the relative error function $re(x) = (p(x) - f(x))/f(x)$ in Algorithm 2 corresponds exactly to the error $e(x) = p_r(x) - f_1(x)$ in Algorithm 1.

Thus, all intermediate points and error values $(y_i, \epsilon_{\max}, \epsilon_{\min})$ are preserved across both algorithms, and their outputs satisfy $p(x) = f(x) \cdot p_r(x)$. As $p_r(x)$ minimizes $\max_{x \in [a,b]} |p_{r,a}(x) - f_1(x)|$ for any $p_{r,a}(x) = \sum_{i=0}^{n} c_{r,a,i} g_i(x)/f(x)$, $p(x)$ minimizes $\max_{x \in [a,b]} |(p_a(x) - f(x))/f(x)|$ for any $p_a(x) = \sum_{i=0}^{n} c_{a,i} g_i(x)$. This implies that $p(x)$ is the minimax relative error approximate polynomial for $f(x)$ on $[a,b]$. □

By applying the relative Remez algorithm, we can obtain an initial guess for non-polynomial functions such as the reciprocal m-th root function $f(x) = x^{-1/m}$ and the exponential function $f(x) = e^x$. Notably, when approximating $f(x) = x^{-\frac{1}{m}}$, we encounter two distinct scenarios: single interval where $x \in [a,b]$ with $b > a > 0$, and dual interval where $x \in [-b, -a] \cup [a, b]$. In the subsequent discussions, we explore the approach for determining the minimax relative error approximate polynomial for $f(x)$ in these scenarios.

$f(x) = x^{-1/m}$ **With Single Interval** For $x \in [a,b]$ where $b > a > 0$ and $m \in \mathbb{Z}^+$, we use Algorithm 2 with basis $\{1, x, \ldots, x^n\}$ to compute the minimax relative error polynomial for $f(x) = x^{-1/m}$. The inputs to the algorithm include the interval $[a,b]$, the chosen basis, the target function $f(x)$, and a precision parameter γ. The following lemma shows that Algorithm 2 returns the optimal approximate polynomial with respect to relative error.

Lemma 1. *If $g(x)$ is continuous and nonzero on the interval $[a,b]$ with $b > a > 0$, and $k \in \mathbb{Z}^+$, then the set $g(x), g(x)x^k, \ldots, g(x)x^{nk}$ is a set of continuous functions on $[a,b]$ that satisfies Haar's condition.*

Proof. It is obvious that the functions $g(x)$, $g(x)x^k$, $\ldots$, $g(x)x^{nk}$ are continuous when $x > 0$. For $n + 1$ distinct points $x_0, \cdots, x_n \in [a, b]$, the determinant

$$D[x_0, \cdots, x_n] = \begin{vmatrix} g(x_0) & \cdots & g(x_0)x_0^{nk} \\ \vdots & \ddots & \vdots \\ g(x_n) & \cdots & g(x_n)x_n^{nk} \end{vmatrix}$$

$$= \prod_{i=0}^{n} g(x_i) \cdot \begin{vmatrix} 1 & \cdots & x_0^{nk} \\ \vdots & \ddots & \vdots \\ 1 & \cdots & x_n^{nk} \end{vmatrix}$$

$$= \prod_{i=0}^{n} g(x_i) \cdot \prod_{0 \le j < i \le n} \left(x_i^k - x_j^k\right).$$

Since $x_0, \ldots, x_n \in [a, b]$ are distinct and $g(x_i) \ne 0$ for all $0 \le i \le n$, the determinant $D[x_0, \cdots, x_n] = \prod_{i=0}^{n} g(x_i) \cdot \prod_{0 \le j < i \le n} \left(x_i^k - x_j^k\right) \ne 0$. This implies that the set $\{g(x), g(x)x^k, \ldots, g(x)x^{nk}\}$ satisfies Haar's condition on $[a, b]$. □

According to Lemma 1, the set $\{1/f(x), \cdots, x^n/f(x)\}$ satisfies Haar's condition on $[a, b]$. Consequently, based on Theorem 3, Algorithm 2 yields the minimax relative error polynomial $p(x) = \sum_{i=0}^{n} c_i x^i$ for $f(x) = x^{-1/m}$ on $[a, b]$. Given this, for any $r \in [a, b]$, the initial guess of $r^{-1/m}$ is $g_0 = p(r)$, which lies in the interval $I(e_0, r^{-1/m})$ where $e_0 = \max_{x \in [a,b]} |(p(x) - f(x))/f(x)|$.

Now consider the constant polynomial $p_a(x) = b^{-1/m}$. For $x \in [a, b]$, $f(x) \in [b^{-1/m}, a^{-1/m}]$. Thus, $max_{x \in [a,b]} |(p_a(x) - f(x))/f(x)| = 1 - \left(\frac{a}{b}\right)^{1/m} \in (0, 1)$. Since $p(x)$ is the minimax relative error approximate polynomial for $f(x)$ on $[a, b]$, $e_0 \in (0, 1)$.

$f(x) = x^{-1/m}$ **With Dual Intervals** For $x \in [-b, -a] \cup [a, b]$ where $b > a > 0$ and $m = 1, 3, \cdots$, we use Algorithm 2 with basis $\{x, x^3, \cdots, x^{2n+1}\}$ to compute the minimax relative error polynomial for $f(x) = x^{-1/m}$. Since both $f(x)$ and the resulting polynomial $p(x)$ are odd functions, when $p(x)$ is the minimax relative error approximate polynomial for $f(x)$ on $[a, b]$, it extends its validity to the dual interval $[-b, -a] \cup [a, b]$. The inputs to the algorithm include the interval $[a, b]$, the chosen basis, the target function $f(x)$, and a precision parameter γ.

According to Lemma 1, the set $\{x/f(x), \cdots, x^{2n+1}/f(x)\}$ satisfies Haar's condition on $[a, b]$. Consequently, based on Theorem 3, Algorithm 2 yields the minimax relative error polynomial $p(x) = \sum_{i=0}^{n} c_i x^i$ for $f(x) = x^{-1/m}$ on $[a, b]$. Since both $p(x)$ and $f(x)$ are odd functions, $p(x)$ is the minimax relative error approximate polynomial for $f(x)$ on $[-b, -a] \cup [a, b]$. Given this, for any $r \in [-b, -a] \cup [a, b]$, the initial guess of $r^{-1/m}$ is $g_0 = p(r)$, which lies in the interval $I(e_0, r^{-1/m})$ where $e_0 = max_{x \in [-b,-a] \cup [a,b]} |(p(x) - f(x))/f(x)|$.

Now consider the polynomial $p_a(x) = b^{-(m+1)/m} x$. For $x \in [-b, -a] \cup [a, b]$, $|p_a(x)/f(x)| \in \left[\left(\frac{a}{b}\right)^{(m+1)/m}, 1\right]$.
Thus, $max_{x \in [-b,-a] \cup [a,b]} |(p_a(x) - f(x))/f(x)| = 1 - \left(\frac{a}{b}\right)^{(m+1)/m} \in (0, 1)$. Since $p(x)$ is the minimax relative error approximate polynomial for $f(x)$ on $[-b, -a] \cup [a, b]$, $e_0 \in (0, 1)$.

$f(x) = e^x$ For $x \in [a, b]$ where $b > a$, we use Algorithm 2 with basis $\{1, \ldots, x^n\}$ to compute the minimax relative error polynomial for $f(x) = e^x$. The inputs to the algorithm include the interval $[a, b]$, the chosen basis, the target function $f(x)$, and a precision parameter γ.

According to Lemma 1, the set $\{1/f(x), \cdots, x^n/f(x)\}$ satisfies Haar's condition on $[a, b]$. Consequently, based on Theorem 3, Algorithm 2 yields the minimax relative error polynomial $p(x) = \sum_{i=0}^{n} c_i x^i$ for $f(x) = e^x$ on $[a, b]$. Given this, for any $r \in [a, b]$, the initial guess of e^r is $g_0 = p(r)$, which lies in the interval $I(e_0, e^r)$ where $e_0 = \max_{x \in [a,b]} |(p(x) - f(x))/f(x)|$.

3.2 Improved Polynomial Approximation for $f(x) = x^{-1/m}$

In Subsect. 3.1, for any real number r in the domain of $f(x)$, we obtain an initial guess $g_0 \in I(e_0, f(r))$ for $f(r)$ using our relative Remez algorithm. While large input ranges demand high-degree polynomials for accuracy, in the CKKS scheme, the ciphertext error increases with both the degree and the size of polynomial coefficients. Therefore, it is crucial to keep these parameters within reasonable bounds.

To address these challenges, for $f(x) = e^x$, we leverage the property $e^x = (e^{x/2^k})^{2^k}$. This allows us to first approximate $e^{x/2^k}$, and then employ k squaring operations to obtain the approximate value of e^x. For $f(x) = x^{-1/m}$, we propose a new type of polynomial $u(x)$ that refines the range of g_0. Since only the ciphertext of r and the bound e_0 are available, we ensure the relative error between $u(x)$ and $r^{-1/m}$ is independent of r, making $u(x)$ universally applicable.

We define $u(x) = \sum_{i=0}^{n} c_i r^i x^{mi+1}$ for $x \in I(e_0, r^{-1/m})$. The relative error between $u(x)$ and $r^{-1/m}$ is: $(u(x) - r^{-1/m})/r^{-1/m} = \sum_{i=0}^{n} c_i r^{(mi+1)/m} x^{mi+1} - 1 = \sum_{i=0}^{n} c_i (r^{1/m} x)^{mi+1} - 1$. Setting $x = tr^{-1/m}$ for $t \in [1 - e_0, 1 + e_0]$, the expression simplifies to $\sum c_i t^{mi+1} - 1$, which is independent of r. Hence, the relative error is uniform for all r in the domain, making $u(x)$ universally effective.

To reduce both depth and non-scalar multiplications, we require $u(x)$ to be the minimax relative error approximation of the constant function $f(x) = r^{-1/m}$ over the interval $I(e_0, r^{-1/m})$. This ensures that $u(x)$ minimizes its output range $I(e_1, r^{-1/m})$, improving overall efficiency.

However, since we only have access to the ciphertext of r and the value of e_0, it is not possible to directly compute $u(x)$ using the relative Remez algorithm. Nevertheless, $u(x)$ should still serve as the minimax relative error polynomial for $f(x)$ over $I(e_0, r^{-1/m})$ for any valid r. To achieve this, we adopt an indirect construction method for the coefficients c_i, as described in the theorem that follows.

Theorem 4. For $x \in I(e_0, r^{-1/m})$, let $t = r^{1/m} x$, which belongs to $[1 - e_0, 1 + e_0]$. Let $v(t) = \sum_{i=0}^{n} c_{v,i} t^{mi+1}$ be the minimax approximate polynomial for $f_1(x) = 1$ on $[1 - e_0, 1 + e_0]$. Let $u(x) = \sum_{i=0}^{n} c_i r^i x^{mi+1}$ be the minimax relative error approximate polynomial for $f(x) = r^{-1/m}$ on $I(e_0, r^{-1/m})$. Then the coefficients $c_{v,i}$ of $v(t)$ are identical to the coefficients c_i of $u(x)$.

Proof. Let $w(t) = \sum_{i=0}^{n} c_i t^{mi+1}$ be the polynomial sharing the same coefficients c_i with $u(x)$. For a general polynomial $u_a(x) = \sum_{i=0}^{n} c_{a,i} r^i x^{mi+1}$, define $w_a(t) = \sum_{i=0}^{n} c_{a,i} t^{mi+1}$. It holds that $u_a(x) = r^{-1/m} \sum_{i=0}^{n} c_{a,i} (r^{1/m} x)^{mi+1} = r^{-1/m} \sum_{i=0}^{n} c_{a,i} t^{mi+1} = r^{-1/m} w_a(t)$. Therefore, for $x \in I(e_0, r^{-1/m})$, the relative error becomes $(u_a(x) - r^{-1/m})/r^{-1/m} = w_a(t) - 1$.

Since $u(x)$ minimizes $max_{x \in I(e_0, r^{-1/m})} |(u_a(x) - r^{-1/m})/r^{-1/m}|$ among all $u_a(x)$, $w(t)$ minimizes $max_{t \in [1-e_0, 1+e_0]} |w_a(t) - 1|$ among all $w_a(t)$. Therefore, $w(t)$ is the minimax approximate polynomial for $f_1(x) = 1$ on $[1 - e_0, 1 + e_0]$. By the uniqueness of minimax approximation, it follows that $w(t) = v(t)$, and hence the coefficients $c_{v,i}$ of $v(t)$ are identical to the coefficients c_i of $u(x)$. □

According to Lemma 1, we can apply the Remez algorithm with the basis $\{x, x^{m+1}, \cdots, x^{mn+1}\}$ to obtain the minimax approximate polynomial $v(t)$ for $f_1(x) = 1$ on $[1 - e_0, 1 + e_0]$. Based on Theorem 4, the coefficients c_i of $u(x)$ are identical to the coefficients $c_{v,i}$ of $v(x)$. By homomorphically computing $g_1 = u(g_0)$ with the ciphertext of g_0 and r, the output range of g_1 becomes $I(e_1, r^{-1/m})$, where $e_1 = max_{x \in I(e_0, r^{-1/m})} |(u(x) - r^{-1/m})/r^{-1/m}|$.

For $u(x) = \sum_{i=0}^{n} c_i r^i x^{mi+1}$, when $n = 0$, the minimax relative error approximate polynomial for $f(x) = r^{-1/m}$ on $I(e_0, r^{-1/m})$ is $u(x) = x$, yielding a maximum relative error $e_1 = e_0$. When $n > 0$, consider the approximate function $w(x) = (h+1)x - hrx^{m+1}$ with real number h. Define $t = r^{1/m} x \in [1-e_0, 1+e_0]$. The relative error between $w(x)$ and $f(x) = r^{-1/m}$ is $e_w = (h+1)t - ht^{m+1} - 1 = (t-1)(1 - ht - ht^2 - \cdots - ht^m)$. The absolute value of e_w is determined by $|e_w| \leq e_0 \cdot |1 - h(t + t^2 + \cdots + t^m)|$. For $t \in [1 - e_0, 1 + e_0]$ where $e_0 \in (0, 1)$, $0 < t + t^2 + \cdots + t^m < 2^{m+1} - 2$. Choosing $0 < h < 1/(2^{m+1} - 2)$ guarantees $|1 - h(t + t^2 + \cdots + t^m)| \in (0, 1)$, and therefore $e' = max|e_w| < e_0$. Since $u(x)$ minimizes the relative error, it follows that $e_1 \leq e' < e_0$.

For $j = 1, \cdots, k$, let $u_j(x) = \sum_{i=0}^{n_j} c_{i,j} r^i x^{mi+1}$ be the minimax relative error approximation of $f(x) = r^{-1/m}$ on $I(e_{j-1}, r^{-1/m})$, where $u_j(I(e_{j-1}, r^{-1/m})) = I(e_j, r^{-1/m})$. It holds $e_k < \cdots < e_1 < e_0$. Let $\alpha = max_{t \in [1-e_0, 1+e_0]} |1 - h(t + t^2 + \cdots + t^m)| \in (0, 1)$. Then the errors are bounded as: $e_k \leq \alpha e_{k-1} \leq \cdots \leq \alpha^k e_0$. By applying the composite polynomial $u_k \circ \cdots \circ u_1$, any desired precision can be achieved. The final approximate value $g_k = u_k \circ \cdots \circ u_1(g_0)$ lies within $I(\mu, r^{-1/m})$. This approach enables high-precision approximation of $r^{-1/m}$ while keeping both the degree and the coefficients of each polynomial within practical bounds.

3.3 Depth and Non-scalar Multiplications

We adopt the relative Remez algorithm and improved polynomial approximation for $f(x) = x^{-\frac{1}{m}}$ (with $m = 1, 2$) within the CKKS scheme to evaluate inverse and square root functions. The same approach is also applied to approximate the exponential function $f(x) = e^x$. To reduce initial error e_0 and approximation accuracy, we maximize the degree of the initial polynomial $p(x)$. This reduces the overall complexity of the composite polynomial $u_k \circ \cdots \circ u_1$ where $u_j = \sum_{i=0}^{n_j} c_{i,j} r^i x^{mi+1}$ for $1 \leq j \leq k$.

We determine two sets of n_j: one minimizing multiplicative depth and the other minimizing non-scalar multiplications. To reduce depth, we precompute $c_{i,j}r^i$ and treat them as ciphertexts. In CKKS, a ciphertext polynomial of degree $mn_j + 1$ with ciphertext coefficients requires a depth $d_j = \lceil log(mn_j + 2) \rceil$.

To further reduce error, we avoid directly computing r^i and x^i, which may yield unstable values. Instead, we compute $t = r \cdot x^m$, and reformulate the polynomial as $u(x) = x \cdot \sum_{i=0}^{n} c_i t^i$. We evaluate this using the Baby-step Giant-step algorithm [18], which reduces non-scalar multiplications compared to naive evaluation. The polynomial is decomposed as $u(x) = t^k p_0(x) + q_0(x)$, with recursive decomposition applied as needed.

To improve efficiency, we adopt the Lazy Baby-step Giant-step algorithm [25], which postpones rescaling and relinearization. Additionally, to reduce the cost of high-modulus-level multiplications, modulus switching is prioritized before multiplications. Finally, we perform a brute-force search to determine the optimal values of n_j that minimize depth or non-scalar multiplications for the composite polynomial $u_k \circ \cdots \circ u_1$.

4 Applications to Non-polynomial Functions

In light of our relative Remez algorithm and improved approximation for $f(x) = x^{-1/m}$, we develop new algorithms for evaluating $inv(x) = \frac{1}{x}$, $sqrt(x) = \sqrt{x}$, and $exp(x) = e^x$. The inverse is approximated directly using our method with $m = 1$, and the square root is obtained via $sqrt(x) = x \cdot invsqrt(x)$. For the exponential function, we apply a minimax polynomial with minimal relative error. These components are further combined to approximate the softmax function. Details are provided in the following subsections.

4.1 Approximate Inverse Algorithm

To approximate the inverse of a real number r, we begin by computing the minimax relative error approximate polynomial $p(x)$ for $inv(x)$ within the interval $[a, b]$ or $[-b, -a] \cup [a, b]$. Consequently, in either scenario, we obtain an initial guess g_0 for $\frac{1}{r}$ such that g_0 falls within $I\left(e_0, \frac{1}{r}\right)$. In subsequent steps, we iteratively determine the minimax relative error approximate polynomial $u_j(x)$ for $f(x) = \frac{1}{r}$ over the interval $I\left(e_{j-1}, \frac{1}{r}\right)$. By amalgamating $p(x)$ with the set of polynomials $\{u_k, \cdots, u_1\}$, Algorithm 3 can be employed to ascertain the approximate value $g_k = u_k \circ \cdots \circ u_1(g_0)$ for $\frac{1}{r}$.

Compared to the method described in [27], our NewInv algorithm can handle a broader range of r values without the restriction of $|r| < 1$. Additionally, for $r \in [-b, -a] \cup [a, b]$, our algorithm computes the approximate value of $1/r$ directly, without the need for an additional comparison operation. In contrast, the previous method could only compute the absolute value $|1/r|$.

Algorithm 3. Approximate Inverse Algorithm NewInv

Require: An minimax relative error approximate polynomial $p(x)$ for $inv(x) = \frac{1}{x}$, a set of polynomials $\{u_k, \cdots, u_1\}$, and a real number r.
Ensure: The approximate value of $\frac{1}{r}$.
1: $g_0 = p(r)$;
2: **for** $1 \leq i \leq k$ **do**
3:     $g_i = u_j(g_{i-1})$;
4: **end for**
5: **return** g_k;

Algorithm 4. Approximate Square Root Algorithm NewSqrt

Require: An minimax relative error approximate polynomial $p(x)$ for $invsqrt(x) = 1/\sqrt{x}$, a set of polynomials $\{u_k, \cdots, u_1\}$, and a real number r.
Ensure: The approximate value of $\sqrt{r}$.
1: $g_0 = p(r)$;
2: **for** $1 \leq i \leq k$ **do**
3:     $g_i = u_j(g_{i-1})$;
4: **end for**
5: $g_s = g_k \cdot r$;
6: **return** g_s;

4.2 Approximate Square Root Algorithm

To approximate the square root of a real number r, we apply our approximation method for $f(x) = x^{-\frac{1}{m}}$ with $m = 2$. This assists us in finding the approximate value of $invsqrt(r) = 1/\sqrt{r}$. In specific, we begin by computing the minimax relative error approximate polynomial $p(x)$ for $invsqrt(x)$ within the interval $[a, b]$. From this, we derive an initial guess g_0 for $1/\sqrt{r}$ such that g_0 falls within $I(e_0, 1/\sqrt{r})$. In subsequent steps, we iteratively determine the minimax relative error approximate polynomial $u_j(x)$ for $f(x) = 1/\sqrt{r}$ over the interval $I(e_{i-1}, 1/\sqrt{r})$. By amalgamating $p(x)$ with the set of polynomials $\{u_k, \cdots, u_1\}$, Algorithm 4 can be employed to ascertain the approximate value $g_k = u_k \circ \cdots \circ u_1(g_0)$ for $1/\sqrt{r}$. The concluding estimation for $\sqrt{r}$ is given by $g_s = g_k \cdot r$.

4.3 Approximate Exponential Algorithm

To approximate the exponential of a real number r, we apply our relative Remez algorithm to the function $f(x) = e^x$. This assists us in finding the approximate value of $exp(r) = e^r$. In Specific, we start by calculating the minimax relative error approximate polynomial $p(x)$ for $exp(x)$ within the interval $[a, b]$. From this, we derive an initial guess g_0 for e^r such that g_0 falls within $I(e_0, e^r)$. By using the previously computed polynomial $p(x)$, Algorithm 5 can be employed to ascertain the approximate value g_0 for e^r.

Algorithm 5. Approximate Exponential Algorithm NewExp

Require: An minimax relative error approximate polynomial $p(x)$ for $exp(x) = e^x$, and a real number r.
Ensure: The approximate value of e^r.
1: $g_0 = p(r)$;
2: **return** g_0;

5 Experimental Results

We conduct the experiments in two parts. The first evaluates the required multiplicative depth and the number of non-scalar multiplications using plaintext inputs. The second measures the runtime on ciphertexts using the Microsoft SEAL library [30]. All experiments are run on a Linux machine with an Intel(R) Xeon(R) Gold 6226R CPU @ 2.90GHz with 16 threads. The code is available at https://github.com/xuchanghong2016/CKKS-NonPolyEval.

5.1 Parameter Selection

We set the dimension $N = 2^{17}$. Using Albrecht's LWE estimator [2], we determine the maximum initial ciphertext modulus q_L to be 2^{1700} in order to achieve 128-bit security. The scaling factor is set to $\Delta = 2^{50}$. In ciphertext experiments, we choose the initial modulus q_L such that the final modulus bits after each homomorphic algorithm are $\log \Delta + 10$.

To ensure compatibility with the requirements of the homomorphic inverse and square root operations described in [27], we define the input range of r as $[2^{-\alpha}, 1]$. Appendix A presents the approximation for the inverse function with dual intervals. For the homomorphic exponential operation, we set the input range of r as $[-1, 1]$. Additionally, the input for the softmax algorithm is configured as a 8-variable vector over a domain of $[-4, 4]^8$.

Assuming that the depth of $p(x)$ is d and the depth of $u_j(x)$ is d_i. Then, the initial modulus for the NewInv algorithm is: $\log q_L = (d + d_1 + \cdots + d_k) \cdot \log \Delta + 2 \log \Delta + 20$. For the NewSqrt algorithm, the initial modulus is: $\log q_L = (d + d_1 + \cdots + d_k) \cdot \log \Delta + 3 \log \Delta + 20$. For the NewExp algorithm, the initial modulus is: $\log q_L = (d + 2) \cdot \log \Delta + 20$.

Due to homomorphic encryption noises, the relative error between $f(x) = r^{-1/m}$ and $u_j \left(I \left(e_{i-1}, r^{-1/m} \right) \right)$ may exceed e_i, causing the output of $u_j(x)$ to fall outside the domain of $u_{j+1}(x)$. To mitigate this, we introduce a margin η to the domain of each $u_j(x)$, ensuring correctness despite homomorphic encryption errors. In our experiments, we set $\eta = 2^{-16}$.

5.2 Performance of Our Algorithms

Approximation of Inverse and Square Root Functions. To ensure precision, we fix the maximum n_j of all $u_j(x)$ at 7. Since running time depends on both depth and non-scalar multiplications, we search for the set of n_j that

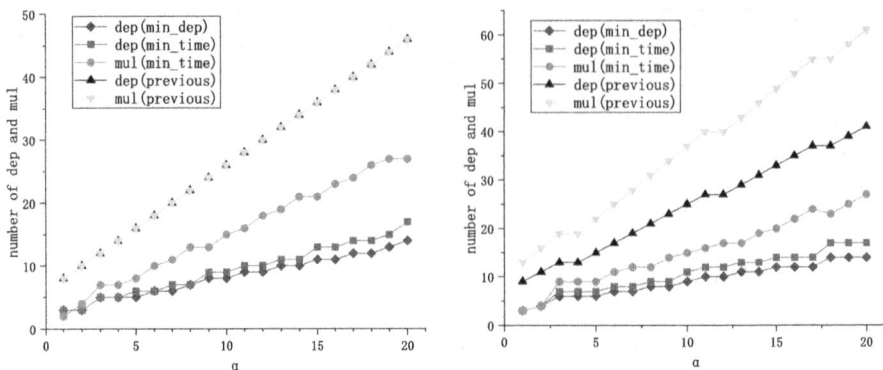

Fig. 1. Depth consumption (optimized for either depth or time) and non-scalar multiplications (optimized for time) for NewInv and NewSqrt algorithms versus Algorithm 1 from [27], across varying α values with an input range of $[2^{-\alpha}, 1]$ and precision $\mu = 2^{-10}$. (a) Inverse. (b) Square Root

Table 1. Comparison of the amortized running time, ciphertext modulus $\log q_L$, and relative error at $2^{-\alpha}$ for our NewInv(x) algorithm and Algorithm 1 from [27] ($n = 1$), evaluated over input range $[2^{-\alpha}, 1]$. Asterisk (*) indicates $\log q_L > 1700$, i.e., less than 128-bit security

	Proposed Method			Previous Method		
α	Time	$\log q_L$	Error	Time	$\log q_L$	Error
4	1.34 s (0.020 ms)	370	5.64e-4	7.70 s (0.12 ms)	820	2.64e-4
8	3.07 s (0.047 ms)	470	6.64e-4	23.25 s (0.35 ms)	1220	4.16e-4
12	6.39 s (0.098 ms)	620	6.65e-4	58.76 s (0.90 ms)	1620	1.70e-3
16	11.23 s (0.17 ms)	770	5.39e-4	101.86 s (1.55 ms)	2020*	2.20e-2
20	22.81 s (0.35 ms)	1030	3.16e-4	177.73 s (2.72 ms)	2420*	2.96e-1

minimizes both. Appendix B lists the optimal n_j sets for NewInv and NewSqrt under various values of $\alpha \in [1, 20]$ and the precision parameter $\mu = 2^{-10}$.

As shown in Fig. 1, which reports the depth and non-scalar multiplication counts of NewInv and NewSqrt across input ranges $[2^{-\alpha}, 1]$, it is evident that our algorithms surpass Algorithm 1 presented in [27] in both aspects. In particular, they require less than 50% of the depth and achieve substantial reductions in non-scalar multiplications. By minimizing both computational depth and cost, our methods offer a notable improvement in the efficiency of homomorphic evaluations.

To further assess the computational efficiency of our algorithms under ciphertext conditions, we measured their running times and initial ciphertext modulus q_L using the SEAL library for various input ranges $[2^{-\alpha}, 1]$. Each experiment was repeated 30 times, and the average running time was amortized over the number of slots $N/2$. As shown in Tables 1 and 2, our NewInv and NewSqrt algorithms

Table 2. Comparison of the amortized running time, ciphertext modulus $\log q_L$, and relative error at $2^{-\alpha}$ for our NewSqrt(x) algorithm and Algorithm 1 from [27] ($n = 2$), evaluated over input range $[2^{-\alpha}, 1]$. Asterisk ($*$) indicates $\log q_L > 1700$, i.e., less than 128-bit security. For $\alpha = 16, 20$, the scaling factor is set to 2^{60} to avoid evaluation error when measuring relative error

	Proposed Method			Previous Method		
α	Time	$\log q_L$	Error	Time	$\log q_L$	Error
4	2.36 s (0.036 ms)	470	4.71e-5	9.30 s (0.12 ms)	770	4.61e-4
8	4.13 s (0.063 ms)	570	4.94e-4	28.42 s (0.43 ms)	1170	1.31e-3
12	7.41 s (0.11 ms)	720	7.52e-4	54.25 s (0.83 ms)	1470	3.45e-2
16	11.72 s (0.18 ms)	820	5.42e-4	104.74 s (1.60 ms)	1870*	2.69e-3
20	18.17 s (0.28 ms)	970	7.70e-4	186.78 s (2.85 ms)	2290*	7.01e-2

Table 3. The running time (amortized running time) and the initial ciphertext modulus q_L of our approximate softmax algorithm and the methods reported by Hong et al. [19] and Lee et al. [26] with the input vector $\boldsymbol{v} = (v_1, \cdots, v_t) \leftarrow [-4,4]^8$. e_{max} and e_{avg} represent the maximum and average absolute errors between the homomorphically computed results and the actual results obtained without encryption

	time	$\log q_L$	e_{max}	e_{avg}
Ours	66.36 s (1.01 ms)	870	0.0116	0.000311
Lee et al.	232.03 s (3.54 ms)	1420	0.127	0.0207
Hong et al.	96.93 s (1.48 ms)	1270	0.0992	0.0122

achieved less than 20% and 15% of the runtime, respectively, compared to the previous method. Additionally, for $\alpha = 16, 20$, the previous method required $\log q_L > 1700$, necessitating a bootstrapping procedure to maintain security in the CKKS scheme, which significantly increases the time cost.

Approximation of Exponential and Softmax Functions. Given that $e^{2x} = (e^x)^2$, we set the input range for the exponential function to $[-1, 1]$ and the output precision as $\mu = 2^{-10}$. Our method employs an approximate polynomial of degree 4, represented as $p(x) \approx 0.999628 + 0.997939x + 0.502899x^2 + 0.176486x^3 + 0.039963x^4$. We evaluated our NewExp algorithm using the SEAL library, which required 0.30 s per operation, averaging 0.0046 milliseconds per slot, with a modulus $q_L = 270$.

To approximate the softmax function for the input vector $\boldsymbol{v} = (v_1, \cdots, v_t) \leftarrow [a, b]^t$, we employ our NewExp and NewInv algorithms to evaluate $softmax(\boldsymbol{v}) = (e^{v_1}, \cdots, e^{v_t}) / \sum_{i=1}^{t} e^{v_i}$. To compare the performance of our softmax algorithm against the methods reported by Hong et al. [19] and Lee et al. [26], we configured the input vector $\boldsymbol{v} = (v_1, \cdots, v_t) \leftarrow [-4, 4]^8$. We randomly sampled this vector and homomorphically evaluated $softmax(\boldsymbol{v})$ using the SEAL library. This operation was performed 30 times with different random input vectors. We calculated both the maximum and average absolute errors between the homomorphically computed results and the actual results obtained without encryption. Additionally, we measured the average running time of these operations, which was then divided by the number of slots $N/2$ to compute the amortized running time. The following parameters were used for this comparison:

- **Hong et al.** [19]: We set $(r, L) = (4, 32)$ for the $AE_{r,L}$ algorithm. Since $x \in [-4, 4]$, the output of $AE_{r,L}(x)$ lies within the interval $[(\frac{3}{8})^{16}, (\frac{5}{8})^{16}]$. Therefore, we set $M = 1$ and $d = 16$ for the inverse operation.
- **Lee et al.** [26]: To compare our results with their initial softmax approximation, we utilize the least-squares method to obtain a polynomial of degree 12 that approximates the exponential function over the interval $[-1, 1]$. We set $B = 4$ based on the equation $e^x = (e^{x/B})^B$. Given that the Goldschmidt method is restricted to input ranges within $(0, 2)$, we choose the scaling factor $R = 512$. Furthermore, the number of iterations d in Goldschmidt's division algorithm for the inverse operation is set to 16.
- **Our methods:** To mitigate the risk of exceedingly large values, we first evaluate $v_i - 4 \in [-8, 0]$. Since $e^{v_i} / \sum_{i=1}^{t} e^{v_i} = e^{v_i - k} / \sum_{i=1}^{t} e^{v_i - k}$, this adjustment does not affect the softmax values. We then employ our approximate algorithms to compute the approximate value of $softmax(\boldsymbol{v})$. The approximate polynomial for the exponential function $f(x) = e^x$ is of degree 9, while the approximate polynomial for the inverse function $f(x) = 1/x$ is of degree 7. The values of n_1, n_2 in u_1, u_2 are set to 7 and 3, respectively.

The results, summarized in Table 3, demonstrate that our NewExp algorithm requires less depth consumption and less than 70% of the time compared to the previous method. Additionally, both the maximum and average errors of our method are significantly smaller than those of the previous method. Furthermore, our method can accommodate a larger input range by applying the domain extension method described in [26].

6 Conclusion

In this paper, we propose a novel method for approximating $f(x) = x^{-\frac{1}{m}}$ and $f(x) = e^x$ within the CKKS scheme. We first obtain an initial approximation using our relative Remez algorithm. For $f(x) = x^{-\frac{1}{m}}$, we further refine the result using a composite polynomial of the form $u_k \circ \cdots \circ u_1$. We also describe the evaluation strategy for each u_j to minimize depth and improve runtime, and provide optimal degree configurations for $u_j(x)$ that reduce either multiplicative depth or overall computation time.

Furthermore, based on our approximation methods, we develop new algorithms for evaluating non-polynomial functions, including inverse, square root, exponential, and softmax. Implemented in the SEAL library, these algorithms demonstrate substantial performance improvements over existing approaches.

Our work enhances the practical utility of homomorphic encryption by enabling the efficient evaluation of essential non-polynomial functions. Improving the efficiency of these functions directly benefits real-world applications. As future work, we plan to integrate our method into larger systems, including privacy-preserving machine learning, to evaluate its performance and robustness in more complex real-world applications.

Acknowledgments. This work was supported by National Cryptographic Science Foundation of China (Grant No. 2025NCSF01001), National Natural Science Foundation of China (Grant No. 62472397), and Innovation Program for Quantum Science and Technology (Grant No. 2021ZD0302902).

A Approximation of Inverse Function with Dual Intervals

For approximation of inverse function with dual intervals, we set the input range as $[-1, -2^{-\alpha}] \cup [2^{-\alpha}, 1]$ for $\alpha = 1, 2, \cdots, 8$. Using our brute-force searching method, the values of degrees are detailed in Table 4. To further assess the computational efficiency of our algorithms under ciphertext conditions, we measured their running times and the initial ciphertext modulus q_L using the SEAL library for $\alpha = 4, 8$. For $\alpha = 4$, our method required 4.45 s per operation, averaging 0.068 milliseconds per slot, with a modulus $q_L = 570$. For $\alpha = 8$, our method required 13.72 s per operation, averaging 0.21 milliseconds per slot, with a modulus $q_L = 820$.

Table 4. Approximation of the inverse function $f(x) = 1/x$ over $[-1, -2^{-\alpha}] \cup [2^{-\alpha}, 1]$ with precision $\mu = 2^{-10}$. We report: polynomial degree n for $p(x) = \sum_{i=0}^{n} c_i x^i$; iteration degrees $\{n_j\}$ for $u_j(x) = \sum_{i=0}^{n_j} r^i x^{i+1}$; multiplicative depth (dep); and non-scalar multiplications (mul). Results are shown for methods minimizing either depth or time

		Minimize Depth		Minimize Time		
α	n	$\{n_1, \cdots, n_k\}$	dep	n	$\{n_1, \cdots, n_k\}$	dep	mul
1	3	{1}	5	3	{1}	5	7
2	3	{3}	6	3	{3}	6	10
3	3	{2, 2}	7	3	{7}	7	13
4	3	{6, 2}	8	3	{3, 3}	9	15
5	3	{5, 5}	9	3	{7, 3}	10	18
6	3	{6, 2, 2}	10	3	{7, 7}	11	21
7	3	{5, 2, 6}	11	3	{7, 1, 7}	13	23
8	3	{5, 6, 5}	12	3	{7, 3, 7}	14	26

B Sets of Values

(Table 5)

Table 5. Comparison of our depth-optimized and multiplication-optimized methods, and the previous method [27], for approximating $f(x) = 1/x$ and $f(x) = 1/\sqrt{x}$ over $[2^{-\alpha}, 1]$ with precision $\mu = 2^{-10}$. Columns show polynomial degree n, degrees $\{n_j\}$, depth, non-scalar multiplications (Mul), and number of iterations (Iter)

α	Function	Minimize Depth		Minimize Multiplications			Previous Method [27]		
		n	$\{n_j\}$	Depth	n	$\{n_j\}$	Depth	Mul	Iter	Depth	Mul
4	Inv	7	{1}	5	7	{1}	5	7	7	14	14
8	Inv	7	{2,2}	7	7	{7}	7	13	11	22	22
12	Inv	7	{5,5}	9	7	{7,3}	10	18	15	30	30
16	Inv	7	{5,2,6}	11	7	{7,1,7}	13	23	19	38	38
20	Inv	7	{6,5,5,2}	14	7	{6,6,1,5}	17	27	23	46	46
4	Sqrt	7	{1}	6	7	{1}	7	9	6	13	19
8	Sqrt	7	{4}	8	7	{4}	9	12	10	21	31
12	Sqrt	7	{3,3}	10	7	{1,6}	12	17	13	27	40
16	Sqrt	7	{5,7}	12	7	{5,7}	14	22	17	35	52
20	Sqrt	7	{3,3,7}	14	7	{3,3,7}	17	27	20	41	61

References

1. Aharoni, E., et al.: Efficient pruning for machine learning under homomorphic encryption. In: Tsudik, G., Conti, M., Liang, K., Smaragdakis, G. (eds.) ESORICS 2023, LNCS, vol. 14347, pp. 204–225. Springer, Cham (2023). https://doi.org/10.1007/978-3-031-51482-1_11
2. Albrecht, M.R., Player, R., Scott, S.: On the concrete hardness of learning with errors. J. Math. Cryptology **9**(3), 169–203 (2015). https://doi.org/10.1515/jmc-2015-0016
3. Blatt, M., Gusev, A., Polyakov, Y., Rohloff, K., Vaikuntanathan, V.: Optimized homomorphic encryption solution for secure genome-wide association studies. BMC Med. Genomics **13**(7), 1–13 (2020). https://doi.org/10.1186/s12920-020-0719-9
4. Boura, C., Gama, N., Georgieva, M., Jetchev, D.: CHIMERA: combining ring-LWE-based fully homomorphic encryption schemes. J. Math. Cryptology **14**(1), 316–338 (2020). https://doi.org/10.1515/jmc-2019-0026
5. Brakerski, Z., Gentry, C., Vaikuntanathan, V.: (Leveled) fully homomorphic encryption without bootstrapping. In: Proceedings of ITCS, pp. 309–325. ACM, New York (2012). https://doi.org/10.1145/2090236.2090262
6. Cheney, E.W.: Introduction to Approximation Theory. McGraw-Hill, Cambridge, UK (1966)

7. Cheon, J.H., Kim, A., Kim, M., Song, Y.: Homomorphic Encryption for arithmetic of approximate numbers. In: Takagi, T., Peyrin, T. (eds.) ASIACRYPT 2017. LNCS, vol. 10624, pp. 409–437. Springer, Cham (2017). https://doi.org/10.1007/978-3-319-70694-8_15
8. Cheon, J.H., Kim, D., Kim, D.: Efficient homomorphic comparison methods with optimal complexity. In: Moriai, S., Wang, H. (eds.) ASIACRYPT 2020. LNCS, vol. 12492, pp. 221–256. Springer, Cham (2020). https://doi.org/10.1007/978-3-030-64834-3_8
9. Cheon, J.H., Kim, W., Park, J.H.: Efficient homomorphic evaluation on large intervals. IEEE Trans. Inf. Forensics Secur. **17**, 2553–2568 (2022). https://doi.org/10.1109/TIFS.2022.3188145
10. Cheon, J.H., Kim, D., Kim, D., Lee, H.H., Lee, K.: Numerical method for comparison on homomorphically encrypted numbers. In: Galbraith, S.D., Moriai, S. (eds.) ASIACRYPT 2019. LNCS, vol. 11922, pp. 415–445. Springer, Cham (2019). https://doi.org/10.1007/978-3-030-34621-8_15
11. Chillotti, I., Gama, N., Georgieva, M., Izabachène, M.: Faster fully homomorphic encryption: bootstrapping in less than 0.1 seconds. In: Cheon, J.H., Takagi, T. (eds.) ASIACRYPT 2016. LNCS, vol. 10031, pp. 3–33. Springer, Heidelberg (2016). https://doi.org/10.1007/978-3-662-53887-6_1
12. Ducas, L., Micciancio, D.: FHEW: bootstrapping homomorphic encryption in less than a second. In: Oswald, E., Fischlin, M. (eds.) EUROCRYPT 2015. LNCS, vol. 9056, pp. 617–640. Springer, Heidelberg (2015). https://doi.org/10.1007/978-3-662-46800-5_24
13. Fan, J., Vercautern, F.: Somewhat practical fully homomorphic encryption. IACR Cryptology ePrint Archive, Report 2012/144 (2012). https://eprint.iacr.org/2012/144
14. Gentry, C.: A fully homomorphic encryption scheme. Ph. D. thesis, Stanford University (2009). http://crypto.stanford.edu/craig
15. Gentry, C., Sahai, A., Waters, B.: Homomorphic encryption from learning with errors: conceptually-simpler, asymptotically-faster, attribute-based. In: Canetti, R., Garay, J.A. (eds.) CRYPTO 2013. LNCS, vol. 8042, pp. 75–92. Springer, Heidelberg (2013). https://doi.org/10.1007/978-3-642-40041-4_5
16. Goldschmidt, R.E.: Applications of division by convergence. Ph. D. thesis, Massachusetts Institute of Technology (1964). http://hdl.handle.net/1721.1/11113
17. Han, K., Hong, S., Cheon, J.H., Park, D.: Logistic regression on homomorphic encrypted data at scale. In: Proceedings of the AAAI Conference on Artificial Intelligence, vol. 33, no. 1, pp. 9466–9471 (2019). https://doi.org/10.1609/aaai.v33i01.33019466
18. Han, K., Ki, D.: Better bootstrapping for approximate homomorphic encryption. In: Jarecki, S. (ed.) CT-RSA 2020. LNCS, vol. 12006, pp. 364–390. Springer, Cham (2020). https://doi.org/10.1007/978-3-030-40186-3_16
19. Hong, S., Park, J.H., Cho, W., Choe, H., Cheon, J.H.: Secure tumor classification by shallow neural network using homomorphic encryption. BMC Genomics **23**(284), 1–19 (2022). https://doi.org/10.1186/s12864-022-08469-w
20. Jutla, C.S., Manohar, N.: Sine series approximation of the Mod function for bootstrapping of approximate HE. In: Dunkelman, O., Dziembowski, S. (eds.) EUROCRYPT 2022, LNCS, vol. 13275, pp. 491–520. Springer, Cham (2022). https://doi.org/10.1007/978-3-031-06944-4_17
21. Kim, M., et al.: Ultrafast homomorphic encryption models enable secure outsourcing of genotype imputation. Cell Syst. **12**(11), 1108-1120.e4 (2021). https://doi.org/10.1016/j.cels.2021.07.010

22. Lee, E., Lee, J.E., No, J.S., Kim, Y.S.: Minimax approximation of sign function by composite polynomial for homomorphic comparison. IEEE Trans. Dependable Secure Comput. **19**(6), 3711–3727 (2022). https://doi.org/10.1109/TDSC.2021.3105111
23. Lee, J.W., et al.: Privacy preserving machine learning with fully homomorphic encryption for deep neural network. IEEE Access **10**, 30039–30054 (2022). https://doi.org/10.1109/ACCESS.2022.3159694
24. Lee, J.-W., Lee, E., Lee, Y., Kim, Y.-S., No, J.-S.: High-precision bootstrapping of RNS-CKKS homomorphic encryption using optimal minimax polynomial approximation and inverse sine function. In: Canteaut, A., Standaert, F.-X. (eds.) EUROCRYPT 2021. LNCS, vol. 12696, pp. 618–647. Springer, Cham (2021). https://doi.org/10.1007/978-3-030-77870-5_22
25. Lee, Y., Lee, J.W., Kim, Y.S., Kim, Y., No, J.S., Kang, H.: High-precision bootstrapping for approximate homomorphic encryption by error variance minimization. In: Dunkelman, O., Dziembowski, S. (eds.) EUROCRYPT 2022, LNCS, vol. 13275, pp. 551–580. Springer, Cham (2022). https://doi.org/10.1007/978-3-031-06944-4_19
26. Lee, S., Lee, G., Kim, J.W., Shin, J., Lee, M.: HETAL: efficient privacy-preserving transfer learning with homomorphic encryption. In: Proceedings of the 40th International Conference on Machine Learning, vol. 202, pp. 19010–19035. JMLR, Honolulu (2023). https://doi.org/10.5555/3618408.3619194
27. Lee, Y., Seo, J., Nam, Y., Chae, J., Cheon, J.H.: Heaan-stat: a privacy-preserving statistical analysis toolkit for large-scale numerical, ordinal, and categorical data. IEEE Trans. Dependable Secure Comput. **21**(3), 1224–1241 (2024). https://doi.org/10.1109/TDSC.2023.3275649
28. Lomont, C.: Fast inverse square root. Tech. rep., Purdue University (2003). http://www.matrix67.com/data/InvSqrt.pdf
29. Lu, W., Huang, Z., Hong, C., Ma, Y., Qu, H.: PEGASUS: bridging polynomial and non-polynomial evaluations in homomorphic encryption. In: 2021 IEEE Symposium on Security and Privacy, pp. 1057–1073. IEEE, San Francisco (2021). https://doi.org/10.1109/SP40001.2021.00043
30. Microsoft SEAL (release 4.1). https://github.com/Microsoft/SEAL. Accessed 12 Apr 2025
31. Remez, E.Y.: Sur la determination des polynomes d'approximation de degre donnee. Comm. Soc. Math. Kharkov **10**(196), 41–63 (1934). https://doi.org/10.1007/BF02401828
32. Rivest, R.L., Adleman, L., Dertouzos, M.L.: On data banks and privacy homomorphisms. Found. Secure Comput. **76**(4), 169–177 (1978)
33. Schraudolph, N.N.: A fast, compact approximation of the exponential function. Neural Comput. **11**(4), 853–862 (1999). https://doi.org/10.1162/089976699300016467
34. Shin, H., Choi, J., Lee, D., Kim, K., Lee, Y.: Fully homomorphic training and inference on binary decision tree and random forest. In: Garcia-Alfaro, J., Kozik, R., Choraś, M., Katsikas, S. (eds.) ESORICS 2024, LNCS, vol. 14984, pp. 217–237. Springer, Cham (2024). https://doi.org/10.1007/978-3-031-70896-1_11

35. Sperling, L., Ratha, N., Ross A., Boddeti, V.N.: HEFT: homomorphically encrypted fusion of biometric templates. In: 2022 IEEE International Joint Conference on Biometrics (IJCB), pp. 1–10. IEEE, Abu Dhabi (2022).https://doi.org/10.1109/IJCB54206.2022.10007995
36. Wilkes, M.V., Wheeler, D.J., Gill, S.: The Preparation of Programs for An Electronic Digital Computer, with Special Reference to the "EDSAC" and the Use of a Library of Subroutines. Addison-Wesley Press (1951)

Athena: Accelerating KeySwitch and Bootstrapping for Fully Homomorphic Encryption on CUDA GPU

Yifan Yang[1], Kexin Zhang[1], Peng Xu[1(✉)], Zhaojun Lu[1], Wei Wang[2], Weiqi Wang[1], and Kaitai Liang[3,4]

[1] School of Cyber Science and Engineering, Hubei Key Laboratory of Distributed System Security, Huazhong University of Science and Technology, Wuhan 430074, China
{yangyifan,zhangkexin,xupeng,lzj_cse,hustweiqiwang}@mail.hust.edu.cn
[2] Cyber-Physical-Social Systems Laboratory, School of Computer Science and Technology, Huazhong University of Science and Technology, Wuhan 430074, China
viviawangwei@hust.edu.cn
[3] Delft University of Technology, Delft, The Netherlands
Kaitai.Liang@tudelft.nl
[4] University of Turku, Turku, Finland
kaitai.liang@utu.fi

Abstract. Fully Homomorphic Encryption (FHE) enables computation over encrypted data, but it faces significant challenges in practical implementation due to its high computational costs, particularly in HMult, HRot, and Bootstrapping operations. This work presents Athena, an accelerated FHE system built on GPUs with a new algorithm-hardware co-design approach. Specifically, to accelerate HMult, HRot, and Bootstrapping, we redesign their common and expensive operation KeySwitch, based on the KLSS method proposed by Kim et al. in CRYPTO'23, and accelerate its core operations, namely NTT, EBConv, and IP. We further optimize the dataflow of Bootstrapping by reducing redundant EBConv and (I)NTT operations, and by improving the global memory I/O in the double-hoisting-based C2S/S2C operation. Moreover, Athena is designed as a general-purpose system that supports various cryptographic parameters. Experimental results demonstrate that Athena significantly improves the performance of KeySwitch and Bootstrapping. In particular, Athena's accelerated KeySwitch optimizes HMult $2.17\times \sim 4.40\times$ and HRot $1.89\times \sim 4.54\times$ compared to TensorFHE (HPCA'23), Poseidon (HPCA'23), and FAB (HPCA'23), respectively. Besides, Athena's Bootstrapping outperforms TensorFHE by nearly $2.74\times$.

Keywords: Fully Homomorphic Encryption · KeySwitch · Bootstrapping · GPU Acceleration

1 Introduction

Fully Homomorphic Encryption (FHE) is an advanced cryptography technique that allows users to perform Turing-complete computations on encrypted data. It carries profound implications across a wide range of applications, e.g., privacy-preserving data analysis and secure cloud computing [3,24]. Since Gentry proposed the first FHE [14], both academia and industry have concentrated on improving FHE schemes in terms of practical performance and functionality. Single-Instruction-Multi-Data (SIMD)-like FHE schemes (e.g., BFV [12], BGV [5], and CKKS [9]) enable computations on multiple plaintext elements and support parallel processing across numerous slots. They require up to 100,000x more computational resources than plaintext-based addition and multiplication.

FHE Accelerating Platforms. Several approaches have been proposed to accelerate FHE using CPU [2,26], General-Purpose Graph Processing Unit (GPU) [13,17,28], Field Programmable Gate Arrays (FPGA), and Application Specific Integrated Circuits (ASICs). Among these, CPU-based solutions provide the worst performance primarily due to the CPU's limited computing units and low instruction throughput. While FPGA-based solutions [1,21,22,29] offer more customized designs for computation and memory systems compared to CPUs and GPUs, their limited on-chip resources (even when using multiple FPGA boards [1]) make it challenging to handle complex FHE workloads effectively [1]. ASIC-based solutions [18,19,25] deliver powerful performance in terms of computation latency and throughput but lack flexibility in supporting various FHE schemes and cryptographic parameters. In comparison, GPUs offer significant advantages, including high parallelism, abundant on-chip resources, and ease of software deployment. Therefore, this work considers leveraging GPUs to accelerate FHE computations.

Performance Bottleneck. Recall that SIMD-like FHE schemes are built around three core operations, namely Homomorphic Multiplication (HMult), Homomorphic Rotation (HRot), and Bootstrapping. They enable homomorphic multiplication between ciphertexts, homomorphic rotation of plaintext slots, and refreshing ciphertexts to restore their multiplicative depth, respectively. We observe that KeySwitch is a common and computationally expensive operation to switch secret keys during the execution of HMult, HRot, and Bootstrapping. For

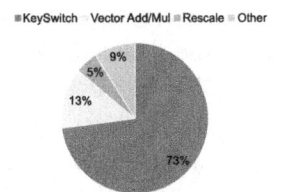

(a) Execution time breakdown of CKKS-based ResNet-20 inference.

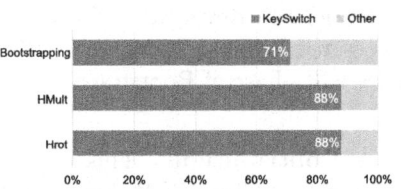

(b) Execution time breakdown of the HMult, HRot, and Bootstrapping.

Fig. 1. Execution time breakdown.

Table 1. Overall comparisons (unit: ms).

Accelerator	Platf.	Modulus	KeySwitch	HMult	HRot	Bootstrapping
100x'21 [17]	NVIDIA V100	64-bit	v2	17.40	16.83	428.93
TensorFHE'23 [13]	NVIDIA A100-40G	32-bit	v2	6.64	6.66	250.45
Phantom'24 [28]	NVIDIA RTX 4090	64-bit	v2	2.29	2.22	×
FAB'23 [1]	Xilinx U280 × 8	64-bit	v2	1.71	1.57	92.4
Poseidon'23 [29]	Xilinx U280	32-bit	v2	3.66	3.31	127.45
Athena	NVIDIA RTX 4090	64-bit	**v3**	**1.51**	**1.47**	**91.46**

Note: (1) Let v2 and v3 denote the Hybrid KeySwitch and the KLSS-based KeySwitch, respectively; (2) All the cryptographic parameters of the above works guarantee at least 128 security level; (3) Athena and Phantom have the same parameters, and we show the best performance of the other works claimed in their papers; (4) Although FAB has the suboptimal performance, its HMult and HRot operations just support 23 multiplication depth, and it just remain 6 multiplicative depth after Bootstrapping; (5) In contrast, all the other works, excluding FAB, support HMult and HRot with ≥ 40 multiplication depth and remain ≥ 16 multiplicative depth after Bootstrapping; (6) The maximum Bootstrapping precision relies on the modulus size, the larger modulus size means that a FHE system can achieve a higher computational accuracy; (7) × means that Phantom does not support Bootstrapping

example, by evaluating the CKKS-based ResNet-20 inference [24] on CIFAR-10 dataset using the OpenFHE [2] library, we see that KeySwitch accounts for over 73% of the total homomorphic inference time, as shown in Fig. 1a. Moreover, KeySwitch also dominates majority time in HMult, HRot, and Bootstrapping as illustrated in Fig. 1b. Therefore, *this work aims to introduce a new perspective to accelerating* KeySwitch *so as to significantly improve FHE performance on GPUs.*

Novelty and Challenge. All prior acceleration efforts, to the best of our knowledge, have focused on the 2nd-generation Hybrid KeySwitch [16]. This type of KeySwitch transforms a ciphertext from a smaller basis to a larger one and then multiplies the transformed ciphertext with a KeySwitch key **swk**. This procedure inevitably requires a large number of (I)NTT operations, resulting in inefficient KeySwitch performance [13,17]. In contrast, this paper adopts the 3rd-generation KLSS KeySwitch [20] to reduce the number of required (I)NTT operations. This reduction comes at the cost of increased computation overhead of EBConv and IP operations in KeySwitch. Moreover, the 3rd-generation KLSS KeySwitch introduces redundant EBConv and (I)NTT operations in the double-hoisting-based C2S/S2C phase of Bootstrapping, which impacts Bootstrapping performance.

Our Contributions. This paper proposes Athena, a GPU-based system for accelerating CKKS FHE computations. Athena focuses on optimizing the core FHE operations KeySwitch and Bootstrapping through an algorithm-hardware co-design approach. Table 1 compares Athena with previous SOTAs, demonstrating that Athena achieves the best performance across HMult, HRot, and Bootstrapping operations. Our main contributions are summarized as follows:

- We redesign KeySwitch based on the KLSS [20] method and optimize the KLSS-based KeySwitch instance to better exploit GPU architectural features. Specifically, we optimize three key computational kernels of the KLSS-based KeySwitch: (1) constructing a pipeline-efficient NTT; (2) reusing intermediate data during EBConv; and (3) alleviating memory bottlenecks in IP.
- We accelerate Bootstrapping by optimizing its C2S/S2C and EvalMod phases. Specifically, we reduce redundant EBConv and (I)NTT operations introduced by the KLSS-based KeySwitch, merge the C2S/S2C's PtMatMultAdd operation into a separate kernel to reduce the Global Memory (GMem) I/O, and reuse the KeySwitch key **swk** in EvalMod phase. In addition, we reduce the plaintext matrix bandwidth by 65.7% in the C2S/S2C phase by encoding the Discrete Fourier Transform (DFT) matrices into KLSS's temporary basis $\mathcal{T}$.
- Finally, we adopt a flexible component-based design to ensure that Athena supports a wide range of cryptographic parameters and evaluate its performance across various GPUs. Athena accelerates HMult by $1.52\times \sim 2.68\times$, $1.93\times \sim 4.40\times$, $1.07\times \sim 2.41\times$, and $2.17\times$ over Phantom [28], TensorFHE [13], Poseidon [29], and FAB [1] on a range of cryptographic parameters, respectively. Similar speedup factors are observed for HRot and HMult, with an execution latency of about 1.5 ms. Furthermore, Athena outperforms the GPU-based SOTA TensorFHE [13] by $2.74\times$ in Bootstrapping under equivalent cryptographic settings.

2 Background

We introduce some fundamental preliminaries, including CKKS, polynomial operations, the KLSS-based KeySwitch [20], and Bootstrapping, which are the core accelerated target of Athena. Table 2 summarizes the frequently used notations.

2.1 CKKS

CKKS supports the computation over encrypted fixed-point complex values without decryption. In CKKS, a plaintext vector $\mathbf{z} = (z_0, z_1, \ldots, z_{N/2-1}) \in \mathbb{C}^{N/2}$ contains $N/2$ elements. The vector $\mathbf{z}$ is encoded into a polynomial $m(X) = \sum_{i=0}^{N-1} a_i X^i \in R_Q$ using Discrete Fourier Transform (DFT) and then scaled up by a factor $\Delta \approx q_i$, where $\{z_i\}$ are called slots, and $\{a_i\}$ are called coefficients in CKKS. A ciphertext, which can be decrypted to m using the secret key s, is represented as a pair of polynomials $\mathbf{ct}(m, s) = (a, b) \in R_Q^2$. CKKS supports numerous homomorphic operations on encrypted data, and we can combine all operations between two ciphertexts flexibly. These operations are as follows:

- CAdd($\mathbf{ct_0}(m_0, s), c$) $\to \mathbf{ct}(m_0 + c, s)$ adds the input plaintext c to the input ciphertext $\mathbf{ct_0}$;

Table 2. Notation Summary

Symbol	Description
λ	Security level
N	Polynomial dimension of R_Q
L	Maximum depth of a ciphertext
l	Current depth of a ciphertext
K	Number of special basis prime modulus
r'	Number of temporary basis prime modulus
γ	Gadget decomposition length of basis $\mathcal{P}Q_L$
$R_Q = \mathbb{Z}_Q[X]/(X^N+1)$	Cyclotomic polynomial ring
$Q_L = \prod_{i=0}^{L} q_i$	Prime modulus product of a ciphertext on max-depth
$Q_l = \prod_{i=0}^{l} q_i$	Prime modulus product of a ciphertext on l-depth
$P = \prod_{i=0}^{K-1} p_i$	Prime modulus product of the special basis
$T = \prod_{i=0}^{r'-1} t_i$	Prime modulus product of the temporary basis
$d = \lceil (L+1)/K \rceil$	Decomposition number on max-depth Q_L
$\beta = \lceil (l+1)/K \rceil$	Decomposition number on Q_l
$d_l = \lceil (l+1+K)/\gamma \rceil$	Gadget decomposition block size of $\mathcal{P}Q_l$
$m, \tilde{m}$	A polynomial in the coefficient or the NTT domain
ξ_{2N}	$2N$-th root unity of $\mathbb{Z}_q$
$\mathcal{I} = \{q_0, \cdots, q_{k-1}\}$	RNS basis $\mathcal{I}$ with k modulus
Δ	Scaling factor of a plaintext
$[a]_\mathcal{I}$	a (a single value or a polynomial) in RNS basis $\mathcal{I}$
ϕ	An automorphism of a polynomial
$radix$	The decompose parameter of the C2S/S2C matrix, where $\log radix = \lceil (\log N - 1)/n \rceil$, and n is the number of decomposed matrix.
$\mathbf{ct}(m, s) = (a, b) \in R_Q^2$	A ciphertext encrypted a plaintext m by the secret key s

- CMult($\mathbf{ct_0}(m_0, s), c$) $\to \mathbf{ct}(m_0 \cdot c, s)$ multiplies the input plaintext c to the input ciphertext $\mathbf{ct_0}$;
- HAdd($\mathbf{ct_0}(m_0, s), \mathbf{ct_1}(m_1, s)$) $\to \mathbf{ct}(m_0 + m_1, s)$ adds two input ciphertexts homomorphically;
- Rescale($\mathbf{ct_0}(m, s)$) $\to \mathbf{ct}(m, s)$ controls the current factor from Δ' to Δ'/q_l and reduces the depth of the input ciphertext by 1;
- HMult($\mathbf{ct_0}(m_0, s), \mathbf{ct_1}(m_1, s)$) $\to \mathbf{ct}(m_0 \cdot m_1, s)$ multiplies two input ciphertexts homomorphically;
- HRot($\mathbf{ct_0}(m, s), r$) $\to \mathbf{ct}(rot_r(m), s)$ rotates the slots of m to the left by r;
- HConj($\mathbf{ct}(m, s)$) $\to \mathbf{ct}(\bar{m}, s)$ computes the conjugation of plaintext m;
- HAuto($\mathbf{ct}(m, s)$) $\to \mathbf{ct}(\phi(m), s)$ computes the automorphism ϕ of plaintext m;
- Bootstrapping($\mathbf{ct_0}(m, s)$) $\to \mathbf{ct}(m, s)$ raises the depth of $\mathbf{ct_0}$ to a new level $l' = L - l_{boot}$ when the multiplication depth of the input ciphertext $\mathbf{ct_0}$ drops to 0, where l_{boot} denotes the multiplication depth cost of Bootstrapping.

Four of these homomorphic operations, e.g. HMult, HRot, HConj, and HAuto, contain the expensive KeySwitch operation. Moreover, HMult and HRot take considerable time in the FHE-based applications. Bootstrapping is the most important and expensive operation in CKKS and is achieved by the composition of various homomorphic operations. Hence, accelerating KeySwitch and Bootstrapping is a major goal of Athena.

2.2 Polynomial Operations

Residue Number System (RNS). The polynomial operations of CKKS rely on cyclotomic polynomial rings $R_Q = \mathbb{Z}_Q[X]/(X^N+1)$, where N is a power of two. We leverage a series of residue rings with small modulus $R_{q_0} \times R_{q_1} \times \ldots \times$

$R_{q_L} \cong R_Q$ to represent R_Q. Thus, a polynomial in R_Q can be represented as an $(L+1) \times N$ matrix of coefficients.

4-Step Number Theory Transform (NTT). NTT is the main operation to handle polynomial multiplications in lattice-based cryptosystems. Given a polynomial ring R_q, suppose that q is a prime integer satisfying $q \equiv 1 \pmod{2N}$, and twiddle factor ξ_{2N} is the $(2N)$-th root of $\mathbb{Z}_q$. NTT achieves the isomorphism transformation $a(X) \to \bar{a} = \{a(\xi_{2N}^i)\}_{i \in [0, N-1]}$ from $a \in R_q$ to $\bar{a} \in \mathbb{Z}_q^N$. The computation formula of NTT can be written as a matrix multiplication, namely

$$\bar{\mathbf{a}} = \mathbf{a}^T \times \mathbf{W} \pmod{q} \text{ and } w_{i,j} = \xi_{2N}^{2ij+j} \in \mathbf{W}.$$

The 4-step NTT [10] is a method to decompose N-NTT to many N_1-NTT and N_2-NTT samples, where $N = N_1 \times N_2$. The 4-step NTT has four steps: (1) N_1-NTT computation; (2) Hadamard product; (3) Matrix transpose; (4) N_2-NTT computation. Specifically, the 4-step NTT views the inputted $\mathbf{a}$ as the form of matrix $\mathbf{A}^{N_1 \times N_2}$ and decomposes the twiddle factor matrix $\mathbf{W}$ to $\mathbf{W}_1 = \{\xi_{2N_1}^{2ij+j}\}$, $\mathbf{W}_2 = \{\xi_{2N}^{2ij+i}\}$, and $\mathbf{W}_3 = \{\xi_{2N_2}^{2ij}\}$, where $N = N_1 \times N_2$, and the dimensions of $\mathbf{W}_1$, $\mathbf{W}_2$, and $\mathbf{W}_3$ are $N_1 \times N_1$, $N_1 \times N_2$, and $N_2 \times N_2$, respectively. In this way, we can compute the 4-step NTT as

$$\bar{\mathbf{A}} = ((\mathbf{A} \times \mathbf{W}_1) \odot \mathbf{W}_2)^T \times \mathbf{W}_3 \pmod{q}.$$

Since both $\mathbf{W}_1$ and $\mathbf{W}_3$ are Vandermond matrices similar as $\mathbf{W}$, we can compute $\times \mathbf{W}_1$ and $\times \mathbf{W}_3$ using the Butterfly method. Compared with the trivial NTT, the 4-step NTT significantly reduces the dependence between internal data. Section 3.1 will describe our 4-step NTT design on GPU in detail.

Exact Basis Conversion (EBConv). EBConv can change the polynomials' basis and was first proposed in [15] without introducing errors. ModUp and ModDown [8] are two basic operations instantiated by EBConv to change and reduce the basis of polynomials, respectively. Since KLSS [20] requires exact basis conversion, we introduce the procedure of EBConv here. Given an input basis $\mathcal{I} = \{q_0, \ldots, q_{r-1}\}$ and an output basis $\mathcal{O} = \{p_0, \ldots, p_{s-1}\}$, $\mathsf{EBConv}_{\mathcal{I} \to \mathcal{O}}([a]_\mathcal{I}) = [a]_\mathcal{O}$ converts the RNS representation $[a]_\mathcal{I} = (a^{(0)}, \ldots, a^{r-1}) \in \mathbb{Z}_{q_0} \times \cdots \times \mathbb{Z}_{q_{r-1}}$ of an integer $a \in \mathbb{Z}_\mathcal{I}$ into $[a]_\mathcal{O} \in \mathbb{Z}_{p_0} \times \cdots \times \mathbb{Z}_{p_{s-1}}$ by computing

$$v = \left\lfloor \sum_{i=0}^{r-1} \frac{[a^{(i)} \cdot \hat{q}_i^{-1}]_{q_i}}{q_i} \right\rceil \in \mathbb{Z} \text{ and}$$

$$\mathsf{EBConv}_{\mathcal{I} \to \mathcal{O}}([a]_\mathcal{I}) = \left(\sum_{i=0}^{r-1} [a^{(i)} \cdot \hat{q}_i^{-1}]_{q_i} \cdot \hat{q}_i - v \cdot [I]_{p_j} \pmod{p_j} \right)_{0 \le j < s},$$

where $\hat{q}_i = \prod_{i' \ne i} q_{i'} \in \mathbb{Z}$.

2.3 The KLSS-Based KeySwitch

KLSS [20] is an efficient KeySwitch method to reduce (I)NTT execution time via 2D gadget decomposition. KLSS has three bases $\mathcal{P} = \{p_0, \cdots, p_{K-1}\}$, $\mathcal{Q}_L = \{q_0, \cdots, q_L\}$, and $\mathcal{T} = \{t_0, \cdots, t_{r'-1}\}$, where $P = \prod_{p_i \in \mathcal{P}} p_i$, $Q_L = \prod_{q_i \in \mathcal{Q}_L} q_i$, and $T = \prod_{t_i \in \mathcal{T}} t_i$.

The main goal of KeySwitch is to multiply a ciphertext c by a KeySwitch key $\mathbf{swk}$, where $\mathbf{swk}$ consists of $d = (L+1)/K$ parts $\mathbf{swk}_i = (a_i, b_i) \in R_{PQ_L}^2$ where $0 \le i < d$. Before executing KeySwitch, each polynomial a_i or b_i in $\mathbf{swk}_i$ is split into $\tilde{d} = (K+L+1)/\gamma$ slices $\mathbf{swk}_i.\mathbf{A}_j$ or $\mathbf{swk}_i.\mathbf{B}_j \in R_{PQ_L[j\cdot\gamma:(j+1)\cdot\gamma]}$, these slices are converted to basis $\mathcal{T}$, and the ciphertext c is similarly divided into d slices $\mathbf{c}_i \in R_{Q_L[i\cdot K:(i+1)\cdot K]}$, where $0 \le i < d$ and $0 \le j < \tilde{d}$.

Figure 2 illustrates the dataflow of the KLSS-based KeySwitch [20]. It transforms the ciphertext slices $\mathbf{c}$ from basis $\mathcal{Q_L}$ to $\mathcal{T}$, computes the Inner Product (IP) between $\mathbf{c}$ and $\mathbf{swk}.\mathbf{A}$ and the IP between $\mathbf{c}$ and $\mathbf{swk}.\mathbf{B}$ both in NTT form, and finally converts the IP results to basis $\mathcal{PQ}_L$ and reduce the converted IP results to basis $\mathcal{Q}_L$ by ModDown, where all basis conversions are executed in coefficient form.

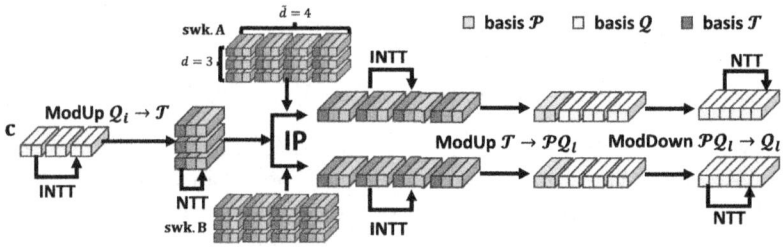

Fig. 2. The KLSS-based KeySwitch dataflow with the parameters $(K, L+1, \gamma, r', d, \tilde{d}) = (2, 6, 2, 3, 3, 4)$. Note that the different colors denote the different bases.

Compared to the Hybrid KeySwitch [16], KLSS significantly improves the performance of KeySwitch by reducing the number of (I)NTT operations. However, its improvement comes at the cost of increased computation overhead on EBConv and IP operations. This paper will design the KLSS-based KeySwitch with high parallelism for significantly enhancing the throughput of KeySwitch on GPU.

2.4 The CKKS Bootstrapping

Bootstrapping is the most critical operation in CKKS to raise the level of a ciphertext from 0 to $L - l_{\text{Boot}}$. It is also the most complex operation in CKKS, as it involves multiple basic homomorphic operations and requires a large amount of memory to store intermediate data. This paper adopts the most advanced Bootstrapping technique [4] to balance the performance, precision, and depth cost. In short, Bootstrapping consists of the following four phases:

- SlotsToCoefficients (S2C) converts the plaintext $m(X)$ from the slots domain to the coefficients domain homomorphically. This phase is equal to multiplying the plaintext DFT matrix and involves $O(radix \log_{radix} N)$ HRot operations by performing the BSGS matrix-vector multiplication [4] with the decomposed DFT matrix [7];
- ModRaise raises the depth of a ciphertext from **ct** to L by bringing the modulus of **ct** from q_0 to Q_L. When decrypting **ct** with the secret key s, we get a different plaintext t satisfying $t(X) = m(X) + q_0 I(X)$;
- CoeffcientsToSlots (C2S) is the inverse of operation S2C to bring the error $I(X)$ introduced in ModRaise from coefficients back to slots;
- EvalMod removes the $q_0 I(X)$ involved by ModRaise. This phase uses the linear polynomial to approximate the nonlinear function $f(x) = \frac{q_0}{2\pi}\sin(\frac{2\pi}{q_0}x) \approx x$ (mod 1) homomorphically.

Moreover, Athena combines C2S/S2C with the feature of KLSS by performing plaintext matrix multiplication on basis $\mathcal{T}$, significantly optimizing the dataflow of Bootstrapping. We will discuss the dataflow optimization in Sect. 3.2.

3 Design of Athena

Figure 3 illustrates an overview of Athena. It includes the polynomial layer, operation layer, and Bootstrapping layer. Athena focuses on optimizing KeySwitch and Bootstrapping. Compared with existing FHE accelerators, Athena accelerates the KLSS-based KeySwitch by redesigning its three important kernels: NTT, EBConv, and IP. Then, Athena optimizes the dataflow of Bootstrapping by combining the C2S/S2C phase with the feature of KLSS and reusing the KeySwitch key of HMult in the EvalMod phase.

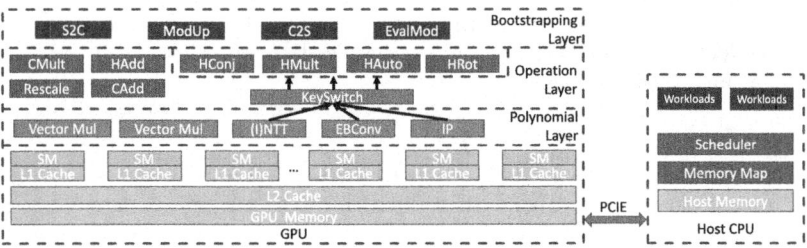

Fig. 3. The system overview of Athena.

3.1 KeySwitch with High Parallelism

Reduce Pipeline Stalls in NTT.

The SOTA GPU-based work TensorFHE (HPCA'23) [13] states that the various pipeline Read After Write (RAW) stalls between iterations are the main bottleneck of trivial NTT implementation on GPU and take more than 40% time of all the (I)NTT execution time. Hence, TensorFHE implements 32-bit modulus NTT by a naive matrix multiplication and uses the emerging Tensor Core Units (TCUs) to carry the matrix multiplication. However, the TCUs-based method increases the computation complexity of NTT from $O(N \log N)$ to $O(N^2)$. Due to the low computation precision of TCUs, TensorFHE is not applicable to large modulus. For example, the TCUs-based 64-bit modulus NTT involves 64 s8 matrix multiplications and increases computational overhead 4× compared to the TCUs-based 32-bit modulus NTT.

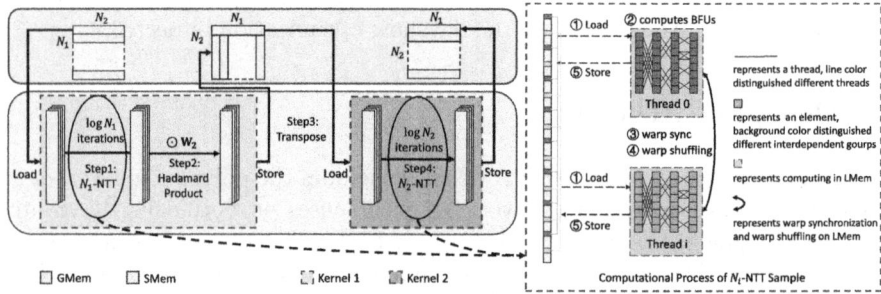

Fig. 4. The 4-step NTT dataflow. Note that: (1) The first three steps are fused into Kernel 1, and the last step occupies Kernel 2; (2) The zoom-in on the right can represent the N_1 and N_2-NTT dataflow; (3) Each warp handles a full N_i-NTT sample, the elements in each N_i-NTT sample are split into different independent groups (eight elements in the same color are in the same group), and each thread processes one interdependent group; (4) Threads are synchronized on warp level, and the data are swapped using warp-shuffling.

Athena addresses the problem of NTT's high RAW stalls on GPU. Specifically, Athena uses 4-step NTT to reduce the data's internal dependence and processes different N_i-NTT on different blocks to achieve NTT pipelines with high performance. To manage the dataflow of N_i-NTT, Athena uses a double-buffering architecture from GLobal Memory (GMem)-Shared Memory (SMem)-Local Memory (LMem) within one block to improve memory access efficiency. To compute N_i-NTT, Athena assigns multiple Butterfly Unit (BFU) based on Shoup modular multiplication tasks of a basic N_i-NTT sample to a single thread and applies the GPU warp-primitive to perform inner-warp data swap. As a result, Athena achieves a highly efficient pipeline across GPU's block-warp-thread level.

We take $N = 2^{16}$ as an example to explain Athena's pipeline-efficient 4-step NTT on the Ada AD102 GPU [23]. Figure 4 shows the procedure of Athena's

4-step NTT. Athena decomposes $N = 2^{16}$ to $N_1 = 2^8$ and $N_2 = 2^8$ and employs two kernels to compute 4-step NTT. It computes N_1-NTT, Hadamard product, and transpose in kernel 1 and computes N_2-NTT in kernel 2. In each kernel, Athena launches 64 blocks, and each block contains 128 threads (equivalent to 4 warps). Athena allocates 1024×8 Bytes SMem for each block and an 8×8 Bytes LMem buffer for each thread to store the intermediate data during the NTT iterations. Athena realizes the four steps of 4-step NTT, mentioned in Sect. 2.2:

- **Step 1**: To compute N_1-NTT, Athena launches kernel 1 and loads four 2^8-NTT samples (containing 1024 elements in total) from GMem to SMem in row-major, and each GPU warp handles one 2^8-NTT sample. Then, each warp sequentially reads its corresponding 2^8-NTT sample, and each thread handles eight elements. During the iterations of N_1-NTT, each thread computes as:
  1. Read its eight dependent elements from SMem to the corresponding LMem buffer;
  2. Execute three times radix-2 butterfly iterations to complete the NTT computation on these eight elements in the LMem buffer;
  3. Synchronize the threads in the same warp via the __syncwarp() GPU instruction to maintain data coherency;
  4. Perform on-the-fly data swap between the threads in the same warp using warp-shuffling primitives;
  5. Continue executing NTT iteration until 2^8-NTT completed and write the data back to the SMem.

  For the BFU computations in the above second step, Athena leverages the thread-level memory instruction cp.async to concurrently transfer NTT twiddle factors alongside BFU computations to overlap the memory transfer latency, thereby enhancing pipeline utilization. Finally, after eight NTT iterations, kernel 1 completes the N_1-NTT computation and stores the four resulted 2^8-NTT samples in LMem.
- **Step 2**: Compute the Hadamard Product between $(\mathbf{A} \times \mathbf{W_1})$ and $\mathbf{W_2}$ in LMem.
- **Step 3**: Compute the transpose of the result in **Step 2**. Since **Step 4** will read data across blocks, **Step 3** writes the data in LMem back to GMem in transposed form and destroys kernel 1.
- **Step 4**: To compute N_2-NTT, Athena launches kernel 2, reads data from GMem to SMem, computes N_2-NTT like **Step 1**, and writes the results back to GMem.

We state that Athena achieves a highly efficient pipeline across three levels:

- **Block-level**: Distribute different N_i-NTT samples to different blocks and use SMem to store the intermediate data during the iterations;
- **Warp-level**: Distribute N_i-NTT samples in the same block to separate warps and adopt warp-level primitives to perform on-the-fly data swaps and ensure data consistency;
- **Thread-level**: Employ double-buffering strategy to achieve NTT data transfer with high throughput and utilize the cp.async instruction to overlap the memory transfer latency of twiddle factors.

Athena achieves parallelism for different modulus and polynomials by launching more blocks. Since the AD102 GPU contains 128 (a multiple of the launched blocks in NTT) Streaming Multiprocessors (SMs), Athena can effectively utilize all SM resources. For other values of N, we adjust the decomposition parameters N_1 and N_2 and the number of sub-NTT samples distributed to each GPU block to obtain the best performance.

Reuse Intermediate Data in EBConv. EBConv contains various computations, like floating-point division FP-Div, 64-bit mulplication u64-Mul, Shoup modular multiplication ModMul, and Barrett reduction ModRed. It is the most complex operation of KeySwitch and introduces many intermediate data to store. Thus, reusing intermediate data in LMem as much as possible is the primary method to improve the performance of EBConv.

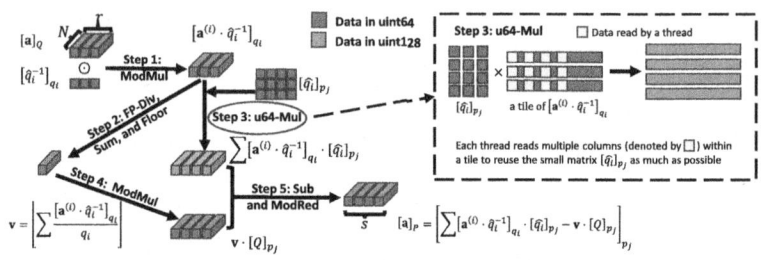

Fig. 5. The EBConv dataflow with high parallelism and data reuse.

Figure 5 illustrates the dataflow of EBConv with an $r \times N$ input matrix $[a]_Q$ and an $s \times N$ output matrix from basis $Q = \{q_0, \cdots, q_{r-1}\}$ to basis $\mathcal{P} = \{p_0, \cdots, p_{s-1}\}$. EBConv consists of five steps:

- **Step 1**: Compute Hadamard product between $[a^{(i)}]_Q$ and $[\hat{q}_i^{-1}]_{q_i}$ by ModMul and output an $r \times N$ matrix;
- **Step 2**: Take the $r \times N$ output matrix of **Step 1** as input, divide the matrix by q_i, sum the r rows of the matrix to obtain an $1 \times N$ matrix, and floor all elements in the $1 \times N$ matrix;
- **Step 3**: Take the $r \times N$ output matrix of **Step 1** as input, multiply the $r \times N$ matrix with the small matrix $[\hat{q}_i]_{p_j}$ by ModMul;
- **Step 4**: Multiply the output of **Step 2** with $[Q]_{p_j}$;
- **Step 5**: Subtract the output of **Step 3** with the output of **Step 4**, apply ModRed to reduce the subtracted result such that all elements are less than p_j, and output $[a]_\mathcal{P}$.

Athena provides high parallelism by partitioning the matrix $\mathbf{a}^{(i)}$ into several tiles with the same size and distributing different tiles to different blocks to balance the parallel workloads. It stores all the intermediate data in the GPU register files to reduce the latency of reading the data as much as possible. In addition, we find that **Step 3** in Fig. 5 involves a small matrix multiplication, where matrix $[\hat{q}_i]_{p_j}$ needs to be loaded many times from GMem. Therefore, Athena lets each thread read multiple columns within a tile to reduce the load times of the matrix $[\hat{q}_i]_{p_j}$.

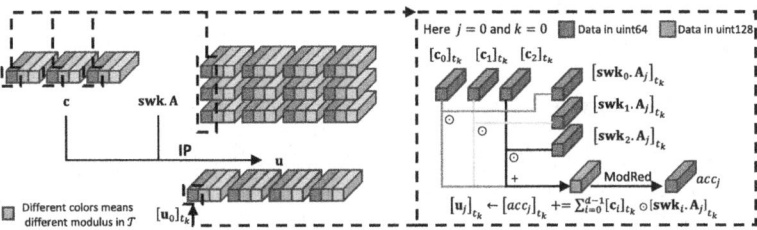

Fig. 6. An example of IP operation. Note that $(d, \tilde{d}, r') = (3, 4, 3)$, $0 \leq i < d$, $0 \leq j < \tilde{d}$, and $0 \leq k < r'$.

Alleviate Memory Bound of IP. Recall that in Sect. 2.3, the KLSS-based KeySwitch adopts IP to compute the Inner Products of the ciphertext polynomial slices **c** with the KeySwitch key slices **swk.A** and **swk.B**, respectively. Figure 6 gives an example to illustrate the IP operation between **c** and **swk.A**. In general, IP reads **c** and **swk** from GMem to LMem and accumulates the i-th product $\mathbf{c}_i \odot \mathbf{swk}_i.\mathbf{A}$ into a 128-bit GPU register acc. After accumulating acc $\beta = \lceil (l+1)/K \rceil$ times, Athena reduces acc by ModRed and writes back the result to GMem, where l is the level of **c**. Athena distributes the workload of IP operation to several smaller blocks to alleviate the memory bound of the SM's L1 cache. In addition, when executing multiple IP operations with the same **swk** (this case will appear when evaluating Chebyshev polynomial in the EvalMod phase of Bootstrapping), Athena can alleviate the memory bound of IP further by reusing the same **swk** that has been loaded in LMem.

GPU Kernel Fusion. Recall that the KLSS-based KeySwitch consists of a series of N-NTT, EBConv, and IP operations. N-NTT is inner-vector data dependent. It means that the input vector of N-NTT must be complete before executing N-NTT. On the contrary, EBConv and IP operations are cross-vector data dependent. It means that a part of the former EBConv's output can be handled by the latter IP operation early if existing the successive EBConv and IP operations. This feature is suitable for fusing the successive EBConv and IP operations. However, in practice, the executing series of N-NTT, EBConv, and IP operations must be INTT $\rightarrow$ EBConv $\rightarrow$ NTT $\rightarrow$ IP $\rightarrow$ INTT $\rightarrow$ EBConv $\rightarrow$ NTT. In other words, an (I)NTT operation must be completely executed before performing EBConv and IP operations. Therefore, Athena splits IP, EBConv, and NTT operations into separate GPU kernels.

To reduce the start and destroy cost of the above kernels and the GMem I/O overhead, Athena fuses the three operations into three separate kernels and parallelizes the workloads on various modulus and polynomials. Specifically, it organizes a 3D GPU grid for each kernel to simplify the computation task of each thread in the kernel. For a 3D grid with (x, y, z) dimensions, the x-dimension handles inner-indexing of a polynomial, the y-dimension parallelizes different modulus, the z-dimension enables executing the operations on different RNS polynomials in batch, and all data are read in row-major to maximize the GPU L2 cache hit rate.

3.2 Bootstrapping with Dataflow Optimization

Recall that Bootstrapping involves four phases (see Sect. 2.4), in which the C2S, EvalMod, and S2C phases take up almost all the time cost of Bootstrapping [17]. Athena focuses on optimizing the dataflow of the C2S/S2C and EvalMod.

Optimize C2S/S2C Phase. Bootstrapping performs a homomorphically linear transformation $\mathbf{A} \cdot \mathbf{ct}(z)$. The only difference between C2S and S2C is the matrix $\mathbf{A}$. Athena uses the (I)DFT matrix decomposition technique to obtain n sparse diagonal matrices and applies the Baby-Step-Giant-Step (BSGS) strategy [7] to reduce the number of HRot operations in each sparse diagonal matrix multiplication. Athena sets $radix = 2^4$ to balance the depth cost and the number of HRot operations, where $\log radix = \lceil (\log N - 1)/n \rceil$. To reduce the computation overhead of sparse diagonal matrix multiplication, Athena applies the double-hoisting strategy [4] with the BSGS parameters of $bs = 2$ and $gs = 16$ to reduce the number of ModDown operations.

Athena combines the double-hoisting strategy with the feature of KLSS. Specifically, Athena performs all plaintext-matrix-multiplication-addition operations PtMatMultAdd in BSGS on basis $\mathcal{T}$ to reduce the number of (I)NTT and EBConv between bases $\mathcal{PQ}_l$ and $\mathcal{T}$. When implementing the C2S/S2C phase, Athena reads the input ciphertext and rotation keys in a permuted order to avoid data permutation across GPU blocks and fuses PtMatMultAdd into a separate GPU kernel to reduce the I/O between LMem and GMem. In addition, it encodes the plaintext matrix to a smaller basis $\mathcal{T}$ rather than basis $\mathcal{PQ}_l$, significantly reducing the plaintext matrix storage and memory bandwidth by $1 - |\mathcal{T}|/|\mathcal{PQ}| = 65.7\%$.

Optimize EvalMod Phase. EvalMod homomorphically computes mod 1 function. Athena applies the Chebyshev approximation [6] and the double-angle iteration to approximate mod 1 function to balance the depth consumption, computation overhead, and precision of EvalMod. Specifically, to realize function $\sin(2\pi x)$, Athena applies the Chebyshev method to approximate function $\cos(2\pi \frac{1}{2^r}(x - 0.25))$ and then computes the double-angle formula $\cos(2x) = 2\cos^2(x) - 1$. To reduce the degree of Chebyshev polynomial and the error caused by Runge's Phenomenon [11], it increases the double-angle iterations to 3 and sets the degree of Chebyshev polynomials to be 32.

Athena merges HMult in the Chebyshev evaluation. Figure 7 illustrates the dataflow of the Chebyshev evaluation. Firstly, it calculates the Chebyshev bases iteratively by computing $T_0(X) = 1$, $T_1(X) = X$, and $T_{2^k}(X) = 2T_{2^{k-1}}^2(X) - 1$.

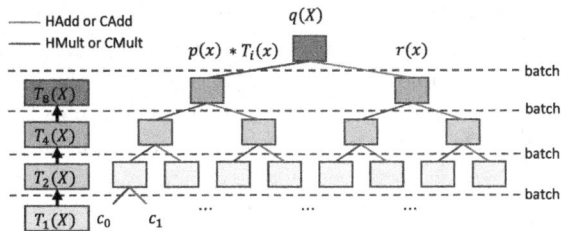

Fig. 7. The dataflow of the 16th-degree Chebyshev evaluation. Note that $T_i(X)$ represents the Chebyshev bases, the binary tree illustrates the computational process, and the tree is evaluated from bottom to top.

Secondly, it constructs a binary tree according to the computation processes of $q(X) = p(X) \cdot T_{2^k}(X) + r(X)$ and adjusts the control flow from the trivial recursive to a bottom-to-top sequential. To enhance the performance of a Chebyshev evaluation, it executes the HMult operations of the same tree level in batch. Specifically, it optimizes the utilization of swk in the IP operations by merging the IP operations of the same tree level into the same GPU kernel.

4 Experiment Settings

4.1 Platforms

We implement Athena based on CUDA 12.4, comprehensively evaluate its performance on the server equipped with NVIDIA RTX 4090 and A100 GPUs, Intel Xeon(R) Gold 6338, and 1024GB host memory (optional). The host OS is Ubuntu 22.04. Note that our experiment results mainly rely on RTX 4090 without special mention. We apply Nsight Compute to analyze the pipeline stalls at the micro-architecture level.

4.2 Methodology

We compare Athena with the SOTA, shown in Table 3, and design the following experiments: (1) Analyze the 4-step NTT performance of Athena and compare

Table 3. The SOTAs and their platforms. Note that Phantom is the only open-sourced, and we evaluate it on RTX 4090 for a fair comparison.

Platf.	Accelerator	Hardware	Platf.	Accelerator	Hardware
CPU	Baseline [25]	AMD Ryzen 3975WX	GPU	100x [17]	NVIDIA Tesla V100
FPGA	Poseidon [29]	Xilinx Alveo U280		Phantom [28]	NVIDIA RTX 4090
	FAB [1]	Xilinx Alveo U280 × 8		TensorFHE [13]	NVIDIA A100-SXM-40G
GPU	Athena	NVIDIA RTX 4090			
		NVIDIA A100-PCIe-80G			

the results with TensorFHE [13] and Poseidon [29] on various dimensions; (2) Provide a comprehensive performance of HRot and HMult on various cryptographic parameters and apple-to-apple comparisons with the previous GPU and FPGA-based works; (3) Analyze the optimization of Athena's Bootstrapping and compare it with the SOTAs on the same parameters settings.

5 Evaluation

5.1 NTT optimization Effectiveness

Athena designs an optimized 4-step NTT with Shoup ModMul. This optimization method is also effective in the 4-step NTT with Barrett ModRed in reducing the pipeline stalls. In Fig. 8, we compare our work with the optimized 4-step NTT with Barrett ModRed and the trivial NTT. The results show that our 4-step NTT optimization method can significantly reduce the pipeline stalls 30.6% for both Shoup ModMul and Barrett ModRed compared with the trivial NTT, and our 4-step NTT with Shoup ModMul saves about 28.6% computational overhead compared with both the optimized 4-step NTT with Barrett ModRed and the trivial NTT. Table 4 compares Athena's NTT throughput on RTX 4090 with a CPU baseline [27], TensorFHE [13], and Poseidon [29]. The $\log N$ represents the logarithm of the degree of the polynomials, and Modulus represents the supported maximum modulus size of these works. The results demonstrate that Athena increases the throughput $1057.87\times$, $1.80\times$, and $1.53\times$ compared with them, respectively.

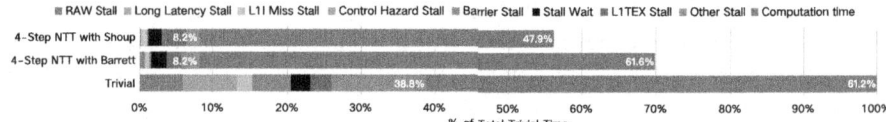

Fig. 8. The pipeline stalls breakdown of three kinds of NTT implementations.

Table 4. (I)NTT throughput on various dimensions (unit: OPS).

	Accelerator	Modulus	$\log N$			
			13	14	15	16
NTT	CPU baseline in [27]	64	6613	3390	1578	769
	TensorFHE [13]	32	3599792	3140055	–	–
	Poseidon [29]	32	–	–	–	548856
	Athena	64	**6410257**	**3606853**	**1562500**	**813504**
INTT	CPU baseline in [27]	64	8695	4118	2057	977
	TensorFHE [13]	32	3592672	3137670	–	–
	Poseidon [29]	32	–	–	–	548856
	Athena	64	**6463341**	**3597122**	**1712329**	**838926**

5.2 KeySwitchOptimization Effectiveness

To accelerate HMult and HRot, Athena focuses on optimizing their key operation KeySwitch. To show the optimization effectiveness more clearly, we compare Athena with the previous works in performing HMult and HRot operations. Table 5 presents the performance of TensorFHE [13], Phantom [28], Poseidon [29], FAB [1], and Athena on various parameters. All these parameters guarantee that CKKS has at least 128-bit security. Since Phantom is the only existing work providing the source code, we evaluate Phantom on all these parameters. The detailed explanation of the parameters is summarized in Table 2. Note that Table 5 does not present the previous work 100x [17] since its performance is much worse than Phantom [28] and TensorFHE [13].

Athena outperforms the state of the art GPU open-source library Phantom [28] $1.52\times \sim 2.68$ and $1.51\times \sim 2.71\times$ in executing HMult and HRot operations, respectively. Compared with the SOTA NVIDIA-GPU work TensorFHE [13], Athena speeds up $\geq 2.90\times$ for both HMult and HRot. When comparing with the SOTA FPGA works Poseidon [29] and FAB [1], Athena outperforms FAB $2.17\times$ and $1.89\times$ for HMult and HRot, respectively. Although FPGA has the customized memory I/O model, which allows FPGA to be much better than GPU in mitigating the memory bound problem, Athena just be slightly slower than Poseidon in executing HRot. Moreover, Athena supports various parameters

Table 5. Comparison: HMult and HRot on various parameters (unit: μs).

Params	Assigned Values							
$\log N$	15		16					
$L+1$	20	23	40	47	44			24
K	4	1	8	1	1			8
γ	8	3	8	3	3			8
r'	8	3	10	3	3			10
Compared Works	Phantom					TensorFHE	Poseidon	FAB
HMult	630.7	1696.2	2289.1	11310.3	10009.4	6648.4	3663.0	1710.0
HRot	615.5	1678.1	2215.2	11218.5	9911.5	6656.3	3311.3	1570.0
Our Work	Athena							
HMult	**318.4**	637.3	**1509.5**	4463.6	3724.3	3440.6 (on A100)		788.1
Speedup	1.98×	**2.66×**	1.52×	2.53×	**2.68×**	1.93×	1.06×	2.17×
HRot	**344.8**	671.8	**1467.4**	4399.0	3657.7	3419.6 (on A100)		830.4
Speedup	1.78×	**2.50×**	1.51×	2.55×	**2.71×**	1.92×	0.97×	1.89×

Note: (1) TensorFHE [13] and Phantom [28] are based on GPU, and Posiedon [29] and FAB [1] are based on FPGA; (2) FAB and Phantom support 64-bit modulus, and TensorFHE and Poseidon only support 32-bit modulus; (3) When comparing with TensorFHE, we evaluate Athena on NVIDIA A100 for a fair comparison, while the other results are based on RTX 4090 (not only the parameters listed in Table 5). In contrast, Poseidon supports only one suit of parameters. In addition, Athena has the best performance on the parameters $(L+1, K, \gamma, r') = (40, 8, 8, 10)$ in the case of $\log N = 16$. In this case, Athena outperforms TensorFHE $4.40\times$ and $4.54\times$ in HMult and HRot, respectively. Compared with Poseidon, Athena's HMult and HRot achieve $2.43\times$ and $2.27\times$ improvement, respectively. In this case, we do not compare Athena with FAB since the latter only supports 23 multiplication depth, which is much less than the former's maximum depth of 39.

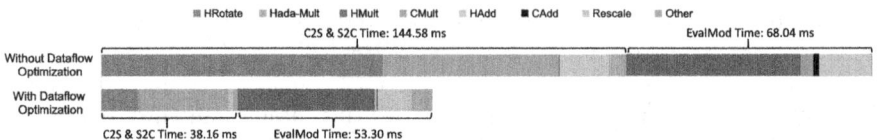

Fig. 9. Homomorphic-operation-level time breakdown of Athena's Bootstrapping on the parameters $(\log N, L+1, K, \gamma, r', radix) = (16, 35, 7, 7, 10, 2^4)$.

5.3 Bootstrapping Optimization Effectiveness

After applying Athena's KeySwitch to realize Bootstrapping, Athena further optimizes the dataflow of Bootstrapping. Figure 9 illustrates the time breakdown analysis of Athena's Bootstrapping with or without the dataflow optimization. The left of the dashed line represents the total time cost of C2S and S2C, and the right part represents the total time cost of EvalMod. The results show that Athena's Bootstrapping with the dataflow optimization achieves $2.32\times$ improvement. Specifically, Athena's dataflow optimization significantly reduces the number of EBConv and (I)NTT operations and memory I/O overhead between GMem and LMem in PtMatMultAdd. And Athena's dataflow optimization also improves the utilization of **swk** in multiple HMult's IP kernels, thereby improving the performance of EvalMod.

Table 6. Bootstrapping comparisons (unit: ms). Note that Set-1 and Set-2 denote the parameters $(\log N, L+1, K, \gamma, r', radix) = (16, 35, 7, 7, 10, 2^4)$ and $(\log N, L+1, K, \gamma, r', radix) = (16, 24, 8, 8, 12, 2^4)$, respectively.

Set-1			Set-2	
Athena	100x [17]	TensorFHE [13]	Athena	FAB [1]
91.46	428.93	250.45	52.23	92.40

Table 6 compares Athena with the previous works in the aspect of Bootstrapping performance. The results show that Athena accelerates Bootstrapping performance 4.68× and 2.74× compared with the GPU-baseline 100x [17] and TensorFHE [13] on the same parameter Set-1, respectively. To compare FAB fairly, we evaluate Athena's Bootstrapping on the parameters Set-2, which FAB provides. Although FAB employs 8 FPGA boards, Athena still achieves 1.77× improvement with relatively limited hardware resources. Note that in this part, we do not compare Athena with Poseidon [29] and Phantom [28], since Poseidon's parameters make Bootstrapping key having a huge and impractical size (≥ 150 GB), and Phantom does not support Bootstrapping.

6 Related Works

The GPU-Based Works. 100x [17] is the first GPU-based work to consider CKKS Bootstrapping and successfully accelerated it to more than 100× compared with CPU. It discusses the performance bottleneck in the 2nd CKKS [16] and achieves good performance. TensorFHE [13] points out that NTT is the performance bottleneck of the CKKS HMult, Bootstrapping, and workloads. It profoundly analyzes the serious pipeline stall problem of naive-NTT on GPU and adopts TCUs to implement matrix-multiplication-like NTT to reduce the pipeline stall. It also focuses on improving the throughput of homomorphic operations through kernel-level batch. Phantom [28] is the first GPU-based open-source library that simultaneously implements the 2nd CKKS scheme on GPU and supports various cryptographic parameters. In summary, these works, except Phantom [28], do not support various cryptographic parameters and explore the parameter selection on hardware overhead, while Phantom [28] does not support Bootstrapping.

The FPGA-Based Works. Several previous works have accelerated FHE on FPGA [1,29]. FPGA offers flexible memory access modes that are well-suited to handling memory-bound workloads caused by the large amount of intermediate data in FHE. With customized computing units, FPGAs often have advantages in optimizing core operations such as modular arithmetic and NTT. However, the limited on-chip resources make it challenging for FPGA to handle complex workloads effectively. Although some FPGA-based works [1,29] achieve performance comparable to the GPU-based works, they are restricted to specific FPGA boards, notably, FAB [1] requires eight FPGA boards to match the performance of a single GPU. Furthermore, upgrading FPGA hardware to improve performance is often complex and costly.

7 Conclusion

FHE has profound implications for various fields, including secure data analytics and cloud computing. This paper presents Athena, a GPU-based FHE system. Athena optimizes the 3rd-generation KeySwitch algorithm KLSS by redesigning its three kernels and optimizes the dataflow of Bootstrapping. The results show that Athena provides the best performance on the core operations HMult, HRot, and Bootstrapping, and provides up to 4.40× and 2.74× improvement over the SOTA GPU-based work in HMult and Bootstrapping performance, respectively.

Acknowledgements. We sincerely thank the anonymous reviewers for their constructive comments. This work was supported by National Key Research and Development Program of China (Grant No. 2022YFB4501500 and 2022YFB4501502). Peng Xu and Zhaojun Lu are co-corresponding authors.

References

1. Agrawal, R., et al.: FAB: an FPGA-based accelerator for bootstrappable fully homomorphic encryption. In: IEEE International Symposium on High-Performance Computer Architecture, HPCA 2023, Montreal, QC, Canada, February 25 – March 1, 2023, pp. 882–895. IEEE (2023)
2. Badawi, A.A., et aal.: Openfhe: open-source fully homomorphic encryption library. Cryptology ePrint Archive, Paper 2022/915 (2022). https://eprint.iacr.org/2022/915
3. Bian, S., et al.: HE3DB: an efficient and elastic encrypted database via arithmetic-and-logic fully homomorphic encryption. In: Meng, W., Jensen, C.D., Cremers, C., Kirda, E. (eds.) Proceedings of the 2023 ACM SIGSAC Conference on Computer and Communications Security, CCS 2023, Copenhagen, Denmark, November 26–30, 2023, pp. 2930–2944. ACM (2023)
4. Bossuat, J.-P., Mouchet, C., Troncoso-Pastoriza, J., Hubaux, J.-P.: Efficient bootstrapping for approximate homomorphic encryption with non-sparse keys. In: Canteaut, A., Standaert, F.-X. (eds.) EUROCRYPT 2021. LNCS, vol. 12696, pp. 587–617. Springer, Cham (2021). https://doi.org/10.1007/978-3-030-77870-5_21
5. Brakerski, Z., Gentry, C., Vaikuntanathan, V.: (leveled) fully homomorphic encryption without bootstrapping. ACM Trans. Comput. Theory **6**(3), 13:1–13:36 (2014)
6. Chen, H., Chillotti, I., Song, Y.: Improved bootstrapping for approximate homomorphic encryption. In: Ishai, Y., Rijmen, V. (eds.) EUROCRYPT 2019. LNCS, vol. 11477, pp. 34–54. Springer, Cham (2019). https://doi.org/10.1007/978-3-030-17656-3_2
7. Cheon, J.H., Han, K., Hhan, M.: Faster homomorphic discrete fourier transforms and improved FHE bootstrapping. IACR Cryptol. ePrint Arch. p. 1073 (2018). https://eprint.iacr.org/2018/1073
8. Cheon, J.H., Han, K., Kim, A., Kim, M., Song, Y.: A full RNS variant of approximate homomorphic encryption. In: Cid, C., Jr., M.J.J. (eds.) Selected Areas in Cryptography - SAC 2018 - 25th International Conference, Calgary, AB, Canada, August 15–17, 2018, Revised Selected Papers. Lecture Notes in Computer Science, vol. 11349, pp. 347–368. Springer (2018). https://doi.org/10.1007/978-3-030-10970-7_16
9. Cheon, J.H., Kim, A., Kim, M., Song, Y.: Homomorphic encryption for arithmetic of approximate numbers. In: Takagi, T., Peyrin, T. (eds.) ASIACRYPT 2017. LNCS, vol. 10624, pp. 409–437. Springer, Cham (2017). https://doi.org/10.1007/978-3-319-70694-8_15
10. Cooley, J.W., Tukey, J.W.: An algorithm for the machine calculation of complex fourier series. Math. Comput. **19**, 297–301 (1965). https://api.semanticscholar.org/CorpusID:121744946

11. Epperson, J.F.: On the runge example. Am. Math. Mon. **94**(4), 329–341 (1987)
12. Fan, J., Vercauteren, F.: Somewhat practical fully homomorphic encryption. IACR Cryptol. ePrint Arch. p. 144 (2012). http://eprint.iacr.org/2012/144
13. Fan, S., Wang, Z., Xu, W., Hou, R., Meng, D., Zhang, M.: Tensorfhe: achieving practical computation on encrypted data using GPGPU. In: IEEE International Symposium on High-Performance Computer Architecture, HPCA 2023, Montreal, QC, Canada, February 25 – March 1, 2023, pp. 922–934. IEEE (2023)
14. Gentry, C.: Fully homomorphic encryption using ideal lattices. In: Proceedings of the Forty-first Annual ACM Symposium on Theory of Computing, pp. 169–178 (2009)
15. Halevi, S., Polyakov, Y., Shoup, V.: An improved RNS variant of the BFV homomorphic encryption scheme. In: Matsui, M. (ed.) CT-RSA 2019. LNCS, vol. 11405, pp. 83–105. Springer, Cham (2019). https://doi.org/10.1007/978-3-030-12612-4_5
16. Han, K., Ki, D.: Better bootstrapping for approximate homomorphic encryption. In: Jarecki, S. (ed.) CT-RSA 2020. LNCS, vol. 12006, pp. 364–390. Springer, Cham (2020). https://doi.org/10.1007/978-3-030-40186-3_16
17. Jung, W., Kim, S., Ahn, J.H., Cheon, J.H., Lee, Y.: Over 100x faster bootstrapping in fully homomorphic encryption through memory-centric optimization with GPUs. IACR Trans. Cryptogr. Hardw. Embed. Syst. **2021**(4), 114–148 (2021)
18. Kim, J., Kim, S., Choi, J., Park, J., Kim, D., Ahn, J.H.: SHARP: a short-word hierarchical accelerator for robust and practical fully homomorphic encryption. In: Solihin, Y., Heinrich, M.A. (eds.) Proceedings of the 50th Annual International Symposium on Computer Architecture, ISCA 2023, Orlando, FL, USA, June 17–21, 2023, pp. 18:1–18:15. ACM (2023)
19. Kim, J., et al.: ARK: fully homomorphic encryption accelerator with runtime data generation and inter-operation key reuse. In: 55th IEEE/ACM International Symposium on Microarchitecture, MICRO 2022, Chicago, IL, USA, October 1–5, 2022, pp. 1237–1254. IEEE (2022)
20. Kim, M., Lee, D., Seo, J., Song, Y.: Accelerating HE operations from key decomposition technique. In: Handschuh, H., Lysyanskaya, A. (eds.) Advances in Cryptology - CRYPTO 2023 - 43rd Annual International Cryptology Conference, CRYPTO 2023, Santa Barbara, CA, USA, August 20–24, 2023, Proceedings, Part IV. Lecture Notes in Computer Science, vol. 14084, pp. 70–92. Springer (2023). https://doi.org/10.1007/978-3-031-38551-3_3
21. Lu, Z., et al.: An FPGA-based key-switching accelerator with ultra-high throughput for FHE. In: Xiong, J., Wille, R. (eds.) Proceedings of the 43rd IEEE/ACM International Conference on Computer-Aided Design, ICCAD 2024, Newark Liberty International Airport Marriott, NJ, USA, October 27–31, 2024, pp. 167:1–167:9. ACM (2024)
22. Lu, Z., Yu, W., Xu, P., Wang, W., Zhang, J., Feng, D.: An NTT/INTT accelerator with ultra-high throughput and area efficiency for FHE. In: De, V. (ed.) Proceedings of the 61st ACM/IEEE Design Automation Conference, DAC 2024, San Francisco, CA, USA, June 23–27, 2024, pp. 158:1–158:6. ACM (2024)
23. NVIDIA: NVIDIA ADA GPU ARCHITECTURE (2023). https://images.nvidia.cn/aem-dam/Solutions/geforce/ada/nvidia-ada-gpu-architecture.pdf
24. Rovida, L., Leporati, A.: Encrypted image classification with low memory footprint using fully homomorphic encryption. Int. J. Neural Syst. **34**(5), 2450025:1–2450025:16 (2024)
25. Samardzic, N., et al.: Craterlake: a hardware accelerator for efficient unbounded computation on encrypted data. In: Salapura, V., Zahran, M., Chong, F., Tang,

L. (eds.) ISCA 2022: The 49th Annual International Symposium on Computer Architecture, New York, New York, USA, June 18 – 22, 2022, pp. 173–187. ACM (2022)
26. Microsoft SEAL (release 4.1) (2023). https://github.com/Microsoft/SEAL, microsoft Research, Redmond, WA
27. Shen, S., Yang, H., Liu, Y., Liu, Z., Zhao, Y.: CARM: CUDA-accelerated RNS multiplication in word-wise homomorphic encryption schemes for internet of things. IEEE Trans. Comput. **72**(7), 1999–2010 (2023)
28. Yang, H., Shen, S., Dai, W., Zhou, L., Liu, Z., Zhao, Y.: Phantom: a CUDA-accelerated word-wise homomorphic encryption library. Cryptology ePrint Archive, Paper 2023/049 (2023)
29. Yang, Y., Zhang, H., Fan, S., Lu, H., Zhang, M., Li, X.: Poseidon: practical homomorphic encryption accelerator. In: IEEE International Symposium on High-Performance Computer Architecture, HPCA 2023, Montreal, QC, Canada, February 25 – March 1, 2023, pp. 870–881. IEEE (2023)

Formally-Verified Security Against Forgery of Remote Attestation Using SSProve

Sara Zain[✉][iD], Jannik Mähn, Stefan Köpsell[iD], and Sebastian Ertel[iD]

Barkhausen Institut, Dresden, Germany
{sara.zain,stefan.koepsell,sebastian.ertel}@barkhauseninstitut.org,
jannik.maehn@ohb.de

Abstract. Remote attestation (RA) is the foundation for trusted execution environments in the cloud and trusted device driver onboarding in operating systems. However, RA misses a rigorous mechanized definition of its security properties in one of the strongest models, i.e., the semantic model. Such a mechanization requires the concept of State-Separating Proofs (SSP). However, SSP was only recently implemented as a foundational framework in the Rocq Prover.

Based on this framework, this paper presents the first mechanized formalization of the fundamental security properties of RA. Our Rocq Prover development first defines digital signatures and formally verifies security against forgery in the strong existential attack model. Based on these results, we define RA and reduce the security of RA to the security of digital signatures.

Our development provides evidence that the RA protocol is secure against forgery. Additionally, we extend our reasoning to the primitives of RA and reduce their security to the security of the primitives of the digital signatures.

Keywords: Formal Verification · Remote Attestation · Digital Signatures · Rocq Prover · SSProve

1 Introduction

Remote attestation (RA) is a fundamental security protocol for establishing authenticity in many digital systems. It is a core building block in systems ranging from embedded IoT devices [2,7,26] to cloud-based trusted execution environments [10,14]. However, despite its central role in establishing trust, RA protocols are often specified without formal cryptographic models, and their security properties—particularly semantic security—remain informally stated or entirely unproven.

The Trusted Platform Module (TPM) specification exemplifies this issue [23]. While TPM specification, for example, outlines key generation and digital signature primitives and defines an attestation flow, it does not formalize the cryptographic properties it relies on, such as semantic security or unforgeability under

© The Author(s), under exclusive license to Springer Nature Switzerland AG 2026
V. Nicomette et al. (Eds.): ESORICS 2025, LNCS 16054, pp. 463–484, 2026.
https://doi.org/10.1007/978-3-032-07891-9_24

chosen-message attacks. It also lacks a formal model of the adversary or a clear representation of what it means for attestation to be indistinguishable from an ideal execution. Existing formal approaches for RA often focus on functional correctness or adopt a Dolev-Yao model to show *symbolic* security [30] but cannot establish *stronger* semantic security. These models can verify correctness but assume cryptographic primitives such as encryption and decryption are correct. VRASED instantiates a hybrid (HW/SW) RA co-design for embedded devices but relies on functional correctness [29]. To prove semantic security is particularly challenging, and appropriate reasoning frameworks were only established recently [18]. A novel methodology called State-Separating Proofs (SSP)[1]. allows reasoning in a modular way about semantic security [8]. Frameworks for cryptographic reasoning like CertiCrypt [5] and (its extension) EasyCrypt [4] have existed for a decade but remained hard to apply.

We provide the first formal proof of semantic security for RA protocols using SSProve. SSProve [1] is a Rocq Prover[2] based framework for game-based cryptographic proofs, and reasonings are done in probabilistic relational Hoare logic (pRHL) [5]. We favored SSProve because it provides access to the rich mathematical components library [27]. We present the generalization of *strong unforgeability* to *perfect indistinguishability* to show that it reduces the security of RA to the security of secure signatures in Sect. 2. In Sect. 3, the RA protocol specifies correctness and indistinguishability properties, and prove the indistinguishability of attestation responses under the chosen-message attack. Our formalization includes an instantiation with RSA signatures, for which we implement and verify key generation (Sect. A), and we ensure that all cryptographic assumptions are captured and mechanized.

Our contribution is publicly available[3].

2 From Unforgeability to Indistinguishability

This section presents the security guarantees of digital signatures, focusing on the transition from strong existential unforgeability (sEUF-CMA) to indistinguishability. We will show how these properties are crucial for RA and are framed within the SSProve methodology, paving the way for a better understanding of RA security. Then, we show how these properties are recast within the SSProve methodology through semantic indistinguishability games.

We begin by recalling the standard textbook definitions of a digital signature scheme and its correctness [9,31], followed by their unforgeability guarantees. Any reference to "textbook definitions" will refer to these references throughout the rest of this paper.

---

[1] While we assume familiarity with foundational frameworks like SSProve and State-Separating Proofs, we summarize the key modeling elements (packages, procedures, state memory) in Sect. 2 and Fig. 1 to support accessibility.
[2] Previously named as Coq.
[3] https://github.com/Barkhausen-Institut/vRATLS/tree/main/theories/examples.

2.1 Digital Signature Schemes

A digital signature scheme $\Sigma = (\text{KeyGen}, \text{Sign}, \text{VerSig})$ defined over a message space $\mathcal{M}$ consists of three probabilistic polynomial-time algorithms:

- **KeyGen** generates a pair of keys (sk, pk), where sk is the secret signing key and pk is the public verification key.
- **Sign** takes the secret signing key sk and a message $m \in \mathcal{M}$ to generate a signature σ on the message.
- **VerSig** uses the public key pk to verify whether a signature σ was generated from a message m.

Functional correctness ensures that the verification process succeeds for legitimate signatures.

Definition 1 (Functional Correctness). *A signature scheme Σ is correct if, for all $m \in \mathcal{M}$ and all key pairs (sk, pk) generated by **KeyGen**, we have:*

$$\textbf{\textit{VerSig}}(pk, m, \textbf{\textit{Sign}}(sk, m)) = true.$$

2.2 Strong Unforgeability

Here, we recall the notion of unforgeability in a digital signature scheme. There are two key notions in digital signature. The first is existential unforgeability under chosen-message attacks (EUF-CMA), where an adversary has to forge a signature of any *new* message, i.e., a message without a previously generated signature [21]. The second is a stricter variant, i.e., strong existential unforgeability (sEUF-CMA) (our research focus), where the adversary has to forge a *new signature* of any message, i.e., including messages with a previously generated signature. The formal definition of sEUF-CMA is as follows:

Definition 2 (sEUF-CMA). *A digital signature scheme Σ is strongly existentially unforgeable under a chosen-message attack if, for any probabilistic polynomial-time adversary $\mathcal{A}$, the probability of forging a new, valid signature for any message—including previously signed messages—is negligible. The advantage of $\mathcal{A}$ in breaking the sEUF-CMA security is*

$$Adv_{\Sigma}^{sEUF\text{-}CMA}(\mathcal{A}) := Pr\big[Exp_{(\Sigma,\mathcal{A})}^{sEUF\text{-}CMA}()\big] < negl$$

where the $Exp_{(\Sigma,\mathcal{A})}^{sEUF\text{-}CMA}$ is defined in Game 1.

In the sEUF-CMA experiment (Game 1), the challenger provides access to a signing oracle while preventing trivial wins. The strong unforgeability condition rules out signature re-randomization or malleability, which is especially critical in RA settings where replay or signature variance can lead to security breaches.

Game 1 $Exp_{(\Sigma,\mathcal{A})}^{sEUF-CMA}()$

- The challenger generates a key pair (sk, pk) using $KeyGen()$ and initializes a set S to keep track of signed message-signature pairs.
- Adversary $\mathcal{A}$ is given access to a signing oracle and the public key (pk). It may query the oracle for arbitrary messages.
- For each query m_i, the challenger computes $\sigma_i \leftarrow Sign(sk, m_i)$, return σ_i to $\mathcal{A}$, and stores (m_i, σ_i) in the set S.
- Finally, $\mathcal{A}$ outputs a candidate forgery (m^*, σ^*). It wins if:
  1. $VerSig(pk, m^*, \sigma^*) = true$, and
  2. $(m^*, \sigma^*) \notin S$, i.e., this exact signature was not returned by the oracle.

2.3 Toward Indistinguishability

In RA, adversaries may interact repeatedly with the signing oracle. We know that sEUF-CMA guarantees that adversaries cannot forge fresh signatures or produce new valid signatures on known messages. Now, we need to ensure that all signing executions appear indistinguishable. That is, the internal behavior of the signing process—such as randomness usage, timing, or subtle variations, should not leak information. Even if forgery remains impossible, the ability to distinguish between different signing behaviors should not threaten RA security.

To address this, we adopt *semantic indistinguishability*: an adversary must fail to forge and be unable to distinguish whether it interacts with a *real* signer or an *idealized* one that leaks no information beyond valid signatures. We formalize this as an indistinguishability game (Fig. 2): the adversary submits signing and verification queries and must guess whether it interacts with the *real* implementation or a simulator enforcing *ideal* behavior. Winning this game must be computationally infeasible. Our formalization is based on game-based proofs [33]. It is an approach to proving cryptographic properties, such as correctness, indistinguishability, and unforgeability, through a sequence of game transitions, with reasoning conducted in probabilistic relational Hoare logic (pRHL) [5]. Each transition ensures that no adversary can distinguish real from ideal executions. We use SSProve, a Rocq Prover-based framework for machine-checked cryptographic proofs, to express and verify the guarantees of indistinguishability. SSProve builds on the State-Separating Proof (SSP) methodology, which structures cryptographic reasoning around packages of procedures that operate over a shared state [8].

Packages and Procedures. Readers familiar with SSP can safely skip this paragraph. A package in SSProve defines a set of procedures operating over a common state. For example, in Fig. 1, package $\mathcal{E}$ may define procedure z, which depends on imported procedure types x and y.

SSProve supports sequential composition $(\mathcal{E}_1 \circ \mathcal{E}_2)$ by inlining procedures, provided the interface matches and states align. Procedures are written using a state monad code to handle randomness and memory [35]. Commands such

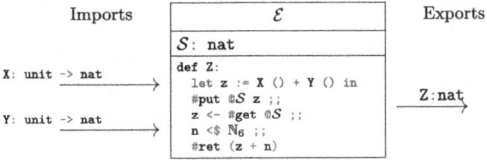

Fig. 1. A package $\mathcal{E}$ in SSProve.

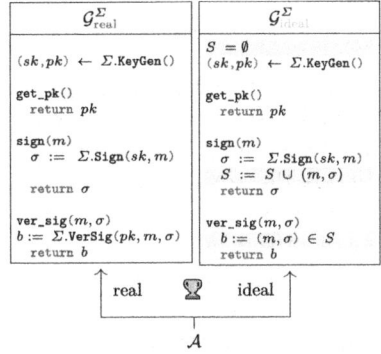

Fig. 2. Game-Pair for indistinguishability ($\mathcal{G}_R^{\Sigma}$)

as get, put, assert, and <$ (for sampling) allow precise control over state and randomness. All procedures are annotated using (#), and memory locations (e.g., @S) abstract away implementation details. A package can define an interface, such as signing and verification procedures, and a stateful implementation

In SSProve, we model the signature process as two distinct packages: one that implements the *real* functionality and the other that provides an *idealized*, abstracted view of signatures (Fig. 2).

The adversary interacts with one of these packages—it can submit signing queries and attempting to verify signatures—and must distinguish whether it interacts with the real or the ideal implementation. Proving that these packages are indistinguishable ensures that signing interactions leak no information beyond what correctness requires.

The *real game* models the real (honest) signature scheme: the adversary may query the signing oracle and later submit a message-signature pair for verification. If the signature is valid, the adversary wins. In the *ideal game*, a simulator responds to signing queries and records issued signatures in a set S. When the adversary attempts to verify a signature, the simulator only accepts message-signature pairs that were previously output by the signing oracle. Any attempt to verify an unissued (potentially forged) signature automatically fails. This technique ensures that guessing a valid signature in the ideal game is infeasible—not because of randomness, but because the simulator enforces a strict policy: only known, previously issued signatures succeed.

The proof of indistinguishability ensures that such forgeries are equally infeasible in the real game—if the two games are indistinguishable, then no such exploit exists. Formally, we express this guarantee using perfect indistinguishability:

Definition 3 (Perfect Indistinguishability ($\approx_0$) [1,9,31]). *Let $\mathcal{G}_1$ and $\mathcal{G}_2$ be two games with the same interface. They are perfectly indistinguishable, denoted $\mathcal{G}_1 \approx_0 \mathcal{G}_2$, if for all probabilistic polynomial-time (PPT) adversaries $\mathcal{A}$,*

$$Adv_{(\mathcal{G}_1,\mathcal{G}_2)}(\mathcal{A}) = \mid Pr[\mathcal{A} \circ \mathcal{G}_1] - Pr[\mathcal{A} \circ \mathcal{G}_2] \mid = 0$$

The $\mathcal{A} \circ \mathcal{G}$ denotes the adversary interacting with game $\mathcal{G}$. Perfect indistinguishability implies that no adversary—regardless of its strategy—can gain any advantage in distinguishing between the real and ideal systems. Unlike indistinguishability, which only needs the advantage to be negligible, perfect indistinguishability ensures exact equality to zero.

In our SSProve development setting, the real and ideal games differ only in their treatment of signature verification. The ideal game maintains an explicit set S of previously signed messages to distinguish genuine queries from forgeries. The real game does not; it verifies signatures as per the signature scheme's definition. If a signature passes verification ($b = true$), the ideal game checks whether it came from the signing oracle ($m \in S$). If yes, the adversary has not forged anything new. If not, it forms a successful forgery attempt. This game-pair structure bridges the conceptual gap between strong unforgeability and indistinguishability, supporting robust reasoning for digital signatures used in protocols like RA. This technique strengthens the security guarantees of RA from correctness toward robust privacy. This shift allows us to move beyond isolated definitions of unforgeability toward composable, black-box security notions essential for verifying RA protocols.

Protocol-Level Reasoning. Our formalization uses SSProve to verify individual primitives and lift these guarantees to the protocol level. The protocol-level abstraction (Fig. 3) treats signatures as black-box functionalities, enabling secure integration into broader systems such as RA. Rather than verifying only functional correctness, this abstraction supports reasoning about composable security, capturing indistinguishability even when the protocol comprises other components. The protocol calls get_pk, sign, and ver_sig as modular components within a single routine, reflecting a structured composition that supports formal, game-based reasoning in SSProve. This technique shows that replacing the signature module with an indistinguishable ideal version leaves the entire protocol indistinguishable from an external adversary. Our formal development

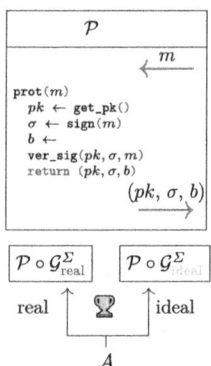

Fig. 3. Protocol.

revealed that even properties like collision resistance at the primitive level become necessary for overall RA security, though not required for correctness.

While SSProve provides essential structure, bridging hand-written cryptographic arguments and machine-verified proofs remains challenging—especially when capturing game transformations and reductions. Our work addresses this by reconciling indistinguishability-based reasoning with formal proofs that scale to realistic protocol security.

Having defined the theoretical foundations of digital signature security, we now present their specification and verification. Since RA builds upon digital signatures, we first formally specify digital signatures. Using the SSProve framework, we modularize key generation, signing, and verification, proving the indistinguishability of *real* and *ideal* signature protocols. This modular development lays the groundwork for the formal security analysis of RA in the next section.

Our formal development of digital signatures is organized around two components: the modular composition of protocol packages and the formal proof of their security properties. Each component is modeled as an SSProve package to support modular and abstract reasoning. Specifically:

- The KeyGen package handles key generation.
- The SigPrim package implements the signing and verification primitives.
- The SigProt package composes these primitives into a complete signature protocol.

The design centers around the KeyGen package, abstracting the key generation process while enabling the specification to be later instantiated with concrete cryptographic algorithms such as RSA or ECDSA. Appendix A provides an example of instantiation for RSA signatures.

Figure 4 illustrates the modular composition. Each box represents an SSProve package, with arrows indicating the composition flow: the KeyGen package generates keys, which SigPrim takes to perform signing and verification operations. SigProt orchestrates these components to implement the full signature protocol. This modular structure suffices to establish strong security guarantees. We formally prove that sEUF-CMA implies indistinguishability between the real and ideal signature protocols. Our development reduces the security of remote attestations to the security of secure signatures. The core intuition behind the proof is rooted in the sEUF-CMA property. Suppose an adversary cannot forge a signature on any new message. In that case, all accepted signatures must have been generated via the signing interface, rendering the behavior of the real and ideal protocols indistinguishable from the adversary's point of view. Conversely, if an adversary could distinguish between the two protocols, it must have found a valid signature on a message not generated by the signing interface, violating strong unforgeability. Thus, indistinguishability and strong unforgeability are tightly linked.

We formalize this reasoning and prove the following results. Theorem 1 establishes Perfect Indistinguishability between the real and ideal digital signature protocols. Theorem 2 establishes a reduction theorem showing that the security of remote attestation is at least as strong as the security of the underlying digital signatures. Theorem 3 combines the two results to conclude that remote attestation satisfies strong existential unforgeability.

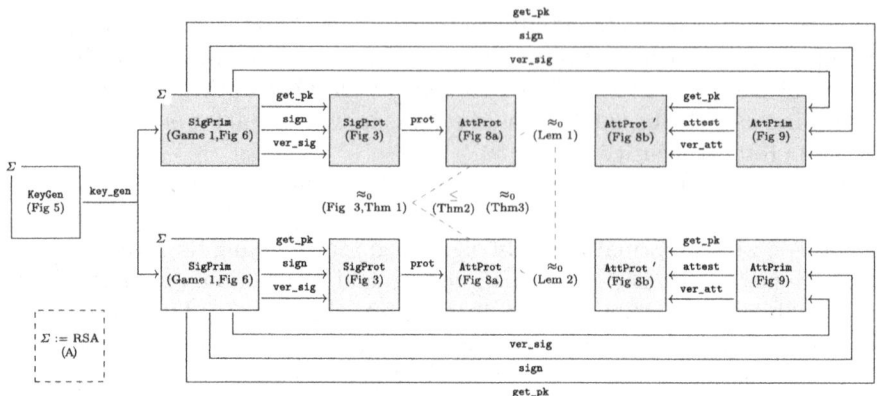

Fig. 4. Modular specification of RA using SSProve package composition. Real-world protocols are depicted in grey, while idealized protocols are shown in yellow. The specification builds upon the modular structure of digital signatures to establish formal security guarantees through indistinguishability proofs. (Color figure online)

2.4 Key Generation

Following the definition of signatures, we formalize key generation. The KeyGen package, abstracts the key generation process over arbitrary finite types for the secret key (SecKey) and public key (PubKey). The package is parameterized by a key generation algorithm Σ.KeyGen, which samples key pairs from a distribution.

Our formalization models key generation as an explicit sampling procedure, which aligns with the sEUF-CMA experiment and simplifies the reduction proofs in SSProve, where key generation produces probabilistically independent keys[4]. This technique ensures the adversary cannot exploit correlations when attempting to forge signatures. This design choice also ensures compatibility with the security game framework, where packages must use explicit

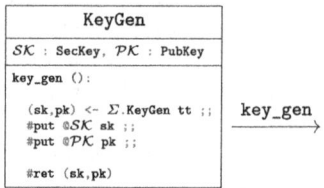

Fig. 5. A KeyGen Package

probabilistic operations and cannot rely on external sources of randomness. Therefore, the KeyGen package exports the procedure key_gen, which samples a key pair using Σ.KeyGen, stores it in the local state, and returns the result. The signing and verification procedures later retrieve this stored key material. Crucially, Σ.KeyGen must be polymorphic in this state, ensuring that the sampling process is side-effect-free for the external state of the composed packages. This technique enables the clean composition of KeyGen with the signature primitives while preserving soundness guarantees.

---

[4] Practical schemes adopt deterministic key derivation for efficiency or side-channel resistance. However, our focus is foundational, and our formalization concentrates only on proving cryptographic soundness right now.

Having defined key generation, we now formalize the signing and verification components.

2.5 Signature Primitives

We now define the signing and verification primitives abstractly over Message and Signature types. The signing function Σ.Sign takes a secret key and a message and outputs a signature. The verification function Σ.VerSig takes a public key, a message, and a signature and outputs a Boolean indicating whether the signature is valid. Both operations are deterministic and do not modify the package state.

The following hypothesis captures the functional correctness of the signature scheme:

Hypothesis 1 (functional correctness) $\forall m \ sk \ pk, ((sk, pk) \leftarrow \Sigma.\text{KeyGen}) \rightarrow \Sigma.\text{VerSig } pk \ (\Sigma.\text{Sign } sk \ m) \ m == true$.

SigPrim $_{\text{real}}$	SigPrim $_{\text{ideal}}$
$\mathcal{SK}$: SecKey, $\mathcal{PK}$: PubKey	$\mathcal{SK}$: SecKey, $\mathcal{PK}$: PubKey, $\mathcal{SIG}$: (S(Message x Signature))
get_pk() := #import key_gen ;; (_,pk) <- key_gen tt ;; #ret pk	get_pk() := #import key_gen ;; (_,pk) <- key_gen tt ;; #ret pk
sign(m) := sk <- #get @$\mathcal{SK}$;; let σ := Σ.Sign sk m ;; #ret σ	sign(m) := sk <- #get @$\mathcal{SK}$;; let s := Σ.Sign sk m ;; S <- #get @$\mathcal{SIG}$;; let S' := S $\cup$ {(m,s)} ;; #put @$\mathcal{SIG}$ S' ;; #ret s
ver_sig(m,s) := pk <- #get @$\mathcal{PK}$;; #ret Σ.VerSig pk s m	ver_sig(m, s) := S <- #get @$\mathcal{SIG}$;; #ret ((m,s) $\in$ S)

Fig. 6. The real and ideal Signature Primitives packages.

That is, for any key pair generated by Σ.KeyGen and any message m, signing, and then verifying should succeed.

We implement two versions of the signature primitive packages (Fig. 6). The real version directly implements the signing and verification operations, invoking Σ.Sign and Σ.VerSig respectively. The ideal version tracks an internal set S of signed messages and accepts a signature during verification only if it corresponds to a message previously signed through the signing interface. Both packages rely on the get_pk procedure from KeyGen to retrieve the pk. With the primitives in place, we now describe the composition of the real and ideal protocols and the security proof that establishes their indistinguishability.

2.6 Indistinguishability Proof

We construct the real and ideal digital signature protocols to formalize the security property by composing the primitives with the key generation package. The composed protocols are defined as follows:

Definition 4 (SigProt$_{\text{real}}$). {package SigProt⊚   SigPrim $_{\text{real}}$ ∘ KeyGen }.

Definition 5 (SigProt$_{\text{ideal}}$). {package SigProt⊚   SigPrim $_{\text{ideal}}$ ∘ KeyGen }.

The wrapper package SigProt relabels the procedures of the signature primitives to provide a unified interface (special notation ⊚). Specifically, it renames the sign operation to challenge and the verification operation ver_sig to verify[5]. This relabeling ensures that the composed packages match the interface and are comparable to the security proof. We then establish our main result:

Theorem 1 (Perfect Indistinguishability of Digital Signatures). *For every adversary $\mathcal{A}$, the advantage to distinguish the packages SigProt $_{\text{real}}$ and SigProt $_{\text{ideal}}$ is 0:*

$$\text{SigProt}_{\text{real}} \approx_0 \text{SigProt}_{\text{ideal}}.$$

Proof. The proof proceeds by establishing an invariant heap_ignore (Fig. 7) that the heap states of the real and ideal packages are identical up to an irrelevant location $\mathcal{SIG}$. As the protocols evolve, this invariant is preserved through every execution step, ensuring that signing and verification operations behave identically from the adversary's perspective. The critical point in the proof is to show that any observable difference between the real and ideal games would require a signature to verify correctly in the real protocol without having been produced by the signing interface in the ideal protocol. However, this is ruled out by the signature scheme's functional correctness property (Definition 1). Note that the real game accepts any syntactically valid signature, and the ideal game only accepts oracle-issued ones. This semantic difference does not make much difference in our formalization because under the sEUF-CMA, the adversary cannot produce a new valid signature on any message, so any accepted signature must have originated from the oracle. Therefore, the adversary gains no distinguishing power. so any accepted signature must have originated from the oracle. However, RA formalization (Sect. 3) assumes injectivity of the hash function $\mathcal{H}$ and ensure that each challenge-state pair maps to a unique message. This prevents adversaries from reusing signatures across different attestation sessions. The combination of injectivity and unforgeability guarantees that an adversary cannot substitute or reapply old signatures for new challenges or states.

---

[5] In SSProve, this is not necessary because procedure names map to a particular natural number. Mapping different procedure names to the same natural numbers establishes the link without an auxiliary package for renaming procedures.

⊢
{ λ (s₁, s₂),
  let inv := heap_ignore {$\mathcal{SIG}$} in
  let h   := inv ⋈ rm_rhs $\mathcal{SIG}$ S in
  let h' := set_rhs $\mathcal{SIG}$ (S ∪ {(Σ.Sign sk m, m)} h in
  let h'' := h' ⋈ rm_rhs $\mathcal{SIG}$ S' in
  h'' (s₁, s₂)) }
ret (pk, Σ.Sign sk m, Σ.VerSig pk (Σ.Sign sk m) m)
≈
ret (pk, Σ.Sign sk m, (Σ.Sign sk m, m) ∈ S')
{ λ (s₁,r₁)
    (s₂,r₂), r₁ = r₂ ∧ heap_ignore {$\mathcal{SIG}$} (s₁, s₂) }

Fig. 7. An invariant heap_ignore.

3 Formal Development of Remote Attestation (RA)

This section formalizes RA and proves its security against forgery. We define packages, describe the protocol, and demonstrate that RA inherits security from digital signatures through a sequence of reductions. By reducing its security to that of the underlying digital signature scheme, we aim to establish perfect indistinguishability for RA.

3.1 Packages

We model the RA setup using SSProve packages that abstract over cryptographic primitives and their interactions with an adversary.

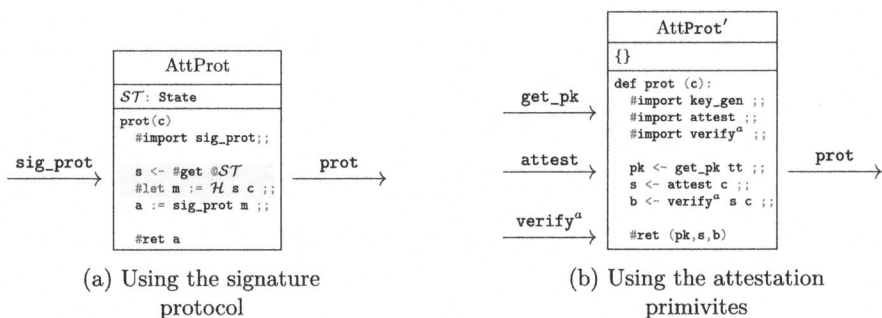

(a) Using the signature protocol

(b) Using the attestation primivites

Fig. 8. Two variants to construct the RA protocol.

Figure 8 defines two packages: AttProt', representing the RA primitives, and AttProt, the RA protocol built atop these primitives. Both packages depend on an abstract State type $\mathcal{ST}$, representing the platform being attested. Their interfaces expose three key operations: first, get_pk[a] for public key access; second, attest for issuing attestations over challenges c, and the last is the verify[a] that a challenge c was attested with a. In Fig. 9, the package AttPrim directly imports the digital signature primitives from SigPrim (Fig. 6). These include key generation, signing, and verification and are parameterized by a cryptographic hash function $\mathcal{H}$ that maps a challenge and system state to a message to be signed. On the other hand, AttProt extends the digital signature protocol (Definitions 4, 5). The attestation is a tuple that contains the hashed state and the respective signature over this state. This design ensures that the attestation is bound to both the current state and a fresh verifier-supplied challenge, thereby preventing replay attacks. The verify^a recomputes the hash internally from c and the current state, assuming the state is fixed—an assumption valid in static RA settings like a secure boot (the system's configuration does not change during the attestation). While more dynamic RA would require verifying against externally supplied hashes, this distinction is irrelevant for indistinguishability: both approaches yield equivalent results in our model. We adopt the constant-state version for simplicity and alignment with common RA setups. Security relies on the indistinguishability of the two packages. If an adversary could distinguish AttProt from AttProt′, the underlying signature scheme would be broken. The reduction leverages collision resistance by assuming *injective* (*uncurry Hash*) in SSProve, ensuring that the hash uniquely binds the challenge and state and preventing forgery via hash collisions.

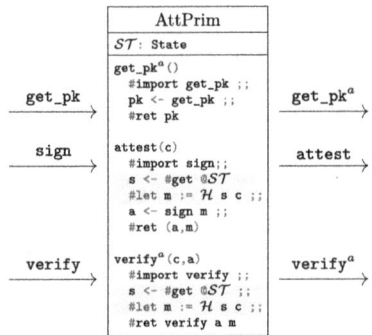

Fig. 9. Package for RA primitives.

3.2 Security Reduction and Indistinguishability (IND) for Protocols

To formally reduce the security of RA to that of digital signatures, we define both real and ideal versions of the attestation protocol by composing the corresponding digital signature packages. In the following definitions, we construct four key packages:

Definition 6 (AttProt$_{real}^{Prim}$). {*package* AttProt′ ⊚ AttPrim ∘ SigPrim$_{real}$ ∘ KeyGen}.

Definition 7 ($\texttt{AttProt}^{Prim}_{ideal}$).
{package $AttProt'$ ⊚ $AttPrim$ ∘ $SigPrim_{ideal}$ ∘ $KeyGen$}.

Definition 8 ($\texttt{AttProt}^{Prot}_{real}$). {package $AttProt$ ⊚ $SigProt_{real}$ }.

Definition 9 ($\texttt{AttProt}^{Prot}_{ideal}$). {package $AttProt$ ⊚ $SigProt_{ideal}$ }.

The first two represent the primitive-level abstraction of remote attestation, composed of real or ideal digital signature primitives. The latter two represent the protocol-level abstraction, containing the full digital signature protocol interface. With these definitions, we establish the indistinguishability of the real and ideal RA protocols, assuming that the underlying signature schemes are indistinguishable. The reduction proceeds through a sequence of games, progressively replacing real components with their ideal counterparts, preserving behavioral equivalence at each step. We formalize this as a refinement between the real and ideal packages:

Lemma 1 (Perfect IND of real Attestation Protocols). *For every adversary $\mathcal{A}$, the advantage of distinguishing the real packages for RA is 0:*

$$AttProt^{Prim}_{real} \approx_0 AttProt^{Prot}_{real}.$$

Proof. First, we will inline the procedures for the RA primitives in $\texttt{AttProt}^{Prim}_{real}$. Afterward, we inline $\texttt{SigProt}$ in the $\texttt{AttProt}^{Prot}_{real}$. Recomputing the hash in $\texttt{verify}^a$ is canceled because $\texttt{SigProt}$ reuses the message, in this case, the hashed state, as input to $\texttt{sign}$ and $\texttt{ver\_sig}$. The rest of the proof is obtained by applying the rules in relational Hoare logic.

Lemma 2 (Perfect IND for ideal Attestation Protocols). *For every adversary $\mathcal{A}$, the advantage of distinguishing the ideal packages for RA is 0:*

$$AttProt^{Prim}_{ideal} \approx_0 AttProt^{Prot}_{ideal}.$$

Proof. The proof reasoning is analogous to the proof of Lemma 1.

Theorem 2 (Security reduction for RA). *For every adversary $\mathcal{A}$, the advantage of distinguishing the packages $AttProt^{Prim}_{real}$ and $AttProt^{Prim}_{ideal}$ is less than or equal to the advantage of distinguishing the packages: $SigProt_{real}$ and $SigProt_{ideal}$*

$$\forall\, \mathcal{A},\ Adv\ \mathcal{A}\ AttProt^{Prim}_{real}\ AttProt^{Prim}_{ideal} \leq$$
$$Adv\ (\mathcal{A} \circ AttProt)\ SigProt_{ideal}\ SigProt_{real}.$$

Proof. SSProve allows us to use the following equalities:

```
1    Adv (A ∘ AttProt) SigProt_ideal  SigProt_real
2  = Adv A (AttProt ∘ SigProt_ideal) (AttProt ∘ SigProt_real)
3  = Adv A AttProt^Prot_real  AttProt^Prot_real
```

The first equality (Line 2) is achieved by reducing the lemma in SSProve (as shown in their Lemma 2.3 [1]). The second equality (Line 3) is, by definition, of the packages for remote attestation (Definitions 6, 7, 8, 9). Our goal then becomes

∀ A, Adv A AttProt$_{real}^{Prim}$ AttProt$_{ideal}^{Prim}$ ≤ Adv A AttProt$_{real}^{Prot}$ AttProt$_{ideal}^{Prot}$.

We define a triangle inequality (as shown in their Lemma 2.2 [1]), and use transitivity of the inequality (≤) to obtain:

Adv A AttProt$_{real}^{Prim}$ AttProt$_{real}^{Prot}$ + Adv A AttProt$_{real}^{Prot}$ AttProt$_{ideal}^{Prot}$

+ Adv A AttProt$_{ideal}^{Prot}$ AttProt$_{ideal}^{Prim}$ ≤ Adv A AttProt$_{real}^{Prot}$ AttProt$_{ideal}^{Prot}$.

By symmetry of games and Lemmas 1 and 2, our goal reduces to:

0 + Adv A AttProt$_{real}^{Prot}$ AttProt$_{ideal}^{Prot}$ + 0 ≤ Adv A AttProt$_{real}^{Prot}$ AttProt$_{ideal}^{Prot}$.

Clearly, this holds by the left and right identity of addition and the definition of ≤ itself.

Based on this result, we claim perfect indistinguishability for the RA protocol.

Theorem 3 (Perfect IND of RA). *For every adversary $\mathcal{A}$, the advantage of distinguishing the packages AttProt$_{real}^{Prim}$ and AttProt$_{ideal}^{Prim}$ is 0:*

$$AttProt_{real}^{Prim} \approx_0 AttProt_{ideal}^{Prim}.$$

Proof. To prove the theorem

Adv A AttProt$_{real}^{Prim}$ AttProt$_{ideal}^{Prim}$ ≤ 0

we apply our Reduction Theorem 2. The goal changes into:

Adv (A ∘ AttProt) SigProt$_{ideal}$ SigProt$_{real}$ ≤ 0

This holds by perfect indistinguishability of digital signatures (Theorem 1), even for an attacker $\mathcal{A}$ that runs the attestation protocol AttProt.

3.3 Security Reduction for Primitives

We refine our reduction by linking the security of RA primitives to that of digital signature primitives. Figure 10 defines the semantics of RA primitives using an auxiliary state $\mathcal{Z}$ that maps challenges c to attestations a.

Definition 10 (SigPrimAtt$_{real}$). *{package AttPrim ∘ SigPrim $_{real}$ ∘ KeyGen }.*

Definition 11 (SigPrimAtt$_{ideal}$). *{package AttPrim ∘ SigPrim $_{ideal}$ ∘ KeyGen }.*

Definition 12 (AttPrimSig$_{real}$).
$$\{package\ AttPrim_{real} \circ SigPrim_{real} \circ KeyGen\ \}.$$

Definition 13 (AttPrimSig$_{ideal}$).
$$\{package\ AttPrim_{ideal} \circ SigPrim_{ideal} \circ KeyGen\ \}.$$

The verify^a procedure queries this mapping. This package, denoted AttPrim$_{real}$, coincides with the earlier AttPrim from Fig. 9. In Definitions 10, 11, 12, 13, we lift digital signature primitives into the RA setting via the AttPrim package and use this to define both real and ideal RA primitive games.

AttPrim $_{real}$	AttPrim $_{ideal}$
$\mathcal{ST}$: State	$\mathcal{ST}$: State, $\mathcal{Z}$: (Challenge x Signature)

get_pk^a()
 #import get_pk ;;
 pk <- get_pk ;;
 #ret pk
	get_pk^a()
	 #import get_pk ;;
	 pk <- get_pk ;;
	 #ret pk

attest(c)
 #import sign;;
 s <- #get @$\mathcal{ST}$
 #let m := $\mathcal{H}$ s c ;;
 a <- sign m ;;
 	
 #ret (a,m)
	attest(c)
	 #import sign ;;
	 s <- #get @$\mathcal{ST}$;;
	 #let m := $\mathcal{H}$ s c ;;
	 a <- sign m ;;
	 Z <- #get @$\mathcal{Z}$;;
	 let Z' := Z ∪ {(c,a)} ;;
	 #put @$\mathcal{Z}$ Z' ;;
	 #ret (a,m)

verify^a(c,a)
 #import verify ;;
 s <- #get @$\mathcal{ST}$;;
 #let m := $\mathcal{H}$ s c ;;
 #ret verify a m
	verify^a(c,a)
	
	 Z <- #get @$\mathcal{Z}$;;
	 #ret ((c,a) ∈ Z)

Fig. 10. Game for RA Primitives

We first establish perfect indistinguishability between RA primitives and their lifted signature counterparts.

Lemma 3 (Perfect IND for real Attestation Primitives). *For every adversary $\mathcal{A}$, the advantage of distinguishing the real packages for RA primitives is 0:*
$$SigPrimAtt_{real} \approx_0 AttPrimSig_{real}.$$

Proof. The proof is by reflexivity on the fact that AttPrim and AttPrim$_{real}$ are equal.

Lemma 4 (Perfect IND for ideal Attestation Primitives). *For every adversary $\mathcal{A}$, the advantage of distinguishing the ideal packages for RA primitives is 0:*

$$\texttt{SigPrimAtt}_{ideal} \approx_0 \texttt{AttPrimSig}_{ideal}.$$

Proof. Instead of discarding the new memory location $\mathcal{Z}$ in $\texttt{AttPrim}_{ideal}$, our proof connects it to the $\mathcal{SIG}$ location in $\texttt{SigPrim}_{ideal}$ with the following invariant:

$\lambda\ (s_1,s_2),\ \texttt{heap\_ignore}\ \{\mathcal{Z}\}\ (s_1,s_2)\ \wedge$
$\quad\quad \texttt{Z\_to\_SIG}\ s_2.\mathcal{Z}\ s_2.\mathcal{ST} = s_1.\mathcal{SIG}.$

The $\texttt{heap\_ignore}$ invariant defines equality on all state location except $\mathcal{Z}$. The function $\texttt{Z\_to\_SIG}$ translates $\mathcal{Z}$ to $\mathcal{SIG}$ via the hash function $\mathcal{H}$.

```
Definition h_to_sig Z ST:
  let s := ST in
  map (λ (c,a), (H c s, a)) Z.
```

The proof consists of three proof obligations, one per procedure. The details are in our proof development. The most interesting part is in the proof obligation for $\texttt{verify}^a$, where we have to establish the following equality:

$(\mathcal{H}\ c_1\ s_1,\ a) \in \mathcal{SIG} = (c,\ a) \in \mathcal{Z}$

By applying our invariant and rewriting the left-hand side, we derive:

$(\mathcal{H}\ c_1\ s_1,\ a) = (\mathcal{H}\ c_2\ s_2,\ a)$

Note that the challenges and the states do not unify immediately because c_2 and s_2 come from the invariant. But unification only arises in the relational Hoare logic reasoning. To solve this goal, we need a vital property of the hash function $\mathcal{H}$; collision-resistance, a.k.a., injectivity.

Hypothesis 2 (Collision-Resistance) *Any hash function $\mathcal{H}$ used in RA must be injective:*

$\forall\ c_1\ s_1\ c_2\ s_2,\ \mathcal{H}\ c_1\ s_1 = \mathcal{H}\ c_2\ s_2 \rightarrow c_1 = c_2 \wedge s_1 = s_2.$

Theorem 4 (Security reduction for RA primitives). *For every adversary $\mathcal{A}$, the advantage of distinguishing the packages $\texttt{AttPrim}_{real}$ and $\texttt{AttPrim}_{ideal}$ is less than or equal to the advantage of distinguishing the packages: $\texttt{SigPrim}_{real}$ and $\texttt{SigPrim}_{ideal}$.*

$\forall\ \mathcal{A},\ \texttt{Adv}\ \mathcal{A}\ \texttt{AttPrim}_{real}\ \texttt{AttPrim}_{ideal} \leq$
$\quad \texttt{Adv}\ (\mathcal{A} \circ \texttt{AttPrim})\ \texttt{SigPrim}_{ideal}\ \texttt{SigPrim}_{real}.$

Proof. The proof follows the same structure as the reduction proof for the protocols (Theorem 2): We use the triangle inequality and apply Lemmas 3 and 4 afterward.

4 Related Work

Early work by Cabodi et al. [11,12] laid the foundation for formalizing hybrid RA properties, analyzing and comparing RA architectures using different model checkers. VRASED [29] extended this by introducing a verified hardware-software co-design for RA, targeting low-end embedded systems and addressing security limitations of hybrid architectures [3,20]. Hybrid RA mechanisms, such as HYDRA [19], further enhanced security by integrating formally verified microkernels, achieving memory isolation while reducing hardware complexity. Formal verification has also been applied to the industry [32] for one of Intel TDX's security-critical processes using ProVerif. Most symbolic approaches (e.g., ProVerif [6] and Tamarin [28]) are used to model attacks [16,24] but offer limited support for computational reductions or indistinguishability arguments. While these tools effectively validate protocol design [36], they cannot capture strong cryptographic assumptions such as unforgeability and negligible advantage. From a cryptographic proof perspective, tools like EasyCrypt [4] support formal game-based security proofs [33]. Recent work in EasyCrypt has been employed to verify existential [17] and strong unforgeability [15], but applying these techniques to RA has not been explored. Our work is the first step toward fully machine-checked, game-based security proofs of RA, formalizing semantic security through perfect indistinguishability in the computational model.

5 Conclusion

We presented a formal verification of semantic security for digital signatures and RA using the SSProve framework in the Rocq Prover. To the best of our knowledge, this is the first work to establish perfect indistinguishability in a machine-checked, game-based setting for RA protocols. This work formalizes and proves security against forgery in RA, providing a foundational guarantee based on sEUF-CMA. Our development reduces the security of RA to the security of secure signatures. We showed that the perfect indistinguishability of signatures can be lifted to prove the security of RA protocols.

In future work, we aim to extend our formalization to verify complex security protocols [13] and strengthen RA's overall security [16,24,34]. Beyond SSProve, we intend to integrate our formalization into the Clutch framework, which supports probabilistic relational reasoning in Iris [25] via ghost state and presampling tapes and may allow formalizing attestation semantics in more expressive systems [22].

Acknowledgements. We appreciate Dr. Carmine Abate and the anonymous reviewers for their valuable feedback. This work has been supported by the Federal Ministry of Research, Technology and Space of Germany through the 6G-ICAS4Mobility project (grant no. 16KISK231) and the 6G-Plattform Germany project (grant no. 16KISK046). Additionally, the authors are also financed based on the budget passed by the Saxonian State Parliament in Germany.

A Appendix

```
1   def RSA.KeyGen ():
2     p <$ P ;;
3     q <$ Q p ;;
4     assert (p != q) ;;
5
6     let φⁿ := (p-1)*(q-1) in
7
8     e <$ E φⁿ ;;
9     let d := e⁻¹ (mod φⁿ) in
10    let ed := e * d in
11    assert (ed == 1) ;;
12
13    let n := p * q in
14    let pk := (n,e) in
15    let sk := (n,d) in
16
17    #ret (pk,sk)
```

Fig. 11. RSA-based Key Generation.

RSA-based Digital Signatures. To make sure that our Hypothesis 1 for functional correctness of digital signatures as stated in Fig. 1 is indeed sufficient, we implement RSA-based digital signatures. RSA-based signatures are one of the schemes from the TPM 2.0 specification. We take full advantage of SSProve and its access to the rich ecosystem of existing developments. A full definition of RSA along with a proof of functional correctness is available in the `mathcomp-extra` library.[6] We placed this proof at the heart of our proof for functional correctness of RSA-based digital signatures. A substantial part of our development then evolves around the setup of the sampling spaces. In Fig. 11, we list a condensed and slightly simplified versioni of the code for Σ.KeyGen. The interested reader can find the full implementation in our Rocq Prover development.

Sample Spaces. The code highlights the three places where we sample values from uniform distributions. In total, we need to sample values for p, q and e (Lines 2,3 and 8). From these values, we calculate d (Line 9) and define the public and the secret key to return (Lines 13–17). Our sampling spaces P, Q and E establish the properties that are need for our functional correctness proof. The space that all three spaces are based upon must obey the following requirements. First, we need to sample prime numbers. Second, there need to exist at least three distinct prime numbers. The following is our mathcomp-based definition:

```
Variable n : ℕ.
Definition 𝔹 : Type := 'I_(n.+6).
Definition primes : finType := {x :𝔹 | prime x}.
Definition P : {set primes} := [set : primes].
```

This definition fulfills both requirement. The set P contains only primes. And P contains at least the primes that are smaller than 6, i.e., 2, 3 and 5.

The sampling space Q now needs to establish the property that p != q (Line 4). That is, Q is depending on the value that was sampled before from P. But Q has to establish yet another property for the space E:

---

[6] https://github.com/thery/mathcomp-extra.

```
Definition Q p :=
  let P' := P :\ p in
  if p == 2
  then P' \ 3
  else if p == 3
       then P' :\ 2
       else P'.
```

In RSA.KeyGen, we use p and q to compute ϕ^n, the Euler totient function (Line 6). This ϕ^n then defines E:

```
Definition E' {m: B * B)} (H: 2<m) :=
  { x : Z_m | 1 < x && coprime m x}.
Definition E {m: B * B)} (H: 2<m) : {set (E' H)} :=
  [set : E' H].
```

E needs to have at least one value to sample e (Line 8). That is, $\phi^n > 3$. And hence, the construction of Q must exclude the two cases where p := 2 and q := 3 or vice versa because

$$\phi^n = (2-1)*(3-1) = 5 \not> 5$$

would not provide a space to sample a coprime number e from.

A.1 Functional Correctness

Based on this sample space construction, we can now proof functional correctness for our digital signature scheme.

Theorem 5 (Functional Correctness for RSA-based Digital Signatures). *Given the definitions of our RSA-based signature scheme* $\Sigma := RSA$, *the following holds:*

```
∀ m sk pk,
  ((sk,pk) <- RSA.KeyGen) ->
  RSA.VerSig pk (RSA.Sign sk m) m == true.
```

Proof. The proof establishes all necessary properties from the construction of the sampling spaces and finally reduces to the functional correctness of RSA itself. Our Rocq Prover development has all the details.

References

1. Abate, C., et al.: Ssprove: a foundational framework for modular cryptographic proofs in coq. In: 2021 IEEE 34th Computer Security Foundations Symposium (CSF), pp. 1–15. IEEE (2021)
2. Angelogianni, A., Politis, I., Xenakis, C.: How many fido protocols are needed? Analysing the technology, security and compliance. ACM Comput. Surv. **56**(8) (2024). https://doi.org/10.1145/3654661
3. Banks, A.S., Kisiel, M., Korsholm, P.: Remote attestation: a literature review. arXiv preprint arXiv:2105.02466 (2021)

4. Barthe, G., Dupressoir, F., Grégoire, B., Kunz, C., Schmidt, B., Strub, P.Y.: Easycrypt: a tutorial. International School on Foundations of Security Analysis and Design, pp. 146–166 (2012)
5. Barthe, G., Grégoire, B., Zanella Béguelin, S.: Formal certification of code-based cryptographic proofs. In: Proceedings of the 36th Annual ACM SIGPLAN-SIGACT Symposium on Principles of Programming Languages, pp. 90–101 (2009)
6. Blanchet, B.: Automatic verification of security protocols in the symbolic model: the verifier proverif. In: International School on Foundations of Security Analysis and Design, pp. 54–87. Springer (2012)
7. Brasser, F., Rasmussen, K.B., Sadeghi, A.R., Tsudik, G.: Remote attestation for low-end embedded devices: the prover's perspective. In: Proceedings of the 53rd Annual Design Automation Conference. DAC 2016. Association for Computing Machinery, New York (2016). https://doi.org/10.1145/2897937.2898083
8. Brzuska, C., Delignat-Lavaud, A., Fournet, C., Kohbrok, K., Kohlweiss, M.: State separation for code-based game-playing proofs. In: Advances in Cryptology– ASIACRYPT 2018: 24th International Conference on the Theory and Application of Cryptology and Information Security, Brisbane, QLD, Australia, 2–6 December 2018, Proceedings, Part III 24, pp. 222–249. Springer (2018)
9. Brzuska, C., Lipiäinen, V.: Companion to cryptographic primitives, protocols and proofs (2021)
10. Buhren, R., Werling, C., Seifert, J.P.: Insecure until proven updated: analyzing AMD SEV's remote attestation. In: Proceedings of the 2019 ACM SIGSAC Conference on Computer and Communications Security, CCS 2019, pp. 1087–1099. Association for Computing Machinery, New York (2019). https://doi.org/10.1145/3319535.3354216
11. Cabodi, G., Camurati, P., Loiacono, C., Pipitone, G., Savarese, F., Vendraminetto, D.: Formal verification of embedded systems for remote attestation. WSEAS Trans. Comput. **14**, 760–769 (2015)
12. Cabodi, G., Camurati, P., Finocchiaro, S.F., Loiacono, C., Savarese, F., Vendraminetto, D.: Secure embedded architectures: taint properties verification. In: 2016 International Conference on Development and Application Systems (DAS), pp. 150–157. IEEE (2016)
13. Camenisch, J., Chen, L., Drijvers, M., Lehmann, A., Novick, D., Urian, R.: One TPM to bind them all: fixing TPM 2.0 for provably secure anonymous attestation. In: 2017 IEEE Symposium on Security and Privacy (SP), pp. 901–920. IEEE (2017)
14. Chen, G., Zhang, Y., Lai, T.H.: Opera: open remote attestation for intel's secure enclaves. In: Proceedings of the 2019 ACM SIGSAC Conference on Computer and Communications Security, CCS 2019, pp. 2317–2331. Association for Computing Machinery, New York (2019). https://doi.org/10.1145/3319535.3354220
15. Cortier, V., Dragan, C.C., Dupressoir, F., Warinschi, B.: Machine-checked proofs for electronic voting: privacy and verifiability for belenios. In: 2018 IEEE 31st Computer Security Foundations Symposium (CSF), pp. 298–312. IEEE (2018)
16. De Oliveira Nunes, I., Jakkamsetti, S., Rattanavipanon, N., Tsudik, G.: On the toctou problem in remote attestation. In: Proceedings of the 2021 ACM SIGSAC Conference on Computer and Communications Security, pp. 2921–2936 (2021)
17. Dupressoir, F., Zain, S.: Machine-checking unforgeability proofs for signature schemes with tight reductions to the computational Diffie-Hellman problem. In: 2021 IEEE 34th Computer Security Foundations Symposium (CSF), pp. 1–15. IEEE (2021)

18. Dupressoir, F., Kohbrok, K., Oechsner, S.: Bringing state-separating proofs to easycrypt a security proof for cryptobox. In: 2022 IEEE 35th Computer Security Foundations Symposium (CSF), pp. 227–242 (2022). https://doi.org/10.1109/CSF54842.2022.9919671
19. Eldefrawy, K., Rattanavipanon, N., Tsudik, G.: Hydra: hybrid design for remote attestation (using a formally verified microkernel). In: Proceedings of the 10th ACM Conference on Security and Privacy in Wireless and Mobile Networks, pp. 99–110 (2017)
20. Francillon, A., Nguyen, Q., Rasmussen, K.B., Tsudik, G.: A minimalist approach to remote attestation. In: 2014 Design, Automation & Test in Europe Conference & Exhibition (DATE), pp. 1–6. IEEE (2014)
21. Goldwasser, S., Micali, S., Rivest, R.L.: A digital signature scheme secure against adaptive chosen-message attacks. SIAM J. Comput. **17**(2), 281–308 (1988)
22. Gregersen, S.O., Aguirre, A., Haselwarter, P.G., Tassarotti, J., Birkedal, L.: Asynchronous probabilistic couplings in higher-order separation logic. Proc. ACM Program. Lang. **8**(POPL), 753–784 (2024)
23. Trusted Platform Module Main Specification (2023). https://trustedcomputinggroup.org/resource/tpm-library-specification/0
24. Ibrahim, A., Sadeghi, A.R., Zeitouni, S.: Seed: secure non-interactive attestation for embedded devices. In: Proceedings of the 10th ACM Conference on Security and Privacy in Wireless and Mobile Networks, pp. 64–74 (2017)
25. Jung, R., et al.: Iris: Monoids and invariants as an orthogonal basis for concurrent reasoning. ACM SIGPLAN Notices **50**(1), 637–650 (2015)
26. Koeberl, P., Schulz, S., Sadeghi, A.R., Varadharajan, V.: Trustlite: a security architecture for tiny embedded devices. In: Proceedings of the Ninth European Conference on Computer Systems. EuroSys 2014. Association for Computing Machinery, New York (2014). https://doi.org/10.1145/2592798.2592824
27. Mahboubi, A., Tassi, E.: Mathematical components. Online book (2021)
28. Meier, S., Schmidt, B., Cremers, C., Basin, D.: The tamarin prover for the symbolic analysis of security protocols. In: Computer Aided Verification: 25th International Conference, CAV 2013, Saint Petersburg, Russia, 13–19 July 2013. Proceedings 25, pp. 696–701. Springer (2013)
29. Nunes, I.D.O., Eldefrawy, K., Rattanavipanon, N., Steiner, M., Tsudik, G.: Vrased: a verified hardware/software co-design for remote attestation. In: USENIX Security Symposium, pp. 1429–1446 (2019)
30. Pornin, T., Stern, J.P.: Digital signatures do not guarantee exclusive ownership. In: Applied Cryptography and Network Security: Third International Conference, ACNS 2005, New York, NY, USA, 7–10 June 2005. Proceedings 3, pp. 138–150. Springer (2005)
31. Rosulek, M.: The Joy of Cryptography. Oregon State University (2021)
32. Sardar, M.U., Musaev, S., Fetzer, C.: Demystifying attestation in intel trust domain extensions via formal verification. IEEE Access **9**, 83067–83079 (2021)
33. Shoup, V.: Sequences of games: a tool for taming complexity in security proofs. cryptology eprint archive (2004)
34. Van Dijk, M., Rhodes, J., Sarmenta, L.F., Devadas, S.: Offline untrusted storage with immediate detection of forking and replay attacks. In: Proceedings of the 2007 ACM Workshop on Scalable Trusted Computing, pp. 41–48 (2007)

35. Wadler, P.: The essence of functional programming. In: Proceedings of the 19th ACM SIGPLAN-SIGACT Symposium on Principles of Programming Languages, POPL 1992, pp. 1–14. Association for Computing Machinery, New York (1992). httpps://doi.org/10.1145/143165.143169
36. Wesemeyer, S., Newton, C.J., Treharne, H., Chen, L., Sasse, R., Whitefield, J.: Formal analysis and implementation of a TPM 2.0-based direct anonymous attestation scheme. In: Proceedings of the 15th ACM Asia Conference on Computer and Communications Security, pp. 784–798 (2020)

SAFEPATH: Encryption-Less On-Demand Input Path Protection for Mobile Devices

Xin Zhang and Yifan Zhang[✉]

Binghamton University, Binghamton, NY 13902, USA
zhangy@binghamton.edu

Abstract. Sensitive data from input devices such as touchscreens and microphones is vulnerable to attackers with OS-level privileges. While prior work has primarily focused on protecting data after it reaches applications, the problem of securing the data path from the device to the application remains underexplored. Existing solutions either use encryption, which incurs significant performance overhead and complexity in key management, or bypass the OS entirely, which reduces compatibility and requires substantial changes to the application.

We present SAFEPATH, a system that secures input data paths without encryption or OS bypass. SAFEPATH leverages ARM memory virtualization to implement a minimal memory hypervisor that intercepts device input data at its entry point into the system, stores it securely, and transmits only lightweight data indices to applications. This design isolates sensitive data from the OS while preserving the native input path structure and requiring minimal modifications to applications. We prototype SAFEPATH on ARM hardware and support six different input devices. Evaluation shows that SAFEPATH blocks OS-level access to input data while preserving system performance. For example, under high system load, it reduces audio frame loss by over 45% compared to encryption-based approaches and maintains over 98% of native throughput across all tested devices. These results demonstrate that SAFEPATH offers strong protection with low overhead and practical deployability.

1 Introduction

Mobile devices increasingly serve as the gateway to sensitive personal services, such as secure messaging, mobile banking, and biometric authentication. These services depend on input from hardware peripherals, such as touchscreens, microphones, fingerprint sensors, and cameras, that often carry highly sensitive data. Unfortunately, this input data is typically exposed to the operating system (OS) before reaching its destination application. On platforms like Android, input data traverses multiple layers and memory buffers before reaching applications, creating a wide attack surface for adversaries with OS-level privileges. As a result, attackers with kernel-level access can intercept or tamper with raw input data in transit, undermining the confidentiality and integrity of the entire interaction. For instance, touch coordinates from a touchscreen could allow an attacker to infer passwords [5,29,54], while audio data from a microphone could expose private conversations [37,41,48]. Even seemingly innocuous sensor readings, such as those from accelerometers, can be exploited to extract sensitive information like voice data [2,7,33,53] or infer touchscreen taps [13,34,36,50].

Existing efforts to protect input data typically fall into two categories. The first category assumes that a trusted input path already exists and focuses on shielding application memory after the data is received. Most existing works fall into this category. A smaller body of work belongs to the second category, which explicitly secures an input path between the data source and the data recipient. They achieve their goals by either *encrypting input data end-to-end* or *bypassing the untrusted OS*. However, both directions suffer from significant limitations: *Encryption-based approaches* introduce substantial performance overhead, which can be prohibitive for latency-sensitive tasks such as voice input or gesture recognition. They also expand the trusted computing base (TCB) to include complex cryptographic modules, which are themselves vulnerable to side-channel leakage. *OS-bypassing solutions*, on the other hand, often require invasive changes to applications and drivers, limit compatibility with standard input processing stacks, and prevent benign in-OS processing operations from being used. A more detailed review of prior work is provided in Sect. 2.

Securing the input path in a way that avoids both encryption and OS bypassing presents several challenges. *First*, the system must prevent a compromised OS from accessing sensitive input data, even though it controls the driver stack and shared memory. *Second*, it must preserve compatibility with the existing input flow, allowing input to pass through standard OS components, so that user applications and in-OS processing can function normally. *Third*, the solution should avoid the overhead and complexity of cryptographic solutions, which are burdensome on resource-constrained devices. *Finally*, the solution should allow applications to selectively enable protection for individual input sessions, without introducing significant development effort or performance cost.

We present SAFEPATH, a system that enables secure input data paths on ARM-based mobile platforms without relying on encryption or bypassing the OS. SAFEPATH uses ARM's hardware memory virtualization support [3,17,20] to construct a minimal hypervisor that intercepts and securely stores input data as it first enters system memory, typically in the driver's initial software-visible buffer. Rather than passing the raw input through the OS, SAFEPATH replaces it with opaque indexes, which propagate through the system's existing input path. Applications later use a controlled hypercall interface to retrieve the original data from the hypervisor, ensuring that only the intended recipient can access the protected input. This index-based indirection model preserves the original data flow and allows in-OS input processing to continue as normal, while preventing even a fully compromised OS from accessing the underlying input data. SAFEPATH supports on-demand protection that can be enabled per device or per session, and it minimizes trusted code by confining all sensitive logic to a small hypervisor with a narrow interface.

It is important to note that SAFEPATH is not intended as a complete end-to-end solution for securing input data throughout its lifecycle. Rather, it complements existing mechanisms, such as trusted execution environments (TEEs) (e.g., Intel SGX [30], ARM TrustZone [42]), that can protect input after it reaches the application. This modular approach allows SAFEPATH to focus on a specific but under-addressed segment of the input data flow: from the device hardware up to the application boundary.

We have implemented a prototype of SAFEPATH on an ODROID-XU4 development board [35] running Android 4.4.4, supporting six types of input devices: touchscreen, microphone, camera, GPS receiver, fingerprint scanner, and accelerometer. Our evaluation shows that SAFEPATH prevents input data leakage in the presence of a fully compromised OS, while incurring negligible performance overhead and requiring minimal changes to applications. Compared to encryption-based approaches, SAFEPATH performs significantly better under high I/O load, and it supports input scenarios, such as OS-mediated processing, that are infeasible for OS-bypassing systems.

In summary, we the following contributions:

- We identify limitations in prior approaches to securing device input paths and motivate the need for a non-encryption, OS-compatible solution.
- We design SAFEPATH, a hypervisor-based system that securely intercepts and delivers input data without disrupting the original input path or requiring cryptographic protection.
- We prototype SAFEPATH on real hardware and demonstrate its effectiveness across diverse input types, with low performance overhead and minimal developer effort.

2 Background and Related Work

Background. Securing device input paths against OS-level attackers is difficult due to the following two primary reasons.

(1) *System and hardware vulnerabilities*: OS-level attackers can exploit numerous classes of vulnerabilities to extract sensitive input data. For example, memory disclosure bugs allow unauthorized access to process and kernel memory [21,22,24,43,46]. Transient-execution attacks such as Spectre, Meltdown, and their variants can leak sensitive information by exploiting speculative behavior in modern processors [9,11,14,31,32,40]. In addition, kernel-level malware such as rootkits can gain full access to kernel memory, including buffers that temporarily store raw input [12,18,27,44,45].

(2) *Wide attack surface in input data paths*: Our analysis of Android source code reveals that input devices have extensive attack surfaces along their input data paths. An *input path* refers to the sequence of memory locations (buffers) through which input device data travels before reaching the application. In Android, these

Table 1. Number of "travel stops" in device input path

	DD	HAL	AF	Total
Touchscreen	8	0	6	14
Microphone	1	1	3	5
Camera	1	3	1	5
Accelerometer	7	3	5	15
GPS receiver	2	4	2	8

DD: Device driver
HAL: Hardware Abstraction Layer
AF: Android Framework

buffers typically span three layers: the device driver layer, the hardware abstraction layer (HAL), and the Android framework layer. Table 1 illustrates the number of "travel stops" in the input paths of various devices. For example, the touchscreen input path has 14 travel stops, each representing a potential vulnerability point where attackers can intercept and misuse sensitive data.

Related Work. Existing solutions fall into two categories depending on when and how they provide input protection. The *first category* assumes the input path is already trusted and focuses on protecting application memory after the input arrives. The *second category* protects the input path itself, ensuring that data can reach applications securely even in the presence of an untrusted OS.

Most prior work belongs to the first category above [1,4,6,8,10,15,16,23,25,26,28,38,47,51,52]. In contrast, only a few systems attempt to secure the path between device and application directly [19,49,55,56]. These systems employ one of two main design philosophies: *OS-bypassing* and *encryption-based methods*.

OS-bypassing approaches establish new trusted channels that route input data around the OS entirely. For example, they may configure hardware devices to deliver data directly to a trusted VM or enclave, bypassing all software components in the untrusted OS [19,55,56]. While effective in principle, these systems suffer from poor compatibility and limited flexibility. They require non-trivial changes to applications and drivers and are unsuitable for use cases where input must be pre-processed by OS components, for instance, gesture detection in touchscreens or audio buffering in HALs.

Encryption-based approaches, on the other hand, protect data by encrypting it at the point of origin and decrypting it only at a trusted endpoint [19,49]. While this allows the reuse of the original data path, it introduces two serious drawbacks. *First*, cryptographic key distribution and protection are non-trivial, especially in adversarial environments. As demonstrated in past work, attackers can extract encryption keys stored in memory via transient execution attacks, even in trusted computing environments like SGX [39]. *Second*, encryption and decryption introduce significant performance overhead, which grows with input volume. In our experiments, encrypting audio streams under system load led to substantial frame loss, in contrast to our optimized SAFEPATH design that maintained performance near native levels.

3 SAFEPATH Design

3.1 Threat Model

SAFEPATH addresses the threat of OS-level compromise on mobile devices. We assume an adversary who has full control over the operating system and can inspect, modify, and replay any data that passes through the OS. Our design makes the following trust and threat assumptions:

(A1) Trusted minimal core for input data protection: SAFEPATH relies on a small, isolated component, introduced later, that operates independently of the compromised OS to manage sensitive input data. We assume this component correctly enforces memory isolation and controls access to protected data, with a minimal code base to facilitate verification.

(A2) Application trust post-data retrieval: SAFEPATH protects input data until it is retrieved by the designated application. After retrieval, securing the data is the application's responsibility, potentially with support from trusted execution environment (TEE) techniques, such as Intel SGX [30] and ARM TrustZone [42]. SAFEPATH does not protect against compromises within the application.

(A3) No physical or side-channel attacks: SAFEPATH does not protect against physical attacks, such as direct hardware probing, nor against side-channel attacks like cache timing or speculative execution leakage. These threats are orthogonal and require complementary defenses.

(A4) Trusted secure boot: We assume the system boots into a trusted initial state, establishing integrity for SAFEPATH's isolated component and preventing adversary control before SAFEPATH's protections are activated.

(A5) Denial-of-service (DoS) attacks are out of scope: SAFEPATH does not attempt to prevent DoS attacks, such as blocking or dropping input data before it reaches applications. Our focus is on protecting the confidentiality of input data against a compromised OS. We assume adversaries prioritize stealth and data exfiltration over causing observable disruptions.

3.2 SAFEPATH Overview

The High Level Idea. We define a device input data path, or simply input path, as the sequence of memory locations (buffers) that hold input device data before it reaches an application. The first buffer in this path is the first memory location in the software stack that captures the data generated by hardware. We refer to this initial location as the **first stop buffer (FSB)**. Because attackers with OS-level privileges can freely access memory content, protecting an input path typically requires a **trusted software entity (TSE)**, which is a component operating at a higher privilege level than the OS, to intercept input data as it is written to the FSB. The TSE then either sends the data directly to the application, bypassing the OS, or encrypts the data and allows it to continue traveling along the original input path.

At first glance, encryption appears to be the only way to preserve the input path while ensuring data confidentiality. However, closer examination shows that encryption-based solutions rely on two roots of trust: the TSE that intercepts and encrypts the data, and the cryptographic algorithms and key management protecting it during transmission. If either is compromised, the confidentiality of input data is at risk.

SAFEPATH adopts a different approach by relying solely on the TSE for data protection. Rather than encrypting and forwarding input data along the original path, the TSE securely stores the data and transmits only indexes, which are opaque references to protected data chunks, through the untrusted OS to the application. Upon receiving these indexes, the application can securely query the TSE to retrieve the original input data.

This design has two major advantages over encryption-based approaches. *First*, SAFEPATH significantly reduces trust dependencies: it relies only on the TSE's memory isolation, eliminating the need to trust cryptographic primitives or key management against OS-level attackers. *Second*, by avoiding cryptographic operations, SAFEPATH achieves substantially lower overhead compared to encryption-based solutions. We analyze the reasons behind these performance gains in Sect. 5 and present detailed evaluation results in Sect. 6.2.

Operations Overview. Figure 1 illustrates the data flow in both the native system and the SAFEPATH-enhanced system. We first describe the baseline operation before presenting the changes introduced by SAFEPATH.

In the native system, when an input device generates data, the device driver writes the data into the first stop buffer (FSB) (Op. ①). The data then flows through multiple OS-managed buffers spanning the Linux kernel and Android framework (Op. ②) before reaching the application (Op. ③). Because these intermediate buffers are exposed to the OS, attackers with OS-level privilege can observe or tamper with the data.

When SAFEPATH protection is enabled, the input flow is modified to secure data confidentiality while preserving OS compatibility. As input data arrives, the device driver attempts to write to the FSB as usual (Op. ❶). However, SAFEPATH's trusted hypervisor, the **Tiny Memory Hypervisor (TMH)**, sets the FSB to be read-only for OS code, causing any driver write to trap to the TMH (Op. ❷). The TMH intercepts the data, partitions it into chunks, assigns indexes, and securely stores the data in protected memory (Op. ❸). Instead of transmitting the original data, the TMH writes the generated indexes back into the FSB (Op. ❹), allowing

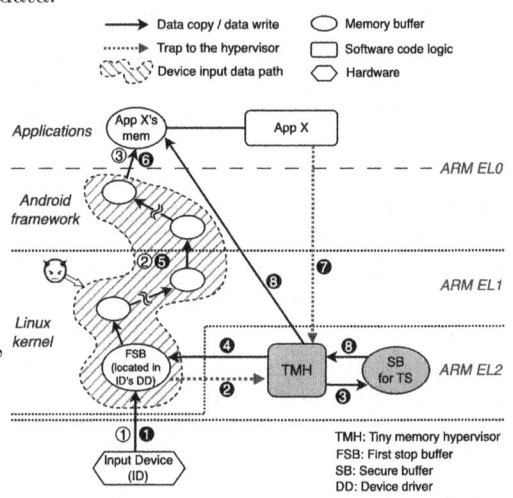

Fig. 1. SAFEPATH operations overview. (Black numbers in white circles mark the sequence of ops when SAFEPATH protection is disabled (i.e., the native system). White numbers in black circles mark the sequence of ops when SAFEPATH protection is enabled.)

the OS to continue handling input events as normal. The indexes propagate through the OS input stack (Op. ❺) and eventually reach the application (Op. ❻). Upon receiving an event containing indexes, the application calls the **Data Retrieval Interface (DRI)** provided by the TMH, supplying the device ID, the indexes, and a buffer to receive the original data (Op. ❼). After validating the request, the TMH retrieves the corresponding data from secure storage and returns it to the application (Op. ❽). Throughout this process, SAFEPATH enforces a one-time-use policy for indexes: any attempt to misuse or replay an index is detected and triggers user alerts about potential breaches. This design secures input data end-to-end against a compromised OS while preserving compatibility with the native event-driven input model.

3.3 The Tiny Memory Hypervisor (TMH)

SAFEPATH's trusted software component, the Tiny Memory Hypervisor (TMH), secures input device data against a compromised OS. The TMH, operating at ARM Exception Level 2 (EL2), above the OS at EL1, realizes the Trusted Software Entity (TSE) introduced earlier and leverages ARM hardware virtualization to enforce memory isolation without disrupting OS execution.

The TMH's primary role is to intercept input data at the FSB (Sect. 3.2) before the OS can access it, securely store the data in protected memory, and mediate its retrieval by applications. To achieve this, the TMH configures the FSB memory pages to be read-only from the OS's perspective (EL1). Any attempt by a device driver to write to the FSB triggers a stage-2 permission fault, trapping execution to the TMH at EL2. Upon trapping, the TMH captures the input data, partitions it into chunks, assigns each chunk a unique index, and stores the data in memory regions protected by stage-2 translation control.

After securing the data, the TMH substitutes the original input in the FSB with the corresponding indexes and returns control to the device driver. From the OS's viewpoint, input event processing proceeds normally, but only opaque indexes traverse the input path instead of sensitive data.

The TMH also mediates application access to protected input data. When an application receives input events containing indexes, it interacts with the TMH through a controlled retrieval interface to obtain the original data. To defend against misuse, the TMH enforces a one-time-use policy: each index can be resolved exactly once, and any attempts at reuse or tampering are detected.

Unlike traditional hypervisors, the TMH focuses solely on securing input paths. It does not manage device emulation, guest scheduling, or general I/O. This narrow scope keeps the TCB small and auditable. By relying on ARM's two-stage memory translation and privilege separation, the TMH provides robust isolation guarantees with minimal system impact.

3.4 Intercepting Input Data at the First Stop Buffer (FSB)

The FSB is the first memory location in software that holds device input after it leaves the hardware. Typically, the FSB resides in the device driver. For devices using direct memory access (DMA), input data initially

```
1   char* ptrFSB = kmalloc(32, GFP_KERNEL);
2   ...
3   kfree(ptrFSB); //when driver is
                    unloaded
```

Fig. 2. FSB redirection illustration: before redirection

lands in a DMA buffer, which could be treated as the FSB. For simplicity, we uniformly consider the driver's first buffer as the FSB, since SAFEPATH's protection mechanism applies equally in either case. We discuss handling DMA devices later in Sect. 4.

To intercept input data at the FSB (Op. ❷ in Fig. 1), the TMH configures the FSB's memory pages as read-only (R/O) for EL1 and EL0 code, using ARM's stage-2 translation control. This ensures that any write to the FSB by the device driver triggers a stage-2 permission fault, trapping execution to the TMH at EL2. However, a challenge arises because stage-2 permissions are enforced at page granularity, typically 4 KB, while an FSB is often much smaller (e.g., tens of bytes). Therefore, marking an entire page as R/O would inadvertently restrict access to unrelated memory contents, causing excessive trapping and performance degradation.

```
1   char* ptrFSB = PAB_alloc(32);
2   ......
3   PAB_free(ptrFSB); //when driver is
         unloaded
```

Fig. 3. FSB redirection illustration: after redirection

To address this challenge, our solution allocates FSBs from a special page-aligned buffer (PAB), which is a contiguous, page-aligned memory region reserved exclusively for storing FSBs of all protected input devices. Device drivers are modified to allocate and free FSBs through wrapper functions, PAB_alloc() and PAB_free(), replacing the standard kmalloc() and kfree() calls (Figs. 2 and 3). Specifically, PAB_alloc() allocates a desired memory region from the PAB, and PAB_free() returns it. This redirection confines FSBs to a easily protected memory region without affecting unrelated memory.

```
1   char * roFSB = ROPAB_alloc(32);
2   char * rwFSB = RWPAB_alloc(32);
3   char * ptrFSB;
4   ...
5   // Line 6-9 is called every time
         the FSB is about to receive
         data from the hardware.
6   if (protectionIsEnabled)
7       ptrFSB = roFSB;
8   else
9       ptrFSB = rwFSB;
10  ...
11  PAB_free(roFSB); //when driver is
         unloaded
12  PAB_free(rwFSB); //when driver is
         unloaded
```

Fig. 4. Dynamic FSB redirection illustration

However, the initial PAB redirection has a drawback: since the PAB stores FSBs for all protected devices, enabling SAFEPATH protection for one device also affects all other devices sharing the same PAB, even if protection is not desired. To support per-device selective protection, SAFEPATH maintains two PABs of equal size: one always configured as read-only (R/O) for protected devices, and the other as read-write (R/W) for unprotected ones. At runtime, the device driver dynamically redirects FSB usage to the appropriate PAB by maintaining two pointers and selecting the correct one before each input transaction based on the user preference (Fig. 4). This dynamic PAB redirection allows SAFEPATH to selectively protect individual input devices with minimal overhead while preserving compatibility with existing driver logic.

3.5 Input Data Partitioning and Indexing

When SAFEPATH protection is enabled, any attempt to write input data to the FSB triggers a trap to the TMH. The TMH captures the original input data and saves it into a secure buffer (Op. ❸ in Fig. 1), while placing indexes corresponding to the input chunks into the FSB (Op. ❹).

Partitioning and indexing are straightforward for devices that generate event-like inputs, such as touchscreen taps, GPS fixes, and motion sensor readings. These events have clear boundaries and consistent sizes, making it easy to partition input data along event boundaries. Each index written to the FSB occupies the same space as the original event, ensuring that the OS input pipeline remains undisturbed. For example, if a touchscreen event is 32 bytes, the TMH writes a 32-byte index into the FSB by padding as needed.

Handling stream input data, such as microphone or camera streams, is more complex because there are no natural boundaries in the incoming data. However, we observe that system components process stream data in well-defined batches. As shown in Fig. 5(a), microphone input flows through the device driver using an 8 KB FSB, is polled by the hardware abstraction layer (HAL) in 4 KB units, and further processed by the `AudioFlinger` service in 1 KB chunks.

Based on this observation, the TMH partitions stream input based on the smallest batch size seen along the processing path. Figure 5(b) illustrates this approach: the TMH partitions incoming audio into 1 KB chunks, stores the chunks securely, and places corresponding indexes into the FSB. As with event-like inputs, each index occupies the same space as its original data chunk—in this case, 1 KB—to preserve compatibility with downstream software.

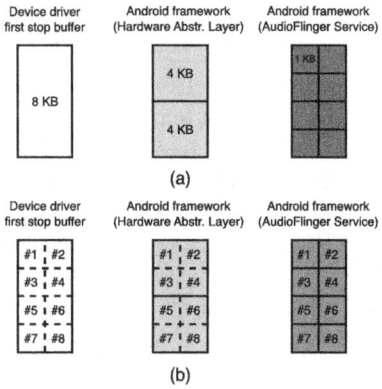

Fig. 5. Partitioning and indexing stream audio data from microphone. (a) In the native system, different software entities process the stream data in different sizes. (b) The tiny memory hypervisor partitions stream audio data based on the smallest processing sizes used in the native system.

3.6 The Data Retrieval Interface (DRI)

The TMH provides the Data Retrieval Interface (DRI) for applications to fetch original input data after receiving input indexes (Op. ❼ in Fig. 1). The DRI is implemented as a hypercall, a direct communication path between the caller and the TMH. However, user applications run at EL0 and cannot directly invoke hypercalls, which are accessible only from EL1 or higher. To bridge this gap, we design the DRI as a sys-hypercall, which is a standard system call that internally issues a hypercall—allowing applications to access TMH services indirectly.

The sys-hypercall DRI requires three input arguments: the device ID, an input data chunk index, and a memory buffer to receive the retrieved data.

Upon invocation, the TMH uses the device ID to locate the correct secure buffer, retrieves the original data chunk based on the index, and writes it to the caller-provided buffer (Op. ❽ in Fig. 1).

Detecting Abusive Usage of the DRI. Security concerns may arise because the sys-hypercall DRI does not require caller authentication. In principle, any process, including malicious ones, could invoke the DRI and attempt to retrieve protected input data.

SAFEPATH mitigates this risk by enforcing a single-use policy for input indexes. For input data intended for one receiving application, such as touchscreen events delivered to a banking app, each index should be resolved exactly once. The TMH tracks usage of all input indexes: if an index is used more than once, the system triggers a security alert, warning the user of a potential compromise and suggesting that the affected input device should be disabled.

An attacker might attempt to bypass this defense by intercepting indexes and preventing them from reaching the legitimate application, ensuring each index is still used only once. However, this approach introduces a new weakness: the receiving application would observe missing inputs, easily detecting the attack. Given our threat model assumption (A3) that attackers seek to avoid detection, such denial-based strategies are unlikely.

Through single-use tracking and anomaly detection, SAFEPATH secures the DRI against unauthorized retrievals without relying on complex caller authentication mechanisms. While our current design enforces a strict single-use policy for each input index, we acknowledge that some advanced scenarios may require legitimate input multicasting to multiple receivers. We discuss how SAFEPATH can be extended to support such cases later in Sect. 4.

3.7 Using SAFEPATH by Application Developers

SAFEPATH provides a switch interface that applications can invoke to enable or disable protection for specific input devices on demand. Like the data retrieval interface (DRI), the switch interface is implemented as a sys-hypercall.

From a developer's perspective, using SAFEPATH is straightforward and requires minimal code changes. Developers define a security policy specifying which input devices to protect and under what conditions, then invoke the switch interface accordingly. For example, a banking app may enable SAFEPATH protection for the touchscreen, accelerometer, and gyroscope while the user is entering a password, and disable it afterward to minimize overhead.

The switch interface is the only SAFEPATH API intended for direct use by applications. Application developers are not required to invoke the DRI manually. Instead, when an application requests input through standard Android services, such as the `InputManager`, the system automatically triggers the DRI if SAFEPATH protection is enabled for the associated device. If protection is disabled, input handling proceeds normally. By integrating DRI invocation into the Android framework rather than exposing it to individual apps, we ensure broad compatibility and minimizes the development burden for application developers.

4 Discussion

4.1 Input Data Multicasting

SAFEPATHs default one-time-use policy for input indexes prevents misuse and replay, assuming input data is intended for a single recipient. However, some scenarios require multicasting, where multiple trusted components need access to the same input.

To support this, SAFEPATH can be extended to allow explicit multicast declarations at the DRI. Instead of consuming an index after one use, the caller can specify how many times it may be used (e.g., via a usage count or recipient list). The TMH enforces this limit, ensuring that input data is accessed only by authorized entities the intended number of times. This extension maintains SAFEPATHs core security properties while providing flexibility for advanced use cases, with misuse still detectable through index overuse.

4.2 Dealing with Input Devices that Use DMA

As discussed in Sect. 3.4, devices using Direct Memory Access (DMA) deliver input data to a dedicated memory buffer (typically allocated by the driver) before software processes it. In these cases, the DMA buffer should be treated as the first stop buffer (FSB). However, our current prototype does not yet support trapping writes to DMA buffers, because ARMs stage-2 translation only applies to CPU-initiated memory access; it cannot interpose on hardware-initiated DMA writes.

We identify two potential solutions to support DMA-based FSBs in SAFEPATH:

(1) *IOMMU virtualization.* By configuring an IOMMU, the hypervisor could monitor and isolate DMA transactions at the device level. This would allow SAFEPATH to trap or redirect input data at the DMA layer, similar to how CPU-accessed FSBs are handled today. While promising, this requires IOMMU support in both hardware and firmware, which is not always present on embedded/mobile platforms.

(2) *Trap-on-read via write-only mapping.* As an alternative, SAFEPATH could mark the DMA buffer as write-only in stage-2 page tables. This would allow DMA writes to proceed unimpeded, but any CPU read, either by the driver or an attacker, would trigger a stage-2 permission fault. When trapped, the hypervisor can inspect the program counter (PC) to determine if the access originated from the legitimate device driver. If so, it emulates the read instruction, performs operations ❸ and ❹ from Fig. 1, and continues SAFEPATHs normal flow. Unauthorized reads from outside the driver would be blocked or logged.

This second approach offers a lightweight alternative to IOMMU-based mediation and may enable SAFEPATH to protect DMA-driven inputs even on devices lacking IOMMU support. We leave the detailed implementation and evaluation of this mechanism to future work.

4.3 Supporting in-OS Processing

A key advantage of SAFEPATH over OS-bypassing input protection techniques is its ability to support in-OS input processing, which is often required in real-world workflows. Many systems rely on trusted OS components to preprocess or filter input data before it reaches user applications, such as gesture smoothing for touchscreen events, noise filtering in audio capture, or sensor fusion in motion tracking.

To support these cases, SAFEPATH allows trusted in-OS components to act as intermediate recipients of protected input. Each such component invokes the same Data Retrieval Interface (DRI) used by applications to securely fetch input data from the TMH. After processing, the component can re-index the result for continued secure transmission. This design treats each legitimate consumer, whether in the OS or in user space, as an authorized participant in its secure input pipeline, requiring use of the DRI and re-indexing interface for access and forwarding.

4.4 Confining Input Writes from Untrusted Drivers

A potential concern in SAFEPATH's threat model is that a compromised OS could instruct the device driver to bypass the FSB and write input data directly to arbitrary memory locations outside the protected path. Since SAFEPATHs enforcement relies on trapping writes to the FSB via stage-2 permissions, it does not prevent such out-of-path memory writes.

However, this behavior would disrupt the expected input flow. Input written outside the FSB would not be processed and delivered to the application via SAFEPATHs pipeline, resulting in dropped or unusable input. This breaks application functionality and violates the attackers objective of remaining stealthy and undetected—an assumption central to our threat model. In other words, SAFEPATH thus relies on the systems functional requirements to constrain attacker behavior: writing input elsewhere results in visible malfunction.

While our current prototype does not confine driver memory writes at runtime, stronger defenses, such as selectively making all driver-accessible memory read-only except for the FSB, could be implemented using stage-2 translation or driver isolation mechanisms. We leave this as future work.

5 System Implementation

We implemented a prototype SAFEPATH system on an ODROID-XU4 development board [35], which features a Samsung Exynos5422 Cortex-A15/Cortex-A7 octa-core CPU and 2 GB of memory. The prototype supports six input devices: touchscreen, microphone, camera, GPS receiver, fingerprint scanner, and accelerometer. The first five are real devices connected via USB, while the accelerometer is a virtual device managed by a real driver. Several notable implementation practices and design strategies are discussed below.

5.1 Identifying the First Stop Buffer (FSB)

To support a new input device, SAFEPATH must first identify the device's FSB within the driver and then apply the dynamic FSB redirection described in Sect. 3.4. Our implementation uses the following strategies to locate the FSB depending on the device's communication model.

For devices that use direct memory access (DMA), we first locate the DMA buffer in the driver source code. This is aided by inspecting common OS kernel functions that assign DMA buffers to bus systems. For example, USB devices typically allocate DMA buffers using the usb_fill_bulk_urb() function. Once the DMA buffer is identified, we trace the data flow from the DMA buffer into driver memory to pinpoint the FSB.

For devices that do not use DMA but communicate via a system bus, we examine how the driver reads input data using bus APIs. For instance, devices connected through I2C often use functions like i2c_smbus_read_word_swapped() to retrieve register values into driver memory. In this case, the destination memory region serves as the FSB.

For devices that do not use formal bus systems, such as those relying on GPIO or UART interfaces, we identify the FSB by analyzing how memory-mapped I/O (MMIO) is set up and used to transfer input data from hardware to driver memory.

5.2 Analyzing and Emulating Trapped Write Instructions

When SAFEPATH protection is enabled, any attempt by a device driver to write to a device's FSB triggers a trap to the TMH. To handle each trap, the TMH must analyze the faulting instruction and obtain the data intended for the write.

This analysis begins by using the saved program counter (PC) from the OS context to locate the faulting machine instruction. The TMH then decodes the instruction according to the ARM architecture specification to determine the type of store operation and extract the data that was being written. The extracted data is then saved into a secure buffer maintained and accessible only by the TMH. To maintain execution consistency, the TMH emulates the original write instruction, but substitutes the real input with the corresponding index in the FSB. Our implementation supports analyzing and emulating all 24 ARM "STORE" instructions that write to memory, ensuring compatibility across diverse device drivers.

5.3 Reducing Trap and Retrieval Overhead

Our original SAFEPATH prototype strictly followed the design described in Sect. 3. However, experiments revealed significant performance overhead compared to the native system. After analysis, we identified two primary causes and implemented corresponding optimizations.

Performance Degradation Reason 1: Trap Overhead for Large Writes. In the original implementation, every write to an R/O FSB triggered a trap to the TMH. This became costly for large memory operations, such as memcpy(), where copying a 1 KB buffer could result in hundreds of traps.

Optimization 1: Bulk Memory Write Recognition and Trap Consolidation. To address this, the TMH attempts to detect if a trapped write originates from a memcpy() function. By using the saved program counter (PC), the TMH locates the faulting machine instruction and inspects a window of surrounding instructions. It matches the observed instruction sequence against known patterns generated by typical memcpy() implementations, such as loops of load-store operations with pointer increments. If a match is found, the TMH extracts the source address, destination address, and data size, and performs the entire copy operation in a single trap, significantly reducing overhead.

Performance Degradation Reason 2: Syscall Overhead at High Input Rates. We also observed poor performance on high-frequency input devices, such as microphones and cameras, especially under system load. When an application invoked the sys-hypercall DRI to retrieve a chunk of input data, there were often many data chunks already buffered and ready, but each DRI call retrieved only one chunk, leading to excessive syscalls.

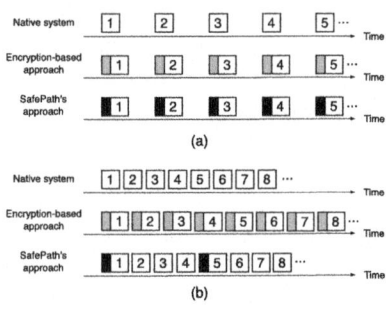

Fig. 6. Input data transmission time analysis. (a) An illustration for the case when input data generation is low. (b) An illustration for the case when input data generation frequency is high.

Optimization 2: Batch Retrieval in DRI. To improve efficiency, we modified the DRI to return all ready data chunks in a single call, including the chunk corresponding to the requested index. This optimization significantly reduces syscall overhead, particularly when input data is generated rapidly.

Notably, this optimization achieves a performance improvement that encryption-based input protection schemes cannot easily replicate. As illustrated in Fig. 6, when input data rates are low, both encryption-based approaches and SAFEPATH introduce comparable overheads (Fig. 6(a)). However, as input rates increase, encryption-based approaches incur linearly growing encryption and decryption costs, while SAFEPATH can amortize retrieval overhead by fetching multiple data chunks per trap (Fig. 6(b)).

6 Evaluation

We conducted extensive experiments to evaluate the effectiveness and performance of our SAFEPATH prototype. The evaluation covers six input devices supported by the system: touchscreen, microphone, camera, GPS receiver, fingerprint scanner, and accelerometer. For each device, we developed a corresponding application to collect input and analyze system behavior under SAFEPATH protection. The accelerometer is a virtual device, but we injected real-world accelerometer traces into the driver to simulate realistic input behavior. These traces traverse the full software stack, following the same data path as inputs from a physical device. All experiments were conducted on Android 4.4.4, the latest version officially supported on the ODROID-XU4 platform used in our prototype.

Our evaluation focuses on two key aspects: (1) the security and functional correctness of SAFEPATHs input protection mechanism, and (2) the performance overhead introduced by enabling SAFEPATH.

6.1 Security and Functional Correctness

We evaluated SAFEPATHs ability to secure the device input path from OS-level attackers by simulating adversaries with direct access to system memory. Specifically, we analyzed whether an attacker could extract meaningful input data from intermediate buffers (i.e., input path buffers or IPBs) when SAFEPATH protection was enabled. We conducted experiments on three input devices carrying distinct data formats to visually assess confidentiality breaches: microphone (audio waveform), camera (video frame), and fingerprint scanner (image).

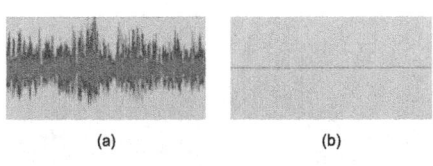

Fig. 7. Effectiveness of secure microphone input path.

Fig. 8. Effectiveness of secure camera input path.

Microphone. Figure 7(a) shows the waveform rendered from data captured at an IPB when SAFEPATH protection was disabled. The waveform clearly reflects a recorded human voice. In contrast, Figure 7(b) illustrates the same buffer under protection: the waveform becomes flat and unrecognizable, confirming that SAFEPATH prevented the attacker from recovering the original audio content.

Camera. Similarly, Fig. 8(a) shows a sharp video frame captured from an unprotected IPB. With SAFEPATH protection enabled (Fig. 8(b)), the frame turns into visual noise, and no useful image information can be extracted. This demonstrates that SAFEPATHs protection also extends to high-bandwidth, frame-based inputs like video.

Fingerprint Scanner. The fingerprint data is especially sensitive and often targeted in biometric attacks. In Fig. 9(a), the unprotected fingerprint buffer reveals a complete and identifiable print. When protection is enabled (Fig. 9(b)), the visual signature is eliminated, validating that no biometric pattern can be reconstructed from the intercepted memory.

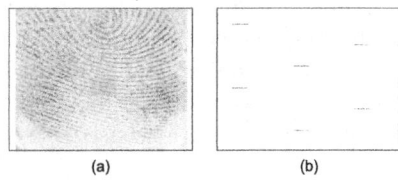

Fig. 9. Effectiveness of secure fingerprint scanner input path.

Across all three devices, these results confirm SAFEPATHs ability to preserve data confidentiality in the presence of a fully compromised operating system. More importantly, the functional correctness of the input delivery is retained. Applications still receive and process user input correctly even though intermediate buffers are sanitized of the actual data.

6.2 Performance Evaluation

We evaluated the runtime performance of the SAFEPATH prototype system across six supported input devices: touchscreen, microphone, camera, GPS receiver, fingerprint scanner, and accelerometer. For each device, we built a simple application to collect input data and measured the performance of SAFEPATH under varying workloads. We compared four configurations: the native system, an encryption-based system, the original SAFEPATH implementation, and the optimized SAFEPATH system.

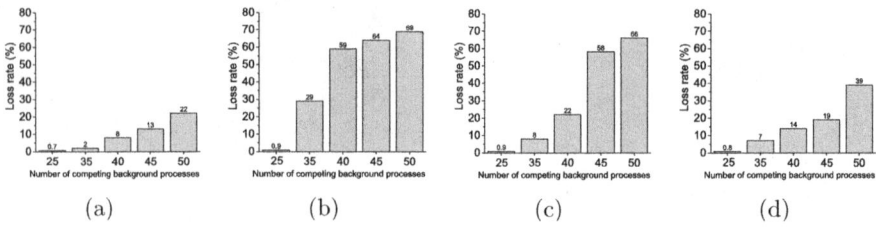

Fig. 10. Microphone input path overhead measured in terms of audio loss rate in percentage when different numbers of background processes competing for the CPU exist. (a) Native system. (b) Encryption-based approach. (c) SAFEPATH Original implementation. (d) SAFEPATH Optimized implementation.

Touchscreen. We evaluated two performance metrics for touchscreen input: (1) end-to-end latency and (2) FSB write time. The end-to-end latency measures the time from when the driver receives a hardware interrupt to when the application callback is invoked. Table 2 shows that SAFEPATH (228 ms) incurs only 3 ms additional latency compared to the native system (225 ms), on par with the encryption-based baseline (227 ms).

Table 2. Touchscreen input path overhead.

	Touch event end-to-end transmission time (milliseconds)	Time to write a touch event to first stop buffer (microseconds)
Native system	225	1
Encryption-based	227	12
SAFEPATH	228	32

For the second metric, we measured the time to write a 4-byte touch event to the FSB. SAFEPATH incurred a higher overhead (32 µs) due to instruction emulation in EL2, but given that the total touch event transmission time operates at the scale of hundreds of milliseconds, this microsecond-level overhead is negligible and does not significantly impact application responsiveness.

Microphone. We evaluated audio recording performance under varying system loads by measuring the audio loss rate. The loss rate is calculated as

$$\frac{HCAF - URAF}{HCAF}, \tag{1}$$

where HCAF denotes the number of hardware-captured audio frames, and URAF denotes the number of user-application-received audio frames. Figure 10 presents the loss rates observed across four system configurations.

In the native system (Fig. 10a), audio loss remained minimal even under heavy CPU load, demonstrating baseline system resilience. The encryption-based system (Fig. 10b) showed severe degradation: the audio loss rate grew linearly with the number of background processes, reaching approximately 69% loss under 50 background tasks. This highlights the high runtime overhead introduced by per-frame encryption and decryption.

The original SAFEPATH implementation (Fig. 10c) performed better than the encryption-based system but still suffered noticeable degradation at higher loads, with a loss rate of around 39% at peak load. This overhead was primarily due to the frequent trapping and handling of small writes without optimization.

After applying our two optimizations, namely bulk memory write Recognition and trap consolidation and batch retrieval in DRI (Sect. 5.3), SAFEPATH achieved performance comparable to the native system, maintaining low audio loss even as background load increased (Fig. 10d). Specifically, the optimized SAFEPATH system exhibited only a 14% loss rate under 50 background processes, versus 8% for the native system. This confirms the effectiveness of both trap consolidation for memcpy() operations and batching multiple audio frames per DRI invocation in reducing runtime overhead under stress.

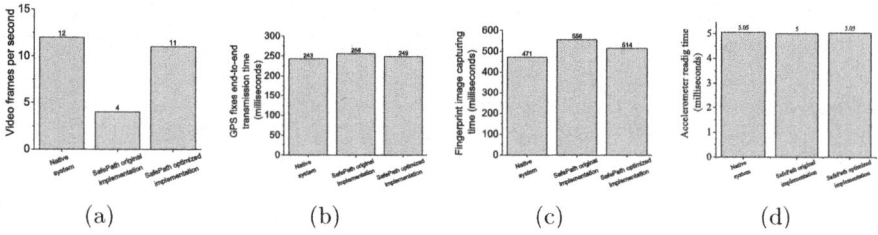

Fig. 11. Input path overhead for different devices: (a) Camera; (b) GPS receiver; (c) Fingerprint scanner; (d) Accelerometer.

Camera. Figure 11a shows that optimized SAFEPATH achieved nearly identical video frame rates as the native system. In contrast, the encryption-based approach introduced severe overhead that disrupted normal operation, preventing usable video recording. This highlights the practical advantage of SAFEPATHs non-cryptographic design when handling continuous, high-throughput data streams.

GPS Receiver. We measured the end-to-end latency of receiving a GPS fix. All three tested systems (i.e., native, original SAFEPATH, and optimized SAFEPATH) performed nearly identically (Fig. 11b), since GPS fix generation is relatively infrequent and latency-insensitive.

Fingerprint Scanner. As shown in Fig. 11c, SAFEPATH optimizations reduced fingerprint capture latency by about 10% over the original implementation, bringing performance in line with the native system. The benefit here stems mainly from faster FSB access management.

Accelerometer. For this virtual device, we measured the time to transmit a sensor reading. Figure 11d demonstrates that the native, original SAFEPATH, and optimized SAFEPATH systems performed almost identically, which is unsurprising given the devices low data rate and lightweight access pattern.

Summary. Our evaluation yields three key takeaways: (1) SAFEPATH's performance optimizations are highly effective, bringing input path performance close to native levels, even for high-frequency devices like microphones and cameras. (2) Encryption-based solutions introduce substantial overhead under heavy load or for streaming inputs, which SAFEPATH avoids by design. (3) For low-frequency or event-driven devices, all approaches perform similarly, reaffirming that SAFEPATHs overhead remains minimal when traps are rare.

7 Conclusion

We presented SAFEPATH, a system that secures device input paths without relying on encryption or OS bypassing. By combining a tiny memory hypervisor with an index-based transmission mechanism, SAFEPATH protects input data while preserving OS compatibility. Our prototype, supporting six input devices, demonstrates that SAFEPATH effectively blocks OS-level attacks with minimal overhead, outperforming encryption-based approaches under high load.

Acknowledgment. We thank the anonymous reviewers for their valuable feedback. This work was supported in part by NSF Award #1566375 and #1943269.

References

1. Ahmad, A., Schultz, A., Lee, B., Fonseca, P.: An extensible orchestration and protection framework for confidential cloud computing. In: USENIX Symposium on Operating Systems Design and Implementation (OSDI) (2023)
2. Anand, S.A., Saxena, N.: Speechless: analyzing the threat to speech privacy from smartphone motion sensors. In: IEEE Symposium on Security and Privacy (S&P) (2018)

3. ARM Limited: ARMV7-a virtualization extensions (2011). https://developer.arm.com/documentation/den0013/d/Virtualization/ARMv7-A-Virtualization-Extensions/Types-of-virtualization
4. Arnautov, S., et al.: SCONE: secure linux containers with intel SGX. In: USENIX Symposium on Operating Systems Design and Implementation (OSDI) (2016)
5. Aviv, A.J., Gibson, K.L., Mossop, E., Blaze, M., Smith, J.M.: Smudge attacks on smartphone touch screens. In: USENIX Workshop on Offensive Technologies (WOOT) (2010)
6. Azab, A.M., et al.: Hypervision across worlds: real-time kernel protection from the ARM trustzone secure world. In: ACM Conference on Computer and Communications Security (CCS) (2014)
7. Ba, Z., et al.: Learning-based practical smartphone eavesdropping with built-in accelerometer. In: Network and Distributed System Security Symposium (NDSS) (2020)
8. Baumann, A., Peinado, M., Hunt, G.C.: Shielding applications from an untrusted cloud with haven. In: USENIX Symposium on Operating Systems Design and Implementation (OSDI) (2014)
9. Borrello, P., Kogler, A., Schwarzl, M., Lipp, M., Gruss, D., Schwarz, M.: Æpic leak: architecturally leaking uninitialized data from the microarchitecture. In: USENIX Security Symposium (2022)
10. Brasser, F., Gens, D., Jauernig, P., Sadeghi, A., Stapf, E.: SANCTUARY: arming trustzone with user-space enclaves. In: Annual Network and Distributed System Security Symposium (NDSS) (2019)
11. Bulck, J.V., et al.: Foreshadow: extracting the keys to the intel SGX kingdom with transient out-of-order execution. In: USENIX Security Symposium (2018)
12. Butler, J.: DKOM: Direct Kernel Object Manipulation. Black Hat USA (2004)
13. Cai, L., Chen, H.: TouchLogger: inferring keystrokes on touch screen from smartphone motion. In: USENIX Workshop on Hot Topics in Security (HotSec) (2011)
14. Canella, C., et al.: A systematic evaluation of transient execution attacks and defenses. In: USENIX Security Symposium (2019)
15. Chen, X., Garfinkel, T., et al.: Overshadow: a virtualization-based approach to retrofitting protection in commodity operating systems. In: ACM Conference on Architectural Support for Programming Languages and Operating Systems (ASPLOS) (2008)
16. Cheng, Y., Ding, X., Deng, R.H.: Efficient virtualization-based application protection against untrusted operating system. In: ACM Asia Conference on Computer and Communications Security (AsiaCCS) (2015)
17. Dall, C., Li, S., Lim, J.T., Nieh, J., Koloventzos, G.: ARM virtualization: performance and architectural implications. In: ACM/IEEE Symposium on Computer Architecture (ISCA) (2016)
18. David, F.M., Chan, E., Carlyle, J.C., Campbell, R.H.: Cloaker: hardware supported rootkit concealment. In: IEEE Symposium on Security and Privacy (S&P) (2008)
19. Dunn, A.M., et al.: Eternal sunshine of the spotless machine: protecting privacy with ephemeral channels. In: USENIX Symposium on Operating Systems Design and Implementation (OSDI) (2012)
20. Fang, Y.: Introduction to the armv8 virtualization system (2020). https://www.openeuler.org/en/blog/yorifang/2020-10-24-arm-virtualization-overview.html
21. Gionta, J., Enck, W., Ning, P.: HideM: protecting the contents of userspace memory in the face of disclosure vulnerabilities. In: ACM Conference on Data and Application Security and Privacy (CODASPY) (2015)

22. Guan, L., Lin, J., Luo, B., Jing, J., Wang, J.: Protecting private keys against memory disclosure attacks using hardware transactional memory. In: IEEE Symposium on Security and Privacy (S&P) (2015)
23. Guan, L., et al.: TrustShadow: secure execution of unmodified applications with ARM trustzone. In: ACM Conference on Mobile Systems, Applications, and Services (MobiSys) (2017)
24. Harrison, K., Xu, S.: Protecting cryptographic keys from memory disclosure attacks. In: IEEE/IFIP Conference on Dependable Systems and Networks (DSN) (2007)
25. Hof, A.V., Nieh, J.: Blackbox: a container security monitor for protecting containers on untrusted operating systems. In: USENIX Symposium on Operating Systems Design and Implementation (OSDI) (2022)
26. Hofmann, O.S., Kim, S., Dunn, A.M., Lee, M.Z., Witchel, E.: InkTag: secure applications on an untrusted operating system. In: ACM Conference on Architectural Support for Programming Languages and Operating Systems (ASPLOS) (2013)
27. Hund, R., Holz, T., Freiling, F.C.: Return-oriented rootkits: bypassing kernel code integrity protection mechanisms. In: USENIX Security Symposium (2009)
28. Hunt, T., Zhu, Z., Xu, Y., Peter, S., Witchel, E.: Ryoan: a distributed sandbox for untrusted computation on secret data. In: USENIX Symposium on Operating Systems Design and Implementation (OSDI) (2016)
29. Incel, Ö.D., et al.: DAKOTA: sensor and touch screen-based continuous authentication on a mobile banking application. IEEE Access **9**, 38943–38960 (2021)
30. Intel Corporation: Intel Software Guard Extensions (nd). https://www.intel.com/content/www/us/en/developer/tools/software-guard-extensions/overview.html
31. Kocher, P., et al.: Spectre attacks: exploiting speculative execution. In: IEEE Symposium on Security and Privacy (S&P) (2019)
32. Lipp, M., et al.: Meltdown: reading kernel memory from user space. In: USENIX Security Symposium (2018)
33. Michalevsky, Y., Boneh, D., Nakibly, G.: Gyrophone: recognizing speech from gyroscope signals. In: USENIX Security Symposium (2014)
34. Miluzzo, E., Varshavsky, A., Balakrishnan, S., Choudhury, R.R.: TapPrints: your finger taps have fingerprints. In: ACM Conference on Mobile Systems, Applications, and Services (MobiSys) (2012)
35. ODROID Wiki: ODROID-XU4 (nd). https://wiki.odroid.com/odroid-xu4/odroid-xu4
36. Owusu, E., Han, J., Das, S., Perrig, A., Zhang, J.: Accessory: password inference using accelerometers on smartphones. In: Workshop on Mobile Computing Systems and Applications (HotMobile) (2012)
37. Petracca, G., Sun, Y., Jaeger, T., Atamli, A.: Audroid: preventing attacks on audio channels in mobile devices. In: Annual Computer Security Applications Conference (ACSAC) (2015)
38. Santos, N., Raj, H., Saroiu, S., Wolman, A.: Using ARM trustzone to build a trusted language runtime for mobile applications. In: Architectural Support for Programming Languages and Operating Systems (ASPLOS) (2014)
39. van Schaik, S., Kwong, A., Genkin, D., Yarom, Y.: SGAxe: how SGX fails in practice (2020). https://sgaxeattack.com/
40. van Schaik, S., Minkin, M., Kwong, A., Genkin, D., Yarom, Y.: CacheOut: leaking data on intel CPUs via cache evictions. In: IEEE Symposium on Security and Privacy (S&P) (2021)

41. Schlegel, R., Zhang, K., Zhou, X., Intwala, M., Kapadia, A., Wang, X.: Sound-Comber: a stealthy and context-aware sound trojan for smartphones. In: Network and Distributed System Security Symposium (NDSS) (2011)
42. Thornton, S.: Arm TrustZone explained (nd). https://www.microcontrollertips.com/embedded-security-brief-arm-trustzone-explained
43. Snow, K.Z., Monrose, F., Davi, L., Dmitrienko, A., Liebchen, C., Sadeghi, A.: Just-in-time code reuse: On the effectiveness of fine-grained address space layout randomization. In: IEEE Symposium on Security and Privacy (S&P) (2013)
44. Song, W., Choi, H., Kim, J., Kim, E., Kim, Y., Kim, J.: Pikit: a new kernel-independent processor-interconnect rootkit. In: USENIX Security Symposium (2016)
45. Sparks, S., Butler, J.: SHADOW WALKER: raising the bar for rootkit raising the bar for rootkit detection detection. Black Hat Japan (2005)
46. Tang, A., Sethumadhavan, S., Stolfo, S.J.: Heisenbyte: thwarting memory disclosure attacks using destructive code reads. In: ACM Conference on Computer and Communications Security (CCS) (2015)
47. Tsai, C., Porter, D.E., Vij, M.: Graphene-SGX: a practical library OS for unmodified applications on SGX. In: USENIX Annual Technical Conference (ATC) (2017)
48. Tung, Y., Shin, K.G.: Exploiting sound masking for audio privacy in smartphones. In: ACM Asia Conference on Computer and Communications Security (AsiaCCS) (2019)
49. Weiser, S., Werner, M.: SGXIO: generic trusted I/O path for intel SGX. In: ACM Conference on Data and Application Security and Privacy (CODASPY) (2017)
50. Xu, Z., Bai, K., Zhu, S.: TapLogger: inferring user inputs on smartphone touchscreens using on-board motion sensors. In: ACM Conference on Security and Privacy in Wireless and Mobile Networks (WiSec) (2012)
51. Yun, M.H., Zhong, L.: Ginseng: keeping secrets in registers when you distrust the operating system. In: Network and Distributed System Security Symposium (NDSS) (2019)
52. Zhang, F., Chen, J., Chen, H., Zang, B.: CloudVisor: retrofitting protection of virtual machines in multi-tenant cloud with nested virtualization. In: ACM Symposium on Operating Systems Principles (SOSP) (2011)
53. Zhang, L., Pathak, P.H., Wu, M., Zhao, Y., Mohapatra, P.: AccelWord: energy efficient hotword detection through accelerometer. In: ACM Conference on Mobile Systems, Applications, and Services (MobiSys) (2015)
54. Zhang, Y., Xia, P., Luo, J., Ling, Z., Liu, B., Fu, X.: Fingerprint attack against touch-enabled devices. In: Workshop on Security and Privacy in Smartphones and Mobile Devices (SPSM) (2012)
55. Zhou, Z., Gligor, V.D., Newsome, J., McCune, J.M.: Building verifiable trusted path on commodity x86 computers. In: IEEE Symposium on Security and Privacy (S&P) (2012)
56. Zhou, Z., Yu, M., Gligor, V.D.: Dancing with giants: Wimpy kernels for on-demand isolated I/O. In: 2014 IEEE Symposium on Security and Privacy (S&P) (2014)

Extending Groth16 for Disjunctive Statements

Xudong Zhu[1,2], Xinxuan Zhang[1,2], Xuyang Song[3], Yi Deng[1,2(✉)], Yuanju Wei[1,2], and Liuyu Yang[1,2]

[1] Key Laboratory of Cyberspace Security Defense, Institute of Information Engineering, CAS, Beijing, China
{zhuxudong,zhangxinxuan,deng,weiyuanju,yangliuyu}@iie.ac.cn
[2] School of Cyber Security, University of Chinese Academy of Sciences, Beijing, China
[3] Anoma, Beijing, China

Abstract. Two most common ways to design non-interactive zero knowledge (NIZK) proofs are based on Sigma (Σ)-protocols (an efficient way to prove algebraic statements) and zero-knowledge succinct non-interactive arguments of knowledge (zk-SNARK) protocols (an efficient way to prove arithmetic statements). However, in the applications of cryptocurrencies such as privacy-preserving credentials, privacy-preserving audits, and blockchain-based voting systems, the zk-SNARKs for general statements are usually implemented with encryption, commitment, or other algebraic cryptographic schemes. Moreover, zk-SNARKs for many different arithmetic statements may also be required to be implemented together. Clearly, a typical solution is to extend the zk-SNARK circuit to include the code for algebraic part. However, complex cryptographic operations in the algebraic algorithms will significantly increase the circuit size, which leads to impractically large proving time and CRS size. Thus, we need a flexible enough proof system for composite statements including both algebraic and arithmetic statements. Unfortunately, while the conjunction of zk-SNARKs is relatively natural and numerous effective solutions are currently available (e.g. by utilizing the commit-and-prove technique), the disjunction of zk-SNARKs is rarely discussed in detail. In this paper, we mainly focus on the disjunctive statements of Groth16, and we propose a Groth16 variant—CompGroth16, which provides a framework for Groth16 to prove the disjunctive statements that consist of a mix of algebraic and arithmetic components. Specifically, we could directly combine CompGroth16 with Σ-protocol or even CompGroth16 with CompGroth16 just like the logical composition of Σ-protocols. From this, we can gain many good properties, such as broader expression, better prover's efficiency and shorter CRS. In addition, for the combination of CompGroth16 and Σ-protocol, we also present two representative application scenarios to demonstrate the practicality of our construction.

Keywords: Zk-SNARK · Sigma protocol · Disjunctive statement · Logical composition

1 Introduction

Zero-knowledge proof (ZKP) allows a prover to convince a verifier that a statement is true without revealing any other information. The introduction of zero-knowledge argument systems [42], particularly non-interactive zero-knowledge (NIZK) systems [19], has greatly impacted cryptography research and applications. Over the last decade, significant advancements have been made in zero-knowledge succinct non-interactive arguments of knowledge (zk-SNARKs). The pairing-based zk-SNARK—Groth16 [45], stands out for its verification efficiency and small proof size. This scheme is widely used in privacy-preserving applications such as verifiable database outsourcing [71], verifiable machine learning [68], privacy-preserving cryptocurrencies [13,16,20,63], electronic voting [72], online auctions [36], and anonymous credentials [33].

Various zk-SNARKs have been developed to prove the non-algebraic statements (e.g. knowledge of preimage of SHA256), which are expressed by arithmetic/boolean circuits supporting general computations in NP. Despite their appeal, these general-purpose schemes can introduce overhead. Separately, there are also algebraic statements which are defined by relations over algebraic structures like prime-order groups. And there are specialized ZKPs for efficiently proving these statements (e.g. knowledge of discrete logarithm). However, the composite statements combining algebraic and non-algebraic statements are common, such as proving a committed value w satisfies both an arithmetic/boolean circuit C (e.g. $\exists w$ s.t. $cm = Com(w) \wedge y = C(w)$). Below we briefly survey ZKPs for different types of statements.

ZKPs for Non-algebraic Statements. zk-SNARKs are general-purpose, efficient ZKPs used for proving non-algebraic statements due to their compactness and efficient verification. Recent advancements have included works [4,12,15,26,43,65,69] based on polynomial interactive oracle proofs (PIOPs), which do not rely on public-key cryptography, require no trusted setup, and offer conjectured post-quantum security. Other works [25,35,58] utilize constant-round PIOPs with KZG [52] polynomial commitment, needing a universal and updatable CRS with constant-size proofs and fast verification. Additionally, works [38,44,45,54] based on linear probabilistic checkable proofs (LPCPs) feature very small proofs and fast verification but are slow on the prover side and require long and "toxic" CRS. By leveraging the KZG polynomial commitment, the recent work [56] combined the ideas of Groth16 and IOPs to trade longer CRS and slower prover's efficiency for concrete smaller proof size and faster verification.

zk-SNARKs can also prove algebraic statements, like the knowledge of discrete-log in a cyclic group, by, for example, representing the exponentiation circuit as Quadratic Arithmetic Programs (QAP). However, proving single exponentiations involves thousands to millions of gates, making zk-SNARKs based on QAP inefficient due to the quasi-linear prover cost and growing CRS size. In contrast, Σ-protocols can prove knowledge of discrete-log with a constant number of exponentiations.

ZKPs for Algebraic Statements. A Σ-protocol is a 3-move public-coin interactive proof system introduced by Cramer [31]. They are commonly used and efficient for proving algebraic statements. For example, Alice can use a Σ-protocol to convince Bob that she knows an a such that $a \cdot G = Y$ for publicly known values $G, Y \in \mathbb{G}$. Σ-protocol-based ZKPs are efficient for these statements, yielding short proofs, requiring a constant number of public-key operations, and not needing trusted CRS generation [32,37,46,47,60,64]. They can also be made non-interactive using the Fiat-Shamir transformation [34]. For more complex statements, Σ-protocols can be combined in parallel to prove compound statements efficiently. Additionally, there are also efficient ZKP compilers [3,57,59] having bridged the gap between Σ-protocol design and working implementations.

While Σ-protocols are efficient for algebraic statements, they are much slower for non-algebraic ones. Consider a cryptographic hash function or block cipher represented by a boolean or arithmetic circuit C. Suppose Alice wants to show that she knows an input w such that $C(w) = y$ for some public y. Alice can treat each gate in C as an algebraic function and prove that the input and output wires of each gate satisfy the related algebraic relation, to show that she indeed knows w. However, this would be prohibitively expensive. The proving and verification time, as well as the proof size, would grow linearly with the circuit size, which for hash functions and block ciphers can be tens of thousands of exponentiations and group elements.

ZKPs for Composite Statements. Composite statements involve both algebraic and non-algebraic components, such as x being a Pedersen commitment to w with $SHA256(w) = y$. ZKPs for these statements have various applications [2,10,24], including proof of solvency for Bitcoin exchanges, anonymous credentials based on RSA and ECDSA signatures, and 2PC with authenticated inputs.

One approach is transforming composite statements into either algebraic or non-algebraic form, using only Σ-protocols or zk-SNARKs. However, this increases proof size and computation. Instead, a better way is to use Σ-protocols for the algebraic part and efficient zk-SNARKs for the non-algebraic part, linking them with customized "glue" protocols. Many works [2,5,21,22,55,61] have constructed such "glue" proofs, featuring low communication costs and efficient verification. Their core idea is to use additional commitments or vector commitments as a bridge to commit the common witness w of two parts, and then use "glue" protocols to prove that the committed values are indeed witness in both two parts. Alternatively, [10] developed transparent ZKPs with a fast prover and linear proof size by linking Σ-protocols with ZKBoo [39]/ZKB++ [23]. Recent work [70] proposed a generic framework of Σ-protocols for algebraic statements from verifiable secret sharing schemes, designing ZKPs for composite statements without "glue" proofs.

ZKPs for Disjunctive Statements. Zero-knowledge techniques for disjunctive statements have a long history [1,32,37]. Disjunctive statements are NP statements composed of a logical "OR" of clauses. For example, Alice can prove to Bob that $x_1 \in \mathcal{L}_1 \vee \cdots \vee x_l \in \mathcal{L}_l$. The witness includes one clause's witness (also called the active clause) and its index. These statements are common in practice, making them crucial for proof optimizations. Disjunctive proofs provide privacy as the verifier cannot determine which clause is satisfied. Applications include membership proofs like ring signatures [62], proving the existence of bugs in a large codebase [50], and proving the correct execution of a processor [14]. Recent interest in optimizing protocols for disjunctions spans zero-knowledge [7,28,40,46,50,53] and secure multiparty computation [11,49,51].

Since a disjunction of NP statements is an NP statement, it can be proved using proof systems for NP-completeness. but this may lead to a significant increase in the complexity. Alternatively, works [7,46,50] have manually modified specific ZKPs to support disjunctive statements, though these rely on individual protocol structures and may not generalize. A more flexible approach is building disjunctive compilers [1,32,40,41], which transform zero-knowledge protocols into disjunctive protocols with sub-linear communication complexity relative to the number of clauses. Recent work [11,48,66] has applied these techniques to the VOLE-based ZK setting.

1.1 Our Contributions

In this paper, we deal with the "OR" composition of the efficient zk-SNARK Groth16 for arithmetic statements (non-algebraic statements) and other Σ-protocols for algebraic statements, or even another Groth16 for arithmetic statements. As we have discussed in introduction section, while the logic composition of Σ-protocols is well-known, most of existing research on zk-SNARKs focuses on "AND" logic composite statements. Using Groth16 to prove disjunctive statements by encoding the entire "OR" statement into the circuit is possible but causes circuit expansion. For the pairing-based Groth16, the CRS length is linear with the circuit size, and the prover's computation is quasi-linear, creating a need for a composition-friendly variant. Our solution separates "OR" logic from the circuit and allows combining two independent proofs for R_1 and R_2 into a proof for $R_1 \vee R_2$ at minimal cost. Additionally, recall that the prover in Σ-OR need to run the entire prover algorithm for the active clause and simulate a transcript for the non-active clause. Therefore, our efficient simulator enables the prover to simulate non-active arithmetic clauses efficiently, improving prover efficiency. The main contributions of this paper are summarized as follows:

Build a Bridge Between zk-SNARKs and Σ- Protocols. By using a Σ-protocol, we create a new zk-SNARK called CompGroth16 in the RO model, which can combine with Σ-protocols to prove disjunctive statements. Specifically, CompGroth16 handle non-algebraic statements and Σ-protocols handle algebraic ones. These can be composed using the classic Σ-OR. Our modular design can work with any Σ-protocol. The main advantage is avoiding the need to encode algebraic parts into the circuit for "OR" statements, increasing efficiency and reducing the size of CRS. For disjunctive statements with an active algebraic clause, a Σ-protocol in Σ-OR can be used. For the arithmetic part, our efficient simulator in Σ-OR eliminates the need to run Groth16's prover algorithm, significantly improving prover's efficiency. We also present two representative applications of our technique for this type of statements.

Construct a New Composition Friendly zk-SNARK. Following the above contribution, we offer a new framework for proving disjunctions of non-algebraic statements. This modular framework allows combining two zk-SNARK implementations for R_1 and R_2 into a zk-SNARK scheme for $R_1 \vee R_2$ without rewriting circuits or regenerating the specific CRS. Using our efficient simulator in Σ-OR, only one Groth16 prover algorithm is needed, with the other simulated efficiently. This means the time to prove $R_1 \vee R_2$ is nearly the same as proving R_1 or R_2, depending on the active clause. Additionally, our solution can be extended to efficiently prove more general disjunctions such as $x_1 \in \mathcal{L}_1 \vee \cdots \vee x_l \in \mathcal{L}_l$ or even conjunctive normal form (CNF) relations by using existing optimizations.

2 Preliminaries

2.1 Notation

If S is a finite set, then $s \leftarrow S$ denotes picking an element uniformly from S and assigning it to s. We use $\lambda \in \mathbb{N}$ to denote a security parameter and 1^λ for its unary representation. "Probabilistic polynomial time" is abbreviated as "PPT". By $y \leftarrow A(x_1, \ldots)$ we mean running algorithm A on inputs $x_1, \ldots$ to output y. $\overline{P}$ and $\overline{V}$ represent the malicious prover and verifier, respectively. A function $negl(n)$ is negligible if it vanishes faster than any inverse polynomial. A disjunctive statement consists of a logical "OR" of clauses. To distinguish between active clauses, we use a horizontal line above $\mathcal{L}$, e.g., $x_1 \in \bar{\mathcal{L}}_1 \vee x_2 \in \mathcal{L}_2$ means the witness of $x_1 \in \mathcal{L}_1$ is the witness for the entire disjunctive statement.

2.2 Bilinear Groups

Following the notation of [45], we work on bilinear groups $(p, \mathbb{G}_1, \mathbb{G}_2, \mathbb{G}_T, e, G, H)$ with the following properties:

- $\mathbb{G}_1, \mathbb{G}_2$ *and* $\mathbb{G}_T$ are elliptic curve groups of prime order p
- Pairing $e: \mathbb{G}_1 \times \mathbb{G}_2 \to \mathbb{G}_T$ is a bilinear map
- G is a generator for $\mathbb{G}_1$, H is a generator for $\mathbb{G}_2$, $e(G, H)$ is a generator for $\mathbb{G}_T$
- There are efficient algorithms for computing the generic group operations.

For $a, b, c \in \mathbb{Z}_p$, we write $[a]_1$ for $a \cdot G$, $[b]_2$ for $b \cdot H$, and $[c]_T$ for $c \cdot e(G, H)$. For notation $G = [1]_1, H = [1]_2$ and $e(G, H) = [1]_T$, whereas the neutral elements are $[0]_1, [0]_2$ and $[0]_T$. Then, we have $[a]_i + [b]_i = [a+b]_i$ for $i \in \{1, 2, T\}$. Given two group elements $[a]_1$ and $[b]_2$, we define their dot product as $[a]_1 \cdot [b]_2 = [ab]_T$, which can be computed efficiently by pairing e. Sometimes we abbreviate $[a]_{i \in \{1,2,T\}}, [b]_{i \in \{1,2,T\}}, \ldots$ as $[a, b, \ldots]_{i \in \{1,2,T\}}$.

2.3 Quadratic Arithmetic Programs

Quadratic Arithmetic Programs (QAP), which was first introduced by Gennaro et al. [38], is a language in which the instances can be verified by using a parallel quadratic check. The efficient reduction between QAP and CIRCUIT-SAT means that when we need an efficient zk-SNARK for CIRCUIT-SAT, we can construct an efficient zk-SNARK for QAP instead. More discussions on encoding an arithmetic circuit to a QAP instance can be found in [38].

Let $\mathbb{F} = \mathbb{Z}_p$. We denote the number of multiplication gates by n and the number of wires by m. QAP instance $\mathcal{Q}_p$ can be specified by $(\mathbb{Z}_p, l, \{u_i(X), v_i(X), w_i(X)\}_{i=0}^m)$, where $1 \leq l \leq m$ is the length of the statement (e.g., public inputs and outputs in an arithmetic circuit); u_i, v_i and w_i are the three sets of polynomials that encode the wires in the target arithmetic circuit. All the polynomials have strictly lower degrees than n and the degree of $t(X)$. QAP instance $\mathcal{Q}_p$ defines the following relation, where we assume that $a_0 = 1$,

$$R = \left\{ (x,w) \middle| \begin{array}{l} x = (a_1, \ldots, a_l) \in \mathbb{Z}_p^l \\ w = (a_{l+1}, \ldots, a_m) \in \mathbb{Z}_p^{m-l} \\ \sum_{i=0}^m a_i u_i(X) \cdot \sum_{i=0}^m a_i v_i(X) \equiv \sum_{i=0}^m a_i w_i(X) \bmod 1 t(X) \end{array} \right\}.$$

Alternatively, $(x, w) \in R$ if there exists (degree $\leq n - 2$) polynomial $h(X)$, such that

$$\left(\sum_{i=0}^m a_i u_i(X) \right) \cdot \left(\sum_{i=0}^m a_i v_i(X) \right) - \sum_{i=0}^m a_i w_i(X) \equiv h(X) t(X),$$

In general, the goal of the prover of a zk-SNARK for QAP is to prove that for public $(a_1, \ldots, a_l)$ and $a_0 = 1$, the prover knows $(a_{l+1}, \ldots, a_m)$ and degree $\leq n - 2$ polynomial $h(X)$, such that the above equation holds.

2.4 zk-SNARKs

We define $\mathcal{R}_\lambda$ as the set of possible NP relations R the relation generator $\mathcal{R}$ may output given 1^λ. $\mathcal{R}$ may also output some side information, an auxiliary input aux, which is given to the adversary. crs, x, w, τ, and π denote the common reference string, statement, witness, simulation trapdoor, and proof, respectively. Language is a set composed of statements. Given the NP relation R, we can define the language with respect to R as $\mathcal{L} = \{x | \exists w \text{ s.t. } (x, w) \in R\}$.

Definition 1. (SNARG). $\Pi = (\mathrm{Setup}, \mathrm{P}, \mathrm{V})$ is a succinct non-interactive argument (SNARG) for $\mathcal{R}_\lambda$ if it satisfies the following three properties:

Completeness: For all $\lambda \in \mathbb{N}, R \in \mathcal{R}_\lambda, (x, w) \in R$,

$$\Pr\left[\mathrm{V}(R, crs, x, \pi) = 1 \,\middle|\, (crs, \tau) \leftarrow \mathrm{Setup}\,(R)\,;\, \pi \leftarrow \mathrm{P}(R, crs, x, w)\right] = 1.$$

Computational Soundness: For all $\lambda \in \mathbb{N}$ and efficient $\overline{\mathrm{P}}$,

$$\Pr\left[\begin{array}{c}\mathrm{V}(R, crs, x, \pi) = 1 \\ \wedge x \notin \mathcal{L}\end{array} \,\middle|\, \begin{array}{c}(R, aux) \leftarrow \mathcal{R}\left(1^\lambda\right)\,;\,(crs, \tau) \leftarrow \mathrm{Setup}\,(R) \\ (x, \pi) \leftarrow \overline{\mathrm{P}}\,(R, aux, crs)\end{array}\right] = negl(\lambda).$$

Succinctness: The length of a proof is given by

$$|\pi| = poly(\lambda) polylog\,(|x| + |w|)\,.$$

Definition 2. (SNARK). A succinct non-interactive argument of knowledge (SNARK) is a SNARG that comes together with an extractor χ. Formally, soundness is replaced by knowledge soundness as follows:

Computational Knowledge Soundness: For all $\lambda \in \mathbb{N}$ and PPT $\overline{\mathrm{P}}$, there exists a PPT extractor $\chi_{\overline{P}}$,

$$\Pr\left[\begin{array}{c}\mathrm{V}(R, crs, x, \pi) = 1 \\ \wedge (x, w) \notin R\end{array} \,\middle|\, \begin{array}{c}(R, aux) \leftarrow \mathcal{R}\left(1^\lambda\right)\,;\,(crs, \tau) \leftarrow \mathrm{Setup}\,(R) \\ ((x, \pi); w) \leftarrow (\overline{\mathrm{P}} \| \chi_{\overline{P}})\,(R, aux, crs)\end{array}\right] = negl(\lambda).$$

Definition 3. (Zero-knowledge SNARK). A SNARK for an NP language $\mathcal{L}$ with a corresponding NP relation R is computationally zero knowledge, if there exists a simulator Sim for all $\lambda \in \mathbb{N}$, $(R, z) \leftarrow \mathcal{R}(1^\lambda)$, $(x, w) \in R$ and every PPT distinguisher D

$$\Pr[(crs, \tau) \leftarrow \mathrm{Setup}(R); \pi \leftarrow \mathrm{P}(R, crs, x, w) : \mathrm{D}(R, aux, crs, \tau, \pi) = 1]$$
$$\approx \Pr[(crs, \tau) \leftarrow \mathrm{Setup}(R); \pi \leftarrow \mathrm{Sim}(R, \tau, x) : \mathrm{D}(R, aux, crs, \tau, \pi) = 1]$$

2.5 Σ-Protocols

Our constructions utilize a special subclass of interactive zero-knowledge proof systems, called Σ-protocols [64]. Therefore, we recall its definition here [40].

Definition 4. (Σ-protocols. Σ-Protocol Π for R is a 3 move protocol between a prover P and a verifier V consisting of a tuple of PPT algorithms $\Pi = (A, Z, \phi)$ with the following interfaces:

- $a \leftarrow A(x, w; r_p)$: On input the statement x, corresponding witness w, such that $R(x, w) = 1$, and prover randomness r_p (we usually omit the randomness r_p as a default input), output the first message a that P sends to V in the first round.

- $c \leftarrow \{0,1\}^\kappa$: Sample a random challenge c that V sends to P in the second round. Note that we use a new flexible parameter κ to describe the distribution. The soundness error directly depends on the selection of κ, the larger κ, the smaller soundness error.
- $z \leftarrow Z(x, w, a, c; r_p)$: On input the statement x, the witness w, the challenge c, and prover randomness r_p, output the message z that P sends to V in the third round.
- $b \leftarrow \phi(x, a, c, z)$: On input the statement x, prover's message a, z, and the challenge c, this algorithm run by V, outputs a bit $b \in \{0, 1\}$.
- $(a, c, z) \leftarrow S(x)$: On input the statement x, this simulator outputs the simulated prover's message a, c, z, where c is randomly sampled from a distribution.

A Σ-protocol has completeness, special soundness, and special honest verifier zero-knowledge properties (HVZK). We recommend referring to [40] for more formal description of these properties. Notably, every Σ-protocol can be transformed into a non-interactive, fully secure zero knowledge proof in the random oracle (RO, denoted by $\mathcal{O}$) model using the Fiat-Shamir heuristic [34], in which the challenge is generated as $c = \mathcal{O}(x, a)$. The extractor $\mathcal{E}$ and simulator S_{NIZK} can make use of rewinding the other party and programming the random oracle.

2.6 Disjunction of Σ-Protocols

The set of relations with Σ-protocols is closed under conjunction and disjunction [32]. The classic protocol for disjunction of Σ-protocols, which we denote Σ-OR, is proposed by Cramer et al. [32]. Then, Ciampi et al. [27] introduced a different Σ-OR protocol with certain advantages over the Cramer et al. construction. We denote Σ_{R_1} and Σ_{R_2} as Σ-protocols for relations R_1 and R_2 respectively. W.l.o.g., we assume that the prover wants to prove the disjunction of the statement $x = (x_1, x_2)$ and knows a witness w_1 showing that $(x_1, w_1) \in R_1$. The proof for relation $R_1 \vee R_2$ is constructed as in Fig. 1.

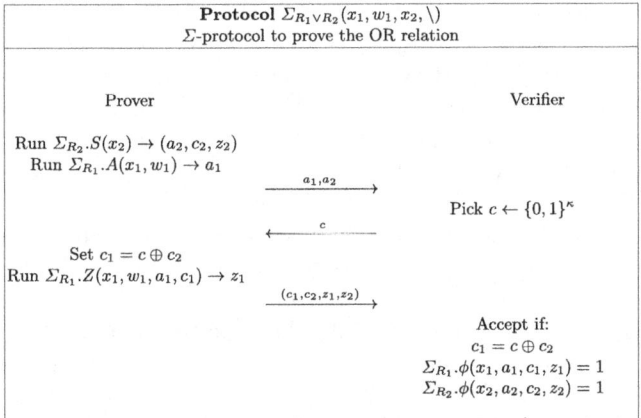

Fig. 1. The *Sigma*-protocol for Relation $R_1 \vee R_2$

The essence of this protocol is that the prover can freely decide one of the challenges from two Σ-protocols, while the other challenge becomes a random challenge due to the influence of the random challenge sent by the verifier. This means that the prover can only simulate the proof for one statement and must then honestly prove the another statement.

3 Framework for Disjunction of Groth16

In this section, we are going to introduce a main construction and a framework. Specifically, in Subsect. 3.1, we review the well-known zk-SNARK scheme—Groth16. In Subsect. 3.2, we introduce a new Groth16 variant scheme—CompGroth16 to prove the disjunction of arithmetic and algebraic statements. And we provide two representative applications for this type of statement. Moreover, we also provide a framework for Groth16 to prove more general disjunctive arithmetic statements. In Subsect. 3.3, we prove the security and analyze the performance of our main construction.

3.1 Groth's Near-Optimal SNARK

The Groth16 [45] is a state-of-the-art scheme for pairing-based zk-SNARKs. Groth16 requires to express the computation as an arithmetic circuit and relies on some trusted setup to prove the circuit satisfiability. Due to its short proof size (3 group elements) and verifier's efficiency (within several milliseconds), Groth16 has become a de facto standard in blockchain projects. This results in a great number of available implementations, code auditing and multiple trusted setup ceremonies run by independent institutions. Therefore, this article takes the construction Groth16 as the starting point. Since our construction is closely related to Groth16, for the convenience of our future discussion, we will briefly review Groth16 in this subsection:

Groth16. Groth16 [45] is a non-universal zk-SNARK for QAP widely used due to its verifier-efficiency. In this paper, we denote the Groth16 scheme by $\Pi_{Groth} =$ (Groth. Setup, Groth. P, Groth. V, Groth. Sim). By m, n and l, we denote the number of wires, multiplication gates and the length of public input of the circuit for $x \in \mathcal{L}$. The statement x and the witness w are expressed as $(a_1, \ldots, a_l)$ and $(a_{l+1}, \ldots, a_m)$ respectively. The Groth16 zk-SNARK scheme, illustrated in Fig. 2, involves a prover generating three group elements: $([A, C]_1, [B]_2)$. The verifier executes a single verification equation that requires the computation of three pairings. Here, $[A]_1$ and $[B]_2$ serve as the commitments to the witness, while $[C]_1$ encodes auxiliary information to prove compliance with the specified public input. The elements in CRS are carefully designed to satisfy the soundness. The Groth16 scheme can be proved to satisfy the computational knowledge soundness in the generic group model (GGM) and perfect zero knowledge. Reference to [45] is recommended for more details.

Groth.Setup(R) :
Sample $\alpha, \beta, \gamma, \delta, \zeta \leftarrow \mathbb{F}^*$ such that $\zeta^n \neq 1$. Let

$$crs_p : \left(\left[\alpha, \beta, \delta, \{\zeta^i\}_{i=0}^{n-1}, \left\{ \frac{\zeta^i t(\zeta)}{\delta} \right\}_{i=0}^{n-2}, \left\{ \frac{\beta u_i(\zeta) + \alpha v_i(\zeta) + w_i(\zeta)}{\delta} \right\}_{i=l+1}^m \right]_1, \right.$$
$$\left. \left[\beta, \delta, \{\zeta^i\}_{i=0}^{n-1} \right]_2 \right)$$

$$crs_v : \left(\left[\left\{ \frac{\beta u_i(\zeta) + \alpha v_i(\zeta) + w_i(\zeta)}{\gamma} \right\}_{i=0}^l \right]_1, [\gamma, \delta]_2, [\alpha\beta]_T \right)$$

$crs = (crs_p, crs_v); td = (\alpha, \beta, \gamma, \delta, \zeta)$
Return (crs, td)

Groth.P($R, crs_p, a_1, \ldots, a_m$) :
$u(X) \leftarrow \sum_{i=0}^m a_i u_i(X); v(X) \leftarrow \sum_{i=0}^m a_i v_i(X); w(X) \leftarrow \sum_{i=0}^m a_i w_i(X);$
$h(X) \leftarrow (u(X)v(X) - w(X))/t(X)$
$(r, s) \leftarrow \mathbb{F}^2; [A]_1 \leftarrow [\alpha]_1 + [u(\zeta)]_1 + r[\delta]_1; [B]_2 \leftarrow [\beta]_2 + [v(\zeta)]_2 + s[\delta]_2$
$[C]_1 = \sum_{i=l+1}^m a_i \left[\frac{\beta u_i(\zeta) + \alpha v_i(\zeta) + w_i(\zeta)}{\delta} \right]_1 + \left[\frac{h(\zeta)t(\zeta)}{\delta} \right]_1 + s[A]_1 + r[B]_1 - rs[\delta]_1$
Return $\pi \leftarrow ([A, C]_1, [B]_2)$

Groth.V($R, crs_v, a_1, \ldots, a_l, \pi = ([A, C]_1, [B]_2)$) :
$[D]_1 = \sum_{i=0}^l a_i \left[\frac{\beta u_i(\zeta) + \alpha v_i(\zeta) + w_i(\zeta)}{\gamma} \right]_1$
Check that $[A]_1 \cdot [B]_2 = [\alpha\beta]_T + [D]_1 \cdot [\gamma]_2 + [C]_1 \cdot [\delta]_2$

Groth.Sim($R, crs, td, a_1, \ldots, a_l$) :
$A \leftarrow \mathbb{F}; B \leftarrow \mathbb{F}; [D]_1 = \sum_{i=0}^l a_i \left[\frac{\beta u_i(\zeta) + \alpha v_i(\zeta) + w_i(\zeta)}{\gamma} \right]_1$
$[C]_1 = \frac{AB[1]_1 - [\alpha\beta]_1 - \gamma[D]_1}{\delta}$
Return $\pi \leftarrow ([A, C]_1, [B]_2)$

Fig. 2. Groth16 construction

3.2 New Groth16 Variant—CompGroth16

Based on logic "AND" and logic "OR", we can divide all the composite statements into two basic categories. Notably, the "AND" composition between statements with unrelated witnesses is straightforward, e.g. proving that two independent statements x_1, x_2 without a common witness satisfy $(x_1, w_1) \in R_1 \wedge (x_2, w_2) \in R_2$ is trivial. This type of statements can be directly proved by proving that $(x_1, w_1) \in R_1$ and $(x_2, w_2) \in R_2$ respectively.

However, the "AND" composition between statements with related witnesses is more involved, e.g. prove that two statements x_1, x_2 with a common witness satisfy $(x_1, w) \in R_1 \wedge (x_2, w) \in R_2$. Fortunately, numerous studies have shown that introducing "glue" protocols can effectively address such problems without expanding the circuit [2,5,21,22,55,61]. On the contrary, the "OR" composition of statements (that is the disjunctive statements) seems to be trickier and has only been well studied for algebraic statements (and for Σ-protocols). For more details, refer to Subsect. 2.6.

Notably, it is very succinct and efficient to prove the algebraic statements with Σ-protocols. As for arithmetic statements, from the Subsect. 3.1, we could learn that Groth16 could also be used to prove them with very fast verification time and very succinct proof size (constant verification time and proof size). However, when considering disjunctive statements involving both algebraic and non-algebraic components, we face two challenges. Firstly, we cannot simply use the Σ-protocol and Groth16 separately. Secondly, because computing a single exponentiation in secp256k1 will incur 95444 constraints [29] (depending on the group, the number of constraints may be greater), and Groth16 has quasi-linear prover time, directly incorporating "OR" logic into the circuit will result in a significant increase in proof time. Moreover, the CRS size of Groth16 is very large, which includes $m + 2n$ elements in $\mathbb{G}_1$ and n elements in $\mathbb{G}_2$, this also implies rapid expansion as the circuit size increases. Additionally, integrating the "OR" logic directly into the circuit essentially requires a complete proof of the entire "OR" statement, and cannot optimize the non-active clauses.

Motivated by these challenges, we formally propose an efficient solution for proving the disjunctive statements involving both algebraic and non-algebraic components. We complete these compositions by establishing a connection between Groth16 and Σ-protocols, and introducing a new scheme—CompGroth16. This scheme then allows us to perform "OR" composition of CompGroth16 and Σ-protocols in the same way as "OR" composition of Σ-protocols, to prove disjunction of arithmetic and algebraic statements. The main difficulty lies in the construction differences between Groth16 and Σ-protocols, which initially prevents us from establishing such a connection. Notably, Groth16 has a large-sized CRS while Σ-protocol does not. Σ-protocol is a 3 move protocol while Groth16 is non-interactive.

Our construction, CompGroth16, stems from the observation that the essential goal of the Groth16 prover is to demonstrate the validity of the pairing check equation: $[A]_1 \cdot [B]_2 = [\alpha\beta]_T + [D]_1 \cdot [\gamma]_2 + [C]_1 \cdot [\delta]_2$.

Notably, all these group elements are public in Groth16. However, we observe that if we consider the element $[B]_2$ as a witness, we can then use a simple Σ-protocol to prove the following relation R_1 (where $pp = (p, \mathbb{G}_1, \mathbb{G}_2, \mathbb{G}_T, e, G, H)$):

$$R_1 = \left\{ \begin{array}{c} (pp, x = ([A,D,C]_1 \in \mathbb{G}_1, [\gamma,\delta]_2 \in \mathbb{G}_2, [\alpha\beta]_T \in \mathbb{G}_T); w = [B]_2 \in \mathbb{G}_2) : \\ [A]_1 \cdot [B]_2 = [\alpha\beta]_T + [D]_1 \cdot [\gamma]_2 + [C]_1 \cdot [\delta]_2 \end{array} \right\}$$

The protocol denoted by Σ_{R_1} is a Σ-protocol for relation R_1. As shown in Fig. 3, this protocol is a public-coin protocol and can be transformed into a non-interactive version using the Fiat-Shamir transformation [34]. We denote the proof of this Σ-protocol (i.e., the transcript $[a]_T, c, [z]_2$) as π_1.

Theorem 1. Σ_{R_1} *is a three-move public-coin protocol for relation R_1. It is perfectly complete, unconditionally special sound, and special honest-verifier zero-knowledge (HVZK).*

The proof of Theorem 1 follows the standard proof method naturally. Specifically, the HVZK simulator Sigma.S picks the challenges $c \leftarrow \mathbb{Z}_p$, generates $[z]_2 \leftarrow \mathbb{G}_2$ and computes $[a]_T = [A]_1 \cdot [z]_2 - c \cdot ([\alpha\beta]_T + [D]_1 \cdot [\gamma]_2 + [C]_1 \cdot [\delta]_2)$. Notably, Σ-protocols can be transformed to be non-interactive in the RO model using the Fiat-Shamir transformation [34]. Knowledge-soundness of the transformed NIZK relies on the special-soundness of the Σ-protocol and therefore requires an extractor to rewind the malicious prover to obtain two transcripts with a shared prefix by programming the RO after rewinding. Zero-knowledge of the NIZK follows from HVZK of the Σ-protocol and programming the RO.

CompGroth16 Construction. Now, we formally present a new zk-SNARK $\Pi_{CompGroth}$, which is based on Groth16 and compatible with Σ-protocols. We

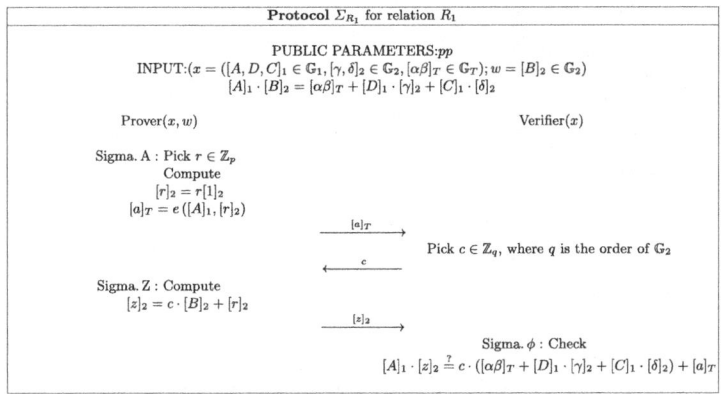

Fig. 3. The Σ-protocol Σ_{R_1} for Relation R_1

implicitly assume the bilinear group parameter is included in R. In addition, we assume that each algorithm checks whether their inputs belong to the correct groups.

Finally, we will describe the main protocol as a non-interactive protocol by using the Fiat-Shamir transformation [34]. Therefore, we denote the concatenation of the statement, elements in the CRS, public input, and proof elements written by the prover up to a certain point in time by *transcript* (this is a common method of simplifying descriptions, just like in [35]). In order to prevent security issues as shown in [17], this definition is necessary.

By the tuple Π_{Groth} = (Groth. Setup, Groth. P, Groth. V, Groth. Sim), we have denoted the well-known Groth16 scheme. Now, for the convenience of discussion, we also denote the Σ-protocol for relation R_1 we have mentioned before in Fig. 3 by Σ_{R_1} = (Sigma. A, Sigma. Z, Sigma. ϕ, Sigma. S). On input QAP relation R, we denote our new construction by $\Pi_{CompGroth}$ = (CompGroth. Setup, CompGroth. P, CompGroth. V, CompGroth. Sim). For simpler expression, we denote the hash function by H. This construction is described in detail in Fig. 4. The core idea of CompGroth16 is that during the process of running Groth16, we can have the prover to prove the pairing check equation with Σ-protocols, and the proof generated by prover includes $([A, C]_1, \pi_1)$ rather than $([A, C]_1, [B]_2)$.

Disjunction of Arithmetic and Algebraic Statements. From the Fig. 4, we can see that the current CompGroth. P algorithm in $\Pi_{CompGroth}$ is actually a Σ-protocol. Therefore, it seems easy to perform "OR" composition of CompGroth16 and other Σ-protocols just as "OR" composition of Σ-protocols to prove disjunction of arithmetic and algebraic statements (just as in Fig. 1). However, there is a detail that needs our attention here. Since we need to consider two protocols now, namely a CompGroth16 protocol and a Σ-protocol, the distribution of challenge spaces for these two protocols may naturally be inconsistent. W.l.o.g., for two prime p, q, we set the challenge from CompGroth16 to be $c_1 \in \mathbb{Z}_p$, and the challenge from Σ-protocol to be $c_2 \in \mathbb{Z}_q$. When we construct

---
CompGroth. Setup(R) :
  Run (crs, td) ← Groth. Setup(R)
  Return (crs, td)

CompGroth. P($R, crs_p, a_1, \ldots, a_m$) :
  Run ($[A, C]_1, [B]_2$) ← Groth. P($R, crs_p, a_1, \ldots, a_m$)
  Run $[a]_T$ ← Sigma. A ($[A, C]_1, [\gamma, \delta]_2, [\alpha\beta]_T; [B]_2$)
  Run c ← $H(transcript)$
  Run $[z]_2$ ← Sigma. Z ($[A, C]_1, [\gamma, \delta]_2, [\alpha\beta]_T, [a]_T, c$)
  Return π ← ($[A, C]_1, [z]_2, [a]_T$)

CompGroth. V ($R, crs_v, a_1, \ldots, a_l, \pi = ([A, C]_1, [z]_2, [a]_T)$) :
  Compute $[D]_1 = \sum_{i=0}^{l} a_i \left[\frac{\beta u_i(\zeta) + \alpha v_i(\zeta) + w_i(\zeta)}{\gamma}\right]_1$
  Run c ← $H(transcript)$
  Run b ← Sigma. ϕ ($[A, D, C]_1, [\gamma, \delta]_2, [\alpha\beta]_T, [a]_T, c, [z]_2$)
  Return b

CompGroth. Sim($R, crs, a_1, \ldots, a_l$) :
  Pick random group elements $[A]_1, [C]_1$ ← $\mathbb{G}_1$.
  Compute $[D]_1 = \sum_{i=0}^{l} a_i \left[\frac{\beta u_i(\zeta) + \alpha v_i(\zeta) + w_i(\zeta)}{\gamma}\right]_1$
  Run $([a]_T, c, [z]_2)$ ← Sigma. S ($[A, D, C]_1, [\gamma, \delta]_2, [\alpha\beta]_T$) (where c ← $\mathbb{Z}_p$)
  Let $c = \mathcal{O}(transcript)$ (To explain non-interactive security, the programmable $\mathcal{O}$ is required in this non-interactive simulation. In Σ-OR, the HVZK simulator Sigma. S is enough to simulate the non-active arithmetic part, so this step can be omitted)
  Return π ← ($[A, C]_1, [z]_2, [a]_T$)

Fig. 4. CompGroth16 construction $\Pi_{CompGroth}$.

the Σ-protocol for "OR" relation just as in Fig. 1, we can just set the c to be a random element in $\mathbb{Z}_{pq}$. Then, with the simulated challenge $c_2 \in \mathbb{Z}_q$, we can compute the $c_1 = (c - c_2) \mod p$. Obviously, given that c is a random element in $\mathbb{Z}_{pq}$, c_1 is also a random element in $\mathbb{Z}_p$. The advantage of OR composition of CompGroth16 and Σ-protocol is to prevent the expansion of the circuit by separating the algebraic part and "OR" logic from the circuit, thereby avoiding CRS regeneration, improving the efficiency of the prover and reducing the size of CRS. Moreover, as we will discussed in Sect. 3.3, our technique can also greatly improve the efficiency of provers when the algebraic clause of the disjunctive statement is an active clause.

Two Representative Applications. As we have discussed in Sect. 1, the general disjunctive statements occur commonly in practice, making them an important target for proof optimizations. For example, disjunctive proofs are often used to give the prover some degree of privacy, as a verifier cannot determine which clause is being satisfied. For the specific disjunction of arithmetic and algebraic statements, we also give two examples of use cases here.

The first application is to directly transform Groth16 into a solution that supports designated-verifier property. Note that in scenarios where proof transfer is not desired, only a specific verifier should know if the proof passes verification, such as anonymous transactions in cryptocurrencies. Of course, we can just obtain the designated-verifier schemes from the well-known and efficient "LIPs to designated-verifier zk-SNARK" transformation mentioned in [18]. In [18], Bitansky et al. proposed that a two-move linear-interactive proof can be combined with pairing-based techniques (or additively homomorphic encryption techniques) to obtain a publicly verifiable (or designated-verifier) zk-SNARK. However, this means that compared to the publicly verifiable scheme, we need a completely different set of new CRS and prove/verify algorithms. In fact, we can let the verifier sample a secret a and publish the $Y = a \cdot G$. Then, the prover only need to prove that $x \in \mathcal{L} \lor \exists\, a\ s.t.\ Y = a \cdot G$. This is clearly a designated-verifier scheme, and this solution can be directly achieved by applying our technique on existing Groth16 proof system anytime. Therefore, our technique provides a plug and play interface for the designated-verifier property of Groth16.

The second application is to construct short-lived proofs. Notably, Arun et al. [6] has provided us a framework to construct short-lived proofs from a standard Σ-protocol and a Σ-protocol for the zero knowledge verifiable delay functions (zkVDF): given a Σ-protocol for R_{zkVDF} and any relation R for which we have a Σ-protocol Σ_R, we can use the standard Σ-OR construction to create a disjunction protocol $\Sigma_{R \lor R_{zkVDF}}$ (See theorem 3 in Sect. 7 of [6] for more details). Now, because that our technique has built a bridge between Groth16 and Σ-protocols, we can generalize the conclusions in [6] to any NP relation with generic zero knowledge proofs instead of just the relation for which we have a Σ-protocol.

Disjunction of Arithmetic and Arithmetic Statements. Inspired by OR composition of CompGroth16 and Σ-protocol, we can also provide a framework to perform OR composition of CompGroth16 and CompGroth16. Suppose that there are two Groth16 proof systems $\Pi_{Groth_1}, \Pi_{Groth_2}$ with crs_1 and crs_2 for R_1 and R_2 respectively. We can transform $\Pi_{Groth_1}, \Pi_{Groth_2}$ into $\Pi_{CompGroth_1}, \Pi_{CompGroth_2}$. And then we can obtain the proof for $R_1 \lor R_2$ directly by using Σ-OR. The main advantage of OR composition of CompGroth16 protocols is to obtain the solution for proving $R_1 \lor R_2$ using existing schemes for proving R_1 and R_2 directly, without rewriting the circuit and regenerating the relation specific CRS. This actually broadens the expression range of Groth16 and to some extent alleviates the deficiency of Groth16 in CRS. Moreover, as we will discussed in Sect. 3.3, our technique can also greatly improve the efficiency of provers for proving this type of statements.

More General Extensions. Notably, for the reason that we have built a bridge between Groth16 and Σ-protocols, it is natural that we could directly utilize a series of optimizations for disjunction of Σ-protocols such as [40,41] to prove the more general disjunction such as $x_1 \in \mathcal{L}_1 \lor \cdots \lor x_l \in \mathcal{L}_l$ efficiently. Recall that [40,41] have built disjunctive compilers, generic approaches that automatically transform large classes of zero-knowledge protocols into disjunctive zero-knowledge protocols with communication complexity sub-linear in the number of clauses. However, the LPCP based zkSNARK Groth16 is not included in these classes. Therefore, from another perspective, our work has expanded the types of protocols that can be applied by these compilers. Moreover, we could also handle statements that contain multiple conjunction and disjunction statements simultaneously. In fact, there are already some optimizations on composition of Σ-protocol for CNF [8,9,40,67]. By building a bridge between Groth16 and Σ-protocols, our technique could also be utilized with these optimizations for handling the general arithmetic CNF. e.g. $(x_1^1 \in \mathcal{L}_1 \lor \cdots \lor x_l^1 \in \mathcal{L}_l) \land \cdots \land (x_1^k \in \mathcal{L}_1 \lor \cdots \lor x_l^k \in \mathcal{L}_l)$ for arithmetic $\{R_i\}_{i \in [1,l]}$.

Notably, our technique may also be extended to other pairing-based non-interactive arguments such as [25, 35]. However, compared to these two schemes, Groth16 requires our technique more urgently. This is because [25, 35] do not depend on circuit-dependent CRS, and the lookup table technique can be applied to these two schemes to alleviate circuit expansion.

3.3 Security and Performance Analysis

Theorem 2. *Protocol $\Pi_{CompGroth}$ is a non-interactive argument with perfect completeness and perfect zero-knowledge in the RO model. It has computational knowledge soundness in the RO model against adversaries that use only the polynomial number of generic bilinear group operations.*

Proof. **Completeness:** The completeness of this construction comes straightly from the completeness of Groth16 and Σ-protocol.

Knowledge Soundness: Notably, the Σ-proof generated by prover can be transformed to be non-interactive in the RO model. Using the forking lemma discussed in [60], if the prover of the Σ-protocol can find, with non-negligible probability, a valid transcript (a, c, z), the prover of the Σ-protocol can also find another transcript (a, c', z'). This yields an extractor with the expected polynomial time to extract $[B]_2$ which satisfies the Groth16's pairing check verification equation $[A]_1 \cdot [B]_2 = [\alpha\beta]_T + [D]_1 \cdot [\gamma]_2 + [C]_1 \cdot [\delta]_2$ with probability 1. Now, we get all the statements and proofs appearing in the original Groth16, and the our CRS is the same as the CRS of Groth16. Then, we can extract the witness by running the extractor of original Groth16 in GGM.

Zero-Knowledge: The simulator CompGroth.Sim is constructed in Fig. 4. On the one hand, our scheme run the Groth.P to obtain the $[A, C]_1$, and from Fig. 2 we can see that the elements $[A]_1$ and $[C]_1$ in real transcript are blinded by factors r and s respectively. Therefore, the elements $[A, C]_1$ in both real and simulated transcript are independent and random. On the other hand, from the ZK property of the Σ_{R_1}, we can directly know that the distributions of the tuple $([z]_2, [a]_T)$ in both real and simulated transcript are the same. Thus, taking into account all the above discussions, the distributions of $([A, C]_1, [z]_2, [a]_T)$ in both real and simulated transcript are the same, and zero knowledge property holds.

Performance Comparison. Notably, our scheme is a specially designed solution for disjunctive statements. Therefore, we give a performance comparison for disjunction of arithmetic and algebraic statements (e.g. $x_1 \in \mathcal{L}_{ari} \vee x_2 \in \mathcal{L}_{alg}$, where $x_2 \in \mathcal{L}_{alg}$ means $\exists\, a$ s.t. $Y = a \cdot G$) in Table 1. By m, n and l, we denote the number of wires, multiplication gates and the length of public input of the circuit for $x \in \mathcal{L}_{ari}$, respectively. By adding a tilde to m, n and l, we want to express the circuit parameters for $x \in \mathcal{L}_{alg}$. In comparison, the number of wires m ($\widetilde{m}$) exceeds the number of multiplication gates n ($\widetilde{n}$), since each gate has an output wire. The statement size l ($\widetilde{l}$) is typical smaller compared to m ($\widetilde{m}$) and n ($\widetilde{n}$). Notably, the exact size of m ($\widetilde{m}$) and n ($\widetilde{n}$) depends on the specific

"OR" statement to be proven. Therefore, compared with the traditional method, although sacrificing a bit of proof size, our solution does not require the heavy generation of a new CRS, has smaller CRS size, and has faster prover efficiency. Additionally, it is worth noting that our approach exhibits significant differences in the efficiency of prover based on which clause is the active clause. In the traditional way, in order to prove the "OR" statement, we have to run Groth16's prover algorithm no matter what. However, in our CompGroth16, if the algebraic clause of the disjunctive statement is an active clause, we can use a very efficient simulator in Σ-OR to simulate the proof transcript of the arithmetic part (just as the CompGroth.Sim shown in Fig. 4). Therefore, by utilizing our technique, we can completely avoid running the expensive Groth16's prover algorithm for such statements. This is a significant improvement in the efficiency of prover.

We also give a performance comparison for disjunction of arithmetic and arithmetic statements (e.g. $x_1 \in \mathcal{L}_1 \vee x_2 \in \mathcal{L}_2$) in Table 2. We use n, m, l and $\bar{n}, \bar{m}, \bar{l}$ to represent the circuit parameters of R_1 and R_2 respectively. Then, we can see from the Table 2 that compared with the traditional method, although sacrificing a bit of proof size and verifier efficiency, our solution has a significantly faster prover efficiency. The main advantage is that our solution does not require the heavy generation of a new CRS, and we directly use the existing CRS for R_1 and R_2 to prove that $R_1 \vee R_2$. Moreover, by utilizing the efficient simulator we have constructed, we can obtain significant efficiency improvements in prover's efficiency from the non-active clause. Suppose that the circuit scales of R_1 and R_2 are the same, anyway, our scheme can save more than half of the proving time when proving the disjunction of arithmetic and arithmetic statements.

Table 1. Theoretical comparison for $x_1 \in \mathcal{L}_{ari} \vee x_2 \in \mathcal{L}_{alg}$

	CRS renew	CRS size	Proof size	Prover comp.	Verifier comp.	PPE
Groth16 for $x_1 \in \mathcal{L}_{ari} \vee x_2 \in \mathcal{L}_{alg}$	Yes	$M + 2N\|\mathbb{G}_1\|, N\|\mathbb{G}_2\|$	$2\|\mathbb{G}_1\|, 1\|\mathbb{G}_2\|$	$M + 3N - LE_1, NE_2, \Theta(N)\mathbb{F}$	$LE_1, 3P$	1
This work for $x_1 \in \mathcal{L}_{ari} \vee x_2 \in \mathcal{L}_{alg}$	No	$m + 2n\|\mathbb{G}_1\|, n\|\mathbb{G}_2\|$	$2\|\mathbb{G}_1\|, 1\|\mathbb{G}_2\|, 1\|\mathbb{G}_T\|, 1\|\mathbb{G}_0\|, 3\|\mathbb{F}\|$	$m + 3n - lE_1, nE_2, \Theta(n)\mathbb{F}$	$lE_1, 3P$	1
This work for $x_1 \in \mathcal{L}_{ari} \vee x_2 \in \mathcal{L}_{alg}$	No	$m + 2n\|\mathbb{G}_1\|, n\|\mathbb{G}_2\|$	$2\|\mathbb{G}_1\|, 1\|\mathbb{G}_2\|, 1\|\mathbb{G}_T\|, 1\|\mathbb{G}_0\|, 3\|\mathbb{F}\|$	$lE_1, 3P$	$lE_1, 3P$	1

This table show us the theoretical performance comparison. By $m(\widetilde{m}), n(\widetilde{n})$ and $l(\widetilde{l})$, we denote the number of wires, multiplication gates and the length of public input, respectively. These parameters satisfy $M = m + \widetilde{m}, N = n + \widetilde{n}, L = l + \widetilde{l}$. We use $\mathbb{G}_0$ to represent a standard elliptic curve group (for algebraic part) and $\mathbb{G}_i$ for $i \in \{1, 2, T\}$ to form the bilinear groups (for non-algebraic part). "E_i" represents exponential computations in group $\mathbb{G}_i$ for $i \in \{1, 2, T\}$. "P" means pairing operations. "PPE" represents the number of pairing product equations used to verify a proof. In "Prover comp." column, "$\mathbb{F}$" represents field operations. When we discuss size, we use $|\cdot|$ notation on groups or field operations to represent corresponding elements. And we have omitted some very small constants in this table. The notation Θ represents quasi-linear

Table 2. Theoretical comparison for $x_1 \in \mathcal{L}_1 \vee x_2 \in \mathcal{L}_2$

	CRS renew	CRS size	Proof size	Prover comp.	Verifier comp.	PPE
Groth16 for $x_1 \in \mathcal{L}_1 \vee x_2 \in \mathcal{L}_2$	Yes	$M+2N|\mathbb{G}_1|, N|\mathbb{G}_2|$	$2|\mathbb{G}_1|, 1|\mathbb{G}_2|$	$M+3N-L\boldsymbol{E}_1, N\boldsymbol{E}_2, \Theta(N)\mathbb{F}$	$L\boldsymbol{E}_1, 3\boldsymbol{P}$	1
This work for $x_1 \in \mathcal{L}_1 \vee x_2 \in \mathcal{L}_2$	No	$M+2N|\mathbb{G}_1|, N|\mathbb{G}_2|$	$4|\mathbb{G}_1|, 2|\mathbb{G}_2|, 2|\mathbb{G}_T|$	$m+3n\boldsymbol{E}_1, n\boldsymbol{E}_2, \Theta(n)\mathbb{F}$	$L\boldsymbol{E}_1, 6P$	2
This work for $x_1 \in \mathcal{L}_1 \vee x_2 \in \mathcal{L}_2$	No	$M+2N|\mathbb{G}_1|, N|\mathbb{G}_2|$	$4|\mathbb{G}_1|, 2|\mathbb{G}_2|, 2|\mathbb{G}_T|$	$\bar{m}+3\bar{n}\boldsymbol{E}_1, \bar{n}\boldsymbol{E}_2, \Theta(\bar{n})\mathbb{F}$	$L\boldsymbol{E}_1, 6P$	2

This table show us the theoretical performance comparison. By $m(\bar{m}), n(\bar{n})$ and $l(\bar{l})$, we denote the number of wires, multiplication gates and the length of public input, respectively. These parameters satisfy $M = m + \bar{m}, N = n + \bar{n}, L = l + \bar{l}$. And other explanations are similar to the explanations of Table 1.

4 Implementation

We also compare the concrete efficiency of Groth's near-optimal zk-SNARK—Groth16 and our zk-SNARK construction (CompGroth16) during implementation in Table 3 and Table 4. In particular, we distinguish between active clauses, and compare their CRS size (denoted by $|CRS|$), CRS generation time (denoted by CG), proof time (denoted by P), and verification time (denoted by V) across different circuit scales. Similar to the pre-existing implementation of Groth's zk-SNARK in the arkworks [30] library, we implemented our zk-SNARKs in the Rust library using low-level subroutines of arkworks. The specific results were measured in a 64-bit Windows 10 Operating System, which was installed on a standard laptop (Victus by HP Laptop 16-d0xxx), with an Intel core i5-11400H 2.70\,GHz CPU and 16GB RAM. Each of our data is obtained by running the corresponding algorithm ten times and taking the average.

Table 3. Performance of the implementations for $x_1 \in \mathcal{L}_{ari} \vee x_2 \in \mathcal{L}_{alg}$

Scales	Groth16				CompGroth16 ($\bar{\mathcal{L}}_{ari}$)				CompGroth16 ($\bar{\mathcal{L}}_{alg}$)			
	$|CRS|$	CG	P	V	$|CRS|$	CG	P	V	$|CRS|$	CG	P	V
$n=2^{14}, \tilde{n}=2^{12}$	2 MB	276 ms	273 ms	3 ms	985 KB	120 ms	112 ms	4 ms	985 KB	120 ms	5 ms	4 ms
$n=2^{14}, \tilde{n}=2^{17}$	12 MB	1.2 s	1.2 s	3 ms	985 KB	120 ms	106 ms	4 ms	985 KB	120 ms	5 ms	4 ms
$n=2^{16}, \tilde{n}=2^{12}$	7 MB	738 ms	691 ms	3 ms	3 MB	425 ms	414 ms	4 ms	3 MB	425 ms	5 ms	4 ms
$n=2^{16}, \tilde{n}=2^{17}$	12 MB	1.3 s	1.4 s	3 ms	3 MB	425 ms	412 ms	4 ms	3 MB	425 ms	5 ms	4 ms
$n=2^{18}, \tilde{n}=2^{12}$	25 MB	2.3 s	2.5 s	3 ms	12 MB	1.5 s	1.5 s	4 ms	12 MB	1.5 s	5 ms	4 ms
$n=2^{18}, \tilde{n}=2^{17}$	24 MB	2.5 s	2.8 s	3 ms	12 MB	1.5 s	1.5 s	4 ms	12 MB	1.5 s	5 ms	4 ms

This table show us the specific performance comparison for $x_1 \in \mathcal{L}_{ari} \vee x_2 \in \mathcal{L}_{alg}$ across different circuit scales (we fix the number of witness to be 2^{10}). For the algebraic statements, we prove that $\exists\, a\; s.t.\; Y = a \cdot G$, where G is selected from a native elliptic curve group $\mathbb{G}$ ($\tilde{n} = 2^{12}$, meaning that the base field of $\mathbb{G}$ is the same as the scalar field of BLS12-381 curve) and a non-native ECDSA group ($\tilde{n} = 2^{17}$, which is the secp256k1 curve) respectively

In summary, for arithmetic-algebraic disjunctions, our solution improves prover efficiency (especially with active algebraic clauses) without new CRS.

Table 4. Performance of the implementations for $x_1 \in \mathcal{L}_1 \vee x_2 \in \mathcal{L}_2$

Scales	Groth16				CompGroth16 ($\bar{\mathcal{L}}_1$)				CompGroth16 ($\bar{\mathcal{L}}_2$)			
	$\|CRS\|$	CG	P	V	$\|CRS\|$	CG	P	V	$\|CRS\|$	CG	P	V
$n = 2^{16}, \bar{n} = 2^{16}$	6 MB	797 ms	780 ms	3 ms	6 MB	871 ms	404 ms	8 ms	6 MB	871 ms	400 ms	8 ms
$n = 2^{16}, \bar{n} = 2^{18}$	24 MB	2.4 s	2.5 s	3 ms	15 MB	2 s	413 ms	8 ms	15 MB	2 s	1.5 s	8 ms
$n = 2^{16}, \bar{n} = 2^{20}$	96 MB	8.5 s	10.2 s	3 ms	51 MB	6.2 s	414 ms	8 ms	51 MB	6.2 s	6.5 s	8 ms
$n = 2^{18}, \bar{n} = 2^{18}$	24 MB	3 s	3.1 s	3 ms	24 MB	2.9 s	1.5 s	8 ms	24 MB	2.9 s	1.5 s	8 ms
$n = 2^{18}, \bar{n} = 2^{20}$	96 MB	9 s	11 s	3 ms	60 MB	7.3 s	1.6 s	8 ms	60 MB	7.3 s	6.4 s	8 ms
$n = 2^{20}, \bar{n} = 2^{20}$	96 MB	12 s	15.8 s	3 ms	96 MB	11.7 s	6.7 s	8 ms	96 MB	11.7 s	6.7 s	8 ms

This table show us the specific performance comparison for $x_1 \in \mathcal{L}_1 \vee x_2 \in \mathcal{L}_2$ across different circuit scales (we fix the number of witness to be 2^{10})

For arithmetic-arithmetic disjunctions, it enables proving multiple statements using existing CRSs, extending Groth16's expressiveness while offering significantly better prover efficiency and acceptable communication.

Acknowldgement. We would like to thank anonymous reviewers from ESORICS 2025 for their valuable suggestions, which have helped us a lot to improve this paper. We are supported by the National Key Research and Development Program of China (Grant No. 2023YFB4503203), the Strategic Priority Research Program of Chinese Academy of Sciences (Grant No. XDB0690200), and the National Natural Science Foundation of China (Grant No. 62372447 and No. 61932019).

References

1. Abe, M., Ohkubo, M., Suzuki, K.: 1-out-of-n signatures from a variety of keys. In: Zheng, Y. (ed.) ASIACRYPT 2002. LNCS, vol. 2501, pp. 415–432. Springer, Heidelberg (2002). https://doi.org/10.1007/3-540-36178-2_26
2. Agrawal, S., Ganesh, C., Mohassel, P.: Non-interactive zero-knowledge proofs for composite statements. In: Shacham, H., Boldyreva, A. (eds.) CRYPTO 2018. LNCS, vol. 10993, pp. 643–673. Springer, Cham (2018). https://doi.org/10.1007/978-3-319-96878-0_22
3. Akinyele, J.A., et al.: Charm: a framework for rapidly prototyping cryptosystems. J. Cryptogr. Eng. **3**(2), 111–128 (2013)
4. Ames, S., Hazay, C., Ishai, Y., Venkitasubramaniam, M.: Ligero: lightweight sublinear arguments without a trusted setup. DCC **91**(11), 3379–3424 (2023)
5. Aranha, D.F., Bennedsen, E.M., Campanelli, M., Ganesh, C., Orlandi, C., Takahashi, A.: ECLIPSE: enhanced compiling method for pedersen-committed zksnark engines. In: PKC 2022. LNCS, vol. 13177, pp. 584–614. Springer (2022)
6. Arun, A., Bonneau, J., Clark, J.: Short-lived zero-knowledge proofs and signatures. In: ASIACRYPT 2022. LNCS, vol. 13793, pp. 487–516. Springer (2022)
7. Attema, T., Cramer, R., Fehr, S.: Compressing proofs of k-out-of-n partial knowledge. In: Malkin, T., Peikert, C. (eds.) CRYPTO 2021. LNCS, vol. 12828, pp. 65–91. Springer, Cham (2021). https://doi.org/10.1007/978-3-030-84259-8_3

8. Avitabile, G., Botta, V., Friolo, D., Venturi, D., Visconti, I.: Compact proofs of partial knowledge for overlapping CNF formulae. J. Cryptol. **38**(1), 7 (2025)
9. Avitabile, G., Botta, V., Friolo, D., Visconti, I.: Efficient proofs of knowledge for threshold relations. In: ESORICS 2022. LNCS, vol. 13556, pp. 42–62. Springer (2022)
10. Backes, M., Hanzlik, L., Herzberg, A., Kate, A., Pryvalov, I.: Efficient non-interactive zero-knowledge proofs in cross-domains without trusted setup. In: Lin, D., Sako, K. (eds.) PKC 2019. LNCS, vol. 11442, pp. 286–313. Springer, Cham (2019). https://doi.org/10.1007/978-3-030-17253-4_10
11. Baum, C., Malozemoff, A.J., Rosen, M.B., Scholl, P.: Mac′n′Cheese: zero-knowledge proofs for boolean and arithmetic circuits with nested disjunctions. In: Malkin, T., Peikert, C. (eds.) CRYPTO 2021. LNCS, vol. 12828, pp. 92–122. Springer, Cham (2021). https://doi.org/10.1007/978-3-030-84259-8_4
12. Ben-Sasson, E., Bentov, I., Horesh, Y., Riabzev, M.: Scalable zero knowledge with no trusted setup. In: Boldyreva, A., Micciancio, D. (eds.) CRYPTO 2019. LNCS, vol. 11694, pp. 701–732. Springer, Cham (2019). https://doi.org/10.1007/978-3-030-26954-8_23
13. Ben Sasson, E., et al.: Zerocash: decentralized anonymous payments from bitcoin. In: 2014 IEEE Symposium on Security and Privacy, pp. 459–474 (2014)
14. Ben-Sasson, E., Chiesa, A., Genkin, D., Tromer, E., Virza, M.: SNARKs for C: verifying program executions succinctly and in zero knowledge. In: Canetti, R., Garay, J.A. (eds.) CRYPTO 2013. LNCS, vol. 8043, pp. 90–108. Springer, Heidelberg (2013). https://doi.org/10.1007/978-3-642-40084-1_6
15. Ben-Sasson, E., Chiesa, A., Riabzev, M., Spooner, N., Virza, M., Ward, N.P.: Aurora: transparent succinct arguments for R1CS. In: Ishai, Y., Rijmen, V. (eds.) EUROCRYPT 2019. LNCS, vol. 11476, pp. 103–128. Springer, Cham (2019). https://doi.org/10.1007/978-3-030-17653-2_4
16. Benet, J., Greco, N.: Filecoin: a decentralized storage network. Protocol Labs, pp. 1–36 (2017)
17. Bernhard, D., Pereira, O., Warinschi, B.: How not to prove yourself: pitfalls of the fiat-shamir heuristic and applications to helios. In: Wang, X., Sako, K. (eds.) ASIACRYPT 2012. LNCS, vol. 7658, pp. 626–643. Springer, Heidelberg (2012). https://doi.org/10.1007/978-3-642-34961-4_38
18. Bitansky, N., Chiesa, A., Ishai, Y., Paneth, O., Ostrovsky, R.: Succinct non-interactive arguments via linear interactive proofs. In: Sahai, A. (ed.) TCC 2013. LNCS, vol. 7785, pp. 315–333. Springer, Heidelberg (2013). https://doi.org/10.1007/978-3-642-36594-2_18
19. Blum, M., Feldman, P., Micali, S.: Non-interactive zero-knowledge and its applications (extended abstract). In: STOC 1988, pp. 103–112. ACM (1988)
20. Bonneau, J., Meckler, I., Rao, V., Shapiro, E.: Coda: decentralized cryptocurrency at scale. IACR Cryptol. ePrint Arch. 352 (2020)
21. Campanelli, M., Faonio, A., Fiore, D., Querol, A., Rodríguez, H.: Lunar: a toolbox for more efficient universal and updatable zkSNARKs and commit-and-prove extensions. In: Tibouchi, M., Wang, H. (eds.) ASIACRYPT 2021. LNCS, vol. 13092, pp. 3–33. Springer, Cham (2021). https://doi.org/10.1007/978-3-030-92078-4_1
22. Campanelli, M., Fiore, D., Querol, A.: Legosnark: modular design and composition of succinct zero-knowledge proofs. In: CCS 2019, pp. 2075–2092. ACM (2019)
23. Chase, M., et al.: Post-quantum zero-knowledge and signatures from symmetric-key primitives. In: CCS 2017, pp. 1825–1842. ACM (2017)

24. Chase, M., Ganesh, C., Mohassel, P.: Efficient zero-knowledge proof of algebraic and non-algebraic statements with applications to privacy preserving credentials. In: Robshaw, M., Katz, J. (eds.) CRYPTO 2016. LNCS, vol. 9816, pp. 499–530. Springer, Heidelberg (2016). https://doi.org/10.1007/978-3-662-53015-3_18
25. Chiesa, A., Hu, Y., Maller, M., Mishra, P., Vesely, N., Ward, N.: Marlin: preprocessing zkSNARKs with universal and updatable SRS. In: Canteaut, A., Ishai, Y. (eds.) EUROCRYPT 2020. LNCS, vol. 12105, pp. 738–768. Springer, Cham (2020). https://doi.org/10.1007/978-3-030-45721-1_26
26. Chiesa, A., Ojha, D., Spooner, N.: FRACTAL: post-quantum and transparent recursive proofs from holography. In: Canteaut, A., Ishai, Y. (eds.) EUROCRYPT 2020. LNCS, vol. 12105, pp. 769–793. Springer, Cham (2020). https://doi.org/10.1007/978-3-030-45721-1_27
27. Ciampi, M., Persiano, G., Scafuro, A., Siniscalchi, L., Visconti, I.: Improved OR-composition of sigma-protocols. In: Kushilevitz, E., Malkin, T. (eds.) TCC 2016. LNCS, vol. 9563, pp. 112–141. Springer, Heidelberg (2016). https://doi.org/10.1007/978-3-662-49099-0_5
28. Ciampi, M., Persiano, G., Scafuro, A., Siniscalchi, L., Visconti, I.: Online/Offline OR composition of sigma protocols. In: Fischlin, M., Coron, J.-S. (eds.) EUROCRYPT 2016. LNCS, vol. 9666, pp. 63–92. Springer, Heidelberg (2016). https://doi.org/10.1007/978-3-662-49896-5_3
29. circom-ecdsa contributors: Implementation of ecdsa operations in circom (2022). https://github.com/0xPARC/circom-ecdsa
30. arkworks contributors: arkworks zksnark ecosystem (2022). https://arkworks.rs
31. Cramer, R.: Modular design of secure yet practical cryptographic protocols (1997). https://api.semanticscholar.org/CorpusID:60892379
32. Cramer, R., Damgård, I., Schoenmakers, B.: Proofs of partial knowledge and simplified design of witness hiding protocols. In: Desmedt, Y.G. (ed.) CRYPTO 1994. LNCS, vol. 839, pp. 174–187. Springer, Heidelberg (1994). https://doi.org/10.1007/3-540-48658-5_19
33. Delignat-Lavaud, A., Fournet, C., Kohlweiss, M., Parno, B.: Cinderella: turning shabby x.509 certificates into elegant anonymous credentials with the magic of verifiable computation. In: 2016 IEEE Symposium on Security and Privacy (SP), pp. 235–254 (2016)
34. Fiat, A., Shamir, A.: How to prove yourself: practical solutions to identification and signature problems. In: Odlyzko, A.M. (ed.) CRYPTO 1986. LNCS, vol. 263, pp. 186–194. Springer, Heidelberg (1987). https://doi.org/10.1007/3-540-47721-7_12
35. Gabizon, A., Williamson, Z.J., Ciobotaru, O.: PLONK: permutations over lagrange-bases for oecumenical noninteractive arguments of knowledge. IACR Cryptol. ePrint Arch. 953 (2019)
36. Galal, H.S., Youssef, A.M.: Verifiable sealed-bid auction on the ethereum blockchain. In: Zohar, A., et al. (eds.) FC 2018. LNCS, vol. 10958, pp. 265–278. Springer, Heidelberg (2019). https://doi.org/10.1007/978-3-662-58820-8_18
37. Garay, J.A., MacKenzie, P., Yang, K.: Strengthening zero-knowledge protocols using signatures. J. Cryptol. **19**(2), 169–209 (2005). https://doi.org/10.1007/s00145-005-0307-3
38. Gennaro, R., Gentry, C., Parno, B., Raykova, M.: Quadratic span programs and succinct NIZKs without PCPs. In: Johansson, T., Nguyen, P.Q. (eds.) EUROCRYPT 2013. LNCS, vol. 7881, pp. 626–645. Springer, Heidelberg (2013). https://doi.org/10.1007/978-3-642-38348-9_37

39. Giacomelli, I., Madsen, J., Orlandi, C.: Zkboo: faster zero-knowledge for boolean circuits. In: 25th USENIX Security Symposium, USENIX Security 2016, pp. 1069–1083. USENIX Association (2016)
40. Goel, A., Green, M., Hall-Andersen, M., Kaptchuk, G.: Stacking sigmas: a framework to compose ς-protocols for disjunctions. In: EUROCRYPT 2022. LNCS, vol. 13276, pp. 458–487. Springer (2022)
41. Goel, A., Hall-Andersen, M., Kaptchuk, G., Spooner, N.: Speed-stacking: fast sublinear zero-knowledge proofs for disjunctions. In: EUROCRYPT 2023. LNCS, vol. 14005, pp. 347–378. Springer (2023)
42. Goldwasser, S., Micali, S., Rackoff, C.: The knowledge complexity of interactive proof systems. SIAM J. Comput. **18**(1), 186–208 (1989)
43. Golovnev, A., Lee, J., Setty, S.T.V., Thaler, J., Wahby, R.S.: Brakedown: linear-time and field-agnostic snarks for R1CS. In: CRYPTO 2023. LNCS, vol. 14082, pp. 193–226. Springer (2023)
44. Groth, J.: Short pairing-based non-interactive zero-knowledge arguments. In: Abe, M. (ed.) ASIACRYPT 2010. LNCS, vol. 6477, pp. 321–340. Springer, Heidelberg (2010). https://doi.org/10.1007/978-3-642-17373-8_19
45. Groth, J.: On the size of pairing-based non-interactive arguments. In: Fischlin, M., Coron, J.-S. (eds.) EUROCRYPT 2016. LNCS, vol. 9666, pp. 305–326. Springer, Heidelberg (2016). https://doi.org/10.1007/978-3-662-49896-5_11
46. Groth, J., Kohlweiss, M.: One-out-of-many proofs: or how to leak a secret and spend a coin. In: Oswald, E., Fischlin, M. (eds.) EUROCRYPT 2015. LNCS, vol. 9057, pp. 253–280. Springer, Heidelberg (2015). https://doi.org/10.1007/978-3-662-46803-6_9
47. Guillou, L.C., Quisquater, J.-J.: A practical zero-knowledge protocol fitted to security microprocessor minimizing both transmission and memory. In: Barstow, D., et al. (eds.) EUROCRYPT 1988. LNCS, vol. 330, pp. 123–128. Springer, Heidelberg (1988). https://doi.org/10.1007/3-540-45961-8_11
48. Hazay, C., Heath, D., Kolesnikov, V., Venkitasubramaniam, M., Yang, Y.: Logrobin++: optimizing proofs of disjunctive statements in vole-based ZK. IACR Cryptol. ePrint Arch. 1427 (2024)
49. Heath, D., Kolesnikov, V.: Stacked garbling. In: Micciancio, D., Ristenpart, T. (eds.) CRYPTO 2020. LNCS, vol. 12171, pp. 763–792. Springer, Cham (2020). https://doi.org/10.1007/978-3-030-56880-1_27
50. Heath, D., Kolesnikov, V.: Stacked garbling for disjunctive zero-knowledge proofs. In: Canteaut, A., Ishai, Y. (eds.) EUROCRYPT 2020. LNCS, vol. 12107, pp. 569–598. Springer, Cham (2020). https://doi.org/10.1007/978-3-030-45727-3_19
51. Heath, D., Kolesnikov, V.: LogStack: stacked garbling with $O(b \log b)$ computation. In: Canteaut, A., Standaert, F.-X. (eds.) EUROCRYPT 2021. LNCS, vol. 12698, pp. 3–32. Springer, Cham (2021). https://doi.org/10.1007/978-3-030-77883-5_1
52. Kate, A., Zaverucha, G.M., Goldberg, I.: Constant-size commitments to polynomials and their applications. In: Abe, M. (ed.) ASIACRYPT 2010. LNCS, vol. 6477, pp. 177–194. Springer, Heidelberg (2010). https://doi.org/10.1007/978-3-642-17373-8_11
53. Kolesnikov, V.: Free IF: How to omit inactive branches and implement $\mathcal{S}$-universal garbled circuit (almost) for free. In: Peyrin, T., Galbraith, S. (eds.) ASIACRYPT 2018. LNCS, vol. 11274, pp. 34–58. Springer, Cham (2018). https://doi.org/10.1007/978-3-030-03332-3_2
54. Lipmaa, H.: Progression-free sets and sublinear pairing-based non-interactive zero-knowledge arguments. In: Cramer, R. (ed.) TCC 2012. LNCS, vol. 7194, pp. 169–189. Springer, Heidelberg (2012). https://doi.org/10.1007/978-3-642-28914-9_10

55. Lipmaa, H.: On black-box knowledge-sound commit-and-prove snarks. In: ASIACRYPT 2023. LNCS, vol. 14439, pp. 41–76. Springer (2023)
56. Lipmaa, H.: Polymath: groth16 is not the limit. In: CRYPTO 2024. LNCS, vol. 14929, pp. 170–206. Springer (2024)
57. Lueks, W., Kulynych, B., Fasquelle, J., Bail-Collet, S.L., Troncoso, C.: zksk: a library for composable zero-knowledge proofs. In: Proceedings of WPES@CCS 2019, pp. 50–54. ACM (2019)
58. Maller, M., Bowe, S., Kohlweiss, M., Meiklejohn, S.: Sonic: zero-knowledge snarks from linear-size universal and updatable structured reference strings. In: Proceedings of the 2019 ACM SIGSAC Conference on CCS 2019, pp. 2111–2128. ACM (2019)
59. Meiklejohn, S., Erway, C.C., Küpçü, A., Hinkle, T., Lysyanskaya, A.: ZKPDL: a language-based system for efficient zero-knowledge proofs and electronic cash. In: 19th USENIX Security Symposium, pp. 193–206. USENIX Association (2010)
60. Pointcheval, D., Stern, J.: Security proofs for signature schemes. In: Maurer, U. (ed.) EUROCRYPT 1996. LNCS, vol. 1070, pp. 387–398. Springer, Heidelberg (1996). https://doi.org/10.1007/3-540-68339-9_33
61. Raymond, M., Evers, G., Ponti, J., Krishnan, D., Fu, X.: Efficient zero knowledge for regular language. IACR Cryptol. ePrint Arch. 907 (2023)
62. Rivest, R.L., Shamir, A., Tauman, Y.: How to leak a secret. In: Boyd, C. (ed.) ASIACRYPT 2001. LNCS, vol. 2248, pp. 552–565. Springer, Heidelberg (2001). https://doi.org/10.1007/3-540-45682-1_32
63. Rondelet, A., Zajac, M.: ZETH: on integrating zerocash on ethereum. CoRR abs/1904.00905 (2019)
64. Schnorr, C.P.: Efficient signature generation by smart cards. J. Cryptol. 4(3), 161–174 (1991). https://doi.org/10.1007/BF00196725
65. Setty, S.: Spartan: efficient and general-purpose zkSNARKs without trusted setup. In: Micciancio, D., Ristenpart, T. (eds.) CRYPTO 2020. LNCS, vol. 12172, pp. 704–737. Springer, Cham (2020). https://doi.org/10.1007/978-3-030-56877-1_25
66. Yang, Y., Heath, D., Hazay, C., Kolesnikov, V., Venkitasubramaniam, M.: Batchman and robin: batched and non-batched branching for interactive ZK. In: Proceedings of the 2023 ACM SIGSAC Conference on CCS 2023, pp. 1452–1466. ACM (2023)
67. Zeng, G., Lai, J., Huang, Z., Wang, Y., Zheng, Z.: Dag-Σ: a DAG-based sigma protocol for relations in CNF. In: ASIACRYPT 2022. LNCS, vol. 13792, pp. 340–370. Springer (2022)
68. Zhang, J., Fang, Z., Zhang, Y., Song, D.: Zero knowledge proofs for decision tree predictions and accuracy. In: Proceedings of the 2020 ACM SIGSAC Conference on Computer and Communications Security, CCS 2020, pp. 2039–2053. ACM (2020)
69. Zhang, J., Xie, T., Zhang, Y., Song, D.: Transparent polynomial delegation and its applications to zero knowledge proof. In: 2020 IEEE Symposium on Security and Privacy, SP 2020, pp. 859–876. IEEE (2020)
70. Zhang, M., Chen, Y., Yao, C., Wang, Z.: Sigma protocols from verifiable secret sharing and their applications. In: ASIACRYPT 2023. LNCS, vol. 14439, pp. 208–242. Springer (2023)
71. Zhang, Y., Genkin, D., Katz, J., Papadopoulos, D., Papamanthou, C.: vSQL: verifying arbitrary SQL queries over dynamic outsourced databases. In: 2017 IEEE Symposium on Security and Privacy (SP), pp. 863–880 (2017)
72. Zhao, Z., Chan, T.-H.H.: How to vote privately using bitcoin. In: Qing, S., Okamoto, E., Kim, K., Liu, D. (eds.) ICICS 2015. LNCS, vol. 9543, pp. 82–96. Springer, Cham (2016). https://doi.org/10.1007/978-3-319-29814-6_8

Author Index

A
Abe, Masayuki 1
Avitabile, Gennaro 22

B
Baek, Joonsang 42
Bao, Chenhao 144
Bian, Bingxue 63
Botta, Vincenzo 22
Boyen, Xavier 262
Brézot, Théophile 84

C
Chakraborty, Suvradip 226
Cheng, Nan 205
Choi, Seongbong 42
Cinal, Adrian 103

D
Damodaran, Aditya 124
de Perthuis, Paola 84
Deng, Yi 400, 506

E
Ertel, Sebastian 463
Escobar, Santiago 186

F
Fan, Qijia 144
Fiore, Dario 22

G
Ghosh, Satrajit 226

H
Haines, Thomas 303
Hamada, Koki 164
Han, Shuai 144, 379

Hébant, Chloé 84
Hernández-Sánchez, Arturo 186
Hu, Honggang 421
Hur, Junbeom 321

J
Jing, Jiwu 282

K
Kaji, Yuichi 247
Kaluđerović, Novak 205
Kim, Doowon 321
Köpsell, Stefan 463
Kubiak, Przemysław 103
Kumar, Chandan 226
Kumazaki, Remma 247
Kutyłowski, Mirosław 103

L
Lamster, Lukas 359
Lee, Hyeonbum 321
Lee, Hyung Tae 42
Lei, Lingguang 282
Li, Qinyi 262
Liang, Kaitai 442
Liu, Jiatao 63
Liu, Shengli 144, 379
Liu, Yuejun 341
Long, Chongyu 282
Lu, Zhaojun 442

M
Mähn, Jannik 463
Mangard, Stefan 359
Mishra, Nimish 226
Mitrokotsa, Aikaterini 205
Mukhopadhyay, Debdeep 226

N
Nanri, Masaya 1

O
Oberhuber, Mathias 359
Ohkubo, Miyako 1

P
Palak, 303
Park, Jaehwan 321
Perez-Kempner, Octavio 1
Pointcheval, David 84

R
Rastikian, Simon 124
Rønne, Peter B. 124
Roy, Partha Sarathi 42
Ryan, Peter Y. A. 124

S
Scherer, Simon 359
Seo, Jae Hong 321
Shao, Mingyao 341
Shao, Yan 341
Shi, Xuanyu 144
Slamanig, Daniel 1
Song, Xuyang 506
Susilo, Willy 42

T
Tibouchi, Mehdi 1

U
Unterguggenberger, Martin 359

W
Wang, Jianfeng 63
Wang, Wei 442
Wang, Weiqi 442
Wang, Yuewu 282
Wechta, Gabriel 103
Wei, Xiaoyang 379
Wei, Yuanju 400, 506
Wu, Zhuo 400

X
Xing, Haoyang 282
Xu, Changhong 421
Xu, Peng 442
Xu, Qiaoer 63

Y
Yang, Liuyu 400, 506
Yang, Yifan 442

Z
Zain, Sara 463
Zhang, Kexin 442
Zhang, Xin 485
Zhang, Xinxuan 400, 506
Zhang, Yifan 485
Zhang, Zhongliang 400
Zhou, Yongbin 341
Zhu, Xudong 506

Made in the USA
Monee, IL
03 May 2026

49438808R00306